Handbook of

Marketing Theory

vPower.com

" ~~calculate~~

" calculate
statical power
from data "

Sample size
calculator

The SAGE
Handbook of

Marketing Theory

Edited by

Pauline Maclaran,
Michael Saren, Barbara Stern
and Mark Tadajewski

Los Angeles • London • New Delhi • Singapore • Washington DC

SAGE Publications Ltd
1 Oliver's Yard
55 City Road
London EC1Y 1SP

SAGE Publications Inc.
2455 Teller Road
Thousand Oaks, California 91320

SAGE Publications India Pvt Ltd
B 1/I 1 Mohan Cooperative Industrial Area
Mathura Road
New Delhi 110 044

SAGE Publications Asia-Pacific Pte Ltd
33 Pekin Street #02-01
Far East Square
Singapore 048763

Library of Congress Control Number: 2009926751

British Library Cataloguing in Publication data

A catalogue record for this book is available from the British Library

ISBN 978-1-4462-7051-6

Typeset by Glyph International, Bangalore, India

This handbook is dedicated to
the memory of our esteemed colleague,
Professor Barbara Stern.

Contents

Notes on Contributors   xi

1   Introduction   1
    Pauline Maclaran, Michael Saren, Barbara Stern, and Mark Tadajewski

SECTION 1   HISTORICAL DEVELOPMENT OF MARKETING THEORY   25

2   The Early Schools of Marketing Thought   27
    Eric H. Shaw, D. G. Brian Jones, and Paula A. McClean

3   The Modern Schools of Marketing Thought   42
    D. G. Brian Jones, Eric H. Shaw, and Paula A. McClean

4   The Emergence of Consumer Research   59
    Harold H. Kassarjian and Ronald C. Goodstein

5   The Evolution of Market Research   74
    David W. Stewart

6   Theorizing Advertising: Managerial, Scientific and Cultural Approaches   89
    Chris Hackley

SECTION 2   PHILOSOPHICAL UNDERPINNINGS OF THEORY   109

7   The Philosophical Foundations of Marketing Research: For Scientific
Realism and Truth   111
    Shelby D. Hunt and Jared M. Hansen

8   Critical Marketing – Marketing in Critical Condition   127
    A. Fuat Fırat and Mark Tadajewski

9   The Marketing Theory or Theories into Marketing? Plurality of Research
Traditions and Paradigms   151
    Kristian Möller, Jaqueline Pels, and Michael Saren

10   Debates Concerning the Scientific Method: Social Science Theory and
     the Philosophy of Science   174
     John O'Shaughnessy

SECTION 3   MAJOR THEORETICAL DEBATES   193

11   Shaping Exchanges, Performing Markets: The Study of Market-ing Practices   195
     Luis Araujo and Hans Kjellberg

12   A Service-Dominant Logic for Marketing   219
     Stephen L. Vargo and Robert F. Lusch

13   Market Ideology, Globalization and Neoliberalism   235
     Robin Wensley

14   The Evolution of Marketing Thought: From Economic to Social
     Exchange and Beyond   244
     Richard P. Bagozzi

15   Metaphorical Myopia: Some Thoughts on Analogical Thinking   266
     Stephen Brown

SECTION 4   THE IMPACT OF THEORY ON REPRESENTATIONS
OF THE CONSUMER   281

16   Representing Global Consumers: Desire, Possession, and Identity   283
     Russell W. Belk

17   Consumer Behavior Analysis   299
     Gordon R. Foxall

18   Consumer Agency and Action   316
     Richard P. Bagozzi

19   Cultural Influences on Representations of the Consumer in Marketing Theory   332
     Pauline Maclaran, Margaret K. Hogg, and Alan Bradshaw

SECTION 5   IMPACT OF THEORY ON REPRESENTATIONS OF
THE MARKETING ORGANISATION   353

20   Interaction in Networks   355
     Lars-Erik Gadde and Håkan Håkansson

21   Practice Perspective of the Marketing Organisation   365
     Roderick J. Brodie, Victoria J. Little, and Richard W. Brookes

22   Orientation and Marketing Metrics   379
     Jonathan Knowles and Tim Ambler

23   Relationship Marketing as Promise Management   397
     Christian Grönroos

**SECTION 6   CONTEMPORARY AND FUTURE ISSUES IN
              MARKETING THEORY**   **413**

24   Marketing Systems, Macromarketing and the Quality of Life   415
     Roger A. Layton

25   The Role of Marketing in Ancient and Contemporary Cultural Evolution 443
     Elizabeth C. Hirschman

26   The Darwinian Underpinnings of Consumption   457
     Gad Saad

27   The Linking Value in Experiential Marketing: Acknowledging
     the Role of Working Consumers   476
     Bernard Cova and Daniele Dalli

28   Technology, Consumers, and Marketing Theory   494
     Nikhilesh Dholakia, Detlev Zwick, and Janice Denegri-Knott

Index   513

Notes on Contributors

Tim Ambler is Senior Fellow in Marketing at London Business School, and a world expert in the fields of the measurement of marketing performance and brand equity. He is the author of four books including *Marketing and the Bottom Line* plus numerous articles in top-tier academic and business journals. Research interests include brand equity, measuring marketing performance, advertising and promotions, and neuro-marketing. Formerly Joint Managing Director of International Distillers and Vintners (now part of Diageo plc), Tim holds Master's degrees in Mathematics from Oxford and Business from the Sloan School (MIT) and is also a qualified accountant.

Luis Araujo is Professor of Industrial Marketing at Lancaster University Management School. His research interests and publications fall mainly in the area of business markets, namely the boundaries of the firm and product-service systems, and practice-based approaches to market studies.

Richard P. Bagozzi is the Dwight F. Benton Professor of Marketing in the Ross School of Business and Professor of Clinical, Social and Administrative Sciences in the College of Pharmacy, both at the University of Michigan. A graduate of the PhD program at Northwestern University, Professor Bagozzi in recent years has received honorary doctorates from the University of Lausanne, Switzerland, and Antwerp University, Belgium. He does basic research in the theory of action and theory of mind, applying ideas derived therefrom to research in consumer behavior, emotions, social identity, sales force behavior, organizational studies, health behavior, self-regulation, and structural equation models.

Russell W. Belk is Kraft Foods Canada Chair in Marketing, Schulich School of Business, York University. He is past president of the International Association of Marketing and Development, and is a fellow, past president, and Film Festival co-founder in the Association for Consumer Research. His awards include the Paul D. Converse Award and the Sheth Foundation/*Journal of Consumer Research* Award for Long Term Contribution to Consumer Research. His research involves the meanings of possessions, collecting, gift-giving, materialism, and global consumer culture.

Alan Bradshaw is a Senior Lecturer in Marketing at Royal Holloway, University of London. His research is concerned with the mediation of cultural dynamics, particularly music, within the sphere of consumption. His work can be found in the *Journal of Macromarketing, European Journal of Marketing, Consumption, Markets & Culture, Marketing Theory* and the *Journal of Marketing Management.*

Roderick J. Brodie is Professor in the Department of Marketing at the University of Auckland of Business School, New Zealand. His publications have appeared in leading international journals including: *Journal of Marketing, Journal of Marketing Research, International Journal of Research in Marketing, Management Science, Journal of Service Research*. He is an area editor of *Marketing Theory* and on the Editorial Boards of the *Journal of Marketing*, the *International Journal of Research in Marketing*, the *Journal of Service Research*, and the *Australasian Journal of Marketing*.

Richard W. Brookes is Associate Professor in the Department of Marketing at The University of Auckland. He has published in various international journals, including *Journal of Business Research, International Journal of Research in Marketing, Psychology and Marketing, Journal of Marketing Management*, and *Journal of Business and Industrial Marketing*. A specialist in international research into automobile buying behavior, he is closely involved with the European Society for Opinion and Marketing Research (ESOMAR), both as a conference speaker and as a judging panel member.

Stephen Brown is Professor of Marketing Research at the University of Ulster. Best known for *Postmodern Marketing*, he has written numerous books including *The Marketing Code, Agents & Dealers, Fail Better!, Free Gift Inside!* and *Wizard! Harry Potter's Brand Magic*. He may not have much of a metaphorical gift, but he's a dab hand with exclamation marks!!

Bernard Cova is Professor of Marketing at Euromed Management, Marseilles and Visiting Professor at Università Bocconi, Milan. A pioneer in the Consumer Tribes field since the early nineties, his internationally influential research has emphasized what he calls 'the Mediterranean approach' of tribal marketing. His work on this topic has been published in the *International Journal of Research in Marketing, The European Journal of Marketing, Marketing Theory*, and *The Journal of Business Research*. He is also known for his groundbreaking research in B2B marketing, especially in the field of project marketing.

Daniele Dalli is Professor of Marketing at the Faculty of Economics in the University of Pisa. His research interests include consumer culture, consumption communities, and consumer resistance. His work has been published in international journals (such as the *International Journal of Market Research*) and presented at international conferences, including those held by the European Marketing Academy and the Association for Consumer Research. He has had chapters in books published by international publishers (Routledge).

Janice Denegri-Knott currently teaches Consumer Culture and Behaviour at undergraduate and postgraduate levels at the Bournemouth Media School. Since 2001, she has been actively researching and publishing in the areas of digital virtual consumption, technology and marketing. Her research interests span from conceptualizing and documenting digital virtual consumption and its practices to consumer producer relations from a power perspective.

Nikhilesh Dholakia is Professor in the College of Business Administration at the University of Rhode Island. His research deals with globalization, technology, innovation, market processes, and consumer culture. His books include *Consuming People: From Political Economy to Theaters of Consumption* (1998) and *M-commerce: Global Experiences and Perspectives* (2006). Dr. Dholakia holds a BTech from Indian Institute of Technology at Delhi, an MBA from Indian Institute of Management at Ahmedabad, and a PhD from the Kellogg School at Northwestern University.

A. Fuat Fırat is Professor and Chair at the Department of Management, Marketing and International Business, University of Texas-Pan American. His research interests cover areas such as macro consumer behavior and macromarketing; postmodern culture; transmodern marketing strategies; gender and consumption; marketing and development; and interorganizational relations. His has won the *Journal of Macromarketing* Charles Slater Award for best article with co-author N. Dholakia, and the *Journal of Consumer Research* best article award with co-author A. Venkatesh. He has published several books including *Consuming People: From Political Economy to Theaters of Consumption*, co-authored by N. Dholakia, and is the founding editor of *Consumption, Markets & Culture*.

Gordon R. Foxall is Distinguished Research Professor at Cardiff University. His chief research interests lie in psychological theories of consumer choice and consumer innovativeness and their relationships to marketing management and the philosophy of psychology. He has published 22 books, over 200 refereed journal papers, and numerous other papers and chapters. He is a graduate of the Universities of Birmingham (PhD Industrial Economics & Business Studies) and Strathclyde (PhD Psychology). He also holds a higher doctorate of the University of Birmingham (DSocSc). He is a Fellow of the British Psychological Society (FBPsS) and the British Academy of Management (FBAM) and an Academician of the Academy of Social Science (AcSS).

Lars-Erik Gadde is Professor of Industrial Marketing at Chalmers University of Technology in Gothenburg. His research is focused on distribution network dynamics and buyer–supplier relationships in industrial networks. He is co-author of a couple of joint publications from the IMP-Group, for example, *Supply Network Strategies and Managing Business Relationships*. Journal publications include *Journal of Business Research, Industrial Marketing Management, International Journal of Research in Marketing, Journal of Management Studies, Marketing Theory*, and *Journal of Purchasing & Supply Management*.

Ronald C. Goodstein received his doctorate in marketing from Duke University 1990 and his Bachelor's from the University of Virginia in 1982. He is an Associate Professor at Georgetown University's McDonough School of Business. His research and teaching are in the areas of customer focus, strategic marketing management and positioning, consumer behavior, and public policy implications of marketing. He also teaches these concepts and strategies to executives around the world.

Christian Grönroos is Professor of Service and Relationship Marketing at Hanken Swedish School of Economics Finland and Chairman of the board of its research and knowledge center CERS – Center for Relationship Marketing and Service Management. His research interests relate to relationship marketing and service management and marketing as well as marketing theory. Recent published books are *Service Management and Marketing, Customer Management in Service Competition, In Search of a New Logic for Marketing* and *Foundations of Contemporary Theory*. He has received international awards and prizes, among them the American Marketing Association's Servsig Career Contribution to the Service Discipline Award and the Scandinavian Ahlsell Award and Erik Kempe Prize for his research and publications as well as the Finnish Pro Oeconomia Prize for best business book. He is a distinguished member of the *Finnish Society of Sciences and Letters.*

Chris Hackley earned his PhD from the University of Strathclyde, Scotland, UK, and is Professor of Marketing at Royal Holloway, University of London. His recent work includes a text book titled *Marketing – A Critical Introduction* (SAGE); a jointly authored article on young people and alcohol in the journal *Sociology*; and occasional journalism and broadcasting comment, most recently in THE and with BBC Radio 4. The second edition of Professor Hackley's textbook *Advertising and Promotion* will be published in late 2009.

Håkan Håkansson has the NEMI Chair of International Management at Norwegian School of Management, BI in Oslo. He is one of the founding members of the IMP group and has been highly involved in the development of the group. Recent publications include Håkansson, H., Waluszewski, A. (eds) (2007) *Knowledge and Innovation in Business and Industry. The Importance of Using Others* (Routledge) and Håkansson, H., Waluszewski, A., Prenkert, F., Baraldi, E. (eds) (2009) *Use of Science and Technology in Business* (Emerald), and two books in print – Håkansson, H., Ford, D., Gadde, L-E., Snehota, I., Waluszewski, A., *Business in Networks* (Wiley) and Håkansson, H., Lind, J., Kraus, K., (eds) *Accounting in Networks* (Routledge).

Jared M. Hansen is Assistant Professor of Marketing at the University of North Carolina, Charlotte. His research investigates methodology and the philosophy of science, pricing and promotions, market structure and competition, and business and society. He has published in several leading journals. He received his PhD from Texas Tech University, an MBA from Brigham Young University, and was a corporate buyer with Walmart prior to the MBA.

Elizabeth C. Hirschman is Professor II of Marketing at the Rutgers School of Business, Rutgers University, New Brunswick, NJ. She has published over 200 academic articles and papers in the marketing, consumer behavior, advertising, psychology, communications, and sociology literatures. Her current research interests include ethnicity, evolution, branding, and consumer production communities.

Margaret K. Hogg is Professor of Consumer Behaviour and Marketing in Lancaster University Management School. Her work has appeared in many international journals including: *Journal of Advertising*; *Journal of Business Research*; *Consumption, Markets and Culture*; *Journal of Marketing Management*; *The European Journal of Marketing*; *The International Journal of Advertising*; and the *Journal of Services Marketing*. She is editor of the SAGE's major works on consumer behaviour and currently holds an award under the French Agence Nationale de la Recherche (ANR/Programme Blanc).

Shelby D. Hunt is the Jerry S. Rawls and P. W. Horn Professor of Marketing at Texas Tech University, Lubbock, Texas. A past editor of the *Journal of Marketing* (1985–87), he is the author of numerous books, including *Foundations of Marketing Theory: Toward a General Theory of Marketing* (M.E. Sharpe, 2002), *Controversy in Marketing Theory: For Reason, Realism, Truth, and Objectivity* (M.E. Sharpe, 2003), and *A General Theory of Competition: Resources, Competences, Productivity, Economic Growth* (SAGE, 2000). One of the 250 most frequently cited researchers in economics and business (Thompson-ISI), he has written numerous articles on competitive theory, strategy, macromarketing, ethics, relationship marketing, channels of distribution, philosophy of science, and marketing theory.

D.G. Brian Jones is Professor of Marketing at Quinnipiac University. His research focuses on the history of marketing thought and has been published in the *Journal of Marketing*, *Journal of the Academy of Marketing Science*, *Journal of Macromarketing*, *Marketing Theory*, and other publications. He is editor of the *Journal of Historical Research in Marketing*.

Harold H. Kassarjian received his doctorate in social psychology from UCLA in 1960. Although he has had several visiting professorships, his academic home before his retirement had always been at UCLA. Upon becoming Professor Emeritus he served as the Dean of the School of Business and Management of the American University of Armenia, and as Adjunct Professor at California State University at Northridge. His interests are in Mass Communications and Consumer Behavior.

Hans Kjellberg is Associate Professor of marketing at Stockholm School of Economics. His research interests concern economic organizing in general and the shaping of markets in particular. He is currently engaged in projects on how marketing practices contribute to shape mundane markets and how investment banks shape the financial markets. Recent articles have appeared in *Consumption, Markets and Culture*, *Industrial Marketing Management*, and *Marketing Theory*.

Jonathan Knowles is the CEO of Type 2 Consulting, a New York-based consultancy that advises companies on how to use brand strategy to enhance business value. He is the author of *Vulcans, Earthlings and Marketing ROI* and many articles on the role of brands in business strategy. Prior to founding Type 2 Consulting in 2006, Jonathan's career path included banking, management consulting, brand strategy consulting, and brand valuation.

Roger A. Layton is an Emeritus Professor in the School of Marketing at the University of New South Wales. He was appointed Foundation Professor of Marketing at UNSW in 1967. His publications have appeared as book chapters and in journals including the *Journal of Macromarketing*, *Journal of Marketing Research*, and *The Service Industries Journal*. He was awarded the Order of Australia for his services to marketing, and is an Honorary Citizen of Guangzhou in recognition of his contribution, to higher education in China.

Victoria Little is Senior Lecturer in the Department of Marketing at the University of Auckland of Business School, New Zealand. Her research interest is in conducting relevant and impactful research at the nexus of marketing research, strategy and practice. She has consulted to a wide range of New Zealand businesses, and is part of the Contemporary Marketing Practice (CMP) Group. She has published in various international conference proceedings, and in the *Journal of Marketing Management*, *Journal of Business & Industrial Marketing*, *Marketing Theory*, and the *International Journal of Learning & Change*.

Robert F. Lusch is the Lisle & Roslyn Payne Professor of Marketing and Head of the Marketing Department in the Eller College of Management at the University of Arizona. His expertise is in the area of marketing strategy, marketing theory, and marketing channels. Professor Lusch has served as Editor of the *Journal of Marketing* and is the author of 125 scholarly articles and 18 books. In 1997, The Academy of Marketing Science awarded him its Distinguished Marketing Educator Award and the American Marketing Association on two occasions (1997 and 2005) presented him the Harold Maynard Award for contributions to marketing theory. In 2001 he received the Louis W. Stern Award from the American Marketing

Association for Outstanding Contributions to the Marketing Channels Literature (2001). The National Association of Accountants awarded him the Lybrand's Bronze Medal for contributions to the accounting literature (1978). The Marketing Management Association awarded him the Lifetime Contributions to Marketing Award in 2006. Professor Lusch has also served as Chairperson of the American Marketing Association, and trustee of the American Marketing Association Foundation.

Pauline Maclaran is Professor of Marketing and Consumer Research at Royal Holloway, University of London. Her publications have been in internationally recognized journals such as, the *Journal of Consumer Research, Psychology and Marketing, Journal of Advertising,* and *Consumption, Markets & Culture.* She is also Editor in Chief of *Marketing Theory,* a journal that promotes alternative and critical perspectives in marketing and consumer behavior.

Paula A. McLean is Visiting Associate Professor in the School of Business at Quinnipiac University. Her research focuses on the history of business education and includes biographies of business scholars.

Kristian Möller is a Research Professor and Director of the Service Factory and the Business Networks Domain at the Helsinki School of Economics. Formerly the President of the European Marketing Academy, Dr. Möller is an active member of the international research network. His current research is focused on business and innovation networks, competence-based marketing, and marketing theory. His work has been published in *California Management Review, Industrial Marketing Management, Journal of Business Research, Journal of Management Studies, Journal of Marketing Management,* and *Marketing Theory.*

John O'Shaughnessy is Emeritus Professor of Business at the Graduate School of Business, Columbia University, New York and was Senior Associate of the Judge Institute, Cambridge University. He has been a marketing research manager, sales manager, and industrial consultant in organization and marketing issues. He has published fourteen books on business topics and has published in many marketing journals including the *Journal of Marketing; Journal of Marketing Science* and the *Journal of Consumer Research.* Throughout his career he has had a special interest in the philosophy of science.

Jaqueline Pels is Marketing Professor at the University Torcuato Di Tella, Buenos Aires, Argentina. Her research experience is in business-to-business marketing, relationship marketing, professional services, and marketing theory. She was Chair of the Relationship Marketing Summit 2007 and of the AMA International Marketing Educators Conference 2000. Her publications have appeared in *European Journal of Marketing, Journal of Business in Industrial Markets, Journal of Relationship Marketing, Journal of Marketing Theory and Practice, Journal of Global Marketing* amongst others. She is Latin America editor for *Marketing Theory* and for the *Academy of Marketing Science-Review* and has served on the Editorial Boards of the *Journal of Marketing, Journal of International Marketing, Journal of Relationship Marketing,* and *Journal of Business in Developing Nations,* amongst others.

Gad Saad is Associate Professor of Marketing, and the holder of the Concordia University Research Chair in Evolutionary Behavioral Sciences and Darwinian Consumption at the John Molson School of Business, Concordia University, Montreal, Quebec, Canada.

Michael Saren is Professor of Marketing at Leicester University, UK. He was a founding editor in 2001 of *Marketing Theory* and co-editor of *Rethinking Marketing* (1999, SAGE). His introductory text is *Marketing Graffiti* (2006, Elsevier). He has also published articles in the *International Journal of Research in Marketing, Consumption, Markets & Culture, Industrial Marketing Management, Journal of Management Studies, European Journal of Marketing, Journal of Business and Industrial Marketing* and *International Business Review*.

Eric H. Shaw is Professor of Marketing at Florida Atlantic University. His research focuses on the history of marketing thought and development of marketing theory, as well as marketing strategy. His research has appeared in the *Journal of the Academy of Marketing Science, Journal of Macromarketing, Decision Sciences, Journal of Marketing Theory and Practice, Marketing Theory*, and *Theoretical Developments in Marketing*, among others. He is Associate Editor of the *Journal of Historical Research in Marketing*.

Barbara Stern was a Professor II of Marketing and Vice-chair of the department at Rutgers Business School. Her research has appeared in the *Journal of Consumer Research, Journal of Marketing, Journal of Advertising, International Journal of Electronic Commerce, Journal of the Academy of Marketing Science (JAMS)*, and other publications. She was the founding co-editor of the journal *Marketing Theory* and received the American Advertising Association Award for Outstanding Contribution to Research in 1997.

David W. Stewart is the Dean of the A. Gary Anderson Graduate School of Management at the University of California, Riverside. Prior to assuming his responsibilities as dean in July 2007, he was a member of the faculty of the Marshall School of Business at the University of Southern California where he held the Robert E. Brooker Chair in Marketing and served as deputy dean of the School for five years. Dr. Stewart is a past editor of both the *Journal of Marketing* and the *Journal of the Academy of Marketing Science*.

Mark Tadajewski is Lecturer in Critical Marketing at the School of Management, University of Leicester. His research has appeared in the *Journal of Marketing Management, Organization, Journal of Macromarketing* and *Marketing Theory* among others. He is the editor of numerous SAGE Major Works, as well as *Critical Marketing: Issues in Contemporary Marketing* (with D. Brownlie, Wiley).

Stephen L. Vargo is a Shidler Distinguished Professor at the University of Hawai'i at Manoa. His primary areas of research are marketing theory and thought and consumers' evaluative reference scales. He has had articles published in the *Journal of Marketing*, the *Journal of the Academy of Marketing Science*, the *Journal of Service Research*, the *Journal of Retailing*, and other major marketing journals and serves on four editorial review boards, including the *Journal of Marketing* and the *Journal of Service Research*. Professor Vargo has been awarded the *Harold H. Maynard Award* by the American Marketing Association for 'significant contribution to marketing theory and thought.'

Robin Wensley is Professor of Policy and Marketing at the Warwick Business School since 1986 and has been Chair of the School, Chair of the Faculty of Social Studies and Chair of the Council of the Tavistock Institute of Human Relations. He was previously with RHM Foods, Tube Investments, and the London Business School and was visiting Professor twice at the

UCLA and University of Florida. Professor Wensley is co-author of *The Handbook of Marketing* (SAGE, 2002, 2006) and is currently Director of the UK Advanced Institute of Management Research (AIM).

Detlev Zwick is Associate Professor of Marketing at the Schulich School of Business, York University, Toronto, Canada. His research focuses on consumer behavior in high-technology and computer-mediated markets, cultural and social theories of consumption, and the critical cultural studies of marketing and management practice. His dissertation entitled *The Speed of Money: Investing as Consumption in the Age of Computer-Mediated Communication*, won a national award from the Marketing Science Institute. He holds a PhD from the University of Rhode Island.

Introduction

Pauline Maclaran, Michael Saren, Barbara Stern,
and Mark Tadajewski

THEORY BUILDING AND THEORISING IN MARKETING

The development of theory is essential, not only for knowledge creation, but also for academic status. Disciplines build their own bodies of theory and apply their own unique lens to particular phenomena. In this respect, marketing is something of a magpie in that it 'borrows' many of its theories from other disciplines, particularly psychology and economics (Mittelstaedt, 1990). The challenge for marketing as an evolving, but relatively young discipline is to build its own distinct body of theory (Murray et al., 1997). To advance as a discipline, marketing needs to acknowledge and, in many cases, reconsider its theoretical foundations and conduct more research that contributes to the nature of knowledge and theory in marketing.

The aim of this handbook is to act as a stimulus for theory development by providing a comprehensive overview of key issues in marketing theory. In so doing, the editors hope to give greater conceptual cohesion to the field, by drawing together many disparate perspectives and presenting contributions from the leading scholars in one volume.

The handbook thus provides a substantive reference point from which to further develop the area by offering a comprehensive and up-to-date treatment of the major approaches, issues and debates and setting these within their historical contexts. Before going on to give a short summary of the six sections and their contents, we will first discuss some of the main issues concerning the development of marketing theory.

There have been many calls from within the marketing academy for a greater emphasis on marketing theory, in relation to both its development and applications (Alderson, 1957, 1965; Alderson and Cox, 1948; Brown, 1948). Notwithstanding many longstanding debates, arguments continue about what this theory should look like, with little resulting agreement (Brownlie et al., 1999; Dholakia and Arndt, 1985; Hunt, 2001, 2003; Sheth, 1992). A major reason why scholars cannot agree on a common definition for theory is because, depending on their philosophical orientation, they have different views of what constitutes theory.

Even so, underpinning all these debates is a steadily more explicit recognition that each way of seeking knowledge will invariably be a partial view, highlighting some features of the object of interest, whilst eliding others (Laughlin, 1995; O'Shaughnessy, 2009), leading some to call for multiple paradigm research (Gioia and Pitre, 1990) which utilises the insights from a range of paradigms in the production of theory (Lewis and Grimes, 1999; Tadajewski, 2008). At the moment, within marketing and consumer research, such exercises have largely been at the methodological rather than metatheoretical level (e.g. Price and Arnould, 1998), and these investigations remain the preserve of a comparatively small group of scholars (see O'Shaughnessy, Möller et al., and Brodie et al., this volume) More generally, we can categorise the main 'ways of seeking knowledge' in marketing theory into very broad ideal types of positivist, interpretive and critical traditions (Hudson and Ozanne, 1988; Murray and Ozanne, 1991; Sherry, 1991), with each discussing what constitutes theory in contrasting ways.

For example, a positivistic researcher (cf. Hunt, 1991) will consider the production of theory to begin with a process of hypothesis postulation, based on a rigorous and objective evaluation of prior scientific research by a scholar who adopts a stance of relative value neutrality and objectivity (e.g. Senior and Lee, 2008; cf. Popper, 1976). Ontologically, therefore, by virtue of utilising the insights of a large range of previous studies, subscribers to this paradigm presume that the social world is largely independent of the idiosyncratic perspective of the researcher (Laughlin, 1995). Epistemologically, these initial hypotheses are subject to rigorous critique through a process of empirical testing and possible refutation (cf. Senior and Lee, 2008). Assuming these hypotheses are not subsequently refuted, the positivist researcher is able to say tentatively that the theory is true (Hunt, 1990). Ideally, such theory will result in the production of 'law-like generalizations' (Hunt, 1991) which enable the prediction of marketplace and consumer behaviour and is thereby used to inform managerial decision-making (Arndt, 1985).

By contrast, an interpretivist researcher questions the possibility of objectivity that is assumed in positivist research (Hudson and Ozanne, 1988). They are likely to contend that the practice of science and by extension theory development can never be an objective or dispassionate exercise. One reason for this is that the researcher is not 'separate' from the world, but an active participant in it and, indeed, the very act of observing can affect the outcome. Secondly, researchers can only view phenomena through their own individual subjective history, life experiences and academic socialisation (e.g. Markin, 1970).

Thus, interpretive researchers stress the 'emergent' nature of research. This means, not simply that findings emerge, but that the research design *per se* may be modified as a result of initial exploratory excursions into the field. Also, research need not necessarily be directed towards the production of nomothetic generalisations given the 'time- and context-specific' nature of interpretive research (Hudson and Ozanne, 1988: 513). For those working through this perspective, contextual 'detail becomes the *theory*' (Laughlin, 1995: 67; cf. Markin, 1970). Consequently, 'theory' is considered more as a story that explains how researchers and informants construct their worlds and the relationship between certain events and actions (Price, 2007). Here, theory is seen more as a process that involves deriving situation-relative insights that might result in analytical abstractions from the study of data-rich research contexts. The theory-practice link in this case is more complex than for positivistic research; some interpretive scholars argue that this type of research can provide managerially useful insights (Elliott and Jankel-Elliott, 2003), while others make a case for this 'scientific style' (Hirschman, 1985) to consider consumption research as an end in itself, not necessarily generating knowledge for marketing managers (Cayla and Eckhardt, 2008; Holbrook, 1985).

A researcher inclined towards the use of Critical Theory will instead view theory production as a historically informed activity that aims to question the existing organisation of society in some respect. Running throughout the work of the Frankfurt School group of scholars was a commitment to 'heighten critical historical consciousness', which in the words of Leo Lowenthal, was their 'theoretical agenda' (Lowenthal, 1987: 70). For scholars in this tradition, theory and practice were inextricably linked in at least two senses. Firstly, they revised their theoretical perspectives on the basis of empirical evidence collected, for example, via observation (Fromm, 1962/2006), interviews and focus groups (Petersen and Willig, 2002). Secondly, they viewed theory production itself as 'adequate practice' (Lowenthal, 1987: 195). This was because it stimulated a critical consciousness among those exposed to it: 'It clashes with and is resisted by the cultural and, in part, political establishment' (Lowenthal, 1987: 195) by revealing 'the gap between the claims of culture and what it claims to offer' (Fromm, 1956/2005). Theory production from a Critical Theory stance, consequently, does not simply try to describe or explain the nature of society, it wants to go beyond this and critique it, offering insights that serve to create a more 'sane society' than one predicated on consumerism (Fromm, 1976/2007) and the continued expansion of the 'dominant social paradigm' (Kilbourne et al., 1997).

Thus, in order to understand developments in marketing theory, we need to understand the philosophy and sociology of science debates that have taken place in marketing and the contexts in which these have evolved, since these have clear implications for the way we understand the development of knowledge about marketing and consumption phenomena. An important role for the handbook is to provide this historical, philosophical, theoretical and conceptual record.

THE NEED FOR THEORY

The earliest calls for the theoretical development of marketing were made by Lyndon Brown (1948) and Wroe Alderson and Reavis Cox (1948). At this time, the latter authors argued 'Only a sound theory of marketing can raise the analysis of such problems above the level of an empirical art and establish truly scientific criteria for setting up hypotheses and selecting the facts by means of which to test them' (1948: 139). Their rationale was that better theory would help identify what problems required solution and thus direct the researcher towards an understanding of which facts to assemble and how to analyse them. Robert Bartels (1951: 325), another early contributor to the debate, claimed that marketing 'can scarcely be said to have attained scientific status' because of its lack of general theories and principles to guide its scholarship. Others reinforced this view (Buzzell, 1963; White, 1940), demonstrating the extent to which marketing researchers were over-reliant on descriptive, qualitative research that remained at the contextual level and failed to achieve analytical generalisability – i.e. theory.

In the late 1950s, this lack of theory was further driven home in the Ford and Carnegie Reports on the state of business education in the US, which pronounced business schools' curricula as based on vocational research, which lacked the utilisation of rigorous research methods and analytical techniques (Tadajewski, 2006a). Both these reports advocated the adoption of more scientific approaches to management education. As a result, the Marketing Science Institute was established in 1961 and this began to emphasise theory to improve business performance, citing three key reasons (Halbert, 1965):

1 Theoretical rules are a prerequisite for developing knowledge. Without a theoretical base we have no base for analysis, nor can we decide what is relevant or not (e.g. Senior and Lee, 2008).
2 Theory can reduce the risk behind taking decisions and can therefore assist practitioners in increasing their productivity.
3 It is not sufficient for marketers to rely on theories developed in other disciplines as theoretical structures from one area are rarely directly applicable to another (e.g. Murray et al., 1997; O'Shaughnessy, 1997).

This early identification of a need for theory stimulated a variety of academics throughout the 1950s and 1960s to rally for various perspectives. These ranged from functionalist conceptualisations of marketing phenomena (e.g. Alderson, 1957, 1965), to empirically grounded and hermeneutic interpretations of consumer behaviours (e.g. Dichter, 1960). Functionalists viewed marketing as an organised behaviour system through which, for example, raw materials such as leather would undergo various assortments and transformation that ultimately result in a given end product, such as a pair of shoes (Alderson and Martin, 1965). Alderson's work was lauded by the Ford Foundation – the most important funding body for marketing research during the 1950s and 1960s (Bartels, 1988) – and was axiologically premised on making the marketing system run both more effectively and efficiently (Alderson, 1957, 1965). However, functionalism never became the central theoretical axis of marketing theory (Wooliscroft et al., 2006). Even at this time, there were multiple theoretical influences waxing and waning. Indeed up to this day, academics continue to argue about what marketing theory should look like with little resulting agreement (see Brown and Fisk, 1984; Brownlie et al., 1999; Dholakia and Arndt, 1985; Greenley, 1995; Hunt, 2002, 2003; McDonagh, 1995; Senior and Lee, 2008).

It has been argued that the need for theory is now even greater, because in an increasingly information-saturated world, knowledge needs to be firmly rooted in order to be distinctive and meaningful. Academics are now, not only producers of marketing knowledge, but also merchandisers, retailers and consumers of it as authors, researchers, teachers and consultants (Brownlie and Saren, 1995). One effect of this process is that the product life cycle of marketing knowledge is shortening and has a shorter shelf life. Under these conditions, higher-level theory can provide an anchor and a referent for the fast moving current generalisations (fmcg) of marketing information in order to differentiate and set them in context.

LEVELS OF THEORY

We consider that it is important to recognise and outline briefly here the different levels at which theories have been conceptualised (Maclaran et al., 2009). They can be classified by level of abstraction along a continuum from metatheory, through grand theory and middle range theory to practice theory, and from high to low levels of abstraction (Van Sell and Kalofissudus, 2007).

Metatheory is theory about theory, i.e. a body of knowledge about a field of study, or about what that field should concern itself with. It remains at a highly conceptual level although it also often incorporates other levels of theory. Much critical theorising takes place at this metatheoretical level in an attempt to deconstruct the field of marketing *per se* thereby overturning fundamental claims and assumptions (see, e.g. Bradshaw and Firat, 2007).

Grand Theory seeks a broad, but slightly less conceptual perspective about the field. Howard and Sheth's (1969) model of buyer behaviour is a good illustration of grand theory in that it tries to account for an overriding theory of how consumers behave in the purchase decision process. One of the reasons that marketing remains self-conscious about its scientific status (Bartels, 1951: 325) is because of its lack of general theories and principles to guide its scholarship (Saad, 2008).

Middle Range Theory was developed by Merton (1968) in order to build a stronger relationship with practice. Middle range theory seeks a less broad scope of phenomena than grand theory and is more specific. Unlike grand theory, it does not try to account for all the range of phenomena in a discipline or sub-field. Rather than trying to theorise abstract entities such as social systems, Merton regards middle range theory as beginning with the collection of observable data from specific and delimited research contexts.

Consumer Culture Theoretics (Arnould and Thompson, 2007) concentrate on the development of theories at the middle range.

Practice Theory tries to explain the way phenomena occur in practice, refusing to prioritise the conceptual importance of *either* individual actors or societal structures (Allen, 2002; Reckwitz, 2002; Whittington, 2006). It neither assumes that individual actors socially construct the world in the absence of societal influences or that societal structures completely determine microlevel action (Whittington, 2006). This type of theorising seeks to achieve a balance between theory and practice without privileging one over the other (Böhm, 2002).

THE ONGOING DEBATES

One of the most enduring debates, which still permeates many discussions today, concerns whether marketing is a science (Alderson and Cox, 1948; Bartels, 1951; Buzzell, 1963; Hunt, 1976), an art (Vaile, 1949) or somewhere in between the two (Stainton, 1952). Scholars have taken up various positions at either end of the art/science continuum (McTier Anderson, 1994). For example, whereas Hutchinson (1952) believed that the nature of marketing meant that it must always remain an art, Hunt (1976) argued strongly for its scientific status. Indeed, by the 1970s marketing science firmly dominated the discipline with a plethora of quantitative analysis techniques. The development of computer technology had increasingly permeated the academy during the 1960s, which enabled researchers to conduct much more complex statistical analyses (Wilkie and Moore, 2003). This concentration on method and technique led to criticism that marketers were too fascinated with 'tool kits', emphasising technology rather than theory (Hunt, 1983).

Another debate concerns the choice of philosophical orientation that is appropriate for marketing theory. According to various scholars, marketing theory should be fallibilistic realist (Hunt, 1984, 2002, 2003), critical realist (Easton, 2002), critical pluralist (Siegel, 1988), critical relativist (Anderson, 1983), critical theoretical (Bradshaw and Fırat, 2007; McDonagh, 2002; Murray and Ozanne, 1991, 1997), feminist (Bristor and Fischer, 1993, 1995; Maclaran and Catterall, 2000), humanist (Monieson, 1988), posthumanist (Campbell et al., 2006), postmodern (Brown, 1995, 1998; Sherry, 1991) and postcolonialist (Jack, 2008) amongst others. These debates are often linked to arguments about appropriate methodologies, ontologies, epistemologies, views of human nature and the value of social change (Anderson, 1986; Calder and Tybout, 1987, 1989; Holbrook and O'Shaughnessy, 1988; Jack and Westwood, 2006; Monieson, 1988; Muncy and Fisk, 1987).

Over the years, these continuing debates have spawned many different classifications of the main schools of thought in marketing, each with particular implications for theory. Carmen (1980) identifies six (microeconomic, persuasion/attitude change, conflict resolution, generalist system, functionalist and social exchange). Fisk and Meyers (1982) propose another six (network flow, market scarcity, competitive marketing management, evolutionary systems change, general systems and dissipative structures). Arndt (1985) has four paradigms (logical empiricist, subjective world, socio-political and liberating). Sheth et al. (1988) list twelve schools (commodity, functional, functionalist, regional, institutional, managerial, buyer behaviour, activist, macromarketing, organisational dynamics, systems and social exchange). Kerin (1996) chooses six metaphors that characterise marketing science and practice in each of the six decades since the launch of the *Journal of Marketing* in 1936 (applied economics, a managerial activity, a quantitative science, a behavioural science, a decision science and an integrative science). More recently, Wilkie and Moore (2003) have identified the '4 eras' of thought development. These are: 1900–1920: 'Founding the Field'; 1920–1950: 'Formalizing the Field'; 1950–1980: 'A Paradigm Shift-Marketing, Management, and the Sciences'; 1980–present; 'The Shift Intensifies – A Fragmentation of the Mainstream'.

Yet, despite such analyses that attempt to group marketing research into coherent streams of knowledge, most commentators recognise the lack of progress in developing marketing theory *per se*. Three key reasons for this have been put forward (Saren, 2000: 31–34):

1   There is a lack of attention to history (Baker, 2001; Greyser, 1997; Levy, 2003). Too often, new generations of marketing scholars reinvent the wheel, ignoring marketing's history and theoretical foundations (Baker, 1995; Tadajewski and Saren, 2008). Fullerton (1987) draws attention to the 'myth of the marketing era' and makes a compelling case that strong evidence of sales and marketing orientations can be found in the production era. Despite these doubts about the four-eras model, it still remains widely used in current introductory textbooks, much to the chagrin of marketing historians. It is not without reason, therefore, that marketing is bemoaned as 'ahistorical' (Fullerton, 1987).
2   There has been an over-emphasis on quantitative methods as part of marketing scholars' quest to claim scientific status. It has been argued that this has led to a lack of new theory generation, because such methods are more suited to theory testing (Bartels, 1988; Venkatesh, 1985). Although much theory generation in consumer research has arisen from interpretivist perspectives during the last twenty years, this has not gained mainstream marketing acceptance (Arnould and Thompson, 2007).
3   The pronounced shift to research specialism from the early 1980s onwards (reflected by the range of new marketing journals) has brought about theoretical fragmentation of the mainstream. It has become more difficult for scholars to engage with others beyond their particular sub-area due to theoretical and conceptual differences (Wilkie and Moore, 2006; cf. Hirschman, 1985), even though some scholars have argued that such a cross-fertilization of ideas would be highly desirable (Davies and Fitchett, 2005; Muncy and Fisk, 1987). This fragmentation has been encouraged by the pluralisation of publication outlets and by journal editors' zealous defence of research specialisms (Easley et al., 2000; Tadajewski, 2008).

This expansion of publication outlets presents a problem for marketing researchers and scholars because of the number of books, journals and articles available and necessary for them to consult. With this in mind, in designing this handbook we have selected leading experts covering the entire range of major theoretical fields. Each author has contributed a new chapter on their topic, which together provides readers with a comprehensive and an up-to-date handbook of marketing theory. The handbook is divided into six sections: (1) *Historical Development of Marketing Theory*; (2) *The Philosophical Underpinnings of Theory*; (3) *Major Theoretical Debates*; (4) *Impact of Theory on Representations of the Consumer*; (5) *Impact of Theory on Representations of the Marketing Organisation*; (6) *Contemporary and Future Issues in Marketing Theory*.

SECTION 1: HISTORICAL DEVELOPMENT OF MARKETING THEORY

The history of marketing theory is a topic that has long merited the attention of a variety of scholars. Building upon the tradition that ranges from the work of Robert Bartels' (1988) to Paul Converse's (1951) the 'Development of Marketing Theory: Fifty Years of Progress' scholars have long considered the development of marketing theory an essential building block for the future progress of the discipline (Alderson and Cox, 1948).

In equal measure, an understanding of the history of marketing theory and thought, which elucidates all of the various 'schools of thought' (Shaw and Jones, 2005), remains important for research students and seasoned academics alike. It goes some way in preventing scholars from reinventing various theoretical, conceptual and methodological wheels that conceivably could occur if theoreticians are historically illiterate (Hollander, 1995). In recognition of the importance of historical studies in foregrounding the further development of marketing theory, the first section of this collection engages with our disciplinary history in all its many facets, ranging from the schools of thought in marketing, the development of consumer and marketing research, to the refinement of advertising theory and practice.

The first contribution by Shaw et al. introduces the development of the earliest schools in marketing thought. By earliest schools we mean, of course, the functional, commodity, institutional and interregional schools of thought. Via a close reading of the development of each of these schools Shaw et al. provide an exceptional orientation device for those new to the development of marketing theory, which is especially important given the fact that some of the work of scholars from these schools is often seen to underpin the most widely subscribed to school in current marketing thought, the marketing management school (Shaw and Jones, 2005; Sheth et al., 1988). Nor should we assume that, simply because these schools of thought are not given so much attention now, such labels can no longer describe the work of a distinct group of academics. As Shaw et al. and Zinn and Johnson (1990) have revealed, the ideas associated with the commodity school, to give one example, continue to be reflected in contemporary literature.

The second contribution by Jones et al. brings the analysis introduced by Shaw et al. to almost the present day. We say 'almost here' because other recent commentators (Lagrosen and Svensson, 2006) have attempted to make the case for introducing a number of further schools of thought, namely, services and relationship marketing schools respectively. Again, whether these form distinct schools of thought is itself debatable. Some have argued, for example, that a 'services dominant logic' underpins or should be viewed as undergirding all marketing theory and practice (Vargo and Lusch, 2004).

Whatever stance one takes on this issue, there are a variety of intellectual sources that can be drawn upon and Chapters 12 and 23 in this collection will introduce the interested reader to the new 'schools' flagged up by Lagrosen and Svensson (2006). Putting these

issues aside, Jones et al.'s chapter charts the development of marketing thought from roughly the 1950s to the present. They introduce a range of schools including the marketing management, marketing systems, consumer behaviour, macromarketing, marketing history and the exchange schools. Each of these schools is dissected by the authors in considerable detail.

The chapter by Kassarjian and Goodstein clearly articulates the development of consumer research as a distinct discipline. In their contribution, Professors Kassarjian and Goodstein take a perceptive and innovative approach to historical research in marketing. They interweave their account of the emergence and subsequent shifts in the theoretical emphases of consumer research with external environmental changes. Such a strategy overcomes a major criticism that the history of consumer research is often depicted in a decontextualised (Schroeder, 2000; Scully, 1996) and ahistorical manner (Tadajewski, 2006b, 2009). Taking us on a journey from the earliest days in the development of marketing and consumer thought, through the Second World War, Kassarjian and Goodstein account for the adoption of the various 'grand theories of human behavior' within the discipline, charting their successes and ultimate declines. The authors draw upon their considerable knowledge of the development of consumer research to clearly delineate the history of the subject (see also Belk, 2009; Levy, 2003; Mittelstaedt, 1990; Tadajewski, 2006b). There is, however, an absence in their chapter that is worth highlighting in the interest of completeness, namely, Kassarjian's own contribution to the discipline, which has been considerable. From 1960 onwards he has played a major role in furthering our understanding of consumer research methods and theory in the areas of consumer perception to name just one topic (e.g. Kassarjian, 1963).

In another extensive historical overview, the next chapter, by David Stewart, includes the prehistory of market research. He documents the informal exchange of various forms of business intelligence from the fourteenth century onwards. Moving closer to the present, Stewart notes the changing nature of the US industrial economy and its implications for the emergence and 'evolution' of marketing research. Naturally enough, with the growing distance between producers and the ultimate consumer, it became increasingly important for producers to understand the nature of consumer needs, wants and desires. Indeed, the history of marketing practice often reveals that producers were cognisant of the value and importance of market research in determining production schedules. Stewart notes the key figures and companies in the history of both marketing theory and practice, highlighting the key techniques and methodological tools that have been adopted during the course of the twentieth and twenty-first centuries.

Rounding off our historical surveys, Chris Hackley sketches the history of advertising thought. Hackley parses the voluminous advertising literature into three key strands: managerial, scientific and cultural approaches. Each of the three approaches that Hackley details can potentially feed into the others and each conceptualises advertising theory and practice in slightly different, but not necessarily incommensurable ways. Managerial and scientific approaches are, he documents, the most prominent strands in the marketing and advertising literatures. More recently, he claims, there has been what can be called an anthropological turn in advertising, with scholars and practitioners alike, beginning to appreciate and apply the methods and insights of cultural anthropology in campaign and theory development.

SECTION 2: THE PHILOSOPHICAL UNDERPINNINGS OF THEORY

As Shelby Hunt and Jared Hansen point out in the first chapter in this section, all research is underpinned by philosophical assumptions. Research reflects a particular way of looking at the world (ontological assumptions) and

possesses a certain orientation that dictates legitimate ways of establishing valid claims to knowledge (epistemological assumptions), all of which will influence the methodology used in consumer and market research (Anderson, 1986). Debates surrounding what constitutes the most appropriate way of seeking knowledge about marketing phenomena are long standing. These range from the first philosophy of science debates that began at the turn of the twentieth century between the *laissez faire* oriented scholars and their German Historical counterparts (Jones and Monieson, 1990), through the empiricist versus interpretive oriented motivation researchers of the 1950s and 1960s (Tadajewski, 2006b), to the 'spirited debate' between the critical relativist (Anderson, 1983, 1986) and scientific realist contingents (Hunt, 1990, 1992).

Hunt and Hansen rally against a variety of forms of relativism. In marketing, critical relativism was initially put forward by Paul Anderson in a series of seminal contributions to the philosophy of marketing thought. He considered the existing logical empiricist emphasis of marketing theory to be seriously problematic. Perhaps the major objection, among many identified by Anderson, is that the objective image of science as a process of hypothetico-deductive reasoning propounded by logical empiricists is not consistent with the actual practice of science. Researchers exhibit varying degrees of tenacity when it comes to their favoured theories and concepts and do not seek to undermine them (Feyerabend, 1975). But more than this, Anderson wanted to question the idea that there was a single scientific method that could be used in the search for knowledge (Anderson, 1986; see also Muncy and Fisk, 1987; O'Shaughnessy, 1997).

By contrast, Hunt and Jared outline the problems that they and a number of philosophers of science perceive with respect to relativism. In an effort to theoretically sensitise marketing scholars to the alternative philosophical perspectives sketched out by philosophers of science, they discuss at length realism and its more recent cousin, scientific realism, explicating this position through recourse to actual case studies in the marketing literature. Scientific realism with its explicit fallibilistic emphasis is, Hunt and Jared claim, the most appropriate philosophy for marketing theory if we are interested in distinguishing 'illusion from reality' (Hunt, 1990: 9). Obviously, not all agree with this interpretation of scientific realism as the most appropriate philosophy for marketing, but this in itself indicates the vitality of marketing theory (e.g. Anderson, 1988; Kavanagh, 1994; Muncy and Fisk, 1987; O'Shaughnessy, 1997, 2009; Peter, 1992).

Following Hunt and Jared, our next contribution by Fuat Fırat and Mark Tadajewski outlines the history and debate surrounding 'critical marketing studies' (Tadajewski and Brownlie, 2008; Tadajewski and Maclaran, 2009). One of the central axes of critical marketing studies is the idea that there is something not quite right with the way marketing is currently conceived and practiced. Gone is the emphasis on distributive justice, critique and a sceptical questioning of the key concepts that are routinely invoked in marketing, with these having been replaced by a relatively uncritical managerial performativity. Theoretical and conceptual touchstones like consumer sovereignty or the marketing concept are accepted as givens, and they are not examined to see whether they have theoretical merit, reflect the present structuring of the marketing system or, indeed, act as ideological veils for inequitable marketplace power relations.

Critical marketing studies, Fırat and Tadajewski assert, try to do exactly this, examining key marketing ideas, concepts and theories, asking questions about whose interests these serve and what power relations they elide. Important in this undertaking is the use of some form of critical social theory such as that associated with Marxism, the Frankfurt School, Feminism, Poststructuralism and others (Saren, 2007). This reference to 'critical' social theory should not, critical marketers tell us, be taken to indicate that critical marketing is totally dismissive of marketing *per se*. But rather that critical marketing is concerned with engaging in a negative activity, which is in turn positive in its own way. As a prominent Critical Theorist, Leo Lowenthal suggested, 'it is exactly the negative [in Critical Theory studies] that was the positive: this consciousness of not going along, the refusal. The essence of Critical Theory is really the inexorable analysis of what is' (Lowenthal, 1987: 62). In other words, as Fırat and Tadajewski explain, we can consider critical marketing studies as an attempt at questioning the status quo or what passes for received wisdom in marketing and consumer research.

Our next chapter, by Kristian Möller, Jacqueline Pels and Michael Saren argues that over the last thirty years, marketing theory and practice has become increasingly heterogeneous. To illustrate this, the authors provide a meta-theoretical interrogation of the domain of marketing theory. They make the case that although paradigms provide us with a way of viewing marketing theory and practices in all their many facets, paradigms also limit what we see. Following the work of Johan Arndt, Möller et al. ask marketing theoreticians to consider the value of exploring marketing using multiple paradigms and concomitantly with a plurality of research methodologies. Drawing from the organisation studies literature, they outline a variety of ways to negotiate the restrictions of incommensurability in an effort to illustrate the benefits of multiple paradigm research, paradigm interplay and metatriangulation, among others.

In the final contribution to section two, John O'Shaughnessy examines the debates surrounding scientific methods and the multiple systems of explanation that marketing scholars can draw upon. In a rigorous, critical analysis, O'Shaughnessy questions the idea that there can be one single scientific method, arguing instead that multiple ways of seeking knowledge are open to marketing and consumer researchers. Indeed, in an analysis that cuts to the heart of many discussions about marketing theory, O'Shaughnessy can be read as suggesting that there never have been, nor are there likely to be any law-like generalisations in marketing theory.

In a seminal review O'Shaughnessy introduces a whole range of key ideas from the philosophy of science including: methodological monism, methodological individualism, methodological exclusivism, methodological pluralism and perspectivism, along with clarifying the ubiquitous term 'paradigm' and the controversy about the incommensurability of paradigms, among others. As an enthusiastic exponent of paradigmatic pluralism himself, like the contributors of our previous chapter, O'Shaughnessy cautions marketing scholars from uncritically subscribing to any one paradigm and in so doing, refusing to consider the perspectives offered by other, perhaps equally compelling – if different – ways of understanding marketing and consumer phenomena.

SECTION 3: MAJOR THEORETICAL DEBATES

This section examines some of the major controversies that have permeated theoretical debates in marketing. The chapters here explore the controversies surrounding different conceptual perspectives in marketing and examine in depth the influence on development of theory of the various schools of thought, which were discussed in Section 1. These schools and their theories are set in their contemporary context and cover major debates about theories concerning the performativity of markets, the concept of networks, debates (and silence) about market ideology and the service dominant logic in marketing.

The first contribution by Luis Araujo and Hans Kjellberg explains how marketing practice and practices influence the operation of markets. Whatever one's opinion of the ontological status of the market, the view that marketing managers take of the nature and scope of the markets in which they consider operating is important, not just epistemologically,

but also teleologically. In other words, the particular definition and understanding of the market that managers adopt itself affects their operations and the outcomes in their chosen, enacted market 'place'. Arajo and Kjellberg discuss the empirical aspects and theoretical implications of this market-making perspective of marketing practice.

The Service Dominant Logic (SDL) approach is outlined by Steve Vargo and Robert Lusch (2004, 2006, 2008) in the next chapter. As a new contender for dominance in marketing theory, in a short time SDL has raised strong interest and discussion about theory development in marketing. The focus of SDL is on marketing as a value co-creation process that is service-based. Marketers can only provide value propositions, embedded in offerings, and their value depends entirely on the experiential evaluation of customers. They contend that service is the fundamental basis of exchange and 'goods are distribution mechanisms for service provision'. Another key aspect is the role of know-how, capabilities and competencies ('operant resources'), which are the key resources for both creating value propositions and extracting value from them as the primary source of competitive advantage. The corollary is that the role of tangible, finite 'operand resources' is to provide the raw material for the pro-active intangible resources to 'activate', as it were.

Central to the SDL approach is its distinction from that referred to by Vargo and Lusch as the historical, still prevailing Goods Dominant Logic (GDL) based on tangible goods and the activities associated with their delivery. The GDL is presented as an antithesis to the SDL, which provides a *'shift in thinking'*:

It represents a shift from thinking about value in terms of *operand resources* — usually tangible, static resources that require some action to make them valuable – to *operant resources* – usually intangible, dynamic resources that are capable of creating value. That is, whereas G-D logic sees services as (somewhat inferior to goods) *units of output*, S-D logic sees service as a *process* - doing something for another party. (Vargo and Lusch 2008: 8)

Vargo and Lusch advocate that the SDL should form the basis of a unified theory of marketing. It can be seen more in terms of an orientation, however; a perspective providing guidelines for how certain existing schools of marketing should be utilised in normative fashion in value creation.

As Djelic (2007) observes, the emergence of the twentieth century neoliberal ideology of politics and markets was indeed a curious blend of economic liberalism, Calvinist doctrine and Spencerian evolutionism. Robin Wensley was one of the earliest marketing academics to question the limits of the extension of the marketing analogy, particularly in the professional and public sector contexts (Wensley, 1990). His chapter in this handbook covers what he regards as the central issues relating to the ideological aspects of markets from two different perspectives. Firstly, in terms of market ideology, he examines the efficacy of the concept of 'the magic of the market' as the solution to problems of welfare and choice associated with Adam Smith's 'invisible hand'. Wensley critically analyses the development and evolution of what has been labelled as the hegemony of neoliberal perspectives on the efficacy of markets and market mechanisms. In the final part of this contribution, he considers global and cultural issues, including issues of identity and how these relate to markets and consumption.

Arguably, the dominant conceptualisation of what is considered a 'marketing phenomenon' in normative marketing theory is centred on the notion of exchange (Bagozzi, 1978). Any marketing ideas or actions involve the *exchange* of products, services, knowledge and money. Thus, in this view, three components must exist as *sine qua non* for an exchange to occur, namely, a seller, a buyer and a product:

- Marketing production
- Products and services
- Buyers and consumption

This conceptualisation of marketing has stimulated some major debates in the decades

since it was first proposed and, in the penultimate chapter in this section, Richard Bagozzi elaborates and reflects on his notion of exchange as fundamental to marketing.

The development of theory and research in marketing is heavily dependent on the language we use and marketing thought and writing is full of metaphors, tropes and figures of speech. The chapter by Stephen Brown opens with an illustration of the power of the metaphor with reference to Levitt's original Harvard Business Review (HBR) article 'Marketing Myopia'. He reminds us that this was published as a reply to motivation researchers such as Ernest Dichter, who were damaging marketing's image at the time (Levitt, 1960). By stressing that 'proper' marketing placed customer needs at the centre of its operation, Brown argues that Levitt's article represented a brilliantly argued refutation of 'the rip-off brigade'. Regarding its core metaphor, however, Brown reminds us that when we re-read *Marketing Myopia* we can see that the myopic trope of the title hardly appears in the text at all. Indeed, short-sightedness hardly gets a mention, even though it is 'perhaps the most famous metaphor in the history of marketing thought' (Brown, 2004).

In his chapter, Brown points to various types of dangers in the over-use in marketing of this 'rolling stone of mossy metaphors'. Much of what passes for marketing 'theory', he argues is 'little more than morbidly obese metaphor'. The crucial question he asks then: are metaphors a good thing? Brown's chapter shows clearly that they are certainly overused; from the metaphorical excesses of management speak to the patented 'metaphor elicitation technique' in marketing. Perhaps they even fulfil a useful function in the era of service dominance. Even if the real, tangible economy is receding fast maybe we do not need it anyway, Brown says, 'because the hyperreal economy, the intangible economy of mental leaps, analogical acumen, and metaphor manufacturing will save the day'. Furthermore, as he points out, metaphors have their dark side too – they blinker our thinking, they conceal as much as they reveal, they shape our discourse and delineate understanding.

SECTION 4: THE IMPACT OF THEORY ON REPRESENTATIONS OF THE CONSUMER

This section looks in detail at the implications of theory for how we conceptualise and undertake research into specific marketing phenomena. We have chosen to focus on consumer behaviour, because conceptions of the customer are central to the development of marketing theory. In addition, consumer behaviour is a research area which has included many diverse perspectives since its emergence in the 1950s as a major sub-area of marketing. This diversity has included concepts drawn from cognitive psychology, psychoanalysis, the mathematical sciences, sociology and cultural anthropology. In the last twenty years, there has been a particularly strong backlash against quantitative perspectives in consumer behaviour especially the information processing view of the consumer (e.g. Belk, 1986) and the (re)emergence of many innovative, interdisciplinary perspectives rooted in the interpretivist paradigm (Levy, 1996), drawing on ethnographic and semiotic methods. The chapters in this section illustrate how different theoretical lenses impact on representations of the consumer.

Critiques often highlight the risk of cultural homogeneity amongst consumers, a homogeneity, they contest, that is driven by increasingly globalised brandscapes. This section commences with a chapter by Russell Belk that unpacks the complexities of the 'global consumer' and refutes the criticism of homogeneity as over-simplistic. Taking a cross-cultural perspective, Belk explores how globalisation affects the three key intersections of desire, possession and identity. In contrast to traditional marketing perspectives that focus on needs and wants, Belk et al.

(2003) conceptualise consumer desires as involving passion and obsession. Belk argues that, on both utilitarian and cultural levels, there are many contextual factors that affect consumer desires and ensure that local meanings and value systems intersect in unique ways with global consumption patterns. Despite the great degree of global interconnectedness in consumer desires, Belk illustrates how consumers from around the world resist or localise the influences of global consumer culture. Examining three specific product categories where consumption is alleged to be global in character, he focuses on Chinese food, American rap music and global Christmas celebrations to show the different shades of meaning that consumers attach to these, depending on utilitarian and cultural contexts.

Consumer desire is looked at through a very different lens in the chapter that follows, by Richard Bagozzi, who identifies it as a key component in consumer decision making processes that lead to consumer action. Highlighting the theoretical gap between consumer behaviour and consumer action, Bagozzi draws on a range of interdisciplinary perspectives from psychology, neuroscience and various applied areas of the social sciences, to augment previous consumer behaviour decision making models. In so doing, he proposes a framework to reconcile this theoretical gap. Taking the variables and processes that influence consumers' reasons for acting, he groups these into four key categories for analysis, namely, the bases for self-regulation of desire, cause of goal desires, causes of action desires and implications of action intentions. Overall, he claims that previous psychological perspectives have been too narrowly focused and, in agreement with other writers in this section, he highlights the need to understand consumers in their everyday lives, rather than through laboratory experiments. Accordingly, Bagozzi argues that his proposed framework to study consumer agency and action moves us from a passive reactive conceptualisation of consumption to an active self-regulatory perspective. As Belk's chapter also shows, consumers are not just acted on by marketing activities and stimuli, but rather they respond creatively, often adapting these to their own advantage.

In contrast to the cognitive stance of dominant psychological perspectives and Belk's cultural lens to analyze global consumer desire, Gordon Foxall has long been at the forefront of behavioural approaches to understand consumer choice in marketing and consumer research (Foxall, 1986, 1990, 1994). He illustrates how his analytic approach, termed 'consumer behavior analysis', can help us understand the complex behaviours that underpin consumers' purchasing and consumption activities. Arguing for a model of consumer choice based on radical behaviourism, he details the theory and research that has guided development of the Behavioural Perspective Model (BPM). Rooted in behavioural economics, which combines experimental economics and operant psychology, the BPM model enables a heightened sensitivity to the effects of environmental contingencies on consumers' actions.

The final chapter in this section returns us to a cultural theoretical lens as Pauline Maclaran, Margaret Hogg and Alan Bradshaw review the field of enquiry commonly referred to as interpretivist consumer research or Consumer Culture Theory (Arnould and Thompson, 2005). As can be seen in the two preceding chapters, the major influences of economics and psychology have meant a strong focus on the purchasing act in consumer behaviour theory. Maclaran, Hogg and Bradshaw document how a cultural perspective shifts this focus towards broader conceptualisations of the experiences embodied in consumer behaviour (Belk, 1995). Building on previous categorisations of this body of interpretivist work, they foreground seven key representations of the consumer: consumers in their cultural contexts; consumers in their subcultural contexts; consumer identities and the meaning of possessions; consumers as gift-givers; consumers and their sense of (market)place; consumers as storytellers and myth-makers; dissatisfied and disadvantaged consumers.

SECTION 5: THE IMPACT OF THEORY ON REPRESENTATIONS OF THE MARKETING ORGANISATION

This section looks in detail at the implications of theory for how we conceptualise the marketing function in the organisation and the role of marketing by and for the organisation. These chapters illustrate how different theoretical lenses impact on representations of the marketing organisation. The traditional view of the firm and how managers conduct marketing activities has evolved significantly over the past twenty years or so. The theoretical basis has shifted from the biological analogy of the autonomous organism operating in a changing business environment, towards an overlapping network of market actors operating in more or less contingent or strategic modes. Some of the research which underpins this shift comes from researchers such as those in the International Marketing and Purchasing (IMP) group and also from renewed attention to the concept of market orientation and its measurement. This section reviews and revisits the theoretical and empirical research developments that have advanced marketing views of the firm, economic theories of the marketing organisation, the social construction of marketing management and behavioural approaches to the organisation of the marketing function.

In 1982, a research project, carried out in five European countries by a group which became known as the IMP, reported how they had developed an approach which challenged traditional ways of examining industrial marketing and purchasing. In business-to-business settings, the IMP study showed that companies, on both the customer and supplier sides, were dominated by some long-term business relationships with a limited number of counterparts. Within the context of these relationships, both marketing and purchasing of industrial goods were seen as 'interaction processes' between the two parties. These researchers also observed that interaction in itself included an important content of its own. In their chapter, Lars-Erik Gadde and Håkan Håkansson review and explain how this concept of interaction in networks challenged prevailing conceptualisations in B2B marketing in four major respects. Firstly, IMP challenged the narrow analysis of single discrete purchases and emphasised the importance of business relationships. Secondly, the view of industrial marketing as manipulation of marketing-mix variables in relation to a passive market was challenged. The third aspect concerned the assumption of an atomistic market structure where buyers and sellers can easily switch business partners. Fourthly, IMP challenged the separation of theoretical and empirical analysis into either the process of purchasing or the process of marketing.

Although this emphasis on the role and importance of business relationships and interaction have been recognised by other schools of thought, Gadde and Håkansson show that there is no general agreement regarding the implications for theories of business (see also Chapter 9 in this volume by Möller et al.). They emphasise that the main objective of the IMP project now is to develop a framework for analysis of business interaction building on an outward-in perspective, implying that the internal organising of a company must reflect its way of approaching business partners. Gadde and Håkansson also explore how interaction is related to the three network layers of activities, resources and actors. In conclusion, they analyze how these conditions, concerning network interaction, may impact on the internal organisation of an enterprise.

Over the last three decades, since the first IMP studies discussed in the foregoing section, a range of alternative, broader perspectives of organisations has emerged in the marketing literature. Greater emphasis is now

placed on marketing organisations' processes, relationships with customers and networks with stakeholders. The next chapter by Roderick Brodie, Vicki Little and Richard Brookes in this section draws on the research undertaken by the Contemporary Marketing Practice (CMP) research group, which develops the case for a multi-theory perspective of the marketing organisation. The chapter examines the conceptual foundations of CMP research, and how it evolved to encompass a multi-theory approach. Brodie et al. then review the empirical evidence about the characteristics and behaviour of contemporary marketing organisations that has been generated since the formation of the CMP group. They follow this with a discussion of how the various conceptual and methodological developments have informed theory development relating to the contemporary marketing organisation. Two of these theoretical and methodological developments are then reviewed – middle range theory, which is an intermediate step between the working hypothesis and unified general theory, and living case studies as co-creative learning with practitioners. The chapter shows how these two key developments of CMP group research have enabled researchers to draw on practice to inform theory and to examine more clearly the relationship between practice and performance.

In the early 1990s, researchers became concerned about the lack of empirical evidence regarding the impact of marketing activities on corporate performance (Kohli and Jaworski, 1990; Narver and Slater, 1990; Ruekert, 1992; Shapiro, 1988). This was partly stimulated by concern over the lack of status and authority of marketing at board level. The notion of market orientation (MO) was developed originally in order to begin to address this issue empirically with the MO construct representing the *implementation* aspects of the marketing concept and the means of measuring marketing performance. Narver and Slater (1990: 24) suggested that market orientation '... consists of three behavioural components – customer orientation, competition orientation, and interfunctional coordination, and two decision criteria long-term focus and profitability'. Kohli and Jaworski (1990: 6) defined MO through three interrelated elements: (i) the organisation wide generation of market intelligence pertaining to current and future customer needs, (ii) dissemination of intelligence across departments and (iii) organisation-wide responsiveness to it. Profitability and performance in general was regarded as a consequence of MO rather than part of the construct. These initial contributions generated many studies on different aspects of market orientation. These explored issues such as whether MO is primarily dominated by customer orientation or represents a multidimensional construct comprising, customer, competitor and market orientation. Another question concerned the passive versus proactive nature of the market orientation construct, i.e. whether it was primarily 'market driven' or included also 'market making' characteristics.

This theme is developed by Jonathan Knowles and Tim Ambler in the following chapter on market orientation and marketing metrics. Initially, they note that market orientation is far from universal among organisations and conclude from this that not all executives agree about the importance of marketing. They assert that this is partly due to different understandings of the term 'marketing', which can be broadly defined as being *both* the whole company's activities designed to satisfy customers and thereby achieve its own objectives, *and* the activities of the functional marketing department (Webster, 1992). A third view defines marketing by the activities that constitute the marketing budget, i.e. marketing research, communications and promotions (Ambler, 2003). The chapter begins by analysing four key marketing performance indicators or 'silver metrics'. It continues with a review of the evolution of marketing metrics and discusses the definition and role of the concept of brand equity as a key construct in the assessment of the productivity of marketing

in financial terms. Knowles and Ambler conclude that no single metric is adequate for performance assessment and therefore none is adequate for planning purposes either. They explain how the four 'silver metrics' that they identify and review should be used in combination with other metrics of marketing performance to provide a compelling portrait of how the company is performing in the market. Finally they argue that we need to better understand the dynamics in changes of orientation and metrics selection itself.

The purpose of the chapter that follows is to analyse how relationship marketing can be conceptualised and managed using a promise management approach. Here Christian Grönroos proposes a marketing definition and approach that helps academics and business practitioners alike to understand and implement a relational strategy in both business-to-business and business-to-consumer contexts. He argues that conventional marketing definitions have become a hindrance for developing marketing in accordance with changes in today's business environment. This is because the focus of traditional definitions is on one function of marketing, i.e. the exchange of pre-produced value without accounting for relationships or dialogue which may add value. Also they postulate a structural set of marketing variables, rather than a marketing *process*. Such definitions have become a straitjacket for marketing practice and for marketing theory. Instead, Grönroos argues that relationship marketing is better viewed as a process-oriented approach to customer management which is best understood as *promise management*; i.e. a process of enabling, making and keeping promises to customers, by meeting the expectations which are created by the promises made. Grönroos bases his analysis mainly, but not entirely, on the Nordic School of thought in marketing research (see Berry and Parasuraman, 1993; Grönroos, 2007).

There are several benefits of the promises management approach to the marketing organisation. It shifts the interest of research into marketing from structure to process. Grönroos argues that previous definitions of marketing have always been over preoccupied with structural elements and neglected the importance of process, which has only been recognised implicitly by them. Also, by emphasising *value-in-use*, it allows for supplier and customer co-production of solutions and thus value co-creation together with customers. Furthermore, viewing marketing as a process includes activities that necessarily go beyond a single marketing function, because the promise management perspective should permeate all organisational functions. Finally, the new definition recognises the fact that everyone involved in interactions with customers are not automatically customer-focused. By focusing on promises, it recognises that part-time marketers exist, whereas conventional marketing approaches do not allow for ways of coping for the part-time marketer, nor trigger any interest in studying them from a marketing perspective. The process of enabling promises explicitly emphasises the need to prepare employees who are not tasked nor trained for their key 'part-time' marketing-related roles.

SECTION 6: CONTEMPORARY AND FUTURE ISSUES IN MARKETING THEORY

Each of the chapters in this final section offers a rethink of some aspect of marketing theory. Overall, the chapters consider the changing sociocultural and political contexts in which theory is developed and highlights contemporary issues likely to impact most on the future development of marketing theory. The authors discuss future research agendas in the light of current trends and, for example, the role of e-marketing and the implications of new technologies are recurrent themes throughout the section. By concluding this handbook with new ways of conceptualising aspects of marketing and

consumer behaviour theory, we hope to leave our readers with inspiration to explore for themselves the many rich avenues for further research into marketing theory.

Macromarketing looks at marketing activities in the context of their wider economic, social, political and ecological environments, and has emerged as a significant area of scholarship where many new theories are required to better understand marketing's impact on society (Fırat and Dholakia, 1982; Kilbourne et al., 1997). Roger Layton's thought-provoking chapter that opens this section takes just such a macro viewpoint in its comprehensive analysis of marketing systems and their theoretical implications. Layton argues that, although contemporary marketing theory offers many insights into the nature of exchange relationships between buyers and sellers, it has not had nearly as much to say about the nature of the networks that these interactions generate. Illustrating how micro decisions create macro outcomes, he discusses the important interconnections between marketing systems, macromarketing and quality of life. These interconnections, he argues, relate particularly strongly to critical problem areas such as obesity, food, finance, energy and environment. Layton enlivens his arguments with an analysis of the marketing system in which a community store in a remote aboriginal township in Central Australia is embedded, showing how complex multi-level structures can emerge from simple, localised exchange.

In the second chapter, Elizabeth Hirschman joins an increasing number of scholars (e.g. Fullerton and Nevett, 1988) who call for a greater acknowledgement of the past as a foundation for understanding the present structure of markets and marketing. Highlighting the analogous relationship between 'marketing-as-process' (Vargo and Lusch, 2004) and the bio-evolutionary process of natural selection, Hirschman explores the role of marketing in cultural evolution. In an ambitious analysis that covers a period of some hundred thousand years, she looks at how marketing activities and social systems have long been intertwined. From this analysis, she proposes a reframing of contemporary marketing theory. Arguing that marketing-as-process has evolved through three concentric cultural cycles, she pinpoints us as now having entered the third, the Era of Consumer Constructed Innovativeness, an era that is enabled by the global availability of creative technologies. Echoing themes that are explored further in the last two chapters of this section, she contends that this is likely to have as dramatic an effect on our culture as did the introduction of agriculture. In conclusion, she identifies three areas of marketing theory that would benefit from this evolutionary perspective: companies as families/tribes; reciprocity versus opportunism in markets; and brands as social markers.

Evolutionary theory is also the theme of the next chapter, but this time from a psychological, rather than a cultural perspective. Gad Saad is the foremost proponent of evolutionary psychology as a lens to better develop theory on consumer behaviour (Saad, 2007). Despite the take-up of Darwinian Theory across a wide range of disciplines in the natural and social sciences as well as in the humanities, to date this perspective has largely remained absent from consumer research. Following a brief discussion of the key tenets of Darwinian Theory in general, and evolutionary psychology in particular, Saad reviews work that has operated at the nexus of evolutionary theory and consumption. He then discusses key epistemological benefits of adopting Darwinian Theory as the organising meta-theoretical framework of consumer research, showing how it can bring many insights to existing interpretations of consumer behaviour and open up many new directions to pursue.

Since Holbrook and Hirschman's (1982) seminal contribution arguing against cognitive information processing models of consumer behaviour, there has been an increasing emphasis on the hedonic and experiential dimensions that surround consumption acts (see also Chapter 19 in this volume). Consistent with this emphasis, experiential marketing has developed not only as a management perspective, but also as a strong research area. The penultimate chapter of this volume, by Bernard Cova and Daniele Dalli, explores theories of experiential marketing, particularly in relation to its linking value and the role of consumers in co-creating that value. Emphasising the strong collective aspects of contemporary consumption, and the fact that 'the link is more important than the thing' (Cova, 1997), they highlight the social bonds that are formed through goods, services and brands, bonds that underpin theories of experiential marketing. An important part of their review shows how, when consumers are active agents in the creation of this linking value, their immaterial labour is being appropriated without financial remuneration (see also Cova and Dalli, 2009). Crucially they argue that current theories of relationship or tribal marketing ignore the role of consumers in creating experiences and actual linking value. Accordingly, Cova and Dalli argue that this significant oversight limits the capability of extant theoretical models to account adequately for the complex and intimate nature of these processes.

The final chapter of the volume explores the intersections of technology, consumers and marketing theory. Nikhilesh Dholakia, Detlev Zwick and Janice Denegri-Knott begin with an overview of how technology has shaped marketing practice and consumer behaviour historically in order to lay the groundwork for the longstanding nexus between marketing and technology from the time of the industrial revolution. They then focus their narrative on the pervasive and deep impacts of new information technologies on marketing practice and theory. To do this, they examine first the distinctive core conceptual elements and main characteristics of new information technologies and why new information technologies often create impacts that are not merely accretive and accelerative, but also radical and transformational.

In subsequent parts of the chapter, focusing strongly on marketing theory, they examine a number of tendencies that have driven marketing and consumer behaviour theories, particularly after the advent of the mass Internet era. In particular, they explore three key issues: (1) is there an emergent theory, or are there emergent theories of information technology marketing? (2) is there an emergent theory, or are there emergent theories of technology consumption and (3) how are high or new information technologies shaping or informing major theories in marketing in areas such as customer relationship management, co-creation, and customer centricism and loci of control in the value creation and consumption process? The chapter ends with a suggestion for a future-oriented research direction about technology and marketing theory.

Overall, the editors of this handbook believe that these six sections together provide a comprehensive reference point for scholars wishing to engage in the development of marketing theory. Having reflected on both historical and contemporary debates, our expert group of authors have also raised many critical concerns for the future development of marketing theory. We hope that doctoral students and new researchers in marketing and consumer behaviour will find this handbook a particularly useful resource to inform them about the complexities of theory development in marketing. After all, the future of marketing theory lies largely with them.

REFERENCES

Alderson, W. (1957) *Marketing Behavior and Executive Action*. Homewood, IL: Richard D. Irwin.

Alderson, W. (1965) *Dynamic Marketing Behavior*. Homewood, IL: Richard D. Irwin.

Alderson, W. and Cox, R. (1948) 'Towards a Theory of Marketing', *The Journal of Marketing*, 13(2): 137–152.

Alderson, W. and Martin, M.W. (1965) 'Toward a Formal Theory of Transactions and Transvections', *Journal of Marketing Research*, 2(2): 117–127.

Allen, D.E. (2002) 'Toward a Theory of Consumer Choice as Sociohistorically Shaped Practical Experience: The Fits-Like-A-Glove (FLAG) Framework', *Journal of Consumer Research*, 28(4): 515–532.

Ambler, T. (2003) *Marketing and the Bottom Line*, Second Edition. London: FT Prentice Hall.

Anderson, P.F. (1983) 'Marketing, Scientific Progress, and the Scientific Method', *Journal of Marketing*, 47(4): 18–31.

Anderson, P.F. (1986) 'On Method in Consumer Research: A Critical Relativist Perspective', *Journal of Consumer Research*, 13(September): 155–173.

Anderson, P.F. (1988) 'Relativism Revidivus: In Defense of Critical Relativism', *Journal of Consumer Research*, 15(December): 403–406.

Arndt, J. (1985) 'The Tyranny of Paradigms: The Case for Paradigmatic Pluralism in Marketing', in N. Dholakia and J. Arndt (eds) *Changing the Course of Marketing: Alternative Paradigms for Widening Marketing Theory*, pp. 3–25. Greenwich: JAI Press.

Arnould, E. and Thompson, C. (2007) 'Consumer Culture Theory (and we really mean theoretics): Dilemmas and Opportunities Posed by an Academic Branding Strategy', in R. W. Belk and J. F. Sherry, Jr. (eds) *Consumer Culture Theory*, Vol. 11 of *Research in Consumer Behavior*. Oxford: Elsevier.

Arnould, E.J. and Thompson, C.J. (2005) 'Consumer Culture Theory (CCT): Twenty Years of Research', *Journal of Consumer Research*, 31(4): 868–882.

Bagozzi, R.P. (1978) 'Marketing as Exchange: A Theory of Transactions in the Market Place', *American Behavioral Scientist*, 21: 535–556.

Baker, M.J. (1995) 'The Future of Marketing', in M.J. Baker (ed.) *Companion Encyclopedia of Marketing*, pp. 1003–1018. London: Routledge.

Baker, M.J. (2001) 'Introduction', in M.J. Baker (ed.) *Marketing: Critical Perspectives on Business and Management*, pp. 1–25. London: Routledge.

Bartels, R. (1951) 'Can Marketing be a Science?', *Journal of Marketing,* 51(1): 319–328.

Bartels, R. (1988) *The History of Marketing Thought,* Third Edition. Columbus: Publishing Horizons.

Belk, R.W. (1986) 'Art Versus Science as Ways of Generating Knowledge About Materialism', in D. Brinberg and R.J. Lutz (eds) *Perspectives on Methodology in Consumer Research,* pp. 3–36. New York: Springer Verlag.

Belk, R.W. (1995) 'Studies in the New Consumer Behaviour', in D. Miller (ed.) *Acknowledging Consumption,* pp. 58–95. London: Routledge.

Belk, R.W. (2009) 'The Modelling-Empiricism Gap: Lessons from the Quantitative-Qualitative Gap in Consumer Research', *Journal of Supply Chain Management,* 45(1): 35–38.

Belk, R.W., Ger, G. and Askegaard, S. (2003) 'The Fire of Desire: A Multi-sited Inquiry into Consumer Passion', *Journal of Consumer Research,* 30 (December): 326–351.

Berry, L.L. and Parasuraman, A. (1993) 'Building a New Academic Field – The Case for Services Marketing', *Journal of Retailing,* 69(1): 13–60.

Böhm, S. (2002), 'Movements of Theory and Practice', *Ephemera,* 2(4), 328–351.

Bradshaw, A. and Fırat, A.F. (2007), 'Rethinking Critical Marketing', in M. Saren, P. Maclaran, C. Goulding, R. Elliott, A. Shankar and M. Catterall (eds) *Critical Marketing: Defining the Field,* pp. 30–43. Oxford: Elsevier.

Bristor, J.M. and Fischer, E. (1993) 'Feminist Thought: Implications for Consumer Research', *Journal of Consumer Research,* 19(March): 518–536.

Bristor, E. and Fischer, E. (1995) 'Exploring Simultaneous Oppressions: Toward the Development of Consumer Research in the Interest of Diverse Women', *American Behavioral Scientist,* 38(4): 526–536.

Brown, L.O. (1948) 'Toward a Profession of Marketing', *Journal of Marketing,* 13(1): 27–31.

Brown, S. (1995) *Postmodern Marketing.* London: Routledge.

Brown, S. (1998) *Postmodern Marketing Two.* London: International Thompson Business Press.

Brown, S. (2004) 'Theodore Levitt: The Ultimate Writing Machine', *Marketing Theory,* 4(3): 209–238.

Brown, S.W. and Fisk, R. (1984) *Marketing Theory: Distinguished Contributions.* New York: John Wiley & Sons.

Brownlie, D. and Saren, M. (1995) 'On the Commodification of Marketing Knowledge', *Journal of Marketing Management,* 11(7): 619–628.

Brownlie, D., Saren, M., Wensley, R. and Whittington, R. (eds) (1999) *Rethinking Marketing: Towards Critical Marketing Accountings.* London: Sage.

Buzzell, R.D. (1963) 'Is Marketing a Science?', *Harvard Business Review,* 41(1): 32–40.

Calder, B.J. and Tybout, A.M. (1987) 'What Consumer Research Is …', *Journal of Consumer Research,* 14(1): 136–140.

Calder, B.J. and Tybout, A.M. (1989) 'Interpretive, Qualitative, and Traditional Scientific Empirical Consumer Behavior Research', in E.C. Hirschman (ed.) *Interpretive Consumer Research,* pp. 199–208. Provo, UT: Association for Consumer Research.

Campbell, N., O'Driscoll, A. and Saren, M. (2006) 'Cyborg Consciousness: A Visual Culture Approach to the Technologised Body', *European Advances in Consumer Research* 7: 344–351.

Carmen, J.M. (1980) 'Paradigms for Marketing Theory', in J.N. Sheth (ed.) *Research in Marketing,* Vol. 3. Greenwich, CT: JAI Press.

Cayla, J. and Eckhardt, G.M. (2008) 'Asian Brands and the Shaping of a Transnational Imagined Community', *Journal of Consumer Research,* 35(August): 216–230.

Converse, P.D. (1951) 'Development of Marketing Theory: Fifty Years of Progress', in H.G. Wales (ed.) *Changing Perspectives in Marketing,* pp. 1–31. Urbana: The University of Illinois Press.

Cova, B. (1997) 'Community and Consumption: Towards a Definition of the Linking Value of Products or Services', *European Journal of Marketing,* 31(3/4): 297–316.

Cova, B. and Dalli, D. (2009) 'Working Consumers: The Next Step in Marketing Theory?', *Marketing Theory,* 9(3): forth-coming.

Davies, A. and Fitchett, J.A. (2005) 'Beyond Incommensurability? Empirical Expansion on

Diversity in Research', *European Journal of Marketing*, 39(3): 272–293.

Dholakia, N. and Arndt, J. (eds) (1985) *Changing the Course of Marketing: Alternative Paradigms for Widening Marketing Theory*. Greenwich: JAI Press.

Dichter, E. (1960) *The Strategy of Desire*. New York: Doubleday.

Djelic Marie-Laure (2007) 'Moral Foundations of Contemporary Capitalism: From Markets to Marketization', Uppsala Lectures.

Easley, R.W., Madden, C.S. and Dunn, M.G. (2000) 'Conducting Marketing Science – The Role of Replication in the Research Process', *Journal of Business Research*, 48(1): 83–92.

Easton, G. (2002) 'Marketing: A Critical Realist Approach', *Journal of Business Research*, 55(2): 103–109.

Elliott, R. and Jankel-Elliott, N. (2003) 'Using Ethnography in Strategic Consumer Research', *Qualitative Market Research: An International Journal*, 6(4): 215–223.

Feyerabend, P. (1975) *Against Method*. London: New Left Books.

Fırat, A.F. and Dholakia, N. (1982) 'Consumption Choices at the Macro Level', *Journal of Macromarketing*, 2(Fall): 6–15.

Fisk, G. and Meyers, P. (1982) 'Macromarketers Guide to Paradigm', in R. Bush and S.D. Hunt (eds) *Marketing Theory: Philosophy of Science Perspectives*. Chicago: American Marketing Association.

Foxall, G.R. (1990) *Consumer Psychology in Behavioral Perspective*. London and New York: Routledge/republished 2004: Frederick, MD: Beard Books.

Foxall, G.R. (1986) 'The Role of Radical Behaviorism in the Explanation of Consumer Choice', *Advances in Consumer Research*, 13, Provo, UT: Association for Consumer Research, pp. 195–201.

Foxall, G.R. (1994) 'Behaviour Analysis and Consumer Psychology', *Journal of Economic Psychology*, 15: 5–91.

Fromm, E. (1956/2005) *The Sane Society*. London: Routledge.

Fromm, E. (1962/2006) *Beyond the Chains of Illusion: My Encounter with Marx and Freud*. New York: Continuum.

Fromm, E. (1976/2007) *To Have Or To Be?* New York: Continuum.

Fullerton, R.A. (1987) 'The Poverty of a Historical Analysis: Present Weaknesses and Future Cure in U.S. Marketing Thought', in A.F. Fırat., N. Dholakia. and R.P. Bagozzi (eds) *Philosophical and Radical Thought in Marketing*, pp. 97–116. Lexington, KY: Lexington Books.

Fullerton, R.A. and Nevett, T. (eds) (1988) *Historical Perspectives in Marketing*. Boston: Lexington Books.

Gioia, D.A. and Pitre, E. (1990) 'Multiparadigm Perspectives on Theory Building', *Academy of Management Review*, 15(4): 584–602.

Greenley, G. (1995) 'A Comment on the Commodification of Marketing Knowledge', *Journal of Marketing Management*, 11(7): 665–670.

Greyser, S.A. (1997) 'Janus and Marketing: The Past, Present, and Prospective Future of Marketing', in D.R. Lehmann and K.E. Jocz (eds) *Reflections on the Futures of Marketing: Practice and Education*, pp. 3–14. Chicago: Marketing Science Institute.

Grönroos, C. (2007) *In Search of a New Logic for Marketing. Foundation of Contemporary Theory*. Chichester: John Wiley & Sons.

Halbert, M. (1965) *The Meaning and Sources of Marketing Theory*. New York: McGraw-Hill.

Hirschman, E.C. (1985) 'Scientific Style and the Conduct of Consumer Research', *Journal of Consumer Research*, 12(September): 225–239.

Holbrook, M.B. and Hirschman, E.C. (1982) 'The Experiential Aspects of Consumption: Consumer Fantasies, Feelings and Fun', *Journal of Consumer Research*, 9(September):132–140.

Holbrook, M.B. (1985) 'Why Business is Bad for Consumer Research: The Three Bears Revisited', in E.C. Hirschman and M.B. Holbrook (eds) *Advances in Consumer Research*, pp. 145–156. 12, Provo, UT: Association for Consumer Research.

Holbrook, M.B. and O'Shaughnessy, J. (1988) 'On the Scientific Status of Consumer Research and the Need for an Interpretive Approach to Studying Consumption Behavior', *Journal of Consumer Research*, 15(3): 398–402.

Hollander, S.C. (1995) 'My Life on Mt. Olympus', *Journal of Macromarketing*, 15(1): 86–106.

Howard, J.A. and Sheth, J.N. (1969) *The Theory of Buyer Behavior*. New York: John Wiley & Sons.

Hudson, L.A. and Ozanne, J.L. (1988) 'Alternative Ways of Seeking Knowledge in Consumer Research', *Journal of Consumer Research*, 14(4): 508–521.

Hunt, S.D. (1976) 'The Nature and Scope of Marketing', *Journal of Marketing*, 40(3): 17–26.

Hunt, S.D. (1983) 'General Theories and the Fundamental Explananda of Marketing', *Journal of Marketing*, 47(4): 9–17.

Hunt, S.D. (1984) 'Should Marketing Adopt Relativism?', in M. Ryan and P.F. Anderson (eds) *Marketing Theory: Philosophy and Sociology of Science Perspectives*, pp. 30–34. Chicago: American Marketing Association.

Hunt, S.D. (1990) 'Truth in Marketing Theory and Research', *Journal of Marketing*, 54(July): 1–15.

Hunt, S.D. (1991) 'Positivism and Paradigm Dominance in Consumer Research', *Journal of Consumer Research*, 18(1): 32–44.

Hunt, S.D. (1992) 'For Reason and Realism in Marketing', *Journal of Marketing*, 56(2): 89–102.

Hunt, S.D. (2001) 'The Influence of Philosophy, Philosophies and Philosophers on a Marketer's Scholarship', *Journal of Marketing*, 64(October): 117–124.

Hunt, S.D. (2002) *Foundations of Marketing Theory: Towards a General Theory of Marketing*. Armonk: M.E. Sharpe.

Hunt, S.D. (2003) *Controversy in Marketing Theory: For Reason, Realism, Truth and Objectivity*. Armonk: M.E. Sharpe.

Hutchinson, K.D. (1952) 'Marketing as Science: An Appraisal', *Journal of Marketing*, 16(January): 286–292.

Jack, G. (2008) 'Postcolonialism and Marketing', in M. Tadajewski and D. Brownlie (eds) *Critical Marketing: Issues in Contemporary Marketing*, pp. 363–384. Chichester: John Wiley.

Jack, G. and Westwood, R. (2006) 'Postcolonialism and the Politics of Qualitative Research in International Business', *Management International Review*, 46(4): 481–501.

Jones, D.G.B. and Monieson, D.D. (1990) 'Early Development in the Philosophy of Marketing Thought', *Journal of Marketing*, 54(1): 1–20113.

Kassarjian, H.H. (1963) 'Voting Intentions and Political Perception', *The Journal of Psychology,* 10: 85–88.

Kavanagh, D. (1994) 'Hunt Versus Anderson: Round 16', *European Journal of Marketing*, 28(3): 26–41.

Kerin, R.A. (1996) 'In Pursuit of an Ideal: The Editorial and Literary History of the Journal of Marketing', *Journal of Marketing*, 60(1): 1–13.

Kilbourne, W., McDonagh, P. and Prothero, A. (1997) 'Sustainable Consumption and the Quality of Life: A Macromarketing Challenge to the Dominant Social Paradigm', *Journal of Macromarketing*, Spring: 4–24.

Kohli, A.K. and Jaworski, B.J. (1990) 'Market Orientation: The Construct, Research Propositions, and Managerial Implications', *Journal of Marketing*, 54(1): 1–18.

Lagrosen, S. and Svensson, G. (2006) 'A Seminal Framework of Marketing Schools: Revisited and Updated', *Journal of Management History*, 12(4): 369–384.

Laughlin, R. (1995) 'Empirical Research in Accounting: Alternative Approaches and a Case for "Middle-Range" Thinking', *Accounting, Auditing & Accountability Journal*, 8(1): 63–87.

Levitt, T. (1960) 'M-R Snake Dance', *Harvard Business Review*, 38(6): 76–84.

Levy, S.J. (1996) 'Stalking the Amphisbaena', *Journal of Consumer Research,* 23(3): 163–176.

Levy, S.J. (2003) 'Roots of Marketing and Consumer Research at the University of Chicago', *Consumption, Markets and Culture*, 6(2): 99–110.

Lewis, M.W. and Grimes, A.J. (1999) 'Metatriangulation: Building Theory from Multiple Paradigms', *Academy of Management Review*, 24(4): 672–690.

Lowenthal, L. (1987) *An Unmastered Past: The Autobiographical Reflections of Leo Lowenthal*. Berkeley: University of California Press.

Lusch, S.L. and Vargo, R.F. (eds) (2006) *The Service Dominant Logic of Marketing: Dialog, Debate and Directions*, New York: M.E. Sharpe.

Maclaran, P. and Catterall, M. (2000) 'Bridging the Knowledge Divide: Issues on the

Feminisation of Marketing Practice', *Journal of Marketing Management*, 16(6): 635–646.

Maclaran, P., Saren, M., Goulding, C. and Stevens, L. (2009) 'Rethinking Theory Building and Theorizing in Marketing', *Proceedings of the 38th European Academy of Marketing Conference*, Nantes, France.

Markin, R.J. (1970) 'Consumer Motivation and Behavior: Essence Vs. Existence', *Business & Society*, 10: 30–36.

McDonagh, P. (1995) 'Radical Change Through Rigorous Review? A Commentary on the Commodification of Marketing Knowledge', *Journal of Marketing Management*, 11(7): 675–679.

McDonagh, P. (2002) 'Communicative Campaigns to Effect Anti-Slavery and Fair Trade: The Cases of Rugmark and Cafédirect', *European Journal of Marketing*, 36(5/6): 642–666.

McTier, A.L. (1994) 'Marketing Science: Where's the Beef?', *Business Horizons*, 37(1): 8–17.

Merton, R.K. (1968) *Social Theory and Social Structure*. New York: The Free Press.

Mittelstaedt, R.A. (1990) 'Economics, Psychology and the Literature of the Subdiscipline of Consumer Behavior', *Journal of the Academy of Marketing Science*, 18(4): 303–311.

Monieson, D.D. (1988) 'Intellectualization in Marketing: A World Disenchanted', *Journal of Macromarketing*, 8(2): 4–10.

Muncy, J.A. and Fisk, R.P. (1987) 'Cognitive Relativism and the Practice of Marketing Science', *Journal of Marketing*, 51(January): 20–33.

Murray, J.B and Ozanne, J.L. (1991) 'The Critical Imagination: Emancipatory Interests in Consumer Research', *Journal of Consumer Research*, 18(2): 129–144.

Murray, J.B. and Ozanne, J.L. (1997) 'A Critical-Emancipatory Sociology of Knowledge: Reflections on the Social Construction of Consumer Research', in R. Belk (ed.) *Research in Consumer Behavior*, pp. 57–92. Greenwich: JAI Press.

Murray, J.B., Evers, D.J. and Janda, S. (1997) 'Marketing, Theory Borrowing and Critical Reflection', *Journal of Macromarketing*, 15(2): 92–106.

Narver, J.C. and Slater, S.F. (1990) 'The Effect of Market Orientation on Business Profitability', *Journal of Marketing*, (10): 20–35.

O'Shaughnessy, J. (1997) 'Temerarious Directions for Marketing', *European Journal of Marketing*, 31(9/10): 677–705.

O'Shaughnessy, J. (2009) *Interpretation in Social Life, Social Science and Marketing*. London: Routledge.

Peter, J.P. (1992) 'Realism or Relativism for Marketing Theory and Research: A Comment on Hunt's "Scientific Realism"', *Journal of Marketing*, 56(April): 72–79.

Petersen, A. and Willig, R. (2002) 'An Interview with Axel Honneth: The Role of Sociology in the Theory of Recognition', *European Journal of Social Theory*, 5(May): 265–277.

Popper, K.R. (1976) 'The Logic of the Social Sciences', in T.W. Adorno, H. Albert, R. Dahrendorf, J. Habermas, H. Pilot and K.R. Popper (eds) *The Positivist Dispute in German Sociology*, Trans G. Adey and D. Frisby, pp. 87–104. London: Heinemann.

Price, L.L. (2007)'That's Interesting, But Now What?', *Presented at the Consumer Culture Theory Qualitative Workshop*, Toronto, May.

Price, L.L. and Arnould, E. (1998) 'Conducting the Choir: Representing Multimethod Consumer Research', in B.B. Stern (ed.) *Representing Consumers: Voices, Views and Visions*, pp. 339–364. London: Routledge.

Reckwitz, A. (2002) 'Towards a Theory of Social Practices: A Development in Culturalist Theorizing', *European Journal of Social Theory*, 5(2): 245–265.

Ruekert, R.W. (1992) 'Developing a Market Orientation: An Organizational Strategy Perspective', *International Research in Marketing*, 9: 225–245.

Saad, G. (2007) *The Evolutionary Bases of Consumption*. Mahwah, NJ: Lawrence Erlbaum.

Saad, G. (2008) 'The Collective Amnesia of Marketing Scholars' Regarding Consumers Biological and Evolutionary Roots', *Marketing Theory*, 8(4): 425–448.

Saren, M. (2000) 'Marketing Theory', in M.J. Baker (ed.) *Marketing Theory – A Student Text*, pp. 21–42. London: Thomson Learning.

Saren, M. (2007) 'Marketing is Everything: The View from the Street', *Marketing Intelligence and Planning*, 25(1): 11–16.

Schroeder, J.E. (2000) 'The Consumer in Society: Utopian Visions Revisited', *Marketing Intelligence and Planning*, 18(6/7): 381–387.

Scully, J.I. (1996) 'Machines Made of Words: The Influence of Engineering Metaphor on Marketing Thought and Practice', *Journal of Macromarketing*, 16(2): 70–83.

Senior, C. and Lee, N. (2008) 'A Manifesto for Neuromarketing Science', *Journal of Consumer Behaviour*, 7: 263–271.

Shapiro, B (1988) 'What the Hell is Market Oriented?', *Harvard Business Review*, (November/December): 119–125.

Shaw, E.H. and Jones, D.G.B. (2005) 'A History of Schools of Marketing Thought', *Marketing Theory*, 5(3): 239–281.

Sherry, J.F. (1991) 'Postmodern Alternatives The Interpretive Turn in Consumer Research', in T.S. Robertson and H.H. Kassarjian (eds) *Handbook of Consumer Research*, pp. 548–591. Englewood Cliffs: Prentice-Hall.

Sheth, J.N. (1992) 'Acrimony in the Ivory Tower: A Retrospective on Consumer Research', *Journal of the Academy of Marketing Science*, 20(4): 345–353.

Sheth, J.N., Gardner, D.M. and Garrett, D.E. (1988) *Marketing Theory: Evolution and Evaluation*. New York: John Wiley & Sons.

Siegel, H. (1988) 'Relativism for Consumer Research (Comments on Anderson)', *Journal of Consumer Research*, 15(1): 129–132.

Stainton, R.S. (1952) 'Science in Marketing', *The Journal of Marketing* 17(1): 64–66.

Tadajewski, M. (2006a) 'The Ordering of Marketing Theory: The Influence of McCarthyism and the Cold War', *Marketing Theory*, 6(2): 163–199.

Tadajewski, M. (2006b) 'Remembering Motivation Research: Toward an Alternative Genealogy of Interpretive Consumer Research', *Marketing Theory*, 6(4): 429–466.

Tadajewski, M. (2008) 'Incommensurable Paradigms, Cognitive Bias and the Politics of Marketing Theory', *Marketing Theory*, 8(3):273–297.

Tadajewski, M. (2009) 'Eventalizing the Marketing Concept', *Journal of Marketing Management*, 25(1–2): 191–217.

Tadajewski, M. and Brownlie, D. (2008) 'Critical Marketing: A Limit Attitude', in M. Tadajewski and D. Brownlie (eds) *Critical Marketing: Issues in Contemporary Marketing*, pp. 1–28. Chichester: John Wiley & Sons.

Tadajewski, M. and Maclaran, P. (eds) (2009) *Critical Marketing Studies*, Vol. I. London: Sage.

Tadajewski, M. and Saren, M. (2008) 'The Past is a Foreign Country: Amnesia and Marketing Theory', *Marketing Theory*, 8(4): 323–338.

Tadajewski, Mark (2006) 'The Ordering of Marketing Theory: The Influence of McCarthyism and the Cold War', *Marketing Theory*, 6(2): 163–199.

Vaile, R. (1949) 'Towards a Theory of Marketing-A Comment', *Journal of Marketing*, 14(April): 520–522.

Van Sell, S.L. and Kalofissudus, I. (2007) 'Formulating Nursing Theory',ww.nursing.gr/theory.html. Last accessed 11 July 2008.

Vargo, S and Lusch, R.F. (2008) 'Service-Dominant Logic: Continuing the Evolution, *Journal of the Academy of Marketing Science*, 36(1):1–10.

Vargo, S.L. and Lusch, R.F. (2004) 'Evolving to a New Dominant Logic for Marketing', *Journal of Marketing*, 68(1): 1–17.

Venkatesh, A. (1985) 'Is Marketing Ready for Kuhn?', in N. Dholakia and J. Arndt (eds) *Changing the Course of Marketing: Alternative Paradigms for Widening Marketing Theory*, pp. 45–67. Greenwich: JAI Press.

Webster, F.E. Jr. (1992) 'The Changing Role of Marketing in the Corporation', *Journal of Marketing*, 56(10): 1–17.

Wensley, R. (1990) '"The Voice of the Consumer?": Speculations on the Limits to the Marketing Analogy', *European Journal of Marketing*, 24(7): 49–60.

White, W.L. (1940) 'Marketing Research', *The Annals of the American Academy of Political and Social Science*, 209: 183–192.

Whittington, R. (2006) 'Completing the Practice Turn in Strategy Research', *Organization Studies,* 27(5): 613–634.

Wilkie, W.L. and Moore, E.S. (2003) 'Scholarly Research in Marketing: Exploring the '4 Eras' of Thought Development', *Journal of Public Policy and Marketing,* 22(2): 116–146.

Wilkie, W.L. and Moore, E.S. (2006) 'Macromarketing as a Pillar of Marketing Thought', *Journal of Macromarketing*, 26(2): 224–232.

Wooliscroft, B., Tamilia, R.D. and Shapiro, S.D. (eds) (2006) *A Twenty-First Century Guide to Aldersonian Marketing Thought*. New York: Springer.

Zaltman, G., LeMasters, K. and Heffring, M. (1982) *Theory Construction in Marketing*. New York: John Wiley & Sons.

Zinn, W. and Johnson, S.D. (1990) 'The Commodity Approach in Marketing: Is It Really Obsolete?', *Journal of the Academy of Marketing Science*, 18(4): 345–353, Holt, Rinehard & Winston.

Historical Development of Marketing Theory

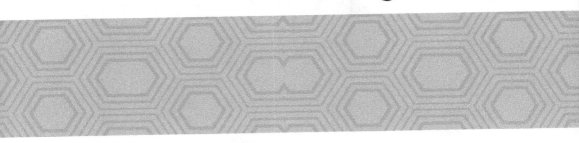

The Early Schools of Marketing Thought

Eric H. Shaw, D.G. Brian Jones,
and Paula A. McLean

INTRODUCTION

In the study of any academic discipline, ideas and issues are discussed and debated. Over the course of time, these concepts and arguments cluster into critical masses that may be described as a means of organizing subject matter, an approach to understanding the discipline or as a school of marketing thought.

Several articles already exist reviewing the early history of individual schools of marketing thought, particularly Hollander (1980) on the institutional school, Hunt and Goolsby (1988) on functions, Murphy and Enis (1986) and Zinn and Johnson (1990) on the commodity school and Savitt (1981) on interregional trade. In addition, the early schools are discussed in two excellent books on the subject of schools of marketing thought and theory: Bartels' (1988) *The History of Marketing Thought*, and Sheth et al.'s (1988) *Marketing Theory: Evolution and Evaluation*. Why yet another history?

Unfortunately, these review articles focus on the history of individual schools and miss the wider landscape of their fit with the other early schools. Also, despite their seminal contributions to the marketing literature, there are some limitations in each of the books. Bartels' (1988) work primarily focuses on subareas of marketing, rather than schools of thought. Although traditional schools are discussed in his general marketing section, the book is a general history of marketing as an academic discipline, organized chronologically, rather than a focus on schools of marketing thought. Sheth et al. (1988) provide the most comprehensive work on schools of marketing thought. Their book mainly centres on the theoretical evaluation of these schools, however, rather than their historical evolution.

The purpose of this work is to broaden and deepen the literature on the early schools of marketing thought. The present chapter provides new insights into the origins and development of the traditional schools and brings their history up to date. It also shows how the traditional schools can be synthesized to create a rudimentary general theory of the marketing process based on channels of distribution.

For purposes of this analysis, a school of marketing thought is defined by three criteria. First, a school represents a substantial body of knowledge. Second, a school is developed by a number of scholars. Third, a school describes or explains at least one aspect of the what, how, who, why, when and where of performing marketing activities.

THE ORIGIN OF MARKETING IN THE ACADEMY

Prior to the academic study of marketing, various thinkers dating back to the ancient Greek Socratic philosophers, Plato and Aristotle, discussed macromarketing issues, such as how marketing was integrated into society (Shaw, 1995). Throughout the Middle Ages, the Medieval schoolmen, from St Augustine of Hippo to St Thomas of Aquinas, wrote about micromarketing concerns, such as how people could practice marketing ethically and without sin (Jones and Shaw, 2002). Most historians agree, however, that marketing as an academic discipline emerged as a branch of applied economics. Various schools of economics provided grist for the marketing mill at that time, particularly the Classical and Neoclassical schools (Bartels, 1988), as well as the German Historical and American Institutional schools (Jones and Monieson, 1990).

In addition to economics as a parent discipline, management also developed as a sister discipline in the early twentieth century. Practical innovations, such as the use of interchangeable parts and assembly lines, were combined with innovative thinking in more efficient management practices. Pioneered by Taylor (1903, 1911) and Gilbreth (1911), 'Scientific Management' studied worker tasks and costs, as well as time and motion, to produce efficiencies on the factory floor. Dramatic improvements in the factory system resulted in mass production, creating the necessity for understanding mass distribution to service mass consumption.

At the turn of the twentieth century, business was bustling in the United States. There was increasing migration to cities, the emergence of national brands and chain stores, rural free mail and package delivery, and growing newspaper and magazine advertising. The completion of the transcontinental railroad generated ever-increasing trunk lines to even small cities, while larger cities developed mass transit, and growing numbers of automobiles and trucks travelled on ever-expanding roadways. These infrastructure developments in transportation and communication connected rural farmers, through agents and brokers, with urban consumers, manufacturers with wholesalers and wholesalers with retailers. These developments helped not just small specialty stores, but also the new mammoth department stores and national mail order houses, to ultimately reach urban and rural household consumers.

The time was ripe for thinking about improvements in market distribution. As academic schools of business arose at the end of the nineteenth century, the first marketing courses in American universities were taught in 1902 (Bartels, 1988). To organize marketing's distinct subject matter, pioneer scholars in the newly emerging discipline developed the first three approaches to the scientific study of marketing phenomena: (1) cataloguing functions, (2) classifying commodities and (3) categorizing institutions. Now known collectively as the traditional approaches to the study of marketing (Bartels, 1988), they were used to argue against the common complaint 'with the large price spread in agricultural products between producers and consumers, and popular criticisms of high costs, waste and inefficiencies in marketing' (Jones and Shaw, 2002: 47). Marketing *functions* demonstrated that the distribution (i.e. storage and transportation) and exchange activities (i.e. buying and selling) performed by specialized marketing *institutions* (trading firms, e.g. wholesaler and retailers, agents and brokers) in moving agricultural and manufacturing *commodities* (i.e. products and services) from sources of supply to places of demand were socially useful and economically valuable (Jones and Shaw, 2002).

MARKETING FUNCTIONS SCHOOL

Marketing functions was the first of the traditional schools to emerge in the embryonic marketing discipline. It addressed the question: what is the work of marketing? The functions approach was described by Converse (1945) as the most significant theoretical development of early marketing thought; indeed he compared it with the discovery of atomic theory, because it sought to identify and catalogue the fundamental elements of the field. Few concepts in the marketing literature have so closely followed such a clearly delineated life cycle. The functional approach to understanding marketing began its introduction during the 1910s, underwent rapid growth in the 1920s, entered early maturity in the 1940s, peaked in the 1950s, began declining in the 1960s and was discarded by the 1970s (roughly paralleling Hunt and Goolsby's 1988 review).

In what historians (Bartels, 1988; Sheth et al., 1988) generally regard as the critical work in the emerging academic discipline of marketing, 'Some Problems in Market Distribution', Arch Shaw (1912: 731) identified five functions of middlemen: '(1) Sharing the risk, (2) Transporting the goods, (3) Financing the operations, (4) Selling the goods, and (5) Assembling, sorting, and reshipping'. In a retrospective letter, Shaw (1950) described how he developed these ideas in 1910 as a student at the Harvard Business School; while studying the historical contribution of merchants to the economy, he searched 'for some simple concept by means of which these functions would fall naturally into definite classifications and their interdependence disclosed. The objective was to give order and usability to the knowledge of market distribution accumulated as of that time'.

L.D.H. Weld recognized that functions are 'universal', often shifting backward and forward in the channel of distribution: 'They are not always performed by middlemen, but often to a greater extent by producers themselves, [and] it should be noted that the final consumer performs part of the marketing functions' (1917: 306). Very similar to Shaw's list, Weld's listing includes seven functions: (1) risk bearing, (2) transportation, (3) financing, (4) selling, (5) assembling, (6) rearrangement (sorting, grading and breaking bulk) and (7) storage. Although arranged and combined somewhat differently, the only new function added is storage.

Although no two authors' lists looked precisely the same, subsequent writers, such as Cherington (1920) with seven functions, Duncan (1920) with eight, Vanderblue (1921) with ten, Ivey (1921) with seven, Converse (1921) with nine and Clark (1922) with seven functions, also entered the competition for best list of functions. Each author added some, dropped others, aggregated several functions into one or disaggregated one function into several others. Clark (1922) ultimately reduced the number to as few as three (with sub-functions): exchange (buying and selling), physical distribution (storage and transportation) and facilitating functions (financing, risk taking and standardization). In the most comprehensive review of the literature to that date, Ryan (1935) expanded the list to more than 120 functions grouped into 16 functions categories. In one historical analysis of the functional approach, Faria (1983) opined that the most useful synthesis and most widely accepted list of marketing functions to 1940 was developed by Maynard et al. in 1927, but Faria offered no evidence in support of his opinion. Maynard et al. (1927) essentially extended Clark's (1922) list of seven functions to eight by adding marketing information. There does not appear to be any basis to argue one author's list of functions versus another list, other than to state the most parsimonious is that of Clark (1922) and the most detailed that of Ryan (1935).

That different writers could produce such varying numbers of functions presents an obvious problem with the concept. By 1948, the American Marketing Association Committee on Definitions expressed their dissatisfaction:

It is probably unfortunate that this term [marketing function] was ever developed. Under it students have sought to squeeze a heterogeneous and non-consistent group of activities.... Such functions as assembling, storage, and transporting, are broad general economic functions, while selling and buying are essentially individual in character. All these discrete groups we attempt to crowd into one class and label marketing functions. (cited in McGarry, 1950: 264)

Attempting to revive the functions approach, McGarry (1950) reconsidered the concept based on the purpose of marketing activity, which he regarded as creating exchanges. McGarry (1950: 269) believed he had arrived at six functions constituting the *sine qua non* of marketing:

Contractual – searching out of buyers and sellers
Merchandising – fitting goods to market requirements
Pricing – the selection of a price
Propaganda – the conditioning of the buyers or of the sellers to a favourable attitude
Physical Distribution – the transporting and storing of the goods
Termination – the consummation of the marketing process

Ironically, in attempting to breathe new life into functions, Hunt and Goolsby astutely observed that McGarry was sowing the 'seeds of its demise'. In their exhaustive search of the literature, they noted that McGarry's list of functions was much closer to the work of marketing managers than older listings of functions, 'McGarry was presaging the rise of the managerial approach to the study of marketing and the demise of the functional approach' (1988: 40). Although there were no new conceptual developments after McGarry, functions could still be found in the revised editions of earlier marketing principles texts, such as Beckman (1927, and subsequent editions through 1973). As the principles texts

died out, so did the functional approach to marketing thought. The functions or work of marketing, however, later re-emerged as channel 'flows' in the institutional school and as managerial tasks in the marketing management school (see Jones et al., this volume).

COMMODITY SCHOOL

The commodity school focused on the distinctive characteristics of goods (i.e. products and services) and addressed the question: how are different classes of goods marketed? Most work in commodities involved categories of goods: 'Classification schemes have always been at the heart of the commodity approach, because they are of critical importance in establishing the differences among various types of commodities' (Zinn and Johnson, 1990: 346). Although he did not use the terms industrial and consumer commodities, Cherington (1920: 21–22) discussed several categories of goods, including raw materials and component parts used in manufacturing and those goods that 'disappear from commerce to go into individual consumption or into household use'. Duncan (1920) distinguished between agricultural and manufactured commodities, noting that the analysis of commodities could be applied to any good, 'whether a material thing or service', anticipating issues of products compared to services (e.g. Judd, 1969; Lovelock, 1981; Rathmell, 1966; Shostack, 1977; Vargo and Lusch, 2004).

In Breyer's (1931) book, *Commodity Marketing*, each chapter followed a common method in describing the marketing of an individual product or service from original producers, through intermediaries, to final users, including such commodities as cotton, cement, coal, petroleum, iron, steel, automobiles, electricity and telephone services. Similarly, in Vaile et al.'s (1952) book, *Marketing in the American Economy*, there was also discussion of how some individual goods are marketed, including used cars and airplanes. In contrast to tracing the movement of individual commodities, Alexander (1951: 34) described the aggregate flow of goods in the United States for 1939, from manufacturing, through manufacturers' sales branches, wholesalers and retailers, to industrial and household consumers. In an even more extensive study, Cox et al. (1965) explored the aggregate flow of goods in the United States for 1947, from agriculture, mining, fisheries and other extractive industries, through wholesalers and other intermediate trade, to manufacturing and construction, to wholesaling and retailing, including imports, public utilities, transportation and services to final users – including exports, government, businesses and households. Most work in the commodity school of thought, however, involved neither individual commodities nor aggregate commodity flows, but rather was focused on the classification of goods.

The most influential classifier of commodities was Copeland (1924). First, he made a clear distinction between industrial and consumer goods based upon who bought the commodity and the use for which it was intended. Copeland recognized the demand for industrial goods was derived from the demand for consumer goods, a distinction largely taken for granted by subsequent scholars. Copeland identified five categories of industrial goods, and later services were added as a sixth category (McCarthy, 1960). Of the six categories, two involve capital goods, two are used in production and two are expense items. Capital goods are generally depreciable and include the two most expensive categories: (1) installations – long-term capital items such as buildings and land and (2) accessory equipment – shorter duration capital items such as trucks and computers. Other goods are used in the production process: (3) raw materials, such as silica, lead oxide and potash heated to 1600 degrees Fahrenheit to produce glass and (4) component parts, for example, rubber tires, metal and plastic body parts, leather seats and glass windows are assembled to produce an automobile. Expense items include categories to maintain

and support the business: (5) supplies for maintenance, repair and operating the business and (6) services to support business operations (e.g. accounting or custodial services). Copeland's industrial goods classification – with the addition of services – has barely changed over the decades of the twentieth century (Perreault and McCarthy, 1996). Although the concept remains the same, the term industrial goods is sometimes replaced with the term business goods or its shorthand expression – B2B (business-to-business marketing).

It is in the area of consumer goods classification, however, that the most extensive developments in the commodity school have occurred. Most work on consumer goods classification is built on Copeland's original three categories: convenience, shopping and specialty goods. Copeland (1924) credited Charles Parlin with suggesting two of the three categories. Gardner cited Parlin's (1912) categories as '(1) convenience goods, those articles of daily purchase required for immediate use, (2) shopping goods, those more important purchases that require comparison as to qualities and price, and (3) emergency goods, those necessary to meet an unexpected occurrence' (1945: 275). Copeland subsumed Parlin's emergency goods in the convenience category.

In another work, cited neither by Copeland nor by Gardner, Parlin (1915: 298) anticipated specialty goods as well, noting those goods for which people 'may go some distance out of their way to find a desired brand'. In another development not cited in the marketing literature, these categories were anticipated by one of Copeland's colleagues at Harvard, Arch W. Shaw, who mentioned convenience and specialty goods. With the former, 'the consumer puts convenience first, either because the amount of money involved is small and values are standardized or because the nature of the product puts a premium on frequent small purchases close at home' (1916: 283). In the latter, 'a specialty [good] is a result of closer adaptation of a product to the needs … of the consumer' (1916: 125).

Thus, Copeland's three categories of goods were in the air, so to speak, at the time he began organizing them into a coherent classification system.

Copeland (1924: 14) clearly defined the three categories. Convenience goods are 'those customarily purchased at easily accessible stores'. Shopping goods include 'those for which a consumer wishes to compare prices, quality, and style at the time of purchase'. There was a third category, however, in which consumers neither travelled to a convenient store location nor made comparisons while shopping. He thought this category so different he called it specialty goods, 'those which have some [special] attraction for the consumer, other than price, which induces him to put forth special effort to visit the store ... and make the purchase without shopping'. Although there were a number of rationales for the three categories of consumer goods, it was the specialty goods category that piqued the most interest and raised the most questions among subsequent authors.

Holton (1958) conceptualized the distinction among the categories based on the benefits resulting from price and quality comparisons relative to searching costs. With convenience goods, the benefits are small and with shopping goods, the benefits are large compared with the cost of search. Specialty goods overlapped the other categories, and the distinction Holton made is that such goods had a small demand thereby requiring a buyer's special effort to find the relatively few outlets carrying them. Luck (1959: 64) rejoined Holton's disparagement of specialty goods by arguing 'the willingness of consumers to make special purchasing efforts is explanatory, consumer oriented and useful'.

Although he used shopping and convenience goods categories, Aspinwall (1958) took a very different approach to Copeland's classification than prior or subsequent authors. Using a continuous colour scheme, where red stands for convenience goods, yellow for shopping goods and shades of orange for goods in between, he related five characteristics of goods to length of channel and type of promotion required based on summing the values on each characteristic. Convenience goods have a high (1) replacement rate, and are low on (2) gross margin, (3) amount of product adjustment or service, (4) time of consumption and (5) search time. Based on these characteristics, such goods require long channels and broadcast advertising. Shopping goods have a low replacement rate and are high on the other four characteristics. These goods require short channels and personal selling. The colours are meant to blend, and shades of orange goods could occur anywhere in between the red and yellow. Orange was more moderate in all characteristics, requiring mid-length channels and some broadcast promotion. The specialty category was not included in Aspinwall's classification.

Several rationales appeared in the literature justifying Copeland's three consumer goods categories. Bucklin (1963), using a decision-making approach, asked the question: prior to purchase, does the consumer have a mental preference map? If the answer is no, then price and quality comparisons are required, indicating a shopping good. If yes, a sub-question must be asked: will the buyer accept substitutes? If yes, then the buyer knows what s/he wants, any close substitute will work, and it is a convenience good. If no, then the buyer knows what s/he wants, will not accept alternatives, and extra search effort is required, indicating a specialty good. Kaish (1967: 31) applied the theory of cognitive dissonance to explain a buyer's willingness to put forth physical or mental energy. Convenience goods are not particularly important to the buyer, any brand will do, no mental cognitive dissonance and minimal physical effort is required. Shopping goods are important and 'arouse high levels of pre-purchase mental anxiety about the possible inappropriateness of the purchase ... [Although anxiety is high] it is reducible by shopping behavior'. Specialty goods are important and also have high pre-purchase anxiety but it is 'not readily reducible' by comparison shopping; their importance requires physical search to locate the special good and reduce the mental anxiety.

Based on product similarity and buyer risk, Bucklin (1976) subdivided shopping goods into two types: low-intensity and high-intensity goods, similar to Krugman's (1965) concept of low-involvement and high-involvement goods. Building on Kaish's work, Holbrook and Howard (1977) developed a two-dimensional map with physical effort on one axis and mental effort on the other. Based on the four quadrants, they also argued for the inclusion of a fourth category of goods, termed preference goods (roughly similar to Krugman's low-involvement or Bucklin's low-intensity shopping goods), requiring some shopping effort, moderate risk and high-brand preference.

Building on these conceptual developments, Enis and Roering (1980) combined two basic buyer considerations – physical effort and mental risk – with the marketer's concern for product differentiation and marketing mix differentiation (although it could be argued that the product is just one element of the marketing mix). This results in a four-way classification relating buyer effort/product differentiation to buyer risk/marketing mix differentiation, with suggestions for marketing strategies relating to each of the convenience, shopping, specialty and preference quadrants.

After an exhaustive literature review of consumer goods categories, Murphy and Enis (1986) organized almost all articles classifying consumer goods, based on Copeland, into a table with two dimensions: effort and risk. Convenience goods are low effort and low risk; and marketers can only employ limited marketing mixes. Compared to convenience goods, preference goods are slightly higher effort and much higher risk; and marketers can use a wider variety of mixes. Shopping goods are still higher on both effort and risk dimensions; here marketers can use the widest range of alternative mixes. Specialty goods are the highest on effort and

risk, but offer marketers the most limited range of alternative mixes. Murphy and Enis (1986: 30) concluded that based on the effort and risk dimensions of price/cost, the four-fold classification is 'superior' to all others. They supported their conclusion with four arguments: (1) it is buyer oriented, (2) it is generalizable across all users [consumer, industrial], sectors [profit, non-profit] and goods categories [products, services], (3) the new classification recognizes the central role of the benefit/cost bundle [benefits must equal or exceed the costs of a transaction], and (4) it has the advantage of using familiar terminology.

From the 1920s to 1980s, Copeland's classification scheme produced one of the longest strings of conceptually building upon and improving an original idea, rather than abandoning a concept to the scrap heap of history or reinventing an old concept with a new name. Nevertheless, there are a number of alternative goods classification schemes in the literature, particularly categorizations featuring bipolar alternatives: low-involvement versus high-involvement goods (Krugman, 1965), products versus services (Lovelock, 1981; Rathmell, 1966; Shostack, 1977; etc.) and many others.

Another classification scheme attracting marketing interest is the work of Nelson (1970, 1974); he separated goods into two categories: search and experience, based on the relative costs of the good versus costs of the search (building on Stigler's (1961) work on the marginal value of information). With search goods, the benefits can be discovered by information search prior to purchase, such as a computer or camcorder. On the other hand, with experience goods, the benefits can only be determined after purchase when the good is utilized, such as toothpaste or fast food restaurants. These goods do not require much search, because they can be purchased inexpensively and discarded for an alternative brand if not satisfactory, or because the cost of search is high relative to the potential benefits. A third category called 'credence goods' was added by Darby and Karni (1973), where the attributes of goods cannot be easily verified before or after purchase. Credence goods require additional information search costs to determine the good's benefits or value, for example, a surgical operation or automobile repair that may not have been necessary. There is some similarity among the goods classification schemas of Copeland (1924) (particularly Bucklin's (1963) version of it), Nelson (1970) and Krugman (1965). Shopping goods and search goods require information search prior to purchase and are typically high involvement, except in the case of preference goods, which are low involvement. Convenience goods and experience goods are inexpensive enough to allow sampling of alternatives or evaluation by purchase, do not require significant information search and are typically low involvement. Specialty goods include, but are not limited to, credence goods and are very high involvement.

INSTITUTIONAL SCHOOL

Marketing institutions refer to those who do the work of marketing, usually marketing middlemen, including wholesalers, agents, brokers and retailers. Sheth et al. (1988: 74) wrote: 'L.D.H. Weld deserves credit as the founding father of the institutional school' based on his discussion of the value of specialized middlemen in performing marketing tasks. Weld (1916: 21) addressed the question: 'Are there too many middlemen?' The foundation of the institutional school is the emphasis on describing and classifying various types of marketing institutions, and later explaining their interactions in what Clark (1922: 8) termed a 'channel of distribution'.

Nystrom's *Economics of Retailing* in 1915 provided the marketing discipline with the earliest discussion of the development of retailing institutions (Bartels, 1988: 91). Nystrom (1915: 11) wrote that one major purpose of the book is to describe 'one link of the distributing system – retailing ... to

determine the most economical routes through which the goods may be transferred from producers to consumer'. Beckman's (1927) *Wholesaling* is credited as the marketing discipline's earliest book on wholesaling institutions (Bartels, 1988: 114). Beckman (1927: v) stated: 'wholesaling occupies a strategic position in the distribution of goods ... the goal of which is a more efficient marketing system'. While retailing and wholesaling middlemen are major links in channels of distribution, both books focus primarily within the institution rather than discussing the linkages between institutions. Further, marketing institutions involve more than retailing and wholesaling middlemen.

Butler and Swinney (1918: 9) defined middlemen to 'include everyone who stands between the prime producer and the ultimate consumer and takes a profit for the risk he runs in addition to being compensated for the cost of his services'. This notion requires a distinction between marketing institutions and middlemen that has often been lost in historical discussions of the institutional approach. The distinction involves the idea of 'functional specialists'. Early on, Duncan (1920: 7) stated that 'functionalized middlemen, or those men, such as railroad men, insurance men, wholesalers, retailers, bankers, who devote their effort to a specialized phase of business activity ... may be called an institution'. Thus, marketing institutions combine what would today be regarded as middlemen (wholesalers, agents, brokers, retailers, etc.) with what was termed functional specialists or facilitating institutions. Clark (1922: 89) dismissed this notion by including only middlemen in marketing institutions and excluding facilitating institutions: 'Functional specialists are agencies which specialize entirely in transportation, storage, risk-taking, and financing. These are not middlemen'. Breyer (1934, 1964) similarly distinguished between:

trading concerns engaged primarily in selling and buying – producers, wholesalers, retailers, brokers, selling agents, commission houses, etc. ... in contrast to non-trading concerns engaged in [facilitating] marketing activity, commercial banks, transportation and storage companies, insurance companies, and so on. (1964: 163)

The institutional school originally emphasized the description and classification of middlemen. Beckman and Engle (1937) and Beckman et al. (1973: 205) may be credited with the most enduring definitions and taxonomy:

> Middlemen stand between prime producers and ultimate consumers. ... All middlemen can be divided into merchant and functional middlemen. ... Merchant middlemen buy the goods outright and necessarily take title to them [e.g. wholesalers and retailers]. ... Functional middlemen assist directly in a change of ownership, but do not take title to the goods [e.g. auctions, brokers, manufacturers' agents, and selling agents].

There are clear definitions for each of the bracketed types of middlemen, and various types of wholesalers, retailers and functional middlemen are further classified and defined. The Beckman and Engle distinction between wholesale and retail is a classic:

> Wholesaling includes all market transactions in which the purchaser is actuated by a profit or business motive in making the purchase, except for transactions that involve a small quantity of goods purchased from a retail establishment for business use, which transactions are considered as retail. (1937: 25)

There were few improvements on Beckman's original definitions and categorization schema, and the school evolved from description and classification of marketing institutions to explaining the economics and behavioural dimensions of channels of distribution.

Clark (1922) appears to have coined the term 'channel of distribution'. Breyer (1934, 1964: 163) characterized the channel as 'the elemental structure' of the marketing institution. Study of channels grew in popularity as several excellent books of readings appeared: Mallen's (1967) *The Marketing Channel: A Conceptual Viewpoint*, Stern's (1969) *Distribution Channels: Behavioral Dimensions*, and Bucklin's (1970) *Vertical*

Marketing Systems, among others. A number of economic and behavioral concepts, such as profit and non-financial rewards, power and dependence, conflict and cooperation, trust and commitment, are found in this rich literature. Several of these concepts are linked in a meta-analysis by Geyskens et al. (1999).

In a foundational theoretical analysis, Lewis (1968) identifies seven theories of marketing channels:

1　McInnes' (1964) 'Theory of Market Separations'
2　Vaile et al.'s (1952) 'Marketing Flows Theory'
3　Aspinwall's (1958) 'Parallel Systems Theory'
4　Aspinwall's (1962) 'Depot Theory'
5　Bucklin's (1965) 'Theory of Postponement and Speculation'
6　Alderson's (1965) 'Theory of Transactions and Transvections'
7　Alderson's (1957) 'Theory of Sorting'

Unfortunately, Lewis did not integrate them in a meta-theoretical analysis.

Some of these represent mid-range theories that are subsumed under higher-level theories. Through much of the discipline's history, scholars have contributed to a rudimentary general theory of the marketing process based on channels of distribution. Although various authors explain it more or less clearly using a variety of differing terminology, the underlying constructs are fundamentally the same. The terms include: 'maladjustments' by Shaw (1916) and Clark (1922), 'obstacles', 'resistances' and 'channel circuits' by Breyer (1934), 'flows' by Vaile et al. (1952), Fisk (1967) and Dixon and Wilkinson (1982), 'discrepancies' by Alderson (1957, 1965) and 'separations' by McInnes (1964).

The terminology by McInnes (1964) and Alderson (1965) is easiest to follow. These authors begin with the relationships between makers and users of goods. It is argued that the potential for market interaction is created when producers become separated from consumers by the division of labour. As specialization increases, the division of labour becomes greater, the gaps created become wider and the network of potential trading relationships becomes more complex.

The potential for exchange, however, is not the same as an actual market transaction. Discrepancies (maladjustments, obstacles, resistances and separations) provide the opportunity for market activity to be performed by middlemen to bridge the gaps (close channel circuits, connect flows) separating original sellers from final buyers, thereby transforming transactional potentialities into actualities.

Simply stated, flows overcome separations. The gaps in the market include: 'space, time, perception (information), ownership and value' (McInnes, 1964: 57–58), and 'assortments' (Alderson, 1965: 78). The flows bridging these gaps are, unfortunately, far more varied. Vaile et al. (1952: 113) proposed eight: three flows from seller to buyer (possession, ownership and promotion), three reciprocal flows between the parties (negotiation, financing and risking), and two flows from buyer to seller (ordering and payment). Fisk (1967) suggested five flows: communication, ownership, finance, physical distribution and risk. Dixon and Wilkinson (1982) reduced the number to three fundamental flows: contact (communication or movement of information), contract (negotiation or movement of use rights) and material fulfilment (physical distribution or movement of products and people).

How fast do flows move to overcome separations and match a seller's small segment of supply with a buyer's small segment of demand? According to Aspinwall's (1962) Depot Theory, goods move towards consumption at a rate established by the final consumer's need for replacement. As detailed in Aspinwall's (1958) Parallel Systems Theory (discussed in the commodity school), replacement rate is inversely related to gross margin, services required, search time and consumption time. Thus, knowing replacement rate provides knowledge of the other characteristics determining rate of flow. The question of which institutional depot (manufacturer, wholesaler, retailer, household, etc.) in the channel will hold and modify inventory is addressed by Bucklin's (1965) 'Theory of Postponement and Speculation'. Alderson (1957) developed the postponement part, arguing that changes in

modifying products and stocking inventory should be postponed to the latest possible point in the marketing flow because of reduced risk. Bucklin (1965) added the corollary theory of speculation that changes in form and holding inventory should be made at the earliest possible point in the marketing flow to take advantage of economies of scale. Thus, speculation takes advantage of the lower costs of modifying goods early to obtain economies of scale resulting in mass production, while postponement deals with reducing risk by modifying goods at the latest point for segmented demand resulting in today's mass customization.

Alderson's (1965) transvection represents one of the most powerful, but underutilized, constructs in marketing thought. A transvection includes all purchases and sales from the original seller of raw materials, through intermediary purchases and sales to the final buyer of a finished product. That is, it links all the institutions (depots) and functions (work performed) in a channel. Alderson (1957, 1965) described what takes place in a channel-transvection in terms of 'Sorts and Transformations'. At each institutional depot, goods are alternatively sorted (sorted-out, accumulated, allocated or assorted) and transformed (modified, merchandised, stored, transported or used). If the channel is regarded as structure, such as the banks of a river, then the transvection represents process, the flow of the river. Therefore, aggregating the set of parallel channel-transvections taking place in a particular economy, such as the USA, for a given time frame, say a year, provides 'an exhaustive description of the marketing process' (Alderson and Miles, 1965: 122). Thus, most partial theories of channels of distribution can be synthesized into a logically coherent whole.

INTERREGIONAL TRADE SCHOOL

There are two approaches to interregional trade, one quantitative and the other conceptual. Their common denominator is a concern with the question of 'where' marketing takes place.

The quantitative approach follows Sir Issac Newton's 1687 'Universal Law of Gravitation'. One body (stars, planets, etc.) is attracted to another by a force that is directly proportional to the masses of the two bodies and inversely proportional to the square of the distance separating them. Using this insight, William Reilly's (1931) book, *The Law of Retail Gravitation*, provides the impetus for bridging the spatial gap in marketing. Following Newton, Reilly's Law states that given a small town between two large cities, each city would attract customers from the small town in direct proportion to the populations [the mass factor] of the two cities and inversely proportional to the square of the distances separating the two cities from the intermediate town.

Converse (1949) made numerous tests of Reilly's formula. Then he extended Reilly's work to define the boundaries of a given trading area:

> A trading center and a town in ... its trade area divide the trade of the town approximately in direct proportion to the population of the two areas and inversely as the square of the distance factors [distance weighted by an empirically determined inertia factor]. (1949: 382)

Converse's modification in the distance factor is significant, making it possible to determine the breaking point between two competing trading centres (which could, in principle, include cities, shopping malls, stores, etc.).

Huff (1964) expanded Converse's work to explain how a buyer chooses among several distant trading centres to purchase products and services. Huff refined both measures in Reilly's and Converse's formulas. He enriched the metric used for the 'size' or 'mass' of the trading centre from population to square footage of selling area. He also improved the measurement for 'distance' from miles to time travelled. Finally, Huff transformed the standard definition of a trading area from a seller's to a buyer's perspective. Huff (1964: 38) criticized the American Marketing Association (AMA) definition of

'trading area' as 'a district whose size is usually determined by the boundaries within which it is economical in terms of volume and cost for a marketing unit to sell and/or deliver a good or service', because it provided 'little insight concerning the nature and scope of a trading area'. Resolving the issue of nature and scope, Huff (1964: 38) defined a trading area as: 'a geographically delineated region, containing potential customers for whom there exists a probability greater than zero of their purchasing a given class of products or services offered for sale by a particular firm or by a particular agglomeration of firms'. Apparently, Huff's work was regarded as definitive, because there have been virtually no additions or criticisms to gravitation models in the marketing literature since his 1964 article; although economists have expanded gravitation models to include additional variables.

E.T. Grether is credited as the major developer of the conceptual side of interregional trade (Savitt, 1981; Sheth et al., 1988). Grether (1950) explored regional exporting and importing based on four factors: (1) resource scarcity, (2) regional affluence, (3) reciprocal demand among regions and the (4) relative competition within regions. Subsequently, in a section of his co-authored book (Vaile et al., 1952: 487–569), Grether refined the characteristics of different geographical regions and their impact on the export and import of products and services. He defined an economic region as a relatively large geographical area with four characteristics: (1) it has more than one centre of economic control, (2) it has greater internal homogeneity (than other areas), (3) it exports a characteristic group of products to other areas and (4) it imports the characteristic products of other areas.

Revzan (1961) provided a number of factors that impact the size of a wholesaler's trade area, such as high product value relative to bulk, transportation rates and available channels of distribution. Savitt (1981: 231) regarded the core of interregional trade as recognition of the importance and interdependence of social and geographic factors that affect a firm and its relationship in channels. Based on the foundation laid by these marketing scholars, the factors affecting interregional trade in today's global economy could easily be replaced by international marketing without any loss of conceptual continuity. Indeed, economists have expanded on the marketing gravity models of Reilly, Converse and Huff by including some of the social and geographic factors identified by Grether, Revzan and Savitt. This modern economic approach expanding interregional trade into international trade has been integrated and reintroduced into the marketing field in a recent marketing dissertation (Sheng, 2007).

CONCLUSION

The early schools of marketing thought developed to answer questions necessary to describe and explain marketing as a scientific field of study. Scholars answered 'What activities make up marketing?' by cataloguing functions. In answer to 'How different types of products and services could be organized?' marketing writers classified commodities and related commodities to functions. The question of 'Who performs marketing functions on commodities?' was answered by categorized marketing institutions. The interregional trade school answered the question 'Where were marketing functions performed on commodities?' Thus, as ideas and issues were discussed and debated, a critical mass developed and coalesced into what became known as 'approaches' to understanding marketing, what we now consider 'schools of marketing thought'.

The early schools answered the questions asked about marketing at that time: what, how, who and where. There still remained, however, questions that were either never addressed or did not develop a critical mass sufficient to be called a school. It would take a paradigm shift to bring these questions to the fore.

REFERENCES

Alderson, W. (1957) *Marketing Behavior and Executive Action*. Homewood, IL: Richard D. Irwin.

Alderson, W. (1965) *Dynamic Marketing Behavior*. Homewood, IL: Richard D. Irwin.

Alderson, W. and Miles, M.W. (1965) 'Toward a Formal Theory of Transactions and Transvections', *Journal of Marketing Research*, 2 (May): 117–127.

Alexander, R.S. (1951) 'Goods for the Market: Industrial Goods', in C.F. Phillips (ed.) *Marketing by Manufacturers*, Homewood, IL: Richard Irwin, pp. 34–58.

Aspinwall, L. (1958) 'The Characteristics of Goods and Parallel Systems Theories', in E.J. Kelley and W. Lazer (eds) *Managerial Marketing*, Homewood, IL: Richard D. Irwin, pp. 434–450.

Aspinwall, L. (1962) 'The Depot Theory', in E.J. Kelley and W. Lazer (eds) *Managerial Marketing*, Homewood, IL: Richard D. Irwin, pp. 652–659.

Bartels, R. (1988) *The History of Marketing Thought*. Columbus, OH: Publishing Horizons.

Beckman, T.N. (1927) *Wholesaling*. New York: Ronald Press.

Beckman, T.N. and Engle, N.H. (1937) *Wholesaling*. New York: Ronald Press.

Beckman, T.N., Davidson, W.R. and Talarzyk, W.W. (1973) *Marketing*. New York: Ronald Press.

Breyer, R.F. (1931) *Commodity Marketing*. New York: McGraw-Hill.

Breyer, R.F. (1934) *The Marketing Institution*. New York: McGraw-Hill.

Breyer, R.F. (1964) 'Some Observations on "Structural" Formation and the Growth of Marketing Channels', in R. Cox, W. Alderson and S. Shapiro (eds) *Theory in Marketing*, second edition, Homewood, IL: Richard D. Irwin, pp. 163–175.

Bucklin, L.P. (1963) 'Retail Strategy and the Classification of Consumer Goods', *Journal of Marketing*, 3(January): 50–55.

Bucklin, L.P. (1965) 'Postponement, Speculation and the Structure of Distribution Channels', *Journal of Marketing Research*, 2(February): 26–31.

Bucklin, L.P. (1970) *Vertical Marketing Systems*. Glenview, IL: Scott Foresman.

Bucklin, L.P. (1976) 'Retrospective Comment on Retail Strategy and the Classification of Consumer Goods', in H.A. Thompson (ed.) *The Great Writings in Marketing*, Plymouth, MI: The Commerce Press, pp. 474–480.

Butler, R.S. and Swinney, J.B. (1918) *Marketing and Merchandising*. New York: Alexander Hamilton Institute.

Cherington, P.T. (1920) *The Elements of Marketing*. New York: Macmillan.

Clark, F. (1922) *Principles of Marketing*. New York: Macmillan.

Converse, P.D. (1921) *Marketing Methods and Policies*. Englewood Cliffs, NJ: Prentice-Hall.

Converse, P.D. (1945) 'The Development of the Science of Marketing – An Exploratory Survey', *Journal of Marketing*, 10(July): 14–23.

Converse, P.D. (1949) 'New Laws of Retail Gravitation', *Journal of Marketing*, 14(October): 379–384.

Copeland, M.T. (1924) *Principles of Merchandising*. Chicago, IL: A.W. Shaw.

Cox, R., Goodman, C.S. and Fichandler, T.C. (1965) *Distribution in a High-Level Economy*. Englewood Cliffs, NJ: Prentice-Hall.

Darby, M.R. and Karni, E. (1973) 'Free Competition and the Optimal Amount of Fraud', *Journal of Law and Economics*, 16(April): 67–86.

Dixon, D.F. and Wilkinson, I.F. (1982) *The Marketing System*. Sydney, Australia: Longman Cheshire.

Duncan, C.S. (1920) *Marketing – Its Problems and Methods*. New York: D. Appleton & Co.

Enis, B.M. and Roering, K.J. (1980) 'Product Classification Taxonomies: Synthesis and Consumer Implications', in C. Lamb, Jr and P.M. Dunne (eds) *Theoretical Developments in Marketing*, Chicago, IL: American Marketing Association, pp. 186–189.

Faria, A.J. (1983) 'The Development of the Functional Approach to the Study of Marketing to 1940', in S.C. Hollander and R. Savitt (eds) *First North American Workshop on Historical Research in Marketing*, Lansing, MI: Michigan State University, pp. 160–169.

Fisk, G. (1967) *Marketing Systems*. New York: Harper & Row.

Gardner, E.H. (1945) 'Consumer Goods Classification', *Journal of Marketing*, 9(January): 275–276.

Geyskens, I., Steenkamp, Jan-Benedict, E.M. and Kumar, N. (1999) 'A Meta-Analysis of Satisfaction in Marketing Channel Relationships', *Journal of Marketing Research*, 36(May): 223–239.

Gilbreth, F.B. (1911) *Motion Study: A Method for Increasing the Efficiency of the Workman*. New York: D. Von Nostron.

Grether, E.T. (1950) 'A Theoretical Approach to the Study of Marketing', in R. Cox and W. Alderson (eds) *Theory in Marketing*, Homewood, IL: Richard D. Irwin, pp. 113–123.

Holbrook, M.B. and Howard, J.A. (1977) 'Frequently Purchased Nondurable Goods and Services', in R. Ferber (ed.) *Selected Aspects of Consumer Behavior*, Washington, DC: NSF, pp. 189–222.

Hollander, S.C. (1980) 'Some Notes on the Difficulty of Identifying the Marketing Thought Contributions of the Early Institutionalists', in C. Lamb, Jr and P. Dunne (eds) *Theoretical Developments in Marketing*, Chicago, IL: American Marketing Association, pp. 45–46.

Holton, R.H. (1958) 'The Distinction Between Convenience Goods, Shopping Goods and Specialty Goods', *Journal of Marketing*, 23(July): 53–56.

Huff, D.L. (1964) 'Defining and Estimating a Trading Area', *Journal of Marketing*, 28(July): 34–38.

Hunt, S.D. and Goolsby, J. (1988) 'The Rise and Fall of the Functional Approach to Marketing: A Paradigm Displacement Perspective', in T. Nevett and R.A. Fullerton (eds) *Historical Perspectives in Marketing: Essays in Honor of Stanley C. Hollander*, Lexington, CT: Lexington Books, pp. 35–52.

Ivey, P.W. (1921) *Principles of Marketing*. New York: Ronald Press.

Jones, D.G.B. and Monieson, D.D. (1990) 'Early Development of the Philosophy of Marketing Thought', *Journal of Marketing*, 54(1): 102–113.

Jones, D.G.B. and Shaw, E.H. (2002) 'A History of Marketing Thought', in Barton A. Weitz and Robin Wensley (eds) *Handbook of Marketing*, London: Sage, pp. 39–66.

Judd, R.C. (1969) 'The Case for Redefining Services', *Journal of Marketing*, 28(January): 58–59.

Kaish, S. (1967) 'Cognitive Dissonance and the Classification of Consumer Goods', *Journal of Marketing*, 31(October): 28–31.

Krugman, H.E. (1965) 'The Impact of Television Advertising: Learning Without Involvement', *Public Opinion Quarterly*, 29(Fall): 349–356.

Lewis, E.H. (1968) *Marketing Channels: Structure and Strategy*. New York: McGraw-Hill.

Lovelock, C.H. (1981) 'Classifying Services to Gain Strategic Marketing Insight', *Journal of Marketing*, 47(July): 9–20.

Luck, D.J. (1959) 'On the Nature of Specialty Goods', *Journal of Marketing*, 24(July): 61–64.

Mallen, B.E. (1967) *The Marketing Channel: A Conceptual Viewpoint*. New York: John Wiley.

Maynard, H.H., Weidler, W.C. and Beckman, T.N. (1927) *Principles of Marketing*. New York: Ronald Press.

McCarthy, E.J. (1960) *Basic Marketing: A Managerial Approach*. Homewood, IL: Richard D. Irwin.

McGarry, E.D. (1950) 'Some Functions of Marketing Reconsidered', in R. Cox and W. Alderson (eds) *Theory in Marketing*, Homewood, IL: Richard D. Irwin, pp. 263–279.

McInnes, W. (1964) 'A Conceptual Approach to Marketing', in Reavis Cox, Wroe Alderson and Stanley Shapiro (eds) *Theory in Marketing*, second edition, Homewood, IL: Richard D. Irwin, pp. 51–67.

Murphy, P.E. and Enis, B.M. (1986) 'Classifying Products Strategically', *Journal of Marketing*, 50(July): 24–42.

Nelson, P.J. (1970) 'Information and Consumer Behavior', *Journal of Political Economy*, 78(March/April): 311–329.

Nelson, P.J. (1974) 'Advertising as Information', *Journal of Political Economy*, 82(July/August): 729–754.

Nystrom, P.H. (1915) *The Economics of Retailing*. New York: Ronald Press.

Parlin, C. (1912) '"Department Store Report" Vol. B, (October) 1912', cited by Edward H. Gardner (1945) 'Consumer Goods Classification', *Journal of Marketing*, 9(January): 275–276.

Parlin, C. (1915) '"The Merchandising of Textiles", A speech delivered to the National Wholesale Dry Goods Association, Philadelphia' in (1964) Hiram C. Barksdale (ed.) *Marketing and Progress*, New York: Holt, Rinehart and Winston, pp. 297–312.

Perrault, W.D, Jr and McCarthy, E.J. (1996) *Basic Marketing: A Global-Managerial Approach*. Homewood, IL: Richard D. Irwin.

Rathmell, J.M. (1966) 'What is Meant by Services?' *Journal of Marketing*, 30(October): 32–36.

Reilly, W.J. (1931) *The Law of Retail Gravitation*. New York: John Wiley.

Revzan, D.A. (1961) *Wholesaling in Marketing Organization*. New York: John Wiley.

Ryan, F.W. (1935) 'Functional Elements in Market Distribution', *Harvard Business Review*, 13(October): 137–143.

Savitt, R. (1981) 'The Theory of Interregional Trade', in F. Balderson, J. Carman and F.M. Nicosia (eds) *Regulation of Marketing and the Public Interest*, New York: Pergamon Press, pp. 229–238.

Shaw, A.W. (1912) 'Some Problems in Market Distribution', *Quarterly Journal of Economics*, 26 (August): 706–765.

Shaw, A.W. (1916) *An Approach to Business Problems*. Cambridge, MA: Harvard University Press.

Shaw, A.W. (1950) 'Correspondence, Arch W. Shaw to Peggy Davies, April 14, Acceptance Speech at the 1950 Converse Award', *Edwin Francis Gay Collection*. San Marino, CA: The Huntington Library.

Shaw, E.H. (1995) 'The First Dialogue on Macromarketing', *Journal of Macromarketing*, 15(Spring): 7–20.

Sheng, S.Y. (2007) 'Foreign Market Opportunity Analysis', PhD dissertation, Florida Atlantic University.

Sheth, J.N., Gardner, D.M. and Garrett, D.E. (1988) *Marketing Theory: Evolution and Evaluation*. New York: John Wiley.

Shostack, G.L. (1977) 'Breaking Free from Product Marketing', *Journal of Marketing*, 41(April): 73–80.

Stern, L. (1969) *Distribution Channels: Behavioral Dimensions*. New York: Houghton Mifflin.

Stigler, G. (1961) 'The Economics of Information', *Journal of Political Economy*, 69(June): 213–224.

Taylor, F.W. (1903) *Shop Management*. New York: Harper.

Taylor, F.W. (1911) *Scientific Management*. New York: Harper.

Vaile, R.S., Grether, E.T. and Cox, R. (1952) *Marketing in the American Economy*. New York: Ronald Press.

Vanderblue, H.B. (1921) 'The Functional Approach to the Study of Marketing', *Journal of Political Economy*, 23(June): 676–683.

Vargo, S. and Lusch, R.F. (2004) 'Evolving to a New Dominant Logic for Marketing', *Journal of Marketing*, 68(1): 1–17.

Weld, L.D.H. (1916) *The Marketing of Farm Products*. New York: Macmillan.

Weld, L.D.H. (1917) 'Marketing Functions and Mercantile Organization', *American Economic Review*, (June): 306–318.

Zinn, W. and Johnson, S.D. (1990) 'The Commodity Approach in Marketing Research: Is It Really Obsolete?', *Journal of the Academy of Marketing Science*, 18(Fall): 345–353.

3

The Modern Schools of Marketing Thought

D.G. Brian Jones, Eric H. Shaw, and Paula A. McLean

INTRODUCTION

For our purposes, here, we follow the previous chapter which defined a school of marketing thought as a substantial body of knowledge developed by a number of scholars describing at least one aspect of the what, how, who, why, when and where of performing marketing activities. During the mid-twentieth century, there was a paradigm shift in marketing thinking that eclipsed the traditional approaches as a number of newer schools developed: marketing management, marketing systems, consumer behaviour, macromarketing, exchange and marketing history. This chapter traces the evolution of these six modern schools of marketing thought.

The paradigm shift from traditional approaches to modern schools of marketing thought resulted from several developments. It was influenced by military advances in mathematical modelling, such as linear programming, during the Second World War. Following the war, the shift in capacity from military production to consumer goods spurred economic growth in the United States

creating supply surpluses and the concomitant necessity for demand generation activities by business firms. The paradigm shift was also affected by the Ford Foundation and Carnegie Foundation reports of 1959 calling for greater relevance in business education and providing foundation funding to produce significant curriculum changes. The most important cause of the paradigm shift in marketing thought, however, was the thinking of the dominant scholar of his time – Wroe Alderson. His numerous articles, marketing theory seminars, newsletters and two seminal books (1957, 1965) resulted in or impacted most modern schools of thought including: marketing management, marketing systems, consumer behaviour, macromarketing, and exchange. Interestingly, Alderson's (1957) *Marketing Behavior and Executive Action* was praised by the Ford Foundation as an exemplar of the direction in which business education needed to go (Tadajewski, 2006).

The first of the modern schools was marketing management, which took a managerial approach to understanding marketing. The marketing systems school was closely related to Alderson's functionalist approach and was developed by a number of Alderson's colleagues and students. The consumer behaviour school was influenced by Alderson's emphasis on the behavioural sciences to supplement economics as a basis of academic research; as a result, scores of psychologists, social psychologists and sociologists were drawn to the study of marketing. With the ascendancy of the marketing management and consumer behaviour schools, and the lessening impact of marketing systems thinking, macromarketing surfaced as a school of thought to deal with the impact and consequences of marketing activities on society and society's impact on marketing, as well as encompassing marketing systems. Still another subfield of marketing pioneered by Alderson is the exchange school, which deals with the interaction of a seller and a buyer in a market transaction and with the interactions of groups of buyers and sellers in channel-transvections. Marketing history provided one of the earliest approaches to the study of marketing, yet only recently emerged as a school of marketing thought.

MARKETING MANAGEMENT SCHOOL

Marketing management addresses the question: How should organizations market their products and services? The school focuses on the practice of marketing viewed from the sellers' perspective. The school originally limited the sellers' perspective to manufacturers, but now includes retailers, service providers and all other types of businesses; and with the paradigm broadening has been extended to all forms of non-business entities as well. This school so dominates the marketing field, it must be included as a school of thought rather than a subarea even though it has only a micromarketing focus. The impetus for a managerial perspective to marketing occurred in a book by Alexander et al. (1940), simply named *Marketing*. Fundamentally, books in this genre are organized around the notion of

a marketing mix. Although less pronounced in this book compared with those that followed, most elements of the marketing mix were covered.

Several emerging concepts in the 1950s and early 1960s form the core of ideas leading to the rapid growth of this new school: Wendell Smith's (1956) notion of 'product differentiation and market segmentation as alternative marketing strategies'; Chester Wasson's (1960) idea of the 'product life cycle'; and Robert Keith's (1960) perspective of a consumer orientation known as the 'marketing concept'. Probably the most important concept is Neil Borden's (1964) expression of the 'marketing mix'. In his classic article about its history, Borden credits James Culliton (1948) with describing the marketing executive as a 'decider', a 'mixer of ingredients'. That notion led Borden, in the 1950s, to the insight that what this mixer of ingredients decided upon was a 'marketing mix'. McCarthy (1960: 52) credits A.W. Frey's *The Effective Marketing Mix* in 1956 with the first marketing mix checklist.

Some of the earliest books titled *Marketing Management* were written by D. Maynard Phelps (1953) and by Keith R. Davis (1961), although both focused on sales management. Another similarly titled book was *Management in Marketing* written by Lazo and Corbin (1961), but it focused on the management functions of planning, organizing and controlling as applied to marketing. None of these books, despite their titles, fit the emerging genre centred on the marketing mix and each soon went out of print. But the marketing management title remained.

Wroe Alderson's (1957) *Marketing Behavior and Executive Action* dealt largely with science, theory and systems, but he devoted the last third of the book to executive decision-making in marketing. It had a monumental impact on the field. According to Bartels (1988: 178), 'Alderson with one sweeping stroke created a new pattern for considering marketing management'. Also influential, and published in the same year as Alderson's work, John Howard's (1957) book, entitled

Marketing Management, emphasized elements of the marketing mix he called 'decision' areas: 'product', 'marketing channel', 'price', 'promotion-advertising', 'promotion-personal selling', and 'location' decisions. This was followed by Kelley and Lazer's (1958) *Managerial Marketing*; a book of readings organized around marketing mix elements termed 'strategic' areas: 'product', 'price', 'distribution channels' and 'communications'. In both books, the basic elements of the marketing mix were then in place. However, it was Eugene McCarthy's (1960) textbook, *Basic Marketing: A Managerial Approach*, that created the marketing mix four P's mnemonic for 'product', 'price', 'promotion' and 'place', which has become the standard for marketing management textbooks since that point in time.

Kelley and Lazer (1958) argued that the title 'Managerial Marketing' made more sense, because management modifies the subject of marketing, suggesting a subarea of marketing, rather than the reverse that suggests marketing is a subarea of management. Nonetheless, the title 'Marketing Management' emerged as the namesake for this new area of study. Taken together, the books written by Alderson, Howard, Kelly and Lazer, and McCarthy provided the critical mass that resulted in marketing management becoming the core course in the marketing curriculum and the dominant school of marketing thought.

Kotler's (1967) sales response model, termed the 'fundamental theorem of market share', provided a logically coherent rationale for the marketing mix. There are two conceptual points. First is the idea that a firm's sales are a direct response to changes in its marketing mix, *ceteris paribus*. The second idea is that a firm's market share responds directly to the effectiveness of its marketing mix and inversely to the marketing mix of the industry (or direct competition). Thus, a firm with an improved product, a reduced price, or more effective promotion or distribution, relative to the industry, will experience an increase in its sales response

and market share. Hence, the marketing manager's job is to find an optimal marketing mix, relative to competition, for a given customer segment.

A major development in conceptual thought occurred when Kotler and Levy (1969) proposed broadening marketing (management) from its original business context to the application of marketing mix techniques to nonprofit organizations. Interestingly, in the same journal issue, Lazer (1969: 3) also proposed broadening marketing management, but in a different direction, to include its societal impact, noting 'that marketing must serve not only business but also the goals of society'. Although both approaches involve broadening marketing, Kotler's version referred to applying management techniques outside the conventional business arena, while Lazer's approach involved the social impact of conventional business (discussed in the macromarketing section that follows). It is the Kotler approach that is discussed here under the rubric of marketing's broadened paradigm.

The issue as to whether marketing was a set of marketing management techniques applicable to all organizations and individuals or, rather, an economic institution designed to achieve social goals was debated during the following decades in various journals and proceedings (e.g. Arndt, 1978; Bartels, 1988; Kotler, 1972, 1975; Luck, 1969, 1974; Sweeney, 1972). But marketing management textbooks also affected academic opinion. During the 1980s, Kotler's *Marketing Management* surpassed McCarthy's *Basic Marketing* for largest share in the textbook market. Thus, in the competition for students' minds, Kotler's line of books came to dominate all segments of the marketing management text market (Cunningham, 2003). This is noteworthy, because McCarthy's book retained marketing's conventional business context, while Kotler's textbooks broadened marketing in the sense of the application of marketing mix techniques to deal with any social or personal cause.

This paradigm broadening dramatically redefined the subject matter of the discipline, because marketing management for laymen and many academics is synonymous with marketing. And the broadened position, according to Kotler (1972: 53), is indeed expansive: 'The marketer is a specialist at understanding human wants and values and determining what it takes for someone to act'. This applies marketing management techniques to any organization or person with something to 'sell', at least in the secondary dictionary meaning of sell 'to persuade or influence' (Merriam-Webster, 1994: 1062). Given this view of marketers, the broadened marketing paradigm was anticipated by Dale Carnegie (1964: i) who advised individuals to employ every word and act to 'win friends, clients and customers' and 'influence people to your way of thinking'.

There is a cost to the broadened paradigm. While the discipline appears broadened by transferring management technology to non-profit entities, Bartels (1988) believed its scope had actually narrowed, by limiting the perspective to individual gain rather than social impact beyond the parties. Sheth and Garrett (1986: 1) concurred with that view, writing: 'The boundary expansions of marketing [management] have resulted in limiting our perception of marketing to selling and promotion'. As these historians remind us, there are more schools to marketing thought than just the single perspective of marketing management, even if many scholars regard it synonymously with marketing.

In his review of marketing management, Webster (1992) also emphasized broadening marketing management, but in a different direction than Kotler. Webster (1992: 13) wrote about 'an expanded view' that addresses 'the role of marketing in firms that go to market through multiple partnerships [channels, strategic alliances and relationships]'. Webster's expansion retains marketing's conventional business context and also links marketing management to the institutional school. Nevertheless, Kotler's version of the broadening concept remains the dominant perspective.

Research in marketing management, despite the popularity of the paradigm broadening, is primarily business oriented and focuses mostly on marketing strategy, segmentation and targeting, or elements of the marketing mix: product, price, promotion, place and market research. One subarea of the mix receiving much research attention is the product 'P'. Ironically, in early definitions of marketing, products were defined out of the field. For example, a fairly common early definition of marketing is 'the creation of place, time, and possession utility' (Converse and Huegy, 1930); and 'form utility' or product is explicitly excluded from marketing and relegated to production (farming or manufacturing). Another irony in the product 'P' is that most related research today is centred on services rather than products (see Fisk et al., 1993; Vargo and Lusch, 2004) as a distinct subarea of marketing management study. Indeed, Vargo and Lusch (2004) make a robust argument that services are more fundamental, because consumers only want the service benefits a product offers. This view – that products only provide delivery vehicles for service benefits – is a position likely to stir considerable debate, analysis of which will have to await future historical hindsight. In any case, marketing management has become so large a school of thought that the number of researchers in some of its subareas such as services or advertising exceed the number of researchers in some of the other schools. Of the first two marketing schools created by Alderson's paradigm shift, management and systems, the latter represents the road less travelled.

MARKETING SYSTEMS SCHOOL

Marketing systems addresses all questions of marketing. For example, What is a marketing system? Why does it exist? Who engages in marketing? Where and when is marketing performed? How does it work? How well is the marketing system performing? The first author to use systems terminology in marketing was Wroe Alderson (1957), whose book *Marketing Behavior and Executive Action* discussed: 'organized behavior systems' (1957: 35), 'survival and growth of systems' (1957: 52), and 'input–output systems' (1957: 65), among some four dozen references to systems concepts. Although not cited, Kenneth Boulding's (1956) 'General Systems Theory: The Skeleton of Science' clearly influenced Alderson. Boulding popularized the notion of a system of systems and specifically credited the name 'General Systems Theory' and the core of his ideas to its founding father – Ludwig Von Bertalanffy's (1951) 'General Systems Theory: A New Approach to a Unity of Science'.

Alderson (1957, 1965) termed his scientific approach to marketing thought as 'Functionalism', but it is better described as 'Systems', even by him:

Functionalism is that approach to science which begins by identifying some *system* of action [e.g. marketing] and then tries to determine how and why it works as it does. Functionalism stresses the whole *system* and undertakes to interpret the parts in terms of how they service the *system*. Some writers ... prefer to speak of the holistic approach because of the emphasis on the *system* as a whole. (Alderson, 1957: 16–17; italics added)

Almost every Alderson reference to the term functionalism uses systems concepts to explain it. Unfortunately, in 1965, Alderson passed away four months prior to the publication of his definitive work, *Dynamic Marketing Behavior*, which was mostly pieced together by colleagues from rough drafts and loose notes (1965: v). It is interesting to speculate that had he lived longer, given his forward thinking, Alderson might have shifted his thinking conceptually from functionalism (entering the decline stage of its life cycle in the social sciences) to general systems theory (beginning its growth stage). There is some basis for this speculation; in one of his last sole authored writings: *A Normative Theory of Marketing Systems*, functionalism is only mentioned briefly in a few sentences, apparently as an afterthought, while Alderson (1964: 105) expresses his 'commitment to the total systems approach'.

While Alderson developed the foundations of marketing systems thinking in his articles, books and marketing theory seminars, the work was carried forward by his students and colleagues. Fisk's (1967) textbook, *Marketing Systems: An Introductory Analysis*, delineated micro- and macro-marketing systems. Dixon (1967), taking a macro perspective, showed how the marketing system was integrated into the larger society of which it forms a part. Boddewyn (1966) developed a framework for comparative marketing systems research focusing on the structure, function, process and environment in which actors engage in marketing. Between the macro and micro, Bucklin's (1970) *Vertical Marketing Systems* described the economics of channels as systems, Stern (1969) described their behavioural dimensions and Mallen (1967) worked on channel interrelationships as 'management decision systems'. At the other end of the spectrum, taking a micro perspective, Lazer (1971) used a systems approach to analyze marketing management. And, of course, Alderson (1957, 1965) originally identified households, as well as firms, as organized behaviour systems.

Any attempt to synthesize schools of marketing thought, or to develop a general theory of marketing, must include systems thinking at least as a superstructure. Nevertheless, discussions of marketing systems, *per se*, declined during the 1970s (although partially re-emerging in macromarketing discussed in a later section) with the rise of marketing management and consumer behaviour.

CONSUMER BEHAVIOUR SCHOOL

Because it deals with human behaviour, consumer behaviour is one of marketing's most eclectic schools of thought. The school initially dealt with questions of buying (search and selection) and consuming (use and disposal). Although buying and consuming are usually lumped together, it is sometimes more fruitful to view them as different roles people play, because there are some notable distinctions between them. For example, a product or service may be bought by one individual and consumed by another, requiring the buyer to anticipate the user's likely satisfaction. The buyer evaluates the deal made for a product or service and the consumer evaluates the satisfaction received, either a bad deal or unsatisfactory experience is less likely to result in repurchase and use (Assael, 1998). Despite the distinctions, buying and using are generally subsumed under the term consumer behaviour, which has also broadened far beyond this traditional domain.

Originally, drawing from the economic notion of 'consumer as utility maximizer', consumer behaviour extended to Freudian psychology 'consumer manipulated by subliminal messages', to Pavlovian psychology 'consumer conditioned by repetitive advertising', to psychophysics 'consumer sensory thresholds sensitized by just noticeable differences', to cognitive psychology 'consumer overwhelmed by information processing and risky decision making', to social psychology 'consumer swayed by opinion leadership and social influence', to sociology 'consumer immersed in social class and subcultures', and even to anthropology 'consumer subject to folklore, ritual, myth and symbolism'.

Prior to the 1950s, there were numerous psychologists, social psychologists, sociologists and economists whose work influenced the early development of consumer behaviour in marketing thought. Sheth et al. (1988) reference such well-known names as Maslow, Festinger, Homans, Rodgers, Osgood, Simon, Katona, Katz and Lazerfield, among many others. During the 1950s, motivation researchers in marketing, such as Ernest Dichter, followed a Freudian bent (Bartos, 1977). They suggested, for example, that women buying cake ingredients rather than premixed were subconsciously giving birth; and men buying red convertibles rather than more traditional cars were subconsciously acquiring mistresses (Bartos, 1977). Although leading to some useful psychological methods such as in-depth interviews, projective techniques and focus groups, conceptually this research largely led to a dead end, and most subsequent scholars prefer to forget the early emphasis on subconscious motivation.

As a school of marketing thought, consumer behaviour began its growth stage in the 1960s with the integration of concepts (including cognitive psychology, risk taking, opinion leadership, information processing and other ideas from psychology to sociology) into comprehensive models of buyer behaviour. These models include environmental and marketing stimuli as inputs, affective and cognitive mental processing, a hierarchy of behavioural outputs leading to purchase and learning providing feedback. Although Nicosia (1966) produced the first model, the two most developed models are those presented in Engel et al.'s (1968) *Consumer Behavior* and Howard and Sheth's (1969) *The Theory of Buyer Behavior*. As the foundation of their textbook, Engel et al.'s model was used mostly for pedagogical purposes. Howard and Sheth's model was more research oriented, was actually tested, received some empirical support (Farley and Ring, 1970) and a partial formalization of constructs was made by Hunt (1976). A metatheoretical analysis of all three models along 16 subjective criteria was published by Zaltman et al. (1973). Despite their lack of clear operational definitions and specification of functional relationships, the component parts of these models provided fertile grounds for subsequent research in consumer behaviour.

The popularity of consumer behaviour spread as several books of readings appeared: Kassarjian and Robertson's (1968) *Perspectives in Consumer Behavior*, Holloway et al.'s (1971) *Consumer Research: Contemporary Research in Action*, and Cohen's (1972) *Behavioral Science Foundations of Consumer Behavior*, to mention a few. In 1969, a Workshop on Consumer Behaviour became the Association for Consumer Research (ACR), and in 1974, the ACR published its first issue of the *Journal of Consumer*

Research (JCR). Having its own association provided researchers with cohesion and networking capability, and the conference and journal offered publication outlets. These events spurred even more research in consumer behaviour.

Designed as a 'medium for interdisciplinary exchange', the *JCR* broadened the boundaries of consumer behaviour far beyond 'purchase, consumption or usage' to virtually any human behaviour, including: 'family planning behavior, occupational choices, mobility, determinants of fertility rates', among many other nonmarket related topics (Frank, 1974: iv). With this broadening, a substantial number of nonbusiness researchers from across the behavioural sciences, particularly psychology, have published in the journal and entered the marketing field. Most of these researchers were not particularly interested in the managerial implications of persuading consumers to purchase products or services. They were more concerned with consumer behaviour as an *end* of study in itself, whether resulting from market purchases or not, rather than a marketing management *means* to a sale (Sheth, 1992). This created another division in marketing thought, a schism so severe that leading scholars such as Kotler (1973) felt compelled to write an article titled: 'Buying is Marketing Too!'. Sheth and Garrett (1986: 221) even predicted a 'divorce between marketing and consumer behavior'. In 1987, Holbrook wrote:

> The field of consumer research ... currently find themselves in a crisis of identity .... [The] *JCR* has lately come to embrace a variety of topics once thought too arcane or abstruse for a scholarly publication devoted to the study of consumer behavior.... It has grown so encrusted with connotations arising from its association with other disciplines that, by now, it stands for everything, which in this case tantamounts to nothing. (1987: 128)

As an indication of how far consumer behaviour has withdrawn from marketing, Wilkie and Moore (2003: 133) noted, 'our count of the nearly 900 articles published by the *Journal of Consumer Research* in its first 20 years showed that the word "marketing"

appeared only three times in an article's title'. Apparently, marketing was not acceptable to nonbusiness researchers, because marketing was not respectable (but this perception is changing; see the exchange school in a later section). Thus, consumer behaviour, like marketing management, has extended beyond the traditional marketing domain to include all behaviour related to consumption from any source, including self production, gift giving, government largess, charity, theft and so on – not just purchase behaviour. This was in spite of the fact that Kotler himself regarded only acquisition from exchange as giving rise to marketing (1980: 20).

After the comprehensive models of the late 1960s, the creation, change, consistency and complexity of attitude, particularly Fishbein's (1967) 'attitude choice model', became the hot topic area during the 1970s. From the 1980s through the 1990s, information processing became the most popular topic of interest (based on the *JCR* index of Volumes 1–20), although consumer behaviour concepts are so numerous that none comes close to dominating.

With its extension beyond purchasing and even consumption, consumer research now covers the spectrum of the social sciences and has almost become an academic discipline in itself, rather than a school of marketing thought. An illustrative but nonexhaustive set of popular topics of this school includes: motivation, personality, influence, selective attention, perception and retention, needs hierarchy, classical and operant learning, emotions, information processing, opinion leadership, hierarchy of effects, diffusion and adoption of innovation, subcultures and cross-cultures, joint decision-making, household gift-giving, buying and consuming, family life cycle, social influence, affect, cognition, intentions and choice, signs, semiotics and symbolism, information search, involvement, memory, persuasion theory, hedonics, imagery, prospect theory, judgement, variety seeking, polarization and deviant behaviour, among others. Among marketing academics, the study of consumer behaviour appears second only to marketing management in popularity.

MACROMARKETING SCHOOL

With the overwhelming focus on marketing management and consumer behaviour, interest waned in the general systems approach. In reaction to the growing micro-oriented schools, and driven by a desire to resurrect Alderson's systems thinking, several scholars sought a return to the larger dimensions of marketing and focused on the part of Fisk's (1967) systems schema involving macromarketing. This school addresses big picture questions, such as: How does the marketing system impact society? How does society impact the marketing system? How productive is the aggregate marketing system?

Although the terminology was different, the fundamental concept of viewing interacting parts in terms of their contribution to the whole, characteristic of macromarketing systems, was anticipated in the works of Breyer's (1934) *The Marketing Institution*, Duddy and Revzan's (1947) *Marketing: An Institutional Approach* and Vaile et al.'s (1952) *Marketing in the American Economy*. For example, Breyer (1934: vi) wrote of the need for a 'unified study of marketing ... not as a device for garnering individual profit but as a social instrument designed to serve the best interests of the public at large'. Duddy and Revzan (1947: vi) viewed the 'marketing structure as an organic whole made up of interrelated parts, subject to growth and change and functioning in a process of distribution that is coordinated by economic and social forces'. But these were voices in the wilderness, outside mainstream marketing thought which at that time was concerned with functions, commodities and institutions. It took Wroe Alderson to bring these ideas to the forefront of marketing thought. But even Alderson (1957), who devoted two-thirds of his pioneering book to science, theory and systems, was recognized by Bartels (1988) for the part devoted to marketing management.

In contrast to micromarketing, which focused on individual firms or households, Fisk (1967) regarded macromarketing as representing an aggregation of these units; and he dedicated his book, the first titled *Marketing Systems*, to Alderson, Breyer and Cox, 'who taught the ABC's of marketing to many grateful students' (1967: v). Lazer (1969) and also Kelley (1969) argued for a greater focus on marketing management's impact on society, because both believed marketing should not be conceived narrowly in terms of individual profit, but in the larger context of social benefit. Subsequently, Bartels and Jenkins emphasized that macromarketing:

> has meant marketing *in general* ... the marketing process *in its entirety*, and the *aggregate* mechanism of institutions performing it. It has meant *systems* and *groups* of micro institutions, such as channels, conglomerates, industries, and associations in contrast to their individual component units ... it has meant the *social context* of micromarketing. ... It has also meant the *uncontrollable environment* of micro firms. (1977: 17; original emphasis)

The first macromarketing conference was held in 1976, during which an association was formed and soon followed by the *Journal of Macromarketing* (*JMM*) in 1981. As in consumer behaviour, the conferences and association generated awareness and offered networking opportunities; additionally, the journal provided research outlets in this new field of macro marketing. But issues immediately arose as to what subject matter constituted macromarketing. In reflecting on the first macromarketing seminar, White (1980: 11) pointed out the importance of systems: 'Use of the term marketing systems or aggregate marketing systems was intended to distinguish macromarketing, which involves groups, networks or subsystems of firms from micromarketing as the study of the firm'.

Perhaps the most widely accepted view of what constitutes its subject matter was Hunt's (1981: 8) definition of macromarketing as the study of marketing systems, their impact on society and society's impact on marketing systems. An extensive examination into what is or should be included in macromarketing, in contrast to micromarketing (marketing management and consumer behaviour), was made by Hunt and Burnett (1982). Based on respondent definitions, it was thought macromarketing should include one or more of: a societal perspective, a high level of aggregation, the consequences of marketing on society, the consequences of society on marketing and anything involving marketing systems (in the aggregate). Currently, the *JMM* includes such topic areas as competition, markets and marketing systems; global policy and environment; marketing and development; marketing history; quality of life, and marketing ethics and distributive justice.

Many scholars noting the academic popularity of the micro areas of marketing management and consumer behaviour decry this lack of attention to bigger societal issues and argue this area of marketing is too important to ignore. After a comprehensive historical analysis of the marketing societal interface, Wilkie and Moore (2003: 142) close with the comment: 'the questions, insights, principles, and discoveries that constitute marketing and society should not be left out of the minds of future marketing thought leaders'.

EXCHANGE SCHOOL

This school focuses on such questions as: Who are the parties to an exchange? What is the motivation of the parties to reach agreement? What is the context of exchange? Most marketing theoreticians have argued that exchange is the heart of marketing (Alderson, 1965; Bagozzi, 1975, 1978; Hunt, 1976; Kotler, 1972; McGarry, 1950; McInnes, 1964; Sheth and Garrett, 1986). As Adam Smith (1776/1937: 17) keenly observed long ago, the division of labour is the fundamental organizing principle of groups and society, and 'given a division of labor there must be exchange'. Given the pervasiveness of

exchange in human interactions, marketing thinkers have raised questions about its nature. As with broadened marketing management and consumer behaviour, the exchange school has also divided into two divergent groups: the traditional one focusing on marketing transactions (i.e. buying and selling) and the broadened path based on generic or social exchange (i.e. generalized giving and receiving).

The initial impetus for the exchange school of marketing was Alderson and Miles' (1965) article (reprinted as a chapter in Alderson's 1965 book) titled: *Toward a Formal Theory of Transactions and Transvections*. Alderson (1965: 83) argued: 'The transaction is a fundamental building block which suggests possibilities for a more rigorous type of marketing theory'. Alderson extended Breyer's (1934) notion of the purchase-sale transaction, whose own conception was built on earlier arguments of 'business practice and legal grounds' developed by John R. Commons (1924: 245), who wrote: 'Marketing is not an *exchange* of commodities – it is a *purchase and sale*' (original emphasis). Commons made the point that marketing is far more than a general exchange of one thing for another; market exchange involves an institutional process of great social value (Shaw, 1995).

Alderson went on to expand the concept of a purchase and sale in an individual market transaction into a theory of market transvections. He regarded the transvection as the set of market transactions from the original seller of raw materials, through all intermediate purchases and sales, to the final buyer of a finished product. Aggregating the set of transvections for a given time period, say a year, in a given place, say the United States, provides an exhaustive description of a society's aggregate marketing process. Although there were a few incremental developments along this route, with the death of Alderson the idea of market or contractual exchange morphed into generic (or social) exchange. That is, the focus of exchange shifted from contractually-oriented market transactions to any form of human exchange, irrespective of context, including gift-giving, the exchange of votes for political promises, or exchanging donations to religious organizations for promises of salvation. According to Kotler's (1972: 48) generic view: '*A transaction is the exchange of values between two parties. The things-of-value need not be limited to goods, services and money; they include other resources such as time, energy, and feelings*' (original emphasis). Four necessary, but not sufficient, conditions for exchange were proposed: (1) at least two parties, (2) each with something of value to the other, (3) capable of communicating and (4) accepting or rejecting the exchange.

Generic exchange deals with 'how' some marketing management techniques, particularly persuasive communication, can be used in a non-business setting, such as social, political, religious or even personal causes. It goes beyond the profit motive or economic value, to encompass any motivations and any values between any parties, including exchanging beliefs, feelings and opinions. The problem posed for marketing thought is that there can be no distinct subject matter without disciplinary boundaries. It appears obvious that almost all human interactions affect people's feelings or opinions to some degree. Consequently, Sheth and Garrett (1986: 773) pointed out: 'marketing must limit itself to exchanges of economic values ... [or] it is likely to be blurred with other disciplines, such as social psychology and group dynamics'. As an illustration of blurring marketing's subject matter, Laczniak and Michie (1979: 220) listed: 'the exchange of wedding vows', 'plea bargaining by a felon' and 'a phone call' among other forms of generic exchanges. According to these critics, such examples of exchange make marketing's subject matter and disciplinary boundaries ambiguous at best and incomprehensible at worst.

Bagozzi (1975, 1978, 1979) undertook the most extensive theoretical work in explaining Kotler's generic exchange concept. The culmination of Bagozzi's work was an attempt to formalize a generic theory of exchange.

He conceptualized three dependent variables (1979: 435–436): 'outcomes, experiences and actions', and four determinants (the first three from his 1978 article): social influence, social actor characteristics, social contingencies and third-party effects. Bagozzi then formalized his theory with a series of structural equations. The formal theory was criticized on several grounds by Ferrell and Perrachione (1980: 158–159): It 'relies on standard economic equations that few, if any, economists have ever been able to empirically test' ... it 'restates exchange theories of other disciplines' but it 'does not qualify as a formal theory (or even the basis for a formal theory) of marketing exchanges ... what Bagozzi has developed is a conceptual framework and some loosely related functional equations'. Essentially, they wrote that there was a disconnection between Bagozzi's conception and formalization. When translating his conceptualization into formal theory, the richness of the concepts are lost, on the one hand, and there is little gain from formalizing economic maximization equations that bear scant resemblance to marketing behaviour on the other.

In attempting a more scientific approach than was previously common, Hunt (1983: 13) proposed: 'marketing is the behavioral science that seeks to explain exchange relationships'. From this definition he deduced four fundamental explananda (phenomena to be explained) 'directed at facilitating or consummating exchanges'. These included: the behaviour of (1) buyers and (2) sellers, (3) the institutional framework in which exchanges between buyers and sellers occur and (4) the consequences on society of the behaviours of 1, 2 and 3. Hunt's four explananda have avoided the criticisms of other conceptual approaches to exchange because of excessive inclusion (all forms of exchange) or critical exclusion (the institutional and social setting for market exchange).

Broadening the notion of a market offering from 'goods and services', Houston and Gassenheimer (1987: 16–17) included: 'ideas, personalities, organizations, media of exchange, places, exchange experiences, and exchange consequences' as potential values in a generic exchange. They concluded: 'exchange can and should serve as the theoretical hub around which other marketing theories connect to form an integrated structure'. Except for goods and services moving through channels, this hub appears to involve any pair of actors, irrespective of the institutional context and social impact, and therefore does not seem to require much other marketing theory than persuasive communication to describe a generic exchange.

Like broadened marketing management, there has also been criticism of generic exchange (e.g. Arndt, 1978; Ferrell and Zey-Ferrell, 1977; Laczniak and Michie, 1979; Luck, 1974; Shaw and Dixon, 1980). Nevertheless, by the early 1980s, the debate was over; social exchange had won hands down (Hunt, 1988), and new generations of marketing students learn the generic concept of exchange as dogma. It is now largely taken for granted.

Moreover, by applying marketing across the social spectrum, no other idea has changed the popular perception of marketing so much as the concept of generic exchange. Many scholars have written about the low esteem, if not contempt, in which marketers were held throughout history (Cassels, 1936; Kelley, 1956; Steiner, 1976). The tag line attached to the tradesman was epitomized in the title of Farmer's (1967) article: 'Would You Want Your Daughter to Marry a Marketing Man?' The answer was a resounding 'No', because marketing did not appear respectable. Certainly that perception has changed with broadened marketing management and generic exchange. Nowadays your daughter might well be a highly regarded marketer employed by either a business firm or charitable organization. By popularizing the notion of marketing (shorthand for marketing management techniques) for all causes, issues and situations, marketing has gone from being bad-mouthed to highly praised. The marketer charged with drumming-up

clients, patients and patrons, often in fund-raising for various causes, is usually named the development officer and applauded for their marketing abilities.

The positive image of generic exchange gave marketers a respectable character rather than being regarded as corrupt or immoral. On the other hand, by expanding marketing practice to virtually all social activity, generic exchange does not fit within the historical context of marketing. Generic exchange might serve as a basis for a general theory of sociology or social psychology, but excluding core business concepts of sellers and buyers, profit motivation and economic valuation, it is hard to conceive of social exchange, *per se*, serving as the foundational hub for a general theory of marketing.

MARKETING HISTORY SCHOOL

Marketing history addresses questions of when practices and techniques, concepts and theories were introduced and developed over time. The first writer to suggest marketing history as a school of thought was E.T. Grether (1976). He examined the *Journal of Marketing* from its origin in 1936 through four decades of publication and divided it into 12 categories, including marketing history. Given its origins in the German Historical School of Economics (Jones and Monieson, 1990), it could be argued that an historical approach existed in marketing before any other school of thought. Yet, it is only since the early 1980s that marketing history has developed a critical mass of active scholars and research publications.

Between 1930 and 1960, historical research in marketing dealt with the development of the discipline (Bartels, 1962; Converse, 1933, 1945, 1959; Hagerty, 1936; Litman, 1950; Maynard, 1941a, 1941b; Weld, 1941) as well as with retailing and wholesaling history (Barger, 1955; Beckman and Engle, 1937; Jones 1936; Marburg, 1951; Nystrom, 1951). There was one general history of marketing distinctive for its scope and historical perspective during this early period, Hotchkiss' (1938) *Milestones of Marketing*.

During the 1960s there was a transition towards more integrative histories of practice and thought (Converse, 1959; Hollander, 1960, 1966) and the publication of more substantive works (Bartels, 1962; Schwartz, 1963; Shapiro and Doody, 1968) that seemed to signal a maturing and growth of interest. It was sporadic, however, and it was not until the early 1980s, under the leadership of Stanley C. Hollander, that historical research in marketing developed the numbers and quality warranting recognition as a school of thought. In 1983, the first North American Workshop on Historical Research in Marketing took place at Michigan State University and has been held biennially since then. By 1989, the proceedings title of the conference proclaimed marketing history as an 'emerging discipline'. This may have been somewhat premature. Yet by the late 1990s, the research presented at the renamed 'CHARM' (Conference on Historical Analysis and Research in Marketing) generated a growth of publications in scholarly books and in leading academic journals, a regular section in the *JMM*, and in 2009, the launch of a new academic periodical dedicated to publishing work in this field – the *Journal of Historical Research in Marketing*. The growing interest in knowledge about marketing history and the history of marketing thought also resulted (in 1999) in the formation of an Association for Historical Research in Marketing, later renamed the CHARM Association. Attendance at the CHARM meetings increasingly represents a broader range of scholars than those working in business schools, as marketing historians build a dialogue with social, economic and business historians. In addition to CHARM, there are parallel history associations, such as the United Kingdom-based CHORD (Centre for the History of Retailing and Distribution) and the Business History Conference which includes historical research in marketing.

Historical research in marketing has matured methodologically (Brown et al., 2001; Golder, 2000; Jones, 1993; Nevett, 1991; Smith and Lux, 1993; Witkowski, 1993; Witkowski and Jones, 2006, 2008); and it has broadened to encompass a wide range of marketing thought and practices. Historical research extends beyond North American borders to describe marketing thought and practice in other countries, and reaches back prior to the twentieth century to describe the ideas of early thinkers and techniques of early practitioners from ancient civilizations to the present. There is also increasing recognition of the way in which marketing thinking was shaped by practitioners, critics and regulators, in addition to scholars. In exploring its past, marketing history appears to have a growing future as a school of marketing thought.

CONCLUSION

At the dawn of the twentieth century, pioneers of marketing thought sought to carve out distinct subject matter for the newly emerging academic discipline of marketing. These early thinkers worked within a common framework of functions, institutions, commodities and later interregional trade, approaches that were considered integral parts of the marketing whole (Shaw et al., in this volume). The paradigm shift of the 1950s brought about a proliferation of new schools: marketing management, marketing systems, consumer behaviour, macromarketing, exchange and marketing history. As the discipline fragmented, most schools have developed a life of their own as scholars narrowly focus within their own specialty with little regard to other schools or their integration into a unified whole (Bartels, 1988).

And yet, the schools are complementary; therefore, early and modern schools may be linked together in at least a rudimentary framework. The marketing functions school identified the work performed in channels of distribution between firms and firms, and between firms and households. The commodity school categorized products and services as the objects of market exchange. The institutional school described the types and behaviour of marketing middlemen (exchange specialists), standing between original producers and final consumers in channels, which in the aggregate provides the institutional context of the marketing system. Marketing management deals with the work of an individual firm in creating profitable sales of products and services. Consumer behaviour includes an individual household's search and selection activities in purchasing assortments of products and services for consumption. The interregional and marketing history schools relate the spatial and temporal aspects of marketing activities, describing places where and occasions when market exchanges occur on a micro scale between individual segments of supply and demand up to the macro scale of aggregate supply and demand. Macromarketing concerns the bidirectional impacts of marketing as an institution with the social system. Marketing systems provides a hierarchical superstructure to integrate firms and households working towards achieving some of their goals through the process of creating stable market transactions and transvections within the institutional channel structure of the aggregate marketing system and the sanctions of society. The exchange school provides a hub linking the elements of the marketing system together in a whole: firms and households as actors playing selling and buying roles directed toward creating market transactions and transvections, linking the objects, locations and occasions for exchange within the institutional channel setting, nested within the aggregate marketing system, which in turn interchanges with other institutions of the total social system. Of course, the more difficult task is formalizing the conceptual linkages among the schools of marketing. But that is a task for future research. And, as we have done in this chapter, marketing historians will document that research and tell the story of its development.

REFERENCES

Alderson, W. (1957) *Marketing Behavior and Executive Action*. Homewood, IL: Richard D. Irwin.

Alderson, W. (1964) 'A Normative Theory of Marketing Systems', in R. Cox, W. Alderson and S.J. Shapiro (eds) *Theory in Marketing*, Homewood, IL: Richard D. Irwin, pp. 92–108.

Alderson, W. (1965) *Dynamic Marketing Behavior*. Homewood, IL: Richard D. Irwin.

Alderson, W. and Miles, M.W. (1965) 'Toward a Formal Theory of Transactions and Transvections', *Journal of Marketing Research*, 2(May): 117–127.

Alexander, R.S., Surface, F.M., Elder, R.F. and Alderson, W. (1940) *Marketing*. New York: Ginn & Company.

Arndt, J. (1978) 'How Broad Should the Marketing Concept Be?', *Journal of Marketing*, 42(January): 101–103.

Assael, H. (1998) *Consumer Behavior*. Cincinnati, OH: Southwestern.

Bagozzi, R.P. (1975) 'Marketing as Exchange', *Journal of Marketing*, 39(October): 32–39.

Bagozzi, R.P. (1978) 'Marketing as Exchange: A Theory of Transactions in the Marketplace', *American Behavioral Scientist*, 21(March/April): 535–556.

Bagozzi, R.P. (1979) 'Toward a Formal Theory of Market Exchanges', in O.C. Ferrell, S. Brown and C. Lamb, Jr (eds) *Conceptual and Theoretical Development in Marketing*, Chicago, IL: American Marketing Association, pp. 431–447.

Barger, H. (1955) *Distribution's Place in the American Economy Since 1869*. Princeton, NJ: Princeton University Press.

Bartels, R. (1962) *The Development of Marketing Thought*. Homewood, IL: Richard D. Irwin.

Bartels, R. (1988) *The History of Marketing Thought*. Columbus, OH: Publishing Horizons.

Bartels, R. and Jenkins, R. (1977) 'Macromarketing', *Journal of Marketing*, 41(October): 17–20.

Bartos, R. (1977) 'Ernest Dichter: Motive Interpreter', *Journal of Advertising Research*, 17(June): 3–9.

Beckman, T.N. and Engle, N.H. (1937) *Wholesaling*. New York: Ronald Press.

Boddewyn, J. (1966) 'A Construct for Comparative Marketing Research', *Journal of Marketing Research*, 3(May): 149–153.

Borden, N.H. (1964) 'The Concept of the Marketing Mix', *Journal of Advertising Research*, 4(June): 2–7.

Boulding, K.E. (1956) 'General Systems Theory: The Skeleton of Science', *Management Science*, 2(April): 197–208.

Breyer, R.F. (1934) *The Marketing Institution*. New York: McGraw-Hill.

Brown, S., Hirschman, E. and Maclaren, P. (2001) 'Always Historicize! Researching Marketing History in a Post-Historical Epoch', *Marketing Theory*, 1(1): 49–90.

Bucklin, L.P. (1970) *Vertical Marketing Systems*. Glenview, IL: Scott Foresman.

Carnegie, D. (1964) *How to Win Friends and Influence People*. New York: Simon and Schuster.

Cassels, J.M. (1936) 'The Significance of Early Economic Thought on Marketing', *Journal of Marketing*, 1(October): 129–133.

Cohen, J. (1972) *Behavioral Science Foundations of Consumer Behavior*. New York: The Free Press.

Commons, J.R. (1924) *Institutional Economics*. New York: Macmillan.

Converse, P.D. (1933) 'The First Decade of Marketing Literature', *NATMA Supplemental Bulletin*, (November): 1–4.

Converse, P.D. (1945) 'The Development of the Science of Marketing – An Exploratory Survey', *Journal of Marketing*, 10(July): 14–23.

Converse, P.D. (1959) *The Beginnings of Marketing Thought in the United States*. Austin, TX: Bureau of Business Research, University of Texas.

Converse, P.D. and Huegy, H.W. (1930) *Elements of Marketing*. New York: Prentice-Hall.

Culliton, J.W. (1948) *The Management of Marketing Costs*. Cambridge, MA: Harvard University Press.

Cunningham, P. (2003) 'The Textbooks of Philip Kotler: Their Role in Defining Marketing Thought and Practice', *Journal of the Academy of Marketing Science*, 31(2): 201–212.

Davis, K.R. (1961) *Marketing Management*. New York: Ronald Press.

Dixon, D.F. (1967) 'A Social Systems Approach to Marketing', *Social Science Quarterly*, 48(September): 164–173.

Duddy, E.A. and Revzan, D.A. (1947) *Marketing: An Institutional Approach*. New York: McGraw-Hill.

Engel, J.F., Kollat, D.T. and Blackwell, R.D. (1968) *Consumer Behavior*. New York: Holt, Rinehart & Winston.

Farley, J.U. and Ring, L.W. (1970) 'An Empirical Test of the Howard Sheth Model of Buyer Behavior', *Journal of Marketing Research*, 7(November): 28–33.

Farmer, R.N. (1967) 'Would You Want Your Daughter to Marry a Marketing Man?', *Journal of Marketing*, 31(January): 1–10.

Ferrell, O.C. and Perrachione, J.R. (1980) 'An Inquiry into Bagozzi's Formal Theory of Marketing Exchanges', in C. Lamb, Jr and P.M. Dunne (eds) *Theoretical Developments in Marketing*, Chicago, IL: American Marketing Association, pp. 158–161.

Ferrell, O.C. and Zey-Ferrell, M. (1977) 'Is All Social Exchange Marketing?', *Journal of the Academy of Marketing Science*, 5(4): 307–314.

Fishbein, M. (1967) 'Attitude and the Prediction of Behavior', in M. Fishbein (ed.) *Readings in Attitude Theory and Measurement*, New York: John Wiley, pp. 477–492.

Fisk, G. (1967) *Marketing Systems: An Introductory Analysis*. New York: Harper & Row.

Fisk, R.P., Brown, S.W. and Bitner, M.J. (1993) 'Tracking the Evolution of the Services Marketing Literature', *Journal of Retailing*, 69(Spring): 61–103.

Frank, R.E. (1974) 'Editor's Comments', *Journal of Consumer Research*, 1(1): iv.

Frey, A.W. (1956) *The Effective Marketing Mix*. Hanover, NH: Dartmouth College.

Golder, P. (2000) 'Historical Method in Marketing Research with New Evidence on Long-term Market Share Stability', *Journal of Marketing Research*, 37(May): 156–172.

Grether, E.T. (1976) 'The First Forty Years', *Journal of Marketing*, 40(July): 63–69.

Hagerty, J.E. (1936) 'Experiences of an Early Marketing Teacher', *Journal of Marketing*, 1(1): 20–27.

Holbrook, M.B. (1987) 'What is Consumer Research?', *Journal of Consumer Research*, 14(June): 128–132.

Hollander, S.C. (1960) 'The Wheel of Retailing', *Journal of Marketing*, 25(July): 37–42.

Hollander, S.C. (1966) 'Note on the Retailing Accordion', *Journal of Retailing*, 42(Summer): 29–40.

Holloway, R.J., Mittelstaedt, R.A. and Venkatesan, M. (1971) *Consumer Research: Contemporary Research in Action*. Boston, MA: Houghton Mifflin Co.

Hotchkiss, G.B. (1938) *Milestones of Marketing*. New York: Macmillan.

Houston, F.S. and Gassenheimer, J.B. (1987) 'Marketing and Exchange', *Journal of Marketing*, 51(October): 3–18.

Howard, J.R. (1957) *Marketing Management: Analysis and Decision*. Homewood, IL: Richard D. Irwin.

Howard, J.R. and Sheth, J.N. (1969) *The Theory of Buyer Behavior*. New York: John Wiley.

Hunt, S.D. (1976) *Marketing Theory: Conceptual Foundations of Research in Marketing*. Columbus, OH: Grid.

Hunt, S.D. (1981) 'Macromarketing as a Multidimensional Concept', *Journal of Macromarketing*, 1(Spring): 7–8.

Hunt, S.D. (1983) 'General Theories and the Fundamental Explananda of Marketing', *Journal of Marketing*, 47(Fall): 9–17.

Hunt, S.D. (1988) *Foundations of Marketing Theory: Toward a General Theory of Marketing*. London: M.E. Sharpe.

Hunt, S.D. and Burnett, J.J. (1982) 'The Macromarketing–Micromarketing Dichotomy: A Taxonomical Model', *Journal of Marketing*, 46(Summer): 11–26.

Jones, D.G.B. (1993) 'Historiographic Paradigms in Marketing', in S.C. Hollander and K. Rassuli (eds) *Marketing, Volume I*, Brookfield, VT: Edward Elgar Publishing, pp. 136–145.

Jones, D.G.B. and Monieson, D.D. (1990) 'Early Development of the Philosophy of Marketing Thought', *Journal of Marketing*, 54(1): 102–113.

Jones, F. (1936) 'Retail Stores in the United States, 1800–1860', *Journal of Marketing*, 1(October): 135–140.

Kassarjian, H.H. and Robertson, T.S. (1968) *Perspectives in Consumer Behavior*. Glenview, IL: Scott, Foresman.

Keith, R.J. (1960) 'The Marketing Revolution', *Journal of Marketing*, 24(1): 35–38.

Kelley, E.J. (1969) 'From the Editor', *Journal of Marketing*, 33(January): 1–2.

Kelley, E.J. and Lazer, W. (1958) *Managerial Marketing: Perspectives and Viewpoints*. Homewood, IL: Richard D. Irwin.

Kelley, W.T. (1956) 'The Development of Early Thought in Marketing', *Journal of Marketing*, 20(July): 62–67.

Kotler, P. (1967) *Marketing Management: Analysis, Planning, and Control*. Englewood Cliffs, NJ: Prentice-Hall.

Kotler, P. (1972) 'A Generic Concept of Marketing', *Journal of Marketing*, 36(April): 46–54.

Kotler, P. (1973) 'Buying is Marketing Too!', *Journal of Marketing*, 37(January): 54–59.

Kotler, P. (1975) *Marketing for Non Profit Organizations*. Englewood Cliffs, NJ: Prentice-Hall.

Kotler, P. (1980) *Marketing Management: Analysis, Planning, and Control*. Englewood Cliffs, NJ: Prentice-Hall.

Kotler, P. and Levy, S.J. (1969) 'Broadening the Concept of Marketing', *Journal of Marketing*, 33(January): 10–15.

Laczniak, G.R. and Michie, D.A. (1979) 'The Social Disorder of the Broadened Concept of Marketing', *Journal of the Academy of Marketing Science*, 7(Summer): 214–229.

Lazer, W. (1969) 'Marketing's Changing Social Relationships', *Journal of Marketing*, 33(January): 3–9.

Lazer, W. (1971) *Marketing Management: A Systems Approach*. New York: John Wiley.

Lazo, H. and Corbin, A. (1961) *Management in Marketing*. New York: McGraw-Hill.

Litman, S. (1950) 'The Beginnings of Teaching Marketing in American Universities', *Journal of Marketing*, 15(October): 220–223.

Luck, D.J. (1969) 'Broadening the Concept of Marketing – Too Far', *Journal of Marketing*, 33(July): 53–55.

Luck, D.J. (1974) 'Social Marketing: Confusion Compounded', *Journal of Marketing*, 38(October): 70–71.

Mallen, B.E. (1967) *The Marketing Channel: A Conceptual Viewpoint*. New York: John Wiley.

Marburg, T. (1951) 'Domestic Trade and Marketing', in H.F. Williamson (ed.) *The Growth of the American Economy*, Englewood Cliffs, NJ: Prentice-Hall, pp. 551–553.

Maynard, H.H. (1941a) 'Marketing Courses Prior to 1910', *Journal of Marketing*, 5(April): 382–384.

Maynard, H.H. (1941b) 'Notes and Communications – Early Teachers of Marketing', *Journal of Marketing*, 7(October): 158–159.

McCarthy, E.J. (1960) *Basic Marketing: A Managerial Approach*. Homewood, IL: Richard D. Irwin.

McGarry, E.D. (1950) 'Some Functions of Marketing Reconsidered', in R. Cox and W. Alderson (eds) *Theory in Marketing*, Homewood, IL: Richard D. Irwin, pp. 263–279.

McInnes, W. (1964) 'A Conceptual Approach to Marketing', in R. Cox, W. Alderson and S. Shapiro (eds) *Theory in Marketing* (second edn.), Homewood, IL: Richard D. Irwin, pp. 51–67.

Merriam-Webster (1994) *Collegiate Dictionary*. Springfield, MA: Merriam-Webster, Inc.

Nevett, T. (1991) 'Historical Investigation and the Practice of Marketing', *Journal of Marketing*, 55(3): 13–23.

Nicosia, F.M. (1966) *Consumer Decision Processes: Marketing and Advertising Implications*. Englewood Cliffs, NJ: Prentice-Hall.

Nystrom, P.H. (1951) 'Retailing in Retrospect and Prospect', in Hugh G. Wales (ed.) *Changing Perspectives in Marketing*, Urbana, IL: University of Illinois Press, pp. 117–138.

Phelps, D.M. (1953) *Marketing Management*. Homewood, IL: Richard D. Irwin.

Schwartz, G. (1963) *Development of Marketing Theory*. Cincinnati, OH: South-Western.

Shapiro, S. and Doody, A. (1968) *Readings in the History of American Marketing*. Homewood, IL: Richard D. Irwin.

Shaw, E.H. (1995) 'The First Dialogue on Macromarketing', *Journal of Macromarketing*, 15(Spring): 7–20.

Shaw, E.H. and Dixon, D.F. (1980) 'Exchange: A Conceptualization', in C. Lamb, Jr and P.M. Dunne (eds) *Theoretical Developments in Marketing*, Chicago, IL: American Marketing Association, pp. 150–153.

Sheth, J.N. (1992) 'Acrimony in the Ivory Tower: A Retrospective on Consumer Research', *Journal of the Academy of Marketing Science*, 20(Fall): 345–353.

Sheth, J.N. and Garrett, D.E. (1986) *Marketing Theory: Classical and Contemporary Readings*. Cincinnati, OH: Southwestern.

Sheth, J.N. Gardner, D.M. and Garrett, D.E. (1988) *Marketing Theory: Evolution and Evaluation*. New York: John Wiley.

Smith, A. (1776/1937) *An Inquiry into the Nature and Causes of the Wealth of Nations*. New York: Modern Library.

Smith, R.A. and Lux, D.S. (1993) 'Historical Method in Consumer Research: Developing Causal Explanations of Change', *Journal of Consumer Research*, 19(4): 595–610.

Smith, W.R. (1956) 'Product Differentiation and Market Segmentation as Alternative Marketing Strategies', *Journal of Marketing*, 21(July): 3–8.

Steiner, R.L. (1976) 'The Prejudice Against Marketing', *Journal of Marketing*, 40(July): 2–42.

Stern, L. (1969) *Distribution Channels: Behavioral Dimensions*. New York: Houghton Mifflin.

Sweeney, D.J. (1972) 'Marketing: Management Technology or Social Process', *Journal of Marketing*, 36(October): 3–10.

Tadajewski, M. (2006) 'The Ordering of Marketing Theory: The Influence of McCarthyism and the Cold War', *Marketing Theory*, 6(2): 163–200.

Vaile, R.S., Grether, E.T. and Cox, R. (1952) *Marketing in the American Economy*. New York: Ronald Press.

Vargo, S. and Lusch, R.F. (2004) 'Evolving to a New Dominant Logic for Marketing', *Journal of Marketing*, 68(1): 1–17.

Von Bertalanffy, L. (1951) 'General Systems Theory: A New Approach to a Unity of Science', *Human Biology*, 23(December): 303–361.

Wasson, C. (1960) 'What is "New" About a New Product?', *Journal of Marketing*, 24(July): 52–56.

Webster, F.E. Jr (1992) 'The Changing Role of Marketing in the Corporation', *Journal of Marketing*, 56(October): 1–17.

Weld, L.D.H. (1941) 'Early Experience in Teaching Courses in Marketing', *Journal of Marketing*, 5(April): 380–381.

White, P.D. (1980) 'The Systems Dimension in the Definition of Macromarketing', *Journal of Macromarketing*, 1(Spring): 11–13.

Wilkie, W. and Moore, E. (2003) 'Scholarly Research in Marketing: Exploring the Four Eras of Thought Development', *Journal of*

Public Policy & Marketing, 22(Fall): 116–146.

Witkowski, T. (1993) 'A Writer's Guide to Historical Research in Marketing', in Stanley C. Hollander and Kathleen Rassuli (eds), *Marketing, Volume I,* Brookfield, VT: Edward Elgar Publishing, pp. 146–155.

Witkowski, T. and Jones, D.G. Brian. (2006) 'Qualitative Historical Research in Marketing', in R.W. Belk (ed.) *Handbook of Qualitative Research Methods in Marketing,* Cheltenham, UK: Edward Elgar Publishing, pp. 70–82.

Witkowski, T. and Jones, D.G. Brian. (2008) 'Historiography in Marketing: Its Growth, Structure of Inquiry, and Disciplinary Status', *Business and Economic History,* 6(June): 1–20.

Zaltman, G., Pinhson, C.R.A. and Angelmar, R. (1973) *Metatheory and Consumer Research.* New York: Holt, Rinehart and Winston.

4

The Emergence of Consumer Research

Harold H. Kassarjian and Ronald C. Goodstein

THE EMERGENCE OF CONSUMER RESEARCH

If you would understand anything, observe its beginning and its development.

Aristotle

Once upon a time a fledgling was born and given the name Consumer Research – the bastard child of marketing and an unknown father variously alleged to be Economics, Psychology, Sociology, Anthropology, Home Economics or occasionally others as well. Despite these humble and ignoble beginnings, the infant developed precociously and was admired, housed, and nurtured by Mother Marketing. It found it had occasionally kind uncles named Business and Government, but the former did not always appreciate the child's talents and the latter tended to favor more legitimate nephews and nieces with names like Art, Science and Medicine .... The child grew and learned. ...

Russell W. Belk (1986)[1]

---

[1] Reprinted with permission from the Association of Consumer Research [Originally appeared as Belk, R.W., (1986) 'What Should ACR Want To Be When It Grows Up,' in R.J. Lutz (ed.) *Advances in Consumer Research*, Vol. 13. Provo, UT: Association for Consumer Research, pp. 423–424.]

Indeed, a half a century has passed since consumer behavior emerged primarily from the field of marketing. And marketing, itself, did not exist as an independent academic endeavor until just a hundred years ago. At the turn of the twentieth century, the area that would become Marketing was embedded as a small unit within the field of economics. The earliest courses were titled Distributive Industries or Distribution of Products (Universities of Michigan, Illinois and California in 1902, Pennsylvania in 1903 and Ohio State in 1905). It took some three decades for marketing to come into its own in the university setting in the United States (Bartels, 1988) and another half century in Europe (Jones and Monieson, 1990).

In those early days, marketing looked different and of course professors were trained in economics rather than what we call modern marketing today: marketing science, consumer behavior and marketing strategy. Academic research was rather impressionistic and often consisted of narrative discussions about the functions of say a wholesaler or rack jobber. Buyer research involved the study of markets, analysis of secondary data and utility theory (see Wilkie and Moore, 2003 for an overview of marketing thought). From this milieu, the foundations of modern consumer behavior emerged.

The purpose of this chapter is to examine those foundations and the emergence of consumer behavior in the early years of development rather than to provide a review of the current state of the field.

WORLD WAR II AND THE POST-WAR DECADE

By the 1940s, two advances occurred that were particularly relevant for the birth of consumer behavior. One was the emergence of Economic Psychology along with several grand theories of human behavior – Freudian Psychoanalytic Theory, Behavioral Learning Theory and Lewinian Field Theory. The other was research on the effects of the mass media and the support of the US Government in wartime research into the effects of propaganda and persuasion on behavior and attitude change (Stouffer et al., 1949).

ECONOMICS – A NEW VIEW

A significant challenge to prevailing economic and marketing thought of that time emerged from George Katona's work on the psychological analysis of economic behavior (Katona, 1951). Katona was not a trained economist but rather an outsider at the time. He had received a law degree from the University of Budapest and a PhD degree in Psychology from Georg Müller's laboratory in Göttingen. He was working as an experimental psychologist in Berlin during the pre-World War II period of hyperinflation. The profound effects of inflation on the behavior of consumers led him to undertake the study of economics and explore Keynesian thinking (Morgan, 1991).

The British economist, John Maynard Keynes, had challenged the prevailing view of economic behavior by emphasizing the role played by government and the expectations of business. Katona felt that consumers'

expectations, attitudes and sentiments also played an active role, and that economists ignored or made naïve assumptions about human behavior. Consumer confidence had to be taken into account to better understand economic fluctuations.

Like so many other scholars at the time, his work was interrupted by the rise of Nazism and he ended up first in New York and then at the University of Michigan. More of an experimental psychologist than an armchair theorist, he was trying to measure the effect that consumer sentiment (optimism, pessimism and confidence) had on economic activity. To do his research and collect data, survey methodology had to be developed. With Rensis Likert, Donald Campbell and other well-known social scientists he established the Survey Research Center at the University of Michigan (Newman, 1983). Today, consumer confidence is considered an important indicator in economic forecasting and survey research permeates the worlds of marketing, politics and most every other aspect of the social sciences. The monthly index of consumer confidence, The Michigan Survey Research Center and the *Journal of Economic Psychology* stand as the legacy of George Katona.

YALE COMMUNICATIONS STUDIES AND EARLY RADIO RESEARCH

The second important advance in the emergence of consumer behavior centered on several communications research programs. During the World War II era, The Yale University Communications Research group started studying the influences of the mass media and in particular its influence on attitude formation and change (e.g. Hovland et al., 1953). 'The Yale group "investigated characteristics of the source of communication (expertise, likeability), the message, (type of appeal, one-sided versus two-sided arguments), and audience characteristics such as sex differences, education, and personality traits such as anxiety and self-esteem"' (Edell, 1993: 197).

Sophisticated research was also appearing in the business sector. The Young and Rubicam advertising agency had hired George Gallup to study the effects of advertising and later to develop the Gallup poll. Other agencies had hired psychologists such as Daniel Starch to better understand how advertising works and impacts the consumer.

Still another psychologist, William Stanton, was an important pioneer in radio research. As a graduate student at the Ohio State University, he had developed a prototype of an audience monitoring device, the forerunner of A.C. Neilson's radio and TV rating audiometers (Maloney, 1987). Eventually, he became a top executive at Columbia Broadcasting System and instigated and abetted the wonderful early audience studies and content analyses of radio programs. Allport's (1935) analyses of soap operas, path breaking studies by Merton (1946) on the Kate Smith War Bond drives, the fascinating research on the effects of the Orson Welles' War of the Worlds radio program (Cantril, 1940) and the wartime studies on rumor (Allport and Postman, 1943) are part of the legacy of CBS and Stanton.

Stanton, with the help of two social psychologists at Princeton – Hadley Cantril and Gordon Alport – was instrumental in bringing to the United States the Austrian contingent. It started with the eminent social scientist, Paul Lazarsfeld, a mathematics PhD from the University of Vienna, who had established a radio research organization in Europe. At Princeton, Lazarsfeld was little appreciated by the administration and had to move his new radio research organization several times until he found a home for it at Columbia University, later to become the Bureau of Applied Social Research (Maloney, 1987).

Like Katona, Lazarsfeld was challenging classical economics with his research by showing that consumers are not rational calculating machines but rather often groped in a fog of half-knowledge and uncertainties. Years before he had completed his classic study on shoe buying in Zurich – with 900 respondents, depth interviews and questionnaires – it was a classic qualitative research project with quantitative support on why the consumer buys. There is more to shoe buying than price and classical economics – attitudes, window displays and personality, along with the erotic effects of female sales people with male customers and vice versa were critical variables (Fullerton, 1990). [Another interesting contribution to this thinking was brought forth from Frank Baum, better known for his *Wizard of Oz* books. He wrote a classic book that examined how store windows could be used to attract customers into dry goods stores (Culver, 1988).]

In due course, Lazarsfeld brought to America his students from the University of Vienna – Ernest Dichter, Herta Herzog, Hans Zeisel and other psychoanalytically oriented researchers who changed the face of the field (Maloney, 1987). Lazarsfeld and his colleagues were bringing back the techniques of introspection as well as introducing qualitative research and small samples to marketing and advertising research (Kassarjian, 1994).

Before long, qualitative research gained a foothold in the research establishment. Solid research was emerging from a number of organizations, particularly the work of Sid Levy and others at Social Research, Inc. and studies commissioned by Pierre Martineau at the *Chicago Tribune*. Their approach was not to measure the percent of consumers that had an opinion about something or read an advertisement, or preferred one brand over another, but rather to explore motivations – why people buy rather than what they buy (Levy, 1991). And, as it turned out, perhaps because of the interest in motivation research, one of the grand theories of human behavior was introduced to the field of marketing and the infant consumer behavior – Freudian Psychology. By the end of World War II, elegant theories of human behavior had become increasingly popular in the humanities and social sciences and their influence had started to seep into the business sector.

MOTIVATION RESEARCH AND FREUDIAN THEORY

The underpinning of psychoanalytic theory is that human behavior is driven by psycho-sexual forces with roots in childhood experiences. The belief was that concepts such as id, ego and super-ego along with childhood psycho-social developmental stages drive most all behavior from psychopathology to shop lifting, from the selection of a spouse to the purchase of a convertible automobile.

By 1957, Ernest Dichter, a major commercial purveyor of qualitative research, 'had appointed himself the "Messiah of Motivation Research" who had rescued the business world from the pathetic ignorance that had prevailed before his advent' (Fullerton and Stern, 1990: 209). He denounced all marketing research as superficial 'nose-counting.' As one might have expected, journalists and the trade press publicized amusing interpretations from Ernest Dichter's reports a convertible car represents a mistress in which one can take a ride once in a while, but when it comes to permanent preference the consumer will choose the sedan. Teenagers use soap to wash their hands to ward off sexual guilt, and baking a cake is analogous to delivering a child. The influence of Sigmund Freud was unmistakable.

To many, Dichter appeared loud and arrogant and just too much for the research establishment to tolerate. The research factories at the advertising agencies and pollsters such as Gallup and Politz lashed back. Marketing academics such as Wroe Alderson, the most profound of American theorists, joined the attack and sessions at professional meetings such as at the American Marketing Association (AMA) often became quite heated as the two sides clashed swords (Fullerton and Stern, 1990). They claimed that Dichter ignored basic social science research and that his findings were neither valid nor reliable. William (Bill) Wells (1956) wrote that some of Dichter's research reports read like a combination of science fiction and *Alice in Wonderland*. In the defense of Dichter, one client shot back, 'I don't care whether Dichter's Chi Squares are everything they should be. I get more useful ideas in talking to Dichter for one day than I ever get out of a hundred tables in a survey report' (Maloney, 1987: 36).

In time, the more inane aspects of the Dichter type of Motivation Research presentations faded away and the quality work of serious researchers survived. Some even ended up as classics to be reprinted again and again. Who today has not read with fascination, Levy's (1959) 'Symbols for Sale,' or heard of Mason Haire's (1950) classic study on Nestlé's Instant Coffee and accepted his interpretation as reasonable.

FIELD THEORY

The second of the elegant theories from the social sciences that impacted on consumer behavior is Kurt Lewin's Field Theory (e.g. 1936). Emerging out of the work of the Gestalt psychologists in Berlin in the early twentieth century, it would be rather difficult to overestimate Lewin's contribution to social psychology and, through psychology, his impact on consumer behavior. His influence permeates the field ranging from studies on group dynamics and sensitivity training, from attitude change to cognitive organization and from balance theories to food eating habits.

The basic characteristic of Lewin's theory is that behavior is a function of the psychological field that exists at the time the behavior occurs. The field is defined as the totality of coexisting facts, including both the person and his psychological environment, all of which are mutually interdependent. Every specific instance of behavior (say the change of attitude about a brand of refrigerator or the purchase of an automobile) must be viewed as the result of the interaction of a variety of influences or vectors impinging upon the person. Since all of these coexisting forces are mutually interdependent, one cannot study any one of them (say influence of the salesman, advertising, personality, social influence or price) independently and expect to be able to reconstruct the act of purchase. This is the familiar Gestalt dictum that the whole is different from if not greater than the sum of the isolated parts. Analysis must begin with the situation as a whole from which the component parts can be differentiated instead of beginning with a study of the isolated elements (Kassarjian, 1973).

The Lewinian approach is ahistoric. Only facts that exist in the present can directly affect present events. Since consumer behavior depends on the forces and influences acting upon the individual at a given moment in time, the moment the behavior itself occurs, past events and future events that do not exist now cannot affect behavior. Only the directly relevant facts from previous behavior that exert an influence on the present are to be considered, rather than many of the childhood experiences or sexual memories used by adherents of Freud or the number of previous trials used by learning theorists or Markov analysts. Further, future events, aspirations and expectations as they are relevant and represented in the present are accounted for by field theory, concepts difficult to deal with in many of the other approaches to consumer behavior (Kassarjian, 1968).

BEHAVIORAL LEARNING THEORIES

The final set of theories that created the infrastructure of consumer behavior is that of behaviorism. The basic view is that behavior is a learned response pattern resulting from experience, usually repeated exposures to a stimulus. It started with John Watson, a psychology professor at Johns Hopkins University and an early regular consultant at J. Walter Thompson Advertising Agency. Watson's contributions relied heavily on classical conditioning and the work of Ivan Pavlov at St. Petersburg in Czarist Russia. Pavlov's dog is well known to most everyone. When a dog is presented with dry meat powder (the unconditioned stimulus – UCS), he naturally salivates (unconditioned response – UCR). If the ringing of a bell (conditioned stimulus – CS) is repeatedly associated with the presentation of the UCS (food), the animal will also salivate (conditioned response – CR). That is,

the dog will soon learn that the ringing of a bell is associated with food (a reward) causing salivation when the UCS is not present. This simple little model, with its subsequent elaborations and sophistication such as the role of rewards and punishment, the number of trials needed, whether the original response is trial and error or cognitively evaluated, etc. form the basis of the variations of learning theories as presented by Hull, Spence, Skinner and so many others (Hilgard, 1956).

Not only were these theories crucial for much of what was to come in main line consumer research but the mathematical off-shoots of learning theory (e.g. Estes et al., 1954a; Bush and Mosteller, 1955) led directly to the to the stochastic and linear learning models of marketing that emerged in the 1960s (e.g. Frank, 1962; Kuehn, 1962 and George Haines, 1969 book, *Consumer Behavior: Learning Models of Purchasing*). It was research on such topics as repetitive purchases, brand loyalty, brand switching, sales estimates and product adoption of that era that were the precursors to Marketing Science as it is defined today.

THE MILIEU OF THE 1960S

Problems cannot all be solved, for, as they are solved, new aspects are continually revealed: the historian opens the way, he does not close it.

Sir Maurice Powicke

During the 1960s and early 1970s, universities were in a growth spurt, scientific knowledge was exploding and the space program was headed to the moon. President Kennedy had introduced the Consumer Bill of Rights, and the country was moving forward on all fronts. The third consumerism wave was in full force (the earlier waves were in the 1900s and 1930s). It was the thousand days of Camelot. It seemed as if there was nothing that could not be accomplished.

Marketing departments along with business schools throughout the land, however, were perceived to be in a dismal state. In an effort to upgrade business schools, the Ford and Carnegie Foundations had issued reports encouraging the schools to incorporate the behavioral sciences, mathematics, statistics and social sciences into teaching, thinking and research. The focus of the reports was remedial in that business education was viewed as a vast 'wasteland of vocationalism ... [that] needed to be transformed into a science based professionalism' (Herbert Simon, quoted in Tadajewski, 2006: 174). As Kernan (1995) pointed out, the charge of these reports to Business Schools was clear and adamant: 'Get Respectable!'

The Ford Foundation was willing to step in with grants and financial backing. In less than a decade, the Ford Foundation had invested in excess of $45 million on business research and educational reform (Tadajewski, 2006). For example, Frank Bass, a traditional marketing professor at the University of Illinois was sent to Harvard to learn mathematics and statistics. Perry Bliss was sent to Harvard to learn psychology and sociology, leading to one of the very early readings books in consumer behavior (Bliss, 1963). Joseph Newman had support for his book on motivation research (1957), as well as Philip Kotler for his work on the use of computer simulation for marketing strategy (1968) and Alan Andreasen for his work on attitudes and innovation diffusion (1965). John Howard was granted a fellowship to write a monograph (1963) that opened the door a bit wider for the behavioral sciences. In time, that monograph morphed into his marketing management text and a bit later into Howard and Sheth's *The Theory of Buyer Behavior* (1969).

Step by step, thinking and ideas from the scientific disciplines began to infiltrate into marketing. Marketing departments here and there began to recruit faculty trained in subjects other than economics: psychology, sociology, operations research, statistics (Myers et al., 1980) and later even geography and chemistry. New ideas and approaches were being introduced – controlled

experiments, computer programming and computer-based data analysis, mathematical models, computer simulation, empiricism and logical positivism – the era of data analysis had arrived. The language of science had reached from the positivists of the Vienna Circle in the 1930s to marketing and the new toddler – consumer behavior. The face and intellectual interests of marketing departments throughout the land were to be permanently changed (Kassarjian, 1994).

THEORIES OF CONSUMER BEHAVIOR SURFACE

Perhaps the most recognized of the newly emerging consumer behavior approaches was one that had morphed from a learning theory background – Howard–Sheth's *The Theory of Buyer Behavior* (1969). Howard and Sheth incorporated aspects of the other major theories of behavior, but it was basically based on learning theories prevalent in psychology at the time – primarily Clark Hull and Kenneth Spence's work on stimulus– response learning.

The Howard–Sheth theory

The Howard and Sheth model focused on the element of repeat buying over time. Given a drive (such as hunger) and the perception of a cue (such as an advertisement), the individual may make a response (purchase), which if reinforced or rewarded, may lead to learning (repeat purchase). Once the buyer is motivated to buy a product class, he is faced with a brand-choice decision. The elements of his decision are (1) a set of motives, (2) several courses of action and (3) decision mediators, by which the motives are matched with the alternatives. Over time, in the face of repetitive brand choice decisions, the consumer simplifies his decision process by storing relevant information and establishing a routine in his decision process (Kassarjian and Robertson, 1968: 440). Howard and Sheth is a fine example of the *Utopian Grand Theories Phase* of consumer behavior development (coined by Ekström, 2003), but there were others.

The Engel, Kollat and Blackwell model

Towards the latter part of the 1960s, several attempts other than Howard–Sheth were seeking an over-arching model of consumer behavior. Arguably, the most widely known of the models at the time was that of Engel et al. (1968). Used as an organizing basis for the first comprehensive textbook in consumer behavior, Engel and his colleagues developed a massive flow chart depicting consumer behavior from the molecular level of basic needs and motives to the molar influences of groups, societies and cultures via several intervening variables. Much like the Howard and Sheth model, this book was widely read and discussed and the model researched by aspiring new academics. The major contribution of this book, however, was that the field now had a 'real' textbook from which consumer behavior courses emerged.

The Nicosia model

Another model at the time, one using computer terminology, was presented by Francesco (Franco) Nicosia (1966). Nicosia used a simulation of the consumer decision process. He took the case of a firm introducing a new product and structured the resulting consumer decision sequence. Nicosia believed that consumer behavior could be diagrammed in a flow chart as a decision sequence similar to computer programs with feedback loops. He then argued that simulation techniques can be used to 'explain in greater depth the structure of a consumer decision process' in order to better predict consumer behavior. The model was one more step toward an encompassing theory of consumer behavior.

MIDDLE-RANGE THEORIES AND THE 1970S

> History, although sometimes made up of the few acts of the great, is more often shaped by the many acts of the small.
>
> Mark Yost

Before much time passed, the grand utopian theories gave way to less complex middle-range theories such as attitudes and information processing (Cohen, 1972). For some years, Tom Robertson had been calling for the development of models on a less grandiose level. He felt that the greatest promise for advancing consumer behavior resided in what Merton had called 'middle-range' theories. These are theoretical or conceptual frameworks which do not constitute full-blown theories that explain all behavior in a grandiose fashion but neither are they merely a set of isolated findings. They suggest explanations and predictions concerning some relatively circumscribed area of inquiry (Ward and Robertson, 1973).

Numerous middle-range theories were being promulgated. Earlier, in Columbia, Lazarsfeld and Katz had stumbled on the idea of the 'Two Step Flow of Communication' and the concept of the 'gatekeeper' – that influence flows from mass media messages to opinion leaders and from opinion leaders to followers, rather than directly from the mass media to the end user (Katz, 1957). Work on the diffusion of innovation was soon to follow (Robertson, 1971; Rogers, 1962). Small group research, reference group theory, attitudes, cognitive dissonance, risk perception, low involvement, attribution theory and information processing were among several other middle-range theories starting to pour forth as researchers joined the cognitive movement and empirically tested facets of the various 'mini-theories.' The cognitive era had arrived in full force and the cognitive consumer was reigning king in the land of consumer research.

These researchers were biting off smaller chunks of behavior to study. For example, employing flow charts, Alan Andreasen (1965) proposed a model of consumer behavior built around attitudes. It too was a decision sequence approach, heavily influenced by Rogers' work on diffusion, but much more from a cognitive point of view. Andreasen's approach was one of the earliest reflections of the cognitive revolution that had arrived in consumer behavior.

Of the middle-range theories, no topic, other than information processing captured a greater interest than attitude formation and change. The interest evolved out of the work of Lazarsfeld and social psychologists of the World War II era, and later from the functional theories of Katz evolving into the expectancy-value approach of Rosenberg and Fishbein (Lutz, 1991) and from these to the highly sophisticated work of today. These researchers had concluded that an attitude (defined as a learned predisposition to respond in a consistently favorable or unfavorable manner with respect to a given object) is the key link in the causal chain between attribute perceptions on the one hand and intentions and behaviors on the other. The influence of Fishbein's model (e.g. Fishbein and Ajzen, 1975) is obviously seen in the multi-attribute models of consumer behavior studied today.

INFORMATION PROCESSING AND CHOICE BEHAVIOR

The other large area of research during the cognitive era and extending to the present was that of information processing. A critical book to emerge on cognitive theories of the consumer was that of Flemming Hansen (1972), *Consumer Choice Behavior: A Cognitive Theory*. Drawing on research conducted both in the United States and in Europe, Hansen constructed a systematic framework for the understanding of choice behavior. The model, along with supporting research, described how an individual attempts to modify available alternatives or

choices so that an acceptable one emerges depending on the amount of conflict that can be tolerated. Appearing on the heels of Nicosia and a bit before Bettman, this book was a milestone in the work to follow on consumer choice and information processing.

With the publication of Bettman's book, *An Information Processing Theory of Consumer Choice* (1979) research on information processing monopolized other topics in the journals and conference proceedings. That book may well have been one of the most cited works at the time and managed to tie together much of the available research in information processing. The central focus is on viewing consumers as cognitively active problem solvers and understanding the strategies and plans used in decision-making, Research has revolved around information search, information acquisition, encoding, storage, retrieval, integration and the processes used in the choice of heuristics. The theory emphasized the role of memory and allowed for flexible processing heuristics and choice mechanisms to a greater extent than previous theories. It explicitly included the construct of processing capacity and discussed specific processing limitations and heuristics in detail.

To sum up this entire line of research, in the words of Shimp (1991: 163), the cognitive orientation views consumer behavior as an 'active process whereby the individual forms hypotheses about consumption alternatives, acquires and encodes information, and integrates the new information with pre-existing beliefs.' This work has had an extremely long period of influence in the field and most certainly has carried through to the present.

EMERGENCE OF THE PROFESSION

The dissemination of scientific findings and intellectual intercourse among the disparate members of the consumer behavior fraternity was a problem at first. Consumer Research was not a topic particularly endearing to social science journals and much of the work did not have an obvious and direct relevance to marketing professionals and marketing journals. To its chagrin, the newly launched *Journal of Marketing Research* was being overwhelmed with papers devoted to consumer research. At other times, researchers presented their work at meetings such as the AMA, American Association for Public Opinion Research, American Psychological Association and at university-sponsored seminars that led to proceedings type edited books (e.g. Newman, 1957; Sommers and Kernan, 1967).

The time was ripe for a professional association and a journal through which researchers could discuss and disseminate their ideas and work. In 1969, at the Ohio State University, a group of individuals met to form what was to become the Association for Consumer Research (ACR). In the following year, the first ACR conference was held on the campus of the University of Massachusetts with about one hundred individuals attending from academia, the mass media, business, consumer organizations and the federal government. That small group has grown such that the North American ACR conference now registers in excess of 1,000 attendees, requiring some 800 plus hotel rooms. In addition, ACR conferences are also held in Europe, Latin America and Asia-Pacific. The birth of the ACR is well documented in numerous publications and need not be repeated here (For example, see the informative papers by Cohen, Engel, Kassarjian, Kernan and Wells in the 1995 ACR proceedings, *Advances in Consumer Research*).

Actually, a few years before the emergence of ACR, psychologists working in industry and advertising agencies, along with academics with similar interests, formed Division 23, the Division of Consumer Psychology, out of the Industrial Psychology arm of the American Psychological Association. A couple of decades later, Division 23 morphed into the Society for Consumer Psychology (SCP) – an organization, primarily of psychologists that specialize in consumer research but which also attracted hundreds of members from marketing departments and business schools. Much like ACR and often with overlapping membership, it has grown rapidly in the following decades. The prestigious *Journal of Consumer Psychology*, edited and owned by SCP, is a major publisher of consumer research since its emergence two decades ago (Schumann et al., 2008).

The premier journal, however, continues to be the *Journal of Consumer Research* (*JCR*). Its history more or less parallels that of ACR. From the very beginning of Consumer Research as a scientific field of endeavor, it was obvious that a major journal was needed and essential. In October 1973, representatives from ten scholarly associations (Association for Consumer Research, AMA, American Psychological Association, American Statistical Association, American Sociological Association and five others) met in Chicago and the new journal was born. In the ensuing months, under the sensitive guidance of Robert Ferber, a policy board was established, a founding editor, Ron Frank from Wharton, appointed and editorial offices established. $50,000 was borrowed from the AMA, repaid within a year, as subscriptions as well as manuscripts flowed in. The first accepted ones were from authors such as George Katona, George Day and Jim Bettman and by Spring 1974, the first issue was mailed to some 7,000 subscribers. Subscriptions came from academics in marketing, psychology, home economics, etc. Also, advertising agencies, corporations, law firms, television networks and governmental agencies were subscribers to a new journal that was about the consumer. Unfortunately, the journal could not be everything for everyone, readership dropped and over the next ten years the journal became what it is today, appealing primarily to academic researchers in the field of consumer behavior. As with ACR, the emergence of the journal has been well documented and need not be repeated here. (See, for example, papers by Ronald Frank and Jerome Kernan in the 1995 Association for Consumer Research Proceedings and the Tenth Anniversary Editorial in the March 1984 issue of *JCR*.)

CONSUMERISM AND PUBLIC POLICY RESEARCH

Meanwhile, in the land of academe, the decade of the 1970s brought serious problems. The country found itself in another war, this one with civilian resistance and unrest. Campuses occasionally looked like a war zone with tear gas, helmeted police and military troops. Enrollment in business school classes dropped precipitously and many business school professors vainly tried to distance themselves from the establishment, the war, and the 'powers that be.' Marketing was being perceived as the handmaiden of the military–industrial complex and, perhaps in self-defense, many marketing professors were promulgating that marketing could be used not only to sell orange juice and tanks but also charities, universities, social causes and hospitals (Kassarjian, 1994). It could be used for the good of society as well as the evils of trade. Kotler and Levy (1969) helped by coining new words: political marketing, social marketing, broadened marketing and even demarketing. The political climate of Kennedy and Johnson was very supportive of buyer oriented rather than seller oriented research (see Andreasen, 2006 for a nice historical review) and the stage was set for developing social marketing, 'an area that would focus on the work of not-for-profit groups and government agencies concerned with effective interventions into social problem areas' (Wilkie and Moore, 2003: 130).

Concerned with consumerists' criticism of marketing practices, a substantial amount of research effort was devoted to investigating such issues as deceptive advertising, counter and corrective advertising, product information, marketplace treatment of disadvantaged and minority consumers and consumer satisfaction, dissatisfaction and complaining behavior (Sheth and Gross, 1988). The latter, consumer satisfaction/ dissatisfaction eventually developed as a subarea (Hunt, 1977). Governmental organizations such as the Federal Trade Commission, the Food and Drug Administration, the White House and the Post Office, along with state attorney generals and district attorneys, had become aware that consumer research could indeed have applications in their spheres of concern. However, the major impact was at the Federal Trade Commission (FTC). 'Beginning in 1971 marketing academics took leave for about a year and moved into the FTC as "in-house consultants".' During the next ten years, some 30 marketing faculty worked in this capacity and contributed significantly to the development of research in the public policy sphere. By the end of the decade, the FTC was spending $1 million per year on marketing research (Wilkie and Moore, 2003). Studies on selling and advertising claims, labeling, product safety, as well as work related to case selection, analysis of evidence, and the development of Trade Regulation Rules poured forth. Consumer research had come into its own as a recognized field of inquiry, not only in industry and academia, but now also in governmental agencies as well as in court rooms. Consumer research, indeed, could be applied to the protection, as well as exploitation, of consumers.

THE SIMPLER CONSUMER AT THE CENTURY END

Writing history is a perpetual exercise in judgment.

Cushing Strout

As the decade of the 1980s arrived, consumer researchers, for the most part, retreated from the halls of government back to their ivied halls. By this time the deep-seated belief in the cognitive man, the thinking, reasoning, problem solving, consumer was being challenged. Of course, in many cases and under many conditions, the consumer appears to behave as a thinking, reasoning, information processing individual, but under other conditions he simply could not care less. Olshavsky and Granbois (1979) had produced data that many purchases do not involve decision making at all. In fact, most purchases require minimal, if any, cognitive activity. Plodding, mindlessness and the 'muddling through' consumer were being recognized as a descriptor of much consumer activity. The concept of involvement and its measurement had important implications (Zaichkowsky, 1985). For example, the assumption that attitudes precede action implies a classical high involvement hierarchy (Petty et al., 1983). Under low involvement conditions the hierarchy of effects is not awareness-attitude-adoption, but rather awareness and minimal comprehension occur first, followed by trial and attitude formation or attitude change in that order (Ray, 1974). Other challengers were promulgating simpler paradigms such as classical conditioning and trial and error learning theories (Nord and Peter 1980; Shimp, 1991). It appeared that Watson, Skinner, Hull and Pavlov were being reincarnated.

The long ignored concept of motivation was also making a comeback. Words such as mood, emotions and affect arousal were beginning to reappear along with exploration into the affective and emotional side of consumer experience.

In Europe, Kroeber-Riel (1979) was claiming that verbal methods of measuring arousal or cognitive activity such as information processing, affect, mood and emotions are either not sensitive enough or involve a needless detour (the measurement of the perception of response) when the response itself can be measured directly. Kroeber-Riel claimed that physiological measures of response are superior approaches.

PHYSIOLOGICAL APPROACH TO CONSUMER BEHAVIOR

Over the years, physiological measures have been used to register emotions, interest, motivations and other responses. Studies use eye movement, pupil dilation, voice pitch analysis as well as galvanic skin response and measurements such as heart rate, respiration and other autonomic nervous system reactions have been promulgated unfortunately with little success or strong experimental support.

Starting in the 1980s, brain lateralization research was appearing in the literature. The basic research involved studies using the electroencephalograph (EEG) on individuals with brain damage, patients emerging from electroconvulsive therapy and by controlled stimulation of the brain hemispheres (Hansen, 1981). These data indicated that among normal individuals, the left hemisphere is primarily responsible for cognitive activities, symbolic representations and sequential analysis. The left brain is causal, logical and argumentative, in contrast to the right brain, which is more diffuse, spatial, intuitive, artistic and musical. Researchers next turned to measurement of brain activity – positron emissions tomography (PET scanning) and functional magnetic resonance image (fMRI) scanning (Hansen and Christensen, 2007). With these brain-scanning techniques, exactly where in the brain activity occurs is being measured (e.g. talking, feeling fear, solving problems, etc.). The work is surely interesting although its level of successful contribution to our knowledge of consumer behavior is yet to be established.

THE QUALITATIVE MOVEMENT

The most widespread challenge to the cognitive approach and laboratory research appeared by the late 1980s under the terms postmodernism, postpositivism, humanism and more recently 'Consumer Culture Theory' (coined by Arnould and Thompson, 2005). Marching in step with postmodern American sociology, anthropology, literary criticism and other scholarly areas as well as postmodern brethren in Western Europe, qualitative research again emerged but with a new twist.

The prologue or preamble of the postmodern work in the US was the consumer behavior odyssey project (Belk, 1991; Belk et al., 1989). A group of consumer researchers traveled across the country interviewing consumers along the way, in little towns, at county fairs and along the road, taking voluminous notes and video recording of consumers behaving in natural settings and real life.

Since then the method has expanded to hundreds of researchers interviewing and taping individuals in a variety of purchase, consumption and disposal situations. These are not controlled experiments in a laboratory with representative samples, or looking at brain activity measures in wired consumers, but real people in the real world in an uncontrolled situation. The data collected in the field is then analyzed, organized and presented in an attempt to better understand what it is that consumers really do and think. To the traditional research establishment, this work was perceived as an attack on the scientific method. It was the puttering of a foolish group of researchers. Of course, many of the postmodern researchers made similar accusations about positivistic research. They felt that controlled laboratory experimentation with subjects placed in unreal situations simply do not represent how consumers really behave (cf. Wells, 1993).

The point is that there are many ways to make contributions to knowledge whether those methods are standard practice or not. Much as Katona challenged traditional economics and introduced survey research, much as the ilk of Dichter rattled the foundations of marketing research, and the cognitive researchers rattled the establishment in the 1960s, so too the postmodern movement has rattled those who work in highly controlled laboratory research or rely on the sometimes unreal assumptions of mathematical modeling. Interestingly, postmodern sociologists, anthropologists and others are now examining consumers as their point of reference.

THE DAWNING OF A NEW CENTURY: BACK TO THE FUTURE

History, by appraising ... [the students] of the past, will enable them to judge of the future.

Thomas Jefferson

As the 1990s arrived, and blended in with the new century, consumer researchers have set their sights on both content and methods once again. While traditional fields such as attitudes, personality, motivation and emotions continue to exist, topics reasonably new to the field have emerged (e.g. behavioral decision theory (BDT) and judgment and decision making (JMD)). Much of the content in the field today, aside from the consumer culture theory work, seems to be towards the BDT side. The applications of BDT researchers turned from brand-based inquiries to people based issues such as greater emphasis on issues related to personal health and well-being.

New methods of inquiry and data presentation have emerged – not only computer imaging such as brain scans, but also from the postmodern realm the presentation of research findings in DVD and streaming video formats. The medium of film has been used as an expression of consumer issues and even poetry has been used as a metaphor for consumer behavior.

With the onset of the 2000s, research in the entire field of consumer behavior simply exploded in size. From a handful of maverick researchers, the number of scholars grew to tens of hundreds. Much as behavioral articles overwhelmed the *Journal of Marketing Research* a few decades earlier, the *Journal of Consumer Research* and the *Journal of Consumer Psychology* were overwhelmed and by the turn of the century, well over a dozen new journals had emerged, publishing the work of hundreds of researchers in dozens of countries. However, as mentioned earlier, our purpose in writing this chapter was not to present the field as it exists today – that we leave to others – but rather to chronicle the development of a scholarly field of endeavor. We hope we have presented an overview of that development that does justice to an exciting field of inquiry that is every bit as important as the fields from which it emerged.

To look back upon history is inevitably to distort it.

Norman Pearson

ACKNOWLEDGEMENTS

The authors would like to thank the editors, reviewers and our colleagues who helped in the preparation of this chapter. We particularly thank Alan Andreasen, Gary Bamossy, Debra R. Kassarjian and Claudia Townsend. Some of the comments in this chapter were presented at the Research Traditions in Marketing Conference during the twentieth anniversary of EIASM in Brussels and at the 2005 Conference on Historical Analysis and Research in Marketing in Long Beach, California.

REFERENCES

Allport, G. (1935) *Psychology of Radio*. New York: Harper Brothers.

Allport, G.W. and Postman, L.J. (1943) *The Psychology of Rumor*. New York: Holt, Rinehard and Winston.

Andreasen, A.R. (1965) 'Attitudes, Customer Behavior and A Decision Model', in L.G. Peterson (ed.) *New Research in Marketing*, Berkeley: University of California, Institute of Business and Economic Research.

Andreasen, A.R. (2006) *Social Marketing in the 21st Century*. London: Sage Publications, Inc.

Arnould, E.J. and Thompson, C.J. (2005) 'Consumer Culture Theory (CCT): Twenty Years of Research', *Journal of Consumer Research*, 31(March): 868–882.

Bartels, R. (1988) *The History of Marketing Thought* third edn., Columbus, OH: Publishing Horizons, Inc. (first edn. published by Richard D. Irwin (1962) as *The Development of Marketing Thought.*)

Belk, R.W. (1986) 'What Should ACR Want To Be When It grows Up', in R.J. Lutz (ed.) *Advances in Consumer Research*, Vol. 13, Provo, UT: Association for Consumer Research, pp. 423–424.

Belk, R.W. (ed.) (1991) *Highways and Buyways: Naturalistic Research from the Consumer Behavior Odyssey*. Provo, UT: Association for Consumer Research.

Belk, R.W., Wallendorf, M. and Sherry, J.F. Jr. (1989) 'The Sacred and the Profane in Consumer Behavior: Theodicy on the Odyssey', *Journal of Consumer Research*, 15(June): 1–38.

Bettman, J.R. (1979) *An Information Processing Theory of Consumer Choice*. Reading, MA: Addison-Wesley.

Bliss, P. (1963) *Marketing and the Behavioral Sciences*. New York: Allyn and Bacon.

Bush, R.R. and Mosteller, F. (1955) *Stochastic Models for Learning*. New York: John Wiley and Sons.

Cantril, H. (1940) *The Invasion from Mars*. Princeton: Princeton University Press.

Cohen, J.B. (ed.) (1972) *Behavioral Science Foundations of Consumer Behavior*. New York: The Free Press.

Culver, S. (1988) 'What Manikins Want: "The Wonderful Wizard of Oz" and "The Art of Decorating Dry Goods Windows"', *Representations*, 21(Winter), 97–116.

Edell, J.A. (1993) 'Advertising Interactions: A Route to Understanding Brand Equity', in A. Mitchell (ed.) *Advertising Exposure, Memory and Choice*, Hillsdale, NJ: L. Erlbaum, pp. 195–208.

Ekström, K.M. (2003) 'Revisiting the Family Tree: Historical and Future Consumer Behavior Research', *Academy of Marketing Science Review*. Vol. 1, pp. 1–29.

Engel, J.F., Kollat, D.T. and Blackwell, R.D. (1968) *Consumer Behavior*. New York: Holt, Rienhard & Winston.

Estes, W.K., Kuch, S., MacCorquodale, K., Meehl, P.E., Mueller, C.G. Jr., Schoenfeld, W.N. and Verplanck, W.S. (1954) *Modern Learning Theory*. New York: Appleton-Century-Crofts.

Fishbein, M. and Ajzen, I. (1975) *Beliefs, Attitudes, Intentions and Behavior: An Introduction to Theory and Research*. Reading, MA: Addison-Wesley.

Frank, R. (1962) 'Brand Choice as Probability Process', *Journal of Business*, 5(1): 43–56.

Fullerton, R.A. (1990) 'The Art of Marketing Research: Selections from Paul F. Lazersfeld's "Shoe Buying in Zurich" (1933)', *Journal of the Academy of Marketing Science*, 18(2): 317–325.

Fullerton, R.A. and Stern, B.B. (1990) 'The Rise and Fall of Ernest Dichter', *Werbeforschung und Praxis* (June), 208–211.

Haines, G. (1969) *Consumer Behavior: Learning Models of Purchasing*. New York: Free Press.

Haire, M. (1950) 'Projective Techniques in Marketing Research', *Journal of Marketing*, 24(2): 649–656.

Hansen, F. (1972) *Consumer Choice Behavior: A Cognitive Theory*, New York: The Free Press.

Hansen, F. (1981) 'Hemispherical Laterization: A Review and a Discussion of its Implications for Consumer Behavior Research', *Journal of Consumer Research*, 8(1): 23–36.

Hansen, F. and Christensen, S.R. (2007) *Emotions, Advertising and Consumer Choice*. Copenhagen: Copenhagen Business School Press.

Hilgard, E.R. (1956) *Theories of Learning*. New York: Appleton-Century-Crofts.

Howard, J.A. (1963) *Marketing: Executive and Buyer Behavior*. New York: Columbia University Press.

Howard, J.A. and Sheth, J. (1969) *The Theory of Buyer Behavior*. New York: John Wiley and Sons.

Hovland, C.I., Janis, I.L. and Kelley, H.H (1953) *Communication and Persuasion*. New Haven: Yale University Press.

Hunt, K. (1977) *Conceptualization and Measurement of Consumer Satisfaction and Dissatisfaction: Proceedings of the Conference Conducted by Marketing Science Institute with Support from the National Science Foundation*, Cambridge, MA: Marketing Science Institute.

Jones, D.B.G. and Monieson, D.D. (1990) 'Early Development of the Philosophy of Marketing Thought', *Journal of Marketing*, 51(1): 102–113.

Kassarjian, H.H. (1968) 'Consumer Behavior: A Field Theoretical Approach', in American Marketing Association Fall Conference Proceedings (Series 28), pp. 285–289.

Kassarjian, H.H. (1973) 'Field Theory in Consumer Behavior', in S. Ward and T.S. Robertson (eds) *Consumer Behavior: Theoretical Sources*. Englewood Cliffs, NJ: Prentice-Hall, Inc.

Kassarjian, H.H. (1994) 'Scholarly Traditions and European Roots of American Consumer Research' in G. Laurent, G.L. Lilien and B. Pras (eds) *Research Traditions in Marketing*, Boston: Kluwer Academic Publishers, pp. 265–279.

Kassarjian, H.H. and Robertson, T.S. (1968) (eds) *Perspectives in Consumer Behavior*. Glenview, IL: Scott, Foresman and Company.

Katona, G. (1951) *Psychological Analysis of Economic Behavior*. New York: McGraw-Hill.

Katz, E. (1957) 'The Two step Flow of Communication: An Up-to-Date Report on an Hypothesis', *Public Opinion Quarterly*, 21(Spring): 61–78.

Kernan, J.B. (1995) 'Framing a Rainbow, Focusing the Light: *JCR*'s First Twenty Years', in F.R. Kardes and M. Sujan (eds) *Advances in Consumer Research*, Vol. 22, Provo, UT: Association for Consumer Research, pp. 488–496.

Kotler, P. (1968) 'Computer Simulation in the Analysis of New-Product Decisions', in F.M Bass, C.W. King, and E.A. Pessemier (eds) *Applications of the Sciences in Marketing Management*. New York: John Wiley and Sons.

Kotler, P. and Levy, S. (1969) 'Broadening the Concept of Marketing', *Journal of Marketing*, 33(January): 10–16.

Kroeber-Riel, W. (1979) 'Activation Research: Psychobiological Approaches in Consumer Research', *Journal of Consumer Research*, 5(3): 240–250.

Kuehn, A.A. (1962) 'Consumer Brand Choice as a Learning Process', *Journal of Advertising Research*, 2(December): 10–17.

Levy, S.J. (1959) 'Symbols for Sale', *Harvard Business Review*, 37(July–August): 117–124.

Levy, S.J. (1991) 'President's Column: A Brief History'. *Association for Consumer Research Newsletter*, (March): 2–6.

Lewin, K. (1936) *Principles of Topological Psychology*. New York: McGraw-Hill Book Co.

Lutz, R.J. (1991) 'The Role of Attitude Theory in Marketing', in Harold H. Kassarjian and Thomas S. Robertson, *Perspectives in Consumer Behavior*, fourth edn., Englewood Cliffs, NJ: Prentice-Hall, Inc.

Maloney, J.C. (1987) 'The First 80 Years of Advertising Research', Paper presented at the Sixth Annual Advertising and Consumer Psychology Conference, Chicago.

Merton, R.K. (1946) *Mass Persuasion: The Social Psychology of a War Bond Drive*. New York: Harper Brothers.

Morgan, J. (1991) Personal (telephone) communication. University of Michigan.

Myers, J.G., Massy, W.F. and Greyser, S.A. (1980) *Marketing Research and Knowledge Development*. Englewood Cliffs, NJ: Prentice-Hall.

Newman, J.W. (1957) *Motivation Research and Marketing Management*. Boston: Divison of Research, Graduate School of Business Administration, Harvard University.

Newman, J. (1983) 'Presentation of the ACR "Fellow in Consumer Behavior Award" to Sidney Levy, Geore Katona and Robert Ferber', in R.P. Bagozzi and A.M. Tybout (eds), *Advances in Consumer 'Behavior, Volume 10*, Provo: UT, Association for Consumer Research, pp. 6–8.

Nicosia, F. (1966) *Consumer Decision Processes: Marketing and Advertising Implications*. Englewood Cliffs, NJ: Prentice-Hall, Inc.

Nord, W.R. and Peter, J.P. (1980) 'Behavior Modification Perspective on Marketing', *Journal of Marketing*, 44(Spring): 36–47.

Olshavsky, R.W. and Granbois, D.H. (1979) 'Consumer Decision Making: Fact or Fiction', *Journal of Consumer Research*, 6(1): 93–100.

Petty, R.E. and Cacioppo, J.T. and Schumann, D. (1983) 'Central and Peripheral Routes to Advertising Effectiveness: The Moderating Role of Involvement', *Journal of Consumer Research*, 10(2): 135–146.

Ray, M.L. (1974) 'Consumer Initial Processing: Definitions, Issues and Applications', in G.D. Hughes and M.L. Ray (eds) *Buyer/Consumer Information Processing*. Chapel Hill, NC: University of North Carolina Press.

Robertson, T.S. (1971) *Innovative Behavior and Communication*. New York: Holt, Rinehard & Winston.

Rogers, E.M. (1962) *Diffusion of Innovation*. New York: The Free Press.

Schumann, D.W., Haugtvedt, C.P. and Davidson, E. (2008) 'History of Consumer Psychology', in C.P. Haugtvedt, P. Herr and F.R. Kardes (eds) *Handbook of Consumer Psychology*. New York: Lawrence Erlbaum.

Sheth, J.N. and Gross, B. (1988) 'Parallel Development of Marketing and Consumer Behavior: A Historical Perspective', in T. Nevett and R.A. Fullerton (eds) *Historical Perspectives in Marketing: Essays in Honor of Stanley C. Hollander*. Lexington, MA: Lexington Books.

Shimp, T.A. (1991) 'Neo-Pavlovian Conditioning and its Implications for Consumer Theory and Research', in T.S. Robertson and H.H. Kassarjian (eds) *Handbook of Consumer Behavior*. Englewood Cliffs, NJ: Prentice-Hall.

Sommers, M.S. and Kernan, J.B. (eds) (1967) *Explorations in Consumer Behavior*. Austin, TX: University of Texas Press.

Stouffer, S.A. and others (1949) *The American Soldier: Studies in Social Psychology in World War II*, Vol. 1–2. New York: John Wiley, Inc.

Tadajewski, M. (2006) 'The Ordering of Marketing Theory: The Influence of McCarthyism and the Cold War', *Marketing Theory*, 6(2): 163–199.

Ward, S. and Robertson, T.S. (1973) *Consumer Behavior: Theoretic Sources*. Englewood Cliffs, NJ: Prentice Hall, Inc.

Wells, W.D. (1956) 'Is Motivation Research Really an Instrument of the Devil', *Journal of Marketing*, 21(October): 196–198.

Wells, W.D. (1993) 'Discovery-Oriented Consumer Behavior', *Journal of Consumer Research*, 19(March): 489–504.

Wilkie, W.L. and Moore, E.S. (2003) 'Scholarly Research in Marketing: Exploring the Four Era', *Journal of Public Policy and Marketing*, 22(2): 116–146.

Zaichkowsky, J.L. (1985) 'Measuring the Involvement Concept', *Journal of Consumer Research*, 12(3): 341–352.

5

The Evolution of Market Research*

David W. Stewart

Modern marketing research has its roots in the complex confluence of many disciplines and the economic affluence that arose in the early twentieth century. The development of statistics, psychometric measurement, public opinion polling, ethnography and individual and group depth interviews – all emerged as important tools during the first half of the twentieth century. At the same time, there was a maturing of the sciences of human behavior, such as psychology, sociology, anthropology and economics, which provided theory and conceptual foundations for understanding human behavior in a market context. These tools and sciences emerged at a time that saw unprecedented growth in the wealth of average consumers, at least in the United States and Europe. This convergence of tools, social sciences and consumer affluence created opportunities and the necessity for the large-scale marketing research industry that emerged in the late 1940s and that has grown and matured subsequently in past 70 years.

The relatively recent advent of formal marketing research does not mean that such research or at least its precursors do not have a long history. In its most basic form, marketing

research is about gathering information about markets, customers and sellers. Defined in this way, marketing research is quite old. It is not difficult to find instances of formal marketing research even in ancient times. For example, the ancient Silk Road was both a trade route and a means for the transfer of information about markets and commodities, as well as for the diffusion of ideas and culture (Franck and Brownstone, 1986). Similarly, efforts at forecasting supply and demand are very old. The ancient Egyptians forecast harvests based on the level of the Nile River during flood season.

While there is no doubt that information about markets has been informally exchanged for thousands of years, it is unlikely that any ancient defined their role in terms of market research. Perhaps the first recorded example of efforts to use information obtained by direct observation of buying and selling and associated business practices are found in business dealings of the prominent and wealthy Fugger family (Ehrenberg, 1928). The Fugger family played a major role in European business and politics for more than 400 years. Over time, members of the family expanded their homes and places of business throughout the political and commercial capitals of Europe. Members of the family exchanged detailed letters about market, trade and financial conditions in their home cities. This systematic exchange of information allowed the family to coordinate its efforts and make decisions based on up-to-date information about local markets and changing economic conditions. It is likely that the Fuggers were not alone among families and business associates who routinely exchanged information about market and business conditions.

Many individuals sought to chronicle local market and business conditions during travels to distant places. Marco Polo had done so during his travels to the Far East. Although better known as a pioneering novelist and the author of *Robinson Crusoe*, Daniel Defoe was also among the first individuals to try to chronicle economic activity in a comprehensive manner. Defoe's book, *A Tour Thro' the Whole island of Great Britain, Divided into Circuits or Journies*, first published in the 1720s and later updated in the 1760s may be regarded as a precursor of the modern economic census. Based on a personal tour and first-hand observation of all of Great Britain, Defoe provided a detailed list of the business and economic activity in every location he visited. The fact that *The Tour* went through nine editions before Defoe's death suggests that his chronicle, or census, was a useful tool for decision makers in business.

This said, the chronicles of travelers were undoubtedly more items of curiosity than tools for business planning among most readers. Nevertheless, as commerce and trade became more global, the need for market information from more distant locations became more important. Informal observation of local business conditions was no longer sufficient. The Industrial Revolution had increased the geographic scope of trade and added to the need for information to inform business decisions. The Industrial Revolution also brought with it the first serious efforts to understand the interdependencies

of markets and economies. Although a number of individuals had written about economics, largely in defense of the global British mercantile trade, the first economic scientist was probably Sir William Petty, who focused on the use of quantitative methods for understanding economic issues. It was Petty who first observed what are today called business cycles. Although able effort went into examination of macroeconomic issues during the period from 1650 to 1900, the advent of what was later to be recognized as market research today, had to wait until almost 1900.

The earliest recorded attempts to forecast the outcome of individual choice behavior occurred in the context of political contests. In 1824, two different newspapers, The *Harrisburg Pennsylvanian* and the *Raleigh Star* used straw polls and canvasses to predict the outcome of forthcoming elections (Lockley, 1950; Robinson, 2002). Such straw polling became common in the United States during the 1800s. The outcome of the *Harrisburg Pennsylvania* poll was prescient; it found Andrew Jackson with a large lead over John Quincy Adams. Although Jackson did win the popular vote, he did not win enough votes in the Electoral College, and the election outcome was then thrown to the US House of Representatives, and Adams was elected President.

THE BEGINNINGS OF FORMAL MARKET RESEARCH

One of the first recorded efforts to apply formal survey research to a marketing problem was carried out by the advertising agency N.W. Ayer & Son. In 1879, the agency wired state officials and publishers throughout the country asking for expectations of grain production in order to assist a client that manufactured agricultural equipment (Bogart, 1957; Lockley, 1950). During this same period, academic researchers in psychology were beginning to create many of the concepts and tools that would form the foundation of modern measurement theory. Gustav Fechner was developing the discipline of psychometrics, along with methods that ultimately found application in sensory testing and the development of measurement scales (Heidelberger, 2004).

Other academic researchers soon followed suit by applying psychological research methods to marketing problems. In 1895, Harlow Gale at the University of Minnesota sent a survey questionnaire to advertising practitioners in an effort to identify what made advertising effective. Following his survey, he also conducted several experiments using his students as subjects, and on the basis of the questionnaire returns, and the results of his own observations of his student subjects, he produced a monograph entitled *On the Psychology of Advertising* in 1900. (Lockley, 1950). At the same time, psychologist Walter Dill Scott of Northwestern University had begun a program of research on advertising (Coolsen, 1947). Scott's research was published in a series of essays that subsequently formed the basis for a research-based book on the psychology of advertising (Scott, 1903). Scott continued his advertising research and produced four revisions of his original book, complete with new research findings, by 1913.

Advertising research was now well on its way to becoming an established and recognized discipline. It primarily focused on both the individual responses of consumers to advertising and its content and the measurement of consumer exposure to advertising. After being hired by Lord & Thomas in 1907, Claude Hopkins developed a set of best practices based on research that were ultimately published in his seminal book, *Scientific Advertising* (1923). Daniel Starch, another psychologist whose contributions have been memorialized by the 'Starch test', a print recognition test, published another research-based book on advertising, *Advertising Principles*, in 1914 (Starch, 1914).

Meanwhile, Charles Coolidge Parlin created a commercial research division at Curtis Publishing in 1911, a division with the charge to develop data to help the company understand the US consumer market, setting off a competition among advertising agencies and other firms to offer market research services (Kay, 2000; Keep et al., 1998). Among the first projects undertaken by Parlin's organization was a census of wholesale and retail distribution for the textile industry (Lockley, 1974). Also in 1911, the Kellogg Company coordinated the efforts of more than 40 members of the Association of National Advertising Managers to conduct the first cooperative magazine readership survey (Bogart, 1957). The need for standardized definitions and common measures related to media use led to the creation of the Audit Bureau of Circulation in 1914 (Advertising Age.com, 2008).

Parlin was also influential in the establishment of a Department of Commercial Research at US Rubber in 1915 and at the Swift and Company in 1916 (Lockley, 1974). Advertising agency, J. Walter Thompson followed suit with the establishment of a marketing research department in 1916 (Advertising Age.com, 2008). By 1916, the *Chicago Tribune* was beginning to publish reports of consumers' buying habits, wants and expectations based on a standardized survey instrument (Bogart, 1957; Lockley, 1974).

As advertising and media research gained recognition as an academic discipline and a useful tool for business decision making, other types of market research were coming into their own. F. I. du Pont de Nemours & Company began to ask sales personnel to estimate the total sales volume for the product(s) they sold, report any new products or processes discussed with customers, estimate future sales and other relevant information. Although other businesses may have been gathering similar data, the du Pont 'Trade Report', as it was called, was the first documented effort by a firm to create a comprehensive analysis of each customer and prospective customer (Pine and Van Gelder, 1927). Not only was du Pont highly successful, during the antitrust trial that resulted in du Pont being ordered to dispose of the Hercules Powder Company and Atlas Company, the judge who ruled in the case did so, in part, because he concluded that no company could possess such detailed information about explosives markets and the explosives industry without commercial espionage (Kerr, 1938).

Marketing research thus began to emerge as a professional discipline after 1910. In 1911, J. George Frederick left his position as editor at *Printers Ink* to establish one of the first marketing research firms, called The Business Bourse. R.O. Eastman left the Kellogg Company to found a marketing research firm in 1916. One of his first clients was General Electric, which commissioned him to estimate the value of the brand name 'Mazda'. This may well have been the first research effort designed to evaluate brand equity (Lockley, 1974). Business schools also began to embrace marketing research during this same period. The Bureau of Business Research was established at Harvard Business School in 1911. Among its first projects was a detailed examination of the operating costs of retail shoe stores. This project ultimately became an annual study of the operating costs of department and specialty stores, performed for the predecessor of the National Retail Merchants Association (Bogart, 1957; Lockley, 1974). Northwestern University's School of Commerce founded a Bureau of Business Research that also examined the operating expenses of various types of retailers (Lockley, 1974).

THE FORMALIZATION OF A MARKETING RESEARCH DISCIPLINE

By 1920, marketing research was well on its way to becoming an identified profession and established academic discipline. Two books, one titled *Business Research and Statistics* (1918) by J. George Frederick, and the other titled *Commercial Research: An Outline of Working Principles* (1919) by University of Chicago Professor C. S. Duncan, then assistant professor at the University of Chicago, sought to document the best practices in marketing research. Percival White's

Market Analysis appeared in 1921. White's book ultimately became the standard textbook on marketing research and went through several editions. Associations of professional marketing researchers, such as the Research Group within The Advertising Club of New York began to form in the 1920s (Lockley, 1974). In 1923, Arthur Charles Nielsen, Jr., established the A.C. Nielsen Company, which initially focused on test marketing new products and in-store measurement of sales to estimate the market share of competitors in various product categories. Nielsen subsequently introduced a national radio index in 1942 and a television rating service in 1950.

A particularly important milestone in the development of marketing research occurred in October of 1926 when the Domestic Commerce Division of the US Department of commerce convened a conference to consider how the Department of Commerce might contribute to marketing research. This conference led to a decision by the Commerce Department to conduct a national census of distribution. The first Census of Distribution was conducted in 1929 and remains a part of the larger Census of Business still conducted every five years by the US Census Bureau.

DEVELOPMENT OF THE TECHNOLOGY OF MARKETING RESEARCH

Although now taken for granted by most marketing researchers, many of the tools and methods for conducting marketing research today were unknown to the pioneers of marketing research. A considerable amount of early market research involved efforts to conduct a census of the relevant market or industry. Probability sampling was largely unknown. Experimental design and the analysis of variance, which have become so important in such contexts as the analysis of alternative marketing actions (e.g. advertising executions, promotions, etc.) and product design (e.g. conjoint analysis), were developed during the 1920s and 1930s and did not become widely known and applied outside of agricultural work until much later.[1] Similarly, much of the work on measurement theory, scale development and data reduction occurred between the 1920s and 1950s.[2] On the qualitative side of the field, the development of focus group depth interviews grew out of work in psychotherapy and communications research after 1920.

Indeed, the period from roughly 1925 to approximately 1980 was a period of rapid development of methods and techniques that now form the basic toolkit of marketing research. Although marketing has added to and refined many of these methods and techniques, most have been borrowed from other disciplines. Specifically four methodological domains emerged as important elements in the evolution of the marketing research toolkit during this period: focus groups, survey research and sampling, experimental design and multivariate data analysis.

Focus group research[3]

Among the most widely used research tools in the social sciences are group depth interviews or focus groups. Originally called 'focused' interviews (Merton and Kendall, 1946), this technique came into vogue after World War II and has been a part of the social scientist's tool kit ever since. Focus groups emerged in behavioral science research as distinctive members of the qualitative research family, which also includes individual depth interviewing, ethnographic participant observation and projective methods, among others. The popularity and status of focus groups has ebbed and flowed over the years, but the use of focus groups in marketing research has grown steadily since the 1970s.

The lineage of focus group research is most commonly and directly traced to studies of persuasive communications and the effects of mass media that were conducted in the early 1940s. Yet, this is only part of the story, as today's focus groups also evolved from three other sources: (1) clinical psychological

uses of group analysis and therapy, (2) sociological and social psychological studies of group dynamics and (3) marketing research uses of focus groups in consumer studies. Consequently, the theoretical underpinnings of focus groups emerged from what pioneer Alfred Goldman describes as a 'rich stew of socio-psychological and psychotherapeutic traditions and techniques' (Goldman and McDonald, 1987: 3).

Sociology's core interest in social groups and group behavior led many researchers to employ group interviews in their research. Both Karl Mannheim (1936) and E. S. Bogardus (1926) report using group interviews in the 1920s. The most prominent, early social psychological uses of focus groups sought to achieve understanding of the effects of media communications such as radio broadcasts, government fund-raising appeals and World War II military training films; and the underlying factors that explained the relative effectiveness and persuasiveness of a particular communication. The most famous and influential impetus to the growth of focus groups sprung from network radio researchers' frustration with their inability to explain why different programs received different likeability scores. Explaining such differences could inform the creative process and help in the creation of programs that are more likely to appeal to an audience Thus, the focused group interview had its origins in the Office of Radio Research at Columbia University in 1941 when Paul Lazarsfeld invited Robert Merton to assist him in the evaluation of audience response to radio programs.[4]

In this early focus group research, members of a mass media studio audience listened to a recorded radio program and were asked to press a red button when they heard anything that evoked a negative response – anger, boredom, disbelief – and to press a green button whenever they had a positive response. These responses and their timing were recorded on a polygraph-like instrument called the Lazarsfeld-Stanton Program Analyzer (a recording device that is quite similar to devices still in use today). At the end of the program, members of the audience were asked to focus on the positive and negative events they recorded and to discuss the reasons for these reactions.

After the outbreak of World War II, Merton applied his technique to the analysis of Army training and morale films for the Research Branch of the United States Army Information and Education Division, which was headed by Samuel Stouffer, one of the leading sociologists of the day and a pioneer in attitude research. Merton later adapted his technique for use in an individual interview and in time, the method, both in group and individual interview settings, became rather widely used. It was also modified and merged with other types of group interviews that did not include the media focus procedure employed by Merton. Thus, what is known as a focus group today takes many different forms and may not follow all of the procedures Merton identified in his book on focused interviews.

Uses of focus groups in psychotherapeutic research emerged from the quite different priorities of clinical diagnosis and treatment. Some of the earliest clinical uses of groups date back to Moreno's (1934) seminal work with psychodrama and play therapy. Compared with groups conducted in the social psychological tradition, the clinical approach was more likely to emphasize interactive group discussions and activities; individuals' deeply seated thoughts and feelings; and extensive, wide-ranging and spontaneous expressions. Researchers influenced by the psychotherapeutic school tend to favor focus groups that are more developmental in orientation and design. Such groups place less emphasis on evaluative tasks and tend to use more indirect ways of asking questions. Also, in contrast to individual patient–therapist psychotherapy, the interactions among participants in clinical group therapy facilitate individuals' treatment processes.

An enduring heritage of focus groups' clinical psychological origins lies in today's cadre of focus group moderators with professional backgrounds in traditional psychotherapy, particularly those forms with early-twentieth-century European origins (Kassarjian, 1994). The earliest and most renowned pioneer who migrated from clinical psychology to marketing research was Paul Lazarsfeld's student Ernest Dichter. Although Dichter tended to prefer individual to group interviews, his consulting company trained a large number of the first generation of focus group researchers. Alfred E. Goldman is the most prominent among the second generation of researchers, who transitioned from clinical to marketing research uses of focus groups, and his article, 'The Group Depth Interview', is widely considered a classic (1962). Many moderators today also have specific ties to newer therapies such as encounter groups, transactional analysis, gestalt therapy, as well as sensitivity training.

The successful uses of focus groups in evaluating World War II morale and training films did not go unnoticed by the marketing research community. The procedures developed by Lazarsfeld and Merton were imported directly into Columbia Broadcasting System's (CBS) research on pilot radio and television programs and are still used today. Although it is likely that some business studies used focus groups in the 1930s (Henderson, 2004), their popularity grew dramatically from the 1950s onward (Leonhard, 1967; Smith, 1954). Today, focus groups are by far the most popular qualitative marketing research tool. Business expenditures on focus groups are estimated to account for at least 80 percent of the more than $1 billion spent annually on qualitative research (Wellner, 2003). In the US alone, over 1,000 focus group facilities have been constructed, and the practice is expanding globally.

Perhaps the most compelling quality of focus groups is their delivery of 'live' consumers for observation by marketing managers. As Axelrod exclaimed in 1975, focus groups provide managers with 'a chance to experience a flesh and blood consumer' (p. 6).

In many ways, market research uses of focus groups reflect both social and clinical psychological traditions, to varying degrees. Their initial emergence in the marketing literature is strongly linked to the so-called 'motivation' researchers of the 1950s (Smith, 1954), who typically had intellectual grounding in Freudian and neo-Freudian thought. Groups conducted in this tradition tend to share the exploratory, interactive, playful and confrontational qualities of clinical psychological groups. By contrast, focus groups rooted in social psychological thinking tend to be more evaluative in purpose, direct in questioning and lower in respondent interaction. Such focus groups are often heavily involved in gathering consumers' reactions to product concepts, marketing communications and competitive brands.

Survey research and sampling

No methodology is more closely identified with marketing research than survey research. Many marketing questions must be addressed at the level of the 'market', that is, at some level of aggregation that represents the market to which a marketer is offering a product or other marketing activity. Answers to such questions require asking standardized questions to one or more groups of consumers who are representative of the larger market. Survey research, defined in the most generic sense, provides such answers. Two critical elements are required for a survey to provide valid answers to such surveys. First, the respondents to a survey must be representative of a larger population. As a result, sampling and sample design has played an important role in the evolution of marketing research. Second, all respondents to a survey must answer the same questions or at least a subset of the same questions. Thus, the design of surveys has been informed and improved by work on question design and scaling techniques.

In many ways, the evolution of marketing research, especially in the period between the 1920s and 1980s, is a story of the development and improvement in sampling methodology. It was readily obvious to early marketing researchers that a census of consumers or distributors was impractical in most cases. Not only is it expensive, but the time required to conduct a census also frequently exceeds the time available to a manager for making a decision. For this reason, samples of consumers were used from the early days of formal market research, as described in the previous section. Public opinion polling and marketing research also emerged during the same period (both the *Journal of Marketing* and *Public Opinion Quarterly* began publication in 1936) and many of the early practitioners of survey research plied their trade in both areas. These early practitioners included such individuals as George Gallup, Paul Lazarsfeld, Elmo Roper and Archibald Crossley (Bogart, 1957). There continues to be broad cross-fertilization of ideas and practices in these fields.

The history of survey research and sample construction is one marked by learning from mistakes. Perhaps the most famous opportunity for learning occurred during the 1936 presidential election when the influential magazine, the *Literary Digest*, predicted that Alfred Landon would defeat Franklin Roosevelt. Early samples in marketing research were believed to be valid representations of the larger market if the percentage distribution of responses did not change as additional data was tabulated (Brown, 1937). This methodology, called stabilization, failed to appreciate the fact that replication of results across successive waves of data collection from a particular sampling frame does not guarantee a representative sample when the sampling frame itself is not representative of the larger population of interest. The *Literary Digest* survey was validated by the stabilization method but failed to correct for bias in the sampling frame from which the sample was selected (Bogart, 1957). The *Literary Digest* sample was very large, ten million potential respondents, but had only a 20 per cent response rate. Even more problematic, the sample was constructed from lists of readers of the *Literary Digest*, owners of automobiles and households with telephones. In the 1930s, such lists included far more affluent, Republican leaning voters than were present the general voter population. As a result of the

Literary Digest failure, stabilization as a means for sample validation fell into disfavor.

Although the 1936 election proved disastrous for the *Literary Digest*, it helped make the reputation of another survey researcher. George Gallup, an employee of Young and Rubicam who had just established the American Institute of Public Opinion, correctly predicted the outcome of the election and the results of the *Literary Digest* survey using a far smaller sample. The reason for Gallup's success was his use of quota sampling; that is, he explicitly recognized that there are significant differences among voters with respect to key demographic characteristics. These characteristics are related to voter preferences. Thus, by constructing his sample to reflect important differences among voters, Gallup created a more representative sample of the population of voters (Babbie, 2007).

Gallup would be involved in another significant learning event in 1948, but with less favorable results for his reputation. Although Gallup has been successful in predicting the presidential contest in 1936 by using a more representative sample than the *Literary Digest*, he did not employ the type of random sample that is common today. Sampling methodologies were not widely introduced in college curricula until the late 1930s and were slow to be taken up by social scientists. The concept of random sampling of people or other units was not well known in survey research even in the late 1940s.

In the 1948 presidential election that pitted Harry Truman and Wendell Willkie against one another, Gallup and all other major pollsters predicted that Willkie would win. There were two reasons these pollsters were wrong, and these served as lessons for future research. First, the sampling approach used was based on quota sampling, rather than random sampling. The failure to predict the election using quota sampling proved to be an important stimulus for the adoption of probability samples using methods of random selection (Mosteller et al., 1949).[5]

The second reason Gallup and other pollsters failed to correctly predict the outcome

of the 1948 election was perhaps even more problematic, but it too provided important lessons for researchers. All of the major pollsters stopped surveying voters about three weeks prior to Election Day under the assumption that voters had made up their minds (Moore, 1995). As a result, the polls missed a significant shift in public opinion during the latter stages of the campaign. The lesson of this failed prediction is that opinion, attitudes and preferences are not always well formed and stable. A weak preference today may give way to a stronger preference tomorrow. This means it is important to continuously measure public opinion and also to capture measures of strength of opinions and preferences.

The capture of the nuances and strength of opinion, attitude and preference was the focus of considerable research activity that paralleled the development of survey research. Drawing on earlier work in psychophysics and his own work on comparative judgment, Louis Thurstone developed the Thurstone Scale in 1928 (Thurstone, 1928). A Thurstone scale consists of statements about a particular issue. Each statement has an associated numerical value indicating how favorable or unfavorable it is judged to be. The numerical value of any given statement is based on careful research involving empirical comparisons of people's responses to the statements. The statements and associated numerical values provided a standardized scale on which people checked each of the statements to which they agreed, and a mean score can be computed that provides a measure of the strength of their attitude. Development of other standardized scales soon followed. In 1932, Rensis Likert introduced a simple bipolar, summative scale that consists of items to which people responded on a five-point scale that ranged from strongly agree to strongly disagree. This scale bears his name and has become a staple of survey research (Likert, 1932).

The next 30 years saw significant attention to scale development with considerable interaction of survey researchers and scale developers. In 1950, Louis Guttman developed the scale that bears his name (Guttman, 1950) and the semantic differential was introduced in 1957 (Osgood et al., 1957). Although not always fully appreciated by practicing marketing research, or even many academic researchers, there are strong theoretical differences in the conceptual foundations of the various scales that have become the mainstay of much survey research. Nevertheless, the development of standard scales for use in survey and marketing research served to accomplish two seemingly incompatible goals. The first goal is to obtain responses from people that are comparable and that can be aggregated for purposes of statistical summary and analysis. The second goal is to capture individual differences in the people's response to specific items. Achieving these two goals while also attending to the practical necessity of making a respondent's task in answering questions relatively simple, comprehensible and time efficient has been a significant achievement for marketing researchers. The art of designing questions that are both useful for a researcher and meaningful to a respondent was well documented in a now classic book, *The Art of Asking Questions* (Payne, 1951).

In addition to survey methodologies related to sampling and question design, marketing researchers focused on improvements in research design by identifying and reducing various biases due to response tendencies unrelated to issue of interest, interviewer characteristics and the design and layout of questions and questionnaires. The globalization of survey research also led to the documentation of cultural differences in response to surveys. Such cultural differences are now routinely recognized in the construction of survey questions. Converse (1987) provides a detailed and comprehensive description of the history and development of survey research to 1960.[6] By the mid-1960s, there was a well-developed literature on the methods of survey research, including treatment of complex sampling designs (Kish, 1965) and questionnaire design (Oppenheim, 1966).

The *Journal of Marketing Research* appeared in 1964 and was largely devoted to the publication of new research techniques, scale development and measurement and statistical methods. Interestingly, the first editorial board consisted of eight members, only three of whom were academics (Wittink, 2004). By the mid-1960s, marketing research experienced the impact of new developments in data analysis, particularly the design and analysis of marketing experiments. Computer technology permitted the storage and analysis of large amounts of data. These new developments enabled marketing research to move beyond small, descriptive studies to analysis of causal relationship and complex interdependencies among variables.

Experimental design

Rudimentary experiments in marketing date from the early work of Scott, Starch and Hopkins, among others. This early work generally took the form of simple comparison between alternatives with respect to some outcome measures. Hopkins (1923) is credited with being one of the first to use split-run, or A/B testing, to evaluate the relative efficacy of alternative media, copy and promotions. Similarly, product comparisons, such as taste tests, have a relatively long history within marketing research. Standardized taste tests date from at least the early part of the twentieth century (Meilgaard et al., 1999) and taste research was widely employed during World War II to help design palatable foods for soldiers (Pangborn, 1964). Use of more formal experimental designs has a much shorter history within marketing research. One of the earliest treatments of controlled experimentation in marketing is found in Appelbaum and Spears (1950). These authors, while calling for greater use of marketing experiments, suggest that the scant literature on marketing experimentation at the time was of questionable validity. Indeed, it was 15 years before marketing experimentation would gain traction in the discipline (Banks, 1965).

This is not to suggest that there were not notable applications of marketing experiments during the intervening period. One such application is the classic 'shopping list' study in which two groups of consumers were exposed to shopping lists that differed only with respect to the presence of instant coffee or regular ground copy (Haire, 1950). While this study is most often remembered as an example of the use of projective measures (the subjective differences that consumers attribute to alternative shopping lists), the reality is that the research design was an experiment in which the independent variable was the shopping list and the dependent variables were the attributions of consumers regarding the type of shopper that would carry each list.

Another notable early application of experimental design in marketing was the work of Edgar Pessemier (1959) who pioneered a simulated shopping environment as the setting for the experimental study of consumer response to changes in the prices of products. In still another example, this time in the context of advertising, Towers, Goodman and Zeisel (1962, 1963) conducted experiments on the effects of television advertising that sought to compare the responses of individuals who were exposed to advertising to the responses of those not exposed in a manner that controlled for the other differences among the individuals.

It is interesting that experimental research in marketing was initially driven by the practitioner community. This was, perhaps, the result of the very specific needs of the business community to evaluate and select from alternative courses of action in an efficient and effective manner (Floyd and Stout, 1970). Nevertheless, by the mid-1970s, experimental research had become the dominant research tool of marketing research, at least among academic researchers. This dominance coincided with the rise of theory-driven research in marketing. Prior to the 1970, most published marketing research in academic journals tended to be descriptive with a focus on consumer characteristics, differences among groups of consumers and institutional practices. This began to change in the early 1970s.

Beginning in the latter half of the 1960s, books appeared that radically altered the way in which marketing scholars approached their work. These books included Nicosia's *Consumer Decision Processes* (1966), Howard and Sheth's *The Theory of Buyer Behavior* (1968) and Engel, Kollat and Blackwell's *Consumer Behavior* (1968). Each of these books proposed 'grand theories' of consumer behavior and attempted to integrate the enormous amount empirical research and theory from many disciplines. The grand theories offered in these books suggested strong causal relationships that begged testing. Such tests required research methods that could identify causal relationships, that is, experimental research. The breadth of these grand theories soon gave rise to frustration at the difficulty of definitive tests, but more specific causal relationships were still amenable to testing in experiments, and, within a decade, more micro-level theoretical treatments, such as Bettman's *An Information Processing Theory of Consumer Choice* (1979), gave renewed vigor to the use of experimental research in the study of consumer behavior.

One of the more important applications of experimental design has been in the context of product design. It is difficult and expensive to create real products to which consumers respond. However, by conceptualizing a product as a bundle of features or benefits, it is possible to present consumers with hypothetical product offerings to which they can respond in terms of preference. Conjoint analysis is the tool by which such hypothetical bundles are created and analyzed (Green and Srinivasan, 1978). Conjoint analysis has been one of the more important innovations in marketing research and has made product design a more efficient and less risky activity for firms.

By the late 1980s, there was a sense among some researchers in the field that the dominance of the experimental method, especially in research that focused on consumer behavior, was too narrow, artificial and limiting. This led to a counter movement within the field that focused on research techniques that provided richer descriptions of consumer behavior in more naturalistic settings. This counter movement emphasized research methods drawn from ethnography, including participant observation. The best-known example of this work is that by Belk et al. (1989). Ethnographic research and other types of qualitative marketing research have also found ready application among marketing research professionals (Elliot and Elliot, 2003). Nevertheless, experimental and ankel survey research remain the dominant forms of marketing research in the twenty-first century.

Multivariate data analysis

The advent of the computer and associated information technologies has had a profound impact on the practice of marketing research. Information technology has provided an opportunity to store, manage and analyze large sets of data. It has also offered the opportunity to apply statistical tools for the analysis of complex relationships.

Statistical tools for the analysis of complex relationships were developed as early as the 1920s. Charles Spearman (1904a, 1904b) developed the original concept of factor analysis, which was further elaborated upon by Thurstone (1934) and others. Similarly, Harold Hotelling developed the early roots of discriminant analysis and canonical correlation (Anderson, 1960). Methods for cluster analysis, which is the most common analytic classification tool for market segmentation, were known as early as the 1930s (Tyron, 1939). Multidimensional scaling techniques, which are now widely employed in product positioning studies (perceptual maps), were introduced by Torgerson in the 1950s (Torgerson, 1958). And, structural equation modeling has deep roots in genetics, economics and psychology.

Although the conceptual foundations of these tools were known for decades, the limitations of computing power prior to the advent of the computer restricted their use to problems involving relatively small sets of variables and researchers who could afford

the small army of research assistants to do the hand analyses. The advent of the computer changed all of this, and the 1970s saw an explosion in the use of multivariate statistical tools in marketing research.

Information technology also facilitated the collection of large volumes of data, as well as the analysis of such data. The modern Universal Product Code was first used for grocery products in 1974. By 1990, 93 percent of mass merchandisers and 94 percent of supermarkets employed scanner technology (*Chain Store Executive*, 1990). The data produced by scanner technology offered rich, longitudinal records of purchases. When combined with other data and the creation of consumer panels that allowed the tracking of individual consumer purchases over time, scanner panel data created a powerful new tool for marketing researchers and the promise of 'single-source' data; that is, a comprehensive set of data on sales, pricing, in-store variables and advertising from a convenient, single source. Market research companies such as IRI and Nielsen offered comprehensive data, analysis and consulting services based on this promise. These data were subsequently provided to academic researchers, sparking an important stream of published literature that applied sophisticated statistical tools and models to these data that lasted from the late 1980s through the turn of the century.

Unfortunately, the initial enthusiasm for single-source data soon met the reality of the limitations of such data. Surprisingly, the electronic data was not error free and, in fact, contained considerable error (Goodstein, 1994). The data provided good indicators of the influence of short-term consumer response to marketing activities, such as price promotions, but offered little insight into longer-term, more persistent changes in the market associated with brand building, product innovation and distribution strategies (Bucklin and Gupta, 1999). Further limiting the utility of scanner panel data was Wal-Mart's decision in 2001 to cease providing its scanner data to third-party commercial data providers. This was a serious blow to marketing researchers interested in product categories where Wal-Mart constitutes a huge share of sales (as much as 40 percent in some cases). While there have been efforts to create indirect substitutes for the Wal-Mart data, the dream of single-source data appears dead.

CONTEMPORARY MARKETING RESEARCH AND ITS FUTURE

By the turn of the twenty-first century, marketing research was a mature discipline. Courses in marketing research are offered in virtually all business schools and are frequently required as part of completing a degree in marketing. Specialized graduate degrees in marketing research are offered by a number of universities. The marketing research industry in the United States alone exceeds $12 billion in annual revenues, and the 200 largest commercial research agencies in the United States employ more than 36,000 people (Honomichl, 2007: H3, H65). On a global level, the industry is expected to grow to $40 billion in revenue by 2009 (*Metrics 2.0*, 2008). Marketing research is a standard tool for decision-making in all industries and has been widely employed by not-for-profit organizations and government agencies.

Marketing research has developed a rich toolbox of research techniques and methods, borrowing from such fields as anthropology, economics, psychology, sociology and statistics, among others. At the same time, marketing research has made significant contributions to research in these basic disciplines, both in terms of methodological and substantive contributions. Over the past decade, there has been a proliferation of new marketing journals that report the growing results of empirical marketing research. Both academic and commercial marketing research is increasingly global in its focus.

Perhaps the most significant new development in marketing research during the past decade is the rise of the Internet. It has provided a new vehicle for data collection, complementing such traditional methods as telephone interviews, personal interviews and mail questionnaires. It has also spawned the creation of new metrics and measurement services designed to capture the behavior of consumers in a Web context. However, the Internet is more than just another communication or distribution channel or another method for obtaining data. Rather, the Internet has created new modes of interaction among consumers and between consumers and marketers. It has added an interactive dimension to the media use experience and created new venues within which consumers interact. These new venues include online social networks, such as *FaceBook* and *MySpace*, and virtual worlds such as *Second Life* (Hoffman and Novak, 2009; Novak, 2008). These new venues not only create opportunities for empirical research but also beg for new theoretical perspectives.

While the discipline of marketing research appears healthy, there are storm clouds on the horizon. In much the same way that other technical disciplines, such as software programming, have become increasingly commoditized, marketing research is becoming a more tactical tool in organizations, focused more on the evaluation of short-term outcomes rather than strategic decisions of the firm (Rainey, 2002). The sophisticated tools that have been developed by marketing researchers often take too long to apply to be useful for guiding decisions, given the pace of change in the marketplace (Constantineau, 1995). The tools are often more helpful for describing the past than for predicting the future. The highly specialized tools for the analysis of consumer response to the individual elements of the marketing mix and for the identification of market segments are less useful for informing the complex decisions related to the management of portfolios of products and markets that now characterize most large business organizations. Marketing research has also done a poor job of linking its activities and measures, and those of marketing in general, to the financial performance of the firm (Association of National Advertisers, 2008; Stewart, 2006, 2008a, 2008b).

These limitations define the challenges and opportunities for the future of marketing research as a discipline. If marketing research is to retain a role in the strategic planning of the firm, it will need to develop tools and methods that provide rapid answers to complex questions that include predictions of future financial performance. This is a noble goal for the next era in the evolution of marketing research.

NOTES

* Portions of this chapter, especially those portions of the chapter that describe the earliest stages of the development of marketing research during the first two decades of the twentieth century, draw heavily from previously published histories of marketing research, including Lockley (1950, 1974), Bogart (1957), and Bartels (1976).

1 Sir Ronald Fisher's first book on the analysis of variance, *Statistical Methods for Research Workers*, did not appear until 1925. Fisher's seminal work, *The Design of Experiments*, did not appear until 1935.

2 This work includes the contributions of Louis Thurstone, Louis Guttman, Rensis Likert and Harold Hotelling. In addition, much of the work on modern personality theory, which has also had a significant influence on consumer research, was still very much in the developmental stage.

3 This section of the chapter draws heavily on Stewart et al. (2007).

4 See Merton (1987) for an interesting recollection of these beginnings as well as how focussed interviewing lost its second 's'.

5 However, see Hansen and Hurwitz (1949) for a cautious defense of the continuing utility of quota sampling.

6 See also Krosnick (1999).

REFERENCES

'Advertising History Timeline' *Advertising Age. com* (http://adage.com/century/timeline/index. html, accessed 3 July, 2008).

Anderson, T.W. (1960) 'Harold Hotelling's Research in Statistics', *The American Statistician*, 14(3): 17–21.

Appelbaum, W. and Spears, R.F. (1950) 'Controlled Experimentation in Marketing Research', *Journal of Marketing*, 14(1): 505–517.

Association of National Advertisers (2008) *The Marketing Organization: Recent Trends and Future Directions*. ANA White Paper, New York: Association of National Advertisers.

Axelrod, M.D. (1975) '10 Essentials for Good Qualitative Research', *Marketing News*, (March 14): 10–11.

Babbie, E.R. (2007) *The Basics of Social Research*. Florence, KY: Wadsworth.

Banks, S. (1965) *Experimentation in Marketing*. New York: McGraw Hill.

Bartels, R. (1976) *The History of Marketing Thought*, 2nd Edition, Columbus, OH: Grid.

Belk, R., Wallendorf, M. and Sherry, J. (1989) 'The Sacred and Profane in Consumer Behavior: The Theodacy of the Odessey', *Journal of Consumer Research*, 15(June): 1–38.

Bettman, J.R. (1979) *An Information Processing Theory of Consumer Choice*, Reading, MA: Addison-Wesley.

Bogardus, E.S. (1926) 'The Group Interview', *Journal of Applied Sociology*, 10: 372–382.

Bogart, L. (1957) 'Opinion Research and Marketing', *The Public Opinion Quarterly*, 21(1): 129–140.

Brown, L.O. (1937) *Market Research and Analysis*. New York: Ronald.

Bucklin, Randolph E. and Gupta, Sunil (1999) 'Commercial Use of UPC Scanner Data: Industry and Academic Perspectives', *Marketing Science*, 18(3): 247–273.

Chain Store Executive (1990) 'MIS Budgets Continue to Rise', August: 70–72.

Constantineau, L.A. (1995) 'Reengineering the Marketing Research Function', *Quirk's Marketing Research Review*, Oct., http:// www.quirks.com/articles/a1995/19951001. aspx?searchID=16185520&sort=5&pg=1, accessed 15 May, 2008.

Converse, J.M. (1987) *Survey Research in the United States: Roots and Emergence 1890– 1960*. Berkeley, CA: University of California Press.

Coolsen, F.G. (1947) 'Pioneers in the Development of Advertising', *Journal of Marketing*, 12(1): 80–86.

Duncan, C.S. (1919), *Commercial Research: An Outline of Working Principles*, New York: MacMillan.

Ehrenberg, R. (1928) *Capital and Finance in the Age of the Renaissance: A Study of the Fuggers and their Connections*. Translated by H.M. Lucas, New York: Harcourt, Brace & Co.

Elliot, R. and Jankel-Elliot, N. (2003) 'Using Ethnography in Strategic Consumer Research',

Journal of Qualitative Marketing Research: An International Journal, 6(4): 215–223.

Engel, J.F., Kollat, D.T. and Blackwell, R.D. (1968) *Consumer Behavior*. New York: Holt, Rinehart, Winston.

Fisher, R. (1925) *Statistical Methods for Research Workers*, New York: MacMillan.

Fisher, R. (1935) *The Design of Experiments*, London: Oliver and Boyd.

Floyd, T.E. and Stout, R.G. (1970) 'Measuring Small Changes in a Market Variable', *Journal of Marketing Research*, 7(1): 114–116.

Franck, I.M. and Brownstone, D.M. (1986) *The Silk Road: A History*. New York: Facts on File Publications.

Frederick, J.G. (1918) *Business Research and Statistics*, New York: D. Appleton and Co.

Goldman, A.E. (1962) 'The Group Depth Interview', *Journal of Marketing*, 26: 61–68.

Goldman, A.E. and McDonald S.S. (1987) *The Group Depth Interview: Principles and Practice*. Englewood Cliffs, NJ: Prentice-Hall, Inc.

Goodstein, R.C. (1994) 'UPC Scanner Pricing Systems: Are they Accurate?', *Journal of Marketing*, 58(2): 20–30.

Green, P. and Srinivasan, S.V. (1978) 'Conjoint Analysis in Consumer Research: Issues and Outlook', *Journal of Consumer Research*, 5(September): 103–123.

Guttman, L. (1950) 'The Basis for Scalogram analysis', in S.A. Stouffer et al. (eds) *Measurement and Prediction. The American Soldier Vol. IV*. New York: Wiley.

Haire, M. (1950) 'Projective Techniques in Marketing Research', *Journal of Marketing*, 14(April): 649–656.

Hansen, M.H. and Hurwitz, W.N. (1949) 'Dependable Samples for Market Surveys', *Journal of Marketing*, 14(October): 363–372.

Heidelberger, M. (2004) *Nature From Within: Gustav Theodor Fechner and his Psychophysical Worldview*. Translated by C. Klohr, Pittsburgh, PA: University of Pittsburgh Press.

Henderson, N. (2004) 'Same Frame, New Game', *Marketing Research*, (Summer): 38–39.

Hoffman, D.L. and Novak, T.P. (2009) 'Flow Online: Lessons Learned and Future Prospects', *Journal of Interactive Marketing*, 23 (1), 23–34.

Honomichl, J. (2007) 'Honomichl Top 50, Business Report on the Marketing Research Industry', *Advertising Age*, Special Section, June 15, H1–H67.

Hopkins, C.C. (1923) *Scientific Advertising*. Reprinted by NTC Business Books.

Howard, J. and Sheth, J.N. (1968) *The Theory of Buyer Behavior*. New York: Wiley.

Hower, R.M. (1939) *The History of an Advertising Agency*. Cambridge, MA: Harvard University Press.

Kassarjian, H.H. (1994) 'Scholarly Traditions and European Roots of American Consumer Research', in G. Laurent, G. Lilien and B. Pras (eds) *Research Traditions in Marketing*, Boston: Kluwer Academic Publishers, pp. 265–287.

Kay, A.S. (2000) 'Roots of Market Research', *DestinationCRM.com*, April 17, (http://www.destinationcrm.com/Articles/News/Daily-News/Roots-of-Market-Research-46416.aspx), accessed 3 July, 2008.

Keep, W.W., Hollander, S.C. and Dickinson, R. (1998) 'Forces Impinging on Long-Term Business-to-Business Relationships in the United States: An Historical Perspective', *Journal of Marketing*, 62(April): 31–45.

Kerr, G. (1938) *DuPont Romance: A Reminiscent Narrative of E.I. Dupont de Nemours and Company*. Wilmington, DE: Du Pont Printing Division.

Kish, L. (1965) *Survey Sampling*. New York: Wiley.

Krosnick, J.A. (1999) 'Survey Research', *Annual Review of Psychology*. Palo Alto, CA: Annual Review, pp. 537–567.

Leonhard, D. (1967) *The Human Equation in Marketing Research*. New York: American Management Association.

Likert, R. (1932) 'A Technique for the Measurement of Attitudes', *Archives of Psychology*, 140: 1–55.

Lockley, L.C. (1950) 'Notes on the History of Marketing Research', *Journal of Marketing*, 14(5): 733–736.

Lockley, L.C. (1974) 'History and Development of Marketing Research', in Robert Ferber (ed.) *Handbook of Marketing Research*, New York: McGraw-Hill, pp.1–3, 1–15.

Mannheim, K. (1936) *Ideology and Utopia: An Introduction to the Sociology of Knowledge*. New York: Harcourt Brace Co.

Morten M., Civille, G.V. and Carr, B.T. (1999) *Sensory Evaluation Techniques*, Third edn. Boca Raton, FL: CRC Press.

Merton, R.K. and Kendall, P.L. (1946) 'The Focussed Interview', *American Journal of Sociology*, 51: 541–557.

Merton, R.K. (1987) 'Focussed Interviews and Focus Groups: Continuities and Discontinuities,' *Public Opinion Quarterly*, 51, 550–566.

Metrics 2.0 (2008) 'Outlook for Market and IT Research – Over 10% Growth to Reach $43 Billion', *Metrics 2.0*, http://www.metrics2.com/blog/2006/10/16/outlook_for_market_and_it_research_over_10_growth.html, accessed 10 July, 2008.

Moore, D.W. (1995) *The Superpollsters: How They Measure and Manipulate Public Opinion in America*. New York: Four Walls Eight Windows.

Moreno, J.L. (1934) *Who Shall Survive?* Washington, D.C.: Nervous and Mental Diseases Publishing Co.

Mosteller, F., Hyman, H., McCarthy, P., Marks, E. and Truman, D. (1949) *The Pre-election Polls of 1948: Report to the Committee on Analysis of Pre-election Polls and Forecasts*. New York: Social Science Research Council.

Nicosia, F.M. (1966) *Consumer Decision Processes*. Englewood Cliffs, NJ: Prentice Hall.

Novak, T.P. (2008) 'eLab City: A Platform for Consumer Behavior Research in Virtual Worlds', Conference on Leveraging Online Media and Online Marketing, Marketing Science Institute, Palm Springs, CA, February 6–8.

Oppenheim, A.N. (1966) *Questionnaire Design and Attitude Measurement*. New York: Basic Books.

Osgood, C.E., Suci, G. and Tannenbaum, P. (1957) *The Measurement of Meaning*. Urbana, IL: University of Illinois Press.

Pangborn, R.M. (1964) 'Sensory Evaluation of Food: A Look Backward and Forward', *Food Technology*, 18: 1309.

Payne, S. (1951) *The Art of Asking Questions*. Princeton, NJ: Princeton University Press.

Pessemier, E.A. (1959) 'A New Way to Determine Buying Decisions', *Journal of Marketing*, 24(2): 41–46.

Pine, A. and Van Gelder, H.S. (1927) *History of the Explosives Industry in America*. New York: Columbia University Press.

Rainey, M.T. (2002) 'Market Research: The Paradox of Influence without Importance', *Market Leader*, 17(Summer): 16–17.

Robinson, S. (2002) 'Polls and Polling', *Mathematics*. Farmington Hills, MI: The Gale Group.

Scott, W.Dill (1903) *The Theory of Advertising: A Simple Exposition of the Principles of Psychology in Their Relation to Successful Advertising*. Boston, MA: George H. Ellis Co.

Smith, G.H. (1954) *Motivation Research in Advertising and Marketing*. New York: McGraw-Hill Book Company.

Spearman, C.E. (1904a) 'General Intelligence Objectively Determined and Measured', *American Journal of Psychology*, 15: 201–293.

Spearman, C.E. (1904b) 'Proof and Measurement of Association between Two Things', *American Journal of Psychology*, 15: 72–101.

Starch, D. (1914) *Advertising Principles*. New York: Scott Foresman.

Stewart, D.W. (2006) 'Putting Financial Discipline in Marketing: A Call to Action', *Corporate Finance Review*, 10(September/October): 14–21.

Stewart, D.W. (2008a) 'How Marketing Contributes to the Bottom Line', *Journal of Advertising Research*, 48(1): 94–105.

Stewart, D.W. (2008b) 'Marketing Accountability: Linking Marketing Actions to Financial Results', *Journal of Business Research*, doi:10.1016/j.jbusres.2008.02.005.

Stewart, D.W., Shamdasani, P. and Rook, D. (2007) *Focus Groups: Theory and Practice*, Second edn. Thousand Oaks, CA: Sage Publications.

Thurstone, L.L. (1928) 'Attitudes can be Measured', *American Journal of Sociology*, 33: 529–554.

Thurstone, L.L. (1934) 'The Vectors of Mind', *Psychological Review*, 41: 1–32.

Torgerson, W.S. (1958) *Theory and Methods of Scaling*. New York: Wiley.

Towers, I., Goodman, L.A. and Zeisel, H. (1962) 'A Method for Measuring the Effects of Television through Controlled Field Experiments', *Studies in Public Communication*, (4): 87–110.

Towers, I., Goodman, L.A. and Zeisel, H. (1963) 'What Could Nonexposure Tell the TV Advertiser', *Journal of Marketing*, 27(3): 52–56.

Tyrone, R.C. (1939) *Cluster Analysis*. Ann Arbor, MI: Edwards Brothers.

Wellner, A.S. (2003) 'The New Science of Focus Groups', *American Demographics*, (March 1): 29–22.

White, P. (1921), *Market Analyis*, New York: McGraw Hill.

Wittink, D.R. (2004) 'Journal of Marketing Research: 2 P's', *Journal of Marketing Research*, 41(February): 1–6.

6

Theorizing Advertising: Managerial, Scientific and Cultural Approaches

Chris Hackley

INTRODUCTION

As one might expect, advertising is a topic which lends itself to theorization from a number of different intellectual perspectives. Advertisements make use of non-advertising ideas and discourses (Cook, 2002; O'Donohoe, 1994), drawing on imagery, narrative styles, genres and techniques from art, aesthetics, movies, television and pop culture, literature, sport and street subcultures, to name but a few. Attempts to theorize about advertising have been no less eclectic in their sources. They have borrowed from the intellectual and scholarly traditions of semiotics, linguistics, mass communications, cognitive science and social psychology, information processing and artificial intelligence, cultural anthropology and ethnography, sociology and literary theory, among others (see, for example, MacInnis and Jaworski, 1989; Mick and Buhl, 1992; O'Barr, 1994; Ritson and Elliott, 1999; Sherry, 1987; Stevens et al., 2003; Tanaka, 1994). This conceptual scope is necessary, because advertising has implications which are hugely significant for the economy but which also impact upon the personal, cultural, ethical, legal and regulatory areas.

Attempts to negotiate a path through this compelling field of thought, writing, research and scholarship must take account of this diversity of interests, methods and perspectives. What is more, accounts of the history of ideas in marketing in general are notoriously contested, subject to amnesiac episodes and exogenous political influences (Hackley, 2009; Tadajewski and Saren, 2008), and often shaded by a narrow Western worldview (Gould, 1991; Jack, 2008). In addition, there is a persistent and continuing debate about the most powerful analogy for management and marketing practice and research. Is it art, or is it science? (see, for example, Belk, 1986; Brown, 1997, 1999: Hirschman, 1983, 1986; Hunt, 1990, 1991, 1992).

In some respects, the debate is more acute in advertising since it is an area of practice in which science and art are forced together in the interests of commerce. The difficult implications of this coexistence are exemplified in the uncomfortable tension and outright conflict which can occur between the creative and account management roles in advertising agencies (Hackley, 2000; Kover and Goldberg, 1995). Creative professionals often use a conceptual vocabulary from art and aesthetics when talking about audience response to advertising (Hackley and Kover, 2007). They see their craft in terms of art. Yet, client marketing executives and agency account managers often use a quite different vocabulary, expressing their understanding of advertising in terms of a technical and scientific worldview (Hackley, 2003a; Kover, 1996). So, rather than ignore these competing visions of advertising or present a one-sided account I propose for the present purpose to separate the field into three main categories. I hope by doing so some of the major questions of the field are clarified somewhat, especially in terms of work which addresses the very same questions but with from quite different terms of reference. The three categories I will divide advertising theory into are managerial, scientific and cultural.

These categories overlap and oversimplify the field, admittedly, but I think they can be useful nonetheless, because they represent three distinct and important strains of work. In addition, I hope that using these categories can create points of engagement between parallel but differing traditions of advertising theory which, generally speaking, do not connect as much as they ought. For example, sociological studies of advertising often neglect highly relevant management literature, while much of the management-oriented research ignores the sociocultural and anthropological studies. Therefore, this scheme is intended as a vehicle for possible integration, as well as a way of distinguishing between different modes of advertising theory.

By managerial theory in advertising, I mean to refer to work which ostensibly supports the aims, values and ends of organizational managers. This presents a problem, because there is an ongoing debate about whether managers are really the intended audience of much academic marketing research, or whether they are used as rhetorical figures to supply an axiological justification for research which is really written for other academics. Managerial relevance is claimed by academic research which, couched in a management vernacular, could plausibly be understood and perhaps applied by practicing managers. Nevertheless, this relevance is also claimed by work which is highly abstract, statistically complex and, no doubt, impenetrable to any but specialists. Advertising, like marketing, enjoys contributions from the full range of theory, from commonsense heuristics or rules-of-thumb, through to highly abstract and specialized sub-branches of social science research.

Advertising management includes each kind of theory, the anecdotal and the scientific. But while both are often managerial in their stated aims, the distinguishing feature of advertising science is that it rests on a scheme or worldview which will account for many advertising phenomena, possibly enabling insight or even prediction. I include work in this category which includes opposing views of what counts as science, since science itself is a category riven with debate and controversy. What this work has in common is a sense of grand theory, a desire to encompass many advertising issues within a set of more or less explicit, but also clear and lasting guiding assumptions.

The third category, cultural theory in advertising, refers to work which analyzes advertising's cultural influence in terms of its impact on self and social identity, relationships, moral development and social values. This category mainly comprises research and scholarship which draws on liberal arts and sociocultural intellectual traditions. Much of this work has managerial relevance, though it may have been pursued from intellectual curiosity alone or from a concern with non-managerial values.

MANAGERIAL THEORY IN ADVERTISING

Popular management theories of advertising

It is important to distinguish between the first published attempts to formalize knowledge of advertising, and the development of the craft itself. Of course, the craft of advertising did not emerge in the 1960s, or even in the 1920s, but long before. Even in the absence of written theory, advertising craft made use of techniques of persuasion from its earliest days. There is a commonly peddled myth that there was a golden age of factual, literal and unpersuasive advertising before it lost its innocence and began corrupting the world with 'lifestyle' appeals. Collins and Skover (1993), for example, imply that in the days of classified advertising it satisfied the conditions for a kind of one-sided Habermassian ideal speech situation, consisting of rational appeals based on product utility. Yet it is difficult to sustain such an argument when advertising archives are looked at in their own historical context. Advertising was, in fact, both persuasive and pervasive from the first days of a mass-market printed media in the 1600s (McFall, 2004). Just because most advertising was classified did not mean it could not tap into aspirations of social status and personal and social identity by using persuasive rhetorical tropes and suggesting identity implications for the consumer. For example, Harbor (2007) details the appeals to class and status in advertisements for London music concerts in the 1700s.

Printing and communications technology developed over time to allow more flexibility in creative executions. But, as early as the 1700s, Victorian entrepreneurs in the UK such as Thomas Holloway were placing billboards in China while Holloway and his contemporaries in the pottery industry were acutely aware of the prestigious effect of having their products placed in royal portraits, books and London stage plays (Hackley, 2005; Quickenden and Kover, 2007).

Marketing and advertising existed, then, long before management was pursued as a distinct field of Western thought and scholarship around the turn of the twentieth century. Early knowledge in marketing was pursued mainly from a desire to improve the managerial efficiency of marketing processes (Wilkie and Moore, 2003). In advertising, knowledge generation began in advertising agencies and focused on practical matters. Later, as advertising grew in importance as an industry, academics began to import concepts from psychology and the other social and statistical sciences to try to create a scientifically based body of advertising knowledge. Advertising, like marketing, developed a genre of popular theory which remains widely known to this day.

American copywriter John E. Kennedy's (1924) is credited with one of the earliest attempts to formalize advertising craft with his widely quoted assertion that advertising is 'salesmanship in print'. Kennedy worked under advertising industry pioneer Albert D. Lasker at the Lord and Thomas advertising agency. He later conceived of 'reason why' advertising. The 'reason why' philosophy advocated persuasive logic in copywriting which, couched in straightforward and easy-to-understand terms for the average consumer, gave concrete reasons why buying this brand of product made sense for the consumer (Fox, 1984). Lasker saw the potential in Kennedy's ideas and formed the first known school of advertising copywriting[1] which taught the principles of persuasive advertising. Several decades later 'reason why' was reborn as the *Unique Selling Proposition* by Rosser Reeves (McDonald and Scott, 2007).

Moving forward to the 1960s, the 'creative revolution' in advertising is often accredited to American advertising pioneer Bill Bernbach, noted for introducing irony in advertising with an iconic campaign for Volkswagen. Many other ideas about advertising effectiveness, advertising research and creativity were popularized by famous practitioners in the 1960s. In addition to Bernbach's groundbreaking ideas on advertising creativity, they included

David Ogilvy's notion of 'brand personality' and Leo Burnett's use of dramatic realism, all of which were counterpoints to the 'hard sell' school of advertising associated with Claude Hopkins (see McDonald and Scott, 2007).

These popular management theories of advertising craft, based mainly on experience and anecdote, remain parts of advertising folklore and still have their followers in many modern agencies. However, the popular theories were supplemented by others which claimed a more robust, indeed a more scientific, rationale.

ADVERTISING MANAGEMENT AND PSYCHOLOGICAL SCIENCE

Science is a powerful word. Political, psychological, anthropological and sociological thinkers such as Marx, Freud, Levi Strauss and Durkheim have all insisted that their work was scientific. Researchers in other fields would say that their claims of scientific knowledge did not meet the essential criteria of science. Debates in the philosophy of science have received a thorough airing in the marketing literature and while advertising research was not immune to these debates, it has, by and large, avoided becoming entrenched in wrangles about philosophy. Instead, advertising research and practice are generally informed by implicit assumptions about epistemology and ontology, the nature of knowledge and essence of social life.

It was not until the modern era, when advertising first emerged as a significant driving force of twentieth-century capitalism, that the application of science to advertising became a serious enterprise. Possibly the most famous and successful exponent was John B. Watson (1924) who applied his psychological theory of behaviourism to a career in advertising at J. Walter Thompson and later the William Esty advertising agencies[2] (Bogart, 1966). Behaviourism still thrives today in some learning systems which

make use of stimulus-response-reinforcement. Nevertheless, by and large, the mental reductionism of Watson's theory has been superseded by theories which model the cognitive and emotional processes involved when consumers engage with persuasive advertising (see O'Shaughnessy and O'Shaughnessy, 2004).

Other attempts to set advertising practice on firmer intellectual grounds made use of pop psychology. Books like Edward Strong's (1929) *The Psychology of Selling and Advertising* and Harry D. Kitson's (1921) *The Mind of the Buyer* set out a sequential model of persuasion which involved getting the consumer's attention, eliciting interest, provoking desire for the product or service and, finally, generating action in the form of a purchase. The acronym A-I-D-A (Attention-Interest-Desire-Action) was adapted by marketing and advertising textbook writers who were persuaded by Kennedy's analogy between selling and advertising. This implied that persuasive communication obeyed the same psychological principles whether communication was conducted face-to-face, as in a sales conversation or through the medium of print or radio.

The theory, boiled down to its applied essentials, was simple enough. Consumers were assumed to be indifferent to the solicitations of marketers until their attention had been attained. The next step was to excite their interest, then stimulate desire for the product and finally persuade them to action, in the form of purchase. At each of these stages, the marketer would encounter resistance. The gradual accumulation of persuasive messages would eventually tip the consumer into each subsequent stage; hence, there was a 'hierarchy of effect' (see discussion in Barry and Howard, 1990).

Does advertising communication require attention?

A-I-D-A remains highly influential in the field for its clarity, economy and universalism. It conveniently treats advertising as just one thing, it assumes that the single desired end of any advertisement is a purchase, and it assumes further that all consumers the world over operate according to very similar cognitive mechanisms. It is the most well known of the 'hierarchy-of-effects' family of theories of advertising persuasion. Conveniently, A-I-D-A maps neatly onto linear theories of communication (Lasswell, 1948; Lazarsfeld, 1941; Schramm, 1948; Shannon, 1948) and links well with information processing models of human cognition.

Today, typical advertising and marketing textbooks use a highly reduced composite of these theories, emphasizing the univocal character of 'the message' and the sequential, rational information processing capability of the human. The linear or 'transmission' model of communication, which posits a sender, an encoding process, a medium, a message, a decoding process and a receiver (see Weaver and Shannon, 1963), is often offered in textbooks as a theoretical basis for the A-I-D-A model of persuasion, though the points of connection between the two are merely incidental (Hackley, 2005). Questions over the pedagogic value and practical relevance of linear communication theories for advertising remain (Buttle, 1995), but a cursory glance at any mainstream marketing communications textbook suggests that their popularity, with authors at least, is undimmed.

Examples of research and theory in advertising which adapt the information processing metaphor of human cognition include Keller et al. (1998), Li et al. (2002) and Mela et al. (1997) who, in their different ways, seek to uncover the generalized cognitive mechanisms underlying the relationship between advertising and attitude, memory and behaviour. MacInnis and Jaworski (1989) seek an integrative scheme for research using the information processing approach to study human responses to advertisements. Note also the thorough going critique of this approach by Heath and Feldwick (2008) who argue that models of advertising communication, which are contingent on the receiver's conscious attention, are seriously misconceived. Heath and Feldwick (2008) argue that marketing

messages and images which are beneath conscious attention register with consumers in important ways. Conversely, they argue, just because a consumer pays attention to a commercial message does not mean that it will necessarily have any effect on his or her attitudes or behaviour.

Ehrenberg et al. (2002) take issue with another assumption underlying the A-I-D-A model. Not only do Ehrenberg et al. (2002) contest the idea that an advertisement is unsuccessful if it does not achieve a sale but they also argue that advertising almost never sells anything, at least not in the short term. According to Ehrenberg (2000), this is a misunderstanding of advertising's role, and it gives ammunition to those who criticize its social influence. He argues that a single advertisement just is not that powerful. Ehrenberg (2000) suggests that advertising seldom generates attitudinal or behavioural change but, rather, reinforces pre-existing brand preferences, reassuring the consumer and encouraging the continuation of the habit of brand preference. Advertising's effect, then, is long term, building presence in the market and credibility for the consumer and leading to enhanced brand 'equity'. Of course, this directly contrasts with the major assumptions of the hierarchy-of-effects family of theories. Indeed, the evident increase, in recent years, in the relative promotional spend allotted to sponsorship, product placement, viral and experiential marketing bears testimony to a practice-based assumption that peripheral routes to the consumer can be as or more powerful than directly engaging them with spot advertising. The notion that advertising acts like publicity to build long-term brand equity has gained much currency.

Active or passive consumers?

Another perceived weakness of the sales-model of advertising is the assumption it seems to make about the passivity of the consumer as receiver of the advertising message.

This assumption is left unstated in 'transmission models' of mass communication, but nevertheless implies that audiences 'receive' information, much as a computer receives data. In contrast, reader response theory, applied from literary to advertising texts, shows that advertising audiences often actively reinterpret advertising texts (e.g. O'Donohoe, 1994; Scott, 1994).

Ernest Dichter (1966), well known for his theories of the now-forgotten discipline of consumer motivation research, demonstrated clearly how actively consumers engage with and use advertising in his work on word-of-mouth advertising. He showed that consumer motivations for talking about brands can be complex and contrary, but the fact that they (we) talk about them is a crucial element in the success of advertising campaigns. Getting talked about, and getting talked about in the right way, is a key measure of an advertisement. Most significantly, Dichter (1966) suggests that advertising is a social experience in which individuals have a personal investment concerning their status or prestige within the peer group. It is perhaps a measure of the domination of the natural science model and the marginalization of motivation research that Ritson and Elliott (1999) had to argue the same points some thirty years later.

The fact that consumers are not machines but individuals who respond to advertisements in widely varying ways has also been noted in scientific advertising research, but in a rather different way. For example, De Pelsmacker et al. (2002) investigate the effect of media context on consumers' attitude to advertisements. It is accepted in discourse and media theory that the medium influences the way the message is interpreted (see Cook, 2002; McLuhan, 1964), but it is widely assumed that the precise influence is too subjective to be predicted or even discovered with accuracy. De Pelsmacker et al. (2002) set out to uncover the relationship between individual characteristics and media influence over the way an ad is perceived. This, of course, is a complex business. Its key assumption is ontological – that is, setting aside sampling

and context issues, it is assumed that cognitive mechanisms are pretty well universal so that the findings can be written of in very general terms as in 'Furthermore, ad content and brand recall is higher for older people when the ad is embedded in a congruent context' (p. 59). This very generalized way of talking (writing) about findings from experimental or survey research is characteristic of the natural science model of research in advertising.

The active consumer is also the topic a paper by Stewart and Pavlou (2002) examining the ways in which consumers respond to interactive advertising. This is evidently an important development given the rising importance of interactive media. It is clearly important now for advertisers to be able to conceive of a two-way flow of communication with consumers. User-led content, evidenced by the rise of social networking websites and other user-driven initiatives is becoming a byword for marketing. Work such as that by Barwise and Strong (2002), examining permission-based mobile advertising, attracts considerable interest from practitioners. Not that spot advertising is redundant: at the time of writing (February 2009), television advertising revenues are falling in absolute terms, but in relative terms, television and print media still take the lion's share of global advertising expenditure.

Critiques of the passive consumer assumption have engaged with the transmission model of communication so prevalent in advertising theory. For example, Stern (1993) undertook a thorough critique of static transmission models of communication in advertising, arguing that the model oversimplifies the communication process. Other work which has indirectly opposed the idea of a passive consumer posits the consumer as an active reader of text, as noted earlier (Scott, 1994), or an interpreter of signs (Mick, 1986). Researchers working from the standpoint of linguistics have pointed out that what is implicit in communication is often more persuasive and telling than what is explicit. When this principle is applied to advertising communication, the limitations of a focus on explicit messages become all-too-apparent. For example, Tanaka (1994) and Cook (2002) have analyzed advertisements in detail to illustrate the rhetorical force of implied connotation and denotation in advertising. Each of these studies, though very different, offers a radical alternative to theories which suppose the consumer to be a passive receiver of information.

It is perhaps too easy to criticize mass communication theory for shortcomings in the ways advertising theorists have expropriated it. Nevertheless, it seems fair to draw attention to a fundamental and long-standing controversy in marketing studies which connects with the transmission theory of communication. Are consumers motivated ultimately by articulated evaluations of product utility? Or, alternatively, by unarticulated, emotional, perhaps visceral responses to stimuli which feature both in conscious and unconscious awareness? Clearly, there are parallels with consumer behaviour research in which there is a dichotomy between the rational model (Howard and Sheth, 1968) and an emotion-driven model of consumer behaviour (Holbrook and Hirschman, 1982). Brand consumption is linked, according to some researchers, with a sense of identity (Elliott and Wattanasuwan, 1998) and motivated by barely articulated emotional, symbolic or unconscious drives (Elliott, 1997). The implications for theories of advertising are clearly considerable.

The importance of the symbolic role of possessions and gift giving had been long acknowledged by anthropologists. Consumption practices in the modern era mimic those of exchange economies in which the ownership and display of certain items denoted the status of an individual in a community's social hierarchy. In marketing scholarship, Sidney Levy (1959) drew on anthropological research to argue that brands carry symbolic meanings which resonate with consumers just as powerfully as their practical utility and value (see also Gardner and Levy, 1955). Authors such as Holt (2004) have continued this line of sociocultural research in marketing. The mainstream of research in marketing,

though, proved resistant to Levy's (1959) ideas, preferring rationality-based models of the consumer (Harris, 2007).

Uses of science in advertising

From the agency perspective, the idea of making advertising effectiveness more predictable and easily measured has been sought like a holy grail. This has led to many attempts to create a scientific advertising management model which reduces risk and uncertainty (Ewing and Jones, 1990; Horsky and Simon, 1983; Lavidge and Steiner, 1961; Lodish et al., 1995; Simon, 1982; Vaughn, 1986). As with the Holy Grail, there is little agreement on the best place to look. Vakratsas and Ambler (1999) comprehensively review the general theories of how advertising 'works'. An open question remains about the status of advertising – is it better to conceive of it as meaning or as information? McCracken (1987) examines this very question, which goes to the heart of debates about advertising as art or science. Cook and Kover (1998) look at the meaning of advertising effectiveness in terms of the very diverse presuppositions which practitioners and academic researchers bring to the idea. They argue, drawing on Wittgenstein, that talk of scientific objectivity in advertising research is part of a 'language game', the rules of which are different for academics and practitioners respectively. Cook and Kover (1998) are not making a practical issue too abstract – on the contrary, they take a resolutely practical perspective. They are simply pointing out that theory is much nearer the surface of everyday concerns than we sometimes think.

The use of the behavioural and social sciences to model the complexities of human motivation dates, as we have seen, from the early part of the 1900s but the work of Ernest Dichter (1949) went further than that of others in integrating science with marketing and advertising. Dichter was the prime mover behind the now-forgotten marketing subdiscipline of motivational research (Tadajewski, 2006). Today, a great deal of published research in advertising draws on theories and assumptions from cognitive science, while the practical fields of copy-testing and advertising research rely substantially on psychological methods and assumptions. Incidentally, the uses of psychological research techniques in advertising excited considerable ethical disquiet some 50 years ago, famously expressed by Vance Packard (1957). The alarm may, though, have been based on a general misunderstanding about the power of psychological research to create advertising which manipulates unwitting consumers (Hackley, 2007). A cynical view would be that the use of psychological ideas in advertising was as much a marketing device, lending plausibility to the theories and building credibility with clients, as a genuine attempt to integrate marketing with social science. After all, the discourse of science is a powerful language in itself – consider the current excitement over neuro-marketing. Separating the substance from the sales pitch (or the sizzle from the sausage) has never been easy in the marketing field (see, for a critique of marketing's uses of social science, O'Shaughnessy, 1997; also readings in Baker (ed.), 2000).

For example, the work of Humanistic psychologist Abraham Maslow (1943; 1954) was widely, if inappropriately, taken up by advertising theorists to conceptualize the status- and emotion-driven motivations behind much consumer purchasing. Maslow suggested that humans have a hierarchy of needs ranging from basic physiological needs for food, warmth and water to needs for social interaction, esteem and, for the fortunate, self-actualization. Yet, the academy misappropriated Maslow's ideas with enduring enthusiasm (Hackley, 2007). Academic marketers had decided that Maslow's scheme could be used to explain universal motivations for consumer behaviour, especially since so many consumers seem to realize a sense of self vicariously by consuming and displaying items associated with prestige and status. This hardly fitted with Maslow's humanistic philosophy – he felt that human potential was best realized not by the consumption of status symbols but through altruism.

Undeterred by such inconsistency, Madison Avenue advertising agencies of the 1960s used Maslow and his hierarchy of needs model to put some intellectual starch in their new pseudoscience of psychographics. Psychographics was the term coined for the segmentation and targeting of consumer markets on the basis of motivations driven by lifestyle aspirations, rather than on the basis of utilitarian needs. In fact, as many successful advertising campaigns showed, agencies could make almost any mundane product aspirational by the suggestive juxtaposition of brand signs with lifestyle images. What does your brand of watch/car/shirt say about you? Maslow's theory fitted agency pitching requirements and textbook formats, because it came with a neat diagram and gave superficial plausibility to psychographics, unlike more apposite but less economical theories of class and status from sociology and cultural anthropology.

MANAGEMENT IN ADVERTISING AGENCIES

Advertising management embraces not only the management of advertising, but also the management of advertising agencies. It is difficult to generalize about this aspect of management in advertising even though the way agencies are organized has striking similarities the world over. In many respects, the work of ad agencies is more like that in other cultural industries like theatre production companies, orchestras or media companies than it is like management in manufacturing, production or customer-service delivery settings. Perhaps there is an analogy with professional services, though unlike universities or legal or medical practices, the raw materials advertising agencies work with are not commonly shared laws or generally agreed bodies of knowledge: their raw materials are people, ideas, insights and creativity. Not only that, but while many agencies have similar working practices, they each apply these in ways which have important differences of emphasis. Most large advertising agencies work across international borders, raising complex issues of cross-cultural communication and management. In advertising agencies, then, more than many other kinds of organization, it is difficult to compare like with like in management practices (Hackley and Tiwsakul, 2008).

Given the managerial and social significance of advertising agencies, there is surprisingly little research which details exactly how campaigns emerge from what can often appear to be a slightly organized chaos. Agencies suffer from stereotyping, with the domineering account executive, the histrionic creative and the exasperated client featuring in many jokes. However, advertising agencies' contribution to the world of marketing is often understated. It is, for example, hard to conceive of the world's most powerful and well-known brands without advertising. In addition to advertising's contribution to economic growth, national competitiveness and brand marketing business, many advertisements have become iconic representations of particular cultural trends or social movements, talked about and even enjoyed as popular entertainment in TV shows and websites.

Yet, as McFall (2004) has pointed out, much of the sociocultural research on advertising completely ignores the crucial but little-known practices of advertising, the things people in ad agencies do to create a campaign. Hackley (2005) has argued that this neglect of the internal dynamics of agencies is also characteristic of much managerial research, a strange omission given the economic and cultural importance of advertising itself. Advertising campaigns are a collective achievement and research such as Hackley (2000), Svensson (2007) and Kelly et al. (2005) are among relatively few empirical studies which have looked at the interpersonal dynamics behind the advertising development process. A small number of others have taken a critical ethnographic approach to study the production of gender in ad agencies, notable examples being Alvesson (1998) and Cronin (2008).

Advertising agencies manage one thing above all else: creativity. Hackley and Kover (2007) have analyzed the angst and insecurity of the creative role, while Kover and Goldberg (1995) described the Machiavellian strategies which creatives need to survive in the unforgiving agency environment. Johar et al. (2001) examined the ways in which creative professionals draw on myths and metaphors to generate ideas in their work. Both Kover (1995) and Hackley (2003b) note that many of the misunderstandings and conflicts in agency account teams arise because the respective account team personnel have fundamentally different ways of looking at the advertising world, but these differing mental models are invariably implicit rather than explicit. This can lead to fundamental conflicts and oppositions. Paul Feldwick (2007), an advertisement industry legend himself and one of very few to publish academic papers, describes the industry's most noted attempt at devising a management system to smooth the politics of account team dynamics, the invention of the account planning discipline.

Turning to other aspects of management in advertising agencies, Mueller (1992), Hite and Fraser (1988) and Onkvisit and Shaw (1987) looked in different ways at the management of advertising executions across national borders. This was a hot topic at the time these papers were published but remains so today and these papers are still cited frequently. What has changed in the past two decades is the increasingly multicultural demography of major world cities, which means that even local advertising now often has to consider multiethnic audiences. This means that research such as Onkvisit and Shaw's (1987) comprehensive review of evidence standardization in international advertising also has a resonance for national campaigns. Onkvisit and Shaw (1987) evaluated the evidence for effectiveness of same creative execution going out the world over versus a localized creative approach with regional variations. Mueller (1992) explored the same topic from a different angle, focusing on the tendency for Western brands and ad agencies to export Western values and creative styles in their advertising, while Hite and Fraser (1988) looked at the approach to international advertising taken by multinational corporations.

Michell et al. (1996) and West and Paliwoda (1996) are examples of the considerable body of research which explores the contentious management relationship between client and agency. For advertising agencies, keeping clients is a challenge and the more successful agencies tend to have more robust and long-lasting client relationships. Michell et al. (1996) analyzed the creative reputation of agencies and the putative influence this has on client confidence, while West and Paliwoda (1996) looked through the other end of the telescope, examining the decision-making structure of clients and the effect this might have on agency relationships. Other research focuses on managerial decision-making, for example in deciding what to do when a celebrity endorser receives negative press attention (Till and Shimp, 1998).

The account planning discipline was one example of a management initiative emerging from the advertising industry, driven by agencies themselves (Feldwick, 2007; Hackley, 2003a). Possibly the only other management trend in advertising to gain wide attention has been Integrated Marketing Communications (IMC), though this has been popularized more by academics than by the industry itself. Schultz and Kitchen (1997) conducted a cross-national study into IMC and the topic still regularly receives attention in the scholarly management literature. Arguably, though, the industry has simply got on with integration of communications planning in a practical way rather than seeing it as something to theorize about.

Another line of managerial theory in advertising has tried to develop practical campaign planning tools. Rossiter et al. (1991) created an advertising planning grid which they claimed was an improvement on the earlier and better-known Foote Cone and Belding (FCB) grid (Vaughn, 1986). Rossiter et al. (1991) argued that advertising strategy is heavily contingent on context, so generalized models such as A-I-D-A offer little practical help to managers. They presented a model premised on brand awareness rather than brand attitude and incorporated more nuanced elements of consumer motivation and purchase involvement in different product categories. By so doing, they suggested that the grid offered a more closely specified practical planning tool for devising creative strategy and tactics.

While this line of managerial theory remains an important part of advertising scholarship and research, there is conflicting evidence regarding the practical efficacy and take-up of academic theories in marketing and advertising. Theoretical constructs such as Rossiter et al.'s (1991) are designed to have a direct and practical managerial relevance, but many other examples of theory in the field are criticized for their inaccessibility. Cornellison and Lock (2002) refer to the 'dearth' of practical advertising theory and argue that advertising practitioners have adapted academic theory to practice in three main ways: instrumental, conceptual and symbolic. The first category, instrumental, is the rarest, because it refers to theories which can be applied directly to practice. Conceptual adaptation means that aspects of academic theories are used as a vocabulary to articulate management problems, while the symbolic or rhetorical use of academic theories legitimizes managerial action. Cornellison and Lock (2002) argue that direct application is not the only legitimate criterion of managerial relevance for academic theory in marketing. This is a point with wider implications, given that relevance remains a highly contested area in the field (see, for example, Wensley, 2007).

CULTURAL PERSPECTIVES ON ADVERTISING

Advertising and consumption are topics of great interest to historians, linguists, sociologists, cultural anthropologists and media or communication scholars. I have already noted sociologist Liz McFall's (2004) work and the linguistics perspectives of Cook (2002) and Tanaka (1994). Other examples include work by O'Barr (1994) and Marchand (1985) on the role of advertising in portraying American culture, Marchand's (1998) work on the role of advertising, public relations and corporate communication in legitimizing corporatism in America, Fowles' (1996) study of advertising and popular culture, deWaal Malefyt and Moeran's (2003) anthropological study of advertising and Blake et al.'s (1996) communication and media studies perspectives, among many other examples.

This strain of work draws attention to advertising's role not only a managerial tool designed to influence attitudes to organizational ends but also as a cultural phenomenon, a form of social communication (Leiss et al., 2005). As such, it reflects and projects prevailing norms, lifestyles and values and taps into wider social themes and trends. Some of this work has offered a cultural critique of advertising, such as Judith Williamson's (1978) work on the semiotics of advertising. Later work by authors such as Wernick (1991) offer a comprehensive outlook on advertising as a phenomenon which drives a promotional culture. This promotional culture frames lives and informs mentalities in important and far-reaching ways and perhaps needs to be resisted as well as understood.

Advertising embodies many issues of human communication and interaction of long-standing interest to anthropologists, including the social status conferred by the ownership and display of objects, gift giving, consumption and symbolic communication. Sherry (1987) has argued that advertising is highly influential but underinvestigated as a cultural document. As noted in the preceding section, the anthropological perspective was advocated in marketing by Levy (1959) but remains largely ignored by management and marketing scholars (Harris, 2007). This disconnection has serious implications for research in the field and its connection with practice. For example, many major international advertising agencies now have departments of researchers with anthropological training, yet there is little research in the management area which evaluates its contribution to advertising effectiveness.

There are also methodological implications to this myopia. Ritson and Elliott's (1999) study, for example, draws attention to the fact that most research into advertising effects assumes that advertising is consumed by individuals in a social vacuum. Their ethnographic research shows that, in fact, advertising is ineluctably a social phenomenon, consumed (as well as produced) in social contexts. Audiences use mass media texts as resources in flexible, imaginative ways, often quite independently from the promoted brands or the agency's intentions. As Dichter (1966) had shown, advertisements are part of a public vocabulary of symbolism which surrounds marketing and consumption. In Ritson and Elliott's (1999) study, adolescents' talk about advertisements was an important part of their social discourse and identity positioning. The prevalence of compilation TV shows of advertisements and the growth in Internet sites offering ads to download for entertainment suggest that it is not only adolescents for whom advertising is an important form of social communication.

Brown et al. (1999) also broaden the methodological base of management research into advertising by deploying literary theory in their analysis of audience responses to advertising. Scott (1990) combines literary with musical signification and adapts the study of rhetoric to show how music evinces meaning in advertising. For advertising professionals, music is a key component in signifying the desired audience segmentation. A particular piece makes the desired audience 'turn their heads' to notice the ad (Hackley, 2005). Scott's (1990) literary analysis shows that the rich and complex meanings of music can be as powerful in conveying meaning and evincing emotion in advertising as in television drama and movies.

Literary analysis and feminist theory are combined in Stevens et al. (2003) and Stern's

(1993) work. Stevens et al. (2003) found that ads targeted at women could generate deeply ambivalent responses. Whether this is good or bad for the client depends on the view taken of how advertising works. If the goal is to stimulate an emotional response and get the brand talked about with the aim of building long-term brand equity and presence, then even strongly negative emotional responses could have a beneficial effect in comparison to indifference. On the other hand, negative or ambivalent responses would be construed very negatively by an account executive or client who felt that advertising should follow the aforementioned A-I-D-A formula.

The literary theory approach, like Sherry's (1987) anthropological work, assumes that advertisements are not merely mediated transmissions of an unequivocal message but rich and ambivalent sites of meaning. The individual advertisement is treated not as a univocal and explicit message but, rather, as an unstable and culturally contingent entity the meaning of which is 'read' differently by different audiences. Mick and Buhl's (1992) classic piece articulates this position with a comprehensive argument drawing on the 'science of signs', semiotics. Semiotics has often been adapted to illustrate the richness and culturally mediated character of advertising meaning (see, for example, Danesi, 2006; and Umiker-Sebeok (ed.), 1987).

O'Donohoe (1994; 1997) illustrates how advertising imagery, narratives and language are part of a connected symbolic scheme which is actively used and adapted by individuals in social interaction. Starting from the advertisement-as-text assumption of the literary and discourse theorists, O'Donohoe (1997) takes Kristeva's notion of inter-textuality and applies it to a postmodern analysis of the ways in which advertisements borrow from and reflect other social texts. Advertising lends itself particularly to such an analysis, because it is the ultimate 'parasitic' (Cook, 2002) discourse, it has no original vocabulary of its own but it reinvents itself by taking ideas from art, popular culture, business and everyday language to try to render promotional

messages relevant and persuasive to consumers. In this sense, advertising reflects reality back at us while combining familiar elements in novel ways.

Advertising – for good or ill?

The cultural dimension of advertising research often raises issues of ethics, public interest and regulation in exploring advertising's role as a form of public communication. Advertising is, according to Cook (2002), still a relatively poorly understood form of discourse. Even where its economic virtues in spreading information, stimulating demand and facilitating competition are known and accepted, advertising's unintended or negative effects still excite vehement debate. Consider the decade-old but still remembered Benetton campaigns which resulted in public protests and frenzied media comment (Giroux, 1994). More recently, controversy still abounds over the advertising and promotion of controversial products and services such as alcohol, foods which are high in fat and sugar, gas-guzzling motor vehicles, pharmaceuticals, weapons and so on.

Internationally, there are striking differences in public notions of what is acceptable or unacceptable in advertising. Certain Benetton advertisements, for example, were banned in some countries but given awards in others, neatly illustrating the contradictions Toscani's work revealed (Hackley, 2005). Nevertheless, in a global marketplace, advertisers have to push the boundaries of acceptability just to get their brand noticed among the cacophony of competition. Controversies over particular advertising campaigns and earnest debates about the rightful role and limits of advertising and the most effective forms of regulation will continue. The vitality of these debates illustrates Cook's (2002) point that advertising has an unstable and contested cultural status. It is, at once, dismissed as a trivial and degraded form of communication, and yet blamed for all manner of social evils. Many people, when asked, will claim that they are not influenced by advertising. Yet, usually, a glance at the brands on their clothes or accessories, or at the car they drive, tells a different story.

An important aspect of sociocultural research in advertising concerns the ethical implications of individual advertising campaigns and of advertising in its totality. There is an ongoing debate about the influence of advertising in general on morals and ethical standards and about the implications for public policy and regulation. Belk and Pollay (1985a) undertook a longitudinal study of the content of American advertising to examine the contention that it portrays 'the good life', the implication being that advertising raises aspirations in an unrealistic or unattainable way. Pollay (1986) expressed the disquiet over advertising in a forthright and highly cited review of the opinions of humanities and social science scholars. They concluded that advertising reinforces materialism and promotes cynicism, irrationality, selfishness and anxiety, among its many other highly undesirable and unintended consequences.

In Pollay et al. (1996), the ethical and policy issues surrounding a specific marketing issue are examined in the study of the effects of cigarette advertising on adolescents' smoking behaviour. These researchers concluded that adolescents were and are particularly susceptible to cigarette advertising and they suggest that arguments that cigarette advertising only causes brand switching among existing users are disingenuous. Many other researchers have looked at public policy issues in advertising regulation, for example Calfee (2002) examined this topic with regard to direct-to-consumer advertising of prescription drugs. Belk and Pollay (1985b) explored the issue of materialism in Japanese advertising culture, while Taylor and Stern (1997) analyzed the extent to which the notoriously male and Caucasian advertising industry stereotypes Asian Americans in advertising portrayals. On the other side of the critical divide, Holbrook (1987) offered a robust rejoinder to Pollay's (1986) bleak assessment of advertising's ethical standards.

Advertising has a profound ideological dimension which, perhaps, goes beyond ethics in important ways. Williamson (1978) and Wernick (1991) are among the authors who alluded to the need to be aware of advertising's ideological potency in order to resist it. Elliott and Ritson (1997) drew on approaches from Critical Theory and poststructuralism to underline the importance of constructing critiques of advertising, while Hackley (2002) looked at the extent to which advertising agencies' surveillance behaviour, in which consumers are often willing participants, amounts (in Bentham's term) to a Panoptic influence which requires resistance. These are examples of work which, to a greater or lesser degree, employ neo-Marxist concepts in a cultural critique of advertising's role. As such, they are controversial within management and marketing research, though they do not necessarily constitute anticapitalistic tirades, as their critics sometimes imply. Rather, they open advertising up to a serious appraisal which, taking account of its essential role in the cultural–economic landscape, offers indications of ways in which its ideological power and social and psychological implications might be better understood.

CONCLUDING COMMENT

This chapter has indicated the wide scope of theory in advertising with examples which fall into three broad and overlapping categories characterized as advertising management, advertising science and advertising culture. The tripartite subdivision is necessary to begin to make sense of the different traditions of theory in the field. The chapter began with an outline of early advertising theory, grounded in the experience of practical advertising professionals and designed to improve practice in ways which could be directly applied. The account moved on to explore the uses of science in advertising theory and the ways in which these have been reflected in theories of advertising management. Finally, sociocultural theories of advertising were discussed.

These three areas overlap with regard to their assumptions, aims and methods but they can, nevertheless, be clearly discerned. What is most important for the purposes of this chapter is not that they overlap, but that they do not overlap enough. Advertising theory development all too often follows three parallel roads, to their mutual impoverishment. For example, sociocultural accounts of advertising might resonate with creative professionals in the field but are often entirely ignored by academics who build their careers exclusively in the advertising science category. Conversely, the use of physical science methods and assumptions in academic theory development is roundly mocked by many advertising practitioners. Another example concerns cultural critique of advertising, which can be flawed by the omission of the material practices of advertising and advertising agencies. This omission seems even stranger in managerial advertising theory which ignores the organizational literature and paints a one-dimensional picture of an advertising development process which is without tension of conflict, and operates objectively on the separate world of consumption. The relative lack of applied advertising commented upon by Cornellison and Lock (2002) can perhaps be attributed to the failure of instrumental theorists to integrate their work with viable theories of organizational process in advertising agencies.

Academic research is a political affair, and different traditions with their preferred aims and methods will inevitably be favoured in particular journals and faculties. The present chapter has attempted to acknowledge these divisions and suggest some points of connection or integration between perspectives that operate from very different, and perhaps philosophically incompatible, assumptions. These include assumptions about the nature of advertising knowledge, about the character of human engagement with mediated advertising and about the right values and aims which should underpin this fascinating and evolving enterprise.

NOTES

1 http://www.anbhf.org/laureates/lasker.html accessed 21 January, 2009.
2 http://www.targetmarket.org/targe_3.htm accessed 20 January, 2009.

REFERENCES

Alvesson, M. (1998) 'Gender Relations and Identity at Work – A Case Study of Masculinities and Femininities in an Advertising Agency', *Human Relations*, 51(8): 969–1005.

Baker, M.J. (2000) (ed.) *Marketing Theory: A Student Text*. London: Thomson Learning Business Press.

Barry, T.E. and Howard, D.J. (1990) 'A Review and Critique of the Hierarchy of Effects in Advertising', *International Journal of Advertising*, 9: 121–135.

Barwise, P. and Strong, C. (2002) 'Permission-Based Mobile Advertising', *Journal of Interactive Marketing*, 16(1): 14–24.

Belk, R. (1986) 'Art Versus Science as Ways of Generating Knowledge About Materialism', in D. Brinberg and R.J. Lutz (eds) *Perspectives on Methodology in Consumer Research*, New York: Springer-Verlag, pp. 3–36.

Belk, R.W. and Pollay, R. (1985a) 'Images of Ourselves – The Good Life in Twentieth Century Advertising', *Journal of Consumer Research*, 11: 887–896.

Belk, R.W. and Pollay, R. (1985b) 'Materialism and Status Appeals in Japanese Advertising', *International Marketing Review*, 13(5): 7–47.

Blake, A., MacRury, I., Nava, M. and Richards, B. (eds) (1996) *Buy This Book: Studies in Advertising and Consumption*, London: Routledge.

Bogart, L. (ed.) (1966) *Psychology in Media Strategy*. Chicago IL: American Marketing Association, p. 3.

Brown, S. (1997) 'Marketing Science in a Postmodern World: Introduction to the Special Issue', *European Journal of Marketing*, 31(3–4): 167–182.

Brown, S. (1999) 'Marketing and Literature – The Anxiety of Academic Influence', *Journal of Marketing*, 63(1): 1–15.

Brown, S., Stevens, L. and Maclaran, P. (1999) 'I Can't Believe It's Not Bakhtin!: Literary

Theory, Postmodern Advertising, and the Gender Agenda', *Journal of Advertising*, 28(1): 11–24.

Buttle, F. (1995) 'Marketing Communications Theory: What Do the Texts Teach Our Students?', *International Journal of Advertising*, 14: 297–313.

Calfee, J.E. (2002) 'Public Policy Issues in Direct-to-Consumer Advertising of Prescription Drugs', *Journal of Public Policy & Marketing*, 21(19): 174–179.

Collins, R.K.L. and Skover, D.M. (1993) 'Commerce and Communication', *Texas Law Review*, 71(4): 697–746.

Cook, G. (2002) *The Discourse of Advertising*. London: Routledge.

Cook, W.A. and Kover, A.J. (1998) 'Research and the meaning of advertising effectiveness: mutual misunderstandings', in W.D. Wells (ed.) *Measuring Advertising Effectiveness*, Hillsdale, NJ: Lawrence Erlbaum Associates, pp. 13–20.

Cornelissen, J.P. and Lock, A.R. (2002). 'Advertising Research and Its Influence upon Managerial Practice: A Review of Perspectives and Approaches', *Journal of Advertising Research*, 42(3): 50–55.

Cronin, A.M. (2008) 'Gender in the Making of Commercial Worlds: Creativity, Vitalism and the Practices of Marketing', *Feminist Theory*, 9(3): 293–312.

Danesi, M. (2006) *Brands*. London and New York: Taylor and Francis and Routledge.

De Pelsmacker, P. Geuens, M. and Anckaert, P. (2002) 'Media Context and Advertising Effectiveness: The Role of Context Appreciation and Context-Ad Similarity', *Journal of Advertising*, 31(2): 49–61.

deWaal Malefyt, T. and Moeran, B. (2003) *Advertising Cultures*. London: Berg.

Dichter, E. (1966) 'How Word-of-Mouth Advertising Works', *Harvard Business Review*, 44(6): 147–157.

Dichter, E. (1949) 'A Psychological View of Advertising Effectiveness', *Journal of Marketing*, 14(1): 61–67.

Ehrenberg, A. (2000), 'Repetitive Advertising and the Consumer', *Journal of Advertising Research*, 40: 39–48.

Ehrenberg, A., Barnard, N., Kennedy, R. and Bloom, H. (2002) 'Brand Advertising and Creative Publicity', *Journal of Advertising Research*, 42(4): 7–18.

Elliott, R. (1997) 'Existential Consumption and Irrational Desire', *European Journal of Marketing*, 34(4): 285–296.

Elliott, R. and Ritson, M. (1997) 'Poststructuralism and the Dialectics of Advertising: Discourse, Ideology, Resistance' in S. Brown and D. Turley (eds) *Consumer Research: Postcards from the Edge*, London: Routledge, pp. 190–219.

Elliott, R. and Wattanasuwan, K. (1998) 'Brands as Symbolic Resources for the Construction of Identity', *International Journal of Advertising*, 17(2): 131–144.

Ewing, M.T. and Jones, J.P. (1990) 'Agency Beliefs in the Power of Advertising', *International Journal of Advertising*, 19(3): 335–348.

Feldwick, P. (2007) 'Account Planning: Its History and Significance for Ad Agencies', in G. Tellis and T. Ambler (eds) *The Sage Handbook of Advertising*, Chapter 3.3, London: Sage, pp.184–198.

Fowles, J. (1996) *Advertising and Popular Culture*. London: Sage.

Fox, S. (1984) *The Mirror Makers: A History of American Advertising and Its Creators*. New York: William Morrow.

Gardner, B. and Levy, S. (1955), 'The Product and the Brand', *Harvard Business Review*, March–April: 33–39.

Giroux, H.A. (1994) 'Consuming Social Change: The United Colors of Benetton', *Cultural Critique*, 26(Winter 1993–1994): 5–32. A version of this piece is reprinted in *Business and Society Review*, 89(Spring): 6–14.

Gould, S.J. (1991) 'The Self-Manipulation of My Pervasive, Perceived Vital Energy Through Product Use – An Introspective-Praxis Perspective', *Journal of Consumer Research*, 18(2): 194–212.

Hackley, C. (2000) Silent Running: Tacit, Discursive and Psychological Aspects of Management in a Top UK Advertising Agency', *British Journal of Management*, 11(3): 239–254.

Hackley, C. (2002) 'The Panoptic Role of Advertising Agencies in the Production of Consumer Culture', *Consumption, Markets and Culture*, 5(3) September: 211–229.

Hackley, C. (2003a) 'How Divergent Beliefs Cause Account Team Conflict', *International Journal of Advertising*, 22(3): 313–332.

Hackley, C. (2003b) 'Account Planning: Current Agency Perspectives on an Advertising Enigma', *Journal of Advertising Research*, 43(2): 235–246.

Hackley, C. (2005) *Advertising and Promotion: Communicating Brands*. London, Sage.

Hackley, C. (2007) 'Marketing Psychology and the Hidden Persuaders', The *Psychologist*, 20(8): 488–490.

Hackley, C. (2009) *Marketing – A Critical Introduction*. London: Sage.

Hackley, C. and Kover, A.J. (2007) 'The Trouble with Creatives: Negotiating Creative Identity in Advertising Agencies', *International Journal of Advertising*, 26(1): 63–78.

Hackley, C. and Tiwsakul, R. (2008) 'Comparative Management Practices in International Advertising Agencies in the UK, Thailand and the USA', in C. Smith, B. McSweeney and R. Fitzgerland (eds) *Remaking Management: Between Global and Local*, Chapter 14, Cambridge: Cambridge University Press, pp. 586–626.

Harbor, C. (2007) 'Pervasive and Persuasive: Advertisements for Concerts in London 1672–1750', *Marketing Theory into Practice, Academy of Marketing Conference*, Hosted by Kingston Business School at Royal Holloway University of London, 3–6 July, 2007 (CD-ROM).

Harris, G.E. (2007) 'Sidney Levy: Challenging the Philosophical Assumptions of Marketing', *Journal of Macromarketing*, 27(1): 7–14.

Heath, R. and Feldwick, P. (2008) '50 Years Using the Wrong Model of Advertising', *International Journal of Advertising*, 50(1): 29–59.

Hirschman, E.C. (1983) 'Aesthetics, Ideologies and the Limits of the Marketing Concept', *Journal of Marketing*, 47(summer): 45–55.

Hirschman, E.C. (1986) 'Humanistic Inquiry in Consumer Research: Philosophy, Method and Criteria', *Journal of Marketing Research*, 23: 237–249.

Hite, R. and Fraser, C. (1988) International Advertising Strategies of Multinational Corporations, *Journal of Advertising Research*, 28(4): 9–18

Holt, D. (2004) *How Brands Become Icons: The Principles of Cultural Branding*. Harvard, MASS: Harvard Business School Press.

Holbrook, M.B. (1987) 'Mirror, Mirror, on the Wall, What's Unfair in the Reflections on Advertising', *Journal of Marketing*, 51: 95–103.

Holbrook, M.B. and Hirschman, E.C. (1982) 'The Experiential Aspects of Consumption: Consumer Fantasies, Feelings and Fun', *Journal of Consumer Research*, 9 (September): 132–140.

Horsky, D. and Simon, S.L. (1983) 'Advertising and the Diffusion of New Products', *Marketing Science*, 2(1): 1–16

Howard, J. and Sheth, J.N. (1968) *Theory of Buyer Behavior*. New York: J. Wiley & Sons.

Hunt, S.D. (1990) 'Truth in Marketing Theory and Research', *Journal of Marketing*, 54(July): 1–15.

Hunt, S.D. (1991) *Modern Marketing Theory: Critical Issues in the Philosophy of Marketing Science*. Cincinnati: Southwestern Publishing Co.

Hunt, S.D. (1992) 'For Reason and Realism in Marketing', *Journal of Marketing*, 56(April): 89–102.

Jack, G. (2008) 'Postcolonialism and Marketing', in M. Tadajewski and D. Brownlie (eds) *Critical Marketing: Issues in Contemporary Marketing*, Chichester: Wiley, pp. 363–383.

Johar, G.V., Holbrook, M.B. and Stern, B.B. (2001) 'The Role of Myth in Creative Advertising Design: Theory, Process, and Outcome', *Journal of Advertising*, 30(Summer): 1–25.

Keller, K.L., Heckler, S.E. and Houston, M.J. (1998) 'Effects of Brand Name Suggestiveness on Advertising Recall', *Journal of Marketing*, 62: 48–57.

Kennedy, J.E. (1924) *Reason Why Advertising Plus Intensive Advertising*. TWI Press, Inc.

Kelly, A., Lawlor, K. and O'Donohoe, S. (2005) 'Encoding Advertisements: The Creative Perspective', *Journal of Marketing Management*, 21: 505–528.

Kitson, H.D. (1921) *The Mind of the Buyer*. New York: MacMillan.

Kover, A.J. (1995) 'Copywriters' Implicit Theories of Communication: An Exploration', *Journal of Consumer Research*, 21(4): 596–611.

Kover, A.J. (1996) 'Why Copywriters Don't Like Advertising Research – And What Kind of Research Might They Accept?', *Journal of Advertising Research*, 36(2) rc: 8–12.

Kover, A.J. and Goldberg S.M (1995) 'The Games Copywriters Play – Conflict, Quasi-Control – A New Proposal', *Journal of Advertising Research*, 35(4): 52–68.

Lazarsfeld, P.F. (1941) 'Remarks on Administrative and Critical Communications

Research', *Studies in Philosophy and Science*, 9: 3–16.

Lasswell, H.D. (1948) 'The Structure and Function of Communication in Society', in L. Bryson (ed.) *The Communication of Ideas*. New York: Harper.

Lavidge, Robert J. and Steiner, G.A. (1961) 'A Model for Predictive Measurements of Advertising Effectiveness', *Journal of Marketing*, 25: 59–62.

Leiss, W., Kline, S., Jhally, S. and Botterill, J. (2005) *Social Communication in Advertising: Consumption in the Mediated Marketplace*. London: Routledge.

Levy, S. (1959) 'Symbols for Sale', *Harvard Business Review*, 37(July): 117–124.

Li, H., Daugherty, T. and Biocca, F. (2002) 'Impact on 3-D Advertising on Product Knowledge, Brand Attitude, and Purchase Intention: The Mediating Role of Presence', *Journal of Advertising*, 31(3): 43–57.

Lodish, L.M., Abraham, M., Kalmenson, S., Livelsberger, J., Lubetkin, B., Richardson, B. and Stevens, M.E. (1995) 'How T.V. Advertising Works: A Meta-Analysis of 389 Real World Split Cable T.V. Advertising Experiments', *Journal of Marketing Research*, 32(2): 125–139.

MacInnis, D.J. and Jaworski, B.J. (1989) 'Information Processing from Advertisements: Toward an Integrative Framework', *Journal of Marketing*, 53: 1–23.

Marchand, R. (1985) *Advertising the American Dream: Making Way for Modernity, 1920–1940*, University of California Press.

Marchand, R. (1998) *Creating the Corporate Soul: The Rise of Public Relations and Corporate Imagery in American Big Business*. Los Angeles: University of California Press.

Maslow, A.H. (1943) 'A Theory of Human Motivation', *Psychological Review*, 50(4): 370–396.

Maslow, A.H. (1954) *Motivation and Personality*, New York: Harper, p. 236.

McDonald, C. and Scott, J. (2007) 'A Brief History of Advertising', in G.Tellis and T. Ambler (eds) *The Sage Handbook of Advertising*, London: Sage, pp. 17–34.

McCracken, G. (1987) 'Advertising – Meaning or Information?', in M. Wallendorf and P. Anderson (eds) *Advances in Consumer Research*, Vol 14, Provo: UT ACR, pp. 121–124.

McFall, L. (2004) *Advertising: A Cultural Economy*. London: Sage.

McLuhan, M. (1964) *Understanding Media*. London: Routledge.

Mela, C.F., Gupta, S. and Lehmann, D.R. (1997) 'The Long-Term Impact of Promotion and Advertising on Consumer Brand Choice', *Journal of Marketing Research*, 34: 248–261.

Michell, P.C.N., Cataquet, H. and Mandry, G.D. (1996) 'Advertising Agency, Creative Reputation and Account Loyalty', *Creativity and Innovation Management*, 5: 38–47.

Mick, D.G. (1986) 'Consumer Research and Semiotics: Exploring the Morphology of Signs, Symbols and Significance', *Journal of Consumer Research*, 13: 196–213.

Mick, D.G. and Buhl, C. (1992) 'A Meaning-Based Model of Advertising Experiences', *Journal of Consumer Research*, 19(3): 317–338.

Mueller, B. (1992) 'Standardization vs Specialization: An Examination of Westernization in Japanese Advertising', *Journal of Advertising Research*, 32(1): 15–24.

O'Barr, W. (1994) *Culture and the Ad: Exploring Otherness in the World of Advertising*. London: Harper Collins.

O'Donohoe, S. (1994) 'Advertising Uses and Gratifications', *European Journal of Marketing*, 28(8/9): 52–75.

O'Donohoe, S. (1997) 'Raiding the Postmodern Pantry – Advertising Intertextuality and the Young Adult Audience', *European Journal of Marketing*, 31(3–4): 234–253.

Onkvisit, S. and Shaw, J.J. (1987) 'Standardized International Advertising: A Review and Critical Evaluation of the Theoretical and Empirical Evidence', *Columbia Journal of World Business*, 39 (6): 19–25.

O'Shaughnessy, J. (1997) 'Temerarious Directions for Marketing', *European Journal of Marketing*, 31(9/10): 677–705.

O'Shaughnessy, J. and O'Shaughnessy, N.J. (2004) *Persuasion in Advertising*. London: Routledge.

Packard, V. (1957) *Hidden Persuaders*. New York, Longmans.

Pollay, R.W. (1986) 'The Distorted Mirror: Reflections on the Unintended Consequences of Advertising', *Journal of Marketing*, 50(April): 18–36.

Pollay, R.W., Siddarth, S., Siegel, M. Haddix, A., Merritt, R.K., Giovino G.K. and Erikson, M.P. (1996) 'The Last Straw? Cigarette Advertising and Realized Market Shares Among Youths and Adults, 1979–1993', *Journal of Marketing*, 60(2): 1–16.

Quickenden, K. and Kover, A.J. (2007) 'Did Boulton Sell Silver Plate to the Middle Class? A Quantitative Study of Luxury Marketing in Late Eighteenth-Century Britain', *Journal of Macromarketing*, 27(March): 51–64.

Ritson, M. and Elliott, R. (1999) 'The Social Uses of Advertising – An Ethnographic Study of Adolescent Advertising Audiences', *Journal of Consumer Research*, 26(3): 260–277.

Rossiter, J.R., Percy, L. and Donovan, R.J. (1991) 'A Better Advertising Planning Grid', *Journal of Advertising Research*, 31(5): 11–21.

Schramm, W. (1948) *Mass Communication*. Urbana, Ill: University of Illinois Press.

Schultz, D.E. and Kitchen, P.J. (1997) 'IMC in US Ad Agencies – An Exploratory Study', *Journal of Advertising Research*, 37(5): 7–18.

Scott, L.M. (1990) 'Understanding Jingles and Needledrop – A Rhetorical Approach to Music in Advertising', *Journal of Consumer Research*, 17: 223–236.

Scott, L.M. (1994) 'The Bridge from Text to Mind: Adapting Reader-Response Theory for Consumer Research', *Journal of Consumer Research*, December: 461–490.

Shannon, C.E. (1948) 'A Mathematical Theory of Communication', *Bell System Technical Journal*, 27(July and October): 379–423, 623–656. http://plan9.bell-labs.com/cm/ms/what/shannonday/shannon1948.pdf.

Sherry, J.F. (1987) 'Advertising as Cultural System', in J. Umiker-Sebeok (ed.) *Marketing and Semiotics*, Berlin: Mouton, pp. 441–462.

Simon, H. (1982) 'ADPULS: An Advertising Model with Wearout and Pulsation', *Journal of Marketing Research*, 19: 352–363.

Stern, B.B. (1993) 'A Revised Communication Model for Advertising: Multiple Dimensions of the Source, the Message, and the Recipient', *Journal of Advertising*, 23: 25–16.

Stern, B.B. (1993) 'Feminist Literary Criticism and the Deconstruction of Ads: A Postmodern

View of Advertising', *Journal of Consumer Research*, 19: 556–566.

Stevens, L., Maclaran, P. and Brown, S. (2003) '"*Red* Time Is Me Time" Advertising, Ambivalence and Women's Magazines', *Journal of Advertising*, 32(1): 35–45.

Stewart, D.W. and Pavlou, P.A. (2002) 'From Consumer Response to Active Consumer: Measuring the Effectiveness of Interactive Media', *Journal of the Academy of Marketing Science*, 30(4): 376–396.

Strong, E.K. (1925) *The Psychology of Selling and Advertising*. New York: McGraw-Hill.

Svensson, S. (2007) 'Producing Marketing: Towards a Social-Phenomenology of Marketing Work', *Marketing Theory*, 7: 271–290.

Tadajewski, M. (2006) 'Remembering Motivation Research: Toward an Alternative Genealogy of Interpretive Consumer Research', *Marketing Theory*, 6(4): 429–466.

Tadajewski, M. and Saren, M. (2008) 'The Past is a Foreign Country: Amnesia and Marketing Theory', *Marketing Theory*, 8(4): 323–338.

Tanaka, K. (1994) *Advertising Language: A Pragmatic Approach to Advertisements in Britain and Japan*. London: Routledge.

Taylor, C.R. and Stern, B.B. (1997) 'Asian-Americans: Television Advertising and the Model Minority Stereotype', *Journal of Advertising*, 26(2): 47–61.

Till, B.D. and Shimp, T.A. (1998) 'Endorsers in Advertising: The Case of Negative Celebrity Information', *Journal of Advertising*, 27(1): 67–82.

Umiker-Sebeok, J. (ed.) (1987) *Marketing and Semiotics*. Berlin: Mouton.

Vakratsas, D. and Ambler, T. (1999) 'How Advertising Works: What Do We Really Know?', *Journal of Marketing*, 26 (January): 26–43.

Vaughn, R. (1986) 'How Advertising Works: A Planning Model Revisited', *Journal of Advertising Research*, 26 (February–March): 57–66.

Watson, J. (1924) *Behaviorism*. Chicago: University of Chicago Press.

Weaver, W. and Shannon, C.E. (1963) *The Mathematical Theory of Communication*. Urbana: University of Illinois Press.

Wensley, J. (2007) 'Relevance of Critique: Can and Should Critical Marketing Influence

Practice and Policy', in M. Saren, P. Maclaren, C. Goulding, R. Elliott, A. Shankar and M. Caterrall (eds) *Critical Marketing: Defining the Field*, Oxford: Elsevier, pp. 233–243.

Wernick, A. (1991) *Promotional Culture, Advertising, Ideology and Symbolic Expression.* London and Newbury Park, CA: Sage.

West, D.C. and Paliwoda, S.J. (1996) 'Advertising Client–Agency Relationships: The Decision-Making Structure of Clients', *European Journal of Marketing*, 30(8): 22–39.

Wilkie, W.S. and Moore, E.S. (2003) 'Scholarly Research in Marketing: Exploring the Four Eras of Thought Development', *Journal of Public Policy and Marketing*, 22(autumn): 116–146.

Williamson, J. (1978) *Decoding Advertisements: Ideology and Meaning in Advertising.* New York: Marion Boyars.

Philosophical Underpinnings of Theory

The Philosophical Foundations of Marketing Research: For Scientific Realism and Truth

Shelby D. Hunt and Jared M. Hansen

INTRODUCTION

All research projects have philosophical foundations. That is, when scholars engage in a research project, there are always underlying assumptions as to what entities exist (i.e. ontological assumptions), what research designs are appropriate for generating new knowledge (i.e. methodological assumptions), and what criteria are appropriate for evaluating knowledge-claims (i.e. epistemological assumptions). Marketing scholars often face a quandary when searching for a philosophical foundation to ground their research. On the one hand, when they consider relativism as a foundation, they recognize that all forms of philosophical relativism lead to nihilism. That is, all forms of philosophical relativism lead to the conclusion that all knowledge claims the researcher can possibly make are equally good, equally bad, equally right, equally wrong, equally ethical and equally unethical. Because most researchers do not wish to be associated with nihilism,

philosophical relativism is unacceptable. On the other hand, when researchers consider logical positivism or logical empiricism as a foundation, they recognize that these positivistic philosophical positions have been thoroughly evaluated in the philosophy of science and have been shown to provide unsatisfactory guidelines for conducting research in both the physical and social sciences.[1]

Philosophy of science researchers addressed their own version of the quandary in the 1970s. After the acknowledgment of the deficiencies of positivistic philosophy of science in the 1960s and the subsequent repudiation of relativism (of both the Kuhnian and Feyerabendian varieties) in the early 1970s, philosophers of science in the latter part of the 1970s turned sharply toward a *realist* orientation: 'Contemporary work in philosophy of science increasingly subscribes to the position that it is a central aim of science to come to knowledge of how the world *really* is, that correspondence between theories and reality is a central aim of science' (Suppe, 1977: 649).

Indeed, by the late 1970s, 'the majority of philosophers of science ... profess to be scientific realists' (Causey, 1979: 192). Nevertheless, as Leplin (1984: 1) observes, 'scientific realism is a majority position whose advocates are so divided as to appear a minority'.

Therefore, contemporary philosophy of science suggests that the quandary that marketing scholars face is more apparent than real. Specifically, contemporary philosophy of science suggests that realism is a viable foundation for all forms of research, including marketing research. Nonetheless, though realism is a majority position in the philosophy of science, the nature of realism, its characteristics, and its implications for marketing research are underdeveloped in marketing. The purpose of this chapter is to review the philosophy of scientific realism and discuss it as an appropriate foundation for marketing research. Specifically, because relativism has been argued in marketing to be a viable alternative to scientific realism, this chapter reviews several reasons why philosophers of science rejected relativism as a foundation for research in the 1970s. Then, the chapter (1) examines the historical development of realism, (2) explicates the four fundamental tenets of modern, scientific realism, and (3) develops a scientific realist model of truth that uses, as a continuing example, the effects of decoys on consumer choice sets, as reported in Heath and Chatterjee (1995). The chapter concludes by reviewing scientific realism's argument for truth as a research objective and regulative ideal in marketing research. This argument relies on the importance of trust and ethics in marketing research.[2]

WHY RELATIVISM WAS REJECTED

To understand why philosophy of science rejected relativism in the 1970s, one needs to know what relativism is. All forms of philosophical relativism embrace two theses: (1) the relativity thesis that something is relative to something else and (2) the nonevaluation thesis that there are no objective standards for evaluating *across* the various kinds of 'something else' (Siegel, 1987). Some standard examples of philosophical relativism, drawn from Hunt (2002a, 2003) will clarify the realism–relativism issue for readers:

1 *Cultural relativism* holds that (a) the elements embodied in a culture are relative to the norms of that culture, and (b) there are no objective, neutral, *or nonarbitrary criteria to evaluate* cultural elements across different cultures.
2 *Ethical relativism* holds that (a) what is ethical can only be evaluated relative to some moral code held by an individual, group, society or culture, and (b) there are no objective, impartial or nonarbitrary standards for evaluating different moral codes across individuals, groups, societies or cultures.
3 *Conceptual framework-relativism* holds that (a) knowledge claims are relative to conceptual frameworks (theories, paradigms, world views or *Weltanschauungen*), and (b) knowledge claims cannot be evaluated objectively, impartially or nonarbitrarily across competing conceptual frameworks.
4 *Reality relativism* (a view often associated with constructionism), holds that (a) what comes to be known as 'reality' in science is constructed by individuals relative to their language (or group, social class, theory, paradigm, culture, world view or *Weltanschauung*), and (b) what comes to count as 'reality' cannot be evaluated objectively, impartially or nonarbitrarily across different languages (or groups, etc.).
5 *Subjectivism* (a position often paired with relativism) holds that there is something basic to the human condition – usually something about human perception and/or language – that categorically prevents objective knowledge about the world.

To understand why relativism and subjectivism are minority views within the philosophy of science, consider how these 'isms' would respond to the following six questions: 'Does the sun revolve around the earth or does the earth revolve around the sun?' Conceptual framework relativism, for example Kuhn's (1962) relativism, implies the following answer: 'First I must know whether you subscribe to the paradigm of Copernicus or Ptolemy, for these paradigms – like all paradigms – are incommensurable and, therefore, there is no *truth* to the matter independent of the paradigm you hold'. And subjectivism implies the following answer: 'Because scientists see what their theories and paradigms tell them is there, the theory-ladenness of observation tells us that an *objective* answer to your query is impossible'.

Question two: 'Was Great Britain morally *right* in leading the drive in the nineteenth century to abolish slavery in cultures throughout the world?' Relativism responds: 'Since slavery is a cultural element that cannot be evaluated independently of the norms of the culture within which it exists, no judgment on this matter can be made – to apply one's own norms elsewhere is simply cultural ethnocentrism'. Question three: 'Should Great Britain work toward the abolition of slavery in the few remaining states in which slavery continues to exist?' Answer: 'See response to previous question'. Question four: 'Did the Holocaust occur?' Answer: 'Since the Holocaust is a "constructed" reality (Lincoln and Guba, 1985: 84), just one of many "multiple realities", the Holocaust's occurrence or nonoccurrence cannot be objectively appraised independent of the world-view of a particular social grouping or culture'.

Question five: 'Is a culture that is tolerant of individuals from other cultures preferable to a culture that oppresses everyone outside the dominant culture?' Answer: 'Although the predisposition toward tolerance is a cultural element that varies widely across different cultures, no judgment can be made across cultures as to the moral superiority of tolerant versus intolerant cultures'. Question six: 'Should an academic discipline be open to the views of those outside the discipline?' Answer: 'Although it is true that different academic disciplines differ in their relative openness to the views of outsiders, no judgment can be made across disciplines as to the relative desirability of such openness'.

It should be easy now to understand why relativism and subjectivism are minority views in the philosophy of science. Relativism does not imply a constructively critical stance toward knowledge claims, nor does it simply imply acknowledging that the knowledge claims of science are fallible. Relativism implies nihilism – the belief that we can never have genuine knowledge about anything. Relativists, incoherently, *know* that no one else can ever know anything. (If it is true that all knowledge is impossible, how can one *know* that 'all knowledge is impossible'?) Furthermore, relativism does not imply a tolerant stance toward outside ideas and other cultures; it implies *indifference* to the norm of tolerance. Moreover, relativism does not imply ethical sensitivity; it implies ethical impotence. Finally, subjectivism (a view usually paired with relativism) does not caution science to work at minimizing bias; it maintains that the human condition makes the very idea of objectivity to be a chimera. Therefore – like truth – objectivity should be abandoned.

For the preceding reasons, among others, philosophy of science rejected relativism in the 1970s. Marketing should too. The next section examines the historical development of realism, the philosophy that this chapter puts forward as appropriate for grounding marketing research.

HISTORICAL DEVELOPMENT OF SCIENTIFIC REALISM

From the very beginnings of the scientific revolution in the sixteenth century, science and philosophy were closely related. Indeed, prior to the nineteenth century, science was a branch of philosophy, and scientists were referred to as 'natural philosophers'.[3] However, this situation changed in the latter half of the nineteenth century when philosophy came to be dominated by Hegel (1770–1883) and his idealism: 'He ruled the philosophical world as indisputably as Goethe the world of literature, and Beethoven the realm of music' (Durant, 1954). Hegel's idealism was hostile to mathematics and unsympathetic to science. Its central tenet was that the external world does not exist unperceived: 'All reality is [for idealism] mental (spiritual, psychical). Matter the physical, does not exist' (Angeles, 1981: 120). Thus, Hegel's 'identity of reason and reality' denied the existence of tangible objects (e.g. rocks and trees) and proclaimed only *reason* to be *real*.

Hegelian idealism's dominance in philosophy began to crack at the turn of the century from the efforts of G. E. Moore (1873–1958) and Bertrand Russell (1872–1970), who offered three major arguments against idealism: First, idealism confuses the act of perception with the object being perceived. Once the object of a mental act is distinguished from the awareness of it, there is no reason to deny the existence of the object independently from its being perceived. Second, idealism uses the concept *real* in ways that violate principles of intelligible discourse. That is, the meaning of the term 'real' derives from such exemplars as 'this table exists'. Denying the fundamental examples that give meaning to a term, while at the same time continuing its use in other contexts, produces unintelligible speech. Third, idealism constitutes sophistry, for the behaviors of idealists are inconsistent with their stated beliefs. Although they claim that objects such as chairs do not exist, when entering rooms, idealists approach and sit on chairs, just as if they believe such chairs *do* exist. The philosophy that Moore and Russell argued for was, in today's terminology, 'classical' or 'common-sense' realism, whose central tenet is that the external world of tangible objects exists independent of perception.

The second crack in idealism's philosophical hegemony developed from a discussion group at the University of Vienna that was formed in 1907 by the mathematician Hans Hahn, the physicist Philipp Frank and the social scientist Otto Neurath. By the 1920s, the 'Vienna Circle' group had added other physicists, including Moritz Schlick (1882–1936), who had studied under Max Planck

and who had already received acclaim for his interpretations of Einsteinian relativity. Under Schlick's leadership, the Vienna Circle sought a philosophy that would (1) heal the rift between science and philosophy and (2) provide a means for interpreting quantum mechanics. The philosophy they developed, 'logical positivism', was not opposed to the common-sense realism of Moore and Russell. Indeed, the positivists were allies with the realists in their philosophical battles with advocates of Hegelian idealism. Schlick's (1934) classic article on the foundations of logical positivism framed the idealism–realism question as: 'If the phrase "external world" is taken with the signification it has in everyday life, … [then] are there, in addition to memories, desires, and ideas, also stars, clouds, plants, animals, and my own body?' He answered: 'It would be simply absurd to answer this question in the negative' (p. 101). Therefore, 'logical positivism and realism are not in opposition; whoever acknowledges our fundamental principle must be an empirical realist' (p. 107).

But if the logical positivists had no problems with according reality status to tangible, observable entities, they strongly questioned giving such status to any 'transcendent world' that allegedly 'stood behind' the observable world, but about which nothing could be verified by observational means. Because the positivists' 'verifiability principle' equated the meaningfulness of a proposition with the possibility of its verification, for Schlick (1934: 107), 'The denial of the existence of a transcendent external world would be just as much a metaphysical statement as its affirmation. Hence, the consistent empiricist does not deny the transcendent world, but shows that both its denial and affirmation are meaningless'. A major reason the positivists questioned the meaningfulness of any proposition in which transcendent or unobservable concepts are included is that they believed that this was the best interpretation of quantum mechanics. Understanding how they came to this conclusion requires at least some understanding of the world implied by quantum mechanics – a world that is anything but commonsensical.

Quantum mechanics, realism and positivism

The development of quantum mechanics began with attempts to solve the 'black body' problem at the turn of the century. A black body is one that perfectly absorbs and then re-emits all radiation falling upon it. In the smoothly continuous world of classical physics, the radiation emitted from a black body would also be perfectly continuous. Max Planck, however, proposed in 1900 that the radiant energy emitted takes place *only* in the form of discrete packets, which he called energy *quanta*. Electromagnetic radiation, he proposed, is made up of a whole number of packets of energy, with each packet having the energy hv, where h is Planck's constant and v is the frequency of oscillation. Einstein used Planck's idea of energy quanta in 1905 to discredit the (then firmly established) view that light is fundamentally wave-like. He theorized that construing light as being made up of individual particles or *photons* would explain how electrons are emitted from metals by an incident beam of light. Thus was born what has become known as the wave-particle duality: light is *simultaneously* both wave-like and particle-like.

In 1911, Ernest Rutherford developed his solar system model of the atom, in which negatively charged electrons orbit a positively charged, nuclear 'sun'. His model, however, had a major problem: if electrons could occupy any of the infinite number of possible orbits, they would spiral ever closer to the nucleus, and the atom would be unstable. A young Dane, Niels Bohr, solved this problem by applying quantum theory. He theorized that electrons could occupy only *discrete* orbits around the nucleus, and he used Planck's constant to identify those specific orbits that would be possible. In 1923, Lewis de Broglie proposed that *all* subatomic particles, not just photons, are actually 'wave-particles' and

developed equations that connected the energy and momentum of any such particle with the frequency of its associated wave. Erwin Schrödinger then used de Broglie's ideas in 1926 as a basis for accommodating the wave-particle duality through his justly-celebrated wave function equation. In 1927, Heisenberg proposed his indeterminacy principle: the experimental act of investigating the position (momentum) of a subatomic particle *necessarily* destroys the possibility of measuring its momentum (position) to arbitrary accuracy. At the limit, if one knows precisely where any subatomic particle is, one has absolutely no idea what it is doing. Dirac then used wave mechanics in 1928 to develop quantum field theory. If interrogated in a particle-like way, the formalism of quantum field theory gives probability predictions of particle behavior; but if interrogated in a wave-like way, the theory gives probability predictions of wave-like behavior.

Since the late 1920s, predictions of quantum mechanics have been confirmed in thousands of experiments. Given its radical break with classical mechanics, its interpretation prompted a great debate between Einstein, who argued for a realist interpretation, and Bohr, who, influenced by the Vienna Circle, argued for a positivist view. Bohr and his positivist allies developed an interpretation of quantum mechanics that is now referred to as the 'Copenhagen interpretation', which is often used interchangeably with 'instrumentalist interpretation' and 'positivist interpretation'. Its basic premise is that what we can know about the quantum world is only the effects we can observe *after* an intervention. As Bohr put it, 'The entire formalism is to be regarded as a tool for deriving predictions ... under experimental conditions' (Bohr, quoted in Polkinghorne, 1984: 79). That is, the uncertainty described in Heisenberg's principle does not reflect science's ignorance of the laws of nature – uncertainty *is* a law of nature. Prior to an act of measurement (observation), it is meaningless speculation even to talk about where a subatomic particle *really* is, or its momentum, or the direction of its spin.

All particles exist in a *superposition* of potential states.

Einstein and his realist allies attacked the Copenhagen view with appeals to (1) rhetoric (e.g. Einstein's famous claim that God does not 'play dice' with the universe), (2) 'hidden variable' theories that posited entities standing behind the wave-particle duality (e.g. David Bohm's hypothesized 'pilot wave'), and (3) numerous 'thought experiments'. Of the thought experiments that attempted to undermine the view that uncertainty is a law of nature, Einstein's most famous one, with Boris Podolsky and Nathan Rosen (hence the 'EPR' experiment), argued that quantum mechanics implied, at times, that the information that a particle is being investigated would be transmitted *instantaneously* to a second particle. Since speeds in excess of the speed of light are impossible, argued EPR, quantum mechanics violates 'local reality' and must be deficient.

Bohr responded to Einstein's rhetoric with the gentle chide that it is not for scientists to prescribe to God how He should run the world. As to the various hidden variable theories, Bohr and his positivist allies argued that such theories were *ad hoc* and, in any case, the hidden variables (e.g. Bohm's 'pilot wave') seemed even more bizarre than the Copenhagen view. The Hungarian mathematician John von Neumann then joined the argument and argued that any hidden variable theory was bound to disagree with some of the verified empirical results of quantum mechanics' experiments. After Bohr et al. had rebutted Einstein's thought experiments, John Bell in the 1960s developed some experimentally testable consequences of the EPR thought experiment. Since then, the results of experiments have tended to favor the Copenhagen interpretation: Einsteinian local reality seems incorrect. As the realist philosopher Putnam (1990: 8) puts it, 'One cannot emphasize too strongly that only a small minority – an extremely small minority – feels any discomfort with the Copenhagen interpretation to the present day'. Indeed, the positivist, Copenhagen view, as unsettling as its nonrealistic interpretation is to many, continues to reign supreme among physicists.

Realism since the 1930s

Realism suffered a heavy blow in the quantum mechanics debate. However, beginning in the 1960s, the 'received view' that *all* theories (and not just quantum mechanics) should be interpreted according to the dictates of positivism began steadily losing ground to the realism now generally referred to as 'scientific realism' (Suppe, 1977). This realism is associated with such philosophers as Maxwell (1962), Sellars (1963), Putnam (1962, 1990), Bhaskar (1979), MacKinnon (1979), (Siegel 1983, 1987), McMullin (1984), Boyd (1984), Levin (1984), Leplin (1984), Harré (1986), Manicas (1987) and Niiniluoto (1999). However, there is no 'grand theory' of science to which all scientific realists ideologically adhere. The absence of a scientific realist grand theory of science notwithstanding, Hunt (1990, 2003) argues that four theses serve as the fundamental tenets of scientific realism, which we shall refer to as classical realism, fallibilistic realism, critical realism and inductive realism.

First, *classical* realism is the commonsense realism of Moore and Russell, which holds that the world exists independently of its being perceived. For example, the 'external realism' advocated by Searle (1995: 150) maintains that 'the world (or alternatively, reality or the universe) exists independently of our representations of it'. As Thagard (2007: 29–30) argues, because the best 'scientific evidence strongly suggests that the universe is over 10 billion years old, but that representations constructed by humans have existed for less than a million, ... we can infer that that there was a world existing independent of human representation for billions of years ... [and] truth is not a purely mental matter'. Thus, classical realism contrasts with idealism and deconstructive, postmodernist relativism, which hold that all reality is 'in here' (the mind) and, therefore, all reality is relative to the mind that knows it. For classical realism, there really is something 'out there' for science to theorize about. To hold otherwise is to make all of science a sham.

Second, scientific realism argues for *fallibilistic* realism, which maintains that, though the job of science is to develop genuine knowledge about the world, such knowledge will never be known with certainty. The concept of 'know with certainty' belongs in theology, not science. For scientific realism, there is no 'God's eye view', nor does science need one to fulfill its goal of being a truth-seeking enterprise. As Siegel (1983: 82) puts it, 'To claim that a scientific proposition is true is not to claim that it is certain; rather, it is to claim that the world is as the proposition says it is'. As Hooker (1985) points out, a consequence of fallibilistic realism is that scientific realism rejects *direct* realism, which is the view that (1) because our perceptual processes necessarily result in a veridical representation of external objects, (2) knowledge about external objects can be known with certainty. Scientific realism rejects (and should reject) direct realism.

Third, scientific realism adopts *critical* realism, which recognizes the fallibility of scientist's perceptual (measurement) processes involved in the testing for the truth-content of knowledge-claims. For scientific realism, all of science's knowledge-claims are provisional, subject to revision on the basis of further evidence. Critical realism stresses the importance of the continuing efforts of science to develop ever-better measures of constructs, research procedures for empirical testing and epistemological norms for developing scientific knowledge.

In current social science, the 'critical' in *critical realism* is used in two very different ways. First, as discussed, scientific realism is critical in that science must both critically (1) evaluate and test its knowledge claims to determine their truth content and (2) evaluate and re-evaluate the methodologies and epistemologies that inform extant scientific practice. Most scientists and realist philosophers of science accept this kind of *critical* realism.

However, the 'critical' in critical realism is also often used in the manner of Sayer (1992: 6), who states, 'Social science must be critical of its object'. For Sayer's and others' version of critical realism, therefore, it is not enough that one be critical of science's knowledge claims, methodologies and epistemologies. Researchers must also be critical of society. Indeed, researchers must become social activists, because social scientists 'should develop a critical awareness in people and, indeed, assist in their emancipation' (Sayer, 1992: 42). Therefore, those researchers who are interested in explaining, predicting and understanding phenomena, but who do *not* want to assume the role of the social activist involved in transforming society, should be cautious about self-describing their research as 'critical realist' in the Sayer sense.

Fourth, scientific realism adopts *inductive* realism, which maintains that 'the long-term success of a scientific theory gives reason to believe that something like the entities and structure postulated by the theory actually exists' McMullin (1984: 26). Because the logical positivists believed that science's implicit acceptance of inductive realism in the nineteenth century had wrongly encouraged it to believe in the absolute truth of Newtonian mechanics, they rejected inductive realism and accepted Humean skepticism's position with respect to unobservable constructs (McMullin, 1984; Stove, 1982; Suppe, 1977). Scientific realism, in contrast, maintains that Humean skepticism, which 'denies that one can progress by logical reasoning from perceptual experience to any genuine knowledge of an external world' (Watkins, 1984: 3), is wrong-headed. For scientific realism, the positivists were 'throwing out the baby with the bath water'. Therefore, for inductive realism, and contrary to logical positivism and logical empiricism, concepts that are *unobservable* are appropriate in theories that purport to explain observable phenomena. Similarly, and contrary to Popperian falsificationism, the positive results of empirical tests – not just falsifications – provide evidence as to the truth content of the theories tested.

A SCIENTIFIC REALIST MODEL OF TRUTH

The preceding section introduced the four basic tenets of scientific realism. This section develops a scientific realist model of truth that focuses on the successes and failures of empirical tests. To articulate the model, we use an example from consumer research. Heath and Chatterjee (1995) review the effects of decoys on consumer choice sets. A decoy is an option introduced into a choice set that causes preference reversals between two other options in the set. These preference reversals are referred to as 'attraction effects theory', and they contradict standard economic models of individual choice, which customarily assume all preferences to be independent of irrelevant alternatives.

Heath and Chatterjee (1995) identify five theoretical issues and assess the extent to which 95 empirical tests (found in 15 articles) support the five hypotheses of attraction effects theory. One hypothesis they examine is: 'Decoys will reduce shares of lower-quality competitors more that they will reduce shares of higher-quality competitors' (p. 270). They report that the 15 articles they review contain 92 tests in which product attribute quality is the independent variable and competitor product market share is the dependent variable (see their Table 1). Of the 92 tests, 'decoys reduced shares of lower-quality competitors 50 per cent of the time (18/36) but reduced shares of higher-quality competitors only 11 per cent of the time (6/56)., Comparing each combination of the higher-quality product share reduction (change in the C^d variable in their Table 1, where $n = 56$) and lower-quality product share reduction (change in the C^d variable in their Table 1, $n = 36$), 1568 of 2016 (78 percent) possible comparisons support the quality hypothesis, 406 of 2016 (20 percent) are counter to the hypothesis, and 42 of 2016 (2 percent) of the possible comparisons show no statistically significant differences. We use the findings of Heath and Chatterjee (1995) on the product attribute-quality hypothesis,

in particular, and the implications of their findings for attraction effects theory, in general, as continuing examples to illustrate the scientific realist model of truth.

The model

Scientific realism, in viewing marketing research as a truth-seeking enterprise, conceptualizes *truth* as not an entity, but an *attribute*. It is an attribute of both beliefs and linguistic expressions. For example, it is an attribute of such linguistic expressions as those denoted by the labels 'theories', 'laws', 'propositions' and 'hypotheses'. Recall that the inductive realism tenet of scientific realism maintains that the long-run success of a theory gives reason to believe that something like the entities and structure postulated by the theory actually exists. Figure 7.1 is a model that explicates the meaning of 'something like theory X is likely true' and 'something like theory X is likely false' in the scientific realism approach to science.

Assume that box 1 in Figure 7.1 contains the linguistic expression denoted by 'attraction effects theory'. Attraction effects theory posits entities (e.g. the entities labeled 'goods', 'brands' and 'people'), attributes of entities (i.e. the identifiable characteristics or properties of goods, brands and people – e.g. loss aversion, higher-quality, lower-quality and market share) and structures (e.g. the proposition that there is a negative relationship between the attribute-quality level of a firm's product and the product's resistance to attacks from competitor's decoys). The theory (i.e. attraction effects theory) posits that the entities, attributes and structures referred to in box 1 exist in the world external to the theory (i.e. box 3). That is, the linguistic expressions that constitute the theory in box 1 are *about* the world in box 3.

Path A, from box 1 to box 2, shows that some theory (e.g. attraction effects theory) has certain implications or outcomes. That is, the theory can be used to explain some phenomena. For example, why did fewer

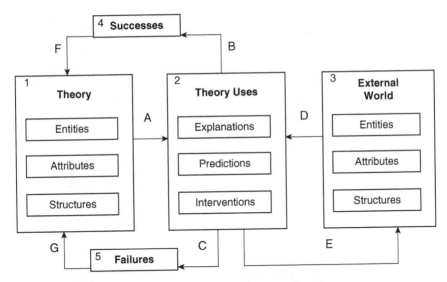

**Figure 7.1   Scientific realism: theory successes, failures and truth.
(Source: Adapted from Hunt 2002b). Reprinted by permission of the author).**

consumers purchase the decoy product when the competitor product was of higher quality? They did so because 'in real world markets, price discounts move consumers from lower-quality to higher-quality brands more than from higher-quality to lower-quality brands ... [and] loss aversion, the tendency for losses to be more unpleasant than equivalent gains are pleasant, appears to be greater for quality than price' (Heath and Chatterjee, 1995: 270). The theory can also be used to predict some phenomena (e.g. 'Decoys will reduce shares of lower-quality competitors more that they will reduce shares of higher-quality competitors'). The theory can also be used to suggest interventions (e.g. to attack competitors' brands, use viable – not dominated – decoys).

Paths B and C show that the theory's outcomes are sometimes successful (box 4) and sometimes not (box 5). For example, as to explanations, some competitors that have lower-quality product attributes lose more market share when decoys are present than competitors with higher-quality product attributes (which would constitute explanatory successes), but other competitors with lower-quality product attributes lose less market share when decoys are present than

competitors with higher-quality product attributes (which would constitute explanatory failures). As to predictions, recall that of the 92 tests reported on by Heath and Chatterjee (1995) with product attribute quality level as the independent variable, 78 percent of the comparisons (of the 2016 higher-quality product versus lower-quality product share changes in the C^d variables in Table 1) were successes (box 4) and 20 per cent were failures (box 5). As to interventions, at times the suggestions of attraction effects theory are right (e.g. sometimes the viable decoys have stronger effects on competitors' market shares), and at times the suggestions are wrong (e.g. sometimes the viable decoys have weaker effects on competitors' market shares). Both the successes and failures are impacted by the entities, attributes and structures that exist in the external world (box 3), as shown by path D. In turn, the outcomes in box 2 impact (by way of path E) the entities, attributes and structures in box 3 (e.g. when managers in firms interpret the outcomes in box 2 as supporting the truth of attraction effects theory, and this belief then guides their future patterns of behavior).

What, then, is the import of a high or low proportion of successes (box 4), and a low or high proportion of failures (box 5)? Paths F and G represent inferences from a theory's successes and failures to the truth-content and falsity-content of a theory. For scientific realism, a high proportion of successes, relative to failures, gives reason to believe that something like the entities, attributes and structures posited by the theory in box 1 (e.g. the hypotheses of attraction effects theory) actually exist in the world external to the theory (i.e. they exist in box 3). That is, we infer that something like the theory posited in box 1 is likely true. The 'something like', then, equates with attraction effects theory being 'approximately true' or 'having truth content'. From a high proportion of failures, relative to successes, we infer that something like the theory (e.g. again, attraction effects theory) is likely false. In a sense, paths F and G depict a 'weighing' of evidence, as Bunge (1967: 319) so aptly puts it. However, scientific realism, as a theory of science, does not imply that 'a high proportion of successes, relative to failures' means 'true with probability "p"'. Likewise, it does not imply that 'a high proportion of failures, relative to successes' means 'false with probability "p"' Indeed, most scientific realists are highly skeptical of efforts that attempt to apply the logic of probability to the weighing of evidence involved in the empirical testing of theories. Also, the realist approach to truth does not equate 'truth' with 'truth with certainty'. As the realist Siegel (1983: 82) puts it, 'To claim that a scientific proposition is true is not to claim that it is certain; rather, it is to claim that the world is as the proposition says it is'.

Returning to the study by Heath and Chatterjee (1995) on the hypotheses of attraction effects theory, note that the authors frame their conclusions consistent with scientific realism. They find that, as an independent variable, higher-quality product attributes seemed to fare best: 'The meta-analysis and experiment add evidence to three lines of research suggesting that it is generally easier to increase share of higher-quality than lower-quality brands' (p. 282).

Furthermore, their findings regarding higher-quality product attributes showed that: 'Decoys increase shares of higher-quality targets more … than they increased shares of lower-quality targets' (p. 274). Moreover, when they, as scientific realism puts it, 'weighed' the total empirical evidence, they conclude:

> The asymmetric decoy effects … parallel three other asymmetries: (1) asymmetric price competition across lower-quality and higher-quality brands in real-world markets … (2) greater loss aversion to quality than to price … and (3) compromise brands drawing a larger share from lower-quality than higher-quality competitions … These disparate research streams converge on the same conclusion: It is generally easier to increase share of higher-quality brands than low-quality brands. (p. 282)

Therefore, Heath and Chatterjee (1995) disagree with Allenby and Rossi's claim (1991) that income effects can explain the attraction effects. Indeed, for them, the empirical evidence to date shows that 'the fact that the populations would have differed on many dimensions makes it difficult to know exactly which factors mediated the effect' (Heath and Chatterjee, 1995: 282).

On the scientific realist model of truth

Readers should note that truth is an attribute of beliefs and linguistic expressions, it is not an entity in the external world (i.e. truth is not in box 3 in Figure 7.1). Therefore, *truth is not an entity that researchers do (or can) study*. To treat truth as an entity in box 3 is to engage in reification, that is, it is 'to postulate as an entity fallaciously' (Levin, 1991: 57). For example, with regard to truth, Anderson (1988: 404) asks, 'Indeed, how would we know truth even if we held it in our hands?' His query is (one suspects) meant to be taken as just an instance of colorful, relativist rhetoric. Nevertheless, his reification of truth vividly illustrates the conceptual danger of treating an unobservable, intangible concept, such as truth, as if it referred to an observable, tangible object, such as an apple. By wrongly leading us to believe that truth could be held in our hands, his reification of truth, absurdly, leads us to inquire how we could recognize it with our eyes.

A common accusation by relativists is that those holding that science should seek true theories must also reify truth. For example, Zinkhan and Hirscheim (1992: 83) maintain that those who hold truth in high regard must assume that 'there is an immutable truth out there which scientists can study'. However, they provide no quotations of realists or any other evidence of instances of reification – and for good reason: it is likely that no such evidence exists. Truth for scientific realists is not an entity for study, let alone, an 'immutable' entity.

The scientific realist model of truth in Figure 7.1 prompts several observations. First, the model seems consistent with the kind of arguments advanced in the review of attraction effects theory by Heath and Chatterjee (1995). This is unsurprising, for many philosophers of science, as well as most philosophically oriented social science researchers, believe that only some version of realism can explain the actual workings of science without reducing it to a shameful charade. For example, because no rational person searches for the characteristics of a nonexisting entity, what other than the warranted belief that the entity labeled 'brands' exists could motivate the search for whether (or not) *decoy* brands prompt consumers to adopt the target's or competitor's brands in choice sets? Are we to believe that researchers say to themselves: 'Even though I do not believe in the existence of decoy brands, I shall pretend they exist and then pretend to investigate whether (or not) such decoy brands impact on the decision to adopt the target's or competitor's brands, whose existence I also shall pretend to believe in?' Although disingenuous activities do take place in science, scientific realism maintains that the totality of research in the physical sciences, social sciences and marketing is not best described as an elaborate charade.

Second, the scientific realist model of truth is inconsistent with logical positivism and logical empiricism. Even though both the logical positivists and logical empiricists held truth in high regard, both were under the spell of Humean skepticism with respect to induction (Stove, 1982). Therefore, both refused to countenance the real existence of entities that were, in principle, unobservable. Because, for the logical empiricists, only observables are real, the concept of 'brands' must be simply a shorthand way of talking about a collection of observable entities. That is, the logical empiricists made a sharp distinction between 'theoretical terms' and 'observation terms', with only the latter referring directly to some aspect of the world. Theoretical terms would have to be given meaning by being defined through 'correspondence rules' with observation terms. However, this posed a major problem for the logical empiricists: the problem of theoretical dispensability. Called the 'theoretician's dilemma' by Hempel (1965), the first half of the dilemma is: if all theoretical terms can be defined through correspondence with observation terms, and if the purpose of science is to determine relationships among observation terms, then theoretical terms are unnecessary in science. The second half of the dilemma is: if theoretical terms *cannot* be defined through correspondence with observation terms, then theoretical terms are meaningless and, *surely*, are unnecessary in science.

For scientific realism, the 'theoretician's dilemma' is no dilemma at all. Scientific realism dismisses the theoretical term/observation term dichotomy as a false dichotomy. That is, scientific realism acknowledges that all the terms in a theory are, properly speaking, 'theoretical terms'. The expression 'theoretical term' means nothing more than 'a term in a theory'. For scientific realism, some terms in a theory may denote something more observable, more detectable and more easily measurable than other terms. In fact, some terms may denote nothing, in principle, observable at all. However, all the terms in a theory (excepting, of course, mathematical and logical terms) can legitimately claim to denote the existence of some entity, such claims being based on (1) the senses (classical realism) and/or (2) the success of a theory (inductive realism).

Third, the model in Figure 7.1 is inconsistent with strict falsificationism. As were the logical empiricists, Popper (1972) was strongly influenced by Humean skepticism (Stove, 1982). For Popper (1972: 86, 88; italics added), 'I regard Hume's formulation and treatment of the logical problem of induction … as a flawless gem … a gem of priceless value … a simple, straightforward, logical refutation of any claim that induction could be a valid argument, *or a justifiable way of reasoning*'. Thus, Popper (1972), by claiming that all *positive* results of a theory test are irrelevant to science (not a 'justifiable way of reasoning'), fell into a form of irrationalism (Stove, 1982). In terms of Figure 7.1, falsificationism would maintain that, whereas the inferences of path F are not a justifiable way of reasoning, the inferences of path G are justifiable. The scientific realist model of truth – in accord with the actual practice of science – maintains that both paths F and G are defensible.

FOR TRUTH AS A RESEARCH OBJECTIVE AND REGULATIVE IDEAL

We turn now to scientific realism's argument for truth as a research objective and regulative ideal. The argument is based on trust. What is trust? Trust exists when one has confidence in another's reliability and integrity (Moorman et al., 1993). In turn, the confidence of the trusting party in the trustworthy party's reliability and integrity is associated with the belief that the trustworthy party has attributes such as consistent, competent, honest, fair, responsible, helpful and benevolent (Dwyer and LaGace, 1986; Larzelere and Huston, 1980; Rotter, 1971). The importance of trust is recognized across disciplines and research traditions.

In the marketing of services, Berry and Parasuraman (1991: 144) find: 'Customer-company relationships require trust'. Indeed, they contend, 'Effective services marketing depends on the management of trust because the customer typically must buy a service before experiencing it' (1991: 107). In marketing education, Huff, Cooper and Jones (2002) find that trust has consequences important to the success of student project groups. In strategic alliances, Sherman (1992: 78) concludes that 'the biggest stumbling block to the success of alliances is the lack of trust'. In retailing, Berry (1993: 1) stresses that 'trust is the basis for loyalty', and Ganesan (1994) finds trust as influencing a retailer's long-term orientation. In relationship marketing, Morgan and Hunt (1994) find that trust promotes cooperation, increases the likelihood that conflict will be of the functional kind and decreases uncertainty. In international marketing, Hewett and Bearden (2001) find that a multinational's subsidiary having trust in the headquarters' marketing function will increase the subsidiary's acquiescence to headquarters' direction. In the brand equity area, Chaudhuri and Holbrook (2001) find brand trust to impact purchase loyalty and attitudinal loyalty. In competition theory, Hunt (2000: 235–237) explicates how resource-advantage theory can explain the relationships among trust, competitive advantage and wealth.

In short, trust is a key concept in many different literatures. What, then, are the relationships among trust, science, realism and ethics?

Trust, science, realism and ethics

Zaltman and Moorman (1988) explore the factors determining whether marketing managers actually use the research generated by marketing research departments. The key factor, they find, is trust: 'Perhaps the single most important factor affecting the use of research is the presence or absence of trust' (1988: 16). Indeed, a major requirement for developing and maintaining trust is 'being a truth teller' (1988: 20). Thus, truth and trust are interrelated.

Scientific realism views trust as a key construct for understanding the dynamics of scientific disciplines. Trust is essential in all disciplines, because scientific knowledge is a shared form of knowledge; it is shared with its clients. The clients of commercial marketing researchers are limited in general to the organizations that purchase the research. However, the clients of academic marketing researchers include not only marketing practitioners, but also students, government officials, consumers, other academicians and members of the general public (Hunt, 2002a; Monroe, 1988). In essence, all researchers who share their research with clients state implicitly: 'Trust me'. Thus, science and trust are interrelated.

One consequence of the importance of trust in science is for those whose research projects are guided by philosophies maintaining that the research does *not* 'touch base' – path D in Figure 7.1 – with a reality external to the researcher's own linguistically encapsulated theory, or paradigm, or research tradition, or worldview. Such philosophies provide no grounds for the client trusting the knowledge claims of the researchers and are self-defeating for practicing researchers who might adopt them at the 'workbench' level.

Trust and ethics

Studies indicate that a difficult ethical problem facing marketing researchers is 'misinterpreting the results of a research project with the objective of supporting a predetermined personal or corporate point of view' (Hunt et al., 1984: 312). Because such biases would destroy trust, marketing associations are paying more attention to marketing's codes of ethics. It has been long recognized that one of the major, distinguishing characteristics that separates professions from other vocations is that all true professions have a degree of self control by means of formal and/or informal codes of ethics. An underlying

tenet of all such codes is that the true professional, when interacting with clients of any kind, is not guided totally by self interest. For example, when people go to physicians, they have a right to expect that their physicians will not adopt methods of treatment based solely on which method will best serve the physicians' interests. Because of the disparity in knowledge of diseases and their respective treatments, the social compact between laypeople and their physicians requires a significant element of *trust*. Scientific realists, philosophers of science, are coming to realize that both *trust* and *ethics* are interrelated keys to understanding scientific communities.

Rom Harré has been at the forefront of those philosophers advocating the importance of, in his terms, 'moral order' in science. Harré (1986) defines scientific knowledge as 'trustworthy knowledge', rather than truth with certainty: 'Science is not a logically coherent body of knowledge in the strict, unforgiving sense of the philosophers' high redefinition, but a cluster of material and cognitive practices, carried on within a distinctive moral order, whose main characteristic is the trust that obtains among its members and [the trust that] should obtain between that community and the larger lay community with which it is interdependent' (1986: 6). What, for him, is trust? 'To trust someone is to be able to rely on them in the matter in question. ... Scientists believe that things personally unknown to them are as *another scientist* says they are'. However, 'trust is not maintained by telling each other only literal truths. Under that constraint the members of the community would perforce remain forever silent. It is enough that they tell each other what they honestly believe to be the truth' (1986: 12). In this regard, Harré is claiming that the moral order of science implies, among other things, the avoidance of sophistry and deception, as well as outright fraud.

Harré points out that trust in all societies is often role-related: 'it is because the trusted one is in the role of parent, guardian, policeman, research supervisor and so on, that the trust is there until something happens to upset it' (Harré, 1986: 21). Therefore, scientists in their role as researchers producing trustworthy belief are required by their peers and by the lay community to maintain a moral order. This moral order is necessary, Harré argues, because researchers are involved in producing 'practically reliable scientific knowledge'. This 'reliance might be existential, concerning what there is or what might be, or it might be practical, concerning what can and cannot be done, or both. The moral quality of the product comes through clearly in the kind of outrage felt by the [scientific] community at the disclosure of scientific fraud' (Harré, 1986: 13). Harré asks: 'Is scientific method ... and scientific morality, the fiduciary act of committing oneself to make one's scientific utterances fiduciary acts, the best way to discipline a community which exists to find out about the natural world?' (Harré, 1986: 26). Harré answers this question affirmatively on the basis that science is committed to referential realism, which holds that 'existence is prior to theory, and ... truth and falsity migrate from the epistemology of science to the morality of its human community' (1986: 6). For Harré, any view of science that claims that scientific knowledge is 'constructed' or 'created' by the scientific community independent of some external reality (Path D in Figure 7.1) is to be rejected on moral grounds. He summarizes his position as follows:

> Science has a special status, not because it is a sure way of producing truths and avoiding falsehood, but because it is a communal practice of a community with a remarkable and rigid morality at the heart of which is a commitment that the products of this community shall be trustworthy.... Science is not just a cluster of material and cognitive practices, but is a moral achievement as well.... Antirealism, which, like it or not, seeps out into the lay world as antiscience, is not only false, but morally obnoxious. (Harré, 1986: 7)

Marketing researchers have numerous clients for the knowledge they produce. Concerning marketing knowledge, its development, and dissemination, does the *trust* that these constituencies have *in* marketing

researchers impose certain special responsibilities *on* them? If so, what is the nature of these responsibilities, and what does it imply about the most appropriate philosophy to guide marketing science? Philosophies based on relativism, constructionism and deconstructive postmodernism would seem to be unlikely candidates for inspiring trust. Most assuredly, no set of philosophical foundations can *guarantee* the production of trustworthy knowledge. Nevertheless, researchers can find comfort in the fact that there exist philosophies of science – such as scientific realism – that, at the minimum, are not antithetical to truth and its surrogate, trustworthy knowledge, and, at the maximum, may (fallibly) yield knowledge that is truly worthy of clients' trust. Although the clients of marketing researchers can ask for no more, they surely deserve no less.

In conclusion, there are numerous 'isms' in the philosophy of science, for example, logical positivism, logical empiricism, idealism, relativism and scientific realism. Of all these 'isms', scientific realism seems to make the most sense for marketing, for no *other* philosophy is coherent (without being dogmatic), is critical (without being nihilistic), is open (without being anarchistic), is tolerant (without being relativistic), is fallible (without being subjectivistic) and – at the same time – can account for the success of science. It is a good candidate for providing a philosophical foundation for marketing research.

NOTES

1 The exception is, of course, quantum mechanics. The 'Copenhagen' interpretation of quantum mechanics, which is the dominant interpretation in physics, is guided by and consistent with positivism. See Hunt (2003) for more on the issue of realism, positivism and quantum mechanics.

2 This chapter draws heavily on Hunt (1990, 2002a, 2003).

3 The historical material in this section, except where noted, draws heavily on the works of Ayer (1959), Bergmann (1967), Hunt (2003), Joergensen (1970), Manicas (1987), Polkinghorne (1984) and Suppe (1977).

REFERENCES

Allenby, G.M. and Rossi, P.E. (1991) 'Quality Perceptions and Asymmetric Switching between Brands', *Marketing Science*, 10(Summer): 185–204.

Anderson, P.F. (1988) 'Relativism Revidivus: In Defense of Critical Relativism', *Journal of Consumer Research*, 15(December): 403–406.

Angeles, P.A. (1981) *Dictionary of Philosophy*. New York: Barnes and Noble Books.

Ayer, A.J. (1959) *Logical Positivism*. Glencoe, Illinois: The Free Press.

Bergmann, G. (1967) *The Metaphysics of Logical Positivism*. Madison, WI: The University of Wisconsin Press.

Berry, L.L. (1993) 'Playing Fair in Retailing', *Arthur Andersen Retailing Issues Newsletter*, 5(March): 2.

Berry, L.L. and Parasuraman, A. (1991) *Marketing Services*. New York: The Free Press.

Bhaskar, R. (1979) *The Possibility of Naturalism*. Brighton, England: Harvester Press.

Boyd, R.N. (1984) 'The Current Status of Scientific Realism', in J. Leplin (ed.) *Scientific Realism*, Berkeley: University of California Press, pp. 41–82.

Bunge, M. (1967) *Scientific Research. Vol. 2: The Search for Truth*. New York: Springer-Verlag.

Causey, R.L. (1979) 'Theory and Observation', in P.D. Asquith and H.E. Kyburg (eds) *Current Research in Philosophy of Science*, East Lansing: Philosophy of Science Association, pp. 187–206.

Chaudhuri, A. and Holbrook, M.B. (2001) 'The Chain of Effects from Brand Trust and Brand Affect to Brand Performance: The Role of Brand Loyalty', *Journal of Marketing*, 65(2): 81–93.

Durant, W. (1954) *The Story of Philosophy*. New York: Simon and Shuster.

Dwyer, F.R. and LaGace, R.R. (1986) 'On the Nature and Role of Buyer-Seller Trust', in T. Shimp et al. (eds) *AMA Summer Educators Conference Proceedings*, Chicago, IL: American Marketing Association, pp. 40–45.

Ganesan, S. (1994) 'Determinants of Long Term Orientation in Buyer-Seller Relationships', *Journal of Marketing*, 58(April): 1–19.

Harré, R. (1986) *Varieties of Realism*. Oxford, UK: Basil Blackwell Ltd.

Heath, T.B. and Chatterjee, S. (1995) 'Asymmetric Decoy Effects on Lower-Quality versus Higher-Quality Brands: Meta-analytic and Experimental Evidence', *Journal of Consumer Research*, 22: 268–284.

Hempel, C.G. (ed.) (1965) *Aspects of Scientific Explanation and Other Essays in the Philosophy of Science*. New York: The Free Press.

Hewett, K. and Bearden, W.O. (2001) 'Dependence, Trust, and Relational Behavior on the Part of Foreign Subsidiary Marketing Operations: Implications for Managing Global Marketing Operations', *Journal of Marketing*, 65(4): 51–66.

Hooker, C.A. (1985) 'Surface Dazzle, Ghostly Depths: An Exposition and Critical Evaluation of van Fraassens' Vindication of Empiricism against Realism', in M.C. Paul and A.H. Clifford (eds) *Images of Science: Essays on Realism and Empiricism*, Chicago: University of Chicago Press, pp. 153–196.

Huff, L.C., Cooper, J. and Jones, W. (2002) 'The Development and Consequences of Trust in Student Project Groups', *Journal of Marketing Education*, 24(1): 24–34.

Hunt, S.D. (1990) 'Truth in Marketing Theory and Research', *Journal of Marketing*, 54(July): 1–15.

Hunt, S.D. (2000) *A General Theory of Competition: Resources, Competences, Productivity, Economic Growth*. Thousand Oaks, CA: Sage Publications.

Hunt, S.D. (2002a) *Foundations of Marketing Theory: Toward a General Theory of Marketing*. Armonk, NY: ME Sharpe.

Hunt, S.D. (2002b) 'Truth and Scientific Realism'. Unpublished working paper. Lubbock, TX: Marketing Department, Texas Tech University.

Hunt, S.D. (2003) *Controversy in Marketing Theory: For Reason, Realism, Truth and Objectivity*. Armonk, NY: M.E. Sharpe.

Hunt, S.D., Chonko, L.B. and Wilcox, J.B. (1984) 'Ethical Problems of Marketing Researchers', *Journal of Marketing Research*, 21(August): 309–324.

Joergensen, J. (1970) 'The Development of Logical Empiricism', in. O. Neurath, R. Carnap and C. Morris (eds), *Foundations of the Unity of Science*, second edn., Chicago: University of Chicago Press.

Kuhn, T.S. (1962) *The Structure of Scientific Revolutions*. Chicago, IL: University of Chicago Press.

Larzelere, R.E. and Huston, T.L. (1980) 'The Dyadic Trust Scale: Toward Understanding Interpersonal Trust in Close Relationships',

Journal of Marriage and the Family, 42(August): 595–604.

Leplin, J. (1984) *Scientific Realism*. Berkeley, CA: University of California Press.

Levin, M.E. (1984) 'What Kind of Explanation is Truth?', in J. Leplin (ed.) *Scientific Realism*, Berkeley, CA: University of California Press, pp. 124–139.

Levin, M.E. (1991) 'The Reification-Realism-Positivism Controversy in Macromarketing: A Philosopher's View', *Journal of Macromarketing*, 11(Spring): 57–65.

Lincoln, Y.S. and Guba, E.G. (1985) *Naturalistic Inquiry*. Beverly Hills, CA: Sage Publications.

MacKinnon, E. (1979) 'Scientific Realism: The New Debates', *Philosophy of Science*, 46(4): 501–532.

Manicas, P.T. (1987) *A History and Philosophy of the Social Sciences*. New York: Basil Blackwell, Inc.

Maxwell, G. (1962) 'The Ontological Status of Theoretical Entities', in H. Feigl and G. Maxwell (eds) *Scientific Explanation: Minnesota Studies in the Philosophy of Science*, Vol. 3, Minneapolis, MN: University of Minnesota, pp. 3–27.

McMullin, E. (1984) 'A Case for Scientific Realism', in J. Leplin (ed.) *Scientific Realism*, Berkeley: University of California Press, pp. 8–40.

Monroe, K.B. (1988) 'Developing, Disseminating, and Utilizing Marketing Knowledge', *Journal of Marketing*, 52(October): 1–25.

Moorman, C., Deshpande, R. and Zaltman, G. (1993) 'Factors Affecting Trust in Market Research Relationships', *Journal of Marketing*, 57(January): 81–101.

Morgan, R.M. and Hunt, S.D. (1994) 'The Commitment-Trust Theory of Relationship Marketing'. *Journal of Marketing*, 58(July): 20–38.

Niiniluoto, I. (1999) *Critical Scientific Realism*. Oxford, UK: Oxford University Press.

Polkinghorne, J.C. (1984) *The Quantum World*. New York: Longman.

Popper, K.R. (1972) *Objective Knowledge*. Oxford: Oxford University Press.

Putnam, H. (1962) 'What Theories are Not', in E. Nagel, P. Suppes and A. Tarski (eds) *Proceedings of the 1960 International Congress*, Stanford, CA: Stanford University Press, pp. 240–251.

Putnam, H. (1990) *Realism with a Human Face*. Cambridge, MA: Harvard University Press.

Rotter, J.B. (1971) 'Generalized Expectancies for Interpersonal Trust'. *American Psychologist*, 26(May): 443–452.

Sayer, A. (1992) *Method in Social Science: A Realist Approach*, second edn., London: Routledge.

Schlick, M. (1934) 'Uber das Fundament der Erkenntnis', *Erkenntnis*, 4. English translation by David Rynin, in A.J. Ayer, (ed.) *Logical Positivism*, Glencoe, IL: The Free Press. (Page numbers refer to English translation.), pp. 209–227.

Searle, J.R. (1995) *The Construction of Social Reality*. New York: Free Press.

Sellars, W. (1963) *Science, Perception and Reality*. New York: Humanities Press.

Sherman, S. (1992) 'Are Strategic Alliances Working?', *Fortune* (September): 77–78.

Siegel, H. (1983) 'Brown on Epistemology and the New Philosophy of Science', *Synthese* 56(1): 61–89.

Siegel, H. (1987) *Relativism Refuted*. Dordrecht: D. Reidel Publishing.

Stove, D. (1982) *Popper and After*. Oxford, UK: Perganon Press.

Suppe, F. (1977) 'Afterword – 1977', in F. Suppe (ed.) *The Structure of Scientific Theories*, second edn, Urbana, IL: University of Illinois Press, pp. 614–730.

Thagard, P. (2007) 'Coherence, Truth and the Development of Scientific Knowledge', *Philosophy of Science*, 74: 28–47.

Watkins, J. (1984) *Science and Skepticism*. Princeton, NJ: Princeton University Press.

Zaltman, G. and Moorman, C. (1988) 'The Importance of Personal Trust in the Use of Research', *Journal of Advertising Research*, 28(5): 16–24.

Zinkhan, G. and Hirschheim, R. (1992) 'Truth in Marketing Theory and Research: An Alternative Perspective', *Journal of Marketing*, 56(2): 80–88.

8

Critical Marketing – Marketing in Critical Condition[1]

A. Fuat Fırat and Mark Tadajewski

INTRODUCTION

Writing a review of critical marketing is a daunting task. It requires settling many a contentious issue, beginning with what critical marketing is. To ensure the widest review, the term 'critical' in critical marketing could be defined in its most general sense; that is, as any position that judgmentally evaluates a body of discourse with the intention to find any faults or problems to be challenged and modified or corrected. When so defined, what is critical and what needs to be criticized are bound to change with time and context. What was a critical reading and perspective during earlier periods of our history is likely to be found to deserve criticism later on, specifically if this once critical paradigm is to gain prominence and find acceptance in the mainstream of the discipline. A review of critical marketing, so defined, would necessitate a historical reading of the erstwhile paradigms in the discipline, detailing how each came to be 'critically' confronted, and how other, once critical, perspectives took center stage as the new paradigm, then becoming the target of critical evaluations themselves.

Another way to think of 'critical' is to link it to a certain perspective or school of thought, such as the Critical Theory (Frankfurt) school (Bradshaw and Fırat, 2007). In this case, the review would require finding literature in the discipline that uses this specific perspective as its point of departure. Only work that has such an orientation would be the focus of the review. Or, to put it another way, the focus is how to be critical. A third way to approach the term 'critical' is to take a system-based approach. In this case, all works that challenge the disciplinary discourse arising in and from a specific cultural (social–economic–political) order of organizing human life – for example, modern capitalism – would be considered 'critical'. Here, the focus is not on how to be critical, but what to be critical of.

In this chapter, we shall try to present as wide a review of critical marketing as possible within page limits, to provide some degree of completeness, but intend to concentrate on the third (system-based) sense of the term 'critical'. Our purpose is to critically explore the nature of modern marketing, as it became constructed within modern capitalism, in order to expose its current character(istics) as we review the critical marketing literature.

A PLURALITY OF VOICES

There has been almost an explosion of interest in critical marketing since the beginning of the twenty-first century (e.g. Burton, 2001; Catterall et al., 2000; Ellis et al., 2010 (forthcoming); Hackley, 2009; Saren et al., 2007; Tadajewski and Brownlie, 2008; Tadajewski and Maclaran, 2009a, b, c, d). Not surprisingly, much of this interest in the English-speaking world comes from the UK and Europe (e.g. Alvesson, 1994; Brownlie et al., 1999; Ellis et al., 2010 (forthcoming); Morgan, 1992, 2003; Skålén et al., 2008; Tadajewski and Brownlie, 2008). There are historical reasons for this distinction in interests between North American and European scholars of marketing. There are, of course, scholars of marketing in other continents and those who represent different voices and forms of critical approaches (e.g. Varman and Vikas, 2007b; Vikas and Varman, 2007). It is unfortunate that their voices are difficult to hear, unless they get published in 'Western' media – journals and conference proceedings especially. In addition, the authors of this chapter are greatly limited to literature that appears in English. We apologize to colleagues and intellectuals who produce critical works in languages other than English for our inability to access their work. Although it is common knowledge, we should mention the hegemony of English language media in the marketing discipline – possibly all business disciplines – and that we do not necessarily think this to be a healthy condition. One critical act will be to break this hegemony, as well as the dominance of literature coming out of North America.

Interest in critical marketing and that it is not led by North American scholars is one step toward breaking the dominance. North America's modern economic success and influence all over the world stifles new theories and practices that are truly critical, preventing them from gaining ground in, especially, North America, as it is harder to let go of what has previously brought 'success' by those who have had this success (Dholakia et al., 1983). New theories and practices are not yet tried and proven, when what has been successful has served to perpetuate the American Way. The problem with this logic and emotion is that things change, and what has been successful will not forever be successful (however we define successful). This is known by all business disciplines leading to discourses on coping with change, turbulence and environmental uncertainty. And yet, these discourses in modern business disciplines are largely about how to maintain the 'principles' of success by modifications in ways they are practiced. Principles are often thought to be universal across time and space and are tightly held on to (see especially Luthra, 1991).

For the successful, modifying the principles because changes require it is usually only possible after fatal shocks to the system and not before, as the present financial crisis stands as testament. This is the current condition of North American corporations; change occurs slowly, if at all. This is why critical thinking regarding norms, principles and the order as a whole, comes not from North America today, but from elsewhere. Furthermore, the political spectrum from far left to far right is much broader and livelier in Europe, making it easier to challenge the dominant systemic paradigm. Maybe, even more importantly, change, whether social change, cultural change, political change, is more prevalent in Europe; thus, Europe feels the pressure to recognize change without dogmatically clinging to principles and practices that once produced dazzling standards of living, but now only reaffirms a commitment to ontological irresponsibility in a world of environmental risk and melting icecaps (Bouchet, 1994).

The emergence of renewed interest in critical marketing at this juncture is auspicious, since paradigms that are currently arising from North America, such as Consumer

Culture Theory (CCT) (Arnould and Thompson, 2005), tend to dilute the critical edge of many works that preceded them in attempting to challenge and redirect marketing (see also Hetrick and Lozada, 1994; Ozanne and Murray, 1995). The so-called critical orientations from North America and elsewhere often propose apologist renditions of the conditions of being a consumer in a market economy[2] (cf. Goulding, 2003). They interpret any and all resistance to corporate formulated signs or attempts at formulating meanings by consumers, as genuine agency (cf. Applbaum, 2000; Clarke et al., 2007; Jhally et al., 1985; Kline and Leiss, 1978; Lippke, 1991; Lynd, 1936; Maxwell, 1996; Sneddon, 2001; Svensson, 2007; Varman and Vikas, 2007a; Varman and Kappiarath, 2008), without sufficient consideration of the systemic construction of subjectivities and impositions plaguing consumers.

In case we have forgotten, the Critical Theorists have for a long time pointed out the 'pseudo-individuality' that the consumption of mass-produced goods provides us with (Horkheimer and Adorno, 2002), the general 'herd instinct' that people possess (Fromm, 1950/1978), and some of the problems associated with 'romantic individualistic' conceptions of agency (Hartmann and Honneth, 2006). Within the marketing literature at least, agency is still routinely conferred by CCT scholars on the basis of consumers demonstrating adherence to an 'achievement ideology' (Featherstone, 1983). This ideology undergirds the neoliberal worldview affirmed by Thatcher and Reagan (see Bauman, 2007; Featherstone, 1983; Harvey, 2007; Schor, 2007; cf. Holt, 1997, 1998). Let us just clarify what we mean here.

In reference to the consumption-oriented *weltanschauung* perpetuated by the types of glossy lifestyle magazines that occupy newsagent shelf space, Featherstone writes:

> Today's readers are introduced to an achievement ideology which holds that age-sets and class backgrounds can be transcended and that in cultivating a stylistic presentation of self and distinct lifestyle they can transform goods from mass produced

commodities into expressions of individuality. Within consumer culture individuals are not only cajoled into a mass conformism through fear of difference, but are also offered the promise of an apparently transcending difference, an individuality in which they speak not only through their clothes but through all their commodities: home, car, leisure equipment and body assembled together into an expressive lifestyle. (Featherstone, 1983: 7–8; see also Bauman, 1983: 40; Marcuse, 1964/1972)

Consumers' chronic and sometimes alienating dependence on the products of the modern capitalist market order, even as they produce allegedly individual meanings (cf. Muñiz and O'Guinn, 2001; Muñiz and Schau, 2005; Schouten and McAlexander, 1995) is too often forgotten in much interpretive and CCT work (e.g. Arnould and Thompson, 2005; Giesler, 2008; Üstüner and Holt, 2007); as is the centrality of work and production relations in the constitution and structuring of individual identity (see Rothstein, 2005; Varman and Vikas, 2007a). Clearly, critical thought has much to do with challenging the norms of the day and the order that these norms uphold (Fromm, 1956/2005). It is a matter of recognizing who and which potential institutionalizations are sanctioned by the reigning order (Fırat, 1987). It is about how what is valued in the reigning order benefits some and not others (see Conca, 2001; Fridell et al., 2008; Varman and Vikas, 2007a).

Value has been central to modern economic theory. It is the construct that is afforded the key role in the distribution of resources – resources flow to that which is valued, or to whomever controls and/or possesses that which is valued. What gets valued in society, therefore, is significant in also indicating the heart of a society. It tells us something about ourselves, when many acting in the movie industry earn millions of dollars in income, at the same time as medical practitioners working for Doctors Without Borders, saving many human lives from death, disease and misery, often putting their own lives at risk, earn a pittance in comparison. It also tells us something about ourselves as disciplinary scholars that not many, if any, studies exist as to why such discrepancies in what is valued occur.

SURVEYING THE CRITICAL TERRAIN

The generally accepted history of marketing is one proposed by Bartels (1988). This history recounts a series of 'orientations' (Jones and Shaw, 2005). The managerial orientation (e.g. Alderson, 1957, 1965) that put exchange at the center of activities attributed to marketing, which were then to be orchestrated and organized to facilitate exchanges, is generally deemed to be the maturation of 'modern marketing'. According to the modern marketing orientation, coined as the 'marketing concept', the consumer must be the starting point of marketing thought; and the satisfaction of consumer needs, in an economically efficient fashion, the purpose of marketing activity. The emergence of such a collective consciousness for those involved in marketing practice and scholarship is often believed to have happened after World War II. Although this proposition has been challenged (Fullerton, 1988; Tadajewski, 2009; Tadajewski and Saren, 2009), it still has some influence within the academy, however erroneous.

Beyond the walls of the marketing academy, as part of a wider-ranging critique of the 'veil of illusion' (Fromm, 1962/2006) cast around production and consumption relations, there have been many critical assessments and indictments of marketing regarding its impact on consumers and society. Included among this material are the books *To Have or To Be* (Fromm, 1976/2007), *The Hidden Persuaders* (Packard, 1957, 1960), *Captains of Consciousness* (Ewen, 1974), *The New Industrial State* (Galbraith, 1967) and *The Poor Pay More* (Caplovitz, 1963), among many others. These works awakened a critical consciousness among marketing academics and some practitioners that marketing, as it was currently practiced, may have detrimental effects on some members of society and

on society as a whole. The response from the marketing academy was the articulation of 'correct' marketing approaches, including the market (customer) orientation and the marketing concept.

Several indictments of general orientations in marketing from within the academy appeared in the 1970s and 1980s (e.g. Firat et al., 1987; Monieson, 1988; Moorman, 1987; Spratlen, 1972). At the same time, marketing practices were beginning to be recognized as a major force in modern culture among philosophers and sociologists, resulting in critiques and assessments from diverse positions (Baudrillard, 1988; Featherstone, 1990; Jameson, 1989) (These critiques have been outlined by various scholars, including Firat and Dholakia (2006), Firat and Venkatesh (1995) and Cherrier and Murray (2007)).

A doctoral dissertation completed at Northwestern University in 1976 (Firat, 1978) suggested that modern marketing was plagued by problems inherent to capitalism. The implication was that these problems could not be solved without radical transformations of capitalism. This research was later published as a chapter in an edited book with philosophical and radical contributions from different scholars; some already established at the time, and others who were young scholars with critical orientations (Firat et al., 1987). Before the publication of this book, *Philosophical and Radical Thought in Marketing*, there had been few publications from within the discipline in the critical marketing genre, although four books that did critically examine the social implications of certain marketing practices should be cited (Dholakia and Arndt, 1985; Fisk, 1974; Ingebrigtsen and Pettersson, 1981; Kangun, 1972).

Very broadly speaking, these books (Dholakia and Arndt, 1985; Fisk, 1974; Ingebrigtsen and Pettersson, 1981; Kangun, 1972) were critical of marketing, noting the detrimental effects of marketing practices and to a slightly lesser extent, explicating marketing's role in affirming unequal power relations in society (i.e. with respect to the power and influence of big business versus consumers and nonconsumers alike). Nevertheless Fisk (1974) held out high hopes that marketing tools and techniques would demonstrate their value in encouraging environmentally sustainable behaviour among consumers and corporations alike. Conversely, many chapters in *Philosophical and Radical Thought in Marketing* considered the problems attributed to particular marketing practices to be systemic, and thus that the structure of market and consumption relations required a radical rethinking.

Although the work that appeared in the Fırat et al. (1987) collection is often suggestive of a Critical Theoretic orientation, inasmuch as the work of Critical Theorists is drawn upon (e.g. Kilbourne, 1987), the reader is generally left to infer the paradigmatic affiliation of many of the chapters. A major step in articulating a research agenda that explicitly aligned itself with Critical Theory was, surprisingly, presented in the *Journal of Consumer Research* (*JCR*) in 1991 by Jeff Murray and Julie Ozanne. We say surprisingly here, because even with the slight pluralization of paradigms that are acceptable to mainstream marketing scholars, the *JCR* was still considered a bastion of positivistic theorizing (Hirschman, 1993; Willmott, 1999).

In their paper, Murray and Ozanne provide a historical overview of the development of Critical Theory, and then proceed to outline a methodological strategy which researchers interested in critical perspectives could adopt and adapt for their own studies. In later work, they have subsequently critiqued their method as too much of a 'straitjacket', and sketched out a poststructural critique of their own work (Murray and Ozanne, 2006). However, recalling the comments by Peter and Olson (1983) that marketing researchers have to market their own findings, ideally making these consistent with the assumption base of the likely audience, Murray and Ozanne arguably watered down the critical edge of the work of the Frankfurt School, for which they were criticized (Hetrick and Lozada, 1994). The most salient aspect of their work that would jar with the views put forward by

critical scholars who associate criticality with nonmanagerial performativity (e.g. Tadajewski and Brownlie, 2008), was that Murray and Ozanne discussed the usefulness of Critical Theory for marketing managers (see also Burton, 2002). This is at odds with a strict interpretation of Critical Theory or critical marketing (e.g. Bradshaw and Fırat, 2007), as it appears to encourage the cooptation of Critical Theory by those closely associated with the status quo, namely elements of the business community. In their words, Murray and Ozanne believed that 'Critical theory can be useful to practitioners. Private interest groups could examine their practices to see if they harm or help the public. Harmful practices should be examined and replaced by practices that resolve contradictions between private and public interests' (Murray and Ozanne, 1991: 140).

To many, this perspective seems perfectly reasonable. The problem is that the interest group Murray and Ozanne wish to help are already influential actors when it comes to the means of ideational distribution (cf. Monieson, 1981, 1988). Providing such groups with a further toolbox for their marketing armoury is not commensurate with the radical skepticism that Critical Theory was meant to encourage (Kellner, 2000), nor with overhauling the ordering of society that Fromm (1956/2005) called for. Murray et al. (1994) have produced a response to this criticism, and other scholars have followed them in arguing that critical perspectives in marketing should, for the sake of intellectual purity, refuse to engage with marketing management (Bradshaw and Fırat, 2007).

Since these articles, which appeared in the consumer research literature or in critical, edited texts, rather than in mainstream marketing outlets, thus indicating a resistance to critical thinking in marketing (Svensson, 2005; Tadajewski, 2008a), there has not been a landslide of critically inflected thought turned on to marketing theory or practice (McDonagh, 1995; Murray and Ozanne, 1997; Sherry, 1991). That is, until renewed interest amongst European scholars.

CRITICAL MARKETING STUDIES

Obviously, 'critical marketing studies' (Tadajewski and Brownlie, 2008) – the umbrella label increasingly given to a broad range of critical perspectives in marketing (Tadajewski and Maclaran, 2009a) – is not a unified movement (Bradshaw and Fırat, 2007). If we are permitted to operate at a very high level of generality, we think that many, if not all, critical scholars see themselves as playing some role in developing 'a systematic critique of social conditions that aims to help people envision a better society' (Murray and Ozanne, 1991: 129). Murray and Ozanne label this an 'emancipatory interest', the central imperative here being the reduction of 'constraints on human freedom and potential' (Murray and Ozanne, 1991: 129). One of the earliest critical marketing commentators, Heede (1985: 148), described the values motivating a number of critical scholars, in terms that echo those enunciated by Murray and Ozanne (see also Benton, 1985a; Kilbourne, 1995).

Much as Kuhn (1970) predicted, many of the most radical thinkers in any given discipline tend to be those who do not have a great deal of intellectual currency invested in the existing status quo. As Heede remarked:

[These early critical scholars] took their degrees in marketing, perhaps by happenstance, because they, as outsiders, wanted to study how the modern society was functioning so that they could change it in accordance with the values they were exposed to in their youth. And they ended up as young professors in marketing departments where they discovered that the marketing system was corrupting them. Therefore they want to change the system from inside by creating a new marketing system suitable for the society they want. (Heede, 1985: 148)

The idea that critical marketing studies might be linked with envisioning a better society, as per the Murray and Ozanne citation, raises an interesting question: Can critical marketing be differentiated from macromarketing, that is, from the group of scholars interested in examining the impact of marketing on society and society on marketing (Shapiro, 2006)? Let us briefly consider this issue.

DIFFERENTIATING CRITICAL MARKETING AND MACROMARKETING

According to recent commentary, macromarketing scholars take a more managerial perspective than those working from a critical marketing position, wanting to transform business practice for the better, or at least modify it in the face of social concern and legal criticism (Böhm and Brei, 2008; Dholakia and Sherry, 1987; Venkatesh, 1999). For most macromarketers, the capitalist system and the economic doctrine of neoliberalism are largely accepted as improving the standard of living of most consumers in the world, without much criticism (Kilbourne, 2004; cf. Fraser, 2003; Nederveen Pieterse, 2004). This lack of criticism of the Western Dominant Social Paradigm (DSP) with its attendant 'ideology of consumerism' has led to the emergence of 'critical macromarketing[3]' (Kilbourne et al., 1997). Critical macromarketing attempts to question the DSP assumptions underpinning the marketing system (i.e. a faith in technology to avert environmental destruction, support for liberal democracy, defense of private property ownership, free markets and limited state intervention in marketplace activities etc.) (Kilbourne, 2004; Kilbourne et al., 2002).

Critical marketing studies, much like critical macromarketing and critical management studies more generally, instead adopts a 'deep skepticism regarding the moral defensibility of prevailing conceptions' of marketing and consumption practices (Adler et al., 2008), highlighting how the way we understand marketing is inextricably linked with the development of the capitalist system, in ways which do not benefit all marketplace participants (Böhm and Brei, 2008; Denzin, 2001; Hill and Dhanda, 2004; Migone, 2007; Pfeiffer et al., 2007; Varman and Belk, 2008; Varman and Vikas, 2007a, b; cf. Lyon, 2007).

Critical marketers are not necessarily critical of marketing *in toto*, dismissing all the benefits that marketing can and does offer people in terms of time, place and possession utilities (Benton, 1987); as dismissing the role of marketing in society without actually scrutinizing marketing practice would be decidedly unreflexive (Catterall et al., 1999, 2002). There is much concern with acknowledging the historical relations that have served to define the political–economic system in certain ways, whilst excluding other ways of thinking about economic relations, at the same time as questioning the logic of forever expanding the market and the application of marketing theory into realms previously beyond its reach (Harvey, 2007). Brownlie (2007: 664) provides a particularly good overview of the developing position of critical marketing, when he notes that:

> For as diverse as the discipline of marketing may appear to be, the reality we inhabit and that inhabits us is clearly the product of a particular group's perspective on markets, marketing, economic development and social consumption. 'Critical' scholars argue that the substance of marketing as an academic discipline is merely how those entities look from the standpoint of particular elites: typically racially and economically privileged straight males – frequently profit-motivated businessmen.

In place of uncritically supporting neoliberal principles which hold that 'human well-being can be best advanced by the maximization of entrepreneurial freedoms within an institutional framework characterized by private property rights ... unencumbered markets, and free trade' (Harvey, 2007: 22), critical marketers question the extent to which corporate power should be unfettered. In line with this, they also doubt whether the massive agglomeration of power, by certain privileged groups, is likely to result in social and marketplace justice and environmental sustainability (Arndt, 1985a; McDonagh and Prothero, 1997; Micheletti and Stolle, 2007; Moisander and Pesonen, 2002). Again, this concern for marketplace justice is one that has long been enunciated by marketing scholars,

and thus it could quite easily be argued – *contra* Alvesson and Willmott (1996) – that marketing has actually been critical for quite some time.

BACK TO THE FUTURE

From the very beginning of academic concern for marketing activities, there was not only an interest in describing and therefore legitimating market institutions and the role of the middleman (e.g. Shaw, 1915), issues of distributive justice[4] were also prominent, especially at the University of Wisconsin, courtesy of Henry Charles Taylor and Edward David Jones (Jones, 1994). To be sure, as marketing has developed and progressively been more closely associated with marketing management and corporate objectives, as a result of the American Marketing Association's definitional predilections, we have moved further and further away from a core concern with social justice and ethical issues (Wilkie and Moore, 2006; cf. Abela and Murphy, 2008).

Whilst the diffusion of critical perspectives in marketing – critical in the sense that it invokes some form of radical social theory, whether derived from Critical Theory (Benton, 1985a, 1987), variants of Marxism (e.g. Arvidsson, 2005, 2008), poststructuralism (e.g. Humphreys, 2006; Moisander and Pesonen, 2002), postcolonialism (e.g. Jack, 2008), critical race theory (e.g. Borgerson and Schroeder, 2002), or feminism (e.g. Bristor and Fischer, 1993; Catterall et al., 2000; Desmond, 1997; McDonagh and Prothero, 1997), when examining some aspect of the study or practice of marketing – is thought to be quite a recent phenomenon, its intellectual genealogy is far longer than many assume (Tadajewski and Brownlie, 2008). For example, an interest in applying critical social theory, in much the same way as contemporary critical marketing scholars, can be traced to Paul Lazarsfeld (1941), who used Critical Theory to examine the potential effects of marketing communications on political activism (Lazarsfeld, 1941). Somewhat later in the 1970s, early 1980s, a number of commentators started to situate their work clearly within 'critical marketing' (Hansen, 1981).

As we pointed out in the foregoing section, European scholars have been prominent figures in developing critical marketing theory and practice. This is perhaps a result of the exposure of these scholars to critical social thought as part of the course of doctoral training in European countries, as well as because of the reverence with which critical thought, in all its many varieties, is treated on the continent. As Arndt (1985a, b), Arnould and Thompson (2007) and Murray and Ozanne (1997) have revealed, the American system of doctoral socialization in marketing works against the greater use of critical perspectives (see Scott, 2007), which the European system seems to foster (cf. Schroeder, 2007).

EUROPEAN CRITIQUE

In the late 1970s, European marketing scholars were beginning to publish studies that utilized the ideas of Marx and the culturally inflected, neo-Marxist work of the Critical Theorists. These marketers included Heede (1981, 1985), Hansen (1981) and Johan Arndt (1985a, b), among others. According to Fleming Hansen, this scholarship was a response to neo-Marxist criticism of marketing. Although Hansen does not actually go into any detail regarding the neo-Marxist work he is referring to, he does describe argumentation that bears the hallmarks of Horkheimer's critique of the unequal nature of exchange relationships, as well as Adorno's destabilization of the notion of consumer sovereignty (Adorno, 1989; Horkheimer, 1972; see also Benton, 1987).

Outlining the terrain of critical marketing in Denmark, Hansen described the work of Heede that examined 'the role of marketing from the point of view of a Marxist and

suggests weaknesses in the functioning of the marketing system' (Hansen, 1981: 215); he then turned to that of Ingebrigtsen and Pettersson which critiqued the prevalence of logical empiricism; as well as scholarship produced by Jull-Sørensen that was 'concerned with the problems inherent in applying modern marketing principles in developing societies' (see also Dholakia, 1984; Luthra, 1991), and took the consumer as their primary stakeholder, 'looking upon the consumer with the consumer's interests in mind, rather than serving the interests of the company' (Hansen, 1981: 21). The value of the Hansen paper lies in its detailing work that had not actually been translated into English at that point.

More influential than Hansen in encouraging scholars to broaden their theoretical toolkit was the work of Arndt (1985a, b). Along with Murray and Ozanne (1991), Arndt has probably done more to encourage a critical literacy among marketing and consumer academics, in view of the fact that his call for paradigmatic pluralism was published in the *Journal of Marketing*; a plea that was further developed and widely circulated in the important text, *Changing the Course of Marketing: Alternative Paradigms for Widening Marketing Theory* (Dholakia and Arndt, 1985).

In his *Journal of Marketing* paper, Arndt was critical of the devotion of marketing scholars to logical empiricism, and their intent on producing knowledge that was of direct relevance for one stakeholder group, namely marketing management (cf. Dobscha and Ozanne, 2008). Paradigms, Arndt pointed out, sensitize us to the social environment, encouraging us to focus on some features of the social world, while excluding others (see also Dholakia and Firat, 1980). It was this latter issue that Arndt was concerned about; if paradigms provide only a partial view of the social environment, then it was desirable for marketing scholars to expand the range of paradigms that they used (cf. Alvesson, 1994):

By limiting itself to the empiricist orientation and logical empiricist paradigms ... marketing has remained essentially a one-dimensional science concerned with technology and problem solving. The subjective world and liberating paradigms [interpretive and critical theory paradigms] challenge the assumptions of empiricism by generating metaphors resulting in the asking of quite different research questions. While no paradigm or metaphor is more than a partial and incomplete truth, the *notion* of paradigms should be viewed as an argument for paradigmatic tolerance and pluralism. The yin and yang of progress in marketing include both the logic, rigor and objectivity of logical empiricism and the socio-political paradigms, and the speculations, visions, and consciousness of the subjective world and liberating paradigms (Arndt, 1985a: 21; emphasis in original)

In line with this argument, other scholars have argued that producing knowledge for marketing managers that enables them to better understand, predict and control consumer behaviour means that marketing is a 'controlling science' (Heede, 1985). By using alternative paradigms, especially those from the critical school, the production of knowledge for consumers gains more importance. Marketing scholarship seen through this critical prism thus becomes a means by which the consumer can liberate themselves, adopting a more critical stance with respect to consumption and marketing practices. Marketing can, in other words, be a 'liberating science' (see also Dobscha and Ozanne, 2008; Ozanne and Murray, 1995).

Now, this discussion of liberation has been developed in a number of different directions. Without doubt, notions of criticality and education are at the forefront of much critical discussion in marketing. Benton (1985b) has made a compelling case for marketing education to take a critical turn, by incorporating lectures and seminar discussion that deal with important critiques of marketing theory and practice. He is quick to say that a critical orientation should not necessarily replace the traditional orientation, but be integrated into a balanced marketing curriculum (the types of work that Benton considers important in a critical marketing education includes texts by Galbraith and Packard, among others). He writes:

If the goal of the marketing system is really to satisfy consumer needs and wants, as consumers themselves define and express them, then students must be made critically aware of the larger social forces that direct their lives, including the effects of marketing activities. The role of the marketing educator should be to provide a variety of viewpoints and sources of information. (Benton, 1985a: 56).

Benton's plea for pedagogic pluralism thus mirrors Arndt's (1985a, b) desire for paradigmatic pluralism (see also Olson, 1982). Other scholars have followed up Benton's arguments with their own calls for 'Critical Reflection in the Marketing Curriculum' (Catterall et al., 1999, 2002).

CRITICAL MARKETING EDUCATION AND HUMAN AGENCY

The reason why growing numbers of critical scholars emphasize education, whether in terms of encouraging students to examine key marketing ideas, like the marketing concept or consumer sovereignty from a critical perspective (e.g. Benton, 1987; Dixon, 2008), is that education can quite literally empower those students who live in a cultural context in which the market acts as a powerful socialization agent (Catterall et al., 2002). Critical marketing education can enable them to make more considered decisions, in the face of marketing communications that may fail to provide full and accurate information about the product concerned. Or, at the very least, be lacking in the amount of information that enables consumers to make 'objective' (Jhally et al., 1985; Kline and Leiss, 1978; Leiss et al., 1985) choices about product qualities when they are faced with the multitude of 'me too' competitor products (Heath, 2000; Kline and Leiss, 1978).

It is hoped that those students able to scrutinize marketing activities using the intellectual skills provided by a critical marketing education will be more likely to make ethically and socially responsible decisions, either in their own consumption or in their place of work. Similar beliefs underlie the creation of 'reflexively defiant' consumers (Ozanne and Murray, 1995).

This can only be a good thing. After all, as marketing theorists are well aware, market-place exchanges are often decidedly asymmetrical (Karlinsky, 1987; Hackley, 2002; Ozanne and Murray, 1995; McDonagh, 2002). And even though government and legal protection of consumers has improved, and there are a growing number of organizations who monitor marketing activities, exposing these where the rhetoric and the reality diverge (e.g. *Which?* Magazine, *New Dream*, *Adbusters* and so forth), 'the buyer–seller exchange [still] does not exhibit general symmetry, because sellers have the upper hand; sellers control the information that is exchanged, have resources to empirically test their claims and have access to the mass media to promote their products' (Ozanne and Murray, 1995: 520).

Ozanne and Murray praise the contribution that periodicals like *Consumer Reports* make in terms of informing the consumer, so that discourse about products becomes less unequal – coming closer in some respects to an ideal speech situation in Habermas' terms – so that each person who wants to enter into discourse about a given product, service or company, is free to do so without being structurally constrained. However, they also note that these reports do not 'encourage reflection on the origins of this culture and which groups in society benefit from this system. In other words, from a traditional public policy perspective, the informed consumer is critical within the bounds of the existing society' (Ozanne and Murray, 1995: 521). The critically reflexive consumer, by contrast, engages in what Tadajewski and Brownlie (2008), following Whittle and Spicer (2008) and Fournier and Grey (2000), have referred to as 'ontological denaturalization'. They refuse to take the present organization of the marketing system as natural, seeing it instead as a historical product which could have developed in other ways (see Fromm, 1956/2005). For Ozanne and Murray:

… a more radical notion of the informed consumer would involve consumers forming a different relationship to the marketplace in which they identify

unquestioned assumptions and challenge the status of existing structures as natural. Through reflection, the consumer may choose to defy or resist traditional notions of consumption, become more independent from acquisition and disposition systems, or define their own needs independent from the marketplace. (Ozanne and Murray, 1995: 522)

Here critical scholars optimistically believe that those currently disempowered in the marketplace (e.g. Adkins and Ozanne, 2005; Ozanne et al., 2005) or who are apathetic about changing the structures of marketplace encounters, as a function of the seeming powerlessness of individual consumers in contrast to powerful corporations (Dholakia and Firat, 2006; Fromm, 1942/2002; Horkheimer, 1993), can be encouraged to enter into a dialogue about how the market-place could be organized along different lines (e.g. Goldman, 1987; Harms and Kellner, 1991; Jhally et al., 1985; Kline and Leiss, 1978; cf. Crane and Desmond, 2002). Related to this point is the notion of consumer agency. Critical perspectives in marketing can be differentiated quite markedly from some of the Consumer Culture Theoretic work (Arnould and Thompson, 2005, 2007) which privileges agency to a point that we think is pretty untenable (see Bradshaw and Holbrook, 2008; Varman and Vikas, 2007a, b).

It should be uncontested that not all people will have the opportunity to enter into the types of discussions about the restructuring of the marketplace that critical marketers idealize. Burrell (2001) has noted that dialogue usually favours the powerful. Certainly there are a variety of different groups that exist on 'the margins of society' (Thompson, 1995) that will find access to the means of marketplace dialogue difficult, if not impossible (cf. Nederveen Pieterse, 2004). Alwitt (1995) and Hill and Stamey (1990) mention the poor and homeless respectively, but there are other groups including the 'young, old, and mentally disabled – inhabiting the margins of society [who] seldom have a voice in the dialogues which form marketing strategies and public policies' (Thompson, 1995: 188).

Consumers are, after all, far from able to adopt those subject positions that they deem desirable (cf. Arnould and Thompson, 2005). For instance, there are numerous structures which frame consumer decision-making (see Gould and Gould, 2003; Tadajewski, 2008b; cf. Allen, 2002), and certain groups are structurally restricted in terms of their consumption behaviours (e.g. Varman and Belk, 2008; Varman and Vikas, 2007b). Accepting this, we can say that subject positions are influenced by 'the total configuration of ... the socioeconomic and political structure of ... society' (Fromm, 1950/1978: 52), as well as by biological and cultural factors (Fromm, 1947/2003). As a case in point, Ozanne et al. (2005) and Adkins and Ozanne (2005) have demonstrated how there are certain structural preconditions, which prevent people from adopting a critical stance in relation to their choice behaviour – lack of education and the subsequent literacy problems that result, being a major factor (Adkins and Ozanne, 2005; Ozanne et al., 2005; Wallendorf, 2001). The fact that many university educated consumers easily buy into the culture of consumption further implies that undertaking years of education does not necessarily stimulate critical consciousness; rather certain forms of education are also necessary for critical consciousness to flourish (see also Benton, 1985a, b; Catterall et al., 1999, 2002). The absence of this insight regarding the condition of the consumer is also reflected in the noncritical approaches in marketing and corresponding depictions of consumption in capitalism.

CONNECTING PRODUCTION AND CONSUMPTION

Unpacking the logic of capitalism is, of course, no simple task. With the growth in 'muckracking' scholarship (e.g. Klein, 2000), as well as work produced by critical scholars such as Desmond (1995, 1999) in marketing,

Billig (1999) in psychology, and Hudson and Hudson (2003) in organization studies, it is becoming increasingly obvious how the contemporary capitalist system works to hide unpleasant relations of production from all, apart from those willing to engage in the most aggressive information search. Behind the polished façade of marketing communications and retailing environments like Niketown, are a whole range of production facilities spread throughout the globe that produce prominently marketed products, at low cost, but in conditions for the workers that resemble the satanic mills that Blake remarked upon in the nineteenth century. Knowledge of such production sites would clearly 'shake the sign' (Goldman and Papson, 1996) of even the most influential brand – after all, 'handmade connotes something entirely different when you know a product is made with child labor' (Tadajewski and Saren, 2008).

Notwithstanding the difficulties of obtaining this type of information, in keeping with the ontological denaturalistic posture adopted by critical scholars, they not only desire to question the present organization of society – whether in terms of production or consumption relations – but also to reveal the 'backstage' workings of marketplace institutions, in the first place, because it is ethical to do so (cf. Brewis and Wray-Bliss, 2008), and secondly as it can encourage consumers to critically reflect on their relationship with brands that use suppliers known to be unethical in their dealings with employees or the natural environment. Connecting production and consumption relations in this way can, naturally enough, be viewed as a theoretical project, but it is very much a project with practical implications. Juliet Schor, for example, is well known for her stinging critiques of economic theory and the structuring of consumption, and she often uses critical social theory in her research (e.g. Schor, 2007). In a practice turn, she has recently cofounded *New Dream*, an organization that provides consumers with information about the backstage of contemporary capitalism, with the political aim of helping people consume in a socially responsible fashion.

Where Desmond (1995, 1998) called attention to the impact of production locations being far removed from the consumers' attention, both in spatial and cognitive terms, *New Dream* tries to reconnect the circuits of production and consumption:

In today's global marketplace, we rarely see what is behind the stuff we buy. Where does a particular product come from? What are the working conditions like for the person or people who created it? We'll connect you to better choices and help you find what you are looking for—whether it's environmentally and socially responsible products, a greater understanding of the issues, or a chance to share helpful information with others. (http:// www.newdream.org/cc/index.php)

Schor's practical work thus functions as a good case study of the kind of muckraking orientation that Thompson (2007) highly values. Thompson says that 'By transgressing conventional boundaries between academics and activism, critically minded researchers can facilitate grassroots political action and empower consumer–citizens with realpolitik knowledge for collectively redressing specific failings, excesses, abuses, and exploitations of a given market system' (Thompson, 2007: 123).

Note that the critically minded scholar/ practitioner/activist serves as a facilitator – consumers are given the information that can help them *determine their own course of action*, which they can debate and discuss with other marketplace groups. The neoliberal paternalism and dubious morality of social marketing is thereby avoided (see Dholakia, 1984; Dholakia and Dholakia, 2001; Pfeiffer, 2004; Witkowski, 2005). What we mean here by 'dubious morality' is the extent to which social marketing has been firmly associated with neoliberalism and structural adjustment programmes, which have been criticized for their negative impact on the stakeholders they were supposed to 'help' (e.g. Pfeiffer, 2004). It is also questionable exactly how social marketing represents a more moral approach than traditional marketing

(e.g. Hastings, 2003), when social marketing represents what Bauman calls an 'antidote' product (in Rojek, 2004), that is, the product that cures the problem caused by the same tools it invokes, namely marketing. Consider the recent comments in *Private Eye*, a UK-based satirical weekly:

JUNK food companies love to get their teeth into any campaign that can link them to healthy eating. Thus a consortium of usual suspects (Coca-Cola, Pepsi, Nestlé, Kellogg's, Cadbury's, etc.) announced its £200m contribution to the latest anti-obesity campaign this summer – even before the government got around to launching the scheme. (*Private Eye*, 2008: 9; emphasis in original)

Of course, irrespective of the preceding criticism of social marketing, it is also easy to point to a number of cases where social marketing has actually been effective in encouraging behavioural change (Witkowski, 2005). Furthermore, any criticism of the lack of reflexivity of social marketing should not be taken to imply that critical marketing studies will have little direct influence on the external world, beyond the ivied walls of the academy. Critical marketers do appreciate the fact that after the requisite critical analyzes have been undertaken that 'expeditious interventions by marketers are required' (McDonagh, 2002: 642).

For us, and we think for the mass of critical marketing scholars, an association with critical marketing studies necessarily indicates some commitment to changing marketplace status quo through a whole range of practical interventions; teaching the next generation of socially engaged scholars and practitioners probably being the primary contribution. Beyond teaching commitments, we find the comments of Callon useful in thinking through the performative dimension of critical marketing studies (see also Spicer, Alvesson and Karreman, 2009)[5]:

If you consider that the organization of markets is a growing concern for numerous groups, the next step is to ask: where will I go in order to participate in an experiment about the organization of markets? ... As social sciences are performative activities, you will influence the course of those experiments. For example, you will probably help some actors who are trying to elaborate rules, or you will allow some groups to participate in the discussion of the market. (Callon in Barry and Slater, 2002: 302)

To summarize the intellectual landscape covered so far, critical marketing studies is characterized by a degree of reflexivity that is largely absent in mainstream marketing theory. Studies that have called for marketing to take a critical turn have questioned the existing ontological and epistemological precepts guiding the production of knowledge in marketing (e.g. Arndt, 1985a, b; Heede, 1985; Moorman, 1987; Murray and Ozanne, 1991). Greater reference is made to the profoundly political nature of both the production of marketing knowledge, as well as its practical application (Applbaum, 2000; Svensson, 2007; Tadajewski and Brownlie, 2008). Marketing, on this reading, is not considered to be apolitical or morally neutral (Benton, 1987; Svensson, 2007) but closely related to the promotion of particular economic ideologies that support corporate marketplace freedom from governmental and legal regulation (Harvey, 2007).

Critical marketing also questions the role of the researcher in the production of knowledge about marketing institutions, and demands that they recognize their complicity in perpetuating the status quo and their responsibility for ensuring social change, where change is necessary and desirable, however piecemeal such change may be (Kellner, 1983; Murray and Ozanne, 1991; Schor, 2007). By way of a conclusion, let us now discuss this in more detail.

THOUGHTS FOR THE FUTURE: CRITICAL SKEPTICISM

Claims made by mainstream marketing scholars regarding the concept of marketing and the status of the consumer (as sovereign in the market) generally ring hollow for the general public, the critics of marketing and students of history (Benton, 1987; Dixon, 2008; Schipper, 2002). Often, the claims are in terms of what ought to be (good) marketing, not in terms of the history of modern society. Also, the context of the study of marketing in the marketing literature is generally limited to the set of phenomena and practices that have come to be identified as marketing. Unfortunately, this ahistorical approach tends to take for granted relations and states that appear natural, when in the light of history, consumer sovereignty, for instance, proves to be socially constructed and delimited.

When, for example, marketing research indicates that consumers desire automobiles or cellular phones or television sets, among other products, these desires are considered as the starting point. Indeed, in this case, if marketing organizations do not provide the qualities that the consumers are looking for, despite all their selling and promotion efforts, they will not succeed in the long term. Even if a few times they can seduce (Smith and Higgins, 2000) consumers to try their products, eventually their success will end. This seems logical and finds evidence in practice. As such, the consumer does appear to be sovereign and marketing, if properly exercised is easily, but unreflexively thought to be the practice of 'listening' to consumer desires and providing for them.

The problem with this modern marketing discourse is that the consumers and their desires are decontextualized, as a result giving the impression that the consumer's desires are inherent and original to the consumer – outside of needs that are conceptualized to be 'natural' and shared by all humans, such as needs for nourishment, security, etc. True, lip service is given to the fact that desires are 'influenced' (rather than constructed) by culture, the economy, technology, the social structure and so forth. Even so, once this is acknowledged, it is almost immediately forgotten. It is the consumer who decides, desires, chooses – witness the long-lasting dominance of the cognitive decision school in consumer research, rather than studies that take the social, environmental, political and biological structuring of consumption as their focus.

For insightful analysis, the consumer must be framed within her or his historical–cultural context. Such framing will provide the grounds for understanding what marketing is and the role(s) it plays at different points in history. With such framing, insights can be gained beyond the relatively superficial information that simple context-bound empirical measures can produce. Yet, to have such framing, a critical school of thought is needed. This critical perspective can enlighten us about the connections and interactions of actors and their actions that together constitute what comes to be known as marketing at different moments of human history.

Marketing, as currently conceptualized and defined, is the product of modern capitalism. A critical understanding of the discipline, therefore, as well as of the practices and theories assigned to marketing, require contextualization within the modern capitalist system. Marketing – or Marcology as Levy (1976) recommended calling it – is founded on the existence and workings of *the market*; its name so betrays it.

THE MARKET[6]

The market can, to be sure, be said to be many things (see Gibson-Graham, 1996, 2006). It is a place, a physical site, if we are talking of the flea market in Boone, NC, that takes place on a certain day of the week, or a produce market in Tangiers, or the fish market in San Francisco, CA. In the sense that classical economists envisioned it, as in the case of Adam Smith's 'invisible hand', it is a mechanism whereby exchanges are realized. In marketing textbooks, the market is defined as a set of potential and actual consumer units. In political partitions of the world's regimes, it is usually assigned the role of the foundation of a political system: The free market system, often presented as an idea(l) (Dholakia and Fırat, 2006).

Which of the aforementioned is the market; or is it even something else, or a combination of all? A 'critical marketing' of the future requires an understanding of this foundation on which the discipline is built. It is interesting that the nature or status of the market is always assumed in the marketing literature; a definition is provided as an axiom without much, if any, epistemological inquiry. This is rather surprising given its centrality in contemporary human lives (although see Layton in this volume).

Obviously, markets existed from very early in human history (Braudel, 1995; Polanyi, 1957). Were they, however, what we know as the market today? It is intriguing that local markets and the activities of merchants in these markets can also be considered detrimental to the success of *the market* (Diawara, 1998). The implication is that multiple markets exist (Venkatesh et al., 2006). The Market, with a capital 'M', one generally implied when modern marketing, as well as economics, scholars say 'the market', constitutes a special phenomenon, one whose existence may threaten local markets. *This* Market calls for a rationale that is not present in markets (Ritzer, 1995). To critically understand marketing, we need to articulate what the Market is (see Gibson-Graham, 1996, 2006), and this needs to be done in its historical context, rather than on the basis of assumptions that universalize it (see also Habermas, 1992, 1993).

Adam Smith and other classical modern economists saw the Market as *the* answer to realizing the modernist project. For them, the Market played the key role in the 'free' exchange of things that human beings thought they needed to progress toward affluent lives that emancipated them from those forces, other than their own free wills. Modernity's intent was to enable humans to take control of their own destiny. This was to be achieved through employing scientific knowledge and technologies that would progressively free them from nature's impositions (Angus, 1989). Modernity was also to free humans from oppression by others. They could 'cultivate' their existence as they cultivated land (agriculture), through *culture* – that is, what they created themselves – instead of submit to *nature* – all that human beings encountered as given in/by the universe. Thus, the project of modernity was to build a grand future, an ideal society where all humans would be nurtured as free-willed individuals realizing their utmost potentials (Dholakia and Fırat, 2006).

For this project to be realized, modern human existence had to be organized based on norms that provided the conditions for such progress (Steuerman, 1992). Habermas, building on Weber's ideas (Foster, 1983), articulated the norms of the discursive domains of human existence as science, art and morality. Each domain had to have its own norms to facilitate progress. Contamination of one domain by the norms of other domains would, according to modern thinkers, impede progress; each domain had to preserve its purity (Fırat, 1995).

Culture, that part of human experience humanly created and through which humans acted upon their world, also became separated into its practical domains. These were the political, the social and the economic domains. Similar to the discursive domains, each developed with its norms, but also institutions or media through which these norms could be exercised; these were the domains of practice. The norms of these practical domains are well known: Democracy is the norm of the political, civility is the norm of the social, and efficient allocation of material resources is the norm of the economic. The institutions or media through which these norms are exercised are equally well familiar: The nation-state for the political, the (nuclear) family – reinforced by legal and educational institutions – for the social, and the Market for the economic.

The economic eventually developed a special place among all the practical domains of culture, becoming the locomotive force in modern society. This is understandable. For modern thought, the conditions that mattered in knowing and taking control of human life and its destiny, lay in the material universe; the material world was the domain of the economic. Therefore, the most significant issues that mattered in realizing the modern project were economic matters. Success of the economy is, therefore, considered of paramount importance, and this is evident in the public discourses that dominate contemporary modern politics. Most necessary is that the Market, the institution of the economic, should operate freely and according to its own norm.

The Market, to conclude, is an institution that is geared to allow and foster the norm of the economic to work. We would emphasize that it is not simply a mechanism, which is meant to facilitate the workings of any and all norms, or the aims of any of its participants. As Alwitt (1995) reminds us in no uncertain terms, there are a variety of actors who are effectively excluded from marketplace exchanges. Irrespective of whether the literature on the marketing concept does admit that not all exchanges will be consummated on the basis of the consumer desiring certain products, it is often far easier for scholars to make vague gestures to the marketing concept, consumer sovereignty and agency, without actually devoting much attention to scrutinizing the theories, concepts and values that we thereby reaffirm without a second glance. Perhaps, then, critical marketing studies represents a call for marketing to become more realistic, highlighting where marketing rhetoric is actually incommensurate with marketplace reality.

This requires that we do not valorize consumer agency uncritically, but realize the extent to which all consumer decision-making is structured by capitalistic relations that have endured for a substantial period. As an institution – that is, an organization of patterns of performances (behaviours), relationships and interactions that maintains and reproduces itself consistently (Cronin, 2008) – the Market is inscribed with an ideology, goals and a system of values; it privileges certain means and ends, and categories (social or otherwise), over others (Fromm, 1956/2005, 1962/2006/1998). The most significant contribution of critical marketing must be to decipher this institution (Cronin, 2008), discover its parti-cularities (see Gibson-Graham, 1996, 2006), thus also illuminating the nature of modern marketing, to thereby critically assess and transform it. It is possible to say, therefore, that critical marketing's mission to remove marketing from its critical condition is not yet complete, nor may it ever be (Brownlie, 2006).

NOTES

1 Both authors contributed equally to this chapter. Author names are listed alphabetically.

2 The work of Craig Thompson is somewhat difficult to associate with this comment. Undoubtedly he is often a co-author on key papers that stress consumer agency and the freedom to shift subject positions that we criticise here. Yet, his earlier work, especially that in relation to marketing ethics, betrays a much more critical stance in relation to marketplace agency (e.g. Thompson, 1995). It will be interesting to watch how his position changes from the CCT position piece (Arnould and Thompson, 2005), the greater the influence of Foucault is on his work and the more prominent position he assumes in the academy.

3 Although the number of scholars that have labelled their work as 'critical macromarketing' is comparatively small – Kilbourne et al. (1997) being the major exemplar – this is an area that has the potential to grow further (cf. Shapiro, 2006; Tadajewski and Jones, 2008) given that the editor of the Journal of Macromarketing has publically expressed his interest in publishing research produced by the 'critical school' (Shultz, 2007)

4 The relationship between critical marketing and macromarketing is an area that is being debated further in a variety of publications currently in progress.

5 This 'performative dimension' of critical scholarship is based on the work of Spicer, Alvesson and Karreman (2009). A copy of that paper can be accessed at: http://64.233.183.104/search?q=cache:UP_dhHf1yFcJ:andre.spicer.googlepages.com/cmsre-submitted.doc±performative±critical±management±studies&hl=en&ct=clnk&cd=6&gl=uk.

6 Elements of this section are drawn from Dholakia and Firat (2006).

REFERENCES

Abela, A.V. and Murphy, P.E. (2008) 'Marketing with Integrity: Ethics and the Service-Dominant Logic for Marketing', Journal of the Academy of Marketing Science, 36: 39–53.

Adkins, N.R. and Ozanne, J.L. (2005) 'Critical Consumer Education: Empowering the Low-Literate Consumer', Journal of Macromarketing, 25(2): 153–162.

Adler, P.S., Forbes, L.C. and Willmott, H. (2008) 'Critical Management Studies', Annals of the Academy of Management, 1: 119–179.

Adorno, T.W. (1989) 'The Culture Industry Revisited', in S.E. Bronner and D.M. Kellner (eds) Critical Theory and Society: A Reader, New York: Routledge, pp. 128–135.

Alderson, W. (1957) Marketing Behavior and Executive Action. Homewood: Richard D. Irwin.

Alderson, W. (1965) Dynamic Marketing Behavior: A Functionalist Theory of Marketing. Illinois: Richard D. Irwin.

Allen, D.E. (2002) 'Toward a Theory of Consumer Choice as Sociohistorically Shaped Practical Experience: The Fits-Like-A-Glove Framework', Journal of Consumer Research, 28(March): 515–532.

Alvesson, M. (1994) 'Critical Theory and Consumer Marketing', Scandinavian Journal of Marketing, 10(3): 291–313.

Alvesson, M. and Willmott, H. (1996) Making Sense of Management: A Critical Introduction. London: Sage.

Alwitt, L.F. (1995) 'Marketing and the Poor', American Behavioral Scientist, 38(4): 564–577.

Angus, I. (1989) 'Circumscribing Postmodern Culture', in I. Angus and S. Jhally (eds) Cultural Politics in Contemporary America, New York: Routledge, pp. 96–107.

Applbaum, K. (2000) 'Crossing Borders: Globalization as Myth and Charter in American Transnational Consumer Marketing', American Ethnologist, 27(2): 257–282.

Arndt, J. (1985a) 'On Making Marketing More Scientific: The Role of Orientations, Metaphors and Problem Solving', Journal of Marketing, 49(Summer): 11–23.

Arndt, J. (1985b) 'The Tyranny of Paradigms: The Case for Paradigmatic Pluralism in Marketing', in N. Dholakia and J. Arndt (eds) Changing the Course of Marketing: Alternative Paradigms for Widening Marketing Theory, Greenwich: JAI Press, pp. 3–25.

Arnould, E.J. and Thompson, C.J. (2005) 'Consumer Culture Theory (CCT): Twenty

Years of Research', *Journal of Consumer Research*, 31(March): 868–882.

Arnould, E.J. and Thompson, C.J. (2007) 'Consumer Culture Theory (And We Really Mean Theoretics): Dilemmas and Opportunities Posed By an Academic Branding Strategy', in R. Belk and J. Sherry (eds) *Consumer Culture Theory*, Oxford: Elsevier, pp. 3–22.

Arvidsson, A. (2005) 'Brands: A Critical Perspective', *Journal of Consumer Culture*, 5(2): 235–258.

Arvidsson, A. (2008) 'The Function of Cultural Studies in Marketing: A New Administrative Science?', in M. Tadajewski and D. Brownlie (eds) *Critical Marketing: Issues in Contemporary Marketing*, Chichester: Wiley, pp. 329–344.

Barry, A. and Slater, D. (2002) 'Technology, Politics and the Market: An Interview with Michel Callon', *Economy and Society*, 31(2): 285–306.

Bartels (1988) *The History of Marketing Thought*, third edn. Columbus: Publishing Horizons.

Baudrillard, J. (1988) 'Consumer Society', in M. Poster (ed.) *Jean Baudrillard: Selected Writings*, Cambridge: Polity Press, pp. 29–56.

Bauman, Z. (1983) 'Industrialism, Consumerism and Power', *Theory, Culture and Society*, 1: 32–43.

Bauman, Z. (2007) 'Collateral Casualties of Consumerism', *Journal of Consumer Culture*, 7(1): 25–56.

Benton, R. (1985a) 'Micro Bias and Macro Prejudice in the Teaching of Marketing', *Journal of Macromarketing*, Fall: 43–58.

Benton, R. (1985b) 'Alternative Approaches to Consumer Behavior', in N. Dholakia and J. Arndt (eds) *Changing the Course of Marketing: Alternative Paradigms for Widening Marketing Theory*, Greenwich: JAI Press, pp. 197–218.

Benton, R. (1987) 'The Practical Domain of Marketing: The Notion of a "Free" Enterprise Economy as a Guise for Institutionalised Marketing Power', *American Journal of Economics and Sociology*, 46(4): 415–430.

Billig, M. (1999) 'Commodity Fetishism and Repression: Reflections on Marx, Freud and the Psychology of Consumer Capitalism', *Theory and Psychology*, 9(3): 313–329.

Böhm, S. and Brei, V. (2008) 'Marketing the Hegemony of Development: Of Pulp Fictions and Green Deserts', *Marketing Theory*, 8(4): 339–366.

Borgerson, J.L. and Schroeder, J.E. (2002) 'Ethical Issues of Global Marketing: Avoiding Bad Faith in Visual Representation', *European Journal of Marketing*, 36(5/6): 570–594.

Bouchet, D. (1994) 'Rails Without Ties. The Social Imaginary and Postmodern Culture. Can Postmodern Consumption Replace Modern Questioning', *International Journal of Research in Marketing*, 11: 405–422.

Bradshaw, A. and Fırat, A.F. (2007) 'Rethinking Critical Marketing', in M. Saren, P. Maclaran, C. Goulding, R. Elliott, R.A. Shankar and M. Catterall (eds) *Critical Marketing: Defining the Field*, Amsterdam: Elsevier, pp. 30–40.

Bradshaw, A. and Holbrook, M.B. (2008) 'Must We Have Muzak Wherever We Go? A Critical Consideration of the Consumer Culture', *Consumption, Markets and Culture*, 11(1): 25–43.

Braudel, F. (1995) *A History of Civilizations*. New York: Penguin (trans. by Mayne, R.).

Brewis, J. and Wray-Bliss, E. (2008) 'Re-searching Ethics: Towards a More Reflexive Critical Management Studies', *Organization Studies*, 29(11): 1–20.

Bristor, J.M. and Fischer, E. (1993) 'Feminist Thought: Implications for Consumer Research', *Journal of Consumer Research*, 19(March): 518–536.

Brownlie, D. (2006) 'Emancipation, Epiphany and Resistance: On the Unimagined and Overdetermined in Critical Marketing', *Journal of Marketing Management*, 22: 505–528.

Brownlie, D. (2007) 'Everything and Nothing: Habits of Simulation in Marketing', *Marketing Intelligence and Planning*, 25(7): 662–667.

Brownlie, D., Saren, M., Wensley, R. and Whittington, R. (1999) *Rethinking Marketing: Towards Critical Marketing Accountings*. London: Sage.

Burrell, G. (2001) '*Ephemera*: Critical Dialogues on Organization', *Ephemera: Critical Dialogues on Organization*, 1(1): 11–29.

Burton, D. (2001) 'Critical Marketing Theory: The Blueprint', *European Journal of Marketing*, 35(5/6): 722–743.

Burton, D. (2002) 'Towards a Critical Multicultural Marketing Theory', *Marketing Theory*, 2(2): 207–236.

Caplovitz, D. (1963) *The Poor Pay More: Consumer Practices of Low Income Families.* New York: The Free Press.

Catterall, M., Maclaran, P. and Stevens, L. (1999) 'Critical Marketing in the Classroom: Possibilities and Challenges', *Marketing Intelligence and Planning*, 17(7): 344–353.

Catterall, M., Maclaran, P. and Stevens, L. (eds.) (2000) Marketing and Feminism: Current Issues and Research. London: Routledge.

Catterall, M., Maclaran, P. and Stevens, L. (2002) 'Critical Reflection in the Marketing Curriculum', *Journal of Marketing Education*, 24(3): 184–192.

Cherrier, H. and Murray, J.B. (2007) 'Reflexive Dispossession and the Self: Constructing a Processual Theory of Identity', *Consumption, Markets and Culture*, 10(1): 1–29.

Clarke, N., Barnett, C., Clike, P. and Malpass, A. (2007) 'Globalising the Consumer: Doing Politics in an Ethical Register', *Political Geography*, 26: 231–249.

Conca, K. (2001) 'Consumption and Environment in a Global Economy', *Global Environmental Politics*, 1(3): 53–71.

Crane, A. and Desmond, J. (2002) 'Societal Marketing and Morality', *European Journal of Marketing*, 36(5/6): 548–569.

Cronin, A. (2008) 'Gender in the Making of Commercial Worlds: Creativity, Vitalism and the Practices of Marketing', *Feminist Theory*, 9(3): 293–312.

Denzin, N.K. (2001) 'The Seventh Moment: Qualitative Inquiry and the Practices of a More Radical Consumer Research', *Journal of Consumer Research*, 28(September): 324–330.

Desmond, J. (1995) 'Reclaiming the Subject: Decommodifying Marketing Knowledge?', *Journal of Marketing Management*, 11: 721–746.

Desmond, J. (1997) 'Marketing and the War Machine', *Marketing Intelligence and Planning*, 15(7): 338–351.

Desmond, J. (1998) 'Marketing and Moral Indifference', in M. Parker (ed.) *Ethics & Organizations*, London: Sage, pp. 173–196.

Desmond, J. (1999) 'Marketing Progress into the 21st Century: Hegel Vs Nietzsche?', paper presented at the 1st Critical Management Studies Conference, UMIST, July.

Dholakia, N. and Arndt, J. eds (1985) *Changing the Course of Marketing: Alternative Paradigms for Widening Marketing Theory.* Greenwich: JAI Press.

Dholakia, N. and Fırat, A.F. (1980) 'A Critical View of the Research Enterprise in Marketing', in R.P. Bagozzi, K.L. Bernhardt, P.S. Busch, D.W. Cravens, J.F. Hair and C.A. Scott (eds), *Marketing in the 80's: Changes & Challenges*, Chicago: American Marketing Association, pp. 316–319.

Dholakia, N. and Fırat, A.F. (2006) 'Global Business Beyond Modernity', *Critical Perspectives on International Business*, 2(2): 147–162.

Dholakia, N. and Sherry, J.F. (1987) 'Marketing and Development: A Resynthesis of Knowledge', in J.N. Sheth (ed.) *Research in Marketing*, Volume 9, Greenwich: JAI Press, pp. 119–143.

Dholakia, N., Fırat, A.F. and R.P. Bagozzi (1983) 'The De-Americanization of Marketing Thought: In Search of a Universal Basis', in C.W. Lamb and P.M. Dunne (eds) *Theoretical Developments in Marketing*, Chicago: American Marketing Association, pp. 25–29.

Dholakia, R.R. (1984) 'A Macromarketing Perspective on Social Marketing: The Case of Family Planning in India', *Journal of Macromarketing*, 4(Spring): 53–61.

Dholakia, R.R. and Dholakia, N. (2001) 'Social Marketing and Development', in P.N. Bloom and G.T. Gundlach (eds) *Handbook of Marketing and Society*, Thousand Oaks: Sage, pp. 486–505.

Diawara, M. (1998) 'Toward a Regional Imaginary in Africa', in F. Jameson and M. Miyoshi (eds) *The Cultures of Globalization*, Durham: Duke University Press. pp. 103–124.

Dixon, D. (2008) 'Consumer Sovereignty, Democracy, and the Marketing Concept: A Macromarketing Perspective', in M. Tadajewski and D. Brownlie (eds) *Critical Marketing: Issues in Contemporary Marketing*, Chichester: Wiley, pp. 67–84.

Dobscha, S. and Ozanne, J.L. (2008) 'An Ecofeminist Analysis of Environmentally Sensitive Women Using Qualitative Methodology: The Emancipatory Potential of an Ecological Life', in M. Tadajewski and D. Brownlie (eds) *Critical Marketing: Issues in Contemporary Marketing*, Chichester: Wiley, pp. 271–300.

Ellis, N., Fitchett, J., Higgins, M., Jack, G., Lim, M., Saren, M. and Tadajewski, M. (forthcoming,

2010) *Marketing: A Critical Textbook*. London: Sage.

Ewen, S. (1974) *Captains of Consciousness: Advertising and the Social Roots of the Consumer Culture*. New York: McGraw-Hill.

Featherstone, M. (1983) 'Consumer Culture: An Introduction', *Theory, Culture & Society*, 1(3): 4–9.

Featherstone, M. (1990) *Consumer Culture and Postmodernism*. London: Sage.

Firat, A.F. (1978) *The Social Construction of Consumption Patterns*. Unpublished Ph.D. Thesis. Northwestern University, Evanston, Illinois (IL).

Firat, A.F. (1987) 'The Social Construction of Consumption Patterns: Understanding Macro Consumption Phenomena', in A.F. Firat, N. Dholakia and R.P. Bagozzi (eds) *Philosophical and Radical Thought in Marketing*, Lexington: Lexington Books, pp. 251–267.

Firat, A.F. (1995) 'Consumption Culture or Culture Consumed?' in J.A. Costa and G. Bamossy (eds) *Marketing in a Multicultural World: Ethnicity, Nationalism, and Cultural Identity*, Thousand Oaks: Sage, pp. 105–125.

Firat, A.F. and Dholakia, N. (2006) 'Theoretical and Philosophical Implications of Postmodern Debates: Some Challenges to Modern Marketing', *Marketing Theory*, 6(3): 123–162.

Firat, A.F. and Venkatesh, A. (1995) 'Liberatory Postmodernism and the Reenchantment of Consumption', *Journal of Consumer Research*, 22(December): 239–267.

Firat, A.F., Dholakia, N. and R.P. Bagozzi (eds) (1987) *Philosophical and Radical Thought in Marketing*. Lexington: Lexington Books.

Fisk, G. (1974) *Marketing and the Ecological Crisis*. New York: Harper & Row.

Foster, H. (1983) 'Postmodernism: A Preface', in H. Foster (ed.) *The Anti-Aesthetic: Essays on Postmodern Culture*, Seattle: Bay Press, pp. ix–xvi.

Fournier, V. and Grey, C. (2000) 'At the Critical Moment: Conditions and Prospects for Critical Management Studies', *Human Relations*, 53(1): 7–32.

Fraser, N. (2003) 'From Discipline to Flexibilization? Rereading Foucault in the Shadow of Globalization', *Constellations*, 10(2): 160–171.

Fridell, M., Hudson, I. And Hudson, M. (2008) 'With Friends Like These: The Corporate Response to Fair Trade Coffee', *Review of Radical Political Economics*, 40(1): 8–34.

Fromm, E. (1942/2002) *The Fear of Freedom*. London: Routledge.

Fromm, E. (1947/2003) *Man For Himself: An Inquiry into the Psychology of Ethics*. London: Routledge.

Fromm, E. (1950/1978) *Psychoanalysis and Religion*. New Haven: Yale University Press.

Fromm, E. (1956/2005) *The Sane Society*. London: Routledge.

Fromm, E. (1962/2006) *Beyond the Chains of Illusion: My Encounter with Marx and Freud*. London: Continuum.

Fromm, E. (1976/2007) *To Have or to Be?* New York: Continuum.

Fromm, E. (1998) *On Being Human*. New York: Continuum.

Fullerton, R.A. (1988) 'How Modern is "Modern" Marketing? Marketing's Evolution and the Myth of the "Production" Era', *Journal of Marketing*, 52(1): 108–125.

Galbraith, J.K. (1967) *The New Industrial State*. London: Hamilton.

Gibson-Graham, J.K. (1996) *The End of Capitalism (As We Knew It): A Feminist Critique of Political Economy*. Oxford: Blackwell.

Gibson-Graham, J.K. (2006) *A Postcapitalist Politics*. Minneapolis: University of Minnesota Press.

Giesler, M. (2008) 'Conflict and Compromise: Drama in Marketplace Evolution', *Journal of Consumer Research*, 34(April): 739–753.

Goldman, R. (1987) 'Marketing Fragrances: Advertising and the Production of Commodity Signs', *Theory, Culture and Society*, 4: 691–725.

Goldman, R. and Papson, S. (1996) *Sign Wars: The Cluttered Landscape of Advertising*. London: Guilford Press.

Gould, E. and Gould, N.J. (2003) 'Blowing Smoke-Rings in the Face of Health ... Class Counts', *Consumption, Markets and Culture*, 6(4): 251–273.

Goulding, C. (2003) 'Issues in Representing the Postmodern Consumer', *Qualitative Market Research: An International Journal*, 6(3): 152–159.

Habermas, J. (1992) 'A Generation Apart from Adorno (An Interview)', *Philosophy & Social Criticism*, 18: 119–124.

Habermas, J. (1993) 'Notes on the Developmental History of Horkheimer's Work', *Theory, Culture and Society*, 10: 61–77.

Hackley, C. (2002) 'The Panoptic Role of Advertising Agencies', *Consumption, Markets and Culture*, 5(3): 211–229.

Hackley, C. (2009) *Marketing: A Critical Introduction*. London: Sage.

Hansen, F. (1981) 'Contemporary Research in Marketing in Denmark', *Journal of Marketing*, Summer: 14–21.

Harms, J. and Kellner, D. (1991) 'Critical Theory and Advertising', *Current Perspectives in Social Theory*, 11: 41–67.

Hartmann, M. and Honneth, A. (2006) 'Paradoxes of Capitalism', *Constellations*, 13(1): 41–58.

Harvey, D. (2007) 'Neoliberalism as Creative Destruction', *The Annals of the American Academy of Political and Social Science*, 610(March): 22–44.

Hastings, G. (2003) 'Relational Paradigms in Social Marketing', *Journal of Macromarketing*, 23(1): 6–15.

Heath, J. (2000) 'Ideology, Irrationality and Collectively Self-Defeating Behavior', *Constellations*, 7(3): 363–371.

Heede, S. (1981) 'Marx and Marketing: A Radical Analysis of the Macro Effects of Marketing', in S. Ingebrigtsen (ed.) *Reflections on Danish Theory of Marketing*, Nyt Nordisk Forlag Arnold Busck, pp. 103–110.

Heede, S. (1985) 'The Conflict Between Ideology and Science', in N. Dholakia and J. Arndt (eds) *Changing the Course of Marketing*, Greenwich: JAI Press, pp. 147–158.

Hetrick, W.P. and Lozada, H.R. (1994) 'Constructing the Critical Imagination: Comments and Necessary Diversions', *Journal of Consumer Research*, 21(3): 548–558.

Hill, R.P. and Dhanda, K.K. (2004) 'Confronting the Environmental Consequences of the High Technology Revolution: Beyond the Guise of Recycling', *Organization & Environment*, 17(2): 254–259.

Hill, R.P. and Stamey, M. (1990) 'The Homeless in America: An Examination of Possessions and Consumption Behaviors', *Journal of Consumer Research*, 17(3): 303–321.

Hirschman, E.C. (1993) 'Ideology in Consumer Research, 1980 and 1990: A Marxist and Feminist Critique', *Journal of Consumer Research*, 19(March): 537–555.

Holt, D.B. (1997) 'Poststructuralist Lifestyle Analysis: Conceptualizing the Social Patterning of Consumption in Postmodernity', *Journal of Consumer Research*, 23(March): 326–350.

Holt, D.B. (1998) 'Does Cultural Capital Structure American Consumption?', *Journal of Consumer Research*, 25(June): 1–25.

Horkheimer, M. (1972) *Critical Theory: Selected Essays*, in M.J. Connell et al. New York: Herder and Herder.

Horkheimer, M. (1993) 'Reason Against Itself: Some Remarks on Enlightenment', *Theory, Culture and Society*, 10: 79–88.

Horkheimer, M. and Adorno, T. (2002) *Dialectic of Enlightenment: Philosophical Fragments*, in G.S. Noerr (ed.), E. Jephcott (tr.), Stanford: Stanford University Press.

Hudson, I. and Hudson, M. (2003) 'Removing the Veil? Commodity Fetishism, Fair Trade and the Environment', *Organization and Environment*, 16(4): 413–430.

Humphreys, A. (2006) 'The Consumer as a Foucauldian "Object of Knowledge"', *Social Science Computer Review*, 24: 296–309.

Ingebrigtsen, S. and Pettersson, M. (1981) 'Epistemological Problems in Marketing', in S. Ingebrigtsen (ed.) *Reflections on Danish Theory of Marketing*, Nyt Nordisk Forlag Arnold Busck, pp. 111–133.

Jack, G. (2008) 'Postcolonialism and Marketing', in M. Tadajewski and D. Brownlie (eds) *Critical Marketing: Issues in Contemporary Marketing*, Chichester: Wiley, pp. 345–362.

Jameson, F. (1989) 'Postmodernism and Consumer Society', in H. Foster (ed.) *The Anti-Aesthetic: Essays on Postmodern Culture*, Seattle: Bay Press, pp. 111–125.

Jhally, S., Kline, S. and Leiss, W. (1985) 'Magic in the Marketplace: An Empirical Test for Commodity Fetishism', *Canadian Journal of Political and Social Theory*, 9(3): 1–22.

Jones, D.G.B. (1994) 'Biography and the History of Marketing Thought', in R.A. Fullerton (ed.) *Explorations in the History of Marketing*, Greenwich: JAI Press, pp. 67–85.

Jones, D.G.B. and Shaw, E. (2005) 'A History of Marketing Thought', in B. Weitz and R. Wensley (eds), *Handbook of Marketing*. London: Sage, pp. 39–65.

Joy, A. and Ross, C.A. (1989) 'Marketing and Development in Third World Contexts: An

Evaluation and Future Directions', *Journal of Macromarketing,* Fall: 17–31.

Kangun, N. (1972) 'Introduction', in N. Kangun (ed.) *Society and Marketing: An Unconventional View*, New York: Harper & Row, pp. 2–4.

Karlinsky, M. (1987) 'Changing Asymmetry in Marketing', in A.F. Fırat, N. Dholakia and R.P. Bagozzi (eds) *Philosophical and Radical Thought in Marketing*, Lexington: Lexington Books, pp. 39–55.

Kellner, D. (1983) 'Critical Theory, Commodities and the Consumer Society', *Theory, Culture and Society*, 1(3): 66–83.

Kellner, D. (2000) 'Marcuse and the Quest for Radical Subjectivity', *Social Thought and Research*, 7(2): 1–24.

Kilbourne, W.E. (1987) 'Self-Actualization and the Consumption Process: Can You Get There From Here', in A.F. Fırat, N. Dholakia and R.P. Bagozzi (eds) *Philosophical and Radical Thought in Marketing*, Lexington: Lexington Books, pp. 217–234.

Kilbourne, W.E. (1995) 'Green Marketing: Salvation or Oxymoron?', *Journal of Advertising*, 24(2): 7–19.

Kilbourne, W.E. (2004) 'Globalization and Development: An Expanded Macromarketing View', *Journal of Macromarketing*, 24(2): 122–135.

Kilbourne, W.E., McDonagh, P. and Prothero, A. (1997) 'Sustainable Consumption and the Quality of Life: A Macromarketing Challenge to the Dominant Social Paradigm', *Journal of Macromarketing*, Spring: 4–24.

Kilbourne, W.E., Beckmann, S.C. and Thelen, E. (2002) 'The Role of the Dominant Social Paradigm in Environmental Attitudes: A Multinational Examination', *Journal of Business Research*, 55: 193–204.

Klein, N. (2000) *No Logo*. London: Flamingo.

Kline, S. and Leiss, W. (1978) 'Advertising, Needs and "Commodity Fetishism"', *Canadian Journal of Political and Social Theory*, 2(1): 5–30.

Kuhn, T.S. (1970) *The Structure of Scientific Revolutions*. Chicago: The University of Chicago Press.

Lazarsfeld, P. (1941) 'Remarks on Administrative and Critical Communications Research', *Studies in Philosophy and Social Science*, 9: 2–16.

Leiss, W., Kline, S. and Jhally, S. (1985) 'The Evolution of Cultural Frames for Goods in the Twentieth Century'. See: http://faculty.quinnipiac.edu/charm/CHARM%20proceedings/CHARM%20article%20archive%20pdf%20format/Volume%202%201985/3%20leiss%20kline%20jhally.pdf

Levy, S. (1976) 'Marcology 101, or the Domain of Marketing', in K.L. Bernhardt (ed.) *Marketing: 1776–1976 and Beyond*, Chicago: American Marketing Association, pp. 577–581.

Lippke, R.L. (1991) 'Advertising and the Social Conditions of Autonomy', *Business and Professional Ethics Journal*, 8(4): 35–58.

Luthra, R. (1991) 'Contraceptive Social Marketing in the Third World: A Case of Multiple Transfer', *International Communication Gazette*, 47: 159–176.

Lynd, R.S. (1936) 'Democracy's Third Estate: The Consumer', *Political Science Quarterly*, 51(4): 481–515.

Lyon, S. (2007) 'Fair Trade Coffee and Human Rights in Guatemala', *Journal of Consumer Policy*, 30: 241–261.

Marcuse, H. (1964/1972) *One Dimensional Man*. London: Abacus.

Maxwell, R. (1996) 'Out of Kindness and Into Difference: The Value of Global Market Research', *Media, Culture and Society*, 18: 105–126.

McDonagh, P. (1995) 'Radical Change Through Rigorous Review? A Commentary on the Commodification of Marketing Knowledge', *Journal of Marketing Management*, 11: 675–679.

McDonagh, P. (2002) 'Communicative Campaigns to Effect Anti-slavery and Fair Trade', *European Journal of Marketing*, 36(5/6): 642–666.

McDonagh, P. and Prothero, A. (1997) 'Leap-Frog Marketing: The Contribution of Ecofeminist Thought in the World of Patriarchal Marketing', *Marketing Intelligence and Planning*, 15(7): 361–368.

Micheletti, M. and Stolle, D. (2007) 'Mobilizing Consumers to Take Responsibility for Global Social Justice', *The Annals of the American Academy of Political and Social Science*, 611: 157–175.

Migone, A. (2007) 'Hedonistic Consumerism: Patterns of Consumption in Contemporary

Capitalism', *Review of Radical Political Economics*, 39(2): 173–200.

Moisander, J. and Pesonen, S. (2002) 'Narratives of Sustainable Ways of Living: Constructing the Self and Other as a Green Consumer', *Management Decision*, 40(4): 329–342.

Monieson, D.D. (1981) 'What Constitutes Usable Knowledge in Macromarketing?', *Journal of Macromarketing*, 1(1): 14–22.

Monieson, D.D. (1988) 'Intellectualization in Marketing: A World Disenchanted', *Journal of Macromarketing*, 8(2): 4–10.

Moorman, C. (1987) 'Marketing as Technique: The Influence of Marketing on the Meanings of Consumption', in A.F. Fιrat, N. Dholakia and R.P. Bagozzi (eds) *Philosophical and Radical Thought in Marketing*, Lexington: Lexington Books, pp. 193–215.

Morgan, G. (1992) 'Marketing Discourse and Practice: Toward a Critical Analysis', in M. Alvesson and H. Willmott (eds) *Critical Management Studies*, London: Sage, pp. 136–158.

Morgan, G. (2003) 'Marketing and Critique: Prospects and Problems', in M. Alvesson and H. Willmott (eds) *Studying Management Critically*, London: Sage, pp. 111–131.

Muñiz, A. Jr. and O'Guinn, T.C. (2001) 'Brand Community', *Journal of Consumer Research*, 18(September): 129–144.

Muñiz, A.M. Jr. and Schau, H.J. (2005) 'Religiosity in the Abandoned Apple Newton Brand Community', *Journal of Consumer Research*, 31(March): 737–747.

Murray, J.B. and Ozanne, J.L. (1991) 'The Critical Imagination: Emancipatory Interests in Consumer Research', *Journal of Consumer Research*, 18(September): 129–144.

Murray, J.B. and Ozanne, J.L. (1997) 'A Critical-Emancipatory Sociology of Knowledge: Reflections on the Social Construction of Consumer Research', in R. Belk (ed.) *Research in Consumer Behavior*, Greenwich, JAI Press, pp. 57–92.

Murray, J.B. and Ozanne, J.L. (2006) 'Rethinking the Critical Imagination', in R.W. Belk (ed.) *Handbook of Qualitative Research Methods in Marketing*, Cheltenham: Edward Elgar, pp. 46–55.

Murray, J.B., Ozanne, J.L. and Shapiro, J.M. (1994) 'Revitalizing the Critical Imagination: Unleashing the Crouched Tiger', *Journal*

of Consumer Research, 21(December): 559–565.

Nederveen Pieterse, J. (2004) 'Neoliberal Empire', *Theory, Culture and Society*, 21(3): 119–140.

Olson, J.C. (1982) 'Presidential Address – 1981: Toward a Science of Consumer Behavior', in A. Mitchell (ed.) *Advances in Consumer Research*, 9, Provo, UT: Association for Consumer Research, pp. v–x.

Ozanne, J.L. and Murray, J.B. (1995) 'Uniting Critical Theory and Public Policy to Create the Reflexively Defiant Consumer', *American Behavioral Scientist*, 38(4): 516–525.

Ozanne, J.L., Adkins, N.R. and Sandlin, J.A. (2005) 'Shopping [For] Power: How Adult Learners Negotiate the Marketplace', *Adult Education Quarterly*, 55(4): 251–268.

Packard, V. (1957/1960) *The Hidden Persuaders*. London: Penguin.

Peter, J.P. and Olson, J.C. (1983) 'Is Science Marketing?', *Journal of Marketing*, 47(4): 111–125.

Pfeiffer, J. (2004) 'Condom Social Marketing, Pentecostalism and Structural Adjustment in Mozambique: A Clash of AIDS Prevention Messages', *Medical Anthropology Quarterly*, 18(1): 77–103.

Pfeiffer, J., Gimbel-Sherr, K. and Augusto, O.J. (2007) 'The Holy Spirit in the Household: Pentecostalism, Gender, and Neoliberalism in Mozambique', *American Anthropologist*, 109(4): 688–700.

Polanyi, K. (1957) *The Great Transformation*. Boston: Beacon Press.

Private Eye (2008) UK, P. 9.

Ritzer, G. (1995) *The McDonaldization of Society: An Investigation into the Changing Character of Contemporary Social Life*. Thousand Oaks: Pine Forge Press.

Rojek, C. (2004) 'The Consumerist Syndrome in Contemporary Society: An Interview with Zygmunt Bauman', *Journal of Consumer Culture*, 4(November): 291–312.

Rothstein, F.A. (2005) 'Challenging Consumption Theory: Production and Consumption in Central Mexico', *Critique of Anthropology*, 25(3): 279–306.

Saren, M., Maclaran, P., Goulding, C., Elliott, R., Shankar, A. and Catterall, M. (eds) (2007) *Critical Marketing: Defining the Field*, Amsterdam: Elsevier, pp. xvii–xxiii.

Schipper, F. (2002) 'The Relevance of Horkheimer's View of the Customer', *European Journal of Marketing*, 36(1/2): 23–35.

Schor, J.B. (2007) 'In Defense of Consumer Critique: Revisiting the Consumption Debates of the Twentieth Century', *The Annals of the American Academy of Political and Social Science*, 611: 16–30.

Schouten, J.W. and McAlexander, J.H. (1995) 'Subcultures of Consumption: An Ethnography of the New Bikers', *Journal of Consumer Research*, 22(June): 43–61.

Schroeder, J.E. (2007) 'Critical Marketing: Insights for Informed Research and Teaching', in M. Saren, P. Maclaran, C. Goulding, R. Elliott, A. Shankar and M. Catterall (eds) *Critical Marketing: Defining the Field*, Amsterdam: Elsevier, pp. 18–29.

Scott, L. (2007) 'Critical Research in Marketing: An Armchair Report', in M. Saren, P. Maclaran, C. Goulding, R. Elliott, A. Shankar and M. Catterall (eds) *Critical Marketing: Defining the Field*, Amsterdam: Elsevier, pp. 3–17.

Shapiro, S.J. (2006) 'Macromarketing: Origins, Development, Current Status and Possible Future Development', *European Business Review*, 18(4): 307–321.

Shaw, A.W. (1915) *Some Problems in Market Distribution*. Cambridge: Harvard University Press.

Sherry, J.F. (1991) 'Postmodern Alternatives: The Interpretive Turn in Consumer Research', in T.S. Robertson and H.H. Kassarjian (eds) *Handbook of Consumer Behavior*, Englewood Cliffs: Prentice Hall, pp. 548–591.

Shultz, C.J. (2007) 'The Unquestioned Marketing Life? Let Us Hope Not', *Journal of Macromarketing*, 27(3): 224.

Skålen, P., Fougère, M. and Fellesson, M. (2008) *Marketing Discourse: A Critical Perspective*. London: Routledge.

Sneddon, A. (2001) 'Advertising and Deep Autonomy', *Journal of Business Ethics*, 33: 15–28.

Smith, W. and Higgins, M. (2000) 'Reconsidering the Relationship Analogy', *Journal of Marketing Management*, 16: 81–94.

Spratlen, T.H. (1972) 'The Challenge of a Humanistic Orientation in Marketing', in N. Kangun (ed.) *Society and Marketing: An Unconventional View*, New York: Harper and Row, pp. 403–413.

Spicer, A., Alvesson, M. and Karreman, D. (2009) 'Critical Performativity: The Unfinished Business of Critical Management Studies', *Human Relations* , 62(4): 537–560.

Steuerman, E. (1992) 'Habermas vs Lyotard: Modernity vs Postmodernity?', in A. Benjamin (ed.) *Judging Lyotard*, London: Routledge, pp. 99–118.

Svensson, G. (2005) 'Ethnocentricity in Top Marketing Journals', *Marketing Intelligence and Planning*, 23(5): 422–434.

Svensson, P. (2007) 'Producing Marketing: Towards a Socio-phenomenology of Marketing Work', *Marketing Theory*, 7(3): 271–290.

Tadajewski, M. (2008a) 'Incommensurable Paradigms, Cognitive Bias and the Politics of Marketing Theory', *Marketing Theory*, 8(3): 273–297.

Tadajewski, M. (2008b) 'Final Thoughts on Amnesia', *Marketing Theory*, 8(4): 465–484.

Tadajewski, M. (2009) 'Eventalizing the Marketing Concept', *Journal of Marketing Management*, 25(1–2): 191–217.

Tadajewski, M. and Brownlie, D. (2008) 'Critical Marketing: A Limit Attitude', in M. Tadajewski and D. Brownlie (eds) *Critical Marketing: Issues in Contemporary Marketing*, Chichester: Wiley, pp. 1–29.

Tadajewski, M. and Jones, D.G.B. (2008) 'The History of Marketing Thought: Introduction and Overview', in M. Tadajewski and D.G.B. Jones (eds.) (2008) *The History of Marketing Thought*, Volume I, London: Sage, pp. xviii–xlii.

Tadajewski, M. and Maclaran, P. (2009a) 'Critical Marketing Studies: Introduction and Overview', in M. Tadajewski and P. Maclaran (eds) *Critical Marketing Studies*, Volume I. London: Sage.

Tadajewski, M. and Maclaran, P. (eds) (2009b) *Critical Marketing Studies*. Volume I. London: Sage.

Tadajewski, M. and Maclaran, P. (eds) (2009c) *Critical Marketing Studies*. Volume II. London: Sage.

Tadajewski, M. and Maclaran, P. (eds) (2009d) *Critical Marketing Studies*. Volume III. London: Sage.

Tadajewski, M. and Saren, M. (2009) 'Rethinking the Emergence of Relationship Marketing', *Journal of Macromarketing*, 29(2): 193–220.

Thompson, C.J. (1995) 'A Contextualist Proposal for the Conceptualization and Study of Marketing Ethics', *Journal of Public Policy and Marketing*, 14(2): 177–191.

Thompson, C.J. (2007) 'A Carnivalesque Approach to the Politics of Consumption (or) Grotesque Realism and the Analytics of the Excretory Economy', *The Annals of the American Academy of Political and Social Science*, 611: 112–125.

Üstüner, T. and Holt, D.B. (2007) 'Dominated Consumer Acculturation: The Social Construction of Poor Migrant Women's Consumer Identity Projects in a Turkish Squatter', *Journal of Consumer Research*, 34(June): 41–56.

Varman, R. and Belk, R. (2008) 'Weaving a Web: Subaltern Consumers, Rising Consumer Culture, and Television', *Marketing Theory*, 8(3): 227–252.

Varman, R. and Kappiarath, G. (2008) 'The Political Economy of Markets and Development: A Case Study of Health Care Consumption in the State of Kerala, India', *Critical Sociology*, 34(1): 81–98.

Varman, R. and Vikas, R.M. (2007a) 'Rising Markets and Failing Health: An Inquiry into Subaltern Health Care Consumption Under Neoliberalism', *Journal of Macromarketing*, 162–172.

Varman, R. and Vikas, R.M. (2007b) 'Freedom and Consumption: Toward Conceptualizing Systemic Constraints for Subaltern Consumers in a Capitalist Society', *Consumption, Markets and Culture*, 10(2): 117–131.

Venkatesh, A. (1999) 'Postmodern Perspectives for Macromarketing: An Inquiry into the Global Information and Sign Economy', *Journal of Macromarketing*, 19(2): 153–169.

Venkatesh, A., Penaloza L. and Firat, A.F. (2006) 'Market as a Sign System and the Logic of the Market', in R.F. Lusch and S.L. Vargo (eds) *The Service Dominant Logic of Marketing: Dialog, Debate and Directions*, Armonk M.E. Sharpe, pp. 251–265.

Vikas, R.M. and Varman, R. (2007) 'Erasing Futures: Ethics of Marketing an Intoxicant to Homeless Children', *Consumption, Markets and Culture*, 10(2): 189–202.

Wallendorf, M. (2001) 'Literally Literacy', *Journal of Consumer Research*, 27(March): 505–511.

Whittle, A. and Spicer, A. (2008) 'Is Actor Network Theory Critique?', *Organization Studies*, 29(4): 611–629.

Wilkie, W.L. and Moore, E.S. (2006) 'Macromarketing as a Pillar of Marketing Thought', *Journal of Macromarketing*, 26(2): 224–232.

Willmott, H. (1999) 'On the Idolization of Markets and the Denigration of Marketers: Some Critical Reflections on a Professional Paradox', in D. Brownlie, M. Saren, R. Wensley and R. Whittington (eds) *Rethinking Marketing: Towards Critical Marketing Accountings*, London: Sage, pp. 205–222.

Witkowski, T. (2005) 'Sources of Immoderation and Proportion in Marketing Thought', *Marketing Theory*, 5(2): 221–231.

9

The Marketing Theory or Theories into Marketing? Plurality of Research Traditions and Paradigms

Kristian Möller, Jaqueline Pels,
and Michael Saren

INTRODUCTION

The evolution of theory is essential for any discipline. This assertion is taken for granted in sciences, but has to be re-emphasized in such an applied social study like marketing where the serious discussion of its scientific nature began to appear in late 1940s (Alderson and Cox, 1948; Bartels, 1951; Converse, 1945). It is also noteworthy that, just two decades ago, prominent scholars debated whether marketing is indeed an 'art or science' (e.g. Sheth et al., 1988). An essential aspect in developing marketing theory is the understanding of our current knowledge base, its relative strengths and weaknesses, and potential white spots. Providing this fundamental knowledge is the objective of this chapter. Given the adoption of multiple paradigmatic positions and the diverse definitions of the

domain of enquiry, this is not straightforward. Marketing seems to have diverse meanings for different researchers.

From a fairly monolithic theoretical position in the 1960s, we have travelled to a world of differentiated and specialized research scenes, involving metatheoretically disparate research traditions. From an initial functional view of marketing, our focus has extended in various directions including the aspects of services marketing, political dimensions of channel management, interaction in business networks, relationship marketing and a service-logic informed theory development. As marketing academics, we should not mind this; the current flux is an indication of the progress of the discipline. Without proper understanding of the various approaches, it is, however, difficult to navigate among the various schools of thought. This point has been emphasized by Burton (2005), who in her 'Marketing Theory Matters' article pointed out the relative lack of researchers interested in theory. We pursue this aim through a comparison of the major theoretical schools in marketing.

The disciplinary diversification of marketing thought has aroused opposing responses. Various authors have raised their voice and argued for a general or universal theory in marketing (e.g. Grönroos, 1994), and some have attempted to develop such a theory (e.g. Bagozzi, 1975; Gummesson, 1999; Hunt, 2002; Vargo and Lusch, 2006). These efforts, however, always seem to fall short (Möller and Halinen, 2000; Prendergast and Berthon, 2000; Woodal, 2007), and some scholars argue that we should actually appreciate the position that marketing, as a complex and layered social domain, cannot be described nor understood by any one research tradition or paradigmatic approach (Anderson, 1986; Arndt, 1985; Brodie et al., 1997; Burton, 2005; Dholakia and Arndt, 1985; Möller, 2007).

In this chapter, we develop this view. Drawing on Scherer (1998), we distinguish between 'pluralism of paradigms' and 'pluralism of theories' and advise marketing scholars to adopt both theoretical and paradigmatic pluralism. It is suggested that each research tradition can only provide a particular and partial view of its focal phenomena, dependent on its ontological and epistemological assumptions as well as the issues it has chosen to take to the foreground, i.e. its intellectual goals (Morgan, 1986). As research traditions, often also called 'schools', play a central role in our examination of the theory development in marketing, it is useful to understand their properties.

Sheth et al. (1988: 19) state that

a school of thought must: (1) have a distinct focus relevant to marketing goals and objectives, specifying *who* will or should benefit from marketing activities and practice, (2) it must also have a perspective on *why* marketing activities are carried out or should be carried out by the stakeholders, finally (3) a school of thought should be associated with a significant number of scholars who have contributed toward the thought process (italics in original).

Research traditions (RTs) offer, not only well-articulated packages of conceptualized marketing knowledge, but programmatic ways of carrying out research within marketing (Arndt, 1985). RTs also contain risks. They are only partial descriptions of the domains of marketing phenomena they address, and the descriptions and suggestions they provide are dependent on their underlying philosophical assumptions. By embracing one marketing tradition, a researcher is framing the marketing phenomena in a way guided by the RT. That is, one is mentally a 'prisoner' of the tradition – i.e. its choice of domain/paradigm. Thus, in order to utilize different traditions efficiently or to challenge them, it is essential to understand their theoretical positions and core philosophical assumptions. We aim to do this through a so-called metatheoretical analysis of the principal marketing research traditions.

Metatheoretical analysis involves describing for each RT its philosophical positions (i.e. the ontological, epistemological and methodological assumptions) as well as its domain (i.e. the core phenomena, the intellectual goals and key research questions). This enables a researcher to rise above the traditions and have a vantage point of a metatheoretical plane. From this position, it is possible to gain and compare the knowledge created by different research traditions, their benefits and limitations, and to understand the position of each tradition in the theoretical map of marketing, as well as to understand how they can potentially be linked. Similarly, addressing a topic from multiple paradigms will often result not just in a more holistic picture but may even change the way in which the subject is viewed and asking quite different research questions.

The chapter is organized as follows. In the next section, we first explain the principles of metatheoretical analysis and how we selected the marketing research traditions to examine.

Next, the chosen traditions are analyzed and their underlying philosophical assumptions, goals and focal marketing phenomena covered are compared and discussed. We contend that none of the RTs individually can cover such a complex and multilayered field as that of the marketing discipline. This position leads us to recommend a multiple theories and multiple paradigms perspective. In the subsequent section, we explore the philosophical issues underlying the plural paradigms view and discuss how the so-called problem of paradigmatic incommensurability can be overcome by using a meta-paradigmatic approach. We conclude with suggestions for the future development of marketing theory.

PLURALISM OF RESEARCH TRADITIONS

Two closely related approaches are generally used in the meta-analysis of research traditions. One tries to derive a restricted number of highly abstract metatheoretical dimensions and employ these to develop a typology of relevant approaches. The other approach defines a set of descriptive criteria and evaluates existing approaches according to these criteria. The former 'typology' approach, exemplified by the work of Burrell and Morgan (1979) and Arndt (1985), is very powerful but necessarily highly abstract. The alternative 'profile' method (e.g. Anderson, 1986; Möller, 1994; Möller and Halinen, 2000) provides a more detailed description but not such an elegant positioning. The profile approach is chosen here, because many of the research traditions in marketing are not monolithic, but include constructs and ideas from more than one disciplinary approach. This requires an in-depth comparison.

On the basis of our investigation of several theoretical comparisons of research traditions and practices within marketing and management (Anderson, 1986; Arndt, 1985; Brodie et al., 1997; Burrell and Morgan,

1979; Burton, 2001; Coviello et al., 1997; Easton, 1995; Easton and Håkansson, 1996; Eiriz and Wilson, 2006; Gioia and Pitre, 1990; Mattsson, 1997; Möller, 1994, 2007; Möller and Halinen, 2000; Pels et al., 2009; Vargo and Lusch, 2004; Walker et al., 1987; Wensley, 1995), we suggest that attention be paid to the following issues when research traditions are compared:

- The basic goals of the tradition, the core marketing phenomena it addresses, what questions it is asking and what it tries to achieve.
  - The disciplinary background and driving forces; i.e. whether the tradition is primarily linked to some theoretical disciplines that provide its focus, or if it is driven by social/managerial questions.
  - The key concepts used in describing the core phenomena.
  - Level of focus, unit of analysis and contextuality; e.g. whether the tradition focuses on personal or organizational behaviour, and if it includes their context.
  - Time orientation and the focus on structure versus process, or both.
- Worldview; what the ontological basis is, or in other words, the assumptions about the nature of marketing phenomena.
  - Explanatory mechanism and methodological orientation; i.e. the kind of mechanism(s) through which tradition aims to produce new knowledge; whether one can recognize a primary mode of empirical analysis within tradition; and what its benefits and limitations are.

A second issue in the meta-analysis is selecting the research traditions to be profiled. In order to understand the present theoretical situation in marketing, one has to examine the developments in the discipline since the 1960s. The 1960s provide a natural starting phase, because during that decade the marriage between the marketing concept (firms exist to satisfy customer wants at a profit – Kotler, 1967) and the perspective of achieving this goal through management of the 'mix' of competitive marketing parameters, the '4 Ps', crystallized into a paradigmatic research approach, which has since influenced the majority of marketing research.

Based on our reading of the extant studies listed in the preceding paragraph, the following traditions are included:

1 Marketing management
2 Services marketing
3 Marketing channels studies
4 Interaction and network approach
5 Relationship marketing
6 Market orientation studies
7 Service-dominant logic approach

To make the analysis of these complex traditions feasible, several limitations must be accepted. Firstly, it is important to recognize that our discussions concerning marketing traditions do not tend to fit very neatly into the themes and categorizations based on more conventional subfields of marketing such as B2B, social marketing, consumer behaviour, not-for-profit and so forth. Talking and writing about marketing in terms of conventional practice-oriented categories for the organization of the study of marketing phenomena limit the possibilities and range of theoretical analysis. To paraphrase Foucault, categories create outcomes. Thus, the conventional managerial functionalist subgroupings are inappropriate as a basic structure for theory; instead, they should be a part of what is subjected to theoretical analysis.

Secondly, the reductionism inherent in the conventional marketing subcategories tends to obscure important overriding and holistic marketing phenomena, which are relevant to but not wholly revealed within partial subareas that are important at the level of theory. These phenomena include general underlying mechanisms, structures and relations as well as more general concepts such as identity, culture and knowledge.

Thirdly, as can be seen from the list, we focus on research adopting the perspective of the firm and its marketing stance and organization. This means excluding consumer behaviour, the theoretical aspects of which are dealt with in some depth elsewhere in this book, and the societal aspects of marketing, comprising the macromarketing studies. This omission is

not meant to represent any value judgement; it is a choice made out of necessity.

Fourth, in order to keep the treatment of the traditions manageable, a high abstraction level in profiling leading to gross simplifications is necessary. This may imply unjustified suggestions, but details must be forsaken for gaining comparative clarity between the research schools; and, finally, this kind of analysis is always interpretative and must be regarded with care. Other researchers making different choices would write another story or paint a different portrait about marketing. Two obvious examples are the paradigmatic view on marketing suggested by Arndt (1985) and the book about theoretical schools within marketing discipline by Sheth et al. (1988).

Marketing research traditions: A contested field

Each of the selected major marketing traditions is briefly assessed by examining the cognitive goals, theoretical driving forces, underlying assumptions, and insights provided for the marketing domain. The aim is not to make judgment on which research approach is better, but rather to develop an understanding of their relative descriptive and explanatory strengths and limitations, as well as on the assumptions on which they are based.

Marketing Management School

The Marketing Management School (MMS) has been seen to form a marriage between the marketing concept (firms exist to satisfy customer wants at a profit) and the perspective of achieving this goal through management of the 'mix' of competitive marketing parameters, the '4 Ps'. During the late 1960s and 70s, the MMS crystallized into a paradigmatic research approach which has been seen to be dominating the majority of research into marketing until the 1990s (Sheth et al., 1988; Vargo and Lusch, 2004). The MMS serves as a good reference point as many of the later approaches have positioned themselves by specifying how they are addressing various limitations and flaws they perceive in the MMS. The MMS can be characterized as trying to solve the following normative problem: how to develop an optimal marketing mix consisting of the Product, Place, Price and Promotion solutions for competing for the preferences of a chosen target segment of consumers, households or organizational buyers. This basic issue involves several subproblems: being able to understand and analyze buyer preferences, choosing the target market, differentiating and positioning the product in relation to the competing product alternatives and estimating the market response. Evolving segmentation and positioning theories and techniques relied on the development of a deeper understanding of consumers' brand choice behaviour. Kotler's (1967) classic textbook on marketing management can be used *ahead* as an exemplar of this school of thought. *of the* *thices*

The MMS and marketing mix approach is primarily rooted in the monopolistic theory of competition, suggesting that both consumer demand and marketers' offerings are essentially heterogeneous, and that competition involves differentiating your offering from that of the competitors using consumers' perceptions and preferences as guiding heuristics (Chamberlin, 1965, first published 1933; Dickson and Ginter, 1987; Dorfman and Steiner, 1954; Kotler, 1967, 1972). In essence, the MMS is a normative theory of the development of optimal marketing management solutions. In solving its key questions (optimal mix, segmentation solution and offering positioning), it relies, besides marginal utility theory, on being informed about customer preferences and responses (through consumer behaviour research and organizational buying behaviour research). Another key assumption of the MMS is working markets with primarily independent, i.e. atomistic, buyers and sellers.

Attention has been drawn to the limitations of MMS (Constantinides, 2006). By assuming primarily independent exchanges between marketers and their customers, the MMS is silent about the buyer–seller interaction and relationships. This is clearly a major limitation.

It does not imply, however, that the approach suggests or supports 'one shot' transactional marketing activities as many of the critics of the MMS approach postulate (Grönroos, 1994). On the contrary, creating customer satisfaction and loyalty through repeated purchasing and consumption experiences was recognized relatively early as one of the key goals of marketing and modelled through learning effects in the so-called brand choice/brand loyalty models (Bass et al., 1961; Kotler, 1972). From this perspective, the so-called 'transactional marketing' and 'product orientation' are largely rhetorical labels invented in the 'paradigm battle' of the 1990s.

The MMS is also silent about the organization of marketing activities. It does not contain any theory-based advice for organizing marketing activities. This limitation concerns, unfortunately, most theory development within marketing. A third major limitation of the MMS is its treatment of strategic issues. Although it covers well the product/brand and segment-level issues (Dickson and Ginter, 1987), it is relatively silent about such questions as: In which fields and specific markets should the firm be? How should the firm compete in these markets? These questions concern, however, corporate and strategy and were never the primary focus of the developers of the MMS approach.

Services marketing school

By the late 1970s, the Marketing Management tradition was beginning to be questioned by researchers interested in services. Their main concern was that the MMS did not provide conceptualizations for describing and managing the service provider–customer relationship. Consumers' quality experiences and subsequent satisfaction towards the service were argued to be an outcome of an interaction relationship between the personnel and the customer, augmented by the traditional marketing communications, institutional image and service delivery technology. The development and maintenance of enduring relationships is emphasized (e.g. Berry and Parasuraman, 1993; Grönroos, 1990; Zeithaml and Bittner, 1996).

Besides the joint production roles and enduring relationships, the Services Marketing School (SMS) stresses the organizational aspects in the successful marketing of services. The whole organization should be targeted and culturally fine-tuned for the service of target customers. This notion was captured via the internal marketing concept, which was suggested for achieving the organizational awareness and skills (Grönroos, 1981). Another prominent construct was the service quality and its operationalization with the ultimate goal of a better management of customer satisfaction (Parasuraman et al., 1985; Zeithaml et al., 1988). This is related to the modelling of the service encounter and factors influencing its success (Norman, 1984).

An early problem with the services research was its relative theoretical shallowness; especially the issues concerning organizing have remained underdeveloped. Much of the services marketing research is driven primarily by empirical issues. Inductive orientation is especially strong among the Nordic researchers. Instead of developing in-depth theory-based understanding, service research seems to aim at broad, managerially oriented frameworks. A stronger theoretical base has been constructed for the customer service expectations and behaviour by drawing from the psychological and social psychological foundations in consumer behaviour. Concerning the service production and interface organizing, the school brought forward relevant issues, but lacking relations to organizational theory, has not developed them up to the potential that they merit. Another noteworthy aspect is the silence concerning the context or environment of service relationships and encounters. The School seems to implicitly assume a market context with multiple customers and service providers.

Channels Research Tradition

In the late 1970s, researchers interested in industrial marketing and marketing channels started to develop frameworks and theories focusing on relationships between business marketers and channel members. Research in the Channels Research Tradition (CRT) examines how actors in a marketing channel behave, and how and why various forms of channels evolve. The basic normative goal is defining efficient relational forms between channel members.

The tradition attempts to combine the economic and behavioural aspects influencing channels relationships (Stern and Reve, 1980). The economic perspective is strongly influenced by the transaction costs economics, which tries to define the efficient governance structure in dyadic exchange relationships by using a set of transaction and market properties (Rindfleisch and Heide, 1997; Williamson, 1985). Its core concepts include asset specificity, uncertainty and the frequency of transaction; under specific combinations of these contingency factors, matching governance structures are postulated.

The behavioural perspective draws from social-exchange theory and organizational sociology and employs political–economy concepts like power and dependency, and social aspects – expectations, cooperation, trust, commitment, communication and conflict behaviour – in analyzing channels relationships (Anderson and Narus, 1990; Dwyer et al., 1987; Emerson, 1962; Frazier, 1983; Gaski, 1984; Heide, 1994).

An essential aspect in the Channels research is its strong programmatic and systemic nature. The inherent dualism – polity and economy – and the contextuality are the dominant features. Driven by the political–economy framework (Stern and Reve, 1980) and utilizing a rich multidisciplinary base, the tradition offers three essential points: (1) both economic and political aspects and their interactions must be considered in examining channel behaviour, (2) a focal channel and a dyadic relationship form the recommended unit(s) of analysis and (3) complex relationships cannot be understood outside of their context or environment, as the 'dyadic behaviour' and 'channel' are reciprocally interrelated (Heide, 1994; Möller, 1994; Möller and Halinen, 2000; Rindfleisch and Heide, 1997; Wathne and Heide, 2004). Key results of the

CRT cluster around the influence of opportunism, trust and commitment, on relationship continuity and performance and on the linkages between the context of the dyad and the relational behaviour in the dyad.

One should note, however, that the channel context/environment–dyadic behaviour linkage, modelled through the political–economy framework, have received relatively little empirical attention (see, however, Wathne and Heide, 2004). Another limitation is the limited empirical research on the development processes of channel relationships and channel structures.

Interaction and network approach

The Interaction and Network Approach is mainly associated with the work centred on the Industrial Marketing and Purchasing (IMP) Group (Anderson et al., 1994; Axelsson and Easton, 1992; Ford, 1990; Håkansson and Snehota, 1995; Möller and Halinen, 1999; Möller and Wilson, 1995). Its birth can be traced to late 1970s and early 1980s when a number of European scholars started to develop a theory of supplier–customer relationships based on extensive multi-country case study (Håkansson, 1982). Relationships were seen essentially as interactive and dynamic. During the 1980s, the emphasis was on understanding how relationships are created and managed. Both parties were seen as active, and the key constructs in describing relationships included interaction processes, adaptation and investments in relationships, actor bonds, resource ties, activity chains, relationship outcomes and phases of relationships see (Ford, 1990, 1997, 2002 for compilations of the IMP research).

The Interaction Approach is influenced by early channels research, resource dependency theory and social exchange theory. As the Channels School, it utilizes economic aspects – the investments into relationships – and behavioural aspects – expectations, relationship atmosphere, mutuality – in analyzing relationships. There is, however, a clear difference in how the Interaction Approach emphasizes the processual character of relationships

and describes these through resource and social exchange processes and adaptations. This dynamic perspective is empirically enabled through case studies, whereas the Channels research is dominated by structural equation modelling.

Since 1990s, the primary focus of the approach has been on understanding business networks and organizational action in network context. This development was led especially by Håkansson (1987, 1989) and Ford (1990); see also Axelsson and Easton (1992); and manifested in the Actors–Resources–Activities (ARA) framework (Håkansson and Snehota, 1995). Three levels of analysis and related goals can be discerned in the IMP-driven network research.

At the microlevel, the question is how individual organizations act in a network context, and how they develop, maintain and dissolute network positions and roles. Relationships have a key role in this research. Relationships exist between different types of actors and are seen as vehicles for accessing and controlling resources and creating new resources in the relationships. A key issue is understanding the kind of capabilities or competences through which organizations and personal actors try to achieve their goals in the relationships and through relationships. This perspective relates the network view to the resource-based theory of the firm and offers a new viewpoint to the strategic thought (Håkansson and Ford, 2002; Mattsson, 1985; Möller and Törrönen, 2003).

The meso-level addresses the issue of how focal networks, also called value nets or strategic nets, evolve and to what extent, and how these structures can be intentionally created and managed (Alajoutsijärvi et al., 1999; Möller and Halinen, 1999). Applications of this view involve analysis of the technological development (Håkansson and Waluszewski, 2002), the nature of the internationalization of firms and international cooperative relationships (Johansson and Mattsson, 1988; Håkansson and Johansson, 1988). Important issues include the goals and structures of specific focal networks (e.g. supply nets, competitive coalitions and R&D and innovation networks) and their governance (Jarillo, 1988; de Man, 2004).

Finally, the macro-level research addresses the questions of how extensive network structures evolve, and what factors influence these dynamics. This view, sometimes called the 'markets as networks' challenges the Industrial Organization view of markets (Porter, 1980). It contends that markets – or industries or clusters – are constructed by complex and interdependent interorganizational relationships not by independent actors (Håkansson and Snehota, 1995; Thompson et al., 1994). The macro network perspective has primarily been employed in examining how technological networks evolve (Håkansson, 1987; Lundgren, 1995; Möller and Svahn, 2009; Powell et al., 1996).

From the point of theoretical assumptions, the Network Approach contains several departures from the mainstream marketing studies. Both relationships and networks form the unit of analysis, and the focus is on both their structures and dynamics. More importantly, the worldview of network studies emphasizes contextuality and time. That is, singular events or relationships cannot be understood without knowledge of their context and evolution. This adoption of historical perspective is related to the primary use of qualitative case analysis. Moreover, the environment is not regarded as transparent, actors are seen to perceive its structure and meanings and learn about them through enactment (Weick, 1985).

The historical explanation view has important consequences for the normative and managerial applications of the network approach. It can only provide relatively broad guidelines of how to manage in a network environment in general. More specific normative suggestions require the historical understanding of the particular network situation and always remain context dependent. This view is being challenged by the more recent 'strategic net(work)' approach, which is interested in networks as quasi-organizations and especially in the management mechanism of different types of strategic nets (Möller and Rajala, 2007; Möller and Svahn, 2006). These researchers generally adopt a more reductionist ontological view of networks and apply contingency-thinking-based frameworks.

Relationship Marketing

The evolution of Relationship Marketing (RM) can be traced to the early 1990s when a number of researchers and marketing consultants began to criticize the Marketing Management tradition as being dominated by product-orientation, not customer orientation, and having a transactional, not relational, view of marketing exchange (Grönroos, 1994).

The key aspect of Relationship Marketing (RM) is the focus on marketer–supplier relationships and the dynamics of these relationships. Both the seller and customer can be active, which is the key to understanding their behaviours and relationship dynamics. The key question is how to manage these relationships. The approach is influenced by services marketing, the interaction approach in business marketing, channels research and the ideas of database and direct marketing (Eiriz and Wilson, 2006; Möller and Halinen, 2000, Pels, 1999; Sheth and Parvatiyar, 2000). In addition, Sheth and Parvatiyar (1995) included aspects of consumer behaviour research as the roots of RM. This variety of roots has consequences for the consistency of the developing RM theory. Möller and Halinen (2000) contend that RM actually consists of two theoretically different and distinctive approaches: market-based RM (MRM) and network-based RM (NRM). We echo this view.

MRM seems to rely on a number of, often silent, assumptions on relationships and their context. Especially data-based marketing and services-oriented relationship research address a market of potential customer relationships with relatively low actor interdependence and interaction intensity and, consequently, with relatively low switching costs. This is reflected in the use of CRM tools for targeting marketing activities, managing the buyer–seller encounters and the customer life-cycle value (Ehret, 2004; Reinartz and Kumar, 2003). Another important theme is the analysis of the relationship value and its antecedents (Flint et al., 1997; Ravald and Grönroos, 1996; Ulaga, 2003; Ulaga and Eggert, 2006) and the role of trust and commitment in relationship performance (Morgan and Hunt, 1994).

Network-based RM assumes a network of interdependent, often reciprocal relationships involving relatively complex buyer–seller interactions, leading to mutual dependence and higher switching costs. Besides social relationships, these involve economic, functional, legal, logistics and processual ties. This perspective is not elaborated here, as its key aspects have been discussed under the Interaction and Networks approach.

The market-based RM does not address the context or environment of the buyer–seller exchange and its influence on the relationship. Competitive markets with several independent buyers and sellers are (silently) assumed. Although emphasizing collaboration in value creation and dialogue as a means of achieving this (Grönroos, 2004; Gummesson, 1997), there is relatively little empirical evidence on the dialogical practices. The tradition examines increasing commitment levels of customer roles (e.g. the 'ladder of loyalty' by Christopher et al., 2002), but the perspective is primarily on marketer's activities. That is, market-based RM has a strong managerial orientation. While network-based RM primarily relies on understanding oriented methodology, the studies in market-based RM tend to employ explanatory, hypothesis-testing methodology (see, e.g. the studies by Morgan and Hunt, 1994; Ulaga and Eggert, 2006). Related to these orientations, the empirical results of the MRM deal mainly with the issue of what factors influence the length and profitability of customer relationships and are silent about the dynamics of these relationships.

Market orientation studies

Interest in the market orientation (MO) of firms commenced during the late 1980s and especially in the beginning of the 1990s. A growing number of researchers became concerned about the lack of empirical evidence regarding the relevance of marketing activities for corporate performance (Kohli and Jaworski, 1990; Narver and Slater, 1990; Ruekert, 1992; Shapiro, 1988). MO studies became anchored in the notion that MO represents the implementation of the marketing concept. Narver and Slater (1990: 24) suggested that MO '… consists of three behavioural components – customer orientation, competition orientation, and interfunctional coordination, and two decision criteria: long-term focus and profitability' (i.e. the MKTOR scale). Kohli and Jaworski (1990: 6), based on both theoretical reviews and interviews of marketing practitioners, defined MO through three interrelated elements: (i) the organization wide generation of market intelligence pertaining to current and future customer needs, (ii) dissemination of intelligence across departments (iii) and organization-wide responsiveness to it (i.e. the MARKOR scale). Profitability and performance, in general, was seen more as a consequence of MO than a part of the construct.

These initial contributions had, by the mid-2000s, generated over 120 studies on different aspects of MO (Kirca et al., 2005). The early discussion on the definition of MO explored whether it is primarily dominated by customer orientation or represents a multidimensional construct comprising, in addition to customer orientation, competitor orientation and MO. Another theme concerned the passive versus proactive nature of the MO construct; whether it was primarily 'market driven' or included also the 'market making' characteristics. This related to the view different scholars had about MO. The current views encompass both these perspectives, as well as the extensive and proactive character of MO (Carillat et al., 2004; Homburg and Pfesser, 2000; Tuominen et al., 2004; van Raaij and Stoelhorst, 2008).

Both scales (MARKOR and MKTOR) provide an MO score that is an unweighted sum of the components. While easy to use for comparing the level of MO across industries and across companies, this approach has several limitations as a diagnostic tool for management. As pointed out by Van Bruggen and Smidts (1995) and van Raaij and Stoelhorst (2008), managers would require information on all relevant dimensions, an idea of their relative importance and linkages, and a view of the meaning of a specific score, how good or bad it is. These issues have been, to a certain extent, addressed by the extensive modelling research on MO.

In a nutshell, MO studies address the following broad questions: What is a market-oriented organization? Which are its antecedents? What does it matter to be market oriented or, in other terms, what are the consequences of MO? It has been shown that the level of MO is generally positively related to such performance variables as customer satisfaction and loyalty, market performance (sales and market share) and financial performance. There is, however, considerable variation in these linkages (González-Benito and González-Benito, 2005).

MO tradition has provided strong evidence of the importance of being able to implement the original marketing concept. The approach contains, however, several issues, which have curtailed its potential. First, although paying some attention to the market construction aspect, MO studies have primarily been focussed on explaining current market behaviour through cross-sectional studies. More importantly, MO research generally assumes not only working markets but also that the MO construct is generic. That is, its components are not expected to be affected by the business field or the business strategy pursued by the firm. This is a strong assumption which, nevertheless, has received some empirical support. The underlying reason for this support, we believe, is based on the operationalization of MO as the level or intensity of MO of a firm (Kohli and Jaworski, 1990). The focus on the intensity of MO has left relatively unexamined the role that the market-related competences or capabilities play in company performance.

Since Day's (1994) seminal study of the marketing capabilities, there is strong reason to believe that it is primarily the underlying firm capabilities that not only determine the level of its MO, but also allow superior performance (Cadogan et al., 2008). There is also strong reason to believe that these capabilities are not generic, like the MO construct, but that the profile and relevance of capabilities or competences vary according to the strategy pursued by the firm (Miles and Snow, 1978, 1983; Miller, 1996). Here, the resource-based view of the firm differs from the rather simplistic MO tradition; it is the historically accumulated resources that form the basis of firm competitiveness (Golfetto and Gibbert, 2006; Srivastava et al., 2001).

Another limitation of the MO tradition is its relatively static nature. Although the learning and processual aspects of MO have been emphasized by Narver and Slater (Slater, 1997; Slater and Narver, 2000), there is relatively little empirical research that systematically examines the processes through which a firm may become market oriented (van Raaij and Stoelhorst, 2008). In sum, it seems that the relevance of the MO tradition could be enhanced by systematically enriching it with the marketing-competence-oriented research, building on the RBV and dynamic capabilities view of the firm and by adopting a more process-oriented research methodology.

Service-dominant logic

The Service-Dominant Logic (SDL) approach represents the latest marketing school (Vargo and Lusch, 2004, 2006, 2008). Its evaluation is difficult for a number of reasons. As the newest contender among the research traditions in marketing, SDL has not had the time to produce much empirical research, and seems to form an orientation or programme which has not had sufficient time to become a 'tradition'. On the other hand, the SDL has raised strong interest and discussion about the theory development in marketing and as such merits our attention.

The focus of SDL is on gaining greater understanding of marketing as a value cocreation process. The approach suggests that all value creation is service-based and grounded on the cocreation of value between the marketer and the customer. Marketers can only provide value propositions, embedded in offerings, and it depends on the motivation and capability of customers to render benefits, i.e. value out of offerings. As such, the approach shares the interaction perspective of customers and suppliers with the Interaction and Network tradition. Another key aspect is the role of capabilities/competencies; these are the key resources ('operant resources') for both creating value propositions and rendering value out of them. Thus, knowledge and capabilities are the core source of competitive advantage. (Barney, 1991; Wernerfelt, 1984). In other words, the resource-based view of the firm and its marketing-related application, resource advantage theory (Hunt, 2002) and the emerging competencies-based view on marketing (Golfetto et al., 2006; Möller, 2006; Srivastava et al., 2001) provide a strong foundation for SDL.

While emphasizing marketing as a social and economic process as a context for the dyadic-level value creation, SDL does not yet articulate this process and its interaction with the dyadic exchange, which is one of the strengths of the Channels Tradition. Vargo and Lusch advocate that the SDL should form the basis of a unified theory of marketing. The SDL has an important role in emphasizing the value creation and especially its cocreation aspect underlying marketing. This notion, which was already in the early recognition of marketing processes, served a bridging function between demand and supply, and which besides a behavioural and functional view, also involved cultural and ecological perspectives (Alderson, 1957, 1963; Cox et al., 1965), had become overlooked by mainstream marketing management However, more than a general theory of marketing, SDL can be interpreted in terms of a broad framework, providing guidelines on how certain existing schools of marketing should be utilized in normative fashion in the value creation processes. In this sense, it 'competes' with its distinguished forerunner, Alderson's 'Analytical Framework for Marketing' (in Wooliscroft et al., 2006), with which it shares several aspects (Wooliscroft, 2008).

Synthesis – marketing as a multilayered and pluralistic field

The metatheoretical analysis of the selected marketing research traditions has significant implications for theory development within marketing. The analysis shows that current marketing research is pluralistic, and that research traditions cannot be integrated or unified because of their distinctive worldviews and distinctive intellectual goals, which, although partly overlapping, include different aspects of the marketing phenomena being addressed. Drawing on the analyzed material, marketing as a research domain seems to consist of several interrelated layers, as described in Figure 9.1.

- Individuals and their behaviours (behaviours of customers and sellers)
- Groups and their behaviours (family buying behaviour, sales teams and buying centres)
- Management (marketing as specialized and institutionalized management)
- Functions and their behaviours (marketing as a function and its interactions with other company functions)
- Organizations or firms and their behaviours (marketing and customer organizations and other relevant actors)
- Interorganizational behaviours (between buyers and sellers)
- Institutional systems and their dynamics (e.g. distribution channels); and
- Markets, industries, cultures and their dynamics (forming the context or environment of marketing and consummating behaviours).

These domains are obviously interrelated or nested. In their totality, they comprise the complex domain of marketing. It is so extensive that none of the research traditions has tried to cover it in its entirety. In fact, it is important to understand the level or part of the marketing domain that a theory is focusing on, and the kind of assumptions it makes about that domain. Actions and behaviours

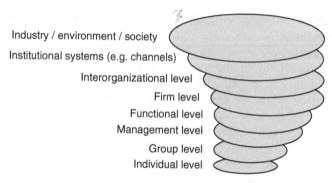

Industry / environment / society

Institutional systems (e.g. channels)

Interorganizational level

Firm level

Functional level

Management level

Group level

Individual level

Figure 9.1   Marketing research domain as a layered system (modified from Möller 2007).

in each domain allow different research approaches in terms of ontological assumptions and methodology. We believe that this extensive and layered character of marketing as a research domain, or more correctly as a 'cluster' of research domains, is one of the underlying reasons for the number and multi-paradigmatic character of research traditions in marketing. Our comparative analysis has clearly shown that none of the major research schools or traditions can provide a 'holistic' or comprehensive representation of the complex and multilayered domain of marketing. This conclusion and the identified differences between the schools have several consequences for marketing researchers. One of them is how to accept and work with this multiparadigmatic landscape.

PLURALISM OF PARADIGMS

'Scholars who talk about pluralism are often satisfied with simply illustrating or categorizing different streams of research. These efforts work quite well for an initial orientation, but are insufficient' (Scherer, 1998: 156). We fully agree with Scherer's position here, because addressing the paradigmatic level is not easy. The difficulty has its origin in the fact that theories have an embedded and paradigmatic position, whereas an RT can have diverse, coexisting and even competing theories. In short, there is no

unequivocal link between a research school and a unique paradigmatic position. This is clearly evidenced by Brodie et al. (2009) when they discuss how the CMP project[1] studies marketing practices from different paradigmatic approaches. Another example is Sheth and Pravatyar's (2000) *Handbook of Relationship Marketing*, in which the diverse relationship marketing views are presented. This difficulty is not unique to the marketing discipline. To quote Willmott (1993: 685), on criticizing Burrell and Morgan's isolationism, 'It may be asked: how often are sets of paradigmatic assumptions articulated in organizational analysis in their pure form?' Accepting the difficulties and limitations, we believe an effort needs to be made in this direction.

In this section, we first explore the philosophical debate in marketing. Then, referring to organizational theory literature, we discuss how the problem of paradigmatic incommensurability can be overcome by using a meta-paradigmatic approach.

In using the often-contested term 'paradigm' without discussing all of its semantic and philosophical interpretations (see Tadajewski, 2008), we follow the original application in the work of Kuhn (1970) where a paradigm specifies a general set of philosophical assumptions about the ontology, epistemology and appropriate methodologies for developing and investigating theory. In marketing, during the 1980s and early 1990s, there was a strong debate as to which should be the dominant research paradigm, with some colleagues taking a more interpretive/relativist approach (Anderson, 1983; Hirschman, 1986; Hudson and Ozanne, 1988; Peter, 1992; Peter and Olson, 1983, 1989) and others a more positivist/realist stance (Bagozzi, 1980; Hunt, 1990, 1991, 1993). As in other managerial disciplines, some marketing academics also argued in favour of paradigmatic pluralism. Arndt made a strong case about the need for pluralism in paradigms when developing marketing theory:

'While paradigms are not theories, they are the foundations of theories but often remain implicit, are taken for granted, and, hence, are usually unquestioned ... By limiting itself to the empiricist orientation and logical empiricist paradigms such as instrumental man, marketing has remained essentially a one-dimensional science concerned with technology and problem solving. Adopting other paradigms and metaphors will result in the asking of quite different research questions. The notion of paradigms should be viewed as an argument for paradigmatic tolerance and pluralism'. (Arndt, 1985: 11)

More recently, the recognition of pluralism in marketing has come from a diverse range of marketing theorists, including Hunt (1991), Thompson et al. (1997), Green (2001), Davies and Fitchett (2005) and Ambler (2006) inter alia. However, this has not resulted in any wider interest in the debate as reflected in the main marketing journals. This contrasts with the other cognate disciplines, notably academics in organizational theory who have maintained a long-term discussion on the issue of paradigms and the vexed issue whether paradigms are inherently incommensurable or irreconcilable (Burrell and Morgan, 1979). Hence, we will draw on this literature to see how this affects the possible ways of studying marketing theory.

Many RTs are explicitly linked to a specific paradigm and, thus, to a given research methodology, e.g. the marketing management tradition. The central methodological problem is that, by taking any one perspective, not only all observations and data become 'boxed' into the explanatory dimensions of the chosen paradigm, but also competing theories are judged and measured according to the others' methodological and ontological assumptions (Pels et al., 2004).

We suggest that domains of inquiry need not be related to a given philosophical paradigm, thus opening the possibility of engaging in a multiparadigm approach and a broad set of research methodologies. In essence, we follow Gioia and Pitre's (1990) invitation to adopt pluralism in both paradigms and methods in order to achieve 'a more comprehensive explanation and understanding of a social phenomenon'. Taking a pluralistic approach requires addressing the central issue of incommensurability. The debate within the organizational theory can be grouped into three positions (see Table 9.1).

Paradigm incommensurability[2] This position suggests that, given the ontological, epistemological and methodological differences, paradigms are mutually exclusive and boundaries should be left intact. In this position, differences are emphasized, allowing for little or no communication between adherents of different paradigmatic standings. Under this perspective, when multi-method research projects are used, they should be undertaken as sequential or parallel studies (i.e. Burrell and Morgan, 1979; Hassard, 1988).

Paradigm integration This position suggests that it is possible to simultaneously assess and synthesize a variety of contributions from different paradigms, thus ignoring the differences between competing approaches and their paradigmatic assumptions (e.g. Reed, 1985; Willmott, 1993). We also position Minger's[3] (2001) critical pluralism approach within the paradigmatic integration view, because Mingers states that 'the argument about paradigm incommensurability has been overstated ... it is possible to detach research methods from a paradigm and use them *critically and knowledgeably*' (italics in original).

Multiparadigm This position focuses on the benefits of a holistic approach (Gioia and Pitre, 1990). Just as Burrell and Morgan (1979) bring the topic of incommensurability onto the forefront of academic debate, Gioia and

Table 9.1 Levels of interplay between paradigms

Paradigms are mutually exclusive Boundaries are left intact	Paradigm boundaries disappear	Holistic approaches to paradigmatic distinctions *Multi-paradigm* Gioia and Pitre (1990)				
Emphasizes differences		**Paradigm boundaries are permeable Emphasizes similarities** *Bridging*[2] (Gioia and Pitre, 1990)			**Meta-level analysis of paradigms Emphasizes similarities and differences** *Meta-paradigm* (Gioia and Pitre, 1990)	
Paradigm incommensurability (Morgan and Burrell 1979[1])	*Paradigm integration* (Willmott, 1993 and Reed, 1985)	*Structuration* Giddens (1979)	*Negotiated order* Strauss (1978)	*Organizing* Weick (1979)	*Interplay* Schultz and Hatch (1996)	*Meta-triangulation* Lewis and Grimes (1999)
Sequential Morgan and Burrell (1979) / *Parallel* Hassard (1988)	Or *Critical pluralism* Mingers (2001)	Interpret/functionalist transition zones	Radical struct./radical humanist transition zone	Radical humanist/interpret transition zone	Researcher moves back and forth between paradigms	Grounded on a 'home paradigm it explores disparities to arrive to an enlarged understanding

[1] Also defined as Bracketing (Lewis and Grimes, 1999) or Isolationism (Mingers, 2001).
[2] Also defined as Paradigm Crossing (Schultz and Hatch, 1996).

Pitre (1990) try to help researchers untangle themselves from the either/or position. In their terms, 'Traditional approaches to theory building on organizational study have tended to produce valuable, but nonetheless incomplete, views of organizational knowledge, mainly because they have been predicated predominantly on the tenets of one major paradigm (Kuhn, 1970) or way of understanding organizational phenomena'. Gioia and Pitre, rather than viewing theory building as a search for *truth*, given their multiparadigm perspective, see theory building as a search for comprehensiveness stemming from different worldviews. In short, Gioia and Pitre seek to recommend a broader approach to theory building that accounts for different paradigmatic assumptions. This view is shared and reinforced by Goles and Hirschheim (2000), who provide a similar categorization of paradigmatic positions.

We believe that this 'call' for a broader approach should be extended to the marketing discipline and following a multiparadigmatic methodology. As Goles and Hirschheim (2000) show, within the multiparadigm position, there are two distinct views. One is the *bridging* or *crossing* perspective, which focuses on the similarities between paradigms and recognizes that paradigm boundaries are permeable. The alternative view is a *meta-paradigmatic* approach, which argues that both similarities *and* differences are relevant and that a higher level of abstraction is needed to 'iron-out' the differences.

- **Bridging:** These are scholars who focus on inter-paradigm similarities. They accept that boundaries can (and must) be crossed but recognize that the central assumptions of the paradigms will be at odds; thus, their aim is to find transition zones. Giddens' (1979) structuration theory, Strauss' (1978) negotiated order and Weick's (1979) organizing scheme all falls into this line of work.
- **Meta-paradigm:** This is the other multiparadigmatic view and the one we would like to encourage. Gioia and Pitre (1990) state that 'looking from a meta-level can allow simultaneous consideration of multiple paradigms and

their transition zones ... a meta-perspective is qualitatively different from cross-boundary considerations. From a meta-perspective the intent is to understand, to accommodate, and if possible, to link views generated from different starting assumptions'. From the meta-paradigmatic perspective, two research approaches were suggested: Schultz and Hatch (1996) invite scholar to use *interplay* and Lewis and Grimes (1999) suggest adopting *meta-triangulation*.

Interplay: This approach considers it critical to recognize the tensions between differences and similarities amongst paradigms. Shultz and Hatch (1996) argue that the acknowledgement of contrasts and connections between paradigms may be equated with the concept of paradox. However, interplay differs significantly from previous uses of paradox in organization theory (e.g. Poole and Van de Ven, 1989) by stressing the interdependent relationship between constitutive oppositions. Schultz and Hatch are not interested in accepting, clarifying or resolving the contradictions of paradoxes, but rather in preserving the tension between contrasts and connections[4] in order to reach new ways of theorizing organizations. The interplay strategy involves two steps: (a) empirical recognition of contrasts and connections, and (b) examination of the implications of recognizing both contrasts and connections by moving between the two paradigms. In short, researchers move back and forth between paradigms so that multiple views are held in tension. Interplay allows cross-fertilization without demanding integration.

Meta-triangulation: Gioia and Pitre (1990) state that 'a multiple-perspective view is not a demand for integration or resolution of disagreements or paradoxes (cf. Poole and Van de Ven, 1989). ... rather, it is an attempt to account for as many representations related to an area of study by linking theories through their common transition zone'. The view of meta-paradigm is roughly analogous to the notion of triangulation. It implies a kind of meta-triangulation, not across method *within* a single theory or paradigm, but *across* theories and paradigms. It implies expanding the concept of triangulation beyond the search for similarities to see differences as well, thus reaching a more comprehensive portrayal. Any meta-paradigm perspective is nonetheless rooted in a specific paradigm, depending on the ground assumptions of the observer.

Lewis and Grimes (1999) develop the idea of meta-triangulation further. They see multi-paradigm theorists as a midpoint between dogmatism and relativism that offers a tremendous, yet unrealized, theory-building potential. These authors suggest meta-triangulation as a map of the theory-building process, where the focus is to use different paradigms to explore disparity and interplay and thereby arrive at an enlarged and enlightened understanding of the phenomena of interest, as well as of the paradigms employed. For example, if we take the topic of value, meta-paradigmatic approaches would invite researchers not only to hop-scotch between qualitative and quantitative research methods, as Woodruff and Flint (2006) suggest, but also essentially invite researchers to go one step further and apply different paradigmatic standings and trying, through the use of different lenses, to shed light at the complex phenomenon of value. In this manner, some scholars might want to take a grounded theory approach and question themselves (independently of the current definitions and previous studies) about what value is for a customer; on the other hand, the same researcher (or another member of the same research team) might engage in a large sample study of how customers relate to different definitions of value (derived form the current definitions found in the literature). In an interplay approach, the researcher would be moving between the results obtained through each method with the aim of expanding its understanding of the phenomenon. Researchers taking a meta-triangulation standing would also conduct both types of research, but would try to identify the 'common ground' and the areas of specificity (e.g. Davies and Fitchett, 2005).

We argue from this brief review of the philosophical issues that, for the marketing discipline, what is required is a much more complex, holistic ontology and approach to methodology. This follows what the other management disciplines, such as organizational management, strategic management and information systems, have realized. In particular, we suggest that the meta-paradigmatic standing identified in the organizational theory literature is potentially fruitful for marketing. Within this, both the meta-triangulation and interplay research approaches provide the basis for fruitful methodologies for further research in marketing theory building. However, there have been few research applications that fully embrace a multiparadigm pluralistic perspective in marketing.

DISCUSSION

Our analysis reveals several major findings about the marketing research traditions that we examined. The RTs are relatively logical configurations where the research focus and practices follow the goals and underlying theoretical assumptions. This does not mean that the schools are equally well developed; there are actually several differences between them in terms of the solidness of the theory development and problem-solving potential. Researchers working within a school do not necessarily recognize the underlying assumptions of the RT and their consequences, because these have often not been explicitly described.

Another aspect is how well the schools cover relevant marketing domains and their research issues. There seem to be clear lacunae concerning our research-based understanding of marketing organizations. This is a logical consequence of the fact that most schools are primarily interested in customers and customer behaviour, exchange relationships and through what means the marketer tries to influence these. MO is the only tradition that fully focuses on the orientation of the marketing organization; and even it has a relatively mechanistic and narrow view of organization. This is a serious limitation.

It seems that mainstream marketing scholars are not interested in research questions like: What kind of marketing organizations exist in different fields/contexts? How does one explain potential differences? How do organizational forms/solutions evolve? What are the performance consequences of different forms, and why? Are we ready to leave these relevant issues organizational researchers. It is interesting to compare this situation to the development of consumer behaviour studies into a new discipline. The most probable reason is, of course, the narrow focus adopted by most research in mainstream marketing on influencing customers. We clearly lack the sociology of marketing organizations. A related 'white area' is studying the marketing management from more sociological than completely normative point of view. We have relatively little knowledge of the organizational positions, values, professional conduct or ethics of the management carrying out marketing activities.

In sum, although our knowledge and perspectives of marketing phenomena have increased encouragingly during the last decades, there is still great potential for stronger theory development. The multilayeredness of the marketing domain(s) is an evidence of the complexity of the task at hand. One option is to focus even more within each RT. There is also another option of broadening the scope. For the reasons we have articulated earlier, the marketing discipline would clearly benefit from research adopting a holistic view. Such an approach requires moving out of the current paradigmatic 'silos' and adopting a multiparadigmatic approach and, in this chapter, we have outlined alternative approaches in order to overcome paradigmatic incommensurability.

NOTES

1 Further details about the participants, research philosophy and other aspects of the CMP research programme are available at http://cmp.auckland.ac.nz. See also the chapter by Brodie et al. in this volume.

2 Also defined as Bracketing (Lewis and Grimes, 1999) or Isolationism (Mingers, 2001).

3 Mingers is an information systems scholar. We have included his critical pluralism approach, because it is a 'new' position and as such deserves being considered.

4 However, the paradox literature has emphasized contrasts defined as simultaneous oppositions.

REFERENCES

Alajoutsijärvi, K., Möller, K. and Rosenbröijer, C.J. (1999) 'Relevance of Focal Nets in Understanding the Dynamics of Business Relationships', *Journal of Business-to-Business Marketing*, 6(3): 3–35.

Alderson, W. and Cox, R. (1948) 'Towards a Theory of Marketing', *The Journal of Marketing*, 13(2): 137–152.

Alderson, W. (1963) 'The Analytical Framework for Marketing', in P. Bliss (ed.) *Marketing and Behavioral Sciences*. Boston, MA: Allyn and Bacon, pp. 25–40.

Alderson, W. (1965) *Dynamic Marketing Behavior: A Functionalist Theory of Marketing*. Homewood, IL: Richard D. Irwin.

Ambler, T. (2006) 'The New Dominant Logic of Marketing: Views of the Elephant', in S.L. Vargo and R.F. Lusch (eds) *The Service-Dominant Logic of Marketing*, Armonk, New York: M. E. Sharpe, pp. 286–296.

Anderson, E., Fornell, C. and Rust, R.T. (1997) 'Customer Satisfaction, Productivity, and Profitability: Differences between Goods and Services', *Marketing Science*, 16(2): 129–145.

Anderson, P.F. (1983) 'Marketing, Scientific Progress and Scientific Method', *Journal of Marketing*, 47(Fall): 18–31.

Anderson, P.F. (1986) 'On Method in Consumer Research: A Critical Relativist Perspective', *Journal of Consumer Research*, 13(9): 155–173.

Anderson, J.C. and Narus, J.A. (1990) 'A Model of the Distributor's Perspective of Distributor-Manufacturer Working Partnerships', *Journal of Marketing*, 54: 42–58.

Anderson, J.C., Håkansson, H. and Johanson, J. (1994) 'Dyadic Business Relationships within a Business Network Context', *Journal of Marketing*, 58: 1–15.

Arndt, J. (1979) 'Toward a Concept of Domesticated Markets', *Journal of Marketing*, 43(4): 65–75.

Arndt, J. (1985) 'On Making Marketing Science More Scientific: Role of Orientations, Paradigms, Metaphors and Puzzle Solving', *Journal of Marketing*, 49: 11–23.

Axelsson, B. and Easton, G. (1992) *Industrial Markets: A New View of Reality*. London: Routledge.

Bagozzi, R.P. (1975) 'Marketing as Exchange', *Journal of Marketing*, 39(10) 4: 32–39.

Bagozzi, R.P. (1980) *Casual Models in Marketing*, New York: John Wiley & Sons, Inc.

Bartels, R. (1951) 'Can Marketing be a Science?', *Journal of Marketing*, 51(1): 319–328.

Bass, F.M., Buzzell, R.D., Greene, M.R., Lazer, W., Pessemier, E.A., Shawver, D.L., Shuchman, A., Theodore, C.A. and Wilson, G.W. (eds) (1961) *Mathematical Models and Methods in Marketing*. Homewood, IL: Richard D. Irwin.

Berry, L.L. and Parasuraman, A. (1993) 'Building a New Academic Field – The Case of Services Marketing', *Journal of Retailing*, 69(1): 13–60.

Brodie, R.J., Coviello, N.E., Brookes, R.W. and Little, V.J. (1997) 'Towards a Paradigm shift in marketing? An examination of current marketing practices', *Journal of Marketing Management*, 13(5): 383–406.

Brown, L.Q. (1948) 'Toward a Profession of Marketing', *Journal of Marketing*, 13(7): 27–31.

Burrell, G. and Morgan, G. (1979) *Sociological Paradigm and Organizational Analysis*. London: Heinemann Books.

Burton, D.E. (2001) 'Critical marketing theory: the blueprint?', *European Journal of Marketing*, 35(N 5/6): 722–743.

Burton, D. (2005) 'Marketing Theory Matters', *British Journal of Management*, 16(1): 5–18.

Buzzell, R. (1963) 'Is Marketing a Science?', *Harvard Business Review*, (01/02): 32–48.

Cadogan, J.W., Souchon, A.L. and Procter, D.B. (2008) 'The Quality of Market-Oriented Behaviors: Formative Index Construction', *Journal of Business Research*, 61: 1263–1277.

Chamberlin, E.H. (1933/1965) *The Theory of Monopolistic Competition*. Cambridge, Mass: Harvard University Press.

Christopher, M., Payne, A. and Ballantyne, D. (2002) *Relationship Marketing: Creating Stakeholder Value*, second edn. Oxford: Butterworth-Heinemann.

Constantinides, E. (2006) 'The Marketing Mix Revisited: Towards the 21st Century Marketing', *Journal of Marketing Management*, 22: 407–438.

Converse, P. (1945) 'The Development of Science of Marketing', *Journal of Marketing*, 10(7): 14–23.

Coviello, N.E., Brodie, Roderick J. and Munro, H.J. (1997) 'Understanding Contemporary Marketing: Development of a Classification Scheme', *Journal of Marketing Management*, 13: 501–522.

Cox, R., Goodman, C.S. and Fichandler, T.C. (1965) *Distribution in a High Level Economy*. Englewood Cliffs, NJ: Prentice Hall, Inc.

Day, G.S. (1994) 'The Capabilities of Market-Driven Organizations', *Journal of Marketing*, (10): 37–52.

de Man, A.P. (2004) *The Network Economy, Strategy, Structure and Management*. Cheltenham, UK: Edward Elgar.

Deshpandé, R. and Farley, J.U. (1996) 'Understanding Market Orientation: A Prospectively Designed Meta-Analysis of Three Market Orientation Scales', MSI Working Paper 96–125, Marketing Science Institute, Cambridge, MA.

Dholakia, N. and Arndt, J. (eds) (1985) *Changing the Course of Marketing: Alternative Paradigms for Widening Marketing Theory* (Research in Marketing Supplement 2). Greenwich, CT: JAI Press.

Dickson, P.R. and Ginter, J.L. (1987) 'Market Segmentation, Product Differentiation and Marketing Strategy', *Journal of Marketing*, (4): 1–10.

Dorfman, R. and Steiner, P.O. (1954) 'Optimal Advertising and Optimal Quality', *The American Economic Review*, 44(12): 826–836.

Dwyer, F.R., Schurr, P.H. and Oh, S. (1987) 'Developing Buyer Seller Relationships', *Journal of Marketing*, 51(4): 11–27.

Easton, G. (1995) 'Methodology and Industrial Networks', in K.E. Möller and Wilson (eds) *Business Marketing: An Interaction and Network Perspective*, D.T., Boston: Kluwer, pp. 411–492.

Easton, G. and Håkansson, H. (1996) 'Markets as Networks' (Editorial introduction), *International Journal of Research in Marketing*, 13(5): 407–413.

Easton, G. (2002) 'Marketing a Critical Realist Approach', *Journal of Business Research*, 55: 103–109.

Ehret, M. (2004) 'Managing the Trade-Off between Relationships and Value Networks. Towards a Value-Based Approach of Customer Relationship Management in Business-To-Business Markets', *Industrial Marketing Management*, 33: 465–473.

Eiriz, V. and Wilson, D. (2006) 'Research in Relationship Marketing: Antecedents, Traditions and Integration', *European Journal of Marketing*, 40(3/4): 275–291.

Emerson, R.M. (1962) 'Power Dependence Relations', *American Sociological Review*, 27(2): 31–40.

Flint, D.J., Woodruff, R.B and Gardial, S.F. (1997) 'Customer Value Change In Industrial Marketing Relationships: A call for New Strategies and Research', *Industrial Marketing Management*, 26(2): 163–176.

Ford, D. (1990) *Understanding Business Markets: Interaction, Relationships, Networks*. London: Academic Press.

Ford, D. (ed.) (1997) *Understanding Business Markets: Interaction, Relationships and Networks*, second edn. Bridgend: The Dryden Press.

Ford, D. (ed.) (2002) *Understanding Business Markets and Purchasing*, third edn. Cornwall: Thomson Learning.

Foucault, M. (1968) 'Response au cercle d'épistémologie', *Cahiers pour l'analyse*, 9: 28–31.

Frazier, G. (1983) 'Interorganizational Exchange Behavior in Marketing Channels: A Broadened Perspective', *Journal of Marketing*, 47(Fall): 68–78.

Gaski, J.F. (1984) 'The Theory of Power and Conflict in Channels of Distribution', *The Journal of Marketing*, 48(3): 9–29.

Giddens, A. (1979) *Central Problems in Social Theory*. Berkeley: University of California Press.

Giddens, A. (1991) *Modernity and Self Identity: Self and Society in the Late Modern Age*. Cambridge: Cambridge Polity Press.

Gioia, D.A. and Pitre, E. (1990) 'Multiparadigm Perspectives on Theory Building', *Academy of Management Review*, 15(4): 584–602.

Goles, T. and Hirschheim, R. (2000) 'The Paradigm is Dead, Long Live the Paradigm: the Legacy of Burrell and Morgan', *Omega: The International Journal of Management Science*, 28: 249–268.

Golfetto, F. and Gibbert, M. (2006) 'Marketing Competencies and the Sources of Customer Value in Business Markets', *Industrial Marketing Management*, 35: 904–912.

González-Benito, Ó. and González-Benito, J. (2005) 'Cultural vs. Operational Market Orientation and Objective vs. Subjective Performance: Perspective of Production and Operations', *Industrial Marketing Management*, 34: 797–829.

Green, P.E. (2001) 'The Vagaries of Becoming (and Remaining) a Marketing Research Methodologist', *Journal of Marketing*, 64(7): 104–108.

Grönroos, C. (1981) 'Internal Marketing – An Integral Part of Marketing Theory', in J.H. Donnelly and W.E. George (eds) *Marketing of Services*, pp. 236–238.

Grönroos, C. (1990) Service Management and Marketing: Managing the Moments of Truth, in *Service Competition*. Lexington, MA: Lexington Books.

Grönroos, C. (1994) 'Quo Vadis, Marketing? Toward a Relationship Marketing Paradigm', *Journal of Marketing Management*, 10: 347–360.

Grönroos, C. (2004) 'The Relationship Marketing Process: Communication, Interaction, Dialogue, Value', *Journal of Business & Industrial Marketing*, 19(2): 99–113.

Guba, E. and Lincoln, Y. (1994) 'Competing Paradigms in Qualitative Research', in N.K. Denzin and Y.S. Licoln, (eds) *Handbook of Qualitative Research*, Thousand Oaks, CA: Sage, pp. 105–117.

Gummesson, E. (1997) 'Relationship Marketing as a Paradigm Shift: Some Conclusions from The 30r Approach', *Management Decision*, 35(4): 267–272.

Gummesson, E. (1999) *Total Relationship Marketing: Rethinking Marketing Management from 4Ps to 30Rs*. Oxford: Butterworth-Heinemann.

Gummesson, E. (2004) 'Return on Relationships (ROR): The Value of Relationship Marketing and CRM in Business-To-Business Contexts', *Journal of Business & Industrial Marketing*, 19(2): 136–148.

Håkansson, H. (ed.) (1982) *International Marketing and Purchasing of Industrial*

Goods. An Interaction Approach. Chichester: John Wiley & Sons.

Håkansson, H. (ed.) (1987) *Industrial Technological Development. A Network Approach*. London: Croom, Helm.

Håkansson, H. (1989) *Corporate Technological Behaviour. Cooperation and Networks*. London: Routledge.

Håkansson, H. and Ford, D. (2002) 'How Should Companies Interact in Business Networks?', *Journal of Business Research*, 55(2): 133–139.

Håkansson, H. and Johanson, J. (1988) 'Formal and Informal Cooperation Strategies in International Industrial Networks', in F.J. Contractor and P. Lorange (eds) *Cooperative Strategies in International Business*. MA: Lexington Books.

Håkansson, H. and Snehota, I. (eds) (1995) *Developing Relationships in Business Networks*. London: Routledge.

Håkansson, H. and Waluszewski, A. (2002) 'Path Dependence: Restricting or Facilitating Technical Development?', *Journal of Business Research*, 55(7): 561–570.

Hassard, J. (1988) 'Overcoming Hermeneutics in Organizational Theory: An Alternative to Paradigm Incommensurability', *Human Relations*, 42: 247–259.

Heide, J.B. (1994) 'Inter-Organizational Governance in Marketing Channels', *Journal of Marketing*, 58(1): 71–98.

Hirschman, E. (1986) 'Humanistic Inquiry in Marketing Research: Philosophy, Method, and Criteria', *Journal of Marketing Research*, 23(8): 237–249.

Homburg, C. and Pflesser, C. (2000) 'A Multiple Layer Model Of Market-Oriented Organizational Culture: Measurement Issues and Performance Outcomes', *Journal of Marketing Research*, 37: 449–462.

Hudson and Ozanne (1988) 'Alternative Ways of Seeking Knowledge in Consumer Research', *Journal of Consumer Research*, 14(4): 508–521.

Hunt, S.D. (1971) 'The Morphology of Theory and the General Theory of Marketing', *Journal of Marketing*, 35(4): 65–68.

Hunt, S.D. (1976) 'The Nature and Scope of Marketing', *Journal of Marketing*, 40(7): 17–28.

Hunt, S.D. (1990) 'Truth in Marketing Theory and Research', *Journal of Marketing*, 54(7): 1–15.

Hunt, S.D. (1991) *Marketing Theory: Conceptual Foundations of Research in Marketing*. Homewood, Illinois: Irwin.

Hunt, S.D. (1993) 'Objectivity in Marketing Theory and Research', *Journal of Marketing*, 57(4): 76–91.

Hunt, S.D. (2002) *Foundations of Marketing Theory: Toward a General Theory of Marketing*. Armonk, NY: M. E. Sharpe.

Hunt, S.D. (2003) *Controversy in Marketing Theory*. Armonk, NY: M. E. Sharpe.

Jarillo, J.C. (1988) 'On Strategic Networks', *Strategic Management Journal*, 9(1): 31–41.

Jaworski, B.J. and Kohli, A.K. (1993) 'Market Orientation: Antecedents and Consequences', *Journal of Marketing*, 53–70.

Jaworski, B.J. and Kohli, A.K. (1996) 'Market Orientation: Review, Refinement, and Roadmap', *Journal of Market-Focused Management*, 1(2): 119–135.

Johanson, J. and Mattsson, L.G. (1988) 'Internationalisation in Industrial Systems. A Network Approach', in N. Hood and J.E. Vahlne (eds) *Strategies in Global Competition*, London: Croom Helm, pp. 287–314.

Kirca, A.H., Jayachandran, S. and Bearden, W.O. (2005) 'Market Orientation: A Meta-Analytic Review and Assessment of Its Antecedents and Impact on Performance', *Journal of Marketing*, 69(2): 24–41.

Kohli, A.K., and Jaworski, B.J. (1990) 'Market Orientation: The Construct, Research Propositions, and Managerial Implications', *Journal of Marketing*, 54(1): 1–18.

Kotler, P. (1967) *Marketing Management: Analysis, Planning and Control*. Englewood Cliffs, New Jersey: Prentice-Hall.

Kotler, P. (1972) 'A Generic Concept of Marketing', *The Journal of Marketing*, 36(2): 46–54.

Kuhn, T.S. (1970) *The Structure of Scientific Revolutions*. Chicago: University of Chicago Press.

Lewis, M.W. and Grimes, A.J. (1999) 'Metatriangulation: Building Theory from Multiple Paradigms', *Academy of Management Review*, 24(4): 672–690.

Lundgren, A. (1995) *Technological innovation and network evolution*. London: Routledge.

Lusch, R.F., and Vargo, S. L. (2006) 'Service-Dominant Logic as a Foundation for General Theory', in R.F. Lusch and S.R. Vargo (eds) *The Service Dominant Logic of Marketing*.

Dialogue, Debate, and Directions. Armonk, NY: M. E. Sharpe.

Mattsson, L-G. (1985) 'An Application of Network Approach to Marketing: Defending and Changing Market Positions', in N. Dholakia and J. Arndt (eds) *Changing the Course of Marketing: Alternative Paradigms for Widening Marketing Theory*. Greenwich, CT: JAI Press.

Mattsson, L.G. (1997) '"Relationship Marketing" and the "Markets-as-Networks Approach" – A Comparative Analysis of Two Evolving Streams of Research', *Journal of Marketing Management*, 13(7): 447–462.

Miles, R.E. and Snow, C.C. (1978) *Organizational Strategy, Structure and Process*. New York: Mc-Graw-Hill.

Miller, D. (1996) 'Configurations Revisited', *Strategic Management Journal*, 17(7): 505–512.

Mingers, J. (2001) 'Combining Research Methods: Towards a Pluralism Methodology', *Information Systems Research*, 12(3): 240–259.

Morgan, G. (1986) *Images of Organization*. California: Sage Publications.

Morgan, R.M. and Hunt, S.D. (1994) 'The Commitment-Trust Theory of Relationship Marketing', *Journal of Marketing*, 58(7): 20–38.

Möller, K. (1994) 'Interorganizational Marketing Exchange: Metatheoretical Analysis of Current Research Approaches', in G. Laurent, G. Lilien and B.P. Kluwer (eds) *Research Traditions in Marketing*, Boston: Kluwer, pp. 348–82.

Möller, K. (2006a) 'Role of Competences in Creating Customer Value: A Value-Creation Logic Approach', *Industrial Marketing Management*, 35(11): 913–924.

Möller, K. (2006b) 'Marketing Mix Discussion – Is the Mix Misleading Us or are We Misreading the Mix? Comment on: The Marketing Mix revisited: Towards the 21st Century Marketing? by E. Constantinides', *Journal of Marketing Management*, 22: 439–450.

Möller, K. (2007) 'Marketing Research Traditions: Toward Theoretical Unification or Pluralism?', *Australasian Marketing Journal*, 15(1): 64–69.

Möller, K. and Halinen, A. (1999) 'Business Relationships and Networks: Managerial Challenge of Network Era', *Industrial Marketing Management*, 28: 413–427.

Möller, K. and Halinen, A. (2000) 'Relationship Marketing Theory: Its roots and Directions', *Journal of Marketing Management*, 16(1–3): 29–54.

Möller, K. and Svahn, S. (2003) 'Managing Strategic Nets: A Capability Perspective', *Marketing Theory*, 3(2): 201–226.

Möller, K. and Svahn, S. (2006) 'Role of Knowledge in Value Creation in Business Nets', *Journal of Management Studies*, 43(5): 985–1007.

Möller, K. and Svahn, S. (2009) 'How to Influence the Birth of New Business Fields – Network Perspective', *Industrial Marketing Management*, 38(4): 450–458.

Möller, K. and Rajala, A. (2007) 'Rise of Strategic Nets – New Modes of Value Creation', *Industrial Marketing Management*, 36(7): 895–908.

Möller, K., Rajala, A. and Svahn, S. (2005) 'Strategic Business Nets – Their Type and Management', *Journal of Business Research*, 58: 1274–1284.

Möller, K. and Törrönen, P. (2003) 'Business Suppliers' Value Creation Potential: A Capability-Based Analysis', *Industrial Marketing Management*, 32: 109–118.

Möller, K. and Wilson, D. (eds) (1995) *Business Marketing: An Interaction and Network Perspective*. Boston/Dordrecht/London: Kluwer Academic Publisher.

Narver, J.C. and Stanley F.S. (1990) 'The Effect of Market Orientation on Business Profitability', *Journal of Marketing*, (10): 20–35.

Parasuraman, A., Zeithaml, V.A. and Berry, L.L. (1985) 'A Conceptual Model of Service Quality and Its Implications for Future Research', *Journal of Marketing*, 49(Fall): 41–50.

Pels, J. (1999) 'Exchange Relationships in Consumer Markets?', *European Journal of Marketing*, 33(1/2): 19–37.

Pels, J., Saren, M, and Brodie, R. (2004) 'Investigating Multiple Marketing Practices: Exploring the Role of Paradigm', *Irish Academy of Management*, Dublin, Ireland, 2–3 September.

Pels, J., Moller, K.E. and Saren, M. (2009) 'Do we Really Understand Business Marketing? Getting Beyond RM-BM Matrimony', *Journal of Business and Industrial Marketing*, 24(5–6).

Peter, J. Paul and Olson, Jerry (1983) 'Is Science Marketing?' *Journal of Marketing*, (Fall): 111.

Peter, J.P. and Olson, J. (1989) 'The Relativist/Constructionist Perspective on Scientific Knowledge and Consumer Research', in

E.C. Hirschman (ed.) *Interpretive Consumer Research*, Provo, UT: Association for Consumer Research, pp. 24–28.

Peter, P. (1992) 'Realism of Relativism for Marketing Theory and Research: A Comment on Hunt's "Scientific Realism"', *Journal of Marketing*, 56(4): 72–79.

Pettigrew, A.M. (1997) 'What Is a Processual Analysis?' *Scandinavian Journal of Management*, 13(4): 337–348.

Poole, M.S and Van de Ven, A.H. (1989) 'Using Paradox to Build Management and Organization Theories', *Academy of Management Review*, 14: 562–578.

Porter, M.E. (1980) *Competitive Strategy*. New York: Free Press.

Porter, M.E. (1985) *Competitive Advantage*. New York: The Free Press.

Powell, W.W., Kogut, K. and Smith-Doerr, L. (1996) 'Interorgnizational Collaboration and the Locus of Innovation: Networks of Learning in Biotechnology', *Administrative Science Quarterly*, 41: 116–145.

Prendergast, A. and Berthon, P. (2000) 'Insights from Ecology: An Ecotone Perspective of Marketing', *European Management Journal*, 18: 223–232.

Ravald, Annika and Grönroos, Christian (1996) 'The Value Concept and Relationship Marketing', *European Journal of Marketing*, 30, 2: 19–30.

Reed, M. (1985) *New Directions in Organizational Analysis*. London: Tavistock.

Reinartz, W.J. and Kumar, V. (2003) 'The Impact of Customer Relationship Characteristics on Profitable Lifetime Duration', *Journal of Marketing*, 67, 1(1): 77–99.

Rindfleisch, A. and Heide, J.B. (1997) 'Transaction Cost Analysis: Past, Present and Future', *Journal of Marketing*, 61(4): 30–54.

Ritter, T., Wilkinson, I.F. and Johnston, W.J. (2004) 'Managing in Complex Business Networks', *Industrial Marketing Management*, 33: 175–183.

Ruekert, R.W. (1992) 'Developing a Market Orientation: An Organizational Strategy Perspective', *International Research in Marketing*, 9: 225–245.

Scherer, A.G. (1998) 'Pluralism and Incommensurability in Strategic Management and Organization Theory: A Problem in Search of a Solution', *In The British Library: The World's Knowledge*, 5(2): 147–168.

Schultz, M. and Hatch, M.J. (1996) 'Living with Multiple Paradigms: The Case of Paradigm Interplay in Organizational Culture Studies', *Academy of Management Review*, (April).

Shapiro, B. (1988) 'What the Hell is Market Oriented?' *Harvard Business Review*, (November/December): 119–125.

Sheth, J.N. (1994) 'The Domain of Relationship Marketing', Unpublished paper, *Second Research Conference on Relationship Marketing*, Centre for Relationship Marketing, Emory University, Atlanta, Georgia.

Sheth, J.N, Gardner, D.M. and Garrett, D.E. (1988) *Marketing Theory: Evolution and Evaluation*. Wiley.

Sheth, J.N. and Parvatiyar, A. (1995) 'Relationship Marketing in Consumer Markets: Antecedents and Consequences', *Journal of the Academy of Marketing Science*, 23(4): 255–271.

Sheth, J.N. and Parvatiyar, A. (2000) *Handbook of Relationship Marketing*. Thousand Oaks: Sage Publications.

Siegel, H. (1988) 'Relativism for Consumer Research? (Comments on Anderson)' *Journal of Consumer Research*, 15(June): 129–132.

Slater, S.F. (1997) 'Developing a customer value-based theory of the firm', *Journal of the Academy of Marketing Science*, 25: 162–167.

Slater, S. and John C.N. (1995) 'Market Orientation and the Learning Organization', *Journal of Marketing*, (July): 63–74.

Slater, S.F. and Narver, J.C. (2000) 'Intelligence Generation and Superior Customer Value', *Journal of the Academy of Marketing Science*, 28(1): 120–127.

Stern, L.W. and Reve, T. (1980) 'Distribution Channels As Political Economies: A Framework for Comparative Analysis', *Journal of Marketing*, (Summer): 52–64.

Tadajewski, M. (2008) 'Incommensurable Paradigms, Cognitive Bias and the Politics of Marketing Theory', *Marketing Theory*, 8(3): 273–297.

Thompson, J.D. (1967) *Organizations in Action: Social Science Bases of Administrative Theory*. New York: McGraw-Hill.

Thompson, C. (1997) 'Exploring the Difference: A Postmodern Approach to Paradigmatic Pluralism in Consumer Research', in S. Brown, and D. Turley, (eds) *Consumer Research: Postcards from the Edge*, London: Routledge, pp. 150–189.

Thompson, G., Frances, J., Levačič R. and Mitchell J. (eds.) (1994) *Markets, Hierarchies and Networks: The Coordination of Social Life.* Thousand Oaks, CA: Sage Publications, Inc.

Tuominen, M., Rajala, A. and Möller K. (2004) 'Market-Driving Versus Market-Driven: Divergent Roles of Market Orientation in Business Relationships', *Industrial Marketing Management*, 33(3): 207–217.

Ulaga, W. (2003) 'Capturing Value Creation in Business Relationships: A Customer Perspective', *Industrial Marketing Management*, 32(8): 677–693.

Ulaga, W. and Eggert, A. (2006) 'Value-Based Differentiation in Business Relationships: Gaining and Sustaining Key Supplier Status', *Journal of Marketing*, 70(1): 118–136.

Van Bruggen, G.H. and Smidts, A. (1995) 'The Assessment of Market Orientation: Evaluating the Measurement Instrument as a Tool for Management', Proceedings of the Annual Conference of the European Marketing Academy, Cergy-Pontoise, May 16–19.

Van den Bulte, C.H. (1991) The Concept of Marketing Mix Revised. A Case Analysis of Metaphor, in *Marketing Theory and Management*. Chent, Belgium: Chent Press.

van Raaij, Erik M. and Stoelhorst, J.W. (2008) 'The Implementation of a Market Orientation', *European Journal of Marketing*, 42(11/12): 1265–1293.

Varadarajan, P.R. (1985) 'A Two-Factor Classification of Competitive Strategy Variables', *Strategic Management Journal*, 6: 357–375.

Vargo, S. and Lusch, R. (2004) 'Evolving to a New Dominant Logic for Marketing', *Journal of Marketing*, 48(January): 1–17.

Vargo, S. and Lusch, R. (2006) *The Service Dominant Logic of Marketing: Dialog, Debate and Directions.* New York: M. E. Sharpe.

Vargo, S. and Lusch, R.F. (2008) 'Service-Dominant Logic: Continuing the Evolution',

Journal of the Academy of Marketing Science, 36(1): 1–10.

Walker, Jr.,O.C., Ruekert, R.W. and Roering, K.J. (1987) 'Picking Proper Paradigms: Alternative Perspectives on Organizational Behavior and Their Implications for Marketing Management Research', in M.J. Houston (ed.) *Review of Marketing*, Chicago: American Marketing Association, pp. 3–36.

Wathne, K.H. and Heide, J.B. (2004) 'Relationship Governance in a Supply Chain Network', *Journal of Marketing*, 68(January): 73–89.

Weick, K. (1979) *The Social Psychology of Organizing.* Reading MA: Addison-Wesley.

Weick, K. (1985) 'The significance of corporate culture', in P. Frost, L. Moore, M. Louis, C. Lundberg and J. Martin (eds) *Organizational Culture*, Beverly Hills, CA: Sage, pp. 381–389.

Wensley, R. (1995) 'A Critical Review of Research in Marketing', *British Journal of Management*, 6: S63–S82.

Wernerfelt, B. (1984) 'A Resource-Based View of the Firm', *Strategic Management Journal*, 5(2): 171–180.

Williamson, O.E. (1985) *The Economic Institutions of Capitalism.* New York, NY: The Free Press.

Willmott, H. (1993) 'Breaking the paradigm Mentality', *Organization Studies*, 14(5): 681–719.

Woodall, T. (2007) 'New Marketing, Improved Marketing, Apocryphal Marketing. Is One Marketing Concept Enough?', *European Journal of Marketing*, 41: 1284–1296.

Wooliscroft, B. (2008) 'Re-inventing Wroe?', *Marketing Theory*, 8(4): 367–385.

Zeithaml, V.A., Berry, L.L. and Parasuraman, A. (1988) 'Communication and Control Processes in the Delivery of Service Quality', *Journal of Marketing*, 52: 35–48.

Zeithaml, V.A. and Bitner, M.J. (1996) *Service Marketing.* New York: McGraw-Hill Companies Inc.

10

Debates Concerning the Scientific Method: Social Science Theory and the Philosophy of Science

John O'Shaughnessy

INTRODUCTION

The philosophy of science deals with questions about science, whether natural science or social science, and not with answering scientific questions, which is the province of science itself. Methodology, in the sense of the methods employed by a discipline to attain knowledge, is a major concern and an area of controversy. The questions addressed are:

1 What methods for seeking knowledge are worth pursuing, given the subject matter being explored?
2 What methods should science use to construct explanatory systems?
3 What criteria should be used in the choice of methods?
4 What are the methods used in applying a scientific paradigm or explanatory system?
5 What distinguishes causal from interpretive methods?

WHAT METHODS FOR SEEKING KNOWLEDGE ARE WORTH PURSUING, GIVEN THE SUBJECT MATTER BEING EXPLORED?

Methodological monism

The answer to this question on methods has traditionally been dominated by the dogma of *methodological monism*, a core thesis of *positivism*, which states that all forms of scientific inquiry must, to be called scientific, follow the methods of the natural sciences. The most extreme version of methodological monism is the twentieth-century brand of positivism known as *logical positivism*, associated with the so-called 'Vienna Circle' in the 1930s. The Vienna Circle understood the following tenets as defining 'good science':

• Science is the search for *descriptive* laws, which are systemized into theory that contains no theoretical entities not defined in observational terms.

- Teleological explanations in terms of goals, functions and purposes are invalid.
- Meaningful statements are either *synthetic* or *analytic* – a synthetic statement (all buyers are subject to conditioning) is an empirical one with observable facts relevant to its truth or falsity, while an analytic statement (a purchasing agent buys on behalf of an organization) is just true through the meaning of the terms used. This distinction was enshrined in the *verifiability principle*, which claimed that, to be scientific, statements must be empirically verifiable. Those that are not verifiable are either analytic or nonsensical. All propositions about religion and ethics are thus unscientific, being nonsensical.
- Methodological monism supports *empiricism* and contrasts with *rationalism*. Empiricism is the claim that what we know, we know only because the empirical evidence so far happens to point that way. Empiricists argue that the only way to understand the world is through observation and experiment. In contrast, followers of rationalism seek to deduce facts about the world through the exercise of reason. Handy and Harwood (1973), supporters of a strong empiricist (positivist) tradition, argue that rationalism is still the dominant orientation among formal model builders, giving rise to models like 'game theory' and 'utility theory' that confuse warranted assertions about the particular model with warranted assertions about some aspect of human behavior. They take model builders to task for not investigating the presumed connections between the model and observed behavior with any degree of thoroughness: typically, it is the *internal* aspects of the model that are examined rather than matching the model to actual behavior. This criticism still applies since it is easy for rationalism in marketing science to sacrifice reality for intellectual rigor. (The real debate, though, in practice is not which to exclude but where the relative dominance lies since empiricism and rationalism inevitably play a part in all scientific inquiry.) In November 2008, in *Scientific American*, the editors made a similar accusation against those physics and mathematics PhDs who crafted the financial software for Wall Street, arguing their naïve, purely rational models helped precipitate the Wall Street collapse.
- Methodological individualism is the claim that social phenomena are wholly explainable in terms of facts about individuals. The logical positivists were *methodological individualists* in that they recognized only individual particulars, denying that general abstract concepts like 'society' or 'market', 'beauty', 'goodness', offer any additional insight onto the world. In contrast, *methodological holism* focuses on social wholes. Whichever approach is adopted in marketing depends on the questions being addressed. Thus, psychologists implicitly adopt methodological individualism while methodological holism has attractions for those social scientists whose interest lie in the behavior of groups. Diffusion theory in marketing focuses on the individual but is quoted in support of the product life cycle (PLC), which is a holistic phenomenon assumed to arise from the individual actions of decision makers.

If we were to accept the tenets of logical positivism, there would be little in *social* science that would pass the logical positivists' criteria for being a science. However, when we speak of positivism or positivists today, we are not talking about those who subscribe to the doctrines of logical positivism but to those who focus on empirical observation, *causal* explanation, experimentation, measurement and testing. The most well-known academic in marketing advocating a positivist philosophy of science is Shelby Hunt (1991).

Although still a very useful distinction, philosophers today deny the sharp division between synthetic and analytic statements with Kripke (in Scott, 2004) adding the concept of *necessary a posteriori* truths, quoting examples that are neither synthetic nor analytic. John L. Austin, a linguistic philosopher, points out that there are classes of utterances that are perfectly meaningful but cannot be said to be either true or false or just definitional. To say, for example, 'I promise I will buy you that bicycle tomorrow' is neither true nor false, neither describing nor evaluating but simply doing or acting. In respect to scientific method generally, Putnam (1981) claims that no philosopher of science accepts that there is just one scientific method or set of methods and this is even more true today. Susan Haack (2003) agrees, arguing there is no magic set of methods we 'baptize as scientific method', distinct from the intellectual tools we employ in our daily lives.

Popper (1959) substituted *falsifiability* for verifiability as the necessary condition for any hypothesis to be potentially scientific on the ground that scientific theories or hypotheses can be falsified but never completely proven. This claim by Popper is still quoted as orthodoxy though Duhem (1954), a French physicist, had early on in the twentieth century demonstrated that the falsifiability of a scientific law in an absolute sense is also not demonstrable. In any case, social science theories do not commonly come along with obvious ways of testing them. Determining how to test a theory may require considerable ingenuity, more than that needed to think of the theory itself. Concepts like cognitive dissonance, frequently quoted in marketing, have resisted all attempts at falsification.

The verifiability principle of the logical positivists goes hand-in-hand with the *correspondence theory of truth*. This asserts that something is true if it corresponds with the 'facts': the idea of the world consisting of unambiguous facts to be objectively observed and generalized about was a central tenet of positivism. Nevertheless, the correspondence theory of truth is less operational than it seems, once we recognize that the notion of truth is *semantic* in that it depends, first and foremost, on the interpretation of the meaning of the expression whose truth is being determined. In any case, we now accept that what we label 'facts' can be theory-determined, or at least concept-dependent.

Methodological monism is still dominant under the headings of *logical empiricism* and *naturalism*. Logical empiricism is a much more sophisticated version of logical positivism with the goal of science being *explanation* (not mere description) but continuing to insist that scientific hypotheses be testable and potentially falsifiable. However, the particular brand of logical empiricism that perhaps holds most sway is naturalism. Nagel (1961) was a logical empiricist who supported the doctrine of *naturalism*, which asserts that whatever occurs, including mental events, is contingent upon the occurrence of physical–chemical–physiological events and structures. For the naturalist, the only scientific explanation is a *causal explanation*. Naturalism has major adherents in philosophy though there are critics (see Rea, 2003). Journal articles in marketing and science generally tend to eschew the word 'cause' as too theory-loaded in favor of functional relationship. Marketing journal articles are more likely to suggest some cause rather than demonstrate it though this may change with the application of structural equation models (SEM) from statistics (Pedhazur, 1997).

Methodological exclusivism

A parallel claim to that of methodological monism is that the study of human beings requires a distinct methodology of its own, borrowing nothing from the methods of the natural sciences. It is argued, for example, that only dogmatic faith allows someone to argue that social science should, to be scientific, depend solely on the methods of the natural sciences. Both methodological monism and the counter claim for distinct methods for studying human action, Roth (1987) categorizes as *methodological exclusivism*.

Methodological exclusivism is not just confined to positivist writers on social science like Rudner (1966) who are methodological monists but those like Winch (1958) who claims the social sciences require a distinct methodology. Methodological exclusivism as applied to the study of human behavior is generally interpretive. Those undertaking ethnographic studies like Belk (1991) in consumer research will naturally lean to this position. Winch argues that, if the objects of study are essentially sensory data, they can typically be studied via the methods of the natural sciences. However, if the object of study is human beings, acting in a way that *expresses* a way-of-life, such a study comes under the heading of the humanities and calls for methods distinct from the natural sciences.

Methodological Pluralism

There is a danger of replacing methodological monism with the claim that the social (human) sciences require a unique methodology of their own. *Methodological pluralism* rejects any claim that there is just one set of methods that gives privileged access to studying and explaining human behavior (O'Shaughnessy, 1997). Whatever the controversy over Feyerabend's (1975) book, *Against Method*, with its antiobjectivism thesis, it has wide appeal in arguing that there is no one best way to conduct successful science and science cannot be restricted to following one set of rules, regardless of subject matter; there are 'different methods for different topics'.

Methodological pluralism accepts a post-positivist conception of science, rejecting the claim that there is any one set of methods that provides a privileged access to reality and truth. Methodological pluralism implies we can be an antipositivist in rejecting methodological monism but still access, when appropriate, the methods of the natural sciences to study human behavior.

WHAT METHODS SHOULD SCIENCE USE TO CONSTRUCT EXPLANATORY SYSTEMS?

Ignoring, for the present, interpretation as a scientific method or arguing interpretation seeks understanding rather than explanatory theory, philosophy of science seeks to describe the way traditional science proceeds to establish truth. Two methods receive central stage. One is *induction* and the other the *hypothetico-deductive* (H-D) *method*. Nevertheless, a third method has become increasingly of interest, namely, *abduction*. All three methods have imperfections.

Induction

In induction, we build up from 'facts'. Once the facts are collected and ordered, inductive generalizations can be made. It is only when numerous observations are compared is it possible to generalize. This passage from the observed facts to generalization is *induction*. Such generalizations, it is argued, may evolve

into 'laws' if they withstand testing. Laws in turn can be related to other laws to form some theory. Science, on this view, is primarily concerned with the collection of data, forming generalizations from these data, with laws and theories later emerging through the testing process.

The rationale of induction needs to justify such statements as: All observed Xs are Ys so all Xs are Ys. Those who accept that induction can be rationally justified are *inductivists*. The problem for the inductivist is to find a method that provides inductive proof, that is, to show how observational evidence can be used to validate laws of wide generality or at least to provide criteria that would certify 'good' inductive inferences. Zaltman and Bonoma (1979) recommend induction as a basis for theory building in marketing though what they recommend has serious limitations (O'Shaughnessy, 2009).

As universal laws cannot be absolutely verified or confirmed by any form of inductive logic, one rationale to justify induction is simply the claim that it works. However, its having worked in one set of circumstances in the past is no guarantee for future success. A second rationale to justify induction is by reference to the uniformity of nature, as opposed to regarding nature as chaotic. However, this assumption seems much less true when it comes to the social world than to the world of physics. Nevertheless, even if nature is uniform this does not imply that the particular uniformities being observed (e.g. in a market) will hold in the future. The uniformity of nature assumption itself relies on induction. A final rationale relates to sampling theory but the theory cannot justify induction, because it depends on induction: sampling theory is in fact an application of induction. Faith in induction as a way to theory building is implicit in social science and marketing studies and manifests itself in an *implicit* belief that, with enough studies, the truth will be out with the evidence being overwhelmingly in support for some resulting theory (Boland, 1982). This relies on faith in the possibility of universals, stability and uniformity of behavior.

Hypothetico-deductive method

This is the method popularized by Karl Popper (1959, 1963). The hypothetico-deductive method claims the first priority is to generate a hypothesis to guide observation and experiment. As Popper says, the simple command to observe cannot be followed since there is an indefinite number of things that might be observed. Observation, he argues, is selective and science is a combination of inspiration and deduction. Hence, he recommends the H-D method. Inspiration is needed to postulate the hypothesis or model, which in turn directs the process of testing. This is the method most commonly set out in marketing journal articles devoted to research, giving the impression that this was the method actually adopted to do the research rather than adopted for writing up the results.

Popper refers to the H-D philosophy as *deductivism* to distinguish it from inductivism. For Popper the H-D method is a method of falsification in that it can falsify a hypothesis but never prove one. Popper argues that the more easily falsified hypothesis should be selected for testing first. The more easily tested hypothesis tends to be wide in scope so that, if it withstands all attempts to falsify it, we learn a great deal. Another reason a hypothesis may be more easily falsified is because it makes precise predictions that are neither vague nor ambiguous. However, the falsification approach can be very elusive. Thus we have yet to test the existence of gravitational waves (ripples in the fabric of space and time, which is one of the predictions of Einstein's general theory of relativity) as the technology for doing so is still being developed.

The more basic question is: What constitutes 'falsification'? Few scientists would throw out a theory just because of a few anomalies, at least not until a better theory comes along. In any case, how do we choose between theories spun off by the different explanatory systems in social science? Popper acknowledged that, while falsification is still best for testing *within* theories to improve them, the evaluation of competing theories (*between* theory choosing) must involve a wider range of criteria since competing theories may survive all feasible types of testing. Popper was later to argue that the competing theories must be assessed together rather than each in isolation, applying all types of criticism but particularly searching for inconsistencies.

The H-D method has come to enjoy wide acceptance among social scientists, because it legitimizes the postulation of unobservable theoretical entities (hypothetical constructs) like 'attitudes' (MacCorquodale and Meehl, 1948). In contrast, the inductive approach to theory building seeks purely observational sciences made up of descriptive regularities. This is strange since even in the eighteenth century some of the most successful theories in physics and chemistry assumed unobservable entities. As Ernest Nagel (1961) argues, no interesting scientific hypothesis restricts itself to what can be directly observed but includes nonobservable constructs (hypothetical constructs) like the electron or self-image. Models in consumer behavior typically employ such hypothetical constructs ('construct' substitutes for 'concept' to indicate it is constructed for the discipline).

While the inductivist views scientific progress as occurring through the steady accumulation of more and more facts leading to theories becoming more and more general in scope, this is not necessarily so with the H-D account. The H-D approach views scientific progress as involving successive formulations, modifications and rejections of theories without any absolute assurance that scientific knowledge will necessarily be steady and cumulative. Although the H-D method has wide acceptance, it is not strictly deductive as the name suggests. If we are assuming the method can lead to knowledge, its success rests upon induction; a fact obscured by Popper's use of the word 'deductivism' to describe the method.

Popper's 'deductivism' went together with his claim that science progresses through the falsification of theories. Nevertheless, as we have seen, critics argue that the hypothetico-deductive method does not circumvent the problem of induction and its justification. The question still remains as to the grounds for expecting unfalsified theories or hypotheses to remain unfalsified and falsified theories or hypotheses to be continually falsified regardless of their domain of application. There is an inductive element in weighing the significance of each falsification or non-falsification and we need some way of rationally defending why so many nonfalsifications in such circumstances lead us to accept the hypothesis. Usually, the criterion is *conventionalist*, which says that we select on the basis of what is conventionally acceptable like the selection of confidence limits in statistics.

Popper is criticized for his views on *within* theory testing and *between* theory choosing. Ernest Nagel (1979), an early critic of Popper, while agreeing that science is an honest search for evidence to eliminate rival hypotheses, rejects Popper's particular conception of the role of falsification in theory development as an over-simplification that is 'close to being a caricature of scientific procedure', while the substance of Popper's later ideas on science, even when understood to be prescriptive, are 'any less dubious than when they are taken to be descriptive' (pp. 76–77). Nagel views Popper's ideas on science as doubtful and his prescriptions to scientists as lacking in substance. In fact, Nagel believes Popper's description of the scientific enterprise is false and his prescriptions superficial.

Popper was inspired by Einstein whose theory of general relativity appeared to be a bold conjecture with Einstein inviting scientists to falsify his claim. However, what Nagel (1979) and others find simplistic about falsificationism is that it fails to show how knowledge can advance through applying tests designed to falsify hypotheses. As Ravetz (1990) says, if the hypothesis is falsified, we gain only the knowledge that some particular hypothesis is false. On the other hand, if the test does not falsify we learn only that the

hypothesis has not yet been proved false. As a principle of method, he regards such an approach as bankrupt.

Abduction

Charles Sanders Peirce (1839–1914) employed the term 'abduction' for the type of reasoning or method of discovery that moves from a given set of facts to an explanatory hypothesis. As a mode of inference, *abduction* proceeds from the observation of unexpected fact(s) to a hypothesis that would explain the fact(s). There is a link between abduction and causal analysis in that the hypothesis could be causal but this is not necessarily so, as demonstrated by Peirce's own example of abduction. This example involves docking at a Turkish seaport and seeing a man on horseback, surrounded by many horsemen holding a canopy over his head. It would be reasonable to infer that this was the governor of the province if unable to think of any other man who would be so honored. Abduction is illustrated in science by the way Kepler reached his hypothesis about the elliptical path of Mars from the observed irregularities in the movement of Mars. We visualize companies using abduction to explain product failures, but this is less common than it should be since, as Karen Arenson (2006) says, institutions 'are not always hungry for more information. Investigations can be costly and they can assign blame'. Mowen (1979) in a discussion of abduction argues that marketers can develop marketing theory through abduction (though he prefers the term retroduction, often used as a synonym).

Lipton (1991) contrasts Popper's all H-D model with abduction, which he views as 'inference to the best explanation' by pointing out that the H-D model is an account of corroborating evidence rather than inference. Inference does rather better since it brings in the competition. Scientists also reject hypotheses, not because the hypothesis is incompatible with the data, but because the hypotheses turn out to be inadequate by way of explaining what we want to explain. As Lipton says, it is a mistake to claim that disconfirmation operates exclusively through refutation, that is, in data being incompatible with the hypotheses. He quotes others in arguing that scientists also reject theories as false because, while they are not refuted by the evidence, they fail to explain salient contrasts. Lipton concludes by arguing that Inference to the best explanation (abduction), linked to contrastive explanations, provides an alternative to the deductive–nomological (D–N) model in its account of (a) the context of discovery (b) the determination of relevant evidence (c) the nature of disconfirmation in that it lends positive support that contrastive experiments provide.

Abduction goes along with using case studies for theory development. Few social scientists and marketing academics have not, at one time or another, reflected on whether cases could not be put to more use than just being instruments for sharpening students' acumen in class discussion. Could not bringing together 'similar' cases contribute to marketing theory? A book by two political scientists, Alexander George and Andrew Bennett (2005), prompted many to think afresh about the potential of case studies for the development of theory. They demonstrated that case studies could be used to develop theory. If we wish to go beyond correlation to causation in decision processes, statistical methods are not very helpful. Case studies, the authors argue, are more efficient at discovering the scope conditions of 'theories' (the range of phenomena to which they apply) and evaluating claims about causal necessity or sufficiency in specific instances. In fact, analysis of a case may show that some alleged cause is neither necessary nor sufficient. Cases are less effective at gauging generalized causal effects or the causal weights of variables across a wide range of cases, at present the province of statistical methods. Cases can supplement whatever theories we possess and deviant cases can uncover new or omitted variables, test

hypotheses or discover causal paths and mechanisms. The usefulness of statistical-correlation findings is considerably reduced when, as is commonly the case, such studies do not identify causal variables that decision-makers can act upon. Established statistical generalizations tend to be undermined when confronted with case histories. We are seemingly always able to think of some exception to any statistical generalization. This is not surprising when we consider the crucial importance of contextual factors in explaining or understanding behavior.

WHAT CRITERIA SHOULD BE USED IN THE CHOICE OF METHODS?

In brief, the criteria to be used in the choice of methods will depend on the particular paradigm adopted and the corresponding questions being addressed. Nevertheless, this brief statement needs to be unpacked by an understanding of the nature of social science and the concept of a paradigm.

There are no methods or processes that will lead to the discovery of universal laws in social science. There are no existing universal laws in social science and no claims that are universally true. Nicholas Humphrey (1983), an experimental psychologist, words it well:

'There are not, and never will be, Newtonian principles of human behavior. Those academic psychologists who have tried to emulate the method and theory of classical physics – who have tried like Clark Hull in the 1930s to write a latter-day *Principia* – have proved what any layman might have told them at the start: the mountain of human complexity cannot be turned into a molehill of scientific laws'. (Humphrey, 1983: 7)

We would all like to believe in the possibility of *nomothetic* (law-like) *explanations* in marketing where the goal often lies in identifying abstract laws for repeatable events and processes. This demands too much. Even though we generally talk of laws in science as being unconditionally universal, the fact is that in many branches of the natural sciences, laws are stated as being universally valid *only* under certain 'ideal' conditions, for pure cases of the phenomena being discussed. The discrepancies, however, between what the laws of science assert and what observation discloses, can be accounted for in terms of fairly well-authenticated discrepancies between the ideal conditions and the actual conditions being observed. This is where the natural sciences score over the social sciences. Even in economics, the discrepancy between the assumed ideal conditions for an economic law to apply and the actual conditions in the market are usually so huge and the conjectures needed to fill the gap are so tricky and complicated that the strategy used by the natural sciences is infeasible.

McGuire (2000) maintains that those who still seek universal laws in psychology find themselves confined to 'testing hypotheses' that are really truisms requiring no investigation to establish their truth, like saying no one likes to be humiliated or that, if I stare at the sky in the street, others will look up also. His alternative to the 'positivist view' is 'perspectivism'. Fay (1996) sees perspectivism as an alternative to positivism with perspectivism arguing that there can be no intellectual activity without an organizing conceptual scheme that reflects some perspective. Perspectivism goes hand-in-hand with methodological pluralism.

Perspectivism acknowledges there are no laws of social behavior or of intentional action and no hypothesis is perfectly true (as we inevitably misrepresent reality to some extent) even if true enough on occasions. McGuire recognizes context moderates against universals being able to explain the individual case but recommends exploring the pattern of contexts in which a hypothesis does or does not obtain and identifying the reasons why it does or does not. To fall back on universals misses the nuances of the situation. Flyvbjerg (2003) and many others similarly deny the possibility of laws in the social sciences on the ground that findings are context-dependent.

Not only some philosophers but also some psychologists argue that what social scientists often regard as empirical hypotheses to be put forward for testing are in fact simply conceptual truths. Smedslund (1995), a professor of psychology at the University of Oslo, claims that all psychological propositions that refer to voluntary behavior (intentional actions) are necessarily true as the relationship between antecedent and consequent is conceptual and not causal. This claim usually rests on the assumption that the relationship between reasons for action and causes is conceptual and not causal (see the following section). Still there are many journal articles that purport to test empirical hypothesis when the hypotheses are just conceptual truths. I provide examples elsewhere (O'Shaughnessy, 2009), but an obvious example is the assertion that 'a high credibility source is more persuasive than a low credibility source'. If it were not, as a matter of definition, it would not be a high credibility source.

If we are able to speak of an overall perspective for a discipline, subdiscipline or research tradition that perspective is termed its *paradigm*, a term popularized by Thomas S. Kuhn (1962). The question arises as to how the term 'perspective' corresponds to the concept of a paradigm. A perspective is a system of integrated beliefs and recalled images that provides a lens through which to interpret what is going on. This is also true of a paradigm as all paradigms embody a perspective. Nevertheless, a paradigm is a perspective within science embodying substance of an explanatory nature.

Kuhn (1962) in his seminal work *The Structure of Scientific Revolutions*, concerned with the historical development of science, moved away from an exclusive focus on theory/model-testing and theory building with this notion of a 'scientific paradigm'. The concept of a paradigm was *substituted* for the concept of theory. A scientific paradigm is an overall conceptualization of the field involving values, concepts, theories, models and applications. The concept of a paradigm and the notion of paradigm shifts made sense to social scientists as psychologists, for example, noted the paradigm of introspective psychology being dislodged by behaviorism and behaviorism displaced by cognitive psychology and perhaps cognitive psychology being submerged by cognitive neuroscience. Kuhn claims that a scientific revolution was needed before the adoption of a new paradigm. Kuhn seemed to view the social sciences as preparadigmatic because of the failure to agree on any one single paradigm though different paradigms in social science are apt to ask different questions or open up different windows onto a problem. That said, for Kuhn, understanding a paradigm does not come about from memorizing laws or theories or models but by mastering applications; being able to solve a certain class of problem and being able to recognize in different situations further applications.

Kuhn's initial (1962) conceptualization of a paradigm was criticized for its ambiguity and vagueness. Later, Kuhn (1974) defined a paradigm as covering two related senses:

First as a disciplinary matrix: 'Disciplinary' because the paradigm is the common possession of some scientific community and a 'matrix' because every paradigm embodies sets of orderly elements like symbolic generalizations or expressions; beliefs and values sought like predictive accuracy, simplicity, consistency; models; exemplars which are the shared set of crucial, striking, successful examples of problem solving application. The concept of a disciplinary matrix comes closer to defining the explanatory systems in psychology and sociology than does the view of a science as being composed of theories along the lines traditionally suggested.

Second, as exemplars: While exemplars (as stated in the foregoing section) are part of the disciplinary matrix, they are also paradigmatic of the field. Exemplars represent the paradigm-as-achievement and so serve as models for future generations of scientists. They represent in the most fundamental sense, the concept of a paradigm. They are the concrete successes attributable to the disciplinary matrix's power. Through familiarity with the field's exemplars, the scientist absorbs the rules to be followed for extending the application of the disciplinary matrix.

A problem raised by Kuhn was that of the *incommensurability* of paradigms. According to Kuhn, choosing between theories within an accepted paradigm is very different from choosing between paradigms. Kuhn claims that the rules for choosing between theories within a paradigm are implicit in the paradigm itself, while there are no operational rules for choosing between the rival paradigms themselves, which are incommensurable, so the scientific community's judgment is the final court of appeal. Incommensurability arises because (a) the paradigms do not deal with the same problems or (b) the terms common to each paradigm differ in meaning or (c) differences in concepts between paradigms may represent different perspectives. Later, Kuhn (1977) was to argue that choice between paradigms is influenced by the commitment of scientists to certain values like predictive accuracy; consistency and coherence to what is already established.

Kuhn denies the criticism that he is suggesting that choice between different paradigms is an irrational act. He is simply asserting that there is no choice process that is logically compelling. While agreeing that the meaning of terms may be theory-dependent, Suppe (1977) argues there is little support for the view that incompatible theories are noncomparable because they are incommensurable. However, Kuhn is not denying the possibility of comparability but denies the possibility of the acceptance of a common vocabulary by which to do it.

Donald Davidson (1984) argues that the very concept of *totally* different frameworks or sets of beliefs is in itself unintelligible. The fact that disagreement takes place at all implies some commonality of standards for evaluation. Fay (1996) points out those differences between paradigms can only be understood against a background of similarities; that competing paradigms in science must be about the same world and share a sufficient vocabulary and methods of inquiry for them to compete.

This is simply saying that scientific paradigms cannot be completely incomparable but can be *incommensurable* in that we may be unable to translate rival paradigms into a common vocabulary. Being incommensurable is something different from paradigms being incomparable. In marketing, Hunt (1991) is strong in endorsing this view.

With the recognition that various social science explanatory systems or paradigms are simply different windows onto a problem or simply answering different questions, many philosophers have accepted 'perspectivism'. Claims about viewpoints being tied to perspectives, contrast with the belief associated with 'positivism' that we can attain knowledge that reflects *Reality as it is* (Fay, 1996). Positivism is commonly contrasted with purely interpretive approaches, but interpretive approaches constitute just one of many perspectives as to ways of tracking truth. That said, open-minded people, within limits, are often capable of shifting from one perspective to another in social science. If other paradigms yield the same conclusions, scientists can have more confidence in the theory. Nevertheless, differing perspectives can lead to conflict. However, such conflict need not be destructive. There can be constructive conflict where debate is vigorous and sharp but polarization and rancor are rare. Marketing should and needs to examine different perspectives or paradigms. As Shweder (2003) says:

'The knowable world is incomplete if seen from any one point of view, incoherent if seen from all points of view at once and empty if seen from nowhere in particular'. (Shweder, 2003: 45)

An interesting example of alternative perspectives is philosophy of science itself. The traditional perspective on the subject was exemplified by Ernest Nagel (1961) in his extremely impressive, *The Structure of Science,* where the perspective was normative in approach, aptly illustrated by examples drawn from most branches of science (including social science). However, along came another perspective, that of Thomas S. Kuhn (1962) where the perspective was historical development. Kuhn's perspective has taken over in the social sciences as being more descriptive of what actually happens. Natural scientists, if they read such books, are more respectful of Nagel, which is a far more demanding book as well as more to their liking. While both perspectives are justified, it is sad that Nagel, who, as a philosopher of science, had such a great deal to say about the philosophy of the social sciences, is now so neglected.

If we accept perspectivism, it makes no sense to say we know 'Reality as it really is' since we view things from a point of view that links to our stock of available concepts, and our belief system with its own assumptions and biases. The identification of the 'facts' may not always be theory-determined, but the process will always be concept-dependent. It was Gilbert Ryle (1949) who said we could only observe a *conceptualized* reality, not because our vocabulary is deficient, but because the very notion of an unconceptualized reality is absurd. The very notion of seeing the world free of any perspective is incoherent. We interpret from a standpoint or perspective. Einstein talked of advances in science as equivalent to climbing a mountain to get a still higher perspective.

Can the various perspectives or paradigms be integrated in some way to provide more explanatory depth? Foxall (2007) is one academic who has sought in his writings to integrate radical behaviorism, cognitive psychology (or at least cognitive psychology that focuses on intentional behavior) and neuroscience. What makes some academics reject perspectivism is when it is interpreted as a form of *relativism* that denies the existence of objective standards for establishing truth. This is a misinterpretation and to avoid such identification, perspectivism is sometimes defined as the 'multiplicity of perspectives' view.

We neither prove nor disprove any theory in any *absolute* sense. This claim about absolute proof and disproof underpins the doctrine of *fallibilism*, which asserts that there is no certainty: all knowledge is subject to modification and change. Factual knowledge at best can only be probable in that we cannot prove the contrary to be absolutely impossible. There are always potential alternatives for any theory we might regard as true. Experiment is not the answer since in a final analysis even in an experiment we can never be certain of distinguishing cause from mere coexistence. As Fay (1996) says, getting out models in social science is analogous to mapmaking in that no mapmaker believes there is a unique premapped world waiting to be discovered. This is a very fine analogy.

Fay argues that the doctrine of fallibilism combined with perspectivism eschews the positivist notion that science must be able to mirror reality. When perspectives or paradigms are deeply rooted, preconceptions may be held as axiomatic truths. This makes it difficult to even temporarily adopt another paradigm. The preconceptions that are an integral part of any perspective are essential for interpreting the world, without which nothing could be discerned. On these grounds, Fay is rightly critical of social scientists who claim they start out without any preconceptions; being epistemologically so self-conscious leads to narcissistic self-display.

The reason for the absence of law-like (universal) generalizations in social science is, as already suggested, that explanations that possess any depth will be context-dependent and context-defined. Moreover, there are just too many contexts to suggest laws while people are not exact tokens of each other, even biologically.

The choice of method will relate to the questions being asked and the paradigm adopted. If the paradigm adopted eschews unobservable mental events as does behaviorism, the questions asked will relate to external influences and methods measuring such influences. Similarly, a cognitive model based on a paradigm derived from the computer metaphor will find it difficult to deal with questions about motivation and emotion and will fall back on laboratory-type methods.

WHAT ARE THE METHODS USED IN APPLYING A SCIENTIFIC PARADIGM OR EXPLANATORY SYSTEM?

The adoption of a specific paradigm implies the adoption of a conceptual lens through which to view the area of interest. A paradigm suggests the questions that might be asked but, most of all, it guides the researcher in interpreting the resulting 'facts' selected. If interpretation is based on a paradigm, model or theory, the term 'imputational interpretation' is used, since we impute onto the behavior of interest a way of behaving in line with the paradigm, model or theory. In imputational interpretation, we take our paradigm and assess how far it explains or can be applied to the relevant behavior or predicts outcomes of interest (Krausz, 1993). We look for congruence between model and data. As different basic social science paradigms or perspectives offer different stances in regard to human behavior, we might ask: Will the evidence tell us which is best? Not necessarily, since the different approaches may be addressing different questions or the evidence does not give an unequivocal answer.

In imputational interpretation, interpretation proceeds by imputing a structure to the behavior, guided by the paradigm or perspective adopted, just as we might interpret all market behavior in terms of exchange theory. When paradigms apply, they enrich understanding by providing a way to interpret behavior that may be otherwise puzzling and seemingly incoherent. However, there are obvious dangers in imputation. Any paradigm, theory or model creates a framework of expectations that is one way of seeing, but also a way of not seeing, since models exercise restrictions on what to look for. They push interpretation to fit the paradigm, theory or model, ignoring inconvenient facts. Thus, the effectiveness of lemon juice as a prophylactic against scurvy was accepted as a fact by seamen from the time of Columbus, but medical men up to the mid-nineteenth century rejected this claim, because their paradigm convinced them that this disease, like all diseases, was caused by either bad air or an imbalance of the humors: a case of bad knowledge driving out good (Wootton, 2006).

If the theory or paradigm adopted always affects interpretation of the facts, this casts doubts on the independence of observation from theory in any scientific investigation. Hence, the claim that observation is theory-driven or theory-determined. Nevertheless, the interpretation of facts cannot be entirely dictated by one's theoretical position since interpretation operates within confines constrained by the material of reality. Nonetheless, there are no *completely* uninterpreted 'givens' that can serve as the foundation of knowledge. However, does the interpretation of facts *always* depend on theories held? This is disputed by Hacking (1983). He does not agree that *all* scientific observations are interpretations in the light of theories held. While agreeing that interpretation is always involved, he argues, for example, that the early development of optics depended solely on noticing surprising phenomena that preceded any formulation of theory.

An explanation may seem perfectly adequate, only because *not* all relevant aspects of the problematic situation have been considered. One of the reasons for encouraging inter-disciplinary research is that this helps in looking for rival hypotheses, plus perspectives from other disciplines. However, cooperation may be resisted on the ground that rival disciplines are entertaining paradigms that are deviant and heretical. It is always a revelation when a journal editor (in ignorance or error) sends an article to a reviewer who does not subscribe to the same paradigm as the author. The reviewer often seems unable to tolerate another perspective, and it is this that makes multiperspective approaches so difficult to orchestrate.

WHAT DISTINGUISHES CAUSAL FROM INTERPRETIVE METHODS?

Performance and competence theories: Not all theories are causal or alternatively interpretive.

Rational choice theory (RCT) in economics is not a *causal* or interpretive theory but a combination of *competence* and *performance theories*. Interpretation will be at work but interpretation is not the focus. Performance theory in RCT consists of theories of instrumental rationality concerned with drawing up rules for choosing the best means to achieve ends. Instrumental rationality in turn draws on competence theories. A person's competence is tied to mastery of the rules or norms of rationality that are applicable to the activity being undertaken. A competence theory thus seeks to specify the capacities and processes of the rational agent who has mastered the relevant rules for the activity being undertaken. It results in criteria to judge the mastery of the rules. In particular, we have decision theory and game theory, which seek rules for identifying utility-maximizing strategies by simulating the thought processes of perfectly rational agents seeking the best course of action. Utility-maximizing, as the core of rational choice theory in economics, comes under rationalism as there is no empirical fact finding. The utility-maximizing concept of rational choice theory has even been the favored approach to considerations of equity in marketing (O'Shaughnessy and O'Shaughnessy, 2005) viewing equity considerations as just a potential cost. Elster (1999) will have none of this arguing that equity issues rest on emotions and emotions cannot be accommodated in any cost/ benefit function.

The instrumentalist doctrine

Instrumentalism, a species of pragmatism associated with logical positivism, justifies science in terms of its ability to predict and control. *Marketing Science*, the marketing journal, has an instrumentalist slant. The obsession in all marketing science with prediction and error functions indicates the pervasiveness of this doctrine. If scientific theories are merely instruments for prediction and control, this leaves no independent explanatory function for theories. Whether or not theories capture hidden aspects of reality is subservient to their predictive ability; theories are not true or false but merely useful or not so useful.

Does successful prediction distinguish science, rather than explanation? Milton Friedman (1953), a Nobel Laureate economist, seems to think so. He endorses the claim that an economic theory's predictions are its vindication and validation; its assumptions are unimportant, even if seemingly unsound or untrue. Instrumentalists regard theories and theoretical terms as simply heuristic (rules of thumb) instruments, which are effective or ineffective. Friedman argues that the ultimate goal of a positive science is a 'theory', which yields valid and meaningful predictions about phenomena not yet observed; that a theory's assumptions should not enter into the assessment of its value, as focusing on the truth of assumptions gets in the way of its predictive capacity, in that efficient prediction depends on simplifying reality. Friedman's view relegates explanation to rationalizations of successful prediction in the non-Freudian sense of rationalization to mean making up an answer to give the impression the explanatory difficulty has been solved. Friedman's view is well argued but it is not one endorsed by philosophers of science or by the scientific community where explanation is the goal of science.

Causal models of explanation

Lipton (1991) raises three objections to causal models of explanation. *First*, we have no analysis of causation that is noncontroversial. This is true though controversies over the exact nature of cause tend not to be a major obstacle. *Second*, there are many noncausal explanations that possess explanatory depth. Mathematical explanations are never causal while philosophers in their explanations seldom resort to causal explanation. *Third*, the causal model is weak in that it seldom provides an account of the selectivity criteria used to select the causally relevant factors.

Whatever cause we might select, we could ask for its cause and so on to an ever-receding (futile) search for a first cause. This is so though most information on the causal history of a phenomenon is not relevant to explaining what we want explained. In fact, we do not so much explain events as *features* of events.

Lipton asks what makes one piece of information about the causal history of an event explanatory and another not. He answers that the causes selected to explain facets of the events will tie to our interests. This reduces the number of factors we need to consider. Beveridge (1950) illustrates this well:

> The cause of an outbreak of plague may be regarded by the bacteriologist as the microbe he finds in the blood of the victims, by the entomologist as the microbe-carrying fleas that spread the disease, by the epidemiologist as the rats that escaped from the ship and brought the infection into the port. (Beveridge, 1950: 126)

We speak not only of causes but also of 'causation' and 'causality' as synonyms for the process of causing. The cause we seek is tied to context and our interests. No causal explanation is a total explanation in that no causal explanation will cite all the necessary antecedent conditions for bringing about the effect. Oxygen is a necessary condition for fire but we do not see the need to say this in asserting the lighting of the match to the dry timber caused the fire. In speaking of X being the cause of Y, we are giving priority to X over other factors or conditions that could have been labeled causal.

The regularity theory of causation, associated with David Hume (1711–1776), asserts that cause refers to a constant or statistical regularity that obtains between some antecedent S-type events and some subsequent Y-type events. Hume's analysis of cause led to a particular account of explanation where the *explicandum* (that which is to be explained) is deduced from a universal law as illustrated by the D-N or covering law model of explanation promoted by Hempel (1965) for example 'X has expanded. This is because X is metal and all metals expand when heated'. The 'law' from which the explicandum is inferred could, of course, be statistical. This gives rise to the inductive-statistical (I-S) version of the covering law model. Since these models predict, as a matter of straight deduction, from a universal or statistical regularity, the claim arose that the aim of any science is captured in the sequence:

(universal) law→prediction→control

This is purely an idealization in the case of the social sciences since there are no universal nontrivial generalizations in social science. As Juarrero (1999) says, even Pavlov's dogs did not salivate when the bell rang unless they were hungry. The sciences, as we have said, tend to eschew the term 'cause' for the notion of a functional relationship. The functional conception of causality where 'if X, then always Y' becomes $Y = \int(X)$ and suggests mathematical certitude though Juarrero argues it is simply a refinement of the regularity theory, without directly mentioning cause.

What is not always made clear is that working back from a problematic situation to identifying cause(s), the researcher cannot do so without some idea as to what to look for. If the researcher does not have a mental store of possible causes or reasons that includes the correct one, she cannot discover the cause. As Fay (1996) says, causal ascription ultimately must be backed by causal theories. If we are to license inferences from alleged causal relations, there is a need to indicate why the alleged cause and effect are more than accidentally related.

The regularity theory contrasts with a *natural necessity view* where some necessity is assumed in X causing Y. While we do take high correlations to suggest the possibility of some sort of causal connection, it is usually only if there are reasons suggesting a causal connection. Even in Philosophy, 101 students will point out that Hume's view fails to distinguish spurious regularities from causal relationships; a distinction that becomes obvious if we manipulate what we believe is the cause. That said, to insist that what we label 'cause' be a *sufficient* factor to

bring about the effect envisions complete determinism. Outside the laboratory, there is no such determinism when it comes to human action, since what determines Y is not just the so-called cause X but X together with an accompanying context of factors. As Bhaskar (1979), a scientific realist, says, causal relationships in the social sciences manifest empirical invariances only under closed conditions as in the laboratory.

Scientific realism contrasts with *idealism*. Idealism claims that reality is in some way mental; that the contents of the mind are all that there is in experience: whatever reality is out there is 'unknowable'; all we have consists of ideas about what the world is like. Idealism asserts there are different ways of looking at reality (that is, different perspectives), none of which is necessarily more correct than the others. Idealism contrasts with scientific realism. While there are various forms of scientific realism, they all involve claims about the actual existence of things: with scientific realism asserting that scientific entities like the electron and/or scientific theories like relativity theory, make claims about real things and must be either true or false because truth is how the world is. Realism should not be confused with positivism and those undertaking qualitative research can subscribe to either idealism or realism.

Bhaskar endorses the *scientific realist* view of causal processes, namely, that generative (causal) mechanisms are normally out of phase with their effects. For the scientific realist, there is an asymmetry between explanation and prediction, except in closed systems like the experimental laboratory. The scientific realist argues that in the real world the expected conjunctions are unlikely to occur because of the presence of intervening factors and countervailing causes. In real life (open systems), several generative structures are apt to be at work to produce the outcomes and we do not know ex-ante which will be at work. This makes the realist search for *causal structures* through abduction (working back from the facts to the causes) rather than testing hypotheses through checking predictions.

Interpretive methods

Interpretation is distinguished from inference. Inference draws valid conclusions from given premises while interpretation is never certain as it always involves a degree of conjecture. Interpretations are always guided by perspective or viewpoint. Human behavior, it is argued, needs a descriptive richness in interpretation that goes beyond that which can be captured by a set of propositions, tested in a context abstracted from real life and context. Behavior needs to be contextually situated for full understanding, yet the search for universal 'laws' ignores context. Leo Bogart (2003) stresses the importance of context with regard to ads:

'What the advertiser transmits is not what the viewer experiences. What the viewer sees at home is not what the client sees in the viewing room. Commercials are experienced in context'. (Bogart, 2003: 232)

Interpretive methods focus both on goal-seeking (purposive) behavior and expressive behavior. Expressive behavior is meaningful behavior that is an end in itself. An exemplar of expressive behavior would be the case of a couple, married many years, renewing their marriage vows. Another example is when we give money to some cause, which we know is lost; simply because it makes us feel we are doing something to promote our moral values. Interpretive methods are concerned with identifying the meaning (significance) of action and/or people's intentions and reasons for action embracing those which are instrumental and expressive. Under the heading of interpretive social sciences come such sub-disciplines as *ethnomethodology* and *symbolic interactionism* (Solomon, 1983), usually founded on *phenomenology*, which centers on reality as experienced by the individual.

Lyons (2001) after reviewing successive theories of mind in psychology claims the most useful and informative explanation of human action will always be because of 'what I believed and wanted'. Interpretive approaches are likely to focus on the search for meaning (significance and/or intent) that positivist social science neglects: understanding generally means understanding the meaning (significance) of the action. Understanding the meaning of action in terms of its significance for the individual relates to the reason-giving explanation, which is couched in terms of wants and beliefs in that to say something is significant for the individual is to say he or she believes it is important to his or her wants.

The term 'hermeneutics' refers to the interpretation of texts, especially Biblical. One claim is that the social sciences are more reflective of the methods of hermeneutics than the natural sciences. What is distinctive about a *full* hermeneutics account, as traditionally envisioned, is that it takes account of context and history. Many attempts have been made to find a set of general principles for the interpretation of texts as a foundation for hermeneutics. Friedrich Schleiermacher (1768–1834) conceived the 'hermeneutic circle' in which the interpretation of each part of a text is carried out by reference to the whole, and the understanding of the whole text by reference to the parts. This raises the problem of where to start. Schleiermacher argued the problem is resolved intuitively by a 'leap' into the circle, moving from parts to whole and whole to parts in an iterative way. The hermeneutic circle constitutes a part of hermeneutics and is one of its most well-known features. However, in itself it is insufficient to determine the meaning of a text.

For Hans-Georg Gadamer no interpreter is entirely neutral but is constrained by the tradition embodied in the text (Warnke, 1987). The interpreter's own perspective on that tradition constitutes part of the interpreter's horizon, which contrasts with the disparate and possibly distant horizon of the text. Gadamer claims there is a need for a *fusion of horizons* – of text tradition and the interpreter's horizon. Gadamer's dominance in twentieth-century hermeneutics was established by his *Truth and Method* (1979). Gadamer does not confine hermeneutics to just the interpretation of texts in literature. He argues persuasively that hermeneutics is dominant in science as well as cultural contexts.

Gadamer rejects the notion of absolute objectivity and open-mindedness in interpreting human action. It is just not possible to interpret in a completely objective way; it is in fact our preconceptions that make understanding of others possible. Understanding others does not arise from discarding our own meanings of things nor will it come from just trying to put ourselves in another's shoes. If there is to be any depth of understanding, it will come from *fusing* or integrating our meanings with those meanings we aim at understanding. This is what Gadamer calls the *fusion of horizons*. Unfortunately, the word 'fusion' carries the notion of the horizons becoming one *single* unity. This is *not* what Gadamer intends. He accepts some discord is likely to remain. This is because whatever is being interpreted stems from a different context and conceptual perspective than that of the interpreter.

Max Weber (1864–1920) used the term *verstehen*, translated into English as empathy. This term was adopted by Collingwood (1946) for the purpose of interpreting history; identifying the meaning of action with trying to relive the thoughts of the agent. However, this is now a minority view. Today, the interpretation of behavior is tending to be conceived, as Fay (1996) says, more like *deciphering* a poem than seeking some inner mental union with the author. Stueber (2005) is an exception. He claims that empathy as traditionally conceived is necessary for our folk-psychological understanding of others and he seeks to rehabilitate the concept as originally proposed. Even though it has limitations, he argues, it is still the central 'default mode' for understanding others. Charles Taylor (1964) endorses the deciphering view but continues to use the term *verstehen* for the deciphering. *He* distinguishes this conception of *verstehen* from the English word empathy defining verstehen as the set of intersubjective meanings that make up social life, to be grasped through interpretation, without resorting to empathy.

There are philosophers who view scientific explanation as causal explanation and seek to demonstrate that even the reason-giving explanation is causal. Brown (2001), a philosopher of science, argues that philosophers today generally hold that 'reasons are causes and reason explanations are causal explanations' of action (p. 152). If this is so, then the reason-giving explanation can be grouped under naturalism, the vision of many philosophers in the field of social science.

However, Fay argues that reasons in themselves cannot possibly be the cause of anything as the content of thought is neither a state, nor an event, nor a process. Some who endorse this view go on to claim that reasons are simply justifications for action. Nevertheless, Fay does not go this route, arguing that the *real* (causal) reasons for action must be understood to mean the *practical reasoning process* that caused the person to act. He acknowledges, however, that the reasoning process that causes the person to act may not always be conscious or amenable to recall or even capable of verbalization. In opposition, Bernard Williams (2002) and many others in the linguistic philosophy insist the relationship between motivational state, conviction and action, is a purely conceptual one, not a causal one and reject the notion of the reason-giving explanation being classified under naturalism.

Conclusion

Philosophy of social science makes us conscious of the philosophical background to all forms of argument and inquiry and highlights considerations that shake up our mental habits to think more clearly about what we are doing, where we are going and where we have come from. Philosophy of social science, like social science itself, provides sensitizing concepts that induce tolerance of alternative perspectives but also provides weapons for demolishing dogmatism when none is justified. All inquiry in social science is directed to tracking truth, and this search can be mishandled by neglecting relevant philosophical considerations.

REFERENCES

Arenson, K.W. (2006) 'What Organizations Don't Want to Know Can Hurt', *The New York Times*, August 22 C1, C4.

Austin, J.L. (1962) *How to do things with words*. London: Oxford University Press.

Belk, R.W. (ed.) (1991) *Highways and Buyways: Naturalistic Research from the Consumer Behavior Odyssey*. Provo, UT: Association for Consumer Research.

Beveridge, W.I. (1950) *The Art of Scientific Investigation,* A Vintage Book, p. 126.

Bhaskar, R. (1979) *The Possibility of Naturalism*. Atlantic Highlands, NJ: Humanities Press.

Bogart L,(2003) *Finding Out: Personal Adventures in Social Research – Discovering What People Think, Say, and Do*. Chicago: Ivan R. Dee.

Boland, L.A. (1982) *The Foundations of Economic Method*. London: George Allen & Unwin.

Brown, J.R. (2001) *Who Rules in Science*. Cambridge, MA: Harvard University Press.

Collingwood, R.G. (1946) *The Idea of History*. Oxford: Oxford University Press.

Davidson, D. (1984) *Inquiries into Truth and Interpretation*. New York: Oxford University Press.

Duhem, P. (1954) *The Aim and Structure of Physical Theory*. Trans. P. Weimer. Princeton: Princeton University Press.

Elster, J. (1999) *Alchemies of the Mind*. Cambridge: Cambridge University Press.

Fay, B. (1996) *Contemporary Philosophy of Science*. Oxford: Blackwell Publishing Co.

Feyerabend, P. (1975) *Against Method*. London: Verso.

Flyvbjerg, B. (2003) *Making Social Science Matter*. Cambridge: Cambridge University Press.

Foxall, G. (2007) 'Intentional Behaviorism', *Behavior and Philosophy*, 35: 1–55.

Friedman, M. (1953) 'The Methodology of Positive Economics', in *Essays on Positive Economics*. Chicago: University of Chicago Press.

Gadamer, H.-G. (1979) *Truth and Method*. J. Cumming and G. Barden (eds), trans. William Glen-Doepel. London: Sheed and Ward.

George, A.L. and Bennett, A. (2005) *Case Studies and Theory Development in the Social Sciences*. Cambridge MA: MIT Press.

Haack, S. (2003) *Defending Science – Within Reason*. Amherst, NY: Prometheus.

Hacking, I. (1983) *Representing and Intervening*. Cambridge: Cambridge University Press.

Handy, R. and Harwood, E.C. (1973) *A Current Appraisal of the Behavioral Sciences*. Great Barrington, MA: Behavioral Research Council.

Hempel, C.G. (1965) *Aspects of Scientific Explanation*. New York: Free Press.

Humphrey, N. (1983) *Consciousness Regained*, Oxford: Oxford University Press, p. 7.

Hunt, S.D. (1991) *Modern Marketing Theory: Critical Issues in the Philosophy of Marketing Science*. Cincinnati, OH.: South-Western Publishing Co.

Juarrero, A. (1999) *Dynamics in Action: Intentional Behavior as a Complex System*. Cambridge, MA: A Bradford Boo, The MIT Press.

Krausz, M. (1993) *Rightness and Reasons: Interpretation in Cultural Practices*. Ithaca, N.Y.: Cornell University Press.

Kuhn, T.S. (1962) *The Structure of Scientific Revolutions*, second edition. 1970. Chicago: University of Chicago Press.

Kuhn, T.S. (1974) 'Second Thoughts on Paradigms' in F. Suppe (eds) *The Structure of Scientific Theories*, Urbana: University of Illinois Press.

Kuhn, T.S. (1977) 'Second Thought on Paradigms', in F. Suppe (ed.) *The Structure of Scientific Theories*. Urbana: University of Illinois Press.

Lipton, P. (1991) *Inference to the Best Explanation*. London and New York: Routledge.

Lyons, W. (2001) *Maters of the Mind*, Edinburgh: Edinburgh University Press, p. 156.

MacCorqudale, K. and Meehl, P./e. (1948) 'Hypothetical Constructs and Intervening Variables', *Psychological Review*, 55: 95–107.

McGuire, W.J. (2000) *Constructing Social Psychology: Creative and Critical Processes*. New York: Cambridge University Press.

Mowen, J.C. (1979) 'Retroduction and the Research Process in Consumer Behavior', in O.C. Farrell, S.W. Brown and C.W. Lamb (eds) *Conceptual and Theoretical Developments in Marketing*. Chicago: American Marketing Association.

Nagel, E. (1961) *The Structure of Science*. New York: Harcourt, Brace and World.

Nagel, E. (1979) *Teleology Revisited*. New York: Columbia University Press, pp. 76–77.

O'Shaughnessy, J. (1997) 'Temerarious Directions for Marketing', *European Journal of Marketing*, 31(9/10): 677–705.

O'Shaughnessy, J. (2009) *Interpretation in Social Life, Social Science and Marketing*. London: Routledge.

O'Shaughnessy, J. and O'Shaughnessy, N.J. (2005) 'Considerations of Equity in Marketing and Nozick's Decision-Value Model', *Academy of Marketing Science Review*. www. Vancouver.wsu.edu/amsrev/theory/oshaughnessy 10-2005 htmi

Pedhazur, E. (1997) *Multiple Regression in Behavioral Research*. New York: Wadsworth.

Peirce, C.S. *Collected Papers*. Vols 1–8 C. Hartshorne, P. Weis and A.W. Burks (eds) (Vol. 11). Cambridge. MA: Harvard University Press.

Popper, K.R. (1959) *The Logic of Scientific Discovery*. London: Hutchinson.

Popper, K.R. (1963) *Conjectures and Refutations*. London: Routledge and Kegan Paul.

Putnam, H. (1981) *Reason, Truth and History*. Cambridge: Cambridge University Press.

Ravetz, J.R. (1990) *The Merger of Knowledge and Power: Essays in Critical Science*. London: Mansell.

Rea, M.C. (2003) *World Without Design: The Ontological Consequences of Naturalism*. Oxford: Oxford University Press.

Roth, P.A. (1987) *Meaning and Method in the Social Sciences*. Ithaca: Cornell University Press.

Rudner, R.S. (1966) *Philosophy of Social Science*. Englewood Cliffs, NJ: Prentice Hall.

Ryle, G. (1949) *The Concept of Mind*. New York: Barnes and Noble.

Scott, S. (2004) *Philosophical Analysis in the 20th Century*. New Jersey: Princeton University Press (Volume I and volume II).

Shweder, R.A. (2003) *Why Do Men Barbecue?* Cambridge MA: Harvard University Press.

Smedslund, J. (1995) 'Commonsense and the Pseudoempirical', in Smith, Harre and Van Langenhove (eds) *Rethinking Psychology*, Sage publications, p. 196.

Solomon, M.R. (1983) 'The Role of Products as Social Stimuli: A Symbolic Interactionism Perspective', *Journal of Consumer Research*, 10(December): 319–329.

Stueber, K.R. (2005) *Rediscovering Empathy: Agency, Folk Psychology and the Human Sciences*. Cambridge MA: The MIT Press.

Suppe, F. (1977) 'Editor's Introduction', in Suppe, F. (ed.) *The Structure of Scientific Theories*. Urbana: University of Illinois Press.

Taylor, C. (1964) *The Explanation of Behavior*. New York: Humanities Press.

Warnke, G. (1987) *Gadamer: Hermeneutics, Tradition and Reason*. Stanford: Stanford University Press.

Williams, B. (2002) *Truth and Truthfulness*. Princeton, NJ: Princeton University Press.

Winch, P.G. (1958) *The Idea of a Social Science*. London: Routledge and Kegan Paul.

Wootton, D. (2006) *Bad Medicine: Doctors Doing Harm since Hippocrates*. Oxford: Oxford University Press.

Zaltman, G. and Bonoma, T.V. (1979) 'The Lack of Heresy in Marketing', in O.C. Farrell, S.W. Brown and C.W. Lamb (eds) *Conceptual and Theoretical Developments in Marketing*, Chicago: American Marketing Association, pp. 474–484.

Major Theoretical Debates

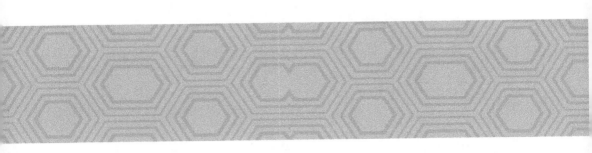

Shaping Exchanges, Performing Markets: The Study of Market-ing Practices

Luis Araujo and Hans Kjellberg

INTRODUCTION

> The primary observable phenomenon for any theory of marketing is the hard practical fact of the market. (McInnes, 1964: 52)

This observation from *Theory in Marketing* (Cox et al., 1964) provides an appropriate historical backdrop to recent calls for a return to the study of markets in Marketing (Kjellberg and Helgesson, 2007a; Peñaloza and Venkatesh, 2006). For early marketing theorists, the market constituted '... the starting point and the checkpoint for all theory' (McInnes, 1964: 67). However, markets faded from center stage into an undistinguished background, reduced to collections of actual and potential buyers and deserving no more than a passing mention in textbooks (Barnhill and Lawson, 1980; Samli and Bahn, 1992; Sissors, 1966). Readers of the *Handbook of Marketing* (Weitz and Wensley, 2002) may find discussions on market segmentation and representation of product–market structures

but will not find much about markets[1]. We may thus feel entitled to ask: Does or should Marketing theory have anything to say about markets?

This chapter provides an overview of theoretical developments and empirical studies in a vital research tradition that for the past decade have sought to reaffirm the connection between Marketing theory and markets, following the trail of early theorists such as Alderson and Cox (1948) and McInnes (1964). The bulk of this work, which we label a practice approach to markets, has been conducted at the intersection of marketing, economic sociology and the sociology of science and technology, following the publication of Callon's (1998a) influential volume *The Laws of the Markets*.

We begin by tracing theoretical developments that contributed to disconnect marketing from its roots in the study of markets. We then introduce the starting points for a practice approach to markets and address its consequences for four issues of particular relevance to Marketing theory: (1) How are market agencies (e.g. buyers and sellers) configured? (2) How do some exchanges become 'economic'? (3) How are objects of exchange shaped and qualified? (4) How do ideas and theories about markets contribute to shape the phenomena they seek to describe? In a subsequent section, we discuss the implications of the approach for our conception of markets and marketing before offering some concluding comments.

RECONNECTING MARKETING TO MARKETS

Why have interest in markets waned as far as Marketing theory is concerned? In this section, we provide a brief overview of how attempts at broadening the concept of marketing during the 1960s and 1970s shifted the focus away from markets. Alderson (1965: 23) starts Chapter 1 of *Dynamic Marketing Behavior* with a crisp statement: 'A theory of marketing explains how markets work'. Although it is widely acknowledged that Marketing theory was originally rooted in markets, specifically in the distributive function (Bartels, 1962), marketing has changed continuously, both as a set of managerial practices and a theoretical domain (Shaw and Jones, 2005; Wilkie and Moore, 2003). There is no stable set of practices or theories that we can unequivocally call 'marketing'.[2]

Theoretical debates and controversies about the nature and scope of marketing have profoundly affected the development of the subject. One of those controversies sprang out of Kotler and Levy's (1969a) award winning paper. If marketing had hitherto been the preserve of business firms and their activities in markets, it should henceforth be understood '... as a societal activity that goes beyond the selling of toothpaste, soap and steel' (ibid.: 10). There is no reason why '... marketing technology should be confined to an organization's transactions with its client group' (Kotler, 1972: 48). Marketing management

could '... be viewed generically as the *problem of regulating the level, timing, and character of demand for one or more products of an organization*' (Kotler, 1973: 42).

The generic marketing concept evoked both enthusiastic and antagonistic reactions. Bartels (1974: 75) framed the controversy succinctly: 'The question, then, is whether marketing is identified by the *field* of economics, in which marketing techniques have been developed and generally applied, or by the so-called marketing *techniques*, wherever they may be applied'. Whereas Kotler and Levy chose *techniques* ahead of *field*, others argued for the opposing viewpoint. Luck (1969: 54), for example, preferred to reserve the label marketing to '... activities whose ultimate result is a *market transaction*', suggesting that '... a particular act must be related to an eventual or intended offer to buy and/or sell a specified good or service [...] or that act is not a *marketing* act'.

The *field* versus *techniques* controversy was quickly settled in favor of techniques (Hunt, 1976: 19).[3] The view of marketing as a set of management tools and techniques was reinforced in a quick succession of moves (see e.g. Dawson, 1971; Kotler and Levy, 1969a, b; Kotler, 1972, 1973; Luck, 1969, 1974; Shuptrine and Osmanski, 1975). A new paradigm emerged, anchoring the discipline in a generic notion of exchange, broken free from its attachments to the market (Hunt, 1976: 25; Kotler, 1972: 48). Bagozzi (1975: 39) framed marketing as 'the discipline of exchange behavior' and marketing management as a 'function of universal applicability'. In the words of Anderson (1983: 28), the broadened concept made it clear that '... marketing is a generic human activity, which may be studied because it is an intrinsically interesting social phenomenon'. Subsequent generations of students were taught the generic concept of marketing as a foundational dogma (Shaw and Jones, 2005).

Ironically, this development appears to have narrowed rather than broadened the scope of the discipline. In an undeservedly neglected contribution, Sweeney (1972: 4) remarked: 'This "broadened" concept of marketing, however, merely extends the range of organizations and relationships to which marketing technology can conceivably be applied. Rather than extend the concept of marketing beyond that of a technology, it reinforces and further defends the idea that marketing is fundamentally a set of organization management skills and techniques'. In short, two outcomes of the 'broadening debate' left a lasting imprint on the discipline. First, the generic concept of marketing meant that all forms of exchange should be covered, not just those happening in markets. Secondly, marketing was cut loose from its origins in markets and made portable across the whole of society by its reconfiguration as a set of tools and techniques. These outcomes were mutually reinforcing. The more marketing found new domains of application, the more it became detached from markets.

In their survey of schools of marketing thought, Shaw and Jones (2005: 272–273) argue that broadening the concept of marketing obfuscated marketing's identity and resulted in a step backward from the tight focus on markets. By attempting to encompass virtually every form of exchange marketing came to represent nothing, they concluded. In a recent paper, Venkatesh et al. (2006: 252) underscore and lament the lost connection to markets: 'Paradoxically, the term market is everywhere and nowhere in our literature'.

Venkatesh and Peñaloza (2006) suggest a shift of emphasis from marketing back to markets. The advantage for marketers is that:

> By viewing themselves as inhabiting the markets they produce, and bringing them about in conjunction with other market agents, as opposed to discovering some pre-existing consumer segment or merely competing with other businesses, marketers are better suited to developing novel ways of conceptualizing what they do. (ibid.: 147)

This broad manifesto brings us back, full circle, to the link between marketing and markets and to Bartels' (1974) dilemma of whether to conceive marketing as rooted in markets or as a set of techniques of general applicability. Our argument echoes Venkatesh and Peñaloza's (2006: 136) call for bringing markets to the foreground of our discipline: 'As we shift our attention to the *market* as the primary focus of our discipline, we recognize that *marketing* is something that takes place within a market system and is therefore derivative of the main focus'.

Thus, we suggest a move from the study of *marketing*, understood as techniques to regulate exchanges, to *market-ing* understood as practices that help perform markets (see Figure 11.1). Two implications follow from this conceptual move. First, we are sensitized to the fact that various practices and forms of expertise other than those implied by the generic concept of *marketing* contribute to

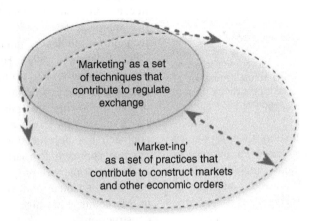

Figure 11.1   Shifting from 'Marketing' to 'Market-ing'.

shape markets, e.g. legislative, regulatory and accounting practices. Secondly, when attending to practices, it becomes clear that marketers perform tasks beyond those implied by the generic concept of *marketing*, i.e. regulating the timing, level and character of demand within pre-existing markets structures. Instead, we suggest that marketing is actively engaged in the production and transformation of markets as well as other economic orders – more about this later. In the next section, we sketch the contours of a practice-based approach to markets.

A PRACTICE APPROACH TO MARKETS

Within social science, we find quite diverse *theories of practice* as well as approaches that attend to practice primarily as a methodological tool. Even within management studies, there are several relatively independent developments, e.g. accounting as practice (Ahrens and Chapman, 2007), strategy as practice (Chia and Holt, 2006), attention to consumption practices (Holt, 1995; Warde, 2005), etc. Very generally, Reckwitz (2002: 244) suggests that practice approaches share an interest in everyday, mundane activities. Thus, a practice approach to markets directs attention once again to the onerous work of making markets function. As Alderson and Cox (1948: 148) put it:

Little thought (perhaps none) is given to the fact [...] that someone has to exert great effort continuously if there is to be the intricate organization required to inform potential buyers and sellers, to bring them together in the actual negotiation of a transaction, and to make it possible for them to carry out all transactions negotiated.

As a first approximation, then, a practice approach to markets takes an interest in how market-ing actions, including those bridging supply and demand, contribute to shape markets. Most *theories of practice* (e.g. those suggested by Bourdieu, 1990; de Certeau, 1984; Schatzki, 2008) share with

other social theories an ambition to explain patterns of human (inter)action, but differ in their primary explanation of these patterns. Rather than resulting from aggregate individual behavior or normative consensus, social order emerges as a consequence of recurrent ways of 'making do' (de Certeau, 1984), routinized behaviors (Reckwitz, 2002) and communal negotiations of meaning (Wenger, 1998). Theories of practice thus offer an alternative to both individualist and societist theories (Reckwitz, 2002; Schatzki, 2005). The crucial point is that practices are made by and through their routine reproduction and recursive ordering (Giddens, 1984).

Elaborating on theories of practices, Reckwitz (2002: 249–250) distinguishes between 'practice' (*praxis*) as a way of describing 'the whole of human action (in contrast to "theory or mere thinking")', and 'a practice' (*praktik*) implying 'a routinized type of behavior which consists of several interconnected elements'. This distinction sheds some light on the term *marketing practice*, which predominantly is used in the first sense, i.e. as a catch-all for what marketing practitioners *do* (Brodie et al., 1997; Coviello et al., 2002). The attention to practice in the sense of interconnected and routinized behavior, though, has made few inroads in marketing (but see Holt, 1995; Korkman, 2006).

In parallel to the various theories of practice, a more methodologically oriented practice approach developed within science and technology studies (Latour, 1987; Lynch, 1993; Pickering, 1992). Here, attention to practice was motivated primarily as a way of studying ongoing ordering, e.g. science in action. Following the publication of *The Laws of the Markets* (Callon, 1998a), this approach has become the most influential practice approach to markets. Also known as the performativity program, the approach has been adapted and further developed in Marketing focusing on the continuous construction of markets (Araujo, 2007; Araujo and Spring, 2006; Azimont and

Araujo, 2007; Kjellberg and Helgesson, 2006, 2007a, b; Rinallo and Golfetto, 2006).

While this approach shares with some of the classic works in marketing an interest in what makes markets work, it does not seek to promote their revival (cf. Brown, 2007). It also fits well with the more recent idea that '... markets are not universal, self-contained entities, but rather take on distinct discursive forms and material practices across various social contexts and over time' (Venkatesh and Peñaloza, 2006: 147). Still, the research program initiated by Callon constitutes a radical break with most traditional approaches to markets found within the Marketing discipline, both old and new.

First, it extends Granovetter's (1985) discussion on embeddedness beyond the social ties that lubricate market exchange, to include the role of objects, apparatus and technologies in making markets work (Callon, 1998b; Muniesa et al., 2007). Empirical inquiries should attend to the practical interactions between different types of entities, incorporating both social and material elements (Latour, 2005). In this respect, a focus on practice involves a consideration of material devices, embodied skills and mental representations as well as the configurations in which they come together to form particular blocks, i.e. attention to *praktik* (Shove and Pantzar, 2005).

Secondly, the approach does not depart from predefined market agencies to understand processes within a wider system, but regards the constitution of agencies and markets as outcomes of a co-configuration process (Callon, 2007). Empirical attention is directed toward understanding processes of economic organizing as they happen; leaving the question of their outcome open rather than starting out with predefined ideal types (e.g. perfectly competitive markets). Compared with other practice approaches, these first two points imply a decentering of human agency.

Thirdly, the approach questions the traditional idea of a radical gap between theory and action, the world of ideas and the world of *praxis*, and argues instead for an interactive link between ideas and actions (Latour, 1995). In so doing, this way of approaching markets shifts our attention from epistemology (how the world is understood) to ontology (how the world is being made). This and the previous point highlight the import of *praxis*, but suggest that it refers to situated performances rather than pure human action.

These three distinctive traits imply a definition of 'market practice' that includes both *praxis* and *praktik*, and in fact suggest that their interrelation is central to our understanding of markets as ongoing constructions. This admittedly broad sweep definition highlights a preference for studying markets as ever-changing performances, rather than as stabilized entities; as nexuses of activities being shaped and routinized by multiple calculative agencies (Callon and Muniesa, 2005; Kjellberg and Helgesson, 2006). How do situated performances become interconnected to form more or less durable nexuses of activities and elements, which partake in the construction of specific market forms?

The view of markets emerging from the growing body of empirical studies in this tradition emphasizes the coordination of action through the establishment of durable associations, the ongoing configuration of actors as calculating agents, and the resolution of conflicts of interest through commensuration of prices and qualities (cf. Callon, 1999). Of these three, calculation and the configuration of calculative agents has received the most thorough treatment. Rather than assuming that calculation is an innate feature of agents, Callon turns the emergence of calculative practices and the socio-technical arrangements making up calculative agents into central empirical puzzles, recognizing that what can and cannot be measured and calculated varies over time and across settings. Basically, calculation relies on technical instruments that translate phenomena into measurable quanta through decontextualization (Power, 2004). This translation also involves transforming characteristics normally represented by different units into common metrics (Espeland

and Stevens, 1998). Measures such as prices, cost–benefit ratios, risk assessments and supplier evaluation scores are all examples of this kind of commensuration (cf. Sjögren and Helgesson, 2007).

In the following sections, we will address four issues that are central to the understanding of markets and marketing from a practice perspective. First, we will discuss the implications of a practice approach for our conception of agency and market actors. Secondly, we will revisit the issue raised by the development of the generic marketing approach as discussed in the preceding section – What makes exchanges *economic*? Thirdly, we will look at how products and services are framed and qualified to become objects of exchange. Fourthly, we will address the issue of how ideas about markets contribute to shape markets, exchanges and objects of exchange.

ISSUE 1: HOW ARE ECONOMIC AGENCIES CONFIGURED?

A practice approach emphasizes that economic organizing and the emergence of economic orders are closely connected to the constitution of economic agencies (for empirical examples see Callon et al., 2007). Attending to how economic agencies are configured in practice rather than what they might be in principle, challenges ideas about those who act in markets. In this section we outline how market actors are conceptualized from a practice perspective.

First, a practice approach directs attention to the concrete interactions between entities as part of some event or situation. Rather than searching for enduring causes of action, attention is directed to how individual practices interlink to form temporally emergent entities such as buyers, sellers, goods and markets. A practice approach is thus highly sensitive to the idea that actors need to be positioned within temporal frames. Emirbayer and Mische (1998) suggest that agency can be analytically decomposed into three distinct

elements with different temporal outlooks: *iterational* (oriented toward the past); *projective* (oriented toward the future); and *practical/ evaluative* (oriented toward the present). A practice perspective emphasizes the latter, focusing on 'real-time accounting' rather than retrospective (because) or prospective (in order to) accounts (cf. Pickering, 1993). Drawing on the idea that action precedes thought (Giddens, 1993; Weick, 1979), a practice approach seeks to account for action-reaction sequences without resorting to models based on the cognitive capacities of actors: 'Sensemaking, intentionality and other such concepts all direct attention away from practice, implying that the sources of agency lie elsewhere, and indeed, that they are already in place when practice starts to unfold' (Andersson et al., 2008: 68).

Secondly, a practice approach brings to centre stage the proposition that actors are emergent outcomes of associations (Belk, 1988; Callon and Latour, 1981; Emirbayer and Goodwin, 1994; Hodgson, 1998). One familiar branch of this argument concerns the malleability of goals and interests (Araujo and Brito, 1998; Granovetter, 1992). Another revolves around the identity of social actors being a temporary achievement; a 'relatively stable construction in an ongoing process of social activity' (Calhoun, 1991: 52). A third branch is concerned with the co-configuration of actors and the contexts in which they are being elaborated, between positions and dispositions (Bourdieu, 1981), e.g. users and machines (Woolgar, 1991). In different ways, these contributions point toward the primacy of social process, of interaction, in understanding the make-up of actors.

Thirdly, and as a consequence of the foregoing, a practice approach questions à priori recognition of differences in size between actors (Callon and Latour, 1981). Instead, the starting point is that actors become actors by being recognized by others (Håkansson and Snehota, 1995; Latour, 1996). As a result, variation in actor size becomes an empirical issue. '*There are* of course macro-actors and micro-actors, but the difference between them is brought about by power relations and the constructions of networks that will *elude analysis* if we presume *a priori* that macro-actors are bigger than or superior to micro-actors' (Callon and Latour, 1981: 280).

Fourthly, the preceding three arguments (real-time accounting, actors as emergent outcomes and recognition by others) decenter the human subject by contemplating the possibility of material agency (Callon and Law, 1995; Latour, 1992; Law, 1994). Most importantly, it highlights that those who act typically are collectives made up of a number of heterogeneous elements including a myriad of 'fixtures and furnishings' such as technical devices, spatial arrangements, metrological systems, contracts, documents, scientific knowledge, etc. (Latour, 2005; Muniesa et al., 2007). Cognition is conceived as a distributed process rather than something that resides in individual minds (Hutchins, 1995). This differentiates the practice approach from those contextual and temporal approaches that are exclusively concerned with *human agency* (Archer, 2002; Emirbayer and Goodwin, 1994; Emirbayer and Mische, 1998; Giddens, 1981; Sewell, 1992; Swanson, 1992). Elaborating on this issue in relation to marketing, Anderson et al. (2008) suggest that the idea of a generalized human agency loses relevance when employing a practice approach. Instead, attention is directed toward the multiplicity of agential configurations that are being enacted as part of unfolding market practices.

This reading of what a practice approach means for our conception of agency and actors, has resulted in a reversal of the traditional critique of *homo œconomicus* as an unrealistic abstraction. In an oft-quoted passage, Callon (1998b: 51) asserted that: 'Yes, *homo œconomicus* really does exist. [...] He is formatted, framed and equipped with prostheses which help him in his calculations and which are, for the most part, produced by economics'. Latour (2005: 209–210) deploys a similar argument when describing how a mass retail scene configures and formats choice:

A supermarket [...] has preformatted you to be a consumer, but only a generic one. To transform

yourself into an active and understanding consumer, you also need to be equipped with an ability to *calculate* and *choose*. [...] Even when one has to make the mundane decision about which kind of slice of ham to choose, you benefit from dozens of measurement instruments that equip you to become a consumer – from labels, trademarks, barcodes, weights and measurement chains, indexes, prices, consumer journals, conversations with fellow shoppers, advertisements and so on. The crucial point is that you are sustaining this mental and cognitive competence as long as you *subscribe* to this equipment. You don't carry it with you: it is not your own property. [emphasis in original]

Cochoy's (2008) ethnography of supermarket shopping shows the role of the mundane shopping cart in linking together market practices. The cart connects predefined choices inscribed in shopping lists with marketing cues such as packaging of products and shelf position in the supermarket. It configures a particular set of social relationships, as shoppers navigate the layout of supermarkets, facing shelves, avoiding each other but also observing each other's carts and their contents. Thus, a shopping cart plays a role as a frame for collective and distributed agency, as well as a template for the mutual adjustment of choices.

We can envisage two basic strategies for realizing sought-after economic agencies (Callon, 2008). The first one assumes that the deficiency is to be found in the make-up of the agent and employs prosthetic devices to repair or re-equip the collective so that it can perform as expected. This approach takes as its starting point a fixed set of ideas about the exchange situation and the tasks that the economic agents are to accomplish therein. The ever larger shopping carts studied by Cochoy are a prime example of such a prosthesis in consumer society, removing as they do an important physical constraint on shopping. The second approach, which Callon calls habilitation, considers the environment to be the source of maladjustment and seeks to transform the exchange situation so that it better fits the capacities of the agents. A good example is the efforts of retail and wholesale representatives to modify the proposed aboli-tion of Resale Price Maintenance (RPM) in Sweden in the 1950s (Kjellberg, 2001). These trade representatives were concerned about the ability of retailers to perform price calculations on their own as required in the event of a ban on RPM. Rather than using prosthetic devices to remedy this shortcom-ing, however, they successfully lobbied for allowing the use of recommended resale prices for those retailers who did not have the calculative capacity to price on their own.

To summarize, a practice-based approach emphasizes that agencies are outcomes of socio-technical configurations relying on associations between social and material entities, rather than residing in individual bodies and minds. A competent economic agent (e.g. consumer, shopper) able to calcu-late and choose as a free-willed individual is not a primitive category but the outcome of multiple and distributed processes of config-uration that may involve both the use of prosthetic devices and efforts at habilitation.

ISSUE 2: WHAT MAKES EXCHANGE ECONOMIC?

While the generic concept of marketing relegated economic exchange to just one domain for the application of marketing tech-niques, the markets-as-practice approach turns economic exchange into a central topic for empirical inquiry. If economic exchanges and markets are provisional achievements requiring continuous work, then it is impera-tive to investigate just how particular forms of exchange are constructed as *economic* and what kinds of supporting devices are required for these constructions to hold.

In order to explicate the conditions for calculation, defined broadly as the capacity to perceive differences and grade them, Callon (1998c) re-employs the term *framing* originally used by Goffman (1974). Framing purports to establish a multidimensional boundary inside of which interactions can

take place independently of their surrounding context. As Callon (1998c: 253) memorably put it: '... framing represents a violent effort to extricate the agents concerned from [the network of interactions in which they are involved] and push them onto a clearly demar-cated stage which has been specially prepared and fitted out'. But framing is always fragile, partial and temporary requiring substantive investments to hold; it brackets the outside world rather than abolishes the links to it. With every included element being a potential conduit, the outside world always threatens to disturb the events unfolding inside the frame (see Figure 11.2). Such disturbances are the counterpart to framing: *overflowing* – the occurrence of something more, less or else than what the framing encases. Overflows are effects of associations that transgress the boundary established through framing. Positive and negative economic externalities (e.g. knowledge spillovers and environmental damages, respectively) are examples of such overflows.

Despite efforts to frame a transaction as a singular event, it can only take place if it fits within a complex set of entanglements on the buyer and seller sides; the processes of framing and overflowing, entangling and disentangling are mutually interdependent. Miller (2002) illustrates this with the interaction between a car salesperson and prospective customer. This scenario can only be understood by reference to the entangled web of the customer's life-style, personal finances and projected use of the car, the salesperson's quota and commis-sions, the relation between the franchised dealership and the manufacturer, etc. As noted by both Miller (2002) and Callon et al. (2002), there are important countervailing forces at play in framing economic exchanges. Business firms tend to focus precisely on how to attach consumers to *their* networks rather than to their competitors' networks. Market practices involve considerable efforts to establish and strengthen the entanglements connecting prac-tices on the supply and demand sides.

These observations led Miller (2002) to criticize Callon for overly emphasizing the

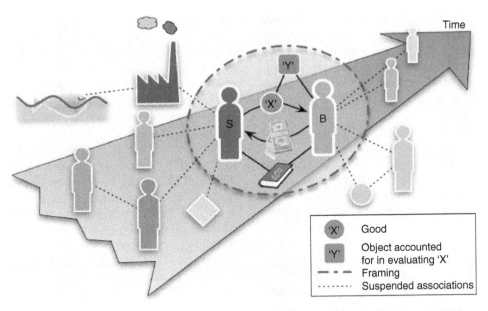

Figure 11.2   Framing an economic exchange. Framing refers to the process of establishing a multidimensional boundary (temporally, spatially and in terms of content), which serves to delimit what is to be taken into account as part of a particular exchange between a seller (S) and a buyer (B).

disentanglement side of transactions. The entanglements and multiple forms of calculation of real market exchanges, he argues, expose the limitations of Callon's approach. Still, the existence of such entanglements does not necessarily dissolve the notion of markets into a generic form of exchange. For instance, it does not compromise the agents' generic roles as buyer and seller in a transaction framing them as essentially strangers to each other. Slater (2002a) instead suggests that disentanglements and calculation are underpinned by the regime of property rights that enables the alienation of goods: '… the stability of legal entities and frameworks allows for reliable and predictable encounters and in this much broader sense allows "calculation"' (ibid.: 238). This argument harks back to the view of market exchange championed by the new institutional economics (e.g. North, 1990). Ménard (1995), for example, defines markets as institutional arrangements that enable the routine and voluntary transfer of property rights on a regular basis.

Although the practice approach to markets shares the sensitivity of institutional approaches to the potential import of normalizing efforts on economic exchanges, there are two important points of distinction. First, institutional approaches tend to assume that rules and regulations matter for how exchanges are conducted. A practice approach emphasizes that framing is an 'expensive outcome' (Callon, 1998c: 252), i.e. that considerable work is necessary for, say, a rule to have import. Secondly, institutional approaches establish at the outset the relation between institutions and markets, e.g.: 'Institutions operate at a higher level of generalization than do markets and organizations: they delineate rules of the game within which such "governance structures" actually operate' (Ménard, 1995: 164). In contrast, a practice perspective recognizes no such differences between normalizing efforts and exchanges. Rules and regulations are either taken into account, which means that they help perform exchanges and consequently operate at the same level as other exchange activities, or they are not.

The preoccupation with framing and overflowing, entangling and disentangling, does not imply that markets are conceived as the home of pure instrumental rationality or as dominated by the formalism of property rights. Objects and actors are involved in multiple worlds, and their identity is never fully captured by the roles scripted for them as part of some specific framing effort (Slater, 2002a). Framing is always liable to be disrupted by the actions of entities on both sides of the intended boundary (e.g. buyers, sellers, competitors, and regulators). Frames are never entirely set in concrete, although, literally speaking, parts of them may very well be (Kjellberg, 2001).

To summarize, a market exchange is enabled by a process of framing allowing distinct agents to come together and agree on prices and conditions for the exchange of goods and money. Markets are 'collective devices that calculate compromises on the value of goods' (Callon and Muniesa, 2005: 1230). They are characterized by the attachment and detachment of property rights, the circulation of goods and exchange mechanisms involving the calculation of prices. They do not, however, share the same form; the idea of the market as unitary entity should be replaced by a plural notion of market forms involving many different attempts at framing economic exchanges.

ISSUE 3: HOW ARE EXCHANGE OBJECTS CONSTRUCTED?

The tensions between framing efforts and entanglements also affect objects of exchange.

This is captured by the notion of *qualification* (Callon et al., 2002), a process that turns products and services into (tradable) goods, thus linking the continued and variegated existence of objects as part of a social reality and their temporarily stabilized characteristics as objects of exchange. To qualify is to temporarily stabilize and detach a product from other objects and processes, ascribing to it a list of essential properties (Slater, 2002b: 100). Consequently, both products and services can be turned into goods – e.g. a car may be sold or rented for a limited period and use. Goods, then, are outcomes of qualification and correspond to states at specific points in time whereas products should be seen as processes, trajectories in time (see Figure 11.3).

If products have temporal trajectories then we can trace their 'careers' and the social meanings they acquire as they move through instances of production, circulation and use. Products may have long and complex biographies that are temporarily interrupted by the attachment and detachment of property rights connected to transactions (Kopytoff, 1986). A car, for example, is a product that is successively transformed as it moves from a design office, to test tracks, to manufacturer catalogs and dealership showrooms. At the same time, it only acquires its familiar meaning as a social object when embedded in complex socio-technical networks comprising public roads, traffic systems, rules regarding the licensing of drivers and cars, systems for the provision and distribution of fuel, access to spare parts and specialized maintenance skills. It is a good when it is first sold, but once in the hands of its first registered

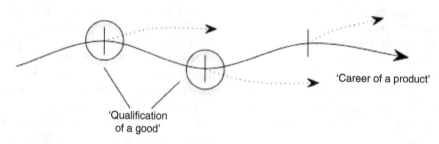

'Career of a product'

'Qualification of a good'

Figure 11.3   The qualification of goods in the career of a product.

owner, it follows a particular trajectory as a product including clocking up miles and going through scheduled services. As it is advertised in used car magazines as a second-hand bargain and finds its way back to dealership courtyards, it is temporarily stabilized as another type of good (Araujo and Spring, 2006). The same product can thus constitute different goods at different stages in its 'career', e.g. as a new, for rent and second-hand car. Products thus link a variety of economic agents, and, '... reciprocally, it is the agents that, by adjustment, iteration and transformation, define its characteristics' (Callon et al., 2002: 198).

The work of qualifying goods is a distributed effort involving a variety of market professionals. Through this process, products are transformed into tradable goods that slot into the worlds of the buyers, becoming entangled in their socio-technical networks (Callon and Muniesa, 2005: 1234). Qualification and requalification processes undertaken by specialist market professionals thus mediate the relationship between products and goods. Housing markets provide more complex examples of qualification and valuation of goods, as documented in detail by Smith et al. (2006). Their study describes the roles of a range of intermediaries in the Edinburgh housing market, namely, solicitors, estate agents, property developers and surveyors who interface with buyers and sellers, providing important market information and advice.

For market professionals engaged in a continuous process of qualification and requalification, the product is a strategic variable rather than a fixed object. Markets change not only because products and services are formulated, but also because of attempts at (re)qualifying goods. Marketing is thus involved in the simultaneous definition and redefinition of both objects of exchange and markets. The success of any such attempt critically depends on performing a particular set of both user and competitive relationships through a variety of practices (e.g. product design, packaging, merchandising and advertising). In summary,

markets are not simply containers within which economic agents act, but are continuously being restructured through the dynamics of qualification and requalification.

ISSUE 4: WHAT IS THE ROLE OF IDEAS IN SHAPING MARKETS?

How do theories, ideas and methods in general and from marketing, in particular, help shape markets? One of Callon's (1998b) contributions was to highlight the role of expert discourses in performing the very phenomena they purportedly describe. In short, Callon (1998b: 2) suggested that '... economics, in the broad sense of the term, performs, shapes and formats the economy, rather than observing how it functions'. A number of subsequent studies have highlighted the import of theories and ideas on the realization of economic orders (Callon et al., 2007; Helgesson, 1999; Kjellberg, 2001; MacKenzie, 2003, 2004; MacKenzie and Millo, 2003; MacKenzie et al., 2007). This has also proven to be the most controversial proposition advanced by this approach (Fine, 2003; Miller, 2002; Mirowski and Nik-Khah, 2007; Nik-Khah, 2006).

A discourse is deemed performative if it contributes to the construction of the reality it describes (Callon, 2007). To increase conceptual clarity, MacKenzie (2004) distinguishes between *generic* and *Austinian* performativity.[4] Generic performativity, he argues, refers to the basic idea that the economy is '... performed by economic practices, including marketing and accountancy, and by the all-pervasive practices of metrology' (MacKenzie, 2004: 305). This signals the starting point for the practice approach we sketched above, i.e. that markets are outcomes of multiple and distributed practices. Austinian performativity, on the other hand, is a stronger claim referring to situations where a specific theory or model brings into being the relations it describes (ibid.). This requires that the multiplicity of socio-technical configurations characterizing empirical markets has been successfully managed by privileging the enactment of one particular version over others within all areas of market practice, i.e. in conducting economic exchanges, in establishing normative guidelines for such exchanges and in generating representations of them (Kjellberg and Helgesson, 2006).

The distinction between generic and Austinian performativity underscores that the notion of performativity refers to ideas in general. Callon has repeatedly used terms such as 'economics at large' (Callon, 2005: 9) and 'economics in the broad sense of the term' (Callon, 1998b: 2) in his discussions of the relation between economics and the economy. His thesis is not – as some critics have implied – that economics as an academic discipline with a set of well-articulated theories, brings about the economy! Rather, the thesis is that ideas, models, techniques, methods and professional practices about the economy do not simply describe but actively shape the economy (Porter, 2008). This important point has been further elaborated through empirical studies. First, the question of which ideas are 'about the economy' can itself be subject to negotiation (Sjögren and Helgesson, 2007). Second, the ideas need not emanate from academics – certainly not only from economists! – at least not in any easily identifiable way. Instead, empirical research indicates other actors, self-interested theorists (Rinallo and Golfetto, 2006), as important sources of ideas, including buyers and sellers (Azimont and Araujo, 2007; Barrey, 2007), and third parties such as consumer magazines (Mallard, 2007).

Several lines of thought within social science relate to performativity and help us identify ways in which ideas contribute to perform phenomena (cf. Callon, 2007). A first and well-known case is Merton's (1996) discussion on the *self-fulfilling prophecy*. Applied to a market setting, we have no difficulty in recognizing how market theories may spread to and influence decisions and subsequent perceptions and actions of economic agents. Similar lines of reasoning can be found in approaches that emphasize the import of sense-making for the organization of markets (Anand and Peterson, 2000; Ford and Redwood, 2005) or how theoretical language slips into the discourse of lay actors (Ferraro et al., 2005).

We also recognize a link between institutional arrangements, or *prescriptions* more generally, and performativity. The role of Industrial Organization theory in the design of antitrust and competition legislation in the Western world is one strong example (Djelic, 2002; Hovenkamp, 1991). By setting up legal rules and competition authorities, national governments seek to ensure that the structural conditions required for market competition are present. Here, economics does not primarily describe reality, '... its mission is to say what the economy is to be and to propose solutions and devices to make it that way' (Callon, 2007: 325). Of course, the prescriptive practices at work may be subtler. Concepts such as 'public opinion' and 'mainstream culture' are brought into being at least in part, by pollsters, market researchers and their arsenals of techniques and tools aimed at extracting opinions from representative samples of populations (Igo, 2007; Osborne and Rose, 1999). Over time, individuals learn how to cooperate in the creation of these phenomena and become the willing subjects of those surveyors, keen to portray themselves as the 'informed consumers' and 'opinioned citizens' which they understand is expected of them.

As argued by Callon (2007), however, there is growing evidence that these two cases cannot account for all the ways in which ideas contribute to enact reality. The self-fulfilling prophecy only requires the actors to believe in the model to bring about the reality it proposes. Similarly, as long as actors follow the prescriptions, the envisioned reality will emerge. What is being suggested by empirical studies of performativity is that the *content* of the ideas matters. Not all ideas are equally feasible. Not all theories are capable of accounting for and forecasting correctly the behavior they trigger, irrespective of peoples' beliefs in them.

In addition, there are important restrictions in terms of what can be done – although these restrictions may not be known in advance, but emerge as part of the process.

This can be seen in a third case, *inscription* (cf. Akrich, 1992), which refers to ways in which ideas are embodied into material arrangements. As an illustration, consider the SIM-cards in our cell phones. These tiny devices and their corresponding slots in the phones assist in enacting the idea of two separate markets where there used to be only one: one market for mobile phone handsets and one market for mobile telephone services. Similarly, in their study of the relation between the Black and Scholes option pricing formula and real option markets, MacKenzie and Millo (2003) note that one way in which the formula gained verisimilitude was by being programmed into calculators (and later into trading software) used by the option traders. One important point about this kind of operation is that it never starts from scratch. Materialization must always take into account what is already there, that which is already being performed, as it were. A second point is that some things are more difficult to create than others. The enactment of reality is far from arbitrary.

One convenient way to think about all these cases is to view statements and their worlds as socio-technical *agencements*, or 'agreements which include the statements that describe them and contribute toward putting them into action' (Callon, 2007: 328). This allows us to observe two processes (Latour, 1999): first, how certain associations are contextualized and made more durable whether through repetitive indoctrination, formal legislation, materialization or all of these; in short, how the world implied by a statement gradually becomes actualized. Second, how some associations through successive transformations are abstracted, divested of materiality and temporality and made increasingly general and mobile until they can be brought together to appear as models, theories or ideas. Rather than the great divide between representations and

realities of markets, we observe the practical transformations of associations that co-produce markets and ideas about markets (Kjellberg and Helgesson, 2006).

IMPLICATIONS FOR MARKETING THEORY

This section will focus on implications of a practice approach for our understanding of markets and Marketing theory. The discussion is organized around two major implications of the practice approach to markets:

1 The conceptualization of market agents and objects of exchange
2 The role of professional expertise in the construction and operation of markets

As far as the first implication is concerned, a practice approach conceives of acting entities as provisional outcomes, as collectives, or networks of associated materials. This line of reasoning has some precursors in marketing, namely in notions such as *organized behavior systems* (Alderson, 1957) and the *extended self*, i.e. the suggestion that the material world, and particularly possessions, contributes symbolically to an individual's sense of self (Belk, 1988). A practice approach does not discard symbolic aspects but is much more attentive to *literal* extensions, i.e. to what some associations of materials can *do* as *agencements* or agential configurations.[5]

This provides a way of addressing the variability as well as the differential capacities of actors. First, we can address the issue of an actor's variable geometry and its ability to coordinate its various engagements. Whilst bringing together several specific collectives generally will enrich an actor's repertoire of responses, it will also increase the number of potential conflicts amongst its constituent collectives. The common denominator of the collectives, which is central to ascribing their actions to the actor in the first place, will also decrease. Hence, co-ordination problems are

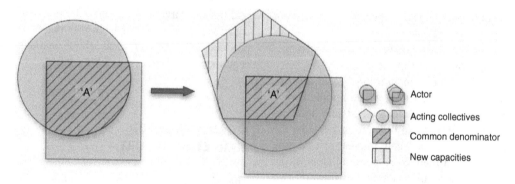

Figure 11.4 The configuration of actors. An additional acting collective (the pentagon) is subsumed under the same actor label ('A') as two other such collectives (circle and square). This expands the actor's capacity to act (area with vertical lines), but reduces the basis for ascribing the actions of the collectives to the same actor (area with diagonal lines).

likely to multiply as the actor grows in size (Andersson et al., 2008). This directs attention to how collectives are held together and to the existence and make-up of a metrological system that allows communication across collectives and between centre and periphery within an actor (Helgesson and Kjellberg, 2005). As an example, consider efforts to centrally coordinate, for example via a key account management system, the ways in which various departments in a buying firm interact with prospective suppliers.

Secondly, we can address the issue of an actor's capacity to act. A number of authors have linked capacity to act to multivocality – i.e. when actions can be coherently interpreted from alternative vantage points (Araujo and Brito, 1998; Friedberg, 1993). By distinguishing between the collectives that act and the actors to which actions are ascribed, an actor's capacity to act can be conceived as a function of the number of collectives whose actions are ascribed to it. Subsuming a number of additional acting collectives will offer an actor a richer repertoire of responses (see Figure 11.4).

A similar approach can be taken to exchange objects and how they are understood. The proposition that goods have meanings beyond their functional characteristics has led to a focus on symbols and the circuits through which they are produced and diffused

(Levy, 1959; McCracken, 1986). Goods become temporary embodiments of meanings, through complex transfers from the cultural sphere to goods and from goods to their users. Markets become 'symbolically malleable entities [...] structured by a logic that can be grasped through quasi-semiotic analysis' (Slater, 2002c: 75). Consumption becomes an exercise in decoding signifiers, as dematerialized goods turn into mediators of meaning and identity (Rosa et al., 1999).

But these approaches tend to focus narrowly on 'highly autonomous individuals preoccupied with symbolic communication' (Warde, 2005: 132), and elide the processes through which the symbolic and material properties of objects are stabilized and destabilized. A practice approach allows us to address a number of ambiguities including the conflation of consumption and purchase. Rather than using the term consumption interchangeably with purchase, Warde (2005: 137) suggests that it should be viewed '... as a process whereby agents engage in appropriation and appreciation, whether for utilitarian, expressive or contemplative purposes, of goods, services, performances, information or ambience, whether purchased or not, over which the agent has some degree of discretion'.

Whereas mass retail provides us with familiar examples of stable and singularized objects of exchange, other market forms present us with contrasting examples. Lindberg and Nordin (2008) illustrate how the organizational buying of complex professional services requires different degrees of objectification of the service at different stages of the buying process. Finch and Acha (2008) address the issue of how to requalify a partly exploited oil and gas field, the Forties in the North Sea, as a good. They demonstrate how a clear distinction between production and exchange activities is difficult to sustain in this setting. The qualities that can be attached to this emerging good depend crucially on the associations that are forged between the field and existing entities within the network of assets that make up the buying company. But, as Finch and Acha emphasize, the qualification process affected the field itself. Whereas the seller performed the Forties as a mature field, both through its production activities and its various re-presentations, the buyer performed it as a second-hand prospect for re-exploration and re-development. Finch and Acha point to the important role of an emerging group of market professionals, reservoir engineers and their calculative tools, in *performing* the Forties as a second-hand field.

Simakova and Neyland's (2008) ethnographic study of the development and launch of a new product, illustrates the crucial role of narratives in constructing putative market relations. These narratives involve the attribution of agency, identities and the assignment of roles to different characters in the story. Simakova and Neyland emphasize that these stories must also be made compelling, i.e. they must succeed in bringing the members of the envisaged constituency to enact the relations articulated in the narrative. There is a danger that the stories will lose their coherence and compelling character, as they are always liable to be challenged before they have a chance to materialize.

Following in the same vein, essentialist distinctions, such as the habitual contrast between products and services need to be superseded by the idea that there is no reason to distinguish between products and services

based on their intrinsic qualities. In the case of products, we have to go beyond their physical properties to look at how their meaning become stabilized as objects in socio-technical networks and in the case of services, we need to bypass their apparent intangibility to examine how they can be turned into discrete and tradable objects (Slater, 2002b: 109). In summary, a practice approach highlights that taken-for-granted categories such as market actors and objects of exchange are accomplished constructions that have been temporarily stabilized through particular configurations of human and material agents. If these supporting devices are withdrawn or transformed, the stability of these constructions is undermined and market agencies and objects of exchange reconfigured as a result.

As far as the second implication is concerned, a practice approach does not regard professional expertise as an external infrastructure to markets, but as deeply implicated in their performance. As discussed earlier, the notion of performativity highlights the role of professional expertise in making economic processes and entities visible and calculable.

The import of expertise on markets can be clearly seen in the wide variety of market devices employed, ranging from accounting and purchasing methods, to contracts and performance monitoring systems (Muniesa et al., 2007). For example, mass retail makes use of a variety of plug-ins such as spatial arrangements, labels, trademarks, packaging, shopping carts, etc., to help configure consumers as calculative, decision-making agents (Barrey et al., 2000). If in mass retail, facing the consumer side, calculative agencies are highly distributed and heavily weighted toward the selling side, business markets provide a sobering counterpoint. In these markets, powerful calculative agencies often reside on the purchasing side (e.g. prequalification of suppliers and supplier evaluation programs). New tools and technologies can often upset the character and relative balance of calculative agencies – for example the introduction of online reverse auctions in business markets (Jap, 2007).

Efforts made to frame exchanges by disentangling the objects and agents of exchange from their networks, are often supported by specific forms of expertise. Contract and property law as well as accounting are examples of professional expertise that assist the cutting up of networks (Strathern, 1996), helping to render visible particular socioeconomic entities (e.g. organizational units and patents) and reshape their relations. Laws provide the regulatory framework under which property rights, contracts and so on, can be exchanged and third party enforcement of rules sustained. Accounting supplies the calculating tools that allow market actors to determine costs and prices, undertake investments and so on. These practices are crucial to enforce the framing and disentanglement processes that Callon (1998c) identifies as necessary to effect market exchange.

Slater (2002a: 247) notes that marketing expertise is just as concerned with entanglements as disentanglements. Marketing is often portrayed as set of techniques (e.g. design and packaging) for entangling goods in customer 'lifeworlds' in order to produce better opportunities for disentangling through market exchanges. As Callon et al. (2002: 293) quip: 'to disentangle, you have to entangle better'. Markets thus require practices that disentangle relations (i.e. that make goods calculable and alienable) as well as practices that embed exchanges in specific contexts (e.g. relate product design to usage). It is this paradoxical nature of market exchanges that allow them be framed both as discrete events, as Callon (1998c) argues, and as activities that produce multiple entanglements between producers and users, as Miller (2002) counterposes.

Marketing's contribution to the reproduction and transformation of markets is thus elusive, multifaceted and indeterminate in its consequences. It is involved in producing both entanglements and disentanglements, is distributed over time and space, and dependent on a hybrid mix of knowledge derived from the social sciences as well as tacit, practical knowledge on the workings of particular market

forms. As Stidsen (1979: 78) noted, '... a marketing plan is not just a plan for entering or exploiting a market – it is also a plan for altering a market'. Alderson and Cox's (1948: 151) early insight concerning market dynamics is worth quoting in this regard:

> An organized behavior system is not a neutral framework or container for the actions and evaluations that take place within it. That is to say that a market changes day by day through the very fact that goods are bought and sold. While evaluation is taking place within a marketing structure, the structure itself is being rendered weaker or stronger and the changes in organization which follow will have an impact on tomorrow's evaluations. Marketing theory will not provide an adequate approach if it ignores this *interaction between the system and the processes which take place within it*. [emphasis added]

A focus on the performativity of marketing should not obscure the fact that there are multiple and often conflicting efforts at performing markets. Take the mundane example of supermarkets. Barrey et al.'s (2000) study demonstrates how these spaces are configured and formatted to interface directly with the final consumer. Product designers, packaging designers and merchandisers all contribute to configure the choice of consumers, drawing on different representations of consumers and their choice processes. The product designer looks at aesthetic and functional elements working at the interface between production, purchasing and use of the product. The packaging designer is concerned with the projection of product characteristics to facilitate choice when consumers face the product in the shopping environment. The merchandiser, finally, is concerned with the configuration of the space in which consumer choices are made, both in terms of its overall layout, allocation and product 'facings'.

The cycle of negotiations between manufacturers and retailers represents an opportunity to question how these retail scenes are formatted, including the allocation of an exact space to each category and product, a particular display for each product, etc. (Azimont and Araujo, 2007). But other agents also contribute to formatting this scene; regulatory and standards agencies, scientific advisors, consumer associations and trade organizations may all seek to affect product formulations, labels, displays, etc. (Slater, 2002b: 105). Several agencies thus contribute to shape a particular economic order, employing alternative calculative devices that may require reconciliation in concrete exchange situations (Kjellberg and Helgesson, 2006).

As Kjellberg's (2007) study of Swedish postwar distribution systems shows, the performation of economic order requires both new calculative algorithms and new economic agencies. Paradoxically, the realization of new agential configurations both draws on and disrupts existing ones. Extant economic orders comprise collective investments displaying varying degrees of resistance to change (Azimont and Araujo, 2007). Implementing changes may thus involve complementary investments in new tools, performance metrics, ways of collecting and analyzing data, etc. The successful advocacy of change requires an acute sense of timing, the imaginative mobilization of facts, forecasts, expert opinions etc., but also the ability to experiment with different calculative devices (e.g. What performance metric will capture the attention of a particular constituency?).

Although the contribution of ideas, theories and methods to the shaping of financial markets has been discussed at length (see MacKenzie et al., 2007), there are still relatively few studies of generic performativity as discussed in the foregoing section. Some theory or other influences the actors engaging in market practice – including both formalized models and know-how constructed 'on the job' – and their actions contribute in important ways to the realization of markets. However, in most markets, we witness multiple and conflicting attempts at shaping and the role of marketers, regulators, consumers and other economic agents in this process is still poorly understood. Given the various charges against marketing for fuelling the spread of a consumerist society – and the counterarguments based on the *give-them-what-they-want* school

of marketing theory and practice (Shankar et al., 2006) – detailed empirical studies of the contribution of marketing ideas to markets remain an important and reflexively challenging task. Such studies may also reinvigorate discussions about relevance in marketing (Brennan and Turnbull, 2002; Brownlie and Saren, 1997), by providing a better understanding of how theories affect action.

CONCLUSIONS

In this chapter, we have introduced a set of arguments in favour of reconnecting Marketing theory to markets informed by a practice-based approach. By conceptualizing marketing as one set of expert contributions to the construction and operation of markets, a practice approach to markets recovers the theoretical tradition in Marketing, which concerned itself with the functioning of markets (Alderson, 1965; Alderson and Cox, 1948). The construction of markets and economic orderings, in general, involves the intervention of multiple bodies of expertise, to turn economic actors into calculating, profit-making agents, employees into competent work-place actors, and buyers into decision-makers capable of choosing among competing offers (Rose, 1999). Markets, then, are outcome of multiple, emergent processes of organizing assisted by expert interventions. Marketing practices play an important role in such processes, but only one role amongst many.

A focus on practices implies both a shift away from marketing as a set of mobile techniques deployable across society at large and a different view of markets. If markets are the outcome of multiple sets of practices, they cannot be reduced to the ideal type of spontaneous self-organization so beloved by neoclassical economists or to the assortment of actual and potential customers embraced by Marketing theory. With no *a priori* distinctions between efforts to shape and exploit markets, a much wider set of issues, agencies and activities can be studied as parties implicated in their construction and operation. To paraphrase Tucker (1974: 31) a practice approach offers tools for studying markets as marine biologists study fish, rather than as fishermen study them.

Reconnecting marketing to markets has a number of implications for Marketing theory. First, it enables us to come to terms with the notion that marketing practices are highly contextual and linked to particular market forms. This does not imply that marketing practices cannot circulate or that the skills, competencies and knowledge deployed in marketing practices are irreducibly tied to particular markets. But it alerts us to the fact that there is no universal and stable toolbox ready to colonize new domains as implied by the generic concept of marketing. Further, it introduces a degree of skepticism toward the idea that if marketing practices are deployed in nonmarket, nonprofit, or public sector settings, commoditization and marketization will necessarily follow. As we have attempted to show, it takes more than a transplant of marketing practices and tools to create fully-fledged markets.

Secondly, associating marketing practices with the shaping of markets inverts Sweeney's (1972) argument on how the broadened concept of marketing crystallized its status as a set of immutable tools and frees the discipline to address topical issues regarding the creation of new markets and the functioning of existing ones. Economists are increasingly concerned about how their expertise can be deployed in designing markets, recognizing that their functioning depends on the adequacy of detailed rules to suit particular purposes (Roth, 2007). In recent times, the application of economic theory has invaded processes of deregulation (Crew and Kleindorfer, 2002) and market creation in novel domains such as welfare and health care (Smith, 2005), carbon trading (Lohmann, 2005) and bodily goods (Almeling, 2007). In all these cases, there is a need for careful empirical investigation of shifting boundaries between different domains that do not necessarily conform to ideal types

(e.g. market, reciprocity or redistributive exchange). So far, though, the discipline of Marketing has had little to say about the creation of new markets and what characterizes the good functioning of markets. And yet, as Callon (2009) reminds us, the process of creating a market – cultivating the characteristics of goods, the modes of exchange and the agencies involved – is a huge undertaking that cannot be delegated to economics experts alone.

Last but not least, a practice approach provides Marketing theory with tools for playing a more salient role in public policy debates regarding the good functioning of markets. The notion of performativity recognizes the influences of multiple market theories on the functioning of markets. One such influence is the normalizing effect of regulatory practices so often regarded as enveloping and constraining market behaviour but not necessarily contributing to the construction of markets. From a practice perspective, marketing should not simply seek to supplement Industrial Organization's deficiencies in its attempts to promote competitive market structures (Gundlach and Phillips, 2002). In short, markets cannot be seen as mere sites where independent and autonomous parties come to perform mutually satisfying exchanges, as the marketing-as-generic exchange school would put it.

As Callon (2009) argued, at the heart of markets we often find debates, burning issues and controversies that cannot be accommodated within existing framings. A well-functioning market is thus not one that closely approximates an ideal template, but one that is able to accommodate ways of detecting and dealing with the overflows it necessarily produces. In this sense, a practice view of markets is well equipped to address the concerns that Sheth and Sisodia (2005) expressed for marketing, namely, its inability to harness and channel the energies of the market system for the benefit of customers, corporations and society. We should temper this observation with a cautionary note. If marketing alone does not possess the power to mould markets, it should not be regarded as holding a privileged position to realign the interests of corporations, customers and society at large. To paraphrase a quote attributed to the French politician Georges Clemenceau: 'markets are too important a business to be left to marketers alone'.

ACKNOWLEDGEMENTS

Earlier versions of this chapter was presented and discussed at the Department of Marketing and Strategy at Stockholm School of Economics and at an IMP Market Studies Workshop in April 2009 hosted by John Finch at the University of Strathclyde. The authors are grateful to the participants for a series of helpful comments and suggestions.

NOTES

1 For a wide-ranging discussion of the notion of markets and its relationship to Management see Snehota (2004).

2 Witness, for example, the controversy surrounding the latest definition of marketing offered by the American Marketing Association and the ensuing debate in the *Journal of Public Policy and Marketing* (Vol. 26, No, 2, 2007).

3 Kotler (2005: 114) reminisced: 'The matter was settled when an overwhelming number of marketing educators said they favored the broadening movement'.

4 The term 'Austinian performativity' explicitly recognizes the link to Austin's work on performative utterances in the philosophy of language (Austin, 1962).

5 The argument is not a traditional materialist one, i.e. that the qualities and capacities of a subject depend on the objects at its disposal. Rather, the subject and object categories are dissolved in favour of hybrid collectives 'which can truly be said to act' and whose capacities and interests are emergent (Latour, 1994: 7). This is reflected in the notion of *agencement* (Muniesa et al., 2007), which emphasizes the distributed and material character of agencies. 'Instead of considering distributed agency as the encounter of (already "agenced") persons and devices, it is always possible to consider it as the very result of these compound agencements' (ibid.: 2).

REFERENCES

Ahrens, T. and Chapman, C.S. (2007) 'Management Accounting as Practice', *Accounting, Organizations and Society*, 32: 1–27.

Akrich, M. (1992) 'The De-Scription of Technical Objects', in W.E. Bijker and J. Law (eds) *Shaping Technology/Building Society*, Cambridge MA: The MIT Press, pp. 205–224.

Alderson, W. (1957) *Marketing Behavior and Executive Action: A Functionalist Approach to Marketing Theory*. Homewood, Ill.: Richard D. Irwin Inc.

Alderson, W. (1965) *Dynamic Marketing Behavior*. Homewood, Ill.: Richard D. Irwin Inc.

Alderson, W. and Cox, R. (1948) 'Towards a Theory of Marketing', *Journal of Marketing*, 13: 137–152.

Almeling, R. (2007) 'Selling Genes, Selling Gender: Egg Agencies, Sperm Banks, and the Medical Market in Genetic Material', *American Sociological Review*, 72: 319–340.

Anand, N. and Peterson, R.A. (2000) 'When Market Information Constitutes Fields: Sensemaking of Markets in the Commercial Music Industry', *Organization Science*, 11: 270–284.

Anderson, P.F. (1983) 'Marketing, Scientific Progress, and Scientific Method', *Journal of Marketing*, 47: 18–31.

Andersson, P., Aspenberg, K. and Kjellberg, H. (2008) 'The configuration of actors in market practice', *Marketing Theory*, 8: 67–90.

Araujo, L. (2007) 'Markets, Market-Making and Marketing', *Marketing Theory*, 7: 211–226.

Araujo, L. and Brito, C. (1998) 'Agency and Constitutional Ordering in Networks – A Case Study of the Port Wine Industry', *International Studies of Management & Organization*, 27: 22–46.

Araujo, L. and Spring, M. (2006) 'Services, products, and the institutional structure of production', *Industrial Marketing Management*, 35: 797–805.

Archer, M.S. (2002) 'Realism and The Problem of Agency', *Journal of Critical Realism (incorporating Alethia)*, 5: 11–20.

Austin, J.L. (1962) *How to do Things with Words*. Oxford, Oxford University Press.

Azimont, F. and Araujo, L. (2007) 'Category Reviews as Market-Shaping Events', *Industrial Marketing Management*, 36: 849–860.

Bagozzi, R. (1975) 'Marketing as Exchange', *Journal of Marketing*, 39: 32–39.

Barnhill, J.A. and Lawson, W.M. (1980). 'Toward a Theory of Modern Markets', *European Journal of Marketing*, 14: 50–60.

Barrey, S. (2007) 'Struggling to be Displayed at the Point of Purchase: The Emergence of Merchandising in French Supermarkets', in M. Callon, Y. Millo and F. Muniesa (eds) *Market Devices*, Oxford: Blackwell, pp. 92–108.

Barrey, S., Cochoy, F. and Dubuisson-Quellier, S. (2000) 'Designer, Packager Et Merchandiser: Trois Professionnels Pour Une Même Scéne Marchande', *Sociologie du Travail*, 42: 457–482.

Bartels, R. (1962) *The Development of Marketing Thought*. Homewood, Ill.: Richard D. Irwin.

Bartels, R. (1974) 'The Identity Crisis in Marketing', *Journal of Marketing*, 38: 73–76.

Belk, R.W. (1988) 'Possessions and the Extended Self', *Journal of Consumer Research*, 15: 139–168.

Bourdieu, P. (1981) 'Men and Machines', in K. Knorr Cetina and A.V. Cicourel (eds) *Advances in Social Theory and Methodology: Toward an Integration of Micro- and Macro-Sociologies*, London: Routledge and Kegan Paul, pp. 304–317.

Bourdieu, P. (1990) *The Logic of Practice*. Cambridge: Polity Press.

Brennan, R. and Turnbull, P.W. (2002) 'Sophistry, Relevance and Technology Transfer in Management Research: An IMP Perspective', *Journal of Business Research*, 55: 595–602.

Brodie, R.J., Coviello, N.E., Brookes, R.W. and Little, V. (1997) 'Towards a Paradigm Shift in Marketing? An Examination of Current Marketing Practices', *Journal of Marketing Management*, 13: 383–406.

Brown, S. (2007) 'Are We Nearly There Yet? On the Retro-Dominant Logic of Marketing', *Marketing Theory*, 7: 291–300.

Brownlie, D. and Saren, M. (1997) 'Beyond the One-Dimensional Marketing Manager: The Discourse of Theory, Practice and Relevance', *International Journal of Research in Marketing*, 14: 147–161.

Calhoun, C. (1991) 'The Problem of Identity in Collective Action', in J. Huber (ed.) *Macro-Micro Linkages in Sociology*, Newbury Park CA.: Sage, pp. 51–75.

Callon, M. (ed.) (1998a) *The Laws of the Markets*. Oxford: Blackwell Publishers/The Sociological Review.

Callon, M. (1998b) 'Introduction: The Embeddedness of Economic Markets in Economics', in M. Callon (ed.) *The Laws of the Markets*, Oxford: Blackwell, pp. 1–57.

Callon, M. (1998c) 'An Essay on Framing and Overflowing: Economic Externalities Revisited by Sociology', in M. Callon (ed.) *The Laws of the Markets*, Oxford: Blackwell, pp. 244–269.

Callon, M. (1999) 'Actor-Network Theory – The Market Test', in J. Law and J. Hassard (eds) *Actor Network Theory and After*, Oxford: Blackwell, pp. 181–195.

Callon, M. (2005) 'Why Virtualism Paves the Way to Political Impotence. A Reply to Daniel Miller's Critique of the Laws of the Markets', *Economic Sociology, the European Electronic Newsletter*, 6: 3–20.

Callon, M. (2007) 'What Does it Mean to Say that Economics is Performative?' in D. MacKenzie, F. Muniesa and L. Siu (eds) *Do Economists Make Markets? On the Performativity of Economics*, Princeton NJ.: Princeton University Press, pp. 311–357.

Callon, M. (2008) 'Economic Markets and the Rise of Interactive *Agencements*: From Prosthetic Agencies to Habilitated Agencies', in T. Pinch and R. Swedberg (eds) *Living in a Material World*, Cambridge MA.: The MIT Press, pp. 29–56.

Callon, M. (2009) 'Civilizing Markets: Carbon Trading Between *In Vitro* and *In Vivo* Experiments', *Accounting, Organizations and Society*, 34: 535–548.

Callon, M. and Latour, B. (1981) 'Unscrewing the Big Leviathan: How Actors Macro-Structure Reality and How Sociologists Help Them To Do So', in K. Knorr Cetina and A.V. Cicourel (eds) *Advances in Social Theory and Methodology: Toward an Integration of Micro- and Macro-Sociologies*, London: Routledge and Kegan Paul, pp. 277–303.

Callon, M. and Law, J. (1995) 'Agency and the Hybrid Collectif', *South Atlantic Quarterly*, 94: 481–507.

Callon, M., Méadel, C. and Rabeharisoa, V. (2002) 'The Economy of Qualities', *Economy and Society*, 31: 194–217.

Callon, M., Millo, Y. and Muniesa, F. (eds) (2007) *Market Devices*. Oxford: Blackwell Publishing/The Sociological Review.

Callon, M. and Muniesa, F. (2005) 'Economic Markets as Calculative Collective Devices', *Organization Studies*, 26: 1229–1250.

Chia, R. and Holt, R. (2006) 'Strategy as Practical Coping: A Heideggerian Perspective', *Organization Studies*, 27: 635–655.

Cochoy, F. (2008) 'Calculation, Qualculation, Calqulation: Shopping Cart Arithmetic, Equipped Cognition and the Clustered Consumer', *Marketing Theory*, 8:15–44.

Coviello, N.E., Brodie, R.J., Danaher, P.J. and Johnston, W.J. (2002) 'How Firms Relate to their Markets: An Empirical Examination of Contemporary Marketing Practices', *Journal of Marketing*, 66: 33–46.

Cox, R., Alderson, W. and Shapiro, S.J. (eds) (1964) *Theory in Marketing*. Homewood, Ill.: Richard D. Irwin Inc.

Crew, M.A. and Kleindorfer, P.R. (2002) 'Regulatory Economics: Twenty Years of Progress?', *Journal of Regulatory Economics*, 21: 5–22.

Dawson, L.M. (1971) 'Marketing Science in the Age of Aquarius', *Journal of Marketing*, 35: 66–72.

de Certeau, M. (1984) *The Practice of Everyday Life*. Berkeley CA.: University of California Press.

Djelic, M.-L. (2002) 'Does Europe mean Americanization? The Case of Competition', *Competition and Change*, 6: 233–250.

Emirbayer, M. and Goodwin, J. (1994) 'Network Analysis and the Problem of Agency', *American Journal of Sociology*, 99: 1411–1454.

Emirbayer, M. and Mische, A. (1998) 'What Is Agency?', *American Journal of Sociology*, 103: 962–1023.

Espeland, W.N. and Stevens, M.L. (1998) 'Commensuration as a Social Process', *Annual Review of Sociology*, 24: 313–343.

Ferraro, F., Pfeffer, J. and Sutton, R.I. (2005) 'Economics Language and Assumptions: How Theories can Become Self-Fulfilling', *Academy of Management Review*, 30: 8–24.

Finch, J.H. and Acha, V.L. (2008) 'Making and Exchanging a Second-Hand Oil Field, Considered in an Industrial Marketing Setting', *Marketing Theory*, 8: 45–66.

Fine, B. (2003) 'Callonistics: A Disentanglement', *Economy and Society*, 32: 478–484.

Ford, D. and Redwood, M. (2005) 'Making Sense of Network Dynamics Through Network Pictures: A Longitudinal Case Study', *Industrial Marketing Management*, 34: 648–657.

Friedberg, E. (1993) 'From Organizations to Concrete Systems of Action', in S.M. Lindenberg and H. Schreuder (eds) *Interdisciplinary Perspectives on Organization Studies*, Oxford: Pergamon, pp. 153–169.

Giddens, A. (1981) 'Agency, Institution, and Time-Space Analysis', in K. Knorr Cetina and A.V. Cicourel (eds) *Advances in Social Theory and Methodology: Toward an Integration of Micro- and Macro-Sociologies*, London: Routledge and Kegan Paul, pp. 161–174

Giddens, A. (1984) *The Constitution of Society, Outline of a Theory of Structuration*. Cambridge, Polity Press.

Giddens, A. (1993) *New Rules of Sociological Method*, second edn. Cambridge: Polity Press.

Goffman, E. (1974) *Frame Analysis. An Essay on the Organization of Experience*. New York: Harper & Row.

Granovetter, M. (1985) 'Economic Action and Social Structure: The Problem of Embeddedness', *American Journal of Sociology*, 91: 481–510.

Granovetter, M. (1992) 'Problems of Explanation in Economic Sociology', in N. Nohria and R. Eccles (eds) *Networks and Organizations*, Cambridge MA.: Harvard Business School Press, pp. 25–56.

Gundlach, G.T. and Phillips, J.M. (2002) 'Marketing in Antitrust: Contributions and Challenges', *Journal of Public Policy and Marketing*, 21: 250–253.

Håkansson, H. and Snehota, I. (1995) *Developing Relationships in Business Networks*, London, Routledge.

Helgesson, C.-F. (1999) 'Making a Natural Monopoly: The Configuration of a Techno-Economic Order in Swedish Telecommunications', PhD thesis, Stockholm, The Economic Research Institute, Stockholm School of Economics.

Helgesson, C.-F. and Kjellberg, H. (2005) 'Macro-Actors and the Sounds of the Silenced', in B. Czarniawska and T. Hernes (eds) *Actor Network Theory and Organizing*, Malmö: Liber & Copenhagen University Press, pp. 175–198.

Hodgson, G.M. (1998) 'The Approach of Institutional Economics', *Journal of Economic Literature*, 36: 166–192.

Holt, D.B. (1995) 'How Consumers Consume: A Typology of Consumption Practices', *The Journal of Consumer Research*, 22: 1–16.

Hovenkamp, H. (1991) *Enterprise and American Law, 1836–1937*. Cambridge MA: Harvard University Press.

Hunt, S.D. (1976) 'The Nature and Scope of Marketing', *Journal of Marketing*, 40: 17–28.

Hutchins, E. (1995) *Cognition in the Wild*. Cambridge MA: The MIT Press.

Igo, S.E. (2007) *The Averaged American. Surveys, Citizens and the Making of a Mass Public*. Cambridge MA: Harvard University Press.

Jap, S.D. (2007) 'The Impact of Online Reverse Auction Design on Buyer-Supplier Relationships', *Journal of Marketing*, 71: 146–159.

Kjellberg, H. (2001) 'Organizing distribution: Hakonbolaget and the efforts to rationalize food distribution, 1940–1960', PhD thesis, Stockholm, The Economic Research Institute, Stockholm School of Economics.

Kjellberg, H. (2007) 'The Death of a Salesman? Reconfiguring Economic Exchange in Swedish Post-War Food Distribution', in M. Callon, Y. Millo and F. Muniesa (eds) *Market Devices*, Oxford: Blackwell, pp. 65–91.

Kjellberg, H. and Helgesson, C.-F. (2006) 'Multiple Versions of Markets: Multiplicity and Performativity in Market Practice', *Industrial Marketing Management*, 35: 839–855.

Kjellberg, H. and Helgesson, C.-F. (2007a) 'On the Nature of Markets and their Practices', *Marketing Theory*, 7: 137–162.

Kjellberg, H. and Helgesson, C.-F. (2007b) 'The Mode of Exchange and Shaping of Markets: Distributor Influence on the Swedish Post-War Food Industry', *Industrial Marketing Management*, 36: 861–878.

Kopytoff, I. (1986) 'The Cultural Biography of Things: Commoditization as Process', in A. Appadurai (ed.) *The Social Life of Things: Commodities in Cultural Perspective*, Cambridge: Cambridge University Press, pp. 64–91.

Korkman, O. (2006) 'Customer value formation in practice. A practice-theoretical approach', PhD thesis, Helsinki, Swedish School of Economics and Business Administration.

Kotler, P. (1972) 'A Generic Concept of Marketing', *Journal of Marketing*, 36: 46–54.

Kotler, P. (1973) 'The Major Tasks of Marketing Management', *Journal of Marketing*, 37: 42–49.

Kotler, P. (2005) 'The Role Played by the Broadening of Marketing Movement in the History of Marketing Thought', *Journal of Public Policy and Marketing*, 24: 114–116.

Kotler, P. and Levy, S.J. (1969a) 'Broadening the Concept of Marketing', *Journal of Marketing*, 33: 10–15.

Kotler, P. and Levy, S.J. (1969b) 'Marketing Notes and Communications. A New Form of Marketing Myopia: Rejoinder to Professor Luck', *Journal of Marketing*, 33: 55–57.

Latour, B. (1987) *Science in Action: How to Follow Scientists and Engineers Through Society*. Cambridge MA: Harvard University Press.

Latour, B. (1992) 'Where Are the Missing Masses? The Sociology of a Few Mundane Artefacts', in W.E. Bijker and J. Law (eds) *Shaping Technology/Building Society. Studies in Sociotechnical Change*, Cambridge MA: The MIT Press, pp. 225–258.

Latour, B. (1994) 'On Technical Mediation – Philosophy, Sociology, Genealogy', *Common Knowledge*, 3: 29–64.

Latour, B. (1995) 'The "Pedofil" of Boa Vista: A Photo-Philosophical Montage', *Common Knowledge*, 4: 144–187.

Latour, B. (1996) *Aramis, or the Love of Technology*. Cambridge MA: Harvard University Press.

Latour, B. (1999) *Pandora's Hope, Essays on the Reality of Science Studies*. Cambridge MA: Harvard University Press.

Latour, B. (2005) *Reassembling the Social. An Introduction to Actor-Network-Theory*. Oxford: Oxford University Press.

Law, J. (1994) *Organizing Modernity*. Oxford: Blackwell.

Levy, S.J. (1959) 'Symbols for Sale', *Harvard Business Review*, 37: 117–124.

Lindberg, N. and Nordin, F. (2008) 'From Products to Services and Back Again: Towards a New Service Procurement Logic ', *Industrial Marketing Management*, 37: 292–300.

Lohmann, L. (2005) 'Marketing and Making Carbon Dumps: Commodification, Calculation and Counterfactuals in Climate Change Mitigation', *Science as Culture*, 14: 203–235.

Luck, D.J. (1969) 'Marketing Notes and Communications: Broadening the Concept of Marketing. Too Far', *Journal of Marketing*, 33: 53–55.

Luck, D.J. (1974) 'Marketing Notes and Communications. Social Marketing: Confusion Compounded', *Journal of Marketing*, 38: 70–72.

Lynch, M. (1993) *Scientific Practice and Ordinary Action: Ethnomethodology and*

Social Studies of Science. Cambridge: Cambridge University Press.

MacKenzie, D. (2003) 'An Equation and its Worlds: Bricolage, Exemplars, Disunity and Performativity in Financial Economics', *Social Studies of Science*, 33: 831–868.

MacKenzie, D. (2004) 'The Big, Bad Wolf and the Rational Market: Portfolio Insurance, the 1987 Crash and the Performativity of Economics', *Economy and Society*, 33: 303–334.

MacKenzie, D. and Millo, Y. (2003) 'Constructing a Market, Performing Theory: The Historical Sociology of a Financial Derivatives Exchange', *American Journal of Sociology*, 109: 107–145.

MacKenzie, D., Muniesa, F. and Siu, L. (eds) (2007) *Do Economists Make Markets? On the Performativity of Economics*. Princeton NJ: Princeton University Press.

Mallard, A. (2007) 'Performance Testing: Dissection of a Consumerist Experiment', in M. Callon, Y. Millo and F. Muniesa (eds) *Market Devices*, Oxford: Blackwell, pp. 154–172.

McCracken, G. (1986) 'Culture and Consumption: A Theoretical Account of the Structure and Movement of the Cultural Meaning of Consumer Goods', *Journal of Consumer Research*, 13: 71–84.

McInnes, W. (1964) 'A Conceptual Approach to Marketing', in R. Cox, W. Alderson and S.J. Shapiro (eds) *Theory in Marketing*, Homewood, Ill.: Richard D. Irwin Inc., pp. 51–67.

Ménard, C. (1995) 'Markets as Institutions Versus Organizations as Markets? Disentangling Some Fundamental Concepts', *Journal of Economic Behavior and Organization*, 28: 161–182.

Merton, R.K. (1996) *On Social Structure and Science*. Chicago: University of Chicago Press.

Miller, D. (2002) 'Turning Callon the Right Way Up', *Economy and Society*, 31: 218–233.

Mirowski, P. and Nik-Khah, E. (2007) 'Markets Made Flesh', in D. MacKenzie, F. Muniesa and L. Siu (eds) *Do Economists Make Markets? On the Performativity of Economics*, Cambridge MA: The MIT Press, pp. 190–224.

Muniesa, F., Callon, M. and Millo, Y. (2007) 'An Introduction to Market Devices', in M. Callon, Y. Millo and F. Muniesa (eds) *Market Devices*, Oxford: Blackwell, pp. 1–12.

Nik-Khah, E. (2006) 'What the FCC Auctions can Tell Us About the Performativity Thesis', *Economic Sociology – The European Electronic Newsletter*, 7: 15–21.

North, D.C. (1990) *Institutions, Institutional Change, and Economic Performance*. Cambridge: Cambridge University Press.

Osborne, T. and Rose, N. (1999) 'Do the Social Sciences Create Phenomena?: The Example of Public Opinion Research', *British Journal of Sociology*, 50: 367–396.

Peñaloza, L. and Venkatesh, A. (2006) 'Further Evolving the New Dominant Logic of Marketing: From Services to the Social Construction of Markets', *Marketing Theory*, 6: 299–316.

Pickering, A. (ed.) (1992) *Science as Practice and Culture*. Chicago: The University of Chicago Press.

Pickering, A. (1993) 'The Mangle of Practice: Agency and Emergence in the Sociology of Science', *American Journal of Sociology*, 99: 559–589.

Porter, T.M. (2008) 'Locating the Domain of Calculation', *Journal of Cultural Economy*, 1: 39–50.

Power, M. (2004) 'Counting, Control and Calculation: Reflections on Measuring and Management', *Human Relations*, 57: 765–783.

Reckwitz, A. (2002) 'Toward a Theory of Social Practices: A Development in Culturalist Theorizing', *European Journal of Social Theory*, 5: 243–263.

Rinallo, D. and Golfetto, F. (2006) 'Representing Markets: The Shaping of Fashion Trends by French and Italian Fabric Companies', *Industrial Marketing Management*, 35: 856–869.

Rosa, J.A., Porac, J.F., Runser-Spanjol, J. and Saxon, M.S. (1999) 'Sociocognitive Dynamics in a Product Market', *Journal of Marketing*, 63: 64–67.

Rose, N. (1999) *Powers of Freedom. Reframing Political Thought*. Cambridge: Cambridge University Press.

Roth, A.E. (2007) 'The Art of Designing Markets', *Harvard Business Review*, 85: 118–126.

Samli, A.C. and Bahn, K.D. (1992) 'The Market Phenomenon: An Alternative Theory and Some Metatheoretical Research Considerations', *Journal of the Academy of Marketing Science*, 20: 143–153.

Schatzki, T.R. (2005) 'Peripheral Vision: The Sites of Organizations', *Organization Studies*, 26: 465–484.

Schatzki, T.R. (2008) *Social Practices. A Wittgensteinian Approach to Human Activity and the Social,* second edition. Cambridge: Cambridge University Press.

Sewell, W.H.J. (1992) 'A Theory of Structure: Duality, Agency, and Transformation', *The American Journal of Sociology,* 98: 1–29.

Shankar, A., Whittaker, J. and Fitchett, J. (2006) 'Heaven Knows I'm Miserable now', *Marketing Theory,* 6: 485–505.

Shaw, E.H. and Jones, D.G.B. (2005) 'A History of Schools of Marketing Thought', *Marketing Theory,* 5; 239–281.

Sheth, J.N. and Sisodia, R.S. (2005) 'A Dangerous Divergence: Marketing and Society', *Journal of Public Policy and Marketing,* 24: 160–162.

Shove, E. and Pantzar, M. (2005) 'Consumers, Producers and Practices: Understanding the Invention and Reinvention of Nordic Walking', *Journal of Consumer Culture,* 5: 43–64.

Shuptrine, F.K. and Osmanski, F.A. (1975) 'Marketing in an Environment of Change. Marketing's Changing Role: Expanding or Contracting?', *Journal of Marketing,* 39: 58–66.

Simakova, E. and Neyland, D. (2008) 'Marketing Mobile Futures: Assembling Constituencies and Creating Compelling Stories for an Emerging Technology', *Marketing Theory,* 8: 91–116.

Sissors, J.Z. (1966) 'What Is a Market?' *Journal of Marketing,* 30: 17–21.

Sjögren, E. and Helgesson, C.-F. (2007) 'The Q(u)ALYfying Hand: Health Economics and Medicine in the Shaping of Swedish Markets for Subsidized Pharmaceuticals', in M. Callon, Y. Millo and F. Muniesa (eds) *Market Devices,* Oxford: Blackwell, pp. 215–240.

Slater, D. (2002a) 'From Calculation to Alienation: Disentangling Economic Abstractions', *Economy and Society,* 31: 234–249.

Slater, D. (2002b) 'Markets, Materiality and the "New Economy"', in J.S. Metcalfe and A. Warde (eds) *Market Relations and the Competitive Process,* Manchester: Manchester University Press, pp. 95–113.

Slater, D. (2002c) 'Capturing Markets from the Economists', in P.D. Gay and M. Pryke (eds) *Cultural Economy: Cultural Analysis and Commercial Life,* London: Sage, pp. 59–77.

Smith, S.J. (2005) 'States, Markets and an Ethic of Care', *Political Geography,* 24: 1–20.

Smith, S.J., Munro, M. and Christie, H. (2006) 'Performing (Housing) Markets', *Urban Studies,* 43: 81–98.

Snehota, I. (2004) 'Perspectives and Theories of Market'. in H. Håkansson, D. Harrison and A. Waluszewski (eds), *Rethinking Marketing. Developing a New Understanding of Markets.* Chichester, John Wiley, pp. 15–32.

Stidsen, B. (1979) '[Toward a Concept of Domesticated Markets]: Comment', *Journal of Marketing,* 43: 76–79.

Strathern, M. (1996) 'Cutting the Network', *The Journal of the Royal Anthropological Institute,* 2: 517–535.

Swanson, G.E. (1992) 'Doing Things Together: Some Basic Forms of Agency and Structure in Collective Action and Some Explanations', *Social Psychology Quarterly,* 55: 94–117.

Sweeney, D.J. (1972) 'Marketing: Management Technology or Social Process?', *Journal of Marketing,* 36: 3–10.

Tucker, W.T. (1974) 'Future Directions in Marketing Theory', *Journal of Marketing,* 38: 30–35.

Venkatesh, A. and Peñaloza, L. (2006) 'From Marketing to the Market. A Call for a Paradigm Shift', in J.N. Sheth and R.S. Sisodia (eds) *Does Marketing Need Reform? Fresh Perspectives on the Future,* Armonk NY: M. E. Sharpe, pp. 134–150.

Venkatesh, A., Peñaloza, L. and Fırat, A.F. (2006) 'The Market as a Sign System and the Logic of the Market', in R.F. Lusch and S.L. Vargo (eds) *The Service-Dominant Logic of Marketing. Dialog, Debate and Directions,* Armonk NY: M. E. Sharpe, pp. 251–265.

Warde, A. (2005) 'Consumption and Theories of Practice', *Journal of Consumer Culture,* 5: 131–153.

Weick, K.E. (1979) *The Social Psychology of Organizing,* second edition. New York: Random House.

Weitz, B.A. and Wensley, R. (2002) *Handbook of Marketing.* Thousand Oaks CA: Sage.

Wenger, E. (1998) *Communities of Practice. Learning, Meaning and Identity.* Cambridge: Cambridge University Press.

Wilkie, W.L. and Moore, E.S. (2003) 'Scholarly Research in Marketing: Exploring the "4 Eras" of Thought Development ', *Journal of Public Policy & Marketing,* 22: 116–146.

Woolgar, S. (1991) 'Configuring the user: the case of usability trials', in J. Law (ed.) *A Sociology of Monsters: Essays on Power, Technology and Domination,* London, Routledge, pp. 58–99.

12

A Service-Dominant Logic for Marketing

Stephen L. Vargo and Robert F. Lusch

INTRODUCTION

Every scientific discipline has an underlying dominant logic, often inherited and shared with related disciplines. These logics are useful, if not essential, to the advancement of the discipline(s). They represent the paradigms that provides the perceptual gestalt used in organizing the phenomena of interest. Marketing inherited its dominant logic from economic science, which in turn inherited its logic from an economic philosophy developed during the Industrial Revolution. We (Vargo and Lusch, 2004a, 2008c) have called this logic goods-dominant (G-D) logic. However, it is not the only logic that has been suggested either for marketing or for economic thought. Indeed, some early economic philosophers and an increasing number of economists, marketing academics and researchers in other business disciplines have argued, directly or indirectly, for an alternative logic based on the exchange of service. We call our vision of the convergence of these alternative logics 'service-dominant (S-D) logic'. The purposes of this chapter are 1) to review briefly the historical roots of G-D logic 2) to outline the foundations of S-D logic, and 3) to point toward developing S-D logic-related research in understanding markets and marketing.[1]

ALTERNATIVE LOGICS OF MARKETS AND MARKETING

Foundations of goods-dominant logic

As implied by the label, G-D logic (Lusch and Vargo, 2006b; Vargo and Lusch, 2004a) focuses on goods, or more generally on 'products' – indicating both tangible (goods) or intangible ('services') units of output. In G-D logic, these products are seen as the bases of exchange. G-D logic can be paraphrased as follows (see Vargo and Lusch, 2004a):

1 Economic exchange is fundamentally concerned with units of output (products).
2 These products are embedded with value during the manufacturing (or agricultural or extraction) process.
3 For efficiency, this production ideally (a) takes place in isolation from the customer and (b) results

in tangible output that is (c) standardized and (d) can be inventoried to even out production cycles in the face of irregular demand.

4   These products can be sold in the market by capturing demand to increase the quantity of units sold, in order to maximize profits.

In short, G-D logic says that the purpose of the firm is to *produce and sell valuable units of output* and, as a corollary, the role of the customer is to purchase and *consume* these units and then buy more. It has also been called the 'neoclassical economics research tradition' (e.g. Hunt, 2000), 'manufacturing logic' (e.g. Normann, 2001), 'old enterprise logic' (Zuboff and Maxmin, 2002) and 'marketing management' (Webster, 1992).

G-D logic is grounded in the economic philosophy that was initially developed by Adam Smith (1776/1937), generally considered the 'father of economics'. Smith did not literally invent economics; in fact, that was not even his intention. Smith was a *moral philosopher* whose purpose – consistent with the title of his seminal work: *An Inquiry into the Nature and Causes of the Wealth of Nations* – was to identify the normative activities that would lead to *national wealth*, rather than to provide a positive foundation for *economic science*.

In (mostly) the early chapters, Smith (1776/1937) actually established a general economic philosophy, based on the foundational proposition of the efficiency of the 'division of labor', resulting in the necessity of 'exchange'. For Smith (1776/1937: 1), labor was the 'fund which originally supplies (the nation) with all the necessities and conveniences of life which it annually consumes'. That is, it is labor – by which Smith meant the application of mental and physical skills, essentially service (see Vargo and Lusch, 2004a, 2008a), rather than just physical labor – that provides the foundation for exchange. He also established *value-in-use* – benefit in relation to the labor required to achieve it – which he referred to as real value, as the central metric. However, having done so, he partially abandoned this general model of economic activity, since he was not inherently concerned

with all of exchange or with economic exchange in general. As noted, he was seeking a normative explanation about which types of service should be promoted in order to advance national wealth. Thus, he shifted his focus to *value-in-exchange* (nominal value, market price), rather than value-in-use, which he felt was easier to understand; it also simplified his task.

In the context of the eighteenth century and the Industrial Revolution, with limitations on personal travel and the nonexistence of electronic communication, Smith (1776/1937) saw the primary route to wealth creation as the export of tangible goods, and the primary source of these goods was manufacturing. Therefore, he created a foundational model centered on *products* – surplus tangible goods that could be exported. This narrowed focus on the exchange value of tangible goods can be seen in his extended discussion of the distinction between '*productive*' and '*unproductive*' activities (see Vargo and Morgan, 2005). For Smith, only those activities that contributed to the creation of surplus tangible goods were deemed 'productive'. Other activities, though useful and essential to individual and national well-being, were called 'unproductive', because they did not create exportable tangible goods and thus did not contribute to national wealth.

A number of economic philosophers, such as Say (1821/1937) and Mill (1929), who followed Smith (1776/1937) generally disagreed with his *productive versus unproductive* distinction, reasoning that all activities that contributed to well-being were productive; however, after doing so, they generally acquiesced to Smith's (1776/1937) productive/ unproductive distinction. This distinction took solid root and, over time, 'products' (tangible goods) became the focus of economics; value morphed from *usefulness* to an *embedded property of goods* (essentially value-in-exchange); *unproductive* morphed into *services* (intangible goods); and a clear distinction between *producers* (creators of value) and *consumers* (destroyers of value) was established.

This product-centered, or goods-centered, model of economic activity also had an additional appeal; it was compatible with the increasing desire of the economists to turn economic philosophy into a science of economics. During this time, the model of 'science' was Newtonian mechanics, a model of matter embedded with properties. A compatible economic model of products embedded with utility was particularly appealing. Thus, partially because of a desire for scientific respectability, the goods-centered paradigm survived and flourished. Economics and, in time, related business disciplines, as well as more general, societal understandings of commerce, developed from this G-D paradigm. *Services* (usually plural), from this G-D perspective, are typically seen as either (1) a restricted type of good (i.e. as intangible units of output, which cannot be standardized, produced separate from the customer or inventoried) or (2) an add-on that enhances the value of a good (e.g. after-sale service).

The presence of a G-D paradigm in marketing is apparent in such diverse literature as Levitt's (1960) general caution about "marketing myopia and Shostack's (1977: 73) statement, 'The classical "marketing mix", the seminal literature, and the language of marketing all derive from the manufacture of physical goods', as well as the terminology used to describe the related marketing phenomena, such as 'producer', 'consumer', 'goods and services', 'supply chains', 'channels of distribution', 'value-added', etc. In the last 30 years, this G-D logic paradigm has increasingly become viewed as restricted, if not flawed, as evidenced by the call for a more encompassing and solid paradigmatic foundation for marketing by a number of scholars (e.g. Gronroos, 1994; Gummesson, 1995; Hunt and Morgan, 1995; Schlesinger and Heskett, 1991; Shostack, 1977).

THE EVOLUTION OF SERVICE-DOMINANT LOGIC

S-D logic represents the convergence of these general calls for a new paradigm, as well as more specific calls for reformulating thought in specific areas of academic interest in business and marketing, such as services and relationship marketing (e.g. Gronroos, 1994; Gummesson, 1995), resource-advantage theory (e.g. Hunt, 2000), core competency theory (e.g. Day, 1994; Prahalad and Hamel, 1990), network theory (e.g. Achrol and Kotler, 1999; Hakansson and Snehota, 1995; Norman and Ramirez, 1993), consumer culture theory (e.g. Arnould and Thompson, 2005) and others, which collectively point toward an alternative logic of the market (for detailed evolution, see Vargo and Lusch, 2004a). It is a logic that implies moving the understanding of markets and marketing from a product or *output-centric* focus to a service or *process-centric* focus.

The most distinguishing difference between G-D logic and S-D logic is the conceptualization of service. In S-D logic, *service* is defined as the application of competences (knowledge and skills) for the benefit of another party (Vargo and Lusch, 2006, 2008a). The use of the singular 'service', as opposed to the plural '*services*' that is traditionally employed in G-D logic, is subtle but critical. It signals a shift from thinking about value creation in terms of *operand resources* – usually tangible, static resources (e.g. natural resources) that require some action to make them valuable – to *operant resources* – usually intangible, dynamic resources (e.g. human knowledge and skills) that are capable of creating value (Constantin and Lusch, 1994; Vargo and Lusch, 2004a). That is, whereas G-D logic sees services as (somewhat inferior to goods) *units of output*, S-D logic sees service as the *process* of doing something for and with another party and thus always dynamic and collaborative.

According to S-D logic, economic exchange is about providing service in order to receive reciprocal service – that is, *service is exchanged for service*. Whereas goods are sometimes involved in this process, they are *appliances* for service provision; they are *conveyors of competences*. Regardless of whether service is provided directly or indirectly, through a good, it is the knowledge and skills (competences – operant resources) of the providers and beneficiaries that represent the essential source of value creation, not goods.

It is important to note that S-D logic represents a shift in the *logic of exchange*, rather than a shift in the *type of product* that is under investigation. That is, S-D logic is not about making services more important than goods, but is about transcending both *goods* and (what have been referred to as) *'services'* with the common denominator, *service* – a process of doing something for and with another party. It is a shift that we (Vargo and Lusch, 2004a) argue is already taking place. As we have suggested, evidence of this 'new logic' can be found in somewhat diverse academic fields such as information technology (e.g. service-oriented architecture), human resources (e.g. organizations as learning systems), marketing (e.g. service and relationship marketing, network theory) and the theory of the firm (e.g. resource-based theories), etc., as well as in practice (e.g. IBM, GE, etc.).

Interestingly, this 'new logic' is actually also an old logic in the sense that it parallels many of the foundational ideas of value creation through the reciprocal application of knowledge and skills for which Smith (1776/1937) argued prior to his abandoning them to discuss more narrow notions of national wealth creation. It is also very similar to the work of Bastiat (1848/1964): 162), the nineteenth-century economist who claimed 'Services are exchanged for services … it is the beginning, the middle, and the end of economic science'. It can also be found in more contemporary work, such as the 'Nordic School's' (e.g. Gronroos, 1994; Gummesson, 1995) approach to service marketing, Normann (2001), Delauny and Gadrey (1992), and elsewhere.

Rather than implying that goods-based models of exchange should be modified to adjust for somewhat-less-than-desirable (compared to goods) service characteristics (i.e. lacking in tangibility, ability to be standardized, ability to be created separate from the customer and incapable of being inventoried), S-D logic suggests that a service-based

foundation, built upon service-driven principles, can provide a generalizable logic for understanding *all economic activity* (i.e. even when goods are involved). S-D logic, therefore, plays a unifying role. It not only accounts for goods in exchange, but also actually gives them a central role. This is notably different from the treatment of service(s) in G-D logic, in which service(s) has traditionally been either almost ignored or, more recently, treated as somewhat inferior, which has resulted in separate research streams in the marketing literature.

More generally, we have argued elsewhere (e.g. Vargo and Lusch, 2008c) that G-D logic has created additional conceptual bifurcations, such as the producer–consumer and the related business-to-consumer versus business-to-business distinctions, and necessitated the development of other (sub)disciplines. Arguably, the necessity for these distinctions largely vanishes in an S-D logic conceptualization of exchange, markets and marketing, making it possible to contemplate a true unified theory of the market, marketing and exchange.

FOUNDATIONAL PREMISES OF S-D LOGIC

In Vargo and Lusch (2004a), S-D logic was captured in eight foundational premises (FPs), which were intended to establish a framework for the service-centered mindset. As noted, many of the concepts (e.g. value co-production/co-creation and operant resources) underlying this mindset, and thus the FPs, are neither exclusive to nor invented by S-D logic itself. Rather, S-D logic captures shifting contemporary marketing thought, in which marketing is seen as a facilitator of ongoing processes of voluntary exchange through collaborative, value-creating relationships among individuals and organizations.

Since the publication of our initial work on S-D logic, 'Evolving …' (Vargo and Lusch, 2004a) and in spirit of co-creation and evolution that underlie S-D logic, the initial eight

Table 12.1 Foundational premises of S-D logic

Premise number	Foundational premise
FP1	Service is the fundamental basis of exchange.
FP2	Indirect exchange masks the fundamental basis of exchange.
FP3	Goods are a distribution mechanism for service provision.
FP4	Operant resources are the fundamental source of competitive advantage.
FP5	All economies are service economies.
FP6	The customer is always a co-creator of value.
FP7	The enterprise cannot deliver value, but only offer value propositions.
FP8	A service-centered view is inherently customer oriented and relational.
FP9	All social and economic actors are resource integrators.
FP10	Value is always uniquely and phenomenologically determined by the beneficiary.

Adapted from Vargo and Lusch, 2008a

premises have been revised and extended through the dialog and discussion among various interested scholars. Minor revisions and one addition (FP9) occurred in *The Service Dominant Logic of Marketing: Dialog, Debate and Directions* (Lusch and Vargo, 2006a; Vargo and Lusch, 2006). A more complete revision and the addition of FP10 were presented in Vargo and Lusch (2008a), the special issue of the *Journal of the Academy of Marketing Science*. The 10 FPs, as modified, are shown in Table 12.1 (Vargo and Lusch, 2008a) and discussed in the following section. Together, they provide the foundation for S-D logic.

One further comment on foundational premises might be appropriate here. As we developed S-D logic, we gave considerable thought to the use of the term 'premise' vs. 'proposition' to describe the ideas, of our own and others, that we were trying to convey. In the philosophy of science, the terms have quite different meanings. A *premise* is a statement that is assumed to be true and upon which further theory is built. On the other hand, a *proposition*, at least from a logical positivist perspective, is a statement that is intended to be tested for its truth content. As developed, the 10 FPs of S-D logic are intended to reflect the former. However, one should expect that if the premises are sufficiently rich, they should provide the foundation upon which to derive propositions that can then undergo scientific investigation and empirical testing. To that end, we began this process by deriving a set of derivative propositions that address how

firms can use service-logic to gain competitive advantage (Lusch et al., 2007).

FP1: Service is the fundamental basis of exchange

FP1 is the central premise of S-D logic: the purpose of exchange is reciprocal service provision. As noted, in S-D logic, 'service', is the process of using one's competences for the benefit of another party. It is thus distinguished from the plural '*services*', which implies a type of good, or unit of output, characterized by (often considered inferior) qualities of intangibility, heterogeneity, inseparability and perishability (e.g. Zeithaml et al., 1985). Thus, economic exchange involves doing something for another party under the condition that the other party will provide mutual service, by applying its own competences. However, as implied by FP2, the complex and indirect nature of economic exchange often makes this rather simple tenet difficult to see.

FP2: Indirect exchange masks the fundamental basis of exchange

Service-for-service exchange typically involves complex, indirect processes and is thus easy to miss. That is, service is often provided through goods (see FP3), but in addition to, or instead of, using these goods to provide service directly, they can also be used as a form of currency – that is, they can exchanged in the market by one party to obtain some alternative service. Similarly, service exchange also often occurs through the combination of the applied competences of internal microspecialists (e.g. assembly line workers) and/or the combination and integration of the microspecializations (e.g. the combination of all of the resources contributed and integrated by the various participants in the value network or constellation).

Furthermore, in monetized exchange, the reciprocal nature of service provision is delayed in relation to the initial transaction until the currency, representing rights to future service, are used in subsequent exchange. However, all of these exchange vehicles (i.e. goods, organizations and networks and money) are intermediaries in complex, service-for-service-exchange processes.

In all cases, these institutions involve individuals applying their competences for the ultimate benefit of another party so that they can receive the benefit of applied competences that they do not possess. That is, regardless of its dynamic and complex structure, the essence of market exchange remains the same; people still exchange their applied competences (e.g. knowledge and skills) for the applied competences of others. They are exchanging service for service.

FP3: Goods are a distribution mechanism for service provision

In S-D logic, the importance of goods does not vanish. Once service is understood as the basis of all exchange, goods can be seen as vehicles or transmitters of competences for service provision. The value of a good is not created in a factory and distributed to the market, but rather value creation takes place and is determined through its contribution to the user's self-service process – its value-in-use in the context of other resources (see FP10). Rather than 'services' representing a special case of 'intangible goods', as they have been conceived under G-D logic, goods are actually a special case of, or a vehicle for, indirect service provision. The basis of exchange is always service provision; goods, when used, are *appliances* for service provision. That is, service is superordinate, not an alternative, to goods.

FP4: Operant resources are the fundamental source of competitive advantage

One of the most central and critical differences between S-D logic (Vargo and Lusch, 2004a, b) and G-D logic is the shift in emphasis from operand to operant resources (Constantin and Lusch, 1994). Operand resources are those which must be acted upon before benefit can be realized, whereas operant resources are those which can cause effects. Operand resources are usually tangible and static, whereas operant resources are usually intangible and dynamic. As the name implies, G-D logic is centered on operand resources, whereas S-D logic refocuses exchange on operant resources by shifting from units of output to value-creation processes as the purpose of exchange – that is, service-for-service (FP1). Therefore the ability to compete in the market is a function of knowledge, both individual and organizational.

This does not reduce the importance of operand resources in human well-being; it just acknowledges that operand resources only become valuable in the context of active resources – for example, through modification, combination and use (see Zimmerman, 1951). It is the firm that can make use of (i.e. acquire and integrate) these various resources in ways that increase their own well-being that provides competitive advantage. This resources-based view of competition is captured and elaborated in the resource-advantage theory of competition (see, Hunt and Madhavaram, 2006). Since S-D logic implies that value is created through activity, it points toward the primacy of the human resources of the firm (Lusch et al., 2007) and emphasizes the necessity of seeing the customer as a co-creator of value (see FP6).

FP5: All economies are service economies

The common perception is that developed countries are in the middle of a 'new service economy'. However, from an S-D logic perspective, service provision is neither just now becoming abundant nor only recently gaining importance, but rather is the basis of all economic exchange (FP1). What is often seen as an emerging 'service economy' is actually an artifact of viewing the world through a manufacturing and agriculture and extraction lens – that is, with a G-D logic perspective. What is currently changing is that the service nature of exchange is becoming increasingly apparent as specialization increases and as less of what is exchanged fits the dominant manufactured-output classifications of economic activity. In S-D logic, there is no 'service revolution'; there is a *revelation in service-centered thinking*. Arguably, this revelation is at least partially driven by a true revolution: an information revolution (see Rust and Thompson, 2006). That is, in part, the apparent increase in service can be understood in terms of the exponential rate of increase in knowledge and the increasing ability to exchange information (i.e. operant resources) in a relatively pure form – without being transported by people and/or matter (liquification in Normann's [2001] terms) – through digitization. This ability to exchange information in pure form and at great distances, through digitization, can be contrasted with the relative requirement in Smith's time to embed it in goods.

FP6: The customer is always the co-creator of value

From a service perspective, the nature of value creation is interactivity. In G-D logic, this vision of interaction is implied, somewhat pejoratively, by 'inseparability' (of production and consumption), as a distinguishing characteristic between goods and services. We (e.g. Vargo and Lusch, 2004a, b) have argued that inseparability is not a useful distinguishing

characteristic of service, whereas it is probably a universal characteristic of value creation. That is, value creation occurs at the intersection of activities of providers and beneficiaries and is always determined by the beneficiary. Alternatively stated, value is always created through use and in context (see FP10), rather than manufactured and then delivered. This use implies the application of the *customer's operant resources* to those applied by the provider. All of this, in turn, implies that the customer is always an active participant of the value creation process – that is, a co-creator of value.

The term 'co-creator' requires some elaboration. In Vargo and Lusch (2004a), the term 'co-producer' was used in discussing FP6. Clearly, '*co-producer*' implies something of a G-D logic perspective. We therefore changed FP6 to the '*co-creator of value*' in Vargo and Lusch (2006), but retained the term co-production, which has a useful S-D logic meaning as well. Whereas 'co-creation of value' describes the process of joint application of operant resources among firms and customers in creating benefit, 'co-production' can be thought of as a subset of co-creation. That is, co-production involves the co-creation of the core offering itself and can occur through shared inventiveness, design and/or production of the firm's value proposition (Vargo and Lusch, 2006). Thus, from an S-D logic perspective, the customer always co-creates value, through use, and *can* also (but not necessarily) be a participant in co-production. This requirement, that value cannot be made by the firm and delivered, but rather co-created, implies that the firm can only propose its creation.

FP7: The enterprise cannot deliver value, but can only offer value propositions

Consistent with FP6, FP7 makes explicit the idea that the firm cannot make and deliver value. That is, because of the collaborative nature of value creation and the role of the customer in value determination, contextually and through use, the firm can initially only make value propositions, and then participate in its co-creation, if that proposition is accepted.

FP8: A service-centered view is inherently customer oriented and relational

In the G-D logic conceptualization of exchange, with its focus on units of output, the metric of exchange is the transaction. From this perspective, 'customer orientation' usually means something like making units that the customer will buy and 'relationship' usually refers to multiple transactions occurring over time. That is, customer orientation and relationship are normative adjustments to G-D logic, which together are necessary for increasing the long-term profitability of the firm through selling more units of output (tangible or intangible).

On the other hand, in S-D logic – with service as the basis of exchange and defined in terms of benefit from the mutual application of operant resources to reciprocally co-create value – exchange is inherently interdependent and relational and customer oriented. That is, in G-D logic, the firm and the customer are separate, with the former seen as a producer of value and the latter as a destroyer; whereas, in S-D logic, value creation is an interactive and collaborative process and, thus, value creation is always relational. Likewise, service, which is defined in terms of customer-perceived benefit, is inherently customer oriented.

Thus, rather than a normative statement, in S-D logic, relationships represent a positive statement about how value is created through the relationships of parties in service-for-service exchange. Customer centricity or, more precisely, mutual centricity (see Gummesson, 2008) and relationships are not options; they are realities of value-creating processes. In (the restatement of) FP9 (Vargo and Lusch, 2006), this relational orientation

is extended to the firm's network of resources in addition to its customers. In fact, the producer and consumer (customer) distinction vanishes.

FP9: All social and economic actors are resource integrators

The premise that value is co-created, implies that value is determined through the integration of both provider-supplied and beneficiary-supplied resources (always operant and sometimes operand). However, these resources, in turn, come from various sources – that is, other market-facing, public and private sources. In the traditional G-D logic-based literature, this integration is most often captured in concepts of supply chains (or more recently, value networks) and manufacturing (i.e. resource assembly). In the (G-D logic-based) 'services' literature, it is partially captured in the observation of the heterogeneity of services. S-D logic extends the manufacturing logic from *making things* to *integrating resources to create 'densities'* (Normann, 2001).

Norman (2001: 27) defines maximum density as a situation which 'the best combination of resources is mobilized for a particular situation – for example for a customer at a given time in a given place – independent of location, to create the optimum value/cost result'. In S-D logic, the integrating of resources to create densities is extended from the concept of provider and supply networks to the service beneficiary (e.g. 'customer') and beneficiary networks. This suggests a network-with (and within)-network model (cf. Gummesson's [2006] 'many-to-many' marketing), in which each actor is combining resources from multiple parties to create value.

The integrative, network-with-network model of value creation can be extended from individuals to all actors and institutions (e.g. families, firms, cities and nations) in their creation of value for themselves through the integration of resources acquired through both economic and social exchange. This foundational premise is a generalized version of the more restricted FP9 introduced by Vargo and Lusch (2006), as modified by Vargo and Lusch (2008a). Implicitly, together with the service-for-service tenet, it suggests that all parties in exchange are resource integrators and thus the producer versus consumer distinction is only a mater of perspective.

FP10: Value is always uniquely and phenomenologically determined by the beneficiary

This tenth foundational premise was added (Vargo and Lusch, 2008a) to capture more explicitly the experiential nature of value. This experiential nature of value creation is implicit in the S-D logic definition of service, various FPs (e.g. FP6, FP8 and FP9) and other, less-formalized, conceptual notions (e.g. consumer's perceptions, meeting higher-level needs and customer's determination). The unique and contextual interpretation of value was made explicit in Vargo and Lusch (2008a). The word 'phenomenological', rather than 'experiential', was used, because the term 'experience' is often interpreted to have positive-only connotations (e.g. something of a 'Disneyworld event' – a 'wow' factor), rather than positive, neutral or negative contextually specific, meanings. This experiential and contextual nature of value creation suggests that a term like '*value-in-context*', might be a better term than the slightly G-D logic friendly term 'value-in-use'.

CONCEPTUAL TRANSITIONS AND CHALLENGES

As we have indicated elsewhere (e.g. Lush and Vargo, 2006b; Vargo and Lusch, 2008a), whereas S-D logic is not a paradigm, since it does not represent a worldview (Hunt, 2002), it is a change in mindset that operates at a pretheoretic, paradigmatic level and, thus, requires a major transition in thinking. That is, it suggests a very different purpose of exchange than G-D logic, which is paradigmatic, and therefore requires transitioning from one mental model to another and, where possible, from one lexicon to another.

Placing service, rather than goods at the center of exchange, the central tenet of S-D logic, moves the focus of exchange, value creation and marketing from tangible (operand) resources to intangible (operant) resources, such as knowledge and skills (Lusch and Vargo, 2006c). Table 12.2 (Lusch and Vargo, 2006c: 286) provides a summary of these and other conceptual transitions associated with moving from the dominant, goods-logic toward the service-logic for marketing.

The G-D logic concepts are the traditional core concepts for understanding business. The S-D logic related concepts represent a *movement toward* the language that is needed to capture a service-centered logic. However, even this lexicon is partially grounded in and has G-D logic connotations. Thus, this lexicon will continue to be revised, refined and elaborated, as has partially taken place over

Table 12.2 Conceptual transitions

Goods-dominant logic concepts	Transitional concepts	Service-dominant logic concepts
Goods	Services	Service
Products	Offerings	Experiences
Feature/attribute	Benefit	Solution
Value-added	Co-production	Co-creation of value
Value-in-exchange	Value-in-use	Value-in-context
Profit maximization	Financial engineering	Financial feedback/learning
Price	Value delivery	Value proposition
Equilibrium systems	Dynamic systems	Complex adaptive systems
Supply Chain	Value-Chain	Value-creation network/constellation
Promotion	Integrated Marketing Communications	Dialog
To Market	Marketing to	Marketing with
Product orientation	Market orientation	Service orientation

(Source: Adapted from Lusch and Vargo, 2006c: 286)

time, as reflected in Vargo and Lusch (2008a), as S-D logic evolves. However, this transition from G-D-logic- to S-D-logic-compatible concepts is a difficult one, partly because the former serves not only as the formal language of the goods-centered model of economic exchange; but also as the vernacular foundation for everyday thought about exchange, marketing and business in general. This leads to difficult, partial transitions – G-D logic interpretations of S-D logic (middle column) – that are especially evident in first attempts (by us and others) at grasping and expressing S-D logic.

Some of the transitions in S-D logic can also be seen in the way that marketing seems to have transitioned to thinking in terms of marketing '*with*', rather than '*to*' customers. The shift in primacy of resources, from operand to operant, has implications for how exchange processes, markets and customers are perceived and, thus, how they are approached. Focusing on the primacy of operant resources, S-D logic views customers as resources that are capable of acting with other resources and collaborating to co-create value with the firm (Vargo and Lusch, 2004a). Thus, S-D logic considers customers to be dynamic, knowledge-generating and value-creating resources. This is a fundamental transition away from G-D logic, which views customers as operand resources that the firm acts upon. From a G-D logic perspective, customers are considered exogenous to the firm and are 'segmented' and 'targeted', and are often considered to be 'manipulated' in the process of value creation. The primary focus of marketing within G-D logic is to identify customers, and market and sell to them. Like other concepts and transitions that characterize S-D logic, we do not claim that we invented the idea of customers as value-(co)creating resources but rather see our treatment of co-creation as the logical extension of more isolated and focused conceptualizations and transitions found in the S-D logic pedigree.

Similar to how G-D logic considers customers to be operand resources, it also treats employees and other network partners as static

resources that need to be 'managed', if not manipulated (Lusch et al., 2007). Alternatively, S-D logic views all exchange partners (customers and 'suppliers') as operant resources that, to some extent, are always collaborators in the value-creation process. From this perspective, employees, customers and other network partners become the source, rather than the object, of a firm's innovation, competence, value and ultimately equity. Similarly, whereas G-D logic assumes that the external environments (legal, competitive, social, physical, technological, etc.) are largely uncontrollable influences to which the firm needs to adapt (McCarthy, 1960), S-D logic and the co-creation and resource-integration foundations challenge this assumption by viewing the external environments as resources the firm draws upon for support by overcoming resistances and co-creating these environments. Figure 12.1 (Lusch et al., 2007: 7) depicts the shift of marketing philosophies and the evolution from a goods- toward a service-dominant logic.

G-D-LOGIC-BASED CHALLENGES FOR S-D LOGIC

As discussed, the deeply rooted influence of a goods-centered lexicon creates difficulties for the conceptualization and communication of the S-D logic for marketing. That is, the dominant G-D logic based lexicon represents more than just words available to talk about marketing; it reflects the underlying paradigm for thinking about and understanding commerce, the market and exchange in general. This is particularly problematic for discussing and describing a counter-paradigmatic view, such as S-D logic, since there are often no alternative, generally acceptable, counter-paradigmatic or even neutral words available. We have previously noted several common misperceptions of S-D logic (e.g. Lusch and Vargo, 2006c; Vargo and Lusch, 2006, 2008a) that can be directly attributable to language limitations, such as the concepts of 'service'

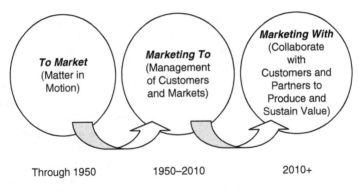

**Figure 12.1   The evolution of marketing.
(Source: Adapted from Lusch et al., 2007: 7).**

versus 'services', 'co-creation' versus 'co-production', and 'use value' versus 'utility'.

The meaning of 'service' as the key designator of S-D logic is the most common, and arguably the most critical, semantic issue surrounding S-D logic. Also arguably, no other issue is as tied to the difficulty of using words that have specific G-D logic meanings for explicating the nuances of S-D logic. Some have suggested that 'service' has too much baggage (e.g. Lehmann, 2006), whereas others, have suggested that the S-D logic definition of service is 'novel' or 'inconsistent' with traditional definitions (e.g. Achrol and Kotler, 2006; Levy, 2006). Still others have argued that it is just the wrong choice and/or it creates a false dichotomy between goods and services (e.g. Brodie et al., 2006).

For the most part, the issues surrounding the use of the term 'service' by S-D logic seem to be tied to the fact that in G-D logic, 'services' has a G-D-logic-specific meaning – usually, units *of output*, intangible goods. As noted, S-D logic, on the other hand, uses the singular term 'service' to refer to a *process*. We (Vargo and Lusch, 2006, 2008b) acknowledge some baggage associated with the term 'services', but argue that the term 'service', as defined by S-D logic, is neither novel nor faulty but, rather, precisely the correct, if not essential term, since there is no other word that better captures the idea of one party using their resources for another party. Additionally, this use of the word 'service'

transcends the old, intractable (see Vargo and Lusch, 2004b) question concerning the difference between goods and 'services' (intangibility, heterogeneity, inseparability and perishability) by reframing the issue to emphasize the *relationship*: service is the *common denominator* of exchange; goods are s*ervice-provision mechanisms*. Thus, as we (e.g. Lusch and Vargo, 2006c) have noted, the notion of a false dichotomy between goods and service(s) (Brodie et al., 2006) is not created by S-D logic, but rather was created by G-D logic and is, arguably, resolved by S-D logic. The appropriateness of the term 'service' is explored in more detail in Vargo and Lusch (2008b).

As partially discussed, the problem of G-D-logic-inspired words being inadvertently used to describe S-D logic is evident in the selection of the term 'co-production' by Vargo and Lusch (2004a) to capture the collaborative nature of value creation. Perhaps at least in part, the use of the term co-production led to the argument that S-D logic does not always apply, because customers do not always want to be active participants (e.g. Wilkie and Moore, 2006; Rust and Thompson, 2006). This argument is probably correct when viewed in the context of co-production but, arguably, vanishes in relation to co-creation of value, the term now used (see Lusch and Vargo, 2006c; Vargo and Lusch, 2006, 2008a). Nonetheless, also as noted, 'co-production' was retained to describe the involvement of the customer in the creation (e.g. co-design, shared production, etc.) of a firm's core offering, an optional subset and of the nonoptional value co-creation. That is, co-creation is the common denominator for value creation and superordinate to co-production in the same way that service is superordinate to goods.

DIRECTIONS: TOWARD A THEORY OF THE MARKET AND MARKETING

S-D logic is, arguably, not a theory since it does not contain the law-like generalizations required of a theory (see Hunt, 2002), at least by some. However, the ten foundational premises of S-D logic are rich in nature and can be used to generate derivative propositions (see e.g. Lusch et al., 2007) that are law-like in nature and empirically testable. As noted, it also is not a paradigm, at least in some senses of the word. As Kuhn (1970: 10) defines paradigms, they are 'accepted examples of actual scientific practice that provide models from which spring particular coherent traditions of scientific research'. Hunt (1991) uses the term in a broad sense to connote a 'worldview'. S-D logic does not presently meet either standard for a paradigm.

Although S-D logic is not a paradigm (Lusch and Vargo, 2006b; Vargo and Lusch, 2006; Vargo, 2007b), it functions at a paradigmatic level and provides an alternative lens, a mindset, through which phenomena can be examined. It is therefore operating at a paradigmatic level of abstraction and is pre-theoretical (see Vargo, 2007b).

Some (e.g. Venkatesh et al., 2006; Wilkie and Moore, 2006) have implied that S-D logic might not go far enough, because it does not move marketing beyond its present managerial or firm-centric orientation and/or does not adequately provide a *market* focus. In part, their observations are possibly well founded, especially as represented solely by the original *Journal of Marketing* article (Vargo and Lusch, 2004a), because it was

intended more as a refocusing effort than a complete redefinition of marketing.

Furthermore, market*ing*, by definition, is essentially a managerial activity, as is appropriate given its origin and initial focus on application. That is, marketing has normative connotations: it implies doing something – going to market, acting on the market, etc. In addition, the *Journal of Marketing*, in which S-D logic was introduced has an editorial policy of managerial relevance. Thus, as Vargo and Lusch (2006) acknowledged, some of their initial presentation of S-D logic was couched in managerial terms, but it is not inherently managerial.

We have suggested (e.g. Lusch and Vargo, 2006b; Vargo and Lusch, 2008c) that S-D logic might provide a foundation for rethinking marketing, perhaps providing a foundation for a general theory. However, we also agree with Venkatesh et al. (2006) and others that what is missing in marketing is an adequate understanding of the market. Thus, perhaps more importantly, we (e.g. Lusch and Vargo, 2006b; see also Vargo, 2007a; Vargo and Lusch, 2008c) have also suggested that S-D logic potentially offers a foundation for a much-needed positive *theory of the market,* on which better normative *theories of marketing* could be based. That is, the basic premise of S-D logic, that service (applied skills and knowledge) is exchanged for service is a more solid foundation for understanding markets and marketing than is the very limited foundation of exchange centered on goods. Therefore, S-D logic might not only lead to better marketing theory, but also could potentially provide a revised, process-oriented theory of economics and society.

We believe that building this theory of the market will require rethinking some of the basic assumptions and models of marketing, many of which were inherited. This is not a new vision. Perhaps Alderson (1957: 69) expressed the need first and best over 50 years ago when he argued, in the context of the debate about the nature of the value created by marketing, 'what is needed is not an interpretation of the utility created by marketing, but a marketing interpretation of the whole process of creating utility'. To that end, some of the major reformulations that we have identified are:

1 Shifting the focus of exchange from goods to service
2 Shifting the unit of analysis from products to value creation
3 Understanding that the essential drivers for all value creation are operant resources, rather than operand resources
4 Elimination of the producer–consumer distinction and adopting a relational, collaborative understanding of value creation
5 Moving from a linear (e.g. supply chain) perspective of value creation to a network perspective
6 Understanding the resource integration, contextual and phenomenological nature of value

Importantly, as we have shown (Vargo and Lusch, 2008c), many of these transitions and reformulations in the way we see markets and marketing have been somewhat stealthily being developed in the subdisciplines of marketing, most notably service marketing and business marketing, and seeping into mainstream marketing. We have tried to synthesize some of these transformations with others taking place outside of marketing in the ongoing development of S-D logic. However, Alderson's admonition mostly remains and will continue to do so until considerably more basic theory is developed – for example, a general theory of the market.

Not only might these transformations and initiatives lead to reformulated marketing science but, arguably, to contributions to the reformulation of economic science. Importantly, many of the same transitions in thought and initiatives can be seen simultaneously developing in economics – for example in growth theory, inframarginal analysis, etc.

Additionally, these reformulations will likely offer insight on social and ethical, legal, societal and ecological issues (Vargo and Lusch, 2008c). Such areas are already being examined (see e.g. Abela and Murphy, 2008) and show initial support for S-D logic

as a more integrative approach for studying ethical and socially beneficial aspects of marketing.

CONCLUSION

For the last several decades, marketing practitioners have been calling for more relevance from marketing academics and marketing academics have been calling for a paradigm shift. More generally, individuals and institutions of all sorts have been calling for more meaningful and informed approaches to common human needs and social issues. Not only does the dominant, G-D logic model of economics not lend itself fully to this need for more relevance, but also it is arguably part of the problem. This should not be entirely surprising. How could a model based solely on the exchange of operand resources, in which one party creates value and another consumes or destroys value and from which the derivative normative purpose is to sell increasingly more (preferably tangible) products inform issues of mutual well-being? We argue that responding to these calls requires frame-breaking perspectives and ideas. Fortunately, many of these perspectives and reconceptualizations can be found in subdisciples and research initiatives of marketing thought, as well as similar divergences outside of marketing. S-D logic is not so much an attempt to *create* a paradigmatic shift as it is to *discover* one in the convergence of these ongoing divergences and then to accelerate its extension. Rather than the creation of a top-down, definitive position, it represents a collaborative work in process.

Although our initial focus is on perspective and the underlying logic of the market, we also recognize the considerable work that needs to be done in theory building and its empirical testing and, ultimately, in establishing and reframing practice, both in marketing and other social institutions. As such, we continue to invite and encourage others to participate with us to co-create S-D logic and to use it to create a unifying theory of the market and, from this theory, a more meaningful and relevant theory of marketing, among other applications.

NOTES

1 This chapter relies heavily on writing we have published elsewhere, including, in some cases, work done with various coauthors.

REFERENCES

Abela, A.V. and Murphy, P.E. (2008) 'Marketing with Integrity: Ethics and the Service Dominant Logic for Marketing', *Journal of the Academy of Marketing Science*, 36(1): 39–53.

Achrol, R. and Kotler, P. (1999) 'Marketing in the Network Economy', *Journal of Marketing*, 63(Special Issue): 146–163.

Achrol, R. and Kotler, P. (2006) 'The Service-Dominant Logic for Marketing: A Critique', in R.F. Lusch and S.L. Vargo (eds) *The Service-Dominant Logic of Marketing: Dialog, Debate, and Directions*, Armonk, New York: M.E. Sharpe, pp. 320–333.

Alderson, W. (1957) *Marketing Behavior and Executive Action: A Functionalist Approach to Marketing Theory*, Homewood, IL: Richard D. Irwin.

Arnould, E.J. and Thompson, C.J. (2005) 'Consumer Culture Theory (CCT): Twenty Years of Research', *Journal of Consumer Research*, 31(March): 868–883.

Bastiat (1848/1964) *Selected Essays on Political Economy*, S. Cain, trans., G.B. de Huzar, ed. Princeton, NJ: D. Van Nordstrand.

Brodie, R.J., Pels, J. and Saren, M. (2006) 'From Goods – Toward Service-Centered Marketing: Dangerous Dichotomy or an Emerging Dominant Logic?', in R.F. Lusch and S.L. Vargo (eds) *The Service-Dominant Logic of Marketing: Dialog, Debate and Directions*, Armonk, New York: M.E. Sharpe, pp. 307–319.

Constantin, J.A. and Lusch, R.F. (1994) *Understanding Resource Management*. Oxford, OH: The Planning Forum.

Day, G.S. (1994) 'The Capabilities of Market-Driven Organization', *Journal of Marketing*, 58(October): 37–52.

Delaunay, J.-C. and Gadrey, J. (1992) 'Services in Economic Thought: Three Centuries of Debate'. Boston: Kluwer Academic Publishers.

Gronroos, C. (1994) 'From Marketing Mix to Relationship Marketing: Towards a Paradigm Shift in Marketing', *Asia-Australia Marketing Journal*, 2(August): 9–29.

Gummesson, E. (1995) 'Relationship Marketing: Its Role in the Service Economy', in W.J. Glynn and J.G. Barnes (eds) *Understanding Services Management*. New York: John Wiley & Sons.

Gummesson, E. (2006) 'Many-to-Many Marketing as Grand Theory', in R.F. Lusch and S.L. Vargo (eds) *The Service-Dominant Logic of Marketing: Dialog, Debate and Directions*, Armonk, New York: M.E. Sharpe, pp. 339–353.

Gummesson, E. (2008) 'Extending the Service-Dominant Logic: from CustomerCentricity to Balanced Centricity', *Journal of the Academy of Marketing Science*, 36(1): 15–17.

Hakansson, H. and Snehota, I. (1995) *Developing Relationships in Business Networks*. London: Routledge.

Hunt, S. (1991) Modern Marketing Theory: Critical Issues in the Philosophy of Marketing Science, Cincinnati: SouthWestern Publishing Co.

Hunt, S. (2000) *A General Theory of Competition: Resources, Competences, Productivity, Economic Growth*. Thousand Oaks, CA: Sage Publications.

Hunt, S. (2002) *Foundations of Marketing Theory: Toward a General Theory of Marketing*. Armonk, NY: M.E. Sharpe.

Hunt, S. and Madhavaram, S. (2006) 'The Service-Dominant Logic of Marketing: Theoretical Foundations, Pedagogy and Resources-Advantage Theory', in R.F. Lusch and S.L. Vargo (eds) *The Service-Dominant Logic of Marketing: Dialog, Debate and Directions*, Armonk, New York: M.E. Sharpe, pp. 67–84.

Hunt, S. and Morgan, R.M. (1995) 'The Comparative Advantage Theory of

Competition', *Journal of Marketing*, 59(April): 1–15.

Kuhn, T.S. (1970) *The Structure of Scientific Revolutions*. Chicago: University of Chicago Press.

Lehmann, D.R. (2006) 'More Dominant Logics for Marketing: Productivity and Growth', in R.F. Lusch and S.L. Vargo (eds) *The Service-Dominant Logic of Marketing: Dialog, Debate, and Directions*, Armonk, New York: M.E. Sharpe, pp. 296–301.

Levitt, T. (1960) 'Marketing Myopia', *Harvard Business Review*, 38(July–August): 26–44, 173–181.

Levy, S.J. (2006) 'How New, How Dominant?', in R.F. Lusch and S.L. Vargo (eds) *The Service-Dominant Logic of Marketing: Dialog, Debate and Directions*, Armonk, New York: M.E. Sharpe, pp. 57–64.

Lusch, R.F. and Vargo, S.L. (eds) (2006a) *The Service-Dominant Logic of Marketing: Dialog, Debate, and Directions*. Armonk, New York: M.E. Sharpe.

Lusch, R.F. and Vargo, S.L. (2006b) 'Service-Dominant Logic as a Foundation for a General Theory', in R.F. Lusch and S.L. Vargo (eds) *The Service-Dominant Logic of Marketing: Dialog, Debate and Directions*, Armonk, New York: M.E. Sharpe, pp. 406–420.

Lusch, R.F. and Vargo, S.L. (2006c) 'Service-dominant logic: reactions, reflections and refinements', *Marketing Theory*, 6(3): 281–288.

Lusch, R.F., Vargo, S.L. and O'Brien, M. (2007) 'Competing Through Service: Insights from Service-Dominant Logic', *Journal of Retailing*, 83(1): 5–18.

McCarthy, E.J. (1960) *Basic Marketing, A Managerial Approach*. Homewood, IL: Richard D. Irwin.

Mill, J. Stuart (1929) *Principles of the Political Economy*, (1885) Reprint, London: Longmans, Green.

Normann, R. (2001) *Reframing Business: When the Map Changes the Landscape*. New York, NY: John Wiley & Sons.

Normann, R. and Ramirez, R. (1993) 'From Value Chain to Value Constellation: Designing Interactive Strategy', *Harvard Business Review*, 71(July–August): 65–77.

Prahalad, C.K. and Hamel G. (1990) 'The Core Competence of the Corporation', *Harvard Business Review*, 68(May–June): 79–91.

Rust, R.T. and Thompson, D.V. (2006) 'How Does Marketing Strategy Change in a Service-Based World' in R.F. Lusch and S.L. Vargo (eds) *The Service-Dominant Logic of Marketing: Dialog, Debate, and Directions*, Armonk, New York: M.E. Sharpe, pp. 381–392.

Say, J.-B. (1821), *A Treatise on the Political Economy*. Boston: Wells and Lilly.

Schlesinger, L.A. and Heskett, J.L. (1991) 'The Service-Driven Company', *Harvard Business Review*, 69(September–October): 71–81.

Shostack, G.L. (1977) 'Breaking Free from Product Marketing', *Journal of Marketing*, 41(April): 73–80.

Smith, A. (1776/1937) *An Inquiry into the Nature and Causes of the Wealth of Nations*. London: W. Strahan and T. Cadell.

Vargo, S.L. (2007a) 'On a Theory of Markets and Marketing: From Positively Normative to Normatively Positive', *Australasian Marketing Journal*, 15(1): 56–63.

Vargo, S.L. (2007b) 'Paradigms, Pluralisms, and Peripheries on the Assessment of the S-D Logic', *Australasian Marketing Journal*, 15(1): 108–111.

Vargo, S.L. and Robert F. Lusch (2004a) 'Evolving to a New Dominant Logic for Marketing', *Journal of Marketing*, 68(1): 1–17.

Vargo, S.L. and Lusch, R.F. (2004b) 'The Four Service Marketing Myths: Remnants of a Goods-Based, Manufacturing Model', *Journal of Service Research*, 6(4): 324–335.

Vargo, S.L. and Lusch, R.F. (2006) 'Service-Dominant Logic: What It Is, What It Is Not, What It Might Be', in R.F. Lusch and S.L. Vargo (eds) *The Service-Dominant Logic of Marketing: Dialog, Debate and Directions*, Armonk, New York: M.E. Sharpe, pp. 43–56.

Vargo, S.L. and Lusch, R.F. (2008a) 'Service-Dominant Logic: Continuing the Evolution', *Journal of the Academy of Marketing Science*, 36(1): 1–10.

Vargo, S.L. and Lusch, R.F. (2008b) 'Why "Service"?', *Journal of the Academy of Marketing Science*, 36(1): 25–38.

Vargo, S.L. and Lusch, R.F. (2008c) 'From Goods to Service(s): Divergences and Convergences of Logics', *Industrial Marketing Management*, 37(May): 254–259.

Vargo, S.L. and Fred W. Morgan (2005) 'Services in Society and Academic Thought: An Historical Analysis', *Journal of Macromarketing*, 25(1): 42–53.

Venkatesh, A., Penaloza, L. and Fırat A.F. (2006) 'The Marketing as a Sign System and the Logic of the Market', in R.F. Lusch and S.L. Vargo (eds) *The Service-Dominant Logic of Marketing: Dialog, Debate and Directions*, Armonk, New York: M.E. Sharpe, pp. 251–265.

Webster, F.E., Jr. (1992) 'The Changing Role of Marketing in the Corporation', *Journal of Marketing*, 56(October): 1–17.

Wilkie, W.L. and Moore, E.S. (2006) 'Examining Marketing Scholarship and the Service-Dominant Logic', in R.F. Lusch and S.L. Vargo (eds) *The Service-Dominant Logic of Marketing: Dialog, Debate and Directions*, Armonk, New York: M.E. Sharpe, pp. 266–278.

Zeithaml, V.A., Parasuraman, A. and Berry, L.L. (1985) 'Problems and Strategies in Services Marketing', *Journal of Marketing*, 49(Spring): 33–46.

Zimmermann, E.W. (1951) *World Resources and Industries*. New York: Harper and Row.

Zuboff, S. and Maxmin, J. (2002) *The Support Economy*. New York: Penguin.

13

Market Ideology, Globalization and Neoliberalism

Robin Wensley

INTRODUCTION

It is rather ironic that this chapter is being written in the middle of what might well become the Great Crash of 2008/9. The twin topics of the culture of consumption (and the way in which non-sustainable levels of debt have facilitated its continued growth) and the need for regulation within markets are very much top of the agenda at the time of writing. By way of some defence against the accusation of just applying 20:20 hindsight, I would like to point out that a significant proportion of this chapter was covered in an earlier Masterclass session given to the Marketing Society (Wensley, 1997)!

In this chapter, we will cover the central issues from two different perspectives. First, in terms of market ideology, we will critically analyse the development and evolution of what might reasonably be termed the hegemony of neoliberal perspectives on the efficacy of markets and market mechanism in a wide range of contexts. Then we will consider what might be termed cultural issues from the primary perspective of issues of identity and how it relates to some of the

issues of global markets. Finally, we will consider how these aspects relate to the broader issue of social welfare.

'THE MAGIC OF THE MARKET'

In public policy, we often associate market ideology with the Ronald Reagan quote 'The magic of the market' although many before him had also seen the solution to problems of welfare and choice in Adam Smith's hidden or, more correctly, invisible hand. In passing, it is worth noting two particular issues about Adam Smith's writing. First, in his Wealth of Nations,[1] as previous commentators have noted, Smith has paid little attention to the notion of the invisible hand – it basically appears in almost a footnote only[2] – and paid much more attention to his concerns relating to the wider public interest and the behaviour of cartels of producers or professionals. Second, he had a clear view that the market or markets operated within the context of a wider set of norms and values.

Market ideology has come to be associated with two related but different aspects of the political economy. First, a belief that the market represents a means of achieving appropriate welfare outcomes through the process of choice and competition, and second that such an approach can be extended to the provision of many domains previously defined by what have been called public services.

We will consider a number of aspects that have arisen particularly in this extension of the market domain. Some of these aspects have been around since Adam Smith's initial observations; others have at the very least come to the fore more recently. To start with the one closely linked to Adam Smith – as Bishop (1995) notes:

> a close reading of the Wealth of Nations reveals that Smith thought the interests of merchants and manufacturers were fundamentally opposed to those of society in general, and that they had an inherent tendency to deceive and oppress society while pursuing their own interests. (p. 165)

Hence, the issue of regulation or intervention is to ensure that the producers do not, either explicitly or implicitly, collude to privilege their individual or collective interests against the public interests of the wider community. As the remit of public services provided by private suppliers has extended in national contexts such as the UK, so has the number and range of regulatory agencies.

Adam Smith and the invisible hand

The logic of the 'invisible hand' is the clear assumption that the individual pursuit of self-interest is much more likely to increase overall social welfare than alternatives such as the actions of governments or politicians (Tobin, 1991, 1992). Of course, this assumption has been subject to a great deal of scrutiny and critical analysis although it is difficult not to conclude that, in the end, most commentators have, not perhaps surprisingly, read their own interpretations into Adam Smith's text. For instance, Tobin (1992) comments:

> Adam Smith is not responsible for the excesses committed in his name. His main purpose was to oppose protectionism and other regulations favouring special interests at the expense of the general public. His important message was that the accumulation of precious metals by contriving trade surpluses was contrary to the national interest, for the true wealth of a nation lay in its capacity to deliver useful goods and services to its citizens. Modern microeconomists of all shades would agree and usually do.
>
> ... The Wealth of Nations is a very down-to-earth book, with a simple thematic moral, a rudimentary theoretical model, an imaginative intuition, a vast collection of historical and institutional material, and a great deal of wisdom and common sense. Perhaps looser claims for the invisible hand, less sweeping. less rigorous and less abstract than general equilibrium models, would be more congenial to Smith. Second-best claims that admit market failures but say governments are worse. (pp. 127–128)

The other side of individual self-interest is the issue of distribution of wealth and the question of individual morality. On both questions, it is important to recognize that Adam Smith placed strong emphasis on a 'god fearing' world in which all was to the Almighty's design. Viner (1927) argued cogently that Smith's belief in an optimistic theology meant that he regarded issues of both wealth distribution and self-interest as relatively unproblematic. In the context of the later, he notes:

> Nowhere in the Wealth of Nations does Smith place any reliance for the proper working of the economic order upon the operation of benevolence and sympathy ... benevolence is not merely as a rule left out of the picture of the economic order, when mentioned it is with the implication that it is a weak reed upon which to depend.

The context of this quotation is, however, itself significant, as it refers to the 'Wealth of Nations' and does not include Adam Smith's other and earlier work, indeed the one on which his reputation initially was established, 'The Theory of Moral Sentiments'. In this case, he uses the notion of the invisible hand in a rather different context to refer more generally to the distribution of means to happiness rather than economic maximization.[3] As Billet comments:

> Smith is severely critical of the pursuit of wealth and power in his work on morality and yet maintains

a positive attitude toward wealth in his political economy. The supposed contradiction can be resolved when one realizes that in the Wealth of Nations, his sympathy towards 'bettering one's condition' expresses the preoccupation of political economy with the subsistence and comfort of the masses, and that he has already provided in his earlier book an explicit and comprehensive critique of 'riches' and the pursuit of power, aimed at admonishing the rich and enlightening the receptive. (Billet, 1976: 302)

Djelic (2005, 2007a and 2007b) has developed a similar analysis in much more thorough and systematic manner to argue that whilst the original notion of the invisible hand as partially developed by Adam Smith recognized a wider social and political context, there was a gradual development of the so-called neoliberal synthesis, with the convergence, particularly in the US political economy, of a number of key influences:

In the twentieth century, the emergence of neoliberalism represented an emerging synthesis. All three bodies of thought – economic liberalism, Calvinist doctrine and Spencerian evolutionism – were present and combined in this synthesis. At the same time, the neoliberal synthesis pushed forward a process already well under way – the disenchantment of economics and economic activity. Rationalization, individualism, utilitarianism, laissez faire and a belief in progress remained as key building blocks.... The profound meaning, though, the legitimacy and the moral backbone that had been understood to sustain economic activity, at least in classical economy and in the Calvinist worldview, had all but disappeared. (Djelic, 2007b: 28)[4]

It is hardly surprising therefore that, in the early nineties, the American Marketing Association (AMA) decided it could do no better than break with its own tradition of change and repeat its annual slogan 'Marketing makes a good life better'!

Different forms of capitalism

There has been much discussion about the extent to which one can identify different forms of capitalism on a national or a regional basis. A key writer in this area has been Richard

Table 13.1   The use of surplus value in capitalism

	Appropriation	Reinvested
Private	Predatory capitalism	'Puritan' capitalism
Collection	Welfare capitalism	State capitalism

Reproduced with permission from Djelic (2007a)

Whitley (1999) who identifies six different forms of capitalism or 'national business systems': Arm's length, Collaborative, State organized, Highly organized, Fragmented and Coordinated industrial district. Amable (2003) adopts a more specific geographic approach to come up with five types: Market-based model, Social-democratic model, Continental European model, Asian model and Mediterranean model.

Djelic (2007a) develops a more conceptual approach to suggest that there are four 'ideal types'. The two dimensions she uses relate to whether value is mostly appropriated for 'unproductive' use or mostly reinvested and whether the value created goes mostly to private interests or to a collective. This leads to four simple ideal types that are presented in Table 13.1.

In her matrix, it is clear that in principle at least she sees an underlying logic, which could result in the existence of different 'forms' of capitalism over extended periods. Whether we regard there as being a specific form that will become dominant as an inevitable process of evolution might be seen as a question analogous to that raised by Fukuyama (1992) in his polemical treatise on 'The end of history'.[5]

However, in the context of the current global political economy, she notes:

Contemporary capitalism clearly falls into the top line; and it has increasingly been moving (back), over the period studied, towards the predatory cell. Fifth, and finally, extreme commodification and a predatory pattern of use of surplus value combine to generate and reinforce imbalances and inequalities – economic, social, cultural, political and geopolitical. In spite of an unmistakable progress of democratization and in spite of facilitating global technologies, our world is not 'flat' (Friedman, 2005). Arguably, the stratification in our world – as measured by differences in wealth and power between those who have most and those who have least – may be historically unprecedented.

Contemporary capitalism comes together with new and strong forms of stratification that increasingly have a transnational and not simply a national scope. (p. 31)

The question therefore remains whether the apparently inexorable trend that she notes towards the model of predatory capitalism now faces a challenge that could mean a halt or indeed even reversal. We may have to rethink the relationship between the wider political economy and the nature of specific markets and consider more critically both the relationship between them and the related doctrine of market failure. In the first case, we may revisit some of the issues raised by Kelner (1984) in his article on the relationship between markets and socialism. In the later case, we need to consider the recent renewal of attacks on the use of the principle of market failure as the sole legitimate justification for market intervention.

The failure of market failure?

There has also been a significant revival in challenges to the hegemony of market-based approaches (often, generally described as the process of marketization) behind critical questioning of the policy doctrine of market failure. Under this doctrine, intervention in the market place is only justified if there is clear evidence of market failure. Both Kay (2007) and Hutton and Schneider (2008) strongly suggest that there needs to be a much clearer recognition that not only do markets rarely reflect the ideal aspects incorporated in neoliberal theory but that it also makes little sense to treat such idealized concepts as a realistic objective for economic policy.

However, we now wish to shift our analysis from the general issues of the nature of the political economy to the developments and concerns around the nature of consumption. Of course, there are links between these two perspectives: indeed some have noted that until recently major parts of the world economy continued to achieve economic growth through a process of 'privatized

Keynesianism' where the banks encouraged more and more private debt rather than the more traditional Keynesian use of public funds (Bellofiore and Halevi, 2008).

The emergence of the BRIC economies

In the last few years, particularly in the financial and investment community, there has been an increasing focus on emerging and developing markets in the BRIC (Brazil, Russia, India and China) economies. The acronym was first coined and prominently used by the bank holding company Goldman Sachs in 2001. Goldman Sachs argued that, since they are developing rapidly, by 2050, the combined economies of the BRICs could eclipse the combined economies of the current richest countries of the world.

Of course, this was a projection about the overall size of the economies themselves, and therefore by implication their importance to the global economy, rather than a comment on their wealth per capita or indeed the distribution of such wealth. In these wider issues of political economies, it is also clear that the likely balance between state, market and civil society (Benington, 2007) in each of the emerging economies will be quite different, which will pose both individually and collectively a further challenge to the neoliberal consensus.

Indeed a closer analysis of the BRIC 'phenomenon' not only helps us to see how a general notion of 'otherness' can be used to mask what are in fact very different types of entity but also that the actual pattern of the further development of a global economy is both more contested and more complex than often represented in debates about such phenomena as global markets.

GLOBALIZATION, CULTURE AND IDENTITY

The neoliberal consensus comes to its final form, at least from a marketing perspective in the notion of unfettered markets and global consumers. This 'utopian' ideal was perhaps characterized from a marketing viewpoint most clearly by Ted Levitt when he asserted:

> The worldwide success of a growing list of products that have become household names is evidence that consumers the world over, despite deep-rooted cultural differences, are becoming more and more alike. (1983)

In consequence, he contended, the traditional multinational corporation strategy of tailoring its products to the needs of multiple markets put it at a severe disadvantage vis-à-vis competitors who applied marketing imagination to the task of developing advanced, functional, reliable and standardized products, at the right price, on a global scale.

Least this sounds a little too much like a supplier-driven process to foist a uniform product or service on the customer,[6] there was also a parallel narrative, which focused on the privileging of a consumer rather than a producer culture.[7] As Paul DuGay (1996) observed:

> Governing economic life in an enterprising manner is intimately bound up with the de-differentiation of economy and culture - with a pronounced blurring between the sphere of 'production' and 'consumption', the 'corporate' and 'culture'. As the language of the market becomes the only valid vocabulary of moral and social calculation, the 'privilege of the producer' is superseded by the 'sovereignty of the consumer', with 'civic culture' gradually giving way to 'consumer culture' as citizens are reconceptualized as 'enterprising consumers'.

It is noteworthy, however, that not only have there been different views proclaimed about the inevitability of such trends: such as the global–local dilemma that Levitt referred to. Slogans such as 'Think Global; Act Local' have acquired considerable currency albeit at some significant loss of specificity! Also, rather ironically, some of those who have proclaimed what they see as the evident benefits in welfare terms for such an outcome have most often been vociferous in their critique of what they see as the opposite trend (see for instance, Epstein, 2004).

More recently, two developments are particularly worthy of additional note: the challenge to what might seen as the 'branding of everything', and the ways in which some of the issues of identity reintroduce what might be broadly termed cultural variables such as religion.

The branding of everything

Naomi Klein (2000) and Conley (2008) both from rather different perspectives have forcefully challenged the extent to which consumer marketing focuses on 'branding'. Klein is particularly concerned by the attempt, as she sees it, to distance the brand image itself from the realities of the production and distribution process in a global economy. For a rather more nuanced and reflective commentary of some of these issues, it is also worth reading Tully (2003), and for a more detailed analysis of some of the issue in the area of food production and consumption, see Roos et al. (2007).

Conley focuses more on the extent to which branding is used as the sole means to achieve authenticity:

> The object of the great phalanx of brand-mongers and "experiential marketers" is to tap into every facet of human contact with the world and manage it so that only that which is marketed seems genuine.

Again, there are strong resonances with some of the issues raised earlier by writers such as Fromm (1990), with his critique of ownership as the prime definition of identity and meaning.

Identity, ethnicity and belief

Lindridge (2005) conducted an interesting empirical study looking at differences in consumption patterns between British consumers, Indian emigrants and Indians. Overall, as the executive summary of his article notes:

> All religions have something to say about consumption either directly or indirectly. The great religions all promote a framework of ethics that

influence what we consume and the manner in which we approach consumption. And as religion becomes less important, individuals get closer to the position Lindridge associates with British Whites where only the shadow of religious association remains. As British Indians see religion as less significant in their lives, their consumption behaviour becomes more similar to that of the majority community.

Some would argue that this could be seen as confirmation of convergent tendencies but only in a very particular manner: by the immigrants towards the consumption pattern of what might be termed the indigenous population. We also need to consider what patterns might emerge for Hindi immigrants to India. On top of this, it is worth remembering the observation by the late Robin Cook on the Britishness of some Indian food:

Chicken Tikka Massala is now a true British national dish, not only because it is the most popular, but because it is a perfect illustration of the way Britain absorbs and adapts external influences. Chicken Tikka is an Indian dish. The Massala sauce was added to satisfy the desire of British people to have their meat served in gravy. (Robin Cook, 2001)

It is therefore far from clear how far in the longer run we are actually witnessing an overall 'homogenization' of consumer tastes or more a parallel set of processes of convergent and divergent trends in different sub-domains. We also referred earlier to the 'End of History' perspective, although we can now see particularly with the advantage of hindsight that, as Fukuyama himself has recognized, his initial treatise severely underestimated the importance of religion and ideology.[8] It is indeed time to revisit these major assertions about the nature of global markets through the further empirical evidence of the last 20–30 years.

Markets and the wider issues of social welfare

The other key area in which the neoliberal consensus is now under critical scrutiny goes back to our original commentary on the wider social welfare aspects. Here again we can see some clear forebodings of the current crisis.

For instance, in a careful summary of the empirical evidence of privatizations of public assets in various countries and particular of the earlier Mexican and Asian financial crises, Bathala and Korukonda (2003) note that:

The discussion and the data analysis ... clearly show that the underlying causes that have led to the Mexican and Asian crises are not due to the existence of free markets per se but are due to their abuse. ... Then important lesson from these crises is that free market benefits come at a cost. In order for the free markets to contribute to social gains and pareto improvements, it is important that the respective governments, regulators, bankers and market participants exercise diligence and restraint. (p. 865)

In a more detailed study, which reviewed the experience in the UK specifically, Taylor-Gooby et al. (2004) concluded:

The experiment in developing a welfare state within a market-orientated public policy has made (some) real progress toward welfare ends. It faces corresponding limitations, most importantly in stimulating and regulating private market provision (in child care, elder care and pensions) and in managing the behaviour of private actors (in seeking to promote employment for workless groups) while it simultaneously pursues market freedom so that regulation is limited and compulsion only deployed against politically weak groups such as young unemployed people. (p. 589)

CONCLUSION

It is difficult to avoid a conclusion that three core assumptions about the wider political economy, often unspoken, which underpinned much of the writing and research in marketing and marketing management, are being subjected to profound critical scrutiny. The neoliberal consensus, the presumed efficacy of an unfettered market system and the gradual convergence towards global markets and global consumers all look at best contentious conclusions. For marketing scholars and researchers this must inevitably mean that such assumptions will need to be examined and considered much more thoroughly in the future.

Surely, marketing should be about studying the nature of markets as they actually operate in broad terms of inputs, choices and outputs. It is clear that, in pursuing this goal, we need to recognize that the process of market evolution and its impact on wider social welfare is a complex and contingent one. There remain challenges between individual interests and collective impacts, between simple single identity choices and complex multiple identities and between seeing the emphasis within the overall economic system as around the improved efficiency of existing modes of activity as compared with the innovation heralded by the Schumpeterian doctrine of creative destruction (1942/2008). Marketing scholars, therefore, cannot avoid implicitly even if not explicitly, engaging both with some of these wider theoretical debates and also engaging with those who adopt the language of marketing itself as rhetorical device for a wider agenda in the overall political economy.

NOTES

1 The common abbreviated version of the full title 'An Inquiry into the Nature and Causes of the Wealth of Nations',

2 The sole reference in Wealth of Nations is in Book IV: Of Systems of Political Economy, within a chapter on 'Chapter II: Of Restraints Upon the Importation From Foreign Countries of Such Goods As Can Be Produced At Home':

'By preferring the support of domestic to that of foreign industry, he intends only his own security; and by directing that industry in such a manner as its produce may be of the greatest value, he intends only his own gain, and he is in this, as in many other cases, led by an invisible hand to promote an end which was no part of his intention.'

(see http://oll.libertyfund.org/?option=com_ staticxt&staticfile=show.php&title=220&chapter=1119 10&layout=html#a_2313856 accessed on 01/03/09),

3 'They (the rich) are led by an invisible hand to make nearly the same distribution of the necessaries of life, which would have been made, had the earth been divided into equal portions among all its inhabitants, and thus without intending it, without knowing it, advance the interest of the society, and afford means to the multiplication of the species' from Theory of Moral Sentiments, Part IV: Of the Effect of Utility Upon the Sentiment of Approbation a Consisting of One Section (from http://oll.liberty-fund.org/?option=com_staticxt&staticfile=show.php %3Ftitle=192&chapter=200135&layout=html&Itemi d=27, on 01/03/09),

4 However, as she then presciently notes:

'Strangely enough, notions like "invisible hand" or "spontaneous market equilibrium" carried with them the shadows and echoes of a lost moral frame. This lost moral frame had originally given meaning to a peculiar form of economic and acquisitive behaviour. It also had placed bounds and limits upon it, through notions like "fellow feeling" as a counterpoint to "self-interest". Without the frame, only pragmatic ethics remained – acute individualism combined with utilitarianism; materialism as the only end; an attachment to laissez faire and competition even when those were leading in fact through their own internal contradictions to a weakening of competition; rationalization and the eviction of pockets of irrationality; finally a profound and undisputed conviction that the evolutionary trend meant Progress'.

5 Of course as others, including Fukuyama himself has recognized his initial treatise severely underestimated the importance of religion and ideology in the evolutionary process.

6 Indeed Wensley (1990) argued that even within marketing itself the rhetoric of customer sovereignty is used to disguise a much less empowering view of the user.

7 Of course, in reality, such processes take place over a long period, and there are strong interactions not only between the supply and demand networks but also with the wider national and international political economy. For a thorough and well-documented historical analysis of how one key product moved from luxury to necessity and the ways in which it was both used and represented in various strata of society (and indeed the complex interaction between the nature and scale of production and the distribution and forms of consumption), see Mintz (1986).

8 Ironically, Marx may prove to be more right than we expected in raising profound questions as to the extent to which predatory capitalism is inevitably driven towards a vicious spiral, which cannot be sustained in the long run. Equally, however, Fukuyama's (1995) somewhat more recent interest in Trust now seems remarkably prescient.

REFERENCES

Amable, B. (2003) *The Diversity of Modern Capitalism*. Oxford: Oxford University Press.

Bathala, C. and Korukonda, A.R. (2003) 'An analysis of social welfare issues in free market environments', *International Journal of Social Economics*, 30(7/8): 854–866.

Bellofiore, R. and Halevi, J.(2008) 'A critique of post-Keynesian economics applied to the political economy of the Eurozone', 10th Anniversary Conference of the Association for Heterodox Economics, Cambridge, 3–6 July, 2008.

Benington, J. (2007) The Reform of Public Services, Stationery Office and National School of Government, London.

Billet, L. (1976) 'The Just Economy: The Moral Basis of the Wealth of Nations', *Review of Social Economy*, 34(3): 295–315.

Bishop, J.D. (1995) 'Adam Smith's invisible hand argument', *Journal of Business Ethics*, 14(3): 165–180.

Conley, L. (2008) 'OBD: Obsessive Branding Disorder: The Illusion of Business and the Business of Illusion', *Public Affairs* (2 June).

Cook, R. (2001) Extracts from a Speech by the Foreign Secretary to the Social Market Foundation in London, Guardian.co.uk, Thursday 19 April, 2001 17.03 BST (available at http://www.guardian.co.uk/world/2001/apr/19/race.britishidentity) on 02/03/09.

Djelic, M.-L. (2005) 'How Capitalism Lost its Soul: From Protestant Ethic to Robber Barons', in Vranceanu and Daianu (eds), *Ethical Boundaries of Capitalism*, Ashgate.

Djelic, M.-L. (2007a) 'Changing Forms of Capitalism, Globalization and the Marketization of (Nearly) Everything?', Uppsala Lectures in Business 2007 – Lecture I, Uppsala University, Department of Business Studies, September 2007.

Djelic, M.-L. (2007b) 'The "Ethics of Competition" or the Moral Foundations of Contemporary Capitalism', in M.-L. Djelic and R. Vranceanu (eds), *Moral Foundations of Management Knowledge*, Cheltenham: Edward Elgar.

DuGay, P. (1996) *Consumption and Identity at Work*. Sage: London.

Epstein, R. (2004) *Free Markets Under Siege: Cartels, Politics and Social Welfare*. London: IEA.

Friedman, T. (2005) *The World is Flat*. New York: Farrar, Straus and Giroux.

Fromm, E. (1990) *To Have or To Be?* London: Abacus.

Fukuyama, F. (1992) *The End of History and the Last Man*. New York NY: The Free Press

Fukuyama, F. (1995) *Trust: The Social Virtues and the Creation of Prosperity*. London: Hamish Hamilton.

Hutton, W. and Schneider, P. (2008) 'The Failure of Market Failure: Towards a 21st Century Keynesianism, Provocation', 08 November 2008, NESTA: London, (http://www.nesta.org.uk/assets/Uploads/pdf/Provocation/market_failure_provocation_NESTA.pdf) on 1/3/09.

Kay, J. (2007) 'The Failure of Market Failure', *Prospect Magazine*, London, 26 July 2007.

Kelner, P. (1984) 'Are Markets Compatible With Socialism?', in Ben Pimlott (ed.) *Fabian Essays In Socialist Thought*, London: Heinemann, pp. 146–156.

Klein, N. (2000) *No Logo*. London: Flamingo.

Lindridge, A. (2005) 'Religiosity and the Construction of a Cultural-Consumption Identity', *The Journal of Consumer Marketing*, 22(2/3): 142–151.

Levitt, T. (1983) 'Globalization of Markets', *Harvard Business Review*, May–June 1983.

Mintz, S.W. (1986) *Sweetness and Power: The Place of Sugar in Modern History*, London: Penguin

Roos, G., Terragni, L. and Torjusen, H. (2007) 'The Local in the Global – Creating Ethical Relations Between Producers and Consumers', *Anthropology of Food*, S2, March 2007 (available at http://aof.revues.org/document489.html on 10/3/09).

Schumpeter, J.A. (1942/2008) *Capitalism, Socialism, and Democracy*, Harper Perennial Modern Classics, New York NY: HarperCollins, first published 1942.

Taylor-Gooby, P., Trine, L. and Kananen, J. (2004) 'Market Means and Welfare Ends: The UK Welfare State Experiment', *Journal of Social Policy*, 33(4): 573–592.

Tobin, J. (1991) 'The Invisible Hand in Modern Macroeconomics', Cowles Foundation Discussion Paper no 996, Yale University, New Haven CN, January 1991 (http://econpapers.repec.org/paper/cwlcwldpp/966.htm on 1/3/09).

Tobin, J. (1992) 'The Invisible Hand in Modern Macroeconomics', in Michael Fry (ed.) *Adam Smith's Legacy: His Place in the Development of Modern Economics*. London: Routledge, pp. 117–129.

Tully, M. (2003) *India in Slow Motion*. London: Penguin.

Viner, J. (1927) 'Adam Smith and Laissez Faire', *Journal of Political Economy*, 35(2): 198–232.

Wensley, R. (1990) '"The Voice of the Consumer?": Speculations on the Limits to the Marketing Analogy', *European Journal of Marketing*, 24(7): 49–60.

Wensley, R. (1997) 'Marketing and Society: Part of the Solution or Part of the Problem?', Marketing Society Midlands Masterclass, Warwick: Warwick University (mimeo).

Whitley, R. (1999) *Divergent Capitalisms*. Oxford, UK: Oxford University Press.

14

The Evolution of Marketing Thought: From Economic to Social Exchange and Beyond

Richard P. Bagozzi

The history of marketing thought is marked by a series of revealing ebbs and flows that suggest considerable ferment and uncertainty as to what marketing is all about. Consider first an early definition:

> Marketing is the performance of *business activities* that direct the flow of goods and services from producers to consumers. (National Association of Marketing Teachers, USA, 1935, emphasis added)

Here we see recognition of both sellers and buyers but with a decidedly one-sided emphasis on the seller and what sellers do. Not until 50 years later was a more explicit two-way relationship recognized between seller and buyer, in a new definition formulated through a process of consensus building by business people and professors:

> Marketing is the process of planning and executing the conception, pricing, promotion, and distribution of ideas, goods and services to create *exchanges* that satisfy individual and organizational objectives. (American Marketing Association, 1985, emphasis added)

This definition reflects a convergence of points of view that emerged about 15 years earlier, where the foundational notion of 'exchange' (e.g. Kotler, 1972) 'won' the 'broadening' debate between those advocating marketing as a discipline concerned with exchanges construed generically and occurring amongst people and organizations subject to economic, social and psychological regulatory processes (e.g. Kotler and Levy, 1969), and those viewing exchanges narrowly as conducted solely by business enterprises subject to regulation via the profit motive (e.g. Luck, 1969). Nevertheless, notice that the 1985 American Marketing Association (AMA) definition still emphasizes more on the seller than the buyer, by starting with the perspective of 'planners' and 'executers' of activities attempting to create exchanges with buyers.

As marketing scholars came to place more emphasis on the *relationship* between buyer and seller (e.g. Sheth and Parvatiyar, 1995a, b) and the *provision of services* to buyers (e.g. Vargo and Lusch, 2004), value creation became a defining feature of the field (e.g. Prahalad and Ramaswamy, 2004):

> Marketing is an organizational function and a set of processes for creating, communicating, and delivering *value* to customers and for *managing customer relationships* in ways that benefit organization and its stakeholders. (AMA, 2004, emphasis added)

Here we see that the concept of exchange has been expunged from the definition of marketing, and stress is placed once again on the point of view of the marketer ('organizational function', 'processes' organizations engage in, 'managing customer relationship'), with a return to profits of marketers seemingly the sole motive and governance of the course of marketer–customer relationships. Calls for co-creation of value by firms and customers have not gone very far to overcome the presence of knowledge, resource and power disparities between buyers and sellers, and decision making remains more under the control of sellers than buyers or entails little formal mutuality in the 2004 AMA definition.

Perhaps reflecting an attitude of avoiding 'throwing out the baby with the bath water', so to speak, industry and academic representatives reintroduced 'exchange' into the most recent AMA definition:

> Marketing is the activity, set of institutions, and processes for creating, communicating, delivering, and *exchanging* offerings that have *value* for customers, clients, partners, and society at large. (AMA, 2007, emphasis added)

This definition still leans toward the point of view of the marketer and conveys a normative tone (see Hunt, 2002 for an interesting perspective on scientific and normative orientations in marketing theory), but it gives some pride of place to the concepts of exchange and value for buyers, albeit through the lens of the marketer. To see that the meaning of marketing continues to pose identity problems for practitioners, scholars and students of marketing, one has only to note that the AMA bylaws now call for a formal revisit of the definition of marketing every five years.

Definitions of few disciplines rest on such shifting sands.

In this chapter, we consider the role of exchange frameworks and theories in marketing thought and research. We begin with a discussion of the foundation of exchange thinking in marketing. Then we briefly summarize the large body of research in marketing contributing to the specification of and evidence for marketing exchange processes. Next, we comment on recent efforts to redirect attention toward relationship marketing, service provision and value creation and co-creation. From the point of view of classic exchange and social exchange theories, and especially from the perspective of contemporary social exchange theories, the recent efforts to shift focus are unconvincing and are already subsumed under new formulations of social exchange in multiple disciplines outside of marketing. Finally, we close with the outline of a new approach to marketing and social exchanges, grounded in plural subject theory. The new approach takes off from existing exchange theories, which are atomistic in the sense of presupposing the separation of needs of exchange partners and building theories predicated on a strong independence between the partners, to propose a holistic framework where needs, goals, decisions and actions are mutually constructed and interdependence is the cornerstone for parties considering, initiating, engaging in and resolving exchanges.

THE CONCEPT OF MARKETING EXCHANGE

Early marketing thought up until about 1970 tended to conceive of marketing exchanges in business or economic terms. Buyers and sellers were presumed to operate from self-interest as the sole motive for engaging in exchanges, and money and products or services were the focal objects in exchanges. Firms set prices and allocated marketing effort to maximize profits subject to cost constraints; buyers chose products and services to maximize utility subject to budget constraints. Economic theory was taken for granted as the framework explaining exchanges, especially in terms of matching supply and demand at the macro level. Loosely connected to these economic explanations of exchange were developments in the science and practice of marketing management at the microlevel, where models were developed to estimate demand, segment markets, allocate resources to advertising, assign salespersons to accounts or territories and so on. Parallel efforts occurred to understand consumers in terms of their motives and decision making. Nevertheless, little was proposed in the way of a formal theory linking buyers and sellers.

Then, about 40 years ago, marketing scholars began searching for concepts and theories accounting for marketing behavior. The developments were primarily at the micro level, focusing separately on firm and buyer behavior. Many marketing management textbooks followed on Kotler's (1967) text, arguably the first one, while Howard and Sheth (1969) proposed the first systematic consideration of buyer behavior. Both trends owed some intellectual debt to prescient thinking by Alderson (1957, 1965, 1968) who seems to have been one of the first to bring business and behavioral ideas together in the field.

Initial attempts to ground marketing in exchange theory were descriptive. Consider first three guiding questions proposed as scientific problems defining the marketing discipline: (1) Why do people and organizations engage in exchange relationships? (2) How are exchanges created, resolved or avoided? and (3) How should exchanges be created, resolved or avoided? (Bagozzi, 1978: 536). By placing emphasis on exchanges and why and how they emerge, transpire and function the way they do, these questions delineate the generic phenomena to be explained and regulated in marketing and define a unique subject matter for the field. Notice also that the questions acknowledge that 'what marketing is' is more than the strategic or instrumental

actions of parties on one side of the exchange or the other, but rather marketing theory must focus on the exchange relationship as its central dependent variable or process under scrutiny. As Popper (1963: 67) suggested, definitions of a subject matter such as reflected in the aforementioned questions often cut across boundaries of disciplines, which are themselves arbitrary to a certain extent. Hence, disciplines invariably overlap and experience ongoing redefinition.

Marketing exchanges tended to be construed in narrow terms and limited to dyadic transactions in most scholarship of the day. A partial exception was work on channels of distribution, which sometimes considered systemic processes and series of transactions with intermediaries functioning between manufacture and consumer. But by and large marketing thought focused on one party in a dyadic exchange or the other and saw the other party as an abstraction or a given and to be treated indirectly and at arm's length.

The descriptive foundation for a theory or theories of marketing exchange considered such topics as the structure or types of exchange, the actors in exchanges, the media and meaning of exchange and the context and processes governing exchanges. Let us briefly consider these, for they provide perspective on the many studies exploding on the scene in the decades following the emergence of marketing exchange thinking.

Three structures or types of exchange have been identified (Bagozzi, 1975). *Restricted exchange* is the traditional or received view and is limited to dyadic relationships: A↔B, where '↔' signifies 'gives to and receives from' and A and B are the parties or actors in the exchange.

A second structure of exchange, *complex exchange*, is common in systems of exchange and has two forms. Complex chain exchanges occur as sequences of direct exchanges and are found, for example, in supply chains: A↔B↔C↔D where A might be a manufacturer, B a wholesaler, C a retailer and D a consumer. Complex circular exchanges consist of each exchange partner linked reciprocally to two others, adjacent to the partner, such that the pattern of relationships is continuous or in a circular pattern: A↔B↔C↔A. Complex exchange can of course involve hybrids such that one or more actors is linked reciprocally with other actors not directly linked to others in the chain or circle or linked to subsets of them. We have in essence networks of exchanges that may exist in innumerable patterns. A majority of organizations and consumers are engaged in many direct and indirect exchanges at any one time, although the most developed theories to date occur for isolated dyads.

A third structure of exchange is termed *generalized exchange* and exhibits univocal reciprocity. Univocal reciprocity occurs 'if the reciprocations involve at least three actors and if the actors do not benefit each other directly but indirectly' (Ekeh, 1974: 48). Diagrammatically one way to depict this is as A→B→C→A. In generalized exchange, the social actors form a system in which each actor gives to another but receives, if at all, from someone other than to whom he or she gave. Generalized exchange has not been studied much in contemporary research but occurs, for instance, when marketers give to charities or social causes or when consumers volunteer their time and efforts to hospitals. A special case of generalized exchange happens inter-generationally when a person gives to his son, who in turn gives to his son and so on. People and institutions give to other people and institutions who in turn benefit others who may or may not be linked inter-generationally with earlier givers.

It is important to consider different structures of exchange, because the motives, decision making, actions and social processes differ across the structures. This implies that different theories must be applied to or developed for the different structures if we are to understand marketing and make policy recommendation effectively.

Early thinking about the *actors in exchange* tended to see the parties in abstract, disembodied ways, and this still tends to be true in many economic and other theories of exchange to this day. Who an actor is, what

one's characteristics are, what processes go on within actors (whether individual persons or organizations) and what relationships actors have to others who are one or more steps removed from the exchange both constrain and facilitate exchanges and need to be incorporated within any formal theory of marketing exchange. But except for haphazard or ad hoc characteristics of organizations (e.g. firm size, perceived trust worthiness) or consumers (e.g. personality traits, information processing and preferences), little has been done to take into account the aforementioned aspects of actors *within the context of exchange relationships*. Moreover, consideration of the specific actions of the key actors in exchanges and their organization has also been haphazard and in need of work. Within firms, this might mean delineation of buying centers and their personnel, policies, procedures and decision processes, as well as authority structures; and specification of networks of decision makers and influence, including patterns of social capital throughout the organization. Likewise, characterization of the key parties in consumer decision making needs consideration, where this might mean understanding such forces as family decision making, cross generational influence, peer pressure, the role of culture and the media in shaping consumer needs and responses, as well as single actor determination of purchase decisions. Unfortunately, little has been done to date relating intra-firm, intra-family and intra-decision-maker attributes to processes of exchange.

The *media and meaning of exchange* are a third descriptive foundation in need of elaboration in the run-up to a theory of marketing exchanges (Bagozzi, 1975). The nature of exchange media has too often been limited to the least common denominator: tangible entities changing hands, such as products, money or on occasion bartered goods or personal services. By media of exchange are meant the vehicles or entities with which people communicate to, and influence, others in the satisfaction of their needs or desires. These vehicles or entities may consist of the main objects of exchange seemingly changing hands, as well as incentives or other shapers of the course of the exchange. For example, common media of exchange include money, persuasion, rhetoric, punishment, rewards, power, inducements, activation of normative or ethical commitments and positive or negative affect.

The meaning of exchange refers to the subjective significance of the media of exchange or the exchange itself, for the actors. A *utilitarian exchange* is one where the parties enter a transaction with the hope of accruing specific tangible benefits. For an organization, the benefit might be added revenue or profit; for a consumer, the benefit might be use or ownership of a product. Utilitarian exchange appears to be what economists have in mind when they refer to 'economic man' (Schneider, 1974). A *symbolic exchange* is one where the meaning of exchange goes beyond utility or use to include the transfer or sharing of psychological, social or other intangible entities between actors. The parties to any exchange often give and receive intangible 'currency', which enriches, and even replaces, the utilitarian character of the exchange. In some instances' the actors come to view the exchange process and outcomes, not so much in terms of giving something(s) up so as to get something(s) of value, but as a process of mutually constructing the significance of the exchange in their lives. In other words, transactions may not be predicated on an explicit quid pro quo accounting, but rather emerge and transpire as psychological and social constructions of reality (Berger and Luckman, 1996; see also Bagozzi, 1976, and Harré and Secord, 1973).

Often everyday marketing exchanges involve both utilitarian and symbolic aspects and might be designated *mixed exchanges.* Thus, we see a need to move away from the strictly narrow version of an 'economic persona', so characteristic of economic theory and some versions of social exchange, to a broader and more valid outlook of a 'marketing persona' rooted in a fuller conceptualization of human behavior. Whereas the economic persona construes actors as rational decision makers attempting to maximize profits or satisfaction under conditions of full or nearly full information and free from external influence and divorced from emotional foibles, marketing behavior is more often characterized by actors who are sometimes rational, sometimes not, and typically have to reconcile conflicting motives; who engage in utilitarian, symbolic and mixed exchanges involving psychological and social forces; who work with the information they have, the best they can, frequently relying on decision heuristics, habit or custom; and who navigate complex internal requisites and conflicts, as well as legal, ethical, normative, competitive, environmental and other constraints and facilitators.

The final descriptive foundation for a theory or theories of exchange has been hinted at in the foregoing section; namely, the need to formulate *processes and factors constraining or facilitating* marketing exchanges or constituting marketing exchanges. Whereas the types, actors and media and meaning of exchange capture descriptive aspects of the exchange milieu, what goes on in the exchange itself and the conditions governing the exchange are at the heart of the subject matter of marketing. Of course, reasons for the initiation and resolution of exchanges are intimately linked to the processes and constraints regulating exchanges and include actor motivation, characteristics of actors (e.g. values, interaction styles and orientation) and other variables. In addition to offers, counter offers and communication going on between actors in an exchange and manifest in or along with the media of exchange, it is important to consider such processes as cooperation, mutually problem solving and conflict. We turn now to a summary of research to date, which addresses processes, constraints and facilitators in marketing exchanges.

EXCHANGE AND MARKETING RESEARCH

Much research has been conducted into marketing exchanges since the 1980s. This research is noteworthy in its quality of theorizing and empirical insights. However, virtually all the research to date has scrutinized specific facets of exchange, rather than comprehensively addressing multiple components of exchange mentioned in the preceding section.

A pioneering study into the antecedents and consequences of relationship commitment was performed by Morgan and Hunt (1994), where the authors use the definition proposed by Moorman, Zaltman and Deshpandé (1992: 316): 'Commitment to the relationship is defined as an enduring desire to maintain a valued relationship'. See also research by Dwyer, Schurr and Oh (1987). Morgan and Hunt examined only one party in the exchange relationship (automobile tire retailers who dealt with suppliers). Although their proposed structural equation model fit the data poorly (comparative fit index = 0.89), and therefore findings should be interpreted cautiously, Morgan and Hunt found support for 12 of 13 hypotheses. The most important for our purposes were significant positive effects of relationship termination costs, shared values with suppliers and trust (confidence in the reliability and integrity of suppliers) on relationship commitment, and significant positive effects of relationship commitment on acquiescence (compliance), propensity to remain in the relationship and cooperation by suppliers. For further research on antecedents of trust, see Moorman et al. (1993) who found that such interpersonal factors as perceived integrity, willingness to reduce uncertainty, confidentiality, expertise, tactfulness, sincerity, congeniality and timeliness were associated with trust. See also Doney and Cannon (1997), Dyer and Chu (2000) and Anderson and Narus (1990).

Many studies have examined the antecedents to relationship commitment in recent years. Anderson and Weitz (1992) investigated 378 pairs of manufacturers and their relationships to industrial distributors. Commitment was found to be influenced by idiosyncratic investments made by partners (e.g. in training, facilities and linking manufacturer and distributer in the customer's mind) and by perceived commitment made by partner. Skarmeas et al. (2002) discovered that relationship commitment in international buyer–seller associations are direct positive functions of transaction – specific investments (in personnel, training programs, effort and facilities) and direct negative functions of opportunism (partner malfeasance), and indirect positive functions of environment volitivity and indirect negative functions of cultural sensitivity through opportunism. For further insights into the control of supplier opportunism in inter-firm relationships, see Stump and Heide (1996). Finally, Geyskens et al. (1996) deepened our understanding of commitment by examining affective and calculative versions and found that both were determined by perceptions of interdependence (measured by dealer dependence and perceptions of dependence) and trust, but in different degrees. Calculative commitment was a function of interdependence more than trust was for Dutch new car dealers and by trust more than interdependence for American dealers. Affective commitment was affected more by trust than interdependence for both Dutch and American dealers.

A number of studies have investigated the consequences of relationship commitment. Gundlach et al. (1995) employed a behavioral simulation of manufacturer–distributor exchange relationships. They found that credibility of partner commitment affected relational social norms (sentiments and behaviors shared by actors) and long-term commitment intentions for both manufacturers and distributors. Perceptions of opportunism of partners were negatively associated with relational social norms for both manufacturers and distributors. Relational social norms also had long-term effects on commitment. The study by Skarmeas et al. (2002) mentioned earlier also found that relationship commitment influenced the performance of the relationship (measured with self-reported success).

It is not possible to discuss all the studies examining exchange in marketing. We simply point here to a sampling of key articles in a variety areas: knowledge utilization within firms (Menon and Varadarajan, 1992); the interrelationships between governance and communication in inter-firm relationships (Mohr et al., 1996); joint competitive advantages in buyer–supplier relationships (Jap, 2001); customer relationship management (Homburg et al., 2002, 2008); power and conflict in channel relationships (Frazier et al., 1989; Johnson et al., 1993; Mohr and Spekman, 1994); perception of long-term orientations in buyer–seller relationships as a function of mutual dependence and trust (Ganesan, 1994); value and performance in inter-firm relations (Palmatier, 2008; Palmatier et al., 2007); interdependency and performance in wholesaler–supplier relationships (Lusch and Brown, 1996).

It can be seen that most research on exchange in marketing has been done on inter-firm or business-to-business relationships. Yet, even here, little has been done in the way of studying influence and other processes, per se. Most work addresses one party in the transaction, and those that have taken dyadic perspectives have not investigated processes transpiring between parties, which require longitudinal designs and scrutiny of actions and counteractions and their meanings for the parties in the exchange.

Likewise, although a wealth of knowledge exists concerning consumer information processing and consumer behavior, research to date has been rather static in orientation and focused on the consumer as a responder or reactor, not on the relationship between consumer and seller and what occurs between them. The last major section of this chapter considers efforts to rectify this neglect by introducing plural subject theory and developing its significance for marketing exchange theory.

RELATIONSHIP MARKETING: A DIVERSIONARY INTERLUDE?

In the early 1990s, marketing scholars began to consider a seemingly new basis for the defining feature of marketing – relationship marketing (e.g. Sheth and Parvatiyar, 1995a, b). Sheth and colleagues criticized the exchange paradigm for its inability 'to explain the relational engagement of firms' and for its focus to date on only 'one role of the sellers, namely that of the supplier' (Sheth and Uslay, 2007: 303). By the first decade of the twenty-first century, other marketing scholars proposed various aspects of value for customers as a new logic for the field. Thus, Vargo and Lusch (2004) claim that 'service provision' is the 'new dominant logic for marketing', where services are defined as 'the application of specialized competences (knowledge and skills) through deeds, processes, and performances for the benefit of another entity or the entity itself' (p. 2; see also Lusch and Vargo, 2006). Vargo and Lusch (2004) advocate a shift from value in exchange, the only value alleged to reside in exchanges, to value in use. Similar to Sheth and colleagues, Vargo and Lusch (2004: 11), speak of 'the inherent focus on the customer and the relationship'. Likewise Prahalad and Ramaswamy (2000, 2004) posit that value co-creation, where firms and consumer co-create value, will be the basis for competition and business relationships in the future, a position largely echoed by Sheth and Uslay (2007: 305) and Vargo and Lusch (2004: 10–11).

Sheth, Lusch and colleagues have done much to develop the centrality of relationships in marketing (for an even earlier specification of marketing relationships, see Bagozzi, 1974a). However, by taking too restricted a perspective on relationships and too narrow a view on exchanges, recent advocacies of focus on relationships and value creation as the basis for marketing have muddied and limited our conceptualization of marketing.

It can be argued that marketing relationships, while important, are subsumed under the concept of social exchange. This occurs with regard to the processes linking the parties to an exchange. So far scholars in marketing have limited the conceptualization of marketing relationships to policy orientations of sellers who attempt to manage customer relations (e.g. key account management) or who view exchange from the perspective of presumed idealized outcomes of exchanges (e.g. co-creation of value). Yet as reflected in applied research to date, many kinds and aspects of exchange relationships have been examined: conflict, power, communication, trust, bargaining and negotiation, compliance, commitment, reciprocity, cooperation, social networks, satisfaction, social identity and social capital. The nature and scope of exchange relationships in marketing need to be specified and done so in a way going beyond the narrow discussions of relationship marketing in recent years. At the same time, it should be recognized that the representation of marketing exchange relationships is but one part of a needed theory or theories of marketing. Such a theory must also link such relationships to characteristics of the actors, including internal processes, the constraining and facilitating conditions in which exchanges are embedded, the media and meaning of exchanges, and the actions taken by actors in relation to each other, which fulfill or thwart exchange relationships.

It would seem appropriate as well to correct deficiencies in current relationship marketing thinking. A glaring problem is the one-sided orientation built into contemporary treatments, where the perspective of the firm and its profits take center stage, with satisfactory outcomes for customers assumed to be a natural consequence of decision making and practices of the firms. Similarly, treatments of co-creation have taken disparities between marketer and customer for granted. Until conceptualizations of both marketing relationships and co-creation practices incorporate differences in interests, knowledge, power and other resources between marketers and customers, and do so in relationship to the economic, environmental, political and social systems in which their interactions take place, we are likely to progress minimally beyond the atomistic and business-dominated frameworks characterizing contemporary marketing thought.

Some progress in thinking has been made in exchange theory by scholars outside of marketing that helps to overcome the narrowness of relationship marketing thinking and promises to ground the exchange paradigm as the basis for a definition and theory of marketing and needed empirical research. We briefly mention these developments here.

Molm and Cook (1995) discuss exchange networks and power in social exchange. They also consider such 'emergent properties' in exchange relationships as justice norms, commitment and affective ties (see also Nahapiet and Ghoshal, 1998). Flynn (2005) shows how social exchange relates to identity orientations, thus linking two heretofore-distinct conceptual traditions. Social identity, we submit, might facilitate exchanges between actors both within and across organizations; social identity might also mediate the relationship between reciprocity and other aspects of exchange and decision making and the nature of individual and joint outcomes for exchange partners. Finally, Lawler (2001: 321) develops a theory of 'how and when emotions, produced by social exchange, generate stronger or weaker ties to relations, groups, or networks'. Current developments in social exchange theory offer new directions for marketing thought by incorporating and going beyond concepts of relationship marketing and co-creation of value. Indeed the latter are subsumed under modern theories of exchange.

SOCIALITY AND MARKETING EXCHANGE

Economic and social exchange theories begin with the individual needs of the parties to an exchange and assume that each party attempts to maximize his or her utility or expected profit from the exchange. As such, although the exchange entails a relationship between two or more persons or organizations and in that sense is social, the social aspects are limited to an inferred relationship as a joint outcome and the offers and counteroffers and social influence that transpire between the parties. In essence, the theories of exchange rest on individualistic assumptions, and any social content in exchange concerns either social constraints on the parties or social implications to a consummated or thwarted exchange, such as emotional or other ties resulting from an exchange. Economic and social exchange theories are atomistic instrumental frameworks, where the benefits and costs associated with a transaction, coupled with intrapersonal or intra-organizational requisites, determine the outcomes. This is fine as far as it goes, but it neglects important kinds and aspects of social action central to marketing, which make exchanges holistic in many instances.

A fundamentally different approach would be one based on mutuality. Early in the development of exchange ideas in marketing, social content was introduced in two senses. Bagozzi (1974b) defined the notion of an 'exchange system', specifying it as 'a set of social actors, their relationships to each other, and the endogenous and exogenous variables affecting the behavior of the social actors in those relationships' (p. 78). He suggested that the prior history of reward mediation, if any, inter-actor attraction, actor intentions in conjunction with resource capabilities, perceived esteem or expertise of the partner, role position (authority or status), credibility of messages communicated between actors and the relative value trade-offs of product and money for the actors all functioned to govern dyadic exchanges. However, this article never developed the notion of mutuality beyond the nature of give and take and its significance for the actors. Building on the new home economics, but revamping it to focus on the shared utility of two actors interacting with each other in relation to a contemplated commercial exchange with a third party, Bagozzi (1978, 1979) proposed a more social model of marketing exchanges. This model also introduced a number of inter-actor variables (e.g. interpersonal attraction, power, conflict and degree of

sharing), but these were all exogenous to the process of exchange and influenced exchange outcomes and thus represented a bare-bones introduction of social content and then primarily only as determinants of exchange outcomes.

Descriptive foundation

To ground a theory of marketing exchanges in social content, and recognizing the fundamental relational nature of marketing exchanges, we begin with plural subject theory from philosophy, then revise and deepen it to fit marketing (see Bagozzi, 2000, 2005). Consider first what a social unit is.

Our starting point is Gilbert's (1989: 152) notion of a *social group*, where 'each of a certain set of persons must correctly view himself and the rest, taken together, as "us*" or "we*"'. 'We' of course refers to the 'self' plus at least one other person, but Gilbert (1989: 465) points out a stronger sense of 'we' that forms a foundation for plural subject theory. For Gilbert, 'we' refers to the self and one or more others 'that share in the action of a verb'. She then maintains that collectivity concepts incorporate the idea of plural subjects into their meaning. In contrast to 'singularism', which she defines as 'the thesis that these [collective] concepts are explainable solely in terms of the conceptual scheme of singular agency', Gilbert advocates 'intentionalism', which she specifies as 'the view that according to our everyday collectivity concepts, individual human beings must see themselves in a particular way in order to constitute a collectivity' (Gilbert, 1989: 12). The requisite to share in an action of a verb, which is Gilbert's main contribution to plural subject theory, means that group members have a collective goal and are jointly committed to achieving the goal together (Gilbert, 2000).

In sum, Gilbert's (1989: 204–236) concept of a social group requires that members think of themselves as 'us', 'we', 'our', etc.; the members are jointly ready to act in a group action to accomplish a group goal; and common knowledge among members exists to this effect. She contrasts her ontology of group wills with tit-for-tat or the commonly accepted view based on 'an "exchange of promises" such that each person unilaterally binds himself to the goal in question, leaving himself beholden for release to someone else upon whom, through this particular transaction, he has no claim' (Gilbert, 1990: 7). Instead, Gilbert (1989: 204) asserts that individual wills of group members are bound to a group 'simultaneously and interdependently' such that 'each expresses a *conditional commitment* of his will, understanding that only if the others express similar commitments are all of the wills jointly committed to accept a certain goal when the time comes' (emphasis in original). In other words, 'only when *everyone* has done similarly [i.e. expressed a conditional commitment] is *anyone* committed' (Gilbert, 1990: 7; emphasis in original). For our purposes, a group or collectivity can mean two or more actors engaged in an exchange relationship, two or more actors within a group or organization interacting in an exchange with an individual actor, or two or more members of a group or organization involved in an exchange with two or more members of another group or organization. Networks of such exchanges may also be construed as collectivities in many instances.

We conceive of collective goals broadly and ranging from (a) total or near total commitment to both a mutual objective and the means to achieve that objective to (b) a more limited commitment to only sharing an objective in common to start. The shared objective might itself be held in common to different degrees. Thus, for example, the former might refer to a joint agreement between a government and various contractors to build a bridge, where a long and complex process of exchange preceded the final agreement. An instance of a looser common commitment at the other end of the continuum might be an agreement between parties to attempt to formulate a joint understanding of what a common goal might be, without yet anticipating how to go about achieving the goal once it is agreed upon. Even in the simple case of an individual consumer entering a store for the purpose of 'shopping around for ideas', an implicit shared goal with the retailer exists, if only to the extent that both allow each other the leeway to consider the possibility of a joint meeting of the minds.

With this as background, it is possible to designate three central forms of sociality in marketing (Bagozzi, 2005). The first is termed *buyer social action*, the second *seller social action*. In both cases, we have two or more individual persons cooperating together to reach collective ends. How they do this will be specified more fully in the following section. The third form of sociality in marketing is termed *buyer–seller social action* and consists of two or more persons interacting personally or as agents of a group so as to become better off by giving up something in exchange for receiving something else in return. Beyond the aforementioned individualistic motives, the possibility of a mutual construction of the end(s) and/or the means of buyer–seller social action is also acknowledged in the sense that the buyer and seller both purposively attempt to meet each others needs as a unit in isolation or as a unit under larger implications for other units, the environment or other social considerations (e.g. social welfare). Indeed, buyer–seller social action might even consist of seemingly one-way selfish (e.g. exploitive) or benevolent (e.g. altruistic) arrangements (e.g. Bagozzi, 1975).

To provide perspective for the theory developed in the next section of the chapter, let us consider a typology of motives and orientations of people engaging in marketing buyer–seller social action. We can identify four such motives and orientations. The first is *selfish buyer–seller social actions*, where the buyer or seller attempts to get as much as possible from the other agent without taking into account the market or needs of the other agent and indeed without acting in accordance with certain social, legal or ethical norms, per se. In terms of the orientation of the buyer or seller, he/she is totally uncommitted to the buyer–seller relationship, per se. Extreme, but not uncommon, examples of selfish buyer–seller social actions occur when a buyer shop-lifts merchandize from a department store or a seller knowingly deceives buyers by selling defective or unsafe goods. To a certain extent, the buyer and seller in these instances operate as brigands or gangsters and set the transaction price and terms of trade themselves. That is, they surreptitiously push the costs onto the other agent while satisfying their own needs and taking unfair advantage of the other.

A second category of motives and orientations is termed, *self-interested buyer–seller social actions*. This is the classic model of marketing assumed by economists and others and consists of the buyer or seller attempting to give as little as possible (e.g. offering the minimum, given what the market will bear) and to receive as much as possible (e.g. to find the best deal or to maximize profits). The orientation of buyer or seller in self-interested buyer–seller social actions is one of limited commitment to the buyer–seller relationship. Market forces in the form of income, costs, and competition constrain the terms of trade to a large extent, subject to the operation of personal desires or utilities of the buyer and seller.

The third category of motives and orientation is *mutual buyer–seller social actions*. Here buyer and seller work consciously and purposively to arrive at joint outcomes, which take into account the requisites of self and other. This might mean following such agreed upon or perhaps implicit rules as 'maximize both parties' gains while minimizing shared costs', 'split the gains and losses such that x per cent goes to buyer and (1–x per cent) goes to the seller', or 'harmonize the relationship of buyer and seller' in some other mutually satisfying way. The orientation of buyer and seller in mutual buyer–seller social actions can be described as one of high shared commitment to the relationship. Long-term buyer–customer relationships in both business-to-business and business-to-consumer markets sometimes exhibit such motives and orientations as

described here. Firm–customer co-creation of value, where the balance of power or resources is relatively equal between actors, might fit this category too.

The fourth category of motives and orientation is *benevolent buyer–seller social actions*. Here, buyer or seller strives to give as much as possible to the other agent without much consideration allowed to costs or gains for the self, per se. We might say that such cases exhibit total or near total commitment of buyer or seller to the relationship. An example might be the patronage of a local hardware store or restaurant by a customer, which is done at least on occasion more to support the retailer out of friendship, pity or loyalty (and despite the presence of more convenient, less expensive or in some other way more satisfying alternatives), than to enact traditional self-serving motives, per se. Citizens of small towns sometimes traffic with certain businesses in this way or out of a vaguely held motive to 'build community' or support native enterprises. Even large corporations have been known now and then to eschew economic gains or accept higher costs by dealing with minority or indigenous suppliers as a matter of policy.

It should be pointed out that the aforementioned four cases do not exhaust the possibilities of buyer–seller social action. Notice that the selfish, self-interested or benevolent buyer–seller social action cases were presented for the instances where buyer *or* seller has the motivation and orientation in question. Of course, both parties may have the same or different motivations and orientations. The most stable and enduring buyer–seller social actions are likely to occur when the motives and orientations are similar. This is especially true for the self-interested and mutual buyer–seller social action cases.

The remainder of this chapter will focus on the first two forms of sociality in marketing mentioned in the preceding section, namely, buyer social action and seller social action, where a group of buyers or sellers has a common goal to engage a third party in an exchange relationship. Many of the ideas developed in the following section in this regard provide a foundation, or at least a starting point, for the mutual buyer–seller social action case, too.

Collective goals, collective commitment and social action

The point of departure describing, accounting for, and showing the implications of sociality in marketing begins with the idea of collective goals. A *collective goal* is an end or objective attributed to a group that a member of the group has. Tuomela (2003) contrasts a collective goal, which he terms a we-mode goal, with the goal that an individual person has (an I-mode goal). Under an I-mode goal, an individual typically believes that he/she can achieve the goal by his/her own actions, and moreover the goal is for oneself. By contrast, under a collective or we-mode goal, the group member believes that he/she alone cannot achieve the goal alone (or at least in certain special cases of groups that we might consider, it is very difficult to achieve the goal alone; while in the majority of group cases it is impossible to do so), rather the group acts in a way to achieve the goal (typically through collective action), and the goal is not for the self but for the group. Tuomela (2003: 97) calls this latter property 'forgroupness' and asserts that this provides a partial reason for the group member to act collectively so as to achieve the goal. Furthermore, Tuomela (2003: 95) maintains that a collective we-mode goal must satisfy the following 'collectivity condition': 'It is true on "quasiconceptual" grounds and hence necessarily that a goal content p is satisfied for (that is, in the case of) a member of a collective g and, indeed, for g if and only if it is satisfied for every member of g'. An I-mode goal does not of course satisfy the collectivity condition, and this shows yet another distinction between I-mode and we-mode goals. By satisfaction of a goal content in the collectivity condition, Tuomela means that the achievement of the collective goal comes about as a consequence of the collective effort of group members. We can relax some of the conditions proposed in the foregoing section for collective goals (e.g. group members can have both collective and individual goals; not every member in the group must hold the collective goal at all times or to the same extent), but these will not be considered here in the interests of brevity.

Our next conceptual building block in constructing a framework for sociality in marketing is the idea of collective commitment. A *collective commitment* is a joint resolution to act as a body, group or whole to achieve a collective goal. Thus, the distinction between a collective goal and a collective commitment is analogous to the difference between a goal intention and an implementation intention, but of course, collective goals and collective commitment apply to the group level, and in particular in the plural subject theory sense, whereas goal and implementation intentions as originally developed are individual level variables (see Bagozzi, 2006, for background on goal and implementation intentions).

Gilbert (2002b) terms what is called collective commitment in the preceding section, as joint commitment, which she characterizes as acting together or doing things with other persons. For her, a joint commitment entails a *collective intention*, which can be defined as follows: 'Persons A and B collectively intend to do x if and only if A and B are jointly committed to intend as a body to do x' (Gilbert 2003: 46). A joint commitment and collective intention have the unique property of requiring, to a certain extent, that either party wishing to act contrary to the intention must ask for permission from the other actor(s) that are party to the joint commitment. By contrast, with a personal commitment, an individual can act unilaterally to break his/her own commitment. A joint commitment has normative force not found necessarily with a personal commitment. In other words, the agents in a joint commitment are answerable to each other such that each has obligations to the others to act in accordance with the commitment, and rights or entitlements to expect that others will act accordingly.[1] To ground these obligations and rights in the social psychology of the agents, it has been proposed that these are manifest in the so-called social or self-conscious emotions (Bagozzi, 2000: 390). Thus, pride, empathy, guilt, shame, embarrassment, jealousy, envy and gratitude function to reinforce and control appropriate rights and responsibilities in acting as plural subjects. Such basic emotions as anger, happiness, sadness and fear can be socially conditioned as well. Moreover, group norms and social identity processes operate to regulate collective goals, commitment and intentions (see Bagozzi, 2006). Gilbert (2002a, b, 2003) considers other aspects of plural subject theory that are relevant here – such as the distinction between dependent individual and personal commitments, the interdependence and simultaneity of dependent commitments, the genesis of joint commitments and the structure of such commitments – but it is beyond the scope of this chapter to discuss these here.

Collective goals, commitment and intentions form the foundation for a theory of *social action*. Elsewhere, a seemingly similar theory has been developed, but this, except for the provision of certain social constraints, was formulated at the individual level and in the context of consumer action (see Bagozzi, 2006). Consider how many of the variables in theories of goal setting and goal striving at the individual level permit us to develop, by analogy, a theory of social action at the group level and for all areas of marketing, not merely consumer action. We postpone to the next section of this chapter how the group level variables (collective goals, commitment, etc.) are formulated, for this requires a rather complex approach at both the conceptual and operational levels of analysis. For now, we propose that group level variables, in the plural subject sense advocated by Gilbert (1989) or in the similar we-mode sense considered by Tuomela (1995, 2000, 2002), can be thought to be linked functionally or causally in a way parallel to that developed in consumer action theory (see Chapter 18 in this volume; and Bagozzi, 2006, Figure 1.2 therein). Specifically,

in skeleton form, we suggest that the central variables (expressed in the plural subject or we-mode sense developed in the next section) and their interconnections can be depicted as shown in Figure 14.1.

Social action can be thought to begin with a joint desire for a goal, which is the immediate precursor to collective goal formation. A joint desire may emerge through normal interactions among members of a group as they socially construct their needs, purpose or mission; it might begin with an internal crisis or external threat where the group must cope with the danger and reach a decision on what ends to pursue; it might arise as a consequence of a task assigned to it by a higher authority; or it may simply entail joint problem solving over which everyday objectives to attain. In any case, the commonly agreed upon or attributed desire will constitute a reason for forming a collective goal, where group members come to jointly intend to strive for the goal.

The collective goal intention then leads to a collective desire to enact one or more means to the end, which is expressed as a desire to act. The desire may be globally formed as a non-specific, generally agreed upon desire simply to act in some way, or it might consist of specific urges or wants to act in particular ways, but without a well-formed determination to so act. The collective desire to act gains focus and resolution through the collaborative decision or intention to act in a specific way, where the group collectively commits itself to act.

In this framework, the collective intention becomes yet more refined through mutual planning (sometimes termed an implementation intention), where consensus or other joint rules are realized as to when, where and how to collectively act. Planning is translated into action via joint efforts to attempt to enact the plans, which typically entail the need to overcome impediments and resist temptations or distractions during the goal striving process, to monitor progress, and to make adjustments accordingly. Successful trying shifts into full-blown joint action at some point when the co-efforts to implement the means successfully set the coordinated actions in motion.

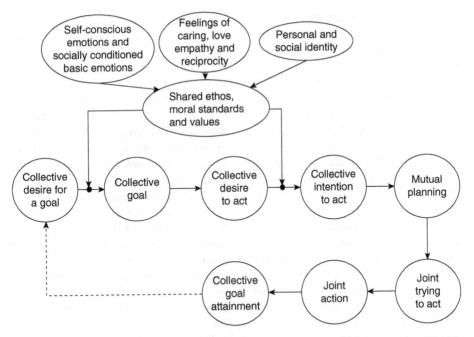

Figure 14.1 Key variables and processes in social action for either buyer social action or seller social action.

Depending on the quality of the joint action, the vulnerability or receptiveness of the anticipated outcome to change and the presence of inhibiting or facilitating conditions in the situation at hand, collective goal attainment will occur.

Two pivotal group control processes serve to regulate the transformation of a collective goal desire into a collective goal intention and a collective desire to act into a collective intention to act (see Figure 14.1). These comprise the shared ethos, moral standards, or values of group members, as attributed to the group, and moderate the two key transitions highlighted in Figure 14.1. That is, it is hypothesized that the shared ethos/moral standards/values interact with the respective desires to influence goal intentions and action intentions, respectively. The social control here is analogous to that characterized as 'self-regulation by second-order desires and personal standards' by Bagozzi (2006) in his theory of consumer action. It can be seen in Figure 14.1 that the shared ethos/moral standards/values are dependent on three learned social forces: (a) self-conscious emotions and

socially conditioned basic emotions, (b) feelings of caring, love, empathy and reciprocity and (c) personal and social identity.

The approach taken here follows the orientation of Gilbert (1989), Tuomela (1995, 2000, 2002) and Velleman (1997), which might be termed, conceptual nonindividualism. Here members of a group see themselves and other members as 'we' and sharing in a propositional attitude[2] or action as plural subjects wherein an agent and one or more other agents in a group join in the action of a verb or the holding of a belief, attitude, desire or intention (see e.g. Gilbert, 1989: 153, 465). We now turn to a formal explication of the representation of the variables shown in Figure 14.1 in this sense of groupness.

THE CONCEPT OF 'WE-NESS' AND ITS ELABORATION

The variables in Figure 14.1 are at one level of thinking 'attitudes', in the sense defined by philosophers. In particular, they are 'we-attitudes' and represent a kind of collective intentionality. Tuomela (2002: 3) defines a we-attitude as follows: 'a person has a we-attitude A (say a goal, intention or belief) if he has A, believes that the others in his collective (group) have A and believes in addition that there is a mutual belief in the collective that the members have A'. For example, persons in a group can be thought to be desiring, having a goal, intending, planning, trying and acting together as a body, unit, group or whole.

We begin with this definition of a we-attitude and develop the conceptual foundations and implications of we-ness in the following section. Tuomela (2002) has not elaborated on the definition of we-attitudes in this way but has focused instead on larger conceptual issues related to we-attitudes. In addition, Tuomela has neglected certain complexities and opportunities that we develop next which are of particular interest to marketers. Moreover, he has not been concerned with operational, measurement and construct validity issues, nor has he addressed the hypotheses and rationales undergirding the processes sketched in Figure 14.1. This is understandable, because these issues are not part of the normal subject matters of philosophers who concentrate on the logical foundations of social facts and related concepts. We wish to consider these issues and will begin by deepening the seemingly simple definition of we-attitudes and drawing out the implications of this amplification.

To do this, we consider the case of a three-person group, which can be extended to larger groups using the rationale developed in the following section. Consider three group members consisting of M (the self or me), person A and person B. For purposes of focus and continuity, we will attend to we-intentions, where consistent with Tuomela's (2003) collectivity condition discussed earlier, the property of collective acceptance is stipulated and concerns the conative proposition, 'We intend to achieve X' (see also Gilbert, 2002b).

Beginning with Tuomela's (2002) definition in the foregoing section of a we-attitude, we can say that each member of the group has three categories of we-intentions: their own we-intention, their estimate of the we-intentions of the other two group members, and their estimates of the mutuality of we-intentions. To capture these aspects of collective we-intentions, it is necessary to consider, not only one's own intention to act together and one's own assessment of the other members' intentions to act together, but also to assess what one thinks each of the other members' self collective intentions are and what the others' assessment of the intentions of their partners are. This provides for the proper self, other and mutual appraisals of we-intentions in the group, which are hinted at by Tuomela (2002) and Gilbert (2002a, 2002b).

To better see this, Table 14.1 presents the nine we-intention appraisals that must be made by each of the three members in the group, where we assume here for ease of exposition that co-members are friends in a friendship group. We have left off specific mention of the group goal or action and the seven-point, 'weak intention' to 'strong intention', scale typically used to record responses of group members and needed to apply the ideas to do an empirical inquiry. We have also omitted the descriptive lead-in to the appraisals that should be used in the beginning of the questionnaire to define the task for respondents as being a study of we-intentions. The items and wording in Table 14.1 are expressed as they might appear on a questionnaire so as to elicit group members' we-intentions. Note that the wording and referents used in the left-most column are from the point of view of each respondent. Thus, persons M, A and B would each be exposed to wording as shown in Table 14.1, and their own we-intentions, as well as their estimates of the we-intentions of co-members and the mutuality of we-intentions in the group.

It can be seen that a single we-attitude category (in this instance a we-intention) entails 27 distinct propositional attitudes derived

Table 14.1 Example of we-intentions for the three-person group case with coded categories of responses

Item	Coded categories for respondents: by Person M	by Person A	by Person B
Estimate of the strength of my intention to participate in …			
a. My estimate of my own intention to participate in …	a^M	a^A	a^B
b. Friend A's estimate of my intention to participate in …	b^M	b^A	b^B
c. Friend B's estimate of my intention to participate in …	c^M	c^A	c^B
Estimate of the strength of friend A's intention to participate in …			
d. My estimate of friend A's intention to participate in …	d^M	d^A	d^B
e. Friend A's estimate of his/her own intention to participate in …	e^M	e^A	e^B
f. Friend B's estimate of friend A's intention to participate in …	f^M	f^A	f^B
Estimate of the strength of friend B's intention to participate in …			
g. My estimate of friend B's intention to participate in …	g^M	g^A	g^B
h. Friend A's estimate of friend B's intention to participate in …	h^M	h^A	h^B
i. Friend B's estimate of his/her own intention to participate in …	i^M	i^A	i^B

from respondents in a 3-person group. Now Tuomela's (2002) three conditions for establishing a we-attitude speak to the following: one's own we-attitude (a, in Table 14.1), one's estimates of the we-attitudes of co-members (d, g), and one's estimate that the we-attitudes are mutually held (b, c, e, f, h, i). This, then, results in a partition of the 27 we-intention expressions into groupings of 3, 6, and 18, respectively. Notice that the latter we-attitudes are in the form of second-order mutual beliefs (e.g. Tuomela, 1995: 41–51). For example, b^M is the estimation of belief that person M has that co-member A believes that M has an intention to participate in the group activity (where this, as for all items, would be expressed as a matter of degree or strength ranging from 1 to 7 on a 'weak intention' to 'strong intention' scale). Schematically, we can

write b^M as $E_M E_A M(HI)$, where E_M = 'M estimates or believes that', E_A = 'A estimates or believes that', M = 'person M' again, and HI = 'has we-intention I'. Table 14.2 presents a reorganization and re-expression of the we-intentions shown in Table 14.1 by use of this new notation. Although people may have mutual beliefs of an order greater than 2, we submit that this occurs relatively infrequently and further that second-order mutual beliefs should suffice as a practical matter for the purposes developed in the following section. Note, too, that instead of each person estimating the we-attitudes of both self and all group members individually, as done in this chapter, it may be sufficient to rely on self estimates and a global estimate of group members overall. This would make the measurement task less unwieldy for larger groups.

Table 14.2 Partition of we-intentions for the three-person group case into self, other(s), and mutual we-intentions (see text for definitions of symbols and an example exposition; see also Table 14.1)

	by Person M	by Person A	by Person B
Self expression of we-intention	M(HI)	A(HI)	B(HI)
Belief that co-members have we-intentions	$E_M A(HI)$	$E_A M(HI)$	$E_B M(HI)$
	$E_M B(HI)$	$E_A B(HI)$	$E_B A(HI)$
Second-order mutual beliefs that group members have we-intentions	$E_M E_A M(HI)$	$E_A E_M A(HI)$	$E_B E_M B(HI)$
	$E_M E_B M(HI)$	$E_A E_B A(HI)$	$E_B E_A B(HI)$
	$E_M E_A A(HI)$	$E_A E_M M(HI)$	$E_B E_M M(HI)$
	$E_M E_B A(HI)$	$E_A E_B M(HI)$	$E_B E_A M(HI)$
	$E_M E_A B(HI)$	$E_A E_M B(HI)$	$E_B E_M A(HI)$
	$E_M E_B B(HI)$	$E_A E_B B(HI)$	$E_B E_A A(HI)$

Given the aforementioned representation of 'we-ness' for intentions in the three-person group, we are now in a position to scrutinize an interesting implication of agreement or convergence in beliefs of group members and interesting implications of divergence or discrimination in beliefs. We will show that these implications can be developed into testable hypotheses. In addition, these representations permit us to make statements about such important group properties as the definition of a group, the degree of solidarity in a group, the presence of deviants in a group, the occurrence of coalitions and so on, but these are not considered here in the interests of brevity.

The first model and set of testable hypotheses I consider is called the *key informant model* of construct validity. Applied to the we-intention items shown in Table 14.1, this model allows us to examine convergent and discriminant validity of the measures of we-intentions for persons M, A and B. To do this and obtain variability in responses, so as to perform the appropriate statistical analyses, we would need to obtain a sample of, say, more

than 100 similar groups with three members from each group. Figure 14.2 illustrates the key informant model, where the so-called correlated uniqueness model is chosen for purposes of exposition, but analogous models could be drawn for the additive trait-method-error model and the direct product model, among others (see Bagozzi et al., 1991, for a discussion of models of construct validity). The circles represent latent variables corresponding to the three respective we-intentions of M, A and B, the boxes stand for the empirical measures (see Table 14.1), the λs are factor loadings, the e_is are error terms, the θ_{ij}s are correlated errors and the ϕ_{kl}s are correlations amongst factors. Convergent validity is achieved when the model fits satisfactorily in a statistical sense; the higher the standardized factor loadings (i.e. the closer the loadings are to 1.00), the greater the degree of convergence. Discriminant validity obtains when the ϕ_{kl}s are significantly less than 1.00. Evidence for random error is found in the variances of the e_is, and the degree of method bias (in this case due to the three classes of key informants) can be seen in the θ_{ij}s. We would like to see

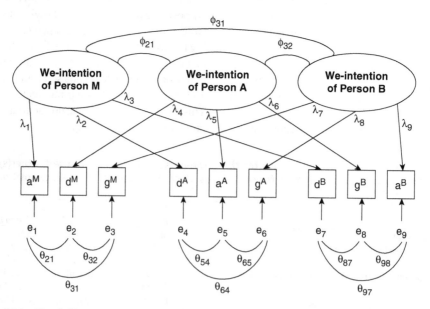

Figure 14.2   Key informant correlated uniqueness model for testing construct validity of measures of we-intentions in a three person group (see Table 14.1 for definitions of measures shown in boxes above).

high factor loadings, because this shows that the group members agree on their assessments of each person's we-intentions. That is, each person's own expressed we-intention converges with the estimate of this person's we-intention as provided by the other two group members. Likewise, we would like to see high correlations amongst factors, because this shows that the three estimated we-intentions for the group members are in agreement.

Notice that the key informant model in Figure 14.2 uses only 9 of the 27 we-intention items shown in Table 14.1. Further, these items refer to each person's own assessment of his/her we-intention, as well as his/her beliefs that the others believe that he/she has the we-intention. The latter of course are a subset of the mutual beliefs. Importantly, the key informant model is at the group level in the sense that the target latent variables capture properties of the group as a whole (as seen by each member, where the measures of each member's we-intention are from the self and each of the two group members). In this sense, the key informant model appears to be consistent with supraindividualism in that the group is directly treated as an intentional subject. The key informant model is consistent also with Gilbert's notion of 'we' under plural subject theory and Tuomela's we-mode thinking.

To test for construct validity and utilize all the measures of we-intentions shown in Table 14.1, and thereby incorporate the full sense of Tuomela's (2002) definition of we-attitudes

as a threefold constellation as presented earlier, there are at least a dozen models that may be scrutinized, depending on whether one looks at we-intentions of each group member separately, as measured by self or persons A or B or by all three members at once, or whether one looks at we-intentions by different kinds of aggregation across group members or within group members. Needless to say there are many complex possibilities here, each with somewhat different meanings and implications.

Figure 14.3 shows a model for testing construct validity, where all measures shown in Table 14.1 are utilized. Taking the first factor as an example, we see that persons M, A and B all provide estimates of person M's we-intentions. The measured responses of persons indicated in each rectangle can be combined or aggregated to provide a measurement of its respective hypothesized factor. In the first rectangle at the left, for instance, person M expresses his/her own we-intention (a^M), his/her estimate of friend A's assessment of M's own we-intention (b^M), and his/her estimate of friend B's assessment of M's own we-intention (c^M). Thus, from the point of view of each group member, each person (1) has a we-intention him or herself, (2) believes or judges that each of his/her partners has the we-intention and (3) believes or judges that all share jointly in the we-intention. The aforementioned three categories yield 3, 6 and 18 judgments, respectively (see Table 14.2).

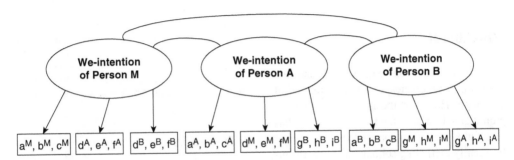

Figure 14.3 Abbreviated model for testing construct validity of measures of we-intentions where self, other, and mutual responses are aggregated in a three person group (see Table 14.1 for definitions of measures shown in boxes).

In addition to using the model of Figure 14.3 to examine reliability and convergent and discriminant validity of measures, we can investigate the following aspects of we-ness in a group in question. We get an indication of convergent and discriminant validity of the we-intentions of each group member. To the extent that loadings are low or fail to confirm a single factor in any case, this would suggest that the member in question is not perceived as a member of the group. Even if the loadings are high and suggest that each member is perceived by self and others as a group member, unless the correlations are high, a member would be perceived as a deviant member; high factor correlations indicate strong mutuality. The factor means can be inspected to get an indication of the average strength of we-intentions *of* group members.

To reiterate, the two models shown in Figures 14.2 and 14.3 cover only a portion of the relevant models that can be scrutinized. Other models can be constructed to investigate different combinations of self, other and mutual estimates of we-ness, and still other models can be used to examine meaningful subsets of the 27 propositional attitudes.

Algesheimer, Bagozzi and Dholakia (2009) applied plural subject theory in a study of 277 three-person teams playing computer games competitively on the internet. The authors tested the models shown in Figures 14.2 and 14.3, as well as other models, and found strong evidence for construct validity. They also tested the predictive validity of we-intentions.

CONCLUSION

A compelling case can be made for construing marketing as the science, art and practice of exchange. However, the notion of exchange promulgated in the field of marketing has been rather narrow and one-sided to date. Most frequently marketing scholars and practitioners have conceived of marketing as a largely economic activity conducted at arm's length. While some marketing exchanges fit this conceptualization, we argue that marketing exchanges are best thought to consist somewhere along a continuum marked by economic-like exchanges on the one end, where the parties to the exchange function as independent actors with individualistic motives and with little or no concern for social aspects of either the exchange relationship itself or the social environment in which the parties are embedded, and mutual exchanges on the other end, where the parties jointly function under the auspices of shared action (according to plural subject theory) and within the constraining and/or facilitating social environment in which the exchange and parties are embedded.

We argue as well that the exchange relationship might best be viewed as an instance of symbiosis, such that the parties to an exchange cooperate in a mutually beneficial relationship. This is not to say that marketing exchanges are not sometimes unbalanced or reveal disparities in resources and power and undergo conflict. Nevertheless, we submit that the most beneficial exchanges for the actors engaged in them, as well as for society as a whole in the long run, are those based on a sharing in the action of a verb.

NOTES

1 In addition to the obligation to do one's part in a collective commitment, Tuomela (1995) notes further that there is the responsibility of group members to help others do their parts. This is similar to the imperative or implication discussed by Muniz and O'Guinn (2001) in their group notion of 'consciousness of kind' for brand communities.

2 A propositional attitude is a kind of state of mind that expresses a relation between a person and a proposition. More formally: 'If a person x thinks that p, desires that p, believes that p, is angry that p, and so on, then he or she is described as having a propositional attitude to p' (Blackburn, 1994, 307).

REFERENCES

Alderson, W. (1957) *Marketing Behavior and Executive Action*. Homewood, IL: Richard D. Irwin.

Alderson, W. (1965) *Dynamic Marketing Behavior*. Homewood, IL: Richard D. Irwin.

Alderson, W. (1968) *Men, Motives, and Market*. Englewood Cliffs, NJ: Prentice Hall.

Algesheimer, R., Bagozzi, R.P., and Dholakia, U. (2009) 'A Framework for Assessing Construct Validity and Predictive Validity in Small Group Research', forthcoming.

American Marketing Association (2007, 2004, 1985) Definition of Marketing, http://www. marketingpower.com/AboutAMA/ Documents/American%20Marketing%20 Association%20Releases%20New%20 Definition%20for%20Marketing.pdf.

Anderson, J.C. and Narus, J.A. (1990). 'A Model of Distributor Firm and Manufacturer Firm Working Partnerships', *Journal of Marketing*, 54: 42–58.

Anderson, E. and Weitz, B. (1992) 'The Use of Pledges to Build and Sustain Commitment in Distribution Channels', *Journal of Marketing Research*, 29: 18–34.

Bagozzi, R.P. (1974a) 'What is Marketing Relationship?', *Der Markt*, 51: 64–69.

Bagozzi, R.P. (1974b) 'Marketing as an Organized Behavioral System of Exchange', *Journal of Marketing*, 38(4): 77–81.

Bagozzi, R.P. (1975) 'Marketing as Exchange', *Journal of Marketing*, 39: 32–39.

Bagozzi, R.P. (1976) 'Science, Politics and the Social Construction of Marketing', in K.L. Bernhardt (ed.) *Marketing: 1776–1976 and Beyond*, Chicago: American Marketing Association, pp. 586–592.

Bagozzi, R.P. (1978) 'Marketing as Exchange: A Theory of Transactions in the Market Place', *American Behavioral Scientist*, 21: 535–556.

Bagozzi, R.P. (1979) 'Toward a Formal Theory of Marketing Exchange', in O.C. Ferrell, S.W. Brown and C.W. Lamb (eds) *Conceptual and Theoretical Developments in Marketing*, Chicago: American Marketing Association, pp. 431–447.

Bagozzi, R.P. (2000) 'On the Concept of Intentional Social Action in Consumer Behavior', *Journal of Consumer Research*, 27: 388–396.

Bagozzi, R.P. (2005) 'Socializing Marketing', *Journal of Marketing*, 1: 101–110.

Bagozzi, R.P. (2006) 'Consumer Action: Automaticity, Purposiveness and Self-Regulation', in N.K. Malhotra (ed.) *Review of Marketing Research*, vol. 2, Armonk, NY: Sharpe, pp. 3–42.

Bagozzi, R.P., Yi, Y. and Phillips, L.W. (1991) 'Assessing Construct Validity in Organizational Research', *Administrative Science Quarterly*, 36: 421–458.

Berger, P.L. and Luckmann, T. (1966) *The Social Construction of Reality: A Treatise in the Sociology of Knowledge*. Garden City, NY: Doubleday.

Blackburn, S. (1994) *The Oxford Dictionary of Philosophy*. Oxford: Oxford University Press.

Doney, P.M. and Cannon, J.P. (1997) 'An Examination of the Nature of Trust in Buyer–Seller Relationships', *Journal of Marketing*, 61: 35–51.

Dwyer, F.R., Schurr, P.H., and Oh, S. (1987) 'Developing Buyer–Seller Relationships', *Journal of Marketing*, 51: 11–27.

Dyer, J.H. and Chu, W. (2000) 'The Determinants of Trust in Supplier–Automaker Relationships in the U.S., Japan and Korea', *Journal of International Business Studies*, 31: 259–285.

Ekeh, P.P. (1974) (article says 1874?) *Social Exchange: The Two Traditions*. Cambridge, MA: Harvard University Press.

Flynn, F.J. (2005) 'Identity Orientations and Forms of Social Exchange in Organizations', *Academy of Management Review*, 30: 737–750.

Frazier, G.L., Gill, J.D., and Kale, S.H. (1989) 'Dealer Dependence Levels and Reciprocal Actions in Channel of Distribution in a Developing Country', *Journal of Marketing*, 53: 50–69.

Ganesan, S. (1994) 'Determinants of Long-Term Orientation in Buyer–Seller Relationships', *Journal of Marketing*, 58: 1–19.

Geyskens, I., Steenkemp, J.E., and Scheer, L.K. (1996) 'The Effects of Trust and Interdependence on Relationship Commitment: A Trans-Atlantic Study', *International Journal of Research in Marketing*, 13: 303–317.

Gilbert, M. (1989) *On Social Facts*. Princeton, NJ: Princeton University Press.

Gilbert, M. (1990). 'Walking Together: A Paradigmatic Social Phenomenon'. *Midwest Studies in Philosophy*, 15 (November): 1–14.

Gilbert, M. (2000) *Sociality and Responsibility: New Essays in Plural Subject Theory*. Lanham, MD: Rowman & Littlefield Publishing, Inc.

Gilbert, M. (2002a) 'Acting Together', in G. Meggle (ed.) *Social Facts and Collective*

Intentionality, Frankfurt am Main: Dr. Hänsel-Hohenhausen, pp. 53–71.

Gilbert, M. (2002b) 'Considerations on Joint Commitment: Responses to Various Comments', in G. Meggle (ed.) *Social Facts and Collective Intentionality*, Frankfurt, pp. 73–101.

Gilbert, M. (2003) 'The Structure of the Social Atom: Joint Commitment as the Foundation of Human Social Behavior', in F.F. Schmitt (ed.) *Socializing Metaphysics: The Nature of Social Reality*, Lanham, pp. 39–64.

Gundlach, G.T., Achrol, R.S., and Mentzer, J.T. (1995) 'The Structure of Commitment in Exchange', *Journal of Marketing*, 59: 78–92.

Harré, R. and Secord, P.F. (1973) *The Explanation of Social Behavior*. Totawa, NJ: Littlefield, Adams & Co.

Homburg, C., Droll, M., and Totzek, D. (2008) 'Customer Priortization: Does it Pay Off, and How Should it be Implemented?', *Journal of Marketing*, 72: 110–130.

Homburg, C., Workman, J. P., and Jensen, O. (2002, January) 'A Configuration Perspective on Key Account Management', *Journal of Marketing*, 66: 38–60.

Howard, J.A. and Sheth, J.N. (1969) *The Theory of Buyer Behavior*. New York, NY: Wiley.

Hunt, S.D. (2002) *Foundations of Marketing Theory: Toward a General Theory of Marketing*. Armonk, NY: M.E. Sharp, Inc.

Jap, S.D. (2001) 'Perspectives on Joint Competitive Advantages in Buyer–Supplier Relationships', *International Journal of Research in Marketing*, 18, 19–35.

Johnson, J.L., Sakano, T., Cote, J.A., and Onzo, N. (1993) 'The Exercise of Interfirm Power and its Repercussions in U.S. – Japanese Channel Relationships', *Journal of Marketing*, 57: 1–10.

Kotler, P. (1967) *Marketing Management Analysis, Planning and Control*. Englewood Cliffs, NJ: Prentice Hall.

Kotler, P. (1972) 'A Generic Concept of Marketing', *Journal of Marketing*, 36: 46–54.

Kotler, P. and Levy, S.J. (1969) 'Broadening the Concept of Marketing', *Journal of Marketing*, 33: 10–15.

Lawler, E.J. (2001) 'An Affect Theory of Social Exchange', *The American Journal of Sociology*, 107: 321–352.

Luck, D. (1969) 'Broadening the Concept of Marketing too Far', *Journal of Marketing*, 33: 53–55.

Lusch, R.F. and Brown, J.R. (1996) 'Interdependency, Contracting, and Relational Behavior in Marketing Channels', *Journal of Marketing*, 60: 19–38.

Lusch, R.F. and Vargo, S.L. (2006) 'Service-Dominant Logic: Reactions, Reflections and Refinements', *Marketing Theory*, 6: 281–288.

Menon, A. and Varadarajan, P.R. (1992) 'A Model of Marketing Knowledge Use within Firms', *Journal of Marketing*, 56: 53–71.

Mohr, J.J., Fisher, R.J., and Nevin, J.R. (1996) 'Collaborative Communication in Interfirm Relationships: Moderating Effects of Integration and Control', *Journal of Marketing*, 60: 103–115.

Mohr, J. and Spekman, R. (1994) 'Characteristics of Partnership Success: Partnership Attributes, Communication Behavior, and Conflict Resolution Techniques', *Strategic Management Journal*, 15: 135–152.

Molm, L. and Cook, K. (1995) 'Social Exchange and Exchange Networks', *Social Perspectives on Social Psychology*, 209–235.

Moorman, C., Zaltman, G., and Deshpandé, R. (1992) 'Relationships Between Providers and Users of Market Research: The Dynamics of Trust Within and Between Organizations', *Journal of Marketing Research*, 29: 314–328.

Moorman, C., Deshpandé, R., and Zaltman, G. (1993) Factors Affecting Trust in Market Research Relationships. *Journal of Marketing*, 57: 81–101.

Morgan, R.M. and Hunt, S.D. (1994, January) 'The Commitment-Trust Theory of Relationship Marketing', *Journal of Marketing*, 58: 20–38.

Muniz Jr., A.M. and O'Guinn, T.C. (2001) Brand Community, *Journal of Consumer Research*, 27: 412–432.

Nahapiet, J. and Ghoshal, S. (1998) 'Social Capital, Intellectual Capital, and the Organizational Advantage', *The Academy of Management Review*, 23: 242–266.

Palmatier, R.W. (2008) 'Interfirm Relational Drivers of Customer Value', *Journal of Marketing*, 72: 76–89.

Palmatier, R.W., Dant, R.P. and Grewal, D. (2007) 'A Comparative Longitudinal Analysis of Theoretical Perspectives of Interorganizational Relationship Performance', *Journal of Marketing*, 71: 172–194.

Popper, K.R. (1963) *Conjectures and Refutations*, New York, NY: Harper & Row, p. 67.

Prahalad, C.K. and Ramaswamy, V. (2004) *The Future of Competition: Co-creating Unique*

Value with Customers, Boston: Harvard Business School Press.

Prahalad, C.K. and Ramaswamy, V. (2000) 'Co-opting Customer Competence', *Harvard Business Review*, 78: 79–87.

Schneider, H.K. (1974) *For a Modern Treatment of Economic Man*. New York, NY: The Free Press.

Sheth, J.N. and Parvatiyar, A. (1995a) 'Antecedents and Consequences of Relationship Marketing in Consumer Markets', *Journal of the Academy of Marketing Science*, 23: 255–271.

Sheth, J.N. and Parvatiyar, A. (1995b) 'The Evolution of Relationship Marketing'. *International Business Review*, 4: 387–418.

Sheth, J.N. and Uslay, C. (2007) 'Implications of the Revised Definition of Marketing: From Exchange to Value Creation', *Journal of Public Policy & Marketing*, 26: 302–307.

Skarmeas, D., Katsikeas, C.S. and Schlegelmilch, B.B. (2002) 'Drivers of Commitment and its Impact on Performance in Cross-Cultural Buyer–Seller Relationships: The Importer's Perspective', *Journal of International Business Studies*, 33: 757–783.

Stump, L.S. and Heide, J.B. (1996) 'Controlling Supplier Opportunism in Industrial Relationships', *Journal of Marketing Research*, 33: 431–441.

Tuomela, R. (1995) *The Importance of US: A Philosophical Study of Basic Social Notions*. Stanford.

Tuomela, R. (2000) *Cooperation: A Philosophical Study*. Dordrecht.

Tuomela, R. (2002) *The Philosophy of Social Practices: A Collective Acceptance View*. Cambridge, UK.

Tuomela, R. (2003) 'The We-Mode and the I-Mode', in F.F. Schmitt (ed.) *Socializing Metaphysics: The Nature of Social Reality*, Lanham, pp. 93–127.

Vargo, S. and Lusch, R.F. (2004) 'Evolving to a New Dominant Logic for Marketing', *Journal of Marketing*, 68: 1–17.

15

Metaphorical Myopia: Some Thoughts on Analogical Thinking

Stephen Brown

INTRODUCTION

A journal rests on my desk. It's the latest issue of *Journal of Marketing Management*, arguably the pre-eminent academic organ in the UK. It's a special issue devoted to 'Marketing Myopia' (Wright et al., 2008). After pausing to kick myself for failing to submit something (because I have written about Ted's classic paper in the past), I skim the contributions. Not one engages with the nitty-gritty of Levitt's (1960a) original article, reputedly the best-selling *Harvard Business Review* reprint of all time and a landmark moment in the history of marketing thought. They're content to make use of the titular metaphor, which famously refers to managers' inability to see what business they are in. I kick myself again. Harder this time.

The metaphor, of course, is all that really matters, all that remains 50 years after 'Marketing Myopia' materialised in Levitt's mind's eye. What a Eureka moment that must have been for an ambitious young economist, newly plucked from obscurity by the pre-eminent business school in the United States. He had to make his name; he had to prove

himself worthy of Harvard's decision to appoint a doctorateless plebeian. And, boy, did Theodore deliver the academic merchandise, merchandise that is still stylish half a century later. As Coco Chanel famously observed, 'fashion changes, style remains' (see Brown, 2008).

Ted Levitt may or may not qualify as the Coco Chanel of marketing thought – cursory examination of their respective biographies suggests several intriguing parallels, though[1] – but there's no doubt that his seminal article remains endlessly fascinating. It is fascinating for three main reasons. Firstly, for its historical context, something contemporary commentators are inclined to overlook. Far from being a stand-alone contribution, Marketing Myopia was published as a riposte to 'the depth men', the motivation researchers who were undermining marketing's image at the time (Levitt, 1960b). In the late fifties, marketing's social standing was at a particularly low ebb, thanks to the subliminal advertising scam and a host of similar incidents (Brown, 2001). However, by stressing that 'proper' marketing placed customer needs at the centre of its operation, Levitt's article represented a brilliantly argued refutation of the rip-off brigade. It rebranded marketing as a boon to humankind, a customer-led and customer-focussed endeavour and, in so doing, Levitt effectively saved our collective bacon and set us on the customer-centric path that still pervades marketing thinking (Kotler, 2008).

Secondly, the golden glow of the so-called 'marketing revolution', the assumption that our academic discipline entered a whole new dispensation in the late 1950s, blinds us to the reality of Marketing Myopia's production and reception. Far from being universally lauded, Levitt's provocative article was condemned for its egregious historical inaccuracies and alleged misrepresentation of the American railroads industry (see Marion, 1993).[2] Such shortcomings, one imagines, would sink most nascent academic careers. But Levitt rode out the storm, not least on account of his incredible writing ability. Cavalier with the facts or not, Ted's way with words ensured that even when he got it wrong, as he often did, his metaphor-engorged papers were always worth reading. And indeed re-reading, because when we re-read Marketing Myopia, it is clear that the 'myopic' trope hardly appears in the body of the article (Brown, 2004a). There is much 'listening' to the customer and 'hearing' what they have to say. Shortsightedness, however, hardly gets a mention, even though it is perhaps the most famous metaphor in the history of marketing thought!

Marketing Myopia, thirdly, is the metaphorical gift that keeps on giving. Apart from the obvious point that the 50-year-old article is still widely cited and anthologised when countless intervening publications have long since been forgotten,[3] subsequent commentators on Levitt's classic article have extended the analogy, arguing that there's also a problem with long-sightedness and managers' lack of peripheral vision (Day and Schoemaker, 2006; Kotler and Singh, 1981; Marion, 1993). The metaphor, in fact, is infinitely adaptable, insofar as it is easy to think of ocular ailments that pertain to contemporary business life – marketing glaucoma, PR cataracts, brand

strabismus, logistics laser surgery, pricing pince-nez, retail store bifocals and, some would say, the registered blindness of the academic establishment (González-Crussi, 2006; Jay, 1994; Levin, 1997).

I see no scholarships.

TALKING TURKEY

Fertile metaphors (like Levitt's) yield an enormous scholarly harvest and most would concede that the granaries of marketing thought are full to overflowing. The merest glance at the marketing textbooks reveals a veritable shed load of corny conceits, tuberous tropes and fruitful figures of speech. The marketing mix (cooking), the 4Ps (alchemy), the Product Life Cycle (biology), brand personality (psychology), the wheel of retailing (transportation), viral marketing (epidemiology), buzz marketing (apiary), guerrilla marketing (warfare), stealth marketing (espionage), relationship marketing (marriage), consumer information processing (computers), the foundations of marketing thought (architecture) and many, many more are testament to the fact that marketing thinking is undeniably bountiful, bordering on superabundant (see Kitchen, 2008).

As I write, for example, brand DNA, emotional branding and the so-called brand gym are attracting enthusiastic attention, and no doubt brand diets, muscle-bound brands, brand obesity, brand botox, brand detox, brand cellulite and the like are girding their loins, preparing to participate in the marketing management beauty pageant, where their ambition is to save the world and do good deeds. The only thing more popular than corporeal tropes is anthropomorphism. According to *The Economist* (2004), animal analogies are essential if one deigns to dash off a management bestseller. Purple cows, black swans, inquisitive squirrels, dancing elephants, cubicle monkeys, indecisive mice, canny rats, lunatic lemmings, silverback CEOs, killer apes (sorry, apps), hares 'n' tortoises, hedgehogs 'n' foxes, spiders 'n' starfish and strangely disembodied long tails are happily cavorting on the corporate Serengeti, where the consultancy waterholes are brimming and the retainer fee forage is inexhaustible, reputedly.[4]

Cynicism aside, the brute reality is that marketing thinking is inherently metaphoric, branding especially. Describing one thing in terms of another is what metaphors do (argument is war, life is a circle, paperwork is mountainous, etc.) and successfully branded products, services, organisations, countries, cities, celebrities and suchlike do exactly the same. Volvo is safety, BMW is performance, Virgin is fun, Marlboro is freedom, Levi's is rugged, Versace is sex, Paris is style, New York is energy, Brazil is samba, Scotland is canny, Madonna is metamorphic, Britney is bonkers (Brown, 2005). Just as metaphors often describe abstract phenomena in concrete terms (time is money, bureaucracy is an iron cage, etc.) so too abstract characteristics become embodied in products and services (magic means Disney, refreshment is Coke, athleticism equals Nike, etc.).[5] Some of these metaphorical transfers may be unanticipated by managers and are therefore decidedly unwelcome (McDonald's is arteriosclerosis, Microsoft is megalomaniacal, Las Vegas is sleazy, etc.), but such figurative imputations are the coin of the marketing realm.

Above and beyond the 'conceptual' metaphors that populate both the brandscape and mainstream marketing's verdant water meadows, day-to-day marketing discourse is dominated by 'conversational' metaphors (see Knowles and Moon, 2006; Kövecses, 2002; Punter, 2007). That is to say, the language routinely employed by marketing commentators, be they journalists, academics or retainer-engorged gurus, is replete with figures of speech, as are the everyday idioms used by managers and consumers (Zaltman, 2003). Many of these are clichés, admittedly, metaphors that have been ground down by the glacier of overuse and deposited on the terminal moraine of meaninglessness (e.g. tip of the iceberg, thin end of the wedge, nail in the

coffin, crying over spilt milk and shutting the stable door after the brand has bolted). The fact remains, nevertheless, that figures of speech figure prominently in marketing communications and great marketing thinkers are often blessed with a gift for the metaphorical *mot juste*.

The aforementioned Ted Levitt, for instance, is particularly partial to personification, attributing human characteristics to inanimate objects. In addition to Marketing Myopia, the infamous remark about marketing's 'step-child' status and his stunningly brilliant articulation of the Product Life Cycle concept, Levitt's lively prose literally lactates with personification: 'The throbbing pulse of the reality the data sought to capture' (Levitt, 1986); 'If entrepreneurship was the hippie youth of the 1980s, then making money was its long hair' (Levitt, 1991a); 'Companies that don't metabolize information right will see small problems and discontinuities metastasize into major maladies' (Levitt, 1991b). He makes use of many other metaphors, of course – music, food, gambling, games and animals, both domestic and wild – and repeatedly extols the virtues of expressive language ('the metaphor makes the sale'). However, the late great Ted Levitt was a personifier first, last and always (Brown, 2004a).

Philip Kotler, by contrast, is nothing if not New Age minded (Brown, 2002a). A child of the sixties, his books and articles are stuffed with similes that reflect the spirit of that memorably forgetful decade. Although Kotler purports to be an exponent of marketing science, his preferred metaphorical repertoire reveals an inordinate fondness for pseudoscience, not to say science fiction. Thus, he gives ample space to 'spectres', 'spirits', 'presences', 'uncontrollable forces', and 'bump in the night' behaviours. He exhibits a conspiracy culture-immersed interest in brain washing, mind control, subliminal messages and secret societies. He mentions magic, mysticism, mythology, soothsaying, foretelling, rebirthing, pyramidology, alchemy, time travel, good luck charms and every other imaginable manifestation of the paranormal.

If not quite the Krishnamurti of marketing scholarship, he is definitely our own, our very own, Koot-Hoomi.[6]

Even the supposedly unreadable writings of Wroe Alderson are a rich repository of metonymy and more (Brown, 2002b). His oeuvre is riddled with personification, anthropomorphism, military analogies, ecological conceits, sporting similes, travelling tropes, artistic allusions, mechanical or meteorological comparisons and suchlike. An eclectic mix, one might say, a mix that is itself a metaphor for Alderson's scholarly Catholicism. True, the former farm boy was unusually fond of agricultural tropes – 'This is a clear case of multiple causation like the contributions of the sun and the rain to a crop of wheat' – but the overwhelming impression is of analogical overkill and intellectual ill discipline. On reading Wroe, one is left with the feeling that Alderson, like Wittgenstein, was just too clever for his own good. At least some of this feeling is attributable to his exhibitionistic expressions, his prodigal prose and his wayward way with words.

HERDING CATS

Whether it be 'conceptual' or 'conversational' conceits, there is no denying that marketing is a rolling stone of mossy metaphors. Much of what passes for marketing 'theory' is little more than morbidly obese metaphor. Many are not even metaphors. The much-vaunted Service-Dominant Logic of Marketing, for example, is actually an elongated, arguably over-extended, chiasmus.[7] Yet, regardless of where marketing theories fit into the figurative family – alongside kid sisters simile and synecdoche, next to big brothers allegory and symbol or in cahoots with crazy cousins myth and archetype, who went to Hollywood and made a fortune as screenwriters – the crucial question has to be asked: Are metaphors a good thing?

Fifty years ago, the answer was clear. Certainly not! Way back then, when metonymical Reds were under the bed and the

unadorned International Style of modern architecture held sway, metaphors were widely considered sinful, depraved, the demon seed of beatniks and similar juvenile delinquents (Ortony, 1993). Strunk and White (1959), the prim protectors of proper literature, warned against extravagant language in general and exuberant metaphors in particular (see also Orwell, 1962). Metaphors were considered unnecessary, unseemly and unfit for humanist consumption. Mixed metaphors, akin to the preceding paragraph, were a serious syntactical faux pas, a sign of intellectual ill breeding. Plain prose, simply put, was the order of the day. This was especially so in an academic discipline that aspired to respectable scientific status in the soul-searching aftermath of the highly critical Ford and Carnegie reports (Brown, 1995).

Come the freewheeling 1980s, however, when it was morning in America and clichés were king, figures of speech came out of the closet. Lakoff and Johnson (1980) led the way, by demonstrating the pervasiveness of metaphorical reasoning and contending that humankind's understanding of the world was metaphor mediated. Even the most common or garden-variety prose, they showed, was blooming with efflorescent analogies. In this regard, it is surely no accident that the 1980s also witnessed the emergence of trope-engorged business blockbusters, principally Peters and Waterman's mega-selling *In Search of Excellence*. Predicated on the archetypal journey or quest metaphor that underpins everything from Homer's *Odyssey* and *The Pilgrim's Progress* to *On the Road* and *Dude, Where's My Car?*, it swept all before it and established the figure-filled template that dominates the business bestseller list to this very day (Peters and Waterman, 1982).[8]

In the quarter century since Peters and Waterman's staggering textual triumph, metaphors have gone from strength to strength. As Hirschman (2007) reveals in her recent overview of the metaphor literature, the topic has attracted considerable attention from marketing and consumer researchers. Studies range from analyses of advertising (Scott, 1994;

Stern, 1988) and art galleries (Joy and Sherry, 2003) to the trope-truffling techniques employed by new product developers (Durgee and Chen, 2006). Gerald Zaltman's 'metaphor elicitation technique' is perhaps the most celebrated contribution – so celebrated it has been granted a US patent – but ZMET is only the tip of the proverbial intellectual iceberg (Zaltman, 2003; Zaltman and Zaltman, 2008). Actually, it is more like an ice pack, because metaphorology is an enormously popular activity practised by every imaginable academic discipline. Thirty years ago, the eminent rhetorician Wayne Booth (1978: 47) wryly predicted that there would soon be more metaphoricians than metaphysicians and that 50 years hence there would be 'more students of metaphor than people'.

Yo, Nostradamus.

WHITE ELEPHANT

If not quite the dog's bollocks, metaphors are the bees' knees nowadays. Metaphors, many believe, are the bits, the bytes, the binary code of the imagination (Pink, 2005). The creative economy, we are reliably informed, is reliant on managers' metaphor-making prowess and analogical thinking generally (Florida, 2003, 2005; Howkins, 2002; Ogle, 2008). Production can be offshored with impunity, as can information processing and routine back office functions like after-sales service. However, heaven help the developed world if figures of speech follow suit. Even mixed metaphors are acceptable these days. As leading literary critic James Wood (2008) reminds us, William Shakespeare and Henry James were not reluctant to mix their metaphors (James coyly called them 'loose' metaphors). The thing that grammarians object to is not mixed metaphors, as such, but mixed clichés akin to Sam Goldwyn's apocryphal 'bite the hand that lays the golden egg' or George Orwell's (1962: 151) ironic classic, 'The Fascist octopus has sung its swan song, the jackboot is thrown into the melting pot'.

In this regard, consider the following passage plucked from a recent essay on marketing theory:

> Yet, in the marketing academy we constantly justify ourselves through recourse to theory, and are at pains to establish our 'theoretical positioning'. Without a strong, substantive and fixed foundation we feel that our work will be ridiculed, or relegated to the 'descriptive' dustbin. And so we wrap our work in theories, but like the story of the emperor's new clothes, we may thereby collude with the emperor in weaving a web of deception, loath to challenge this appearance of academic rigour and respectability, or to design an alternative and better-fitting mode of academic 'dress'. (Maclaran and Stevens, 2008: 346)

Every single sentence in this passage contains a mixed metaphor: geographical and corporeal in the first one (pains, positioning); architectural and receptacle in the second (foundation, dustbin); apparel and arachnid in the third (emperor clothes story and weaving web of deception). The rest of the article is equally metaphor laden. However, such is the prevalence of metaphor nowadays that Maclaran and Stevens' admixture does not jar, let alone appal. On the contrary, it comes across as refreshingly lively writing.

Still, if marketing teaches us anything, it is that once something is universally lauded, universal loathing is not far behind. Ubiquity is the beginning of obloquy. Triumph is a harbinger of disaster. These truisms are as true for cool brands, breakthrough products, exemplary organizations and management fads as they are for theories, concepts, frameworks and, yes, figurative language. Most marketing academics roll their eyes at the mere mention of the 4Ps (and as for the multi-P extensions – enough already!). Peters and Waterman's *In Search of Excellence* is now a standing joke within the management community (though Peters' confession that he fudged his data didn't help). The metaphorical excesses of management speak, everything from out of the box thinking to running things up the flagpole, are regularly excoriated by incandescent lovers of language (Humphrys, 2005; Watson, 2004; Whichelow and Murray, 2007).[9] Even Gerry Zaltman's much-lauded metaphor elicitation technique has been cruelly described as 'The mutant lovechild of Ernest Dichter and Walt Disney'.

Conversely, when one considers the enthusiasm surrounding concepts like 'experiential' marketing, 'emotional' branding, 'service-dominant' logic or the (frankly, ludicrous) fabrication of 'authenticity' (Gilmore and Pine, 2007), it is hard not to conclude that some kind of collective defence mechanism is at work. The real economy – the tangible economy – may be disappearing over the eastern horizon but, hey, we don't need it anyway, because the hyperreal economy, the intangible economy of mental leaps, analogical acumen and metaphor manufacturing will save the day. They have the numbers. We have the smarts. They have the sweatshops. We have the synapses. Or something like that.

Defence mechanisms, most might concede, are dangerously delusional at the best of times, but the rationalisations of western capitalism are potentially ruinous. Metaphors will not save us, no matter how many we tropes we turn out. Metaphors have their dark side too. They conceal as much as they reveal. They blinker our thinking. They shape our discourse. The essentially metaphorical idea of 'equilibrium' affects huge swathes of micro- and macro-economic theorizing – recent advances in behavioural economics notwithstanding (Lunn, 2008) – and cognitive psychology is inextricably mired in the brain-as-computer analogy, with all the attendant terminology of storage, memory, parallel processing, cerebral software, et cetera.

As every literary theorist knows, however, metaphors both highlight and hide certain aspects of the compared domains and the more vivid the metaphor the more marked is this figure/ground contrast (Lewontin, 1993). When someone – Steve Jobs, say, the iconic CEO of Apple Inc – is described as a lion, people tend to think of savagery, ferocity and alpha male carnivorousness, not the lazy feline that spends most of the day lolling around, licking its incisors and snoozing contentedly in the sunshine. Likewise, the commonplace

metaphor that illness is warfare – the idea that we battle disease, fight for life, are attacked by viruses, and the like – is deeply and dangerously distorting (Sontag, 1991). True, the trope is beloved by Big Pharma, because it helps perpetuate the pills-kill-ills belief system and assists with the sale of silver-bullet palliatives (Law, 2006). However, it also leads to a situation where, for instance, cancer sufferers are held responsible for their failure to 'fight' the affliction with sufficient vigour. If the disease carries you off, well, it's because of your cowardice in the face of the enemy. You are to blame. It's your own fault, you pathetic creature.

SHOOT THE PUPPY

The same is true of an even more deeply embedded metaphor: business is war. This comparison has been made so often that it almost falls into the corporate cliché category (Allard, 2004; James, 1985). Nevertheless, the construct is regularly conscripted by the captains of industry – just think of all those books on Sun-Tzu, Genghis Khan and the leadership secrets of Robert E. Lee – even though the comparison is riddled with holes. As Mark Joyner (2008), a former Special Forces operative, points out in his detailed deconstruction of the warfare metaphor, there's is a fundamental difference between marketers and marines. The latter, by and large, try to blend into the background and remain as inconspicuous as possible. Camouflage is king. Low profile is all. The former aims to be as conspicuous as possible and stand out from the me-too mass. Anonymity is anathema. High profile is ideal.

Metaphors not only shape our worldview but they also shape our worldview of our worldview. What, after all, is a 'paradigm shift' but a terrifically sticky trope that no amount of scraping and nit-picking can remove from the rubber sole of scholarship? Allegedly dead metaphors are the stickiest figures of all, because we are inclined to forget that they are metaphors and therefore subject to the short-comings of figurative language. Undead met-aphors is perhaps a better way to describe them, since they are parasitic, vampiric, the bloodsuckers of thought and the Count Draculas of discourse. At the risk of over-stretching an already strained metaphor, they are linguistic leeches that leave us weakened, debilitated, unable to hold a mirror up to ourselves and ripe for a garlic-garlanded stake through the heart.

If ever a metaphor were ripe for the staking, that metaphor is 'marketing science'. For the past half century, or thereabouts, the source domain 'marketing' has been mapped onto the target domain 'science'. The map and the territory have fused, in fact. They are insepa-rable in most people's minds. However, a moment's reflection reveals that many other target domains are conceivable. These include marketing as 'conversation', 'dance', 'gam-bling', 'magic', 'religion', 'technology' and, of course, 'art'. Some of these have been tried, or argued for at least, though none has seriously challenged science's supremacy (Brown, 1996a). Given the standing of science in western culture – most would agree that it is one of our towering achievements; many believe it is *the* towering achievement – this state of affairs is hardly surprising, especially when physicists are the Brahmins and mar-keters are the Untouchables of the academic caste system.

Having said that, it is necessary to constantly remind ourselves that 'marketing science' is a figure of speech, the transposition of one domain onto another. The upshot of this transposition process is that marketing has embraced the symbols and language and ethos of science – logic, rigour, experimenta-tion, hypothesis testing, model building, the search for general theories, the idea of dis-passionate endeavour untainted by researcher subjectivity, the past-tense, passive-voiced rhetoric of academic articles etc., etc. – and having done so it is moving ever further away from what the discipline of marketing was originally designed to do: assist practitioners and prospective practitioners (Tapp, 2005).

As Bennis and O'Toole (2005) point out in their devastating critique of contemporary business schools, the metaphor that manage-ment is science (rather than, say, a craft, calling or community service) is having a deleterious impact on the character, curriculum and recruit-ment policies of leading business schools. Many faculty, they contend, are so preoccupied with the purportedly objective approach of management science that they have no idea of what real business actually involves, the down 'n' dirty, day 'n' daily determination to make the sale, move the merchandise, manage the inventory and, ideally, massacre the com-petition. 'Today', they ruefully observe, 'it is possible to find tenured professors of manage-ment who have never set foot inside a real business, except as customers' (Bennis and O'Toole, 2005: 100).

Irrespective of where one stands on the managerial 'relevance' debate – our duty is to serve or our duty is to critique – it's undeniable that the marketing science model is affecting academics' behaviour, distorting our discipline and driving a wedge between B-school based thinkers and real-world emplaced practitioners (Tadajewski and Brownlie, 2008). The latter, by and large, do not subscribe to the market-ing is science metaphor. They adhere, rather, to a technology trope, a toolkit analogy, a widget worldview, if you will. They expect help, not hypotheses. Forced, furthermore, to choose between rigorous, carefully qualified articles in impenetrable journals and the sparkling, if superficial, similes sold by fast-talking man-agement consultants, who can blame managers for choosing saccharine over science?

In many ways, marketing managers and marketing academics live in different meta-phorical worlds.

PIG IN THE PYTHON

Another metaphor that has been well and truly naturalised is 'the customer is king' (Dixon, 2008). To be sure, the notion of customer sov-ereignty long predates the modern marketing concept and even the most put-upon marketing manager might concede that customers are a pretty important part of the commercial equation (Brown, 2004b). What's more, if there is one thing students take away from their many and varied marketing courses, be they undergraduate or post-experience, it is the divine right of customers. Everything flows from king customer, long to reign over us, happy and glorious. Heaven be praised.

Customer is king may be modern marketing's core metaphor, but it's a core that, if not quite rotten, is definitely decidedly dodgy. It insinuates that managers are subservient, that consumers are omniscient, that bowing and scraping and prostration and genuflection and worshipful adoration before His Royal Highness King Customer are right and proper, the done thing, the way to behave. Yet, the empirical evidence clearly shows that consumers are not omniscient, that they are prone to errors of judgement, that they are often completely wrong headed, that their hidebound views can seriously inhibit innovation and, not least, that sovereign consumers' awareness of their elevated position is giving them delusions of grandeur (Christensen, 1997; Franklin, 2003). Now, this does not mean that the consumer as emperor metaphor has no clothes. Nor does it mean that sovereign consumers can be safely dethroned, much less defenestrated. It simply means that obsequious deference to the monarch's every whim is injudicious at best and injurious at worst. An alternative constitutional conceit is required.

Some, of course, will contend that customer is king is ancient history, that an egalitarian 'relationship' increasingly pertains between ruler and ruled. However, relationship marketing's marriage metaphor is just as distorted as the monarchical alternative, not least because marketers' desire to establish 'relationships' with numerous customers carries connotations of polygamy (Blythe, 2006; Tynan, 1997). And even if the relationship is construed as social rather than marital – we're your best buddy, someone you can rely on – this too is problematic, especially when broken (Zuboff and Maxmin, 2003). According to Ariely

(2008), there is a profound difference between social and business relationships. When CRM-committed organisations break their social contract, as many 'friendly' financial institutions tend to do when credit gets tight, they are loathed even more fiercely than when impersonal arrangements prevail. Consumers accept that business is business but when blood-brother bonds are betrayed it's blood on the carpet time:

> In the past few decades companies have tried to market themselves as social companions – that is, they'd like us to think that they and we are family, or at least friends who live on the same cul-de-sac. 'Like a good neighbour, State Farm is there' is one familiar slogan. Another is Home Depot's gentle urging: 'You can do it. We can help'.
>
> Whoever started the movement to treat customers socially had a great idea. If customers and a company are family, then the company gets several benefits. Loyalty is paramount. Minor infractions – screwing up your bill and even imposing a modest hike in your insurance rates – are accommodated. Relationships of course have ups and downs, but overall they're a pretty good thing.
>
> But here's what I find strange: although companies have poured billions of dollars into marketing and advertising to create social relationships – or at least an impression of social relationships – they don't seem to understand the nature of a social relationship, and in particular its risks.
>
> For example, what happens when a customer's check bounces? If the relationship is based on market norms, the bank charges a fee, and the customer shakes it off. Business is business. While the fee is annoying, it's nonetheless acceptable. In a social relationship, however, a hefty late fee – rather than a friendly call from the manager or an automatic fee waiver – is not only a relationship killer; it's a stab in the back. Consumers will take personal offense. They'll leave the bank angry and spend hours complaining to their friends about this awful bank. After all, this was a relationship framed as a social exchange. No matter how many cookies, slogans, and tokens of friendship a bank provides, one violation of the social exchange means that the consumer is back to the market exchange. It can happen that quickly. (Ariely, 2008: 78–79)

The relationship metaphor may be lumbering toward the elephant graveyard of outworn marketing expressions, but there's a frisky new tusker in town: 'customer co-creation'

(Jaworski and Kohli, 2006; Tapscott and Williams, 2006). The basis of this customer-marketer arrangement is even more easy-going than the marital trope, since it presumes some kind of creative give and take. Consumers contribute to product development and distribution; meanwhile marketers allow consumers to take charge, if not control, and everyone is pretty cool about it. Clearly, this notion is related to the 'network' metaphor that's causing so much excitement among social scientists, itself a reflection of new technology's on-going role as a master metaphor. Just as the computer, the atom bomb, the telephone exchange, the motor car, the cinema and the steam engine were employed by past generations of thinkers, today's equivalent is the world wide web, the wisdom of crowds, the emergent science of complexity, the power of networks, the co-creating consumer (Ball, 2005; Surowiecki, 2005; Watts, 2003).

It may be some time before this undeniably popular trope is pulled apart, though for me it carries crazy connotations of happy-clappy consumer elves in Santa's corporate grotto, working for no reward other than the joy on little children's cherubic faces come crisp and even Christmas morn. All say 'aaahhh'. Capitalism's face ceases to shine, however, when the happy-clappy consumer elves get above themselves and start to think they own the place, the product and the brand. Just ask the over-enthusiastic Harry Potter fans who have been sued by J.K. Warner Brothers for breach of copyright (Brown, 2005). Co-consumer, one suspects, is a misnomer, akin to friendly fire. Cyber slave labour is a better descriptor. As Brock (2008) observes in his review of Charles Leadbeater's *We Think*, a wide-eyed endorsement of customer co-creation: 'what has been called the wisdom of crowds often turns out to be control by a digitally adept elite, which sifts and edits'. Design guru Stephen Bayley is equally dismissive:

We have had the web for about 15 years and long-range electronic collaboration has yet to design anything (still less produce a literary masterpiece).

Moreover, there is nothing new here: the design of complicated building, cars and products is way beyond the scope of an individual's expertise. It has always been a collaborative process. Ideas have always been freely distributed among design teams. It's just that they used to be called drawings. Frankly, I'd prefer experts at BMW to design my car, not a freely-sweating amateur geek on a laptop.

There's an attractive, enlightened liberalism about the We-Think ideology. It posits a world in which the ruthless globalization of Microsoft and Coke can be undermined by a subversive, file-sharing democracy. Unfortunately for the theory, the new consumers in China and India seem very happy to sign up to the old values and old belief systems that we are all so busy rejecting. (Bayley, 2008: 12)

Regardless of such neo-Luddite reactions, it's evident that an e-ristocracy rules the web and the workers of the wiki-world remain enchained, in thrall to false consciousness 2.0.

JUMPING THE SHARK

If the bad news is that root metaphors are difficult to root out, the good news is that management metaphors have a life cycle just like products, brands and organisations. A figure of speech that starts off *striking* soon becomes *standard*, then increasingly *stale* and, in the fullness of time, a *stiff* or dead metaphor. Breaking out of the box is a classic case in point. Once illuminating, latterly ridiculed, it is now in the box – the coffin – of discourse. Pushing the envelope is pushing up daisies. Running things up the flagpole is flying at half-mast. The tipping point has reached its tripping point. Shoot the puppy has not only been put down but it is also decomposing alongside the dead whale that is being kicked up the beach by an 800-lb gorilla.

Be that as it may, the lifecycle of management metaphors is enormously variable. Some are like fireflies, a brief burst of illumination on a sultry summer's night (those that announce revolutions or crises are inherently short lived), others are akin to cicadas, chirping incessantly at the edge of corporate consciousness (those that extol the 'simply better' benefits of 'built to last' consistency, for instance). Yet others are veritable home runs on their home turf only to strike out ignominiously in less congenial cultural contexts (baseball metaphors outside America and Japan). Timing is an important consideration too, because there is a tide in the affairs of metaphor, which taken at the flood leads to the Fortune 500 (business as war analogies have surrendered in the aftermath of Iraq, whereas going green is the new red, white and blue).

Despite the enormous variation in life expectancy, the very best metaphors appear to enjoy an innings of approximately 10 years (Gummesson, 2001). *In Search of Excellence* and *Good to Great* are fairly typical in this regard. Not only are they predicated on the archetypal quest metaphor, but also the primary vehicle is composed of subordinate conceits. The chapter titles of *In Search of Excellence* include 'Stick to the Knitting', 'Close to the Customer' and 'Hands-on, Value-driven'. *Good to Great* is made up of 'The Hedgehog Concept', 'Level Five Leadership' and 'The Flywheel and the Doom Loop', among others. Business bestsellers, it seems, are a bit like Russian dolls, with figures within figures of speech. It remains to be seen whether *Good to Great* will last as long as its excellent predecessor, but the same heady mix of trope-inflated contents suggests that, if and when it stalls in due course, it won't be for lack of metaphorical horsepower (Rosenzweig, 2007).

Longevity is one thing, of course, lifestyle is something else again, insofar as the metaphorical persona that characterised an organisation or brand or institution in its salad days may alter considerably as its waistline thickens and middle-aged spread sets in. Enron evolved from the smartest guys in the room to the biggest crooks on the planet. Ryanair switched from an endearingly aggressive upstart to a big belligerent bully who pummelled all who stood in its path. Wal-Mart mutated from an affable Southern gentleman, who greeted everyone on entry, to a descendent of Dr Evil intent on total global domination. Nike began as a dedicated athlete who played for the love of the sport but was so determined to win that

it dabbled in dubious sweatshop practices. Google set out hoping to 'do no harm' but ended up as a spineless cybercensor for the People's Republic of China. Sony slipped from a sagacious Eastern guru, intuitively in tune with the needs of the market, to a forgetful senior citizen who sets laptops on fire and fails to deliver Playstations on schedule. The business school, according to Khurana's (2007) critical history of the institution, commenced as a knight in shining armour, aiming to raise the standards of dubious social activities, only to turn into a Mephistophelean schemer, who induces MBAs to sell their souls for infernal share options.

Marketing's customer-facing metaphor has likewise put on poundage in the 50 years since it emerged, mewling and puking, from Ted Levitt's overactive imagination. The search for 'satisfied' customers has been superseded by 'delighted' customers, which has been trumped in turn by 'enchanted' customers, 'enthralled' customers, 'enraptured' customers, et cetera. One wonders if marketing's middle-aged heart can continue to take the ventricular strain, especially given its diet of saccharine similes and anthropomorphic road-kill. The 'orgasmic' customer, which is surely the next natural step, will be the death of it, analogical defibrillation notwithstanding (Brown, 2002).

Change, clearly, comes with the metaphorical territory. Some metaphors develop, others turn to dust, yet others limp along, unloved and unlovable. Stage-type similes are a good example of the latter category, where the historical trajectory of a phenomenon is likened to a three- or four-phase process. The classic instance is the so-called three eras schema (production era/sales era/marketing era) beloved of introductory marketing textbooks and condemned for its historical inaccuracies by generation after generation of archive aficionados (Fullerton, 1988; Tadajewski, 2006; Wilkie and Moore, 2003). Yet, it refuses to go away. Why is that? Is it because textbook writers are lazy or incompetent? Is it because pedagogic tractability always takes precedence over historical accuracy? Is it because no one really cares that much about the past, since marketing is basically a forward-facing discipline (and practice)? Is it because the archive trufflers tend to adopt a hectoring, finger-wagging tone towards their irredeemably ignorant readership?

Speaking personally, I'm not sure that any of these propositions hold water. What I do believe is that humankind is awfully partial to stage-type analogies. Whether it be Stone Age/Bronze Age/Iron Age or Ancient/Medieval/Modern or thesis/antithesis/synthesis or indeed the multi-phase periodicities posited by Schiller, Lessing, Fichte, Vico, Comte, Marx and many more, intellectual history is replete with 'stagy' constructs (Brown, 1996b). These stages are doubtless just as dubious as marketing's three-era version but they persist despite the best efforts of hectoring archive hounds. I suspect, therefore, that we are in the presence of what Lakoff and Johnston term an 'experiential' metaphor, a deep-seated figure of speech predicated on humankind's corporeal existence, in this case the various well-defined phases of life's rich journey (see Zaltman and Zaltman, 2008). Or maybe, as socio-biologists believe, it has something to do with the limbic brain and humankind's hunting, gathering, slashing, burning, storytelling past on the primeval, post-Pleistocene plains of mother Africa. On the other hand, maybe it's all down to those pesky mega-metaphors called narratives, myths, allegories and archetypes.

THREE LITTLE PIGGIES

Irrespective of whether nature or nurture is at work, the mutability of metaphors is incontestable. Nevertheless, what are the mechanisms of metaphorical change? Are marketing metaphors Malthusian, whereby they increase exponentially while demand increases arithmetically and the upshot of the imbalance is war, famine, disease or death? Are marketing metaphors Veblenian, the corporate equivalent of conspicuous consumption, Tiffanyesque trinkets that are acquired

as a signifier of success, only to be cast aside as they trickle down to the hoi polloi? Are marketing metaphors Marxian, fluffy-bunny forms of false consciousness, the figurative face of exploitation, despoliation, waste, symbols of the internal contradictions of collapsing hyper-capitalism? Are marketing metaphors Porterian, a competitive arena where the five forces of substitutes, suppliers, rivals, new entrants and buyer power prevail, where the value chain metaphor captures the value of metaphors and where low cost tropes co-exist with differentiated expressions and focussed figures of speech?

A compelling case, no doubt, can be made for any or all of the aforementioned forces. However, the most plausible mechanism – or, rather, the mechanism that most marketers might subscribe to – is Darwinian. The fittest metaphors survive. Those that are best adapted to the managerial/academic environment are selected and reproduce successfully. Those that aren't die early and unloved. Many similes survive in specialist niches (dogs and cows in the Boston box), some are stranded when the environment changes (tsunami tropes in the aftermath of the Indian Ocean tragedy), yet others are able to adjust thanks to a lucky mutation (long an unpretentious paragon of purity, Dove soap is thriving as an unadulterated ambassador for 'real' beauty). Nevertheless, all battle it out in a bloody world of no-holds-barred competition, where tropes are red in tooth and claw and cliché. The ascent of management demands nothing less.

If metaphors are Darwinian and anthropomorphism in all its furry, finny, flighty forms is the single most popular conceit (Morris Holbrook, take a bow), there remains a profound philosophical conundrum for the learned zoologists of our discipline. What kind of animal is marketing theory, exactly? Much of course depends on what is meant, exactly, by 'theory', because the past half century of marketing science has failed to establish whether theory is a genus or a species or an order.

We can still enquire, though, whether marketing theory is a rare, wonderful or indeed endangered species like the panda, polar bear or bird of paradise. Is it, as many suspect, a mythical creature akin to the unicorn or the werewolf or the Loch Ness Monster? Is it a domestic herd animal of the cow, sheep or pig persuasion (i.e., a fancy word for vague but generally accepted rules of thumb)? Alternatively, is it, as the existence of this anthology implies, the elephant in the room, a gigantic reminder that prodigious amounts of marketing science have very few full-blown theories to show for 50 years of superhuman effort?

When push comes to shove – not easy with an elephant in the room – my theory is that theories are serpents.[10] They are enticing, enchanting, persuasive, pernicious, dangerous and deadly. They reside in the Tree of Knowledge and promise innocent academics the earth. They shed their skin, they speak with forked tongue and their venom is a hallucinogenic narcotic. Many marketing academics, unfortunately, are addicted to the snake extract called theory. They truly believe that with the aid of the scientific method, we can return to the Garden of Eden known as General Theory. They're deluding themselves. They're in postmodern Purgatory and they don't even know it. They're suffering from metaphorical myopia.

Thanks Ted.

NOTES

1 Like Levitt, Chanel was a whiz with aphorisms. Like Levitt, Coco had an irascible streak. Like Levitt, she was an outsider who became the ultimate insider (Madsen, 1990).

2 So fierce was the criticism that when 'Marketing Myopia' was first republished, in a 1962 anthology called *Innovation in Marketing*, it contained a lengthy, self-justifying footnote on the history of the railroad industry. This footnote, interestingly, mysteriously disappeared from subsequent republications (though it was replaced with a *mea culpa* on the citations front, where Levitt finally acknowledged his sources, while failing to mention his most obvious intellectual influences, Malcolm P. McNair and David Riesman among them). Quite a guy, our Ted.

3 Marketing Myopia has been reprinted at least four times in *HBR*, and it features in all manner of anthologised marketing 'classics'. Ted was never averse to recycling it in his own books, all of which were lightly reworked versions of previously published articles (see Brown, 2004).

4 J.R.R. Tolkien (1964: 15) termed these 'beast fables'. They include the works of Aesop, Aristophanes, Chaucer, Swift, Kafka and Kipling, as well as Orwell's *Animal Farm*, Adams' *Watership Down* and Potter's *Peter Rabbit* (consider also the cinematic oeuvres of Disney and Dreamworks).

5 The technical term for this is 'hypostasis'. The study of metaphor is full of technical terms and hair-splitting distinctions between figures of speech (Kövecses, 2002). For most practical purposes, the crucial distinctions are between metaphor (where one thing is described as another), simile (where one thing is 'like' something else) and metonymy (where the part stands for the whole).

6 The New Agers among you will know that Jiddu Krishnamurti (1895–1985) was an enormously famous sage of the inter-war era and that Koot-Hoomi was one of the so-called 'hidden masters' whose spiritual ideas were channelled through that charlatan nonpareil, Madame Blavatsky (see Roland, 1995).

7 As Morner and Rausch (1995) explain, chiasmus is a form of antithesis where the second half of a statement inverts the first half (e.g. 'Ask not what your country can do for you; ask what you can do for your country'.). SDL, in a nutshell, argues that marketing is less about products plus service than service plus products (Vargo and Lusch, 2004).

8 The 1980s also witnessed the eruption of post-structuralism, which had much to say on metaphor, not to mention Levi-Strauss's classic cogitations on totemism.

9 For all the execration, it cannot be denied that management-speak is an enormously fecund fount of figurative language.

10 Serpents are one of the oldest and most revered/feared human symbols (Becker, 1994). In addition to the Garden of Eden story, they are important in innumerable cultures, ranging from ancient Egypt (the cobra goddess) and Central America (the feathered serpent) to their manifestations in Indian and Norse mythology (Kundalini and Midgard serpents, respectively). For a detailed discussion of serpent symbolism, see Narby (1999).

REFERENCES

Allard, K. (2004) *Business as War: Battling for Competitive Advantage*. New York: John Wiley.

Ariely, D. (2008) *Predictably Irrational: The Hidden Forces That Shape Our Decisions*. London: HarperCollins.

Ball, P. (2005) *Critical Mass: How One Thing Leads to Another*. New York: Arrow.

Bayley, S. (2008) 'Unravelled by Technical Hitches', *The Times*, 5 April, 12.

Becker, U. (1994) *The Element Encyclopedia of Symbols*. Shaftesbury: Element.

Bennis, W.G. and O'Toole, J. (2005) 'How Business Schools Lost Their Way', *Harvard Business Review*, 83(5): 96–104.

Blythe, J. (2006) *A Very Short, Fairly Interesting and Reasonably Cheap Book About Studying Marketing*. London: Sage.

Booth, W.C. (1978) 'Metaphor as rhetoric: the problem of evaluation', in S. Sacks (ed.) *On Metaphor*, Chicago: University of Chicago Press, pp. 47–70.

Brock, G. (2008) 'Over to Me', *Times Literary Supplement*, 4 April, 14.

Brown, S. (1995) *Postmodern Marketing*. London: Routledge.

Brown, S. (1996a) 'Art or Science? Fifty Years of Marketing Debate', *Journal of Marketing Management*, 12(4): 243–267.

Brown, S. (1996b) 'Trinitarianism, the Eternal Evangel and the Three Eras Schema', in S. Brown, J. Bell and D. Carson (eds) *Marketing Apocalypse: Eschatology, Escapology and the Illusion of the End*, London: Routledge, pp. 23–43.

Brown, S. (2001) *Marketing – The Retro Revolution*. London: Sage.

Brown, S. (2002a) 'The Specter of Kotlerism: A Literary Appreciation', *European Journal of Management*, 20(2): 129–146.

Brown, S. (2002b) 'Reading Wroe: On the Biopoetics of Alderson's Functionalism', *Marketing Theory*, 2(3): 243–271.

Brown, S. (2004a) 'Theodore Levitt: The Ultimate Writing Machine', *Marketing Theory*, 4(3): 209–238.

Brown, S. (2004b) 'O Customer, Where Art Thou?' *Business Horizons*, 47(4): 61–70.

Brown, S. (2005) *Wizard! Harry Potter's Brand Magic*. London: Cyan.

Brown, S. (2008) *Fail Better! Stumbling to Success in Sales and Marketing*. London: Cyan.

Christensen, C.M. (1997) *The Innovator's Dilemma: When New Technologies Cause Great Firms to Fail*. Boston: Harvard Business School Press.

Day, G.S. and Schoemaker, P. (2006) *Peripheral Vision: Detecting the Weak Signals That Will Make or Break Your Company*. Boston: Harvard Business School Press.

Dixon, D.F. (2008) 'Consumer Sovereignty, Democracy, and the Marketing Concept: A Macromarketing Perspective', in M. Tadajewski and D. Brownlie (eds) *Critical Marketing: Issues in Contemporary Marketing*, Chichester: Wiley, pp. 67–83.

Durgee, J.F. and Chen, M. (2006) 'Metaphors, Needs and New Product Ideation', in R.W. Belk (ed.) *Handbook of Qualitative Research Methods in Marketing*, Cheltenham: Edward Elgar, pp. 291–302.

Florida, R.L. (2003) *The Rise of the Creative Class and How It's Transforming Work, Leisure, Community and Everyday Life*. New York: Basic Books.

Florida, R.L. (2005) *The Flight of the Creative Class: The New Global Competition for Talent*. New York: HarperCollins.

Franklin, C. (2003) *Why Innovation Fails: Hard-Won Lessons for Business*. London: Spiro Press.

Fullerton, R. (1988) 'How Modern is 'Modern' Marketing? Marketing's Evolution and the Myth of the Production Era', *Journal of Marketing*, 52(1): 7–32.

Gilmore, J.H. and Pine, B.J. (2007) *Authenticity: What Consumers Really Want*. Boston: Harvard Business School Press.

González-Crussi, F. (2006) *On Seeing: Things Seen, Unseen, and Obscene*. London: Duckworth.

Gummesson, E. (2001) 'Are Current Research Approaches in Marketing Leading Us Astray?', *Marketing Theory*, 1(1): 27–48.

Hirschman, E.C. (2007) 'Metaphor in the Marketplace', *Marketing Theory*, 7(3): 227–248.

Howkins, J. (2002) *The Creative Economy: How People Make Money From Ideas*. London: Penguin.

Humphrys, J. (2005) *Lost for Words: The Mangling and Manipulating of the English Language*. London: Hodder & Staughton.

James, B.G. (1985) *Business Wargames: Business Strategy for Executives in the Trenches of Market Warfare*. Harmondsworth: Penguin.

Jaworski, B. and Kohli, A.K. (2006) 'Co-creating the voice of the consumer', in R.F. Lusch and

S.L. Vargo (eds) *The Service-Dominant Logic of Marketing: Dialog, Debate, and Directions*, Armonk: M.E. Sharpe, pp. 109–117.

Jay, M. (1994) *Downcast Eyes: The Denigration of Vision in Twentieth-Century French Thought*. Berkeley: University of California Press.

Joy, A. and Sherry, J.F., Jr. (2003) 'Speaking of Art as Embodied Imagination: A Multi-Sensory Approach to Understanding Aesthetic Experience', *Journal of Consumer Research*, 30(September): 259–282.

Joyner, M. (2008) *Mind Control Marketing: How Everyday People are Using Forbidden Mind Control Psychology and Ruthless Military Tactics to Make Millions Online*. New York: Steel Icarus.

Khurana, R. (2007) *From Higher Aims to Hired Hands: The Social Transformation of American Business Schools and the Unfulfilled Promise of Management as a Profession*. Princeton: Princeton University Press.

Kitchen, P.J. (2008) *Marketing: Metaphors and Metamorphosis*. Basingstoke: Palgrave Macmillan.

Knowles, M. and Moon, R. (2006) *Introducing Metaphor*. Abingdon: Routledge.

Kotler, P. (2008) *FAQs on Marketing. Answered by the Guru of Marketing*. London: Marshall Cavendish Business.

Kotler, P. and Singh, R. (1981) 'Marketing Warfare in the 1980s', *Journal of Business Strategy*, (Winter), 30–41.

Kövecses, Z. (2002) *Metaphor: A Practical Introduction*. Oxford: Oxford University Press.

Lakoff, G. and Johnson, M. (1980) *Metaphors We Live By*. Chicago: University of Chicago Press.

Law, J. (2006) *Big Pharma: How the World's Biggest Drug Companies Control Illness*. London: Constable & Robinson.

Levin, D.M. (1997) *Sites of Visison: The Discursive Construction of Sight in the History of Philosophy*. Boston: MIT Press.

Levitt, T. (1960a) 'Marketing Myopia', *Harvard Business Review*, 38(4): 45–56.

Levitt, T. (1960b) 'M-R Snake Dance', *Harvard Business Review*, 38(6): 76–84.

Levitt, T. (1986) 'The Marketing Imagination', in *The Marketing Imagination, New Expanded Edition*, New York: Free Press, pp. 127–140.

Levitt, T. (1991a) *Thinking About Management*. New York: Free Press.

Levitt, T. (1991b) 'Fast History', in *Thinking About Management*, New York: Free Press, pp. 70–72.

Lewontin, R.C. (1993) *Biology as Ideology: The Doctrine of DNA*. New York: HarperPerennial.

Lunn, P. (2008) *Basic Instincts: Human Nature and the New Economics*. London: Marshall Cavendish Business.

Maclaran, P. and Stevens, L. (2008) 'Thinking Through Theory: Materialising the Oppositional Imagination', in M. Tadajewski and D. Brownlie (eds) *Critical Marketing: Issues in Contemporary Marketing*, Chichester: Wiley, pp. 345–361.

Madsen, A. (1990) *Chanel: A Woman of Her Own*. New York: Henry Holt.

Marion, G. (1993) 'The Marketing Management Discourse: What's New Since the 1960s?' in M.J. Baker (ed.) *Perspectives on Marketing Mnagement*, Volume 3, Chichester: Wiley, pp. 143–168.

Morner, K. and Rausch, R. (1995) *NTC's Dictionary of Literary Terms*. Lincolnwood: NTC Publishing.

Narby, J. (1999) *The Cosmic Serpent: DNA and the Origins of Knowledge*. New York: Putnam.

Ogle, R. (2008) *Smart World: Breakthrough Creativity and the New Science of Ideas*. London: Marshall Cavendish Business.

Ortony, A. (1993) *Metaphor and Thought*. Cambridge: Cambridge University Press.

Orwell, G. (1962) 'Politics and the English language', in *Inside the Whale and Other Essays*, London: Penguin, pp. 143–157.

Peters, T. and Waterman, R.H. (1982) *In Search of Excellence: Lessons From America's Best-Run Companies*. New York: HarperBusiness.

Pink, D.H. (2005) *A Whole New Mind: Moving From the Information Age to the Conceptual Age*. New York: Riverhead Books.

Punter, D. (2007) *Metaphor*. Abingdon: Routledge.

Roland, P. (1995) *Revelations: Wisdom of the Ages*. Berkeley: Ulysses Press.

Rosenzweig, P. (2007) *The Halo Effect ... and the Eight Other Business Delusions That Deceive Managers*. New York: Free Press.

Scott, L.M. (1994) 'Images in Advertising: The Need for a Theory of Visual Rhetoric', *Journal of Consumer Research*, 21(2): 252–274.

Sontag, S. (1991) *Illness as Metaphor: AIDS and Its Metaphors*. London: Penguin.

Stern, B.B. (1988) 'Medieval Allegory: Roots of Advertising Strategy for the Mass Market', *Journal of Marketing*, 52(3): 84–94.

Strunk, W. and White, E.B. (1959) *The Elements of Style*. New York: Longman.

Surowiecki, J. (2005) *The Wisdom of Crowds: Why the Many are Smarter Than the Few*. London: Abacus.

Tadajewski, M. (2006) 'Remembering Motivation Research: Toward an Alternative Genealogy of Interpretive Consumer Research', *Marketing. Theory*, 6(4): 429–466.

Tadajewski, M. and Brownlie, D. (2008) *Critical Marketing: Issues in Contemporary Marketing*. Chichester: Wiley.

Tapp, A. (2005) 'Why Practitioners Don't Read Our Articles and What We Should Do About It', *The Marketing Review*, 5(1): 3–13.

Tapscott, D. and Williams, A.D. (2006) *Wikinomics: How Mass Collaboration Changes Everything*. New York: Portfolio.

The Economist (2004) 'How 51 Gorillas Can Make You Seriously Rich', *The Economist*, August 21: 77.

Tolkien, J.R.R. (1964) *Tree and Leaf*. London: HarperCollins.

Tynan, C. (1997) 'A Review of the Marriage Analogy in Relationship Marketing', *Journal of Marketing Management*, 13(7): 695–703.

Vargo, S.L. and Lusch, R.F. (2004) 'Evolving to a New Dominant Logic for Marketing', *Journal of Marketing*, 68(1): 1–17.

Watson, D. (2004) *Gobbledygook: How Clichés, Sludge and Management-Speak Are Strangling Our Public Language*. London: Atlantic Books.

Watts, D.J. (2003) *Six Degrees: The Science of a Connected Age*. London: William Heinemann.

Whichelow, C. and Murray, H. (2007) *It's Not Rocket Science and Other Irritating Modern Clichés*. London: Piatkus.

Wilkie, W.L. and Moore, E.S. (2003) 'Scholarly Research in Marketing: Exploring the '4 Eras' of Thought Development', *Journal of Public Policy and Marketing*, 22(Fall): 116–146.

Wood, J. (2008) *How Fiction Works*. London: Jonathan Cape.

Wright, L.T., Jayawardhena, C. and Dennis, C. (2008) 'Editorial: Marketing Myopia', *Journal of Marketing Management*, 24(1–2): 131–134.

Zaltman, G. (2003) *How Customers Think: Essential Insights Into the Mind of the Market*. Boston: Harvard Business School Press.

Zaltman, G. and Zaltman, L. (2008) *Marketing Metaphoria: What Deep Metaphors Reveal About the Minds of Consumers*. Boston: Harvard Business School Press.

Zuboff, S. and Maxmin, J. (2003) *The Support Economy: Why Corporations Are Failing Individuals and the Next Episode of Capitalism*. London: Allen Lane.

The Impact of Theory on Representations of the Consumer

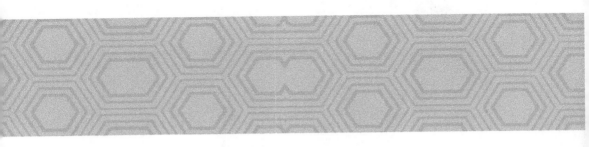

Representing Global Consumers: Desire, Possession, and Identity

Russell W. Belk

INTRODUCTION

Three themes that reverberate throughout world consumption are desire (wanting things), possession (having things) and identity (being a certain kind of person through the things we have). Together, these are the engines of consumer culture. They are ancient and modern, ubiquitous and personal, benign and invidious. Even though these behavioural processes are pervasive, this need not mean that they involve the same consumer goods or have the same impact everywhere. Therefore, besides considering the nature of these three phenomena, this chapter will consider the degree and nature of cultural variations affecting them. This discussion requires a consideration of globalization as it affects consumption. The aim is to better understand how globalization affects desire, possession, and identity. At stake here is not only the degree to which the world's consumers want the same brands and styles, but also larger questions such as whether, through consumption, the cultures of the world are homogenizing. Can there be such a thing as global cinema? Are standards of beauty converging on a world standard?

Are there global cuisines? Is world music truly global? With increasingly global Christmas celebrations, are we beginning to see the emergence of global consumption holidays? And if the answers to some of these questions are in the negative, then – What are the processes of resisting, localizing or otherwise dealing with these global influences?

DESIRE

Consumer desire is a passionate emotion that differs from want and need in several significant ways (Belk et al., 2003). The model that underlies need conceptualizations is that of natural urges like hunger and thirst. In such views, these needs decline in urgency once they are satisfied and they can be satisfied by a variety of things serving a particular category of needs. Thus, a variety of foods can satisfy our hunger, and a variety of beverages can satisfy our thirst. Because needs are seen as natural, their satisfaction is regarded as a matter of necessity, even when they are in the realm that Maslow (1970) called higher-order needs – needs for such things as love and status. In contrast to needs, wants and wishes are regarded as less imperative and may focus either on a general category of things, such as a vacation, or a specific object like a particular model of automobile. Rather than appearing to be natural and bodily, wants are thought to originate in the mind and are regarded as a matter of personal preference. In contrast to the imperial necessities of needs and the fanciful wishes of consumer wants, consumer desires instead involve a passionate fixation on a particular object. Our desires are both felt at the bodily level as well as envisioned in mental images. In distinguishing desire from needs and wants, Belk et al. (2000: 99) contrast their use in English vernacular:

> We burn and are aflame with desire, we are pierced by or riddled with desire; we are sick or ache with desire; we are seized, ravished, and overcome by desire; we are mad, crazy, insane, giddy, blinded, or delirious with desire; we are enraptured, enchanted, suffused, and enveloped by desire; our desire is fierce, hot, intense, passionate, incandescent, and irresistible; and we pine, languish, waste away, or die of unfulfilled desire. Try substituting need or want in any of these metaphors and the distinction becomes immediately apparent. Needs are anticipated, controlled, denied, postponed, prioritized, planned for, addressed, satisfied, fulfilled, and gratified through logical instrumental processes. Desires, on the other hand, are overpowering; something we give in to; something that takes control of us and totally dominates our thoughts, feelings, and actions. Desire awakens, seizes teases, titillates, and arouses. We battle, resist, and struggle with, or succumb, surrender to and indulge our desires. Passionate potential consumers are consumed by desire.

The focus here is on desire for material objects of consumption, but the same emotions are found in passionate romantic love towards a particular person (Ahuvia, 2005).

Besides its compelling intensity, desire in consumer societies has been found to be a state of anxious anticipation that is itself pleasurable and desirable (Belk et al., 2003). That is, we desire to desire things and become despondent if we have nothing that we long for. We use magazines, the Internet and window shopping to help fuel our desire

for new things in consumption categories that interest us. However, desire is also perceived to be dangerous if we let it take too much control of our behaviour. Therefore, there is a tension between the seductive possibilities of things desired and the moral forces keeping these desires in check (Belk et al., 2003).

Consumer desires have arguably become the dominant focus of our hope for a better future within consumer cultures. These material hopes can become not only aspirational markers of personal achievements, belonging, and status, but also can act as ends in themselves regardless of their transformative potential. This is seen vividly, for example, in the use of rich white suburban brands like Tommy Hilfiger by poor black inner-city youth to claim social status, as well as use by white suburban kids of cool inner-city brands like Phat Farm to claim hip status (Kotlowitz, 1999). Although pursuing hope and happiness through human relationships, occupational achievements, or religious fulfilment may ultimately be more conducive to actually achieving happiness, these pursuits increasingly appear to take a back seat to material desires (Wuthnow, 1994).

POSSESSION AND IDENTITY

Within a consumer culture, it is difficult to separate possession and identity. The dictum that you are what you have becomes an implicit creed in such a culture and supports the notion that we have an extended self that includes certain of our possessions, whether as individuals, families or larger groups of owners (Belk, 1988). Once we come to regard something as ours we are reluctant to give it up for what it is worth or even for several times what it might cost to replace it. Experimental researchers call this the endowment effect and explain it in terms of irrationally valuing what we have more than others do (e.g. Kahneman et al., 1990). Nevertheless, through the notion of extended self, we can appreciate a more reasonable explanation for such valuations than the irrational quirks that some suggest (e.g. Ariely, 2008). When we commit to and subsequently live with a possession, even for a short length of time, it not only serves as a symbol of our tastes and judgement, but it also absorbs our memories and histories that have been lived out with this possession. Consider a puppy that we buy from a breeder. At the moment of choice, we may well be relatively indifferent to one puppy versus others in the same litter. However, two weeks later, the situation is likely to be very different. Not only have we invested time and love in caring for and beginning to train the dog, but chances are we also have begun to regard it as having a distinct and unique personality. We have given the dog a name, fed it, cleaned up after it, and held it in our arms. It has become endearing by virtue of its dependence on us and we have also bonded with it and become attached (Belk, 1996a). Similar feelings of attachment are not restricted to living possessions like a companion animal and can also be evoked by inanimate objects (Kleine and Baker, 2004). In related conceptualizations, Kopytoff (1986) calls such objects 'singular' rather than 'commodities', and Belk et al. (1989) call them 'sacred' rather than 'profane'.

As McCracken (1986) theorizes, we do not gain a sense of possession of things simply by purchasing and taking physical control of them. Rather, we often must perform possession rituals that may include cleaning, showing off, photographing, and talking about our new acquisition. A 'new' used car or apartment may be symbolically scrubbed, no matter what state of cleanliness we receive it in. We also personalize these objects by placing our stuff in them in order to make them truly our own. We thereby remove traces of former owners and impose our own identity on the possession. However, it is not necessarily just a matter of us marking the object as ours. For certain objects like new skis, a new kayak, or a new book, in order to feel that it is ours and a part of our extended self, we may well also need to gain some sense of competency and control, if not mastery, of the possession (Belk, 1988).

The initial formulation of the self extended through our possessions envisioned a concentric set of levels of self surrounding a core, unextended, self (Belk, 1988). These concentric circles included not only possessions that are progressively less central to self, but also aggregate levels of self progressing from the individual to the family to more distant groups with which we identify. At the aggregate level of nation, we incorporate such shared national symbols as flags, anthems, national parks, and monuments as part of our extended self. More recently, Tian and Belk (2005) found that rather than this seamless progression from individual to aggregate selves, there may also be competing selves across group contexts. In particular, they found that for professionals, the work self and the home or family self may vie for centrality in our awareness through the presence of material objects signifying one or the other. The work self may extend into the home and family via cell phones, pagers, e-mail, computers, and other ways in which we bring work home. At the same time, home and family self may extend into the workplace though photos, mementos, and creations such as children's drawings, as well as the same telephones and e-mail devices that link us in the other direction to our work self at home.

It is clear that most of our possessions become something more than they were when they left the factory or shop door. They become embedded in our aspirations, our thoughts, and our lives. They are a primary vehicle through which we express ourselves and make various identity claims. They may represent our hopes and ideals through the process that McCracken (1988) calls 'displaced meaning'. When we envision our life as vastly better in another place or time – either past or future – we often anchor it to an object or set of objects. Looking backward or to another place, we may treasure a photograph, souvenir, or other reminder of this time or place (Belk, 1991a; Csikszentmihalyi and Rochberg-Halton, 1981; Stewart, 1984). Looking forward, which we are more prone to do when we are younger, we may represent a future time and place through other representations or in terms of a concrete aspirational object, as in 'When I get my Porsche/house/spouse ...'. The implied consequence here is that everything will be wonderful and I will experience a Cinderella-like total transformation. This is often made manifest for young couples in the lavish dream wedding (e.g. Leeds-Hurwitz, 2002; Otnes and Pleck, 2003) as well as the set of elaborate desires made concrete in the wedding gift registry that has come to characterize Western weddings (Purbrick, 2007).

Belk (1991b) discusses numerous additional categories of possessions in which we often invest intense meanings, including perfumes, jewellery, clothing, foods, homes, vehicles, grave goods, religious icons, medicines, gifts, collections, money, and pornography. He suggests five indicants that we have elevated the meaning of a possession to a numinous level: (1) unwillingness to sell for market value; (2) willingness to buy with little regard for price; (3) nonsubstitutability; (4) unwillingness to discard; and (5) feelings of elation/depression due to having or not having the object. All of this suggests a highly personal relationship between us and at least certain of our things. Nevertheless, as Belk (1988) points out, object relations are seldom this isolated and almost always involve other people, either as audience, rival, or co-owner of meaningful possessions. Rather than person–thing relationships, our material relations are therefore person–thing–person relationships. One vivid illustration of this person–thing–person triangle is in the phenomenon of conspicuous consumption (Mason, 1999; Veblen, 1899). Here we show off not for ourselves but for others. However, there is also the interpersonal issue of other's envy of our possessions to contend with. Although consumer envy is likely to be more 'benign' than 'malicious' (wishing the owner of the desired object harm), we nevertheless have to walk a line between provoking and avoiding others' envy if we do not want to be resented and regarded as being overly ostentatious and superficially focused on consumption

(Belk, 2008). Other types of interpersonal object relations such as communication through gift giving and sharing our possessions with others (Belk, 1996b, 2007) are focused more on the aggregate extended self rather than the core individual self. These processes embrace the person–thing–person relationship less egoistically.

GLOBAL CONSUMPTION

Global and local consumers

I think it appropriate to entitle this section 'Global Consumption' rather than something like 'The Global Consumer', in order to avoid implying that in a high-level global economy, we all want and aspire to the same things. For this is what is often implied by the use of the terms 'consumer culture' or 'consumer society' (e.g. Glickman, 1999; Goodwin et al., 1997; Schor and Holt, 2000; Strasser et al., 1998), as well as by many treatments of 'globalization' (e.g. Bauman, 1998; Canclini, 2001; Ritzer, 2004; Rollin, 1989). Indeed, Keyfitz (1982) suggested that consumers of the world are increasingly desirous of acquiring a 'standard package' of goods that includes a house, a car, a refrigerator, a television, and the ability to travel. Although there appears to be some truth to this contention at the scale proposed, for most middle-class consumers this is a bare minimum on a list of desiderata that includes a revolving host of brand name luxury goods in categories such as clothes, jewellery, perfumes, handbags, fountain pens, watches, alcohol, cellular phones, electronics, cars, and more. Still, there are several levels at which the claim of global consumer desires breaks down. At a strictly utilitarian level, climate, geography, bodily differences, income differences, and varied infrastructures will preclude uniformity in a number of areas of consumption. We can expect to see few snow skis in Fiji and few surfboards in Nepal, for example.

At a more cultural level, factors such as religious prescriptions and proscriptions, languages, cultural values and norms, and other such traditions further restrict cross-cultural homogeneity in consumer preferences. For example, dietary rules and dress norms among Hindus, Muslims, and Jews will affect some food preferences and clothing selections. However, this has not stopped McDonald's from modifying its menu to appeal to Hindus (Watson, 1997) or haute couture designers from making clothing for covered women (Balasescu, 2003; Jones, 2007). And, at a more subtle level, consumers in various cultures may superficially adopt the same entertainment programmes, theme parks, and soft drinks and yet interpret them and fit them into local cultures in quite different ways than consumers in other cultures do (e.g. Brannen, 1992; Foster, 2008; Ger and Belk, 1996; Hendry, 2000; Liebes and Katz, 1990; Miller, 1998; Wilk, 1993). For example, Russian immigrants to Israel watched the American television series *Dallas*, but rather than watching in awe of the wealthy Texas family it portrayed, the viewers used the programme to critique and ridicule American values. Cultural norms also matter. In both the West and the East, the consumption of luxury designer brands is popular. From a Western perspective, we think of this as a means of conspicuous consumption, of standing out, and of showing off our wealth. Nevertheless, according to one study of women in their 20s in Tokyo, 94 per cent owned at least one Louis Vuitton item, 92 per cent owned at least one Gucci piece, and more than 50 per cent of the sample also owned Prada and Chanel (Chadha and Husband, 2006: 1). With such a preponderance of people owning these items, it would be conspicuous and make someone stand out if they did NOT own such goods. Owning them is more a matter of fitting in than standing out in this cultural context.

Global and local consumption

The degree and nature of global versus local consumer desires and consumption may be best seen in examining a few specific product categories where consumption is alleged to be global in character. I will briefly consider three such categories: food, music, and holidays, with a narrower focus on Chinese food, American rap music, and global Christmas celebrations.

Chinese food

Food is highly expressive of culture and one of the things emigrants miss most when they move to a new culture. Food is sufficiently important in China that, rather than greet people by asking 'How are you?', it is more common to ask 'Have you eaten yet?' (Farquhar, 2002). In the past 200 years, thanks both to European colonialism and the Chinese diaspora, 'Chinese food' has spread throughout much of the world. In some cases, different Chinese cuisines are featured such as Cantonese, Sichuan, and Shandong. A familiar lament of overseas Chinese (like immigrants from other cultures encountering foreign restaurant versions of their home cuisines) is that it is not 'real' Chinese food, but has instead been modified to suit local tastes and expectations. For instance, chop suey and chow mein are Chinese–American dishes originally made from leftovers, and the fortune cookie is virtually unknown in China, Taiwan, and Hong Kong.

Nevertheless, even in Chinese homelands, culinary arts are an invented tradition, and Chinese food has globalized via creolization within China just as it has globalized in non-Chinese cultures. For example, Hong Kong Chinese pride themselves on a particular form of dim sum called *yumcha* (literally 'drink tea' in Cantonese), but have incorporated within it things like sashimi from Japan, chicken feet from Thailand, fresh cream cakes from the West, black glutinous rice from Singapore, lotus seed cakes from Malaysia, and Japanese-style salmon salad (Tam, 2001). In addition, a 'Cantonese' *yumcha* may include Sichuan clams, Beijing red-bean cake, Shanghai dumplings, and Xiamen vermicelli rolls. None of this impedes the perception that *yumcha* is distinctly Hongkongese.

Likewise, the alteration of Chinese foods in cultures as diverse as Hawaii and Papua New Guinea does nothing to deter these foods from being perceived as markers of Chineseness by Chinese immigrants and expatriates (Wu, 2002; Wu and Cheung, 2002). Class is further demarcated within Chinese food and beverages, and these gradations are used, for instance, within Hong Kong to distinguish Hong Kong people from visiting mainland Chinese (Belk and Groves, 1998; Ma, 2001).

The counterpart of Chinese food outside of China is Western food within China. While McDonald's, Kentucky Fried Chicken, and Pizza Hut are all popular Western fast foods in Chinese cities, they are commonly regarded as not 'real food', and their consumption as not considered 'real eating' (Wu and Cheebeng, 2001). Adult consumers often report that they find the taste of hamburgers to be unappealing and strange (Watson, 2005). But one thing is clear: these restaurants represent Westernness, modernity, and hip status (Yan, 2000). And while adults raised on Chinese food may disdain hamburgers, Chinese children are learning to love them. The younger generation of only children or 'little emperors' are increasingly affluent and are learning to order their own food (to the initial shock of older Chinese) at as young an age as three or four (Jing, 2000; Watson, 2005). Furthermore, as argued in the preceding section, within China, adaptation has taken place, and McDonald's in China is not the same as McDonald's elsewhere. Critiques that see this as akin to America's earlier brand imperialism in Europe (De Grazia, 2005; Domosh, 2006) are too facile. There have been adaptations to McDonald's menu in China, like offering rice and red-bean pies, as well as more fundamental alterations like changing from a policy of quick table turnover to a place to leisurely pass time and feel safe (Yan, 2000).

Rap music

In considering the global spread of African American rap music, we should first note that like the spread of clothing brands, this music has spread within the United States from the poor black inner city to the affluent white suburbs (Kitwana, 2005). Can this same diffusion extend to more distant cultures? In order to answer this question, we must first consider that nature of rap music and its ties to other types of consumption. Rap is a part of hip-hop culture, which originated among African American and Afro-Caribbean youth in the South Bronx of New York City. It also includes wild-style graffiti or 'tagging', break dancing, certain styles of dress and language, and deejays 'scratching' or mixing music (Hebdige, 2004; Rose, 1994). Rap itself is a form of rhymed toasting and boasting to the beat of highly syncopated electronic music. In the popular variant of gangsta rap, it draws on pimp ('mack') toasting, which may be seen as a variant of the trickster motif (Quinn, 2005). It is a form of signifying that involves aphoristic phrasing, punning, word play, spontaneity, improvisation, metaphor, braggadocio, indirection, circumlocution, and suggestiveness (Smitherman, 1977: 94). Rap is primarily a masculine or hypermasculine musical form (Perry, 2004).

Rap music and the hip-hop culture from which it emerged are generally accepted to be the latest instantiation of coolness (e.g. Kitwana, 2005). Rap music embraces the basic character of cool rebelliousness. Gangsta rap joins a long tradition of romanticizing the outlaw and trickster. The related culture of hip-hop has given us distinctive fashions and grooming styles that act as 'marker goods' (Douglas and Isherwood, 1979) signalling coolness. Even sunglasses that became a part of the cool jazz persona in the 1930s continue among rap artists and fans as part of the cool mask. And rap is nothing if not an attitude and style of nonconformity that opposes the mainstream. Ironically, this same rebellious nonconformity sells products, especially to teenagers seeking to break free of family influence and establish their independence and identity. Sometimes a company gets lucky enough to have their brand become cool with no effort on their part, as with the 1986 rap hit 'My Adidas' by Run-DMC (Longville and Leone, 2006) or when the

British skinheads and subsequent youth subcultures adopted Dr. (Doc) Martens boots (Roach, 2003). Klein (2000) reports that brands like Nike, Pony, and Stussy were so anxious to have cool kids and rap musicians wear their clothing that they gave them free clothing and did not attempt to stop counterfeiting of their brands. With rap, cool has also shifted from being disdainful of consumption to celebrating consumption. Bling bling (the ostentatious consumption first popularized by rap musician Brian 'Baby Birdman' Williams in 1999) is anything but subtle. High-end brands like Cristal champagne (although now fallen from the grace of coolness), Gucci, and Mercedes are mentioned with great frequency in rap lyrics (Hip Hop, 2003). Advertisers also borrow bling to lend cool status to their brands. For example, an ad for The Game athletic shoes by 310 that appeared in the hip-hop magazine *Vibe*, in April 2006, showed the shoes draped around the neck of a heavily tattooed young black male standing with a menacing look in front of a Bentley Continental GT Coupe (see Belk, 2006: 85).

At first glance, it appears that rap music has globalized with both sales of American rap musicians and local rap artists in countries around the world. In addition, the baggy trousers, oversized shirts, and baseball caps worn backwards by American rap groups have been adopted by youth cultures abroad, including Polish teens (Antoszek, 2003). But many American rap words and phrases like 'the hood', 'homies', 'the yard', and 'yo', translated badly into Polish rap. And although hip-hop culture is also quite popular in the Netherlands, gangsta rap is not. The reasons lie in the welfare structure of the country and the absence of inner-city ghettos or 'hoods', gang violence, and guns, all of which make it hard to identify with the themes of American gangsta rap (Krims, 2002). As a result, a new hybrid form of music and culture called Nederhop has arisen on the Dutch rap scene (Sansone, 1995). Furthermore, rap and some of its related products may be globally adopted, but their meanings are locally adapted. Thanks in part to such localization, the spread of rap

has hardly been limited to North American suburbs and Europe. Youth subcultures in India (Karkaria, 2004), Australia (Martino, 2000), New Zealand (Mitchell, 2001), Greenland (Kjeldgaard and Askegaard, 2006), Japan (Condry, 2001), China (Wang, 2005), and Korea (Morelli, 2001), for example, have also embraced the music and its associated consumption patterns. In each case, there is also local adaptation of cool consumption, as for example with Greenlandic youth coveting cool snowmobiles. This suggests that the status that rap-related coolness conveys is not a universal currency that can be used anywhere. Rather, it is a microcultural capital that can only be converted into economic, social, and sexual capital largely within the peer group to whom one is cool. But commonalities remain. To gain this sort of cool capital, it is necessary not only to stand out and be different, but also to be, or at least appear to be, indifferent to the opinions of others. Milner (2004: 60) notes that such pursuit of power through indifference to worldly sanctions is otherwise reserved for saints or holy men. But unlike saints, the cool need not renounce worldly pleasures; they only need to seem indifferent towards them. If such cool indifference towards the consumption commodities we once longed for is instead real and the unemotional mask of coolness is no longer a mask, this may be a metaphor for jaded consumer culture generally.

Christmas

A third consumption context in which to consider global consumption representation is the spread of holidays and especially that of Christmas. Christmas has become a key ritual celebrating consumption, and it appears to increasingly transcend religious and geographic boundaries. It is no longer only a Christian celebration, but is increasingly found in Muslim, Jewish, Hindu, and Buddhist cultures as well. It is celebrated in such non-Christian countries as Japan, China, Turkey, Thailand, India, and Egypt. This global diffusion of Christmas is possible, because it is the secular rather than the religious aspects of the festival that have become dominant. These include Christmas decorations, gift-giving, Christmas cards, Christmas foods, carols, and icons like Christmas trees, Santa Claus, snowmen, and reindeer. Historically, Christmas emerged from earlier holidays marking the Northern Hemisphere winter solstice. The Roman festivals of Kalends and Saturnalia were among the predecessors of Christmas, as was the Persian celebration of the sun god Mithras. In the second and third centuries AD, the Christian church sought to co-opt these 'pagan' celebrations by inventing Christmas (Count and Count, 1997). Even the yearly criticisms of contemporary secular celebrations of Christmas as orgies of consumption excess are not new. Libanius (1977) reported strong criticism of the lavish feasting, gift-giving, decorations, spending, and gambling associated with Kalends and Saturnalia in ancient Rome (Miller, 1993). Thus, recent criticisms of the consumerization of Christmas (e.g. Flynn, 1993; Horsley and Tracy, 2001) are hardly new.

Celebrating Christmas may be a sign of joining global consumer culture. It was also a sign of becoming American among some Jewish immigrants (Heinze 1990; Schandler and Weintraub, 2007). But rather than being consumer-driven, it appears that it is retail merchants and manufacturers who have largely driven the popularity of global Christmas as a way to increase sales and profits (Santino, 1996; Schmidt, 1995). For many, Christmas sales have become the key determinant of whether the year is profitable. By encouraging consumers to join the festivities by buying luxurious gifts for family and friends, it is hoped that normal caution will be thrown to the wind and the exuberance of the season will lead to spending with abandon.

The fact that Christmas is now being celebrated globally need not mean that it is celebrated in a uniform way. In Japan and China, for example, Christmas is a couples' holiday in much the same way that Valentine's Day is in the West (and in these countries too, for that matter). Japanese and Chinese young couples go to restaurants, bars, and hotels for Christmas rather than gathering around the family hearth at home (Belk and Kimura, 2005; Moeran and Skov, 1993; Zhao and Belk, 2005). Japanese Christmas gifts are sold in different sections of department stores than gifts for Seibo, a key Japanese holiday that occurs about the same time of year. The merchandise is different (e.g. different foods and liquors are decorated and sold as Christmas gifts versus Seibo gifts), and there is strong emphasis on buying a Christmas cake. Among these cakes, there are different European traditions such as Italian, German, and Austrian Christmas cakes, even if the tradition is dying in these countries. And unlike the hybrid American Santa Claus, the Japanese Santas are national as well with distinct figures identified as Norwegian, Finnish, or Swedish (Bowler, 2005; Curtis, 1995; Nissenbaum, 1996; Van Renterghem, 1995; Restad, 1995; Siefker, 1997). Still, the conflict between Santa Claus and his European predecessor figures is not as evident in Japan as it sometimes is in Europe (Belk, 1987, 1993). In the Netherlands, the competition between Santa Claus and the Dutch figure of Sinter Klaus (and his sinister assistant, Zwarte Piet) led to a gradual replacement of Sinter Klaus by Santa in advertising and iconography. In order to preserve the tradition of Sinter Klaus Eve on 5 December, the Dutch banned advertising with Santa until after Sinter Klaus arrived on his white horse.

Like all invented traditions, Christmas continues to evolve. But rather than being led by folklore, Christmas is now more of a marketing and media-driven phenomenon (Golby and Purdue, 1986; Kirschenblatt-Gimblatt, 1983; Marling, 2000; Schmidt, 1995). The Western view of Christmas as a family holiday is alive and well in North American and European traditions (e.g. Barnett, 1954; Gillis, 1996; Waits, 1993), but not those of Asia, outside of the Philippines and a few other Asian Christian enclaves. Elsewhere in Asia, the lunar New Year is instead the time for family to come together, a tradition that is especially strong in China.

A BRIEF HISTORY OF
GLOBAL CONSUMPTION

The broader question concerning consumption and global consumers is the degree to which we are all becoming part of a global ethos – a global consumer society in which we measure ourselves and others based on our material possessions. Besides considering this question across geographic regions, it is also useful to consider how consumer culture has spread over time. To examine this question requires recognizing that consumerism is embedded in what is today called 'globalism'. Hopkins (2002) suggests that we can distinguish four different versions of globalization in world history. He calls the first 'archaic globalization' and uses the term to include the broad period of history before industrialization and the nation state. Great kings and warriors sought to expand their empires in this era, and China and Southeast Asia were one of the most important staging grounds for such globalization. A combination of consumers desiring precious goods and medicines, merchant princes seeking profit, and adventurers, religious zealots, and pilgrims, all helped expand trade routes in these eras, primarily focusing on luxury goods and preservatives such as salt (Stearns, 2001). These luxuries included gems, precious metals, high-quality cloth and clothing, exotic beverages such as tea, as well as spices and perfumes. The second era of globalization that Hopkins (2002) delineates is 'proto-globalization', which he places between approximately 1600 and 1800 in Europe, Asia, and parts of Africa. During this period, nation states, banks, and pre-industrial manufacturing emerged, and nations simultaneously pursued political and economic objectives through military might. Sugar, tobacco, tea, coffee, and opium helped fuel international trade, and global consumer desires and trade patterns covered larger expanses of the world. Hopkins' (2002) third era of globalism is entitled 'modern globalization' and is marked by industrialization and further growth of the nation state. A global division of labour began to emerge,

relying first on colonialism and slavery and later on migration. Manufactured goods were traded from industrialized nations, primarily in Europe and North America, to other parts of the world that provided commodities and labour. Developments in transportation, eventually including motorized ships, cars, trains, planes, airports, and highways facilitated faster shipment of goods and allowed perishable goods to travel from their origins to all parts of the world. This era lasted until the 1950s, when postcolonial globalization became the order that we know today (Hopkins, 2002). Especially after the end of communism in the former Soviet Union and Eastern Europe and the embrace of capitalism by China and India, it was clear that capitalist enterprises and global flows of people, money, communications, technology, and ideas were triumphant (Appadurai, 1996). Transnational corporations, brands, logos, and demonstrations against the unequal effects of postmodern globalism are hallmarks of the current era, along with interlocking global communications and entertainment networks.

Although modern colonialism and industrialism originated in Europe, these activities had their heaviest impact on the production side of the global economy. On the consumption side, the growth of consumerism was even more widespread. Nevertheless, most histories of consumerism concentrate on Europe (especially England, the Netherlands, and France) and America and envision rampant consumption as migrating to the rest of the world in imitation (e.g. Brewer and Porter, 1993; Campbell, 1987; Fox and Lears, 1983; Leach, 1994; Lears, 1994; McCracken, 1988; McKendrick et al., 1982; Mukerji, 1983; Sassatelli, 2007; Schama, 1987; Strasser, 1989; Williams, 1982). Stearns (2001) offers the beginning of a correction to this picture by emphasizing the historic role of East Asia, Russia, Africa, and the Middle East in the rise of consumerism. The thrust of the argument started by McKendrick et al. (1982) is that the economic growth and consumption that has traditionally been treated as stemming from the Industrial Revolution may be more properly seen as stemming from a Consumer Revolution that preceded it. Rather than quibble about where exactly consumerism began, McCracken (1988) usefully suggests that the development of consumer desire in various parts of the world can be seen as explosions that became more and more sustained and widespread.

In asking whether consumer desire is induced by marketers or an innate tendency on the part of consumers, Rassuli and Hollander (1986) probably put too much emphasis on the agency of both parties and ignore the mutually reinforcing environment created when consumer desire and marketer promotion combine in an atmosphere of growing abundance. But they are insightful in suggesting four criteria for a 'culture of consumption':

- People (or some very substantial segment of the population) consume at a level substantially above that of crude, survival-level subsistence.
- People obtain goods and services for consumption through exchange rather than self-production.
- Consumption is seen as an acceptable and appropriate activity.
- People, in fact, tend to judge others and perhaps themselves in terms of their consuming lifestyles (Rassuli and Hollander, 1986: 5).

Despite some limitations, this definition of consumer culture is helpful in its specification of the second and third criteria suggesting that more than economic preconditions are needed for a consumer culture to exist. It is also necessary that consumption is venerated and used to make social judgements. A big limitation, however, is that the first criterion clings too closely to Maslow's (1970) hierarchy of needs – at least as it is commonly but inaccurately understood to stipulate that lower-order needs must be satisfied before higher-order needs can be addressed. Rather than this sequential opening and closing of the floodgates of different desires, Maslow actually stipulated that the needs he hypothesized ebb and flow in importance in a more continual fashion, which allows a number of possible hierarchies in the strength of various

desires. But even this more complex understanding cannot account for what I have termed 'leaping luxuries' (Belk, 1999). Drawing largely on post-communist consumption patterns in Russia and Eastern Europe and post-Mao consumption in China, I present evidence of consumers sacrificing 'necessities' in order to afford 'luxuries'. For example, consumers in Romania were found to forgo adequate food in order to afford a refrigerator into which they could not then afford to put food (Belk, 1997). Consumers in the favelas of Rio di Janero were found to buy television antennas for their roofs to impress their neighbours, even though they had no electricity, much less a television. And cave paintings, grave goods, and collections of interesting pebbles have been found in 30,000–80,000-year-old caves in Europe – a time when skeletons and other evidence suggests that life was nasty, brutish, and short, as Hobbes phrased it in *Leviathan* (Belk, 1995). Clearly, these are not the patterns that Maslow would have predicted.

CONCLUSION

There is obviously far more to the history of global consumption than can be summarized here. Some of the other contexts that I currently find interesting are pre-Communist China (e.g. Dikötter, 2006; Gerth, 2003; Zhao and Belk, 2008), postprotectionist India (e.g. Cayla, 2008; Mazzarella, 2003; Varman and Belk, 2008, forthcoming), and the oil-rich Arab Gulf States (e.g. Belk and Sobh, 2008; Vogel, 2003; Yaqin, 2007). But there remain many more unique cultural contexts that need to be examined before a full portrait of global consumption representations can be drawn. And because these contexts extend forward and backward in time in a linked way, this ongoing project can never be complete. We need to understand more about the roles of cultures and multiculturalism, gender and gender bending, religion and materialism, voluntary and involuntary simplicity, wealth and poverty, economic growth and decline, and many other factors affecting consumption around the globe. As we move through another economic turmoil, coupled with global warming, declining fossil fuels, and global shifts in economic power, the challenge will become more and more interesting as well as more and more important.

Although consuming nonlocal objects is nearly as old as humankind, the degree of global interconnectedness in our consumer desires and consumption patterns has never been greater than it is today. This interconnectedness is sometimes quite visible (e.g. K-pop and world music, Hollywood and Bollywood films, Japanese manga and anime) and sometimes relatively invisible (e.g. back-office service providers in Bengaluru, counterfeit Louis Vuitton handbags from China, Toyotas made in the US with parts from who knows where). At a broader level, with the collapse of the former Soviet Union and the Iron Curtain, the rise of the Internet, the economic ascendance of Asia, and global media like CNN and al Jazeera, consumer lifestyles and aspirations are increasingly interconnected as well. As we have seen, this does not mean we will all eat the same foods, watch the same films, listen to the same music, or drive the same cars. Consumer research suggests that, for all our globalization, we can simultaneously observe that nationalism, regionalism, cultural and economic backlash, 'anti-globalization' movements, regional subcultures, and other local consumption patterns are growing as well. It is well to remember that, despite the current explosion of interest in globalization, the term only emerged in the swirl of changes that occurred in the world in the late 1980s and 1990s (Hopkins, 2002). It is fair to say that its meanings and our understandings of the concept will continue to develop.

This chapter has discussed some alternatives to global homogenization based on research in marketing and other disciplines. But it has only been able to introduce a few of the relevant takes on the broad topic of globalization. I have tried to provide ample suggestive references for those who wish to explore global consumption more fully. But I have largely ignored a host related concepts that might be brought into the discussion, including glocalization, grobalization, coca-colonization, cultural hegemony, cultural imperialism, hybridity, world systems theory, global structures of common difference, nothingness, core and periphery, McWorld, global youth culture, and cultural fusion. Concerns with globalism are not new, even if new technologies and new means of resistance raise fresh concerns. Ultimately, issues of global identities demand an otherness against which to compare ourselves. Just how this desire for otherness is worked out has enormous implications for us all. Consumer desire, envy, materialism, and corporate marketing are critical forces that will shape the character of global consumerism. These acquisitive, egoistic, and expansive forces can also be balanced or countered by localism, sharing, downshifting, gift-giving, aid, cooperation, compassion, and collaboration. It remains to be seen how these two sides to global interdependency will play out in the twenty-first century.

REFERENCES

Ahuvia, A. (2005) 'Beyond the Extended Self: Loved Objects and Consumers' Identity Narratives', *Journal of Consumer Research*, 32(June): 171–184.

Antoszek, A. (2003) 'Hopping on the Hype: Double Ontology of (Contemporary) American Rap Music', in P. Boi and S. Broeck (eds) *CrossRoutes – The Meanings of 'Race' for the 21st Century*, Munich: Lit Verlag, pp. 239–253.

Appadurai, A. (1996) *Modernity at Large: Cultural Dimensions of Globalization*. Minneapolis, MN: University of Minnesota Press.

Ariely, D. (2008) *Predictably Irrational: The Hidden Forces that Shape Our Decisions*. New York: Harper.

Balasescu, A. (2003) 'Tehran Chic: Islamic Headscarves, Fashion Designers, and New Geographies of Modernity', *Fashion Theory*, 7(1): 39–56.

Barnett, J.H. (1954) *The American Christmas*. New York: Macmillan.

Bauman, Z. (1998) *Globalization: The Human Consequences*. New York: Columbia University Press.

Belk, R.W. (1987) 'A Child's Christmas in America: Santa Claus as Deity, Consumption as Religion', *Journal of American Culture*, 10(Spring): 87–100.

Belk, R. (1988) 'Possessions and the Extended Self', *Journal of Consumer Research*, 15(September): 139–168.

Belk, R. (1991a) 'Possessions and the Sense of Past', in Russell W. Belk (ed.) *Highways and Buyways: Naturalistic Research from the Consumer Behavior Odyssey*, Provo, Utah: Association for Consumer Research, pp. 114–130.

Belk, R. (1991b) 'The Ineluctable Mystery of Possessions', *Journal of Social Behavior and Personality*, 6(June): 17–55.

Belk, R. (1993) 'Materialism and the Making of the Modern American Christmas', in D. Miller (ed.) *Unwrapping Christmas*, Oxford: Oxford University Press, pp. 75–104.

Belk, R. (1995) *Collecting in a Consumer Society*. London: Routledge.

Belk, R. (1996a) 'Metaphoric Relationships with Pets', *Society and Animals*, 4(2): 121–146 also available at http://www.psyeta.org/sa/sa4.2/belk.html.

Belk, R. (1996b) 'The Perfect Gift', in Cele Otnes and Richard F. Beltramini (eds) *Gift Giving: A Research Anthology*, Bowling Green, OH: Bowling Green University Popular Press, pp. 59–84.

Belk, R. (1997) 'Romanian Consumer Desires and Feelings of Deservingness', in Lavinia Stan (ed.) *Romania in Transition*, Aldershot, UK: Dartmouth, pp. 191–208.

Belk, R. (1999) 'Leaping Luxuries', in R. Batra (ed.) *Marketing Issues in Transitional Economies*, Boston: Kluwer Academic Publishers, pp. 39–54.

Belk, R. (2006) 'Coola Skor, Cool Identitet', (Cool Shoes, Cool Identity), in A.M. Dahlberg (ed.) *Skor Ger Mer: Makt Flärd Magi*, Stockholm: Swedish Royal Armoury, pp. 77–90.

Belk, R. (2007) 'Why Not Share Rather than Own?', *Annals of the American Academy of Political and Social Science*, 611(May): 126–140.

Belk, R. (2008) 'Marketing and Envy', in R.H. Smith (ed.) *Envy: Theory and Research*, Oxford: Oxford University Press, pp. 211–226.

Belk, R., Ger, G. and Askegaard, S. (2000) 'The Missing Streetcar Called Desire', in S. Ratneshwar, D.G. Mick, and C. Huffman (eds) *The Why of Consumption*, London: Routledge, pp. 98–119.

Belk, R., Ger, G. and Askegaard, S. (2003) 'The Fire of Desire: A Multi-sited Inquiry into Consumer Passion', *Journal of Consumer Research*, 30(December): 326–351.

Belk, R. and Groves, R. (1998) 'Luxury Beverage Consumption in Hong Kong', in K. Hung and K.B. Monroe (eds) *Asia Pacific Advances in Consumer Research*, Vol. 3, Provo, Ut: Association for Consumer Research, pp. 36–37.

Belk, R. and Kimura, J. (2005) 'Christmas in Japan: Globalization versus Localization', *Consumption, Markets and Culture*, 8(September): 325–338.

Belk, R. and Sobh, R. (2008) 'Behind the Closed Doors: Gendered Home Spaces in a Gulf Arab State', with Rana Sobh, 21:50 minute video, Toronto: Odyssey Films.

Belk, R., Wallendorf, M. and Sherry, J.F. Jr. (1989) 'The Sacred and the Profane in Consumer Behavior: Theodicy on the Odyssey', *Journal of Consumer Research*, 16(June): 1–38.

Bowler, G. (2005) *Santa Claus: A Biography*. Toronto: McClelland and Stewart.

Brannen, M.Y. (1992) '"Bwana Mickey": Construction Cultural Consumption at Tokyo Disneyland', in J.J., Tobin (ed.) *Re-Made in Japan: Everyday OLife and Consumer Taste in a Changing Society*, New Haven, CT: Yale University Press, pp. 216–234.

Brewer, J. and Porter, R. (eds) (1993) *Consumption and the World of Goods*. London: Routledge.

Campbell, C. (1987) *The Romantic Ethic and the Spirit of Modern Consumerism*. Oxford: Blackwell.

Canclini, N.G. (2001) *Consumers and Citizens: Globalization and Multicultural Conflicts*. Minneapolis, MN: University of Minnesota Press.

Cayla, J. (2008) 'Following the Endorser: Shah Rukh Khan and the Creation of the Cosmopolitan Indian Male', *Advertising and Society Review*, 9(2): 35–45.

Chadha, R. and Husband, P. (2006) *The Cult of the Luxury Brand: Inside Asia's Love Affair with Luxury*. London: Nicholas Brealey.

Condry, I. (2001) 'A History of Japanese Hip-Hop: Street Dance, Club Scene, Pop Market', in T. Mitchell (ed.) *Global Noise: Rap and Hip-Hop Outside the USA*, Middletown, CT: Wesleyan University Press, pp. 222–247.

Count, E.W. and Count, A.L. (1997) *4000 Years of Christmas: A Gift from the Ages*. Berkeley, CA: Ulysses Press.

Csikszentmihalyi, M. and Rochberg-Halton, E. (1981) *The Meaning of Things: Domestic Symbols and the Self*. Cambridge: University of Cambridge Press.

Curtis, B. (1995) 'The Strange Birth of Santa Claus: From Artemis the Goddess and Nicholas the Saint', *Journal of American Culture*, 18(4): 17–32.

De Grazia, V. (2005) *Irresistible Empire: America's Advance through 20th-Century Europe*. Cambridge, MA: Belknap Press.

Dikötter, F. (2006) *Exotic Commodities: Modern Objects and Everyday Life in China*. New York: Columbia University Press.

Domosh, M. (2006) *American Commodities in an Age of Empire*. London: Routledge.

Douglas, M. and Isherwood, B. (1979) *The World of Goods: Towards an Anthropology of Consumption*. New York: W. W. Norton.

Farquhar, J. (2002) *Appetites: Food and Sex in Post-Socialist China*. Durham, NC: Duke University Press.

Flynn, T. (1993) *The Trouble with Christmas*. Buffalo, NY: Prometheus Press.

Foster, R.J. (2008) *Coca-Globalization: Following Soft Drinks from New York to New Guinea*. New York: Plagrave MacMillan.

Fox, R.W. and Lears, T.J.J.(eds) (1983) *The Culture of Consumption: Critical Essays in American History: 1880–1980*. New York: Pantheon.

Ger, G. and Belk, R. (1996), 'I'd Like to Buy the World a Coke: Consumptionscapes of the Less Affluent World', *Journal of Consumer Policy*, 19: 271–304.

Gerth, K. (2003) *China Made: Consumer Culture and the Creation of the Nation*. Cambridge, MA: Harvard University Asia Center.

Gillis, J.R. (1996) *A World of Their Own making: Myth, Ritual, and the Quest for Family Values*. New York: Basic Books.

Glickman, L. (ed.) (1999) Ithica, *Consumer Society in American History: A Reader*. NY: Cornell University Press.

Golby, J.M. and Purdue, A.W. (1986) *The Making of the Modern Christmas*. Athens: University of Georgia Press.

Goodwin, N.R., Ackerman, F. and Kiron, D. (eds) (1997) *The Consumer Society*. Washington, DC: Island Press.

Hebdige, D. (2004) 'Rap and Hip-Hop: The New York Connection', in Murray Forman and Mark Anthony (eds) *That's the Joint! The Hip-Hop Studies Reader*, New York: Routledge, pp. 223–232.

Heinze, A.R. (1990) *Adapting to Abundance: Jewish Immigrants, Mass Consumption, and the Search for American Identity*. New York: Columbia University Press.

Hendry, J. (2000) *The Orient Strikes Back: A Global View of Cultural Display*. Oxford: Berg.

Hip Hop (2003), 'Product Mentions in Rap Music', http://www.uic.edu/orgs/kbc/hiphop/mentions.htm.

Hopkins, A.G. (2002) 'Introduction: Globalization – An Agenda for Historians', in A.G. Hopkins (ed.) *Globalization in World History*, pp. 1–10. London: Pimlico.

Horsley, R. and Tracy, J. (eds) (2001) *Christmas Unwrapped: Consumerism, Christ, and Culture*. Harrisburg, PA: Trinity Press.

Jing, J. (2000) 'Introduction: Food, Children, and Social Change in Contemporary China', in *Feeding China's Little Emperors: Food, Children, and Social Change*, Stanford, CA: Stanford University Press, pp. 1–26.

Jones, C. (2007) 'Fashion and Faith in Urban Indonesia', *Fashion Theory*, 11(2/3): 211–232.

Kahneman, D., Knetsch, J. and Thaler, R.H. (1990) 'Experimental Tests of the Endowment Effect and the Coase Theorem', *Journal of Political Economy*, 98(December): 1325–1348.

Karkaria, B. (2004) 'Hinduism and India Cool', *The Times of India*, February 27, online edition.

Keyfitz, N. (1982) 'Development and the Elimination of Poverty', *Economic Development and Cultural Change*, 30: 649–470.

Kirshenblatt-Gimblatt, B. (1983) 'The Future of Folklore Studies in America: The Urban Frontier', *Folklore Forum*, 16(2): 175–234.

Kitwana, B. (2005) *Why White Kids Love Hip-Hop: Wankstas, Wiggers, Wannabes, and the New Reality of Race in America*. New York: Basic Civitas Books.

Kjeldgaard, D. and Askegaard, S. (2006) 'The Glocalization of Youth Culture: The Global Youth Segment as Structures of Common Difference', *Journal of Consumer Research*, 33(September): 231–247.

Klein, N. (2000) *No Logo! Taking Aim at the Brand Bullies*. New York: Picador.

Kleine, S.S. and Baker, S.M. (2004) 'An Integrative Review of Material Possession Attachment', *Academy of Marketing Science Review*, 1: 1–39.

Kopytoff, I. (1986) 'The Cultural Biography of Things: Commoditization as Process', in A. Appadurai (ed.) *The Social Life of Things: Commodities in Cultural Perspective*, Cambridge: Cambridge University Press, pp. 64–91.

Kotlowitz, A. (1999) 'False Connections', in Roger Rosenblatt (ed.) *Consuming Desire: Consumption, Culture, and the Pursuit of Happiness*, New York: Island Press, pp. 65–72.

Krims, A. (2002) 'Rap, Race, the "Local", and Urban Geography in Amsterdam', in R. Young (ed.) *Music Popular Culture Identities*, Amsterdam: Rodopi, pp. 181–196.

Leach, W. (1994) *Land of Desire: Merchants, Power, and the Rise of a New American Culture*. New York: Vintage.

Lears, J. (1994) *Fables of Abundance: A Cultural History of Advertising in America*. New York: Basic Books.

Leeds-Hurwitz, W. (2002) *Wedding as Text: Communicating Cultural Identities Through Ritual*. Mahwah, NJ: Lawrence Erlbaum.

Libanius (1977) *Selected Works*, Vol. 3. Cambridge, MA: Harvard University Press.

Liebes, T. and Katz, E. (1990) *The Export of Meaning: Cross-Cultural Readings of Dallas*. New York: Oxford University Press.

Longville, de T. and Leone, L. (directors) (2006) 'Just for Kicks', 81-minute DVD. New York: CAID.

Ma, E.K. (2001) 'The Hierarchy of Drinks: Alcohol and Social Class in Hong Kong', in G. Mathews and T. Lui (eds) *Consuming Hong Kong*, Hong Kong: University of Hong Kong Press, pp. 117–139.

Marling, K.A. (2000) *Merry Christmas! Celebrating America's Greatest Holiday*. Cambridge, MA: Harvard University Press.

Martino, W. (2000) 'Mucking Around in Class, Giving Crap, and Acting Cool: Adolescent Boys Enacting Masculinity in School', *Canadian Journal of Education*, 25: 102-112.

Maslow, A. (1970) *Motivation and Personality*, second edition. New York: Harper & Row.

Mason, R. (1999) *The Economics of Conspicuous Consumption*. Mahwah, NJ: Edward Elgar.

Mazzarella, W. (2003) *Shoveling Smoke: Advertising and Globalization in Contemporary India*. Durham, NC: Duke University Press.

McCracken, G. (1986) 'Culture and Consumption: A Theoretical Account of the Structure and Movement of the Cultural Meaning of Consumer Goods', *Journal of Consumer Research*, 13(June): 71–84.

McCracken, G. (1988) *Culture and Consumption: New Approaches to the Symbolic Character of Consumer Goods and Activities*. Bloomington, IN: Indiana University Press.

McKendrick, N., Brewer, J. and Plumb, J.H. (eds) (1982) *The Birth of a Consumer Society: The Commercialization of Eighteenth Century England*. Bloomington, IN: Indiana University Press.

Miller, D. (1993) 'A Theory of Christmas', in D. Miller (ed.) *Unwrapping Christmas*, Oxford: Oxford University Press, pp. 3–37.

Miller, D. (1998) 'Coca-Cola: A Black Sweet Drink from Trinidad', in Daniel Miller (ed.) *Material Cultures: Why Some Things Matter*, Chicago: University of Chicago Press, pp. 169–187.

Milner, M., Jr. (2004) *Freaks, Geeks, and Cool Kids*. New York: Routledge.

Mitchell, T. (2001) 'Kia Kaha! (Be Strong!): Maori and Pacific Islander Hip-Hop in Aotearoa – New Zealand', in Tony Mitchell (ed.) *Global Noise: Rap and Hip-Hop Outside the USA*, Middletown, CT: Wesleyan University Press, pp. 280–305.

Moeran, B. and Skov, L. (1993) 'Cinderella Christmas: Kitsch, Consumerism, and Youth in Japan', in D. Miller (ed.) *Unwrapping Christmas*, Oxford: Oxford University Press, pp. 105–133.

Morelli, S. (2001) '"Who is a Dancing Hero?" Rap, Hip-Hop and Dance in Korean Popular Culture', in T. Mitchell (ed.) *Global Noise: Rap and Hip-Hop Outside the USA*, Middletown, CT: Wesleyan University Press, pp. 248–258.

Mukerji, C. (1983) *From Graven Images: Patterns of Modern Materialism*. New York: Columbia University Press.

Nissenbaum, S. (1996) *The Battle for Christmas*. New York: Alfred A. Knopf.

Otnes, C.C. and Pleck, E. (2003) *Cinderella Dreams: The Allure of the Lavish Wedding*. Berkeley, CA: University of California Press.

Perry, I. (2004) *Prophets of the Hood: Politics and Poetics in Hip Hop*. Durham, NC: Duke University Press.

Purbrick, L. (2007) *The Wedding Present: Domestic Life Beyond Consumption*. Aldershot, UK: Ashgate.

Quinn, E. (2005) *Nuthin' but a 'G' Thang: The Culture and Commerce of Gangsta Rap*. New York: Columbia University Press.

Rassuli, K.M. and Hollander, S.C. (1986) 'Desire – Induced, Innate, Insatiable?', *Journal of Marcomarketing*, 6(Fall): 4–24.

Restad, P.L. (1995) *Christmas in America: A History*. Oxford: Oxford University Press.

Ritzer, G. (2004) *The Globalization of Nothingness*. Thousand Oaks, CA: Pine Forge Press.

Roach, M. (2003) *Dr. Martens: The Story of an Icon*. London: Chrysalis.

Rollin R. (ed.) (1989) *The Americanization of the Global Village: Essays in Comparative Popular Culture*. Bowling Green, OH: Bowling Green State University Popular Press.

Rose, T. (1994) *Black Noise: Rap Music and Black Culture in Contemporary America*. Hanover, NH: University Press of New England.

Sansone, L. (1995) 'The Making of a Black Youth Culture: Lower-class Young Men of Surinamese Origin in Amsterdam', in V. Amit-Taliai and H. Wulff, (eds) *Youth Cultures: A Cross-cultural Perspective*, London: Routledge, pp. 114–143.

Santino, J. (1996) *New Old Fashioned Ways: Holidays and Popular Culture*. Knoxville, TN: University of Tennessee Press.

Sassatelli, R. (2007) *Consumer Culture: History, Theory and Politics*. Los Angeles, CA: Sage.

Schama, S. (1987) *The Embarrassment of Riches: An Interpretation of Dutch Culture in the Golden Age*. New York: Knopf.

Schandler, J. and Weintraub, A. (2007) '"Santa, Schmanta": Greeting Cards for the December Dilemma', *Material Religion*, 3(November): 380–403.

Schmidt, L.E. (1995) *Consumer Rites: The Buying and Selling of American Holidays*. Princeton, NJ: Princeton University Press.

Schor, J.B. and Holt, D.B. (eds) (2000) *The Consumer Society Reader*. New York: New Press.

Siefker, P. (1997) *Santa Claus: Last of the Wild Men*. Jefferson, NC: McFarland & Company.

Smitherman, G. (1977) *Talkin and Testifyin: The Language of Black America*. Boston: Houghton Mifflin.

Stearns, P.N. (2001) *Consumerism in World History: The Global Transformation of Desire*. London: Routledge.

Stewart, S. (1984) *On Longing: Narratives of the Miniature, the Gigantic, the Souvenir, the Collection*. Baltimore, MD: John Hopkins University Press.

Strasser, S. (1989) *Satisfaction Guaranteed: The Making of the American Mass Market*. New York: Pantheon.

Strasser, S., McGovern, C. and Judt, M. (eds) (1998) *Getting and Spending: European and American Consumer Societies in the Twentieth Century*. Cambridge: Cambridge University Press.

Tam, S.M. (2001) 'Lost, and Found?: Reconstructing Hong Kong Identity in the Idiosyncrasy and Syncreticism of *Yumcha*', in D.Y.H. Wu and Tan Chee-being (eds) *Changing Foodways in Asia*, Hong Kong: Hong Kong University Press, pp. 49–69.

Tian, K. and Belk, R. (2005) 'Extended Self and Possessions in the Workplace', *Journal of Consumer Research*, 32(September): 297–310.

Van Renterghem, T. (1995), *When Santa was a Shaman*. St. Paul, MN: Llewellyn Publications.

Varman, R. and Belk, R. (2008) 'Weaving a Web: Subaltern Consumers, Rising Consumer Culture, and Television', *Marketing Theory*, 8(September): 227–252.

Varman, R. and Belk, R. (forthcoming), 'The Making of Reflexive Local Discourse: Local and Global Articulations of Anti-Consumption Movements', *Journal of Consumer Research*, forthcoming.

Veblen, T. (1899) *The Theory of the Leisure Class*. New York: MacMillan.

Vogel, F.E. (2003) 'The Public and the Private in Saudi Arabia: Restrictions on the Power of Committees for Ordering the Good and

Forbidding the Evil', *Social Research*, 70(Fall): 749–768.

Waits, W.B. (1993) *The Modern Christmas in America*. New York: New York University Press.

Wang, J. (2005) 'Bourgeois Bohemians in China? Neo-Tribes and the Urban Imaginary', *The China Quarterly*, 183: 532–548.

Watson, J. (ed.) (1997) *Golden Arches East: McDonald's in East Asia*. Stanford, CA: Stanford University Press.

Watson, J. (2005) 'China's Big Mac Attack', in James L. Watson and Melissa L. Caldwell (eds) *The Cultural Politics of Food and Eating: A Reader*, Malden, MA: Blackwell, pp. 70–79.

Wilk, R. (1993) '"It's Destroying a Whole Generation": Television and Moral Discourse in Belize', *Visual Anthropology Review*, 10(1): 94–102.

Williams, R.H. (1982) *Dream Worlds: Mass Consumption in Late Nineteenth Century France*. Berkeley, CA: University of California Press.

Wu, D.Y.H. (2002) 'Improvising Chinese Cuisine Overseas', in D.Y.H. Wu and S.C.H. Cheung (eds) *The Globalization of Chinese Food*, Honolulu: University of Hawaii Press, pp. 56–66.

Wu, David Y.H. and Chee-beng, T. (2001) 'Introduction' in D.Y.H. Wu and T. Chee-being (eds) *Changing Foodways in Asia*, Hong Kong: Hong Kong University Press, pp. 1–15.

Wu, D.Y.H. and Cheung, S.C.H. (2002) 'The Globalization of Chinese Food and Culture: Markers and Breakers of Cultural Barriers', in D.Y.H. Wu and S.C.H. Cheung (eds) *The Globalization of Chinese Food*, Honolulu: University of Hawaii Press, pp. 1–18.

Wuthnow, R. (1994) *God and Mammon in America*. New York: Free Press.

Yan, X. (2000) 'Of Hamburger and Social Space: Consuming McDonald's in Beijing', in D.S. Davis (ed.) *The Consumer Revolution in Urban China*, Berkeley, CA: University of California Press, pp. 201–225.

Yaqin, A. (2007) 'Islamic Barbie: The Politics of Gender and Performativity', *Fashion Theory*, 11(2/3): 173–188.

Zhao, X. and Belk, R. (2005) 'Sinolization of a Western Holiday: The Sweethearts' Christmas', in *Advances in Consumer Research*, 32(8).

Zhao, X. and Belk, R. (2008) 'Advertising Consumer Culture in 1930s' Shanghai: Globalization and Localization in Yue Fen Pai', *Journal of Advertising*, 37(Summer): 45–56.

17

Consumer Behavior Analysis

Gordon R. Foxall

INTRODUCTION

Consumer psychology is usually cognitive in orientation. Scores of consumer behavior texts assume this theoretical position without considering the philosophical implications of the concepts on which they rely to explain choice, let alone offering any philosophical justification for the cognitive stance itself. It is rare for the writers of these texts, as it is for consumer psychologists generally, to consider that an alternative paradigm, behavior analysis, can assist in the explanation of consumer choice (Foxall, 2003). Yet, there is a large volume of evidence to show that economic behavior is reliably sensitive to environmental contingencies. Specifically, the subdiscipline of *behavioral economics* is concerned with the combination of experimental economics and operant psychology to elucidate economic relationships. Much of the work in behavioral economics has been concerned with nonhuman animals, though there is an increasing tendency to apply the methods developed in the operant chamber to a wide range of applied human problems. *Consumer behavior analysis* is the application of behavioral economics to the sphere of human consumer choice, particularly in the context of advanced

marketing-oriented economies (Foxall, 2002). Now, marketing brings a further level of complexity to what is already a multi-disciplinary exercise. There are considerations stemming from human marketing activity that are never encountered in the laboratory regardless of whether the subjects are human or nonhuman. The very concept of exchange, for instance, is either nonexistent in the nonmarketing environment or very much less complicated. Considerations of price, which are easily replicable in experiments, are compounded by those of advertising, distribution, and subtleties of product characteristics, as well as by issues of status consumption and interpersonal effects that are absent from behavioral economics work in nonmarketing environments. It is the aim of consumer behavior analysis to comprehend marketing-led consumer choice in terms of behavior analysis: to understand how far the methods of behavioral economics can be transferred from their original contexts to the marketing sphere, to recognize differences in human marketing behavior that require behavioral economics to be modified, to arrive at the boundaries of a behavior analytical interpretation of complex human behavior.

Despite its connections with marketing science as an academic approach, this research program has always had strong intellectual underpinnings: its aim has been to examine whether a model of consumer choice based on behavior analysis can be formulated at all, and, if so, to determine the epistemological nature of such a model (Foxall, 1994). A particular concern from the outset has been the nature of radical behaviorist interpretation, the depiction of complex human behavior – understood as that which is not amenable to direct experimental investigation – in terms derived from laboratory-based behavior analysis. This framework has always permitted – indeed, promoted – inter-disciplinarity, methodological pluralism, an explorative and critical approach to behavior analysis and economic choice, and, above all, an approach that is determined to reveal how useful behavior analysis can be in understanding consumer behavior rather than assuming a priori that it is the sole perspective thereon.

This chapter describes the theory and research, which has guided the development of consumer behavior analysis, particularly the Behavioral Perspective Model (BPM), initially an interpretive device, which resulted from the logical application of the principles of the experimental analysis of behavior to the realm of consumer choice, and its testing and evaluation as a source of empirical evidence on the nature and scope of a behavioral perspective on economic choice. The derivation of the model has been described previously (Foxall, 1990/2004, 1996, 1998a)

and its subsequent refinement and application to consumer research have also been extensively described (DiClemente and Hantula, 2003a; Foxall, 2005, 2007a; Foxall et al., 2007). In addition, the philosophical and theoretical implications of the application of behavior analysis to complex choice have been addressed (Foxall, 2004, 2007b, c). Consumer behavior analysis itself has been the subject of a comprehensive selection of chapters, which describe the development and early application of the BPM in the context of behavior analysis and behavioral economics, and marketing research (Foxall, 2002).

THE BEHAVIORAL PERSPECTIVE MODEL

The BPM is an elaboration of the three-term contingency, modified to take into account the complexities introduced by social and economic institutional arrangements that govern marketing activity (Figure 17.1; Foxall, 1990/2004). Consumer choice takes place at the intersection of the consumer's learning history and the current consumer behavior setting, i.e. where the experience of consumption meets an opportunity to consume anew. This intersection of time and space forms the consumer situation, the immediate shaper of approach – avoidance responses

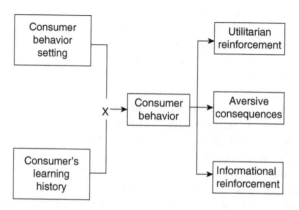

Figure 17.1 Summative Behavioral Perspective Model.

involved in purchase and consumption. The *consumer behavior setting* is composed of the stimulus antecedents of that behavior, some of which will have been present on earlier consumption occasions. In the presence of the individual's learning history, these initially neutral stimuli are transformed into the discriminative stimuli that set the occasion for current choice; in particular, his or her consumption history invests them with kind of meaning, i.e. the capacity to generate specific kinds of approach and/or avoidance behaviors, which produce consequences that regulate the rate of recurrence of the behaviors that produced them. The consumer situation consists also of motivating operations (MOs) such as rules (Michael, 1982, 1993; see also Agnew, 1998; Fagerstrøm et al., in press) that invest the consequences inherent in the discriminative stimuli with additional motivating or inhibitory power by making the consequences of radical behaviorism appear more or less reinforcing, more or less punishing.

Consumer behavior settings

Like the three-term contingency, then, the BPM specifies behaviorally antecedent stimulus conditions (the behavior setting) but combines the concepts of discriminative stimuli and MOs by means of the construct of behavior setting *scope*, the extent to which these setting elements encourage or inhibit the behavior predicted to occur in such settings. The most closed setting likely to be encountered in reality is that of the animal laboratory where the experimental subject has no alternative but to be present and where its behavioral repertoire is severely restricted to serve the purposes of the researcher (see Schwartz and Lacey, 1988). More open than this, but still toward the closed pole of the continuum, is the human operant experiment, which the subject is comparatively free to leave at any time even though the social and physical pressures of the experimental space may well act against this. Toward the other end of the continuum, settings of purchase

and consumption are all relatively open compared to this, but still differ from one another along a restricted continuum of closed–open consumer behavior settings (Foxall, 1990/2004). Hence, standing in line at the bank to pay in a check takes place in a relatively closed consumer behavior setting: there is probably no alternative to being there and waiting until a teller becomes available, standing in an orderly fashion is encouraged both by the physical style of the building and by the social arrangements, deviation from the established behavior program of the setting is likely to be punished by stares or glares or, if one's fellow customers have succumbed to the latest assertiveness training fad by more direct, and potentially socially embarrassing action. Depending on their learning histories, some customers may actually seek such social disapproval and arrange for calls on their mobile phones to come in at this time but most of us seem to be sufficiently conditioned to conform fairly closely to the behavior patterns laid down by the designers of this closed consumer behavior setting. An open consumer behavior setting encourages a wider range of alternative behaviors. In a bar, for instance, all manner of beverages and snacks may be available, there may be TV to watch, talking loudly may not be discouraged and even singing and dancing may be possible. The customer is free to leave at any time, even if only to go to another bar in the vicinity – at least far freer than he or she would be to leave the bank and find another at which to present the check.

The idea of consumer behavior setting scope finds parallels in Hursh's concept of open and closed economies. Hursh (1980) argues that, 'A behavioral experiment is an economic system and its characteristics can strongly determine the results'. In what he calls an *open economy*, daily total consumption is independent of response level since food is made available to the organism outside the experimental period; demand is highly elastic with respect to price (response rate declines as price increases), while in a *closed economy*, elasticity of demand is low for an essential commodity like food. However, if behavior analysts are to understand complex human behavior such as real world consumer choice, they need additional theoretical constructs. The scope of consumer behavior settings, from the most open to the most closed, represents the range of behavioral options available to the consumer in a situation of purchase or consumption, and thereby enhances the capacity of the would-be interpreter of her/his behavior to render it intelligible. Unlike open–closed economies, which comprise a dichotomous classification, open–closed behavior settings form a continuum, though they are often treated for ease of exposition and research as binary variables. More importantly, open–closed economies reflect only one element of the marketing mix – price–quantity relationships and, hence, elasticity of demand – while consumer behavior settings necessarily involve the other mix elements as well as word-of-mouth and other forms of interpersonal influence – i.e. the very *plasticity* of demand (Penrose, 1959). Behavior setting scope is conceptualized as a continuum from closed to open in which the former type of setting permits one or at best a very few behaviors to be enacted within its confines, while the latter type permits a whole range of often competing behaviors to be enacted.

Patterns of reinforcement

The consequences of economic behavior fall into three types: utilitarian reinforcement, which consists in the functional outcomes of behavior, informational reinforcement, which stems from the symbolic outcomes, principally performance feedback, and aversive/punishing consequences, the costs of purchase and consumption. Such aversive outcomes can themselves be subdivided into those that are utilitarian in nature and those that are symbolic. In summary, we are looking at consumer behavior as a function of utilitarian reinforcement, informational reinforcement, and aversive consequences (Foxall and Schrezenmaier, 2003). Utilitarian reinforcement consists in

the direct usable, economic and technical benefits of owning and consuming a product or service, while informational reinforcement inheres in benefits of ownership and consumption, which are usually social in nature and consist in the prestige or status as well as the self-esteem generated by ownership and consumption. The driver of a Lada, for instance, is principally concerned with the utilitarian benefits that all cars provide: the most obvious is getting from A to B, door-to-door transportation. Informational reinforcement, on the other hand, is more likely to involve a lifestyle statement by which the consumer seeks to convey his or her social status or to bolster esteem and/or reported feelings of self-esteem. The driver of a Porsche clearly gets from A to B in it but, in addition, gains the social esteem and status provided by friends and acquaintances who admire these prestige products and from members of the general public who see him or her driving around in a socially desirable vehicle. The social status and esteem that driver is accorded are the symbolic rewards of consumption. Most products have an element of both the instrumental and the symbolic. A mobile phone not only provides communications services when and where the consumer wants them; because it is a Nokia and therefore has interchangeable colored cases, it may also signal to that consumer's social group that he or she is 'cool' (or, a year or so later, 'not so cool').

These considerations reflect the *plasticity* of demand: the sensitivity of demand not only to price but also to all four generic elements of the marketing mix (product, price, promotion, and place) and their interactions and their global influence. Within the context of orthodox behavioral economics, Hursh (1980) comments that, 'Reinforcers can be distinguished by a functional property called elasticity of demand that is independent of relative value'. However – and this is a second rule of interpretation drawn from the BPM analysis – patterns of reinforcement can be distinguished according to the degree of utility (functionality) and information (symbolism) they provide. Consumer behavior analysis contends that the *pattern of reinforcement* assumes the place occupied by the *schedule of reinforcement* in the closed setting of the operant laboratory when one turns to the interpretation of complex behavior. It also adds complexity to the idea of the elasticity of demand by defining characteristics of demand plasticity.

By establishing the pattern of reinforcement, arrived at by combining high and low levels of utilitarian reinforcement and high and low levels of informational reinforcement, we can posit four operant classes of consumer behavior as shown in Figure 17.2. This figure represents at this stage no more than a hypothesis and the labels attached to the four classes of consumer behavior are purely arbitrary – though they have proved very useful in subsequent research. The four broad classes of consumer behavior, which can be inferred from the pattern of high/low utilitarian and informational reinforcement that maintains them are as follows. Accomplishment is consumer behavior reflecting social and economic achievement: acquisition and conspicuous consumption of status goods, displaying products and services that signal personal attainment. Hedonism includes such activities as the consumption of popular entertainment. Accumulation includes the consumer behaviors involved in certain kinds of saving, collecting, and installment buying. Finally, Maintenance consists of activities necessary for the consumer's physical survival and welfare (e.g. food) and the fulfillment of the minimal obligations entailed in membership of a social

system (e.g. paying taxes). Note that both types of reinforcer figure in the maintenance of each of the four classes, though to differing extents.

The BPM contingency matrix

Adding in the scope of the current behavior setting, leads to the eightfold way depicted in Figure 17.3, which shows the variety of contingency categories that exclusively constitute a functional analysis of consumer behavior. Let us take a closer look at the four broad operant classes of consumer behavior with the added complexity of consumer behavior setting scope added in.

Accomplishment

Accomplishment in an open setting consists in general in the *purchase and consumption of status goods*. A familiar instance is prepurchase consumer behavior for luxuries and radical innovations such as exotic vacations and iPhones. These behaviors, including window-shopping and browsing, involve search for and comparative evaluation of information about many products and services. Most of the items in question are possessed and used for the pleasure or ease of living they confer, the wellbeing they make possible for the individual: they thereby provide extensive hedonic rewards. Nevertheless, they are often status symbols and their conspicuous consumption also strengthens the behavior in question. They attest directly, and often publicly and unambiguously, to the consumer's attainments, especially economic. Goods in

	High utilitarian Reinforcement	Low utilitarian reinforcement
High informational reinforcement	ACCOMPLISHMENT	ACCUMULATION
Low informational reinforcement	HEDONISM	MAINTENENCE

Figure 17.2 Patterns of Reinforcement defining Operant Classes of Consumer Behavior.

Behavior-setting scope

	Closed	Open
ACCOMPLISHMENT	CC2 Fulfillment	CC1 Status consumption
HEDONISM	CC4 Inescapable entertainment	CC3 Popular entertainment
ACCUMULATION	CC6 Token-based consumption	CC5 Saving and collecting
MAINTENANCE	CC8 Mandatory consumption	CC7 Routine purchasing

Figure 17.3   The BPM Contingency Matrix.

this category are usually highly differentiated – by novel function in the case of innovations, by branding in the case of luxuries. In a closed setting, Accomplishment can be generally described as *fulfillment*. In such a context, it comprises personal attainments gained through leisure, often with a strong element of recreation or excitement as well as achievement. This category refers to the material contribution to *fulfillment* and could include both the completion of a personal development seminar such as Insight and gambling in a casino. Gambling in so closed a setting is an activity maintained by both utilitarian and informational consequences. In addition, few consumer behaviors are maintained so thoroughly by social rules. All these elements of the setting unambiguously signal both the positive consequences of approved approach behaviors and the potentially punishing implications of escape or avoidance responses, which flout established rules and gaming conventions. Although several games may be available in the casino, there is one principal reinforcer: winning. Pleasure and social approval stem mainly from success, though a certain amount of enjoyment and prestige may be derived from being part of

a somewhat exclusive social group and conforming to its code of behavior. Closely defined acts must be performed in order to participate, including obtaining membership, dressing appropriately, entering the game at the right time, and in an acceptable manner.

Hedonism

In an open setting, this behavior generally consists of *popular entertainment*. Obvious examples are watching television game shows, which provide near-constant utilitarian reward, and the reading of mass fiction, which contains a sensation on almost every page. iPods and DVDs have made such reinforcement more immediate to the point of its being ubiquitous. Mass culture presents frequent and predictable, relatively strong and continuous hedonic rewards, which are not contingent on long periods of concentrated effort. Indeed, the arrangement of reinforcers is such that viewing, listening, or reading for even a short interval is likely to be rewarded. Informational feedback is more obvious on some occasions than others, as when game shows allow the audience to pit their own performances against that of the competing participants, but it is not the main source of reward. Hedonism in closed settings consists as a generalization of inescapable entertainment and amelioration. The behaviors in question are potentially pleasurable but – in this context – may be irksome, because they are unavoidable. As a result, consumption of these products and services may be passive rather than active. An example is the situation in which long distance airline passengers must purchase meals and movies along with their travel. The meals are usually consumed, like the in-flight movies, which follow them, without alternative. The setting, which cannot be other than highly restrictive if one is to arrive safely, is further closed by the pulling of blinds, the disappearance of cabin staff, the impossibility of moving around the plane, and the attention of one's fellow passengers to the movie. To try to read or engage in other activities may even invite censure.

Accumulation

In an open setting, Accumulation is generally described as *saving and collecting*. For example, purchases for which payments are made prior to consumption – installments for a holiday, which can only be taken once the full amount has been paid. Another example is payments into a Christmas club. Discretionary saving with the intention of making a large purchase once a certain amount has accumulated would fall into this category too. Promotional deals requiring the accumulation of coupons or other tokens before a product or service can be obtained also belong here. The important reward, in every case, is informational, feedback on how much one has accumulated, how close one is to the ultimate reinforcer. Accumulation occurring in a closed setting may be described, in general terms, as *token-based buying*. This also involves collecting – through schemes in which payment for one item provides tokens, which will pay for another. Although some examples of this are quite recent, the practice is simply an extension of the familiar prize schemes open to collectors of cigarette cards or trading stamps. For example, the 'air-miles' earned by frequent flyers on domestic and

international airlines constitute informational reinforcers (Foxall, 1997b). Some hotels also offer gifts to customers who accumulate points by staying there frequently. The collection of these tokens is reinforced by gaining additional free air travel or hospitality, or by access to different types of reinforcer such as prizes. Purchase and consumption of the basic product, the air travel or accommodation originally demanded are maintained by both the intrinsic hedonic rewards they embody and the feedback on progress that is being made toward the ultimate incentive. The setting is relatively closed, because the first item would probably be purchased anyway in some form or other and the consumer's income constraint makes it likely that the second or backup reinforcer would be obtained only in this way.

Maintenance

In an open setting, Maintenance may be generally described as *routine purchasing and consumption*. This includes the regular buying of goods necessary for survival. For example, the habitual purchasing of grocery items at a supermarket. Consumer behavior in these circumstances is indeed routine: it occurs as if reinforcement were available only at fixed intervals. Further, contrary to the usual depiction, the frequent consumer, of say, baked beans, is highly rational, having tried and evaluated many brands in the relevant product class. However, his or her behavior is not static: again, in contrast to the received wisdom of the marketing texts, comparatively few such consumers are brand loyal in the sense of always choosing the identical brand in a long sequence of shopping trips. There is so much choice that the consumer enjoys considerable discretion among versions of the product (Ehrenberg, 1988/1972). Maintenance is generally characterized in closed settings as *mandatory purchase and consumption*. It includes all forms of consumer behavior necessary to remain a citizen: the payment of taxes for public and collective goods, for instance; less extremely, it includes payments into pension schemes linked to employment and payments of endowment insurance premiums linked to mortgages. To this extent, Maintenance is the consumer behavior inherent in pursuing the normal business of citizenship. In the workplace, it may include the enforced use of areas under smoking bans, which, for smokers, represent a severe limitation on behavior (though for nonsmokers, particularly the allergic, they constitute an opening of the setting, a measure that permits a wider range of behaviors).

RESEARCH

The first applications of the BPM were as an interpretive device; issues central to consumer research were examined not within the usual cognitive framework but from a behavioral perspective: the relationship between consumers' attitudes and behavior (Foxall, 1983), the adoption and diffusion of innovations (Foxall, 1986), spending, consuming and saving (Foxall, 1994), 'green' consumption (Foxall, 1996), and the nature and influence of marketing management (Foxall, 1998a) were interpreted within the new framework (see also Foxall, 1996). Most of this work was conducted within an ambience of testing out behavior analysis by comparing it with the conventional information processing accounts of consumer choice, a desire to promote a clash of competing explanations in a Feyerabendian spirit (Feyerabend, 1975). The scientific evaluation of the model as a means of predicting more specific aspects of consumer choice came later and continues today.

Three strands of research exemplify the consequent attempts to test the model: the prediction of verbal behavior with respect to consumers' emotional responses to retail and consumption environments, the application of matching and maximization techniques to consumer choice, and the analysis of consumer demand. In addition, there is continuing work to extend the methodological basis of consumer behavior analysis through experimentation and case study analysis, and there is a strong program of conceptual development and theoretical advance.

Verbal behavior and emotional response

The first aim was to test the model as a whole, to understand whether (and if so how) the three structural variables of setting scope, utilitarian reinforcement, and informational reinforcement interacted. The first study, undertaken in England, employed a tripartite classification of verbal responses to the emotions engendered by different environments, based on Mehrabian and Russell's theory of environmental psychology (Foxall, 1997a). The three dominant emotions are *pleasure*, *arousal*, and *dominance*. The verbal measures of these emotions were interpreted as predictable in various consumer contexts defined by the BPM. Utilitarian reinforcement was proposed as engendering the verbal responses that Mehrabian and Russell proposed to measure *pleasure*, which implied satisfaction and utility. Informational reinforcement, the verbal responses related to *arousal*, which emphasize environmental feedback and the monitoring of changing circumstances. Mehrabian (1980) argues for this configuration of attitudes, and Foxall (2005) makes the case for their inclusion in consumer research. The scope of the consumer behavior setting was assumed to correspond to the verbalizations that Mehrabian and Russell linked to dominance (being in control as opposed to being subject to another). This is not the kind of research framework that experimental behavior analysis would enjoin upon us, but it seems particularly appropriate for the testing of what is essentially an interpretive device for understanding complex human behavior rather than an experimental technique for use in the closed settings of the operant laboratory (for a fuller discussion of this kind of methodology and its relevance to radical behaviorist interpretation, see Foxall, 1998b).

The results of this work confirm the predictions. The expectations of a larger *pleasure* score for higher utilitarian reinforcement; similarly, a larger *arousal* score was found for greater informational reinforcement; and a larger *dominance* score characterized a more open consumer behavior setting scope. The results indicate that by using the pleasure, arousal, and dominance measures as predicted verbal responses to the consumer situations defined by the BPM contingency matrix, it is possible to make useful predictions of consumer behavior. The robustness of these findings is affirmed by work, which has replicated the research in Venezuela, in Spanish, with similar results (Foxall and Yani-de-Soriano, 2005; Soriano et al., 2002). As a result, we have data that support the expectation that economic choice, or at least its verbal description, is predictable from stimuli that represent the structural variables of the BPM in varying combinations.

Theoretical questions about the interpretation of findings inevitably arise from these investigations, as they do from all applied work. Mehrabian and Russell claim to be tapping emotions, not use of words, albeit through verbally based measurements. Moreover, they accord a causal role to emotion in the determination of responses to physical and social environments. By claiming to do no more than predict verbal behavior, our initial studies attempted to keep in line with radical behaviorist principles by which causation is interpreted in terms of functional relationships between overt responding and variables in the extrapersonal environment.

Matching and maximization

We turn now to a research area much closer to the heart of behavior analysis and behavioral economics. An important debate in the evolution of behavioral economics has been – and to some extent remains – the question whether consumers maximize in some sense or follow some other decision rule such as satisficing. Controversy has long surrounded economists'

assumption that consumer behavior maximizes utility (or the satisfactions obtained from owning and using economic products and services).

While distinguished economists such as Friedman (1953) argued that maximization was a feasible assumption as long as it contributed to predictive accuracy, equally distinguished behavioral scientists such as Simon (1959) decried the lack of empirical support for the assumption and argued that consumers, like other economic actors, are content to achieve a satisfactory rather than maximal level of return for their efforts, i.e. to satisfice. The advent of experimental economics brought empirical data to bear on the question of maximization through controlled studies of animal behavior in which responses (key pecking or bar pressing) are analogous to money, food pellets, or other items of reward to goods, and the ratio of responses to rewards to price. Two intellectual communities have grown up around this research, each associated with its own set of conclusions: the behavioral economists, exemplified by Kagel et al. (1995), whose experiments satisfy them of maximization, and the behavioral psychologists, exemplified by Herrnstein (1997), whose work provides them with evidence for an alternative decision process, melioration, in which the consumer selects at each choice point the more rewarding option without necessarily maximizing overall returns. A more precise formulation than satisficing, melioration refers to the choice of whatever option (e.g. one of a number of products) provides the consumer with the greater/greatest immediate satisfaction; while he or she can be said to maximize returns at each choice point in a sequence of purchase decisions, there is no reason to expect that the behavior involved will maximize overall return as economic theory predicts. Despite protracted debate, no solution to the problem has been found, which satisfies both camps. However, as marketing scientists, we can safely leave the protagonists, as Guthrie characterized Tolman's rats, 'lost in thought'.

Failure to generate definitive experimental data has not deterred these behavioral scientists from suggesting, in the absence of any direct evidence, how the behavior of human consumers is related to the system of rewards that ostensibly maintains it. The application has, however, devised and tested a method of obtaining data on consumers' purchase choices over time, which have direct relevance to our understanding more clearly how consumer choice is distributed over a sequence of purchase occasions and when such behavior can be said to maximize.

Matching refers to the tendency of animals and humans to distribute their responses between two choices in proportion to the patterns of reward programmed to be contingent on each choice. Herrnstein discovered, defined, and built upon this phenomenon. Defining choice not as an internal deliberative process but as a *rate* of intersubjectively observable events that are temporally distributed, Herrnstein's dependent variable was not the single response that needed contextual explication in terms of a single contingent reinforcer: it was the relative frequency of responding, which he explained by reference to the relative rate of reinforcement obtained from the behavior. Animals presented with two opportunities to respond (pecking key A or key B), each of which delivers reinforcers (food pellets) on its own variable interval (VI) schedule, allocate their responses on A and B in proportion to the rates of reward they obtain from A and B. This phenomenon, known as 'matching', has been replicated in numerous species including humans and has found applications in behavior modification and organizational behavior management, to name but two relevant fields. In particular, it provides a framework for the behavioral analysis of consumption (Rachlin, 1989, 2000a, b). The phenomenon is particularly well researched in contexts that require an individual to allocate a limited period between two choices, each scheduled to produce reward at a different rate.

Most choices for human consumers require the allocation of a fixed income between alternative choices, each of which exacts a different monetary sacrifice. In this case,

responses take the form of surrendering money in varying amounts, while the reward is the receipt of a fixed amount of the good in question. Price is the ratio of units of money that must be exchanged for units of the good. Both matching and maximizing theories make a similar prediction of behavior on such schedules: the individual will maximize by exclusively selecting the schedule that provides the higher return. Studies of animal choice confirm this prediction. The reason is that, given the parameters of matching in the context of consumer choice, where the schedules that govern performance are close analog of the ratio schedules imposed in the operant laboratory, both maximization and matching theories predict a similar pattern of choice, one that eventuates in maximization and matching by virtue of the expectation that consumers will always select the cheapest alternative when selecting among brands. The expected behavior pattern is, therefore, exclusive choice of the more favorable schedule. Although there is some evidence that this is generally the case, there are frequent exceptions in that consumers sometimes buy the most expensive option or, on the same shopping trip, purchase both cheaper and dearer versions of the same product, something that animal experiments, which demand discrete choices in each time frame, do not permit their subjects. In other words, the marketing system adds complications to the analysis that cannot be anticipated within the original context of the behavioral economics research program. Even behavioral economics research with human consumers in real time situations of purchase and consumption (token economies and field experiments) have not been able to incorporate such influences on choice as a dynamic bilateral market system of competing producers who seek mutually satisfying exchanges with consumers whose high levels of discretionary income make their selection suppliers not only routine but also relatively cost-free. Behavioral economics experiments with human consumers have at best been able to incorporate only a portion of the full marketing mix influence on consumer choice. It has typically been possible to employ price as a marketing variable but not the full panoply of product differentiation, advertising and other promotional activities, and competing distribution strategies, which are the dominant features of the modern consumer-oriented economy. Moreover, because it is the marketing mix, rather than any of its elements acting in isolation from the rest, that influences consumer choice, such experiments have been unable to capture the effect of this multiplex stimulus on purchasing and consumption.

By and large, our analyses found that brand competition was generally marked by ideal matching, while product choices, as demonstrated here by wine and cola purchases by some degree of under-, over- or anti-matching. Relative demand curves were generally downward sloping. Again, with some exceptions, consumers maximized by purchasing the least expensive of the brands composing their considerations sets. Where there were exceptions from the predictions of matching and maximizing theories, they occurred for reasons peculiar to the marketing context: first, because the composition of consumers' consideration sets often meant that their selections were among premium priced, higher quality brands, or at least those more highly differentiated through promotional activity, rather than among all of the brands that made up the product category. As a result, their selecting the least expensive brand refers only to their choosing within the limitations of this subset of available product versions. A second source of exception was that some consumers bought more than one brand on a single shopping trip, often adding a rather more expensive brand to the cheapest within their consideration set. No doubt, the different brands were intended for distinct situations of usage, as when a standard and less expensive fruit juice is purchased for consumption by children of the household in the course of the day and a more expensive version is obtained for the family's use at breakfast. The sheer desire for variety sometimes led consumers to select a more expensive brand on occasion, either in addition to or instead of the cheapest alternative. In the qualitative phase of the research, one respondent reported that she 'just had to' buy a distinctively flavored brand of butter from time to time; another, that she would purchase a cheaper store brand sometimes even though this was not part of her regular repertoire simply as a result of the convenience of shopping at a different supermarket. Nevertheless, apart from these predictable exceptions, the predictions of both matching and maximization theories were fulfilled. Although matching is a truism in the case of consumer choice – the more one buys, the more one spends, and at more or less constant prices the relative amount spent on one brand will be proportionally similar to the relative amount of it that is bought – these studies have clarified a number of matters in marketing and consumer research.

An interesting outcome of the application of matching theory to consumer choice is the finding that brands can be defined in terms of their substitutability as revealed by estimates of the s parameter that approach unity, while product groupings and categories whose members are independent or complementary are indicated by under-, over- or anti-matching (Romero et al., 2006). Foxall, James, Chang and Oliveira-Castro (in press) present further evidence on this. The third conclusion drawn by Hursh (1980) is that, 'Reinforcers may interact as complements, as well as substitutes'. We benefit here from making a distinction between utilitarian and informational or symbolic reinforcement, which goes beyond the usual distinction between primary and secondary reinforcers (Foxall, 1997a). In the case of brands, it is inevitable that they will tend to be substitutes in so far as they are functionally similar (almost identical in terms of physical formulation), i.e. in terms of utilitarian reinforcement, and complements in so far as they are differentiated by branding, i.e. in terms of informational reinforcement or social symbolism. Branding is an attempt to reduce the perceived substitutability of brands by altering their value to the consumer on the basis of their social significance (e.g. increasing the status of their owners and users) or psychological significance (e.g. enhancing the self-esteem of those who own and use them).

Hursh (1980) also argues that 'because reinforcers differ in elasticity and because reinforcers can be complementary, no simple, unidimensional choice rule such as matching can account for all choice behavior'. The *pattern of reinforcement* (the pattern of low-to-high utilitarian reinforcement and low-to-high informational reinforcement produced by buying or using a product) is an analytical category that takes the place in interpretive behaviorism occupied by that of the schedule of reinforcement in the experimental analysis, of behavior. Because patterns of reinforcement differ and because informational reinforcement increases the complementarity of brands within a product category, nonprice elements of the marketing mix come to the fore. The study of brand choice indicates that the multi-disciplinarity of behavioral economics can usefully be extended by the inclusion of results and perspectives from marketing research. Behavioral economics is supported by the research in that its analyses, and conclusions are shown to apply to human consumers in situations of free choice; behavioral economists should appreciate, however, the conclusions of marketing researchers to the effect that most consumers are multi-brand purchasers, and that marketing considerations other than price influence choice. Marketing researchers may need to take note of the import of price differentials in brand choice. The behavioral mechanism of choice that underlies the molar patterns of consumer choice depicted here appears to be momentary maximization of benefit, a result that is consistent with melioration or overall maximization. However, the lesson of the research is that brand choice is reinforced by two sources of reward, *utilitarian*, which derives from the functional benefits of the good, and *informational* or *symbolic*, which derives from the psychological and cultural meanings, which goods acquire through their

participation in social interactions and, by derivation, through advertising and other means to branding. The recognition of both sources of reinforcement is the key requirement for both marketing researchers and behavioral economists.

Consumer demand analysis

The point of the discussion of pattern of reinforcement and plasticity of demand is not to dismiss such stalwarts of economic analysis as elasticity of demand. Rather, having established the usefulness of the former types of interpretive construct to consumer behavior analysis, the aim should be to operationalize them and relate them to the standard constructs. This has been one of the tasks of work on consumer demand analysis within the BPM context. Much of the work on demand analysis has involved comparison of the buying patterns of consumers grouped by their predominant purchasing of brands having specific patterns of informational and utilitarian reinforcement.

The observed decreases in the quantity bought with increases in prices, indicated by negative elasticity coefficients, may, however, have been associated with different response patterns by different groups. The tendency to buy larger quantities when prices are lower may be related to one or more of the following three patterns: (1) buying larger quantities of a product when its price was below its usual, average, price rather than when its price was above its average price (i.e. intra-brand or absolute elasticity); (2) buying larger quantities when buying brands belonging to cheaper, lower informational levels than when buying brands belonging to more expensive, higher informational levels (i.e. informational inter-brand or relative elasticity); and (3) buying larger quantities when buying brands belonging to cheaper, lower utilitarian levels than when buying brands belonging to more expensive, higher utilitarian levels (i.e. utilitarian inter-brand or relative elasticity). These phenomena have been investigated in two studies, employing different sets of consumer panel data, which have borne out these extensions to matching analysis in the context of consumer choice (Oliveira-Castro et al., 2006, in press).

The possibility of combining matching and elasticity of demand analyses has led, most recently, to the testing of an equation that relates amount spent to quantity bought, utilitarian reinforcement obtained, informational reinforcement obtained, and price paid (which detects promotions). The results, which are discussed in the chapter by Oliveira-Castro et al., (in press) are highly encouraging for the view that economic demand is influenced, in addition to the amount purchased, by all three of the variables posited by the BPM – utilitarian reinforcement, informational reinforcement, and aversive consequences – can be shown to influence amount spent.

Experimental analyses

Numerous studies in the experimental analysis of behavior are relevant to the development of consumer behavior analysis (see, inter alia, Foxall, 2003). However, several recent approaches to the experimental analysis of consumer behavior are of particular interest to the progress of the model and research program. The first is Hantula's use of simulated shopping malls to test predictions of matching theory in a consumer context. In a series of experiments, Hantula and his colleagues have investigated the influence of various marketing elements (e.g. price and service level measured in terms of delay) on the spending behavior of buyers of consumer products (DiClemente and Hantula, 2003b; Hantula et al., 2001; Rajala and Hantula, 2000; Smith and Hantula, 2003; see also Hantula et al., in press). This work is significant not only for its contribution to consumer behavior analysis but also for its insights into the nature of economic psychology, i.e. the manner in which the all-too-often-separated disciplines of economics and psychology,

and biobehavioral consumer research might be integrated. The integration is achieved in this case through foraging theory. A central emphasis has been on the relevance of the delay reduction hypothesis (DRH; Fantino, 1969) to consumer decision-making. This hypothesis has been supported in the simulated context of online shopping for consumer goods (DiClemente and Hantula, 2003b; Rajala and Hantula, 2000). Increasing realism has been achieved by studies in which the monetary cost of products has been the independent variable (Smith and Hantula, 2003). Smith and Hantula argue that cost can be conceptualized in terms of a temporal constraint on foraging since time expended on working for money is an initial phase of the period spent foraging. Hence, the DRH should provide an account of the effects of price on preference during the consumption phase. 'The DRH predicts that the organism should prefer the stimulus associated with the shortest time to reinforcement, and that increasing delay to conditioned reinforcement should be associated with reduced preference for the corresponding response option. Accordingly, less expensive items should be selected with greater frequency from among several because they are most profitable from the standpoint of E/T [energy expenditure, E, per unit time spent foraging, T], consistent with optimal foraging theory and classical utility theory' (Smith and Hantula, 2003: 657). The findings of the research indicate that in general, increases in price have a similar effect on consumer preferences to delay. Although it is only one of a number of important outcomes of this kind of investigation, the finding that the price of a product may be viewed as a temporal factor by which foraging may be understood is valuable for further research that treats temporally extended consumption by humans in terms of foraging.

The constant need in experimental work that is designed to have some impact on the interpretation of complex behavior is to move gradually closer to empirical investigations of choice that permit field experimentation; in this way, the rigor of experimental manipulations and the links with the principles of behavior analysis can be retained while the focus of research more closely resembles the kinds of day-to-day behavior exhibited by consumers in natural settings. An interesting approach to this is found in the experimental work of Oliveira-Castro (e.g. 2003) on the influence of the base price of products on the amount of time prospective consumers spend on search. Oliveira-Castro's observations of consumers during the prepurchase phase of their purchase sequence not only permits in-store methodologies to be evaluated in the context of consumer behavior analysis but also yields the result that search behavior is more extensive for higher-priced items.

Sigurdsson has pioneered in-store experimentation within the consumer behavior analysis framework (Sigurdsson et al., in press; Sigurdsson et al., in press). In addition, Fagerstrøm has integrated an experimental approach with conjoint analysis to test the effects of both utilitarian reinforcement and informational reinforcement on consumer preference (Fagerstrøm et al., in press).

DEVELOPMENT

In conclusion, I should like to mention briefly a few of the developments in consumer behavior analysis that are currently underway. Any depiction of theory development and empirical research that portrays them as necessarily sequential or unidirectional is alien to the consumer behavior analysis research program in which theoretical, philosophical, and empirical concerns interact continuously. Each component of the program informs, shapes, and reshapes the others.

A key area to which consumer behavior analysis offers entry is the strategic behavior of the firm. These are things that behavioral economics as we know it (as a derivative of experimental economics and behavior analysis) has scarcely touched upon. Not to have marketing considerations, especially as they are related to the overall governance of the

economic enterprise, been addressed. Consumer behavior analysis, with its unique mélange of economics, psychology, and marketing is well placed to answer these concerns. A beginning has been made with an outline of *the marketing firm* (Foxall, 1999) that seeks to formulate the substantive functions and contributions of marketing management and the theory of the firm in terms of behavior analysis and behavioral economics. The firm emerges as necessarily a marketing enterprise, the goals of which are to influence consumer demand by the closure of the consumer behavior setting and the manipulation of patterns of reinforcement. Little progress has to date been made in this area, and it is therefore a pleasure to welcome the paper by Xiao and Nicholson (in press), which extends this thinking into a specific area of consumer and managerial interactivity. Consumer behavior analysis is poised to make a strong contribution to understanding the nature of the firm and of producing a theory of the firm to stand alongside those of economics and behavioral science, one which uniquely emphasizes the concerns of marketing and strategy, which have traditionally been the focus of management and marketing science.

Another dimension to the attempt to present consumer behavior and managerial behavior in similar terms, something of which marketing and business studies in general stands in need, is suggested by the work on the population ecology of firms (e.g. Hannan and Freeman, 1977). Current work in the CBAR Group includes modeling consumer choice patterns in terms of inter-species foraging – the pioneering approach of Hantula and his colleagues has already been mentioned – and the forging of an intellection connection between work on the life cycles and behaviors of groups of consumers ('species') and those of the organizations that provide their patches is a logical outcome of these interests.

The extension of the philosophy of science underlying consumer behavior analysis is also a major preoccupation. The purpose of this research program has been overwhelmingly epistemological: to discover the extent to which behavior analysis could provide a convincing explanation of consumer choice in the context of the affluent marketing-oriented economy. The strategy was to build simple models of consumer behavior based on unreconstructed radical behaviorism and to test them, first by exploring their interpretive capacity and later by reference to new empirical research. Whether radical behaviorism would succeed wholly in the task of explaining complex choice was always an open question but the order of procedure began with the assumption that it be tested on its own merits to the full. Additional strands of explanation would be incorporated only as required (Foxall, 1996, 1998). The answer as to whether radical behaviorism can provide the lead to the accurate prediction of consumer choice is positive. The common tie provided by the principle of 'selection by consequences' (Skinner, 1981) brings strength to this approach to consumer research. The BPM, like behavior analysis and natural selection, is a selectionist system: the integration of all three into a standpoint from which to explain consumer choice promises to provide a major area within both the theoretical and the applied analyses of human behavior.

REFERENCES

Agnew, J. (1998) 'The Establishing Operation in Organizational Behavior Management', *Journal of Organizational Behavior Management*, 18(1): 7–19.

Baum, W.M. (1974) 'On Two Types of Deviation from the Matching Law', *Journal of the Experimental Analysis of Behavior*, 22: 231–242.

Baum, W.M. (1979) 'Matching, Undermatching and Overmatching in Studies of Choice', *Journal of the Experimental Analysis of Behavior*, 32: 269–281.

DiClemente, D.F. and Hantula, D.A. (2003a) 'Applied Behavioral Economics and Consumer Choice', *Journal of Economic Psychology*, 23: 589–602.

DiClemente, D.F. and Hantula, D.A. (2003b) 'Optimal Foraging Online: Increasing Sensitivity to Delay', *Psychology and Marketing*, 20: 785–810.

Ehrenberg, A.S.C. (1972/1988) *Repeat Buying*. North Holland, Amsterdam. Reprinted 1988, London: Griffin.

Fagerstrøm, A., Foxall, G.R. and Arntzen, E. (in press) 'Implications of motivating operations for the functional analysis of consumer behavior'. *Journal of Organizational Behavior Management*.

Fantino, E. (1969) 'Choice and Rate of Reinforcement', *Journal of the Experimental Analysis of Behavior*, 12: 723–730.

Feyerabend, P. (1975) *Against Method*. London: NLB.

Foxall, G.R. (1983) *Consumer Choice*. London and New York: Macmillan.

Foxall, G.R. (1986) 'The Role of Radical Behaviorism in the Explanation of Consumer Choice', *Advances in Consumer Research*, 13: 195–201.

Foxall, G.R. (1990/2004) *Consumer Psychology in Behavioral Perspective*. London and New York: Routledge. Republished 2004, Frederick, MD: Beard Books.

Foxall, G.R. (1994) 'Behaviour Analysis and Consumer Psychology', *Journal of Economic Psychology*, 15: 5–91.

Foxall, G.R. (1996) *Consumers in Context: The BPM Research Program*. London and New York: Routledge.

Foxall, G.R. (1997a) *Marketing Psychology: The Paradigm in the Wings*. London: Macmillan; New York: St. Martin's.

Foxall, G.R. (1997b) 'Affective Responses to Consumer Situations', *International Review of Retail, Distribution and Consumer Research*, 7: 191–225.

Foxall, G.R. (1998a) 'The Marketing Firm', *Journal of Economic Psychology*, 20: 207–234.

Foxall, G.R. (1998b) 'Radical Behaviorist Interpretation: Generating and Evaluating an Account of Consumer Behavior', *The Behavior Analyst*, 21: 321–354.

Foxall, G.R. (1999a) 'The Marketing Firm', *Journal of Economic Psychology*, 20: 207–234.

Foxall, G.R. (1999b) 'The Contextual Stance', *Philosophical Psychology*, 12: 25–46.

Foxall, G.R. (1999c) 'The Substitutability of Brands', *Managerial and Decision Economics*, 20: 241–257.

Foxall, G.R. (2002) *Consumer Behaviour Analysis: Critical Perspectives in Business and Management*. London and New York: Routledge.

Foxall, G.R. (2003) 'The Behavior Analysis of Consumer Choice', *Journal of Economic Psychology*, 24: 581–588.

Foxall, G.R. (2004) *Context and Cognition: Interpreting Complex Behavior*. Reno, NV: Context Press.

Foxall, G.R. (2005) *Understanding Consumer Choice*. London and New York: Palgrave Macmillan.

Foxall, G.R. (2007a) *Explaining Consumer Choice*. London and New York: Palgrave Macmillan.

Foxall, G.R. (2007b) 'Intentional Behaviorism', *Behavior and Philosophy*, 35: 1–55.

Foxall, G.R. (2007c) 'Explaining Consumer Choice: Coming to Terms with Intentionality', *Behavioural Processes*, 75: 129–145.

Foxall, G.R. and James, V.K. (2002) 'The Behavioral Analysis of Consumer Brand Choice: A Preliminary Analysis', *European Journal of Behavior Analysis*, 2: 209–220.

Foxall, G.R. and James, V.K. (2003) 'The Behavioral Ecology of Brand Choice: How and What do Consumers Maximize?', *Marketing and Psychology*, 20: 811–836.

Foxall, G.R., Oliveira-Castro, J.M., James, V.K. and Schrezenmaier, T.C. (2007) *The Behavioral Economics of Brand Choice*. London and New York: Palgrave Macmillan.

Foxall, G.R. and Oliveira-Castro, J.M. (in press) 'Intentional Consequences of Self-Instruction', *Behavior and Philosophy*.

Foxall, G.R. and Schrezenmaier, T.C. (2003) 'The Behavioral Economics of Consumer Brand Choice: Establishing a Methodology', *Journal of Economic Psychology*, 24: 675–695.

Foxall, G.R., Oliveira-Castro, J.M. and Schrezenmaier, T.C. (2004) 'The Behavioral Economics of Consumer Brand Choice: Patterns of Reinforcement and Utility Maximization', *Behavioural Processes*, 65: 235–260.

Foxall, G.R. and Yani-de-Soriano, M.M. (2005) 'Situational Influences on Consumers' Attitudes and Behavior', *Journal of Business Research*, 58: 518–525.

Foxall, G.R., James, V.K., Chang, J. and Oliveira-Castro, J.M. (in press) 'Substitutability and Independence: Matching analyses of brands and products', *Journal of Organizational Behavior Management*.

Friedman, M. (1953) *Essays in Positive Economics*. Chicago: University of Chicago Press.

Green, L. and Freed, D.E. (1993) 'The Substitutability of Reinforcers', *Journal of the Experimental Analysis of Behavior*, 60: 141–158.

Hannan, M.T and Freeman, J. (1977) 'The Population Ecology of Organizations', *American Journal of Sociology*, 82: 929–964.

Hantula, D.A., DiClemente, D.F., and Rajala, A.K. (2001) 'Outside the Box: The Analysis of Consumer Behavior', in L. Hayes, J. Austin, and R. Flemming (eds) *Organizational Change*, pp. 203–233. Reno, NV: Context Press.

Hantula, D.A., Brockman, D. and Smith, C. (in press). 'Online Shopping as Foraging: The Effects of Increasing Delays on Purchase and Patch Residence', *IEEE Transactions on Professional Communication*.

Herrnstein, R.J. (1961) 'Relative and Absolute Strength of Response as a Function of Frequency of Reinforcement', *Journal of the Experimental Analysis of Behavior*, 4: 267–272.

Herrnstein, R.J. (1982) 'Melioration as Behavioral Dynamism', in M.L. Commons, R.J. Herrnstein, and H. Rachlin (eds) *Quantitative Analyses of Behavior*, Vol. II, pp. 433–458. Cambridge, MA: Ballinger.

Herrnstein, R.J. (1997) In H. Rachlin and D.I. Laibson (eds) *The Matching Law: Chapters in Psychology and Economics*. New York: Russell Sage Foundation.

Herrnstein, R.J. and Loveland, D.H. (1975) 'Maximizing and Matching on Concurrent Ratio Schedules', *Journal of the Experimental Analysis of Behavior*, 24: 107–116.

Herrnstein, R.J. and Vaughan, W. (1980) 'Melioration and Behavioral Allocation', in J.E.R. Staddon (ed.) *Limits to Action: The Allocation of Individual Behavior*, pp. 143–176. New York: Academic Press.

Hursh, S.R. (1980) 'Economic Concepts for the Analysis of Behavior', *Journal of the Experimental Analysis of Behavior*, 34: 219–238.

Kagel, J.H., Battalio, R.C. and Green, L. (1995) *Economic Choice Theory: An Experimental Analysis of Animal Behavior*. Cambridge: Cambridge University Press.

Mehrabian, A. (1980) *Basic Dimensions for a General Psychological Theory: Implications for Personality, Social, Environmental and*

Developmental Studies. Cambridge, MA: Oelgeschlager, Gunn and Hain.

Mehrabian, A. and Russell, J.A. (1974) *An Approach to Environmental Psychology.* Cambridge, MA: MIT Press.

Michael, J. (1982) 'Distinguishing between Discriminative and Motivational Functions of Stimuli'. *Journal of the Experimental Analysis of Behavior*, 37: 149–155.

Michael, J. (1993) 'Establishing Operations'. *The Behavior Analyst*, 16: 191–206.

Oliveira-Castro, J.M. (2003) 'Effects of Base Price Upon Search Behavior of Consumers in a Supermarket: An Operant Analysis', *Journal of Economic Psychology*, 24: 637–652.

Oliveira-Castro, J.M., Ferreira, D.C.S., Foxall, G.R., and Schrezenmaier, T.C. (2005a) 'Dynamics of Repeat Buying for Packaged Food Products', *Journal of Marketing Management*, 21: 37–61.

Oliveira-Castro, J.M., Foxall, G.R., and Schrezenmaier, T.C. (2005b) 'Patterns of Consumer Response to Retail Price Differentials', *Service Industries Journal*, 25: 309–327.

Oliveira-Castro, J.M., Foxall, G.R. and Schrezenmaier, T.C. (2006) 'Consumer Brand Choice: Individual and Group Analyses of Demand Elasticity', *Journal of the Experimental Analysis of Behavior*, 85: 147–166.

Oliveira-Castro. J. M., Foxall, G. R. and James, V. K. (in press) 'Consumer Brand Choice: Allocation of Expenditure as a Function of Pattern of Reinforcement and Response Cost'. *Journal of Organizational Behavior Management.*

Penrose, E. (1959) *The Economic Theory of the Growth of the Firm.* Oxford: Blackwell.

Rachlin, H. (1989) *Judgment, Decision and Choice.* New York: Freeman.

Rachlin, H. (2000a) *The Science of Self Control.* Harvard University Press, Cambridge, MA.

Rachlin, H. (2000b) 'Teleological Behaviorism', in W. O'Donohue and R. Kitchener (eds), *Handbook of Behaviorism* Academic Press, San Diego, pp. 195–215.

Rajala, A.K. and Hantula, D.A. (2000) 'Towards a Behavioral Ecology of Consumption: Delay-Reduction Effects on Foraging in a Simulated Internet Mall', *Managerial and Decision Economics*, 21: 145–158.

Romero, S., Foxall, G.R., Schrezenmaier, T.C., Oliveira-Castro, J.,and James, V.K. (2006) 'Deviations from Matching in Consumer Choice', *European Journal of Behavior Analysis*, 7: 15–40.

Schwartz, B. and Lacey, H. (1988) 'What Applied Studies of Human Operant Conditioning Tell Us About Humans and About Operant Conditioning', in G. Davey and C. Cullen (eds) *Human Operant Conditioning and Behavior Modification*, pp. 27–42. Chichester: Wiley.

Sigurdsson, V., Saevarsson, H. and Foxall, G.R. (in press a) 'Brand-Placement and Consumer Choice: An In-Store Experiment', *Journal of Applied Behavior Analysis.*

Sigurdsson, V., Foxall, G. R. and Saevarsson, H. (in press b) 'In-Store Experimental Approach to Pricing and Consumer Behavior', *Journal of Organizational Behavior Management.*

Sigurdsson, V., Engilbertsson, H. and Foxall, G. R. (in press c) 'The Effects of a Point-of-Purchase Display on Relative Sales: An In-Store Experimental Evaluation', *Journal of Organizational Behavior Management.*

Simon, H. (1959) 'Theories of Decision Making in Economics and Behavioral Science', *American Economic Review*, 49: 223–283.

Skinner, B.F. (1981) 'Selection by Consequences', *Science*, 213(4507): 501–504.

Smith, C.L. and Hantula, D.A. (2003) 'Pricing Effects on Foraging in a Simulated Internet Shopping Mall', *Journal of Economic Psychology*, 23: 653–674.

Soriano, M.Y., Foxall, G.R. and Pearson, G.J. (2002) 'Emotional Responses to Consumers' Environments: An Empirical Examination of the Behavioral Perspective Model in a Latin American Context', *Journal of Consumer Behaviour*, 2: 138–154.

Xiao, S. and Nicholson, M. (in press) 'Trick or Treat? An Examination of Marketing Relationships in a Non-deceptive Counterfeit Market', *Journal of Organizational Behavior Management.*

Yani-de-Soriano, M.M. and Foxall, G.R. (2006) 'The Emotional Power of Place: The Fall and Rise of Dominance in Retail Research', *Journal of Retailing and Consumer Services*, 13: 403–416.

18

Consumer Agency and Action

Richard P. Bagozzi

[An agent is] one who acts. The central problem of agency is to understand the difference between events happening in me or to me, and my taking control of events, or doing things. (Blackburn, 1994: 9)[1]

Considerable progress has been made in consumer research in the past few decades (see Chapter 4 in this book, and Payne and Bettman, 2004). Most of this research focuses on how consumers process market-related information (e.g. prices, product/service attributes and performance, brand names, advertising appeals, and store environments). A wealth of information has emerged in this regard that might be categorized under such headings as attention processes, perception, memory, information search, categorization, cognitive schemas, judgment and evaluation, inference drawing, and choice.

The vast majority of research, and indeed the theories driving this research, draw upon psychology, particularly cognitive psychology and social psychology. Both in consumer research and psychological research, emphasis to date has been on the behavior of individuals

---

in the sense of what occurs inside the minds of decision makers. Cognitive responses, and to a lesser extent emotional responses, to marketing stimuli are the phenomena under study in much of contemporary consumer research. Hence the characterization of the focus of consumer research as consumer *behavior*, where behavior refers to psychological variables and processes. Even the dependent variables in most studies are decidedly psychological (e.g. attitudes, preferences, and intentions).

Much less attention has been devoted to what consumers do and why they do the things they do (i.e. consumer *action*), where of course information processing and consumer behavior play a role particularly in the initial stages of decision making but also possibly following a decision to act (Bagozzi, 2006a, 2006b). Yet, the role of consumer behavior *in* consumer action has been given scant consideration. Save for occasional mention or testing of correlations between psychological states and purchase outcomes or predictions of such outcomes, actual consumer actions have been neglected. What are lacking are theories of how psychological processes constituting consumer behavior lead to or guide consumer action. The gap between consumer behavior and consumer action equires specification of complex, multifaceted processes and not merely investigation of empirical links between mental states (e.g. current preferences or attitudes) and observed action (e.g. subsequent purchases).

To grasp what I mean by action, consider Aristotle's (2000: 104) claim: 'The first principle of action – its moving cause, not its goal – is rational choice, and that of rational choice is desire, and goal-directed reason'. We might say that action is what one does as an agent either as an end in and of itself or as a means to achieving a goal. Moreover, this action is determined proximally by choice (roughly comprised of such volitional processes as decision making and intention formation), whereas choice is determined by desire, and desire by goal-directed reasoning, where the latter encompasses in part cognitive and emotional processes and more broadly what might be termed *reasons for acting*. In a nutshell, we might summarize intentional or purposive action in this regard as follows: reasons for acting→desire to act→decision making/choice/intention to act→action (as an end or means)→achievement of an end or not→collateral outcomes (for self, others, and surroundings).

The processes outlined in the aforementioned schematic of action are largely deliberative or reasoned. Nevertheless, it is important to acknowledge that the determinants of action sometimes function automatically below conscious awareness. Thus, the need to consider dual-process models (e.g. Strack and Deutsch, 2004) and social neuroscience (e.g. Harmon-Jones and Winkielman, 2007). In this chapter, I present a framework for consumer action, and use it to draw-in research from psychology, neuroscience, consumer behavior, and various applied areas of the social sciences. Both the framework and supporting research are works in progress, because researchers in economics, psychology, neuroscience, and marketing are only now beginning to see the connections binding together the ideas and findings from the theory of mind, neuroscience, psychology, and the theory of action, where these developments are literally exploding daily on the scene (e.g. Camerer et al., 2005; Dietvorst

et al., 2009; Harmon-Jones and Winkielman, 2007; Yoon et al., 2006).

The review begins with a discussion of the consumer decision making core, which presents the key variables and processes linking, and regulating, reasons for acting to action. Then the variables and processes that influence the core and emanate from it are considered in four subsections: the bases for self-regulation of desires, causes of goal desires, causes of action desires, and implications of action intentions.

THE CONSUMER DECISION MAKING CORE

We can represent consumer decision making in terms of the central motivation, cognitions, and volitions a person engages in as he/she is exposed to, and processes, either marketing stimuli or internal stimuli related to consumption needs and opportunities. In a sense, the consumer decision making core constitutes everyday folk psychological processes regulating one's responses to external and internal marketing-related stimuli. Yet, the folk psychology can be grounded in basic psychological and neuroscience principles.

Figure 18.1 presents a bare bones rendition of the consumer decision making core. The heart of the core is the throughput processes consisting of goal desire→goal intention→action desire→action intention. This captures the largely deterministic stages starting with goal formation, where a desire to pursue a goal emerges, leading to a commitment to pursue the goal and manifest in a goal intention, followed by establishment of a desire to do what is necessary to achieve the goal, and ending with a commitment to a specific course of action (i.e. an action intention), as a means to the desired end.

The throughput processes are considered deterministic in two senses. First, each of the three paths in the center of Figure 18.1 reflects learned responses or routines that either occur automatically or else are connected to thoughts or feelings activated by the psychological state or event at the origin of each

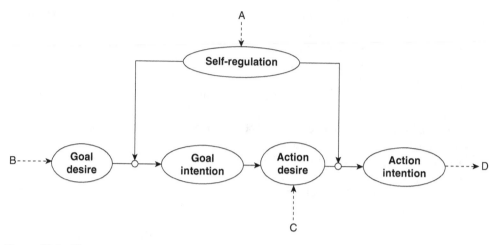

Figure 18.1   The consumer decision making core (after Bagozzi, 2006a, b).

path, which then function deterministically according to psychological laws to activate the psychological state or event at the head of each arrow. Second, as represented by B and C in Figure 18.1, psychological states or events in the form of reasons for acting activate goal or action desires, respectively, in a deterministic way, again according to psychological laws.

An example of a deterministic link between goal intention and action desire might occur when I form an intention to replenish my supply of breakfast cereal after eating the last helping of it in the box one morning, and this leads me to desire to take a small detour to the local supermarket at the end of the work day as I return home. Notice that, at this point in the morning, I might not have formed a specific action intention, only an action desire to do the means needed to achieve the goal. I may realize that I need to be open or flexible throughout the day should something come up to make it unfeasible for me to go to the supermarket. Hence, it is possible for my action desire to be activated but for my action intention to be tentative or contingent on later considerations. Of course, the action desire might under some circumstances lead straightaway to an action intention to make a trip to the store or to go to the store at the end of the day; the latter would be an example of the present formation of an

intention to act at a later time. An instance of a deterministic initiation of an action desire in the second sense mentioned earlier (i.e. path C in Figure 18.1) might be the energization of an action desire by the development or retrieval of a strong attitude to act, such as occurs when upon hearing a particularly persuasive argument made by a politician, I form a favorable attitude toward voting on an issue, and this, perhaps along with other criteria, enlivens my desire to vote (i.e. my action desire).

Although seldom explicitly recognizing the metaphysical assumptions in their studies, most researchers in psychology and consumer research assume deterministic processes along the lines described in the preceding section, albeit amongst different mental states or events. Whether one, say, performs an experiment, by manipulating information and observing attitude change or conducts a survey, where attitudes, subjective norms, perceived behavioral control, and intentions are measured, the statistically inferred causal or functional connections are implicitly presumed to be deterministic. Can consumers self-regulate their actions in non- or quasi-deterministic ways? Does the concept of willpower apply in consumer action?

Although some researchers categorically rule out self-regulation in a willful sense (e.g. Wegner, 2002), I wish to leave room for self-control of seemingly deterministic processes.

This is shown in Figure 18.1 through the role of self-regulation of desires by the operation of personal moral or self-evaluative standards. By self-regulation, I mean the indirect effects of three classes of human agency on self-evaluative standards, which function as moderators of the effects of goal desires on goal intentions and the effects of action desires on action intentions (see Figure 18.1): (1) social and self-conscious emotions, (2) feelings of caring, love, empathy, or reciprocity, and (3) personal and social identity (see next main section of chapter).

There are two broad categories of self-regulation: reflectivity and reflexivity (Bagozzi, 2006b). *Reflective self-regulation*, for me, means the active imposition of personal moral or self-evaluative standards to a felt or possible goal desire or action desire (Bagozzi, 2006a, b). That is, decision makers evaluate their desires and then reason and decide whether they want to have or want to not have the desires they experience and scrutinize. They do this in such a way as to cancel, override, modify, or postpone further consideration or implementation of the desire to act. More specifically, I propose that, when thinking about one's desire to act (or one's goal desire), a decision maker asks him/herself such questions as the following: Am I the kind of person who should have this desire? Am I the kind of person who acts on this kind of desire? Is the desire consistent with the kind of person I wish to be? Will acting on this desire lead to personal flourishing? What effect will acting on this desire have on other people important to me, other people whom I might not even know, or social welfare writ large? In answering the question of what to decide or do, the decision maker brings to bear reasons for deciding or for acting or not (e.g. duty, obligations, or other personal standards and social requisites). Such reasons both justify and motivate the decision or action. Thus, self-regulatory reasoning comes to interact with our desires to influence our intentions and through intentions action. In a parallel manner, I suggest that a decision maker can reflect upon his/her lack of felt desire for a goal or to act in a particular decision context. Here the person considers whether to accept, embrace, or construct a desire for a goal or to act; questions analogous to those noted in the foregoing section could be posed self-reflectively with regard to self-perceived lack of felt desire (e.g. 'Is my not feeling a desire to act consistent with the type of person I wish to be?').

Therefore, self-regulation serves to moderate the effects, if any, of desires on intentions, and the processes are reflective ones based on reasoning. Note that desires, intentions, and their antecedents are empirical in the sense that they can be measured or manipulated as physical phenomena. The reasoning processes in self-regulation, by contrast, are largely composed of ideals and constitute transcendental-type concepts, although we leave open the possibility that some or at least part of such reasoning processes can be represented empirically as well. Thus, decision makers can exercise a certain degree of control over their desires and intentions. Left by themselves, desires operate deterministically to influence intentions. However, by the willful imposition of self-evaluative standards one can stop the effect of a desire on decisions or create or activate a desire to influence intentions where no such desire currently exists.

Note further that self-regulation can also occur *reflexively*. That is, learned values, dispositions, traits, virtues, and vices can function as moderators of the effects of desires on intentions (Bagozzi, 2006b; Sekerka and Bagozzi, 2007). An example would be a virtuous consumer deciding seemingly spontaneously to resist his/her personal desire to purchase a product that harms the environment. Here, the virtue is presumably internalized and has been operating for a while as a personal policy that is activated later upon being confronted with the possibility of purchasing a product. Finally, I wish to stress that another way that people self-regulate their desires is by being thankful or expressing their gratitude for that which they have, by limiting their wants through regular self-examination, by consciously resisting the persuasive effects of advertising, peer pressure, and the larger culture pressing one to consume or in other ways expand one's wants, and by, in general, being satisfied with or appreciative of much of what one already has.

The consumer decision making core has not been tested in its entirety to date, although pieces of it have been subjected to empirical research; however, the linkages referred to by A, B, C, and D in Figure 18.1 have received considerable examination in consumer research. Empirical research testing the throughput processes in the consumer core can be found in Bagozzi et al. (2003) and Dholakia et al. (2007). The consumer decision making core provides a new way of looking at consumer action; it also integrates much of the fragmented research in consumer behavior and psychology by suggesting how the reasons for acting and other processes are linked to the core through A, B, C, and D. We turn now to the research in this regard, while also pointing out how social neuroscience might inform research in this respect.

SELF-REGULATION

Self-regulation has been defined as 'any efforts by the human self to alter any of its own inner states or responses' (Vohs and Baumeister, 2004: 2) and is often used interchangeably with self-control. However, it can be argued that much research falling under the label 'self-regulation' or 'self-control' (e.g. Baumeister and Vohs, 2004; Carver and Scheier, 1998; Higgins, 1997) is not self-regulatory in a strict sense and in fact represents variants of deterministic processes. That is, most research done to date into self-regulation manipulates conditions for decision making and observes deterministic responses, where the intervening cognitive responses are themselves deterministic and presumed to constitute self-regulation.

Another way to look at self-regulation is as the exercise of a kind of human agency that is neither impulsive, compulsive, habitual, coerced, nor reinforced via rewards but rather is an intentional response to the question, 'How shall I act?'. One answers this question through the self-reflective or self-reflexive processes considered in the preceding section. Nevertheless, how explicitly does self-regulation in this sense happen? I submit that the self-reflective and self-reflexive processes are incited by the three mechanisms mentioned earlier and shown in Figure 18.2.

One central determinant of self-regulation resides in the self-conscious or social emotions: pride, gratitude, embarrassment, guilt, shame, envy, jealousy, and social anxiety. Self-conscious emotions function as consumers'

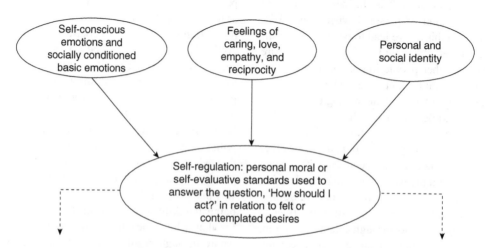

Figure 18.2   Factors grounding or instigating self-regulation (see Figure 18.1).

situational sensors to scrutinize whether they or their behavior, action, goals, or desires fit a significant social group or particular social setting based on evaluative signals from members of the target group or based on internalized emotional dispositions to react in a particular way. These emotions shape, instigate, or condition the consumer's self-evaluative standards used to answer the question, 'How should I act?'. Such other basic emotions as disgust or anger can ground or initiate self-regulation, too, when linked to relevant social situations. Emotional groundings of self-reflective and self-reflexive self-regulatory processes have biological and genetic foundations, yet are subject to developmental socialization and cultural forces.

Not much research to date has investigated the role of self-conscious emotions and socially conditioned basic emotions in the self-regulation of consumer action, but recent developments in psychology and in sales force behavior provide a basis for considering such processes. Haidt (2001) proposes that affectively valenced (i.e. polarized) mental states nondeliberatively influence moral judgments. He has found that disgust (Wheatley and Haidt, 2005) and 'elevation' (a kind of positive emotional response to moral beauty, Haidt, 2003) affect moral judgments. Verbeke et al. (2004) found that pride, a common emotion felt by salespeople in their everyday work settings, must be self-regulated if salespeople are to avoid negative social and personal consequences and are to succeed. Pride is self-regulated differently and has different consequences for salespeople in group versus individualistic cultures (Bagozzi et al., 2009). Coping with social anxiety has also been found to affect self-regulatory-like actions by salespeople (Belschak et al., 2006), and embarrassment appears to have important self-regulator consequences as well (Verbeke and Bagozzi, 2003). Finally, felt shame is coped with differently in-group versus individualistic cultures and leads to altruistic actions toward co-workers and higher performance in the former (Bagozzi et al., 2003). These and other self-conscious

emotions deserve specific scrutiny as they relate to consumer self-regulation (cf. Louro et al., 2005). Recent research points to a greater role for emotional than reasoned processes in moral decision making and has identified distinct neuro-processes in this regard (Greene and Haidt, 2002).

A second source and grounding of self-regulatory processes shown in Figure 18.2 are feelings of caring, love, empathy, and reciprocity. Two broad neuro systems seem to undergird these influences on self-regulation. One of these is termed theory of mind (ToM) and is defined as the ability to understand others as intentional agents in the sense of inferring the beliefs, desires, intentions, and other mental states or events of other people, so as to explain or predict their decisions or actions (e.g. Baron-Cohen et al., 2000; Dennett, 1987; Wellman, 1990).

A certain level of expertise in ToM processes seems to be necessary for effective interpersonal communication and the acquisition and use of appropriate emotional knowledge and skills functioning in interpersonal contexts. To the best of our knowledge, ToM processes have not been studied in consumer research, but have been recently scrutinized in marketing with respect to salespeople. Dietvorst et al. (2009) developed a paper and pencil scale to measure four aspects of ToM (which the authors termed, interpersonal mentalizing) that capture abilities demarcating higher versus lower performing salespersons: building rapport, detecting key nonverbal cues, taking a bird's eye view, and shaping interpersonal interactions to one's advantage. Importantly, for our purposes, and consistent with recent research on autism (e.g. Amodio and Frith, 2006), the regions of the brain that were activated more highly for people high versus low in ToM skills were the medial prefrontal cortex (MPFC) and the temporo-parietal junction (TPJ). Salespersons scoring both high and low on ToM skills showed equally high activation of the temporal poles (TP) regions of the brain. In addition to the demonstration of brain activation by use of functional magnetic resonance imaging (fMRI), a field study showed that rapport building had an indirect effect on performance through the person's ability to cope with social anxiety, whereas detecting nonverbal cues, taking a bird's eye view, and shaping interactions had direct effects on performance. The study of ToM skills in consumers would seem fruitful for understanding how consumers comprehend, and are influenced by, persuasive communications and how interactions with salespersons affect decision making and purchases. Personal and moral standards underlying the self-regulation of consumer action are likely to be dependent on the ability of ToM skills to mediate the effects of self-conscious and other emotions; feelings of caring, love, empathy, and reciprocity; and personal and social identity.

Feelings of caring, love, empathy, and reciprocity play out in face-to-face interactions and in mediated communications such as advertising. For people with normal levels of morality or well-developed personal standards subject to ethical concerns, such feelings are likely to shape or serve as input or criteria to self-regulation. For example, persons watching a television commercial, where the effects of poverty are demonstrated, may empathize with the victims, struggle with competing desires to purchase a product meeting needs for personal indulgence versus altruistic urges, and decide to donate money to the sponsor. Recent research in neuroscience suggests that the deliberative and nondeliberative processes underlying such decisions are more complex than meet the eye.

Consider recent research in this regard into the actions of salespersons scoring high versus low in Machiavellianism, which is a personality trait that can be used to study empathy and its effects (Bagozzi et al., 2009). Machiavellians have worldviews marked by cynicism and mistrust of others. They enter exchanges with an orientation to act first to exploit others before they, themselves, will be exploited. Common interpersonal tactics used by Machiavellians include deception, flattery, and manipulation. Unlike non-Machiavellians who are more trusting and

prone to be subject to feelings of guilt and shame, Machiavellians face little self-regulatory restraints and, if not unmoral, are at best amoral. They also show greater than average tendencies for psychopathic or sociopathic behaviors. Some paper-and-pencil research and considerable speculation by researchers in recent years imply that Machiavellians should be high in ToM skills, as well as empathy. Yet research findings tend to be contradictory.

By use of fMRI experiments, Bagozzi et al. (2009) found that salespeople scoring high versus low in Machiavellianism had significantly less activation in the MPFC, TPJ, and precuneus regions of the brain, and significantly greater activation of the insula and pars opercularis regions of the brain. What this suggests is that Machiavellianisms in fact score low on ToM skills and on taking the perspectives of people with whom they interact. Perspective taking is a key component of empathy, and is at least partially a top-down deliberative process. If Machiavellians lack ToM skills and lack empathy in a perspective taking sense, then why is it that they are successful in some personal selling jobs? An answer to this question can be found in Bagozzi et al.'s (2009) findings. Machiavellians showed greater activation of the insula and pars opercularis regions of the brain than non-Machiavellians. This means that Machiavellians show greater mirror neuron activation, which supports the conclusion that they are more emotionally attuned to interaction partners in the sense of displaying greater emotional contagion and motor mimicry skills than non-Machiavellians. Such mirror neuron activity represents automatic, bottom-up aspects of empathy. Thus, Machiavellians, while lacking in ToM and perspective taking skills, have the ability to be more sensitized to nondeliberative aspects of emotional content in interactions. Coupled with their tendency to strike first and attempt to manipulate others in deceptive ways, such emotional attunement gives them strategic advantages over non-Machiavellians in certain situations.

By use of field surveys, Bagozzi et al. (2009) also found that Machiavellians work best when the social situation or managerial control is loose. Many sales settings fit this condition.

New research in the neuroscience underpinnings of empathy in the actions of salespeople has implications for consumer research. Unlike Machiavellian salespeople who score low on perspective taking, and thus lack a basis for developing conscious empathic feelings, it is likely that most consumers will be receptive to empathic experiences, and these will occur to the extent that the insula, pars opercularis, and precuneus regions of the brain are activated. Interestingly, the neural circuits involved entail a kind of shared or synchronized representation of self and other, and this occurs even vicariously when a person watches other people interacting. Such processes mean that empathy may be a key factor in social influence, not only in actual face-to-face transactions, but also in the modeling of interactions in advertisements, in group purchase contexts such as family decision making, and when one is a target of persuasive communications where such feelings as tenderness, compassion, pity, caring, and love are conveyed in meaningful ways. Such empathic messages might have direct deliberative effects on goal and action desires (paths B and C in Figure 18.1). However, they may also have more indirect and nondeliberative effects through their role in self-regulation, such as found in moral behavior or in the application of personal standards of conduct in consumption settings, where competing desires must be reconciled or the lack of felt desire might be overcome.

The final source of, and grounding for, self-regulatory processes shown in Figure 18.2 are personal and social identities. Our moral and self-evaluative standards emerge or are activated by the identities we wish to express or maintain. Sometimes consumers see products and services as extensions of their personal or independent-based selves (e.g. Belk, 1988). Their possessions may be used to express their uniqueness and standout from others (e.g. Simonson and Nowlis, 2000; Tian et al., 2001). Alternatively, group, communal, or collective behavior may be salient, and consumers may select purchases so as to fit-in or identify with the social entities or companies that are important to them (e.g. Ahearne et al., 2005; Bagozzi and Dholakia, 2006a, b; Bhattacharya and Sen, 2003). Indeed, in some social situations, consumption is itself socially performed. In either the personal or social identification cases, self-regulation of desires may track closely the extent that one attempts to follow an ideal or hoped-for self, an ought self, a core or presented self, or some other self from one's repertoire of multiple selves (e.g. Markus and Nurius, 1986; Wilson and Ross, 2001).

The antecedents to self-regulation discussed in the preceding section and shown in Figure 18.2 provide deterministic accounts of the origins of self-regulation as the application of personal standards to felt desires. The aforementioned antecedents, themselves, can be explained by yet deeper social psychological processes and/or genetic processes. For example, self-conscious emotions have been proposed to arise from threats to or elevations of self-representations in relation to identity-goal relevance and identity-goal congruence, where people make attributions as to the locus, stability, controllability, and globality of the threats or elevations (e.g. Tracy and Robins, 2004).

ANTECEDENTS TO GOAL DESIRES

Desires have been conceived in at least two senses in consumer research. One tradition sees desires in a narrow biological sense, roughly equivalent to what is meant by lust. Belk and colleagues have investigated this sense of desire (e.g. 'passionate and fanciful consumer desire') thoroughly (e.g. Belk et al., 2002). The sense of desire conceived in this chapter and reflected in goal desires and action desires is broader and follows a different tradition that is consistent with Aristotle's usage mentioned earlier, as well as contemporary philosophers (e.g. Schroeder, 2004; Schueler,

1995), neuroscientists (e.g. Baron-Cohen et al., 2000), and developmental psychologists (e.g. Astington, 1996). Desire herein is defined as a specific category of feelings that have motivational force and exist in appetitive and volitive forms (Bagozzi, 2006a, b). They function to motivate goal and action intentions and exhibit aspects of bodily appraisals similar to that described by Damasio's somatic-marker hypothesis (Damasio, 1999). We also propose that desires perform an integrative function to summarize a decision maker's overall felt urge to pursue a goal or to act, by transforming many potentially experienced reasons for acting into the motivation to act.

A strength of consumer research to date is the uncovering of literally dozens of cognitive responses and a few emotional responses to marketing stimuli that are grounded in experimental research. These developments parallel and often overlap with similar knowledge generated in psychology, where perhaps hundreds of different cognitive responses and the conditions governing their operation and a dozen or so emotions have been identified. Cognitive and emotional responses can be thought of as reasons for acting that serve as inputs to decision making en route to consumer action. They therefore enter the consumer decision making core through points B and C in Figure 18.1 (they also function at different stages in action implementation at point D, as developed in the last major section of the chapter).

Because there are so many cognitive and emotional responses, it is difficult to specify a cogent, coherent explanation for consumer action based on these, so the field of consumer research remains rather fragmented. An integration of the vast research findings to date seems beyond the grasp of the field, at least in the short to medium run, and a viable alternative is needed. One approach is to focus on everyday psychological reactions and processes in a folk psychology sense. There are at least four senses of folk psychology (Ravenscroft, 2004), but for my purposes, I use folk psychology in a slightly looser sense than posited by contemporary philosophers.

By folk psychology, I mean theories of human behavior and action that a researcher proposes, which are based on variables and processes that lay people espouse in their everyday situations, either explicitly or implicitly, and which researchers use to understand, explain, and predict behavior and action in empirical research. Such theories need not necessarily correspond completely with, or formally simulate, the actual causal processes determining or constituting human behavior and action, but to the extent that such theories receive empirical support, they may be claimed (tentatively) to represent psychological laws. The objective is to specify a relatively small number of fundamental mental states or events that can serve researchers well to explain consumer action. By 'small number ...' and 'open-ended', I mean that the list of mental states or events should be parsimonious, yet based on sound theory and empirical research, and exemplars on the list should be removed and added, as knowledge grows accordingly.

In this spirit, I propose that an initial list of determinants of goal desires should include cognitive goal schemas, positive and negative anticipated and anticipatory emotions, and affect toward the means (see Figure 18.3). These operate in a manner akin to goal setting to create new goal desires or to activate latent or stored goal desires.

Cognitive schemas express the network of values, motives, or subgoals initiating or reinforcing goal desires (e.g. Bagozzi et al., 2003; Bagozzi and Sekerka, 2009). D'Andrade captures the nature and function of such schemas aptly as follows:

> To understand people one needs to understand what leads them to act as they do, and to understand what leads them to act as they do one needs to know their goals, and to understand their goals one must understand their overall interpretive system, part of which constitutes and interrelates those goals, and to understand their interpretive system - their schemas - one must understand something about the hierarchical relations among their schemas. (1992: 31).

Both the individual values/motives/subgoals and relationships amongst values/motives/

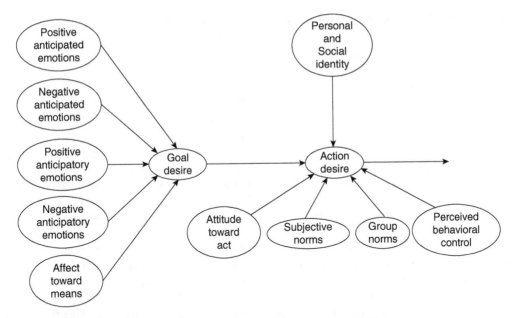

Figure 18.3 Antecedents to goal and action desires (see Figure 18.1).

subgoals have been shown to influence goal desires and decision making. Cognitive schemas have been used in consumer research to study goal setting in such contexts as consumption recycling (Bagozzi and Dabholkar, 1994), body weight maintenance (Bagozzi and Edwards, 1998; Pieters et al., 1995), voting (Bagozzi and Dabholkar, 2000), self-regulation of hypertension (e.g. Taylor et al., 2006), and private equity financing (Moradin et al., 2006).

Cognitive schemas are thinking-based representations of a person's motivational reasons for choosing a goal or not. They are thought to function in largely deliberative ways in the sense that they conjure up, and are used to weigh, pros and cons of a prospective goal. More automatic and nondeliberative aspects of motivation behind a person's goal desires can be represented in three aspects of goal-directed emotions. Anticipated positive and negative emotions of imagined consequences of goal success and goal failure, respectively, support goal desires and inaugurate the formation and commitment to goals (Bagozzi et al., 1998; Bagozzi and Dholakia, 2006a; Perugini and Bagozzi, 2001). They do this by connecting

anticipated consequences of goal achievement and goal disappointment to basic and self-conscious emotions, and in this sense reflect a kind of automaticity in their effects on goal desires. Anticipatory positive and negative emotions function similarly to initiate goal setting, but instead of focusing on outcomes associated with goal attainment/ goal frustration, they emphasize present feelings of having a goal in the here and now (Baumgartner et al., 2008). Such emotions are limited in the positive sense to hope and the negative to worry or anxiety, whereas any of a number of categories of positive and negative emotions can signify anticipated emotions. The final emotion impacting goal-setting and goal desires is affect toward the means. Whereas anticipated and anticipatory emotions deal with the consequences or outcomes of goal achievement/goal frustration, affect toward the means is directed toward the processes leading up to goal outcomes. Affect toward the means has been found to influence consumer decision making with regard to coupon usage and exercising and dieting in the service of regulating body weight (Bagozzi et al., 1992; Bagozzi and Edwards, 2000).

ANTECEDENTS TO ACTION DESIRES

Action desires are shown in the consumer decision making core (Figure 18.1) to be dependent on goal intentions. Once a consumer commits to pursuing a goal, the desire for a particular means often follows automatically. This is because a particular means may have been learned and function habitually, once a goal intention forms, or only one means is available or one means dominates all others, or the means has been preselected by social pressure or a governing authority in an organization to which one belongs. However, in cases where a goal commitment is tentative or uncertainty in goal attainment clouds one's judgments, the initiation of action desires may occur via the operation of action-focused mental events. A number of candidate mental events in a folk psychology sense might function in this regard. We identify one here: the theory of planned behavior and its abridgements (see Figure 18.3). The theory of planned behavior posits that action intentions are functions of attitude toward an act, felt subjective normative pressure to act, and perceived behavioral control over the act. We posit that the antecedents to intentions typically lack motivational import in and of themselves, and to influence decisions, such reasons for acting must gain emotive significance (Bagozzi, 1992). Emotive significance occurs through the integrative, embodied appraisal, and transformative properties of action desires (e.g. Bagozzi et al., 2003; Bagozzi and Dholakia, 2006a). Hence entry to the consumer decision making core through path C in Figure 18.1. Further, because subjective norms are limited to compliance processes in social behavior and neglect internalization and identification social processes, influence on action desires should include paths from group norms and social identity. Many studies of late confirm the central intervening role of action desires on action intentions for the variables in the theory of planned behavior plus group norms and social identity (e.g. Bagozzi and Dholokia, 2006a, 2006b; Bagozzi et al., 2003; Bagozzi

et al., 2007; Perugini and Bagozzi, 2001; Taylor et al., 2005).

ACTION IMPLEMENTATION PROCESSES

The consumer decision making core 'ends' with the effects of action intentions (path D in Figure 18.1). After an action intention has been formed, action might be initiated straightaway, as occurs for some spontaneous and everyday decisions. An example of direct action might be an impulsive purchase of a candy bar in the supermarket in response to arousal of a desire and activation of an intention to 'grab the bar', while waiting in line to empty a basket of groceries. Alternatively, after examining and comparing digital cameras on a website, I might decide on the spot to by an attractive brand through one of the vendors conveniently advertised on the page and begin the purchase process accordingly.

More common, for many decisions, action intentions either will be formed at one point in time and activated later to enact a particular action or else will entail performance of many thinking exercises, perhaps over multiple steps and points in time, and possibly including multiple motor instantiations interspersed between thinking and volitional processes, before a terminal action will be performed. One important set of processes early on, following upon formation of action intentions, is planning. Gollwitzer (1996) proposed that planning about when, where, and how to act is a key stage in goal striving, and he termed such planning, implementation intentions. Because planning will in the normal case, follow a decision to act, I prefer not calling planning, implementation intentions. Rather, action intentions, I claim, lead to planning. These processes have been tested by Bagozzi et al. (2003) and Dholakia et al. (2007).

Following planning (Figure 18.4), another complex stage of action initiation occurs: trying. By trying, I mean such mental and physical activities as activation of motor

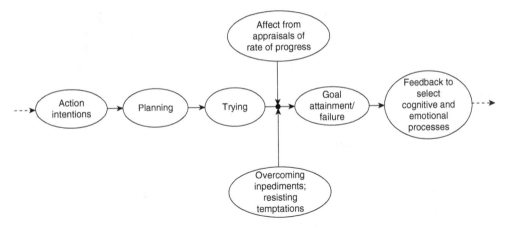

Figure 18.4 Implications of action intentions (see Figure 18.1).

responses leading up to a final action, allocation of time and mental and physical energy, monitoring of progress, resistance of temptations deflecting one away from goal striving, overcoming impediments to goal attainment, changing plans and making new plans as needed, maintaining willpower and sustaining self-discipline, and reassessing commitments to a goal and a chosen course of action when required. A number of these aspects of trying have been tested in such self-regulatory contexts as body weight maintenance, exercising and dieting, and blood pressure control (e.g. Bagozzi et al., 2003; Bagozzi and Edwards, 2000; Dholakia et al., 2007; Taylor et al., 2005).

Figure 18.4 shows two aspects of trying that moderate the effects of effort expended in pursuit of a goal on goal attainment/failure: approach and avoidance processes. One set of such processes consists of affective responses occurring in reaction to evaluations of a consumer's goal progress such that, when the rate of progress is below a reference value, negative affect happens, and when the rate of progress is at or above the reference value, positive affect results (e.g. Carver and Scheier, 1998). When progress is made in pursuit of either a sought-for incentive or avoidance of a threat, a consumer will feel elated or relieved, respectively, and the action implication is to stay the course. When progress wanes in pursuit of an incentive or avoidance of a threat,

one feels sad or anxious, respectively, and the action implication is to try harder to achieve the goal. Of course, when consumers try to achieve a consumption goal, they sometimes alter the target goal or their definition of success or failure; indeed, they even might abandon goal striving in certain cases.

The effects of effort on goal attainment/failure can also be moderated by impediments or temptations faced during goal pursuit. Here, goal achievement will be facilitated to the extent that the striver attempts to overcome the former or resist the latter. Fortuitous or unplanned happenings can also augment or interfere with goal striving.

The action implementation process 'ends' with actual goal attainment or failure. Nevertheless, as shown in Figure 18.4, cognitive responses and emotional reactions therefrom feedback to selected variables and processes in the consumer decision making core or in the antecedents that interface with the core and discussed herein in relation to A, B, and C in Figure 18.1.

CONCLUSION

The study of consumer agency and action is a recent focus of inquiry and complements past and present emphasis on consumer behavior, which has taken a narrow psychological turn and generated an impressive but largely unintegrated body of research. It might be argued that consumer agency and action are the main subject areas in need of elucidation, if we are to understand consumers in their everyday lives and inform corporate and public policy in this regard.

Consumer behavior research certainly provides inputs to the study of consumer agency and action, but at the same time, a need exists to branch out from laboratory experiments to investigate alternative methods, such as naturalistic field experiments, surveys, and qualitative procedures. Laboratory methods may be too limiting as the primary method upon which to rely. It is unknown to what degree the control attained in the laboratory corresponds to everyday consumer behavior, agency, and action. The conditions needed to manipulate two or three factors, say, and indeed the magnitudes of the manipulations themselves needed to produce desired effects, may seldom occur in the marketplace. If the stimuli consumers regularly face are many in number, reveal themselves in unexpected ways, and occur at levels of intensity less than that proffered in the laboratory, and at the same time transpire in environments with numerous, common distractions and are presented to consumers who have on average less motivation and cognitive skills than the typical student respondent, we may be deceiving ourselves as to the relevance and external and ecological validities of our laboratory findings. At least the effects found in the laboratory may be weaker and less numerous in the real world than we are led to believe. Moreover, everyday consumption situations may harbor resources, forces, etc. that shape consumer behavior, agency, and action in ways that regularly counteract the psychological outcomes we take for granted as law-like. On the other hand, one suspects that some consumption contexts contain conditions that reinforce or accentuate the conditions producing law like consumer behavior, agency, and action. We simply do not know the answers to such questions, as a lacuna exists between knowledge from the laboratory and natural consumption.

The study of consumer agency and action can close the gap between laboratory knowledge of consumption and real-world manifestations. That is, by focusing on agency and action, we move from a passive, reactive conceptualization of consumption, to an active, self-regulatory perspective. Consumers are not merely shaped by market-related stimuli and the conditions under which information processing occurs, but rather consumers, at least on occasion, are capable of changing the environment to advantage, self-regulating their urges, and in general responding creatively. The framework presented in this chapter provides one way to investigate such agent-centered courses of action.

REFERENCES

Ahearne, M., Bhattacharya, C.B. and Grues, T. (2005) 'Antecedents and Consequences of Customer-Company Identification: Expanding the Role of Relationship Marketing', *Journal of Applied Psychology*, 90: 574–585.

Amodio, D.M. and Frith, C.D. (2006) 'Meeting of Minds: The Medial Frontal Cortex and Social Cognition', *Nature Reviews*, 7: 268–277.

Aristotle (2000) *Nicomachaen Ethics*, trans. and ed. by R. Crisp. Cambridge, UK: Cambridge University Press.

Astington, J.W. (1996) 'What is Theoretical about the Child's Theory of Mind?: A Vygotskian View of its Development', in P. Carruthers and P.K. Smith (eds) *Theories of Theories of Mind*. Cambridge: Cambridge University Press.

Bagozzi, R.P. (1992) 'The Self-Regulation of Attitudes, Intentions, and Behavior', *Social Psychology Quarterly*, 55: 178–204.

Bagozzi, R.P. (2006a) 'Explaining Consumer Behavior and Consumer Action: From Fragmentation to Unity', *Seoul Journal of Business*, 12(2): 111–143.

Bagozzi, R.P. (2006b) 'Consumer Action: Automaticity, Purposiveness, and Self-Regulation', in N.K. Malhotra (ed.) *Review of Marketing Research*. Armonk: Sharpe.

Bagozzi, R.P. and Dabholkar, P.A. (1994) 'Consumer Recycling Goals and their Effect on Decisions to Recycle: A Means-End

Chain Analysis', *Psychology & Marketing*, 11: 313–340.

Bagozzi, R.P. and Dabholkar, P.A. (2000) 'Discursive Psychology: An Alternative Conceptual Foundation to Means-End Chain Theory', *Psychology & Marketing*, 17: 535–586.

Bagozzi, R.P. and Dholakia, U.M. (2006a) 'Antecedents and Purchase Consequences of Customer Participation in Small Group Brand Communities', *International Journal of Research in Marketing*, 23: 45–61.

Bagozzi, R.P. and Dholakia, U.M. (2006b) 'Open Source Software User Communities: A Study of Participation in Linux User Groups', *Management Science*, 52: 1099–1115.

Bagozzi, R.P. and Edwards, E.A. (1998) 'Goal Setting and Goal Pursuit in the Regulation of Body Weight', *Psychology and Health*, 13: 593–621.

Bagozzi, R.P. and Edwards, E.A. (2000) 'Goal-Striving and the Implementation of Goal Intentions in the Regulation of Body Weight', *Psychology and Health*, 15: 255–270.

Bagozzi, R.P. and Sekerka, L.E. (2009) 'Moral Judgments in Management: Hierarchical Motive Structures Drive Moral Choice', Unpublished working paper, Ross School, University of Michigan.

Bagozzi, R.P., Baumgartner, H. and Pieters, R. (1998) 'Goal-Directed Emotions', *Cognition and Emotion*, 12: 1–26.

Bagozzi, R.P., Baumgartner, H. and Yi, Y. (1992) 'Appraisal Processes in the Enactment of Intentions to Use Coupons', *Psychology and Marketing*, 9: 469–486.

Bagozzi, R.P., Bergami, M. and Leone, L. (2003) 'Hierarchical Representation of Motives in Goal-Setting', *Journal of Applied Psychology*, 88: 915–943.

Bagozzi, R.P., Dholakia, U.M. and Basuroy, S. (2003) 'How Effortful Decisions Get Enacted: The Motivating Role of Decision Processes, Desires, and Anticipated Emotions', *Journal of Behavioral Decision Making*, 16: 273–295.

Bagozzi, R.P., Dholakia, U.M. and Pearo, L.R. (2007) 'Antecedents and Consequences of Online Social Interactions', *Media Psychology*, 9: 77–114.

Bagozzi, R.P., Verbeke, W. and Gavino, Jr., J.C. (2003) 'Culture Moderates the Self-Regulation of Shame and its Effects on Performance: The Case of Salespersons in

the Netherlands and the Philippines', *Journal of Applied Psychology*, 88: 219–233.

Bagozzi, R.P., Belschak, F., Verbeke, W. and Gavino, Jr, J.C. (2009) 'Cultural Differences in the Self-Regulation of Pride and its Effects on Adaptability, Effort, and Company Citizenship Behaviors: The Case of Salespeople in the Netherlands and the Philippines, Unpublished working paper, Ross School, University of Michigan.

Bagozzi, R.P., Verbeke, W., Dietvorst, R.C., Belschak, F.D., and Schraa-Tam, C. (2009) Empathy by Managers: When Perspective Taking and Empathic Concern are Decoupled. Unpublished working paper, Ross School, University of Michigan.

Baron-Cohen, S., Tager-Flusberg, H. and Cohen, D. (2000) *Understanding Other Minds: Perspectives from Developmental Cognitive Neuroscience*, second edition. Oxford: Oxford University Press.

Baumgartner, H., Pieters, R. and Bagozzi, R.P. (2008) 'Future-Oriented Emotions: Conceptualization and Behavioral Effects', *European Journal of Social Psychology*, 38: 685–696.

Baumeister, R.F. and Vohs, K.D. (eds) (2004) *Handbook of Self-Regulation: Research, Theory and Applications*. New York: Guilford Press.

Belk, R.W. (1988) 'Possessions and the Extended Self', *Journal of Consumer Research*, 15(2): 139–168.

Belk, R.W., Ger, G. and Askegaard, S. (2002) 'The Fire of Desire: A Multisited Inquiry into Consumer Passion', Working paper, University of Utah.

Belschak, F., Verbeke, W. and Bagozzi, R.P. (2006) 'Coping with Sales Call Anxiety: The Role of Sale Perseverance and Task Concentration Strategies', *Journal of the Academy of Marketing Science*, 34: 403–418.

Bhattacharya, C.B. and Sen, S. (2003) 'Consumer-Company Identification: A Framework for Understanding Consumers' Relationships with Companies', *Journal of Marketing*, 67: 76–88.

Blackburn, S. (1994) *The Oxford Dictionary of Philosophy*. Oxford: Oxford University Press.

Camerer, C., Loewenstein, G. and Prelec, D. (2005) 'Neuroeconomics: How Neuroscience Can Inform Economics', *Journal of Economic Literature*, 49: 9–64.

Carver, C.S. and Scheier, M.F. (1998) *On the Self-Regulation of Behavior*. Cambridge: Cambridge University Press.

D'Andrade, R.G. (1992) 'Schemas and Motivation', in R.G. D'Andrade and C. Strauss (eds) *Human Motives and Cultural Models*. Cambridge: Cambridge University Press.

Damasio, A.R. (1999) *The Feeling of What Happens: Body and Emotion in the Making of Consciousness*. New York: Harcourt Brace.

Dennett, D. (1987) *The Intentional Stance*. Cambridge, MA: Bradford Books/MIT Press.

Dholakia, U.M., Bagozzi, R.P. and Gopinath, M. (2007) 'How Formulating Implementation Plans and Remembering Past Actions Facilitate the Enactment of Effortful Decisions', *Journal of Behavioral Decision Making*, 20: 343–364.

Dietvorst, R.C., Verbeke, W., Bagozzi, R.P., Yoon, C., Smits, M. and vander Lugt, A., (2009) 'A Salesforce-Specific Theory of Mind Scale: Tests of its Validity by Multitrait-Multimethod Matrix, Confirmatory Factor Analysis, Structural Equation Models, and Functional Magnetic Resonance Imaging', *Journal of Marketing Research* (forthcoming).

Gollwitzer, P.M. (1996) 'The Volitional Benefits of Planning', in P.M. Gollwitzer and J.A. Bargh (eds) *The Psychology of Action: Linking Cognition and Motivation to Behavior*. New York: Guilford.

Greene, J. and Haidt, J. (2002) 'How (and Where) Does Moral Judgment Work?', *TRENDS in Cognitive Science*, 6(12): 517–523.

Haidt, J. (2001) 'The Emotional Dog and its Rational Tail: A Social Intuitionist Approach to Moral Judgment', *Psychological Review*, 108: 814–834.

Haidt, J. (2003) 'Elevation and the Positive Psychology of Morality', in C.L.M. Keyes and J. Haidt (eds) *Flourishing: Positive Psychology and the Life Well-Lived*. Washington, D.C: American Psychological Association.

Harmon-Jones, E. and Winkielman, P. (2007) *Social Neuroscience: Integrating Biological and Psychological Explanations of Social Behavior*. New York: Guilford Press.

Higgins, E.T. (1997) 'Beyond Pleasure and Pain', *American Psychologist*, 52: 1280–1300.

Louro, M.J., Pieters, R. and Zeelenberg, M. (2005) 'Negative Returns on Positive Emotions: The Influence of Pride and Self-Regulatory Goals on Repurchase Decisions, *Journal of Consumer Research*, 31: 833–840.

Markus, H. and Nurius, P. (1986) 'Possible Selves', *American Psychologist*, 41: 954–969.

Morandin, G., Bagozzi, R.P. and Bergami, M. (2006) 'The Hierarchical Cognitive Structure of Entrepreneur Motivation Toward Private Equity Financing', *Venture Capital: An International Journal of Entrepreneurial Finance*, 8: 253–271.

Payne, J.W. and Bettman, J.R. (2004) 'Walking with the Scarecrow: The Information-Processing Approach to Decision Research', in D. Koehler and N. Harvey (eds) *Blackwell Handbook of Judgment and Decision Making*. Malden, MA: Blackwell Publishing Ltd.

Perugini, M. and Bagozzi, R.P. (2001) 'The Role of Desires and Anticipated Emotions in Goal-Directed Behaviors: Broadening and Deepening the Theory of Planned Behavior', *British Journal of Social Psychology*, 40: 79–98.

Pieters, R., Baumgartner, H. and Allen, D. (1995) 'A Means-End Chain Conceptualization of Consumers' Goal Structures', *International Journal of Research in Marketing*, 12: 227–244.

Ravenscroft, I. (2004) 'Folk Psychology as a Theory', *Stanford Encyclopedia of Philosophy*, viewed 10 September, 2008, <http://plato. Stanford.edu/entries/folkpsych-theory/>.

Schroeder, T. (2004) *Three Faces of Desire*. Oxford: Oxford University Press.

Schueler, G.F. (1995) *Desire: Its Role is Practical Reason and the Explanation of Action*. Cambridge, MA: Bradford/MIT Press.

Sekerka, L.E. and Bagozzi, R.P. (2007) 'Moral Courage in the Workplace: Moving To and From the Desire and Decision to Act', *Business Ethics: A European Review*, 16: 132–149.

Simonson, I. and Nowlis, S.M. (2000) 'The Role of Explanations and Need for Uniqueness in Consumer Decision Making: Unconventional Choices Based on Reasons', *Journal of Consumer Research*, 27: 49–68.

Strack, F. and Deutsch, R. (2004) 'Reflective and Impulsive Determinants of Social Behavior', *Personality and Social Review*, 8: 220–248.

Taylor, S.D., Bagozzi, R.P. and Gaither, C.A. (2005) 'Decision Making and Effort in the Self-Regulation of Hypertension: Testing Two Competing Theories', *British Journal of Health Psychology*, 10: 505–530.

Taylor, S.D., Bagozzi, R.P., Gaither, C.A. and. Jamerson, K.A. (2006) 'The Bases of Goal

Setting in the Self-Regulation of Hypertension', *Journal of Health Psychology*, 11: 141–162.

Tian, K.T., Bearden, W.O. and Hunter, G.L. (2001) 'Consumers' Need for Uniqueness: Scale Development and Validation', *Journal of Consumer Research*, 28: 50–66.

Tracy, J.L. and Robins, R.W. (2004) 'Putting the Self into Self-Conscious Emotions: A Theoretical Model', *Psychological Inquiry*, 15: 103–125.

Verbeke, W. and Bagozzi, R.P. (2003) 'Exploring the Role of Self- and Customer-Provoked Embarrassment in Personal Selling', *International Journal of Research in Marketing*, 20: 233–258.

Verbeke, W., Belschak, F. and Bagozzi, R.P. (2004) 'The Adaptive Consequences of Pride in Personal Selling', *Journal of the Academy of Marketing Science*, 32: 386–402.

Vohs, K.D. and Baumeister, R.F. (2004) 'Understanding Self-Regulation: An Introduction', in R.F. Baumeister and K.D. Vohs (eds) *Handbook of Self-Regulation: Research, Theory, and Applications*. New York: Guilford Press.

Wellman, H. (1990) *The Child's Theory of Mind*. Cambridge, MA: MIT Press.

Wegner, D.M. (2002) *The Illusion of Conscious Will*. Cambridge, MA: MIT Press.

Wheatley, T. and Haidt, J. (2005) 'Hypnotically Induced Disgust Makes More Judgments More Severe', *Psychological Science*, 16: 780–784.

Wilson, A.E. and Ross, M. (2001) 'From Chump to Champ: People's Appraisals of their Earlier and Presented Selves, *Journal of Personality and Social Psychology*, 80: 572–584.

Yoon, C., Gutchess, A.H., Feinberg, F. and Polk, T.A. (2006) 'A Functional Magnetic Resonance Imagining Study of Neural Dissociations between Brand and Person Judgments', *Journal of Consumer Research*, 33: 31–40.

19

Cultural Influences on Representations of the Consumer in Marketing Theory

Pauline Maclaran, Margaret K. Hogg, and Alan Bradshaw

INTRODUCTION

Traditional theories of consumer behaviour research stem from cognitive, behavioural or trait schools of thinking and are heavily influenced by economics and psychology (Mittlestaedt, 1990). These theories tend to portray consumers as passive individuals who simply respond to environmental or biological forces that operate largely beyond their control (Hirschman, 1993), implying that the predictive mechanics of purchase decisions are somehow made in isolation from a social world. This orientation has been interpreted as researchers engaged with achieving scientific credibility for marketing scholarship following damning reports from the Ford and Carnegie Foundations (see Tadajewski, 2006 and Chapters 3 and 4 in this volume) However, in recent years, the influence of post-structuralism and general multidisciplinary approaches have created space within consumer research for investigating cultural components that provide rich accounts of the lived experiences that regularly define consumption. This cultural perspective shifts the focus from a narrow concern with purchasing acts towards broader conceptualizations of the experiences embodied in consumer behaviour (Belk, 1995).

This chapter presents an overview of key theoretical cultural perspectives and their influence on how we conceptualize, represent and understand consumers. We have chosen seven key strands in interpretive consumer research that each contribute to how we understand consumers and their relationship to consumption. As per any attempt towards categorization, it is important to acknowledge that many of the categories we discuss overlap, whilst such a major review must also carry the health warning that gross over-simplifications occur, as, indeed, does the overlooking of seminal works. However, this chapter is intended to serve as a useful point on introduction to cultural perspectives of the consumer, and we urge readers to explore the bibliography with a view to continue the literature review herein initiated. Our groupings embrace both established and emerging theoretical areas and include: consumers in their cultural contexts; consumers in their subcultural contexts; consumer identities and the meaning of possessions; consumers as gift-givers; consumers and their sense of (market)place; consumers as storytellers and myth-makers; dissatisfied and disadvantaged consumers. This overview does not take into account the more macro level conditioning of consumer behaviour, an important area that is explored further by Fırat and Tadajewski's Chapter 8 in this volume.

Before we discuss these representations of consumers in more detail, we first give a general overview of the background to cultural approaches in consumer research and highlight important theoretical milestones.

BACKGROUND AND OVERVIEW OF A CULTURAL APPROACH TO UNDERSTANDING CONSUMERS

During the 1980s, a group of researchers generally associated with the fringes of the *Association of Consumer Research* (ACR) and the *Journal of Consumer Research* (JCR) pushed an agenda broadly conceived as 'post-positivist, naturalistic, interpretive, and post-modern' (Lutz, 1989). This agenda was concerned with 'the value of research which does *not* begin with a theory to be tested but rather a phenomenon to be understood; research that treats consumers as *informants* rather than *subjects;* research that examines consumer behaviour from the perspective of the consumer rather than that of the marketing manager; research that seeks *understanding* rather than causal explanation; in short, research that differs from 'traditional' consumer research on almost every dimension of importance' (Lutz, 1989). Since then, interpretive research has represented about 20 per cent of the articles published in *JCR* from 1990 onwards (Simonson et al., 2001: 259).

This movement of interpretivist studies did not gain a foothold in consumer research without considerable paradigm arguments between established and up-and-coming consumer behaviour researchers (see Wilkie and Moore, 2003: 127ff for a good summary). *Advances in Consumer Research* also provides useful windows into the flurry of debates around the conference floor and in various addresses (see, for instance, Cohen, 1995; Engel, 1995; Kardes and Sujan, 1995; Kassarjian, 1995; Kernan, 1995; Wells, 1995). The struggle to establish interpretivist research within consumer behaviour involved philosophical (and thus epistemological, ontological and methodological) issues (see Chapter 4 in this volume). Some of the voices in the debate included Anderson, 1983; Arndt, 1985; Deshpande, 1983; Fırat et al., 1987; Fırat and Venkatesh, 1995; Hunt, 1983, 1990, 1992; Peter, 1992; Peter and Olson, 1983; Zinkhan and Hirschheim, 1992 and Brownlie et al., 1999. The variety of positions can be seen *inter alia* in Arnould and Thompson, 2005; Calder and Tybout, 1987; Fırat et al., 1987; Hirschman, 1991; Holbrook, 1987; Holbrook and O'Shaughnessy, 1988; Levy, 2005; Sherry 1990a and Tybout, 1995. These paradigm debates continue to the present day (Levy 2003) with specific examples from the cultural end of consumer research seen in philosophical discussions of hermeneutics (Arnold and Fischer, 1994); phenomenology (Thompson et al., 1989); semiotics (Mick, 1986); through to feminism (Bristor and Fischer, 1993).

A seminal study in the creation of interpretive consumer research was provided by Holbrook and Hirschman (1982). They argued against the dominant mechanical models that framed consumer behaviour as a series of rational decisions and towards acknowledging the fantasies, feelings and fun that underlie hedonic consumption experiences. A methodological shift was initiated and a series of interpretive pathways emerged, such as introspection, and a consequent commitment to deploying more lyrical descriptions of consumer behaviour, better able to capture rich experiential dynamics (Holbrook, 1990). This entailed a rejection of the strictures of conventional scientific approaches, as consumer researchers embraced creative expression and started to adopt a discourse of 'weird science' (Belk, 1991). Soon studies appeared which incorporated methods from humanities, phenomenology, hermeneutics and semiotics (Holbrook and Grayson, 1986; Scott, 1994a; Stern, 1989). With such canonical pieces as Belk's (1988) investigation of possessions and the extended self, a new imperative for studying consumer behaviour arose, which shifted away from managerialist concerns with understanding purchasing decisions towards a drive to understand consumption as a subject in its own right.

The 'Consumer Behavior Odyssey'

One particular work led the way in respect of studying consumers in their everyday environments, a work that has been described by Wells (1991: iii) as 'putting the joy of discovery back into its proper place' and by Bradshaw and Brown as the 'self-styled crazy gang's carnivalesque cross-country expedition' (2008: 1400). This was the *Consumer Behavior Odyssey* embarked upon by Belk and his comrades in the summer of 1986. Over twenty consumer researchers conducted qualitative research as they travelled between the East and West US coast in a giant recreational vehicle (Belk, 1991). This epic adventure ambitiously sought fresh ways of acquiring knowledge about the nature and experiences of consumer behaviour and did so in rich contexts from which to generate new theories about: marketplace interactions (Belk et al., 1988; Heisley et al., 1991); brand communities (O'Guinn, 1991); the power of the past in terms of memories and collections (Belk, 1990, 1991; Belk et al., 1991); the consumption patterns of upper middle class females (Durgee et al., 1991); and, the most famous work to originate from the project, a study of the secularization and sacralization processes

at work in contemporary society (Belk et al., 1989). The Odyssey might be regarded as revolutionary in that it broke boundaries and stimulated substantive theoretical insights through the use of innovative research methods. As argued by Bradshaw and Brown (2008), the exercise was an empirical rejection of narrow managerial concerns, a methodological rejection of quantitative, experimental and sample based studies, a metaphorical rejection of information-processing, cognitive–affect–behaviour modelling paradigms and a rhetorical pioneering of new forms of research representation including photos and films. The voyage celebrated new empirical concerns with collecting, gift-giving and cultural experiences; alternative methodologies grounded in depth interviews and naturalistic qualitative methods; and contextually the Odyssey pushed inquiry away from mainstream sites, such as shops, malls and the home, towards the remote fringes of consumer culture. Moreover, the study rejected the mechanical computer-like framing of the consumer in favour of 'a socially and culturally embedded notion of consumer as communicator, disseminator, hedonist, explorer, itinerant and storytelling shape-shifter' (Bradshaw and Brown, 2008: 1400). The sheer extremity of the project contributed to a polarisation of the field between the conventional and 'weird scientists' and brought into focus the 'different incommensurate underlying philosophies of science' (Belk, 2009), which has resulted in a diversion of interests and the creation of a new margin, rather than an overall shift in consumer research.

The experiential/subjective aspects of consumption

As Holbrook (1992) reminds us, whilst the original Odyssey conceived of human life using the metaphor of a large boat, conventional consumer research has tended to conceive of humans like a computer, where mechanical thought processes can be mapped, analysed and predicted. In opposition, Holbrook and

Hirschman (1982) argue that consumption is an inherently subjective experience grounded in emotions. Hence, rationalistic models for explaining consumer behaviour were held to overlook daydreaming and fantasies, and the general spirit of hedonism at the heart of consumer behaviour. Their paper marked a convergence between consumer research and sociology, with Campbell (1987) also arguing that a romantic impulse lies at the heart of consumption. These claims were further researched in the edited volume *Romancing the Market* (Brown et al., 1998). As part of this acknowledging of the wider dynamics of consumption experience, there was a re-inquiry into consumer value, which challenged its conventional framing bound to simple definitions of utility, and understood relative to such prosaic terms as 'wants' and 'needs'. Instead, value came to be framed as including aesthetic, ethical and spiritual dimensions (Holbrook, 1998). Continuing this romanticist trajectory was the framing of consumption as mediated by a passionate and fanciful pursuit of desire (Belk et al., 2003).

A further seminal inquiry into the multi-dynamism of consumption was presented by Holt's (1995) typology, which he derived from a longitudinal study of baseball spectators in Chicago. Further to the hedonic categorisation of consumption, Holt noted that consumption could also be a form of integration as consumers manipulate the meaning of objects and use these objects to classify themselves and others. Consumption was also demonstrated as a form of play; for example, Arnould and Price's (1993) study of white river rafting is one of the earliest papers in consumer research to examine the autotelic aspects of consumption as play.

The postmodern turn

As per many subject areas, postmodernity has left a strong impression on interpretive consumer research and caused many axiomatic foundations to be questioned. Perhaps most significantly within consumer research was the postmodern challenge to the demarcation between production and consumption; a challenge which shifted the emphasis to the consumer as producer of meanings through his or her consumption acts (Brown, 1995; Fırat and Dholakia, 1998). Reconceptualising the consumer as a symbolic communicator and a type of text to be interpreted, the postmodern turn led to the importation of forms of analysis associated with literary theory and semiotics, which were concerned with reading texts. Hence, consumer objects could be read as texts that help understand productive forces, whilst productive objects, such as advertisements, were read in order to mine insights for the benefit of understanding consumption. For example, whilst Belk (1986) argues that art ought to be used to gain fresh insights into consumption and materialism, Holbrook and Grayson (1986) interpret the film *Out of Africa* in order to explore how symbolic consumption can convey artistic meaning. Holbrook and Hirschman (1993) extend this method to other texts, including the TV series *Dallas* and the movie, *Gremlins* whilst Holbrook (2004, 2005a, b, 2008) pioneers the method of ambi-diegetic and music analysis in order to explore the use of soundtrack in plot development. Similarly Brown (1997) reviews fiction and interprets *Harry Potter* as a celebration of marketing activity (Brown, 2005), Schroeder and Borgerson (2002) review the commerciality of Renaissance art, whilst Schroeder (2002) argues that people now consume aesthetic objects as part of an 'image economy', which leads to an understanding of art within a much broader consumptionscape.

Not only are cultural texts read for insights into consumer culture, but consumption objects and advertisements are also interpreted as texts. For example, Schroeder (2002) argues the case for consumer researchers to be equipped with knowledge of art history and provides an analysis of a Calvin Klein advert with reference to Dutch group portraiture and contemporary androgyny discourse. Elsewhere, literary criticism yields influential perspectives from Stern who argued that scholars could view advertisements as meaningful cultural artefacts (1989). Hence, literary critical analyses of Ivory Flakes adverts reveal a complex portrait of the American woman as a consumer of products, advertising and culture. Stern (1993) included gendered readings of advertising texts as part of a feminist postmodern approach that included analyses of the dramatic structure of adverts in order to affect persuasion through the elicitation of empathy and sympathy (1994), and the extensive use of myths within advertising texts (1995). Meanwhile, Scott deepens the conversation between consumer research and literary theory by revealing the role of musical and visual rhetoric in advertising (1990, 1994b) and also by adapting reader–response theory to consumer research (1994a). Not only have alternative approaches such as art history and literary theory come to the fore as scholars seek to interpret, understand and locate brand references to culture, but also scholars increasingly think of the condition of branding as fundamentally linked to the aesthetic condition of contemporary living in a brand culture (see Schroeder and Salzer-Morling, 2006; Venkatesh and Meamber, 2006).

Meaning transfer processes

Another important theoretical milestone was McCracken's (1986) meaning transfer model in which he moves the relationship between the consumer and culture to centre stage in his influential structuralist interpretation of the movement of meaning via consumption. He identifies a series of cultural categories and principles that provide the basis for establishing distinctions (e.g. 'of time, space, nature and person' McCracken, 1986: 72) in the social world. McCracken's model maps the transfer of meaning from the culturally constituted world, to goods and then to individuals. Whilst this one-way linear transfer of meaning has attracted critiques (e.g. Ritson and Elliott, 1999), McCracken's framework remains a turning point in our understanding

of consumers and how meaning is created and mediated through consumption.

In contrast to McCracken (1986), Holt (1997) adopts a poststructuralist approach in his examination of the social patterning of consumption, and argues that the interrelationship between cultural frameworks and social contexts is central to understanding patterns of consumption. Similarly, our knowledge of the role of consumer rituals in the meaning transfer process has been developed considerably since McCracken (see Otnes and Lowrey, 2003). In particular, the process of meaning creation takes on added significance in the framing of brands as resources for constructing identity and group formation. Whilst Holt (2004) locates brand meaning as emanating from cultural anxieties, there has been increasing recognition of the contestation of brand meaning between brand managers and groups of tribal consumers (Cova et al., 2007).

Categorisations of interpretive consumer research

Whilst good overviews and categorisations of the general interpretive consumer research body of work already exist (Arnould and Thompson, 2005; Belk, 1995), we specifically seek to identify studies concerned with cultural representations of the consumer. Hence, we intend these categories to augment categories identified by Belk (1995) including consumption symbolism; property and possessions; collections (acquisition and disposition); subcultures/cultures of consumption; consumption festivals and rituals and gifts and gift-giving. The review also augments the four Consumer Culture Theory (CCT) research programmes identified by Arnould and Thompson (2005): consumer identity projects; marketplace cultures; the sociohistoric patterning of consumption; and mass-mediated marketplace ideologies and consumers' interpretive strategies (871: 874). In the overview that follows, we highlight how key theoretical foci in interpretive consumer research represent the consumer. For more detail on the broader body of this research, interested readers should consult both afore-mentioned works.

Consumers in their cultural contexts

Interpretive consumer research has long rec-ognised that theoretical frameworks of con-sumer behaviour are not globally applicable, particularly in the context of developing and non-Western economies. A series of studies investigate consumer concepts in different cultural settings and establish the importance of cross-cultural variation and highlight the insights that can be gained by studying cul-tural contexts of consumer experiences.

Japan and China have proved to be the source of important cross-cultural comparisons. For example, Applbaum and Jordt (1996) provide one of the earliest studies to identify the potential value of exploring categories cross-culturally. They identify how different cultures construct different relationships between individuals and their consumer goods. Joy's (2001) study of gift giving in Hong Kong points to the significance of the familial over personal identity in Chinese culture. These latter insights served as the harbinger for subsequent work on family identity in Western cultures (Epp and Price, 2008). Similarly, Zhao and Belk's (2008) examination of the rise of consumer society in a former communist state allows the authors to extend Barthes' myth model beyond its traditional focus on the transfer of cultural meanings into an explanation of ideological shifts in different societies. Meanwhile Bonsu and Belk (2003) use Ghana as a context for investigating death rituals, noting how the bereaved in Ashante society use 'conspicuous consumption rituals' (p. 41) to create new social identities for themselves and for the deceased. Another example of a cross-cultural study is provided by Ger and Belk's (1999) research into the lifestyles of consumers across four cultures in order to discover why materialism is spreading on a global basis.

Immigrant consumers have also provided a focus for interpretivist researchers in relation to their transitions and how they use con-sumption to acculturate (or not) to their host country. Peñaloza (1994: 32) explores the outcomes of the acculturation processes experienced by Mexican immigrants living in the US, whilst Askegaard et al. (2005) extend this framework to a non-US context (Greenlandic immigrants into Denmark) and report similar identity positions. A further phenomenon revealed by Askegaard et al. and also in Oswald's (1999) earlier study is how ethnic consumers 'culture swap'; using goods to move between one identity and another as they negotiate relations between home and host cultures (p. 303). The metaphor of border-crossing was used to delineate how South Asian women in Britain navigate imag-ined multiple worlds between household and societal contexts (Lindridge et al., 2004). British Asian family life also provided a context for examining how gender, culture and consumption are negotiated in family settings (Lindridge and Hogg 2006). Another study of acculturation (Ustuner and Holt, 2007) explores a Turkish squat to examine how poor migrant women necessarily engage with the dominant consumer culture through a variety of means including by reconstitut-ing their village culture in the city, and by pursuing the dominant ideology as a myth through ritualised consumption. Finally, from a material culture perspective, immigrants sometimes consume jeans not to produce dif-ferentiated identities but rather to produce an 'ordinary' identity, which facilitates integration (Borgerson, 2009).

Consumers in their subcultural contexts

Although consumption is frequently accused of contributing to individualisation, paradoxi-cally much consumption is about being a member of a group constructed according to shared values. Interpretive consumer research-ers contribute greatly to our knowledge of how consumption creates community. Indeed by the early 1990s, Badot et al. (1993) had already suggested that the word 'societing' could more appropriately replace the term 'marketing'. During the 1990s, Bernard Cova's work that drew on the sociology of the gift and Maffesoli's (1996) concept of postmodern tribalism to highlight the search for community in consumption. Cova theorises the 'linking value' of products and services (Cova, 1996, 1997, 1999) and deploys a tribal metaphor, showing that the link between members of a group is often more important than the actual product or service being utilised (see also Chapter 27 in this volume). This sense of community is especially powerful when consumers engage in high involvement leisure activities such as skydiving (Celsi et al., 1993), in-line roller-skating (Cova and Cova, 2001, 2002), white-water rafting (Arnould and Price, 1993) and dancing (Goulding et al., 2002, 2009).

Communities that form around particular products or services were later termed 'subcultures of consumption' by Schouten and McAlexander (1995) in their study of Harley-Davidson motorcycle owners. Schouten and McAlexander foreground the important role of subcultures of consumption in understanding consumers' experiential relationships with brands, an understanding complemented by later self–brand relationship studies (e.g. Escalas and Bettman, 2005; Fournier, 1998). Nelson et al. (1992) challenge the term 'subcultures' within the context of leisure activities on the grounds that leisure groupings do not exhibit sufficient experiential social depth, and style (Hebdige, 1979), to demonstrate that they are a way of life. In a further critique, Holt (1997: 345–346) argues that Schouten and Alexander's (1995) use of the term 'subcultures' ignores important social categories such as ethnicity, gender, social class and age; categories that create different product/brand meanings for particular groups within the same subculture. Similarly, Kates (2002) also shows how different 'interpretive communities' exist within a subculture. Kozinets (2001) prefers

the term 'culture of consumption', believing that this more accurately conveys interconnections between media, marketer and consumer narratives and images. However they are framed, these microcultures provide alternative ways of theorizing 'distinct patterns of socially shared meanings and practices' (Thompson and Troester, 2002: 551) amongst consumer groups (see Hughes, 2009, for more in-depth discussion of the differences between these various 'collective' terms).

Although the consumers in Schouten and McAlexander's study also cohered around a particular brand (Harley-Davidson), it was not until Muniz and O'Guinn's study (2001) that the term 'brand community' was introduced. Muniz and O'Guinn define a brand community as a 'structured set of social relationships, among users of a brand, whose affinity, history and culture are derived from the consumption of that brand' (p. 1). Drawing from sociology, these authors identified three markers of community: namely consciousness of kind, moral responsibility and shared rituals and traditions. This conceptualization offers insights into the complex relationship between marketers, consumers and brands, insights further developed in subsequent studies on brand communities (Cova et al., 2007; McAlexander et al., 2002; Muniz and Schau, 2005) and the evolution of brand culture more generally (Holt, 2004; Schroeder and Salzer-Moerling, 2006). Cayla and Eckhardt's (2008) work on Asian brands demonstrates how marketing creates transnational imagined communities, that parallels the creation of imagined communities by other media. However, marketers may have difficulties controlling meanings that evolve around a brand and consumers may even take over or co-create brand meaning, as in the case of the Apple Newton, a product discontinued by Apple Macintosh but still maintained by a community of loyal customers (Muniz and Schau, 2005). Such loyalty to a brand can be so fervent that it is like a religion, or a cult (Belk and Tumbat, 2005; Muniz and Schau, 2005).

Consumer identities and the meaning of possessions

Levy's (1959) paper on 'Symbols for Sale' can justifiably be regarded as the forerunner to a stream of research in consumer behaviour that concentrates on how individuals use consumption as identity seekers and identity makers. Belk's (1988) exploration of the relationship between possessions and the extended self initiated a plethora of studies around identity, self and consumption. Ahuvia's (2005) re-examination of Belk's (1988) original propositions critiques the notion of the metaphor of a 'core-self' underlying the notional extended self. Meanwhile Miller (1998) calls for a framing of the materiality of consumption in which the meaning of both consumers and the object are simultaneously created in the act of consumption. He argues that this materiality is essential for understanding not only identity, but also intimate relationships between people. The investment of meaning in possessions has attracted significant attention, for example, Grayson and Shulman (2000) use semiotics to trace how possessions represent important links to events, people, places and values because of their indexical value in verifying 'important moments of personal history' (Grayson and Shulman, 2000: 19). Curasi et al. (2004) also explore the semiotic qualities of products in their examination of how cherished possessions come to represent inalienable wealth within families through the layering of meanings. Fournier (1998) identifies the ecology of self-brand relationships in consumers' lives as active partners, characterised by love, self-connectedness, commitment and intimacy.

Coupland (2005) deals with mundane consumption, or what she terms 'invisible brands' in a household. In this case, brand meanings do not derive from the relationship with a consumer's identity, or from the consumer–brand relationship. Rather these mundane brands are rendered invisible by their very ordinariness; and their meaningfulness derives from the process of brand storage, which Coupland likens to animal camouflage

in natural environments. In contrast, other studies examine what Coupland (2005: 115) terms 'heroic or important brands' (e.g. Schouten and McAlexander, 1995) where the significance of brand meaning derives from the brand's role in creating, maintaining or reinforcing different aspects of the self and self-identity.

Wooten (2000) contributes to our understanding of how symbolic consumption fits into consumer socialization processes, particularly as peers gain increasing influence (as family influences wane) on adolescent consumers. As Miller (1998) argues, the entire relationship web of a family is partly produced through consumption so that the act of shopping for a family can be regarded as 'making love in the supermarket'. Family transitions proved to be invaluable contexts for understanding the changing relationship between consumption, identity and the self over time (what Arnould and Thompson (2005) describe as identity projects).

Consumer as gift-givers

Certain consumption activities, such as the Burning Man Festival (Kozinets, 2002), and the music file-sharing service, Napster (Giesler, 2006; Giesler and Pohlman, 2003), are best understood in terms of the gift economy rather than the exchange economy that so traditionally underpins marketing theory. Whereas the exchange economy accords status to those who *have* the most, a gift economy accords status to those who *give* the most (Hyde, 1979). Gifts are related to play, enchantment and art, and, as such, they emphasise connection and fantasy, rather than division and rationality (Kozinets, 2002). Burning Man and Napster represent countercultural trends that seek a larger community-driven sense of self, harnessing contemporary Internet technology to enhance their communicative powers and, particularly in the case of Napster, their sharing abilities.

Gift-giving underpins many sociocultural rituals and celebrations such as birthdays and

Christmas and is used to reinforce relationships and family bonds. Gifts perform a communicative role. For example, gifts may be used to communicate hope and best wishes during life stage transitions such as marriage, retirement, a housewarming, a new baby and other experiences accompanied by uncertainty (Ruth, 1996). Gift-givers frequently go to great lengths to select appropriate gifts that will convey the right symbolic meaning (Wooten, 2000). Indeed, the symbolic meanings that may be conveyed through the process of gift-giving may even change or reformulate interpersonal relationships (Ruth et al., 1999; Sherry, 1983). It is common for messages such as love, affection and esteem for the recipient to be communicated during gift-giving at Christmas and on St Valentine's Day (Fischer and Arnold, 1990; Otnes et al., 1993; Ruth, 1996). Whereas many studies assume an exchange basis (either economic, social or romantic) for gift-giving, Belk and Coon (1993) highlight the agapic love paradigm that is based on a more altruistic and spontaneous emotional response where the giver does not seek anything in exchange.

On account of the communicative power of gifts, there may also be anxiety involved in gift-giving and a worry that the right message will not be conveyed, or indeed, that offence or disappointment may result (Green and Alden, 1988; Ruth, 1996; Wooten, 2000). Gifts may even engender interpersonal conflict when consumers use them to provoke a calculated response, such as guilt, in the recipient (Sherry et al., 1993). There are also cross-cultural differences in gift-giving. Joy (2001) illustrates how consumers in Hong Kong have more nuanced gift-giving practices than their Western counterparts. Consumers in Hong Kong made more subtle distinctions based on a continuum of how intimate a relationship was perceived to be, distinctions that were guided by important cultural rules such as reciprocity, sentiment and face.

Consumers often indulge in self-gifts. This conceptualization can even apply to fairly mundane products such as women's magazines

(Stevens et al., 2007). Monadic gift-giving of this nature is often engaged in as a reward for work done or as a therapy to provide an escape from daily pressures (Mick and DeMoss, 1990a, b, 1993). Sherry et al.'s (1995: 408) studies of monadic gift giving reveal that such behaviour is motivated by a need for 'volitional ceremonial self-care'.

Consumers and their sense of (market) place

Whereas traditional marketing management approaches focus on the, tangible elements of consumptionscapes (shopping centres, restaurants etc.), interpretive consumer researchers are more interested in the cultural meanings created as consumers experience particular consumptionscapes. A number of pioneering ethnographic studies explore consumers' sense of (market) place (Belk et al., 1988; McGrath, 1989; McGrath et al., 1993; Sherry, 1990b, c, 1998b) and reveal the cultural dynamics that inhere in sites for consumption. For example, shopping malls and retail outlets, such as flagship brand stores, provide consumers with material and symbolic resources for identity creation (Csaba and Askegaard, 1999; Sandikci and Holt, 1998). Contemporary thematised and spectacularised commercial venues combine the incorporation of brand meanings not only with entertainment, but also with therapeutics and spirituality (Kozinets et al., 2002, 2004; Peñaloza, 1999), and even encourage utopian experiences (Maclaran and Brown, 2005). The study of consumers in contexts such as religious theme parks (O'Guinn and Belk, 1989) helps us understand the increasingly blurred relationship between commerce and religion and how both may contain sacred rites. Locations for what McAlexander et al. (2002) term 'brandfests' reveal subtle marketer–consumer dynamics where brand meanings may be both reinforced and simultaneously renegotiated. Similarly, cybermarketscapes are virtual spaces where tensions are played out between marketers' quest for commercial gain and consumers' search for freedom and identity creation (Venkatesh, 1998). The development of commercial spaces through time has also been examined in some detail (e.g. McGrath, 1989; Wallendorf et al., 1998).

Together with Sherry's (1998a) study of servicescapes, these studies reveal multifaceted experiential dimensions of marketplace behaviour, of 'being-in-the-marketplace' (Sherry, 1998a: 9). In bringing to life the everyday worlds of consumers and showing how consumers' experiences interweave with marketing activity, theories are generated around the joint (marketer/consumer) production of cultural spaces. Significantly too, they show how the relationship between consumer cultures and marketing cultures is a continually evolving and interactive process (Holt, 2002; Peñaloza, 2001; Sherry, 1998b). Marketers maintain an important social role in the organization of commercial spaces and enhance their relationships with consumers by sensitive use of marketing activities within the spaces concerned. Maclaran and Brown's (2005) study of a refurbishment of a festival marketplace showed what could happen when marketers overlook this role and how consumers could experience acute disillusionment when their utopian imaginings, generated by the venue, were destroyed. Emotional attachments may also be formed for commercial locations that are less spectacular and less branded, for example, Borghini et al. (2006) show how consumers develop strong bonds with more ordinary places such as small independent shops, restaurants or bars.

Other studies focus on consumers' attempts to seek temporary escapes from the market altogether (Belk and Costa, 1998a; Kozinets, 2002), creating spaces free from commercial interests and marketers' interventions. These types of spaces offer opportunities for transformative play and fantasy creation where consumers can enact alternative realities. The Burning Man Festival, for example, is revealed as an extraordinary site in terms of consumer creativity (Kozinets, 2002).

Consumers as storytellers and myth-makers

From a cultural perspective, consumers are conceived of as storytellers and mythmakers (Durgee, 1988; Holt, 2003, 2004; Levy, 1982). Humankind has long held an amazing propensity for storytelling. The use of stories as entertainment and as a way of passing on information is a very ancient method of communication. Cultural myths can be distinguished from stories in usually performing a more didactic and moral function that often also has sacred connotations (Gabriel, 2004). Collective folklore and myths contribute to a society's cohesion and sense of identity (Levy, 1981), Contemporary consumers weave stories around themselves in pursuit of their individual and family identity projects (Epp et al., 2005); they tell each other stories about their experiences of particular products and services (facilitated by the burgeoning of Internet discussion forums); and, likewise, they are drawn to the commercial myths that marketers create around brand images and through marketing communications, especially advertising (Arnould, 2008; Luedicke and Giesler, 2008; Thompson, 2004). An important interpretivist contribution here has been an understanding of the role that myths play in the marketplace.

Marketing draws on mythology in order to endow products and services with deeper meanings that communicate with consumers in powerful, often unconscious, ways and develop a strong brand culture (Schroeder and Salzer-Morling, 2006). Cultural myths use archetypal images and themes that help us make sense of our experiences and indicate appropriate ways for us to behave (Hirschman, 2000). Traditionally, myths make us aware of oppositions that they progressively mediate, such as good/evil, life/death, science/nature, male/female and so forth (Levy, 1982). In taking on life's central contradictions and the complexities of being human, they also often speak across cultures (Fraser, 1922/1985), Myths help us resolve cultural contradictions and understanding their role is particularly important for marketers, given that many brands now compete in 'myth markets', rather than product markets (Holt, 2004: 39). Mythic representations are continually being created and recreated, presented and re-presented in the marketplace as they evolve in response to the needs of particular social groups and specific market structures (Thompson, 2004). Whereas in bygone times myths were most frequently religious and circulated by word-of-mouth, nowadays myths are likely to be commercially mediated, and circulated through marketplace phenomena such as films, television, brands and advertising (Arnould, 2008; Holt, 2004). For example, Holt and Thompson's (2004) analysis of American men's consumption practices reveals how the man-of-action hero, idealised in American mass culture, reconciles two opposing myths of masculinity in American culture: 'the rebel' and 'the breadwinner'. Commercial myths develop new mythic ideals that often draw on many existing cultural myths to achieve their unique 'syncretic blending of narrative and imagistic elements' (Thompson and Tian, 2008). This work extends previous meaning transfer models and theorises the historic, competitive and ideological influences on commercial myth-making and how this transforms popular memory.

Dissatisfied and disadvantaged consumers

The alienation of consumers from the market-place, for economic or personal reasons, remains an under-investigated area in both mainstream and interpretive consumer research. In a hedonistic marketplace, driven by what Campbell (1987) describes as a 'rest-less dissatisfaction', there are many areas of consumption where consumers have to exercise self-control in their consumption practices, such as the consumption of food, drink and drugs. Excessive consumption of these can lead to overeating, alcohol or nicotine abuse, drug addiction and consequences

that are detrimental to health (e.g. Borrowman and Costa, 2004; Hirschman, 1992a). To have too much choice in these areas may actually be disempowering, as it merely leads to greater temptation to indulge in over-consumption. As consumer appetites are constantly fuelled by excessive consumption environments and promotional messages, there is also the concomitant need for greater self-control.

Feelings of regret and even self-disgust may be strong whenever consumers do not exercise sufficient self-control and experience a bad outcome from their excessive consumption. Every act of self-indulgent and excessive consumption has its flipside. Consumers, supposedly luxuriating in a narrative that condones excessive consumption and indulgence, are then offered antidotes to their over-indulgence, as evidenced by the boom in slimming and exercise-related products. Thus, consumers oscillate between their particular poison and its antidote, an oscillation that produces ambivalence in relation to their consumption of products (O'Donohoe, 2002; Otnes et al., 1997). Moreover, the overall focus on self that consumer culture encourages can result in guilt and conflicting emotions. Stevens et al. (2003) explore the guilt experienced by women in relation to magazine reading and 'me-time'; Sherry et al. (1995) refer to the bittersweet nature and 'dialectical tension' of self-gifting or monadic giving (p. 408); and Belk and Costa (1998b) describe the 'emotionally charged' nature of women's chocolate consumption (p. 189).

The concept of 'retail therapy' is now common parlance in consumer culture, as is compensatory consumption (Woodruffe, 1997). Interpretive consumer researchers have theorised the compulsive and addictive, i.e. 'the dark side of consumer choice', a phrase coined by Hirschman (1991). In certain cases, consumers may lose control altogether, and it is now widely recognised that there can be an addictive dimension to consumption behaviour (Elliott, 1994). The addictive shopper obtains a high through purchasing, and is unable to restrict his or her purchasing behaviour (Elliott et al., 1996; Hirschman,

1992b; O'Guinn and Faber, 1989). Although an addict may feel in control temporarily while engaging in the actual shopping activity (Eccles et al., 1999), the long-term effects are likely to include financial problems, and even alienation from loved ones, due to the secretive behaviours that addictive consumption encourage (e.g. concealed purchases). At its extreme, addictive consumption takes a pathological form, as in the increasing prevalence of eating disorders and alcohol and drug abuse.

The sense of consumer agency, which underlies the notion of consumer identity projects is also called into question by work on vulnerable consumers (Adkins and Ozanne, 2005), which shows how important skills such as managing identity are not necessarily available to all consumer groups. Many adults have low literacy and numeracy skills and this makes it difficult for them to locate and assess goods and service information, and to calculate the total cost of even a few everyday purchases. Wallendorf (2001) highlights how brand loyalty may be a type of coping strategy for low-literacy consumers, because brand names may indicate certain product types (i.e. washing up liquid), thereby lessening the risks involved in making choices. Low-income consumers are another vulnerable group (Hill, 1991, 2001). Poorer consumers pay more for goods and services, often face choices of lower quality products and are increasingly being excluded from access to them (Hamilton, 2007; Hamilton and Catterall, 2006a). Limited product availability can be a problem for low-income consumers (Hill and Stephens, 1997). Hill (2002) and Hamilton and Catterall (2006b) explore the survival strategies that enable low-income consumers to cope within a culture of poverty.

CONCLUSION

Having documented major theoretical milestones, we have structured our review of cultural influences on representations of the consumer in marketing theory around seven key theoretical foci. Like all categorizations, we aimed to simplify sufficiently in order to make some sense and render some order to this complex area. We claim no definitive status for the categories we have chosen and, indeed, we realise that certain categories are somewhat controversial, as, for example, that in relation to consumer disadvantage. We think it important to highlight this under-researched area, however, as one of the major criticisms of interpretive research is that, too often, it uses higher income (and, frequently US-based) consumers in its purposive, judgement related sampling. In doing so, it ignores a vast number of consumers who are less able to relate to consumer culture in positive ways, and are also less easily accessed for research purposes (e.g. the homeless and the addicted). There is much scope for future research in this area, research that has the potential to enhance our knowledge of marketing's societal impact and help us explain why more choice has not made consumers any happier (Shankar et al., 2006). As marketing activities become increasingly questioned and critiqued by a wider public (e.g. Klein, 2000), this knowledge gap becomes increasingly evident.

We have already identified the importance of the virtual world (e.g. Muniz and Schau, 2005), and it is within the context of virtual worlds and the electronic landscape that we sense some of the fastest and, potentially, most important changes, are emerging (see Chapter 28 for a fuller review of the many theoretical implications). This is particularly in relation to the blurring of online and offline and how consumers transfer meaning between the two environments, especially given the proliferation of social networking sites and virtual worlds such as *Second Life*. A final area that we wish to flag up for future research is the need to explore more fully the material dimensions of markets and draw insights from the burgeoning studies on material culture (Borgerson 2005; Dant, 2005; Miller 2005; Parsons, 2009). Rather than seeing material objects as passive and filled with meaning by the consumer, we need to understand more about the agentic effects of material goods and how consumer meaning creation is co-produced by the material world in which consumers exist. This whole area opens up many new and exciting perspectives from which to reconceptualise representations of consumers within consumer research. We thus add material culture studies to the many other multi-disciplinary bases that have informed interpretivist researchers, such as sociology, anthropology, literary theory, art history, social psychology and media/cultural studies. As our foregoing review illustrates, these disciplines have all greatly enriched our knowledge of the consumer and stand in sharp contrast to applied psychology, which remains the foundational discipline for much of the academic work published in consumer research. Consumer culture is continually shifting and changing, caught in a continual dance with marketers and their activities in the marketplace. Therefore, if we, as consumer researchers, wish to join this dance, we also need to continually adapt and adopt new perspectives and ways of understanding.

REFERENCES

Adkins, N.R. and Ozanne, J.L. (2005) 'The Low Literate Consumer', *Journal of Consumer Research*, 32(June): 93–105.

Ahuvia, A.C. (2005) 'Beyond the Extended Self: Loved Objects and Consumers' Identity Narratives', *Journal of Consumer Research*, 32(June): 171–184.

Anderson, P.F. (1983) 'Marketing, Scientific Progress and Scientific Method', *Journal of Marketing*, 47(Fall): 18–31.

Applbaum, K. and Jordt, I. (1996) 'Notes Towards an Application of McCracken's "Cultural Categories" for Cross Cultural Consumer Research', *Journal of Consumer Research*, 23(December): 204–218.

Arndt, J. (1985) 'On Making Marketing Science More Scientific: Role of Orientations,

Paradigms, Metaphors, and Puzzle Solving', *Journal of Marketing*, (Summer): 11–23.

Arnold, S.J. and Fischer, E. (1994) 'Hermeneutics and Consumer Research', *Journal of Consumer Research*, 21(June): 55–70.

Arnould, E. (2008) 'Commercial Mythology and the Global Organization of Consumption,' *Advances in Consumer Research*, Volume 35, Dunluth, MN: Association for Consumer Research, pp. 67–71.

Arnould, E.J. and Price, L.L. (1993) 'River Magic: Extraordinary Experiences and the Extended Service Encounter', *Journal of Consumer Research*, 20(June): 24–45.

Arnould, E.J. and Thompson, C.J. (2005) 'Consumer Culture Theory (CCT): Twenty Years of Research', *Journal of Consumer Research*, 31(March): 868–882.

Askegaard, S., Arnould, E.J. and Kjeldgaard, D. (2005) 'Postassimilationist Ethnic Consumer Research: Qualifications and Extensions', *Journal of Consumer Research*, 32(June): 160–170.

Badot, O., Bucci, A. and Cova, B. (1993) 'Societing: The Managerial Response to the European Aestheticization of Everyday Life', *European Management Journal*, May: 48–56.

Belk, R.W. (1986) 'Art Versus Science as Ways of Generating Knowledge about Materialism', in D. Brinberg and R.J. Lutz (eds) *Perspectives on Methodology in Consumer Research*, New York: Springer Verlag, pp. 3–36.

Belk, R.W. (1988) 'Possessions and the Extended Self', *Journal of Consumer Research*, 15: 139–168.

Belk, R.W. (1990) 'The Role of Possessions in Constructing and Maintaining a Sense of Past', *Advances in Consumer Research*, Volume. *17*, Provo, UT: Association for Consumer Research, pp. 669–676.

Belk, R.W. (1991) 'Possessions and Sense of Past', in R.W. Belk (ed.) *Highways and Buyways*, Provo, UT: Association for Consumer Research, pp. 114–130.

Belk, R.W. (1995) 'Studies in the New Consumer Behaviour', in D. Miller (ed.) *Acknowledging Consumption*, London: Routledge, pp. 58–95.

Belk, R.W. (2009) 'The Modeling-Empiricism Gap: Lessons from the Qualitative-Quantitative Gap in Consumer Research', *Journal of Supply Chain Management*, 45(1): 35–38.

Belk, R.W. and Coon, G.S. (1993) 'Gift-Giving as Agapic Love: An Alternative to the

Exchange Paradigm Based on Dating Experiences', *Journal of Consumer Research*, 20(December): 393–417.

Belk, R.W. and Costa, J.A. (1998a) 'The Mountain Man Myth: A Contemporary Consuming Fantasy', *Journal of Consumer Research*, 25(December): 218–240.

Belk, R.W. and Costa, J.A. (1998b) 'Chocolate Delights: Gender and Consumer Indulgences', in E. Fischer and D.L. Wardlow (eds) in *Proceedings of the Fourth Conference on Gender, Marketing and Consumer Behavior*, San Francisco: Association for Consumer Research, pp.179–193.

Belk, R.W. and Tumbat, T. (2005) 'The Cult of Macintosh', *Consumption, Markets and Culture*, 8(3): 205–218.

Belk, R.W., Sherry, J.F. and Wallendorf, M. (1988) 'A Naturalistic Inquiry into Buyer and Seller Behavior at a Swap Meet', *Journal of Consumer Research*, 14(March), 449–470.

Belk, R.W., Wallendorf, M. and Sherry, J.F. (1989) 'The Sacred and the Profane in Consumer Behavior: Theodicy on the Odyssey', *Journal of Consumer Research*, 16: 1–28.

Belk, R.W., Ger, G. and Askegaard, S. (2003) 'The Fire Of Desire: A Multi-Sited Inquiry Into Consumer Passion', *Journal of Consumer Research*, 30(December): 326–351.

Belk, R.W., Wallendorf, M., Sherry, J.F. and Holbrook, M.B. (1991) 'Collecting in a Consumer Culture', in R.W. Belk (ed.) *Highways and Buyways: Naturalistic Research from the Consumer Behaviour Odyssey*. Provo, UT: Association for Consumer Research, pp. 178–215.

Belk, R.W., Wallendorf, M., Sherry, J.F., Holbrook, M.B. and Scotts, R. (1988) 'Collectors and Collecting,' *Advances in Consumer Research,* Vol. 15, Provo, UT: Association for Consumer Research.

Bonsu, S. and Belk, R.W. (2003) 'Do Not Go Cheaply into that Good Night: Death Ritual Consumption in Asante, Ghana', *Journal of Consumer Research*, 30(June): 41–55.

Borgerson, J.L. (2005) 'Materiality, Agency, and the Constitution of Consuming Subjects: Insights for Consumer Research', *Advances in Consumer Research*, Vol. 32, Dunluth, MN: Association for Consumer Research, pp. 439–443.

Borgerson, J. (2009) 'Materiality and the Comfort of Things: Drinks, Dining, and Discussion with Daniel Miller', *Consumption, Markets and Culture*, 12(2): 155–170.

Borrowman, M.A and Costa, J.A. (2004) 'Consuming Illicit Drugs: Disproportionate Disadvantage and Poor Women of Color', in *Proceedings of the 7th Gender, Marketing and Consumer Behavior Conference*.

Bradshaw, A. and Brown, S. (2008) 'Scholars Who Stare at Goats: The Collaborative Circle Cycle in Creative Consumer Research', *European Journal of Marketing*, 42(11/12): 1396–1414.

Bristor, J.M. and Fischer, E. (1993) 'Feminist Thought: Implications for Consumer Research', *Journal of Consumer Research*, 19(March): 518–536.

Brown, S. (1995) *Postmodern Marketing*. London: Routledge.

Brown, S. (1997) *Postmodern Marketing 2*. London/Boston: Thomson Business Press.

Brown, S. (2005) *Wizard!: Harry Potter's Brand Magic*. London: Cyan Books.

Brown, S., Doherty, A-M, and Clarke, W. (1998) *Romancing the Market*. London: Routledge.

Brownlie, D., Saren, M., Wensley, R. and Whittington, R. (1999) *Rethinking Marketing: Towards Critical Marketing Accountings*. London: Sage.

Borghini, S., Sherry, J.F. Jr. and Joy, A. (2006) 'Marketplace Attachment in the Realm of Ordinary Spaces', *Proceedings of the Consumer Culture Theory Conference*.

Calder, B. and Tybout, A.M. (1987) 'What Consumer Research Is', *Journal of Consumer Research*, 14(1): 136–140.

Campbell, C. (1987) *The Romantic Ethic and the Spirit of Modern Consumerism*. Oxford: Basil Blackwell.

Cayla, J. and Eckhardt, G.M. (2008) 'Asian Brands and the Shaping of Transnational Imagined Community', *Journal of Consumer Research*, 35: 216–230.

Celsi, R., Rose, R.L. and Leigh, T.W. (1993) 'An Exploration of High-Risk Leisure Consumption through Skydiving', *Journal of Consumer Research*, 20(June): 1–23.

Cohen, J.B. (1995) 'Abbott and Costello Meet Frankenstein: An ACR Retrospective', *Advances in Consumer Research,* Vol. 22, Provo, UT: Association for Consumer Research, pp. 545–547.

Coupland, J.C. (2005) 'Invisible Brands: An Ethnography of Households and their Brands in their Kitchen Pantries', *Journal of Consumer Research*, 32(June): 106–118.

Cova, B. (1996) 'The Postmodern Explained to Managers: Implications for Marketing', *Business Horizons*, 39(6): 15–23.

Cova, B. (1997) 'Community and Consumption: Towards a Definition of the Linking Value of Products or Services', *European Journal of Marketing*, 31(3/4): 297–316.

Cova, B. (1999) 'From Marketing to Societing: When the Link is More Important Than the Thing', in D. Brownlie, M. Saren, R. Wensley and R. Whittington (eds) *Rethinking Marketing*, London: Sage, pp. 64–83.

Cova, B. and Cova, V. (2001) 'Tribal Aspects of Postmodern Consumption Research: the Case of French In-Line Roller Skaters', *Journal of Consumer Behaviour*, 1(1): 67–76.

Cova, B. and Cova, V. (2002) 'Tribal Marketing: The Tribalisation of Society and its Impact on the Conduct of Marketing', *European Journal of Marketing*, 36(5/6): 595–620.

Cova, B., Kozinets, R.V. and Shankar, A. (2007) *Consumer Tribes*. Oxford: Elsevier.

Csaba, F.F. and Askegaard, S. (1999) 'Malls and the Orchestration of the Shopping Experience in a Historical Perspective', in E.J. Arnould and L.M. Scott (eds) *Advances in Consumer Research*, Vol. 26, Provo, UT: Association for Consumer Research, pp. 34–40.

Curasi, C., Price, L.L. and Arnould, E.J. (2004) 'How Individuals' Cherished Possessions Become Families' Inalienable Wealth', *Journal of Consumer Research*, 31(December): 609–622.

Dant, T. (2005) *Materiality and Society*. Maidenhead, UK: Open University Press.

Deshpande, R. (1983) 'Paradigms Lost: On Theory and Method in Research in Marketing', *Journal of Marketing*, 47(Fall): 101–110.

Durgee, J.F. (1988) 'Interpreting Consumer Mythology: A Literary Criticism Approach to Odyssey Informant Stories', *Advances in Consumer Research*, Vol. 15, Provo, UT: Association for Consumer Research, pp. 531–536.

Durgee, J.F., Holbrook, M.B. and Wallendorf, M. (1991) 'The Wives of Woodville', in R.W. Belk (ed.) *Highways and Buyways: Naturalistic Research from the Consumer Behavior Odyssey*, Provo, UT: Association for Consumer Research, pp. 167–177.

Eccles, S., Hamilton, E. and Elliott, R. (1999) 'Voices of Control: Researching the Lived Experiences of Addictive Consumers', *Proceedings of the International Conference on Critical Management Studies*, July, UMIST.

Elliott, R. (1994) 'Addictive Consumption: Function and Fragmentation in Postmodernity', *Journal of Consumer Policy*, 17(2):159–179.

Elliott, R., Eccles, S. and Gournay, K. (1996) 'Revenge, Existential Choice, and Addictive Consumption', *Psychology and Marketing*, 13(8): 753–768.

Engel, J.F. (1995) 'ACR's 25th Anniversary: How It All Began', *Advances in Consumer Research*, Vol. 22, Provo UT: Association for Consumer Research, pp. 548–549.

Epp, A. and Price, L.L. (2008) 'Family Identity: A Framework of Identity Interplay in Consumption Practices', *Journal of Consumer Research*, 35(June): 50–70.

Escalas, J.E. and Bettman, J.R. (2005) 'Self-Construals, Reference Groups and Brand Meaning', *Journal of Consumer Research*, 32(December): 378–389.

Firat, F.A, Dholakia, N. and Bagozzi, R.P. (1987) *Philosophical and Radical Thought in Marketing*. Massachusetts: Lexington Books.

Firat, A.F. and Venkatesh, A. (1995) 'Liberatory Postmodernism and the Re-Enchantment of Consumption', *Journal of Consumer Research*, 22(December): 239–267.

Firat, F.A and Dholakia, N. (1998) *Consuming People: From Political Economy to Theaters of Consumption*. New York: Routledge.

Fischer, E. and Arnold, S. (1990) 'More than a Labor of Love: Gender Roles and Christmas Gift Shopping', *Journal of Consumer Research*, 17(3): 333–345.

Fischer, E. and Arnold, S. (1994) 'Hermeneutics and Consumer Research', *Journal of Consumer Research*, 21(1): 55–71.

Fournier, S. (1998) 'Consumers and their Brands: Developing Relationship Theory in Consumer Research', *Journal of Consumer Research*, 24(March): 343–373.

Fraser, J.G. (1922/1985) *The Golden Bough: A Study in Magic and Religion*. New York: Macmillan.

Gabriel, Y. (ed.) (2004) *Myths, Stories and Organizations: Premodern Narratives for Our Times*. Oxford: Oxford University Press.

Ger, G. and Belk, R.W. (1999) 'Accounting for Materialism in Four Cultures', *Journal of Material Culture*, 4(July): 183–204.

Giesler, M. (2006) 'Consumer Gift Systems', *Journal of Consumer Research*, 33(September): 283–290.

Giesler, M. and Pohlmann, M. (2003) 'The Anthropology of File Sharing: Consuming Napster as a Gift,' in P. Keller and D.W. Rook (eds) *Advances in Consumer Research*, Vol. 30, Provo, UT: Association for Consumer Research, pp. 94–100.

Goulding, C., Shankar, A. and Elliott, R. (2002) 'Working Weeks, Rave Weekends: Identity Fragmentation and the Emergence of New Communities', *Consumption, Markets and Culture*, 5(4): 261–284.

Goulding, C., Shankar, A., Elliott R. and Canniford, R. (2009) 'The Marketplace Management of Illicit Pleasure', *Journal of Consumer Research*, 35(5): 759–771.

Grayson, K. and Schulman, D. (2000) 'Impression Management in Services Marketing', in T.A. Swartz and D. Iacobucci (eds) *Handbook of Services Marketing and Management*, Newbury Park, CA: Sage, pp. 51–67.

Green, R.T. and Alden, D.L. (1988) 'Functional Equivalence in Cross-Cultural Gift-Giving in Japan and the United States', *Psychology and Marketing*, 5(Summer): 155–168.

Hamilton K. (2007) 'Making Sense of Consumer Disadvantage', in M. Saren, P. Maclaran, C. Goulding, R. Elliott, A. Shankar and M. Catterall (eds) *Critical Marketing: Defining the Field*, Oxford: Elsevier, pp. 178–192.

Hamilton, K. and Catterall, M. (2006a) 'Consuming Love in Poor Families: Children's Influence on Consumption Decisions,' *Journal of Marketing Management*, 22(9/10): 1031–1052.

Hamilton, K. and Catterall, M. (2006b) 'Transitions into Poverty: An Exploratory Study into How Families Cope When Faced with Income Reduction and Limited Consumption Opportunities', *The Marketing Review*, 6(2): 123–136.

Hebdige, D. (1979) *Subculture: The Meaning of Style*. London: Methuen.

Heisley, D.D., McGrath, M.A. and Sherry, J.F. (1991) 'To Everything There Is a Season: A Photo Essay of a Farmers' Market', in R.W. Belk (ed.) *Highways and Buyways: Naturalistic Research from the Consumer Behavior Odyssey*, Provo, UT: Association for Consumer Research, pp. 131–140.

Hill, R.P. (1991) 'Homeless Women, Special Possessions, and the Meaning of "Home": An Ethnographic Case Study', *Journal of Consumer Research*, 18(3): 298–310.

Hill, R.P. (2001) *Surviving in a Material World*. Notre Dame, Indiana: University of Notre Dame Press.

Hill, R.P. (2002) 'Consumer Culture and the Culture of Poverty: Implications for Marketing Theory and Practice', *Marketing Theory*, 2(September): 273–293.

Hill, R.P. and Stephens, D.L. (1997) 'Impoverished Consumers and Consumer Behavior: The Case of Afdc Mothers', *Journal of Macromarketing*, 17(2): 32–48.

Hirschman, E.C. (1991) 'Secular Mortality and the Dark Side of Consumer Behavior: Or How Semiotics Saved My Life', *Advances in Consumer Research*, Vol. 18, Provo, Utah: Association for Consumer Research, pp. 1–4.

Hirschman, E.C. (1992a) 'Recovering from Drug Addiction: A Phenomenological Account', in J.F. Sherry, Jr. and B. Sternthal (eds) *Advances in Consumer Research*, Vol. 19, Provo, UT: Association for Consumer Research, pp. 541–549.

Hirschman, E.C. (1992b) 'The Consciousness of Addiction: Toward a General Theory of Compulsive Consumption', *Journal of Consumer Research*, 19(2): 155.

Hirschman, E.C. (1993) 'Ideology in Consumer Research, 1980–1990: A Marxist and Feminist Critique', *Journal of Consumer Research*, 19(March): 537.

Hirschman, E.C. (2000) *Heroes, Monster, and Messiahs: Movies and Television Shows as the Mythology of American Culture*. Kansas City: Andrews McMeel Publishing.

Holbrook M.B. (1987) 'What is Consumer Research?', *Journal of Consumer Research*, 14(June):128–132.

Holbrook, M.B. (1990) 'Presidential Address; The Role of Lyricism in Research on Consumer Emotions: "Skylark, Have You Anything To Say To Me?"', *Advances in Consumer Research*, Vol.17, Provo, UT: Association for Consumer Research, pp. 1–18.

Holbrook, M.B. (1992) *Consumer Research: Introspective Essays on the Study of Consumption*. California: Sage.

Holbrook, M.B. (1998) *Consumer Value: A Framework for Analysis and Research*. London: Routledge.

Holbrook, M.B. (2004) 'Ambi-Diegetic Music in Films as a Product-Design and Placement

Strategy: The Sweet Smell of Success', *Marketing Theory*, 4(3): 1–28.

Holbrook, M.B. (2005a) 'The Ambi-Diegesis of "My Funny Valentine"', in S. Lannin and M. Caley (eds) *Pop Fiction: The Song in Cinema*. Bristol: Intellect.

Holbrook, M.B. (2005b) 'Art Versus Commerce as a Macromarketing Theme in Three Films from the Young-Man-with-a-Horn Genre', *Journal of Macromarketing*, 25(1): 22–31.

Holbrook, M.B. (2008) 'Music Meanings in Movies: The Case of the Crime-Plus-Jazz Genre', *Consumption, Markets and Culture*, 11(4): 307–328.

Holbrook, M.B. and Grayson, M.W. (1986) 'The Semiology of Cinematic Consumption: Symbolic Consumer Behaviour in Out of Africa', *Journal of Consumer Research*, 13: 374–381.

Holbrook, M.B. and Hirschman, E.C. (1982) 'The Experiential Aspects of Consumption: Consumer Fantasies, Feelings and Fun', *Journal of Consumer Research*, 9(September):132–140.

Holbrook, M.B. and Hirschman, E.C. (1993) *The Semiotics of Consumption: Interpreting Symbolic Consumer Behavior in Popular Culture and Works of Art*. New York: Mouton de Gruyter.

Holbrook M.B. and O'Shaughnessy, J. (1988) 'On the Scientific Status of Consumer Research and the Need for an Interpretive Approach to Studying Consumption Behavior', *Journal of Consumer Research*, 15(December):398–402.

Holt, D.B. (1995) 'How Consumers Consume: A Typology of Consumption Practices', *Journal of Consumer Research*, 22(June):1–16.

Holt, D.B. (1997) 'Poststructuralist Lifestyle Analysis: Conceptualizing the Social Patterning of Consumption in Postmodernity', *Journal of Consumer Research*, 23(March): 326–350.

Holt, D.B. (2002) 'Why Do Brands Cause Trouble: A Dialectical Theory of Consumer Culture and Branding', *Journal of Consumer Research*, 29(June): 70–90.

Holt, D.B. (2003) 'What Becomes an Icon Most?', *Harvard Business Review*, 81(3): 43–50.

Holt, D.B. (2004) *How Brands Become Icons – The Principles of Cultural Branding*. Boston: Harvard Business School Press.

Holt, D.B. and Thompson, C.J. (2004) '"Man-of-Action-Heroes": The Pursuit of Heroic

Masculinity in Everyday Consumption', *Journal of Consumer Research*, 31(September): 425–440.

Hughes, N. (2009) 'Consumer Collectives', in E. Parsons and P. Maclaran (eds) *Contemporary Issues in Marketing and Consumer Research*, Oxford: Elsevier, pp. 89–103.

Hunt, S.D. (1983) 'General Theories and the Fundamental Explananda of Marketing', *Journal of Marketing*, 47(Fall): 9–17.

Hunt, S.D. (1990) 'Truth in Marketing Theory and Research', *Journal of Marketing*, 54(July): 1–15.

Hunt, S.D. (1992) 'For Reasons and Realism in Marketing', *Journal of Marketing*, 56(April): 89–102.

Hyde, L. (1979) *The Gift: Imagination and the Erotic Life of Property*. New York: Vintage.

Joy, A. (2001) 'Gift Giving in Hong Kong and the Continuum of Social Ties', *Journal of Consumer Research*, 28(September): 239–256.

Kates, S.M. (2002) 'The Protean Quality of Subcultural Consumption: An Ethnographic Account of Gay Consumer', *Journal of Consumer Research*, 29(December): 383–399.

Kardes, F.R. and Sujan, M. (1995) (eds) *Advances in Consumer Research*, Vol. 22, Provo UT: Association for Consumer Research.

Kassarjian, H.H. (1995) 'Some Recollections from a Quarter Century Ago', *Advances in Consumer Research*, Vol. 22, Provo UT: Association for Consumer Research, pp. 550–552.

Kernan, J.B. (1995) 'Declaring a Discipline: Reflections on ACR's Silver Anniversary', *Advances in Consumer Research*, Vol. 22, Provo UT: Association for Consumer Research, pp. 553–560.

Klein, N. (2000) *No Logo: Taking Aim at the Brand Bullies*. London: Flamingo.

Kozinets, R.V. (2001) 'The Field Behind the Screen: Using the Method of Netnography to Research Market-Oriented Virtual Communities', *Journal of Marketing Research*, 39(1): 61–72.

Kozinets, R.V. (2002) 'Can Consumers Escape the Market? Emancipatory Illuminations from Burning Man', *Journal of Consumer Research*, 29(June): 20–38.

Kozinets, R.V., Sherry, J.F. Jr., Storm, D., Duhachek, A., Nuttavuthisit, K. and DeBerry-Spence, B. (2002) 'Themed Flagship Brand Stores in the New Millennium: Theory, Practice, Prospects', *Journal of Retailing*, 78(1): 17–29.

Kozinets, R.V., Sherry, J. F. Jr., Storm, D., Duhachek, A., Nuttavuthisit, K. and DeBerry-Spence, B. (2004) 'Ludic Agency and Retail Spectacle', *Journal of Consumer Research*, 31(December): 658–672.

Kozinets, R.V., Sherry, J.F., McGrath, M.A., Borghini, S., Diamond, N., Kahle, L. and Kennedy, P. (2005) '"My Nana, My Mom and I Went to American Girl": Brand Experience in the Construction of Family Mythology', in K.M. Ekstrom and H. Brembeck (eds) *European Advances in Consumer Research*, Vol. 7, Goteborg, Sweden: Association for Consumer Research, pp. 155–159.

Levy, S.J. (1959) 'Symbols for Sale', *Harvard Business Review*, 37(July): 117–124.

Levy, S.J. (1981) 'Interpreting Consumer Mythology: A Structural Approach to Consumer Behavior', *Journal of Marketing*, 45: 49–61.

Levy, S.J. (1982) 'Presidential Address: Constructing Consumer Behavior: A Grand Template', *Advances in Consumer Research*, Vol. 19, Provo, UT: Association for Consumer Research, pp. 1–6.

Levy, S.J. (2003) 'Roots of Marketing and Consumer Research at the University of Chicago', *Consumption, Markets and Culture*, 6(2): 99–110.

Levy, S.J. (2005) 'The Evolution of Qualitative Research in Consumer Behaviour', *Journal of Business Research*, 58: 341–347.

Lindridge, A.M. and Hogg, M.K. (2006) 'Paternal Gatekeeping in Diasporic Indian Families: Examining the Intersection of Culture, Gender and Consumption', *Journal of Marketing Management*, 22(9–10): 979–1008.

Lindridge, A.M., Hogg, M.K. and Shah, M. (2004) 'Imagined Multiple Worlds: How South Asian Women in Britain Use Family and Friends to Navigate the "Border Crossings" Between Household and Societal Contexts', *Consumption, Markets and Culture*, 7(3): 211–238.

Luedicke, M.K. and Giesler, M. (2008) 'Towards a Narratology of Brands?', *European Advances in Consumer Research*, Vol. 8, Dunluth, MN: Association for Consumer Research, pp. 419–420.

Lutz, R.J (1989) 'Positivism, Naturalism and Pluralism in Consumer Research: Paradigms in Paradise', *Advances in Consumer Research*, Vol. 16, Provo, Utah: Association of Consumer Research, pp. 1–7.

Maclaran, P. and Brown, S. (2005) 'The Center Cannot Hold: Consuming the Utopian Marketplace', *Journal of Consumer Research*, 32(September): 311–323.

Maffesoli, M. (1996) *The Time of the Tribes*. London: Sage.

McAlexander, J.H., Schouten, J.W. and Koenig, H.F. (2002) 'Building Brand Community', *Journal of Marketing*, 66(January): 38–54.

McCracken, G.C. (1986) 'Culture and Consumption: A Theoretical Account of the Structure and Movement of the Cultural Meaning of Consumer Goods', *Journal of Consumer Research*, 13(June): 71–84.

McGrath, M.A. (1989) 'An Ethnography of a Gift Store: Trappings, Wrappings, and Rapture', *Journal of Retailing*, 65(4): 421–449.

McGrath, M.A., Sherry, J.F. and Heisley, D.D. (1993) 'An Ethnographic Study of an Urban Periodic Marketplace: Lessons from the Midville Farmers' Market', *Journal of Retailing*, 69(3): 280–319.

Mick, D.G. (1986) 'Consumer Research and Semiotics: Exploring the Morphology of Signs, Symbols and Significance', *Journal of Consumer Research*, 13(September): 196–213.

Mick, D.G. and DeMoss, M. (1990a) 'To Me from Me: A Descriptive Phenomenology of Self-Gifts', *Advances in Consumer Research*, Vol. 17, Provo, UT: Association for Consumer Research, pp. 677–682.

Mick, D.G. and DeMoss, M. (1990b) 'Self-Gifts: Phenomenological Insights from Four Contexts', *Journal of Consumer Research*, 17(December): 322–332.

Mick, D.G. and DeMoss, M. (1993) 'Further Findings on Self-Gifts: Products, Qualities, and Socioeconomic Correlates', in J.F. Sherry and B. Sternthal (eds) *Advances in Consumer Research*, Vol. 20, Provo, UT: Association for Consumer Research. pp. 140–146.

Miller, D. (1998) *A Theory of Shopping*. Cambridge: Polity Press.

Miller, D. (2005) *Materiality*. Duke University Press.

Mittelstaedt, R.A. (1990) 'Economics, Psychology, and the Literature of the Sub-Discipline of Consumer Behavior', *Journal of the Academy of Marketing Science*, 18(4): 303–311.

Muniz, A. and O'Guinn, T. (2001) 'Brand Community', *Journal of Consumer Research*, 27(March): 412–432.

Muniz, A.M. and Schau, H.J. (2005) 'Religiosity in the Abandoned Apple Newton Brand Community', *Journal of Consumer Research*, 31(4): 737–747.

Nelson, C., Treichler, P. and Grossberg, L. (1992) 'Cultural Studies: An Introduction', in L. Grossberg et al. (eds) *Cultural Studies*, New York: Routledge, pp. 1–22.

O'Donohoe, S. (2002) 'Living with Ambivalence: Attitudes to Advertising in Postmodern Times', *Marketing Theory*, 1(1): 91–108.

O'Guinn, T.C. (1991) 'Touching Greatness: the Central Midwest Barry Manilow Fan Club', in R.W. Belk (ed.) *Highways and Buyways: Naturalistic Research from the Consumer Behavior Odyssey*, Provo, UT: Association for Consumer Research, pp. 102–111.

O'Guinn, T.C. and Belk, R.W. (1989) 'Heaven on Earth: Consumption at Heritage Village, USA', *Journal of Consumer Research*, 16(September): 227–238.

O'Guinn, T.C. and Faber, R.J. (1989) 'Compulsive Buying: A Phenomenological Exploration, *Journal of Consumer Research*, 16(September): 147–157.

Oswald, L.R. (1999) 'Culture Swapping: Consumption and the Ethnogenesis of Middle-Class Haitian Immigrants', *Journal of Consumer Research,* 25(March): 303–318.

Otnes, C.C. and Lowrey, T.M. (2003) *Contemporary Consumption Rituals: A Research Anthology*. Mahwah, NJ: Lawrence Erlbaum Associates.

Otnes, C.C., Lowrey, T.M. and Kim, Y.C. (1993) 'Gift Giving for "Easy" and "Difficult" Recipients: A Social Roles Interpretation', *Journal of Consumer Research*, 20 (September): 229–244.

Otnes, C.C., Lowrey, T.M. and Shrum, L.J. (1997) 'Toward an Understanding of Consumer Ambivalence', *Journal of Consumer Research*, 24(June): 80–93.

Parsons, E. (2009) 'What Things Do: Examining Things that 'Matter' in Consumer Research', *Advances in Consumer Research,* Vol. 36, Duluth, MN: Association for Consumer Research.

Peñaloza, L. (1994) 'Atravesando Fronteras/Border Crossings: A Critical Ethnographic Exploration of the Consumer Acculturation of Mexican Immigrants', *Journal of Consumer Research*, 21(June): 32–54.

Peñaloza, L. (1999) 'Just Doing It: A Visual Ethnographic Study of Spectacular Consumption Behavior at Nike Town', *Consumption, Markets and Culture*, 2(4): 337–400.

Peñaloza, L. (2001) 'Consuming the West: Animating Cultural Meaning and Memory at a Stock Show and Rodeo', *Journal of Consumer Research*, 28(3): 369–398.

Peter, J.P. (1992) 'Realism or Relativism for Marketing Theory and Research: A Comment on Hunt's "Scientific Realism"', *Journal of Marketing*, 56(April): 72–79.

Peter, J.P. and Olson J.C (1983) 'Is Science Marketing?', *Journal of Marketing*, 47(Fall): 111–125.

Ritson, M. and Elliott, R. (1999) 'The Social Uses of Advertising: An Ethnographic Study of Adolescent Advertising Audience', *Journal of Consumer Research,* 26(December): 260–277.

Ruth, J.A. (1996) '"It's the Feeling that Counts": Toward a Framework for Understanding Emotion and its Influence on Gift-Exchange Processes', in C. Otnes and R.F. Betramini (eds) *Gift Giving: A Research Anthology*, Bowling Green, OH: Bowling Green University Popular Press, pp. 195–214.

Ruth, J.A., Otnes, C.C. and Brunel, F. (1999) 'Gift Receipt and the Reformulation of Interpersonal Relationships', *Journal of Consumer Research*, 25(4): 385–402.

Sandikci, O. and Holt, D.B. (1998) 'Malling Society: Mall Consumption Practices and the Future of Public Space', in J.F. Sherry, Jr. (ed.) *Servicescapes: The Concept of Place in Contemporary Markets*, Chicago: NTC Business Books, pp. 305–336.

Schouten, J.W. and McAlexander, J.H. (1995) 'Subcultures of Consumption: An Ethnography of the New Bikers', *Journal of Consumer Research*, 22(June): 43–61.

Schroeder, J. (2002) *Visual Consumption*. London: Routledge.

Schroeder, J. and Borgerson, J. (2002) 'Innovations in Information Technology: Insights from Italian Renaissance Art', *Consumption, Markets and Culture*, 5(2): 153–169.

Schroeder, J. and Salzer-Morling, M. (2006) *Brand Culture*. London: Routledge.

Scott, L. (1990) 'Understanding Jingles and Needle Drop: A Rhetorical Approach to

Music in Advertising', *Journal of Consumer Research*, 17(September): 223–236.

Scott, L.M. (1994a) 'The Bridge from Text to Mind: Adapting Reader-Response Theory to Consumer Research', *Journal of Consumer Research*, 21(Dec): 461–480.

Scott, L.M. (1994b) 'Images in Advertising: The Need for a Theory of Visual Rhetoric', *Journal of Consumer Research*, 21(September): 252–273.

Shankar, A., Whittaker, J. and Fitchett, J.A. (2006) 'Heaven Knows I'm Miserable Now', *Marketing Theory*, 6(December): 485–505.

Sherry, J.F., Jr. (1983) 'Gift Giving in Anthropological Perspective, *Journal of Consumer Research*, 10(2): 157–168.

Sherry, J.F. (1990a) 'Postmodern Alternatives: The Interpretive Turn in Consumer Research', in H.H. Kassarjian and T.S.Robertson (eds) *Handbook of Consumer Research*, Englewood Cliffs, NJ: Prentice-Hall, pp. 549–591.

Sherry, J.F., Jr. (1990b) 'A Sociocultural Analysis of a Midwestern Flea Market', *Journal of Consumer Research*, 17(June): 13–30.

Sherry, J.F. (1990c) 'Dealers and Dealing in a Periodic Market: Informal Retailing in Ethnographic Perspective', *Journal of Retailing*, 66(2): 174–200.

Sherry, J.F., Jr. (1998a), *Servicescapes*. Lincolnwood, IL: NTC Business Books.

Sherry, J.F., Jr. (1998b) 'The Soul of the Company Store: Nike Town Chicago and the Emplaced Brandscape,' in J.F. Sherry Jr. (ed.) *Servicescapes: The Concept of Place in Contemporary Markets*, Lincolnwood, IL: NTC Business Books, pp. 109–146.

Sherry, J.F., Jr. (2000) 'Place, Technology and Representation', *Journal of Consumer Research*, 27(2): 273–278.

Sherry, J.F., Jr. McGrath, M.A. and Levy, S.J. (1993) 'The Dark Side of the Gift', *Journal of Business Research*, 28(November): 225–244.

Sherry, J.F., McGrath, M.A. and Levy, S.J. (1995) 'Monadic Giving: Anatomy of Gifts Given to the Self', in J.F. Sherry (ed.) *Contemporary Marketing and Consumer Behavior*, Thousand Oaks, CA: Sage, pp. 399–432.

Simonson, I., Carmon, Z., Dhar, R., Drolet, A. and Nowlis, S.M. (2001) 'Consumer Research: In Search of Identity', *Annual Reviews in Psychology*, 52: 249–275.

Stern, B.B. (1989) 'Literary Criticism and Consumer Research: Overview and Illustrative Analysis', *Journal of Consumer Research*, 16(Dec): 322–334.

Stern, B.B. (1993) 'Feminist Literary Criticism and the Deconstruction of Ads: A Postmodern View of Advertising and Consumer Responses', *Journal of Consumer Research*, 19(Mar): 556–566.

Stern, B.B. (1994) 'Classical and Vignette Television Advertising Dramas: Structural Models, Formal Analysis and Consumer Effects', *Journal of Consumer Research*, 20(March): 601–615.

Stern, B.B. (1995) 'Consumer Myths: Frye's Taxonomy and the Structural Analysis of Consumption Text', *Journal of Consumer Research*, 22(September): 165–185.

Stevens, L., Maclaran, P. and Brown, S. (2003) ''Red Time is Me Time': Advertising, Ambivalence, and Women's Magazines', *Journal of Advertising*, 32(1): 35–45.

Stevens, L., Maclaran, P. and Catterall, M. (2007) 'A Space of One's Own: Women's Magazine Consumption Within Family Life', *Journal of Consumer Behavior*, 6(July/August): 236–252.

Tadajewski, M. (2006) 'Remembering Motivation Research: Toward an Alternative Genealogy of Interpretive Consumer Research', *Marketing Theory*, 6(4): 429–466.

Thompson, C.J. (2004) 'Marketplace Mythology and Discourses of Power', *Journal of Consumer Research*, 31(June): 162–180.

Thompson, C.J., Locander, W.B. and Pollio, H.R. (1989), 'Putting Consumer Experience Back into Consumer Research: The Philosophy and Method of Existential-Phenomenology', *Journal of Consumer Research*, 16(September): 133–146.

Thompson, C. J. and Troester, M. (2002) 'Consumer Value Systems in the Age of Postmodern Fragmentation: The Case of the Natural Health Microculture', *Journal of Consumer Research*, 28(4): 550–571.

Thompson, C.J. and Tian, K. (2008) 'Reconstructing the South: How Commercial Myths Compete for Identity Value through the Ideological Shaping of Popular Memories and Countermemories', *Journal of Consumer Research*, 34(February): 519–613.

Tybout, A. (1995) 'The Value of Theory in Consumer Research', Presidential address in *Advances in Consumer Research*, Vol. 22, Provo, Utah: Association for Consumer Research, pp.1–8.

Ustuner, T. and Holt, D.B. (2007) 'Dominated Consumer Acculturation: The Social Construction of Poor Migrant Women's Consumer Identity Projects in a Turkish Squatter', *Journal of Consumer Research*, 34(June): 41–56.

Venkatesh, A. (1998) 'Cyberscapes and Consumer Freedoms and Identities', *European Journal of Marketing*, 32(7/8): 664–676.

Venkatesh, A. and Meamber, L.A. (2006) 'Arts and Aesthetics: Marketing and Cultural Production', *Marketing Theory*, 6(1): 11–40.

Wallendorf, M. (2001) 'Literally Literacy', *Journal of Consumer Research*, 27(4): 505–511.

Wallendorf, M., Lindsey-Mullikin, J. and Pimentel, R. (1998) 'Gorilla Marketing: Customer Animation and Regional Embeddedness of a Toy Store Servicescape', in J.F. Sherry, Jr. (ed.) *Servicescapes: The Concept of Place in Contemporary Markets*, Chicago: NTC Business Books, pp. 151–198.

Wells, W.D. (1991) 'Preface', in Belk, R.W. (ed.) *Highways and Buyways: Naturalistic Research from the Consumer Behavior Odyssey*, Provo, UT: Association for Consumer Research, p.iii.

Wells, W.D. (1995) 'What Do We Want To Be When We Grow Up', *Advances in Consumer Research*, Vol. 22, Provo UT: Association for Consumer Research. pp. 561–563.

Wilkie, W.L. and Moore, E.S. (2003) 'Scholarly Research in Marketing: Exploring the "4 Eras" of Thought Development', *Journal of Public Policy and Marketing*, 22(2): 116–146.

Woodruffe, H.R. (1997) 'Compensatory Consumption: Why Women Go Shopping When They're Fed Up and Other Stories', *Marketing Intelligence and Planning*, 15(7): 325–334.

Wooten, D.B. (2000) 'Qualitative Steps Toward an Expanded Model of Anxiety in Gift-Giving', *Journal of Consumer Research*, 27(June): 84–95.

Zhao, X. and Belk, R.W. (2008) 'Politicizing Consumer Culture: Advertising's Appropriation of Political Ideology in China's Social Transition', *Journal of Consumer Research*, 35(August): 231–244.

Zinkhan, G.M. and Hirschheim, R. (1992) 'Truth in Marketing Theory and Research: An Alternative Perspective', *Journal of Marketing*, 56(April): 80–88.

Impact of Theory on Representations of the Marketing Organisation

20

Interaction in Networks

Lars-Erik Gadde and Håkan Håkansson

INTRODUCTION

In 1982, a research project, carried out in five European countries (the IMP-study), was reported in a book 'based on an approach which challenges traditional ways of examining industrial marketing and purchasing' (Håkansson, 1982: 1). The analysis was solidly founded in empirical observations in this study as well as in several minor research projects before. The empirical observation concerned the role and importance of business relationships.

In business-to-business settings, the IMP study showed that companies on both the customer and supplier sides were dominated by some long-term business relationships with a limited number of counterparts. The relationships were long term – in average 12.5 years – they involved huge number of people from each side, including technicians, and were often characterized by mutual adaptations. Within the frame of these ongoing relationships, both marketing and purchasing of industrial goods were 'seen as interaction processes between the two parties' (ibid.: 15). The interaction between the parties in these processes was extensive considering the number of people involved and the longevity of the relationships. It even seemed to be the

case that interaction in itself included an important content of its own (later on identified as a 'substance' in Håkansson and Snehota, 1995).

These conditions were quite different from what could be expected according to the mainstream view of the features of transactions between buyers and sellers, where 'market exchange' was supposed to rule the game. In the book, the challenges in relation to prevailing conceptualizations covered four issues. Firstly, IMP challenged the narrow analysis of single discrete purchases and emphasized the importance of business relationships. Secondly, the view of industrial marketing as manipulation of marketing-mix variables in relation to a passive market was challenged. IMP rather stressed the interaction between individual buyers and sellers. The third challenge concerned the view implying an atomistic market structure where buyers and sellers easily could switch to new business partners, while IMP called the attention to the stability and longevity of business relationships. Fourthly, IMP challenged the separation, which had occurred in analyzing either the process of purchasing or the process of marketing. Instead, IMP claimed, the understanding of the processes of marketing and purchasing requires simultaneous analysis of the buying and selling sides of the relationship where interaction plays a crucial role.

The aforementioned conditions concerning relationships and interaction have been confirmed in a large number of empirical studies covering various countries, industries and cultures. The findings of the studies concern both the content of interaction and explanations of the consequences of the variety in interaction (for overviews, see Håkansson et al., 2009 and Wilkinson, 2008).

AIM AND OUTLINE OF THE CHAPTER

Over time, the role and importance of business relationships and interaction have been recognized by other schools-of-thought. As shown in the coming section, there is no general agreement regarding the implications for theories of business. In order to provide a foundation for such implications, we rely on an analogy to organization theory where theories X, Y and Z have been used to explore the relationship between an individual and the organization in which it is involved. Our main objective is to develop a framework for analysis of business interaction building on an outward-in perspective, implying that the internal organizing of a company must reflect its way of approaching business partners. On this basis, we explore how interaction is related to the three network layers of activities, resources and actors. We conclude the paper by analyzing how these conditions concerning network interaction may impact on the internal organizing of a company.

THEORETICAL CONSEQUENCES OF THE EMPIRICAL OBSERVATION

The empirical observation of the significance of relationships and interaction described in the preceding section is no longer questioned. It is generally acknowledged that business relationships play an important role in the business landscape. However, there is no consensus concerning the conceptualization and analysis of these relationships (Ford and Håkansson, 2006). Over time, the empirical findings concerning relationships and interaction have created a debate regarding the implications for theory. A number of alternative theoretical approaches have been advocated such as transaction cost analysis (Heide, 1994; Rindfleisch and Heide, 1997; Williamson, 1985), relational exchange theory (Macneil, 1980) and agency theory (e.g. Eisenhardt, 1989).

Relationships and their inherent interaction can thus be modeled in different ways. In order to provide a perspective on interaction in business-to-business settings, we relate to the debate in organizational theory concerning theories X and Y regarding how individuals can be seen in relation to the organization they represent. Theories X and Y were presented by McGregor (1960) in order to identify two different psychological models behind people's behavior in organizations. According to theory X, individuals are assumed to dislike work and will seek to avoid it. Actually, 'the average human being prefers to be directed, wishes to avoid responsibility, has relatively little ambition, wants security above all' (McGregor, 1960: 33–34). The basic prescription for handling individuals consequently is that most people must be coerced, controlled and directed in order to secure adequate performance. Theory Y contrasts this view in arguing that most individuals do not 'inherently dislike work' and therefore 'external control and threat of punishment are not the only means for bringing about effort toward organizational objectives' (ibid.: 47). In some situations, thus, theory Y would be more appropriate for explaining the behavior and functioning of individuals. Both these psychological models have an inside-out perspective on the individual, implying that the features of the individual determine the relation with the organization.

Theories X and Y were later supplemented and/or challenged by theory Z (Ouchi, 1981), based on a combination of ideas from Japanese companies and American management tradition. Theory Z represents a humanistic approach to management and despite some similarities with theory Y, it breaks away from McGregor's basic frame. Theory Y is a largely psychological perspective focusing on individual dyads of employer–employee relationships. Theory Z changes the level of analysis by considering in which way the individual is embedded into the entire organization, thus taking situations outside the actual workplace into consideration. This holistic concern for what is going on between employer and employee thus signifies an outside-in explanation of individuals' behavior and functioning.

The basic characteristics of these three models of the relationship between individuals and organizations are translated in the following section to illustrate how interaction in business-to-business settings can be analyzed.

THEORIES FOR ANALYZING INTERACTION

The basic point of departure for understanding interaction between companies is the classical market model, which can be seen as the X-model for interaction. In the market model, the interaction with others is described as very 'thin' and lacking a substance of its own (Swedberg, 1994). According to this view, interaction functions merely as an instrument – the market mechanism for efficient transactions. Under the governance of this mechanism, actors avoid to become dependent on their business partners since they appreciate the freedom to interact at each moment with the one providing the best business conditions. Furthermore, and which is an important argument for the market mechanism, this mechanism saves the society from some not-so-positive human features that are assumed to characterize the individual actor – it forces all actors despite these features to behave in a way that is positive for the totality.

The mechanism works as long as it provides opportunities for suppliers and customers to switch freely among potential business partners.

For the market mechanism to function as intended, interaction should be free from friction or transaction costs so each actor directly can react on price signals. Given this general mechanism, the company is within its ownership boundary free to use and combine resources as it wants, in terms of innovation, production and organization. The external interaction does not constrain what can be done internally. However, the outcome of what is done internally must be efficient owing to the ruling invisible hand – the market mechanism. Consequently, external interaction is not hindered through specific limitations due to internal conditions. The company is free to design its way of acting toward all potential counterparts on both the purchasing and marketing sides. It is free to make any decision about who to interact with as interaction in itself is totally standardized. There is no need for relationships in interaction based on similar assumptions as theory X.

Nevertheless, the empirical findings presented in the preceding section indicate that there are relationships out there. These features of business reality must in some way be taken into consideration. This is also done in other schools of thought, for example, transaction cost analysis (TCA). The main objective of TCA is to identify what is the appropriate governance mode for various types of transactions, and particularly whether these should take place via the market or be integrated within the hierarchy. When it comes to the view of business relationships and interaction, TCA can be used as a relevant illustration of theory Y. The transaction cost approach is founded in the basic market theory that we described earlier. However, TCA acknowledges that in some situations, specific reasons will lead to 'market failures' where neither the market nor the firm is the most appropriate governance mode. In those situations, other mechanisms for governance can be used, for example, business relationships. Thus, under specific conditions, business relationships will lead to lower transaction costs than that of the market or the hierarchy. In these situations, (e.g. a limited number of market players, high asset specificity and low frequency of transactions) a relationship approach will be favored by the economic actors. The content of relationships is no big issue since interaction builds primarily on 'trust'. These conditions explain the popularity and usefulness of the transaction cost approach. TCA builds on classic market theory and considers business relationship as an additional feature. The content of this relationship is restricted to a specific behavioral aspect (trust) – which is mainly 'psychological'. It is not necessary to change other assumptions concerning the behavior of the company – it should still behave as an independent actor and only rely on relationships when other mechanisms are not appropriate. In this respect, it is similar to theory Y's explanation concerning the relationship between the individual and the organization.

The 'pure' market theory and transaction cost theory thus build on the same basic assumptions. TCA recognizes interaction as a governance mechanism but apply an inside-out perspective. Actors are supposed to use interaction for the provision of benefits that cannot be obtained through the two other governance modes. Actors are supposed to be in full control of the interaction processes, and they are assumed to be able to influence the interaction with regard to their own objectives. Interaction is thus a means for the actors.

The main ambition with this paper is to explore what implications for interaction a theory Z-approach would provide. This means that we are searching for an outside-in perspective on interaction. By taking theory Z as the inspiration for a theory of interaction, we have to consider a broad view where the interaction processes are part of a holistic context. We need therefore to take the point of departure in the overall business landscape where companies are involved in complex industrial settings. From this perspective, interaction is a reflection of features of this industrial setting in a number of dimensions, in the same way as the relationship between the individual and the organization in theory Z. According to this view, interaction will be an

effect of the setting rather than of the characteristics of the individual company. It is appealing to use this analogy since the relationship between the individual and the organization according to theory Z is characterized by longevity, consensual decision-making and informal methods of control. These features have been identified as important characteristics of business relationships.

Following the foregoing discussion, the analysis requires a holistic perspective. In this respect, we rely on the industrial network model (Håkansson and Snehota, 1995). This model emphasizes the role of business relationships and how these relationships are connected in network structures. These networks are analyzed in three layers: activities, resources and actors, each providing part of the substance in the interaction in business relationships. This substance in terms of activity links, resource ties and actor bonds is connected to what the involved companies are doing internally in terms of activities and resources. The substance in a particular relationship sometimes is connected to substances in other relationships in which the two companies are involved. Consequently, there are certain connections between the internal organizing of resources and activities within a company and its external interaction. A more substantive interaction with others makes the single 'business unit' less of an independent island and more of a part of a mainland (Håkansson and Snehota, 1989). Interaction will therefore, in an indirect way, include others, and it will also be multi-dimensional from a content point of view, which is illustrated in the following three sections concerning interaction in relation to resource constellations, activity patterns and actor webs, respectively.

RESOURCE CONSTELLATIONS AND INTERACTION

Any industrial setting involves a huge number of resources connected in intricate constellations. These constellations have been built up over long time and consist of combinations of tangible and intangible resources. Some resources are physical and clearly visible and represented by, for example, machines, buildings, infrastructures for communication and transportation, equipment and vehicles. Other resources may be less visible, but as important as the physical, including human capabilities and competencies and other organizational resources. Resource constellations have significant economic consequences since they are costly to design, operate and maintain.

Any resource appears in a constellation where it is combined with other resources. The features of the individual resource are affected by the principles of combining. This combining can be more or less systematic, more or less conscious, and more or less active. Irrespective of which of these conditions are to hand the actual principle of combining relates the resources to each other. It is through this process that interfaces among resources evolve and provide relationships with substances in terms of resource ties across the boundaries of firms. This substance is to a large extent determined by the content of the interaction. Through intensified interaction, companies can find ways to connect their resources so that they fit better together. One of the main findings in the first IMP-study concerned the significant impact of adaptations. Any adaptation is a modification in the features of a resource in relation to one or several resources of the business partner. Such modifications tie the resources to each other and can concern adaptations between physical resources, between organizational resources or between physical and organizational resources.

Resource combining and adaptations have particular spatial consequences. Adaptations exploit the inherent heterogeneity of resources implying that the value of a resource is not predetermined. The economic value of a specific resource is contingent on its connections to other resources. Moreover, the value is dependent on how well the resources function in relation to each other. The better the two resources fit together – the better the financial outcome. The greater the adaptations – the better the resources will fit together. Since adaptations increasingly span the boundaries of firms, interaction is critical to the outcome. What is ongoing in the interaction in a particular relationship thus impacts on other interaction processes. Therefore, the modifications of a resource owing to adaptations in a relationship will impact on the opportunities for combining in other relationships. The greater the 'resource' content of the interaction among business partners the more systematically related will be the collective resource constellation of all connected resources.

In this way, the development of individual resources is strongly related to the evolvement over time of the resource constellation in which the particular resource is involved. Studies of technical development clearly indicate that technologies are characterized by path-dependency (David, 1985; Dosi et al., 1988; Rosenberg, 1994). The development of a resource along a specific path is strongly contingent on its interaction with other resources in various applications over time. Therefore, any adaptation and modification of a resource can have far-reaching consequences, since it may evolve into a new technological trajectory and a modified resource path.

A company's resource combining efforts must take these spatial and timely consequences into consideration. In its 'resourcing' efforts, a firm must coordinate the handling of internal resources with both the interaction process in relation to a specific counterpart and how this affects other interactions of the two parties. Resource combining is thus to a large extent an organizational process where internal and external resources become related and interaction is crucial for the outcome of these efforts. Interaction is not merely about connecting resources. The ways in which interaction is handled is in fact a value generation process. Over time, the interaction with the counterpart creates a resource in itself. Interaction is thus a very special resource, since it is functioning as an interface between other resources. With this view, interaction becomes a resource organizing other resources.

ACTIVITY PATTERNS AND INTERACTION

The activity layer of the network shares its properties with the resource layer. The business landscape is full of activities: manufacturing, distribution, design and usage of offerings, planning, information exchange, research and development and so on. These activities are connected into a larger setting identified as an activity pattern. Within this overall pattern, various activity configurations can be identified. An activity configuration consists of those activities that are necessary for the creation of a particular end product, such as a PC, a logistics service or an information system. The activities involved in a specific configuration are normally allocated to different firms through division of labor. The ways in which activities are organized into actual configurations have profound economic implications. The efficiency in a particular set-up of activities is contingent on the efficiency in the undertaking of individual activities and on the coordination of these single activities.

The main feature of the activity layer is the inherent interdependency among activities since an activity normally builds on other activities and leads to yet others. Activities are serially interdependent and have thus to be conducted in a specific order, which calls for planning and synchronization. Other activities have been adjusted in relation to each other in order to improve their joint performance, for example, the outbound operations of a logistics service provider and the assembly activities of a manufacturing company. These adjustments, in order to handle the dependence between two activities, in turn create interdependences between the activities.

Activities within the boundary of a company are usually very closely integrated while activities performed in different companies can be more or less related. The nature of the connection is determined by the interaction between the companies and the substance of this interaction is identified as 'activity links'. These activity links connect production, transportation, warehousing and other activities on the two sides and for the outcome of these processes, interaction is crucial. An activity conducted by a company can, in this way, be linked to one or several activities of a business partner and through this connection, linked to other companies. Consequently, these linkages in the spatial dimension will affect the way an activity is conducted and thereby make it more or less integrated with other internal and external activities.

The adjustment of two activities will thus impact on a number of other activities conducted by different companies. A particular adjustment is thus beneficial not only for the two companies involved but also for the overall pattern and therefore may lead to further adjustments across company boundaries. In the time dimension, single activities and activity configurations thus tend to evolve in processes of mutual adjustments. We identify this development as specialization. The activity pattern involving several actors is likely to become increasingly specialized. Individual actors build specialization through adjustments into their activities relative to others as their interactions evolve. Adjustments and specialization involve significant costs for the actors but are critical for the development of business relationships and combinations of relationships. Specialization is neither a simple nor an uncontroversial process since activity adjustments affect many others – positively or negatively.

In conclusion, interaction is an activity organizing other activities. Activity organizing within a company must take the interdependencies to other internal activities into consideration, as well as the interdependencies to the activities of its business partners, which in turn will impose indirect interdependencies to other firms.

ACTOR WEBS AND INTERACTION

In the two previous sections, we have discussed the role of interaction in resource combining and activity configuration. Obviously, these processes are not self-generating, but require the active involvement of actors. Actors in business have intent – they combine resources and configure activities with certain ambitions and motives in mind. The intent of actors is based on knowledge of their own resources and activities as well as on knowledge of other actors and their resources and activities. Owing to the enormous number of actors populating the business landscape, it would be impossible for an actor to be aware of all these actors, the resources they control and the activities they perform.

Actors therefore tend to focus their attention to a limited number of business partners to which they can be closely related. Through such relationships with other actors, it is possible to identify what benefits may be provided through activity links and resource ties. The outcome of this interactive analysis is what leads to adaptations among resources and adjustments of activities. These adaptations and adjustments tend to extend the connections also in the actor layer through the actor bonds that evolve between actors over time, which represents the third substance of interactive relationships. This means that an actor is not a self-contained entity, nor can it exist in isolation. Any actor is connected to other actors and formed by its interaction with these. We refer to this connection as 'jointness' in the space dimension of the business landscape. Jointness is a characteristic of the specific relationship between any two actors in relation to all other actors and is a central feature of business networks where interaction is a key attribute. Jointness may appear in various forms such as collaborative product development, synchronized delivery systems and openness in information exchange. Similar to the interdependences in activity patterns, jointness in actor webs not only provides opportunities but also constrains the autonomy of actors.

A significant feature in the web of actors is that companies evolve over time. Actors change with respect to the activities they perform, the resources they control and what actors they interact with. The jointness with other actors is an important determinant of these changes implying that the evolution of a single actor is never an individual course of action. On the contrary, it is a process taking place interactively with others and thus in co-evolution with these actors. This co-evolution of actors is strongly connected to the emerging paths in resource constellations and the specialization of activity patterns.

Interaction may appear to take place between only two actors. However, the intentions of those actors, the content and outcome of their interaction may have widespread impact since both parties are simultaneously involved in interaction with others. Sometimes intentions and outcomes of these processes are contradictory and cause tensions between the parties. In other situations, various interaction processes may reinforce each other and thus further strengthen both the jointness and the co-evolution in the web of actors.

INTERACTION AND NETWORKS

The sections analyzing interaction in resource constellations, activity patterns and actor webs all provide an outside-in view of interaction and thereby also on business relationships. The resource constellations, activity patterns and actor webs are three main layers of the business landscape. In relation to each of these, we have found that interaction has a major role, as it is highly involved in shaping the business landscape. Our analysis is summarized in Figure 20.1.

Interaction processes within and among resources, activities and actors are important ingredients in the functionality and evolvement of the business landscape. At the same time, the three layers are affected through their mutual interaction in both the space and time dimension. Through interaction, the resources

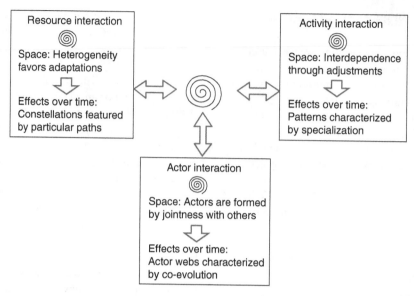

Figure 20.1   Interaction in the business landscape.

controlled by different companies may be tied together in order to take advantage of heterogeneity and development paths. Through these processes, the usage, and thereby the value, of each resource can be enhanced (Gadde and Håkansson, 2008; Håkansson and Waluszewski, 2007). In the same way, interaction may link the activities performed by different companies to each other by exploiting interdependencies and making specialization possible over time. Both these factors will in turn positively affect the performance of the involved companies in relation to each other (Araujo et al., 2003; Gadde and Snehota, 2000). Finally, through interaction the involved actors (companies or parts of companies) can gain advantages from co-evolution over time at the same time that they can develop jointness with specific business partners, which increases their importance for these actors (Ritter and Gemünden, 2003).

A significant consequence of these characteristics is that interaction becomes the main building process in the business landscape by creating the specific features in the three network layers. The direction of this process will be determined by the substance in the interaction. If the involved actors together

are creating a large number of extensive resource ties between each other, the resource constellation will be affected in a considerable way. The resources will become more valuable as they are related to each other in a systematic way. If the involved actors together are creating a large number of extensive activity links, this will significantly affect the total activity pattern. Again, we can expect improved efficiency, for example, through an activity pattern where supply chains become systematically related to each other. Finally, if the involved actors are creating a large number of extensive actor bonds a business landscape will be formed where companies are very knowledgeable about some specific others, which in turn will enhance further cooperation in order to benefit from co-evolution. An interesting empirical illustration is given in Bocconcelli and Håkansson (2008).

In the preceding section, we have identified important positive aspects following from increasing interaction substance. However, these benefits are also accompanied by certain drawbacks. The network lacks the automatic regulating mechanism of the market. The substance in the interaction will not appear automatically, neither is it necessarily directed toward something good from the society point of view. The actual effect of the substance depends on the ways individuals (managers, technicians, accountants and others) are behaving. Resource ties, activity links and actor bonds can be created only through people. The substance will not appear by itself but is the result of all the ambitions and competence of the people involved. Therefore, interaction will mirror the ambitions of those that are mostly involved in the process. The network will be more efficient and innovative for them than for anybody else. This is an important conclusion in relation to industrial policy issues. A network should never be left alone and allowed to follow its own route, but instead always be influenced. Without such influencing efforts, the network will evolve in directions that are not beneficial to some of the actors involved. The forces residing in powerful actors must be balanced by organized mobilization among weaker actors. In these processes, interaction will have a major role to play.

CONCLUSION

Coming back to our analogy with organization theory, the main differential between theory Z and the other two concerned a shift from an inside-out perspective towards an outside-in perspective. By looking at interaction from an outside-in view, we found that the basic processes in the three network layers are directed by interaction. We also showed that these processes provide interaction with particular content through the activity links, resource ties and actor bonds that evolve between the actors in business relationships. This substance shapes the features of activities, resources and actors, and over time contributes to the dynamics in the three network layers. However, there is no automatic mechanism directing the development of the network.

As soon as we acknowledge that interaction has a substance we have to reinterpret the meaning of interaction. In such a frame, interaction becomes an organizing process where it is possible for the most involved actors to achieve major benefits from both a technological and a commercial point of view. However, this also means that all others have to become involved in this organizing if they want to influence their situation. The network evolves through these organizing efforts, which contain two different processes of importance to any company. The first regards the interaction and organizing in relation to other companies in the overall business landscape that we have focused in this chapter. The second concerns the internal organizing within each of the involved companies (Håkansson and Lind, 2004). This internal organizing is crucial since it determines how the individual company can interact with others, what issues that will be dealt with and what substance that will be created. If we aim at creating resource ties, the key resources have to become involved in the interaction; if we want to establish activity links, the key activities must be involved and so on. Moreover, the substance created through external interaction processes must in some way be anchored in the internal organizing of the interacting companies. The main conclusion of our exploration is therefore that interaction should be seen as an organizing process with two important roles. On the one hand, interaction may be seen as an organizing process relating a number of company-based organizing processes to each other. On the other hand, interaction may be seen as an organizing process where the internal organizing of each company is related to the overall interaction processes in the network.

REFERENCES

Araujo, L., Dubois, A., and Gadde, L.-E. (2003) 'The Multiple Boundaries of the Firm', *Journal of Management Studies*, 40(3): 1255–1277.

Bocconcelli, R. and Håkansson, H. (2008) 'External Interaction as a Means of Making Changes in a Company: The Role of

Purchasing in a Major Turnaround for Ducati', *IMP Journal*, 2(2): 25–37.

David, P.A. (1985) 'Clio and the Economics of QWERTY', *The American Economic Review*, 75(2): 332–337.

Dosi, G., Freeman, C., Nelson, R., and Soete, L. (eds) (1988) *Technical Change and Economic Theory*. London: Pinter.

Eisenhardt, K. (1989) 'Making Fast Strategic Decisions in High-Velocity Environments', *Academy of Management Journal*, 32(3): 543–576.

Ford, D. and Håkansson, H. (2006) 'The Idea of Interaction', *IMP Journal*, 1(1): 4–27.

Gadde, L-E. and Snehota, I. (2000) 'Making the Most of Supplier Relationships', *Industrial Marketing Management*, 29: 305–316.

Gadde, L-E. and Håkansson, H. (2008) 'Business Relationships and Resource Combining', *IMP Journal*, 2(1): 31–45.

Håkansson, H. (ed.) (1982) *International Marketing and Purchasing of Industrial Goods – An Interaction Approach*. New York: Wiley.

Håkansson, H. and Lind, J. (2004) 'Accounting and Network Coordination', *Accounting, Organization and Society*, 29: 51–72.

Håkansson, H. and Snehota, I. (1989) 'No Business is an Island', *Scandinavian Journal of Management*, 5(3): 187–200.

Håkansson H. and Snehota, I. (eds) (1995) *Developing Relationships in Business Networks*, London: International Thomson.

Håkansson, H. and Waluszewski, A. (eds) (2007) *Knowledge and Innovation in Business and Industry. The Importance of Using Others*. London: Routledge.

Håkansson, H., Ford, D., Gadde, L-E., Snehota, I., and Waluszewski, A. (2009) *Business in Networks*. London and New York: Wiley.

Heide, J. (1994) 'Interorganizational Governance in Marketing Channels' *Journal of Marketing*, 58(1): 71–85.

Macneil, I.R. (1980) *The New Social Contract: An Inquiry into Modern Contractual Relations*. New Haven: Yale University Press.

McGregor, D. (1960) *The Human Side of Enterprise*. New York: Mc Graw-Hill.

Ouchi, W.G. (1981) *Theory Z*. Reading, Mass: Addison-Wesley.

Rindfleish, A. and Heide, J.B. (1997) 'Transaction Cost Analysis: Past Present and Future Applications', *Journal of Marketing*, 61: 30–54.

Ritter, T. and Gemünden, H.G. (2003) 'Network Competence: Its Impact on Innovation Success and its Antecedents', *Journal of Business Research*, 56(9): 745–755.

Rosenberg, N. (1994) *Exploring the Black Box: Technology, Economics, History*. Cambridge: Cambridge University Press.

Swedberg, R. (1994) 'Markets as Social Structures', in Smelser, N.J. and Swedberg, R. (eds) *The Handbook of Economic Sociology*. Princeton, NJ: Princeton University Press.

Williamson, O.E. (1985) *The Economic Institutions of Capitalism*. New York: The Free Press.

Wilkinson, I. (2008) *Business Relating Business. Managing Organisational Relations and Networks*. Cheltenham, UK: Edwar Elgar.

21

Practice Perspective of the Marketing Organisation

Roderick J. Brodie, Victoria J. Little,
and Richard W. Brookes

INTRODUCTION

Since the 1970s, Webster (1992) and other scholars have observed a number of subtle changes in the way marketing is practiced. Reflecting a knowledge-rich and turbulent operating environment, mainstream marketing thinking about the nature and role of the marketing function has changed. Greater emphasis is now placed on the social and economic processes undertaken by the marketing organisation (Vargo and Lusch, 2004; Wilkie and Moore, 2003). Organisations have adapted to environmental change, shifting away from large bureaucratic, hierarchical forms to new organisational types such as strategic partnerships and networks (Webster, 1992). Key characteristics of these newer organisational forms are flexibility, specialisation, and an emphasis on relationships rather than market transactions. These relationships are not only with customers, but also with other stakeholders including suppliers, channel intermediaries, and other market contacts. In this 'networked' view of organisations, specialised firms are tied together in collaborative, value-creating exchange relationships (Achrol, 1997; Axelsson and Easton, 1992; Achrol and Kotler, 1999).

While considerable discussion has focused on the types of emerging organisational forms, less attention has been given to the impact of theory on representations of the marketing organisation. The purpose of this chapter is to provide insight into this issue, by drawing on a decade of research undertaken by the Contemporary Marketing Practices (CMP) research group. In doing so, the chapter develops the case for adopting a multi-theory-practice-based perspective of the marketing organisation. The approach to theorising is compatible with contemporary theorising in organisational science (Weick, 1989). Both have a focus on developing middle-range theory, serving as a bridge between the development of general theories and empirical research about the practices of organisations (Pinder and Moore, 1979).

The next section outlines the conceptual foundations of CMP research, and the resultant development of a configuration approach for understanding the marketing practices of organisations. A review of the empirical evidence generated over the years follows. The review leads to a discussion of how various conceptual and methodological developments have informed theory about the contemporary marketing organisation. In the following section, the process of middle-range theorising is discussed, to illuminate the interface between theory and practice. This discussion is followed by consideration of the role of 'living' case studies in understanding the marketing organisations' practices. The final section discusses the results of recent studies linking practice to performance, and offers conclusions relating to the contribution of a multi-lensed configuration approach to understanding the contemporary marketing organisation.

CMP MULTI-THEORY APPROACH

In the 1990s, a new programme of research emerged at the University of Auckland, New Zealand. The genesis of the programme came from several faculty members who were engaged in executive teaching. Through a combination of in-class discussions and reportage by mid-career managers about the organisations they worked for, the faculty members observed an apparent gap between the academic discourse and the marketing practice. For example, in the 1990s, strong academic arguments were being made for a 'paradigm shift', away from the traditional marketing management approach and towards a relational-based approach (e.g. Christopher et al., 1991; Grönroos, 1990; Gummeson, 1987; Sheth et al., 1988). However, in their interactions with practicing executives, faculty noticed that managers were not 'shifting'; rather, they were integrating relationship approaches with their existing approaches. They were doing so in response to increasing environmental pressures to grow, improve profits, and cut costs. This observation stimulated the group to reconsider the relevance of the then-current

academic literature. The result was the launch of a formal research programme in 1996, now known as Contemporary Marketing Practices (CMP)[1]. The original objectives were to *profile marketing practices in a contemporary environment, and to examine the relevance of relational marketing in different organisational, economic, and cultural contexts*. The programme adopted an empirically-based middle-range theorising approach and had a strong emphasis on the interface between theory and marketing practice.

In parallel to the conceptual developments emerging from the group at the University of Auckland, Jaqueline Pels from the Universidad Torcuato di Tella in Buenos Aires, Argentina, was arriving at similar conclusions about the need for a multi-theoretical view. The research undertaken in New Zealand and by Pels (1999) in Argentina indicated that *all* the firms studied employed an approach to marketing that involved a combination of classic transactional practices *and* a range of different relational practices. While the research findings indicated that practices are continually evolving, the notion of paradigm shift or having a new logic guiding the evolution of practice was not supported (Brodie et al., 1997).

Over the last 10 years, the research programme has grown to include core researchers in New Zealand, the USA, the UK, and Argentina, and more recently a broader network of researchers throughout the world. Nearly 50 CMP-derived journal publications have been highly cited and, as a corpus, provide considerable insight to the theory and practice of contemporary marketing organisations. The original conceptual and empirical papers published in the *Journal of Marketing Management* (Brodie et al., 1997; Coviello et al., 1997) and the more recent *Journal of Marketing* paper that generalises the initial empirical findings (Coviello et al., 2002) are the most highly cited. More recently, the paper by Brodie, Coviello, and Winklhofer (2008) in a special issue of the *Journal of Business and Industrial Marketing* provides an overview of the CMP approach to theory development, and an assessment of the programme's overall contribution to marketing knowledge.

A typology of marketing practices derived from various theoretical perspectives in the academic literature provides the theoretical grounding for the research programme (Coviello et al., 1997). The typology recognises the fragmentation of mainstream marketing, and the greater emphasis on economic and social processes leading to more flexible organisational structures. Six general theoretical frameworks that relate to these economic and social processes serve as a foundation for the CMP classification scheme. They are: services marketing, inter-organisational exchange relationships, channels, networks, strategic management and value chain, and information technology within and between organisations. These align closely with the seven general theoretical frameworks identified by Vargo and Lusch (2004): market orientation, services marketing, relationship marketing, quality management, value chain management, supply chain management, and network analysis.

A content analysis of the then-prevailing marketing and broader management literature forms the basis of the classification scheme. Distinction are drawn between the use of the concepts associated with market activity, and concepts associated with management activities. The five concepts/dimensions relating to external or market activity are: purpose of exchange; nature of communication; type of contact; duration of exchange; and formality of exchange. The four concepts or dimensions relating to internal or management activity are, managerial intent, managerial focus, managerial investment; and managerial level of implementation. The literature was re-analysed based on these dimensions to identify various types of marketing practiced by organisations. Four discrete perspectives of marketing practice were subsequently identified, one *transactional* and three relational (*database, interaction, and network*). Tables 21.1 and 21.2 illustrate how these dimensions of market-related and management-related activity translate into the four perspectives of marketing practice.

Firstly, Table 21.1 details how the five market-related dimensions distinguish between the four types of marketing practice (transactional, database, interaction, and network).

Secondly, Table 21.2 details how the four management-related dimensions distinguish between the four types of marketing practice.

The typology is comprehensive and encompasses a range of organisational practices.

Table 21.1 CMP classification scheme of market activities

| Dimension | Type of Marketing Practice | | | |
	Transactional	Database	Interaction	Network
Purpose of Exchange	Generating a profit or other 'financial' measure(s) of performance	Acquiring customer information	Building a long-term relationship with a specific customer	Forming strong relationships with a number of organisations in market(s) or wider marketing system
Nature of Communication	Communicating to the mass market	Targeting a specifically identified segment(s) or customer(s)	Individuals at various levels in the organisation personally interacting with their individual customers	Senior managers networking with other managers from organisations in the market(s) or wider marketing system
Type of Contact	Impersonal (e.g. no individualised or personal contact)	Somewhat personalised (e.g. by direct mail)	Interpersonal (e.g. involving one-to-one interaction between people)	Interpersonal (e.g. involving one-to-one interaction between people)
Duration of Exchange	No future personalised contact with us	Some future personalised contact with us	One-to-one personal contact with us	One-to-one personal contact with people in the organisation and wider marketing system
Formality in Exchange	Mainly at a formal, business level	Mainly at an informal, social level	At both a formal, business and informal, social level	At both a formal, business and informal, social level

Table 21.2 CMP classification scheme marketing management activities

Dimension	Types of marketing practice			
	Transaction	Database	Interaction	Network
Managerial intent	Attract new customers	Retain existing customers	Develop cooperative relationships with the customers	Coordinate activities between the organisations, customers, and other parties in the wider marketing system
Managerial focus	Our product /service offering	Customers in our market(s)	Specific customers in our market(s), or individuals in organisations we deal with	The network of relationships between individuals and organisations in the wider marketing system
Managerial investment	Product, promotion, price, and distribution activities (or some combination of these)	Technology to improve communication with our customers	Establishing and building personal relationships with individual customers	Developing our organisation's network relationships within the market(s) or wider marketing system
Managerial level	Functional marketers (e.g. marketing manager, sales manager, and major account manager)	Specialist marketers (e.g. customer service manager and loyalty manager)	Non-marketers who have responsibility for marketing and other aspects of the business	The Managing Director or CEO

Importantly, because the classification scheme works with theory at the middle range and embraces a multi-theoretical approach, the richness of organisations' marketing practices is captured in a commensurately rich theoretical result – well beyond a simple dichotomy. This development was possible because CMP researchers took the view that the alternative practices are not mutually exclusive. Based on their on-going discussions with practicing managers, they realised that a multi-theory position obviated the need to draw distinct boundaries, or to assume each practice is independent and mutually exclusive. The approach highlighted the similarities and differences between each practice, as determined by the market and marketing dimensions derived from the literature. Thus, the classification scheme used multiple perspectives to broaden the view of markets and marketing management to identify, recognise, and categorise a 'rich and thick' range of relevant empirical phenomena (Geertz, 1973).

The theoretical classification scheme acknowledged possible multiple perspectives, and therefore allowed empirical research to identify different configurations of types of marketing practices of organisations. Coviello et al.'s (2002) *Journal of Marketing* implications of this approach. This study examined 308 firms in the US and four other Western countries, aiming to explain how different types of firms relate to their markets. Confirming the classification scheme, the research identified three groups of firms: those whose organisational practices were predominantly transactional, those whose organisational practices were predominantly relational/network-based and those whose organisational practices were both transactional *and* relational/network-based. Subsequent research found these results also generalised to emerging markets including Argentina (Pels et al., 2004), West Africa (Dadzie et al., 2008), and Russia (Wagner, 2005).

CMP'S METHODOLOGICAL APPROACH

By embracing this multi-theoretical perspective coupled with multi-method approaches, the CMP group has sought to encourage an interplay that involves applying both positivist and interpretative methods. Pels and Saren (2005) and Moller, Pels and Saren in Chapter 9 of this volume provide a fuller discussion of this topic and how this philosophy underpins the approach. Methodologically, one of the early and defining characteristics of the research was the diversity in methodological expertise of the research group. The range was broad, from those who preferred working with standardised questionnaires and large samples, to those who preferred working with in-depth case studies and participant–observer case vignettes. There were a number of less traditional approaches, for example the use of a group decision support system in an interactive/online environment. Table 21.3 provides an overview of the potential armamentarium of research methods and the coverage of these methods among CMP researchers.

The research as a whole therefore draws on a broad range of research philosophies and methodological approaches. This leads to 'team-research pluralism', allowing the group to achieve a more nuanced understanding of marketing practices in various international market contexts. The philosophy is that the multi-lensed approach is commensurate with the complexity of marketing organisations practices. Complex phenomena require a commensurate approach, so traditional views challenged in a dispassionate and robust manner.

In applying multi-method research, the group initially used sequential designs with alternative methods being employed in stages, feeding results from one stage into the next stage in the sequence. For example, the initial interpretive research based on Nicole Coviello's PhD (Coviello, 1996) helped develop the CMP framework and subsequent survey research. The preferred approach now, however, is to use a 'parallel design' where enquiries are carried out in parallel, with results informing and enriching each other simultaneously. For example, most surveys involved middle managers, who act as participant observers for their organisations. In addition to responding to a structured questionnaire, they are required to reflect on the practices in their organisations and in so doing, provide qualitative assessments of their marketing practices, changes to marketing practice in general, and influences on these practices. When analysing the results, researchers toggle between statistical analysis of the quantitative data and the qualitative analysis of individual responses and groups of cases. When the research is reported, text units and other qualitative summaries of groups of cases are used to augment the quantitative findings (or vice versa).

Importantly, as the group's understanding of marketing practices within the group evolved, so too has the application of methodological

Table 21.3   Matching research purpose with research methodology (adapted from Voss, Tsikriktsis, and Frohlich, 2002)

Purpose	Research question	Research methods	CMP usage
Exploration	Is there something interesting enough	In-depth case studies	Yes
Uncover areas for research	to justify research?	Unique/exemplary cases	Yes
and theory development		Unfocused, longitudinal field study	Yes
Theory building	What are the key variables?	Few focused case studies	Yes
Identify/describe key	What are the patterns or linkages	In-depth field studies	Yes
variables	between variables?	Multi-site case studies	Yes
	Why should these relationships exist?	Best-in-class case studies	No
Theory testing	Are the theories we have generated able	Experiment	No
Test theories developed	to survive the test of empirical data?	Quasi-experiment	Yes
in previous stages	Did we get the behaviour predicted by	Multiple case studies	Yes
Predict future outcomes	the theory or did we observe another	Large-scale sample of population	Yes
	unanticipated behaviour?		
Theory extension/	How generalisable is the theory?	Experiment	No
refinement	Where does the theory apply?	Quasi-experiment	Yes
To better structure theories in		Case studies	Yes
light of observed results		Large-scale sample of population	Yes

approaches. For example, qualitative research has moved beyond the traditional case method to apply action research with 'living case studies' (Little et al., 2006), successfully facilitating both theory-focused knowledge development and student-focused learning outcomes (Little et al., 2006a). The section titled 'Using Practice to Inform Theory about the Organisation', later in this chapter, provides a more detailed discussion of the living case approach.

CMP's approach to data collection and analysis now incorporates the living case approach, the survey instrument and other method-based innovations. For example, while the survey data has traditionally been collected from executive students as part of their coursework (allowing for a large number of reliable responses), a growing interest in sector-specific studies has led to the development and use of an online email survey (e.g. Brady and Palmer, 2004), and data collection through a website (Coviello, Winklhofer, and Hamilton, 2006). In addition, some research now takes a more traditional approach to data collection by analysing random samples of marketing managers in a sector, rather than gathering data from executive students.

MIDDLE-RANGE THEORISING

The middle-range theorising approach to knowledge creation was referred to at the outset of this chapter, and discussed as a linchpin of the CMP approach. The initial idea about the need for middle-range theorising in the social sciences came from Merton (1967) in sociology. He defines middle-range theories as:

> ... theories that lie between the minor but necessary working hypotheses that evolve in abundance during day-to-day research and all-inclusive systematic efforts to develop a unified theory that will explain all the uniformities of social behaviour, social organisation and social change.
>
> (Merton, 1967: 39)

Thus, rather than attempting to explain everything about a general subject (e.g. marketing or the motion of objects), the theoretical focus is on a subset of phenomena relevant to a particular industry or organisational context. Middle-range theory is concerned with explicit, testable statements about the relationships between specific variables (Pondy, 1980). Grand or general theories were viewed as being too broad to generate those statements (whether hypotheses or propositions)[2].

Bluedorn and Evered (1980) place middle-range theory in context with empirical generalisation and general theory. The overall theorising process, according to this representation, could commence either at the point of empirical generalisation or at the middle-range theory level, or at the general theory point. In all cases, a process of refinement delivers more explicit generalisations – whether middle-range theory or general theory – and migrates the scope of the theory or generalisation from narrow to broad. Thus, the middle-range theorising approach connects ideas to reality through a process of systematic refinement. Rather than connecting 'general' theory to empirical data, middle-range theory provides the middle ground. As Bluedorn and Evered (1980: 22) argue, 'general' theories 'lack the necessary conceptual and propositional integration to produce testable hypotheses that would ground them in the empirical world'.

Following Merton (1967), Weick (1995) argues that theorising might serve as a means to further development, where the process of theorising consists of activities like 'abstracting, generalizing, relating, selecting, synthesizing, and idealizing' (p. 389). Thus, the process develops and contributes by combining findings and drawing on general theories from within the management disciplines and also from the social sciences (e.g. economics, political theory, and cognitive psychology). This leads to middle-range theories that are inherently interdisciplinary in nature and are not constrained by a dominant general theory.

CMP research has evolved an empirically based middle-range theorising approach that

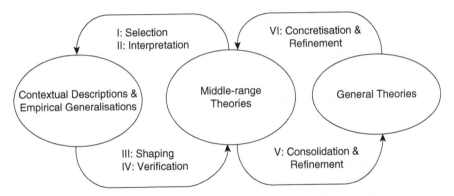

Figure 21.1   Bridging role of middle-range theory (adapted from Pondy, 1980).

draws on multiple theories and paradigms. The approach is driven by placing a strong emphasis on actual practices within markets and what managers and organisations do rather than on developing a general theory. Middle-range theorising underpins this practice-based process. Saren and Pels (2008) explore how this approach underpins the CMP methodological approach. More recently, Brodie et al. (2009) use the notion of the scientific circle of enquiry to elaborate further on the bridging role middle-range theory (Figure 21.1).

The first circle of enquiry follows what Hunt (1983) refers to as 'discovery' context and 'justification' context. In the 'discovery' stage, middle-range theories select and interpret contextual descriptions as well as empirical generalisations. This 'justification' stage follows where contextual description and empirical generalisations are used to shape and verify theories. The second circle of enquiry is between middle-range theories and general theories. Here, middle-range theories consolidate general theories by expanding their scope and making them more explicit. In turn, general theories make middle-range theories more concrete and hence explicit.

An important characteristic of middle-range theorising is that it focuses on the interface between theory and practice. Thus, it directs attention to managerial issues and concerns. The living case approach facilitates the interface between theories and marketing practices, as discussed in the previous section,

providing the problem-solving context for the middle-range theorising process.

USING PRACTICE TO INFORM THEORY ABOUT THE ORGANISATION

The living case approach builds on both case research and case teaching traditions, creating direct linkages between the case or research site and the researchers. The case data is sourced directly from the business contexts of middle managers who are part-time executive students, completing postgraduate and postexperience diplomas in marketing, or an MBA. The case approach encourages these executives to critically examine and reflect on their business contexts and practices through a process of facilitated learning. The outcome is constructed and refined theory that interprets and explains these phenomena and provides a framework for managerial decisions and practices. Thus, the living case approach fits with the theory discovery stage that involves the selection and interpretation of middle-range theories, in turn leading to contextual descriptions as well as empirical generalisations.

By working closely with executive students who are also practicing managers, the living case approach enables research directly relating to particular phenomena based on the managers' multiple and individual contexts and understandings. This approach allows managers to apply marketing theory to their own day-to-day contexts, and in so doing, to enhance their learning. It also allows for theory development relating to complex process-based phenomena, a traditionally less tractable area of enquiry. Living case studies also create a 'zone of mutuality' – a nexus between research cases and teaching cases (Little et al., 2008). Thus, the requirement for pedagogical quality is satisfied, while the research cases have a clear research method rather than being solely a pedagogical tool. The result is advancement of both theoretical knowledge and student learning.

Following the principle of middle-range theorising, the research case is motivated by a particular management problem in a theoretical setting and not only by classroom needs. The characteristics of 'good' living cases follow the principles of good research. This includes a writing style appropriate to the research paradigm, ensuring a chain of evidence to identify address and make explicit where alternative interpretations and conclusion. Consistent with the CMP approach, living cases use multiple methods. Quantitative methods provide insight into the wider context by profiling current marketing practices across different firm types and industries. Qualitative methods provide a deeper and richer understanding at the individual manager and firm level. This pluralistic approach facilitates the development of a more comprehensive understanding of the nature of marketing practice, and provides requisite variety by matching the complexity and multi-dimensionality of the contemporary business environment faced by managers.

Integration of research with executive teaching and the use of action learning and living case studies as a research vehicle is a key aspect of the CMP research approach. Action learning is a problem solving approach initially developed for managers in industry (Revans, 1998). This involves identifying that a complex problem is identified, and then a defined group embarks on continuous cycles of action and reflection, in order to arrive at a solution. The cases are alive and evolving, in that they are based on executive students' experiences in their own organisations. Another characteristic of the living case study approach and action learning is that the underlying philosophy is the democratic creation of knowledge. The collegial interaction by faculty with the practicing managers taking executive courses promotes mutual exchange of ideas and sharing of experiences, through fostering longitudinal, trusting, and productive partnerships. The mutual learning process is iterative, conducted over multiple stages, or cycles. Furthermore, the executives benefit from information, as they draw upon input from colleagues within their firms, from colleagues within their learning group. This may also include wider stakeholder groups (e.g. customers and distributors).

EXAMPLES OF LIVING CASE STUDIES

Table 21.4 shows two examples of the CMP living case approach to understanding marketing practices, relating to information technology (IT) adoption and customer value creation and delivery processes. These projects took place in a series of executive courses at the University of Auckland, New Zealand, and at Cranfield University, United Kingdom. A new cohort of managers is involved in each stage.

There are several differences and similarities between the two living cases. Common characteristics are an underlying action learning philosophy, a three stage longitudinal and iterative approach, a self-completion survey completed by executive students and based on their firms, in-depth reportage and reflection by participant–managers, and an iterative approach. In each case, the managers were directly involved with the day-to-day operations of their firms, and participating in MBA or postexperience executive programmes, taught by some members of the research team. The managers were encouraged to use a variety of data sources within their firms (including their executive colleagues and observation) to gather information. The standard CMP questionnaire

Table 21.4   Comparison of approaches in two CMP living cases

Stage	Living Case A	Living Case B
Research focus	IT adoption processes and e-marketing	Customer value creation and delivery
Stage one	149 executive students/ managers, NZ and UK as participant observers of their organisations	152 executive students/managers, NZ as participant observers of their organisations
	Standard CMP self-completion questionnaire, augmented with IT based items	Standard CMP self-completion questionnaire, augmented with customer value based items
	Completed by managers in consultation with colleagues in situ in their firms, as a take-home assignment	Each question framed with theory, discussed in class. Survey answered either in-class or as take home assignment in consultation with colleagues in their firms
	Results analysed, reported back, and discussed in-class	Results analysed, reported back, and discussed in-class
Stage two	In-depth interviews with managers	Executive student project briefing, incorporating discussion of theory and implications for marketing practice
		Executive students conduct fieldwork in own firms, assessing and evaluating their firms' approach to customer value creation and delivery with support of relevant theory
	Individual discussion and feedback on project findings	Individual discussion and feedback on project findings
	Classroom discussion of aggregated results	Classroom discussion of aggregated results
Stage three	In-class focus group with key informants from focal firm in process of new IT adoption. (NZ)	Longitudinal single firm case. Interviews, observation, workshops, archival analysis. Series of cycles of investigation and reflection in close consultation with the CEO and management team
	Creation of new frameworks for IT adoption based on this data	

was used, enabling classification of the managers' organisations on the basis of general approach to marketing practice (transaction marketing, database marketing, e-marketing, interaction marketing, and network marketing) (Coviello et al., 2002). However, the two living case approaches are also different. Teaching, learning and research processes are customised to meet student requirements, curriculum requirements, and faculty's research interests and strengths. This is an advantage of the living case approach, as it offers a flexible method of creating knowledge and achieving learning outcomes based on available resources and the teaching and learning environment.

Living case study A focuses on the impact of IT on marketing practices. In Stage One, the standard CMP questionnaire enabled profiling of marketing practices and assessment of the use of IT of all the firms in the executive classes. The impact of IT was determined by a five-point scale asking for an assessment of the current level of IT usage, expected

level of IT use in 5 years' time, and whether IT took a reinforcing, enhancing, or transforming role in the organisation (Orlikowski, 2000). The students are then required to reflect on expected and actual uses of IT in their organisations. The results are collated, summarised, then reported back and discussed in class.

The second stage used in-depth interviews and self-reflection. These managers had participated in the survey of their own company in a previous class, and were taking a subsequent class to that in which the survey was undertaken. Managers were equipped with an a priori body of knowledge (the survey results from the previous class) upon which to reflect and to compare and contrast the results from their research into their own firms. The researchers and managers benefited from shared knowledge and insights, further enriching the results and enhancing learning In terms of the adoption of IT-enabled interactivity, 'no one view prevails' (Brookes et al., 2004). As summarised in Brookes et al.

(2004: 258) and in Brady et al. (2008: 110), and based on Orlikowsky's (2000) three categories, 'different levels of IT integration and deployment in organisations have particular implications for marketing practices'. For example, consumer goods companies are slightly more likely to be found adopting IT-enabled interactivity in reinforcing or enhancing roles, while business-to-business service firms are slightly more likely to be adopting IT-enabled interactivity in transformational roles. Brodie et al. (2007) also found a high positive relationship between e-marketing penetration and performance in terms of both customer acquisition and customer retention. In other words, marketing practices and IT-enabled interactivity initiatives are related, context is critical, and therefore a variety of approaches and practices are to be observed. The call for middle-range theory development is thus consistent with finding such as these.

The third stage was undertaken in another group of managers, in a small class setting (<20 students). Students explored the nature of IT adoption processes in more depth, through a single living case: a firm currently adopting mobile digital technologies. A student within the class was a member of this firm and recruited his fellow managers into the project. The instructors and students could compare and contrast theoretical models of IT adoption with this live case. Executives from the case firm participated in an in-class focus group, and these findings are applied by the students to extant conceptual frameworks. Student teams then developed models of the IT adoption process based on their interpretation of the theoretical constructs and data from the focus group. All models were then presented back to the class by each student group, reflected upon and discussed by the class, and finally aggregated by the group into a meta-model (or middle-range theory) of the contemporary marketing organisation (Little et al., 2008).

Living case study B also features multiple stages and multiple methods. The first two stages took place at the Business School in executive classes, while the third took place within a firm, where the senior management team was comprised primarily of past and present executive students. In Stage One, the standard CMP questionnaire profiled marketing practices across student firms in four executive classes. Further items assessed the managers' views of their firms' customer value creation and delivery.

In Stage Two, managers in a smaller class assessed and critiqued their firms' approach to customer value creation and delivery. The cases were co-constructed, taking the form of written reports authored by the students and refined with the help of the instructor. The cases described and analysed their firms' approaches to customer value creation and delivery. The cases are also solved by the students, in the sense that problems were identified and alternative solutions or recommendations developed as outputs of the analysis process.

In the third stage, the researcher entered a single industrial electronics firm headed by one of the managers in a previous class, and worked with the management team in that firm to understand (and improve) that firm's approaches to creating and delivering customer value. Notably, several managers within that firm had undertaken postexperience courses taught by the instructor. The case initially developed from discussions with managers. The content of these discussions was subsequently synthesised, refined, presented, and discussed in two workshops designed to examine and challenge the firm's current practice. The case solution is arrived at consultatively by both the instructor and the managers over a period of some months, and took the form of new understandings and new organisational approaches to practice and the development of a middle-range theory. This consisted of a series of conceptual frameworks articulating various approaches to customer value creation and delivery, including the identification of four types of customer value (Little, 2004; Little et al., 2006b).

A middle range theorising process of marketing organisations informs theory through the agency of the two living cases. The outcomes of the research were further depth and description of customer value postures, explaining alternative approaches to customer value creation and delivery. These postures were refined and developed over all three stages, resulting in 'rich and thick' (Geertz, 1973) description of customer value creation and delivery. In both living cases and over all three stages, both researchers and executives benefited from shared knowledge and insights, enriching the results and enhancing joint learning. The pluralistic process enabled the identification of knowledge gaps, stimulated ongoing reflection and learning by both faculty and managers, and resulted in iterative knowledge building following an evolving circle of enquiry.

CONCLUSIONS

This chapter has drawn on the experience CMP research programme to develop the case for adopting a configuration perspective to understand the representation of the contemporary organisation. A discussion of various conceptual and methodological developments has informed this theoretical perspective. The configuration perspective provides explanation for the range of marketing practices identified in the empirical research. Some organisations have predominantly transactional practices, some organisations predominantly relational/network practices, while some organisations' practices were both transactional *and* relational/ network practice. Hence, there is range of organisational structures to accommodate different configurations of practice. What are of particular interest are the hybrid structures for organisations adopting pluralistic practices that integrate transactions, relationships, and networks. These findings suggest the need for a broader configuration perspective of organisations. Vorhies and Morgan

(2003) initially explored this perspective in marketing, with the objective of building understanding of how different strategies shape organisations. Recently, Pels and Lefaix-Durand (2009) integrate the CMP practice perspective with configuration theory. They draw pioneering work of Miller (1987) and Meyer et al. (1993) in organisation theory.

The CMP research programme has benefited from using a multi-theory practice-based approach that is underpins a process of middle-range theorising, pluralistic methods, and living case studies. Such an approach has enabled the research group to create a closer interface between theory and practice and to support practical problem solving by managers in their organisations. It is suggested that theorising at the middle range has an essential role to play in the process of further refining knowledge about configurations of marketing organisations. Through a systematic process of discovery and verification and shaping, the research evolves, so it both balances and challenges refining empirical generalisations and emerging general theories. In the process, as Pondy (1980: 22) notes, we can perhaps consider middle-range theorising as a 'means to the ends of creating theories of ever-increasing scope'.

In the middle-range theory research process, the evolving action learning approach enables researchers to provide an interface between what has been termed 'the academic–practitioner divide' in marketing (Brennan, 2004). As demonstrated throughout this chapter, the research is not designed primarily 'to serve the faculty's interests at the expense of students and the firms that employ them' (Mitra and Golden, 2008:.31). Rather, it has been a collaborative, iterative, and productive process that involves the furthering of our understanding of the configurations of marketing practices that shape organisation. Thus, the theorising process provides a pragmatic understanding of the use of theory to understand and represent the contemporary marketing organisation and to ultimately inform general theory.

NOTES

1 Further details about the participants, research philosophy and other aspects of the CMP research programme are available at http://cmp.auckland.ac.nz.

2 Pinder and Moore's (1980) book essays *Middle Range Theory and the Study of Organizations* provide excellent guidance addressing questions about 'what is middle range theory', and 'why and how does middle range theory develop'. The collection of essays also provides examples of the application of middle-range theorising. These applications demonstrate how the process of middle-range theorising provides a bridge between empirical generalisations and general theories.

REFERENCES

Achrol, R. (1997) 'Changes in the Theory of Interorganisational Relations in Marketing: Toward a Network Paradigm', *Journal of the Academy of Marketing Science*, 25(1): 56–71.

Achrol, R.S. and Kotler, P. (1999) 'Marketing in the Network Economy', *Journal of Marketing(Special Issue)*, 63: 146–163.

Axelsson, B. and Easton, G. (eds) (1992) *Industrial Networks: A New View of Reality*. London: Routledge.

Bluedorn A.C. and Evered, R. (1980) 'Middle Range Theory and the Strategies of Theory Construction', *Middle Range Theory and the Study of Organisations*, Boston: Martinnus Nijhoff Publishing, pp. 61–71.

Brady, M. and Palmer, R. (2004) 'What Are They Doing? A Study of Contemporary Marketing Practice in Ireland', *Irish Journal of Management*, 25(1): 125–136.

Brady, M., Fellenz, M. and Brookes, R.W. (2008) 'Researching the Role of Information Communication Technologies in Contemporary Marketing Practices', *Journal of Business and Industrial Marketing*, 23(2): 108–114.

Brennan, R. (2004) 'Should We Worry About an "Academic–Practitioner Divide" in Marketing?', *Market Intelligence and Planning*, 22(5): 492–500.

Brodie, R., Saren, M. and Pels, J.P. (2009) 'The SD Logic and Theorizing About Markets and Marketing: The Case for Middle Range Theory', Working paper, Department of Marketing, University of Auckland.

Brodie, R.A., Coviello, N.E. and Winklhofer, H.M. (2008) 'Reviewing the Contemporary Marketing Practices (CMP) Research Program: 1996–2006', *Journal of Business and Industrial Marketing*, 23(2): 84–94.

Brodie, R.J., Coviello, N., Brookes, R. and Little, V. (1997) 'Towards a Paradigm Shift in Marketing? An Examination of Current Marketing Practices', *Journal of Marketing Management*, 13: 383–406.

Brodie, R.J. Winklhofer, H., Coviello, N.E. and Johnston, W.J. (2007) 'Is e-Marketing Coming of Age? An Examination of the Penetration of eM and Firm Performance', *Journal of Interactive Marketing*, 21(1): 2–21.

Brookes, R.W., Brodie, R.J., Coviello, N.E. and Palmer, R.A. (2004) 'How Managers Perceive the Impacts of Information Technologies on Contemporary Practices: Reinforcing Enhancing or Transforming', *Journal of Relationship Marketing*, 3(4): 7–26.

Child, J. (1972) 'Organisational Structure, Environment and Performance: The Role of Strategic Choice', *Sociology*, 6(1): 1–22.

Christopher, M., Payne, A. and Ballantyne, D. (1991) *Relationship Marketing: Bringing Quality, Customer Service and Marketing Together*. Oxford: Butterworth Heinemann.

Coviello, N. (1996) *Internationalising the Entrepreneurial High Technology, Knowledge-Intensive Firm*. Unpublished PhD, University of Auckland, Auckland.

Coviello, N., Brodie, R.J. and Munro, H. (1997) 'Understanding Contemporary Marketing: Development of a Classification Scheme', *Journal of Marketing Management*, 13(6): 501–522.

Coviello, N.E., Brodie, R.J., Danaher, P.J. and Johnston, W.J. (2002) 'How Firms Relate to Their Markets: An Empirical Examination of Contemporary Marketing Practices', *Journal of Marketing*, 66: 33–46.

Coviello, N.E., Winklhofer, H. and Hamilton, K. (2006) 'Marketing Practices and Performance of Small Service Firms: An Examination in the Tourism Accommodation Sector', *Journal of Service Research*, 9(1): 38–58.

Dadzie, K., Johnston, W. and Pels, J. (2008) 'Business to Business Marketing Practices in Emerging Economies: West Africa and Argentina Compared with the United States', *Journal of Business and Industrial Marketing*, 23(2): 115–123.

Geertz, C. (1973) 'Thick Description: Towards an Interpretive Theory of Culture', in C. Geertz (ed.) *The Interpretation of Cultures*, pp. 3–30. New York: Basic Books.

Gummesson, E. (1987) 'The New Marketing: Developing Long-term Interactive Relationships', *Long Range Planning*, 20(4): 10–20.

Grönroos, C. (1990) *Service Management and Marketing: Managing the Moments of Truth in Service Competition*. Lexington, MA: Lexington Books.

Hunt, S.D. (1983) *Marketing Theory: The Philosophy of Marketing Science*. London: Irwin.

Little, V.J. (2004) *Understanding Customer Value: An Action-Research Based Study of Contemporary Marketing Practice*. Unpublished PhD, University of Auckland, Auckland, New Zealand.

Little, V.J., Brookes, R. and Brodie, R.J. (2006) *Action Inquiry in the Business School: Enlisting Managers to Develop Theory and Improve Practice in Their Organisational Contexts*. Paper presented at the ALARPM 7th and PAR 11th World Congress in Action Research, 21–24 August, 2006, University of Groningen, Groningen, The Netherlands.

Little, V.J., Brookes, R.W. and Palmer, R. (2008) 'Research Informed Teaching and Teaching Informed Research: The CMP "Living Case Study" Approach to Understanding Contemporary Marketing Practice', *Journal of Business and Industrial Marketing*, 23(2): 124–134.

Little, V.J., Motion, J. and Brodie, R.J. (2006a) 'Advancing Understanding: The Contribution of Multi-Method Action Research-Based Approaches to Knowledge Creation', *International Journal of Learning and Change*, 1(2): 217–228.

Little, V.J., Motion, J. and Brodie, R.J. (2006b) *Discovering Different Perspectives of Customer Value: Implications for Marketing Theory and Practice*. Paper presented at the Australian and NZ Marketing Academy (ANZMAC) Conference, University of Queensland, Brisbane, Australia.

Lusch, R.F. and Vargo, S.L. (eds) (2006) *The Service-Dominant Logic of Marketing: Dialog, Debate, And Directions*. Armonk, NY: M E Sharpe.

Meyer, A.D., Tsui, A.S. and Hinings, C.R. (1993) 'Configuration Approaches to Organisation Analysis', *Academy of Management Journal*, 36(5): 1175–1195.

Merton, R.K. (1948) 'The Self-Fulfilling Prophecy', *The Antioch Review*, 8: 193–210.

Merton, R.K. (1967) *On Theoretical Sociology: Five Essays, Old and New*. New York: Free Press.

Miller, D. (1987) 'The Genesis of Configuration', *Academy of Management Review*, 12(4): 670–687.

Mitra, D. and Golder, P.N. (2008) 'Does Academic Research Help or Hurt MBA Programs?', *Journal of Marketing*, 72(5): 31–47.

Orlikowski, W.J. (2000) 'Using Technology and Constituting Structures: A Practice Lens for Studying Technology in Organisations', *Organisation Science*, 11(4): 404–428.

Pels, J. (1999) "Exchange Relationships in Consumer Markets", *European Journal of Marketing*, 33(1-2): 19–37.

Pels, J., Brodie, R. and Saren, M. (2004) 'Investigating Multiple Marketing Practices: Exploring the Role of Paradigm', *Proceedings of the Irish Academy of Management Conference*. Dublin, Ireland.

Pels, J., Coviello, N. and Brodie, R.J. (1999) *Transactions Versus Relationships? The Risk of Missing the Real Issue*. Paper presented at the 15th IMP Conference, Dublin.

Pels, J. and Lefaix-Durand, A. (2009) 'Introducing Managers in Marketing Practice Studies: A Configuration Approach to the Way Organisations Relate to their Markets'. *Proceedings of the 38th European of Academy of Marketing Conference*. Nantes, France.

Pels, J. and Saren, M. (2005) 'The 4Ps of Relational Marketing: Perspectives, Perceptions, Paradoxes and Paradigms: Learnings from Organisational Theory and the Strategy Literature', *Journal of Relationship Marketing*, 4(3/4): 59–84.

Pinder, C.C. and Moore, L.F. (1979) 'The Resurrection of Taxonomy to Aid the Development of Middle Range Theories of Organisational Behavior', *Administrative Science Quarterly*, 24: 99–118.

Pinder, C.C. and Moore L.F., (1980) *Middle Range Theory and the Study of Organisations*. Boston: Martinnus Nijhoff Publishing.

Pondy, L.R. (1980) 'The Circle of Enquiry', *Middle Range Theory and the Study of*

Organisations, Boston: Martinnus Nijhoff Publishing, pp. 61–71.

Revans, R.W. (1998) *The ABC of Action Learning*. London: Lemos and Crane.

Ruekert, R.W., Walker Jnr, O.C. and Roering, K.J. (1985) 'The Organisation of Marketing Activities: A Contingency Theory of Structure and Performance', *Journal of Marketing*, Winter: 13–25.

Saren, M. and Pels, J.P. (2008) 'A Comment on Paradox and Middle-Range Theory', *Journal of Business and Industrial Marketing*, 23(2): 105–107.

Sheth, J.N., Gardner, D.M. and Garrett, D.E. (1988) *Marketing Theory: Evolution and Evaluation*. New York: John Wiley.

Vargo, S.L. and Lusch, R.F. (2004) 'Evolving to a New Dominant Logic for Marketing', *Journal of Marketing*, 68(Jan): 1–17.

Vorhies, D.W. and Morgan, N.A. (2003) 'A Configuration Theory Assessment of Marketing Organisation Fit with Business Strategy and its Relationship with Marketing Performance', *Journal of Marketing*, 67(Jan): 100–115.

Voss, C., Tsikriktsis, N. and Frohlich, M. (2002) 'Case Research in Operations Management', *International Journal of Operations and Production Management*, 22(2): 195–220.

Wagner, R. (2005) 'Contemporary Marketing Practices in Russia', *European Journal of Marketing*, 39(1/2): 199–215.

Webster, F.E., (1992) 'The Changing Role of Marketing in the Corporation', *Journal of Marketing*, 56(Oct): 1–17.

Weick, K.E. (1988) 'Enacted Sensemaking in Crisis Situation', *Journal of Management Studies*, 25(4): 305–317.

Weick, K.E. (1989) 'Theory Construction as Disciplined Imagination', *Academy of Management Review*, 14(4): 516–531.

Weick, K.E. (1995) *Sensemaking in Organisations*. Thousand Oaks, CA: Sage.

Weick, K.E. (2007) 'The Generative Properties of Richness', *Academy of Management Journal*, 50(1): 14–19.

Wilkie, W.L. and Moore, E.S. (2003) 'Scholarly Research in Marketing: Exploring the "4 Eras" of Thought Development', *Journal of Public Policy and Marketing*, 22(2): 116–146.

22

Orientation and Marketing Metrics

Jonathan Knowles and Tim Ambler

INTRODUCTION

Most business disciplines vie for more attention from senior management. Their claims are based on competing views about the management orientation most likely to deliver business success (e.g. a financial orientation versus a production orientation). Marketers claim that marketing, as the sourcing and harvesting of cash flow, is the lifeblood of any organisation. A market orientation leads to the development of customer and distribution channel franchises (Day and Wensley, 1983) and is likely to enhance profitability (Kotler, 1997; Narver and Slater, 1990; Slater and Narver, 2000). Market driven organisations achieve this success through the skills of market sensing and customer linking (Day, 1994).

Since market orientation is far from universal among organisations, we can conclude that not all executives agree about the importance of marketing. Part of this is due to different understandings of the word 'marketing'. Marketing can be broadly defined as being *both* the whole company's activities designed to satisfy customers and achieve its own objectives thereby ('pan company marketing')

and the activities of the functional marketing department (Webster, 1992). A third view defines marketing by the activities that constitute the marketing budget, i.e. marketing research, communications and promotions (Ambler, 2003).

The nature of an organisation's orientation determines the type of metrics to which it attaches the greatest importance. This chapter begins by analysing the four factors that influence the selection of marketing metrics – in other words, the key marketing performance indicators. It continues with a review of the evolution of marketing metrics and discusses the emergence of the concept of brand equity – possibly the most important concept for marketing in the last 50 years – and discusses its role as a key construct in the assessment of the productivity of marketing in financial terms. We examine the different ways in which brand equity can be defined and valued.

We then review four metrics that claim to be the single or dominant indicator of performance (what we term 'silver metrics'). We draw the conclusion that no single metric is adequate for performance assessment and therefore none is adequate for planning purposes either. We note that these 'silver metrics' can often be used in combination with other metrics of marketing performance to provide a compelling portrait of how the company is performing in the market – these combinations create a market or marketing dashboard.

We conclude with a discussion of the limitations of our work, suggest a number of areas for future research, and highlight our main conclusions.

INFLUENCES ON THE SELECTION OF MARKETING METRICS

In this section, we outline the four factors that influence the selection of the marketing metrics that an organisation chooses to track for the purpose of planning and/or performance monitoring.

The mandate for marketing

What companies mean by 'marketing' will largely determine the metrics they use to measure its performance and how it is planned. Narver and Slater (1990) were the first to develop a robust definition of market orientation and to articulate the three mechanisms through which a market orientation was linked to enhanced business performance:

1 Customer perspective: Assessing the benefits from the customer's point of view as distinct from a purely internal perspective (e.g. realising supply efficiencies or immediate profit-making).
2 Long-term perspective: Emphasising long-run profitability through building customer relationships, not just achieving immediate transactions.
3 Comprehensive perspective: Adopting a firmwide, cross-functional perspective to create and sustain customer satisfaction and thereby long-run profitability.

These findings were reinforced by their replication study a decade later (Slater and

Narver, 2000) and by a meta-analysis of 56 studies (58 samples) in 28 countries, which showed that, although market orientation is a consistent predictor of firm performance, stronger effects were found for studies set in large, mature markets, such as the USA, relative to emergent cultures (Deshpandé and Farley, 2004). Market orientation using the Kohli et al. (1993) MARKOR scale gave stronger results (Ellis, 2006).

It is ironic that the definition of marketing success as synonymous with business success is not always embraced by its own practitioners. For example, the American Marketing Association (AMA) has only recently changed its preference for defining marketing in terms of 'process' in favour of a definition of marketing in terms of satisfying stakeholders at large.

The AMA has revised its formal definition of marketing four times during its 75-year history. We extend the analysis of Wilkie and Moore (2006) and Darroch et al. (2004) who in turn extended Cooke et al. (1992) to include the 2007 definition:

> 1935 – Marketing as Push (AMA 1948, 1960)
> 'The performance of business activities that direct the flow of goods and services from producers to consumers'.
> 1985 – Marketing as the 4 Ps (Sevier, 2005)
> 'The process of planning and executing the conception, pricing, promotion and distribution of ideas, goods and services to create exchanges that satisfy individual and organizational objectives'.
> 2004 – Marketing as Management (Keefe, 2004: 17; Sevier, 2005)
> 'Marketing is an organizational function and a set of processes for creating, communicating and delivering value to customers and for managing customer relationships in ways that benefit the organization and its stakeholders'.
> 2007 – Marketing as Social Benefit (AMA, 2008)
> 'Marketing is the activity, set of institutions, and processes for creating, communicating, delivering, and exchanging offerings that have value for customers, clients, partners, and society at large'.

The evolution of the AMA's definition of marketing provides insight into the changing priorities for marketing. In the earlier decades, the focus was on production and the processes to follow. By 2004, the definition had become both customer-focused and longer-term, emphasising the need to build relationships rather than manage transactions. By 2007, sensitivity to the public debate about corporate social responsibility (Holder-Webb et al., 2009) and to the exclusive focus on the manager's, or marketer's point of view (Wilkie and Moore, 2006) resulted in the excision of any reference to the conduct of marketing in order to benefit the company itself, its employees and shareholders. Meanings change with time; marketing was originally framed in terms of what the customer did, i.e. go to the market. Today, we usually, but not exclusively, see marketing as what the firm, or provider of goods and/ or services, does. The coming years will no doubt witness an increasing emphasis on the engagement and community dimensions of marketing as social media technologies enter the business mainstream.

The perspective in this chapter is of the provider seeking to exchange the goods and/ or services for cash, i.e. the 'pan company marketing' perspective (Webster, 1992) of achieving profits from meeting customer needs (Kotler and Keller, 2006).

This is consistent with the definition of marketing adopted by the UK Chartered Institute of Marketing (CIM, 2008) as the '... management process of anticipating, identifying and satisfying customer requirements profitably'.

Business model and metric selection

The second major influence on the selection of planning and performance metrics is the firm's business model. A firm is interested in measuring those variables that best capture the links between management actions and the eventual financial outcomes. These will differ both across industries and within industries. The marketing metrics relevant to a producer of industrial steel will differ from those relevant

to an airline; and metric selection for an airline with a 'hub and spoke' strategy will differ from those appropriate to an airline with a 'point to point' strategy. The role of marketing metrics is to monitor the performance of the company on those dimensions most critical to the strategy it has selected for exploiting its differential advantage in creating, and capturing, value.

Measurement does not itself improve performance. Rather, metrics should be seen as part of a learning process that enhances future profits by improving the planning and implementation process. As we note in the conclusion of this chapter, we consider the linkage of measurement to performance improvement to be an important topic for future research.

Goals and metric selection

A third influence on the selection of metrics is the firm's perception of its marketing goals and the stages towards those goals. The most common goal, and sometimes the only explicit goal, is to achieve a certain level of financial performance, typically expressed as shareholder value (Rust et al., 2004a). While articulating a financial objective for the company is helpful, it does not clarify the particular strengths and distinctiveness of the business that enables this financial performance; nor does it separate the short from the long term; nor give employees anything to believe in. As Collins and Porras (1995) have shown, long-term success needs more than financial goals; employees and customers need to understand the vision/mission of the business and the values to which they believe the company holds firm.

Metric selection should therefore be a function of what intermediary processes and functions the company views as critical to generating sustainable financial success. The popularity of the concept of the 'Balanced Scorecard' (Kaplan and Norton, 1993) reflects this appreciation that market success is a function of how effectively the company manages the health of a number of resources critical to generating that success (the Kaplan and Norton framework encourages managers to view their business health from four perspectives: financial, customer, internal business process, and learning and growth).

The timeframe relevant to marketing measurement

The fourth influence on the selection of marketing metrics is the timeframe over which performance should be evaluated. If marketing activities are believed to impact only the short-term performance of the business, then each reporting period can be treated as a discrete entity. If it is believed that financial performance in any given reporting period benefits from a combination of marketing activity within that period and the influence of marketing activity in prior periods, then a more sophisticated set of metrics is required.

For example, suppose we pick the last calendar year as the evaluation period. We could take the accumulated cash as our performance measure, but this would be both simplistic and potentially misleading. An accountant would first want to know the amount of cash held at the start of the year. Finishing with £1 million is impressive if we started with £200,000 but less impressive if we started with £2 million. The accountant would also want to know what receipts and payments came in during our year but were due for the previous year. Similarly, he will want to know what net cash flow is due to us at the year end. This reflects the accounting principle of 'matching' – ensuring that the revenues and expenses of the business refer to the same period.

Effective business management requires an understanding of how the period under review is methodically separated from the periods before and after for the purpose of performance evaluation. Any business with a long sales cycle, or for which corporate reputation is important, should seek to quantify the benefits generated in the current period but which will not generate cash flow until future time periods.

The issue of the appropriate timeframe for performance measurement is particularly important for marketing, because human choice behaviour is a complex function of many different influences, and that our predisposition to buy from certain companies may reflect many years of exposure to their products and communications. As we discuss later, the concept of brand equity is therefore a critical component of performance evaluation from the marketing metrics perspective.

THE EVOLUTION OF MARKETING METRICS

In this section, we review how metrics have evolved largely in practice and then why there has been so little dependence on theory.

Marketing performance measurement has been an elusive goal for over 100 years. Ever since John Wanamaker, the US department store magnate, allegedly remarked that 'I know that half of my advertising is wasted – I just wish I knew which half' (a remark also widely attributed to William Hesketh Lever, the founder of what is now Unilever), marketers have been challenged to demonstrate the business impact of their activities.

The connotation of the remark is negative, but it is worth remembering that both Wanamaker and Lever were extremely financially successful. Marketers often fail to appreciate that the remark can be made in respect of any activity that combines uncertainty, risk, and reward. When advertising a vacant position, the company pays for a readership of 10,000. Yet, only one person gets the job. If that was the most efficient medium to reach the unknown future employee, none of the money was wasted, and certainly not 99.99 per cent. In similar vein, a drilling company is not admonished simply because a proportion of its test wells prove to be dry.

There are two reasons why the productivity of marketing investments needs to be judged for its overall effectiveness, rather than the efficiency of any one tactic:

- First, there is often a complex interaction of factors that lead a customer to buy a given product or service via a certain channel (an online purchase may well be the result of favourable in-store experience and vice versa).
- Second, the evaluation of the productivity of marketing investments is complicated by the fact that conspicuous waste may add to the perceived quality of the brand (Ambler and Hollier, 2004).

The Wanamaker remark exemplifies the need to define goals and terms with some care. The demonstration of marketing effectiveness has to deal with three specific challenges:

1 Defining goals with sufficient precision to make comparisons possible.
2 Distinguishing between 'effectiveness' (achieving the goals at whatever the cost) and 'efficiency' (the ratio of return to cost). Considerations of efficiency may well require a firm to moderate its goals or the resources provided, as there is little point in setting goals that cannot be achieved with the given resources.
3 Collecting the data to measure performance versus the goals and also diagnostics, e.g. stages towards those goals and explanations for variances.

The history of marketing metrics

The measurement of marketing performance, and especially advertising, has traditionally focused on the impact on sales (Lehmann and Reibstein, 2006), although some earlier work included measures of profit and/or cash flow (Day and Fahey, 1988; Feder, 1965; Sevin, 1965). From an academic perspective, the predominance of sales-based approaches reflects the fact that sales data are accessible whereas profit data generally are not.

The focus of marketing performance measurement shifted in the 1980s to market share as the predictor of cash flow and profitability (Buzzell and Gale, 1987). This relationship was subsequently modified (Gale, 1994) to show that both share and profits were driven by perceived quality, although the interaction

between perceived and actual quality was problematic.

The importance of perceived quality was further demonstrated by Aaker and Jacobson (1994) who demonstrated that movements in stock prices could be better explained by a combination of changes in return on investment (ROI) and brand equity (the latter defined as 'perceived product quality') than by changes in ROI alone.

Firms' ability to maintain a competitive advantage in product quality has subsequently declined due to the increasing convergence of quality standards that resulted from the widespread adoption of Six Sigma (a management process for identifying and removing defects and errors in the production process) and TQM (Total Quality Management). This 'commoditisation' of quality resulted in the emergence of a number of other factors that had hitherto been secondary or tertiary variables in the algorithm of business success. These variables expressed the nature of the customer's relationship with the product, service, or provider and the quality of the overall user experience. Notable examples are customer loyalty (Dick and Basu, 1994), brand equity (see Keller, 1998 for review) and customer satisfaction (Ittner and Larcker, 1998; Szymanski and Henard, 2001). Ittner and Larcker (1998: 2) found that 'the relationship between customer satisfaction and future accounting performance generally is positive and statistically significant'.

This evolution in marketing measurement was a reflection of the wider trend in business towards supplementing financial analysis with a more broadly based, future-facing analysis of the determinants of business success. As noted previously, this trend was popularised and accelerated by the emergence of the 'Balanced Scorecard' (Kaplan and Norton, 1993) that offered a way to translate business strategy into objectives and measures across four perspectives.

The understanding of business performance as a function of the interplay of a variety of resources was enhanced by Srivastava et al. (1998). Their depiction of brand equity and trade networks as forms of relationship assets with demonstrable market value was instrumental in a reassessment of what had hitherto been seen as 'soft' factors in the algorithm of marketplace success.

In similar vein, Clark (1999) showed how financial measures (profit, sales, and cash flow) could be supplemented with nonfinancial indicators (market share, quality, customer satisfaction, loyalty, and brand equity), input (marketing audit, implementation, and orientation) and output (marketing audit, efficiency/effectiveness, and multivariate analysis) measures.

This broadened definition of the metrics relevant to marketing performance measurement has been helpful, as it reflects the reality of the influences on customer purchase behaviour. However, it has also led to an explosion of choice.

Meyer (1998: xvi) claimed that 'firms are swamped with measures' and that some have over 100 metrics. This variety makes comparison difficult between results of different studies (Murphy et al., 1996). A literature search of five leading marketing journals yielded 19 different measures of marketing 'success', the most popular of which were sales, market share, profit contribution, and purchase intention (Ambler and Kokkinaki, 1997).

This plethora of metrics is damaging to marketing's credibility among those that do not recognise that marketing is contextual. Firms compete using different strategies, skills, and resources. The metrics relevant to one firm's approach may not be relevant to another's. Standardisation is helpful for shared understanding and comparisons across companies, but the business context and the need for competitive differentiation will result in a variety of relevant metrics. This is especially true when the market environment is evolving rapidly as a result of new technology, such as is currently the case with social media technology platforms. Part of the skill in marketing is identifying which metrics will most help with planning and performance evaluation.

The competing requirements for standardisation and insight have led to the creation of 'dashboards' (McGovern et al., 2004; Reibstein et al., 2005) that combine the key metrics required to manage the business into a single display. Typically, they provide specific data on the relevant intermediary steps between the marketing activities and the financial returns to the company.

There appears to be a common pattern in the evolution of marketing metrics and the development of the marketing dashboard for senior management (Clark, 1999):

- little awareness of the need for marketing metrics at top executive level;
- seeking the solution exclusively from financial metrics;
- broadening the portfolio of metrics to include a miscellany of nonfinancial metrics; and
- finding some rationale to reduce the number of metrics to a manageable set of about 25 or less (Unilever, 1998).

Marketing metrics theory

'Perhaps no other concept in marketing's short history has proven as stubbornly resistant to conceptualization, definition, or application as that of marketing performance' (Bonoma and Clark, 1988: 1). This situation has arguably persisted over the ensuing 20 years; metrics seem to be led by practice, with theory post-rationalising practice. Many other sciences advance in this way and, in this section, we discuss the limited theoretic approaches, firstly, in terms of context and then through the use of five theoretical perspectives.

Marketing performance assessment can be understood as a sub-area of the broader field of marketing information use. Marketing information use has been examined from multiple perspectives including the organisational view of knowledge utilisation (Menon and Varadarajan, 1992); market information processes (Moorman, 1995); learning organisation (Baker and Sinkula, 1999; Slater and Narver, 1995; Sinkula, 1994, 2002; Sinkula et al., 1997) and systems theory (Wright and Ashill, 1996).

Ambler et al. (2004) identified five theoretical perspectives that could be said to underlie metrics selection: control, agency, institutional, market orientation (the perspective of this chapter) and brand equity (discussed in depth in the next section).

Control theory: this is essentially the accountant's perspective that the appropriate metrics are those which measure deviation from plan and encourage marketers to return to plan. If the plan is created only with financial numbers, then they will be the dominant metrics.

Agency theory: this uses the economics approach to the transmission of information up and down the firm's hierarchy. Positive (for the agent) information will be communicated upwards to the extent that the gain obtained from its disclosure does not exceed the cost of gathering and processing the information. Metrics requirements will be communicated downwards by the higher levels in order to induce the required behaviour by the lower levels.

Institutional theory: this sees metrics selection as a symptom of, so to speak, club membership. As executives move from firm to firm within a sector, they will bring the metrics they are used to and share the metrics used by the firm they are joining. In other words, metric selection can be as much a function of social networking as a part of the firm's rational strategy.

One consequence of market orientation is a requirement to measure the market that management sees and to analyse the firm's place within it. Whilst all the aforementioned theories contribute to the understanding of metrics, this chapter is primarily concerned with the consistency of marketing orientation, performance, and the metrics to demonstrate that performance and/or variances from it. This perspective shares common ground with control theory – the difference being that control theory looks inwards and largely to accounting whereas market orientation looks outwards to customers, consumers, and competitors.

As noted earlier, performance assessment involves two main types of metrics: those that describe short-term performance (i.e. between the beginning and end of the period in question), and those that describe future performance. Brand equity is critical to the latter, as it refers to the asset built by good marketing that represents a reservoir of future cash flow that will accrue to the business (Ambler, 2003). We cannot measure the future, but we usually can identify today's metrics, which either because of theory or past experience can be expected to predict future performance. Performance metrics selection and brand equity metrics selection are therefore very similar.

BRAND EQUITY

The term 'brand equity' first emerged in the marketing literature of the late 1980s and was popularised initially by Aaker (1991, 1996) and later by Keller (1993, 1998). The idea that marketing creates an asset which could be valued, bought, and sold resonated in a business environment in which purchases and sales of intangible assets were gaining prominence and where the buyers might wish to add the acquired assets to their balance sheets. The UK firm Interbrand pioneered the independent valuation of brands, helping Rank Hovis McDougall defend itself against a hostile takeover from Goodman Fielder Wattie in 1988 (Lindemann, 2003: 31). Soon after, in 1989, GrandMet bought Heublein and needed to put some of the brands, notably Smirnoff vodka, on its balance sheet in order to avoid the appearance of insolvency (Simms, 1997). Other companies that took advantage of the opportunity to add the value of acquired brands to their balance sheets included Nestlé (which bought Rowntree), Philip Morris (which bought Kraft General Foods), Ladbrokes (which acquired Hilton), and GrandMet (which acquired Pillsbury) (Salinas and Ambler, 2008).

These developments prompted a debate about whether intangible assets should be reported on the balance sheet. In essence (and in most countries worldwide), companies are allowed to record the *cost* of *acquired* brands on their balance sheets, but if they do so, they have to conduct an annual review to confirm that the *value* of the asset is higher than the figure on the balance sheet (this is technically known as an 'impairment test') (Harding, 1997). Further review of the accounting treatment of brands is beyond the scope of this chapter.

For a wider business audience, the balance sheet issue should have no relevance. Companies may, if they wish, report the valuation of their brands, both acquired and homegrown, in the narrative sections of their annual reports and, in the UK at least, are encouraged so to do (ASB [Accounting Standards Board], 2006). To an investor, whether the figures appear on one page or another is immaterial; auditors still have to warrant that the narrative section is a reasonable representation of the company's financial position.

The growing business appreciation of the economic significance of brands fuelled, and was fuelled by, the emergence of a number of 'league tables', ranking the world's most valuable brands. Pioneered in 1994 by the (now defunct) *Financial World* magazine, the tables indicated that brands (on average) represented nearly 20 per cent of their parents' market values. Certain consumer and luxury goods brands accounted for more than 50 per cent of their parents' market values. The scale of these numbers established brand equity as a mainstream business topic.

Whilst the new specialist brand valuation sector was establishing its methodologies and approaches, market research agencies were developing ways to define and measure their nonfinancial version of brand equity. Their interest was not in establishing the financial value of a brand; it was on devising approaches that more accurately characterised the nature and strength of a customer's relationship with that brand. This led to research methodologies such as Research International's Equity Engine, Young and Rubicam's BrandAsset Valuator, Ipsos' Equity Builder, and Millward Brown's BrandDynamics. Each of these

involves identifying the sources of brand equity (typically aggregated into categories such as functional, economic, and psychological equity) and/or measuring the strength of customer engagement with the brand.

Lehmann and Reibstein (2006) identify two classes of metrics: consumer behavioural measures, such as loyalty and market share, and 'intermediate' measures, such as awareness and intention to purchase (Park and Srinivasan, 1994). Keller (1993: 8) defines customer-based brand equity as 'the differential effect of brand knowledge on consumer response to the marketing of the brand', and thus focuses on intermediate measures that he suggests have two components: brand awareness and brand image.

Agarwal and Rao (1996) found that ten popular brand equity measures (such as perceptions and attitudes, preferences, choice intentions, and actual choice) were convergent. Perceptions, preference, and intentions (that represented five of the ten metrics) predicted market share, but more dimensions of brand equity are needed to predict behaviour: 'It may not be necessary to subject respondents to difficult questions in order to obtain accurate measures of brand equity. Simple, appropriately worded, single-item scales may do just as well' (Agarwal and Rao, 1996: 246). Customer-based measures, however, are limited by the inability of consumer surveys to elicit accurate information about the store environment in terms of prices and promotions of different brands (Park and Srinivasan, 1994).

Until recently, the problem of multiple definitions of brand equity was mitigated by the limited interaction between the marketing, finance, and accounting functions. Two developments in recent years have changed that:

1   the growing appreciation of the importance of intangible assets, and
2   the demand for higher levels of marketing accountability.

The business case for marketing depends in no small part on developing a credible way of quantifying the proportion of intangible value that is attributable to brands, and demonstrating the role of marketing in building the value of the brand asset. Note that we define 'brand equity' as an asset and distinguish it from the financial worth of that asset, i.e. brand value or valuation. An asset may have different values for different purposes for different people, but it is still the same asset. Brand equity may be measured in many ways, financially and nonfinancially. As brand equity is essentially multidimensional (Keller, 2003), firms need multiple measures to describe it.

Even if the goal is not to ascribe a single financial number to the brand asset, it is important for marketers to be able to describe the mechanisms by which brand equity results in increased cash flows to the business. Srivastava and Shocker (1991: 5) define brand equity as 'a set of associations and behaviours on the part of a brand's customers, channel members and parent corporation that permits the brand to earn greater volume or greater margins than it could without the brand name, and that gives a strong, sustainable and differential advantage'. Brand equity reflects consumer loyalty and the volume of their purchases and/or willingness to pay a premium price for the brand and/or willingness to continue to purchase. Ailawadi et al. (2003) suggest these factors could be combined as 'revenue premium', i.e. the additional price times the additional volume of the brand relative to an unbranded similar product.

If a firm has built up large intangible assets, it can expect a continuing flow of sales and profits without further investment, at least for a time. Brand equity thus helps to predict future business prospects (Balasubramanian et al., 2005; Jacobson, 1990) and the creation of shareholder value (Madden et al., 2006).

Based on a sample of 275 companies, Mizik and Jacobson (2008) found a direct relationship between perceived levels of brand differentiation and the level of stock returns one year later. They also isolated the metrics most strongly related to improvements in current earnings (quality, familiarity, and dif-

ferentiation), and those most predictive of future earnings (relevance and vitality). They established a useful rule of thumb – that when brand equity changes, one third of the impact shows up in current earnings, and two thirds in future earnings. This finding supports the notion of brand equity as an asset in the financial sense of the term, namely as a source of cash flow in future periods.

Brand equity can also be seen as 'sustainable competitive advantage because it creates meaningful competitive barriers' (Yoo et al., 2000: 208), including the opportunity for successful extensions, resilience against competitors' promotional pressures, and the creation of barriers to competitive entry (Farquhar, 1989; Keller, 1993).

Brand value

It would clearly be convenient if brand equity could be measured with a single financial number. If that was the case, then the contribution of marketing to business value in any given period could be expressed as the profit or net cash flow generated in that period plus the difference in brand valuation from the beginning to the end of the period. A single number for performance, or 'silver metric', would simplify management.

There have been a number of approaches to brand valuation – see Salinas and Ambler (2008) for a comprehensive review. A common approach is to equate brand equity with the residual of market value, once the value of the other identified assets of the business have been deducted (Simon and Sullivan, 1993).

Kerin and Sethuraman (1998: 260) also employ the relationship between stock market prices and a firm's intangible assets: 'From a financial perspective, tangible wealth emanated from the incremental capitalized earnings and cash flows achieved by linking a successful, established brand name to a product or service'.

These approaches are inadequate in that they are not able to identify the proportion of intangible value that is attributable to brands as opposed to other forms of intangible asset. Lev (2001) tried to address this issue by proposing a taxonomy of intangible assets. His approach was superseded by the International Accounting Standards Board, which put forward five categories of intangible assets based on the underlying forms of intellectual property (such as patent, contract, copyright, or trademark). These are outlined in the guidance notes to International Financial Reporting Standard 3 (2004), which covers the treatment of goodwill arising from business combinations.

In principle, the market value of a company could then be expressed in terms of its net tangible assets (expressed at market prices) plus the net present value of the cash flows that are expected to flow from its current stock of intangible assets. This approach is consistent with 'efficient market theory' that says that current stock prices are determined by expectations about the future based on current information (Lane and Jacobson, 1995). Brand value could be estimated as part of this process and would represent the present value of the cash flows anticipated as a result of brand equity.

The methodologies used by brand valuation practitioners are based on a variant of this approach. Technically known as 'economic use' approaches, they involve the direct estimation of the incremental cash flows that accrue to a company as a result of having a brand. The most commonly used of these is the 'earnings split' approach whereby the earnings of the business are divided between the assets that support them. Incremental earnings above those that are earned by a commodity product are credited to a variety of intangible assets, of which brand equity is one. These separate earnings streams are then expressed as a net present value using discounted cash flow (Arthur Andersen, 1992; Perrier, 1997). Variations of this Discounted Cash Flow (DCF) methodology are used in the calculation of Customer Lifetime Value (CLV) (Gupta and Lehmann, 2005; Venkatesan and Kumar, 2004) and customer equity (Rust et al., 2004b).

A second, widely used approach is 'the relief from royalty' approach – especially common for justifying internal transfer pricing within international companies. This method begins from an assumption that the business does not own its brand but licenses it from another business at a market rate. What royalty would it pay for the use of the brand? Under this method brand value is the net present value of the royalty payments made (Salinas and Ambler, 2008). This methodology is favoured by the fiscal authorities and the courts, because it calculates brand value by reference to documented, third-party transactions involving brands of equivalent strength in equivalent industries.

Brand valuation is definitely required for certain tax and transactional purposes but its use for marketing performance assessment is more controversial (Ambler and Barwise, 1998). They cite seven reasons:

1 the difficulty of distinguishing between the future cash flow that is due to past marketing actions from those due to future marketing actions;
2 subjectivity;
3 coarse grain (brand valuation cannot be fine tuned enough to pick up short term results);
4 temporal shift of assumptions (the underlying forecast assumptions are not like for like);
5 blinkered or narrow vision of the future;
6 lack of theoretical underpinning or market comparability; and
7 the use of any single number for a multidimensional concept.

Financial performance measures may therefore be a necessary part of, but are not in themselves sufficient for, defining overall business performance. The exclusive use of financial measures may actually undermine long-term performance (Collins and Porras, 1995).

'SILVER METRICS'

The importance of accountability has led to the emergence of a number of metrics whose respective sponsors claim that each represents the only metric needed – the 'silver metric' for marketers. We briefly report the merits of three candidates: Return on Customer; ROI; and variants of DCF such as customer equity or CLV. All of these are discussed more fully in Ambler and Roberts (2006). We also examine the merits of Net Promoter Score.

Return on Customer

Peppers and Rogers (2005: 16) define Return on Customer (ROC) as 'a firm's current-period cash flow from its customers plus any changes in the underlying customer equity, divided by the total customer equity at the beginning of the period'. Reviewing both the change in short-term cash flow and the change in the marketing asset makes sense but whether two such different things should be added together is another matter.

The algebraic analysis is laid out in Ambler and Roberts (2006), but the bottom line is that ROC does not measure performance at all. It reports the *accuracy* of the previous year's forecast of cash flow in the period just ended, together with the *consistency* of the two sets of forecasts, i.e. those made last year and this year, across the two forecasting dates.

This highlights a generic problem of performance evaluation and the key distinction between a 'forecast' and a 'plan'. A plan is what one intends to do and the desired consequences; a forecast is what one expects will happen. One can plan to picnic for a sunny day but then forecast rain. If the day turns out grey but not wet, it is above forecast but worse than plan. Whether it was ever a good plan would be a matter for discussion.

If a forecast fails to materialise, it is a bad forecast. Better than forecast performance says little about how well the business has done, but plenty about the quality of the forecast. Therefore, we can never say that performance was good or bad, only that it was better than plan, or last year, or forecast, or competitors. Performance is relative and the comparators matter.

Return on Investment

ROI has become a fashionable term for marketing productivity – but marketers rarely mean ROI when they say 'ROI'. Return on investment is correctly defined as the net incremental cash received as a ratio of the net incremental cash outflow employed in obtaining that return. Finance people adhere to a strict definition of the term and do not appreciate its usage as a catchall term for marketing accountability and/or various forms of marketing measurement.

In 2005, the American Marketing Association issued a White Paper on marketing accountability (American Marketing Association, 2005: 8) that identified six 'ROI Measures Currently Used':

- incremental sales revenue;
- ratio of cost to revenue;
- cost per sale generated;
- changes of financial value of sales generated;
- cost of new customer (sic); and
- cost of old customer retention.

Note that none of these six measures corresponds to the correct definition of ROI. If marketers' goal in espousing ROI is to convince their finance colleagues that they are serious about accountability, it is counterproductive to define ROI in a way that their finance colleagues do not recognise.

Srivastava and Reibstein (2005) drew attention to a logical flaw with using ROI for performance evaluation, i.e. *dividing* the profit by expenditure whereas all other net benefit metrics are calculated by *subtracting* expenditure. Division rather than subtraction creates a conflict between cash flow or profit (subtraction) and the ROI ratio (division). Marketing's mandate is to generate the maximum cash flow for the business, not to maximise the efficiency of any one form of investment. The profit or economic value added or increase in shareholder value from marketing all require the costs to be *subtracted* from sales revenue along with the other costs.

The law of diminishing returns explains why pursuing ROI causes underperformance and suboptimal levels of activity. After ROI is maximised, further sales will still make profits but at a diminishing rate until the response curve crosses the expenditure line to yield incremental losses. That is the point of maximum profitability (in terms of the quantum of profits).

Other problems with ROI as a performance measure include:

- Knowing what the performance would have been without the marketing activity being considered. In other words, what is the baseline used for comparison?
- Looking only at short-term performance and ignoring changes in brand equity (that is necessary to adjust for inherited and postponed effects).
- Marketing expenditure is not necessarily 'investment' as the use of ROI implies. It is expensed through the Profit and Loss (P&L) Account and not added to the Balance Sheet.

DCF methods

Discounted Cash Flow (DCF) methods are based on comparing the cash flow for the year plus the Net Present Value (NPV) of future years' cash flow with the NPV at the beginning of the period. The same approach has been used for at least 70 years (Williams, 1938) although variants are introduced at regular intervals, notably Shareholder Value (Rappaport, 1986), Brand Value (see the preceding section), Customer Lifetime Value (Gupta and Lehmann, 2005; Venkatesan and Kumar, 2004) and Customer Equity (Rust et al., 2004b).

The case for using DCF to compare alternative strategies when the plan is being crafted is strong, not least because the environmental variables can be standardised across the options. Some of the problems dealt next, such as the quality of forecasting and subjectivity, still apply but to a lesser extent than when one set of people compare their NPV calculations with another set of people's NPV calculations prepared in a different context a year earlier.

In other words, the use of any DCF method as a silver metric for performance evaluation is flawed for the following five reasons:

1 NPVs, calculated at different points in time, confuse variances in managerial performance with contextual variances outside their control.
2 Performance variances versus forecast are certainly due to poor forecasting whereas variances versus plan confound forecasting with execution successes/errors.
3 Using DCF takes credit now for future marketing activities, which, as they have not yet happened, should not be included in the evaluation of past performance.
4 We can estimate the future in various ways, but we cannot measure it.
5 If forecasts are used for performance assessment, then those being assessed, and the assessors, might have difficulty judging their reliability, given the incentives for those involved in their preparation to create forecasts that show their performance in the best possible light.

If a firm had reliable, shared 20–20 foresight, then the long-term improvement in DCF, with suitable controls for the consistency of future-year variables, would be a valid indicator of marketing performance, along with short-term cash flow. However, such is not reality.

Net promoter score

Reichheld (2003) has asserted that the 'Net Promoter Score' (the percentage of people willing to recommend a brand minus those who are not) is an accurate predictor of a company's growth prospects. He suggests that this one metric can replace a whole battery of attitudinal and behavioural questions that appear in most research questionnaires and that it is, without qualification, the one number that every company should seek to grow.

Because of its radical simplicity, the Net Promoter Score approach has been widely adopted by companies. At the same time, it has been widely criticised by academics and market researchers on a number of counts. In the first place, Reichheld and the *Harvard Business Review* appear to have refused to release his data for independent analysis, as is common practice. Secondly, other researchers have not been able to replicate his findings (Keiningham et al., 2007; Schneider et al., 2007). Thirdly his findings are inherently implausible for the same reason as his 'loyalty effect' (Reichheld, 2001) has been found wanting (East et al., 2006), i.e. for putting the emphasis on customer retention rather than acquisition (Reichheld, 2001). In that earlier work he claimed that brand users become increasingly loyal over time and therefore increasingly more likely to pass on that enthusiasm via word of mouth. That may be true under specific circumstances, but as East et al. have demonstrated, recent converts are more likely to share their new enthusiasm than long-term brand users. Initial delight with a service may prompt customers to be active in their recommendation; ongoing satisfaction is not generally something that people make an active effort to publicise.

The fallacy of the 'silver metric'

Theory and business practice shows that there can be no single set of metrics, which suits all sectors and firms, still less a single metric. Contextual determinants include the sector, the size and age of the business, the strategy selected, and the rate of change of the firm's commercial environment. To the extent that metrics represent milestones on the firm's chosen strategic path, strategy should determine which metrics are used. In particular, each firm will have, explicitly or implicitly, a business model linking the use of resources with performance. As firms are increasingly recognising, they need a dashboard of key metrics to drive the business in the product marketplace (Clark et al., 2006; Reibstein et al., 2005).

AREAS FOR FURTHER STUDY

A key area of interest for practitioners is the relationship between metrics development and

performance. The causality could run either way – better performance could provide resources for more metrics development, or more metrics development could drive better performance. Some limited research in that area (Clark et al., 2006) showed no direct relationship between metrics, or the use of metrics, and performance, but the relationship was mediated by organisational learning. In other words, metrics should be seen as part of the process of learning, which has long-term performance benefit even if it has short-term net cost. This is consistent with the observation that fast-moving managers are reluctant radically to improve their metrics systems. This area for future research should be integrated with future dashboard research.

Swartz et al. (1996) showed that firms tend to perform better on those measures which are most visibly tracked. In other words, companies tend to get what they measure. Market share, for example, tends to increase where that is the dominant focus, and customer satisfaction where that is the most actively tracked measure. If this were borne out by further research, then it would imply that firms need to monitor a representative set of metrics of the whole business model in order to maximise the bottom line: selective measurement leads to skewed business results.

One particular area for further research is the development of appropriate metrics to characterise a firm's position in the emerging social media landscape. To date, marketing metrics have reflected a broadcast media environment in which customers have been largely passive recipients of marketing stimuli. Valuable work can be done to determine the nature of the marketing metrics best suited to monitoring marketing performance in an environment of peer networks and customer communities.

Finally, we have not been able fully to answer the questions surrounding market orientation and the marketing metrics that senior management regard as most significant. Those two are closely linked, not least because metrics usage is itself an indication of orientation. Context affects the drivers of orientation and/or metrics selection. For example, if a certain orientation, within a sector, is more productive, we need to understand why some senior sector management adopt it, and some do not. Moreover, we need to understand the dynamics in changes of orientation and metrics selection.

CONCLUSIONS

The linkage between market orientation and business performance has been established by a number of researchers across different industry contexts and for firms of different size (Kara et al., 2005; Narver and Slater, 1990; Slater and Narver, 2000). However, the connection between market orientation and the discipline of marketing is weakened whenever marketing is understood to refer to a limited set of activities, for example just marketing communications.

The restoration of marketing to its strategic role of the sourcing and harvesting of cash flow can only be achieved when marketers articulate the strategic mandate for marketing and embrace the challenge of demonstrating how, and by how much, marketing is able to enhance overall business performance and value. Quantification, preferably in financial terms, of plans and performance is strongly demanded (Clark, 1999; Moorman and Rust, 1999; Marketing Science Institute, 2000; Shaw and Mazur, 1997). Reflecting this, the Marketing Science Institute has rated marketing metrics as a top tier project in recent years (Lehmann and Reibstein, 2006; Marketing Science Institute, 2000).

This chapter has concluded that using purely financial metrics for marketing measurement is inadequate, because they do not express the multidimensional nature of the marketing asset – i.e. brand equity. This asset is crucial in both planning and performance evaluation as it expresses the quantum of marketing's impact on the future cash flows of the business. Since these cash flows cannot be measured today, performance has to be judged by short-term profit, or cash flow, together with any change in brand equity.

Brand equity measurement requires nonfinancial as well as financial metrics. Together, these metrics must accurately characterise the brand's ability to generate future cash flows. As yet, no single metric has emerged that meets this requirement. This, together with the importance of contextual factors in determining marketing strategy and performance, means that marketing measurement will always require a suite of metrics rather than a single one.

REFERENCES

Aaker, D.A. (1991) *Managing Brand Equity*. New York: Free Press.

Aaker, D.A. (1996) *Building Strong Brands*. New York: Free Press.

Aaker, D.A. and Jacobson, R. (1994) 'The Financial Information Content of Perceived Quality', *Journal of Marketing Research*, 31(2): 191–201.

Agarwal, M.K. and Rao, V.R. (1996) 'An Empirical Comparison of Consumer-Based Measures of Brand Equity', *Marketing Letters*, 7(3): 237–247.

Ailawadi, K.L., Lehmann, D.R., and Neslin, S.A. (2003) 'Revenue Premium as an Outcome Measure of Brand Equity', *Journal of Marketing*, 67(4 October): 1–17.

AMA (1948) 'Report of the Definitions Committee', *Journal of Marketing*, 13(2): 202.

AMA (1960) *Marketing Definitions – A Glossary of Marketing Terms*. Chicago: American Marketing Association.

AMA (2005) '*Marketing Accountability Study: White Paper*', Chicago: American Marketing Association.

AMA (2008) 'New Definition of Marketing,' http://www.marketingpower.com/Community/ARC/Pages/Additional/Definition/default.aspx accessed 5 September, 2008.

Ambler, T. (2003) *Marketing and the Bottom Line*, second edition. London: FT Prentice Hall.

Ambler, T. and Barwise, P. (1998) 'The Trouble with Brand Valuation', *Journal of Brand Management*, 5(5 May): 367–377.

Ambler, T. and Hollier, E.A. (2004) 'The Waste in Advertising is the Part that Works', *Journal of Advertising Research*, 44(December): 375–389.

Ambler, T. and Kokkinaki, F. (1997) 'Measures of Marketing Success', *Journal of Marketing Management*, 13(October): 665–678.

Ambler, T. and Puntoni, S. (2003) 'Measuring Marketing Performance', in Susan Hart (ed.) Chapter 15 in *Marketing Changes*, London: Thomson, pp. 289–309.

Ambler, T., Puntoni, S. and Kokkinaki, F. (2004) 'Assessing Marketing Performance: Reasons for Metrics Selection', *Journal of Marketing Management*, 20(3/4): 475-498.

Ambler, T. and Roberts, J. (2006) 'Beware the Silver Metric: Marketing Performance Measurement has to be Multidimensional', *MSI Reports* [06-113].

Andersen, A. (1992) *The Valuation of Intangible Assets*, Special Report # P254, London: The Economist Intelligence Unit.

ASB (2006) *Reporting Statement: Operating and Financial Review*, January. London: Accounting Standards Board.

Baker, W.E. and Sinkula, J.M. (1999) 'The Synergistic Effect of Market Orientation and Learning Orientation on Organizational Performance', *Journal of the Academy of Marketing Science*, 27(4): 411–427.

Baker, W.E. and Sinkula, J.M. (2002) 'Market Orientation, Learning Orientation and Product Innovation: Delving into the Organization's Black Box', *Journal of Market-Focused Management*, 5(Spring): 5–23.

Baker, W.E. and Sinkula, J.M. (2005) 'Marketing Orientation and the New Product Paradox', *Journal of Product Innovation Management*, 22(6): 483–502.

Balasubramanian, S.K., Mathur, I. and Thakur, R. (2005) 'The Impact of High-Quality Firm Achievements on Shareholder Value: Focus on Malcolm Baldridge and J. D. Power and Associates Awards', *Journal of the Academy of Marketing Science* 33(4): 413–422.

Bonoma, T.V. and Clark, B.C. (1988) *Marketing Performance Assessment*. Boston: Harvard Business School Press.

Buzzell, R.D. and Gale, B.T. (1987) *The PIMS Principles: Linking Strategy to Performance*. New York: Free Press.

CIM (2008) 'Definition of marketing,' http://www.cim.co.uk/learningzone2008/guest/new2marketing/Home.aspx accessed 5 September, 2008.

Clark, B.H. (1999) 'Marketing Performance Measures: History and Interrelationships', *Journal of Marketing Management*, 15(8): 711–732.

Clark, B.H., Abela, A. and Ambler, T. (2006) 'Behind the Wheel', *Marketing Management*, 15(3 May–June): 18–23.

Collins, J.C. and Porras, J.I. (1995) *Built to Last*. London: Century.

Cooke, E.F., Raybum, J.M. and Abercrombie, C.L. (1992) 'The History of Marketing Thought as Reflected in the Definitions of Marketing', *Journal of Marketing Theory and Practice*, 1(1): 10–20.

Darroch, J., Miles, M.P., Jardine, A. and Cooke, E.F (2004) 'The 2004 AMA Definition of Marketing and its Relationship to a Market Orientation: An Extension of Cooke, Rayburn, and Abercrombie (1992)', *Journal of Marketing Theory and Practice*, 12(4): 29–38.

Day, G.S. (1994) 'The Capabilities of Market-Driven Organizations', *Journal of Marketing*, 58(4 October): 37–52.

Day, G.S. and Fahey, L. (1988) 'Valuing Market Strategies', *Journal of Marketing*, 52(3): 45–57.

Day, G.S. and Wensley, R. (1983) 'Marketing Theory with a Strategic Orientation', *Journal of Marketing*, 47(4): 79–89.

Deshpandé, R. and Farley, J.U. (2004) 'Organizational Culture, Market Orientation, Innovativeness and Firm Performance: An International Research Odyssey', *International Journal of Research in Marketing*: 3–22.

Dick, A.S. and Basu, K. (1994) 'Customer Loyalty: Towards an Integrated Conceptual Framework',' *Journal of the Academy of Marketing Science*, 28(5): 5–16.

East, R., Hammond, K., and Gendall, P. (2006) 'Fact and Fallacy in Retention Marketing', *Journal of Marketing Management*, 22(1/2): 5–23.

Ellis, P.D. (2006) 'Market Orientation and Performance: A Meta-Analysis and Cross-National Comparisons', *Journal of Management Studies*, 43(5 July): 1089–1107.

Farquhar, P.H. (1989) 'Managing Brand Equity', *Marketing Research*, 1(3): 24–33.

Feder, R.A. (1965) 'How to Measure Marketing Performance', *Harvard Business Review*, 43(3 May/June): 132–142.

Gale, B.T. (1994) 'The Importance of Market-Perceived Quality', in P. Stobart (ed.) *Brand Power*. London and Basingstoke: Macmillan.

Gupta, S. and Lehmann, D.R. (2005) *Managing Customers as Investments*. Upper Saddle River, NJ: Wharton School Press.

Harding, T. (1997) 'Brands from the Standard Setter's Perspective', in R. Perrier (ed.) Chapter 9 in *Brand Valuation*, London: Premier Books.

Holder-Webb, L., Cohen, J., Nath, L. and Wood, D. (2009) 'The Supply of Corporate Social Responsibility Disclosures among U.S. Firms', *Journal of Business Ethics*, 84(4): 497–527.

IASB (2004) 'International Financial Reporting Standard 3 – Business Combinations', March, International Accounting Standards Board.

Ittner, C.D. and Larcker, D.F. (1998) 'Are Nonfinancial Measures Leading Indicators of Financial Performance? An Analysis of Customer Satisfaction', *Journal of Accounting Research*, 36(3): 1–35.

Jacobson, R.T. (1990) 'Unobservable Effects and Business Performance', *Marketing Science*, 9(1): 74–85.

Jaworski, B.J. and Kohli, A.K. (1993) 'Market Orientation: Antecedents and Consequences', *Journal of Marketing*, 57(3): 53–70.

Kaplan, R.S. and Norton, D.P. (1993) *The Balanced Scorecard*. Boston, Mass.: Harvard Business School Press.

Kara, A., Spillan, J.E., and DeShields, O. (2005) 'The Effect of Market Orientation on Business Performance: A Study of Small-Sized Service Retailers', *Journal of Small Business Management*, 43(2): 105–118.

Keefe, L. (2004) 'What is the Meaning of "Marketing"?', *Marketing News*, September 15, American Marketing Association, Chicago: 17–18.

Keiningham, T.L., Cooil, B., Andreassen, T.W. and Aksoy, L. (2007) 'A Longitudinal Examination of Net Promoter and Firm Revenue Growth', *Journal of Marketing*, 71(3): 39–51.

Keller, K.L. (1993) 'Conceptualizing, Measuring, and Managing Customer-Based Brand Equity', *Journal of Marketing*, 57(1 January): 1–22.

Keller, K.L. (1998) *Strategic Brand Management: Building, Measuring and Managing Brand Equity*. Upper Saddle River, NJ: Prentice-Hall.

Keller, K.L. (2003) 'Brand Synthesis: The Multidimensionality of Brand Knowledge', *Journal of Consumer Research*, 29(4): 595–600.

Kerin, R.A. and Sethuraman, R. (1998) 'Exploring the Brand Value-Shareholder Value Nexus for Consumer Goods Companies', *Journal of the Academy of Marketing Science*, 26(4): 260–273.

Knowles, J. (2005) 'In Search of a Reliable Measure of Brand Equity', *MarketingNPV*, 2(3): 16–19.

Knowles, J. (2008) 'Varying Perspectives on Brand Equity', *Marketing Management*, 17(4): 20–26.

Knowles, J. (2009) 'My Brand's Bigger Than Your Brand', *MarketingNPV*, 5(3): 6–8.

Kohli, A.K., Jaworski, B.J and Kumar, A. (1993) 'MARKOR: A Measure of Market Orientation', *Journal of Marketing Research*, 30(November): 467–477.

Kotler, P. (1997) *Marketing Management: Analysis, Planning Implementation and Control*, ninth edition. Englewood Cliffs, NJ: Prentice Hall.

Kotler, P. and Keller, K.L. (2006) *Marketing Management*, twelfth edition. Upper Saddle River, NJ: Pearson Prentice Hall.

Lane, V. and Jacobson, R. (1995) 'Stock Market Reactions to Brand Extension Announcements: The Effects of Brand Attitude and Familiarity', *Journal of Marketing*, 59(1): 63–77.

Lehmann, D.R. and Reibstein, D.J. (2006) *Marketing Metrics and Financial Performance*. Cambridge, Mass: Marketing Science Institute.

Lev, B. (2001) *Intangibles: Management, Measurement, and Reporting*. Brookings Institution Press.

Lindemann, J. (2003) 'The Financial Value of Brands', in R. Clifton and J. Simmons (eds) *Brands and Branding*, London: Profile Books, pp. 27–45.

Madden, T.R., Fehle, F. and Fournier, S. (2006) 'Brands Matter -An Empirical Investigation of Brand Building and the Creation of Shareholder Value', *Journal of the Academy of Marketing Science*, 34(2): 224–235.

Marketing Science Institute (2000) *2000–2002 Research Priorities: A Guide to MSI Research Programs and Procedures*. Cambridge, MA: Marketing Science Institute.

McGovern, G.J, Court, D., Quelch, J. and Crawford, B. (2004) 'Bringing Customers into the Boardroom', *Harvard Business Review*, 82(11 November): 70–80.

Menon, A. and Varadarajan, P.R. (1992) 'A Model of Marketing Knowledge Use Within Firms', *Journal of Marketing*, 56(October): 53–71.

Meyer, M.W. (1998) 'Finding Performance: The New Discipline in Management', *Performance Measurement – Theory and Practice*, Vol. 1, Cambridge, UK: Centre for Business Performance, pp. xiv–xxi.

Mizik, N. and Jacobson, R. (2008) 'The Financial Value Impact of Perceptual Brand Attributes', *Journal of Marketing Research*, 45(1): 15–32.

Moorman, C. (1995) 'Organizational Market Information Processes: Cultural Antecedents and New Product Outcomes', *Journal of Marketing Research*, 32(August): 318–335.

Moorman, C. and Rust, R.T. (1999) 'The Role of Marketing', *Journal of Marketing*, 63(4): 180–197.

Murphy, G.B., Trailer, J.W., and Hill, R.C. (1996) 'Measuring Performance in Entrepreneurship Research', *Journal of Business Research*, 36(1): 15–23.

Narver, J.C. and Slater, S.F. (1990) 'The Effect of a Market Orientation on Business Profitability', *Journal of Marketing*, 54(4): 20–35.

Park, C.S. and Srinivasan, V. (1994) 'A Survey-Based Method for Measuring and Understanding Brand Equity and Its Extendibility', *Journal of Marketing Research*, 31(2): 271–288.

Pauwels, K., Ambler, T., Clark, B., LaPointe, P., Reibstein, D.J., Skiera, B., Wierenga, B. and Wiesel, T. (2008) 'Dashboards and Marketing: Why, What, How and What Research Is Needed?', *MSI Special Report* [08-203].

Peppers, D. and Rogers, M. (2005) *Return on Customer: Creating Maximum Value from Your Scarcest Resource*. New York: Currency (Doubleday).

Perrier, R. (ed.) (1997) *Brand Valuation*, third edition. London: Premier Books.

Rappaport, A. (1986) *Creating Shareholder Value: The New Standard for Business Performance*. New York: Free Press.

Reibstein, D.J., Norton, D.P., Joshi, Y. and Farris, P. (2005) 'Marketing Dashboards: A Decision Support System for Assessing Marketing Productivity', Philadelphia, Penn: Wharton School Working Paper.

Reichheld, F.F. (2001) *Loyalty Rules!: How Today's Leaders Build Lasting Relationships*. Boston, MA: Harvard Business School Press Books.

Reichheld, F.F. (2003) 'The One Number You Need to Grow', *Harvard Business Review*, 81(12): 46–54.

Rust, R.T., Ambler, T., Carpenter, G.S., Kumar, V. and Srivastava, R.K. (2004a) 'Measuring Marketing Productivity: Current Knowledge and Future Directions', *Journal of Marketing*, 68(3 October): 76–89.

Rust, R.T., Lemon, K.N., and Zeithaml, V.A. (2004b) 'Return on Marketing: Using Customer Equity to Focus Marketing Strategy', *Journal of Marketing*, 68(1): 109–127.

Rutherford, D. and Knowles, J. (2008) *Vulcans, Earthlings and Marketing ROI*. Wilfrid Laurier University Press.

Salinas, G. and Ambler, T. (2008) 'A Taxonomy of Brand Valuation Methodologies: How Different Types of Methodologies can help to Answer Different Types of Questions', Electronic Working Paper 08-204. Cambridge, MA: Marketing Science Institute.

Schneider, D., Berent, M., Randall, T. and Krosnick, J. (2007) 'Measuring Customer Satisfaction and Loyalty: Improving the "Net-Promoter' Score", Paper Presented at the Annual Conference of the World Association for Public Opinion Research (WAPOR), Berlin.

Sevier, R. (2005) 'A New Definition of Marketing: the AMA's Update can Mean Enormous Opportunities for Higher Education', *University Business*, March. http://www.universitybusiness.com/ViewArticle.aspx?articleid=425 accessed 5 September, 2008.

Sevin, C.H. (1965) *Marketing Productivity Analysis*. New York: McGraw-Hill.

Shaw, R. and Mazur, L. (1997) *Marketing Accountability: Improving Business Performance*. London: *Financial Times*, Retail and Consumer Publishing.

Simms, J. (1997) 'Accounting for Brands: An Industry Perspective', in R. Perrier (ed.) *Brand Valuation*, third edition, London: Premier Books, pp. 99–108.

Simon, C.J. and Sullivan, M.W. (1993) 'The Measurement and Determinants of Brand Equity: A Financial Approach', *Marketing Science*, 12(1): 28–51.

Sinkula, J.M. (1994) 'Market Information Processing and Organizational Learning', *Journal of Marketing*, 58(1 January): 35–45.

Sinkula, J.M. (2002) 'Market-based Success, Organizational Routines, and Unlearning', *Journal of Business and Industrial Marketing*, 17(4): 253–269.

Sinkula, J.M., Baker, W.E. and Noordewier, T. (1997) 'A Framework for Market-Based Organizational Learning: Linking Values, Knowledge, and Behavior', *Journal of the Academy of Marketing Science*, 25(4): 305–318.

Slater, S.F. and Narver, J.C. (1995) 'Market Orientation and the Learning Organization', *Journal of Marketing*, 59(3): 63–74.

Slater, S.F. and Narver, J.C. (2000) 'The Positive Effect of a Market Orientation on Business Profitability: A Balanced Replication', *Journal of Business Research*, 48(1): 69–73.

Srivastava, R.K. and Shocker, A.D. (1991) 'Brand Equity: A Perspective on its Meaning and Measurement', Working Paper 91-124. Cambridge, MA: Marketing Science Institute.

Srivastava, R.K. and Reibstein, D.J. (2005) 'Metrics for Linking Marketing to Financial Performance', Working Paper 05-200. Cambridge, MA: Marketing Science Institute.

Srivastava, R.K., Shervani, T. and Fahey, L. (1998) 'Market-Based Assets and Shareholder Value', *Journal of Marketing*, 62(1): 2–18.

Swartz, G., Hardie, B., Grayson, K. and Ambler, T. (1996) *Value for Money? The Relationships between Marketing Expenditure and Business Performance in the UK Financial Services Industry*. Cookham, Berks: Chartered Institute of Marketing.

Szymanski, D.M. and Henard, D.H. (2001) 'Customer Satisfaction: A Meta-Analysis of the Empirical Evidence', *Journal of the Academy of Marketing Science*, 29(1): 16–35.

Unilever (1998) Presentation to the Marketing Council Seminar on Measuring Marketing, London. December 2.

Venkatesan, R. and Kumar, V. (2004) 'A Customer Lifetime Value Framework for Customer Selection and Resource Allocation Strategy', *Journal of Marketing*, 68(4): 106–125.

Webster, F.E. Jr. (1992) 'The Changing Role of Marketing in the Corporation', *Journal of Marketing*, 56(10): 1–17.

Wilkie, W.L. and Moore, E.S. (2006) 'Macromarketing as a Pillar of Marketing Thought', *Journal of Macromarketing*, 26(2 December): 224–232.

Williams, J.B. (1938) *The Theory of Investment Value*. Cambridge, Mass.: Harvard University Press.

Wright, M. and Ashill, N. (1996) 'A Contingency Model of Marketing Information', *European Journal of Marketing*, 32(1/2): 125–144.

Yoo, B., Donthu, N. and Lee, S. (2000) 'An Examination of Selected Marketing Mix Elements and Brand Equity', *Journal of the Academy of Marketing Science*, 28(2): 195–211.

23

Relationship Marketing as Promise Management

Christian Grönroos

INTRODUCTION

This chapter is based on the assumption that, both from academic and practitioner perspectives, relationship marketing, as a process-oriented approach to customer management in a meaningful way, is understood as *promise management*, i.e. as a process of enabling promises to customers, making promises to them and keeping promises by meeting expectations created by promises that have been made. Consequently, the *purpose* of the present chapter is to analyse how relationship marketing can be conceptualized and managed using a promise management approach. The analysis aims at developing a marketing definition that helps academics and business practitioners alike to understand and implement a relational strategy in both business-to-business and business-to-consumer contexts. As the analysis draws to a large extent, but not entirely, on the Nordic School of thought in marketing research (see, for example, Grönroos, 2007, and Berry and Parasuraman, 1993), it is also based on the view that relationship marketing and understanding

how to manage services are intertwined. Services are inherently relational, and relational marketing requires the adoption of a service logic (Grönroos, 2007).

DEFINITIONS OF RELATIONSHIP MARKETING IN THE LITERATURE

In the literature, there seems to be no agreement on how relationship marketing is best defined (see chapters in this handbook by Gadde and Håkansson, Moller et al., and Brodie et al.). In his analysis of relationship marketing definitions, Harker (1999) found that the one definition that included the most common elements of what then could be found in the scholarly literature was the following (Grönroos, 1997, slightly modified)[1]:

Relationship marketing is to identify and establish, maintain and enhance, and when necessary terminate relationships with customers (and other parties) so that the objectives regarding economic and other variables of all parties are met. This is achieved through a mutual making and fulfilment of promises.

During the time period since Harker's analysis, research does not seem to have changed the fact that this definition is the one that best covers the field (cf. Harker and Egan, 2006).

The definition includes two strengths: first, it takes a process approach to marketing, and second, it indicates by what means this process proceeds. The process moves from identifying relationships over establishing and maintaining them to enhancing and possibly dissolving them. The means of pursuing this process is making promises and keeping promises that have been made. This part of the definition draws on Calonius's (1983, 1986, 2006) suggestion of the *promise concept* as a key construct in marketing. However, as with all relationship-marketing definitions, this definition does not specify in any detail how the marketing process proceeds beyond the notion of establishing, maintaining, and enhancing relationships. In the present chapter, the progress of this process will be analysed in detail. Due to the comprehensive nature of Grönroos's definition quoted in the foregoing section, which already includes the promise concept, it seems only natural to build upon it and expand it.

VALUE CREATION AS THE GOAL FOR MARKETING

Traditionally, *exchange* has been considered the fundamental construct in marketing (see, for example, Baggozzi, 1975; Hunt, 1976; Kotler, 1972; Pyle, 1931). According to this view, the goal of marketing is to create exchange of goods and services for money or the equivalent. However, concentrating on marketing as exchange draws the marketers' attention to short-term value-in-exchange and away from customers' value creation (cf. for example, Sheth and Uslay, 2007), and this conceals the importance of customers' creation of value-in-use to long-term marketing success (Grönroos, 2007, 2008). Moreover, focusing on exchange takes marketing's

interest away from developing customer relationships and makes marketing focused on transactions (Grönroos, 2007). As Kotler noted, '... the core of marketing is transaction. A transaction is the exchange of values between two parties' (1972: 48). A distinction between direct and indirect exchange, as suggested by Vargo and Lusch (2008) in the discussion of service-dominant logic, does not change this in any fundamental way. On the contrary, using the term 'exchange' metaphorically weakens the exchange construct's base in economic theory and, more or less, makes its meaning and role even more elusive and difficult to use for analysis and planning.

Sheth and Uslay (2007) have suggested that, instead of focusing on exchange, marketing should take the creation of value for customers as its goal. This is not a new view voiced in the marketing literature. However, until now, it has been silenced by marketing's transaction-oriented traditions and models and marketing scholars' preoccupation with exchange. In the 1990s, Holbrook (1994) stated that the value concept is '... the fundamental basis for all marketing activity' (p. 22) and Rust and Oliver (1994) claimed that '... ultimately it is perceived value that attracts a customer or lures away a customer from a competitor' (p. 7). Directly in a relationship marketing context, Grönroos (1997) observes that 'marketing in a relational context is seen as a process that should support the creation of perceived value for customers over time' (p. 407), and Eggert et al. (2006) state that 'offering superior value to customers is essential for creating and maintaining long-term customer–supplier relationships' (p. 20). Also, American Marketing Association's (AMA's) new marketing definition, published in 2004 and renewed in 2007, emphasizes the importance of value creation for marketing. Although the underpinning logic of AMA's attempt to define marketing has been criticized as conventional, outdated and geared towards value-in-exchange (Grönroos, 2006b), the reorientation towards value creation as such follows a general trend in business and marketing.

However, when taking value creation for customers as the goal for marketing, a focus on exchange as the foundational marketing construct is no longer supportable (Grönroos, 2007; Sheth and Uslay, 2007) but an outdated and too restrictive concept to focus on (see also Sheth and Parvatiyar, 1995; Webster, 1992). Instead, the interaction concept central to both a service and relationship marketing logic is a more productive option. As Ballantyne and Varey (2006) put it, interaction is a 'generator of service experience and value-in-use' (p. 336), and service experiences are intertwined with the development and maintenance of relationships. Furthermore, interactions help firms gain and deepen their information about customers and their preferences (Srinivasan et al., 2002).

The key advantage of customer–firm interactions for the supplier is the opportunities for the supplier to engage itself with the customers' processes that such interactions offer (Grönroos, 2008). In these interactions, the customer's processes and activities get exposed to the supplier, which enables the supplier to directly and actively take part in these processes and activities and influence the value creation that takes place in them. The supplier gets an opportunity to directly influence the customers' creation of value, something that is not possible without such interactions (Grönroos, 2008). In ongong relationships with customers, exchange still take place, of course, but focusing on exchange as a basically transaction-oriented concept does not make it possible to capture the essence of relationship development and maintenance and of value creation as value-in-use. Interaction makes this possible.

In conclusion, two concepts are of central importance for the analysis in the present chapter, viz. *value creation* and *promise management*. Hence, first of all, the marketing approach developed in this report is based on the notion that through customer–firm interactions and outcomes of these interactions, marketing aims at supporting customers' value creation. Secondly, the promise concept and promise management is a key concept for an understanding of relationship marketing. The promise concept has been developed into a promise management approach to marketing (Grönroos, 2006b)[2].

WHAT IS CUSTOMER VALUE? WHO CREATES IT AND WHO CO-CREATES?

In management literature and in management jargon, it is claimed that value is delivered to customers. However, the phrase 'deliver value to customers' implies that value is embedded in the product (goods, service activities, ideas, information, or any type of solutions) which is delivered to customers for their use. This is a *value-in-exchange* concept, where the exchange of ready-made value embedded in the products for money is considered the central phenomenon to study. The growing importance to marketing success of interactions between customers and a set of resources of the firm is neglected.

The current research into customer value shows a clear trend away from a value-in-exchange view towards a notion of value being produced not by the supplier, but by the customer when using goods and services and when interacting with the suppliers. According to this research, there is no value for customers until they can make use of a good or a service. Value is not what goes into goods and service activities, it is what customers get out of them; i.e. value emerges in the customers' space rather than in the producer's space (Vandermerwe, 1996). Customers assess the value of goods and services based on what is received and what is sacrificed (Zeithaml, 1988). The notion that only customers can assess value to goods and services was expressed by Levitt (1983) already in the early 1980s. However, this thought was largely ignored by the academic and business communities alike. From the beginning of the 1990s onward, this *value-in-use* notion (see Woodruff and Gardial, 1996), as opposed to a value-in-exchange view, has been put forward in the marketing and management literature (see, for example, Grönroos, 2000; Gummesson, 2002; Holbrook, 1994; Jüttner and Wehrli, 1994; Monroe, 1991; Normann, 2001; Norman and Ramirez, 1993; Ravald and Grönroos, 1996; Sheth and Parvatiyar, 1995; Storbacka and Lehtinen, 2001; Vandermerwe, 1996; Wikström, 1996; Woodruff and Gardial, 1996).

Fifty years ago, Wroe Alderson (1957), whose arguments for a functionalist theory of marketing were geared towards a value-in-use concept (Dixon, 1990: 337–338 and Vargo and Lusch, 2004: 5), made the point that what marketing needs is a 'marketing interpretation of the whole process of creating value' (p. 69). He pointed out the superior role of value-in-use: 'Goods do not really have utility from the consumer viewpoint until they come into the possession of the ultimate user and form a part of his assortment' (Alderson, 1957: 70). In 1979, in a service marketing context, Grönroos concluded that 'it is ... reasonable to consider both goods and services to be bought by consumers in order to give some service or value satisfaction', and that 'a good represents potential value (or utility) for the consumer. He purchases the good and subsequently he has to initiate and implement the activities required to transform this potential value into real value for him. ... A service is in itself an activity ... with in-built ability to transform the potential value (or utility) for the consumer into real value for him' (Grönroos, 1979: 86).

Hence, value is not created in the service provider's processes of designing, delivering and pricing services, but in the customer's *value-generating processes* (Grönroos, 2000) where services and goods are consumed and used (compare Becker, 1965, who treats the household as a production unit). Value is either created by the customer in isolation or in interactions with the service provider (Grönroos, 1979, 2008; Normann and Ramirez, 1993; Prahalad and Ramaswamy, 2004; Vargo and Lusch, 2007). In the service provider's processes, *value propositions* are

developed, whereas *real value* for customers is created in a customer's value-creating processes (see also Gummesson, 2007).

Co-creation demands co-production efforts of the firm and its customers. In these joint processes, if they are well handled, both customers and the firm can be expected to gain. The firm can make use of the customer's knowledge and skills to improve the quality of services as perceived by the customer and, in addition, feed the knowledge obtained in this way into its development processes (compare Schneider and Bowen, 1995). Hence, both the customer's value perception and the firm's ability to create value propositions and to support value fulfilment will benefit. In addition, the productivity of a firm's operations can benefit from co-production (Lovelock and Young, 1979) at the same time as the customers learn how to use a product and thereby both boosts productivity and their own value creation (Grönroos and Ojasalo, 2004).

A value proposition is a *suggested value* that has not been realized yet (compare Gummesson, 2007), whereas customer value is *perceived value*. At least when accepting the value-in-use notion as a better description of how customer value emerges, *delivering value to customers* is not an accurate description of reality. What marketers can do is to develop value propositions or suggested value in the form of various types of offerings and communicate them to customers and then assist customers in their value creation. 'Delivering value to customers' is based on the value-in-exchange notion and contradictory to the notion of value-in-use and the view of the customer as value creator.

Based on a value-in-use notion it is not the customer who gets engaged with the supplier's processes and becomes a value co-creator with a supplier. Rather, it is the supplier which, by developing firm–customer interactions as part of its market offerings, gets opportunities to engage itself with the customers' processes and become a co-creator of value with its customers (Grönroos, 2008). As Storbacka and Lehtinen (2001) observe, customers produce value for themselves independently, but suppliers may offer assistance. Co-creation opportunities that suppliers have are strategic options for creating value (Payne et al., 2008).

In conclusion, suppliers do not deliver value to customers; as *value facilitators* (Grönroos, 2008: 307) they support or *assist customers' value creation* and *possibly get involved in co-creation of value with customers*, by providing them with *resources* such as service processes with service employees, goods and other tangible items as well as with ideas, information, call centre advice, service recovery, payment and invoicing procedures, a whole host of various resources needed by customers (compare Grönroos, 1997).

The analysis of value for customers in a marketing context leads to the following propositions for the understanding of marketing:

Proposition 1a: *Value is not delivered by a firm to customers but created in customer processes through assistance to those processes and through the firm's co-creation in interactions with customers.*
   Proposition 1b: *The role of marketing is, on one hand, to develop and communicate value propositions to customers, and on the other hand, to assist customers' value creation through goods, services, information, and other resources as well as through interactions where co-creation of value with the customers can take place.*

THE ROLE OF CUSTOMER RELATIONSHIPS IN MARKETING

Relationship marketing is, of course, a matter of managing customer relationships. However, as the literature on relationship marketing demonstrates, research into this field and studies of relationship marketing in practice show a variety of different views on the subject. The literature demonstrates a scale of notions of what managing customer relationships is, ranging from creating a mutual commitment and understanding of the supplier and the customer and a win-win situation (see

Håkansson and Snehota, 1995; Morgan and Hunt, 1994; Sheth and Parvatiyar, 1995; Grönroos, 1999; and Gummesson, 2002) as a basis for marketing, to having customers who show a repetitive buying behaviour (see Liljander and Strandvik, 1995) to managing relationship marketing instruments such as loyalty programmes and direct mailings (Verhoef, 2003) and relationship marketing tactics (Leong and Qing, 2006) and relationships as yet another variable in the marketing mix toolbox used to manipulate customers (see the criticism of relationship marketing in practice in Fournier et al., 1998).

Moreover, as Ryals (2005) indicate, a relationship marketing approach with the goal to increase customer retention may not always be a profitable strategy, because the costs of retaining customers may be higher than the benefits to be gained from such a strategy (see also Reinartz and Kumar, 2002).

In marketing and management jargon, the term 'customer relationship' is also used in a multitude of ways. For some, it means customers with whom a behavioural *and* emotional connection and a mutual sense of connectedness (Lindberg-Repo and Grönroos, 2004) have been developed. Repeat purchasing behaviour and a larger share of customers' wallet is not enough for a relationship to have been established with a customer (a behavioural component), in addition a larger share of *their heart and mind* is also required (an emotional or attitudinal component) (Storbacka and Lehtinen, 2001). For others, every customer who has shown up at least twice or even every customer regardless of their purchasing behaviour is called a customer relationship.

Only customers can decide whether they have, or want to have, a relationship with a firm, i.e. whether a customer relationship exists or not. It seems quite obvious that all customers do not want to be in a relationship with firms whose services they are using. Customers can be in transactional modes as well as in relational modes (Grönroos, 1997; Sääksjärvi et al., 2007), and the same customer may probably shift from one mode to another depending on type of products, or supplier, or even situation. There is no research yet that would demonstrate when a customer recognizes a relationship to exist, wants a relationship to exist or shifts from a transactional to a relational mode. In fact, relationship marketing and customer relationships have mostly been studied from a management perspective based on the assumption that marketers decide whether relationships exist or not. There is not much knowledge about customers' interests in relational behaviour and about their reactions to relational approaches. The only thing we definitely seem to know is that unless the most simple and meaningless definition of customer relationships is applied, i.e. a customer that buys two or three times is a customer relationship *or* any customer is a customer relationship, all customers cannot be managed as relationships.

In addition, the research on 'Contemporary Marketing Practices' that has been published demonstrates that firms across cultures use a variety of marketing approaches, some of which can be described as relational, some of which cannot (see, for example, Coviello et al., 2002).

As a conclusion, one can note that in the literature and in management practice customer relationships and relationship marketing is considered to include a variety of levels of customer and firm commitment. To make a definition of relationship marketing useful in as wide array of situations as possible, the relational aspect should be included in a marketing definition in an implicit way only. This leads to the following propositions:

Proposition 2a: *Customers can be in relational as well as nonrelational modes, thus they do not always appreciate being approached in a relational manner by firms, and hence, even though managing customers as relationship often may be effective, it cannot be considered a generic approach to relating a customer to the firm.*

Proposition 2b: *In an implicit way, a marketing definition must allow both for relational and nonrelational marketing strategies and activities.*

MARKETING TRANSCENDS ORGANIZATIONAL BORDERS

According to conventional views, marketing is seen as one function among other organizational functions. Marketing is considered to be most efficiently and effectively planned and implemented by a separate department. In the marketing literature, the terms 'marketing', 'marketing function', and 'marketing department' are also most frequently used interchangeably, almost as synonyms. Inevitably, this approach to understanding marketing has been very successful for consumer goods. However, already in consumer durables where delivering, installing, and repairing equipment as well as customer advice may be important to success in the marketplace, the marketing department and a separate marketing function will find it difficult to manage or even influence all customer contacts. In services and business-to-business, often with enduring customer relationships, this is even more evident. Alone, a marketing function and marketing department cannot support the customers' value-creating processes or even develop solutions and take total responsibility for the fulfilment of value propositions (compare Brown, 2005: 3). Other processes, such as service interactions, repair and maintenance, logistics, call centres, service recovery, and complaints handling, have an often-critical responsibility for supporting customers' value creation. Few of these processes, often none of them are part of the marketing function and the responsibility of the marketing department, and the marketing department/marketing function has limited or no means of influencing how they are planned and implemented.

Both relationship marketing (e.g. Christopher et al., 1991; Grönroos, 1999; Gummesson, 2002) and service marketing (e.g. Booms and Bitner, 1982; Brown and Bitner, 2006; Grönroos, 2000; Gummesson, 1979; Zeithaml et al., 1988) as well as the IMP approach to business-to-business marketing in networks (e.g. Håkansson, 1982; Håkansson and Snehota, 1995) show that marketing cannot be separated into one function and be the responsibility of one department only. In service marketing, the links between marketing, operations, and human resources has for a long time already been recognized (Gummesson, 1979; Booms and Bitner, 1982; Eiglier and Langeard, 1975; Langeard and Eiglier, 1987; Grönroos, 2000; Lovelock, 2000). Relationship marketing and the IMP approach have come to similar conclusions (Christopher et al., 1991; Håkansson and Snehota, 1995; Grönroos, 1999; Gummesson, 2002). In addition, in his studies, Webster has pointed out the need for dispersing a marketing competence outside the marketing department and across the organization (Webster, Jr., 1992; Webster Jr. et al., 2005). Value propositions may be communicated by a separate function, but the supplier's engagement with the fulfilment of these propositions cannot. A number of other organizational functions get involved, and if those other functions do not take a customer focus, value will not emerge in the customers' processes, and marketing will probably fail.

Hence, relationship marketing cannot be viewed as a one-function process only. First of all, it can be stated that marketing as a *phenomenon* is related to the customers and to the *return* on the customers or segments of customers a firm serves over time. Hence, marketing requires a *customer focus*. Secondly, to get the best possible return, regardless of what they do and of which function or department they belong to, the people, systems, and processes that have an impact on the return of customers have to make sure that these customers perceive such a value in their processes that they are satisfied enough and prefer to buy again. Hence, for value to emerge in the customers' processes, everyone who is involved in both communicating value propositions and providing value support to customers' processes have to take a *customer focus* in planning and implementing what they are doing. People in the marketing department, including sales, focus on the customer is a full-time duty. For people in other departments and

processes, such as operations, logistics, repair and maintenance, service recovery and complaints handling, service development, human resource management, investment, IT, and others, other duties are equally important, sometimes more important and most often perceived as more important. However, irrespective of whether, in a given situation, taking a customer focus is of substantial or marginal importance for them, it should always be part of their duties, not on a full-time scale but as Gummesson (1991) puts it as *part-time marketers*.

Hence, it can be concluded that a customer focus is part of not only what in the traditional marketing literature and vocabulary is called the marketing function, but also of many other organizational functions as well (compare Brown, 2005; Brown and Bitner, 2006; Grönroos, 1999; Gummesson, 1987; Piercy, 1985). Defining marketing as a duty for one organizational function will only work in special cases where the value support to customers' processes is embedded in standardized goods. In other situations, marketing cannot be the responsibility of one separate function only.

In conclusion, the analysis of the organizational home of relationship marketing leads to the following propositions:

Proposition 3a: *Marketing cannot be implemented by one organizational function of marketing specialists, the full-time marketers, only.*

Propositions 3b: *Marketing needs a customer focus throughout the organization, thus involving both full-time marketers totally or predominantly trained to take a customer focus and part-time marketers, who when performing their tasks from the outset are not at all or only partly trained to take a customer focus.*

Proposition 3c: *To be effective marketing also requires that technologies, information systems and other systems are designed and function in a customer-focused manner.*

Proposition 3d: *As customers participate in interactions with the firm's resources and, therefore, influence the customer orientation of these interactions, they actively participate in marketing as well. Hence, customers' role as a marketing resource, in addition to their roles as buyers and consumers and users has to be recognized in marketing.*

ELEMENTS OF A MARKETING PROCESS

This chapter takes the position that marketing's goal is to assist customers' value creation. In other words, the goal for marketing is *to engage the firm with the customers' processes* with an aim to support value creation in those processes, in a mutually beneficial way (Grönroos, 2009: 353). The traditional elements of marketing mix-based definitions, for example, creating products and services, pricing, promoting, and delivering, are not enough to help marketing reach this goal. Relationship marketing, as marketing in general, is a process, and therefore, for example, promoting and pricing goods and services do not by themselves take customers from an *off* state of not having value to an *on* state of having value. There must be a process from the *off* state to the *on* state with at least some intermediate state that is facilitated by marketing. There has to be some general guidelines indicating *how* marketing activities and processes should be planned and implemented in order to achieve this move from one state to another.

Here, the promise concept provides support. The seller makes a set of promises concerning, for example, physical goods, services, financial solutions, information, interactions, and a range of future commitments. Then, if a relationship is expected to be maintained and enhanced, these promises have to be kept. Berry (1995) claims that the fulfilment of promises made to customers is the foundation for retaining customers and maintaining relationships with them. Also, in the service marketing literature, promises have been explicitly used (e.g. Bitner, 1995; Grönroos, 2000).

The *promise concept* introduced in the early 1980s in the marketing literature by Henrik Calonius is partly founded on an observation by Levitt (1981): 'When prospective customers can't experience the product in advance, they are asked to buy what are essentially promises – promises of satisfaction. Even tangible, testable, feelable, smellable products are, before they are bought, largely just promises' (p. 96). Calonius defines promises as 'a more or less explicitly expressed conditional declaration or assurance made to another party, or to oneself, with respect to the future, stating that one will do or refrain from some specific act, or that one will give or bestow some specific thing' (1986: 518; 2006: 422).

Some of the marketing activities and processes, such as communicating and pricing, aim at making promises. Of course, customers' past experiences may also influence their perception of future promises about value propositions made to them. Promises are kept by, for example, deliveries, usage of goods and service activities, recovery of problems and mistakes, and call centre advice. As Bitner (1995) observes, promises cannot be expected to be successfully kept unless the organization is prepared to do so. Enabling promises is, therefore, an integral part of making and keeping promises. *Internal marketing*, a concept originating in service marketing research (e.g. Eiglier and Langeard, 1976; Berry, 1981; Grönroos, 1981) and later also in relationship marketing (e.g. Ballantyne, 2003; Dunne and Barnes, 2000), becomes important for marketing success. Employees involved in the fulfilment of promises, regardless of their position in the organization, have to take a customer focus. However, enabling promises also means that resources other than employees, such as goods, IT and other systems, physical resources and information, and also including as a resource external people such as the customer himself or herself and network partner employees, have to be developed in ways that support the fulfilment of promises (Grönroos, 2000).

Some marketing activities are mainly *promise making*, whereas others are mainly *promise keeping*. As research into relationship marketing and service marketing demonstrates, traditional marketing activities performed by a marketing function and full-time marketers are mainly promise making, whereas the promise-keeping activities are mainly the responsibility of other

organizational functions and part-time marketers (Gummesson, 1991, 2002; see also Bitner,
1995; Grönroos, 2000). However, as Brown
(2005) states in his analysis of the current
state of marketing based on a discussion
among management team members in large
companies, '... marketing and sales often
have a major role in making promises to customers and in generating new business',
whereas keeping promises is the responsibility
of others in an organization' (p. 3).

However, making and keeping promises is
not a straightforward issue. Promises made are
perceived by customers, thus creating expectations regarding what should be delivered by
a firm. Such expectation may vary from
person to person and even from situation to
situation. As Ojasalo (2001) has pointed out
in a study of professional services relationships, customers have *implicit* expectations
among explicit ones, and customers easily
expect that these should be fulfilled as well.
In addition, there may be *fuzzy* expectations
that customers have and which do not transform into explicit ones until customers experience the product. Moreover, some expectations
are *unrealistic* and, if such expectations are
not made realistic, customers are bound to
become disappointed (Ojasalo, 2001). Hence,
it is not the promises made as such that should
be kept, but the individual expectations created
by these promises.

In conclusion, the analysis of how value propositions lead to customers' value perceptions
and to suppliers' responsibility for keeping
promises lead to the following propositions:

*Proposition 4a: Customers have explicit as well
as implicit, unrealistic and fuzzy expectations
and these expectations should be fulfilled by the
performance of the firm.*

*Proposition 4b: Fulfilment of promises in a
customer-focused manner requires internal marketing efforts as promise enablers.*

*Proposition 4c: Customer-focused technologies,
information systems, and other systems as well as
appropriate leadership are also required to support
a customer-focused performance by part-time
marketers.*

*Proposition 4d: Helping customers to participate
in customer–firm interactions in ways that has a*

*favourable marketing impact on them is also
required for marketing to be successful.*

*Proposition 4e: Making promises, supported by
internal activities, such as internal marketing
geared towards the fulfilment of expectations
created by promises made, as well as technology,
systems, and leadership support, and fulfilling
expectations created by promises made, form a
firm's marketing process.*

CONCLUSION: MARKETING IN RELATIONAL SITUATIONS

Drawing on the discussion of recent
research into customer value, relationship
marketing, service marketing, and service
logic as well as on the promise concept in the
previous sections, the following promise
management definition for marketing in relational situations can be formulated (Grönroos,
2006b: 407):

Marketing is a customer focus that permeates
organizational functions and processes, and is
geared towards making promises through value
proposition, enabling the fulfilment of individual
expectations created by such promises and fulfilling
such expectations through assistance to customers'
value-generating processes, thereby supporting
value creation in the firm's a well as its customers'
and other stakeholders' processes.

This definition is based on viewing value
creation as the goal for marketing and interaction as a foundational construct in marketing as well as on the promise concept and is,
therefore, labelled a *promise management
definition* (Grönroos, 2006). The definition
could also include a specification of by what
means promises are made (e.g. by developing,
pricing, and communicating value propositions), how promises are enabled (e.g. by
internal marketing and the development of
customer-focused goods and other tangible
items, service processes, technologies, information systems, and other systems as well as
appropriate leadership and by helping customers to use goods and service activities
that have been delivered as well as to take
part in the customer–firm interactions in a
way that supports a favourable marketing

impact on them) and how expectations created by promises are kept by providing assistance to customers' value creation (by providing resources and processes – goods, services, information and people, systems, infrastructures, and physical resources – and interactions between the customer and these resources and processes as well as by mobilizing customers as a resource in the purchasing and consumption and usage processes). However, because these clarifications are inherent in the definition, to keep the definition as short as possible they have been omitted.

The underpinning logic of the suggested marketing definition is the following:

First of all, the definition is based on the notion that marketing's goal is to support customers' value creation. Furthermore, it builds upon the *value-in-use* concept, according to which customer value is created by the customer in customers' value-creating processes. With a set of resources, processes, and interactions, firms *provide assistance to* customers' value creation. This value-in-use approach to customer value is clearly more relevant to marketing than the value-in-exchange view, which has characterized mainstream marketing research.

Secondly, because customers probably do not always want relationships with firms and firms do not always consider creating relationships with customers as the foundation of the best possible business strategy, and the level of supplier and customer commitment sought may vary, managing customer relationships as a phrase is not explicitly included in this definition. Moreover, research today does not provide a clear enough definition or even description of what a relationship is in a commercial context. However, this definition implicitly includes a potential for developing customer relationships. By successfully assisting customers' value creation and doing so in a way which meets individual expectations created by promises that have been made, the likelihood that customers who are in a *relational mode* will want to develop an emotional connection with the firm will increase. *In these cases, relationships will develop.* Moreover, customers who are in a nonrelational mode will probably consider doing repeat business with a firm which performs in the way outlined in the preceding section without getting relationally involved.

Thirdly, as research, for example, into relationship marketing and service marketing as well as research into business-to-business marketing according to the IMP approach demonstrate, as soon as the products provided to customers are more complicated and include more content than standardized goods, one single organizational function cannot take responsibility for total marketing. Therefore, the definition states that several organizational functions have to take a customer focus and take a responsibility for marketing. What traditionally is called the marketing function, including for example market research, advertising and other means of marketing communication, as well as sales will be to 100 percent focused on the customer, whereas other functions such as R&D, product and service development, manufacturing and service operations, logistics, procurement, repair and maintenance, call centre activities, service recovery and complaints handling wherever they are located in the organization, and human resource management and finance will have to be part-time focused on customers. Hence, marketing as a customer focus is a dimension, among others, of the planning and implementing of the tasks of these functions.

Fourthly, unlike the 4 Ps of the marketing mix, the definition does not include a list of variables that are *the* decision-making areas of marketing. Any list such as the 4 Ps endorsed by a reliable source easily becomes a law-like guideline (Kent, 1986). Hence, the promise management definition approaches what should be planned and implemented as marketing as anything that supports value formation in customers' processes by making promises, enabling these processes, and fulfilling expectations created by them. What it takes to do so efficiently and effectively will vary, sometimes less, sometimes more, from industry to industry, context to context, market to market, customer to customer, culture to culture, and even from one point in time to another.

Fifthly, enabling promises is explicitly included in the definition. If this internal support is missing or not taken care of in an adequate manner, it will be difficult to support customers' value-creating processes in a proper way, and marketing will fail.

Sixthly, the definition takes into account the role of expectations (Miller, 1977; see also Rust et al., 1994; Ojasalo, 2001) and of expectancy disconfirmation in marketing (e.g. Oliver, 1980). Communicating value propositions and making promises set expectations and the way such expectations are met by the value support provided has a decisive impact on the success of marketing. As customers' perceptions of similar promises differ, it is not the promises as such that are met but rather the customers' individual expectations created by these promises.

Finally, the definition does not explicitly include the phrases 'relationship marketing' or 'customer relationships', which makes it possible to use the definition in a variety of marketing context.

IMPLICATIONS FOR MARKETING RESEARCH

The promise management definition has several advantages for marketing research (see Grönroos, 2006b). First of all, it is based on current research into customer value, according to which value for customers is created in the customer's processes, *value-in-use*, and it allows for supplier and customer co-production of solutions, and, moreover, for suppliers' value co-creation together with their customers.

Secondly, the suggested definition is geared towards the very nature of marketing as a process, and thus it shifts the interest of research into marketing from structure to process. Other definitions have always been overly preoccupied with structural elements and neglected the importance of process. The process nature has been recognized implicitly only. Of course,

structural elements from traditional marketing definitions such as price and marketing communication are still important to study, but they need to be put into a process perspective.

Thirdly, the alternative definition opens up the *black box of consumption*. The consumption process becomes an integral part of marketing and the marketing process (Grönroos, 2006a). Traditionally, marketing ends with the purchase decision. Goods and services are supposed to be developed and designed so that they automatically meet the expectations of customers. According to the promise management approach, the customer's *interactions* with the resources provided by the firm become a foundational element in marketing and for marketing research. The customer may, for example, interact with service processes, a call centre, an ATM or a vending machine, an Internet web site, a telecommunication infrastructure, a delivery, installation, repair and maintenance service, a service recovery or complaints handling process, and with people, technologies, systems, information, tangible goods, and servicescapes (Bitner, 1992) involved in such interactions. Moreover, in all these interactions, the customers are present as resources, thereby being creators of value for themselves, sometimes as *sole value creators* (Grönroos, 2009: 354) using resources provided by the supplier in isolation from the supplier, sometimes together with the supplier in its capacity as co-creator of value.

Focusing on the interactions and consumption also demonstrates the need for viewing marketing as a process, including activities that go beyond a single marketing function. From a promise management perspective, marketing becomes a customer focus that should permeate organizational functions. The conventional approaches to marketing are based on a view that marketing is one function alongside other functions and, therefore, such other functions easily are perceived as nonmarketing. This view has become a straitjacket for marketing research, where at least mainstream research has not been able to cope with the changes that have taken place in the customer interfaces. Today, the content of customer interfaces has grown far beyond what a one-function marketing approach can take responsibility for.

Finally, the promise management approach recognizes the fact that everyone involved in interactions with customers are not automatically customer focused. Traditionally, marketing activities are supposed to be performed by marketing professionals only. Hence, preparing marketers for their duties has not been a central issue for marketing and for marketing research. Part-time marketers are not expected to exist and, therefore, conventional marketing approaches neither include ways of coping with them, nor trigger any interest in studying them from a marketing perspective. Enabling promises, including internal marketing, explicitly points out the need to prepare employees who are not trained as marketers and whose main task is not marketing for their marketing-related duties.

CONCLUDING REMARKS

The conventional marketing definitions with their focus on one function, exchange of pre-produced value and a structure, a set of marketing variables, rather than process, have become a hindrance for developing marketing in accordance with changes in today's business environment, at least for relationship marketing contexts. They have become equally much a straitjacket for marketing practice as for marketing research. The promise management approach helps marketing to break free from the one-function, marketing-department-based view where only full-time marketers are recognized. Its process nature helps locate the firm's true marketing resources and activities and guides planning and budgeting procedures to include all these resources and activities and not only what the marketing department (and sales) is doing. In this way, marketing becomes more relevant for the customers of a firm. If this is the case, marketing also becomes more relevant for

top management and, in the final analysis, for the firm's shareholders as well.

Finally, the marketing-as-promises-management definition is derived and formulated in such a way that it fits marketing to customers who are in nonrelational modes as well. Hence, it is not restricted to relational contexts only.

NOTES

1 As an example of another way of defining relationship marketing, Gummesson's definition, according to which relationship marketing is *marketing based on interactions, relationships and networks* (Gummesson, 2002), can be mentioned. This definition also takes a process-oriented view; following a set of interactions between customers and a firm and/or its network partners, relationships emerge, and this process may take place in a network.

2 The marketing definition for relationship marketing developed in this report is to a large extent based on Grönroos, Christian: On defining marketing: finding a new roadmap for marketing. *Marketing Theory*, 6(4) 2006b: 395–417, where the definition and its underpinning logic as well as the set of propositions have been previously published.

REFERENCES

Alderson, W. (1957) *Marketing Behavior and Executive Action: A Functionalist Approach to Marketing Theory*. Homewood, IL: Richard D. Irwin.

Bagozzi, R.P. (1975) 'Marketing as Exchange', *Journal of Marketing*, 39(October): 32–39.

Ballantyne, D. (2003) 'A Relationship-Mediated Theory of Internal Marketing', *European Journal of Marketing*, 37(9): 1242–1260.

Becker, G.S. (1965): 'A Theory of Allocation of Time', *The Economic Journal* 75(299): 493–517.

Berry, L.L. (1981) 'The Employee as Customer', *Journal of Retailing*, 3(March): 33–40.

Berry, L.L. (1995) 'Relationship Marketing of Services – Growing Interest, Emerging Perspectives', *Journal of the Academy of Marketing Science*, 23(4): 236–245.

Berry, L.L. and Parasuraman, A. (1993) 'Building a New Academic Field – The Case for Services Marketing', *Journal of Retailing*, 69(1): 13–60.

Bitner, M.J. (1992) 'Servicescapes: The Impact of Physical Surroundings on Customers and Employees', *Journal of Marketing*, 56(April): 57–71.

Bitner, M.J. (1995) 'Building Service Relationships: It's All About Promises', *Journal of the Academy of Marketing Science*. 23(4): 246–251.

Booms, B.H. and Bitner, M.J. (1982) 'Marketing Structures and Organization Structures for Service Firms', in J.H. Donnelly and W.R. George (eds) *Marketing of Services*, Chicago, IL: American Marketing Association, pp. 47–51.

Brown, S.W. (2005) 'When Executives Speak, We Should Listen and Act Differently', *Journal of Marketing*, 69(October): 2–4.

Brown, S.W. and Bitner, M.J. (2006) 'Mandating a Service Revolution for Marketing', in R.F. Lusch and S.L. Vargo (eds) *The Service-Dominant Logic of Marketing: Dialog, Debate, and Directions*, Armonk, NY: M.E. Sharpe, pp. 393–405.

Calonius, H. (1983) 'On the Promise Concept', Unpublished discussion paper. Helsinki: Hanken Swedish School of Economics Finland.

Calonius, H. (1986) 'A Market Behaviour Framework', in K. Möller and M. Paltschik (eds) *Contemporary Research in Marketing*. Proceedings from the XV Annual Conference of the European Marketing Academy, pp. 515–524. Helsinki School of Economics and Hanken Swedish School of Economics Finland (republished in 2006 in *Marketing Theory*, 6(4): 419–428.

Christopher, M., Payne, A. and Ballantyne, D. (1991) *Relationship Marketing*. Oxford: Butterworth Heinemann.

Coviello, N.E., Brodie, R.J., Danaher, P.J. and Johnston, W.J. (2002) 'How Firms Relate to Their Markets: An Empirical Examination of Contemporary Marketing Practice', *Journal of Marketing*, 66(July): 33–46.

Dixon, D.F. (1990) 'Marketing as Production: The Development of a Concept', *Journal of the Academy of Marketing Science*, 18(Fall): 337–343.

Dunne, P.A. and Barnes, J.G. (2000) 'Internal Marketing: A Relationships and Value Creation View', in R. Varey and B. Lewis (eds) *Internal Marketing: Directions for Management*. London: Routledge.

Eggert, A., Ulaga, W. and Schultz, F. (2006) 'Value Creation in the Relationship Life Cycle: A Quasi-Longitudinal Analysis', *Industrial Marketing Management*, 35: 20–37.

Eiglier, P. and Langeard, E. (1975) 'Une Approche Nouvelle du Marketing des Services', *Revue Francaise de Gestion*, 2(Novembre).

Eiglier, P. and Langeard, E. (1976) '*Principe de Politique Marketing Pour les Enterprises de Service*', Working Paper. Institute d'Administration des Enterprises, Université d'Aix-Marseille.

Fournier, S., Dobscha, S. and Mick, D.G. (1998) 'Preventing the Premature Death of Relationship Marketing', *Harvard Business Review*, 76(January–February): 42–51.

Grönroos, C (1979): *Service Marketing. A Study of the Marketing Function in Service Firms* (in Swedish with an English summary). Diss., Stockholm and Helsinki: Akademilitteratur, Marketing Technique Centre and Hanken Swedish School of Economics, Finland.

Grönroos, C. (1981) 'Internal Marketing – An Integral Part of Marketing Theory', in J.H. Donnelly and W.R. George (eds) *Marketing of Services*, Chicago, IL.: American Marketing Association, pp. 238–238.

Grönroos, C. (1982) 'An Applied Service Marketing Theory', *European Journal of Marketing*, 16(7): 30–41.

Grönroos, C. (1990) 'Relationship Approach to Marketing in Service Contexts: The Marketing and Organizational Behavior Interface', *Journal of Business Research*, 20(1): 3–11.

Grönroos, C. (1997) 'Value-Driven Relational Marketing: From Products to Resources and Competencies', *Journal of Marketing Management*, 13(5):407–419.

Grönroos, C. (1999) 'Relationship Marketing: Challenges for the Organization', *Journal of Business Research*, 46(3): 327–335.

Grönroos, C. (2000) *Service Management and Marketing. A Customer Relationship Management Approach*. Chichester: John Wiley & Sons.

Grönroos, C. (2006a) 'Adopting a Service Logic for Marketing' *Marketing Theory*, 6(3): 317–333.

Grönroos, C. (2006b): 'On Defining Marketing: Finding a New Roadmap for Marketing', *Marketing Theory*, 6(4): 395–417.

Grönroos, C. (2007) *In Search of a New Logic for Marketing. Foundation of Contemporary Theory*. Chichester: John Wiley & Co.

Grönroos, C. (2008) 'Service-Dominant Logic Revisited: Who Creates Value? And Who Co-Creates?', *European Business Review*, 20(4): forthcoming.

Grönroos, C. (2009) 'Marketing as promise management: regaining customer management for marketing', *The Journal of Business & Industrial Marketing*, 24(5/6): 351–359.

Grönroos, C. and Ojasalo, K. (2004) 'Service Productivity: Toward a Conceptualization of the Transformation of Inputs into Economic Results in Services', *Journal of Business Research*, 57(4): 414–423.

Gummesson, E. (1979) 'The Marketing of Professional Services – An Organizational Dilemma', *European Journal of Marketing*, 13(5): 308–318.

Gummesson, E. (1987) 'The New Marketing – Developing Long-Term Interactive Relationships', *Long Range Planning*, 20(4): 10–21.

Gummesson, E. (1991) 'Marketing Revisited: The Crucial Role of the Part-Time Marketer', *European Journal of Marketing*, 25(2): 60–67.

Gummesson, E. (2002) *Total Relationship Marketing*. Oxford: Butterworth Heinemann.

Gummesson, E. (2007) 'Exit *Services* Marketing – Enter *Service* Marketing', *Journal of Customer Behaviour*, 6(2): 113–141.

Håkansson, H. (ed.) (1982) *International Marketing and Purchasing of Industrial Goods*. New York: John Wiley & Co.

Håkansson, H. and Snehota, I. (1995) *Developing Relationships in Business Networks*. Routledge: London.

Harker, M.J. (1999) 'Relationship Marketing Defined? An Examination of Current Relationship Marketing Definitions', *Marketing Intelligence and Planning*, 17(1): 13–20.

Harker M.J. and Egan, J. (2006) 'The Past, Present and Future of Relationship Marketing', *Journal of Marketing Management*, 22(1–2): 215–242.

Holbrook, M.B. (1994) 'The Nature of Customer Value – An Axiology of Services in the Consumption Experience', in R.T. Rust, and O.R. Oliver (eds) *Service Quality: New Directions in Theory and Practice*. Thousand Oaks, CA: Sage Publications.

Hunt, S.D. (1976) 'The Nature and Scope of Marketing', *Journal of Marketing*, 40(July): 17–28.

Jüttner, U. and Wehrli, H.P. (1994) 'Relationship Marketing from a Value Perspective', *International Journal of Service Industry Management*, 5(5): 54–73.

Kent, R.A. (1986) 'Faith in Four Ps: an Alternative', *Journal of Marketing Management*, 2(2): 145–154.

Kotler, P. (1972) 'A Generic Concept of Marketing', *Journal of Marketing*, 36(2): 46–54.

Langeard, E. and Eiglier, P. (1987) *Servuction. Le marketing des services*. Paris: John Wiley & Sons.

Leong Y.P. and Quing W. (2006) 'Impact of Relationship Marketing Tactics (RMTs) on Switchers and Stayers in a Competitive Service Industry', *Journal of Marketing Management*, 22(1–2): 25–59.

Levitt, T. (1981) 'Marketing Intangible Products and Product Intangibles', *Harvard Business Review*, 59(May–June): 94–102.

Levitt, T. (1983) After The Sale Is Over, *Harvard Business Review*, 61 (September/October): 87–93.

Levitt, T. (1986) *The Marketing Imagination*. New York: The Free Press.

Liljander, V. and Strandvik, T. (1995) 'The Nature of Customer Relationships in Services', in T.A. Swartz, D.E. Bowen and S.W. Brown (eds) *Advances in Services Marketing and Management*, Vol. 4, Greenwich, CT: JAI Press, pp. 141–167.

Lindberg-Repo, K. and Grönroos, C. (2004) 'Conceptualising Communications Strategy from a Relational Perspective', *Industrial Marketing Management*, 33: 229–239.

Lovelock, C.H. (2000) 'Functional Integration in Services. Understanding the Links Between Marketing, Operations, and Human Resources', in T.A. Swartz and D. Iacobucci (eds) *Handbook of Services Marketing & Management*, Thousand Oaks, CA: Sage, pp. 421–437.

Lovelock, C.H. and Young, R.F. (1979) 'Look to Consumers to Increase Productivity', *Harvard Business Review*, 57(May–June): 168–178.

Lusch, R.F. and Vargo, S.L. (eds) (2006) *The Service-Dominant Logic of Marketing. Dialog, Debate, and Directions*. Armonk, N.Y.: M.E. Sharpe.

Lusch, R.F., Vargo, S.L., and O'Brien, M. (2007) 'Competing Through Service: Insights from Service-Dominant Logic', *Journal of Retailing*, 83(1): 5–18.

Marketing Renaissance (2005) 'Opportunities and Imperatives for Improving Marketing Thought, Practice, and Infrastructure', *Journal of Marketing*, 69(October): 1–25.

Miller, J.A. (1977) 'Studying Satisfaction, Modifying Models, Eliciting Expectations, Posing Problems and Making Meaningful Measurements', in H.K. Junt (ed.) *Conceptualization and Measurement of Consumer Satisfaction and Dissatisfaction*, Cambridge, Mass.: Marketing Science Institute, pp. 72–91.

Monroe, K.B. (1991) *Pricing – Making Profitable Decisions*. New York: McGraw-Hill.

Morgan, R.M. and Hunt, S.D. (1994) 'The Commitment-Trust Theory of Relationship Marketing', *Journal of Marketing*, 58(January): 20–38.

Normann, R. (2001) *Reframing Business. When the Map Changes the Landscape*. Chichester, UK: John Wiley & Sons.

Normann, R. and Ramirez, R. (1993) 'From Value Chain to Value Constellation: Designing Interactive Strategy', *Harvard Business Review*, 71(July–August): 65–77.

Ojasalo, J. (2001) 'Managing Customer Expectations in Professional Services', *Managing Service Quality*, 11(3): 200–212.

Oliver, R.L. (1980) 'A Cognitive Model of the Antecedents and Consequences of Satisfaction Decisions', *Journal of Marketing Research*, 17(November): 460–469.

Payne, A.F., Storbacka, K. and Frow, P. (2008) 'Managing the Co-Creation of Value', *Journal of the Academy of Marketing Science*, 36(1): 83–96.

Piercy, N.F. (1985) *Marketing Organization. Ana Analysis of Information Processing, Power, and Politics*. London: George Allen & Unwin.

Prahalad, C.K. and Ramaswamy, V. (2004) *The Future of Competition: Co-Creating Unique Value with Customers*. Boston, MA: Harvard Business School Press.

Pyle, J.F. (1931) *Marketing Principles*. New York: McGraw-Hill.

Ravald, A. and Grönroos, C. (1996) 'The Value Concept and Relationship Marketing', *European Journal of Marketing*, 30(2): 19–30.

Reinartz, W. and Kumar, V. (2002) 'The Mismanagement of Customer Loyalty', *Harvard Business Review*, 80(July–September): 4–12.

Rust, R.T. and Oliver, R.L. (1994) Service Quality: Insights and managerial Implications from the Frontier. In R.T. Rust and R.L. Oliver (eds) *Service Quality: New Directions for Theory and Practice*, Thousand Oaks, CA: Sage, pp.1–20.

Rust, R.T., Zahorik, A.J. and Keiningham, T.L. (1994) *Return on Quality: Measuring the Financial Impact of Your Company's Quest for Quality*. Chicago, IL: Richard D. Irwin.

Ryals, L. (2005) 'Making Customer Relationship Management Work: The Measurement and Profitable Management of Customer Relationships', *Journal of Marketing*, 69(October): 252–261.

Sääksjärvi, M., Hellén, K., Gummerus, J. and Grönroos, C. (2007) 'Love at First Sight or a Long-Term Affair? Different Relationship Levels as Predictors of Customer Commitment', *Journal of Relationship Marketing*, 6(1): 45–61.

Schneider, B. and Bowen, D.E. (1995) *Winning the Service Game*. Boston, MA: Harvard Business School Press.

Sheth, J.N. and Parvatiyar, A. (1995) 'The Evolution of Relationship Marketing', *International Business Review*, 4(4): 397–418.

Sheth, J.N. and Uslay, C. (2007) 'Implications of the Revised Definition of Marketing: From Exchange to Value Creation', *Journal of Public Policy and Marketing*, 26(2): 302–307.

Srinivasan, S.S., Anderson, R. and Ponnavolu, K. (2002) 'Customer Loyalty in E-Commerce: An Exploration of Its Antecedents and Consequences', *Journal of Retailing*, 78(1): 41–50.

Storbacka, K. and Lehtinen, J.R. (2001) *Customer Relationship Management*. Singapore: McGraw-Hill.

Strandvik, T. (2000) 'Relationsmarknadsföringens arbetsfält (The relationship marketing field)', in C. Grönroos and R. Järvinen (eds) *Palvelut ja Asiakassuhteet Markkinoinnin Polttopisteessä (Marketing: Services and Customer Relationships in Focus)*, Helsinki, Finland: Kauppakaari, pp. 164–77.

Vandermerwe, S. (1996) 'Becoming a Customer "Owning" Company', *Long Range Planning*, 29(6): 770–782.

Vargo, S.L. and Lusch, R.F. (2004) 'Evolving to a new dominant logic for marketing', *Journal of Marketing*, 68(January): 1–17.

Vargo, S.L. and Lusch, R.F. (2008) Service Dominant Logic: Continuing the Evolution. *Journal of the Academy of Marketing Science*, 36(1):1–10.

Verhoef, P.C. (2003) 'Understanding the Effect of Customer Relationship Management Efforts on Customer Retention and Customer Share Development', *Journal of Marketing*, 67(October): 30–45.

Webster Jr., F.E. (1992) 'The Changing Role of Marketing in the Corporation', *Journal of Marketing*, 56(October): 1–17.

Webster Jr., F.E., Malter, A.J., and Ganesan, S. (2005) 'The Decline and Dispersion of

Marketing Competence', *MIT Sloan Management Review*, 46(4): 35–43.

Wikström, S. (1996) 'Value Creation by Company–Consumer Interaction', *Journal of Marketing Management*, 12: 359–374.

Woodruff, R.B. and Gardial, S. (1996) *Know Your Customers – New Approaches to Understanding Customer Value and Satisfaction*. Oxford: Blackwell Publishers.

Zeithaml, V.A. (1988) 'Consumer Perception of Price, Quality and Value: A Means-End Model and a Synthesis of Evidence', *Journal of Marketing*, 52(July): 2–22.

Zeithaml, V.A., Parasuraman, A., and Berry, L.L. (1988) 'Communication and Control Processes in the Delivery of Service Quality', *Journal of Marketing*, 64(April): 35–49.

APPENDIX

Marketing as promise management – the underpinning logic and definition

Propositions based on the underpinning logic of the promise management approach:

1a: *Value is not delivered by a firm to customers but created in customer processes through assistance to those processes and through the firm's co-creation in interactions with customers.*

1b: *The role of marketing is, on one hand, to develop and communicate value propositions to customers, and on the other hand, to assist customers' value creation through goods, service activities, information, and other resources as well as through interactions where co-creation of value with the customers can take place.*

2a: *Customers can be in relational as well as nonrelational modes, thus they do not always appreciate being approached in a relational manner by firms, and hence, even though managing customers as relationship often may be effective, it cannot be considered a generic approach to relating a customer to the firm.*

2b: *In an implicit way, a marketing definition must allow both for relational and nonrelational marketing strategies and activities.*

3a: *Marketing cannot be implemented by one organizational function of marketing specialists, the full-time marketers, only.*

3b: *Marketing needs a customer focus throughout the organization, thus involving both full-time marketers totally or predominantly trained to take a customer focus and part-time marketers, who when performing their tasks from the outset are not at all or only partly trained to take a customer focus.*

3c: *To be effective, marketing also requires that technologies, information systems and other*

systems are designed and function in a customer-focused manner.

3d: *As customers participate in interactions with the firm's resources and, therefore, influence the customer orientation of these interactions, they actively participate in marketing as well. Hence, customers' role as a marketing resource, in addition to their roles as buyers and consumers and users has to be recognized in marketing.*

4a: *Customers have explicit as well as implicit, unrealistic and fuzzy expectations and these expectations should be fulfilled by the performance of the firm.*

4b: *Fulfilment of promises in a customer-focused manner requires internal marketing efforts as promise enablers.*

4c: *Customer-focused technologies, information systems, and other systems as well as appropriate leadership are also required to support a customer-focused performance by part-time marketers.*

4d: *Helping customers to participate in customer–firm interactions in ways that have a favourable marketing impact on them is also required for marketing to be successful.*

4e: *Making promises, supported by internal activities, such as internal marketing geared towards the fulfilment of expectations created by promises made, as well as technology, systems and leadership support, and fulfilling expectations created by promises made, form a firm's marketing process.*

Marketing as promise management – definition

Marketing is a customer focus that permeates organizational functions and processes, and is geared towards making promises through value proposition, enabling the fulfilment of individual expectations created by such promises and fulfilling such expectations through assistance to customers' value-generating processes, thereby supporting value creation in the firm's as well as its customers' and other stakeholders' processes. (Grönroos, 2006b: 407)

Contemporary and Future Issues in Marketing Theory

Marketing Systems, Macromarketing and the Quality of Life

Roger A. Layton

'No man is an island, entire of itself'.

John Donne, *Meditation* XVII

This chapter is about marketing systems, the networked structures and the assortments generated that emerge from voluntary exchanges between sellers and buyers. It is about the emergence of distribution channels and supply chains, of industry clusters, business ecosystems and shopping malls, of traditional marketplaces and sophisticated auction mechanisms, of 'silk roads' and trading empires. Contemporary marketing theory provides us with rich insights into the decision processes of the sellers and buyers who participate in economic exchange but has had relatively little to say about the nature of the networks that emerge from these interactions. Not only are these emergent networks of interest in their own right, but they also suggest how we might think about the way micro decisions create macro outcomes in marketing. If marketing is indeed about the 'creation and delivery of a standard of living'

then an understanding of the micro–macro interface is central to our discipline.

The concept of a marketing system also acts as a bridge between contemporary marketing theory and practice, and the field of macromarketing. In 1977, Shelby Hunt defined macromarketing as 'the study of (a) marketing systems, (b) the impact and consequences of marketing systems on society and (c) the impact and consequences of society on marketing systems'. This perspective is taking on fresh urgency as we attempt to understand the interaction between day-to-day marketing decisions, consumer choices and critical problem areas such as obesity, food, finance, energy and environment.

Just what is a marketing system? The 'road map' set out in Figure 24.1 shows the logical structure of this chapter as it suggests an answer to this question and goes on to explore the interdependencies between the structure and dynamics of marketing systems, the wider institutional/technological or knowledge environment, and the resulting impacts on

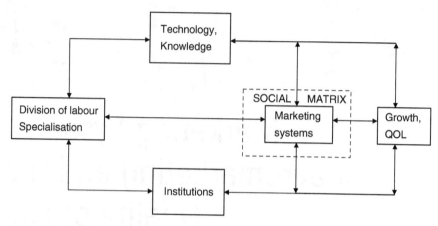

Figure 24.1 The road map.

regional or national economic growth, quality of life and happiness. Marketing systems provide an important, often overlooked, link between specialisation and division of labour and the realities of economic growth and quality of life. Where there is specialisation and division of labour, there is also diversity in the goods and services offered for trade, and where there is trade there are markets and thus marketing systems. The efficiency and effectiveness with which these systems do what they do is central to the creation and delivery of quality of life.

We begin with a somewhat unusual example of a marketing system – that of a community store in a remote aboriginal township in Central Australia. The isolation of the store brings many aspects of a marketing system into stark relief and it will serve as an ongoing example throughout the chapter. In particular, an appreciation of the social matrix in which the store is embedded is essential in understanding the choices made by both managers and customers.

A definition of a marketing system is then set out, and consideration given to the ways in which marketing systems can emerge from otherwise autarchic or isolated exchange. The basic idea goes back to Adam Smith, whose insights into specialisation and the division of labour as essential drivers of economic growth were pivotal. However, division of labour also implies the need for markets where specialised

outputs can be exchanged. For these to develop and succeed, there is a need for an underlying stable, efficient and fair social contract or common understanding that facilitates economic exchange. From this starting point, several streams of thought show how complex multilevel structures can emerge from simple, localised exchange. These insights flow from interdisciplinary studies in fields including the new institutional economics, evolutionary game theory and the agent-based modelling of complex adaptive systems, and from research in economic sociology and anthropology. From this work, four distinctive types of marketing system are identified – autarchic or random, emergent, structured and purposeful. Over time, in response to external and internal change autarchic systems shift to emergent, emergent systems may become structured or purposeful, and these all may co-exist, collapse or morph into new higher order structures. All of these changes will be deeply influenced by the social matrix in which the marketing system of interest is embedded. Marketing systems have emerged in many societies and at many points in time and, while reflecting the unique social matrix in which each is embedded, all have much in common. Questions of structure, function and dynamics, efficiency and effectiveness, adaptation and evolution, resilience and collapse, are just some of the issues that now take on new significance.

This leads directly to a closer examination of the elements making up a marketing system. These include the mix of exchange logics and contexts or settings characterising exchange in a marketing system; the flows of ownership, possession, finance, risk and information that link system participants; the changing roles filled by participants in these flows; the structure and function of the resulting exchange networks; the existence (or lack of) an underlying organising principle; the assortments of goods, services, experiences and ideas that are created and made available in response to perceived customer interests; and the customers or customer groups that may appear at several points in a marketing system.

The links between marketing systems, their structure and dynamics, and economic growth and quality of life outcomes are then considered. This opens up questions as to just what drives regional or local economic growth, an area of considerable interest and uncertainty at present. It is suggested that in addition to the drivers of knowledge/technology/invention and innovation highlighted, for example, by economists including Scherer (1999), Baumol (2002), Mokyr (2002) and the institutional/cultural drivers identified by historians such as North (2005), Grief (2006). There is a third important driver of growth inherent in the successful operation of marketing systems, for within a given institutional framework, these translate technology into assortments of goods, services, experiences and ideas, that in turn provide the basis for quality of life. As the road map suggests, both the knowledge/technology and institutional drivers are themselves modified by a complex network of feedback relationships that work through the marketing systems holding the overall economy together. In this sense, the drivers are in part endogenous, determined by system outcomes, and in part exogenous, influenced by external environmental forces.

By reasserting the importance of the marketing systems within which voluntary economic exchange is embedded, the chapter provides a basis for the extension of marketing theory beyond the specifics of contemporary management to a consideration of the wider possibilities inherent in the emergence of marketing as a social discipline or science concerned with the distinctive aspects of exchange embodied in a study of marketing systems.

MARKETING IN A FRONTIER ECONOMY

Yuendumu is not quite at the end of the road, but close. It is a small desert township of some 900 people, located on traditional aboriginal lands in the centre of Australia about 300 kilometres northwest of Alice Springs along the Tanami Track. The next small settlement along the Tanami is at Rabbit Flat, several hundred kilometres further along the dirt road.

Yuendumu is a service and administrative centre for the local aboriginal community and for a scattering of cattle stations located up to 150 kilometres away. There are perhaps 100 houses, not counting bush shanty dwellings on the outskirts, a community centre, a welfare agency, a small shale and gravel mine operated by the Yuendumu Mining Company, an airstrip, post office, museum, school, Baptist Church, and two stores, one operated by the Yuendumu Social Club and the other by Yuendumu Mining. While English is spoken, the most common language is Warlpiri.

The town had its origin as a ration depot for local aboriginal tribes in 1946. Before then, relations between the black and white communities had been difficult, arising from ongoing conflict between cattle station operators and traditional landowners. In the years since 1946, while traditional land rights have been recognised, the interaction between the white and black communities has not been easy. For the black community, which is by far the most numerous, problems stemming from unemployment, poor education, dependence on public funding, alcohol, drugs and petrol sniffing, combined with large numbers of younger people who have at least partly rejected traditional lifestyles, have created an in-between world of uncertainty, doubt and often despair.

This is the setting for these two retail stores, deeply embedded in a distinctive social matrix, historically and culturally determined, and similar to the settings of most remote area stores in the Northern Territory. These stores operate in a 'frontier economy' (McDonnell and Martin, 2002), at the intersection of Western, developed, competitive market practices, and those where traditional community or group aboriginal values and practices are dominant. As McDonnell and Martin point out, 'aboriginal people bring values and practices to bear on their choices and actions as consumers which derive their forms and meanings from within the aboriginal community' (p. 3). The outcome is a market place where a shifting compromise between new and old ways is essential, where performance criteria reflect both traditional and Western values, and where decision processes are often based less on self interest than on group or family values and needs.

The more important of the two stores is the community store operated by the Yuendumu Social Club. This is typical of over 150 similar stores operated by local community groups in many parts of remote Australia. Average annual sales of these stores are around US$1 million, with gross margins of 30 per cent and net profit margins of between 3.0 per cent and 3.5 per cent (McDonnell and Martin, 2002: 19). The stores carry a range of food and non-food items, provide support services in the form of banking facilities, cooperate in the provision of welfare and other payments, and share profits with the community at large.

Superficially, there is little here to suggest anything other than normal retail outcomes. Looking a little closer, however, the operation of community stores raise a wide range of managerial and social challenges to conventional retail practice, with implications for even wider issues in the economic and social development of aboriginal communities across Australia. These challenges include

the tensions between the cultural obligations of the aboriginals and the legal obligations under Australian law that emerge in the governance of community stores; the balance to be struck in assessing store performance between commercial viability and the generation of social capital through the fostering of social relationships and alliances. Cultural obligations are at risk in managing the implications of demand sharing ('humbugging') where pressure is placed on the store owners/managers to share access to assets and equipment such as cars within kinship groups or where conflicts arise between 'aboriginal hierarchies of power and authority and the business hierarchy of the store' (McDonnell and Martin, 2002: 26) when elders seek to overrule the business decisions of younger kin. In some situations, money is replaced by a social calculus in which 'value in use' can supersede 'value in exchange' to the point where price is irrelevant. These and similar concerns are strengthened when, as often, levels of literacy and numeracy are low. Brand loyalty is high reflecting dependency on pictorial representation and demand is often price inelastic. Packaging changes can lead to dramatic drops in sales. Prices are often high, reflecting not only distance but also lack of competition. This is the world of a frontier economy where the community store, its management and its customers sit uneasily between two contrasting ways of life.

The community store in Yuendumu together with its suppliers and customers is an example of a marketing system. The individual transactions between the store and its customers, or between distributors, suppliers and the store, are examples of marketing systems in a disaggregated or microform. At a higher level of aggregation, the store in Yuendumu is part of a marketing system comprising all 150 or so similar stores across remote areas of Australia. These in turn can be thought of as part of a still wider system of retail distribution in Australia. Returning to Yuendumu, a more inclusive marketing system can be defined in terms of all retailing in the town, comprising the two retail stores, their suppliers and customers, and, depending on the interests of the analyst, illegal 'back door' sales of products such as petrol, alcohol, drugs and pornography. Specific product centered marketing systems at differing levels of aggregation can be identified for each major commodity or service group – such as petrol, alcohol, food, clothing, aboriginal art originating in the town and financial services – with the Yuendumu store as a participant in most.

Intersecting and overlapping marketing systems like these can be identified in most, if not all, human communities, and provide the immediate context or environment for the myriad of detailed management decisions and consumer choices that are central to contemporary marketing theory and practice. Moreover, just as the Yuendumu community store is embedded in a defining social matrix, so too, are the marketing systems found in every human community. It is an understanding of interacting, multilevel marketing systems like those found in Yuendumu that links micro with macro in the study of markets and marketing.

Marketing systems are ubiquitous. They form and reform over time, in much the same way as eddies come and go in a fast moving current of water. They emerge, grow, change, adapt and evolve in response to the immediate and more distant environments in which they are located. They compete, sometimes merging, sometimes collapsing and disappearing. They are dynamic, rarely in equilibrium. They are multilevel in nature, with systems forming and reforming within systems, interacting with systems at higher and lower levels of aggregation. They occupy the middle ground between individual buyer and seller decision processes and outcomes, and the aggregate marketing system (Wilkie and Moore, 1999). Above all, the efficiency and effectiveness with which each individual system does what it does, is essential to the realisation of improving standards of living in human communities in all societies, linking the multitude of daily transactions that are indeed 'the structures of everyday life' (Braudel, 1979) through complex social and marketing hierarchies of

systems, with overall economic performance and quality of life.

MARKETING SYSTEMS DEFINED

Adapting slightly the definition suggested by Layton (2007), a marketing system can be defined as follows:

A marketing system is:

(a) A network of individuals, groups and/or entities
(b) Embedded in a social matrix
(c) Linked directly or indirectly through sequential or shared participation in economic exchange
(d) Which jointly creates, assembles, transforms and makes available
(e) Assortments of products, services, experiences and ideas
(f) Provided in response to customer demand

Does the Yuendumu community store fit this pattern? The first step is to identify the individuals, groups and entities that comprise the focal system and those that comprise any related or overlapping systems needed to understand the focal system. For the Yuendumu community store, the focal system centres on the store itself, and includes at least the agents/suppliers/distributors located primarily in Alice Springs and Darwin, the community store, and the customers – individuals, households, family or kinship groups.

Relationships between the store and each of these individuals or entities are largely defined by the aboriginal culture of the Warlpiri people, together with the social structures associated with the operation of the townships' administrative, welfare, education, religious, mining and art centres. Although the participants in the community store marketing system are linked in many ways, social and cultural, it is the links grounded in economic exchange that define the marketing system. With few exceptions, economic exchange in this system involves the offer and purchase of goods and services on the part of the store and its customers, or between the store and its suppliers. Some transactions may involve barter between two or more parties, some might require careful and skilful bargaining and some are complex deals that turn on an understanding of the social and economic tradeoffs each party has to make. Most, however, will be routine purchases filling shopping baskets or finalising regular supply orders with distributors. Underlying all these transactions are flows of ownership (such as direct or leased sale), possession (involving transport and storage providers), finance (where credit provision or welfare payments and the 'book up' system in Yuendumu are important), risk (insurance and product safety) and perhaps most important the flows of information between each and all of the participants.

The primary role of the marketing system is to put in place assortments of goods, services, experiences and ideas. In Yuendumu, the community store has a relatively wide range of goods, food and nonfood available, provides a range of support services including product advice, some counselling, banking and welfare administration, and in the spirit of Oldenburg's (2001) 'third place', serves as an essential facility for the community at large. It holds the collection of sporting trophies won by the local football team, provides a meeting place where needed, in this way, offering 'experiences' and perhaps 'ideas' as well as the usual retail facilities. Many of the benefits offered in this way are in practice jointly created and/or co-produced as suggested by Vargo and Lusch (2004).

Finally, the system as a whole is responsive to customer demand. If goods and services sought by customers are not offered then the gap is usually filled, and for those goods or services offered, for which there is little demand, a deletion usually occurs. There may be lags, often substantial, involved, but overall the system adapts to changing patterns of customer needs. The mechanism underlying these processes was identified by Alderson (1965), as one where perceived discrepancy drives adaptation.

Once the marketing system or systems of interest have been identified, the social matrix in which the system and/or its major components are embedded can be specified. For the

community store in Yuendumu, this is relatively straightforward, but for the wider system of community stores across remote Australia, it may be important to see the social matrix as comprising the many separate, related, communities making up the outback way of life in the Northern Territory.

Other examples of embedded marketing systems where the importance of the social matrix is evident can be found in the study by Rabo (2005) of merchants in the *souk* of Aleppo, the historical analysis of the trans-Sahara caravans by Lydon (2008) where each caravan is in effect a moving or mobile marketing system, or the early work of Dewey (1962) in a study of peasant marketing systems in Java. Varman and Costa (2008) highlight the importance of embedding a marketing system in a social context in a detailed study of the Bijoygarth marketplace in Calcutta, reconstructing 'the market as a socially embedded institution in which community ties are formed and sustained' (p. 141).

MARKETS AND MARKETING SYSTEMS

The economic exchange that is of interest in the emergence of marketing systems refers to socially embedded exchange transactions that are voluntary, in that each party has a power of veto and freely agrees to the terms, and which involve an economic quid pro quo. This, to an extent, excludes situations where instead of relying on exchange through markets, community needs are satisfied though reciprocative or redistributive social mechanisms. However, as Polanyi in Polanyi et al (1957) notes, there is usually a mixture of these three mechanisms with one being dominant. We are concerned here with situations where market exchange is the dominant, although not always the only mechanism.

Alderson (1965) suggested that exchange will occur if both parties are able to improve the value or potency of the assortments each hold as a result. To the extent that interest centres on the buyer–seller transaction *per se* the linkage in the marketing system is direct; where interest extends beyond the immediate transaction to the wider context in which it occurs, where participants in the transaction benefit from shared costs, risks, infrastructure or information, shared across many sellers and buyers, the relevant linkages are indirect as well as direct. In either case, the strength of the linkages may range from the transitory or casual to long-term relationships reflecting shared social, economic or political interests or commitments.

A market is a forum for carrying out such exchanges (McMillan, 2002) and will often in itself constitute a marketing system. While a market may simply emerge as a consequence of a flow of exchange transactions over time, it may also be considered to be a social construction that can be subject to purposeful design. McMillan suggests that market design would be concerned with 'the mechanisms that organise buying and selling; channels for the flow of information; state-set laws and regulations that define property rights and sustain contracting; and the market's culture, its self-regulating norms, codes and conventions' (McMillan, 2002: 9).

A marketing system will often link many such markets in the creation, assembly, transformation and dispersion of assortments in response to customer demand. Parallel marketing systems are found where structurally distinct marketing systems coexist in serving the same or similar sets of needs. Examples include food marketing systems where an informal marketing system parallels a formal, modern supermarket system; the shadow economy, which emerged in Zimbabwe as a result of hyper-inflation in 2007 (Gappah, 2008); and the growth of cyberspace marketing alternatives to the bricks and mortar of the shopping mall that was in turn an alternative to the local mom-and-pop stores. In many of these situations, the relation between the parallel systems is changing, with one gradually supplanting the other. This is the case with the introduction of supermarket retailing in many countries such as China, where both the state-owned distribution system and informal peasant markets are being gradually replaced by supermarkets, with the old 'wet markets' being auctioned off to regional supermarket chains (Ho, 2005). The interface between the formal and informal economies in a developing community is often a continuing source of friction, where regulation, high interest rates, inaccessible property rights and poor intersector mobility are critical drivers (Arnould and Mohr, 2005; De Soto, 2000; Guha-Khasnobis et al, 2006; Layton, 1988; Rosa and Viswanathan, 2007).

MARKETING SYSTEMS: THE EMERGENCE OF STRUCTURE

Marketing systems can be thought of as multilevel, complex adaptive systems, growing, adapting, emerging and evolving in environments driven by institutional and knowledge-based change. It is this point of view that opens the door to an understanding of the dynamic role that marketing systems can and do play in the processes of economic growth, both nationally and locally. Contemporary growth economics highlights the importance of institutions ('the rules of the game') interacting with knowledge, embodied in entrepreneurial innovation, as drivers of economic growth (Helpman, 2004). However, both sets of factors take effect through multilevel marketing systems that create and deliver on an everyday basis the assortments of goods, services, experiences and ideas that underpin growth in quality of life. These are the 'structures of everyday life' described so eloquently by Braudel (1979), that in turn contribute to and shape the institutional and knowledge-based drivers of growth.

A logical starting point for the emergence of structure in marketing systems outlined in the foregoing section can be found in the ideas of Adam Smith (1776). For Smith, wealth generation flowed from specialisation and the division of labour. These benefits, however, were limited by the extent of the market and that in turn was strongly influenced by transportation costs and population size (Buchanan, 2004). In 1928, Young took matters further with what has come to be called the Smith-Young theorem on the network effects of specialisation (Cheng and Yang, 2004), stating that not only does the division of labour depend on the extent of the market, but also the extent of the market also depends on the division of labour. Young noted that while individuals were free to choose the level of specialisation that was best suited to their needs, the benefits that flowed would depend on the extent of the market, on both the number of participants and the number of different goods on offer. The feedback loop introduced in this way opened the door to the idea of a 'moving' or dynamic equilibrium and endogenised the number of goods on offer. The extent of the market now was not simply measured by the size of the relevant population, but also by the number of goods and the proportion of all goods that were traded. Growth in the extent of the market offered increased gains from trade and opened the door to further economic growth, which in turn led to increased market diversity. Increases in role complexity arising from increased social division of labour were then reflected in the emergence of institutions that led to the generation of new wealth. This way of thinking, which focuses on growth rather than allocation is central to the new classical school of economists (Yang, 2001) and raises many questions about the detailed processes involved, such as the time periods likely to be needed under differing environmental conditions; the likelihoods of growth, equilibrium, or collapse; and the staged development of both the primitive and sophisticated marketing systems found in the world today.

This brief overview highlights the pivotal role of assortment or diversity in traded goods (and services) as specialisation grows. For both producers and consumers the decision to trade, in principle, involves much more than a single commodity. Consumers seek and acquire assortments that match their needs,

and producers will seek to put together product combinations that build on accessing the distinctive competences needed to reap the benefits of specialisation through increasing returns. In this world view, technology and the growth of knowledge, as well as the emergence of supporting institutions, play essential roles in reducing or managing transaction and coordination costs, in facilitating the transactions needed for the system to function, in creating successive waves of innovation, and in creating new sets of needs on the part of consumers as they become aware of the opportunities generated by new knowledge (Bharadwaj et al., 2005).

With increasing specialisation, the networks of trade connections linking sellers and buyers become increasingly dense and the emergence of macro patterns more likely. Since exchange is not cost-free and increasing returns are often available, further specialisation in trade related roles and function is also likely. This will in turn lead to increasing specialisation within markets, and more generally in the structure and functioning of marketing systems. A further consequence is that role specialisation within the emerging patterns may itself lead to a next generation of patterns or emergent structures in which the elements or agents are themselves marketing systems. These effects will be heightened by factors including changes in technology, improvements in 'learning by doing', and institutional or infrastructure development. Finally, it should be noted that the same element or agent (producer or consumer) may participate in many more than one marketing system at any one time. Depending on the specification (including boundaries) of the marketing system or systems of interest, multiple participations may bring with it important spillover effects. An example may be found in remote aboriginal communities such as Yuendumu where the tensions between alcohol (a quasi-legal marketing system) and food/grocery purchasing for a family can often be devastating.

An alternative, complementary approach to the emergence of structure as marketing systems grow and change has its roots in economic sociology and anthropology. It is micro in nature and focuses on the individual choices made by producers and consumers as they deal with each other through voluntary economic exchange. From a starting point where each individual in a society is aware of but independent of all others, living an isolated self-sufficient life, is it possible for the kind of social contract to emerge (Seabright, 2004; Skyrms, 1996, 2004) needed to underpin complex exchange? Binmore (2005) shows, using simple models from evolutionary game theory, that a social contract, 'a set of common understandings that allow the citizens of a society to coordinate their efforts' (p. 3) can indeed emerge. For our purposes this matters, as such a social contract would facilitate the growth of individual barter or exchange and over time allow for the growth of primitive marketing systems.

Binmore suggests that three criteria must be satisfied if a social contract is to be acceptable to participants. These are stability, efficiency and fairness. Stability or equilibrium is essential for survival; efficiency in the sense that nothing is wasted, is essential if a social contract is to compete successfully with other options; and fairness, he suggests, 'is evolution's solution to the equilibrium selection problem of our game of life' (p. 14). His approach to an understanding of a social contract begins with a study of the relationships between two participants captured in a generalised, two-person, evolutionary game framework. Applying these ideas to exchange between two individuals he shows that the evolutionary games considered will often have multiple (Nash) equilibria, each potentially differing in terms of quality of life outcomes. At one extreme, as Bowles et al. (2006) point out, the equilibrium may in fact be a poverty trap arising from factors such as initial inequalities, limited access to education, health etc. resources, and the problems of unchecked criminality, all combining to force a society into a low level equilibrium, which is difficult to escape. Binmore goes on to suggest that higher-level

equilibria, however, may be achievable through the exercise of altruism, and that reciprocal altruism may be sufficient in a situation where participants are engaged in repeated, long term games, to bring about a workable social contract. Stability, in the sense of a Nash equilibrium, is possible, and efficiency likely as individuals strive to better their position.

Fairness is a little more difficult. While noting that the fairness norms implicit in a social contract may vary widely across primitive and advanced human societies they do exist, reflecting both cultural and genetic factors. Binmore (p. 15) argues for their origin in the 'original position' proposed by Rawls (1972), where members of a society 'are asked to envisage the social contract to which they would agree if their current roles were concealed from them behind a veil of ignorance'. Where all three criteria are satisfied, a continuing social contract is likely to form leading to the emergence of marketing systems.

A third approach uses simulation through agent-based modelling to examine the possibility of emergent structures appearing in initially autarchic or random marketplaces. Beginning with a simple simulation environment, in which heterogeneous agents with limited cognitive abilities interact with each other and the environment, Epstein and Axtell (1996) show the emergence of patterns similar to those observed in the real world. Inequality in the ownership of scarce resources emerged quickly. In a simulated world where there were at least two kinds of goods, and trade was allowed, limited optimisation of agent choice yielded outcomes where a primitive form of money came into existence, specialist traders evolved, credit networks of lenders and borrowers established, and price convergence, initially localised, became widespread. More recently, Axtell (1999) explored the conditions under which clusters of agents form into firms and showed that properties of these clusters such as firm size and growth rates, were similar to empirical distributions.

MARKETING SYSTEMS: GROWTH, EVOLUTION AND COLLAPSE

Looking back over the examples of marketing systems that were noted earlier in this chapter four broad recurring patterns could be identified. These are labelled autarchic, emergent, structured and purposeful.

The first, autarchic systems, are found in the early stages of market development where individuals or households are largely self-sufficient, poorly informed outside the immediate family or group, and include barter, sharing or reciprocity within and between households within a community, or the limited boundary exchanges found among neighbouring tribes or groups. While the obvious example of autarchic marketing systems is to be found among foraging or subsistence societies, it is also possible that disaster, whether due to causes such as nature, war, disease, or simply a consequence of a 'tragedy of the commons' (Diamond, 2005), may reduce a sophisticated marketing system to something close to autarchy.

Although the four patterns are separately identified, in practice there is a degree of overlap as one pattern evolves or drifts towards another. Autarchic systems drift towards emergent systems, as an informal patterning emerges from the interactions of individual traders, due initially to specialisation and heterogeneity in needs, influenced by kin or tribal relationships, intensification of resource use, scarcity due perhaps to unexpected climate change, increasing diversity over time of household needs and wants, population growth and agglomeration (Brookfield, 1969; Firth, 1966; Gudeman, 2001). In this process, competition is increasingly substituted for regulated or socially controlled outcomes. Trade within and between communities grows and assortments offered and sought widen and deepen. An acceptable medium of exchange is identified and measurements standardised leading to coherent price structures. With the formalisation of these basic elements, repetitive trading links are established and transitory marketplaces become

fixed with increasing trade volumes. Hawkers, street vendors and other mobile traders grow in importance and regional markets emerge. An important phase is initiated when groups of traders form into firms, associations or networks to reduce costs and exploit increasing returns; when product differentiation and local brands take root, specialist markets develop and specialist roles such as those associated with retailing, wholesaling, brokers or agents, information sources, and enforcement emerge. Where and when some or all of these patterns can be identified, the marketing system can be called emergent.

The specific path that this development takes is deeply influenced by the formal and informal rules, beliefs, and norms held by the community within which the marketing system is changing (Gudeman, 2001). Sociocultural factors including social structure and/or hierarchy; the powers, attitudes and interests of rulers, government leaders, politicians and officials; attitudes towards innovation and entrepreneurship; the existence of a common language and effective communication channels; respect for and access to property rights; and the existence of a stable, efficient and (potentially) fair social contract referred to earlier are all examples of important institutional factors. Added to this list are the constraints and opportunities created by geography, history and physical infrastructure such as distance or isolation; ease of access by sea, river or land; resource endowments; and the cumulative effects of history. For the most part, factors such as these change slowly, establishing the 'limits of the possible' in the growth and operation of marketing systems at all levels of aggregation (Clark, 2007).

A second set of factors that shape the development path taken by a marketing system lie in the changing physical and social technologies open to system participants. These may change swiftly or abruptly and have far-reaching consequences, facilitating the evolution of new organisational forms, widening and deepening assortments offered and sought, linking markets otherwise separate, and changing perceptions of costs, time and distance. The impact of these external factors is often significant in initiating or facilitating the transition from an emergent system to one that is structured or purposeful. This shift is one that transforms traditional market structures into systems capable of rapid growth and sustained transformation. The critical driver in this transformation is the emergence of corporate entities. With the passage of time, dealing with factors such as a complex institutional environment, or exploiting new technologies that often required increased scale, leads to organisational forms enabling centralised control and communication. Multidivisional firms become ubiquitous in many marketing systems, and managers begin to experiment with new organisational forms based on alliances or networks of cooperating enterprises that would further enhance a fit between organisational design, competitive strategy and environment (Roberts, 2004). In this way, emerging marketing systems begin the transition to structured or purposeful systems. The resulting structured marketing systems typically comprise many corporate entities, each of which in isolation could be considered a purposeful or a structured system, that may range in size from small to very large, and include single firms, as well as alliances or networks of firms cooperating in production, distribution or innovation.

In a purposeful marketing system, the distinguishing characteristic is the use of economic or political power to direct flows of transactions in ways that contribute to the goals of the entity exercising power. Most vertically integrated marketing systems fall into this group. Somewhere between purposeful and structured marketing systems, depending on the degree of centralised control, are the business ecosystems discussed by Moore (1996) and Iansiti and Levien (2004), typically comprising a large number of loosely connected participants, often individually purposeful, acting as a community, each relying for mutual effectiveness and survival on each other through a complex web of interdependencies.

Can marketing systems decline, disintegrate or fail? This is clearly possible in the face of natural or political catastrophes such as the recent tsunami in Aceh, the wars in the Balkans (Shultz et al., 2005), or the collapse of the Zimbabwean economy in 2007. In each case, the relevant marketing systems revert to near autarchy and growth begins again. Since path dependence is a common characteristic of complex systems, the structure and dynamics of the resulting marketing systems may differ considerably from the historical patterns. This leaves open the possibility that a marketing system might decline, disintegrate or fail not only as a result of catastrophe, but also as a consequence of the interaction of internal and external factors, raising the now important question of sustainability. Holling (2001) explored this possibility in the context of multilevel economic, ecological and social systems, suggesting that sustainable growth for a system such as a marketing system might be achievable through the fostering of adaptive capabilities and the creation of opportunity. He saw sustainable growth being achieved in a multilevel systemic context, where each level operated 'at its own pace, protected from above by slower, larger levels, but invigorated from below by smaller, faster cycles of innovation' (p. 390).

An ability to generate and test innovations within a level is an essential element in Holling's model. He points to an 'adaptive cycle' where the interaction over time of three variables – wealth or capability, connectedness and resilience – leads to a repetitive cycle beginning with longer term or slow growth where 'skills, networks of human relationships, and mutual trust are developed incrementally and integrated' (p. 394). This, in turn, leads to a phase where systemic connectedness grows to the point where the system becomes increasingly rigid, losing resilience, and thus the ability to absorb external change, becoming 'an accident waiting to happen', Finally, a phase begins of rapid, often far-reaching reorganisation, novelty and experiment, similar to the 'creative

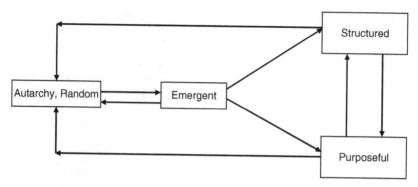

Figure 24.2   Growth, emergence and evolution in marketing systems.

destruction' described by Schumpeter. The cycle begins again with a phase where the potential for growth is re-established, the accumulation of resources is recommenced, interconnectedness is low, resilience is high, leading in turn once again into the growth phase. This new start may simply repeat an earlier cycle, morph or evolve into a new systemic structure, or perhaps fall into a low level 'poverty trap' (Gunderson and Holling, 2001; Homer-Dixon, 2006).

The dynamics of marketing system, growth, adaptation and evolution sketched in the preceding section are depicted in Figure 24.2.

It will be evident that the concept of a marketing system goes much beyond the traditional interest in channel structures, supply chains, logistics systems, and retailing found in much of the marketing literature. Figure 24.3 maps many of the systems considered in this chapter where systems vary in structure and in the level of aggregation, with the latter split into three levels - micro, meso and macro (Liljenstrom and Svedin, 2005). In this grouping, the meso level is of special interest, as it is here that the interface between micro and macro exists, and the level where a study of the marketing systems found might help us to understand micro and macro systems interact to produce the outcomes found in the real world of markets. The conventional focus, however, is on systems in or near the box at the bottom left of the Figure 24.3, including single firm offers to a market (Fisk, 1967; Kotler, 1980 and later), distribution

channels and vertical marketing systems (Bucklin 1967, 1970), and supply chains (Reddy and Reddy, 2001). In this sense, the concept of a marketing system points to a significant generalisation of marketing that has both managerial and theoretical implications.

MARKETING SYSTEMS – LOOKING INSIDE THE SYSTEM

Returning to the road map outlined in Figure 24.1, we begin with a closer look at the essential components of a marketing system embedded within a social matrix. These are identified in Figure 24.4.

The six interdependent elements all play essential roles in the operation of a marketing system, beginning with an explicit or implicit specification of the transaction set that is of interest, the mix of exchange logics that underlie these transactions, and the contexts or settings within which these transactions occur. This initial step leads directly to an identification of the individuals, groups or entities involved, and the roles played by each participant. Together, these two steps go a long way towards specifying the relevant system boundaries. The individuals, groups or entities comprising a marketing system are linked through their participation in or contribution to one or more of the flows of ownership, possession, finance, risk and information that are inherent in the functioning of

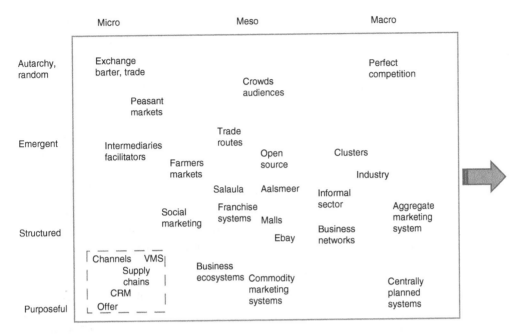

**Figure 24.3   Mapping marketing systems.
(Source: Adapted from Layton 2008b).**

a marketing system. The next two components are concerned with the structure and
dynamics of the resulting interlinked networks and the nature (or existence) of an
organising principle imposing some degree of
order or focus on the operation of the system.
The interaction of these four components
generates the assortments of goods, services,
experiences and ideas that are responsive to
the needs and wants of the customer groups
served by the marketing system.

In considering the general characteristics of
a marketing system, where relevant attributes
include responsiveness, resilience in the face
of external or internal shock, 'health' or
capacity to benefit specific segments or communities, it is important to keep in mind that
a marketing system is often best thought of
as a multilayered or multilevel system, where
the individual agents or actors may themselves

be marketing systems with similar or perhaps
quite different sets of structures and functions. The properties of the whole at any one
level of aggregation flow not just from the
system under study but also from systems
above and below. At the level where decisions
or choices are made by managers or by customers, the decision and choice processes
are shaped by perceptions of the immediate
marketing system in which the actors or
agents are embedded, and in many cases, by
the emergent characteristics of the system or
systems at the next higher levels. In this
sense, system becomes environment and an
understanding of the structural/functional
characteristics of the relevant systems is an
essential input into strategic and operational
marketing decision processes.

We now go on to consider each of the six
components in more detail. In doing so, it is

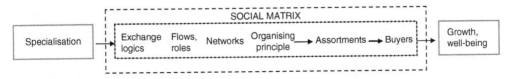

Figure 24.4   The essential components.

important to keep in mind the wide variety of multilevel marketing systems – from the *souks* or medinas of the Middle East, to the shopping malls of Europe and America, to the complex business ecosystems in automobile, oil or pharmaceutical markets, or to global food distribution networks.

Exchange logics, contexts (Figure 24.5)

There are many ways in which a marketing system can be specified. Sometimes it might be in terms of the products, services, experiences or ideas that are the subject of the relevant exchanges. Sometimes it will be specified in terms of space or location, sometimes in terms of history or time, sometimes by the level of aggregation involved, and sometimes by any or all of these. In each case, the specification leads to a transaction set – the transactions, or exchanges, that are at the centre of the focal system.

The transactions or exchanges thus specified can range from the silent trade practised by primitive communities dealing with each other across a common frontier, to the barter found in more developed trading groups (and still found in international trade today in the form of counter trade), to the complex multiparty negotiations required for major investments in resource development. In most, but not all, money plays a central facilitating role. The content of the exchange includes products, services, experiences and ideas, sometimes individually, often in bundled or structured formats offered over time and space. In many such exchanges, close cooperation between buyers and sellers is needed if the desired values are to be created (Prahalad and Krishnan, 2008; Vargo and Lusch, 2004). Beyond the specifics of an exchange, the contexts within which the exchange takes place are also often important. Shopping can be a pleasurable social experience, not only in a peasant marketplace, but also in contemporary shopping malls where owners strive to make shopping more than a

necessary household activity, providing meeting places and facilities for community activity (Mikunda, 2004; Oldenburg, 2001). Safety, hygiene, access and communication are also important factors influencing the viability of an exchange context. In each case, the choices made and the social matrix within which they are embedded, will determine the transaction set, the exchange logic(s) that will apply and the exchange contexts within which the transactions are carried out.

The transaction costs incurred by the participants (including both sellers and buyers) are important in considering the efficiency with which a marketing system creates and delivers assortments. These costs vary with the logics and contexts of the exchanges characterising a marketing system, and are 'the economic equivalent of friction in physical systems' (Williamson, 1985: 18–19). Williamson goes on to note that as such transactions costs can be distinguished from production costs. The distinction has been highlighted by Langlois (2005) who considers the various costs of establishing, maintaining and transferring property rights, suggesting that the latter two sets of costs could be labelled 'mundane transaction costs'. From a marketing systems point of view, many of the costs of interest are mundane but important. For sellers these include the costs of regulation, quality control, transportation and storage, leakages, the search costs involved in finding and bringing parties together, participation in bargaining, the costs of information, fees, bribes, insurance, queuing and delays in general. For buyers, the important costs are often hidden and include time, travel, access generally, as well as the opportunity costs of uncertainty and lack of knowledge. In the longer run, other costs, which are closer to fixed in nature become important for all participants – these include the establishment of a system of property rights, the creation and administration of standards, contract enforcement, the maintenance of such assets, the construction of infrastructure including transport, storage, communication and the facilities for market exchange. Although the

- *Exchange logics, contexts*
  - Products, services, experiences, ideas
  - Offer components – benefits, costs, availability, communication
  - Tangible, intangible
  - Separable, co-production
  - Simple, complex offer
  - Unitary, bundled, tied
  - Isolated, system embedded
  - Typical transaction size, structure
  - Once off, repeated
  - Contemporary, future
  - Low risk, high risk
  - Costs involved
  - Addictive, non-addictive

  - B2C, B2B, C2C

  - Technology mix
  - Obligation, gift, barter, sale
  - Fixed price, auction, negotiated
  - Economic, non-economic values and tradeoffs

  - Legal, illegal
  - Honest, corrupt
  - Bilateral, multilateral

- *Flows*
  - Ownership
  - Possession
  - Finance
  - Risk
  - Information

- *Roles (some examples ...)*
  - Creating, transforming
  - Assembling
  - Storing, transporting
  - Assorting, offering
  - Buying, exchanging
  - Funding
  - Communicating
  - Informing
  - Delivering
  - Recording
  - Facilitating, insuring
  - Agents, brokering
  - Influencing
  - Gatekeeping, allowing
  - Protecting, policing, enforcing
  - Judging, regulating

**Figure 24.5   Marketing system components (A).
(Source: Adapted from Layton 2008a).**

distinction between production and transactions costs is attractive, it may be misleading when an increasing proportion of transactions involve both sellers and buyers in the co-creation and co-production of value. More generally, the search for efficiency in the design and operation of marketing systems will increasingly turn on tradeoffs within and between each of the major cost categories, including production costs (cf. North, 2005: 15, note 3). In the context of evolving institutional and knowledge environments, frequency, uncertainty and asset specificity emerge as playing a critical role in the resolution of these tradeoffs amongst the major cost categories.

Flows (Figure 24.5)

Fisk (1967), drawing on the earlier work of the functional and institutional schools in marketing, identified five distinct flows associated with the operation of a marketing system.

These are the flows of ownership, possession, finance, risk and information (for an earlier and slightly larger listing see Vaile et al., 1952). The flows arise from the sequence of exchanges or transvections (Alderson, 1965) linking buyers, sellers and facilitators in a marketing system where each flow contributes to frictional or transaction costs.

Underpinning these flows are the economic, social, cultural and physical characteristics of the social matrix in which the marketing system is embedded. These characteristics in turn will reflect the wider evolving or changing environments of institutions and knowledge. Ownership, for example, may or may not transfer within the system depending on the nature of the products involved. As a case in point, aboriginal trade may involve access to inalienable assets such as land, water or food sources without granting ownership rights; in contemporary markets, leasing is common, and the problems associated with the transfer or preservation of intellectual property are well known.

Codes of conduct, cultural norms and legal rules are essential elements in defining ownership. As Pryor (2005: 8) notes, 'rules of property are found in human societies at all stages of development'. Possession may or may not coincide with ownership and adds a logistics dimension (transport, storage, transformation, display and despatch) to the operation of a marketing system. Physical infrastructure is an essential element in the flow of possession and does much to determine efficiency and effectiveness. The Food and Agriculture Organization (FAO) of the United Nations has, for example (Abbott, 1963, 1968; Balbo et al., 2002), been concerned for many years with logistics and system design issues in developing countries, such as the design and operation of wholesale market centres, or the loss of rice in a complex distribution system due to storage and transport defects.

Underlying most if not all, exchange in monetised markets is a flow of finance. From the back alley informal banking networks of China (Tsai, 2002), to the microfinance networks of banks such as the Grameen Bank in Bangladesh (De Aghion and Morduch, 2005), to the complex financing of contemporary international trade, credit for producers, traders and customers is essential to the operation of a marketing system. Closely linked to but separate from the flow of finance is the management of risk within the marketing system. This can be handled through the careful selection of trading partners and the creation of reciprocal relationships on social or economic grounds (e.g., *guanxi* in Chinese business networks, relationship management in Western marketing, or a considered choice between cooperation and competition), or more formally through insurance and risk management.

The last of the five flows is concerned with the flow of information in the marketing system. Although less than is the norm for most transactions within a marketing system, asymmetric information is often seen as a problem. This arises when some of the parties to a transaction are better informed than others are and are able to favourably influence present or future outcomes. The problems arising from asymmetric information especially in (but not limited to) subsistence marketplaces have been explored by Rosa and Viswanathan (2007). On the seller side, where the costs of being wrong are high, specialist providers emerge to manage information flows. Advertising agencies, market research firms, public relations specialists, search agencies, venture capitalists and government bureaux, are some of the ways that deficiencies in information flows are addressed. On the buyer side, the diffusion of information through public agencies, non-governmental organisations (NGOs), social networks and cooperative structures continues to be a major area of research in marketing, behavioural economics and economic sociology.

Role specialisation (Figure 24.5)

The evolution of marketing systems from the relatively primitive forms found in autarchy through emergent systems to complex, multi-level structured or purposeful systems generates increasingly complex flows, of ownership, possession, finance, risk and information, each of which leads to growing role specialisation based on distinctive resources, learned skills and acquired network capabilities.

In an emergent system, the roles of a retailer and/or wholesaler emerge early in the evolutionary process, sometimes in the form of hawkers that link outlying districts with markets (Brookfield, 1969), sometimes as market place specialists in a specific commodity, and as trade volumes grow, as specialist wholesalers linking separate markets in higher order networks. In a structured marketing system, the roles associated with ownership and possession become much more complex ranging from supply chain specialists, to warehouse and transport providers, and including a range of specialist advisors in systems design and operation. Flows of finance also create their own sets of specialist roles. In an autarchic or emergent marketing system, money as a medium of exchange rapidly becomes essential if trade is to develop beyond barter transactions. Providing access to funds is the role of the microfinanciers in India and Bangladesh, one of the roles of the community store in Yuendumu, and quickly generalises to encompass the sophisticated financial institutions. Risk associated with poor product quality, transaction failures, lack of or incorrect information, theft, or similar causes is endemic to systems at all levels of development and handled in ways that respond to the social or institutional context. Insurance, performance monitoring, regulation and enforcement roles are examples of the specialised roles needed. Finally, the flow of information through a marketing system is essential to its continued operation and specialised roles in developed marketing systems respond to this need. These include consultants, market research agencies, advertising and public relations specialists, consumer associations, the media, and a wide range of informal communication networks all of whom have a role to play. In an emerging marketing system, information is just as important as in a developed marketing system but more likely to flow through informal networks (family, kinship groups, trade partners or associates, *guanxi* links etc.) than through formal, regulated channels. Identifying the specialist roles supporting each of these flows and an evaluation of short- and long-term incentives, actions taken and outcomes achieved, may provide important insights into system performance.

As well as the direct participants – buyers, sellers and facilitators – there will be others who have a stakeholding in the outcomes of the exchanges or transactions, whose interests may need to be considered. These include businesses whose activities are directly affected by the outcome of the transactions involved (suppliers, service providers etc.), communities dependent on or influenced by trade outcomes, politicians, lobbyists and regulators concerned with social implications, and many others.

- *Networks –structure, dynamic*
  - Boundaries –open, closed; focal aggregation level
  - Participants –individuals, families, entities, systems; endowments, capabilities, interests, limitations; entry and exit flows
  - Value flows overall, and contributed by each participant
  - Network demographics –number etc.
  - Real and/or virtual
  - Spatial factors, location, infrastructure
  - Physical design, structure, facilities

  - Linkages, interaction, relationships, guanxi
  - Power, influence, trust
  - Density, connectivity, centralisation, stability, complexity, resilience

  - Alliances, cooperation, competition, within & between system participants; strength, basis of competition –price, assortment ...

  - Single, intersecting, multi-network focus
  - Layering –single, multilevel systems
  - Parallel systems

  - Dynamics –past, present, future
  - Equilibrium, punctuated equilibrium, disequilibrium, chaos, collapse

- *Organising principle –for each level of aggregation*
  - Underlying social contract
    - Stable, efficient, fair

  - Reciprocative
  - Redistributive
  - Market/Exchange
    - Random, autarchic
    - Emergent
    - Structured
    - Purposeful

  - Profit/Not for profit

  - Capitalism archetypes
    - State guided
    - Oligarchic
    - Big firm
    - Entrepreneurial

  - White, grey, black markets

  - Informal, formal, blended

  - Sustainability

Figure 24.6 Marketing system components (B).
(Source: Adapted from Layton 2008a).

Networks – structure and dynamics (Figure 24.6)

As specialisation grows the network of linkages between buyers and sellers becomes more complex, specialists emerge and take on buyer–seller roles in the process adding to the complexity of the network. Linkages become relationships and may crystallise into alliances, mergers and acquisitions. Networks develop based on shared or common interests. System boundaries become more diffuse and porous, more difficult to define. Physical or spatial limitations give way in the face of lower cost flows of information, possession and ownership. In all these ways, the truth of John Donne's aphorism is clear. Both individuals and organisations need to be seen in context, embedded in an immediate social matrix, relating to each other through economic exchange, in increasingly complex patterns of trade. Identifying these patterns and their consequences is an important step towards understanding a marketing system.

An early step in the study of a marketing system lies in a specification of the system boundaries. While sometimes straightforward, it is always to an extent arbitrary, depending on underlying purpose and can change as that purpose changes. It can be framed in terms of a transaction set, or a set of participants or actors; it might be spatial and will often require a specification of relevant time horizons. Implicitly or explicitly, a focal or primary level of aggregation will be involved. Although a specification of boundary may lead to a sense of closure, most of the marketing systems of interest will be open systems, influencing and being influenced by the environment within which the system operates.

The participants in a marketing system range from individuals or households, to entities (e.g., firms, agencies and cooperatives), to marketing systems (markets, clusters, networks, alliances, partnerships etc.) and will usually include the entities providing the essential support services associated with each of the flows of ownership, possession, finance, risk and information. Within the context of a marketing system, participants may cooperate or compete, directly or indirectly, on one or more of several dimensions including price and assortment (Baumol, 2002: 11). Each participant brings to the marketing system a growth dynamic, resource endowments and capabilities, assortments and customer groups (Hunt, 2000). Where the participant is a purposeful system, or an individual business, trader or supplier, participation brings with it the possibility of goal directed (survival perhaps, growth or profit), strategically focussed, planned decision making, as additional drivers of systemic change. The number, size and mix of characteristics of the participants will vary by level of aggregation as will the value contributed by each to the system overall. Size might also be thought of in terms of total sales or value added overall and by sector or subsystem (Cox et al., 1965; Layton, 1981a, b; Sybrandy et al., 1991). A more detailed picture of the participants in a marketing system can be found using the techniques of corporate demography (Carroll and Hannan, 2000) including growth (entry and exit patterns), size–age interaction, density, competitive intensity, inertia and change.

The linkages between and within participants in a (multilevel) marketing system are important factors influencing function and system dynamics. Typically, the linkages are multidimensional, based often on direct trade relationships, but also involving power, influence, trust, and resting on bases including expertise and knowledge, network access, mutual understanding, kinship and family relationships, *guanxi* or obligation. In order to gain a deeper understanding of a marketing system, the linkages characterising the system can be modelled as network or flow graphs, the former focussing on the linkages *per se* and the latter on the flows through the links. A network graph approach leads directly to a consideration of graph characteristics such as centrality, connectivity, density and, in a dynamic context, to stability, equilibria and resilience (Benkler, 2006; Epstein, 2006).

Organising principle (Figure 24.6)

The fourth element in a mapping of a marketing system is concerned with the overall organising principle governing the operation of the system. A starting point here is the nature and extent of the social contract (Binmore, 2005) or consensus that underpins the exchanges central to the marketing system. An understanding of the specific nature of this social contract and the supporting institutions is an essential first step in understanding the organising principle underpinning a marketing system.

There are many ways in which the detail of the social contract supporting economic exchange can be worked out. One of the best known classifications is that due to Polanyi in Polanyi et al. (1957) who suggested that the social problem of providing people with desired assortments could be solved in one of three ways: (1) reciprocity, usually involving families, kinship groups or neighbourhoods, in a 'give and take of equivalent value over time' (Johnson and Earle, 2000: 48); (2) redistribution, usually through allocations made by a central authority; and (3) exchange, in which distribution is achieved through price-making in markets.

In keeping with the transitions noted earlier, reciprocative and redistributive patterns are more likely to be found in autarchic or early emerging marketing systems, (Johnson and Earle, 2000) where trade shifts from a situation in which each individual is more or less self-sufficient, perhaps with some barter between producers, to one where specialisation develops, with each producer participating in the market as both producer and consumer (a form of autarchy), to one where some pattern or order emerges in roles, location in space or time, and relationships (an emergent system). This will arise for example in a search for ways of reducing transaction costs through the introduction of intermediaries, and as producers seek market niches, where specialisation can lead to competitive advantage (White, 2002). At this point, the generalised patterns give way to the formation of firms, groups or alliances and concentration

of market power begins to develop (cf. Carroll and Hannan, 2000). With this concentration of market power comes an increasing variety of goods, services, experiences and ideas as firms seek to capitalise on economies of scope as well as scale. A (purposeful) alternative to this sequence can be found in the central planning found in the socialist states of Eastern Europe and North Korea, and which still exists in a much-modified form, blended with market exchange, in China today.

Taking a top–down view of an aggregate marketing system, Baumol, Litan and Schramm (2007) focus on the role of the entrepreneur as an innovator, who initiates and carries through the Schumpeterian processes of creative destruction, who upsets and disorganises (p. 3), suggesting that it is this activity that is the critical driver of economic growth. They go on to explore alternative forms of capitalism, ranging from state guided (China, Japan, Korea etc.), oligarchic (Russia), big firm (US mid-century, Europe), to a small firm, entrepreneurial system. Each of these forms provides a distinctive environment for the evolution of marketing systems.

Assortments

Marketing systems have one primary social function and that is to provide assortments that will serve the needs and interests of the buyers and sellers comprising the system. In this context, an assortment is a set of products, services, experiences and ideas, differentiated by attributes, location in space and time, and by factors such as cost, price, brand or quality. A physically identical product, offered for sale at two different locations or at different points in time or at different prices, might, depending on the level of aggregation, be treated as two distinct members of an assortment.

Examples of the assortments offered within a marketing system include the products and services offered by a contemporary supermarket, the set of destinations offered by a tourism marketing system, the set of shops and ancillary services made available in a

- *Assortments*

    - Location in system, contexts, hierarchies, physical characteristics, overlapping assortments . .

    - Presentation/display –place, shop, mall, ...,colour, smell, impacts. .

    - Type
        - Offered (including fiat)
        - Sought
        - Accessible
        - Acquired
        - Accumulated

    - Characteristics
        - Membership –type, counts (width, depth), dimensions
        - Single, multi-level assortments
        - Size distribution, entropy, information
        - Pareto, power law qualities
        - Cross elasticities, complexity measures
        - Dynamics - additions, deletions, rates and drivers of change: merged, and demerged assortments

    - Contexts

    - Discrepancy levels, gaps, drivers
        - Offered/sought
        - Sought/accessible
        - Accessible/acquired
        - Acquired/accumulated

- *Customers/Buyers/ Stakeholders*

    - Specification, description
        - Aggregation levels
        - Composition, buying centers, social structures
        - Roles

    - Demographics (social, industrial)
        - Basics
        - Handicaps –poverty, literacy, access
        - Lifestyles, strategies
        - Adaptation, evolution

    - Decision processes
        - Expectations, hopes
        - Goals, benefits sought, tradeoffs
        - Individual, family, group factors
        - Search, screening, evaluation, choice, post choice processes

    - Group identification
        - Isolates, participants, leaders, iinfluentials. .
        - Relationship effects

    - Segmentation

    - Value in use; cost benefit perceptions

Figure 24.7   Marketing system components (C). (Source: Adapted from Layton 2008a).

shopping mall, the mix of rides in an amusement park, the offerings on eBay on a specific day and time, the range of services offered by a community health centre, or the product and service range mix offered by a supplier.

In a multilevel system, assortments will usually arise at the many points where sellers and buyers interact in each of the different levels. Physical presentation will often be an important factor, or failing that, the ability to communicate the depth and width of an assortment through catalogue displays, or through internet access will play an important part. Assortments may be looked at in terms of what is offered, what customers are looking for, what is in fact accessible to potential customers, and then in terms of what is acquired and accumulated. Not all participants in a marketing system will have access to the full assortment generated by the system. An accessible assortment then is specific to each participant in the marketing system and may

vary by place and time. The existence of a difference between an accessible assortment and a desired assortment is a major factor influencing both the efficiency and effectiveness of a marketing system, and the inability of some (marginal or vulnerable) participants to access a desired assortment is a major source of concern on equity grounds (Hill, 2004). From the point of view of a participant who may see only part of the wider assortment generated by the marketing system, perceptions of the variety offered by the accessible assortment are important factors influencing purchase decisions (Hoch et al., 1999; Van Herpen and Pieters, 2002). Variety, in this setting, is one aspect of the value or 'potency' of the assortment held by a participant, concepts introduced by Alderson (1965) and explored in some depth by Houston et al. (1992).

As Alderson goes on to suggest (Alderson, 1965; Wooliscroft et al., 2006) markets may be discrepant, in that products desired by customers as part of an accessible assortment may not be offered, or products are offered that are not sought by customers. Where this occurs, markets become dynamic, with assortment changing over time as suppliers in the system innovate, adding new products and deleting existing products. Discrepant markets today are a commonplace and assortments are continually changing. It has not always been thus, as Baumol (2002: 3) notes 'even the most well off consumers in pre-industrial revolution society had virtually no goods at their disposal that had not been available in ancient Rome'. In his terms, it is innovation, particularly routinised innovation that is the central driver of contemporary economic growth, responding to or initiating the opportunities and threats created by fast moving assortment discrepancies. Under these circumstances, emergent systems quickly morph into structured/purposeful multilevel composite systems. Is it inevitable then that assortments generated by a marketing system will over time widen and deepen, confronting us with the paradox of (unwanted) choice (Schwartz, 2004) in a world where sustainability is an increasingly urgent concern?

Perhaps the most complex aspect of the concept of assortment lies in measurement. Although Alderson (1965) was aware of the problem, his solution involving a sortability scale added little to the conventional measurements of width and depth. Hart and Rafiq (2006) suggest a hierarchical approach be taken where the width of an assortment refers to the number of categories or classes carried, breadth to the number of distinct lines offered in a category, and depth to the number of variants offered within each product line. Hart and Rafiq go on to add consistency as a further measure that captures some aspects of buyer perceptions of relatedness but note that this is indeed hard to measure. An alternative approach to buyer perceptions of assortment arises in the study of shopping baskets as acquired assortments yielding insights into complementarity and substitution links within offered assortments (Seetharaman et al., 2005).

Another approach focuses on the variety or diversity of an assortment. The economics of product variety were explored by Lancaster (1990) and measures of variety suggested by Gans and Hill (1997). Ecologists concerned with biological diversity have suggested the need to consider both variety/richness and the relative abundance/evenness of species (Huston, 1994), and have developed a wide range of measures many of which are based on the concept of entropy. Entropy also plays a central role in the study of complex systems (Ay et al., 2006), with specific application to the modelling of complexity in marketing systems. If discrepancy gaps are indeed drivers of marketing system growth and change, then measures of assortment that lead to acceptable measures of discrepancy are much needed.

Focussing on assortment in this way also brings into play one of the most obvious characteristics of marketing systems wherever they arise – the scale, scope, colours, smells and sounds of markets at work. Whether it is the medina in Fez or a WalMart store, it is the impact of the assortment of goods, services, experiences and ideas on offer that provides the most vivid memories of a visit. From a slightly different point of view, Stuart Kauffman (2000: 212) noted that 'one of the most striking facts about current economic theory is that it has no account of this persistent secular explosion of diversity of goods, services and ways of making a living'. Much the same could be said of marketing.

Customers, buyers and stakeholders

The last of the six elements of a marketing system is concerned with an identification of the customers or customer groups associated with the system. These will often not be end users but depending on the specification of the level of aggregation and the boundaries of the marketing system of interest, may also include intermediate purchasers of both goods and services. Customers may at one level be thought of as individuals, households or managers, or at another level be considered in aggregate as segments, groups, or perhaps communities or regions. Purchasing may be considered in terms of individual or single purchases of goods or services, or in the form of 'shopping baskets' created to meet diverse needs. Where the purchase involves strong elements of co-production or co-creation of value, these will often be prime determinants of the nature and function of the marketing system. The heterogeneity of the resource endowments or capabilities of purchasers, including capacity to pay, will be another important determinant of system functions and structure. In a negative sense, the consequences of lack of capability such as might be experienced by the functionally illiterate or disabled purchasers are also important factors in system design (Viswanathan et al., 2005). This leads directly to a review of demographics and of decision processes both at the individual and group level. Finally, it is often the case that purchasing is not an isolated event. Rather it is an occasion for social interchange and as such, the physical settings become important providing a distinctive set of benefits (Oldenburg, 2001; Mikunda, 2004; Underhill, 2004).

OUTCOMES – GROWTH, QUALITY OF LIFE AND EXTERNALITIES

Although economic growth is typically measured in terms of changes in per capita real income levels, this is much too narrow a measure for use in the study of marketing systems, where success or failure is ultimately concerned with the delivery of a standard of living or quality of life to the participants and the communities of which they are part, and this in turn is a consequence of the affordability, quality, relevance and accessibility of the assortments created by the marketing system. For each of the individual participants – producers or consumers, individuals, groups or organisations, facilitators or intermediaries – specific survival, surplus, profit or utility goals will govern

their involvement with the marketing system. If these goals are not satisfied, the marketing system will fail, in part or in whole, to deliver the necessary assortments. The overall health of the system thus depends on performance both in a narrow economic sense and in a wider social sense. Both sets of indicators are listed in Figure 24.8. The growth set is concerned with direct measures of system performance, including those relating directly to economic growth and related outcomes, while the second, a well-being set, is more focussed on wider social outcomes and externalities. The two sets are treated separately to highlight the differences – growth may or may not lead to well-being.

Although some of the indicator variables in the growth set can often be measured directly (the performance indicators, value added, satisfaction levels and some aspects of assortment) we lack good or even approximate measures of the remainder. Although efficiency in the narrow sense of reducing transaction costs while keeping assortments constant is achievable, particularly for purposeful marketing systems, efficiency in a wider dynamic sense of reducing costs in the face of continual change in technologies and institutions is much more troublesome, depending on the lags and leads built into the operations of a marketing system. Similarly, the effectiveness of a marketing system in matching offered assortments with desired assortments continuously across a range of market segments is difficult to assess particularly for complex structured marketing systems where satisfaction measures are often too general to be helpful.

In particular, we are challenged to produce useful measures of the health, responsiveness and resilience of a marketing system. Intuitively, the systems embodied in the medina in Fez, the Aalsmeer flower auctions or the aggregate marketing system described by Wilkie and Moore are in some sense 'healthy' and responsive or adaptive, while the collapse of conventional retailing in Zimbabwe, or the disintegration that followed the tsunami in Sumatra, would all be classed as 'not healthy' and nonresponsive, although

Growth	Quality of Life

• Performance
 – Survival, stability
 – Volume, growth
 – Surplus, profitability, ROI, ROA
 – Efficiency – transaction costs
 – Effectiveness
 	
• Assortments
 – Location, size
 – Access, coverage
 – Affordability, relevance
 – Changes – width, depth, diversity . .
 – Discrepancy management
 	
• Value added, created, invested
• Responsiveness to invention, innovation
• Reward allocation within, between systems among participants
• Power locations within the system
• Satisfaction/dissatisfaction levels
• Strengths, weaknesses
• Health, responsiveness, resilience indicators
	• Cultural, religious, economic value impacts
	 – Communication and its consequences
	 – Consumerism, materialism etc
	 – Secular, economy effects
	• Happiness
	 – Choice – too little, too much
	 – QOL, well-being
	 – Impacts on relativities
	 – Failure outcomes? Left behind?
	 – Winners, losers?
	• Distributive justice, fairness
	 – Within systems
	   • Exclusions, inequalities
	 – Within society, culture
	   • Exclusions, inequalities
	• Externalities
	 – Sustainability, environmental impacts
	 – Network effects
	 – Institutional impacts
	 – Technology change
	 – Marketing system change

Figure 24.8   Marketing system outcomes – growth, quality of life. (Source: Adapted from Layton 2008a).

each may be self sustaining in a kind of low level equilibrium. As Nordstrom (2007: 153) points out, 'informal economies pick up where the legitimate economy doesn't deliver'.

A similar although even more complex set of problems arise in finding usable measures of well-being resulting from the operations of a marketing system. The search for 'quality of life' measures in this context is discussed in detail by Sirgy (2001) in a groundbreaking review of the field. Lee at al. (2002) note that consumer well-being is a function of satisfaction with the acquisition, possession, consumption, maintenance and disposition of consumer goods and services. Walker et al. (2007) suggest that 'consumer well-being and welfare may also be influenced by the extent to which one feels an integrated, influential, and connected part of a community' (p. 380). These views are consistent with the earlier suggestion that marketing systems must be considered as embedded in a social matrix and are supported by the Indian study of Varman and Costa (2008). It is clear that much more than the traditional measures of performance are needed if we are to judge the effectiveness of a marketing system.

From a slightly different point of view, economists such as Layard (2005), Bruni and Porta (2005) and Frey (2008) explore the economics of happiness, with Frey in particular suggesting that 'happiness economics' has the potential to change economics substantially. His argument is based not only on a growing acceptance of sound proxy measures for experienced utility, new insights such as the understanding that 'individuals derive utility not only from income (as is implied in much received theory), but also from highly valued social relations and from self-determination, as well as using their own competence' (p. x), and an awareness of the significant policy consequences that flow from the research.

Social critics such as Paul Stiles (2005), point to the deficiencies of the 'market' as it is experienced in countries such as America. Questions of distributive justice abound, particularly in regard to disadvantaged or excluded sectors in a community are becoming increasingly important. Examples occur in the treatment of remote aboriginal communities such as Yuendumu, where access to appropriate assortments of food, groceries and other household necessities is often restricted and costly, or in the refugee camps found in many parts of Africa. In each case the idea of fairness inherent in an acceptable social contract, and which was the starting point for our understanding of the way marketing systems emerged, has largely disappeared. Could the evolutionary processes involved have been better designed and better managed?

LOOKING BACK AND LOOKING FORWARD

Although marketing systems have been part of the marketing literature for many years, relatively little has been done to breathe life into the concept and what has been done is often to be found in the work of scientists, consultants and managers marginally connected to marketing as a field of research. Examples include the practical studies of distribution systems in developing countries carried out by the UN and national aid agencies (Abbott, 1963, 1968; Balbo et al., 2002; Slater et al., 1979), the welfare concerns of NGO's dealing with community segments underserved by conventional marketing systems, action research undertaken by social scientists concerned to lift living standards (e.g., Spriggs and Chambers, 2005). An insight into marketing systems offers the hope of drawing these disparate studies into a coherent framework where knowledge is cumulative rather than episodic. Just as important, or from our point of view perhaps more so, is to bring the rich insights into decision making and choice outcomes gained from many years of research into managerial marketing and consumer studies into an overall framework of theory and practice.

REFERENCES

Abbott, J.C. (1963) 'Marketing and Area Development Studies', in S.A. Greyser (ed.) *Toward Scientific Marketing*. Proceedings of the American Marketing Association, Boston, Chicago: American Marketing Association.

Abbott, J.C. (1968) 'Marketing Issues in Agricultural Development Planning', in R. Moyer and S.C. Hollander (eds) *Markets and Marketing in Developing Economies*, Homewood, IL: Richard D. Irwin, pp. 87–116.

Acemoglu, D., Johnson, S. and Robinson, J. (2004) 'Institutions as the Fundamental Causes of Long-Run Growth', in P. Aghion and S. Durlauf (eds) *Handbook of Economic Growth*.

Alderson, W. (1965) *Dynamic Marketing Behavior: A Functionalist Theory of Marketing*. Homewood, IL: Richard D. Irwin, Inc.

Alexander, J. (1987) *Trade, Traders and Trading in Rural Java*. Singapore: Oxford University Press.

Arnould, E.J. and Mohr, J.J. (2005) 'Dynamic Transformations for Base-of-the-Pyramid Market Clusters', *Journal of the Academy of Marketing Science*, 33(3): 254–274.

Axtell, R. (1999) 'The Emergence of Firms in a Population of Agents: Local Increasing Returns, Unstable Nash Equilibria, and Power Law Size Distributions', *Center on Social and Economic Dynamics*, Working Paper No 3. Brookings Institution.

Ay, N., Olbrich, E., Bertschinger, N. and Jost, J. (2006) 'A Unifying Framework for Complexity Measures of Finite Systems', *Working Papers, Santa Fe Institute*, 06-08-028.

Balbo, M., Visser, C. and Argenti, O. (2002) *Food Supply and Distribution to Cities in Developing Countries: A Guide for Urban Planners and Managers* (draft). FAO Rome.

Baumol, W.J. (2002) *The Free Market Machine: Analyzing the Economic Growth of Capitalism*. Princeton: Princeton University Press.

Baumol, W.J., Litan, R.E. and Schramm, C.J. (2007) *Good Capitalism, Bad Capitalism, and the Economics of Growth and Prosperity*. New Haven: Yale University Press.

Benkler, Y. (2006) *The Wealth of Networks: How Social Production Transforms Markets and Freedom*. New Haven: Yale University Press.

Bharadwaj, S., Clark, T. and Kulviwat, S.(2005) 'Marketing, Market Growth, and Endogenous Growth Theory: An Inquiry into the Causes of Market Growth', *Journal of the Academy of Marketing Science*, 33(3): 347–359.

Binmore, K. (2005) *Natural Justice*. Oxford: Oxford University Press.

Bowles, S., Durlauf, S.N. and Huff, K. (2006) *Poverty Traps*. Princeton: Princeton University Press.

Braudel, F. (1979) *The Structures of Everyday Life – Civilization and Capitalism 15–18th Century, The Limits of the Possible.* Vol 1. New York: Harper & Row.

Brookfield, H.C. (1969) *Pacific Market-places.* Canberra: Australian National University Press.

Bruni, L. and Porta, P.L. (2005) *Economics and Happiness: Framing the Analysis.* Oxford: Oxford University Press.

Buchanan, J.M. (2004) 'Natural Equality, Increasing Returns, and Economic Progress: A Reinterpretation of Adam Smith's System', *Division of Labor and Transaction Costs,* 1(1): 57–66.

Bucklin, L.P. (1967) 'The Economic Structure of Channels of Distribution', in B. Mallen (ed.) *The Marketing Channel.* New York: John Wiley.

Bucklin, L.P. (ed.) (1970) *Vertical Marketing Systems.* Glenview, IL: Scott Foresman.

Carroll, G.B. and Hannan, M.J. (2000) *The Demography of Corporations and Industries.* Princeton: Princeton University Press.

Cheng, W and Yang, X.(2004) 'Inframarginal Analysis of Division of Labor: A Survey', *Journal of Economic Behavior and Organization,* 55: 137–174.

Clark, G. (2007) *A Farewell to Alms: A Brief Economic History of the World.* Princeton: Princeton University Press.

Cox, R., Goodman, C.S. and Fichandler, T.C. (1965) *Distribution in a High Level Economy.* Englewood Cliffs, NJ: Prentice Hall.

De Aghion, B.A. and Morduch, J. (2005) *The Economics of Microfinance.* Boston: The MIT Press.

De Soto, H. (2000) *The Mystery of Capital – Why Capitalism Triumphs in the West and Fails Everywhere Else.* London: Bantam Press.

Dewey, A.G. (1962) *Peasant Marketing in Java.* New York: Free Press.

Diamond, J. (2005) *Collapse: How Societies Chose to Fail or Survive.* New York: Viking Penguin.

Epstein, J.M. (2006) *Generative Social Science: Studies in Agent Based Computational Modelling.* Princeton: Princeton University Press.

Epstein, J.M. and Axtell, R. (1996) *Growing Artificial Societies: Social Science from the Bottom Up.* Washington: Brookings Institution Press.

Firth, R. (1966) *Malay Fishermen: Their Peasant Economy.* New York: WW Norton.

Fisk, G. (1967) *Marketing Systems, An Introductory Analysis.* New York: Harper & Row.

Frey, B.S. (2008) *Happiness: A Revolution in Economics.* Boston: MIT Press.

Gans, J.S. and R.J. Hill (1997) 'Measuring Product Diversity', *Economics Letters,* 55(1): 145–150.

Gappah, P. (2008) 'A Day in Harare', *The Australian Financial Review,* 3(January): 42.

Granovetter, M. (1985) 'Economic Action and Social Structure: The Problem of Embeddedness', *American Journal of Sociology,* 91(November): 481–510.

Granovetter, M. (1995) 'Coase Revisited: Business Groups in the Modern Economy', *Industrial and Corporate Change,* 4(1): 93–130.

Grief, A., (2006) *Institutions and the Path to the Modern Economy: Lessons from Medieval Trade.* Princeton: Princeton University Press

Gudeman, S. (2001) *The Anthropology of Economy.* Oxford. Blackwell.

Guha-Khasnobis, B., Kanbur, R.and Ostrom, E. (2006) *Linking the Formal and Informal Economies.* Oxford: Oxford University Press.

Gunderson, L. and Holling, C.S. (eds) (2002) *Panarchy: Understanding Transformations in Human and Natural Systems.* Washington: Island Press.

Hart, C. and Rafiq, M. (2006) 'The Dimensions of Assortment: A Proposed Hierarchy of Assortment Decision Making', *International Review of Retail, Distribution and Consumer Research,* 16(3): 333–351.

Helpman, E. (2004) *The Mystery of Economic Growth.* Cambridge: Mass. Harvard University Press.

Hill, R.P. (2004) 'Do the Poor Deserve Less Than Surfers? An Essay for the Special Issues on Vulnerable Consumers', *Journal of Macromarketing,* 25(2): 215–218.

Ho, S-C. (2005) 'Evolution Versus Tradition in Marketing Systems: The Hong Kong Food-Retailing Experience', *Journal of Public Policy and Marketing,* 24(1): 90–99.

Hoch, S.J., Bradlow, E.T. and Wansink, B. (1999) 'The Variety of an Assortment', *Marketing Science,* 18(4): 527–546.

Holling, C.S. (2001) 'Understanding the Complexity of Economic, Ecological and Social Systems', *Ecosystems,* 4: 390–405.

Homer-Dixon, T. (2006) *The Upside of Down: Catastrophe, Creativity and the Renewal of Civiilization.* Melbourne: The Text Publishing Company.

Houston, F.S., Gassenheimer, J.B. and Maskulla, J.M. (1992) *Marketing Exchange Transactions and Relationships*. Westport: Quorum.

Hunt, S.D. (1977) 'The Three Dichotomies Models of Marketing: An Elaboration of the Issues', in C.C. Slater (ed.) *Macromarketing: Distributive Processes from a Societal Perspective*, Boulder CO: Business Research Division, University of Colorado, pp. 52–56.

Hunt, S.D. (2000) *A General Theory of Competition: Resources, Competencies, Productivity, Economic Growth*. Thousand Oak: Sage Publications.

Huston, M.A. (1994) *Biological Diversity: The Coexistence of Species on Changing Landscapes*. Cambridge: Cambridge University Press.

Iansiti, M. and Levien, R. (2004) *The Keystone Advantage – What the New Dynamics of Business Mean for Strategy, Innovation and Sustainability*. Boston: Harvard Business School Press.

Johnson, A.W and Earle, T. (2000) *The Evolution of Human Societies: From Foraging Group to Agrarian State*, second edition. Stanford: Stanford University Press.

Kauffman, S. (2000) *Investigations*. Oxford: Oxford University Press.

Kotler, P. (1980) *Marketing Management*, fourth edition. New Jersey: Prentice-Hall Inc.

Kraybill, D.B. and Nolt, S.M. (2004) *Amish Enterprise: From Plows to Profits*, second edition. Baltimore: Johns Hopkins University Press.

Lancaster, K. (1990) 'The Economics of Product Variety: A Survey', *Marketing Science*, 9(3): 189–206.

Langlois, R.N. (2005) 'The Secret Life of Mundane Transaction Costs', *Department of Economics Working Paper*, 2005–49. University of Connecticut.

Layard, R. (2005) *Happiness: Lessons from a New Science*. New York: Penguin Books.

Layton, R.A. (1981a) 'Trade Flows in Macromarketing Systems. Part 1: A Macromodel of Trade Flows', *Journal of Macromarketing*, 1(1): 35–48.

Layton, R.A. (1981b) 'Trade Flows in Macromarketing Systems. Part 2: Transforming Input–Output Tables into Trade Flow Tables', *Journal of Macromarketing*, 1(2): 48–55.

Layton, R.A. (1988) 'Industrial Development and Traditional Distribution: Are They Compatible?', Research in Marketing, Supplement 4. *Marketing and Development: Toward Broader Dimensions*. JAI Press: 173–199.

Layton, R.A. (1989) 'Measures of Structural Change in Macromarketing Systems', *Journal of Macromarketing*, 9(1): 5–15.

Layton, R.A. (2007) 'Marketing Systems: A Core Macromarketing Concept', *Journal of Macromarketing*, 27(2): 193–213.

Layton, R.A. (2008a) 'On Economic Growth, Marketing Systems, and Quality of Life', in W.E. Kilbourne and J.D. Mittelstaedt (eds) *Macromarketing: Systems, Causes and Consequences*, Papers of the 33rd Annual Macromarketing Conference, Clemson, South Carolina, pp. 84–104.

Layton, R.A. (2008b) 'The Search for a Dominant Logic: A Macromarketing Perspective', *Journal of Macromarketing*, 28(3) (forthcoming).

Lee, D. and Sirgy, M.J. (2004) 'Quality-of-Life (QOL) Marketing: Proposed Antecedents and Consequences', *Journal of Macromarketing*, 24(1): 44–58.

Lee, D., Sirgy, M.J., Larsen, V. and Wright, N.D. (2002) 'Developing a Subjective Measure of Consumer Well-Being', *Journal of Macromarketing*, 22(2): 158–169.

Liljenstrom, H. and Svedin, U. (eds)(2005) *Micro, Meso, Macro: Addressing Complex Systems Couplings*. Singapore: World Scientific Publishing.

Lusch, R.F. (1987) 'General Theories, Fundamental Explananda, and Fundamental Axioms of Marketing', D. Sudharsan and F. Winter (eds) *Proceedings of the Twelfth Paul D. Converse Marketing Symposium*, Chicago: American Marketing Association, pp. 75–93.

Lydon, G. (2008) 'Contracting Caravans: Partnership and Profit in Nineteenth-Century Trans-Saharan Trade', *Journal of Global History*, 3: 89–113.

McDonnell, S. and Martin, D.F. (2002) 'Indigenous Community Stores in the "Frontier Economy": Some Competition and Consumer Issues', *Centre for Aboriginal Economic Policy Research*, Working Paper 234.

McMillan, J. (2002) *Reinventing the Bazaar – A Natural History of Markets*. New York: W.W. Norton & Company.

Ménard, C. and Shirle, M.M. (2005) *Handbook of New Institutional Economics*. Dordrecht: Springer.

Mikunda, C. (2004) *Brand Lands, Hot Spots & Cool Spaces*. London: Kogan Page.

Mittelstaedt, R.A. and Stassen, R.E. (1994) 'Structural Changes in the Phonograph Record Industry and its Channels of Distribution, 1946–1966', *Journal of Macromarketing*, 14(1): 31–44.

Mokyr, J. (2002) *The Gifts of Athena: Historical Origins of the Knowledge Economy*. Princeton: Princeton University Press.

Moore, J.F. (1996) *The Death of Competition – Leadership and Strategy in the Age of Business Eco-Systems*. Chichester: John Wiley & Sons.

Nordstrom C. (2007) *Global Outlaws: Crime, Money and Power in the Contemporary World*. Berkeley: University of California Press.

North, D.C. (1990) *Institutions, Institutional Change, and Economic Performance*. Cambridge: Cambridge University Press.

North, D.C. (2005) *Understanding the Process of Economic Change*. Princeton: Princeton University Press.

Oldenburg, R. (2001) *Celebrating the Third Place*. New York: Marlowe and Company.

Polanyi, K. (1944) *The Great Transformation: The Political and Economic Origins of Our Time*. New York: Farrar and Rinehart.

Polanyi, K., Arensberg, C.M. and Pearson, H.W. (eds) (1957) *Trade and Markets in the Early Empire*. Chicago: Henry Regnery Company.

Prahalad, C.K. and Krishnan, M.S. (2008) *The New Age of Innovation*. New York: McGraw Hill.

Pryor, F.L. (2005) *Economic Systems of Foraging, Agricultural, and Industrial Societies*. Cambridge: Cambridge University Press.

Pryor, S. and Grossbart, S. (2005) 'Ethnography of an American Main Street', *International Journal of Retail and Distribution Management* (forthcoming).

Rabo, A. (2005) *A Shop of One's Own: Independence and Reputation among Traders in Aleppo*. London: I.B. Tauris.

Rawls, J. (1972). *A Theory of Justice*. Oxford: Oxford University Press

Reddy, R. and Reddy, S. (2001) *Supply Chains to Virtual Integration*. New York: McGraw Hill.

Roberts, J.D. (2004) *The Modern Firm*. Oxford: Oxford University Press.

Romer, P. (1986) 'Increasing Returns and Long Run Growth' *Journal of Political Economy*, 94(October): 1002–1037.

Rosa, J.A. and Viswanathan, M. (eds) (2007) *Product and Market Development for Subsistence Marketplaces*. Amsterdam: JAI Press.

Scherer, F.M. (1999) *New Perspectives on Economic Growth and Technological Innovation*. Washington: Brookings Institution.

Schwartz, B. (2004) *The Paradox of Choice: Why More is Less*. New York: HarperCollins.

Seabright, P. (2004) *The Company of Strangers: A Natural History of Economic Life*. Princeton: Princeton University Press.

Seetharaman, P.B., Club, S., Ainslie, A., Boatwright, P., Chan, T., Gupta, S., Mehta, N., Rao, V. and Strijnev, A. (2005) 'Models of Multi-Category Choice Behavior', *Marketing Letters* 16(3): 239–254.

Shultz, C.J. II., Burkink, T.J., Grabac, B. and Renko, N. (2005) 'When Policies and Marketing Systems Explode: An Assessment of Food Marketing in the War-Ravaged Balkans and Implications for Recovery, Sustainable Peace, and Prosperity', *Journal of Public Policy and Marketing*, 24(1): 24–37.

Sirgy, M.J. (2001) *Handbook of Quality of Life Research: An Ethical Marketing Perspective*. Dordrecht: Kluwer Academic Publishers.

Skyrms, B. (1996) *The Evolution of the Social Contract*. Cambridge: Cambridge University Press.

Skyrms, B. (2004) *The Stag Hunt and the Evolution of Social Structure*. Cambridge: Cambridge University Press.

Slater, C.G., Jenkins, D.G., Pook, L.A. and Dahringer, L.D. (1979) *Easing Transition in Southern Africa: New Techniques for Policy Planning*. Boulder: Westview Press.

Smith, A. (1776) *An Inquiry into the Nature and Causes of the Wealth of Nations*. Chicago: University of Chicago Press, 1976.

Spriggs, J. and Chambers, B. (2005) 'Connecting People in Cross-Culture Agribusiness: The Case of the Fresh Produce Supply Chain in Papua New Guinea', *Connecting People and Places: Challenges and Opportunities for Development*. Development Studies Association Annual Conference 2005 Milton Keynes, UK.

Stiles, P. (2005) *Is the American Dream Killing You? How 'The Market' Rules our Lives*. New York: HarperCollins.

Sybrandy, A., Pirog, S.E. III, and Tuninga, R.S. (1991) 'The Output of Distributive Systems:

A Conceptual Framework', *Journal of Macromarketing*, 11(2): 19–28.

Tsai, K.S. (2002) *Back-Alley Banking: Private Entrepreneurs in China*. Ithaca: Cornell University Press.

Underhill, P. (2004) *The Call of the Mall*. New York: Simon Schuster.

Vaile, R.S., Grether, E.T. and Cox, R. (1952) *Marketing in the American Economy*. New York: Ronald Press.

Van Herpen, E. and Pieters, R. (2002) 'The Variety of an Assortment: An Extension to the Attribute-Based Approach', *Marketing Science*, 21(3): 331–341.

Vargo, S.L. and Lusch, R.F. (2004) 'Evolving to a New Dominant Logic for Marketing', *Journal of Marketing*, 68(1): 1–17.

Varman, R. and Arnold Costa, J. (2008) 'Embedded Markets, Communities, and the Invisible Hand of Social Norms', *Journal of Macromarketing*, 28(2): 141–156.

Viswanathan, M., Rosa, J.A. and Harris, J.E. (2005) 'Decision Making and Coping of Functionally Illiterate Consumers and Some Implications for Marketing Management', *Journal of Marketing*, 69(January): 15–31.

Walker, R.H., Byrne, G. and Johnson, L.W. (2007) 'Developing a Quality of Life Measure to Assess the Impact of Community Services: The Case of Australian Community Banks', *Journal of Macromarketing*, 27(4): 380–388.

Welch, E. (2005) *Shopping in the Renaissance: Consumer Cultures in Italy 1400–1600*. New Haven: Yale University Press.

White, H.C. (2002) *Markets From Networks – Sociometric Models of Production*. Princeton: Princeton University Press.

Wilkie, W.L. and Moore, E.S. (1999) 'Marketing's Contributions to Society', *Journal of Marketing*, 63(Special Issue): 198–218.

Wilkinson, I.F. (2001) 'A History of Network and Channels Thinking in Marketing in the 20th Century', *Australasian Marketing Journal*, 9(2): 23–52.

Wilkinson, I.F. (2008) *Business Relating Business*. Cheltenham: Edward Elgar.

Williamson, O.E. (1985) *The Economic Institutions of Capitalism*. New York: The Free Press.

Wooliscroft, B., Tamilia, R.D. and Shapiro, S.J. (eds) (2006) *A Twenty-First Century Guide to Aldersonian Marketing Thought*. Boston: Kluwer Academic Publishers.

Yang, X. (2001) *New Classical Versus Neoclassical Frameworks*. Malden: Blackwell Publishers.

Young, A. (1928) 'Increasing Returns and Economic Progress', *Economic Journal*, 38: 527–542.

25

The Role of Marketing in Ancient and Contemporary Cultural Evolution

Elizabeth C. Hirschman

INTRODUCTION

We have not had to leave the confines of adaptationist assumptions to show how the properties of
culture play a fundamental role in human evolution.
(Boyd and Richerson, 2005: 6)

Marketing theory is undergoing a remarkable
revolution. In less than a decade, the field is
being reconceptualized as an interpersonal
process of transmitting ideas, ways of thinking,
and expertise. As Vargo and Lusch (2004: 2)
state, 'marketing has moved from a goods-
dominant view, in which tangible output and
discrete transactions were central, to a service-
dominant view, in which intangibility,
exchange processes and relationships are central'. Emerging from *core competency theory*
(Day, 1994; Prahalad and Hamel, 1990), the
new paradigm of marketing focuses on the
knowledge, skills and practices providing a
competitive advantage in the existing cultural
environment. Viewed in this way, marketing-
as-process is essentially the ideological
equivalent of the bio-evolutionary process of

natural selection, in which those individual
members of each species best adapted to their
surrounding environment survive to reproduce; those members not having the requisite
adaptations for survival, perish.

This evolutionary analogy has not been lost
on marketing scholars who have incorporated
it into theorization and research efforts (see
Eyoboglu and Buja, 2007, Lambkin and Day,
1989). Lambkin and Day (1989) provide an
overview of this approach:

The theory of *natural selection* ... predicts that the
species best 'fitted' to the contingencies of the
environment will survive and prosper, and their
less fit rivals will fail and disappear, because of
their inability to secure adequate resources ...
Marketers have long recognized the potential of
the paradigm for understanding competition in
commercial markets ... but only recently has significant progress been made in realizing its potential
for studying market evolution. (Lambkin and Day,
1989: 9)

More recently, Eyuboglu and Buja (2007)
argued that a 'quasi-Darwinian' selection

process is operative in marketing relationships. As they put it (p. 48), 'Risk and failure in marketing relationships ... are of theoretical importance because they lend themselves as a bridge to the paradigm of Darwinian selection. Casting [relationship] failure as selection opens up the toolbox of Darwinian theory that ... includes the concepts of variation, survival, and adaptation'.

In the present essay, I will explore these ideas within the context of cultural evolution; in other words, casting the metaphoric net at a macro (i.e., social system) level rather than at a micro (i.e., individual firm or industry) level of observation. Further, I will take Vargo and Lusch (2004) at their word and utilize their marketing-as-process model – taken to mean the interpersonal transfer of intangible resources (e.g., information and skills) – as the focal construct.

The period covered in the analysis extends from the late Paleolithic/Early Holocene (i.e., 100,000–30,000 years ago) up to the present time. Discussion focuses on four geneti-cultural coevolutionary phenomena:

1   The development of abstract thought and self-consciousness in modern humans (*homo sapiens*), which made possible the use of symbolic markers to construct self and group identities. I propose that these markers are the cultural foundation upon which brand identity is ultimately grounded.
2   The advent of agriculture, circa 10,000 years ago, permitted economic surpluses to accumulate and long distance trade routes to be established among human populations. With the advent of economic surplus came the possibility of exchanging goods, practices, and ideas across wide distances; this constitutes *innovation diffusion* and is analogous to marketing-as-process as envisioned by Vargo and Lusch (2004).
3   The rise of hierarchically organized, status-differentiated city-states, which enabled artisans and crafts persons to create aesthetically distinctive and functionally innovative goods. These came to serve as status identifiers among both individuals and social groups.
4   The bio-cultural adaptation of humans to experience self-consciousness with regard to behavior in social groups. Several researchers have proposed

that this enabled the development of cooperative behaviors beyond the confines of the tribe and ultimately led to global cooperative networks (Cohen et al., 2002; Riolo et al., 2001); Simon, 1990). At the present time, these networks permit the diffusion of both aesthetic and utilitarian innovations with little temporal delay and provide the socially adaptive underpinning necessary for all marketing relationships.

The discussion next proposes a potential reframing of contemporary marketing theory. I argue that marketing-as-process has evolved through three concentric cultural cycles. First, that marketing functioned as a geographically restricted process of innovation exchange, largely focused on tangible goods and cultural practices (e.g., crop irrigation and harvesting techniques, animal domestication and selective breeding). Second, marketing-as-process then developed into a geographically widespread phenomenon of information transfer and diffusion across cultures, carrying, for example, such key intellectual innovations as monotheism, literacy, and democracy and applied innovations such as the printing press, sailing ships, iron smelting, and gunpowder.

Third, I discuss the current proposal that we now have entered the era of Consumer Constructed Innovativeness (Franke and Shah, 2003; Fuller and Von Hippel, 2007; Fuller et al., 2006; Kozinets, 2002; McAlexander et al., 2002; Muniz and Schau, 2005; Sawhney and Prandetti, 2000; Shah, 2006; Von Hippel, 2005). This marketing-as-process stage is enabled by the global availability of creative technologies operable by individuals who now bring their own creative 'wares' to the marketplace in the form of software, videos, music, poetry, and cultural commentary. I argue that consumers, themselves, are now empowered by novel communications technology to market not only themselves and their creativity, but also to serve as potent sources of cultural change for a worldwide audience, pre-empting in part the historic dominance of both the state and corporations as drivers of the evolution of culture.

SELF CONSCIOUSNESS AND ABSTRACT THOUGHT

Archaeologists and paleontologists propose that human capacity for advanced cognition developed rapidly during the Pleistocene (Boyd and Richerson, 2005), a period punctuated by rapid, large-scale shifts in climate. Both overall brain size and frontal lobe capacity in humans increased markedly during this period. It is theorized by evolutionary psychologists that the simultaneous emergence of representational and abstract art, bodily adornments, cosmetics, music, and religious/supernatural rituals are indicators of the arrival of symbolic reasoning, circa 60,000 to 30,000 years ago (Mithen, 1999).

The birth of symbolic thought was a precondition to marketing behavior, as it made possible the diffusion of ideological innovations and the use of symbolic markers to indicate tribal identity, social rank, and cultural roles. Without the capacity for symbolic thought, human social development likely would have halted with functional tool production at an individual or tribal level. As evolutionary theorists (Boyd and Richerson, 2005: 15) speculate,

> The correlation of brain size with climate variation favors an *external explanation* (i.e., ecological events) for the timing of the evolution of culture in humans ... These are the time scales of variation that [evolutionary] models suggest should favor a cultural system that can mix and match the conservatism of faithful transmission with the flexibility of individual learning to generate rapidly evolving traditions adapted to a rapidly changing environment. Variability on short time scales probably also favors individual behavioral flexibility.

Similarly, Lorquin and Stone (2007: 117) propose that:

> The deterioration of climates during the last few million years would have dramatically increased selection for traits increasing animals' abilities to cope with more variable environments ... Humans responded to climate change with dramatically altered change in both brain size and complexity. This suggests that humans' problem-solving capacity

is enhanced in response to external challenges. Analogously then, we may expect the technological challenges of contemporary culture to exert selection pressures, as well.

Thus, the process of both individual and cultural evolution is an ongoing process, continuing into the present day. One causal explanation suggested by evolutionary theory for the rapid increase in human encephalization during prehistoric times was the origination of *intergenerational cultural transmission* within human groups, which created strong selective pressures for social learning capabilities. The implications of this for marketing theory and practice are significant and straightforward: the transfer of information, products, and services across generations and over millennia substantially altered the course of human evolution. People evolved in ways influenced by the ideas, artifacts, and practices of their ancestors. As these were passed forward to their children and their children's children, these descendants' lives and subsequent evolution were directly impacted. Thus, marketing-as-process helped to *create* the varied human cultures found in modern times and the behaviors of the consumers and marketers within them. Lorquin and Stone (2007: 86) attribute this phenomenon to the inherent plasticity of human cognition, which relies upon postnatal learning, rather than innate response tendencies:

> Donald Campbell emphasized the general similarities of all knowledge-acquiring processes ... [and] Edelman's theory of neuronal group selection is based on the argument that developmental processes cannot specify the fine details of the development of complex brains and hence that a lot of environmental feedback is necessary just to form the basic categories that complex cognition needs to work. ... If cognition is to be complex, it must be built using structures that are *underdetermined* at birth.

An extension of this reasoning by the same theorists suggests that most marketing-as-process creativity and diffusion will occur in tribal-sized groups and communities. This is because direct observation and interpersonal communication lead to very rapid social learning. These communities need not be face-to-face in nature, but could likely be constructed in electronic formats. As our ancestors gained greater cognitive capacity and flexibility, they were able to act upon both their social and natural environments more effectively. As Lorquin and Stone (2007: 245) write concerning human productivity during the Pleistocene:

> There is no question that tool use ... is related to increased brain size and changes in brain structure. It is clear that a connection between brain development and tool technology is one of the earliest gene–culture interactions in evolutionary history. As [humans] began to rely more on culture for their adaptations, that culture began to alter them physically and cognitively.

Body types evolved in response to culturally transmitted knowledge, as well. As human groups developed projectile weapons, such as spears and bows with arrows, together with the ability to cooperatively hunt, they became able to kill large game at safer distances and with greater effectiveness. This permitted our formerly very robust (large and heavyset) body types to become more energy efficient – a smaller more, gracile human body type emerged.

Around 35,000 years ago, human culture and cognition had evolved to include permanent housing, apparel, language, religion, art, and music. Tribal membership now could be marked by symbols, such as tattoos, jewelry, hairstyles, and clothing. From this point in evolutionary history forward, it is probably accurate to say that all the social and symbolic aspects characterizing modern marketing-as-process practices were present in human culture. Importantly, the exchange of ideas, goods and services over long distances was now commonplace. Cultural evolution increased in both speed and complexity. In some cases, the raw materials used for tools and jewelry were transported from distances over 300 kilometers away. Further, humans had gained religious consciousness and were now burying their dead with the accoutrements believed to

be needed in an afterlife – tools, red ocher, figurines, jewelry, and clothing.

At this point in our evolutionary history, the branding of self and community identity existed in ways that echo the same functions and complexity found in the modern marketplace. The arrival of symbolic thought granted our ancestors the ability to see beyond the concrete and immediate tangible realities of their lives and to imagine future places (e.g., an afterlife, paradise, and hell), beauty and magic, the transformation of animals and humans into one another, and the possibility of remaking the self. In many, perhaps most, ways their hopes and fears may have been quite similar to our own.

AGRICULTURE ENABLES ECONOMIC SURPLUS TO ACCUMULATE

Approximately 10,000 years ago, humans began cultivating grains and domesticating animals (e.g., sheep, goats, and cattle) in the geographic region now encompassed by modern-day Syria, Iraq, and Turkey (Anatolia). As Wallace (2005: 41) notes, 'The agricultural frontier and subsequent cultural revolution took about 4,000 years to unfold from localized garden farming to sophisticated high-output agriculture'. The ability to grow and store grains and produce meat and leather enhanced the development of trade with neighboring communities, while the taming of horses and cattle made possible long-distance travel and the transport of both people (with their novel ideas and practices) and their goods. This resulted in marketing-as-process diffusing both functional and aesthetic creativity across tribal groups and cultures.

Lorquin and Stone (2007) describe agriculture as a *radically discontinuous innovation*, which revolutionized both the social stratification and fertility of human populations. Ultimately, the agricultural revolution led to the development of the city-state (Lorquin and Stone, 2007). Yet, like many innovations, this one was not without its costs. Humans now had to engage in more intensive labor than previously, their diets were restricted to what was grown and harvested, and the increased density of human populations proved a fertile breeding ground for epidemic diseases. Politically, the greatest impact of the advent of agriculture was the emergence of a ruling class and the institutionalization of social inequality.

Cavalli-Sforza and Ammerman (1971), examining the archaeological evidence for the spread of agriculture, found a gradient between the oldest and the newest agricultural sites. The data indicated the diffusion of agriculture was accomplished throughout Europe from the Middle East in about 4,000 years. This constituted the first large-scale occurrence of marketing-as-process in human evolutionary history. At its basis, agriculture represented the replacement of one set of cultural consumption practices (e.g., nomadic hunting and gathering) with another.

The spread of this cultural innovation is also instructive, because it illustrates the close interplay between human culture and the natural climate. For example, only certain areas could support the grain crops needed for large-scale urban development; those that were too wet, or dry, or cold did not experience the same rate of cultural development. Further, the domestication of large food and transportation animals, for example, cattle, camels, and horses, greatly impacted the speed at which cultural knowledge could be carried (literally) across large land masses. The Silk Road of Central Asia, for example, was the primary trade route developed by ancient peoples; its existence was made possible by the natural availability of appropriate transport animals, for example, horses, donkeys, and dromedary camels, without which goods could not have been carried over the widely varying terrain from China to Europe. Nevertheless, perhaps even more fundamental was the opportunity for humans, for the first time, to begin to pursue specific intellectual activities and creative projects. Persons gifted in, say, art, music, mathematics, or astronomy, now had time for reflection and experimentation, making possible dramatic progress in the arts and sciences.

Thus, we see that one primary cultural innovation, i.e., agriculture, led to *a cascading revolution in human culture and consumption.* It is very likely that the current rapidity of information exchange via various electronic media (e.g., the Internet) will have the same dramatic culture-altering impact; this topic will be discussed in the third section of the chapter.

THE RISE OF THE CITY-STATE AND ORIGINS OF SOCIAL STRATIFICATION

The Fertile Crescent not only originated agriculture, it was also the first population site on earth to evolve to the cultural level of the city-state. Babylon, Sumeria, Assyria, and Persia came to power in an economic–political environment based on the specialization of labor, the use of standing armies, and centralized (often despotic) political authority. Rapid population growth led to greatly increased per capita wealth and the generation of new forms of transportation and technology. A significant engineering innovation, aqueducts, directed water from rivers to dry, but arable, land nearby the cities, permitting the accumulation of storable and tradable food supplies.

Ritualized interpersonal relationships and the construction and enforcement of social hierarchies (including slavery) created the need for visible markers of position and rank. Caste systems were embedded in an ideology of rationalized personal worth, consistent with capitalistic consumption as it is practiced today. Cuneiform writing – an innovation that would permit long distance accounting communication – reduced the need for direct person-to-person negotiation and permitted extended networks of trust and cooperation to be formed. Letters of credit now could be carried within trading networks for the first time, enabling trade channels to expand thousands of miles over both land and sea routes.

Wallace (2007: 173) writes of these events:

The valleys' ... flat terrain made it possible to build *irrigation canals* that enlarged the productive areas. ... They originated in Babylon, where truly large surpluses of food were produced. ... With cities came well-organized governments and religions, monumental buildings and other public works, royal tombs, standing armies, and extensive trade routes.

PROSOCIAL BEHAVIOR, COOPERATION, ALTRUISM, AND IN-GROUP IDENTIFICATION

Cities also became the birthplace of the third evolutionary stage of marketing-as-practice, following the origination of human abstract/symbolic consciousness and the spread of agriculture. The innovation was the advent of highly complex *systems of social markers*, which communicated one's roles and statuses in society. Notably, the modern marketing research practice of grouping consumers according to their possessions, values, and social economic status could have been applied as validly to populations at this stage of cultural evolution as it is to, say, US consumers of the present day. Richerson and Boyd (2005: 234) explain why this is so:

High population density, the division of labor, and improved communication give rise to *symbolic systems* adapted to simulate the badges and rituals of tribal membership. Complex societies make use of the *symbolic in-group instinct* to delimit a diverse array of culturally defined subgroups, within which a good deal of cooperation is routinely achieved. [For example], military organizations generally mark a set of middle-level, tribal-scale units with conspicuous badges of membership ... companies, regiments, and divisions are made real by symbolic marking.

Importantly for modern-day marketing efforts, these propositions suggest that humans will, *by their evolved nature*, seek to organize themselves into relatively small, tribal-sized groupings, and that purposeful, symbolically supported efforts must be undertaken to group them into larger units. Brand subcultures and

consumption communities would seem to be a direct expression of these evolutionary impulses (e.g., McAlexander et al., 2005; Muniz and Schau, 2005; Von Hippel, 2005).

As these cognitive, economic and political alterations were occurring, their success was enhanced by the concurrent genetic evolution of prosocial behavior. According to Hamilton (1976), *kin selection/inclusive fitness* initially evolved to support cooperation among genetically related persons, usually dwelling in families, clans or tribes. Perhaps in the early Holocene, this prosocial orientation became selected-for in larger units of distantly or unrelated persons, permitting cross-tribal cooperation to take place.

Boyd and Richerson (2005) propose that two elements were crucial to this evolved adaptation. First, individuals within the group had to be willing to assist one another in large-scale cooperative endeavors, rather than selfishly hoarding labor and resources within the immediate family. Second, freeloaders, cheats, and opportunists had to be identified and negatively sanctioned to prevent them from siphoning off valuable community-generated resources. Altruism in the absence of sanctions against cheaters would lead to weakened group-level survival rates. I believe that the historic and current development of marketing distribution channels is built upon the biological underpinning of prosocial mores in complex cultures. As Richerson and Boyd (2005: 214–215) state this proposition:

Human culture encourages the rapid, cumulative evolution of complex adaptations and is particularly adaptive in variable environments .... Group selection gives rise to culturally transmitted cooperative, group-oriented norms, and systems of rewards and punishments to ensure that such norms are obeyed.

Thus, both ancient and modern distribution channels would have been enabled by these gene-culture co-evolutionary patterns. If we view channel participants as 'tribes' who are choosing to cooperate with one another to achieve a large-scale undertaking that could not have been accomplished alone, we are seeing the fruition of inter-group cooperative dynamics that were set in motion several millennia ago.

Further, the individuals within each participating unit or tribe are motivated by:

> ... two sets of social instincts. The first is ... *kin selection and reciprocity*, enabling humans to have a complex family life and frequently form strong bonds of friendship with others. The second is *tribal instincts* that allow us to interact cooperatively with a large, symbolically marked set of people or tribe Richerson and Boyd, 2007: 202).

This suggests that the bonds among market channel members likely can be strengthened by purposeful efforts at symbolic uniformity spanning the channel. For example, this might involve personnel and equipment being labeled with similar logos or insignia, which communicate shared goals, and business interests. Modern-day brand communities, ethnic subcultures, and corporations are all manifestations of the second form of human grouping impulse (see e.g., Selnes and Sallis, 2003; Von Hippel, 2005).

MARKETING AS THE TRANSFER OF INNOVATIONS

Stone and Lorquin (2007: 43) state that 40,000 years ago Europeans originated a novel culture characterized by a number of innovative tool developments:

> They fashioned many tools – spear points, awls, and needles – from ivory, bone and antler. They made nets for small game and ... they constructed bows with arrows ...
>
> These artifacts represented what marketers would now term *product innovations* and evolutionary theorists term *cultural mutations*; that is, they were alterations in what had been accepted practice within the culture and became widely accepted, because they were found to provide superior problem-solving performance. Though such tools may appear to us as simple manual constructions, they represented an early example of marketing as the creation and transfer of ideas, skills and knowledge through culture.

Similarly, at a much later point in human development populations in the Fertile

Crescent originated several innovations that were to have profound impact on both culture and economics.

> Writing was the major innovation of this early civilization. First ... was the cuneiform writing of Babylon; then Egyptian hieroglyphics and Chinese script followed ... (Wallace, 2007: 229)

Because cultural innovations provide *power* to their originators, they were frequently used by one culture to dominate another. Further, within a given culture, subcultures arose, which carefully guarded their technologies, crafts, and knowledge. For example, knowledge of sea navigation, iron smelting, tobacco cultivation, and papermaking are all innovations that lent their originating cultures (or the conquerors of those cultures) great economic power.

Typically innovations spread first within their originating culture and then outward to other cultures through interpersonal communication channels and social observation. Boyd and Richerson (2005: 41) mathematically modeled this ancient innovation diffusion process:

> The better [practice or idea] spreads because people imitate their more-successful neighbors .... Our results suggest that group-beneficial beliefs spread in a wide range of conditions ... [and that] such spread can be rapid. Roughly speaking, it takes about twice as long for a group-beneficial trait to spread across groups, as it does for an individually beneficial trait to spread within a group.

Culture and genetic coevolution has led to strong selection for human abilities to be both individually creative and to imitate the successful behaviors of others. This behavior would seem to be directly related to the diffusion of brand popularity among various subcultures in modern societies. As contemporary subcultures gain social, political and/or economic stature, the goods, services, and activities they consume become incrementally attractive to those in other subcultures. As marketers well know, producing and selling these culturally attractive items is not only profitable, but also fast moving, as imitators may quickly move on to what appear to be superior symbols. Thus, sociological phenomena such as *upward mobility* and *role acquisition* may be understood in evolutionary terms as selected-for traits within the population. Boyd and Richerson (2005: 41) additionally note that:

> People often imitate the successful ... [because] our attraction to the successful makes adaptive sense. ... By imitating the successful, you have a chance of acquiring the behaviors that cause success. ... We grant prestige, and the favors that go with it, to people we perceive as having superior cultural variants as a means of compensating them for the privilege of their company and the opportunity to imitate them.

Thus, the evolutionary perspective provides a novel observation point for conceptualizing not only social mobility and prestige, but also the phenomena of celebrity endorsements and diachronic shifts in brand meaning. As brands are adopted by more/less successful groups or individuals within a culture, their extrinsic value as symbols of various types of success may be altered.

MARKETING AS CONSUMER-DIRECTED AND CONSUMER-PRODUCED INNOVATION

As noted at the outset of this essay, Vargo and Lusch (2004) titled their article 'Evolving to a new Dominant Logic for Marketing', arguing that contemporary marketing practice (and theory) should be focused upon 'intangible resources, the co-creation of value, and relationships (p. 1)', a viewpoint with which evolutionary theory would agree. They cite several authors in the marketing management literature as envisioning marketing as an innovative or adaptive force (e.g., Day and Montgomery, 1999). Indeed, marketing technologies have now reached a level permitting individuals to construct and market their own innovativeness, both in commercial and noncommercial settings (Fuller and von Hippel, 2008).

Multiple examples can be found within popular culture news media. For instance,

Levy (2007, *Newsweek*: 16) describes how consumers 'unlocked' their iPhones to permit themselves to operate on communication networks other than the tied-in AT&T service. An article by Tyrangiel (*Time*, 2007: 60) recounts how a rock music group, Radiohead, made available their most recent album, *In Rainbows*, on the band's website, thereby eliminating the usual manufacturer – wholesaler – retailer delivery channel.

Moreover, ironically, some current innovations are actually revivals of ancient, even prehistoric, practices. For example, a retired geneticist, Wes Jackson, is developing crops modeled on preagricultural grasses and grains, which use water more efficiently and conserve soil nutrients more effectively than current crops (*Time*, 2007). Similarly, Caryl (*Newsweek*, Oct. 1, 2007) reports that the inhabitants of Qara Province, Rajasthan, have been reintroduced by a Dutch anthropologist to their 1,500 year old stone lined aqueducts originally built under Persian rule. The result is that 'today pistachios and fruit trees are flourishing again in Qara, watered by a technology that was perfected while the Iron Age was reaching Europe' (p. 71). (It is interesting to consider this as a *product relaunch*. It would indeed be ironic if the rapidly declining environment (caused by human technological innovations, e.g., the internal combustion engine) leads to the rebirth of innovations originated during the Stone Age, i.e., Pleistocene).

Some theorists see a dramatic change underway in cultural–environmental coevolution; specifically they propose that *diachronic, generation-to-generation* innovation transmission is rapidly giving way to *synchronic, within-generational* innovation transmission. Boyd and Richerson state (2005: 66):

> Social learning through horizontal transmission [may be] more adaptive in rapidly changing environments. Hominid niche construction led to a stable constructed environment, which assured that certain tool technologies, methods of food preparation, and so on would be advantageous from one generation to the next ... However, in postindustrial times the reverse may be occurring: oblique and

horizontal transmission are favored ... Modern culturally constructed environments appear to be changing so rapidly that vertically transmitted information between parents and offspring is too slow to be of sufficient adaptive value.

This possibility has already been recognized by some marketing researchers. For example, Fuller and von Hippel (2008: 2) discuss the origin of some recent intra-generational product innovations and the online consumer communities ('tribes' in evolutionary parlance) that supported their initial diffusion:

> Products like the snowboard, mountain bike, and Apache web server are well-known innovation examples, which have been innovated by users. Such creative consumers often meet in online communities where they collaboratively develop new products. In the virtual café *alt.coffee*, for example, coffee connoisseurs discuss how coffee machines and bean roasters can be improved [by their owners] in order to achieve the optimal 'coffee experience'. Members of the online community *ilounge.com* are dedicated to the apple iPod. They try to resolve product shortcomings of existing iPods, such as the short lifespan of the iPod battery, and develop innovative new designs for the next generation of portable mp3 players. Our research findings show that, on average, around 10 per cent of community members frequently deal with and are dedicated to innovations.

They also discuss the interpersonal (i.e., prosocial) cooperative communication that underlies much of this *communal innovativeness*:

> The main reason why consumers innovate in cooperation with their friends, peers, relatives, and acquaintances is because they look for the complementary knowledge and skills necessary to bring their new product ideas closer to realization. Since consumers benefit from using their innovation and not from selling it, ... often they share their innovation *within communities*. Free revealing offers several benefits to them: network effects, improvement of reputation, related innovations revealed by others...
>
> Being confronted with a member's new product, discussing it, and providing feedback on it creates a common understanding about the innovation.... Through intense interactions a new product may result that is superior to if it were innovated by a single user.

All these examples – from the most technologically advanced to newly rediscovered ancestral practices – are consistent with the notion of marketing as an agent of cultural evolution. Selective cultural adaptation favors practices that show robustness as compared to available alternatives. If we envision marketing as the mechanism that *introduces these innovations to the culture and then tests them against competitors*, we can glimpse the extraordinary and essential role of marketing-as-process over a vast expanse of human endeavor.

APPLYING EVOLUTIONARY THEORY TO CURRENT MARKETING THEORY

Browsing through recent issues of the *Journal of Marketing* and *Journal of Marketing Research*, I identified three topics of inquiry that could benefit from the introduction of an evolutionary perspective: (1) companies as families/tribes, (2) reciprocity versus opportunism in company-to-company and company-to-consumer relationships, and (3) brands as social markers. These are discussed in the following section.

Companies as tribes and families

In both a metaphoric and literal sense, companies function in ways similar to tribes and families. Their members have a sense of belonging and commitment to a shared ideology and set of goals. Overall company welfare is dependent upon cooperation among employees and, conversely, the welfare of individual employees is dependent upon overall corporate performance.

Yet evolutionary theory lets us take this analogy a bit deeper and consider the notion that companies must also identify and adapt to environmentally appropriate niches, if they want to survive over time. As with families and tribes, companies must also distribute resources internally in ways that are deemed equitable by their members, or risk dissension and hoarding/reprisal by individual members.

Further, novel adaptive skills and practices must be rapidly communicated to all members (and perhaps kept hidden from other tribes).

An example of this way of conceptualizing the company is provided by White et al. (2003: 63) who state, 'To survive and prosper in a competitive marketplace, an organization must respond continuously to opportunities and threats posed by a changing environment'. Their research showed (p. 74), 'Marketing managers who perceive their organizational culture as more of an adhocracy or clan are more likely to perceive that they can control the outcome'.

Steenkamp and Guyskens (2006) extended the tribal/family metaphor to the consideration of organizations at a national level. They propose that *consumer ethnocentrism* may be viewed as a manifestation of loyalty to one's country and its production system to the exclusion or rejection of products manufactured by other tribes (i.e., countries). For example, encouraging consumers to 'buy American' or to boycott products and services from various countries with whom the US has political conflicts are inherently rooted in the evolutionary appeal to intra-tribal support and reciprocity.

Marinova (2004: 1) provides a strong empirical example of the tribe/family concept in her work on innovation diffusion *within* the company, 'An organization's ability to recognize the value of new information, assimilate it, and use it strategically is regarded as crucial for its ability to innovate. ... In practice, organizations implement a team approach for developing new products to ensure organization-wide knowledge acquisition and dissemination. [It is hoped] that information that resides in isolated pockets in the organization will become shared over time, leading to better decision making'.

Her results indicated that while the intra-firm diffusion of market knowledge positively enhanced firm innovativeness, when members became too satisfied with their prior performance, inertia could set in and future innovativeness was hindered, i.e., corporate complacency reduces risk taking. From an evolutionary perspective, this is consistent with the finding that an overly stable environment reduces risk-taking by the family or tribal group.

Johnson et al. (2004) also adopt a firm-as-tribe evolutionary perspective noting that, 'Firms often operate in an ever-changing environment, [so] we investigated the moderating effect of environmental turbulence'. Recalling Richerson and Boyd's proposal that more innovative tribes and individuals are better adapted to survive in rapidly changing environments, these authors examined how capable a firm was in absorbing knowledge from current experiences. They found that knowledge obtained about how to interact with other firms was especially valuable for profitability. They also found that at extremely high levels of environmental change ('turbulence'), pre-existing functional knowledge was not adequate to permit appropriate responses. Consistent with Richerson and Boyd, only firms capable of marked innovative learning and adaptational abilities were able to survive.

A final example is provided by Ross and Robertson (2007) who apply the tribe/family analogy to inter-tribal (i.e., inter-organizational) relationships. As they state (p. 118), 'repeated ties between firms over time build commitment and trust which can serve as a safeguard against opportunism. ... Reputation is critical to a firm's ability to enter into relationships with other firms. ... [An opportunistic reputation] may lead to a firm having an organizational life that, in Hobbe's terms, is nasty, poor, brutish and short'. In other words, a firm that mistreats its business partners risks ostracism and banishment from the industry or marketplace in which it competes.

Reciprocity versus opportunism in company–company and company–consumer relationships

This brings us to a second topic currently of interest in marketing theory: relationship creation and maintenance. As Selnes and

Sallis (2003: 81)state, 'Relationship learning [is] a joint activity in which the parties strive to create more value together than they would create individually or with other parties'. Their research indicated, consistent with evolutionary theory, that relationship learning 'can be promoted and accelerated through collaborative commitment (p. 91)'.

However, they also found two costs to the development of these interpersonal bonds, both of which would be predicted by evolutionary theory (Boyd and Richerson, 2005). First, once friendships are established between firms, mutual monitoring for 'cheating' or opportunism decreases, making possible selfish actions by one or both parties (and see also Jap, 2003). Second, inertia and over reliance on the status quo can prevent the parties from exploring even better solutions to joint issues. Moderate and even high levels of cultural turbulence are likely to lead to higher levels of creativity and company adaptiveness. One hypothesis to emerge from this is that companies operating in markets, which are highly competitive and fast-moving technologically (or aesthetically, e.g., fashion) are likely to be the most efficient and effective at exploiting environmental opportunities.

Heide and Wathne (2006) studied relationships between corporate partners in which *opportunism* ('self-interest seeking with guile') was present. They concluded that the short-term rewards of opportunism were less profitable than the long-term return from establishing trust and reciprocity with partner business firms. Similarly, Ross and Robertson (2007), also investigating opportunism, observed that companies typically will punish and negatively sanction business partners that engage in opportunistic behavior.

Among the sanctions used was the refusal to engage in repeat business with the errant partner and also engaging in negative word of mouth with other firms about the opportunistic firm's behavior. Analogously, negative word of mouth by consumers concerning opportunistic and dishonest behavior by firms had a damaging effect on the company's stock prices – thereby reducing capital inflow to the errant firm (Luo, 2007). In evolutionary terms, opportunistic companies are seen by their channel (i.e., tribal) partners and by consumers as behaving in antisocial ways - ways that are destructive to *collective* interests. The companies engaging in such behaviors will be punished much as Boyd and Richerson (2005) described.

Klein et al. (2004) studied why consumers chose to boycott given companies; boycotts are an example of retaliation against a partner/ tribe member who has engaged in inappropriate or selfish conduct. As they comment (p. 96), 'Boycott participation is prompted by the belief that a firm has engaged in conduct that is strikingly wrong and that has negative and possible harmful consequences for various parties (e.g., workers, consumers, and society at large)'. In keeping with evolutionary theory, they found that, 'Boycotters may have an instrumental motivation to change the target firm's behavior and/or to signal to the firm and others the necessity of appropriate conduct (p. 96)'.

Brands as tribal and social markers

Recall that Richerson and Boyd (2005) and other evolutionary theorists (e.g., Mithen, 1999) commented on the appearance of symbolic consciousness in humans around 35,000 years ago. Coincident with this was the use of visual and verbal 'markers' to identify tribal affiliation. Visual markers such as physical appearance, hairstyle, tattoos, scarification, and jewelry were used to create not only personal identity, but also to announce membership in a particular clan or community. Verbal markers such as dialect and accent also helped rapid identification of group members versus 'outsiders' or imitators hoping to gain access to group resources.

The use of such social symbols grew substantially more diverse and intricate with the rise of status hierarchies within the city-state. Rules regulating dress and appearance (e.g., head coverings, apparel designs, facial hair, and color usage, e.g., royal blue) became necessary to enable the rapid and accurate identification not so much of friend or foe, but rather of social rank and occupation. In Imperial Rome, for instance, while all male citizens wore the toga, only senators were permitted to wear the *latus clavus* toga, which featured a wide purple stripe. The emperor and triumphant generals wore the toga *picta*, which was crimson with gold embroidery. Women of noble birth wore the *stola* over their tunics, often in silk or muslin fabrics.

From these evolutionary origins, it is but a tiny conceptual 'leap' to viewing contemporary brands and styles as culturally adaptive signifiers of tribal identity based on various social affiliations and statuses. An article by Kozinets (2002), for example, discusses how the Starbucks brand is viewed by highly involved coffee connoisseurs as 'mechanistic, dispassionate, oppressive, overly large, and lacking humanity', and therefore, is rejected as a desirable social signifier by these consumers.

Brown et al. (2003) in research on 'retro-marketing' also describe the large role which particular brands play as generational affiliation markers, 'The brand must have a virtual essence, that is, it must have existed as an important icon during a specific developmental stage for a particular generation or cohort … The retro-brand must be capable of mobilizing a utopian vision, of engendering longing for an idealized past or community' (p. 30). Thus brand managers and marketing theorists, alike, would do well to recognize that the concept of 'branding' originated not with capitalism and the industrial revolution, but rather with the evolutionary human need for communicating group identity.

CONCLUSIONS

The purpose of the present chapter has been to cast the past in evolutionary terms and to suggest that the current conceptualization of marketing-as-process – especially a process implying the diffusion of innovations across human groups – is consistent with the biocultural coevolutionary models of some theorists, most especially Boyd and Richerson.

The present author is certainly indebted to the prior work of marketing historians, for example Ronald Fullerton (see e.g., Fullerton and Nevett, 1988), who have long called for a greater acknowledgment of the past as a foundation for the present structure of markets and marketing.

The incremental step that I hope the present essay makes, however, is to grasp the significance of the past in a much larger, fuller way. Humans – consumers, marketers, and consumer–marketers – have evolved over *millennia* to reach their current status. During that time, the evolution of our human-constructed culture has deeply affected how we conceptualize ourselves and others, it has impacted how we form ourselves into groups and how we seek to create identities within and through those groups. The evolution of culture has impacted how we respond to those organizations and groups and individuals believed to not be 'playing fair', to not be contributing to the collective welfare. It has made us cognizant of social differences and status differentials.

The present chapter is also highly indebted to the foundational work of scholars such as Muniz and Schau (2005), McAlexander et al. (2002), and Shankar et al. (2007) who have forcefully argued for the view that all consumption is *inherently social*; that we consume not as individuals acting atomistically and independently, but rather as social beings constantly embedded in a mesh of group and subcultural memberships. Our species' evolved characteristics make this so; humans are tribal beings; the personal is always, inescapably, the *interpersonal*.

Yet, as Von Hippel (2005) and others (e.g., Sawhney and Prandetti, 2000) remind us, the 'loss' of the myth of individuality comes with the promise of more empowered consumer–producers acting within democratic groups of like-minded persons. In some important ways, culture – and technology – now seem to have evolved to make it possible to bypass for-profit marketing (and for-profit marketers) and enable groups to produce some of their own goods and services. If this trend continues and intensifies in the future, it will indeed be an ironic return to the most basic form of marketing-as-process – the self-sufficient, group-level productivity of our earliest human ancestors.

REFERENCES

Bowman, D. and Das, N. (2004) 'Linking Customer Management Effort to Customer Profitability in Business Markets', *Journal of Marketing Research*, 41(November): 433–447.

Boyd, R. and Peter, J.R. (2005) *The Origin and Evolution of Cultures*. Oxford: Oxford University Press.

Brown, S., Kozinets, R.V. and Sherry J.F. (2003) 'Teaching Old Brands New Tricks', *Journal of Marketing*, 67(3) July: 19–33.

Caryl, C. (2007) 'Cool, Clear Water', *Newsweek*, October 1: 71.

Dawkins, R. (1976) *The Selfish Gene*. Oxford: Oxford University Press.

Todd, D.D., Brown, T.J. and Mowen, J.C. (2004) 'Internal Benefits of Service-Worker Customer Orientation', *Journal of Marketing*, 68(1) January: 128–146.

Eyuboglu, N. and Buja, A. (2007) 'Quasi-Darwinian Selection in Marketing Relationships', *Journal of Marketing*, 71(4) October: 48–62.

Franke, N. and Shah, S. (2003) 'How Communities Support Innovative Activities', *Research Policy*, 32 (1): 157–178.

Fullerton, R.A. and Nevett, T. (1988) *Historical Perspectives in Marketing*, Boston, MA: Lexington Books.

Grayson, K. (2007) 'Friendship Versus Business in Marketing Relationships', *Journal of Marketing*, 71(4) October: 121–139.

Heide, J.B. and Wathne, K. (2006) 'Friends, Businesspeople and Relationship Roles', *Journal of Marketing*, 70(3) July: 90–103.

Heide, J.B., Wathne, K. and Rokkan, A. (2007) 'Inter-Firm Monitoring, Social Contacts and Relationship Outcomes', *Journal of Marketing Research*, 44(August): 425–433.

Hemetsberger, A. (2001) 'Fostering Cooperation on the Internet', *Advances in Consumer Research*, 29: 354–356.

Jap, S. (2003) 'An Exploratory Study of Online Reverse Auctions', *Journal of Marketing*, 67(3) July: 96–107.

Johnson, J.L., Sohi, R. and Grewal, R. (2004) 'The Role of Relational Knowledge Stores in Interfirm Partnering', *Journal of Marketing*, 68(3) July: 21–36.

Klein, J.N., Smith, C. and John, A. (2004) 'Why We Boycott', *Journal of Marketing*, 68(3) July: 92–109.

Kozinets, R.V. (2002) 'The Field Behind the Screen', *Journal of Marketing Research*, 39 February: 61–72.

Lambkin, M. and Day, G. (1989) 'Evolutionary Processes in Competitive Markets', *Journal of Marketing*, 53(July): 4–20.

Levy, S. (2007) 'Honey, I Bricked the New Mobile Phone!', *Newsweek*, October 15: 16.

Luo, X. (2007) 'Consumer Negative Voice and Firm Stock Returns', *Journal of Marketing*, 71(3) July: 78–88.

Marinova, D. (2004) 'Actualizing Innovation Effort', *Journal of Marketing*, 68(3) July: 1–20.

McAlexander, J., Schouten, J. and Koenig, H. (2002) 'Building Brand Community', *Journal of Marketing*, 66(1): 38–54.

Muniz, A.M. and Schau, H.J. (2005) 'Religiosity in the Abandoned Apple Newton Brand Community', *Journal of Consumer Research*, 31(March): 737–747.

Das, N. and Kasturi Rangan, V. (2004) 'Building and Sustaining Buyer–Seller Relationships', *Journal of Marketing*, 68(3) July: 63–77.

Richerson, P.J. and Boyd, R. (2005) *Not By Genes Alone: How Culture Transformed Human Evolution*. Chicago: University of Chicago Press.

Ross, W.T. and Robertson, D.C. (2007) 'Compound Relationships Between Firms', *Journal of Marketing*, 71(3) July: 108–123.

Sawhney, M. and Prandetti, E. (2000) 'Communities of Creation', *California Management Review*, 42(4): 24–54.

Sawhney, M., Verona, G. and Prandelli, E. (2005) 'Collaborating to Create', *Journal of Interactive Marketing*, 19(4): 23–35.

Selnes, F. and Sallis, J. (2003) 'Promoting Relationship Learning', *Journal of Marketing*, 67(3) July: 80–95.

Shankar, A., Cova, B. and Kozinets, R. (2007) *Consumer Tribes*. Oxford, UK: Butterworth-Heinemann.

Steenkamp, J.B. and Geyskens, I. (2006) 'How Country Characteristics Affect the Perceived Value of Web Sites', *Journal of Marketing*, 70(3) July: 139–151.

Stone, L. and Lurquin, P. (2007) *Genes, Culture and Human Evolution*. Malden, Mass: Blackwell Publishing.

Tadajewski, M. (2009 forthcoming), 'The Foundations of Relationship Marketing: Reciprocity and Trade Relations', *Marketing Theory*.

Tyrangiel, J. (2007) 'Radical Remix', *Time*, October 15: 60.

Vargo, S.L. and Lusch, R.F. (2004) 'Evolving to a New Dominant Logic for Marketing', *Journal of Marketing*, 68(1) January: 1–17.

Von Hippel, E. (2005) *Democratizing Innovation*. Cambridge, MA: MIT Press.

Wallace, W.M. (2007) *Techno-Cultural Evolution: Cycles of Creation and Conflict*. Washington, DC: Potomac Books.

Wathne, K.H. and Heide, J.B. (2004) 'Relationship Governance in a Supply Chain Network', *Journal of Marketing*, 68(1) January: 71–89.

26

The Darwinian Underpinnings of Consumption

Gad Saad

INTRODUCTION

Most scientists and scholars alike rank Darwinian theory as perhaps the most important and influential theory within the accumulated pantheon of human knowledge. Evolutionary theory is at the cornerstone of the biological sciences. Irrespective of whether a biologist is studying phenomena at the molecular, genetic, cellular, organismic, group, population, species, ecological, or phylogenetic levels, Darwinian theory permeates across all units of analysis. The parsimony and explanatory power of evolutionary theory is such that it has made contributions to a wide range of otherwise disparate disciplines, including art/aesthetics, architecture, agriculture, ecology, neuroscience, gastronomy, literature, history, philosophy, medicine, physiology, immunology, politics and international relations, law, sociology, economics, anthropology, computer science, biomimetics, education, and psychology (see Saad, 2007a, Table 2.3, pp. 57–58 for some relevant references). Even religion, which many individuals would qualify as antithetical to evolutionary theory, has been investigated using Darwinian principles

(cf. Boyer and Bergstrom, 2008). That said, the marketing discipline in general, and the consumer research sub-discipline in particular, has largely ignored evolutionary theory within its respective theoretical toolboxes and empirical edifices (Saad, 2008a). The overriding objectives of the current chapter will accordingly be twofold: (1) to provide a discussion of key tenets of evolutionary theory; (2) to subsequently demonstrate ways by which the field of consumer research benefits from a rapprochement with Darwinian and biological-based principles.

I begin with a brief historical overview of the evolution of Darwinian theory over the past 150 years or so. Included here are discussions of natural and sexual selection as originally espoused by Charles Darwin, the Modern Synthesis of the 1930s and 1940s, the growth of sociobiology, human ethology, human behavioral ecology, and Darwinian anthropology in the 1970s, and finally the founding of evolutionary psychology (EP) in the late 1980s and early 1990s. Defining principles of EP are covered, including the recognition that the human mind does not start off as a blank slate, and that it is comprised not only of domain-general mechanisms but also domain-specific computational systems. Furthermore, a crucial epistemological insight from evolutionary theory is addressed, namely that biological organisms (including humans) can be studied at two distinct levels – the proximate and ultimate levels of analysis. Key evolutionary theories and concepts including kin selection, reciprocal altruism, the parental investment hypothesis, paternity uncertainty, Zahavian signaling, and the EP position regarding the nature–nurture debate are described. I then provide explicit links between the central evolutionary principles covered and a broad range of consumption/marketing phenomena. I demonstrate how the great majority of consumption acts that we engage in are rooted in our biological heritage be it the foods that we eat, the toys that we play with as children, the gifts that we offer to close friends, family members, and mates, the advertisements that appeal to us, and the products that we use to beautify ourselves in the mating market, to name but a few examples. In the concluding section of the chapter, I identify at least four important epistemological benefits that the marketing and consumer research disciplines can reap by incorporating evolutionary theory within their theoretical toolboxes.

HISTORICAL SYNOPSIS OF DARWINIAN THEORY

In his seminal book, Darwin (1859) described the process of natural selection, namely the mechanisms by which species evolve in a manner that makes them highly adapted to their ecological niches. Specifically, natural selection recognizes that, as a result of competition (e.g., population growth is bounded by the scarcity of food resources), only those individuals that are best adapted to their environments will survive. This is achieved via three distinct steps: (1) random mutations arise and are manifested within an organism's phenotype; (2) if the random mutation yields

a fitness advantage resulting in an increased chance for the organism possessing the mutation to survive and reproduce; and (3) if the mutation is heritable, then the selective forces of natural selection will be operative. Whereas Darwin recognized the importance of the heritability of traits as a central element of natural selection, he was unaware of the specific mechanisms of heredity. The Modern Synthesis of the 1930s and 1940s solved this problem by incorporating Mendelian genetics within natural selection.

In a subsequent book, Darwin (1871) introduced the parallel process of sexual selection, which explained the evolution of morphological traits and behaviors that could not have evolved via natural selection. For example, a peacock's long, heavy, and ornate tail could not have evolved via natural selection, as its large size is detrimental to the peacock's likelihood of survival (increased chance of predation). Instead, the tail has evolved as a result of female mate choice. In other words, a peacock's tail is a means of wooing hens into mating with a particular individual. Other morphological traits have evolved not as a means for inter-sexual wooing, but rather for intra-sexual combat. For example, rams possess thick cranial bones that permit them to engage in vicious head butting combats, with the winning ram claiming monopolistic sexual access to the females within his territory. In this case, sexual selection is driven by direct intra-sexual rivalry. Zahavi (1975) introduced an important extension to sexual selection, which he termed the 'handicap principle'. He argued that sexual signals must be costly (as per the peacock's tail) in order for these to serve as honest and hence diagnostic cues of an organism's quality, otherwise it would be easy for suboptimal competitors to fake the signal (see also Zahavi and Zahavi, 1997).

Numerous lay people and scholars alike, who are otherwise unfamiliar with the scope of Darwinian theory, mistakenly believe that it is largely restricted to a description of the evolution of an animal's morphological traits. Darwin himself had recognized the importance of evolutionary theory in understanding the psychology of an organism. He famously stated, 'In the distant future, I see open fields for far more important researches. Psychology will be based on a new foundation, that of the necessary acquirement of each mental power and capacity by gradation. Light will be thrown on the origin of man and his history' (Darwin, 1859: 488). With the exception of a few disciplines such as biological anthropology and comparative psychology, the great majority of the social sciences have historically built their knowledge bases whilst fully ignoring the fact that human behavior has been shaped by evolutionary forces. It was not until the 1960s and 1970s that distinct disciplines were founded, which specifically investigated human behavior from a Darwinian perspective. These included human ethology (Eibl-Eibesfeldt, 1989), human sociobiology (Alcock, 2001, Chapter 8; Wilson, 1975, Chapter 26), and human behavioral ecology (Winterhalder and Smith, 2000). Some scholars have merged these approaches under the umbrella of Darwinian anthropology. By the late 1980s and early 1990s, EP was founded as a distinct scientific discipline, of which the key tenets will be discussed in detail in the ensuing section. The interested reader can refer to Smith et al. (2001), Laland and Brown (2002), and Mysterud (2004) for a discussion of the conceptual differences between these varied evolutionary approaches.

Natural selection, as espoused by Charles Darwin, assumed that the unit of selection was the individual organism. This posed a challenge to evolutionists as altruistic behaviors that are otherwise potentially harmful to the altruist have been documented across a very broad range of species (including humans). Altruistic acts can be divided into two categories as a function of the recipients of such beneficent acts: kin or non-kin. By incorporating a gene-centric selectionist perspective, Hamilton (1964) demonstrated that individuals could increase their inclusive fitness by engaging in altruistic acts toward their kin. This form of selection known as kin selection has become one of the cornerstones

of modern evolutionary theory, as it explains a broad range of kin-based altruistic behaviors across a wide range of species. From a gene's perspective, an individual who dies in the commission of saving four of his siblings has actually increased his/her inclusive fitness. What about altruistic acts toward non-kin? Trivers (1971) provided the evolutionary conditions that would make such acts adaptive, a phenomenon known as reciprocal altruism. Needless to say, much of human sociality is driven by the forging and maintenance of reciprocal-based alliances (e.g., friendships and coalitions).

One of the greatest epistemological benefits of evolutionary theory is that it generates explanations that are extraordinarily grand in their scope. Take, for example, Trivers' (1972) parental investment hypothesis. It predicts specific patterns of sexual dimorphisms as a function of the parental cost that is borne by each of the two sexes within a particular sexually reproducing species. For example, the sexual coyness, physical size, and level of aggression of a given sex are perfectly predicted by the parental investment hypothesis. Specifically, the sex that bears the greater parental cost will be smaller, less aggressive, and more sexually coy. For most animals, females provide greater parental investment and, accordingly, they tend to be smaller, less aggressive, and more sexually discriminating (as the costs of a suboptimal mate choice loom larger for them). Incredibly, in species where males engage in greater parental investment (this typically occurs in species where gestation and/or fertilization is external as is the case with fish and birds), the sexual dimorphisms are exactly reversed (e.g., the jacanas and phalaropes in bird species; the praying mantis and the black widow spider in insects; some North Sea pipefish; see Eens and Pinxten, 2000). The parental investment hypothesis is able not only to explain universal human sex differences that transcend cultural settings and epochs, but it also correctly predicts the sex roles across a bewildering number of species spanning numerous phyla. Contrary to a popular lay misconception, this example demonstrates that evolutionary theory posits very specific predictions that are falsifiable. The datum that would falsify the parental investment hypothesis is indeed quite clear. The interested reader is referred to Andrews et al. (2002), Conway and Schaller (2002), Ketelaar and Ellis (2000), and Hagen (2005) for thorough rebuttals to many of the most common misconceptions about evolutionary theory in general and EP in particular. Incidentally, Americans are among the most fervent disbelievers in evolution (Mazur, 2005), in part due to their religious faiths (see Shanks, 2006, and Sober, 2007, for critiques of intelligent design, the latest mutation of creationist thinking).

KEY PRINCIPLES OF EP

Homicide by Daly and Wilson (1988) is one of the early seminal books of EP. This book is profoundly influential, as it demonstrates the explanatory power and theoretical parsimony of evolutionary-based theorizing. The authors in question showed that certain forms of criminality occur in extraordinarily predictable manners, irrespective of cultural setting and/or historical context, as they are driven by universal factors linked to our biological heritage. For example, women are overwhelmingly likely to be killed by their lovers for one key reason: suspected and/or realized sexual infidelity. This tragic reality is due to two simple biological facts: Given that humans are a biparental species, and in light of the fact that only men experience parental uncertainty, the threat of cuckoldry looms large in men's psyches. Men who were willing to invest substantially in a child without any assurances that the child was theirs did not pass on their genes as successfully as those who were more vigilant. This basic evolutionary fact has been borne by a broad range of data.

Another foundational EP source is the edited book by Barkow et al. (1992). The first chapter by Tooby and Cosmides (1992) lays the conceptual differences between EP and the framework to which most social scientists ascribe, namely the Standard Social Science Model (SSSM). One important tenet of EP is the recognition that the human mind consists of domain-specific computational systems that have each evolved to solve recurring challenges, not unlike the fact that each of our organs (e.g., lungs, pancreas, spleen, or liver) is an evolutionary solution to an adaptive challenge. Some of these recurring ancestral problems that have shaped the evolution of the human mind include food foraging, mate choice, kin investments, predator avoidance, and coalition formations. Hence, rather than viewing the human mind as a domain-general processor capable of applying the same algorithm across any context (e.g., the cost–benefit framework or classical conditioning), evolutionary psychologists recognize the evolutionary forces that would give rise to domain-specific computational algorithms. Furthermore, evolutionary psychologists reject the premise that is central to the SSSM, namely that the human mind begins as a blank slate that is subsequently shaped by socialization (see Pinker, 2002, for a critique of the blank slate view of the human mind). In so doing, EP explicitly acknowledges that humans are indeed endowed with a biological-based universal human nature (see Brown, 1991, for an exhaustive list of human universals, and Norenzayan and Heine, 2005, for a discussion of psychological universals).

Implicit to evolutionary theory is the recognition that any phenomenon that involves biological organisms can be explained at two levels, namely the proximate and the ultimate (Mayr, 1961; Tinbergen, 1963). The former refers to a mechanistic explanation of *how* a phenomenon operates and/or *what* factors affect its workings. Ultimate explanations refer to the Darwinian *why* – namely, they seek to elucidate why a phenomenon would have evolved to be of this particular form. A classic example that highlights this distinction is pregnancy sickness. Women have experienced the unpleasant symptoms associated with pregnancy sickness in universally similar ways. Proximate explorations might include the smells that trigger the symptoms of pregnancy sickness, and/or hormonal (e.g., oestrogen) and blood pressure changes that are associated with pregnancy sickness. An ultimate analysis seeks to understand the adaptive problem that pregnancy sickness solves. This ailment coincides with organogenesis, namely the period where the organs are forming in utero. During this ontogenetic process, it is crucially important that the developing embryo not be exposed to any pathogens. Accordingly, pregnancy sickness with its associated nausea and vomiting is an adaptive mechanism meant to expel teratogens (e.g., food pathogens) that a mother might have ingested (Flaxman and Sherman, 2000; Pepper and Roberts, 2006; Profet, 1992). The unique insight from this ultimate Darwinian perspective is that pregnancy sickness is a beneficial ailment as evidenced by the fact that it appears to greatly reduce the likelihood of a miscarriage. Note that the ultimate and proximate explanations do not compete with one another, nor are they contradictory. Rather, both levels of analyses are essential for a complete understanding of a given phenomenon.

Contrary to another popular albeit erroneous misconception, evolutionists do not purport that all human behavior is inscribed in one's genes. Rather, evolutionary theory posits that humans are an inextricable mix of their biological heritage, their individual genes, and their unique environments and life experiences, a position known as interactionism. Hence, from an evolutionary perspective, the nature–nurture debate is somewhat moot. Incidentally, the central mechanisms of Darwinian theory recognize the importance of the environment in defining the operative selective pressures within a particular ecological niche. That said, evolutionists acknowledge that to simply state that a phenomenon is due to culture, learning, or socialization, as is typically the case with most SSSM-based explanations, carries little explanatory power. Rather, one must provide an ultimate explanation as to why many socialization agents typically occur in universally similar manners irrespective of cultural setting or temporal period. A diverse group of evolutionists have applied evolutionary principles in explaining culture (cf. Alvard, 2003; Kanazawa, 2006), perhaps none as exhaustively as Richerson and Boyd (2005) via their gene-culture co-evolution approach (also known as the dual-inheritance model). See Saad (2007, Chapter 5) for an enumeration of ways by which culture is studied from an evolutionary perspective including memetic theory (Blackmore, 1999; Dawkins, 1976).

As mentioned in the introduction of this chapter, evolutionary theory in general and EP in particular have been successfully applied in an extraordinarily broad range of disciplines across the natural and social sciences, as well as in the humanities (see Buss, 2005, and Crawford and Krebs, 2008, for two recent compendia of work within the EP discipline). With that in mind, the Darwinian revolution has yet to make substantial inroads within the marketing and consumer behavior disciplines. In the ensuing section, I provide an overview of evolutionary-based works that have been tackled within the latter two disciplines. I focus mainly on EP-based approaches in the consumption setting, although other evolutionary perspectives have been applied, including in understanding product evolution (Massey, 1999), relationship marketing (Eyuboglu and Buja, 2007; Palmer, 2000), evolution of a preference for sweeteners (Ruprecht, 2005), brand positioning via memetic theory (Marsden, 2002), shopping and brand choice as forms of foraging (DiClemente and Hantula, 2003; Foxall and James, 2003), product design among other design issues (Whyte, 2007), and consumer choice via an evolutionary-based form of operant conditioning (Foxall, 1994a, b, 2007).

EP IN THE CONSUMPTION SETTING

Marketing scholars have developed a rich empirical literature replete with methodologically and theoretically sophisticated approaches, albeit almost exclusively within the proximate realm (Saad, 2006a, 2007a, 2008a; Saad and Gill, 2000). The lack of biological-based and evolutionary-informed research within the marketing discipline seeps its way into the textbooks that marketing students learn from. For example, most consumer behavior textbooks are largely homogeneous in their contents, typically including chapters on key functional areas of relevance to the study of consumption including perception, motivation, personality, decision-making, culture, emotions, learning, and attitude formation and attitude change. Each of these areas exists within its insular paradigmatic walls, void of a common and overarching meta-framework. In the ensuing section, I demonstrate how evolutionary theory serves as the consilient framework across a wide range of these functional areas.

Darwinizing the functional areas of consumer research

I recently provided an overview of the key functional areas tackled by consumer scholars (Saad, 2007a, Chapter 2). In so doing, I demonstrated that all such investigations have occurred at the proximate level whilst purporting that the human mind consists of general-purpose domain-independent processes (e.g., classical conditioning, the elaboration likelihood model, and the theory of reasoned action). That marketing scholars have restricted their focus to proximate issues does not invalidate their work, rather it ensures that it is at best incomplete. Our sensorial system, our emotions, our learning mechanisms, our personalities, our cognitive systems, and our cultural heritage do not arise out of thin air nor do they materialize via arbitrary socialization processes. They are integral elements of our evolved biology, which has been shaped by the dual forces of natural and sexual selection. I went on to highlight ways by which each of the functional areas of interest to marketing scholars might be infused with ultimate-level explorations.

Take for example human olfaction. Milinski and Wedekind (2001) found that individuals'

self-preferences for perfumes were linked to their immunogenetic profiles (as measured by their markers along the major histocompatibility complex). Specifically, people prefer to wear perfumes that maximize their ability to advertise their scents within the mating market (i.e., that are congruent with their unique body chemistry). In this case, a product preference is intimately linked to a perceptual process (olfaction) that is otherwise driven by sexual selection. Hence, whereas marketing scholars might focus on the effects of a perfume's branding, promotion, and packaging on its subsequent sales, Milinski and Wedekind have shown that a key driver of this particular product choice is rooted in one's genetic makeup. Of course, an evolutionary lens is required for a full understanding of each of our four other senses. For example, many visual preferences are innate as they are rooted in our biological heritage. These include color perceptions (Crozier, 1999; Hill and Barton, 2005), and a penchant for symmetric configurations as manifested with both animate as well as inanimate objects (Cárdenas and Harris, 2006).

As a second example, let us explore attitude formation toward a new product/service from an ultimate perspective. This is precisely what Hayward and Rohwer (2004) did when they sought to determine individuals' attitudes toward paternity testing at hospitals. With the advances of DNA technology, why not offer such a service? The attitudinal difference between the two sexes was quite revealing and fully expected from an evolutionary perspective. Women held much less favorable attitudes toward this service and this had nothing to do with any existing attitudinal theory that is espoused by marketing scholars. Instead, cuckoldry is an adaptive strategy that is strictly beneficial to women whilst being solely detrimental to men's reproductive interests. This evolutionary fact bore the subsequent sex difference in attitudes toward paternity testing[1]. Incidentally, emotions are central to the attitudinal positions held by individuals. Of note, consumer scholars have largely ignored the evolutionary underpinnings of our affective system. Generally speaking, key emotions including fear, happiness, envy, disgust, guilt, shame, and love, have evolved as adaptive solutions to evolutionarily relevant problems (Cosmides and Tooby, 2000; Haselton and Ketelaar, 2006).

As a third example, I discuss information search, a process that is central to consumer decision-making. Is there a sex difference when it comes to the extent of search that is carried out prior to making a choice? Marketing scholars have posited a main effect for sex irrespective of the domain in question. Hence, whether choosing a mate, a mutual fund, or a clothing item, women are assumed to be the more comprehensive searchers (known as the selectivity hypothesis; cf. Meyers-Levy and Maheswaran, 1991). Saad et al. (2009) demonstrated the fallacy of such a domain-general approach to information search. They explored sex differences in the extent of mate search prior to either choosing or rejecting prospective suitors. In some instances, women acquired fewer attribute information such as when rejecting a pair of prospective suitors (study 1), whereas when choosing a winning suitor from a large set of competing mates, they evaluated a greater number of prospects (study 2). Hence, the domain in question (mate choice here) along with the inherent tasks (choosing versus rejecting) within the particular domain determines which of the two sexes will engage in greater search. In this particular case, mate search is driven by a biological-based mechanism rooted in the parental investment model (an erroneous mate choice looms larger for women, hence they reject suboptimal suitors more quickly and choose a winning suitor more carefully).

It is worth noting that, for other forms of search (e.g., food foraging), the domain-specific computational systems that are operative are radically different from those used for mate search. For example, certain spatial tasks (e.g., pathfinding versus object location memory) yield recurring universal sex differences, these being rooted in part in the differential division of labor that the two sexes have faced in our evolutionary history

(see Stenstrom et al., 2008, for a review). These sex-specific adaptive differences have been applied in exploring the shopping styles of men and women (Dennis and McCall, 2005), their food foraging strategies in a farmer's market (New et al., 2007), as well as their sex-specific design preferences (Moss et al., 2007).

It is oftentimes wrongly assumed that EP solely explores phenomena that are universally similar across individuals. However, evolutionary theory also seeks to explain why some traits remain highly heterogeneous within a given population. Personality is one such phenomenon. Numerous evolutionary-based arguments have been proposed to explain the maintenance of heterogeneous personality types (cf. Penke et al., 2007; Saad, 2007b), several of which recognize explicitly the importance of the environment in shaping individuals' personalities (i.e., evolutionary theory is not tantamount to biological determinism). Sibling rivalry is one such environmental factor purported to influence an individual's personality. Sibling rivalry exists in countless species. The means by which a given organism navigates through this form of competition varies greatly. Its most extreme form is siblicide, which can be instantiated in a myriad of ways (e.g., brood reduction in some Avian species or in utero cannabilistic siblicide in some shark species). Fortunately, for humans, most sibling rivalries are not nearly as violent. That notwithstanding sibling rivalry is one of the first adaptive problems that a child faces. According to Sulloway's (1996) Darwinian niche partitioning hypothesis, human children seek to maximize the parental investment that is imparted to them by occupying a unique niche in their parents' eyes (e.g., the 'I am an obedient child' versus 'I am a non-conforming rebel' niches). As one goes down a sibship, there are fewer unoccupied niches that are available to choose from. Accordingly, Sulloway argued that this developmental challenge has a profound effect on a child's personality yielding several consistent birth order effects on personality including that laterborns are more likely to be open to novel ideas, experiences, and beliefs. Sulloway demonstrated that of the 28 most radical scientific theories ever espoused, 23 yielded the postulated birth order effect. Specifically, laterborns were more likely to have developed and/or supported the radical scientific theories whereas firstborns were more likely to be fervent supporters of the status quo. Recently, Saad et al. (2005) applied Sulloway's hypothesis in the consumption setting. Specifically, they replicated the latter birth order effect albeit regarding consumers' propensity to be conforming and their likelihood to adopt new product innovations.

Advertising content as fossils of the human mind

As mentioned earlier, the SSSM and EP hold diametrically opposed positions regarding the blank slate premise of the human mind. SSSM-based marketing scholars view marketing-related messages (e.g., advertising content) as crucial socialization agents that are instrumental in forming minds that are otherwise born as empty slates. Evolutionists on the other hand propose that cultural products exist in their particular forms, because they are instantiations of our biological-based universal human nature. One such cultural product is the advertising content that consumers are exposed to. Several scholars have explored advertising content from an evolutionary perspective. I investigated the manner by which female escorts are advertised online (Saad, 2008b). Using data from 48 countries spanning the globe, it was shown that a woman's waist-to-hip ratio (WHR) was universally used as a key selling point. Furthermore, the mean WHR across the full sample was 0.72. This is particularly telling, as evolutionary psychologists have shown that men possess a near-universal WHR preference of 0.70, as this serves as a reliable indicator of nubility and fertility. Elsewhere, I have argued that some advertising contents occur in universally recurring manners, because they cater to evolutionary-derived

visual preferences (Saad, 2004, 2007a, Chapter 4). For example, that women are much more likely to be used in decorative roles, in all countries wherein this issue has been studied, does not point to a global patriarchal conspiracy. Rather, advertisers who happen to be Darwinian beings are fully aware that this strategy is more effective when targeting male consumers. Both Cary (2000) and Colarelli and Dettman (2003) have contended that effective advertisements are those that recognize consumers' human nature. Along those lines, Griskevicius et al. (2009) demonstrated that the efficacy of two persuasive messages (social proof versus scarcity) depended on which of two Darwinian concerns was primed (survival versus mating). When mating was primed, individuals were more receptive to the scarcity appeal (one wishes to be perceived as unique in the mating market), whereas when one's survival was primed, the social proof appeal was preferred (when threatened, there is safety in numbers). Finally, using the costly signaling framework, Ambler and Hollier (2004) argued that wasteful advertising is an honest signal of a brand's health, in the same way that a peacock's 'wasteful' tail is a signal of his fitness.

One of the most frequently used dependent measures when evaluating the efficacy of an advertisement is memory recall. Marketing scholars have explored countless copy variables that might affect a consumer's ad recall, although in no instance was there recognition of the adaptive nature of human memory. Several evolutionary behavioral scientists have recently demonstrated that evolutionarily relevant stimuli (e.g., words that are fitness-related; beautiful faces) are much more likely to be recalled (Becker et al., 2005; Nairne et al., 2007; Weinstein et al., 2008), highlighting the domain-specificity of human memory.

Consumption as lekking

A lek is a physical space where males typically congregate and engage in various forms of sexual signaling under the watchful eyes of discriminating females (Höglund and Alatalo, 1995). Lekking behavior occurs in numerous taxa including birds, reptiles, fish, and mammals. I have argued that numerous consumption acts are instantiations of lekking (Saad, 2007a, Chapter 3; see also Griskevicius et al., 2007; Lycett and Dunbar, 2000; Miller, 2000). When it comes to lekking, humans are unique, in that both sexes engage in the behavior. This is in part due to the fact that humans are a biparental species, resulting in some less-pronounced behavioral dimorphisms. That said, whereas men are much more likely to engage in status-related lekking (e.g., driving a Ferrari), women engage in beautification-related lekking (e.g., scantily clad dress attire, cosmetic surgeries, other beautification practices). Saad and Vongas (2009) explored the effects of conspicuous consumption on men's testosterone levels. Specifically, using a within-Ss design, men drove two cars (very expensive Porsche and an old sedan) in two environments, namely in the center of a major city or on a more isolated highway (i.e., lek and non-lek). Six salivary assays were collected from each participant corresponding to the four experimental conditions as well as two baseline measures taken at the start and end of the experiment. In line with evolutionary predictions, men's testosterone levels increased when driving the Porsche, although the lekking condition did not moderate the increase of testosterone when driving the Porsche. Ultimately, luxury sports cars are male-based forms of sexual signaling, analogous to the peacock's tail. Other studies that have recently investigated men's testosterone levels within business settings include Coates and Herbert (2008), who found that male traders' morning testosterone levels affect their subsequent financial profitability for that day, and White, Thornhill, and Hampson (2006), who uncovered that male entrepreneurs had higher basal testosterone levels than their male counterparts who had not been involved in entrepreneurial activities.

Dress attire can be a form of lekking, and as such has been explored from an evolutionary perspective in several distinct ways. In some instances, scholars have shown that societal changes in fashion trends (e.g., conservative or provocative attire) are in part driven by macro-level variables such as economic conditions, divorce rates, and sex ratios, all of which affect the level of competition in the mating market (Barber, 1999; Hill et al., 2005). Dress attire is affected by more immediate situational variables including a woman's menstrual cycle. Specifically, as is expected from an evolutionary perspective, women are more likely to advertise themselves via their clothing choices when maximally fertile (Grammer et al., 2004; Haselton et al., 2007; Saad and Stenstrom, 2008). Note that such a hypothesis could never have been generated, were it not approached using an evolutionary lens. Other beautification-related issues of relevance to consumer scholars that have been investigated from an evolutionary perspective include hairstyles (Hinsz et al., 2001; Mesko and Bereczkei, 2004), mustaches (Barber, 2001), high heels (Smith, 1999), cosmetic surgery (Sarwer et al., 2004; Singh and Randall, 2007), and acne (Bloom, 2004; Kellett and Gawkrodger, 1999; Kellett and Gilbert, 2001).

Gift giving

Gift giving is a universal human practice, abounding with economic and social consequences. In 2006, the amount spent on gifts by American consumer units was over $137 billion (US Census Bureau, 2006). The ubiquity of this ritual in the animal kingdom (e.g., nuptial gifts) suggests that it is a behavioral homology between numerous species (see Kruger, 2008, for a few species-specific examples). Whereas numerous marketing scholars have investigated gift-giving practices, few have explored the biological and evolutionary underpinnings of this phenomenon. Using kin selection, Saad and Gill (2003) found a positive correlation between expected patterns of gift expenditures and the genetic relatedness of the gift recipients and gift givers. Relatedly, maternal grandmothers and paternal grandfathers are the most and least likely, respectively, to invest in their grandchildren due to their differential levels of parental uncertainty, namely none for the former and two sources for the latter (Pollet et al., 2007). Saad and Gill also demonstrated that gift expenditures spent on close friends were greater than those spent on more distant kin, highlighting the fact that friendships, with their corresponding rituals of non-kin-based reciprocity, are central elements of human sociality. Finally, they explored sex differences in the motives for offering gifts to one's partner. Men were much more likely to use gifts for tactical purposes (e.g., to seduce or to impress). Furthermore, whereas men thought that both sexes offered gifts to one another for the same set of motives, women were aware of the discrepancy of motives. Saad and Gill argued that to the extent that the mating costs of misreading the signals associated with the gift-giving ritual loom much larger for women, it makes evolutionary sense that they would have evolved the superior capacity to navigate successfully through this particular ritual.

Other EP-based studies of gift giving have investigated specific gifts to uncover their evolutionary underpinnings. For example, Haviland-Jones et al. (2005) showed that humans exhibit an innate positive emotional response (e.g., a Duchenne smile) when offered flowers. Not surprisingly, not only are flowers an integral element of the mating ritual across numerous human cultures but also they are used by other species (e.g., the male Bower Bird in decorating his bower)[2]. Cronk and Dunham (2007) found that the amount spent on engagement rings, a form of costly signal meant to demonstrate a man's resources and investment in the prospective bride, was affected by the quality of the two mates. In other words, this particular consumption choice is largely driven by a biological metric of great relevance in the mating market.

Toys constitute one of the most ubiquitous gifts offered to children. The 2005 retail sales of toys in the American market were $21.3 billion (US Toy Industry Association, as cited by the US Department of Commerce Industry Outlook, 2006). In addition to their economic impact, toy preferences are particularly interesting to explore as social constructivists construe toys as a defining socialization agent of gender roles. The SSSM argument proposes that one of the ways by which boys and girls learn their respective gender roles is via the parental reinforcements that they receive when interacting with toys. Little Johnny is praised for rough-and-tumble play with the blue truck whilst Little Suzy is commended for interacting gently with the Barbie doll wearing the pink outfit. These apparent socialization episodes serve as catalysts to a life-long process of gender-specific socialization. The blank slate premise is manifest yet again. Children are born with empty minds, which in this case are subsequently shaped by the toy gifts that they are encouraged to play with. A biological-based perspective falsifies the notion quite convincingly. For example, Berenbaum and Hines (1992) demonstrated that little girls suffering from congenital adrenal hyperplasia, which yields in this instance a masculinization of morphological and behavioral traits, displayed an increased (decreased) penchant for male-specific (female-specific) toys. Alexander and Hines (2002) found that vervet monkeys displayed the same sex-specific toy preferences as that of human children (see also, Alexander, 2003), and Hassett et al. (2008) replicated the sex-specificity of toy preferences with rhesus monkeys. These findings render the socialization-based argument tenuous at best. This last example highlights the richness of data that can be used when testing evolutionary-based hypotheses. In this case, comparative psychology underscores a homologous preference between humans and two species of monkeys[3].

Transformative consumer research

Transformative consumer research is a recent laudable initiative set up by the Association for Consumer Research to study problems that affect consumers' well-being. By and large, much of the research that has been conducted on such matters within the marketing literature has made two explicit assumptions: (1) environmental forces are to blame (e.g., the media causes anorexia); (2) consumers' lack of information drives their poor choices (e.g., lack of knowledge about dietary choices). In reality, many consumption acts that have a deleterious effect on a consumer's welfare possess Darwinian etiologies (Saad, 2007a, Chapter 6). Some of these phenomena occur in universally sex-specific manners irrespective of cultural setting or temporal period. For example, men are much more likely to be pathological gamblers, pornography addicts, and excessive risk-takers (e.g., day traders, reckless drivers, and participants in extreme sports). On the other hand, women are overwhelmingly more likely to be compulsive buyers, sufferers of eating disorders (e.g., bulimia and anorexia nervosa), and excessive sun tanners.

The SSSM position regarding each of these dark side consumption acts is predictable. It is apparently due to one or more socialization agents. For example, social constructivists have blamed the media both for the endemic obesity that is plaguing the American populace (e.g., exposure to ads for fatty foods), whilst at the same time also arguing that it is the causative agent of anorexia and bulimia (e.g., exposure to images of beautiful women). In reality, the media has very little to do with obesity (Saad, 2006b). Rather, obesity is largely due to the incongruence between our evolved gustatory preferences (an adaptation to caloric scarcity and caloric uncertainty) and today's environment of plenty. If eating disorders are due to the media, one would have to explain why women have been the majority of sufferers for close to 2,500 years (cf. the description of the disorder by Hippocrates, the father of modern medicine); why of 100 women that are exposed to the same media images only two to three will develop eating disorders; and why the disease seems to afflict largely women irrespective of cultural context.

Whereas there are several related evolutionary explanations for the incidence of eating disorders (cf. Faer et al., 2005; Gatward, 2007; Salmon et al., 2008), the general idea is that these are an instantiation of the reproductive suppression model (Wasser and Barash, 1983). Specifically, across a wide range of mammalian species, females can shut down their reproductive system if the ecological conditions are not ideal for the successful rearing of an offspring. The mechanism can be triggered at several temporal points including via a delaying of menarche (first menses), shutting off of the menses (secondary amenorrhea), in utero via a miscarriage (non-consciously), or via infanticide. One of the important sequela of eating disorders is secondary amenorrhea suggesting that the disorder is intimately linked to a woman's reproductive strategy. The practical implications are clear. Women who face uncertain ecological environments (in the reproductive sense), be it real or imagined, are at greater risk of developing eating disorders.

Hardcore pornography is largely geared to men. In all cities around the world where strip clubs are legal, the overwhelming majority of these cater to heterosexual men. Incidentally, Miller et al. (2007) found that the tips that female strippers garnered were linked to their ovulatory cycles. Specifically, the tips were larger when the dancers were most fertile. It is difficult to imagine how this finding might have ever been uncovered without recognizing the biological underpinnings driving this particular service encounter. Prostitution, the world's oldest profession, has always existed in mainly one form, irrespective of the cultural setting. Women exchange sex for resources. Addicts of pornography are largely men. The SSSM explanations for these universal sex differences are banal, including that men are socialized to be more sexually daring, and/or that there has always existed a patriarchal conspiracy of female oppression (which in this case is instantiated via the sex trade). As postulated by the parental investment hypothesis, men and women have evolved different mating strategies. These differences manifest themselves in countless ways including in men's greater libidinal drives, greater desire for varied sexual partners, and quicker ability to become sexually aroused by visual stimuli. Hence, to the extent that prostitution, pornographic movies, and strip clubs, are services and products that cater to men's evolved sexuality much more so than that of women, one would expect the universal sex-specificity of male-based consumption (see Malamuth, 1996, and Pound, 2002, for explorations of pornography from an evolutionary perspective). Since sexual stimuli (e.g., pornographic clips on the Internet) are differentially addictive to the two sexes, it is not surprising that men constitute the large majority of pornographic addicts.

Saad and Peng (2006) scoured the sun tanning literature to identify key behavioral and/ or demographic trends regarding excessive sunbathers. Armed with an evolutionary lens, they provided coherence to an otherwise disjointed set of findings. Specifically, they demonstrated that the main results map onto the mating module. These included that single young women constituted the majority of excessive sunbathers, and that individuals discount the potential future costs of sunbathing (e.g., melanoma) whilst focusing on the corresponding immediate benefits (e.g., looking beautiful at tonight's social gathering; see Daly and Wilson, 2005, for an adaptationist account of discounting; see also Van den Bergh et al., 2008, who found that when men were exposed to images of women in bikinis, their discounting rates for monetary rewards increased). Incidentally, women have been found to be more knowledgeable about the deleterious effects of sun exposure, hence the 'lack of information' premise fails in this case.

Each of the disorders discussed so far possesses a robust sex-specificity in its manifestation. In some instances, evolutionary theory predicts that some predilections should occur with equal likelihood across the sexes. For example, men and women are equally likely to succumb to the allure of cocaine or heroin (National Institute on Drug Abuse, 2000). There are no evolutionary-based reasons that would have caused the brain of one sex to be

more pharmacologically pleased by a substance that tickles the brain's pleasure center. See Lende and Smith (2002) for an evolutionary account of addiction, and Eaton et al. (2002) for a discussion of evolutionary health promotion. Other issues of relevance to transformative consumer research that have been tackled from an evolutionary/biological perspective include gambling (Gray, 2004; Spinella, 2003), the desire for money (Briers et al., 2006; Lea and Webley, 2006), and sustainable consumption (Jackson, 2005).

To conclude, many consumption phenomena that affect a consumer's well-being cannot be fully understood without recognizing the biological forces that drive our preferences and behaviors. Ultimately, transformative consumer research is about maximizing happiness, the Darwinian roots of which have been clearly shown by several evolutionary scientists (cf. Buss, 2000; Grinde, 2004).

EPISTEMOLOGICAL ADVANTAGES IN ADOPTING EVOLUTIONARY THEORY WITHIN MARKETING

Evolutionary theory achieves at least four important epistemological objectives. First, it provides ultimate explanations for marketing/ consumption phenomena that have heretofore been solely tackled at the proximate level (e.g., the adaptive reasons that drive consumers around the world to prefer highly caloric foods). Second, it permits for the positing of novel hypotheses and the uncovering of new phenomena that otherwise might remain imperceptible to the scholar who is solely operating at the proximate level. For example, Brown et al. (2005) uncovered that young men's dance abilities are correlated with their bodily symmetry. In other words, physical ability as manifested via dance movements is linked to phenotypic quality. On a related note, Salter et al. (2005) applied an ethological approach in investigating how male and female customers interact with male bouncers who otherwise serve as the entrance gatekeepers to dance clubs. Third, evolutionary theory permits for the tackling of proximate phenomena using evolutionary-based theorizing (e.g., the evolutionary mechanism that drives the relationship between men's testosterone levels and conspicuous consumption). Fourth, it serves as a consilient framework in integrating an otherwise disjointed and incoherent knowledge base (see Wilson, 1998, for a thorough discussion of consilience; and Garcia and Saad, 2008 for an exposé of how Darwinian theory can yield greater consilience within neuromarketing).

The consilient power of evolutionary theory is evident in that consumption phenomena can be mapped onto one of four key Darwinian meta-pursuits, namely the survival, reproductive, kin, and reciprocity modules (Saad, 2007a, Chapter 3; see Bernard et al., 2005, for a discussion of motivation from an evolutionary perspective). The integrative power of evolutionary theory is further manifested in its ability to delineate the effect of culture on consumption into three mutually exclusive categories (see Saad, 2007c, for additional details): (a) cross-cultural similarities rooted in a universal human nature (e.g., that men react more favorably to sexual stimuli irrespective of cultural setting); (b) cross-cultural differences that serve as adaptations to local niches (e.g., the extent to which individuals consume salt, spices, vegetables, or meat as part of their culinary tradition, is in part determined by a country's ambient temperature; cf. Sherman and Billing, 1999; Sherman and Hash, 2001); and (c) cross-cultural differences that are emic-based and hence outside the purview of evolutionary theory (e.g., culture-specific musical instruments such as the Arabic Oud, the Chinese Pipa, and the Indian Sitar).

Evolutionary theory should not be construed as the panacea of all of the marketing discipline's epistemological challenges. However, to the extent that the most prestigious scientific disciplines all possess meta-frameworks that provide consilience to their core knowledge, marketing scholars cannot continue to operate in disjointed, incoherent,

and contradictory paradigms. The perceived maturity, prestige, and influence of our discipline, rests in our ability to incorporate Darwinian tenets within our theoretical and conceptual toolboxes.

CONCLUSION

Consumer scholars have tackled innumerable scientific problems of import, replete with practical implications, using highly varied and sophisticated methodological approaches. If anything, the discipline is reputed for its epistemological pluralism (e.g., the coexistence of the traditional behavioral–quantitative dichotomy along with more recent and influential approaches such as consumer culture theory; see Arnould and Thompson, 2005). However, despite its avowed pluralistic penchant, the field has largely rejected evolutionary theory as relevant in explaining consumption phenomena. I hope to have provided the reader with a compelling exposé of the ways by which evolutionary theory and related biological formalisms might contribute to our field. Ultimately, *Homo consumericus* is a voracious consummatory species shaped by a long Darwinian phylogenetic history.

ACKNOWLEDGMENTS

I thank the editors as well as an anonymous reviewer for their valuable feedback on an earlier draft of this chapter.

NOTES

1 There are several other ways by which a biological-based framework can be used to investigate attitudes. For example, some scholars have discussed the heritability of attitudes in general (Bohner and Wanke, 2002, Chapter 4), and of political attitudes in particular (Alford and Hibbing, 2008). Others have shown that political attitudes are shaped by evolutionarily relevant ontogenetic causes (Thornhill and Fincher,

2007) and/or recurring ecological variables such as the prevalence of parasites (Thornhill et al., 2009). Finally, a domain-specific adaptationist calculus shapes one's attitudes toward various forms of risk taking (Weber et al., 2002).

2 Incidentally, that humans possess a favorable disposition toward nature and the living organisms contained within has been coined the biophilia hypothesis (Wilson, 1984). The hypothesis has recently been applied in the context of man-made environments such as in architectural design (Joye, 2007). Generally speaking, individuals react positively to urban, architectural, or store designs that are congruent with universal evolved landscape preferences.

3 For a similar approach albeit in the context of decisional biases using capuchin monkeys, see Chen et al. (2006). More generally, Gosling and Graybeal (2007) provide a meta-framework for the integration of comparative data in psychological research. To the extent that humans are only one of many consummatory animals, comparative psychology might provide some novel approaches in the study of human consumption.

REFERENCES

Alcock, J. (2001) *The Triumph of Sociobiology*. New York: Oxford University Press.

Alexander, G.M. (2003) 'An Evolutionary Perspective of Sex-Typed Toy Preferences: Pink, Blue, and the Brain', *Archives of Sexual Behavior*, 32: 7–14.

Alexander, G.M. and Hines, M. (2002) 'Sex Differences in Response to Children's Toys in Nonhuman Primates (*Cercopithecus aethiops sabaeus*)', *Evolution and Human Behavior*, 23: 467–479.

Alford, J.R. and Hibbing, J.R. (2008) 'The New Empirical Biopolitics', *Annual Review of Political Science*, 11: 183–203.

Alvard, M.S. (2003) 'The Adaptive Nature of Culture', *Evolutionary Anthropology*, 12: 136–149.

Ambler, T. and Hollier, E. A. (2004) 'The Waste in Advertising is the Part that Works', *Journal of Advertising Research*, 44: 375–389.

Andrews, P.W., Gangestad, S.W., and Matthews, D. (2002) 'Adaptationism – How to Carry an Exaptationist Program', *Behavioral and Brain Sciences*, 25: 489–504.

Arnould, E.J. and Thompson, C.J. (2005) 'Consumer Culture Theory (CCT): Twenty Years of Research', *Journal of Consumer Research*, 31: 868–882.

Barber, N. (1999) 'Women's Dress Fashions as a Function of Reproductive Strategy', *Sex Roles*, 40: 459–471.

Barber, N. (2001) 'Mustache Fashion Covaries with a Good Marriage Market for Women', *Journal of Nonverbal Behavior*, 25: 261–272.

Barkow, J.H., Cosmides, L., and Tooby, J. (eds) (1992) *The Adapted Mind: Evolutionary Psychology and the Generation of Culture*. New York: Oxford University Press.

Becker, D.V., Kenrick, D.T., Guerin, S., and Maner, J.K. (2005) 'Concentrating on Beauty: Sexual Selection and Sociospatial Memory', *Personality and Social Psychology Bulletin*, 31: 1643–1652.

Berenbaum, S.A. and Hines, M. (1992) 'Early Androgens are Related to Childhood Sex-Typed Toy Preferences', *Psychological Science*, 3: 203–206.

Bernard, L.C., Mills, M., Swenson, L., and Walsh, R.P. (2005) 'An Evolutionary Theory of Human Motivation', *Genetic, Social, and General Psychology Monographs*, 131: 129–184.

Blackmore, S. (1999) *The Meme Machine*. Oxford, England: Oxford University Press.

Bloom, D.F. (2004) 'Is Acne Really a Disease?: A Theory of Acne as an Evolutionarily Significant, High-Order Psychoneuroimmune Interaction Timed to Cortical Development with a Crucial Role in Mate Choice', *Medical Hypotheses*, 62: 462–469.

Bohner, G. and Wanke, M. (2002) *Attitudes and Attitude Change*. New York: Taylor & Francis.

Boyer, P. and Bergstrom, B. (2008) 'Evolutionary Perspectives on Religion', *Annual Review of Anthropology*, 37: 111–130.

Briers, B., Pandelaere, M., Dewitte, S., and Warlop, L. (2006) 'Hungry for Money: The Desire for Caloric Resources Increases the Desire for Financial Resources and Vice Versa', *Psychological Science*, 17: 939–943.

Brown, D.E. (1991) *Human Universals*. New York: McGraw Hill.

Brown, W.M., Cronk, L., Grochow, K., Jacobson, A., Liu, C.K., Popovic, Z., and Trivers, R. (2005) 'Dance Reveals Symmetry Especially in Young Men', *Nature*, 438: 1148–1150.

Buss, D.M. (2000) 'The Evolution of Happiness', *American Psychologist*, 55: 15–23.

Buss, D.M. (ed.) (2005) *The Handbook of Evolutionary Psychology*. New York: Wiley.

Cárdenas, R.A. and Harris, L.J. (2006) 'Symmetrical Decorations Enhance the

Attractiveness of Faces and Abstract Designs', *Evolution and Human Behavior*, 27: 1–18.

Cary, M.S. (2000) 'Ad Strategy and the Stone Age Brain', *Journal of Advertising Research*, 40: 103–106.

Chen, M.K., Lakshminarayanan, V., and Santos, L.R. (2006) 'How Basic are Behavioral Biases? Evidence from Capuchin Monkey Trading Behavior', *Journal of Political Economy*, 114: 517–537.

Coates, J.M. and Herbert, J. (2008) 'Endogenous Steroids and Financial Risk Taking on a London Trading Floor', *Proceedings of the National Academy of Sciences of the United States of America*, 105: 6167–6172.

Colarelli, S.M. and Dettman, J.R. (2003) 'Intuitive Evolutionary Perspectives in Marketing Practices', *Psychology & Marketing*, 20: 837–865.

Conway, III, L.G. and Schaller, M. (2002) 'On the Verifiability of Evolutionary Psychological Theories: An Analysis of the Psychology of Scientific Persuasion', *Personality and Social Psychology Review*, 6: 152–166.

Cosmides, L. and Tooby, J. (2000) 'Evolutionary Psychology and the Emotions', in M. Lewis and J.M. Haviland-Jones (eds), *Handbook of Emotions*, 2nd Edition, New York: Guilford, pp. 91–115.

Crawford, C. and Krebs, D. (eds) (2008) *Foundations of Evolutionary Psychology.* Mahwah, NJ: Lawrence Erlbaum.

Cronk, L. and Dunham, B. (2007) 'Amounts Spent on Engagement Rings Reflect Aspects of Male and Female Quality', *Human Nature*, 18: 329–333.

Crozier, W.R. (1999) 'The Meanings of Colour: Preferences Among Hues', *Pigment and Resin Technology*, 28: 6–14.

Daly, M. and Wilson, M. (1988) *Homicide.* New York: Aldine de Gruyter.

Daly, M. and Wilson, M. (2005) 'Carpe Diem: Adaptation and Devaluing the Future', *The Quarterly Review of Biology*, 80: 55–60.

Darwin, C. (1859). *On the Origin of Species by Means of Natural Selection, or the Preservation of Favoured Races in the Struggle for Life.* London: John Murray. [first edition is available online at http://darwin-online.org.uk/]

Darwin, C. (1871) *The Descent of Man, and Selection in Relation to Sex* (2 vols.). London: John Murray.

Dawkins, R. (1976) *The Selfish Gene.* New York: Oxford University Press.

Dennis, C. and McCall, A. (2005) 'The Savannah Hypothesis of Shopping', *Business Strategy Review*, 16: 12–16.

DiClemente, D.F. and Hantula, D.A. (2003) 'Optimal Foraging Online: Increasing Sensitivity to Delay', *Psychology & Marketing*, 20: 785–809.

Eaton, S.B., Cordain, L., and Lindeberg, S. (2002) 'Evolutionary Health Promotion: A Consideration of Common Counterarguments', *Preventive Medicine*, 34: 119–123.

Eens, M. and Pinxten, R. (2000) 'Sex-Role Reversal in Vertebrates: Behavioural and Endocrinological Accounts', *Behavioural Processes*, 51: 135–147.

Eibl-Eibesfeldt, I. (1989) *Human Ethology.* New York: Aldine de Gruyter.

Eyuboglu, N. and Buja, A. (2007) 'Quasi-Darwinian Selection in Marketing Relationships', *Journal of Marketing*, 71: 48–62.

Faer, L.M., Hendriks, A., Abed, R.T., and Figueredo, A.J. (2005) 'The Evolutionary Psychology of Eating Disorders: Female Competition for Mates or for Status?', *Psychology and Psychotherapy: Theory, Research and Practice*, 78: 397–417.

Flaxman, S.M. and Sherman, P.W. (2000) 'Morning Sickness: A Mechanism for Protecting Mother and Embryo', *The Quarterly Review of Biology*, 75: 113–148.

Foxall, G.R. (1994a) 'Behaviour Analysis and Consumer Psychology', *Journal of Economic Psychology*, 15: 5–91.

Foxall, G.R. (1994b) 'Consumer Choice as an Evolutionary Process: An Operant Interpretation of Adopter Behavior', in C.T. Allen and D.R. John (eds) *Advances in Consumer Research*, Vol. 21, Provo, UT: Association for Consumer Research, pp. 312–317.

Foxall, G.R. (2007) *Explaining Consumer Choice.* Hampshire, UK: Palgrave Macmillan.

Foxall, G.R. and James, V.K. (2003) 'The Behavioral Ecology of Brand Choice: How and What Do Consumers Maximize?', *Psychology & Marketing*, 20: 811–836.

Garcia, J. and Saad, G. (2008) 'Evolutionary Neuromarketing: Darwinizing the Neuroimaging Paradigm for Consumer Behavior', *Journal of Consumer Behaviour*, 7: 397–414.

Gatward, N. (2007) 'Anorexia Nervosa: An Evolutionary Puzzle', *European Eating Disorders Review*, 15: 1–12.

Gosling, S.D. and Graybeal, A. (2007) 'Tree Thinking: A New Paradigm for Integrating Comparative Data in Psychology', *The Journal of General Psychology*, 134: 259–277.

Grammer, K., Renninger, L., and Fischer, B. (2004) 'Disco Clothing, Female Sexual Motivation, and Relationship Status: Is She Dressed to Impress?', *Journal of Sex Research*, 41: 66–74.

Gray, P.B. (2004) 'Evolutionary and Cross-Cultural Perspectives on Gambling', *Journal of Gambling Studies*, 20: 347–371.

Grinde, B. (2004) 'Darwinian Happiness: Can the Evolutionary Perspective on Well-Being Help Us Improve Society?', *World Futures*, 60: 317–329.

Griskevicius, V., Goldstein, N.J., Mortensen, C.R., Sundie, J.M., Cialdini, R.B., and Kenrick, D.T. (2009) 'Fear and Loving in Las Vegas: Evolution, Emotion, and Persuasion', *Journal of Marketing Research*, XLVI: 384–395.

Griskevicius, V., Tybur, J.M., Sundie, J.M., Cialdini, R.B., Miller, G.F., and Kenrick, D.T. (2007) 'Blatant Benevolence and Conspicuous Consumption: When Romantic Motives Elicit Strategic Costly Signals', *Journal of Personality and Social Psychology*, 93: 85–102.

Hagen, E.H. (2005) 'Controversial Issues in Evolutionary Psychology', in D.M. Buss (ed.) *The Handbook of Evolutionary Psychology*, New York: Wiley, pp. 145–173.

Hamilton, W.D. (1964) 'The Genetical Evolution of Social Behaviour', *Journal of Theoretical Biology*, 7: 1–52.

Haselton, M.G. and Ketelaar, T. (2006) 'Irrational Emotions or Emotional Wisdom? The Evolutionary Psychology of Emotions and Behavior', in J.P. Forgas (ed.) *Affect in Social Thinking and Behavior*, New York: Psychology Press, pp. 21–39.

Haselton, M.G., Mortezaie, M., Pillsworth, E.G., Bleske-Rechek, A., and Frederick, D.A. (2007) 'Ovulatory Shifts in Human Female Ornamentation: Near Ovulation, Women Dress to Impress', *Hormones and Behavior*, 51: 40–45.

Hassett, J.M., Siebert, E.R., and Wallen, K. (2008) 'Sex Differences in Rhesus Monkey Toy Preferences Parallel Those of Children', *Hormones and Behavior*, 54: 359–364.

Haviland-Jones, J., Rosario, H.H., Wilson, P., and McGuire, T.R. (2005) 'An Environmental Approach to Positive Emotion: Flowers', *Evolutionary Psychology*, 3: 104–132.

Hayward, L.S. and Rohwer, S. (2004) 'Sex Differences in Attitudes Toward Paternity Testing', *Evolution and Human Behavior*, 25: 242–248.

Hill, R.A. and Barton, R.A. (2005) 'Red Enhances Human Performance in Contests', *Nature*, 435 (May 19): 293.

Hill, R.A., Donovan, S., and Koyama, N.F. (2005) 'Female Sexual Advertisement Reflects Resource Availability in Twentieth-Century UK Society', *Human Nature*, 16: 266–277.

Hinsz, V.B., Matz, D.C., and Patience, R.A. (2001) 'Does Women's Hair Signal Reproductive Potential?', *Journal of Experimental Social Psychology*, 37: 166–172.

Höglund, J. and Alatalo, R.V. (1995) *Leks*. Princeton, NJ: Princeton University Press.

Jackson, T. (2005) 'Live Better by Consuming Less? Is There a "Double Dividend" in Sustainable Consumption?', *Journal of Industrial Ecology*, 9: 19–36.

Joye, Y. (2007) 'Architectural Lessons from Environmental Psychology: The Case of Biophilic Architecture', *Review of General Psychology*, 11: 305–328.

Kanazawa, S. (2006) 'Where Do Cultures Come From?', *Cross-Cultural Research*, 40, 152–176.

Kellett, S.C. and Gawkrodger, D.J. (1999) 'The Psychological and Emotional Impact of Acne and the Effect of Treatment with Isotretinoin', *British Journal of Dermatology*, 140: 273–282.

Kellett, S. and Gilbert, P. (2001) 'Acne: A Biopsychosocial and Evolutionary Perspective with a Focus on Shame', *British Journal of Health Psychology*, 6: 1–24.

Ketelaar, T. and Ellis, B.J. (2000) 'Are Evolutionary Explanations Unfalsifiable? Evolutionary Psychology and the Lakatosian Philosophy of Science', *Psychological Inquiry*, 11: 1–21.

Kruger, D.J. (2008) 'Young Adults Attempt Exchanges in Reproductively Relevant Currencies', *Evolutionary Psychology*, 6: 204–212.

Laland, K.N. and Brown, G.R. (2002) *Sense and Nonsense: Evolutionary Perspectives on Human Behaviour*. Oxford, UK: Oxford University Press.

Lea, S.E.G. and Webley, P. (2006) 'Money as a Tool, Money as Drug: The Biological

Psychology of a Strong Incentive', *Behavioral and Brain Sciences*, 29: 161–176.

Lende, D.H. and Smith, E.O. (2002) 'Evolution Meets Biopsychosociality: An Analysis of Addictive Behavior', *Addiction*, 97: 447–458.

Lycett, J.E. and Dunbar, R.I.M. (2000) 'Mobile Phones as Lekking Devices Among Human Males', *Human Nature*, 11: 93–104.

Malamuth, N.M. (1996) 'Sexually Explicit Media, Gender Differences, and Evolutionary Theory', *Journal of Communication*, 46: 8–31.

Marsden, P. (2002) 'Brand Positioning: Meme's the Word', *Marketing Intelligence & Planning*, 20: 307–312.

Massey, G.R. (1999) 'Product Evolution: A Darwinian or Lamarckian Phenomenon?', *The Journal of Product and Brand Management*, 8: 301–318.

Mayr, E. (1961) 'Cause and Effect in Biology', *Science*, 134: 1501–1506.

Mazur, A. (2005) 'Believers and Disbelievers in Evolution', *Politics and the Life Sciences*, 23: 55–61.

Mesko, N. and Bereczkei, T. (2004) 'Hairstyle as an Adaptive Means of Displaying Phenotypic Quality', *Human Nature*, 15: 251–270.

Meyers-Levy, J. and Maheswaran, D. (1991) 'Exploring Differences in Males' and Females' Processing Strategies', *Journal of Consumer Research*, 18: 63–70.

Milinski, M. and Wedekind, C. (2001) 'Evidence for MHC-Correlated Perfume Preferences in Humans', *Behavioral Ecology*, 12: 140–149.

Miller, G.F. (2000) *The Mating Mind: How Sexual Choice Shaped the Evolution of Human Nature*. New York: Doubleday.

Miller, G., Tybur, J.M., and Jordan, B.D. (2007) 'Ovulatory Cycle Effects on Tip Earnings by Lap Dancers: Economic Evidence for Human Estrus?', *Evolution and Human Behavior*, 28: 375–381.

Moss, G., Hamilton, C., and Neave, N. (2007) 'Evolutionary Factors in Design Preferences', *Journal of Brand Management*, 14: 313–323.

Mysterud, I. (2004) 'One Name for the Evolutionary Baby? A Preliminary Guide for Everyone Confused by the Chaos of Names', *Social Science Information*, 43: 95–114.

Nairne, J.S., Thompson, S.R., and Pandeirada, J.N.S. (2007) 'Adaptive Memory: Survival Processing Enhances Retention', *Journal of Experimental Psychology: Learning, Memory, and Cognition*, 33: 263–273.

National Institute on Drug Abuse (2000) 'Gender Differences in Drug Abuse Risks and Treatment', *NIDA Notes*, 15, accessed at http://www.nida.nih.gov/NIDA_Notes/NNVol15N4/tearoff.html on 13 July, 2008.

New, J., Krasnow, M.M., Truxaw, D., and Gaulin, S.J.C. (2007) 'Spatial Adaptations for Plant Foraging: Women Excel and Calories Count', *Proceedings of the Royal Society B: Biological Sciences*, 274: 2679–2684.

Norenzayan, A. and Heine, S.J. (2005) 'Psychological Universals: What are They and How Can We Know?', *Psychological Bulletin*, 131: 763–784.

Palmer, A. (2000) 'Co-Operation and Competition: A Darwinian Synthesis of Relationship Marketing', *European Journal of Marketing*, 34: 687–704.

Penke, L., Denissen, J.J.A., and Miller, G.F. (2007) 'The Evolutionary Genetics of Personality', *European Journal of Personality*, 21: 549–587.

Pepper, G.V. and Roberts, S.C. (2006) 'Rates of Nausea and Vomiting in Pregnancy and Dietary Characteristics Across Populations', *Proceedings of the Royal Society B: Biological Sciences*, 273: 2675–2679.

Pinker, S. (2002) *The Blank Slate: The Modern Denial of Human Nature*. New York: Viking.

Pollet, T.V., Nettle, D., and Nelissen, M. (2007) 'Maternal Grandmothers Do Go the Extra Mile: Factoring Distance and Lineage into Differential Contact with Grandchildren', *Evolutionary Psychology*, 5: 832–843.

Pound, N. (2002) 'Male Interest in Visual Cues of Sperm Competition Risk', *Evolution and Human Behavior*, 23: 443–466.

Profet, M. (1992) 'Pregnancy Sickness as Adaptation: A Deterrent to Maternal Ingestion of Teratogens', in J.H. Barkow, L. Cosmides, and J. Tooby (eds) *The Adapted Mind: Evolutionary Psychology and the Generation of Culture*, New York: Oxford University Press, pp. 327–365.

Richerson, P.J. and Boyd, R. (2005) *Not by Genes Alone: How Culture Transformed Human Evolution*. Chicago: University of Chicago Press.

Ruprecht, W. (2005) 'The Historical Development of the Consumption of Sweeteners – A Learning Approach', *Journal of Evolutionary Economics*, 15: 247–272.

Saad, G. (2004) 'Applying Evolutionary Psychology in Understanding the Representation of Women in Advertisements', *Psychology & Marketing*, 21: 593–612.

Saad, G. (2006a) 'Applying Evolutionary Psychology in Understanding the Darwinian Roots of Consumption Phenomena', *Managerial and Decision Economics*, 27: 189–201.

Saad, G. (2006b) 'Blame Our Evolved Gustatory Preferences', *Young Consumers*, 7: 72–75.

Saad, G. (2007a) *The Evolutionary Bases of Consumption*. Mahwah, NJ: Lawrence Erlbaum.

Saad, G. (2007b) 'A Multitude of *Environments* for a Consilient Darwinian Meta-Theory of Personality: The Environment of Evolutionary Adaptedness, Local Niches, the Ontogenetic Environment and Situational Contexts', *European Journal of Personality*, 21: 624–626.

Saad, G. (2007c) *Homo Consumericus*: Consumption Phenomena as Universals, as Cross-Cultural Adaptations, or as Emic Cultural Instantiations. Submitted for publication.

Saad, G. (2008a) 'The Collective Amnesia of Marketing Scholars Regarding Consumers' Biological and Evolutionary Roots', *Marketing Theory*, 8: 425–448.

Saad, G. (2008b) 'Advertised Waist-to-Hip Ratios of Online Female Escorts: An Evolutionary Perspective', *International Journal of e-Collaboration*, 4: 40–50.

Saad, G., Eba, A., and Sejean, R. (2009) 'Sex Differences When Searching for a Mate: A Process-Tracing Approach', *Journal of Behavioral Decision Making*, 22: 171–190.

Saad, G. and Gill, T. (2000) 'Applications of Evolutionary Psychology in Marketing', *Psychology & Marketing*, 17: 1005–1034.

Saad, G. and Gill, T. (2003) 'An Evolutionary Psychology Perspective on Gift Giving Among Young Adults', *Psychology & Marketing*, 20: 765–784.

Saad, G., Gill, T., and Nataraajan, R. (2005) Are Laterborns More Innovative and Non-Conforming Consumers than Firstborns? A Darwinian Perspective', *Journal of Business Research*, 58: 902–909.

Saad, G. and Peng, A. (2006) 'Applying Darwinian Principles in Designing Effective Intervention Strategies: The Case of Sun Tanning', *Psychology & Marketing*, 23: 617–638.

Saad, G. and Stenstrom, E. (2008) 'The Effect of the Menstrual Cycle on Consumption Patterns', Working paper, Concordia University.

Saad, G. and Vongas, J.G. (2009) 'The Effect of Conspicuous Consumption on Men's Testosterone Levels', *Organizational Behavior and Human Decision Processes*, doi:10.1016/j.obhdp.2009.06.001.

Salmon, C., Crawford, C.B., and Walters, S. (2008) 'Anorexic Behavior, Female Competition and Stress: Developing the Female Competition Stress Test', *Evolutionary Psychology*, 6: 96–112.

Salter, F., Grammer, K., and Rikowski, A. (2005) 'Sex Differences in Negotiating with Powerful Males: An Ethological Analysis of Approaches to Nightclub Doormen', *Human Nature*, 16: 306–321.

Sarwer, D.B., Magee, L., and Clark, V. (2004) 'Physical Appearance and Cosmetic Medical Treatments: Physiological and Socio-Cultural Influences', *Journal of Cosmetic Dermatology*, 2: 29–39.

Shanks, N. (2006) *God, the Devil, and Darwin: A Critique of Intelligent Design Theory*. New York: Oxford University Press.

Sherman, P.W. and Billing, J. (1999) 'Darwinian Gastronomy: Why We Use Spices', *BioScience*, 49: 453–463.

Sherman, P.W. and Hash, G.A. (2001) 'Why Vegetable Recipes Are Not Very Spicy', *Evolution and Human Behavior*, 22: 147–163.

Singh, D. and Randall, P.K. (2007) 'Beauty Is in the Eye of the Plastic Surgeon: Waist-Hip Ratio (WHR) and Women's Attractiveness', *Personality and Individual Differences*, 43: 329–340.

Smith, E.A., Borgerhoff Mulder, M., and Hill, K. (2001) 'Controversies in the Evolutionary Social Sciences: A Guide for the Perplexed', *Trends in Ecology and Evolution*, 16: 128–135.

Smith, E.O. (1999) 'High Heels and Evolution: Natural Selection, Sexual Selection and High Heels', *Psychology, Evolution and Gender*, 1: 245–277.

Sober, E. (2007) 'What is Wrong with Intelligent Design?', *The Quarterly Review of Biology*, 82: 3–8.

Spinella, M. (2003) 'Evolutionary Mismatch, Neural Reward Circuits, and Pathological

Gambling', *International Journal of Neuroscience*, 113: 503–512.

Stenstrom, E., Stenstrom, P., Saad, G., and Cheikhrouhou, S. (2008) 'Online Hunting and Gathering: An Evolutionary Perspective on Sex Differences in Website Preferences and Navigation', *IEEE Transactions on Professional Communication*, 51: 155–168.

Sulloway, F.J. (1996) *Born to Rebel: Birth Order, Family Dynamics and Creative Lives.* New York: Pantheon.

Thornhill, R. and Fincher, C.L. (2007) 'What is the Relevance of Attachment and Life History to Political Values?', *Evolution and Human Behavior*, 28: 215–222.

Thornhill, R., Fincher, C.L., and Aran, D. (2009) 'Parasites, Democratization, and the Liberalization of Values Across Contemporary Countries', *Biological Reviews*, 84: 113–131.

Tinbergen, N. (1963) 'On Aims and Methods of Ethology', *Zeitschrift für Tierpsychologie*, 20: 410–433.

Tooby, J. and Cosmides, L. (1992) 'Psychological Foundations of Culture', in J.H. Barkow, L. Cosmides, and J. Tooby (eds) *The Adapted Mind: Evolutionary Psychology and the Generation of Culture*, New York: Oxford University Press, pp. 19–136.

Trivers, R.L. (1971) 'The Evolution of Reciprocal Altruism', *The Quarterly Review of Biology*, 46: 35–57.

Trivers, R.L. (1972) 'Parental Investment and Sexual Selection', in B. Campbell (ed.) *Sexual Selection and Descent of Man: 1871–1971*, Chicago: Aldine, pp. 136–179.

US Census Bureau (2006) 'Consumer Expenditure Survey', Accessed at http://146.142.4.22/cex/2006/Standard/age.pdf on 13 July, 2008.

US Department of Commerce Industry Outlook (2006). Dolls, Toys, Games, and Children's Vehicles NAICS Code 33993. Accessed at http://www.trade.gov/td/ocg/outlook06_toys.pdf on 13 July, 2008.

Van den Bergh, B., Dewitte, S., and Warlop, L. (2008) 'Bikinis Instigate Generalized Impatience in Intertemporal Choice', *Journal of Consumer Research*, 35: 85–97.

Wasser, S.K. and Barash, D.P. (1983) 'Reproductive Suppression Among Female Mammals: Implications for Biomedicine and Sexual Selection Theory'. *The Quarterly Review of Biology*, 58: 513–538.

Weber, E.U., Blais, A.-R., and Betz, N.E. (2002) 'A Domain-Specific Risk-Attitude Scale: Measuring Risk Perceptions and Risk Behaviors', *Journal of Behavioral Decision Making*, 15: 263–290.

Weinstein, Y., Bugg, J.M., and Roediger, III, H.L. (2008) 'Can the Survival Recall Advantage be Explained by Basic Memory Processes?', *Memory and Cognition*, 36: 913–919.

White, R.E., Thornhill, S., and Hampson, E. (2006) 'Entrepreneurs and Evolutionary Biology: The Relationship Between Testosterone and New Venture Creation', *Organizational Behavior and Human Decision Processes*, 100: 21–34.

Whyte, J. (2007) 'Evolutionary Theories and Design Practices', *Design Issues*, 23: 46–54.

Wilson, E.O. (1975) *Sociobiology: A New Synthesis*. Cambridge, MA: Belknap Press of Harvard University Press.

Wilson, E.O. (1984) *Biophilia: The Human Bond with Other Species*. Cambridge, MA: Harvard University Press.

Wilson, E.O. (1998) *Consilience: The Unity of Knowledge*. London: Abacus.

Winterhalder, B. and Smith, E.A. (2000) 'Analyzing Adaptive Strategies: Human Behavioral Ecology at Twenty-Five', *Evolutionary Anthropology*, 9: 51–72.

Zahavi, A. (1975) 'Mate Selection: A Selection for a Handicap', *Journal of Theoretical Biology*, 53: 205–214.

Zahavi, A. and Zahavi, A. (1997) *The Handicap Principle: A Missing Piece of Darwin's Puzzle*. New York: Oxford University Press.

27

The Linking Value in Experiential Marketing: Acknowledging the Role of Working Consumers

Bernard Cova and Daniele Dalli

INTRODUCTION

Experiential marketing has developed as a research area, as well as a management perspective aimed at emphasizing the importance of consumption experiences in consumer pleasure generation. Consumers access pleasure when they perceive a positive and self-fulfilling experience in the consumption of goods, services, and brands. The role of the consumer is very important in the pursuit of positive experiences; it is (also) the consumer who is responsible for developing a pleasurable consumption experience. In fact, consumers create the meanings associated with such experiences; they activate the resources that the market provides in order to co-create their experiences.

One of the most important elements in creating positive consumption experiences is the collective dimension. From this perspective, consumers do not ask for goods and services as they are – on the contrary – searching for social bonds. That is, '*the link is more important than the thing*' (Cova, 1997). Consumers are pleased if they are immersed in a positive, warm, and social context; a context in which they feel welcome, protected, and included. It is in that sense that we can speak of the linking value of goods, services, and brands in experiential marketing. Their linking value is the value of this product/service/brand for the construction, development or maintenance of interpersonal links – even ephemeral ones.

However, this socio-experiential approach must take into account that consumers are active agents in the creation of this linking value: they act as one another's partners and creatively and subjectively take advantage of the relational resources provided by the market. Conventional approaches to experiential marketing and related marketing processes such as relationship marketing should be considered critically, mainly because they usually ignore the role of consumers in creating experiences and actual linking value. This is relevant from both the theoretical as well as the managerial point of view. Disregarding the role of consumers in creating meaningful consumption experiences limits extant theoretical models' capability to actually capture the intimate nature of these processes. From the managerial perspective, companies should support consumers to develop their experiences, but without exploiting them, and appropriating the value that they create.

THE EXPERIENTIAL PERSPECTIVE ON CONSUMPTION

Since the 1960s and 1970s, consumption has progressively disengaged from its essentially utilitarian conception, which was based on products' and services' use value. Consumption has become an activity that entails the production of meaning, as well as a field of symbolic exchanges. See Chapter 17 for a thorough review of the interpretive turn and its impact for the study of the experiential aspects of consumption. Within this tradition, the salient attributes of experiential consumption are (Carù and Cova, 2003, 2007):

- Consumers are not only consumers
- Consumers act within situations
- Consumers seek meaning
- Consumption involves more than mere purchasing

From the experiential perspective, the consumption experience is no longer limited to pre-purchase activities (stimulation of a need, search for information, estimation, etc.) or to post-purchase activities (assessment of satisfaction), but includes a series of other activities that influence consumers' decisions and future actions. As such, consuming experiences are spread over a period that can be divided into four major stages (Arnould et al., 2002):

- The pre-consumption experience, which involves searching for, planning, day-dreaming about, and foreseeing or imagining the experience
- The purchasing experience, which involves choosing the item, payment, packaging, and the encounter with the service and the environment

- The core consumption experience, which involves sensation, satiety, satisfaction/dissatisfaction, irritation/flow, and transformation
- The remembered consumption experience and the nostalgia experience, wherein photos, movies, and other memorabilia means are used to relive a past experience based on narratives and arguments with friends about the past, something that tends toward the classification of memories

As a result, the consuming experience is more than a mere shopping experience, that is, an individual's experience at a point-of-sale (also called a service encounter in service research). Since the 1970s, this concept of a shopping experience has been based on a series of studies that have looked at purchasing behavior at the point-of-sale and tried to supersede the hypothesis of consumer rationality. These studies first revealed a re-creative type of consumer. Subsequent broader studies highlighted hedonistic behavior in most consumers, thus diverting attention away from the utilitarian to the hedonistic value of shopping. In these studies, the consumer is regarded as an individual who is emotionally involved in a shopping process in which multisensory, imaginary, and emotional aspects are specifically sought and appreciated (Sherry, 1998). At this point, retailing research converged with sociological studies that focused on the same issues (Falk and Campbell, 1997; Miller, 1995), the assumption being that the enjoyment derived from shopping does not stem from buying, wanting, or desiring products, but that shopping is a socioeconomic means of socializing and enjoying oneself and the company of others whilst making purchases. Examples of such shopping experiences range from cultural consumption in a museum to spectacular consumption at Nike Town Chicago (Sherry, 1998).

Although shopping was initially deemed to constitute the main field of experiential consumption, today appears as if the explosion of subjectivity has been generalized throughout Western society, thereby extending the experiential domain to all sectors of consumption. Some researchers (Thompson, 2000) would even characterize postmodern consumption as something akin to the pleasure of being immersed in McDisneyfied banalities.

There is, nevertheless, little agreement on the source and level of pleasure that consumers derive from such experiences. For some observers (particularly for specialists in what has been called 'retail re-enchantment'), pleasure stems from a McDonald's-type experiential shaping of daily banalities. They say that the re-enchantment of our daily lives entails a whole succession of micropleasures, recurring affordable microtreats that derive from in-store consuming experiences. Through a number of poly-sensorial stimulations, consumption is transformed into an entertainment opportunity and a hedonic experience. For other analysts, notably the proponents of postmodern marketing (Fırat and Dholakia, 1998), pleasure offers a total immersion in an original experience. Here, the emphasis is on modern consumers' growing quest for immersion in varied experiences with the aim of exploring the multiplicity of new meanings that they can inject into their lives. The idea is that a consumer comes to market to produce his/her identity, so that s/he is in fact seeking the experience of being immersed in a thematized framework rather than a mere encounter with a finished product. These immersions in enclavized and secure contexts are in contrast with the stress of people's daily lives, sometimes even helping them to live other persons' experiences. This immersion in a consuming experience is tantamount to diving into a framework that has been totally thematized, enclavized, and made secure. One notable example of this is Rainforest Café (Kozinets et al., 2004).

THE PRODUCTION OF EXPERIENCES

Although, within an experiential perspective, it is widely accepted that consumers are not passive agents reacting to stimuli, but are instead the actors and producers of their own consuming experiences (however hyper-real these may be), firms have nevertheless worked

hard to facilitate the production of such experiences. The methods advanced to enable firms to (co)-produce experiences on consumers' behalf have one point in common – they try to create a theatre and a stage for both the consumer and the company's offering (Fırat and Dholakia, 1998). This is achieved through in-depth work on the decor, i.e., on the environmental design and the atmosphere at the point-of-sale.

When a firm or a brand only delivers products and not services, it should create its own premises (theatres of consumption) so that the consumer can experience its products without the intrusion of any competing influences. This occurs in Nike Towns and in other concept or flagship stores. Further examples include Nutella restaurants or Nespresso cafés. Such commercial premises' design must therefore be managed consistently, all the way down to the smallest detail, if the firm wants to air the brand's theme accurately and stimulate all five senses of the individual for whose benefit this staging is taking place. Opinions differ, however, with regard to which elements can be used to complete this staging. Some pundits stress active customer participation, as well as the importance of offering a 'memorabilia mix' (Pine and Gilmore, 1999). Others twin this notion of active customer participation with the facilitators' staging actions, which can involve the presence of specific types of contact personnel to guide the consumer through the experience (Gupta and Vajic, 2000). Other analysts emphasize the product's narrative, i.e., the intrigue or the story that the company offers and the consumer will be enacting (Filser, 2002).

All in all, the production of experiences should include three main facets:

- Decor, design, and staging, with special attention being paid to multisensorial stimulation
- Active participation by the consumer, supported by all kinds of facilitators who specify each party's role in all of the rituals set up in the orbit of the company's offering
- The narrative, story, and intrigues that are created, the most important of which is the creation of memories, usually in the form of derivative products

Toward the late 1990s, a specific marketing school of thought returned to these incipient approaches to the production of experiences and turned them into the basis of a complete managerial approach in which the experiential perspective was totally reversed. In experiential marketing, experience has become a new type of company offer alongside commodities, products, and services (Pine and Gilmore, 1999). It is a fourth category and one that is particularly well adapted to the needs of the postmodern consumer.

In this vision, a good experience must be unforgettable, if not extraordinary. Reintegrating the idea of immersion (Fırat and Dholakia, 1998), experiential marketing then suggested that consumption be turned into a series of extraordinary immersions for the consumer, who could then engage in the unforgettable processes that constitute the experience, or better yet, be transformed due to these experiences. Experiential marketing experts believe that the shift from a commodity to a transformation increases the economic value of a company's offer (Pine and Gilmore, 1999). Consequently, this school of thought appropriates the experience studies by the famous psychologist Csikszentmihalyi (1997), in which the best experience is considered to be a *flow* one, i.e., an exceptional moment during which what we feel, desire, and think are in total harmony. Although only a small fraction of consumer experiences can be classified as flow activities, they are pivotal for marketing, as they represent peak experiences (Arnould et al., 2002). As such, it is indeed this specific flow vision of the consumption experience that has become the foundation of the entire experiential approach in marketing. To achieve this type of flow experience, marketing has recycled and implemented Baudrillard's notion of hyperreality: an experience becomes extraordinary due to increasingly spectacular and surprising decors, as well as the ever-greater scope of the extravagances and simulations in which the consumer will be immersed (Ritzer, 2005).

EXPERIENTIAL MARKETING VERSUS CONSUMING EXPERIENCES

The achievement of these extraordinary experiences has been the main area of discussion for various experts (La Salle and Britton, 2003; Pine and Gilmore, 1999; Schmitt, 1999, 2003) who developed different experiential marketing approaches. The main point is that experiences must be memorable and must involve the individual's personal sphere: experts answered the question on how to create this kind of experiences in different ways, always trying to identify a sequence of steps or activities useful to reach that goal.

According to Pine and Gilmore (1999), the staging is the core of extraordinary experiences' creation, as the production and the supply are the core of goods and services production respectively. They identify specific actions for the experience staging: the first one is the preparation of the stage, which varies according to the different areas of the experience (entertainment, education, desire to escape, and aesthetic experience) and to the different opportunities offered by each area; the second one is turning experience into a show, by giving it a specific theme: for this purpose, they identify a list of possible functional themes. Again, it is necessary to personalize the experience, to search for a sole value for the customer, which is based on the ability of surprising him/her. In this extraordinary experience creation process, the metaphor evoked is the one of theatre, which, in its various forms, represents the reference model.

In the title of his first book, *Experiential Marketing: How to Get Customers to Sense, Feel, Think, Act and Relate to Your Company and Brands*, Schmitt (1999) makes clear the idea that the goal of experiences' creation is to induce specific customer behaviors and reactions. Thus, CEM, Customer Experience Management (Schmitt, 2003) is the process of strategically managing a customer's entire experience with a product or a company, a process that has five basic steps: analyzing the experiential world of the customer, building the experiential platform, designing the brand experience, structuring the customer interface and engaging in continuous innovation.

La Salle and Britton (2003) shift the attention to customer's decision process in order to spot the actions to be undertaken by the company in each phase. The consumer's decision process is made up of five steps – discover, evaluate, acquire, integrate, and extend – through which the consumer moves during consumption. By examining these stages, a business can see rewards and sacrifices through its customers' eyes, thus uncovering the real value of an offering.

Whereas consumer research has tended to adopt a conceptualization that views experience as a subjective episode in an individual's construction/transformation (thus stressing emotional and sensorial dimensions to the detriment of a cognitive dimension), experiential marketing has imbued experience with a more objective meaning. Experiential marketing thus focuses on the company's planning and implementation of what it is offering, whilst accentuating the idea that the outcome should be something that is very significant and unforgettable for the consumer living through this experience. In just a few years, experiential marketing has changed the status of consumption experiences, displacing them from what consumers have personally gone through to participation in a consumption festival dominated by excess, extravagance, magic, spectacularity, and simulation (Carù and Cova, 2007).

In fact, there has been a great deal of criticism of the limited and planned nature of the marketing experiences, which are very manipulative and predetermined and therefore meet with resistance from some consumers. Indeed, such experiences leave the consumer very little room to really participate in their conception and construction. Consumers only become actors insofar as they are allowed to do this, i.e., when they fulfill their role as a consumer overwhelmed by the experience's context. Yet, consumers seemingly not only want to be immerged in their experiences but also seek to design and actively produce them. For many consumers,

an experience is more than the simple acceptance of a prepackaged offer revolving around a theme that has been chosen by the firm (thematization of the experience) – some of it must also be left unorganized so that it can become appropriable. A good example of the appropriation of experience in the daily life of our hypermodern contemporaries is the consumption of holidays. Seventy percent of all Europeans produce their own holidays. This is a way for them to appropriate their vacations.

To an experience that has been organized and planned by the firm, the consumer can oppose a creation of experiences that is very different in nature, one that can be described as the art of living since it is characterized by the art of diverting commercial experiences (de Certeau, 1984). The consumer, acting alone or in a group, diverts the product, service, and especially the pre-planned experience away from its original intention (as determined by the existing market system) in an attempt to reappropriate it in accordance with his/her own rules. By so doing, s/he prepares a new prism for analyzing the event, one that can be noncommercial and even anticommercial in tone. This also means getting involved on a local scale in a system whose imposition the consumer refuses to accept. There are many examples of such diversions today. Relatively organized and dominated by a protest attitude, they seek to create an opposition to the omnipotence of certain world companies, with examples including McDonald and 'Pigeon McNuggets' actions or Danone and the famous 'I boycott danone.com' website. Along these same lines, we also find pub destroyers and other 'adbusters', not to mention England's 'Reclaim The Streets' movement. All of these groups signify our contemporaries' crucial need to reappropriate their daily experiences.

At the same time, many collective experiences have tended to reappropriate products and services found in the market system without this being part of a conscious protest. Examples include fan associations that dig up and pamper yesterday's products like the old GM car (Leigh et al., 2006) or Newton Apple pad (Muniz and Schau, 2005). The meanings and practices that these groups are associating with such products differ from what was originally intended. Moreover, this building of meaning through experience and shared emotion constitutes a daily episode in the creation, consolidation, and preservation of a communitarian sentiment within such groups. What all of these actions have in common is that they comprise experiences that help the product or service to evolve beyond its simple status as a merchandise, thereby enabling consumers to have an experience that is not totally commercial in nature whilst continuing to function within a commercial framework, i.e., one that is defined by the interactions that brands and companies have initiated.

All in all, we can outline a continuum of consuming experiences (Carù and Cova, 2007) that consumers go through:

- At one extreme are experiences that have largely been developed by companies and where consumers are immerged in a context that is frequently hyper-real in nature. Here the firm is pursuing a total experiential marketing approach and plans all details of the experience on the consumers' behalf. Nowadays fashion and sports brands, as well as toys and other forms of entertainment, specialize in this approach.
- At the other extreme, we find experiences that are mainly constructed by the consumers and which can involve company provided products or services. Here the firm is pursuing a traditional product or service marketing approach and it is the consumer who organizes his/her own experience. Traditional products like pasta, the small items that comprise our daily life and most particularly organic products and nonprofit or local associations are prime examples here.
- In the middle, we find experiences that have been codeveloped by companies and consumers. Here the firm provides an experiential platform based on which the consumer can develop his/her own experience. The firms imbues the experience with a potential, turning it into a veritable raw material comprised of certain diffuse elements that the consumer can mould, and which will therefore assume the shape of his/her own experience. Sports tourism or adventure packages, rock concerts, and cultural events are part of this approach.

A SOCIO-EXPERIENTIAL APPROACH TO CONSUMPTION

From both perspectives – consumer research and experiential marketing – it is important to acknowledge the collective dimension in creating pleasant consumption experiences. *Brand fests*, such as the various celebrations and outings that Harley-Davidson or Ducati have organized to encourage a *festival experience*, are paradigmatic types of this collective dimension of the consumer experience. These brand-related events are opportunities for consumers to have an embodied experience of the brand by enjoying direct contact with the staff and other consumers (McAlexander and Schouten, 1998). Riding and socializing with other Harley owners connect people of a similar mindset, congregating and engaging in a way of life that revolves around the consumption of Harley-Davidson (Schembri, 2008). This collective experience involves the development and preservation of communitarian-flavored connections within an experiential context, thereby allowing mutual learning and shared emotions in a socio-experiential approach (Hemetsberger and Reinhardt, 2006). Scholars and managers who think in terms of an individual consumer's behavior often neglect the importance of the collective dimension of the consumption experience. Yet, the consumption experience needs to be made explicit, explained, and shared if it is to really exist, since the attribution of meaning to an individual experience calls for the creation of a narrative that implies the ability and the power to create new texts. An experience is never really complete if it has not been expressed, i.e., as long as it has not been communicated in linguistic or other forms. Whether one has the experience at home or elsewhere, it cannot be separated from ideas like sharing and collective enjoyment (Venkatesh, 1998).

This search for the collective dimension of the consumption experience can be related to the postmodern quest for alternative social arrangements and new communities (Goulding et al., 2002). Consumers are increasingly gathering in multiple and ephemeral groups. Such social, proximate groupings have an important influence on their behavior. In fact, the social dynamics, which are characteristic of our postmodern era, can be defined well by the word 'tribalism' (Bauman, 1990; Cova, 1997; Cova and Cova, 2001; Maffesoli, 1996). The postmodern society appears to be a network of societal microgroups in which individuals entertain strong emotional bonds, experiences, and common passions (Firat and Dholakia, 2006). In postmodernity, the important point is not the project that we build by contractually bonding with others, but the ephemeral fate that we undergo together. All this gives meaning to the collective dimension of existence, leading the individual to lose him/herself in multiple social bodies: sports, music, and religious gatherings that underline the merger or the social confusion. Each postmodern individual is therefore a member of several microgroups in which s/he plays roles that sometimes differ greatly, wearing different masks each time. Belonging to these microgroups has become more important for the individual than belonging to modern day aggregations such as corporations, parties, etc. This is an organic, not a rational, conception of society, which reminds us of archaic blood ties and attachment to the same land; it justifies a metaphorical recourse to the pre-modern notion of a tribe, while knowing that, although '*opposite of what generally sparks off this notion, postmodern tribalism may be perfectly ephemeral, and organized on the occasions to be presented*' (Maffesoli, 2000a: 247). Postmodern tribalism is, indeed '*the search for all passing passions, all things which are lived cyclically and intensively as we know the ephemeral form of the cycle*' (Maffesoli, 2000b: 60).

THE LINKING VALUE CONCEPT

Starting with the postmodern premise of tribalism, some marketing researchers (Cova and

Cova, 2002) introduced the concept of linking value. In the field of marketing, the linking value of a product or a service usually refers to the product's or service's contribution to establishing and/or reinforcing bonds between individuals (Cova, 1995, 1997). Marketing researchers have, however, borrowed this concept from the sociology of the gift (Godbout and Caillé, 1992). Consumption is not perceived as the primary level of interaction. The economic dimension is not seen as the most important, compared to the social one. On the contrary, consumption is considered a secondary level of interaction and it is considered instrumental for the development and maintenance of social interaction. From this perspective, gifts are seen as means for social bonding: the (social) link is more important than the thing; i.e., the things – goods and services – are only the societal support of the links between people. In this view, the gifts exchanged between two individuals nourish their mutual debt, which does not have to be settled (Belk and Coon, 1993; Godbout and Caillé, 1992). The goods and services given in this way have a linking value for both individuals. Thus, the linking value is the intersubjective value of the gift (Godbout, 2007).

Mediterranean marketing researchers twisted this concept somewhat in order to apply it to the understanding of postmodern consumption phenomena (Cova and Cova, 2002). They maintain that the postmodern individual values the social aspects of life at the cost of consumption and the use of goods and services. The goods and services that are valued are mainly those which, through their linking value, permit and support social interaction of the communal type. A product or a service would thus be able to play the societal role in the support of postmodern tribes (Maffesoli, 1996). Such a product or service would be a support for copresence – effective copresence, not solitude in a lonely crowd! This reinforces the idea of a postmodern individual who regards consumption less as a direct way of giving meaning to life than as a way to form links with others in the context of one or several tribes, thus giving meaning to his/her life: *'To satisfy their desire for communities, postmodern individuals seek products and services less for their use value than for their linking value'* (Cova, 1997: 307). In this view, the company is able to introduce a potential for linkage in its offering and the customers will enact it. This could be at the level of the material function of the product (a mobile phone, for example) or at the level of the immaterial meaning of the brand (Ducati, for example) or a blend of both. The linking value of a product/service/brand is its value for the construction, development, or maintenance of interpersonal links – even ephemeral ones.

During the last decade, consumption and marketing researchers from both Europe and the US embraced the concept of the linking value when they examined how consumers forge more ephemeral collective identifications and participate in rituals of solidarity that are grounded in common lifestyle interests and leisure avocations (Arnould and Thompson, 2005). From Cova (1995) to Mathwick et al. (2008), these researchers endeavored to understand *'why and how certain consumption objects and activities have the potential to exert linking value'* (Ostberg, 2007: 94). For example, Jones (2002) shows that, boosted by networking technologies, people's desire for community is satisfied in new ways. Nowhere is this more evident than in text messaging, which highlights a high liking value for kids. In another example, Ostberg (2007) details how the linking value of the Stockholm Brats' particular rendition of style develops the recognition of the Brats by external sources, such as the media and popular culture. Mathwick et al. (2008: 832) conclude that there is *'a fundamental shift from the use value of products or services to consumption motivated by the desire to reinforce consumer-to-consumer (or peer-to-peer) bonds that deliver what he (Cova) refers to as "linking value"'*.

Many recent textbooks on consumption (Szmigin, 2003), marketing (Gummesson, 2002), and qualitative research in marketing (Belk, 2006; Moisander and Valtonen, 2006) emphasize the usefulness of using the specific angle of the linking value instead of the use value in order to understand today's consumption and marketing. Remy and Kopel (2002) introduced the concept of linking services to detail the type of services that present a high linking value. According to these authors, the highest linking value is to be found in services such as leisure ones (gyms and fitness clubs) that *'function on friendly, convivial bases'* (Remy and Kopel, 2002: 51). Ponsonby-McCabe and Boyle (2006: 182) argue that the linking value *'can be formal or informal, stimulated or supported by a firm's marketing endeavours or independently by a number of independent consumers. It can be physical, in the form of organized events and/or conventions in particular locations, or it can be symbolic and assumed – that is, consumers assume that other owners/consumers of the product or service feel in some way linked to them'*. On the whole, two major characteristics seem of paramount importance when trying to understand the unique features of the linking value of products, services, or brands (Cova and Rémy, 2001):

- The linking value can only be experienced during interaction between people. It does not exist before or after such interaction. It is co-constructed during interaction between consumers, which is why it is collective by nature and not individual. Thus, the linking value could be said to escape the object in order to be close to the subjects: it is no longer the wine of brand X that we share during a specific evening, but the wine of our group of persons ABCDE. However, some products or brands have a potential for linking value that others do not. This could be due to the functions of the product (cellular phone, website, etc.) or service (restaurant, pub, etc.) or to the myth of the brand (Apple, Ducati, Nutella, etc.) that brings people together, even if it is just in one's imagination.
- The linking value is not instantaneous. It requires time to come into existence: the time dedicated to reappropriate the product, service or brand in order to make it ours. This time is the time of the rituals that we enact and which help to reintroduce the market offer into our temporal network.

In their analysis of the value that *pasta* has for young Italians, Dalli and Romani (2007) demonstrate how the preparation of pasta creates conditions for the development of an emotional relationship. The complex pasta preparation–consumption ritual is intimately linked to social relationships, while its economic aspects are lost. Thus, the linking value requires a sacrifice to exist: the sacrifice of the time necessary to relocate the market system's offer into the social system driven by a gift-giving logic (Belk and Coon, 1993).

According to Kates (2006: 96), '*the linking value reaches its most organized expressions in brand configurations such as brand communities, subcultures of consumption and cultures of consumption*'. Indeed, Muniz and O'Guinn's (2001) study of brand community provides evidence of this sort of linking value. The research they carried out in the neighborhood of Fairlawn in Bloomingdale, a small Midwestern town in the USA, revealed (among other things) the informal, assumed, and symbolic linking value of the Saab brand for Saab drivers and of the Bronco brand for Bronco drivers there. This communal view of brand experiences has been mainly supported by Mediterranean researchers (Cova and Cova, 2002) who have built a view of branding as a vector of the tribal link. More specifically, these researchers who have hypothesized that consumers value the brands that, through their linking value, permit and support social interaction of a tribal type, i.e., that support AB and not A or B as such. Ephemeral tribes that need to consolidate and affirm their union are, in fact, on the lookout for anything that can facilitate and support communion and the collective. Thus, to satisfy their desire for community, consumers seek brands less for their use value than for their linking value. Consequently, Mediterranean researchers regard branding as the activity of designing and creating experiences in order to facilitate the copresence and the communal gathering of individuals in the tribes' time: a kind of tribal marketing (Cova and Cova, 2002). The *credo* of this 'tribal' marketing is that currently consumers are not only looking for experiences that enable them to be freer, but also experiences that can link them to others, to a tribe – even a small and ephemeral one.

The proponents of experiential marketing implicitly promoted the idea of linking value when they emphasized the social or collective dimension of the experience, which is said to enhance the pleasure lived by the consumer (Pine and Gilmore, 1999). Indeed, the symbolic (re)construction or (re)possession of meanings through shared experiences provides the consumer with strong hedonic and emotional benefits (Elliott, 1997). From this perspective, the immersion of the consumer into a brand experience is not independent of his/her belonging to a brand community (Muniz and O'Guinn, 2001). The feeling of 'we-ness' experienced with an iconic brand and its cult products (Broderick et al., 2003) creates value for the consumer, a linking value (Schembri, 2008). Today, through a host of different approaches such as brand communities, brand fests, brand plants, brand sites, etc., experiential marketing is trying to leverage the linking value of the brand in order to provide consumers with an extraordinary experience. McAlexander et al. (2002) show that participation in brand fests led to a significant increase in overall feelings of integration into the Jeep brand community, and positive feelings about the product category and brand. Thus, researchers infer that the participants derived a linking value from the brand experience (Algesheimer et al., 2005; Bagozzi and Dholakia, 2006). This value is enhanced when consumers are asked to participate in the design of new products (Franke and Piller, 2004; Füller et al., 2006; Sawhney et al., 2005).

These communal ideas upon consumer experiences are related to the debate about the need for a shift in the marketing logic: from product to services then to service. In particular, the linking value and its role in the coproduction of market value is a fundamental element for the evolution of marketing described by Vargo and Lusch in this book (see Figure 12.1, Chapter 12). It is the linking value perceived by consumers that acts as an incentive in promoting consumers' involvement and collaboration in the process of market value creation: they collaborate with companies because, by this means, they have the possibility of interacting with other consumers. This is why consumers can be considered as co-creators of value: they co-create because, in so doing, they perceive a positive outcome (linking value) from the interaction with other consumers involved in the same activity (Chapter 12, pp. 502–503). This holds for various activities, such as pure consumption, collaboration in product innovation, service production and distribution, etc. And, this is why consumers are willing to provide their own resources (Chapter 12, pp. 504–505), integrating them with those from other parties (companies as well) and – mostly important – other consumers. The difference between Vargo and Lusch argument and the point we make in this chapter is that SD logic sees the relationship between the company and the consumer as the focal point in value co-creation, while we consider the consumer-to-consumer interaction as the core process for (linking) value creation. In fact, as we have seen in the preceding discussion, consumers ask for relationships, community, linking value, and togetherness. Moreover, consumers are subjects who greatly contribute to the creation and maintenance of such resources: they both co-create and use the linking value. From the first point of view (co-creation), there is no linking value without consumers' active involvement. From the second point of view (use), the linking value is 'valued' by consumers: consumers confer actual value on community, relationships, etc. In the following sections, this point will be further developed and critical issues will be addressed.

THE DISPUTE ON THE PRODUCER OF LINKING VALUE

The discussion about the linking value in experiential marketing is strictly related to the debate about consumers' involvement in the production of market value. Such a debate follows the publication of Vargo and Lusch (2004) seminal paper about the Service Dominant logic. According to Cova and Dalli (2009), several theories of actual consumer involvement in co-creation are available and, among these, the role of consumers in creating consumption experiences and their involvement in consumption communities (tribes) are of major relevance. In these settings, it is the consumer that is the subject of the production of the experience and – at the same time – of the linking value. In fact, linking value is not out there waiting for consumers to be exploited. Linking value has to be produced, and at present companies invest significant resources in this. However, companies cannot produce linking value without the support of consumers who 'work' – very hard – at producing it:

- Consumers are both creators and users of linking value: the most important resource in brand fests and events is 'the crowd'. The more people participate, the greater the opportunities to interact and develop relationships: it is consumers who 'create' the community through their participation.
- Consumers create the linking value that is then attached to the good, which is consequently perceived as more valuable. New products emerge as a 'community product': the more consumers participate in the new product development process, the more they perceive the product's value, because they regard it as 'their' product, from both the individual and the community point of view (Franke and Piller, 2004).
- Consumers create communal relationships and, hence, linking value even without the participation of companies: services (Couchsurfing), second hand markets (Bookcrossing), treasure hunting (Geocaching), vintage cars, and discarded products (Apple Newton) are examples of settings in which consumers have created opportunities for interaction and community (Dalli and Corciolani, 2008; Leigh et al., 2006; Muniz and Schau, 2005). Furthermore, consumers are able to 'capture' some value from companies and share this, thus developing linking value at the expense of the market, as in peer-to-peer networks.

These and other examples are evidence of consumers' active role in the creation of linking value. At this point, however, appropriate theoretical roots have to be found for this evidence. Originally developed to explain the role of the worker in the manufacturing process, immaterial labor (Lazzarato, 1997) is useful for describing and explaining consumers' primary role in the production of (linking) value. From this perspective, consumers provide two types of value (Hardt and Negri, 2000, 2004):

- Affective value. Consumers produce and use communal relationships and create feelings of ease, well being, satisfaction, excitement, and passion that permeate the products and services with which they deal, which are, subsequently, redistributed among these consumers.
- Cultural value. Consumers are responsible for selecting ideas, symbols, codes, texts, linguistic figures, and images that are then put into products and services. Once the products and brands have received this value, the consumer perceives it and bestows value on it.

Two aspects have to be considered regarding the first type of value (affective immaterial value): (a) consumer-to-consumer interaction and (b) emotional load.

First, in many ways, consumers are active agents in the production of linking value, but the most important moment in this process is that of consumer-to-consumer interaction, although this is usually mediated by companies' resources and services. Through websites and their services (for example, the MyNutella the Community for Nutella), as well as through off-line, direct interaction (for example, the WDW, World Ducati Week, for Ducati.), consumers are the main source of linking value at the very moment in which they both produce and exploit it. Linking means direct relationships between individuals who are both providers and end users of this value. When consumers meet with one another, they exchange positive emotions and feelings and contribute to the development of a positive atmosphere that reverts to all of those who participate in the event (on and off line). In this activity, the product is not relevant: consumers produce value from their interactions. Through direct interactions, consumers develop the network that is necessary (for them as users) to actually exploit linking value.

Second, we must consider the emotional load related to the individual contribution to the intrinsic affective value of goods: individuals contribute to brands and products in term of affective commitment and emotional devotion. It is due to the individual willingness to engage in, for example, positive word-of-mouth, as well as in blog development and maintenance that awareness and attitude toward brands are enhanced. Posting personal experiences, pictures, and other textual materials enhance the affective value of the brand, which is then perceived as the 'property' of many individuals. Even without interacting directly with one another, individual consumers can thus bestow affective value on brands. The case of MyNutella and other brand communities can be considered from this perspective: members develop their personal pages in order to express their devotion to the brand, telling stories about themselves and the product, uploading pictures, etc. Companies often consider these materials their own property: something that witnesses the inherent value of the result of such labor.[1]

Regarding the second type of value (cultural immaterial value), we should note that every consumer is capable of providing support in this direction. It is, in fact, just what every consumer does every day when telling stories about brands and personal experiences, when transforming products according to personal preferences, even when discussing the distinctive properties of one brand versus another. In all of these moments, consumers give substantial, symbolic, linguistic, and – more in general – cultural meaning to products and brands. Sometimes this process is 'institutionalized' in brand community forums and companies can use these chunks of meaning, employing them for marketing strategy planning and implementation. In special cases, it is the company that initiates and manages the process even before the product is put on the market. Consider the case of 500Wantsyou.com, the campaign developed by Fiat for the launch of the new Fiat 500 on July 4, 2007. 500 days before the launch, the company developed a dedicated website as the core element in the development of the brand community for the new product. Several competitions were organized to stimulate consumers to contribute ideas, proposals, and personal opinions about the product in the final phase of its development. Consumers provided thousands of submissions, which the company not only employed in the technical development (design, styling, accessories, etc.), but also in the communication strategy (jingles, videos, photos, and other artwork). Those who participated received tangible benefits (prizes) and social consideration. Consumers' gave the company pieces of knowledge that supported the intrinsic value of the market offering: first, consumers saw that the product had been developed according to their suggestions, which stimulated their commitment to the product and the company. Second, regardless of their subjective evaluations, consumers gave the company a huge amount of free material. This material entered the product, increasing its value.

In sum, linking value is created by consumers in terms of inter-personal interaction, emotional load, and cultural value. Marketing theory needs a more thorough account of the role of 'working' consumers in producing a part (the larger part?) of the linking value associated with products and brands. The sociology of work (Dujarier, 2008; Gorz, 2003) and the sociology of media (Arvidsson, 2006) have addressed this topic as did some works in consumer research (Cova and Dalli, 2009; Humphreys and Grayson, 2008; Zwick et al., 2008).

WORKING CONSUMERS, LINKING VALUE, AND EXPERIENTIAL MARKETING

If we consider the role of the consumer as one of the main sources of linking value, some questions arise quite spontaneously:

- Given that consumers contribute to the linking value that companies employ when implementing their marketing strategies, how do consumers benefit? Is this limited to the self-gratification they perceive when they are integrated into relational/tribal programs? Are recognition and acknowledgment enough? Is being considered a partner, a comrade, a supporter, or even a fan, enough?
- Is there any possibility of compensating consumers for their support in economic terms? Money? Coupons? Other forms of credit?
- Is it possible to esteem the extent to which consumers actually contribute to the linking value? What if they stop producing linking value? What happens if they do not provide their immaterial labor?
- Which role do communities play in the production of linking value? Do companies always control individuals and communities? Are communities able to appropriate the economic benefits of linking value?

To answer these questions, some of the building blocks of the theory and practice of experiential marketing should be reconsidered. The role of consumers in exploiting consumption experiences has to be reconsidered. Several authors have addressed the problem from at least two perspectives. First, consumers are responsible for activating and making the most of their 'immersion' in the consumption experience (Firat and Dholakia, 1998). In so doing, consumers transform goods and services and are able to appropriate the result of their consumption activity in terms of satisfaction and control (Filser, 2002; Ladwein, 2002). They are subject of the consumption process: they produce the real value that they consume. However, they still have to pay for the goods and services they need. Second, the role of end users in the development of effective and satisfactory consumption experiences has also been analyzed in the service sector. The consumer's active role in the service encounter is necessary to realize satisfactory performances, mainly in terms of personalization (Solomon et al., 1985; Surprenant and Salomon, 1987): the more the customer is involved in the process of service production and delivery, the greater the perceived value and satisfaction. Consumers collaborate for a better service. In so doing, they interact among themselves and with sales personnel: the more the interaction, the more the personalization and the greater the perceived value (Bitner et al., 2000, Moore et al., 2005). In sum, experiential marketing and related practices are based on the assumption that consumers appreciate commitment, interaction, etc. However, the fact that consumers create the value added that they appreciate and then have to pay for it has been neglected. In economic terms, they produce positive externalities that are appropriated by the companies that sell 'value added' goods and services.

When scrutinizing the postmodern perspective on consumption experience (Fırat and Dholakia, 2006; Fırat and Venkatesh, 1993, 1995), it appears that consumers are active producers of cultural value. Meanings do not grow spontaneously in goods, services, brands, and companies. Meanings grow inside consumers. The locus of meaning production is in ordinary people who actively process stimuli arising from society and mass communication and attach them to goods and brands. It is true that companies invest huge resources to enrich their goods from a symbolic and cultural point of view, but the very locus in which these symbols obtain value is where consumers actually interact with them and express their feelings. If they like them, they buy the product and pay for it. In sum, the postmodern production of value is inherently symbolic and cultural and consumers are the subjects of this process.

The vast majority of authors in the field of experiential marketing take it for granted that consumers should be involved in the development of satisfactory consumption experiences (Gupta and Vajic, 2000; Pine and Gilmore, 1999). The more they are involved, the better satisfied they are. This is precisely because it is the consumer who produces the experience and, hence, the product or service. Consumers know that the experience is going to be satisfactory, because they produce it. What happens when consumers realize that they are the actual source of their consumption? What happens when they understand that the actual specific, idiosyncratic, and

irreducible elements of their pleasure consist of their own identity? The product, the service, the company, and even the market can be substituted with something different. The linking value that companies seek in tribal marketing programs (Cova and Cova, 2002) can be regarded from this point of view: linking value is produced by consumers. Consumers do not need goods and services, they need linking value, and they produce it by interacting with one another, enriching goods and services with emotional and cultural components. The more they are involved in this process, the more they are satisfied on both the individual (goods and services that are enriched by linking value are more appreciated) and collective level (the community grows). Even in this case, the company could be regarded as an accessory, or a tool that proves to be useful in terms of coordination, facilitation, etc. However, consumers develop the core values of the linking/tribal marketing through their interactions.

Consumer tribes (Cova et al., 2007) and brand communities (Muniz and O'Guinn, 2001) develop due to the interpersonal interaction between consumers (see also Chapter 19 in this volume). Companies provide the technology that facilitates interaction, but they seem to be standing in the wings. Consumers occupy center stage; they are the main characters in this play, because they are the source of value for themselves. This value comprises relationships and affective/cultural elements provided by consumers' immaterial labor. When studying this phenomenon's community level, interesting cases do emerge: communities grow without any support from companies. They are able to produce value and attach it to products and services. They do not need any 'traditional' market to appropriate this value, because they can employ alternative exchange systems such as open source ones (Pitt et al., 2006). In addition, they are sometimes able to sell this value to companies and/or to prohibit companies to capture this value if they do not respect the rights of consumers/producers. In these instances, communities of consumers become the repository of value. The larger and stronger the community, the easier is to manage the production, distribution, and protection of the value.

It is here that we can use the framework proposed by Caillé (2000) between primary and secondary sociality: primary sociality has to do with face-to-face and interpersonal relationships developed within the family, neighborhood, or in friendships when secondary sociality is the domain of impersonal relationships, the sociality of the market (Caillé, 2000). Communities of consumers produce the linking value at the primary level of sociality. But, they protect, control, and even redistribute tangible benefits, acting at the secondary sociality level. In this sense, communities can perform different roles (protection, security, entrepreneurship, etc.) and prevent consumers from being exploited when transferring the value they have produced from the primary to the secondary level of sociality. This perspective was inscribed in the very origins of tribal marketing Cova (1997) suggests that companies should not try to 'create' new tribes. Tribes are out there, and companies (as well as other institutions) should find them and provide goods and services that they (the companies) are able to realize together with tribe members. Tribes are out there, because the most important need of postmodern consumers is interaction and community. The linking value is therefore spontaneously produced by consumers while interacting at the primary level of sociality (Godbout and Caillé, 1992). Companies can exploit this value by moving primary relationships toward the secondary level of sociality (the market); i.e., selling consumers goods and services that are tailored to the needs and characteristics of the tribe. Furthermore, companies sell consumers technologies that enable them to fully exploit their tribal relationships. In this process, companies often exploit consumers and consumption communities: they appropriate the economic benefits that arise from the activities that are performed by consumers. Further, companies exploit consumers when

they 'create' links, relationships, and communities that are not rooted in spontaneous, native, authentic interactions. Companies also exploit communities when they only support them in the perspective of appropriating economic benefits. In fact, if communities (tribes) are strong enough, they can establish rules to prevent exploitation and to protect the value they produce.

CONCLUSION

The linking value construct can be viewed from a critical perspective and could still prove to be of value for a better understanding of consumer culture and a more effective marketing practice. If viewed from the perspective of immaterial labor, linking value should be considered a property of consumers. Consumers produce linking value during the experience and they have to be considered in this light. They are not partners, nor collaborators, or co-creators, but workers and/or suppliers. Workers and suppliers are usually paid, because the market appreciates the value they produce. Consequently, consumers have to be acknowledged by something more than recognition. This holds true not only in terms of the redistribution of economic benefits, but also from an ethical point of view: it is not the company that provides consumers with the opportunity for satisfactory consumption experiences. It is the consumer (at the individual and community level) who provides the company with the basic elements (relationships, affect, and culture) to realize successful goods and services – and even with the money to buy them. As such, the consumer should be better respected.

However, we should be wary of a heroic picture of working consumers. As suggested by Sassatelli (2007: 197), *'volumes of sale do not describe what consumers do, yet they are pretty much what producers are professionally asked to be looking for'*. Indeed, the effect of consumers' activities on value production is mediated through the cultures of the business world. Even if the processes of production of the linking value need to draw on the active work done by consumers, the asymmetry between producers and (working) consumers still remains. People inside companies will take a long time to admit that communities of consumers co-create but also co-own the linking value of their brands.

NOTES

1 Companies do not necessarily succeed in capturing such a value and the opposite happens: the beloved brand is hijacked by consumers and companies are no longer able to control it (Wipperfürth, 2005).

REFERENCES

Algesheimer, R., Dholakia, U.M. and Hermann, A. (2005) 'The Social Influence of Brand Community: Evidence from European Car Clubs', *Journal of Marketing*, 69(3): 19–34.

Arnould, E.J. and Thompson, C.J. (2005) 'Consumer Culture Theory (CCT): Twenty Years of Research', *Journal of Consumer Research*, 31(4): 868–882.

Arnould, E., Price, L. and Zinkhan, G. (2002) *Consumers*. New York: McGraw-Hill.

Arvidsson, A. (2006) *Brands. Meaning and Value in Media Culture*. Oxon: Routledge.

Bagozzi, R.P. and Dholakia, U.M. (2006) 'Open Source Software User Communities: A Study of Participation in Linux User Groups', *Management Science*, 52(7): 1099–1115.

Bauman, Z. (1990) *Thinking Sociologically*. Oxford: Blackwell.

Belk, R.W., (ed.) (2006) *Handbook of Qualitative Research Methods in Marketing*. Cheltenham: Edward Elgar.

Belk, R.W. and Coon, G.S. (1993) 'Gift Giving as Agapic Love – An Alternative to the Exchange Paradigm – Based on Dating Experiences', *Journal of Consumer Research*, 20(3): 393–417.

Bitner, M.J., Brown, S.W. and Meuter, M.L. (2000) 'Technology Infusion in Service Encounters', *Journal of the Academy of Marketing Science*, 28(1): 138–149.

Broderick, A., Maclaran, P. and Ma, P. (2003) 'Brand Meaning Negotiation and the Role of the Online Community: A Mini Case Study', *Journal of Customer Behaviour*, 2(1): 75–104.

Caillé, A. (2000) *L'Anthropologie du Don. Le Tiers Paradigme*. Paris: Desclée de Brouwer.

Carù, A. and Cova, B. (2003) 'Revisiting Consumption Experience: A More Humble but Complete View of the Concept', *Marketing Theory*, 3(2): 267–286.

Carù, A. and Cova, B. (2007) 'Consuming Experiences. An Introduction', in A. Carù, and B. Cova (eds) *Consuming Experience*, Oxon: Routledge, pp. 3–16.

de Certeau, M. (1984) *The Practice of Everyday Life*. Berkeley: University of California Press.

Cova, B. (1995) *Au delà du Marché. quand le Lien Importe plus que le Bien*. Paris: L'Harmattan.

Cova, B. (1997) 'Community and Consumption: Towards a Definition of the Linking Value of Products or Services', *European Journal of Marketing*, 31(3/4): 297–316.

Cova, B. and Cova, V. (2001) 'Tribal Aspects of Postmodern Consumption Research: The Case of French in-Line Roller Skates', *Journal of Consumer Behaviour*, 1(1): 67–76.

Cova, B. and Cova, V. (2002) 'Tribal Marketing: The Tribalisation of Society and Its Impact on the Conduct of Marketing', *European Journal of Marketing*, 36(5/6): 595–620.

Cova, B. and Dalli, D. (2009), 'Working Consumers: The Next Step in Marketing Theory?', *Marketing Theory*, 9(3): 315–339.

Cova, B., Kozinets, R.V. and Shankar, A. (eds) (2007) *Consumer Tribes*. Burlington: Butterworth-Heinemann.

Cova, B. and Rémy, E. (2001) 'Comment et où Classer la Valeur de lien En Marketing', Proceedings of the 17th AFM Congress, Deauville, May.

Csikszentmihalyi, M. (1997) *Finding Flow: The Psychology of Engagement with Everyday Life*. New York: Basic Books.

Dalli, D. and Corciolani, M. (2008) 'Collective Forms of Resistance: The Transformative Power of Moderate Communities. Evidence from the Bookcrossing Case', *International Journal of Market Research*, 50(6): 757–775.

Dalli, D. and Romani, S. (2007) 'Consumption Experiences and Product Meanings: Pasta for Young Italian Consumers', in A. Carù and

B. Cova (eds) *Consuming Experience*. Oxon: Routledge, pp. 65–78.

Dujarier, M.A. (2008) *Le Travail du Consommateur: De McDo à Ebay, Comment nous Coproduisons ce que nous Achetons*. Paris: La Découverte.

Elliott, R. (1997) 'Existential Consumption and Irrational Desire', *European Journal of Marketing*, 31(3/4): 285–296.

Falk, P. and Campbell, C. (eds) (1997) *The Shopping Experience*. London: Routledge.

Filser, M. (2002), 'Le Marketing de la Production d'Expériences: Statut Théorique et Implications Managériales', *Décisions Marketing*, 28(Oct–Dec): 13–22.

Firat, A.F. and Dholakia, N. (1998) *Consuming People: From Political Economy to Theaters of Consumption*. London, New York: Routledge.

Firat, A.F. and Dholakia, N. (2006) 'Theoretical and Philosophical Implications of Post-modern Debates: Some Challenges to Modern Marketing', *Marketing Theory*, 6(2): 123–162.

Firat, A.F. and Venkatesh, A. (1993) 'Postmodernity: The Age of Marketing', *International Journal of Research in Marketing*, 10(3): 227–249.

Firat, A.F. and Venkatesh, A. (1995) 'Liberatory Postmodernism and the Re-Enchantment of Consumption', *Journal of Consumer Research*, 22(3): 239–267.

Franke, N. and Piller, F. (2004) 'Value Creation by Toolkits for User Innovation and Design: The Case of the Watch Market', *Journal of Product Innovation Management*, 21(6): 401–415.

Füller, J., Jawecki, G. and Mülbacher, H. (2006) 'Innovation Creation by Online Basketball Communities', *Journal of Business Research*, 60(1): 60–71.

Godbout, J.T. (2007) *Ce qui Circule entre nous*. Paris: Seuil.

Godbout, J.T. and Caillé, A. (1992) *L'esprit du Don*. Paris: La Découverte.

Gorz, A. (2003) *L'immatériel-Connaissance, Valeur et Capital*. Paris: Galilée.

Goulding, C., Shankar, A. and Elliott, R. (2002) 'Working Weeks, Rave Weekends: Identity Fragmentation and the Emergence of New Communities', *Consumption, Markets and Culture*, 5(4): 261–284.

Gummesson, E. (2002) *Total Relationship Marketing*. Oxford: Butterworth-Heinemann.

Gupta, S. and Vajic, M. (2000) 'The Contextual and Dialectical Nature of Experiences. New Service Development', in J.A. Fitzimmons and M.J. Fitzimmons (eds) *Creating Memorable Experiences*. Thousand Oaks: Sage, pp. 33–51.

Hardt, M.and Negri, A. (2000) *Empire*. Cambridge, Mass.: Harvard University Press.

Hardt, M. and Negri, A. (2004) *Multitude*. New York: Penguin.

Hemetsberger, A. and Reinhardt, C. (2006) 'Learning and Knowledge-Building in Open-Source Communities: A Social-Experiential Approach', *Management Learning*, 37(2): 187–214.

Humphreys, A. and Grayson, K. (2008) 'The Intersecting Roles of Consumer and Producer: A Critical Perspective on Co-Production, Co-Creation and Prosumption', *Sociology Compass*, 2(3): 963–980.

Jones A. (2002) 'Wireless Marketing: The Linking Value of Text Messaging', *Young Consumers: Insights and Ideas for Responsible Marketers*, 3(2): 39–44.

Kates, S. (2006) 'Researching Brands Ethnologically: An Interpretive Community Approach', in R.W. Belk (ed.) *Handbook of Qualitative Research Methods in Marketing*, Cheltenham: Edward Elgar, pp. 94–105.

Kozinets, R.V., Sherry Jr, J.F., Storm, D., Duhachek, A., Nuttavuthisit, K. and Deberry-Spence, B. (2004) 'Ludic Agency and Retail Spectacle', *Journal of Consumer Research*, 31(3): 658–672.

Ladwein, R. (2002) 'Voyage à Tikidad: De l'Accès à l'Expérience de Consommation', *Décisions Marketing*, 28(Oct–Dec): 53–63.

La Salle, D. and Britton T.A. (2003) *Priceless: Turning Ordinary Products into Extraordinary Experiences*. Boston: Harvard Business School Press.

Lazzarato, M. (1997) *Lavoro Immateriale, Forme di Vita e Produzione di Soggettività*. Verona: Ombre Corte.

Leigh, T.W., Peters, C. and Shelton, J. (2006) 'The Consumer Quest for Authenticity: The Multiplicity of Meanings within the MG Subculture of Consumption', *Journal of the Academy of Marketing Science*, 34(4): 481–493.

Maffesoli, M. (1996) *The Time of the Tribes*. Sage: London.

Maffesoli, M. (2000a) 'Trouver les mots', Foreword to the 3rd Edition of *Le Temps des*

Tribus. Le Déclin de l'Individualisme dans les Sociétés Postmodernes. Paris: La Table Ronde.

Maffesoli, M. (2000b) *L'instant Éternel. Le Retour du Tragique dans les Sociétés Postmodernes.* Paris: Denoël.

Mathwick, C., Wiertz, C. and De Ruyter, K. (2008) 'Social Capital Production in a Virtual P3 Community', *Journal of Consumer Research*, 34(6): 832–849.

McAlexander, J.H. and Schouten, J.W. (1998) 'Brandfests: Servicescapes for the Cultivation of Brand Equity', in J.F. Sherry, Jr. (ed.) *Servicescape: The Concept of Place in Contemporary Markets*, Lincolnwood, Ill.: NTC Business Books, pp. 377–401.

McAlexander, J.H., Schouten, J.W. and Koenig, H.F. (2002) 'Building Brand Community', *Journal of Marketing*, 66(January): 38–54.

Miller, D. (1995) *Acknowledging Consumption: A Review of New Studies.* London-New York: Routledge.

Moisander, J. and Valtonen, A. (2006) *Qualitative Marketing Research: A Cultural Approach.* London: Sage.

Moore, R., Moore, M.L. and Capella, M. (2005) 'The Impact of Customer-to-Customer Interactions in a High Personal Contact Service Setting', *Journal of Services Marketing*, 19(7): 482–491.

Muniz, A.M. and O'Guinn, T.C. (2001) 'Brand Community', *Journal of Consumer Research*, 27(4): 412–432.

Muniz, A.M. and Schau, H.J. (2005) 'Religiosity in the Abandoned Apple Newton Brand Community', *Journal of Consumer Research*, 31(4): 737–747.

Ostberg, J. (2007) 'The Linking Value of Subcultural Capital: Constructing the Stockholm Brat Enclave', in B. Cova, R.V. Kozinets, and A. Shankar (eds) *Consumer Tribes*, Oxford: Butterworth-Heinemann, pp. 93–106.

Pine, B.J. and Gilmore, J.H. (1999) *The Experience Economy – Work is Theatre and Every Business a Stage.* Harvard: HBS Press.

Pitt, L.F., Watson, R.T., Berthon, P., Wynn, D. and Zinkhan, G. (2006) 'The Penguin's Window: Corporate Brands from an Open-Source Perspective', *Journal of the Academy of Marketing Science*, 34(2): 115–127.

Ponsonby-McCabe, S. and Boyle, E. (2006) 'Understanding Brands as Experiential Spaces: Axiological Implications for Marketing Strategists', *Journal of Strategic Marketing*, 14(2): 175–189.

Remy, E. and Kopel, S. (2002) 'Social Linking and Human Resources Management in the Service Sector', *Service Industries Journal*, 22(1): 35–56.

Ritzer, G. (2005) *Enchanting a Disenchanted World: Revolutionizing the Means of Consumption.* Thousand Oaks, Calif.: Pine Forge Press.

Sawhney, M., Verona, G. and Prandelli, E. (2005) 'Collaborating to Create: The Internet as a Platform for Customer Engagement in Product Innovation', *Journal of Interactive Marketing*, 19(4): 4–17.

Sassatelli, R. (2007) *Consumer Culture. History, Theory and Politics.* London: Sage.

Schembri, S. (2008) 'The Paradox of a Legend: A Visual Ethnography of Harley Davidson in Australia', *Journal of Management & Organization*, 14(4): 386–398.

Schmitt, B.H. (1999) *Experiential Marketing: How to Get Customers to Sense, Feel, Think, Act and Relate to Your Company and Brands.* New York: The Free Press.

Schmitt, B.H. (2003) *Customer Experience Management.* New Jersey: Wiley & Sons.

Sherry, J.F., Jr. (1998) 'The Soul of the Company Store: Nike Town Chicago and the Emplaced Brandscape', in J.F. Sherry, Jr. (ed.) *Servicescapes: The Concept of Place in Contemporary Markets*, Lincolnwood, IL: NTC Business Books, pp. 109–150.

Solomon, M.R., Surprenant, C., Czepiel, J.A. and Gutman, E.G. (1985) 'A Role Theory Perspective on Dyadic Interactions: The Service Encounter', *Journal of Marketing*, 49(1): 99–111.

Surprenant, C.F. and Solomon, M.R. (1987) 'Predictability and Personalization in the Service Encounter', *Journal of Marketing*, 51(2): 86–96.

Szmigin, I. (2003) *Understanding the Consumer.* London: Sage.

Thompson, C.J. (2000) 'Postmodern Consumer Goals Made Easy!!!!', in S. Ratneshwar, D.G. Mick and C. Huffman (eds) *The Why of Consumption*, London: Routledge, pp. 120–139.

Thompson, C.J., Locander, W.B. and Pollio, H.R. (1989) 'Putting Consumer Experience Back into Consumer Research: The Philosophy and Method of Existential-Phenomenology', *Journal of Consumer Research*, 16(2): 133–146.

Vargo, S.L. and Lusch, R.F. (2004) 'Evolving to a New Dominant Logic for Marketing', *Journal of Marketing*, 68(1): 1–17.

Venkatesh, A. (1998) 'Cybermarketscapes and Consumer Freedoms and Identities',

European Journal of Marketing, 32(7/8): 664–676.

Wipperfürth, A. (2005) *Brand Hijack: Marketing Without Marketing*. New York: Portfolio.

Zwick, D., Bonsu, S.K. and Darmody, A. (2008) 'Putting Consumers to Work: Co-Creation and New Marketing Govern-Mentality' *Journal of Consumer Culture*, 8(2): 163–196.

28

Technology, Consumers, and Marketing Theory

Nikhilesh Dholakia, Detlev Zwick,
and Janice Denegri-Knott

INTRODUCTION

Technology-related turning points that reshape the direction of marketing usually become apparent only in the clear light of hindsight. Sometimes, though, market and commerce-shaping technological breakthroughs are foreseen in prescient ways. Prior to the famed 'Golden Spike' at Promontory Point in Utah that linked the East and West of continental United States by railroad in 1869, three other commemorative spikes were driven. The one from the territory of Arizona bore this inscription: 'Ribbed with iron clad in silver and crowned with gold Arizona presents her offering to the enterprise that has banded a continent and dictated a pathway to commerce'.[1] This inscription foresaw the momentous promise, if not the exact pattern, of continental commerce unfolding with railroads.

From telegraph, railways, and automobiles to television, jets, and the Internet, technologies that reshape and transform markets seem to appear every few decades. This chapter explores the interplay between technology, consumers, and marketing – particularly

marketing theory. Our approach is based on a theory of technology that aligns itself with a 'soft' form technological determinism (see Smith and Marx, 1994). This view holds that changing technologies will always be only one factor among many others – including political, cultural, and economic ones – responsible for changing economic and marketing processes. Soft technological determinism thus overcomes the simplicity of 'hard' technological determinism that proposes a simple cause–effect relationship between technological change and changes in social, economic, or managerial practices (MacKenzie and Wajcman, 1999). In essence, our view of technology – probably best represented by Winner's (1986, 1999) idea of 'political technology' – states that by adopting a particular technology a person, business, or institution may be opting for a lot more in terms of social, political, economic, and cultural implications than a straightforward assessment of the technology's 'objective' instrumental capabilities would suggest. Thus, not all implications of a technological choice, such as the adoption of a new customer relationship management (CRM) system, may be aligned with the user's initial need for the technology. Such a statement – in fact our entire argument – does not at all exclude the possibility that the adoption of technologies such as CRM or Radio Frequency Identification (RFID) provides functional advantages and important operational efficiencies. However, such a purely instrumental perspective limits the analysis to how technology is adopted and used. Our approach to marketing and information technology, while encompassing adoption and usage, also stresses the aspects of how to *shape* technology and how *technology shapes marketing practice* (cf. MacKenzie and Wajcman, 1999). After a brief historical excursus into the nexus between marketing and technology, we turn to new information technologies from the mid-1990s onwards.[2]

To establish a conceptual base for the chapter, we first examine the core characteristics of new information and communication technology that usher in accretive and accelerative impacts on consumers and markets, trigger major transformations, or do both. We then focus on three issues: (1) Is there an emergent theory, or are there emergent theories of information technology marketing? (2) Is there an emergent theory or are there emergent theories of technology consumption? and (3) How do new information technologies shape or inform major theories in marketing in areas such as customer relationship management, co-creation, customer centricity, and loci of control in the value creation and consumption process? The chapter ends with some suggestions for a future-oriented research agenda about technology and marketing theory.

BRIEF HISTORICAL EXCURSUS

Technology adoption processes have held the interest of researchers in marketing and social sciences for several decades (Gatignon and Robertson, 1985). Technology also has been recognized as a key factor driving

strategy – not only R&D aspects but also marketing and product portfolios – of many firms (Capon and Glazer, 1987).

By the 1980s, there was a realization in some of the writings related to marketing and consumer behavior that in products and services infused with significant doses of advanced technology (or 'high technology'), the managerial practices as well as consumer behaviors were different than for conventional consumer or industrial products and services (see Dholakia et al., 1991; Ford and Ryan, 1981; Higgins and Shanklin, 1992; Shanklin and Ryans, 1984; Venkatesh and Vitalari, 1987). For consumer high-tech products, for example, it came to be recognized that adoption becomes just a first step in a process of change that could alter household dynamics (Venkatesh and Vitalari, 1987), the emotional coping mechanisms of consumers (Mick and Fournier, 1998), and psychological experiential states (Hoffman and Novak, 1996).

For high technology in general and information technology in particular, there is evidence of the ongoing erasure of the boundary between the spheres of production and consumption (Vargo and Lusch, 2004) and also increasing available research-based insights about the transforming impacts that consumers have on the application ranges of technological products and services they adopt and use (Shih and Venkatesh, 2004).

The warp of technology is getting steadily interwoven into the weft of commercial processes that connect marketers and consumers and of processes within consumers' lifeworlds. The former, the commercial side interweaving of technology, has led to great interest in the methods and impacts of electronic commerce and mobile commerce (Dholakia et al., 2002; Dholakia et al., 2006). The latter, the focus on technology in consumer lifeworlds, is spawning studies of technology consumption as object–subject theater and of intersubjective performative processes wherein connected consumers rely on technological platforms in attempts to play David – like heroic roles in the Goliath – webs of networked technologies (Zwick and Dholakia, 2006a,b).

As technology penetrates deeper into peoples' lifeworlds, the studies of technology – from marketing and consumer research perspectives – are expanding from adoption and post-adoption issues, and including larger concerns. Such studies are beginning to explore the transformative nature of the market economy and of the cultural spaces that consumers inhabit. For example, from a sweeping review of technology and consumption, Kozinets (2008) concludes that:

> ... although we know much about the general macrosocial and cultural conditions surrounding technology consumption, we discover a surprising gap in our knowledge about the nature and processes by which these conditions form into ideologies and how these ideologies influence consumers' thoughts, narratives, and actions regarding technology. (p. 865)

Based on extensive interviews with technology users, Kozinets (2008) concludes that the 'ideologies of technology have become interwoven with almost every realm of human endeavor and imagination: mundane and lofty, work and play, sex and food, progress and improvement, communication and pleasure ... there seems very little ideological space left for consumers to construct a viable oppositional viewpoint. Indeed, most solutions to social and environmental problems now involve adaptations of technology ...' (p. 879).

From an instrumental position, technology has come to assume an enveloping character – many commercial processes and consumption processes have become so suffused with technology that it is impossible to separate the impacts of technology from the phenomena being studied.

CONCEPTUALIZING HIGH TECHNOLOGY

Especially since the 1980s, information and communication technologies (ICTs) – customer databases, e-commerce methods, information systems, mobile communication devices, and the Internet – have increased dramatically in their global reach and social impact (Castells, 1996; Lyotard, 1984). ICTs represent one of the main driving forces behind major economic, social, and cultural shifts from the modern to the postmodern, from local to global markets, from production to consumption, and from industrial to informational economies.

Two of the most important contemporary transformative processes – the rise in information-producing, information-manipulating, information-distributing, and information-consuming technologies; and the increasing globalization of markets accompanied by the growing prominence of global (including 'glocal') marketing activities – are in a symbiotic embrace. Information, technology, the market, and marketing have become dominant metaphors of the discourses of affluent societies as well as the emerging and developing nations.

With affordable ICTs pervading the planet, consumption experiences and marketing are increasingly represented through the concept of 'data'. Information, more than at any time before, has become the essence of the market (Knorr Cetina and Preda, 2005). Organic and innocuous sounding descriptions of information as 'flowing and circulating' mask the dramatically growing quantity, intensity, complexity, and opacity of informational processes. Consumers often feel overwhelmed and intimidated by the sheer volume of information available for consumption. Marketers have responded to information overload with 'solutions' that seem to mimic the problem: a deluge of search tools, buying guides, top-ten lists, and direct marketing formats offering highly targeted (and hence presumably more relevant) digests, summaries, and 'deals of the week' (Cohen and Rutsky, 2005).

On the production and supply side, ICTs enable arcane repackaging of data into transactable intangibles – creating pyramidal structures of derivative products and services. From the perspective of marketing and consumption, then, the impact of high technology and ICTs has been the transformation of physical marketspaces into datascapes encompassing not only an increasing percentage of customer transactions but also, for example, the real-time tracking of the global movement of commodities and their many components. Changing customer preferences appear on the informational market map as intensifying and diminishing data streams and in a more general sense, the understanding of market and marketing objects (perceived value, goods, segment, communication, consumer, need, supplier, etc.) has been recoded as the exposure to various and always changing patterns of data. This model thus involves, at least in theory that the productive decision actually comes after and in reaction to the market decision. Hence, communication and information play a newly central role in production. 'One might say that instrumental action and communicative action have become intimately interwoven in informationalized industrial processes' (Hardt, 1999). The result is a more or less seamless and extremely fast cybernetic system of stimulus, feedback, and reaction, with a subsequent stimulus reproducing the cybernetic loop. Put differently, the contemporary mode of information marketing must be understood as a dynamic process where existing information systems and customer data continuously inform each other with each new interaction between the system and the customer. Hence, flexibility becomes a very instructive concept to express the effect of the interaction of information technology and marketing theory and practice. By mapping the flows of goods, finances, ideas, and individual consumption in a comprehensive electronic data system the foundation is laid for circular, recursive, and self-reproducing strategies of marketing power aimed at forecasting future customer positions 'in an increasingly dispersed and automated infoscape' (Elmer, 2004: 44; see also Bogard, 1996).

A cybernetic approach that centers on the notion of flexibility recognizes the need for information technology marketers to actively solicit consumers for information. This produces a state of affairs where the building, mining, updating, and distribution of customer data is a key component in the management and modulation of all other elements of marketing strategy. It is therefore fair to say that the increasingly tightly knit liaison between contemporary ICTs and the theory and practice of modern marketing raises new questions about what it means 'to market' – but also 'to consume' – in the age of information- and communication-driven market spaces (Cohen and Rutsky, 2005; Rayport and Sviokla, 1994; Zwick and Dholakia, 2004b). We now turn to a review of two key concerns, which have been dominant in the marketing literature – the distillation of both accretive and accelerative impacts of ICTs on marketing practice by way of situating and contrasting emerging theories on technology, marketing, and consumption.

Accretive and accelerative impacts

Technologies have historically accelerated market-related processes and have added to the productivity and capacity of organizations at steady or even declining costs. The inaugural speech of Abraham Lincoln took two weeks to reach from Washington, DC to the western coast of the still-evolving United States. The inaugural address of Barack Obama was not only heard and seen instantly the world over, in select locations telepresence technologies created real-time, three-dimensional simulations of the oath-taking ceremony. Over time, technologies have increased the speed, capacity, dimensionality, and vividness – and decreased costs – of communication and transaction processes. ICTs continue to play this traditional role of technologies in terms of enhancing marketing processes while increasing their efficiency. Combined with globalization, ICTs are now deployed over globe-spanning interorganizational fields to push down costs of front-end marketing processes such as call centers and tech support, mid-chain processes such as customer relationship management, and back-end processes such as mining of customer data warehouses (Dholakia and Dholakia 2009).

Much research to date has highlighted the role of technology in accelerating and expanding marketing functions, by way of heralding a more efficient and integrative role for marketing practice within organizations (Achrol and Kotler, 1999; Bruce et al., 1996; Piercy, 1985). That marketing has become more central to the functioning of organizations has generally been founded upon the mantra that information is a corporate asset and that its acquisition, management, and distribution are tasks that marketing is best positioned to do (Achrol and Kotler, 1999; Capon and Glazer, 1987; Piercy, 1985). This has been said to be especially true in dynamic, knowledge rich environments, where organizations operating as networks of internal suppliers, distributors, and consumers, require a timely and coordinated approach (Achrol and Kotler, 1999). In that equation, ICTs enable the marketing department to operate as a key resource of the organization by expediting the analysis of market intelligence and monitoring trends, by producing virtually instantaneous matches between product offerings and consumer needs, and by more accurately evaluating the effectiveness of any marketing program. It follows then, that the process of 'doing marketing' is accelerated and enhanced with smart systems connecting various nodes of the value chain such as suppliers, inbound logistics, production processes with outbound logistics, as well as sales and marketing (Archol and Kotler, 1999; Capon and Glazer, 1987; Rayport and Sviokla, 1995, 1999).

That line of analyses has only been accentuated with the growing popularity of the Internet and other digitized media, like digital TV, Global Positioning System (GPS) tracking devices, and mobile phone technology for commercial purposes. Studies in e-commerce and interactive marketing for some time have been pointing out the benefits of ICT adoption including increased speed and reach in communication at lower costs (Hoffman and Novak, 1996; Watson et al., 2000), the potential to add value through information enabled services like product tracking and customization (Rayport and Sviokla, 1995; Watson et al., 2000), improved flexibility in pricing, more

efficient processing of enquiries and orders, and superior customization of products and services (Shugan, 2004). In addition, information and communication technologies have been credited with gifting marketing practice with a completely new set of capabilities that make it possible to deal with dynamic demand conditions through flexible production regimes, stock management, interactive price mechanisms, and adaptable product marketing strategies including bundling, temporary sales, and forward sales.

Early analyses of the impact of internet technology on marketing practice ushered in a new dawn for the discipline characterized by its global reach, increased information symmetries between consumer and company, multi-directional nature of market communication, digital delivery of goods and services, and possibilities to study and know consumers (Hoffman and Novak, 1996; Kozinets, 1999; Zwick and Dholakia, 2004a). In particular the database-driven Internet should be singled out as a revolutionary marketing technology, because its ability to generate, store, and analyze customer data renders the consumer a more accessible and actionable subject for marketing intervention (Arvidsson, 2004; Zwick and Dholakia, 2004b). As consumer behavior in online communities and marketplaces can be immediately captured, modeled, analyzed, and fed back to the virtual consumer, a closed loop of manifested consumer behavior, real-time analysis, and modulated marketing interventions and tactics is established (Blattberg et al., 1994; Elmer, 2004).

Marketing research has documented the emergence and integration of technology into marketing practice as an evolutionary process where gains in efficiency are achieved initially through process automation and later in the accruement of innovative practices aimed at creating increasingly fluid and constant interactions between the front, mid, and back process of marketing (Achrol and Kotler, 1999; Brady et al., 2001; Haeckel, 1985; Nolan, 1973). Early research concentrated on the effects of newly available computational speeds and efficiencies. Nolan (1973, 1979) wrote about the automation and administration of databases, Hedberg (1980) explained ways in which increased data processing capabilities can be integrated into organizational production and marketing processes, and later Long's (1984) work illustrated the progression of change and efficiency in the automation of sales management and selling processes through telecommunication technologies. As Haeckel (1985) points out, inventory record keeping systems of the late 1950s and early 1960s were later transformed into inventory management systems and then real-time market systems. In the 1990s, emphasis was placed on how databases could be used not only to realize sales but increasingly also to improve how the marketer would relate to customers on a one-to-one basis (Stump and Sriram, 1997). Such enthusiasm filtered into the relationship marketing literature, where technological determinist accolades for ICTs where recurring themes for describing how relationship building and maintenance in consumer and business contexts were enhanced with the use of a wide range of technologies, including databases, emails, websites, telephone interaction, and loyalty cards (Berry, 1983; Hammer and Mangurian, 1987; Stump and Sriram, 1997). The argument coming out of this research is that intelligent and integrative ICTs platforms give organizations control and operational effectiveness in areas such as pricing, product development, customer service, customer relationship management, branding, stock inventory management, and marketing information systems. Invariably, the aforementioned research has also gestured the role of ICT as a catalyst of transformational processes, where the ultimate commodity is data produced about the consumer and we may now add, produced by the consumer.

Transformational processes

At the leading edges of ICTs, especially the virtual social space-creating technologies, evidence is building up of uncertain and potentially potent transformational marketing processes and consumption settings.

There is a sobering realization that powerful transformative forces have been unleashed by such ICTs, and that – from the perspective of corporations – ways must be found to bend such forces in the service of capitalism (Parise and Guinan, 2008).

From a production perspective, information and communication technologies have been theorized as product and producer of a more general economic transformation from an energy-intensive to an information-intensive economic system characterized by advances in the technological base, changes in the nature of commodities, and dramatic time–space compression (Harvey, 1989; Kumar, 1995; Liagouras, 2005).

The electronic and information revolutions of the last two decades not only affect how work gets done but also what kind of work generates the bulk of surplus value (see e.g., Allen and Scott Morton, 1994). The emphasis is no longer on the development of technologies that have the ability to replicate and replace hard physical labor but on machines that allow for the manipulation of symbols and for the production and representation of information (Joschner, 1994; Kumar, 1995). In short, postindustrial technologies do not replicate manual labor as much as they enable and automate knowledge work. Consequently, the dominant strategy of value creation in information capitalism is focused on expanding, proliferating, and improving symbolic and communicative systems, rather than on the mass production of physical goods (Castells, 1996; Hardt, 1999; Liagouras, 2005: 21). Put differently, the manufacturing of material components of commodities has become less value-added (and hence less strategically important for the company) than the production of emotional, intellectual, communicative, and aesthetic components (Lash and Urry, 1994). When value generation is the outcome of such informationalized production processes – what Gorz (2004) has eloquently conceptualized as 'immaterial labor' in the context of the knowledge society (see also Hardt and Negri, 2000; Lazzarato, 1996; Virno, 2004) – economic value becomes a function of the degree to which time and space can be compressed in the production cycle (Harvey, 1989).

Usually notions of time–space compression refer to the discussion about the acceleration of global capitalism (e.g., Gee et al., 1996). As Castells (1996: 92) puts it, '[T]he informational economy is global.[…] It is an economy with the capacity to work as a unit in real time on a planetary scale'. While the new realities brought about by the worldwide real-time interconnectivity of complex and spatially dispersed production systems has garnered most of the attention of theorists of information capitalism, there are other ways in which advanced economies rely on time and space compression to produce value. They are related to the shift from the production of capital-intensive, tangible commodities to the production of knowledge-intensive, 'intangible' value such as market information, business intelligence, patents, brands, and community (Arvidsson, 2006; Hardt and Negri, 2004; Lury, 2004). The focus here is on the accelerated interaction between consumption and production traditionally expressed in management concepts such as Toyotism, just-in-time, and lean manufacturing (Thrift, 2005) and more recently in marketing practices that utilize the Internet to establish even more immediate and productive relationships involving consumers directly in co-creation and innovation processes through more or less managed mass collaboration systems (Kozinets et al., 2008; Tapscott and Williams, 2006; Zwick et al., 2008). Hence, and as we describe in more detail in the following section, perhaps the most profound outcome of the information revolution is that the spheres of production and consumption become increasingly difficult to differentiate and may ultimately collapse into each other.

EMERGING THEORIES OF TECHNOLOGY AND MARKETING

The questions that scholars of marketing and consumption now confront are whether, and if so, to what extent and how new ICTs create markets in which consumers with highly dissimilar economic, cultural, and intellectual resources can join the world of business in general, and goods and services in particular. As Arvidsson (2005: 43) points out, '[I]nformation provides an interface on which marketing can act'. Information, however, also provides an interface on which consumers, micro entrepreneurs, and communities can act vis-à-vis large and powerful marketing systems, contesting and changing existing ones or establishing new, innovative, and locally more relevant ones (Kozinets et al., 2008; Tapscott and Williams, 2006). Large-scale, deep transformations in the development, distribution, and deployment of ICTs we have witnessed since the 1980s – including their dramatic acceleration since 2000 – lead to a significant extension of the ways marketing is able to effect systemic–managerial changes.

While much has been written about marketing, technology, public policy, and consumption – with few exceptions – such works have taken the notions and categories of marketing (and consumption) for granted. Marketing, in other words, is regarded as an *a priori* category onto which new technologies are simply overlaid as they come along. As our summary of accretive and accelerative impacts revealed, new ICTs are discussed in terms of either the ability of companies to improve production, marketing, and distribution, or the capacity of consumers to process information and make decisions. The focus of such analyses is on the exploration of instrumental, strategic, and economic outcomes of inserting new information technology into the marketing processes.

From this functionalist perspective of marketing (Zwick and Dholakia, 2004a), information technologies are evaluated, analyzed, and discussed almost exclusively in terms of their ability to optimize the effect of the marketing mix, provide competitive advantages, and support strategic tasks such as segmentation, targeting, and positioning. Notions about the transformative impacts of ICTs on the marketing systems – but also the mode of consumption – rarely figure in any serious conceptual manner.

The instrumentalist–functionalist views of ICTs in marketing are not particularly well suited when the focus is on marketing as a system of provision and consumption as a mode of collaboration, social innovation, and peer production (Arvidsson, 2008; Surowiecki, 2004). In our view, then, the dominant discourses in the discipline that have traditionally provided the basis for understanding the relationship between marketing and technology have not been able to reveal the changed conditions of the cultural and technological 'production of marketing' as a customer relationship technique (for a critical discussion, see Zwick et al., 2008; Zwick and Dholakia, 2004a). In particular, the majority in the marketing academy still holds on to the traditional view that consumers aspire to maximize the consumption of material goods (even as these goods contain more 'knowledge' and eventually become a service, as argued by Vargo and Lusch [2004]) and that ICTs merely facilitate this mode of consumption as material accumulation.

This view has been suspect for a while now (Baudrillard, 1981, 1988; Firat and Venkatesh, 1995) and recently become almost absurd, especially in the affluent world where consumers chase symbols, recognition, information, and what Li and Bernhoff (2008) call psychic income, rather than 'stuff' (Arvidsson, 2008; Bauman, 2008). More to the point, though, the traditional view of marketing insists that production and consumption are two separate, indeed opposed, facets of the exchange coin,[3] yet what marketing practitioners and theorists are beginning to recognize is that with the advent of socially networked ICTs entirely new and uncertain arenas of mass collaboration, innovation, creativity, and play have opened up (Molesworth and Denegri-Knott, 2008), which collectively have the potential to transform current processes of value creation and in the process, redraw the contours of contemporary capitalism.

From the vantage point of many companies, value creation depends increasingly on the work of dispersed, external, and often unpaid human resources. Hence, the challenge for marketing is quickly becoming one of providing technology-enabled platforms and ambiences that channel the productive work of these individuals (often the company's consumers) into a productive, valuable direction (Arvidsson, 2006; Lury, 2004). In marketing and management thought, recently popularized notions such as value co-creation (Prahalad and Ramaswamy, 2000, 2002, 2004a, 2004b) and the concept of a service-dominant logic of marketing (Lusch and Vargo, 2006; Vargo and Lusch, 2004) may be able to provide formal theoretical foundations from which a theory of information technology and marketing could emerge, since both contain in principle the idea that the generation of customer value depends on providing sophisticated managed and interactive platforms for consumer participation (Zwick et al., 2008).

THEORIES OF CONSUMPTION IN THE AGE OF TECHNOLOGY

ICTs have a quixotic duality: information overpowers, and yet it empowers. Even as its volume explodes, information empowers consumers in markets for goods, services, experiences, and ideas. Tools that summon, gather, summarize, and arrange information for the purpose of consumption are getting better, i.e., more easily consumable. People, including consumers and marketers, have access to 'meta-textual means by which information on a topic can be filtered, collected, and presented for consumption' (Cohen and Rutsky, 2005: 2). One of the significant implications, then, of the rise of ICTs and the concomitant production, reproduction, distribution, and endless consumption of information is that it has become almost impossible to distinguish between the consumption of information and the acquisition of knowledge. In other words, a culture increasingly permeated and diffused by ICTs gives birth to situations where every interaction with information (and data) is as much a type of consumption as is the purchasing of a product. As ICTs continue to diffuse throughout social, cultural, and economic institutions, the 'informational reach of marketing' (Arvidsson, 2005: 42), driven by advanced market research techniques, new communication techniques, information distribution channels, and data collection, storage, and mining capabilities has expanded in ways unimaginable even in the 1980s (Poster, 1995; Zwick and Dholakia, 2004b).

TECHNOLOGY AS SHAPER OF MARKETING THEORY

In a technology suffused world, where technology is no longer an instrumental device that aids the processes of marketing but is instead an envelope that surrounds commerce and consumption (as well as an ingredient that saturates these fields), it is not surprising that technology has become a major influence on theories of marketing and consumption. In this section, we examine several ways in which contemporary marketing theory is being shaped by technology.

Customer relationships

Customer relationship management is increasingly taking center stage in organizations' corporate strategies (Greenberg, 2002; Swift, 2001). CRM, closely related to notions of relationship and database marketing, aims at creating, developing, and enhancing personal and valuable relationships with customers by providing personalized and customized products and services (McKim, 2002; Rigby et al., 2002). For it to work, a CRM system relies on its ability to identify and interpret individual customer records. Underlying organizational CRM systems are massive customer databases. Fueled by the steady and steep decline in the cost of data storage and handling over the past thirty years, organizations invested in creating increasingly detailed profiles of their customers and non-customers, despite the fact that such information is not necessary for billing and service-delivery purposes. From bookstores to supermarkets to large chemical manufacturers, organizations make efforts to bestow individual customers with a unique and graspable *identity* (Fayyad and Uthurusamy, 2002; Roberts, 1999). Information technologies such as the customer database represent a powerful response to the fast-changing tastes and fluid identities of the postmodern consumer elites (Featherstone, 1991). By capturing consumer actions and activities in ubiquitous fashion and minute detail, databases become repositories of complex consumer lives by turning behavior into abstract aggregates of individualized and individualizing data points. Once consumption has been dematerialized and made available as coded, standardized, and malleable data, there are no more limits to the construction of difference, to classification, and to social sorting (Lyon, 2001).

A good example of how technology affects marketing practice and theory is presented by the emergence and proliferation of the customer database, a technology that has given rise to techniques, competences, expert systems, and productive units aiming not only at the supervision, administration, and simulation of consumption but also at the flexible production of customers as information commodities (Zwick and Denegri-Knott, 2009). In other words, the reterritorialization and recoding of decoded and deterritorialized flows of customer information – resulting in customer profiles that potentially contain, for each individual, thousands of transactional data points in addition to detailed demographic, psychographic, and geographic information – is not merely a matter of understanding consumer preferences and behaviors to configure flexible and efficient, global production systems. Rather, the massively combinatorial capabilities of the database allow for the restructuring of the gaze of marketers who recognize that new instruments of knowledge also contain the possibility for new forms of production, value creation, and profitability.

Reducing the effects of panoptic techniques to improvements in consumer discipline and control (typically expressed as improved market segmentation and targeting capabilities, customization, one-on-one relationships, interactivity, etc.) ignores the economic innovations brought about by the integration of database technology into existing informational modes of production. We argue that the constant and compounding growth in the volume of data coupled with rising analytical powers of computers has endowed the customer database with an immediate strategic importance in a company's economic value creation process. In short, because of the massive informatization of consumers, it is now more efficient (faster, more flexible, and cheaper) to manufacture customers as modular configurations of propensities, as calculations of possible future values, and as purified groupings of selective homogeneity. Customer classifications are becoming real-time modulations. Put differently, in the age of information capitalism we need to conceive of customer databases as the factories of the twenty-first century.

Customer centricity and co-creation

In an era where information has come to dominate value creation, the separation of production and consumption has become blurred. Manipulation and reproduction of information by consumers increasingly drives the conversion of information into market-exchangeable value. Marketers increasingly provide – for a price – the conditions of production by customers. In such settings, notions of market systems come into productive confrontation with analyses of information and communication technologies. ICTs, on the one hand, transform marketing practices; and on the other hand, represent themselves as active forces of social, cultural, and economic transformation. In other words, ICTs are reshaping the meanings, metaphors,

and practices of marketing even as they continue to mold and refine the methods and techniques of managing a firm's customer relationships.

Value co-creation is the latest of what seems to be a continuous flow of popular management techniques (Ritzer, 1993, 1998). The term was coined by C.K. Prahalad, director of the 'Center for Experience Co-Creation' at the University of Michigan, and describes a situation in which market exchanges are the result of collaborative consumers and marketers creating innovative experiences together. In such collaborative arrangements, the distinction between marketing and buying, production, and consumption collapses and makes way for the hybridization of consumption and production activities turning consumers into active actors of the marketing process. From this perspective, the market democratizes the extraction of value as consumers are promoted to be creative participants in the production process. Consumer involvement is undeniable during the use of automated teller machine, the gas pump, and the supermarket checkout, for example, but such instances do not provide true co-creation moments, because 'the firm is still in charge of the overall orchestration of the experience' (Prahalad and Ramaswamy, 2004: 8). Here, as in what Ritzer (1998) labels McDonaldization, the involvement of the customer is structured by the firm to suit the demands of its supply chain 'rather than fulfill a customer's unique desires and preferences'.

A parallel to Prahalad and Ramaswamy's value co-creation concept is offered in the marketing domain by scholars Stephen Vargo and Robert Lusch (2004 and Chapter 12 in this volume) who suggest that the discipline's progression from a concern with the efficient production and distribution of goods to what they believe to be a necessary preoccupation with devising, marketing, and delivering services. The authors explain that goods are *not* what companies *really* end up with for the exchange process. Rather, the commodities that companies produce for sale are no more than 'intermediate "products"' that consumers use as 'appliances in value-creation processes' (Vargo and Lusch, 2004: 7). This notion of the commodity as a resource echoes Prahalad and Ramaswamy's idea of the commodity as value proposition. The significance of this reframing of commodities as services lies in the role reserved for the consumer in this plot. The way marketing theorists distinguish services from goods has a lot to do with the consumer's participation level during the service production process. In other words, the successful production and commodification of a service requires the active participation of the consumer, while that of goods does not. Therefore, if everything – *including* goods – becomes a service then the consumer becomes enlisted as a permanent member of the company's production and marketing project.

From a marketing theoretical perspective, then, co-creation strategies are no longer designed to control demand in the traditional way by first scrutinizing and then satisfying customer needs. Rather, the idea is for marketing to position itself as a mere facilitator and partner of consumer ingenuity and agency, letting individuals find their own places for playful production in their own consumption experiences, as demonstrated by the popularity of many gaming, open-source hacker, and fan communities (e.g., Dyer-Witheford, 2003; Kline et al., 2003; Kozinets, 2001). It is this productive fervor of the *common*, to use Hardt and Negri's (2000) term, that creates meanings, commodities, and experiences corporations are unable to (re)produce within their own rationalized systems of production. On the lookout for new ideas, marketers must seek ways to appropriate, control, and valorize the creativity of the common and the co-creation concept describes such an approach to marketing. Co-creation affords companies at least two crucial forms of payback: competitive advantage in a consumer culture characterized by fast-changing and fragmented demand (Gabriel and Lang, 1995; Turow, 2000) and a new modular form of control (Deleuze, 1986, 1992a, 1992b) that is well suited for managing the productivity of a virtually free and autonomous consumer workforce, dispersed throughout cyberspace and connected only by a common (and often momentary) desire to collaborate (cf. Arvidsson, 2005). Co-creation then, has become a dominant form of production with the advent of open source models and mass collaboration platforms where consumers can join forces and function as an extension of an organization's workforce (Benkler, 2006; Kozinets et al., 2008; Tapscott and Williams, 2006).

Playful and experiential consumptionscapes

For decades, technologies have aided in the creation of experiential spaces that enchant consumers, at least temporarily (Firat and Dholakia, 1998; Firat and Vicdan, 2008). Until the dawn of the twenty-first century, such experiential spaces were anchored in physical places – consumers had to be transported to such places to partake of the available consumption experiences (Ulusoy and Firat, 2009). ICTs have untethered experiential spaces from physical, locational anchors (Firat and Vicdan, 2008). Based on a study of eBay and extending their analysis to electronic social networking spaces in general, Molesworth and Denegri-Knott (2008) argue that the key task for marketing is to consider its role in the creation and maintenance of play. Experiential marketing denies routine, consistency, and possibly even permanence. It could well be that for a sector of the market – the part that is at the leading trajectory of experiential consumption – there is a requirement not just for built in obsolesces in products but in business models and businesses themselves such that the inevitable transience of any game created is recognized. Yet marketers must do this in a way that does not accelerate what Barber (2007) calls infantilization, the regression of the consumer to a childlike state of relative suspension of reason due to aggressive and pervasive marketing assaults. *eBay*, *Facebook*, and *Second Life* produce new games and therefore pleasures for consumers, but they may still be criticized as superficial in the context of Barber's global political concerns.

Yet, the answer is not to prevent play but rather to align consumer play with the creation of meaningful community, responsible social sensitivities, and tolerance for the other in a lifeworld characterized by difference. An answer to Barber's complaints may therefore be for marketing to attempt to re-focus the types of game that consumers enjoy.

The removal from the physical and material coupled with the hyper-realism and engagement afforded by digital technology produce fantastic, out of the ordinary consumer experiences not possible in other consumer theaters (Molesworth and Denegri-Knott, 2004, 2007). Put differently, websites, virtual worlds, videogames, as liminal or intermediary spaces, have the potential to actualize consumer fantasy beyond what was previously probable even in the elaborate experiential economy of developed cities with their exotic malls and tourist locations (Featherstone, 1998). Consumers can customize and drive unaffordable cars in websites and video games, build palatial homes for their avatars in *Second Life*, become budding sellers on *eBay*, purchase designer clothing for their *Neo-pets* and improve their digital lives with rare and expensive magic artifacts in videogames like *Everquest*, or *World of Warcraft*. Such experiences stretch the theoretical straightjacket of 'Classical' theories of consumption that reduce consumption to the satisfaction rational needs or economic utility (Baudrillard, 1998; Campbell, 1987; Firat and Dholakia's explanation, 1998). Fundamentally, consumer experiences in a digitized arena, which are deprived of a physical container, are best described as playful since they feed from a consumer imagination seeking thrill and excitement and not mere economic exchange. The salient characteristics of such consumer practices are akin to what has been observed in the sociology of play (Caillois, 1958) – competition, chance, role playing and thrill. Consumers compete in online auction sites for desired goods and for popularity in social networking sites like *Facebook* as well as for status in online communities and user-generation sites like *YouTube*. Chance is delved by online auction houses, which endlessly tease consumers with the chance that a desired good may be had, for example, eBay with over 115 million new listing at any one day, offers endlesspossibilities of the rare and the exotic. The potential for role play is vast – from identity experimentation in online communities, transformation in role and status, from consumer seller or broadcaster in auction sites and user-generated websites (Denegri-Knott and Molesworth, 2009), to otherworldly performances as knights and car thieves in videogames (Molesworth and Denegri-Knott, 2004, 2007).

We can see such consumer excursions as the latest development toward the dematerialization of consumption in favor of its playful properties. Such a reading acknowledges the historical trajectory that produced such possibilities, namely the transition from Fordism to post-Fordism. This has been explained elsewhere in terms of a departure from Fordism and its focus on commodity accumulation, to consumption forms that endlessly produce novel experiences (Campbell, 1987; Featherstone, 1991; Lee, 1993; Slater, 1997). Consumers' desire for the new and out of the ordinary has been met with the development of novel business models aiming to profit from consumers' playful behavior. However, the imperative of businesses to maximize profits through increased regulation and professionalization of play produces the very conditions of apathy and boredom (Shankar et al., 2006), that consumers' sought escape from. Therefore, based on the study of virtual consumption spaces such as *eBay* and *Second Life*, we would suggest that reproduction of consumption as meaningful play may emerge as the chief narrative of consumer culture in the twenty-first century.

Marketing at crossroads: consumer serving, capital supporting

With evolving socially networking and globally connecting ICTs, marketing processes and consumption practices are at a crossroads. The social prospects of fully empowered co-creating consumers are exciting but often come into conflict with the private needs of enterprise capital accumulation.

Many new information technologies seem to open new windows into potential democratization of consumption space. At the same time, other technologies enter the fields of production and consumption that offer ever-greater panoptic power to the marketers. The technologies of rebellious democratization seem to get co-opted quickly into corporate marketing and brand promotion programs.

The idea of managing one's life *without* technology is disappearing. Even in the developing world, basic technologies such as mobile telecommunications and the Internet are making rapid inroads among the poor and disadvantaged social segments – and some technology firms are taking major steps to connect the billions who are still not connected.[4] This makes it imperative to keep exploring the apertures and actions where consumers seem to take charge with the aid of technology. While capital resources would remain concentrated with global corporations that would at best number in the thousands, the proliferation of connectivity – in ways that reach a vast majority of the nearly seven billion people on the planet – could create a tipping point. Capital resources favor the well-financed brand marketers but global democratic access to basic electronic connectivity has the potential to create so much in terms of diverse content that the tsunami of user-generated consumptive options could wash over branded consumptive options in some cases. These types of consumer-led actions, in diverse global settings, need to come increasingly on the research radar screens of those working in the fields of marketing and consumption studies.

interwoven with marketing strategy and consumption processes in inextricable ways. Tearing away technology from marketing and consumption would indeed tear apart the very fabric of contemporary commerce and daily life. In this chapter, we examined the distinctive core conceptual elements and main characteristics of new information technologies and why new information technologies are often creating impacts that are not merely accretive and accelerative but radical and transformational. The recent passage from an industrial to an information economy involves dramatic changes in the theoretical and practical elements of marketing the most salient of which is the collapse of the traditional structure of communication between production and consumption – the fundamental domain of the marketing function in business. In other words, the flexibility of new ICTs deployed on both sides of the market exchange equation entails not simply a more rapid feedback loop between production and consumption to the point where production comes after (in reaction to) a market decision. Flexibility of technology means that consumption and production are becoming indistinguishable from one another as general consumer activities become ever more a direct force of production. Therefore, in the age of advanced information and communication technologies, we see the role of marketing in providing a platform to consumers to exchange services, share knowledge, generate communication, and build community. Marketers that find ways to harness and profit from the productive activities of consumers will thrive in the high-tech marketplace.

CONCLUDING OBSERVATIONS

Technology has shaped marketing practice and consumer behavior historically. Especially with the emergence of new connective information technologies and intensive technology-suffused lifeworlds, technology has become

NOTES

1 'The Last Spike', Available at: http://www.nps.gov/archive/gosp/history/spike.html, accessed 18 February, 2008.

2 We employ the terms 'technology', 'high technology', 'new technology', and 'new information technology' interchangeably when referring to information

and communication technologies from the 1990s onwards.

3 This stance has only been remedied partly by the recent discussion on the service – dominant logic (see, e.g., Aitken et al., 2006).

4 An organization called O3b – funded by Google, Liberty Global, and HSBC – plans to employ satellite technology to connect 'the other 3 billion', those in the developing world with no Internet connectivity.

REFERENCES

Achrol, R.S., and Kotler, P. (1999) 'Marketing in the Network Economy', *Journal of Marketing*, 63:146–63.

Aitken, R., Ballantyne, D., Osborne, P. and Williams, J. (2006) 'Introduction to the Special Issue on the Service-Dominant Logic of Marketing: Insights from The Otago Forum', *Marketing Theory*, 6(3): 275–280.

Allen, T.J. and Scott Morton, M.S. (1994) *Information Technology and the Corporation of the 1990s*. New York: Oxford University Press.

Arvidsson, A. (2004) 'On the "Pre-History of the Panoptic Sort": Mobility in Market Research', *Surveillance & Society*, 1(4): 456–474.

Arvidsson, A. (2005) 'Brands: A Critical Perspective', *Journal of Consumer Culture*, 5(2): 235–258.

Arvidsson, A. (2006) *Brands – Meaning and Value in Media Culture*. London: Routledge.

Arvidsson, A. (2008) 'The Ethical Economy of Customer Coproduction', *Journal of Macromarketing*, 28(4): 326–338.

Barber, B. (2007) *Consumed: How Markets Corrupt Children, Infantilize Adults and Swallow Citizens Whole*. New York: W.W. Norton.

Baudrillard, J. (1981) *For a Critique of the Political Economy of the Sign*. St. Louis: Telos Press.

Baudrillard, J. (1988) 'The System of Objects', in M. Poster (ed.) *Jean Baudrillard: Selected Writings*, pp. 10–28. Stanford University Press: Stanford, CA.

Baudrillard, J. (1998) *The Consumer Society: Myths and Structures*. London: Sage.

Bauman, Z. (2008) *Does Ethics Have a Chance in a World of Consumers?* Cambridge, Mass.: Harvard University Press.

Benkler, Y. (2006) *The Wealth of Networks – How Social Production Transforms Markets and Freedom*. New Haven, CT: Yale University Press.

Berry, D. (1983) 'How Marketers Use Microcomputers Now and in the Future', *Business Marketing*, 52(3): 48–53.

Blattberg, R.C., Glazer, R. and Little, J.D.C. (1994) *The Marketing Information Revolution*. Boston, Mass.: Harvard Business School Press.

Bogard, W. (1996) *The Simulation of Surveillance: Hypercontrol in Telematic Societies*. Cambridge, Mass.: Cambridge University Press.

Brady, M., Saren, M. and Tzokas, N. (2001) 'Integrating Information Technology in Marketing Practice – The IT Reality of Contemporary Marketing Practice', *Journal of Marketing Management*, 18(5/6): 555–557.

Bruce, M., Leverick, F., Littler, D. and Wilson, D. (1996) 'The Changing Scope and Substance of Marketing – The Impact of IT', in Conference Proceedings from the *European Academy of Marketing Conference – Marketing for an Expanding Europe*, Vol. 1, Budapest University of Economic Science, pp. 185–204.

Caillois, R. 1958. *Les Jeux et Les Hommes*. Paris: Gallimard.

Campbell, C. (1987) *The Romantic Ethic and the Spirit of Modern Consumerism*. New York, NY: Basil Blackwell.

Capon, N. and Glazer, R. (1987) 'Marketing and Technology: A Strategic Co alignment', *Journal of Marketing*, 51(3): 1–14.

Castells, M. (1996) *The Rise of the Network Society*. Malden, MA: Blackwell.

Chatterjee, P. Hoffman, D. and Novak, T.P (2003) 'Modeling the Clickstream: Implications for Web-Based Advertising Efforts', *Marketing Science*, 22(4): 520–541.

Cohen, S. and Rutsky, R.L. (2005) *Consumption in an Age of Information*. Oxford; New York: Berg.

Cova, B. and Dalli, D. (Forthcoming) 'Working Consumers: The Next Step in Marketing Theory?' *Marketing Theory*.

Deleuze, G. (1986) *Foucault*. Minneapolis, MN: University of Minnesota Press.

Deleuze, G. (1992a) 'Postscript on the Societies of Control', *October* 59(Winter): 3–7.

Deleuze, G. (1992b) 'What is a Dispositif?' in T.J. Armstrong (ed.) *Michel Foucault: Philosopher*, pp. 159–68. Routledge: London.

Denegri-Knott, J. and Molesworth, M. (2005) 'The Ontological Function of eBay as the Actualisation of Consumers' Imagination', *Cultures of eBay Conference*. Essex, UK, August 24–25, 2005.

Denegri-Knott, J. and Molesworth, M. (2009) 'I'll Sell This and Buy Them That', *Journal of Consumer Behaviour*, 8(6).

Dholakia, N. and Dholakia, R.R. (2009) 'Global E-Organization', in G. Salvendy and W. Karwowski (eds) *Introduction to Service Engineering*, New York: Wiley (forthcoming).

Dholakia, R.R., Dholakia, N. and Della Bitta, A.J. (1991) 'Acquisition of Telecommunications Products and Services: An Examination of Inter-Sector Differences', *IEEE Transactions on Engineering Management*, 38(4): 328–335.

Dholakia, N., Fritz, W., Dholakia, R.R. and Mundorf, N. (eds) (2002) *Worldwide E-Commerce and Online Marketing: Watching the Evolution*. Westport CT: Quorum Books.

Dholakia, N., Rask, M. and Dholakia, R.R. (eds) (2006) *M-commerce: Global Experiences and Perspectives*. Hershey PA: Idea Group Publishing.

Dyer-Witheford, N. (2003) 'Sim Capital: General Intellect, World Market, Species Being, and the Video Game', *Electronic Book Review*: [<http://www.electronicbookreview.com/thread/technocapitalism/marxinalia>, accessed October 13, 2007].

Elmer, G. (2004) *Profiling Machines: Mapping the Personal Information Economy*. Cambridge, MA: MIT Press.

Fayyad, U. and Uthurusamy, R. (2002) 'Evolving Data Mining into Solutions for Insights', *Communications of the ACM*, 45(8): 28–31.

Featherstone, M. (1991) *Consumer Culture and Postmodernism*. London: Sage.

Featherstone, M. (1998) 'The Flaneur, the City and Virtual Public Life', *Urban Studies*, 35(5/6): 909–926.

Firat, F. A. and N. Dholakia (1998) *Consuming People: From Political Economy to Theatres of Consumption*. London: Routledge.

Firat, F.A. and Venkatesh, A. (1995) 'Liberatory Postmodernism and the Re-enchantement of Consumption', *Journal of Consumer Research*, 22(December): 239–267.

Firat, A. F. and Vicdan, H. (2008) 'A New World of Literacy, Information Technologies, and the Incorporeal Selves', *Journal of Macromarketing*, 28 (4), 381-396.

Ford, D. and Ryan, C. (1981) 'Taking Technology to Market', *Harvard Business Review*, 59(March/April): 117–126.

Gabriel, Y. and Lang, T. (1995) *The Unmanageable Consumer: Contemporary Consumption and its Fragmentations*. London and Thousand Oaks, CA: Sage.

Gatignon, H. and Robertson, T.S. (1985) 'A Propositional Inventory for New Diffusion Research', *Journal of Consumer Research*, 11(March): 849–867.

Gee, J.P., Hull, G.A. and Lankshear, C. (1996) *The New Work Order: Behind the Language of the New Capitalism*. Boulder, CO: Westview Press.

Giesler, M. (2006) 'Consumer Gift System: Netnographic Insights from Napster', *Journal of Consumer Research*, 33(2): 283–290.

Gorz, A. (2004) *Wissen, Wert und Kapital: Zur Kritik der Wissensökonomie*. Zürich: Rotpunktverlag.

Greenberg, P. (2002) *CRM at the Speed of Light: Capturing and Keeping Customers in Internet Real Time*. Berkeley and London: McGraw-Hill.

Hardt, M. (1999) 'Affective Labor', *Boundary2*, 26(2): 89–100.

Hardt, M. and Negri, A. (2000) *Empire*. Cambridge, Mass.: Harvard University Press.

Hardt, M. and Negri, A. (2004) *Multitude: War and Democracy in the Age of Empire*. New York: The Penguin Press.

Haeckel, S. (1985) 'Strategies for Marketing the New Technologies', in R.D. Buzzell (ed.) *Marketing in an Electronic Age*, Harvard Business School Research Colloquium, Boston. pp. 231–326.

Hammer, M. and Mangurian, G.E. (1987) 'The Changing Value of Communications Technology', *Sloan Management Review*, Winter, pp. 65–71.

Harvey, D. (1989) *The Condition of Postmodernity*. Cambridge, MA: Blackwell.

Hedberg, B. (1980) 'The Design and Impact of Real-Time Computer Systems', in N. Bjorn-Anderson, B. Hedberg, D. Mercer, E. Mumford, and A. Sole. (eds)

Higgins, S.H. and Shanklin, W.L. (1992) 'Seeking Mass Market Acceptance for High-Technology Consumer Products', *Journal of Consumer Marketing*, 9(1): 5–14.

Hoffman, D.L. and Novak, T.P. (1996) 'Marketing in Hypermedia Computer-Mediated

Environments: Conceptual Foundations', *Journal of Marketing*, 60(July): 50–68.

Joschner, C. (1994) 'An Economic Study of Information Technology Revolution', in T.J. Allen and M.S. Scott Morton (ed.) *Information Technology and the Corporation of the 1990s*, pp. 5–42. Oxford University Press: New York.

Kline, S., Dyer-Witheford, N. and De Peuter, G. (2003) *Digital Play: The Interaction of Technology, Culture, and Marketing*. Montreal and Ithaca, NY: McGill-Queen's University Press.

Knorr Cetina, K.D. and Preda, A. (2005) *The Sociology of Financial Markets*. Oxford and New York: Oxford University Press.

Kozinets, R.V. (1999) 'E-tribalized Marketing?: The Strategic Implications of Virtual Communities of Consumption', *European Management Journal*, 17(3): 252–264.

Kozinets, R.V. (2001) 'Utopian Enterprise: Articulating the Meanings of Star Trek's Culture of Consumption', *Journal of Consumer Research*, 28(June): 67–88.

Kozinets, R.V. (2008) 'Technology/Ideology: How Ideological Fields Influence Consumers' Technology Narratives', *Journal of Consumer Research*, 34(April): 865–881.

Kozinets, R.V., Hemetsberger, A. and Jensen Schau, H. (2008) 'The Wisdom of Consumer Crowds – Collective Innovation in the Age of Networked Marketing', *Journal of Macromarketing*, 28(4): 339–354.

Kumar, K. (1995) *From Post-Industrial to Post-Modern Society*. Oxford, England: Blackwell Publishers.

Lash, S. and Urry, J. (1994) *Economies of Signs and Space*. London: Sage.

Lazzarato, M. (1996) 'Immaterial Labour', in P. Virno and M. Hardt (ed.) *Radical Thought in Italy: A Potential Politics*, Minneapolis: University of Minnesota Press. pp.

Lee, M.J. (1993) *Consumer Culture Reborn: The Cultural Politics of Consumption*. London: Routledge.

Li, C. and Bernoff, J. (2008) *Groundswell: Winning in a World Transformed by Social Technologies*. Boston, MA: Harvard Business Press.

Liagouras, G. (2005) 'The Political Economy of Post-Industrial Capitalism', *Thesis Eleven*, 81(1): 20–35.

Long, R. (1984) 'The Application of Microelectronics to the Office; Organizational

and Human Implications', in N. Piercy (ed.) *The Management Implications of New Information Technology*. Beckenham: Croom Helm.

Lury, C. (2004) *Brands: The Logos of the Global Economy*. London: Routledge.

Lusch, R. F. and S. L. Vargo (2006) *The service-dominant logic of marketing: Dialog, debate, and directions*. Armonk, NY: M.E. Sharpe.

Lyon, D. (2001) *Surveillance Society: Monitoring Everyday Life*. Buckingham and Philadelphia, PA: Open University.

Lyotard, J.-F. (1984) *The Postmodern Condition: A Report on Knowledge*. Minneapolis: University of Minnesota Press.

MacKenzie, D.A. and Wajcman, J. (1999) *The Social Shaping of Technology*. Buckingham and Philadelphia: Open University Press.

McKim, B. (2002) 'CRM: Beyond the hoopla', *Target Marketing*, 25(7): 38 ff.

Mick, D.G. and Forunier, S. (1998) 'Paradoxes of Technology: Consumer Coginizance, Emotions, and Coping Strategies', *Journal of Consumer Research*, 25(September): 123–143.

Molesworth, M and Denegri-Knott, J. (2004) 'Desire for Commodities and Fantastic Consumption in Digital Games', *Academy of Marketing Annual Conference*, Cheltenham, UK.

Molesworth, M. and Denegri-Knott, J. (2007) 'Digital Play and the Actualization of Consumer Imagination', *Games and Culture*, 2(2): 114–133.

Molesworth, M. and Denegri-Knott, J. (2008) 'The Playfulness of eBay and the Implications for Business as a Game-Maker', *Journal of Macromarketing*, 28(4): 369–380.

Nolan, R. (1973) 'Managing the Computer Resource: A Stage Hypothesis', *Communications of the ACM*, 16(7): 399–405.

Nolan, R. (1979) 'Managing the Crisis in Data Processing', *Harvard Business Review* 57: 3–4.

Parise, S. and Guinan, P.J. (2008) 'Marketing Using Web 2.0', Proceedings of the 41st Annual Hawaii International Conference on System Sciences (HICSS 2008).

Piercy, N. (1985) 'The Impact of New Technology on Services Marketing', *Services Industries Journal*, 4(3): 193–204.

Poster, M. (1995) 'Databases as Discourse, or Electronic Interpellations', in P. Heelas, S.

Lash and P. Morris (eds) *Detraditionalization*, Blackwell: Oxford, pp. 277–293.

Prahalad, C.K. and Ramaswamy, V. (2000) 'Co-opting Customer Competence.' *Harvard Business Review*, 78(January-February): 79–87.

Prahalad, C.K. and Ramaswamy, V. (2002) 'The Cocreation Connection' *Strategy and Business*, 27(2): 51–60.

Prahalad, C.K. and Ramaswamy, V. (2004a) 'Co-creation Experiences: The Next Practice in Value Creation.' *Journal of Interactive Marketing*, 18(3): 5–14.

Prahalad, C.K. and Ramaswamy, V. (2004b) *The Future of Competition: Co-creating Unique Value with Customers*. Boston, Mass.: Harvard Business School.

Rayport, J.F. and Sviokla, J.J. (1994) 'Managing in the Marketspace', *Harvard Business Review*, 72(6): 141–150.

Rayport, J. and Sviokla, J. (1995) 'Exploiting the Virtual Value Chain', *Harvard Business Review*, 73(6): 75–85.

Rayport, J.F. and Sviokla, J.J. (1999) 'Exploiting the Virtual Value Chain', in D. Tapscott (ed.) *Creating Value in the Network Economy*. Boston: Harvard Business School Publishing.

Rigby, D.K., Reichheld, F.F. and Schefter, P. (2002) 'Avoid the Four Perils of CRM', *Harvard Business Review*, 80(2): 101–109.

Ritzer, G. (1993) *The McDonaldization of Society: An Investigation into the Changing Character of Contemporary Social Life*. Newbury Park, CA: Pine Forge Press.

Ritzer, G. (1998) *The McDonaldization Thesis: Explorations and Extensions*. London and Thousand Oaks, CA: Sage.

Roberts, M. (1999) 'Transforming the Role of Marketing in the Chemical Industry: New Information, New Opportunities', *Chemical Week*, 161(45): S18–S20.

Shankar, A., Whittaker, J. and Fitchett, J. (2006) 'Heavens Knows I'm Miserable Now', *Marketing Theory*, 6(4): 485–505.

Shanklin, W.L. and Ryans, Jr., J.K. (1984) *Marketing High Technology*. Lexington, Mass.: Lexington Books.

Shih, C.-F. and Venkatesh, A. (2004) 'Beyond Adoption: Development and Application of a Use-Diffusion Model', *Journal of Marketing*, 68(January): 59–72.

Shugan, S. (2004) 'The Impact of Advancing Technology on Marketing and Academic Research', *Marketing Science*, 23(4): 469–475.

Slater, D. (1997) *Consumer Culture and Modernity*. Cambridge, UK: Polity Press.

Smith, M.R. and Marx, L. (1994) *Does Technology Drive History?: The Dilemma of Technological Determinism*. Cambridge, Mass.: MIT Press.

Stump, R.L. and Sriram, V. (1997) 'Employing Information Technology in Purchasing: Buyer-Supplier Relationships and Size of the Supplier Base', *Industrial Marketing Management*, 26(2): 127–136.

Surowiecki, J. (2004) *The Wisdom of Crowds: Why the Many Are Smarter than the Few and How Collective Wisdom Shapes Business, Economies, Societies, and Nations*. New York: Doubleday.

Swift, R.S. (2001) *Accelerating Customer Relationships: Using CRM and Relationship Technologies*. Upper Saddle River, NJ: Prentice Hall.

Tapscott, D. and Williams, A.D. (2006) *Wikinomics: How Mass Collaboration Changes Everything*. New York: Portfolio.

Thrift, N.J. (2005) *Knowing Capitalism*. London: Sage.

Turow, J. (2000) 'Segmenting, Signally and Tailoring: Probing the Dark Side of Target Marketing', in R. Anderson and L. Strate (eds) *Critical Studies in Media Commercialism*, Oxford: Oxford University Press, pp. 239–249.

Ulusoy, E. and Firat, A.F. (2009) 'Incorporating the Visual into Qualitative Research: Living a Theme as an Illustrative Example', *Der Markt*, 48 (May), 41–46.

Vargo, S.L. and Lusch, R.F. (2004) 'Evolving to a New Dominant Logic for Marketing', *Journal of Marketing*, 68(January): 1–17.

Venkatesh, A. and Vitalari, N. (1987) 'A Post-Adoption Analysis of Computing in the Home', *Journal of Economic Psychology*, 8: 161–180.

Virno, P. (2004) *A Grammar of the Multitude for an Analysis of Contemporary Forms of Life*. Cambridge, Mass.: Semiotext(e) and MIT Press.

Watson, R.T, Zinkhan, G.M. and Pitt, L.F. (2000) Integrated Internet Marketing. *Communications of the ACM*, 43(6): 97–102.

Winner, L. (1986) *The Whale and the Reactor: A Search for Limits in an Age of High Technology.* Chicago: University of Chicago Press.

Winner, L. (1999) 'Do artifacts have politics?' in D.A. MacKenzie and J. Wajcman (eds) *The social shaping of technology,* Open University Press: Buckingham and Philadelphia, pp. 28–40.

Zwick, D., Bonsu, S.K. and Darmody, A. (2008) 'Putting Consumers to Work: "Co-Creation" and New Marketing Govern-mentality', *Journal of Consumer Culture,* 8(2): 163–196.

Zwick, D. and Denegri-Knott, J. (forthcoming) 'Manufacturing Customers: The Database as New Means of Production', *Journal of Consumer Culture.*

Zwick, D. and Dholakia, N. (2004a) 'Consumer Subjectivity in the Age of Internet: The Radical Concept of Marketing Control Through Customer Relationship Management', *Information and Organization,* 14(3): 211–236.

Zwick, D. and Dholakia, N. (2004b) 'Whose Identity is it Anyway? Consumer Representation in the Age of Database Marketing', *Journal of Macromarketing,* 24(1): 31–43.

Zwick, D. and Dholakia, N. (2006a) 'Bringing the Market to Life: Screen Aesthetics and the Epistemic Object', *Marketing Theory,* 6(1): 41–62.

Zwick, D. and Dholakia, N. (2006b) 'The Epistemic Consumption Object and Postsocial Consumption: Expanding Consumer-Object Theory in Consumer Research', *Consumptions, Markets and Culture,* 9(1): 17–43.

Zwick, D. and Denegri-Knott, J. (2009) 'Manufacturing customers: the database as new means of production', *Journal of Consumer Culture,* 9(2): 221–247.

Index

Figures in **bold**; Tables in *italics*

abduction 177–80, 187
abstract thought 444
actor
    bonds 157, 358, 361–3
    interaction **362**
    webs 361–2
advertising
    agencies (*see* advertising agencies)
    branding (*see* branding)
    communication 92–3
    content 464
    cultural theory in 90
    culture and 98–102 (*see also* culture)
    ethics 100–1 (*see also* ethics: marketing and)
    managerial theory 91–2
    practices in 92, 97
    research 76, 91–2, 94, 96, 100 (*see also*
        marketing research)
    science in 95–6
    scope of 99
    vocabulary 90
advertising agencies
    management in 96–8 (*see also* advertising
        management)
    psychologists in 67
    research by 62
    See also advertising
advertising management
    accounts and 90, 98, 208, 251
    international aspects of 97–8
    psychological science and 92–6
    theory 91–2
    See also advertising
agriculture
    cultural effects of 446–7
    economic surplus and 446
    origins of 444
AIDA 92–3, 98, 100
Alderson, W. 1, 3–6, 35–6, 42–6, 49–50, 62, 130, 151,
    161, 195–6, 198, 207, 210–11, 230–1, 246, 269,
    400, 420, 429, 434–5
altruism 96, 423, 448, 458–9

American Marketing Association (AMA) 37, 62, 67,
    244–5, 380
anthropology
    consumer behavior and 47
    cultural 8, 12, 89, 96
    Darwinian 457, 459
    marketing and 85, 423
applied economics 5, 28
Association of Consumer Research
    (ACR) 47, 67, 333
assortments
    consumers and 422, 434
    diversity of 435
    dynamics of 435
    examples 433
    of goods 417
    marketing systems and 419–21, **427**, 428, 433,
        434, 437
    measurement of 435
    origin of 434
    of services 417
attention-interest-desire-action (AIDA) 92–3, 98, 100
attraction effects theory 118–21

Bartel, R. 3–6, 27–9, 34, 43–4, 49, 52–3, 59,
    130, 151, 196–7
behavior
    altruism 96, 423, 448, 458–9
    analysis of (*see* behavioral analysis)
    gifts and gift giving 95, 286, 336–7, 339–40,
        465–6, 482, 484
    kin selection and 448–9, 458–9, 465
    lekking 464–5
    prosocial 448–9, 454
behavioral analysis
    demand and 310–11
    development of 312–13
    experimental 311–12
    matching in 307–10
    maximization in 307–10
    See also behavioral perspective model;
        consumer behavior

behavioral decision theory (BDT) 70
behavioral perspective model (BPM)
    accomplishment in 303–4, **303**, **304**
    accumulation in **303**, **304**, 305
    components of 300–1, **300**
    consumer behavior settings **300**, 301–2
    contingency matrix 303–6
    emotional responses and 306–7
    hedonism in **303**, 304–5, **304**
    maintenance in **303**, **304**, 305
    patterns of reinforcement in 302–3
    research and 306–12
    verbal behavior and 306–7
behavioural learning theories 63
Bernbach, Bill 91
Bogart, L. 75–7, 80, 86, 92, 188
Bohr, Neils 115–16
Booth, W. 270
Borden, N. 43
brand
    community 262, 334, 338, 449, 484, 486–8
    competition 309
    creation (*see* branding)
    culture 336, 338, 341, 448
    emotional value of 486
    equity 15, 77, 93, 100, 122, 379, 382–8,
        390, 392
    fests 481
    as tribal and social markers 453–4
    value 387–8, 390
branding 239, 267–8, 271, 304, 309–10, 336, 446,
    454, 462, 484. *See also* advertising
Brazil, Russia, India and China (BRIC)
    economies 238
Brown, L. 1, 3–5, 9, 11, 53, 80, 89, 99,189, 199, 250,
    266–9, 272–3, 275–6, 334–5, 340–1, 386, 402–3,
    405, 454, 459–60, 468
Brownlie, D. 1, 4, 11, 128, 131–3, 136, 142, 211, 272,
    333
Boulding, K.E. 46
Bryer, R.F. 30, 34–5, 38, 49–50, 55
Bucklin, L.P. 32–5, 85, 426
business performance 3–4, 383, 388, 392
business schools
    curricula 3, 85
    history of 28, 63–4, 68, 77, 275
    marketing departments 15, 63–4, 67, 132, 379,
        402–3, 408, 498
buyer(s)
    behavior 4, 32, 37, 47, 64, 245–6
    marketing systems and 435–6
    risk 33
    -seller interactions 155, 159–60, **203**, 244,
        253–4, **257**, 355, 421, 428, 432, 434, **434**
        (*see also* buyer(s): social action)
    social action 253–5, **257** (*see also* buyer(s): -seller
        interactions)
    See also consumer(s)

calculative agencies 199, 209
capacity to act 208, **208**
capitalism
    archetypes **431**
    categories of *237*, 237–8
    hyper- 276
    information 499, 500, 503
    predatory *237*, 237–8, 241
    puritan *237*
    state *237*
    welfare *237*
Carnegie Foundation 4, 64, 322
causal explanation 175–6, 186–7, 189, 333
Christmas 274, 283, 287, 289–90, 340
city-state
    marketing and 448
    rise of 444, 447–8
    social stratification and 447–8
companies. *See* firms
competence theory 185
competition
    advertising and 100
    brand 309
    legislation 206
    marketing management school and 155
    theory 122, 155, 224
    See also competitive advantage
competitive advantage 10, 122, 261, *223*, 223–4, 250,
    383, 387, 433, 443, 500, 504
consumer(s)
    action desires 12, 317–19, 323, **325**, 326, **327**
    action implementation 324, 326–7, **327**
    assortments and 422, 434 (*see also* assortments)
    behavior (*see* consumer behavior)
    characteristics 137, 140
    goods 30–2, 42, 283, 311, 337, 374, 402, 437
    cultural context of 140, 284, 337–8
    decision-making 12, 65, 137, 141, 247, 311,
        317–18, 320, 324–7, 427, 480
    desire 12–13, 139, 283–4, 286–7, 293, 323–5, **325**
        (*see also* consumer(s): action desires)
    dissatisfied 342–3
    empathy in 189, 256–7, **257**, 319, 321–3
    ethnocentrism 452
    experience production and 478–9
    experiences 481
    firms and 452–3 (*see also* firms)
    gatherings 482
    as gift-giver 339 (*see also* gifts and gift-giving)
    global 286–7
    identities 339
    linking value and 485–7
    local 286–7
    love in 257, **257**, 284–5, 319, **320**, 321–3,
        339–40, 463
    motivation (*see* motivation)
    as mythmakers 341–2
    place and 340–1

possessions 285–6, 339
psychology 299
reciprocity in 17, 212, 247, 251, 257, 319–22,
    340, 424, 433, 449, 451–2, 453, 466
representations of 12–13
self-regulation by 12, 257, 317–23, **320**, 342
shopping (*see* shopping)
as storytellers 341–2
virtual world and 343, 504–5
See also buyer(s); customer
consumer behavior
    active/passive nature of 93–5
    analysis of (*see* behavioral analysis)
    behavioral perspective model of (*see* behavioral
        perspective model)
    consumerism and 3, 63, 68, 132, 291–3
    Engel model of 65
    Howard–Sheth theory of 4, 47, 64–5, 83, 95, 246
    information processing and 66
    learning history and **300**
    marketing and 139 (*see also* marketing)
    mid-range theories of 65–6
    models for 48, 65
    perspective model of (*see* behavioral
        perspective model)
    physiological approach to 69
    qualitative approach to 69–70
    reinforcement in **300**
    research 48, 328, 332
    scope of 47
    theories 64–6, 332
    See also consumer(s)
consumer behavior marketing school 46–8
consumer culture theory (CCT) 4, 13, 69–70,
    129, 136, 336
consumer demand analysis 310–11
consumer decision making core 317–20, **318**, 326
consumerism 3, 63, 68, 132, 291–3
consumer research
    behavioural learning theories and 63
    characteristics of 480
    categories of 336
    cultural approach to 333
    emergence of 59–60, 66–8
    evolutionary psychology and 462–4 (*see also*
        evolutionary psychology)
    field theory and 60, 62–3, 115
    focus of 316
    interpretive 332–3, 336–7, 342
    motivation research and 61–2 (*see also*
        motivation)
    postmodernism in 335–6
    public policy and 68
    transformative 466–8
    World War II and Post-War decade 60
    Yale University Communications
        Research and 60–1
    See also consumer behavior

consumption
    agents and 208
    culture of 137, 235, 283, 290–2, 338
    experiential aspects of 334–5, 477–9, 481–2
        (*see also* experiential marketing)
    global (*see* global consumption)
    lekking and 464–5
    local 287–90
    postmodern 488
    production and 137–9
    rewards of 478
    theories and technology 501–2
    See also consumer(s)
contemporary marketing practices (CMP)
    case studies in 372–5, *373*
    development of 365–6
    marketing management and 367, *368*
    methodologies in 369–70, *369*
    multi-theory approach of 366, 375
    networks and 367–8, *367*, *368*
    theory in 369–71, *369*, **371**, 375
Converse, P. 6, 29, 37–8, 45, 52–3, 82, 151
core competency theory 221, 443
Cox, R. 1, 3, 5–6, 31, 49, 151, 161, 195,
    198, 210, 432
critical culture theory 128–9
critical marketing
    characteristics of 139
    critical culture theory and 128–9
    critical theory and 127, 131, 133, 135
        (*see also* critical theory)
    critique of 134–5
    definition of 127
    education 135–7
    European scholars and 134
    human agency and 135–7
    interest in 128–9
    macromarketing and 132–3
    origins of 128
    scholars 133, 138
    studies 132
critical social theory 9, 133, 137
critical theory 2–3, 9, 101, 127, 131, 133, 135
culture
    advertising 101
    brand 336, 338, 341, 448
    consumption 137, 235, 283, 290–2, 338
        (*see also* consumer culture theory)
    creativity and 449
    definition of 141
    intergenerational transmission of 445
    marketing and creation of 445
    origin and evolution of 445–7, 449, 454
    youth 289, 293
customer
    centricity 503–4
    as co-creator of value *223*, 225, 503–4
    marketing systems and 435–6

customer (*Cont'd*)
    relationships 502–3
    See also buyer(s); consumer(s)
customer relationship management (CRM) 158, 273,
    427, 502

Darwin, C. 457–9. *See also* evolutionary theory
Darwinian theory. *See* evolutionary theory
Defoe, D. 75
determinism 187, 463, 494
Dichter, E. 11, 47, 61–2, 70, 79, 94–5
discounted cash flows (DCF) 388–90

economic(s)
    actor/agents 201–2, 205–6, 211, 223, 226, 307, 358
    behavioural 13, 271, 299–300, 302, 307–8,
        310, 312, 430
    emergence of 60
    exchange 202–3, **203**, 221
    experimental 13, 299, 307, 312
    frontier 417–19
    growth and (*see* economy: growth of)
    macro- 75, 271
    micro- 5, 236
    philosophy 219–21
    rational choice theory in 185
    service 25, *223*, 225
    theory 129, 137, 186, 212, 246, 248, 307, 398, 435
    See also economy
economic agencies 200–2, 211
economists 60, 140, 212, 248, 307, 310, 437
economy
    BRIC 238
    closed 301
    exchange 339
    gift 339
    global 38, 238–9, 286, 291
    growth of 42, 97, 238, 291, 293, 416–17, 421–2,
        433, 436, **437**
    hyperreal 11, 271
    market 129, 496
    political 156–7, 236–8
    of scale 36
    service 25, *223*, 225
    See also economic(s)
Einstein, A. 114–16, 178–9, 183
empiricism 64, 124, 117, 121, 124, 134–5, 175–6
endowment effect 284
ethics
    advertising and 100–1
    international differences in 100
    marketing and 28, 50
    marketing research and 112, 122–3
    trust and 123–4
    See also relativism: ethical
evolutionary psychology (EP)
    advertising content and 464
    consumption and 461–8

    principles of 460–1
    scope of 463
evolutionary theory
    history of 458–60
    impact of 457
    marketing epistemology and 468–9
    marketing theory and 451–4
exchange
    actors in 247
    categories of 248
    complex 246–7
    conditions for 51
    definition of 246
    economics and 202–3, **203**, 221
    exchange marketing school (*see* exchange
        marketing school)
    generalized 247
    generic 51–2, 212
    indirect 223–4, *223*, 247, 398
    logic of 222
    marketing research and 248–50
    marketing theory and 52, 245–8 (*see also*
        marketing theory)
    meaning of 248
    media of 247
    networks 251, 253, 417
    objects 204–8
    restricted 246
    social actions in 251–7
    theory 156–7, 245, 251–2
exchange marketing school
    early literature on 50
    origin of 50
    scope 43, 50
    See also marketing schools
executive(s)
    decision making 43
    marketing attitudes and 15
    teaching 366, 370–4, *373*
experiential marketing
    characteristics of 476, 480
    consumer participation in 488
    consuming experiences and 479–81
    criticism of 480
    emergence of 479
    linking value and 484 (*see also* linking value)

Facebook 86, 504–5
fallibilism 183–4
falsificationism 122
feminist theory 99–100
field theory 60, 62–3, 115
firms
    consumer experience and 478–9
    consumer relationships and 452–3
    as tribes and families 451–2
    value and 225–6
Fisk, G. 4–6, 8, 20, 36, 46, 49, 130–1, 426, 429

focus groups, market research and 78–80
Ford Foundation 4, 42, 64
framing 140, 152, 202–4, **203**, 335
Freudian theory 47, 60–1, 80
Friedman, M. 86, 237, 307
Frey, A.W. 43
Fromm, E. 3, 20, 129–30, 136

gifts and gift giving 95, 286, 336–7, 339–40, 465–6,
        482, 484
global consumption
        Christmas and 289–90 (*see also* Christmas)
        food and 287–8
        global consumers in 286
        history of 291–2
        rap music 288–9
        survey research and 82
        See also consumption
globalization
        consumerism and 291
        consumption and 283 (*see also* global
                consumption)
        culture and 238–40
        history of 291–2
        identity and 238–40
        marketing and 238–40
Goldman, A. 78–9
goods
        business 31
        capital 31
        categories 30–2
        characteristics of 30
        consumer 30–2, 42, 283, 311, 337, 374, 402, 437
        convenience 31–3
        creation of 204
        definition of 204
        dominant logic (*see* goods-dominant logic)
        flow of 31, 244, 380
        industrial 14, 31, 355
        intangible 220, 224, 229
        luxury 286, 291, 386
        marketing of 30
        products and 204–5 (*see also* product(s))
        service provision and 224
        shopping 31–4
        specialty 31–4
        status 303
        tangible 10, 220, 407
        transportation of 29
goods-dominant logic
        characteristics of 220
        definition of 219–20
        origins of 220–1
        service-dominant logic and 227, 227–8
        services in 221
        See also service-dominant logic
grand theory 4, 90, 116
Guttman, L. 82, 86

Haire, M. 62, 83
Hanson, F. 66, 69, 72, 86, 134
Heede, S. 132, 134–5, 139
Heisenberg uncertainty principle 115
Hollander, S. 6, 20, 27, 53, 292
Howard, J. 4, 43–4, 47, 64–5, 83, 95, 246
Howard–Sheth theory of consumer behavior 4, 47,
        64–5, 83, 95, 246

idealism 113–14, 187
identity
        ethnicity and 239
        individual 129
        personal 337, 453
        possession and 284–6
        social 90–1, 251, 256–7, 319–20, 326
induction 121–2, 177–9
industrial marketing and purchasing (IMP) 157
Industrial Revolution 17, 75, 219–20, 454
information and communication technology (ICT).
        See information technology
information technology (IT) 87, 339, 372–4, 403–4,
        497–506
innovation
        consumer-produced 450–1
        cultural 447, 449
        diffusion of 64–5, 306, 444, 452
        discontinuous 446
        ideological 445
        intellectual 444
        product 85, 449, 464, 485
        technological 450 (*see also* technology)
        transfer of 449–50
inscription 207
interaction
        activity patterns and 360, **362**
        actor webs and 140, 361, **362**
        linking value and 483 (*see also* linking value)
        market(ing) 14, 35, 85, 155, 158, 323, 355–6,
                367–8, **362**, *367*, *368*, 383, 399, 405, 407,
                412, 486, 501
        networks and 14, 154, 157–8, 161, 361–3
                (*see also* networks)
        resource constellations and 358–60, **362**
        social 96, 100, 256, 310, 482, 484
        theories for analysis of 357–8
interactionism 188, 461
international marketing and purchasing (IMP) 13, 213,
        355, 402–3, 406

Journal of Consumer Research (JCR) 48, 67, 131, 333

Katona, G. 47, 60, 67, 70
Kelley, E.J. 44, 49, 52
Kotler, P. 44–5, 48, 5–1, 64, 68, 153, 155, 196, 229,
        244, 246–7, 267–8, 365, 379, 381, 398, 426, 498
kin selection 448–9, 458–9, 465
Kuhn, T. 112, 132, 162, 165, 181–3, 230

Lasker, A. 91
Lazarsfeld, P. 61, 65–6, 78–80, 105, 133–4
lekking 464–5
Levitt, T. 11, 239, 266–8, 275
Levy, S. 62, 68, 73, 95, 99, 103, 140, 147, 196, 208,
    216, 339, 341
linking value
    consumer interaction and 17, 483
    consumption researchers and 483
    definition of 476, 482–3
    marketing research and 483
    production of 17, 485–8
    time course of 483–4
literary analysis 99
Lockley, L.C. 75–7

macromarketing
    critical marketing and 132–3
    definition of 415
    incommensurability of 182
    school (see macromarketing school)
macromarketing school
    definition of 49–50
    early literature on 49
    origin of 49–50
    scope of 49
Mallen, B.E. 35, 46
management
    advertising (see advertising management)
    customer relationship (CRM) 158, 273, 427, 502
    education 3
    marketing (see marketing management)
    practice 28, 97, 402
    promise 15–16, 397, 399, 405–8, 410, 412
    research 99
    senior 367, 374, 379, 384
    system 97, 208, 499
    technology 45
    theories 91–2
market(s)
    characteristics 199
    construction of 211
    data and 496
    definition of 140–1, 197, **197**, 405–6
    exchange 203–4, **204**
    failure 236, 238, 357
    history 140
    logics of (see goods-dominant logic;
        service-dominant logic)
    marketing and 196–8, 210, 212, 497–9 (see also
        marketing)
    marketing systems and 420–1 (see also marketing
        systems)
    practice approach to 198–200, 203, 212
    purpose of 235–6
    segmentation 43, 84, 195, 503
    self-fulfilling prophecy in 206
    self-interest and 236–7

    shaping 205–7, 212
    social welfare and 240 (see also social welfare)
market-based relationship marketing 158–9
marketing
    academy and 28–9
    activities (see marketing practice)
    categories 154
    channels 35
    critical (see critical marketing)
    culture creation and 445 (see also culture)
    customer relationship and 401–2
    definition of 51–2, 140, 197–98, **197**, 210,
        244–5, 379, 405–7, 412
    evolution of 229, **229**
    evolutionary theory and (see evolutionary theory)
    exchange (see exchange)
    experiential (see experiential marketing)
    expertise 209–10
    globalization and 238–40 (see also globalization)
    goals of 241
    history 43, 50, 52–5, 130
    innovation and 449–51 (see also innovation)
    logics of (see goods-dominant logic;
        service-dominant logic)
    management activities 367, 368
    marketing manager 2, 10, 430, 44, 122, 131, 135,
        142, 272–3, 333, 368, 370, 452
    markets and 196–8, 210, 212
    metrics (see marketing metrics)
    micro- 28, 43, 49–50
    narratives in 209
    organizational borders and 402–3
    perspectives 380
    pluralism of 161, 163
    popularization of 52
    practice (see marketing practice)
    process for 404–5
    promise concept in 404
    relationship (RM) (see relationship marketing)
    research (see marketing research)
    research traditions (see research traditions)
    scientific study of 5, 28
    scholars 6, 8–10, 83, 99, 111, 132–4, 139, 246,
        250, 461–3
    schools (see marketing schools)
    systems (see marketing systems)
    technology and 499–7
    theoretical debates in 10–12
    theory (see marketing theory)
    transactional 155
    transvections 36, 43, 50, 54, 429
    trust and 112, 249, **431**
    value creation in 223, 225, 373, 374–5, 398–401,
        404, 406, 412, 503–4 (see also value creation)
marketing history school 52–3
marketing management
    contemporary marketing practices and 368 (see
        also contemporary marketing practices)

school (*see* marketing management school)
techniques 44, 51
textbooks 43–4, 155, 246
marketing management school (MMS)
  characteristics of 154–5
  competition and 155
  early literature on 43–5
  origin of 42–5
  research on 45
marketing metrics
  discounted cash flows (DCF) 390
  evolution 382–5
  history of 383–4
  net promoter score 390–1
  return on customer 389
  return on investment and 389–90 (*see also* return
    on investment)
  selection of 380–2
  theory 384–5
  timeframe of 382
Marketing Myopia (Levitt) 11, 266–8, 277
marketing organisation theory 13–16
marketing practice
  classification 367, *367*
  contemporary (*see* contemporary marketing
    practices)
  database *367*
  emergence of 365
  information technology and 372–4
  interaction *367*
  network *367*
  technology and 495–7 (*see also* technology)
  transactional *367*
marketing research
  advertising research and 76, 91–2, 94, 96, 100
  ethics and 112, 123 (*see also* ethics)
  exchange and 248–50
  experimental design in 82–4
  focus groups in 78–80
  formalization of 77
  future of 85
  as layered system 161, **162**
  linking value and 483 (*see also* linking value)
  multivariate data analysis in 84–5
  origin of 74–7
  promise management and 407–8
  survey research and sampling in 80–2
  technology of 77–86 (*see also* technology)
marketing schools
  commodity 30–4
  conceptual linkages among 54
  consumer behavior 46–8
  definition of 42
  exchange (*see* exchange marketing school)
  functions 28–30
  history of 42, 53
  history school 52–3
  institutional school 34–6

interregional trade 36–8
macromarketing (*see* macromarketing school)
management (*see* marketing management school)
services (SMS) 155–6
survey of 197
systems (*see* marketing systems school)
marketing systems
  assortments and (*see* assortments: marketing
    systems and)
  characteristics 415–16, **416**
  components of 426–8, **427**, *429*
  definition of 415–16, 419–20
  economic growth and 436, **437**
  evolution of 425–6, *426*
  examples of 419
  exchange logics of 428, **429**
  flows in 429–30, **429**
  markets and 420–1
  maturation of 424–6, **426**
  measurements of 436
  networks in 430, **431**, 432
  organizing principles of **431**, 433–5, **434**
  outcomes of 436, **437**
  quality of life and 436, **437**
  role specialization 430–1, **431**
  school (*see* marketing systems school)
  structure in 421–3
marketing systems school
  definition of 46
  early literature on 45–6
  scope of 45–6
marketing theory
  development of 6–8, 151, 196–7
  metaphors in 267–77
  obstacles to 6
  philosophical orientation of 5
  practice approach to 207, 212 (*see also* marketing
    practice)
  service-dominant logic and 230–1
  technology and 500–6
  See also model; theory
market research. *See* marketing research
MARKOR scale 159, 380
Marxism 9, 133
Maslow, A.H. 96, 283, 292
mass communication 89, 94–5, 488
mass retail 201, 208–9
McFall, L. 91, 97, 99
meaning transfer model 336
Merton, R.K. 4, 61, 65, 78–9, 86, 206, 370
metatheoretical analysis 47, 152–3, 161
metatheory 4. *See also* metatheoretical analysis
methodology
  causal 185
  criteria for choosing 180–5
  empirical observation 356–7
  exclusivism 176
  interpretive 185

methodology (*Cont'd*)
    monism 10, 174–7
    multivariate analysis 78, 84–5, 384
    pluralism 176–7
    qualitative 334, 372
    quantitative 6, 75, 372
    sampling 80
    survey 60
micromarketing 28, 43, 49–50
middle range theory. *See* theory: middle range
MKTOR scale 159
model
    behavioral perspective (*see* behavioral
        perspective model)
    consumer behavior 48, 65
    meaning transfer 336
    standard social science (SSSM) 460–1, 464, 466–7
    truth 112, 118, **119**, 120–1
Moore, G.E. 114, 116
motivation
    Freudian theory and 61–2
    profit 52
    research 8, 11, 47, 61–2, 80, 94, 266
    subconscious 47
multivariate data analysis in 78, 84–5, 384

natural section theory. *See* evolutionary theory
Nelson, P.J. 33–4, 338
neoliberalism 132, 138, 237
net promoter score 390–1
network-based relationship marketing 158–9. *See also*
    research traditions: relationship marketing)
networking 48–9, 94, 343, 367, 385, 483, 504–5. *See*
    also networks: social
networks
    activity layers of 360
    banking 430
    business 151, 157, 202, 361, **427**
    communication 431, 450
    contemporary marketing practices and 367–8,
        367, 368
    exchange 251, 253, 417
    interaction and 14, 154, 157–8, 161, 361–3 (*see*
        also interaction)
    in marketing systems 430, **431**, 432
    relationship marketing and 158–9
    social 85, 94, 204–5, 209, 251, 343, 385, 482,
        501, 504–5
    technology and 483, 495
    theory 221–2, 226, 422
    value 224, 226, *227*, 324

organisations
    adaptability of 365
    marketing 13–14, 365–6, 375
    organizing principles of 433
    practice/theory relationships in 371–2
    See also firms
Orwell, G. 269–70

Packard, V. 96, 135
paradigms
    definition of 181–2
    exemplars and 182
    impacts of 185
    science and 181, 185
performativity
    Austinian 205–6, 213
    generic 205–6, 211
perspectivism 10, 181, 183–4
Penrose, E. 302
Pessemier, E. 83
philosophy
    economic 220
    of science, 10, 92, 111–13, 174–5, 177,
        183, 223, 312
    of social science 189
Planck, M. 114–15
Polanyi, K. 140, 148, 420, 433
Popper, K.R. 122, 176, 178–9, 246
popular entertainment 97, 303–4
positivism
    logical 64, 111, 114, 117, 121, 123, 174–6, 185
    methodological monism and 174
    perspectivism as alternate to 181
    -post 69
    tenets of 176
    theory interpretation and 116
possessions 13, 95, 284–6, 323, 339. *See also* gifts and
    gift giving; goods
practice
    advertising 92, 97
    management 28, 97, 402
    marketing (*see* contemporary marketing practices;
        marketing practice)
    theory 4–5, 198, 207, 212 (*see also* theory)
product(s)
    advertising (*see* advertising)
    categories 12, 77, 85, 98, 287, 309–10, 484
    design 78, 83, 205, 210, 461
    differentiation 33, 43, 309, 424
    goods and 204–5 (*see also* goods*)*
    life cycle 4, 43, 175
    market 195, 342, 391, 498 (*see also* market(s))
    marketing (*see* marketing)
    placement 93
    safety 68, 420
production
    costs 428–9
    facilities 137
    knowledge 135, 139, 500
    mass 28, 36, 499
    service 156, 485, 487, 504
promise management 15–16, 397, 399, 405–8,
    410, 412
psychology
    cognitive 12, 47, 182–3, 271, 316, 370
    Freudian 47, 60–1
    Pavlovian 47

psychophysics and 47, 81
  social 47, 256, 316
public policy 68, 101, 136, 212, 235, 240, 500

quantum mechanics 114–16, 124

rap music 12, 287–9
rational choice theory 185
rationalism 175, 185
realism
  classical 116–17, 122
  critical 116–17
  direct 117
  fallibilistic realism 116–17
  inductive 116–18, 122
  philosophers and 116
  quantum mechanics and 116 (*see also* quantum
    mechanics)
  scientific (*see* scientific realism)
relationship marketing (RM)
  criticism of 250–1
  definition of 397–8
  evolution of 158–9
  market-based 158–9
  promise management and 15–16, 397, 399,
    405–8, 410, 412
  See also marketing
relativism
  characteristics of 113
  critical 8
  cultural 112
  ethical 112, 122
  nihilism and 111, 113
  perspectivism and 183
  philosophy of science and 113
  reality 112
  rejection of 112–13
  scientific realism and 112 (*see also* scientific
    realism)
  subjectivism and 112
research
  advertising 76, 91–2, 94, 96, 100 (*see also*
    marketing research)
  by advertising agencies 62
  behavioral perspective model and 306–12
  consumer (*see* consumer research)
  consumer behavior 48, 328, 332
  marketing (*see* marketing research)
  motivation 8, 11, 47, 61–2, 80, 94, 266
  survey (*see* survey research and sampling)
  traditions (*see* research traditions)
  trust and 122
research traditions (RTs)
  channels (CRT) 156–7
  characteristics of 152
  comparison of 153
  interaction and network approach 157–8
  market-based relationship marketing 158–9
  market orientation (MO) studies 159–60

metatheoretical analysis and 152–3, 161
  network-based relationship marketing 158–9
  paradigms for 162–6, *164*
  pluralism of 153–61
  relationship marketing (RM) 158–9
  service-dominant logic (SDL) 10–11, 160–1 (*see
    also* service-dominant logic)
  See also marketing schools
resource(s)
  -advantage theory 122, 221
  constellations 358–61
  distribution 129, 141, 451
  human 222, 224, 403, 406, 501
  integrators *223*, 226
  interaction **362**
  operand 10, 221, 224, 227–8, 231
  operant 10, 161, 221–8, *223*, 231
  scarcity 37
return on investment (ROI) 383, 389–90, 437, 454,
  468, 489, 495
Russell, B. 114, 306

schools. *See* marketing schools; research traditions
science
  abduction and 177–80, 187
  advertising and 95–6
  definition of 174
  fallibilism and 183–4
  hypothetico-deductive method in 178
  induction and 177–9 (*see also* induction;
    Popper, K. R.)
  instrumentalism and 185–6
  marketing as 5
  method choices for 177–80, 184 (*see also*
    scientific method)
  paradigms and 181, 185
  philosophy of 8, 10, 92, 111–13, 174–5, 177, 183,
    223, 312
  realism and (*see* scientific realism)
  trust of 123
scientific management 26, 28
scientific method 8, 70, 175–7, 277
scientific realism
  critical realism and 117
  failures of 118–19, **119**
  positivists and 117
  historical development of 113–15
  idealism and 187
  marketing theory and 9
  theory successes of 118–19, **119**
  trust and 123
  truth and 118–22, **119**
self consciousness 444
service
  benefits 45
  consulting 84
  customer 96, 156, *223*, 226, 368, 499
  definition of 221, 229
  -dominant logic (*see* service-dominant logic)

service (*Cont'd*)
    economy 25, *223*, 225
    exchange and 223–4, 226 (*see also* exchange)
    financial 419
    marketing 221, 231, 400, 402–6, 481
    provider 43, 155, 293, 360, 400, 431
    provision 10, 221, 223–5, 229, 245, 250
    public 236
    quality 156
    reciprocal 221, 223
    telephone 30, 207
service-dominant logic (SDL)
    conceptual transitions in *227*, 227–8
    criticism of 228–9, 269
    evolution of 221
    focus of 160, 222–7, *223*
    marketing theory and 230–1
    research tradition 10–11, 160–1
    services in 221
    See also goods-dominant logic
shopping
    goods 31–3
    malls 37, 311, 415, 421, 428, 434
Simon, H. 106, 307, 315
Smith, Adam 11, 50, 140, 220, 235–7, 242,
    416, 421, 439
Smith, W. 43, 79–80
social actions
    buyer-seller 253–4
    collective goal in 255–7, **257**
    key variables in 257, **257**
    theory of 256
social exchange theory 156–7, 245, 251–2
social groups 78, 113, 252, 302, 304, 321, 342, 444
social welfare 235–6, 240–2, 253, 319
sociology
    consumer research and (*see also* consumer
      research)
    economic 423, 430
    group interviews and 78
    marketing organizations and 167
    organizational 156
Spearman, C.E. 84
standard social science model (SSSM) 460–1, 464,
    466–7
Stanton, W. 61
Stouffer, S. 79
survey research and sampling 60, 70, 75, 78, 80–2, 84,
    94, 369

technology
    communications 91, 444
    computer 5
    conceptualization of 496–500
    consumption 18
    determinism and 494
    high (advanced) 495–6, 506
    history of 495

    information (IT) 87, 339, 372–4, 403–4, 497–506
    knowledge 417, **416**
    marketing 17, 196–7, **429**, **437**, 495, 506
    marketing research and 77–86
    marketing theories and 500–1
    studies of 496
    systems 405, 412
    in transforming processes 499–500
theoretician's dilemma 121
theory
    attraction effects 118–21
    behavioral decision (BDT) 70
    behavioural learning 63
    building 1–3
    competence 185
    competition 122, 155, 224
    consumer culture (CCT) 4, 13, 69–70,
      129, 136, 336
    consumption 501–2
    contemporary marketing practices and 369–71,
      369, **371**
    core competency 221, 443
    critical 2–3, 9, 101, 127, 131, 133, 135
    critical culture 128–9
    Darwinian (*see* evolutionary theory)
    economic 129, 137, 186, 212, 246, 248,
      307, 398, 435
    evolutionary 17, 445, 449–51, 453, 457–63,
      468–9
    evolution of 151
    exchange 156–7, 245, 251–2
    feminist 99
    field 60, 62–3, 115
    Freudian 47, 60–1, 80
    grand 4, 90, 116
    importance of 2
    levels of 4–5
    marketing (*see* marketing theory)
    -meta 4
    middle range 4, 14, 365, 370–1, **371**, 374–5
    natural section (*see* evolutionary theory)
    network 221–2, 226, 422
    philosophical underpinnings of 8–10
    practice 4–5
    rational choice 185
    social action 256 (*see also* social actions)
    truth 176
    See also model
Torgerson, W.S. 84
transaction
    analysis 79
    context for 202
    cost 156, 254, 428–9, 433, 436, *437*
    cost analysis (TCA) 356–8
    definition of 51
    exchange 420–1
    market 43, 50, 54, 155, 196, 365–6, *368*
    property rights of 204

research use of 70
tribalism 338, 482
trust
    definition of 122
    ethics and 123–4
    importance of 122
    in marketing 112, 249, **431**
truth
    axiomatic 184
    conceptual 181
    correspondence theory of 176
    models of 112, 118, **119**, 120–1
    positivism and 121 (*see also* positivism)
    as research objective 122–4
    scientific realist model of 118–22, **119**

value
    affective 486
    brand 387–8, 390, 486
    creation (*see* value creation)
    cultural 486
    customer 399–401
    determination of *223*, 227

economic theory and 129
firms and 225–6
linking (*see* linking value)
marketing and 398–9
value creation
    collaborative nature of 229–30
    conditions for 225–6
    customer and *223*, 225, *373*, 374–5, 398–401,
        404, 406, 412, 503–4
    inseparability and 225
    resources and 221–2
    service basis of 160
    service-dominant logic in 160–1, *227* (*see also*
        service-dominant logic)
Von Bertalanffy, L. 46

Wal-Mart 85, 275
we-attitudes and we-attentions 258–60, *259*, **260**
Weber, Max 141, 189
Weld, L.D.H. 29, 34
Wells, W.D. 62, 67, 70, 333

Yale University Communications Research 60–1

INDEX

Supporting researchers for more than forty years

Research methods have always been at the core of SAGE's publishing. Sara Miller McCune founded SAGE in 1965 and soon after, she published SAGE's first methods book, *Public Policy Evaluation*. A few years later, she launched the Quantitative Applications in the Social Sciences series – affectionately known as the 'little green books'.

Always at the forefront of developing and supporting new approaches in methods, SAGE published early groundbreaking texts and journals in the fields of qualitative methods and evaluation.

Today, more than forty years and two million little green books later, SAGE continues to push the boundaries with a growing list of more than 1,200 research methods books, journals, and reference works across the social, behavioural, and health sciences.

From qualitative, quantitative and mixed methods to evaluation, SAGE is the essential resource for academics and practitioners looking for the latest in methods by leading scholars.

www.sagepublications.com

The Qualitative Research Kit

Edited by Uwe Flick

Read sample chapters online now!

www.sagepub.co.uk

CPSIA information can be obtained
at www.ICGtesting.com
Printed in the USA
FSHW021850171219
65066FS